UNDERSTANDING CIVIL PROCEDURE

Fourth Edition

UNDERSTANDING CIVIL PROCEDURE

FOURTH EDITION

Gene R. Shreve
Richard S. Melvin Professor of Law
Maurer School of Law
Indiana University — Bloomington

Peter Raven-Hansen
Glen Earl Weston Research Professor of Law
George Washington University Law School

Library of Congress Card Number:

ISBN 978-1-4224-0712-7

Library of Congress Cataloging-in-Publication Data
Shreve, Gene R. Understanding civil procedure / Gene R. Shreve, Peter Raven-Hansen. -- 4th ed. p. cm. Includes index. ISBN 978-1-4224-0712-7 (soft cover) 1. Civil procedure--United States. I. Raven-Hansen, Peter, 1946- II. Title. KF8840.S484 2009 347.73'5--dc22
2009005230

Editorial Offices
744 Broad Street, Newark, NJ 07102 (973) 820-2000
201 Mission St., San Francisco, CA 94105-1831 (415) 908-3200
www.lexisnexis.com

MATTHEW◆BENDER

Preface to Fourth Edition

The systematic "stylistic" revision of the Federal Rules of Civil Procedure that went into effect on December 1, 2007, created a transitional nightmare for Civil Procedure teachers and students alike. Many of their materials still quote the old rules. This edition has replaced them with the restyled rules. But most of the case law and secondary literature interpreting the rules predates the restyled rules. This edition therefore still cites these cases and authorities and sometimes quotes them in the interpretation of the restyled rules. It will be years before this rat passes through the snake, but if the restyled rules are true to the accompanying Advisory Committee Notes, "[t]he changes are intended to be stylistic only," and the prior precedent should therefore still be good, even if sometimes confusing because of minute differences in wording and numbering.

Of course, Civil Procedure has also seen some more substantial changes since the third edition. First, the Supreme Court answered some of the questions presented by the supplemental jurisdiction statute, 28 U.S.C. § 1367. Second, by contrast, the Court opened questions about the sufficiency of pleading under the federal rules and perhaps interred "notice pleading" by its decision in *Bell Atlantic Corp. v. Twombly*, 127 S. Ct. 1955 (U.S. 2007). Third, Congress enacted the Class Action Fairness act of 2005 to address alleged forum-shopping in class actions. Fourth, the discovery rules were revised to address special problems posed by the discovery of electronic data, essentially authorizing the courts to innovate as they were doing already in an increasing number of decisions about the parameters of electronic discovery. Finally, many new lower court decisions informed the application of the rules, as well as common law civil procedure doctrines, sometimes warranting mention in the new edition. We have tried to give appropriate attention to all these developments, and, after the fashion of prior editions, to identify opposing perspectives on questions that are still open.

In preparing this edition, we benefitted enormously from the generous suggestions from our colleagues in law teaching and from our students. In particular, we would like to express our gratitude to Professor James Joseph Duane of Regent University School of Law, for his extensive and meticulous corrections and suggestions to the third edition. We tried to adopt almost all of them and trust that the new edition will be better for it.

Finally, Peter Raven-Hansen would like to thank George Washington University Law School students or graduates Sara T. Nazi, Justin T. Ryan, Brian K. Sung, and Tara L. Ward (who carried the brunt of the "stylistic revision" necessitated by the restyled rules). Gene R. Shreve would like to thank Tina Clark, IU-Bloomington Law Class of 2008, and Peter Day and Sean Hirschten Class of 2010. As always, we both also thank our spouses for their support for what has become nearly a lifetime project. And, finally, we'd like to thank our readers for selecting our book. Please let us know of corrections or suggestions for improvement.

Bloomington, Indiana
Washington, D.C.
April 2009

Preface to First Edition

This text treats the entire subject of civil procedure. It is primarily intended as a reference for law school civil procedure students. However, its treatment of recent developments in areas like Federal Rules of Civil Procedure 11, 16 and 26, personal jurisdiction and res judicata may make it useful to some practitioners as well.

If the law of contracts, torts or property reflects the substantive values of our society, civil procedure is the process for making those values real. The law of civil procedure governs the manner in which cases enter, transit, and leave the judicial process. It establishes the authority of courts to hear cases, opportunities for litigants to create and use a record of decision, and the force and effect of judgments.

We believe that the key to understanding the principles of civil procedure is knowing why: why they were created and why they are invoked. To these ends we have used a variety of means. History is the key to personal jurisdiction and the Erie doctrine, and we have explained them accordingly by tracing their historical evolution. Pragmatic concerns chiefly shape the civil procedure of pretrial discovery and motion practice, as well as trial practice, and we start discussion of these subjects by assessing why a lawyer is interested in them.

Federal Rule 11, discovery controls under Federal Rules 26(b)(1), 26(f), and 26(g), and expanded pretrial management under Federal Rule 16, are subjects so new that neither history nor pragmatic considerations are sufficient to anticipate their development. Using theory as well as both reported and unreported opinions available through early 1988, we have compensated by giving more prominence to these subjects than they presently enjoy in the typical civil procedure curriculum. This reflects our conviction that the subjects will grow in importance over the next few years. Finally, throughout the book we identify the latest sources which will enable readers with specialized needs to supplement the information we provide.

We have followed the practice of almost all civil procedure courses in using the Federal Rules of Civil Procedure as our model. However, we have also referred to different state rules and doctrines where appropriate, striving to use a representative cross-section of state models. We have also referred frequently to major civil procedure treatises, using a short form for citations explained in § 5.

Bloomington, Indiana

Washington, D.C.

May, 1988

TABLE OF CONTENTS

Chapter 9   COMPLEX PLEADING AND PRACTICE 279

Chapter 1

INTRODUCTION

§ 1.01 WHAT IS CIVIL PROCEDURE?

[1]   Approaching the Subject

Like all law, the law of civil procedure can be seen as a series of expedients to influence, punish, reward, and authoritatively explain human behavior. Perhaps the reason that beginning students sometimes find civil procedure especially difficult is that it is preoccupied with *litigation* behavior, and students come to the course with little sense of what litigation is.

Litigation is often described as a game. Litigants are like players and judges are like umpires. The litigation game is remorselessly competitive and is often thought to have winners and losers. Its rules, like those of many other games, are difficult to understand in the abstract. They are given life and meaning by the experience of the game itself. Thus, the more we understand the phenomenon of civil litigation, the easier it will be to understand civil procedure.

Litigation differs from most games, however, in at least two important respects.

First, most games exist for the pleasure they give to participants or spectators. So long as they are relatively harmless, they are not difficult to justify. In contrast, the litigation game carries a heavy burden of justification. The game may impose onerous costs upon the parties, the court and the public, and frequently has only one enthusiastic player — the plaintiff.

Civil procedure cases and problems can therefore appropriately be considered from the perspective of cost control or resource allocation. Could the factual dispute between the parties have been resolved by any means that would have eliminated the need for litigation? Should particular tactics employed by litigants be viewed as legitimate procedural means to substantive ends, or unreasonably burdensome means that are disproportionate to the ends? What should the balance be between litigant autonomy and judicial control?

Inquiry about the most appropriate use of judicial resources also requires a developing appreciation of the different roles trial and appellate courts play. The law of civil procedure recognizes that some issues resolved by trial judges should rarely, if ever, be reviewed,[1] because appellate courts have an inferior

---

[1] When the losing party can appeal a trial judge's procedural order and does so, the appellate

vantage point or because redecision does not seem to justify expenditure of scarce appellate resources. Where and how the line should be drawn between matters freely reviewable and matters committed to the trial court's discretion (hence, largely unreviewable) is a recurring question in the civil procedure course.

A second difference between litigation and most games is that games are usually not of central importance to (at least amateur) participants or to society. In contrast, the plaintiff may be forced to play the litigation game in order to avert or recover from a crushing setback in life. To deny claimants opportunities to become effective players in the litigation game might make meaningless the rights secured by substantive law (*e.g.*, torts, contracts, civil rights).

Readers of Dickens' *Bleak House* will recall how the redundant and prolonged Chancery procedure consumed the merits of the case. And, as Kafka's *The Trial* suggests, too little procedure can be just as bad. At its worst, procedure displaces or blocks substance. This can happen either when the expense and delay of too much procedure makes it impossible for a player to stay in the game long enough to reach the merits, or when potential players are shut out of the game because there is too little procedure. We must also be sensitive to possible differences between rules in theory and in application. As Anatole France observed, "the law in its majestic equality forbids the rich as well as the poor to sleep under bridges, to beg in the streets and to steal bread."

Ultimately, then, the game analogy must be used cautiously because it risks trivializing both the costs and the stakes of litigation. Unlike a game, civil litigation does not exist for its own sake. Civil Procedure works best when it validates substantive law (the merits) in the most expeditious, accessible, and unobtrusive way possible.[2]

[2]   Substance and Procedure

The study of the formation and content of substantive rules of decision — the standards by which society controls and affects "primary decisions respecting human conduct"[3] — is the subject of the traditional first year law courses of contracts, torts, property, and substantive criminal law. Civil procedure concerns itself with enforcing substantive rules through civil lawsuits. Roughly speaking, substantive rules of decision control conduct outside the courtroom, and procedural rules control conduct within.[4]

---

court must decide whether the order under review should be upheld. Whatever it decides, the appellate court acts by issuing an order of its own, *e.g.*, to affirm, to reverse, or to vacate and remand for further proceedings. It often explains its order in an accompanying opinion. Most of the edited opinions civil procedure students read are appellate rather than trial court opinions.

[2] *See, e.g.*, Fed. R. Civ. P. 1, which provides that the federal rules of civil procedure "should be construed and administered to secure the just, speedy, and inexpensive determination of every action and proceeding." Hereinafter we will cite to a Federal Rule of Civil Procedure as "Rule."

[3] *Hanna v. Plumer*, 380 U.S. 460, 475 (1965) (Harlan, J., concurring).

[4] For a detailed and illuminating discussion of distinctions between the two, see Walter Wheeler

The latter determine in what courts lawyers file lawsuits; how they frame claims, denials and defenses; how the lawsuits progress from commencement to judgment; and the effect judgments have on subsequent lawsuits.

[3]   Civil Procedure in the United States

Civil procedure in the United States has three distinctive features. First, it follows an adversarial model of dispute resolution. Parties initiate and propel litigation in this model, and the judge, historically and at least in theory, plays the relatively passive role of umpire. The burden is on the parties to present their grievances and defenses. Unlike in so-called *inquisitorial* models of dispute resolution,[5] the judge rarely makes independent inquiries. The burden is also on the parties to prosecute their grievances and defenses; litigation stops unless the parties pursue it. Indeed, some scholars have argued that recent procedural rule changes have "undermined judicial evaluation of the merits of lawsuits and thereby vastly expanded attorneys' opportunities to twist procedure and substance on behalf of their clients."[6] These characteristics of our system of dispute resolution place on lawyers a heavy responsibility for assuring justice and mastering civil procedure.

Second, civil procedure in the United States is dominated by *positive law*: codified rules enacted by legislatures or their delegates. In contrast, the substantive rules of decision taught in the other traditional first year courses are more often doctrinal: declared by courts as part of the *common law*.

One difference between positive and common law lies in the materials containing the legal rules. The common-law materials are almost entirely judicial opinions, and the appropriate inquiry is: what rule best fits the case? In contrast, positive law materials are enacted laws or procedural rules and legislative history. Emphasis in administering the latter is on their plain words and (sometimes) legislative intent, in recognition of the superior lawmaking authority of legislatures and their delegates.

It is not always easy for the first year student to subordinate the comparatively freewheeling policy-oriented analysis of common law taught in many substantive courses to the plain language of positive law, principles of statutory construction, and reading of legislative history. But mastery of the latter lays the groundwork not just for understanding much of civil procedure, but also for understanding upper level law courses. Significantly, practicing lawyers rank "knowledge of statutory law" as the most important knowledge for practice, just ahead of "knowledge of procedural rules."[7]

Cook, *"Substance" and "Procedure" in the Conflict of Laws*, 42 YALE L.J. 333 (1933).

[5] *See, e.g.*, John H. Langbein, *The German Advantage in Civil Procedure*, 52 U. CHI. L. REV. 823 (1985).

[6] Jonathan T. Molot, *How Changes in the Legal Profession Reflect Changes in Civil Procedure*, 84 VA. L. REV. 955, 958 (1998).

[7] Leonard L. Baird, *A Survey of the Relevance of Legal Training to Law School Graduates*, 29 J. LEGAL EDUC. 264, 273 (1978) (explaining that knowledge of common law, constitutional law, ethics, and regulations were all ranked lower by practitioners).

Finally, the purpose of civil procedure is, as the Federal Rules of Civil Procedure state, "to secure the just, speedy, and inexpensive determination of every action and proceeding."[8] Presumably, decisions are more likely to be just when they reach the merits. But the adversarial character of civil dispute resolution in the United States, the number of lawyers, and perhaps a national tendency to look too readily for judicial resolution of matters that other societies settle politically, administratively or privately,[9] have made the goals of "speedy and inexpensive" determinations increasingly difficult to attain.[10] As a result, there is constant pressure for more active judicial management of litigation and for judicial intervention to dispose of the litigation without trial, if possible. Thus, the 1993 amendment to Rule 1 requires the rules to be "administered" — as well as "construed" (the original term) — "to secure just, speedy, and inexpensive determination of every action and proceeding." No one foresees the replacement of our adversarial model by the inquisitorial model of dispute resolution, yet the former is undergoing significant change in response to widespread criticisms of the cost and efficiency of civil litigation.

[4]   Some Common Misperceptions of Civil Procedure

The study of civil procedure is often impeded by misperceptions formed before law school or by comparison of civil procedure with the substantive first year courses.

One is that civil procedure is, as scholars once labeled it, strictly *adjective* law that "exists for the sake of something else."[11] However, while it is true that civil procedure is not an end in itself,[12] it does not follow that procedural law is

---

[8] Rule 1.

[9] *See* Patrick M. Garry, A Nation of Adversaries: How the Litigation Explosion is Reshaping America (1997); Walter K. Olson, The Litigation Explosion: What Happened When America Unleashed the Lawsuit (1991); Jethro Koller Lieberman, The Litigious Society (1983). We say "perhaps," because scholars have raised serious doubts whether the data support claims of a "litigation explosion," especially when one considers the number of lawsuits in proportion to the world's largest economy. *See, e.g.*, Arthur R. Miller, *The Pretrial Rush to Judgment: Are the "Litigation Explosion," "Liability Crisis," and Efficiency Clichés Eroding Our Day in Court and Jury Trial Commitments?*, 78 N.Y.U. L. Rev. 982 (2003); Marc S. Galanter, *The Day After the Litigation Explosion*, 46 Md. L. Rev. 3 (1986).

[10] *See, e.g.*, Arthur R. Miller, *The Adversary System: Dinosaur or Phoenix*, 69 Minn. L. Rev. 1 (1984); David M. Trubek *et al.*, *The Costs of Ordinary Litigation*, 31 U.C.L.A. L. Rev. 72 (1983); Rand Inst., *The Costs of Asbestos Litigation* (1983), *excerpted in* Legal Times of Washington, Aug. 8, 1983, at 26, Table 6.2 (reporting that of every dollar expended per claim, 37 cents were attributable to defendant's litigation expenses, 26 cents attributable to plaintiff's litigation expenses, and 37 cents attributable to net compensation to plaintiffs). Litigation delays vary tremendously between courts. In federal trial courts, the median time between commencement of civil litigation and disposition at trial was 9.5 months, with 2% of the dispositions at trial taking more than 20 months. 2005 Admin. Office U.S. Courts Annual Report of the Dir., Table C-5.

[11] Charles M. Hepburn, The Historical Development of Code Pleading in America and England with Special Reference to the Codes of New York, Missouri, California, Kentucky, Iowa, Minnesota, Indiana, Ohio, Oregon, Washington, Nebraska, Wisconsin, Kansas, Nevada, North Dakota, South Dakota, Idaho, Montana, Arizona, North Carolina, South Carolina, Arkansas, Wyoming, Utah, Colorado, Connecticut, and Oklahoma (1897).

[12] *See* § 1.01[1], *supra*.

less significant than substantive law. At least one federal appellate court has suggested that procedures can have value independent of the merits, such that a lawyer's negligent waiver of the procedure may give rise to malpractice liability even when the procedure would not necessarily have improved the outcome.[13] The appellate cases (the chief vehicle by which substantive law is taught in law school) all reach courts by procedural initiatives, and the procedural posture in which the issues were presented to the appellate court often determines how much attention they will receive.[14] Moreover, courts sometimes use procedure to reach "just" results without changing inhospitable substantive law.[15] Procedure also interacts with substantive law outside the courtroom, as illustrated by the effect of the procedural device of class actions[16] on the substantive elements of securities fraud claims,[17] and the effect of the procedural requirement that plaintiffs pay for notice to class members on the effective enforcement of consumer laws.[18] Law has not escaped "the tendency of all modern scientific and philosophic thought . . . to emphasize the importance of method, process, or procedure."[19]

Another common misperception is that civil procedure is nothing more than the unimaginative and routine application of black-letter law to dry procedural issues. This may be a law student's initial reaction to the positive law materials from which civil procedure is primarily taught.[20] Yet positive law is more dynamic than the black letter of a rule or statute might indicate. Moreover, important parts of civil procedure, including personal jurisdiction (court's power to bind particular defendants) and *res judicata* (the effect of prior judgments on subsequent litigation), are based primarily on judicial doctrine.

It is important to understand that statutes or codified rules governing most procedural questions are not self-applying. Problems often elude solution by plain-language tests or application of simple canons of statutory construction. Statutes over time acquire their own judicial gloss. The legislative product may

---

[13] *Jones Motor Co. v. Holtkamp, Liese, Beckemeier & Childress P.C.*, 197 F.3d 1190 (7th Cir. 1999) (asserting that failure to perfect jury demand may be such a procedure, but affirming judgment for malpractice defendant because plaintiffs had not proven resulting damages to a reasonable certainty).

[14] *See* §§ 13.09 & 13.10 (scope and intensity of review), *infra*.

[15] FLEMING JAMES JR. ET AL., CIVIL PROCEDURE § 1.1 (4th ed. 1992) (quotation marks supplied) (hereinafter JAMES, HAZARD, & LEUBSDORF). *See* Robert M. Cover, *For James Wm. Moore: Some Reflections on a Reading of the Rules*, 84 YALE L.J. 718 (1975).

[16] Suits which may be brought by representative parties on behalf of a defined class of members who are not themselves participants in the litigation but may be bound by its outcome. *See* § 9.09 (class actions), *infra*.

[17] *See* Hal S. Scott, Comment, *The Impact of Class Actions on Rule 10b-5*, 38 U. CHI. L. REV. 337, 338 (1971) (arguing that class actions permit some class members to recover who would fail to satisfy reliance and materiality requirements in individual actions for securities fraud).

[18] *See* Kenneth E. Scott, *Two Models of the Civil Process*, 27 STAN. L. REV. 937, 944 (1975) (noting that the expense of such notice dooms most consumer actions because the expense of individual lawsuits exceeds the benefits that they could confer on individual plaintiffs).

[19] Morris R. Cohen, *The Process of Judicial Legislation*, *in* LAW AND THE SOCIAL ORDER: ESSAYS IN LEGAL PHILOSOPHY 112 (2001).

[20] *See* § 1.01[2], *supra*.

be inarticulate, forcing courts to finish the lawmaking process. Or the legislature may deliberately create a rule that can never be completed in the abstract. Rules of the latter kind place courts at procedural crossroads, supplying general criteria for decision and leaving the result to courts' appreciation of the facts in particular cases.[21]

Furthermore, many, if not most, procedural questions are susceptible to more than one answer. Civil procedure, hence effective litigation, consists less of finding black-letter answers than of making choices among tactical options. These choices turn not just on the rules and procedural posture of litigation, but also on the relative strengths and attitudes of the parties, the relationships between lawyers and judge, and all the other subtle factors that make lawyering an art as well as a profession.

A third misperception is that civil procedure is trial practice.[22] This may cause some law students who cannot picture themselves as trial lawyers to approach their civil procedure course with less enthusiasm. But even a brief glance at litigation statistics refutes this perception. For example, of all the federal civil actions terminated in the year ending Sept. 30, 2000, 72% ended before the pretrial conference that often precedes trial in federal court[23] (one in four of these ended without court action of any kind), 8% ended during or after pretrial, and only 1.4% made it to trial.[24] Just under one third of these were tried to a judge rather than a jury,[25] calling upon far different lawyering skills than jury trial practice. State civil disposition statistics[26] send the same message: civil procedure is not about trial. Litigation in the United States is predominantly *pretrial* practice. In this phase of litigation, it is not theatrics, charisma or trial tactics that carry the day, but mastery of pretrial procedure, the ability to communicate effectively to the court, and a command of the details of the lawsuit.

§ 1.02   SOURCES OF CIVIL PROCEDURE

Constitutional law sets the outer limits of civil procedure. The United States Constitution limits the subject matter of the cases that federal courts may hear,[27] determines the effect courts of one state must give to the judgments of

---

[21] *See, e.g.*, § 9.05 (discussing Rules 19 and 20 dealing with compulsory and permissive joinder), *infra.*

[22] For treatment of trial practice (jury selection, opening statements, presentation of evidence, closing argument, jury deliberation, and preservation of points for appeal), see Thomas A. Mauet, Trial Techniques (4th ed. 1996); James W. Jeans, Trial Advocacy (1975).

[23] *See* § 12.03 (pretrial conference), *infra.*

[24] 2005 Admin. Office U.S. Courts Annual Report of the Dir., note 10, *supra*, Table C-4A.

[25] 2005 Admin. Office U.S. Courts Annual Report of the Dir., note 10, *supra*, Table C-4A.

[26] Only 2% of tort cases terminated in United States district courts from 2002–2003 were terminated by trial, and 30% of those terminated by trial were tried to the bench, not a jury. Bureau of Justice Statistics, U.S. Dept. of Justice (last modified Aug. 29, 2008) http://www.ojp.usdoj.gov/bjs/civil.htm. An even smaller percentage of property and contract cases reach trial.

[27] U.S. Const. art. III. *See* Ch. 5 (subject matter jurisdiction), *infra.*

another,[28] and preserves the right to jury trial in certain categories of cases in federal court.[29] In addition, the Due Process Clause of the Fifth Amendment to the United States Constitution guarantees some minimum level of process to litigants in federal courts, and the Due Process Clause of the Fourteenth Amendment gives a comparable guarantee to litigants in state courts. Due process has helped shape procedural requirements for personal jurisdiction (judicial power to enter binding judgments with respect to particular defendants or property),[30] notice, and the opportunity to be heard in litigation.[31] Given their potential procedural reach, in fact, it is curious that the Due Process Clauses have not been invoked more frequently as sources of procedure.[32]

Statutes are a second source of positive procedural law. In both the federal and state systems, they define the power of various courts to hear particular cases[33] and the convenient forums for litigation.[34] In all states, statutes also help define the personal jurisdiction of state courts.[35] In addition, a declining minority of states[36] have enacted statutory procedural codes.[37]

The most important sources of positive procedural law, however, are formally adopted rules of civil procedure. The federal courts and forty states have adopted them, usually by a judicial rulemaking process authorized by a statute.[38] As of 1986, twenty-three states had copied, with minor modifications, the Federal Rules of Civil Procedure,[39] and almost two-thirds of the states based their procedures substantially on the federal model (although several of

---

[28] U.S. CONST. art. IV. *See* §§ 15.10–15.11 (full faith and credit and inter-system preclusion), *infra*.

[29] U.S. CONST. amend. VII. *See* § 12.07[1] (right to a jury), *infra*. Most state constitutions have analogous procedural provisions governing state courts.

[30] *See* Ch. 3 (personal jurisdiction), *infra*.

[31] *See* Ch. 4 (notice and opportunity to be heard) & § 9.09[4] (due process requirements in class actions), *infra*.

[32] *See* John Leubsdorf, *Constitutional Civil Procedure*, 63 TEX. L. REV. 579 (1984).

[33] *See* §§ 5.01[2] (citing federal statutes illustratively), 13.02–13.04 (federal appeals), *infra*.

[34] *See* Ch. 6 (venue), *infra*.

[35] *See* § 3.07[1] (long-arm statutes), *infra*.

[36] *See* John B. Oakley & Arthur F. Coon, *The Federal Rules in State Courts: A Survey of State Court Systems of Civil Procedure*, 61 WASH. L. REV. 1367, 1378 (1986) (listing California, Connecticut, Georgia, Illinois, Kansas, Louisiana, Nebraska, New York, North Carolina, and Oklahoma as the then remaining states with procedural codes).

[37] *See* § 8.03 (history and problems of code pleading), *infra*.

[38] Oakley & Coon, note 36, *supra*, at 1378.

[39] Oakley & Coon, note 36, *supra*, at 1377 (listing Alabama, Alaska, Arizona, Colorado, District of Columbia, Hawaii, Indiana, Kentucky, Maine, Massachusetts, Minnesota, Montana, New Mexico, North Dakota, Ohio, Rhode Island, South Dakota, Tennessee, Utah, Vermont, Washington, West Virginia, and Wyoming). This statement tends to understate the influence of the federal rules, because four of the states with statutory procedural codes have codified versions of the federal rules (Georgia, Kansas, North Carolina, and Oklahoma), and three other states have rules that "show strong affinity to the content and organization of the Federal Rules . . . ." (Idaho, Michigan, and Nevada). Oakley & Coon, at 1377. *See* Kenneth W. Graham Jr., *State Adaptation of the Federal Rules: The Pros and Cons*, 43 OKLA. L. REV. 293 (1990). Even states that replicated the federal rules have not necessarily kept pace with federal rule amendments, however. *See* Stephen N. Subrin,

the most populated states — including New York and California — substantially diverged from it).[40] As a result, almost all first year civil procedure courses and casebooks focus primarily on the federal rules, as we will here. At the same time, you should remember that the rules of the state in which you eventually practice may well differ, and that you cannot assume that even a state rule that is apparently modeled on a federal rule is the same as the federal "source" rule, or that it has been interpreted the same way as a matter of state law.

Some understanding of the federal rulemaking process[41] is essential to understanding the effect of the Federal Rules of Civil Procedure in federal courts. The Rules Enabling Act delegates lawmaking authority to the Supreme Court to make rules governing "general rules of practice and procedure" for cases in the federal courts.[42] The Judicial Conference of the United States, comprised of the Chief Justice of the Supreme Court and designated judges from other federal courts, oversees the rulemaking process. The Advisory Committee on Civil Rules to the Judicial Conference's Standing Committee on Rules of Practice and Procedure is charged with the actual work of drafting and recommending rules of civil procedure. The Advisory Committee is comprised of judges, practitioners and law professors. The Chief Justice appoints a Reporter who monitors developments in the field and aids the Advisory Committee.

Federal procedural rulemaking typically begins when the Advisory Committee notes a procedural need or problem. If the Committee so directs, the Reporter prepares a preliminary draft of responsive rule changes with "committee notes" explaining their purpose. The Committee meets and revises these materials and then reports them to the Standing Committee. If the Standing Committee approves the draft for publication, it is published in the *Federal Register* and the federal reporters[43] for public comment. In addition, the Advisory Committee usually holds public hearings on the draft in diverse locations. After reviewing public comments, the Committee may make revisions

---

Federal Rules, Local Rules, and States Rules: Uniformity, Divergence and Emerging Procedural Patterns, 137 U. PA. L. REV. 1999, 2037 (1989).

[40] Oakley & Coon, note 36, *supra*, at 1428–31; *see also* John B. Oakley, *A Fresh Look at the Federal Rules in State Courts*, 3 NEV. L.J. 354 (2003).

[41] *See generally* Thomas E. Baker, *An Introduction to Federal Court Rulemaking Procedure*, 22 TEX. TECH. L. REV. 323 (1991); WINIFRED R. BROWN, FEDERAL RULEMAKING: PROBLEMS AND POSSIBILITIES (Federal Judicial Center 1981); Benjamin Kaplan, *Amendments of the Federal Rules of Civil Procedure 1961–1963 (I)*, 77 HARV. L. REV. 601, 601–02 (1964); Laurens Walker, *A Comprehensive Reform for Federal Civil Rulemaking*, 61 GEO. WASH. L. REV. 455 (1993).

[42] 28 U.S.C. §§ 2071–2074. *See generally* Stephen B. Burbank, *The Rules Enabling Act of 1934*, 130 U. PA. L. REV. 1015 (1982). The Act expressly mandates that such rules "shall not abridge, enlarge or modify any substantive right," thus reserving substantive lawmaking to the Congress and to the state legislatures within their proper spheres. *See generally* §§ 7.01–7.04 (the laws applied in federal courts and the applicability of federal procedural rules), *infra. See also* Paul D. Carrington, *"Substance" and "Procedure" in the Rules Enabling Act*, 1989 DUKE L.J. 281 (1989).

[43] Selected opinions of federal courts are published in the *Federal Supplement* (district courts), *Federal Reporter* (courts of appeals), and *United States Reporter* (Supreme Court).

and then submit the proposed rule changes and final comments[44] to the Standing Committee of the Judicial Conference. The latter reviews and ultimately forwards the proposal, revised if necessary, to the members of the Judicial Conference.

If the Conference approves the proposal, it sends the rule changes to the Supreme Court. In theory, the Supreme Court conducts a substantive review of the change. In fact, the Justices have differed about their true role. Justice Douglas, for example, described it as "merely perfunctory" and the Court as "a mere conduit" for transmittal of the rules to Congress.[45] Individual justices may make statements concerning the rule changes. The Court then transmits the changes to Congress no later than May 1 of the year in which they are to become effective. The change becomes effective no earlier than December 1 of that year, unless Congress by statute modifies or rejects the rule.[46] At this writing, the most recent rule change made in this fashion is also, quantitatively at least, one of the most extensive. All of the rules were rewritten to "clarify and simplify them without changing their substantive meaning,"[47] the changes going into effect on December 1, 2007. For lawyers and law students alike, the comprehensive style change may prove a mixed blessing in the short term, as nearly every pre-December 1, 2007, decision quoting a federal rule will become partly anachronistic: the quoted part of the rule may have been "re-styled" out of easy identification or even out of existence, although the analysis of the rule is intended to be unchanged. Whether, as a practical matter, a rule *can* be re-styled without changing its meaning, or inviting an argument that it has been changed, remains to be seen.

However, not all written rules governing federal practice are promulgated in this fashion. Rule 83 authorizes a majority of the judges of each district court to promulgate local rules "consistent" with the formal federal rules of civil

---

[44] When rule changes are adopted, the advisory committee's notes become an important source of legislative history for construing the changes. They are published in the *Federal Rules Decisions*, the principal civil procedure treatises, and in many rulebooks.

[45] *See* Statement of Douglas, 409 U.S. 1132 (1972) (Douglas, J., dissenting). More recently, Justice White has said that the Court's role "is to transmit the Judicial Conference's recommendations without change and without careful study, as long as there is no suggestion that the committee system has not operated with integrity." Statement of J. White, 113 S. Ct. CCC, CCCIV (1993).

[46] Except for rules affecting an evidentiary privilege, Section 2074 contemplates (but does not require) a passive role for Congress: "[i]nertia means approval." David D. Siegel, 28 U.S.C.A. § 2074 commentary (1988). Congress usually remains silent, but has shown a greater tendency to become active in recent years. *Cf.* John Hart Ely, *The Irrepressible Myth of Erie*, 87 Harv. L. Rev. 693, 693–94 (1974) (describing congressional resistance to the Court's proposed federal rules of evidence), and § 4.03[1] (describing congressional substitution of its own enactment for the Court's proposed amendment to Rule 4), *infra*. Congress' constitutional authority to change the rules is not undisputed. *Compare* Linda S. Mullinex, *Judicial Power and the Rules Enabling Act*, 46 Mercer L. Rev. 733 (1995) (questioning such authority to supercede procedural rulemaking by the judiciary), *with* Martin H. Redish, *Federal Judicial Independence: Constitutional and Political Perspectives*, 46 Mercer L. Rev. 697 (1995) (supporting such authority on majoritarian principles).

[47] Report of the Judicial Conference, Committee on Rules of Practice and Procedure, to the Chief Justice of the United States and Members of the Judicial Conference of the United States 3 (September 19, 2006).

.ocedure. Many district courts have exercised this authority to issue house-keeping rules governing the length of briefs and the availability of oral hearings, attorney admissions, procedures for submitting requests for attorneys' fees, and other matters.[48] The result has been a proliferation of local rules, some of them contradicting or altering the uniform federal rules in apparent disregard of Rule 83's insistence on consistency.[49] Indeed, one civil procedure scholar lamented that "[p]rocedural anarchy is now the order of the day."[50]

Individual judges may also establish rules governing procedures for scheduling and argument in their courtrooms. Rule 83 expressly provides that when there is no controlling law, a judge "may regulate practice in any manner consistent with federal law, rules adopted under 28 U.S.C. §§ 2072 and 2075, and the district's local rules."[51] Furthermore, judges always have what has been called "individual calendar" discretion over scheduling and hearing practice in a particular case.[52]

The parties themselves can also be an important source of procedural rules often overlooked by law students. A few federal rules expressly authorize parties themselves to stipulate to departures from the rules,[53] and parties can make other agreements that supplement and sometimes modify positive procedural law. They often agree by contract, for example, to the appropriate forum for litigation under the contract, the mode of service of the complaint and summons, or the applicable substantive law for such litigation, superseding the otherwise applicable law.[54] At a more mundane level, litigation counsel schedule many pretrial activities among themselves.

---

[48] *See* CHARLES ALAN WRIGHT & ARTHUR R. MILLER, FEDERAL PRACTICE AND PROCEDURE § 3154 (giving examples). The scope of local rulemaking authority is a matter of continuing debate. *See, e.g.*, Steven Flanders, *Local Rules in Federal District Courts: Usurpation, Legislation, or Information?*, 14 LOY. L.A. L. REV. 213 (1981); A. Leo Levin, *Local Rules as Experiments: A Study in the Division of Power*, 139 U. PA. L. REV. 1567 (1991). In 1988, Congress acted to subject such rulemaking to closer scrutiny. *See* 28 U.S.C. § 2071; David D. Siegel, 28 U.S.C.A. § 2071 commentary (1988).

[49] *See* Stephen N. Subrin, *Federal Rules, Local Rules, and State Rules: Uniformity, Divergence, and Emerging Procedural Patterns*, 137 U. PA. L. REV. 1999 (1989).

[50] Charles Alan Wright, *Forward: The Malaise of Federal Rulemaking*, 14 REV. LITIG. 1, 11 (1994).

[51] *See, e.g.*, William W. Schwarzer (J., N.D. Cal.), *Guidelines for Discovery, Motion Practice and Trial*, 117 F.R.D. 273 (1987). Judge Schwarzer's *Guidelines* admonish counsel to observe not only the Federal Rules of Civil Procedure and the District Court's Local Rules, but also "the rules and practices of the particular judge to whom the case is assigned." The latter are available "[b]y obtaining from the judge's courtroom deputy copies of the standing orders used by that judge; and [b]y inquiring of the deputy (not the law clerks) how the judge wants things done." Schwarzer, at 273.

[52] David D. Siegel, 28 U.S.C.A. § 2077 commentary (1988).

[53] *See* Rules 15(a) (stipulation in lieu of court permission to amend pleadings), 26(f) (changes in discovery limitations), and Rule 29 (stipulation of discovery procedure).

[54] *See, e.g.*, *National Equip. Rental, Ltd. v. Szukhent*, 375 U.S. 311 (1964) (enforcing contract that designated agent to receive service).

Finally, ethical rules bearing on civil litigation are promulgated as codes of professional responsibility or rules of the bar by courts acting in conjunction with bar associations. The American Bar Association's *Model Rules of Professional Conduct*,[55] substantially adopted by the majority of the states,[56] contain several rules concerning the zeal with which a lawyer may represent a client in litigation.[57] Although historically there have been serious doubts concerning the organized bar's capacity for self-enforcement of such rules,[58] it is probable that the majority of lawyers abide by them. Moreover, several Federal Rules of Civil Procedure underscore professional responsibilities in federal courts and may become a vehicle for enforcement of some of the ethical rules adopted by the bar.[59]

§ 1.03 BRIEFING A CIVIL PROCEDURE CASE

The primary vehicles for class discussion in most civil procedure courses are assigned cases. These are judicial opinions, usually written by judges to accompany their orders (rulings) on civil procedure motions. An *order* may dispose of the lawsuit or simply resolve a skirmish between the litigants and leave the lawsuit to continue. Typically, the order simply says who won — for example: "Plaintiff's motion for summary judgment is granted [denied]." The *opinion* is written by the judge to accompany the order and to explain why the judge decided to rule in favor of the prevailing party (or, in appellate opinions, why the ruling below was reversed or affirmed).

Virtually all the orders in cases we consider were on contested matters. That is to say, the parties urged upon the court opposing choices of judicial conduct before the court decided how to rule in the order. Not all orders are accompanied by opinions, and not all opinions are designated by the court for publication. Opinions are most likely to accompany orders which decide contested matters, because judges feel greater pressure to justify what they have done under such circumstances. In this sense, judges are advocates, too. The judicial opinions we read are the judges' means of arguing that their orders reflect decisions most likely to advance the rule and logic of civil procedure and to do justice in the individual case.

The central purpose of case briefing is to enable students to get the most out of class. Briefing helps students prepare by giving structure to their consideration of cases before class begins. It also provides a working paper during class, making it easier for students to follow developments and to advance the discussion when called upon by the professor. On the other hand, briefs may not

---

[55] AMERICAN BAR ASS'N, MODEL RULES OF PROFESSIONAL CONDUCT AND CODE OF JUDICIAL CONDUCT (2007).

[56] *See* ABA CENTER FOR PROFESSIONAL CONDUCT, STATUS OF STATE REVIEW OF PROFESSIONAL CONDUCT RULES (chart), *available at* http://www.abanet.org/cpr/jclr/ethics_20000_status_chart.pfd (current as of Oct. 17, 2007).

[57] *See, e.g.*, MODEL RULES 3.1–3.6, note 55, *supra*.

[58] AMERICAN BAR ASS'N, SPECIAL COMMITTEE ON EVALUATION AND DISCIPLINARY ENFORCEMENT, PROBLEMS AND RECOMMENDATIONS ON DISCIPLINARY ENFORCEMENT 1 (final draft, 1970).

[59] *See* Rule 11, *discussed in* § 8.05[2] *infra*, and Rule 26(g), *discussed in* § 10.13[1] *infra*.

be terribly useful tools for course review. This is because they are made before class, before thoughts about the material have matured. Comments and addenda students make on their briefs during and after classroom discussion of the case are likely to be far more useful for exam study.

Casebooks and study aids suggest how to brief a case, and many students are taught briefing in first semester orientation lectures or legal methods classes. Our concern here is to explain how the generic briefing technique should be adapted for civil procedure cases.

Most briefs and many reported judicial opinions begin with a *recitation of the pre-litigation facts* which gave rise to the claims or defenses in the litigation. These are always important, if for no other reason than to remind the reader of the real world, flesh-and-blood implications of the legal issues put by the case. But they are often of less significance in civil procedure decisions than in those focusing on points of substantive law.

Instead, the crucial facts for us are *procedural facts*: what happened to the case after it was filed. The chronology of procedural steps taken by the litigants and the court is often important. For example, the pattern might be commencement of the litigation by the filing of a complaint, defendant's filing of a motion to dismiss the complaint for some reason, argument on the motion leading to its denial, fact-finding by the parties, trial, judgment for the plaintiff, and appeal by defendant (raising, among others, the same issue presented previously by motion). Retracing procedural steps is essential to understanding who's who, what has happened in the case, and how ripe procedural rulings are for review. It is also important to an appreciation of the tactical aspects of litigation.[60] It facilitates reconstruction of the alternatives available to the parties as the litigation progresses.

Thus, while an elaborate general fact description may be unnecessary in briefing most civil procedure cases, students should include a full statement of facts setting the *procedural posture* of the case. This statement should ordinarily indicate who is suing whom, facts which may be easier to diagram in the margin of the brief or the casebook itself. The student might use arrows to represent claims (and sometimes defenses) instead of describing the process narratively. Here is an illustration:

---

[60] *See* § 1.01[1], *supra.*

Figure 1-1

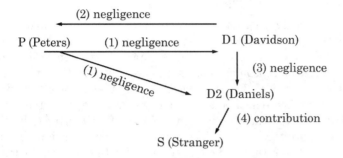

(Diagram shows that (1) Peters sued Davidson and Daniels for negligence, whereupon (2) Davidson counterclaimed against Peters and (3) cross-claimed against Daniels for negligence, and (4) Daniels impleaded Stranger on a theory of contribution.)

The chronology of procedural facts can be suggested by numbering the facts in the brief (as illustrated above) or in the case excerpt itself.

Next, it is useful to *identify the statutes or rules involved in the case*. Some study aids omit this step in briefing because they are geared primarily to briefing cases applying common law, not positive law (statutes or codified rules of procedure).[61]

For example, when you encounter positive federal law, consider the following approach. Read the cited statute or rule carefully, going to your rulebook if the text is not reproduced in the case itself. Is it clear from a reading of the provision how Congress intended to apply it to the case at hand? If so, has the court's decision given it that application? If it is not clear from a reading of the provision how Congress intended it to apply to the case at hand, has the court resolved the provision's ambiguity in a satisfactory way?

Third, the brief should *frame the issues presented by the case*. Many opinions do this expressly, but when the opinion is unclear, framing the issue is often the crucial step towards understanding the court's decision and its reasoning.

Fourth, the brief should *describe the court's decision on the issue at two levels*. The court will both supply an *answer* to the issue put by the case and make a formal *disposition* of the case, as noted often in the final paragraph. For example, when the issue is whether the plaintiff's complaint has stated a claim upon which relief can be granted, the court may decide that it does not and then grant the motion to dismiss and enter an order of dismissal. But this latter

---

[61] Since procedural decisions often turn on rules of positive law, a routine search for this material is a good briefing step. Note, on the other hand, that it is not useful and may even be harmful to attempt to paraphrase applicable positive law. Here there simply is no substitute for the actual language of the statute or rule. Nor is it enough to consider this kind of material in the abstract or in bulk at sporadic intervals during the semester. Students can best learn and understand statutes and rules of procedure in the context of particular case applications. It goes without saying that cases must be read with the rulebook close at hand.

disposition — an order of dismissal — need not go hand-in-hand with the decision of the issue. The court might instead grant the motion to dismiss with leave to plaintiff to amend his complaint.

Fifth, the brief should *describe and critique the reasoning articulated for the decision.* In describing the reasoning, the student should take full advantage of dissenting and concurring opinions, sometimes expressly written to limit the applicability of the court's reasoning. Presumptuous as it might seem at first, you must also evaluate the court's reasoning. This may take some effort, since students often arrive at law school believing that the laws they will study exist as part of a static natural order — like laws of physics. Unfortunately, this attitude permits no more than a superficial grasp of the law in civil procedure or other courses. It makes the student easy prey for the rhetoric in many judicial opinions that the result reached by the court is obvious. On the contrary, many cases — particularly those selected for casebook treatment — pose close and difficult questions. Great jurists may produce illuminating opinions, but they cannot make hard cases easy. What one often finds is "not a matter of right against wrong, but of right against right."[62]

This critical side of analysis and discussion is a good deal of what makes the course (and the professor) tick. Civil procedure professors strive to illustrate and teach the proposition that civil procedure involves hard choices. In turn, answers to examination questions must reflect judgment seasoned by an appreciation of both sides of the issue.[63] To respond, students cannot afford a passive approach to assigned materials.

The critique of the court's reasoning will be the most ambitious portion of your brief, the part most likely to require revision during and after civil procedure class. Don't worry. As noted earlier, unrevised case briefs are ultimately unreliable, anyway. The purpose of briefing is to enable you to get the most out of class and to stimulate (and ultimately reward) your critical thought. A marked up brief is evidence that the purpose was accomplished.

§ 1.04   OUTLINING IN CIVIL PROCEDURE

Outlining in preparation for examinations is an art that goes beyond the scope of this book. But a few principles of that art are especially pertinent to Civil Procedure.

First, a descriptive outline that paraphrases rules, summarizes cases, and condenses lecture notes in more or less chronological order may help you prepare for classes, but is unlikely to be very useful in preparing for exams. It may, more or less, describe the black letter law, but it does not help you

---

[62] Maurice Rosenberg, *Devising Procedures That Are Civil to Promote Justice That Is Civilized*, 69 MICH. L. REV. 797, 797 (1971).

[63] Contrary to what beginning students might assume, outright mistakes by students are fairly uncommon, at least in essay examinations. The difference between an "A" and a "C" examination more often lies in the imagination and agility demonstrated in applying course rules and concepts in a new setting, than in differences in bottom line conclusions. This demonstration is possible only with an approach to civil procedure that is both descriptive *and* critical.

"operationalize" it — synthesize it into an orderly process or template for solving problems. Even if you make a descriptive outline for day-to-day classes, you would need to reorganize (and probably shorten) it to make it a useful tool for problem-solving on exams. What is more useful is an "attack outline" — often consisting of a sequential series of inquiries or steps, or, for the engineers among you, even a flow chart or decision tree — for each particular type of problem (e.g., amendment; motions to dismiss for lack of personal jurisdiction; choice of federal or state law) in the course. To determine the proper inquiries or steps and their logical order, you need to synthesize rules and principles of cases and reorganize them after your own fashion. The process is arduous but rewarding. It will not only provide an approach to the kind of problems that are posed in exam questions (especially essay questions), and a guide to identifying the relevant facts, but also an outline for writing your answer.

Second, an attack outline should not simply paraphrase a rule. In the first place, it is always dangerous to paraphrase positive law — the plain words matter and often control; your paraphrases do not. You should always consult the actual language of pertinent rules and statutes instead of relying on a paraphrase or summary. In addition, the rules are not themselves always organized operationally — that is, in the sequence of steps by which they are applied — and sometimes key factors in the application of the rules are found not in the rule itself, but in the judicial gloss on the rule. You will therefore often need to reorganize a rule and add to it from the cases in order to operationalize it.

Finally, even if you choose not to outline or decide to outline in a different fashion, you should realize that you unavoidably do it anyway when you apply the rules to solve a civil litigation problem. The written attack outline is simply a map of a logical thought process or decision tree that informs legal analysis of a problem.

§ 1.05 RESEARCH AND DRAFTING IN CIVIL PROCEDURE

The starting point for research on any legal problem is to frame the issue tentatively, something that students rehearse in their preparation of case briefs.[64] For law students and beginning lawyers, even this step will sometimes prove difficult. When it does, it may be helpful to consult a civil procedure treatise like this one to frame the issue correctly and to identify relevant statutes or rules.

The second step is to read carefully any statutes or rules of procedure involved in your problem, noting when necessary any time frame for acting under them. It is difficult to overstate the importance of rereading the text of a rule or statute with each succeeding problem. This is because these provisions are drafted to cover a variety of situations arising in cases. A subsequent case thus may be governed by the same rule of procedure, yet the demands of the new controversy may illuminate a different portion of the text. As a result, even

---

[64] *See* § 1.03, *supra.*

experienced lawyers take the trouble to reread rules and statutes carefully.

For federal civil procedure problems, the third step is to consult the two federal practice treatises: J. Moore, *Moore's Federal Practice* (Matthew Bender) and C. Wright & A. Miller *et al.*, *Federal Practice and Procedure* (West). Both are organized primarily by federal rule number, providing easy access when the problem involves the federal rules.[65] Both also reproduce the Advisory Committee's notes that accompanied the rule and represent most of its legislative history. Federal courts often cite analyses and conclusions from these treatises, in recognition of their thoroughness and quality. Finally, both supply voluminous case citations, updated in pocket parts or inserts. Coverage overlaps considerably; yet style, analysis, and case coverage in the two are sufficiently distinct to justify examination of both in researching the typical problem of federal civil procedure. For the typical federal procedural issue, it is rarely wise to go to the cases directly without reading the relevant sections of the treatises. Their unusual thoroughness and authority sometimes supplies an answer without need of additional case research, and they will at least focus the case search and thus ultimately save time for the issues that they address.

Treatises on state procedural law also exist, although they tend to be less thorough and to be updated less frequently. When state statutes bear on the issue, one can review annotations to the relevant statutory code.[66] These steps will help reframe the problem, suggest a more or less detailed analysis, and generate lists of possibly relevant cases for further research. Another method of locating recent case authority for federal civil procedural rules is to use the *Federal Rules Service* (Callaghan), which digests cases by rule number.

With the development of computerized law research, however, the best way to generate a current case list and to review it is to use Lexis or Westlaw. Civil procedure problems that turn on statutes or rules are particularly well-suited to computer research, because it is easy to frame a search request around the statute or rule number. Students are cautioned, however, that there is no uniformity in judicial citation to such procedural law, and a complete search request must include in the alternative all of the likely variants. With regard to the Federal Rules of Civil Procedure, for example, these variants include at least "FRCP," "F. R. C. P.," "Fed. R. Civ. P.," "Rule," and "R." with the relevant number, and, ideally, some generic phrase to help exclude like-numbered federal rules of appellate or criminal procedure from the search.

For drafting problems involving the Federal Rules of Civil Procedure, students should consult the official appendix of forms immediately following the rules. These forms have been declared sufficient in federal practice by Rule 84. Students may also wish to examine unofficial forms. These may offer guidance in both state and federal practice.[67] They are collections of prior pleadings,

---

[65] These treatises also cover some statutory issues of federal procedure, including, notably, jurisdiction.

[66] Annotations for federal rules of procedure and federal procedural statutes may also be helpful. Most can be found in Title 28 of the *United States Code Annotated*.

[67] *See, e.g.*, AMERICAN JURISPRUDENCE PLEADING AND PRACTICE FORMS ANNOTATED (Lawyers Co-op.); LOUIS R. FRUMER & IRWIN HALL ET AL., BENDER'S FEDERAL PRACTICE FORMS (Matthew Bender);

motions or discovery requests. Most have passed muster at some time in a relevant court and may therefore serve as a form for current papers of the same kind.

For several reasons, such form books must be used with extreme caution and a heavy dose of common sense. First, unlike those in the official appendix to the federal rules, most published forms do not carry the imprimatur of any court system. All that stands behind many items memorialized as forms is that they worked once in a case. Close perusal of the fine print in the form books that give citations may reveal that the most recent approval of a particular form came in the nineteenth century. Arcane and dated wording in forms provides another danger signal. Second, because forms were originally created to meet the facts and demands of a different case, substantial adaptation is often necessary to make forms usable. Finally, a form may not have been selected for its brilliance, but for its (one-time) sufficiency. It may represent no more than the lowest common denominator. Still, form books (and, particularly in large law firms today, internally-generated forms and prior papers) are often a helpful starting point for procedural drafting.

§ 1.06 CIVIL PROCEDURE BIBLIOGRAPHY AND SHORT FORM CITATIONS

We cite in footnotes to the textbooks and articles on civil procedure that are useful sources for further reading. Several are cited often enough to warrant use of a short form citation. The following list gives the full citation for each such work, followed by the manner in which we cite it. We supply only the section numbers for these sources because the page numbers vary with succeeding editions.

I. *Hornbooks*

RICHARD D. FREER, INTRODUCTION TO CIVIL PROCEDURE (Aspen 2006) (*FREER*).

JACK H. FRIEDENTHAL, MARY KAY KANE & ARTHUR R. MILLER, CIVIL PROCEDURE (West 3d ed. 1999) (*FRIEDENTHAL, KANE, & MILLER*).

FLEMING JAMES, JR., JOHN LEUBSDORF, & GEOFFREY C. HAZARD, JR., CIVIL PROCEDURE (Little Brown 4th ed. 1992) (*JAMES, HAZARD, & LEUBSDORF*).

LARRY L. TEPLY & RALPH U. WHITTEN, CIVIL PROCEDURE (Foundation Press 3d ed. 2004) (*TEPLY & WHITTEN*).

CHARLES ALAN WRIGHT, LAW OF FEDERAL COURTS (West 5th ed. 1994) (*WRIGHT*).

BENDER'S FORMS OF DISCOVERY (Matthew Bender); FEDERAL PROCEDURAL FORMS LAWYERS EDITION (Lawyers Co-op); NICHOLS CYCLOPEDIA OF FEDERAL PROCEDURE FORMS (Callaghan); WEST'S FEDERAL FORMS (West).

II. *Treatises*

CHARLES ALAN WRIGHT & ARTHUR R. MILLER, FEDERAL PRACTICE AND PROCE-DURE (West) (*WRIGHT & MILLER*; volume number omitted because section numbers are unique). In rare cases where quoted material is taken from a prior edition, we have left a full citation.

JAMES WM. MOORE, MOORE'S FEDERAL PRACTICE (Matthew Bender 3d ed.) (*MOORE*; volume number omitted where section number is keyed to a Federal Rule of Civil Procedure). In rare cases where quoted material is taken from a prior edition of *MOORE*, we have left a full citation.

Chapter 2

SELECTING A COURT — AN INTRODUCTION

§ 2.01 THE CHOICES: STATE AND FEDERAL JUDICIAL SYSTEMS

After a lawyer has agreed to represent a prospective plaintiff and tentatively identified one or more legal "theory" of recovery, she must select the court in which to sue. This decision is enriched and complicated in the United States by the existence not only of fifty-one separate state judicial systems,[1] but also of the federal judicial system. Before we can introduce the factors that affect the choice, we need to describe these alternatives.

It is easiest to start with the federal system, because it is simplest. There are three layers of federal courts. At the bottom lie the federal district courts. These are courts of *original jurisdiction*, so called because they are where judicial cases originate — where they are filed and initially tried.[2] The district courts, like all federal courts, are also courts of *limited subject matter jurisdiction*, in that statutes authorize them to hear only certain kinds of cases.[3] The most important are those involving questions of federal law ("federal question cases") and those involving state law claims valued at more than $75,000 between citizens of different states ("diversity cases").[4] The district courts are assigned to districts whose geographic boundaries correspond with those of the smallest states or with parts of the larger states.[5] For example, the federal trial courts for New York are the United States District Courts for the Southern, Eastern, Western and Northern Districts of New York.

United States Courts of Appeals make up the middle layer.[6] They are courts of *appellate jurisdiction*, so called because they are authorized only to review decisions which come to them on appeal from district courts,[7] certain special-

---

[1] The District of Columbia was given its own judicial system by District of Columbia Court Reform and Criminal Procedure Act of 1970, Pub. L. 91-358, 84 Stat. 473 (codified in scattered sections of 28 U.S.C.).

[2] Cases may also originate in administrative agencies or in certain specialized courts created by Congress. *E.g.*, 28 U.S.C. §§ 171–179 (Court of Federal Claims); 28 U.S.C. §§ 1581–1585 (Court of International Trade).

[3] *See* § 5.01 (subject matter jurisdiction), *infra*.

[4] *See* § 5.01[2] (federal jurisdiction in general); §§ 5.02–5.06 (particulars of federal question and diversity jurisdiction), *infra*.

[5] *See* 28 U.S.C. § 133.

[6] On appellate systems generally, see § 13.07, *infra*.

[7] *See* 28 U.S.C. §§ 1291–1292.

ized federal courts, or federal administrative agencies. The country is divided into twelve geographic circuits,[8] and appeals from the district courts in each circuit are taken to the court of appeals for that circuit. Appeals from many of the administrative agencies go to the Court of Appeals for the D.C. Circuit, while appeals from various specialized federal courts[9] are taken to a thirteenth circuit called the Court of Appeals for the Federal Circuit.[10]

The United States Supreme Court sits atop the federal system. It has original jurisdiction over cases affecting ambassadors and in which states are parties, and appellate jurisdiction in all others.[11] While most appellate jurisdiction exercised by federal courts of appeal is *mandatory*, meaning that a court of appeals must accept a properly filed appeal, the Supreme Court's appellate jurisdiction is chiefly discretionary, meaning that it is free to decide whether to hear an appeal by granting a party's petition to it for a writ of certiorari ("granting cert").[12]

State judicial systems have three or four layers. At the bottom are usually a variety of courts of *limited or special subject matter jurisdiction*, authorized, for example, to hear only traffic, landlord-tenant, small claims or probate cases. All states also have one court of original and *general jurisdiction* that hears all claims not exclusively vested in courts of limited jurisdiction. These claims may include state claims and nonexclusive federal question claims that also could have been brought in federal district courts. State courts of general jurisdiction often exist at the county level, but their designations differ widely. In the District of Columbia, for example, they are called the superior courts, in Virginia circuit courts, and in New York (somewhat perversely) supreme courts. To add to the confusion, in some states these courts also enjoy some form of appellate jurisdiction over cases originally brought in state courts of limited jurisdiction.

State systems have at least one more layer, a court of exclusively or predominantly appellate jurisdiction at the top of their judicial systems, variously called the supreme court, the court of appeals, or, in Massachusetts, the Supreme Judicial Court. Many more populous states also have an intermediate appellate layer, roughly corresponding to courts of appeals in the federal system. Most of these intermediate state appellate courts were created to relieve the caseload burden on the highest state courts. Jurisdiction in inferior state appellate courts is usually mandatory, leaving the highest state court in the system to exercise considerable discretion in selecting cases for further review, much like the United States Supreme Court.[13]

On matters of state law, the highest state court has the last word. However, the United States Supreme Court has the authority to review state court

---

[8] *See* 28 U.S.C. § 41.

[9] *See* note 2, *supra*.

[10] *See* 28 U.S.C §§ 1292(c), 1295.

[11] U.S. Const. art. III, § 2.

[12] On appellate systems generally, *see* § 13.07, *infra*.

[13] On appellate systems generally, see § 13.07, *infra*.

rulings on the meaning and application of federal law. This creates the possibility of a level above state high courts in federal question adjudications. In practice, the possibility is remote because the Supreme Court usually denies review.[14] This means that the highest state courts, as well as the federal courts of appeal, are, as a practical matter, courts of last resort in many federal question cases.[15]

The coexistence of state and federal judicial systems may present the claimant with a choice of forums. A federal court option exists if the claim exceeds $75,000, and the prospective plaintiff and defendants are from different states,[16] or if the claim involves certain questions of federal law.[17] The option of trial in state court is less restricted, available except in the relatively few situations where federal courts enjoy exclusive subject matter jurisdiction.[18] And, as we shall examine in the next section, geographic affiliations of the parties or claims may offer the claimant the choice of state and federal courts in more than one state.

§ 2.02   FACTORS INFLUENCING THE SELECTION OF A COURT

Every first year law student intuitively senses that it would be unfair to require a Vermonter who has never been to or had contact with Alaska to defend a lawsuit brought there. The law acknowledges that unfairness by limiting a court's *personal jurisdiction* (the power to issue a judgment binding a person or affecting his property), requiring some voluntary contact or

---

[14] The Supreme Court has traditionally kept abreast of its workload. Yet the Court has managed this in recent years only by refusing to review a large number of cases properly within its appellate jurisdiction. *See generally* Erwin N. Griswold, *Rationing Justice — The Supreme Court's Caseload and What the Court Does Not Do*, 60 CORNELL L. REV. 335 (1975).

[15] Due to its sparing exercise of its discretionary certiorari jurisdiction, the Supreme Court hears only a small number of federal question cases. Even in 1976, scholars asserted that "Supreme Court review has become an exceedingly unlikely event in most federal litigation." PAUL D. CARRINGTON, DANIEL J. MEADOR & MAURICE ROSENBERG, JUSTICE ON APPEAL 209 (1976) (citations omitted). The numbers still bear this out. In 2006, the Supreme Court reviewed only 0.39% of federal appeals court dispositions of civil suits, and only 1.3% of cases in which petitions for certiorari were filed. Of almost 12,000 appeals terminated, petitions were filed in 3452 cases, and granted in 79, of which only 47 resulted in actual reviews. *See* ADMINISTRATIVE OFFICE OF U.S. COURTS, JUDICIAL BUSINESS OF THE UNITED STATES COURTS, *IN* ANNUAL REPORT OF THE DIRECTOR, ADMINISTRATIVE OFFICE OF THE U.S. COURTS, tables B-1A, B-2 (2006). This has placed federal courts of appeal in a position "to create and to balkanize national law." Alan Betten, *Institutional Reform in the Federal Courts*, 52 IND. L.J. 63, 68 (1976). Fewer data exist on Supreme Court supervision of federal question decisions in state courts, but the lack of effective supervision there appears to be at least as pronounced. *See generally* Preble Stolz, *Federal Review of State Court Decisions of Federal Questions: The Need for Additional Appellate Capacity*, 64 CALIF. L. REV. 943 (1976).

[16] *See* §§ 5.04–5.06 (diversity jurisdiction), *infra*.

[17] *See* § 5.03 *infra*.

[18] Plaintiffs can bring certain cases (federal antitrust, patent and copyright, bankruptcy, etc.) only in federal court. For a discussion of the scope and intended purposes of exclusive federal jurisdiction, see MARTIN H. REDISH, FEDERAL JURISDICTION: TENSIONS IN THE ALLOCATION OF JUDICIAL POWER 149–56 (2d ed. 1990); ALI, STUDY OF THE DIVISION OF JURISDICTION BETWEEN STATE AND FEDERAL COURTS 182–86 (1969).

political affiliation between the defendant and the *forum state* in which the action is brought. Historically, the principal basis for and limitation upon personal jurisdiction was territorial, hence our adoption of the term *territorial jurisdiction* as a generic description for this requirement. Chapter 3 discusses this essential factor in selecting a court.

We considered in the last section how the coexistence of state and federal judicial systems creates the possibility of choice within the same geographical area, choice limited by the constraints of *subject matter* jurisdiction. Chapter 5 discusses this factor. Of obvious interest to the plaintiff's lawyer, it also controls opportunities for the defendant to *remove* the action against him from state to federal court, as discussed in § 5.07.

The defendant's concerns over the convenience of the forum selected by plaintiff are also entitled to recognition. Beyond that, the judicial system as a whole has an efficiency interest in shifting litigation to the most generally convenient locations. These interests are served by the law of *venue*, discussed in Chapter 6.

Lawyers take these legal constraints into account in deciding where to file suit. They also consider a variety of tactical factors.[19] When legal constraints permit a choice, tactical factors should control the decision where to file.

One obvious tactical factor is the identity of the judge who will preside over the litigation. The manner in which cases are assigned to particular judges is often too random to permit accurate prediction. Yet lawyers frequently can make useful comparisons about the quality of judges in different kinds of courts. Some have argued, for example, that the kinds of cases brought in federal court, as well as the appointment process, life tenure, prestige, salary, and research resources of federal judges attract persons to the federal bench who are more capable and less susceptible to majoritarian pressures than those attracted to the state bench.[20] Lawyers given a choice thus tend to file civil rights actions in federal rather than state courts.[21]

The court's calendar can also be a tactical concern. In 2006, for example, the median time from commencement of a civil action to disposition at trial in

---

[19] *See generally* James A. Dooley, *Selecting the Forum — Plaintiff's Position*, 3 AM. JUR. TRIALS 553 (1963); Victor E. Flango, *Attorneys' Perspectives on Choice of Forum in Diversity Cases*, 25 AKRON L. REV. 41 (1991); Josh H. Groce, *Selecting the Forum — Defendant's Position*, 3 AM. JUR. TRIALS 611 (1963); RALPH C. MCCULLOUGH & JAMES L. UNDERWOOD, CIVIL TRIAL MANUAL 2 at 89–140 (2d ed. 1980); Marvin R. Summers, *Analysis of Factors That Influence Choice of Forum in Diversity Cases*, 47 IOWA L. REV. 933 (1962); Note, *Forum Shopping Reconsidered*, 103 HARV. L. REV. 1677 (1990).

[20] *Compare, e.g.*, Thomas B. Marvell, *The Rationales for Federal Question Jurisdiction: An Empirical Examination of Student Rights Litigation*, 1984 WIS. L. REV. 1315 (lawyers representing students select federal courts because they are more protective of student rights), *and* Burt Neuborne, *The Myth of Parity*, 90 HARV. L. REV. 1105 (1977) (federal courts are superior to state courts in protecting federal rights), *with* Michael E. Solimine & James L. Walker, *Constitutional Litigation in Federal and State Courts: An Empirical Analysis of Judicial Parity*, 10 HASTINGS CONST. L.Q. 213 (1983) (state courts are no more hostile to vindication of federal rights than federal courts).

[21] *See, e.g.*, Neuborne, note 20, *supra*.

federal district courts ranged from one month in the fastest district to almost twenty-three months in the slowest.[22] A plaintiff's lawyer anxious to move the case through trial might file it in one of the faster federal district courts or opt instead for a state court with a better trial calendar.

Sundry procedural differences between courts may also influence court selection.[23] Extensive provision in the federal rules for discovery — court-supported fact-gathering by the parties — may attract some lawyers who need discovery to develop their cases and discourage others who already command the facts or whose clients are averse to discovery of *their* facts. Many other procedural factors — including the availability of jury trial, the composition of jury panels, the required level of agreement for verdicts, the applicable rules of evidence, and the availability of appellate review — can influence court selection. Of course, a lawyer's familiarity with procedures of particular courts also influences her choice of court.

Client characteristics may also be an important consideration in choice of court. Some lawyers prefer federal courts when their client is from outside the state.[24] One study suggests that client characteristics along with quality of judges and convenience, in fact, are the most important reasons lawyers choose one forum over another, outweighing procedural considerations.[25]

Finally, the substantive law that courts will apply can be a crucial factor in forum choice. Although there is much support in modern choice-of-law theory for the idea that the law chosen in a case should not vary according to where the case is tried, local choice-of-law ("conflicts") rules and the manner in which they are applied do not always reflect this idea. This can be an enormous incentive for interstate forum-shopping in search of favorable substantive law.[26] Chapter 7 discusses the choice of applicable law in federal court, while the conflict of laws in general is treated in a companion to this volume.[27]

Although every plaintiff shops for a forum in selecting a court in which to sue (given a choice), courts sometimes decry "forum-shopping," almost imbuing it with a sense of impropriety. But as long as the intersection of jurisdictional rules and venue results in forum choices, parties will necessarily have to make them. Indeed, the *Model Rules of Professional Conduct* comment that a lawyer has a "duty to use legal procedure for the fullest benefit of the client's cause,"[28] leading one scholar to assert that this duty "may include selecting a forum with little connection to the events giving rise to a cause of action if that forum is an

---

[22] 2006 ADMIN. OFF. U.S. COURTS ANNUAL REPORT OF THE DIR. Table C-5.

[23] *See generally* Dooley, note 19, *supra*, §§ 19–39; Groce, note 19, *supra*, §§ 9–15.

[24] *See* Flango, note 19, *supra*, at 105. *See* § 5.04, *infra*.

[25] Flango, note 19, *supra*, at 105.

[26] For a survey of developments, see Gene R. Shreve, *Choice of Law and the Forgiving Constitution*, 71 IND. L.J. 271 (1996).

[27] *See generally* WILLIAM M. RICHMAN & WILLIAM L. REYNOLDS, UNDERSTANDING CONFLICT OF LAWS Ch. 4 (3d ed. 2002).

[28] AMERICAN BAR ASS'N, MODEL RULES OF PROFESSIONAL CONDUCT AND CODE OF JUDICIAL CONDUCT Rule 3.1 cmt. 1 (1983).

acceptable forum under the law, despite the fact that the attorney may be accused of taking advantage of 'loopholes' or 'technicalities.' "[29] To put it in terms of our analogy in Chapter One of litigation to a game, "The rules in litigation include the plaintiff's ability to choose which set of rules will govern the game" by choosing the forum.[30] These rules guard against any resulting unfairness, as we shall see. If they waste resources by providing too many choices, the best solution is probably to go after the rules, not the lawyers who use them.

---

[29] Mary Garvey Algero, *In Defense of Forum Shopping: A Realistic Look at Selecting a Venue*, 78 Neb. L. Rev. 79, 106 (1999).

[30] Debra Lyn Bassett, *The Forum Game*, 84 N.C. L. Rev. 333, 336 (2006).

Chapter 3

A COURT WITH JURISDICTION OVER PERSONS AND THINGS

§ 3.01 PRELIMINARY OBSERVATIONS

[1] How and Why Problems of Territorial Jurisdiction Arise

The function of civil litigation is to dispose of controversies by subjecting them to a formal, authoritative process. The process works by ultimately producing binding judgments.[1] For reasons that shall become clear, however, courts cannot be free to issue binding judgments in every civil action filed — no matter where the cause of action arose and no matter where the defendant resides. They are restrained by limitations on *territorial jurisdiction*[2] (courts' jurisdiction over persons and things). We will frequently substitute for territorial jurisdiction a narrower term, *personal jurisdiction* (jurisdiction over persons only).[3]

---

[1] *See generally* Chapter 15, *infra*. This is true unless the case settles or is dismissed without prejudice prior to final judgment.

[2] "Other names for this or similar concepts include judicial jurisdiction, adjudicatory jurisdiction, adjudicatory authority, amenability, nexus, and substantive due process." Kevin M. Clermont, *Restating Territorial Jurisdiction and Venue for State and Federal Courts*, 66 CORNELL L. REV. 411, 412 n.5 (1981). Many courts also use amenability to service of process or "subject to service" as a synonym for territorial jurisdiction, and Congress has sometimes used the terminology of "process" to confer nationwide territorial jurisdiction on federal courts for certain claims. *See, e.g.,* 28 U.S.C. § 2361 (interpleader); 15 U.S.C. § 77V(a) (Securities Act of 1933). The latter terminology can be confusing because service of process can often technically be accomplished (by certified mail, special process server or conformity with foreign service procedures) even in the absence of territorial jurisdiction. Fed. R. Civ. P. 12(b) reflects this possibility by separately listing the defenses of lack of personal jurisdiction and improper service.

On differences between the American law of personal jurisdiction and equivalent rules abroad, see, *e.g.,* Patrick J. Borchers, *Comparing Personal Jurisdiction in the United States and the European Community: Lessons for American Reform*, 40 AM. J. COMP. L. 121 (1992); Linda Silberman, *Comparative Jurisdiction in the International Context*, 52 DEPAUL L. REV. 319 (2002); Kevin M. Clermont, *A Global Law of Jurisdiction and Judgments*, 37 CORNELL INT'L L.J. 1 (2004).

[3] The term "personal jurisdiction" derives from *in personam* jurisdiction, one of three traditional categories of territorial jurisdiction. The other two are *in rem* and *quasi in rem* jurisdiction. *See* § 3.02, *infra*. By far the largest number of cases entertained by courts are founded on personal jurisdiction. The Supreme Court's decisions setting limits on personal jurisdiction have added importance because it has extended them to all forms of territorial jurisdiction. *See* § 3.08, *infra*. These developments have encouraged interchangeable use of the terms territorial jurisdiction and personal jurisdiction. We will follow this approach in the text when the context permits.

Consider the following example. A, a citizen of Hawaii, travels to New York City on business. A steps off of a curb into the path of an automobile driven by B. A receives medical treatment in New York, returns to Hawaii and files suit there for medical expenses incurred in New York resulting from the accident. Service of process in the Hawaii case reaches B in New York by mail. B is a lifetime citizen of New York state. He does no business in Hawaii, owns no property there, and has never visited the state.

Can a Hawaii court entertain this case? No. The Hawaii court would clearly lack personal jurisdiction. Even without benefit of details of the law of personal jurisdiction which follow, we can see why a Hawaii court should not have the power to hear the case. It would add substantially to B's burden of being a defendant for him to have to defend against A's claim in far-away Hawaii. Neither B nor the facts of the controversy have any connection with Hawaii which would suggest that imposition of Hawaii jurisdiction would not be justified. B could go to Hawaii and question the Hawaii court's personal jurisdiction there, but even this would unfairly burden him. The law of personal jurisdiction should and does permit B to sit tight in New York, take no part in the Hawaii proceeding, and successfully resist a Hawaii default judgment[4] if A ever presents it for enforcement in New York.[5]

But what if we change the facts of the example? Suppose that B (not A) was the traveler, that B struck A while B was driving a rented car in Hawaii. Now the Hawaii court clearly has personal jurisdiction. Can you see why?[6] Or suppose we leave the accident in New York, but give B a condominium in Hawaii. Could B as safely assume that the Hawaii court lacked jurisdiction?[7] Even if B had a substantial personal jurisdiction argument to make, would it still be wise for him to refuse to appear and raise it in the Hawaii case?[8]

[2] Law Which Limits the Reach of Courts' Territorial Jurisdiction

[a] State Courts

The primary restraint on the territorial jurisdiction of state courts is the Due Process Clause of the Fourteenth Amendment to the United States Constitution. In "opaque few words,"[9] the Clause provides that "[n]o State shall . . . deprive any person of life, liberty, or property, without due process of law. . . . " A claim is "property" within the meaning of the Clause, which

---

[4] A default judgment may be entered when a defendant fails to respond to the complaint in any manner. *See* FED. R. CIV. P. 55.

[5] *See* § 3.04 (the jurisdictional challenge), *infra.*

[6] Hawaii's authority to impose jurisdiction on B derives from a regulatory concern over acts committed in the forum state. *See* § 3.10 (specific jurisdiction), *infra.*

[7] Maybe not. *See* § 3.11 (general jurisdiction), *infra.*

[8] No. *See* § 3.04[3][b] (tactical considerations in collateral attack), *infra.*

[9] Kevin M. Clermont, *A Global Law of Jurisdiction and Judgments: Views from the United States and Japan*, 37 CORNELL INT'L L.J. 1, 2 (2004).

cannot be forfeited through state proceedings lacking due process.[10] The protections of due process are similarly available to those against whom claims are made.[11]

The Due Process Clause also affords litigants rights to notice and the opportunity to be heard in state court.[12] These rights, however, are secured by a branch of due process doctrine separate and distinct from that which governs territorial jurisdiction.[13]

The concerns which give the Due Process Clause life in the territorial jurisdiction setting are more elusive and less agreed upon by courts and commentators.[14]

There is agreement, however, that the Due Process Clause should protect the nonresident[15] defendant from suffering unreasonably from plaintiff's choice of forum. To uphold jurisdiction in the state forum selected by plaintiff at the very least forces the defendant to go there and move for a *forum non conveniens* dismissal — a dismissal on the ground that there is a more convenient place for the litigation.[16] When a court exercises its considerable discretion to deny the motion, defendant is forced to litigate the merits in the courts of that state.

State law may set additional limits on the reach of state courts' territorial jurisdiction.[17] Most state courts enjoy only as much territorial jurisdiction over nonresident defendants as their legislatures have chosen to confer by statute.

---

[10] *Logan v. Zimmerman Brush Co.*, 455 U.S. 422, 428–29 (1982).

[11] "Any claim asserted by a plaintiff is simply the reverse side of what is at stake to the defendant; the same property is at stake for both." James R. Pielemeier, *Due Process Limitations on the Application of Collateral Estoppel Against Nonparties to Prior Litigation*, 63 B.U. L. Rev. 383, 398 (1983).

[12] *See* Chapter 4, *infra*.

[13] The Supreme Court explained and compared the two branches of due process doctrine in *Phillips Petroleum Co. v. Shutts*, 472 U.S. 797 (1985), concluding that the passive members of plaintiffs' nationwide class were entitled to due process protections of notice and the opportunity to be heard, but that the minimum contacts constraint imposed by due process on personal jurisdiction did not apply to their claims. For discussions of the case, see Arthur R. Miller & David Crump, *Jurisdiction and Choice of Law in Multistate Class Actions*, 96 Yale L.J. 1 (1986); John E. Kennedy, *The Supreme Court Meets the Bride of Frankenstein: Phillips Petroleum Co. v. Shutts and the Multistate State Class Action*, 34 Kan. L. Rev. 255 (1985); § 9.09[3][b], *infra*.

[14] Critics include A. Benjamin Spencer, *Jurisdiction to Adjudicate: A Revised Analysis*, 73 U. Chi. L. Rev. 617, 618 (2006) ("[T]he law of personal jurisdiction has blossomed into an incoherent and precarious doctrine that many commentators have long vilified as being in need of reform."), and Linda S. Simard, *Meeting Expectations: Two Profiles for Specific Jurisdiction*, 38 Ind. L. Rev. 343, 344 (2005) ("[T]he doctrine of personal jurisdiction is largely in a state of disarray.").

[15] Most significant territorial jurisdiction cases involve defendants who do not reside in the forum state. The distinction between the concepts of *residence* and *citizenship* is unclear. *See* § 3.03[1] (suit in defendant's home state), *infra*. However, it is at least true that the Due Process Clause poses no significant obstacle to the forum state's exercise of territorial jurisdiction over its own citizens.

[16] *See* § 6.02[1], *infra*.

[17] For a discussion of state law regulation of personal jurisdiction, see § 3.07[1] (state long-arm statutes), *infra*.

It is therefore possible that the statutory scheme could leave the courts of a state short of the full scope of authority over nonresident defendants permitted under federal constitutional law. In practice, however, this does not seem to be much of a problem. All states now have so-called *long-arm statutes* which endow their courts with all or nearly all the jurisdictional authority permitted by due process.[18]

[b]   Federal Courts

The Fourteenth Amendment does not apply to federal courts. The authority of federal courts is limited by the Due Process Clause appearing in the Fifth Amendment to the Constitution. But the Constitution does not limit federal courts to the same degree. It is at least arguable that the Fifth Amendment permits federal courts to exercise territorial jurisdiction over all United States citizens,[19] permitting greater geographical reach than the Fourteenth Amendment permits state courts.[20]

The current difference in the reach of process, however, is not great. This is because federal courts are as dependent as their state counterparts on the legislative branch to delegate their powers by statute,[21] and Congress has created nationwide territorial jurisdiction for federal courts in only a few special circumstances.[22] Absent such a statute, federal courts will in most cases be limited to the jurisdictional reach of a local state court. This limitation results from Rule 4's provision that service or waiver of service will establish jurisdiction over any defendant "who is subject to the [territorial] jurisdiction of a court of general [subject matter] jurisdiction in the state where the district

---

[18] § 3.07[1] (state long-arm statutes), *infra*.

[19] The principle that defendants submit to territorial jurisdiction in exchange for the benefits of forum citizenship is most fully developed in the law of state court jurisdiction. *See* § 3.03[1] (suit in defendant's home state), *infra*. But the Supreme Court has also applied the principle to uphold a federal court's territorial jurisdiction over a United States citizen. *Blackmer v. United States*, 284 U.S. 421 (1932).

[20] For differing views, compare Robert H. Abrams, *Power, Convenience, and the Elimination of Personal Jurisdiction in the Federal Courts*, 58 IND. L.J. 1 (1982) (supporting the point), JAMES, HAZARD & LEUBSDORF § 2.34 (same), with Maryellen Fullerton, *Constitutional Limits on Nationwide Personal Jurisdiction in the Federal Courts*, 79 NW. U. L. REV. 1 (1984) (questioning whether the Fifth Amendment should permit a federal court to exercise territorial jurisdiction if the Fourteenth Amendment would prevent exercise of territorial jurisdiction by a state court in the same locale), and Lea Brilmayer & Charles Norchi, *Federal Extraterritoriality and Fifth Amendment Due Process*, 105 HARV. L. REV. 1217, 1262 (1992) (arguing that Fifth Amendment constraints should in significant part be "parallel to those of the Fourteenth Amendment").

[21] G.W. Foster, Jr., *Long-Arm Jurisdiction in Federal Courts*, 1969 WIS. L. REV. 9, 11. *Cf.* Note, *Alien Corporations and Aggregate Contacts: A Genuinely Federal Jurisdictional Standard*, 95 HARV. L. REV. 470, 470 (1981) ("[I]n federal cases it is for Congress to determine whether a defendant is amenable to service and to establish the manner in which process may be served."). *Accord, Omni Capital Int'l v. Rudolf Wolff & Co., Ltd.*, 484 U.S. 97 (1987).

[22] Thus, 28 U.S.C. § 2361 permits nationwide service of process in federal statutory interpleader proceedings. For a discussion of additional federal statutes authorizing nationwide service of process, see Jon Heller, Note, *Pendent Personal Jurisdiction and Nationwide Service of Process*, 64 N.Y.U. L. REV. 113 (1989).

court is located . . . ."[23] This provision effectively incorporates the forum state's law of personal jurisdiction, as well as the constitutional limitations upon it. By this indirect route, federal judges usually find themselves laboring under the same Fourteenth Amendment due process and state law limitations as their state court counterparts.[24] This means that federal courts often do not direct their concerns over territorial jurisdiction to a body of distinctly federal law.[25] This is in marked contrast to the preeminent role federal law plays in resolving questions of federal subject matter jurisdiction.[26]

The situation described above changed to a slight degree with the 1993 amendment of Rule 4 authorizing nationwide service of process in some cases brought under federal courts' federal question jurisdiction.[27] Relatively few cases, however, are likely to be affected by the amendment. It represents a "narrow extension of the federal reach. . . ."[28]

---

[23] Rule 4(k)(1)(A). In limited circumstances involving parties added by impleader or compulsory joinder, Rule 4(k)(1)(B) permits service of process up to 100 miles from the federal court — whether or not the same service would have been possible in a local state case.

[24] *See generally* Robert C. Casad, *Personal Jurisdiction in Federal Question Cases*, 70 TEX. L. REV. 1589 (1992). With a limited exception discussed *infra*, Rule 4 makes no distinction between federal diversity and federal question cases. While incorporation of state court jurisdictional limitations has been applauded in the former, Arthur T. von Mehren & Donald T. Trautman, *Jurisdiction to Adjudicate: A Suggested Analysis*, 79 HARV. L. REV. 1121, 1123–25 n.6 (1966), it has been criticized as too confining in federal question cases, particularly those involving alien defendants. *Alien Corporations*, note 21, *supra*; Ronan E. Degnan & Mary K. Kane, *The Exercise of Jurisdiction Over and Enforcement of Judgments Against Alien Defendants*, 39 HASTINGS L.J. 799 (1988); Brian B. Frasch, Comment, *National Contacts as a Basis for In Personam Jurisdiction Over Aliens in Federal Question Suits*, 70 CAL. L. REV. 686 (1982).

[25] *See, e.g., Burger King v. Rudzewicz*, 471 U.S. 462 (1985) (sufficiency of a federal court's territorial jurisdiction measured under Florida's long-arm statute); *Keeton v. Hustler Magazine*, 465 U.S. 770 (1984) (the same under New Hampshire's long-arm statute).

[26] For a particularly helpful discussion of the differences between territorial jurisdiction and subject matter jurisdiction in the federal courts, see *Insurance Corp. of Ireland, Ltd. v. Compagnie des Bauxites de Guinee*, 456 U.S. 694 (1982).

[27] Rule 4(k)(2) now states:

For a claim that arises under federal law, serving a summons or filing a waiver of service establishes personal jurisdiction over a defendant if: (A) the defendant is not subject to jurisdiction in any state's courts of general jurisdiction; and (B) exercising jurisdiction is consistent with the United States Constitution and laws.

[28] Rule 4 Advisory Committee notes (1993). The relative unimportance of the change can be explained as follows. Since defendants incorporated in or citizens of a state are subject to jurisdiction in that state, *see* § 3.03[1], *infra*, only aliens appear to fit within the category created in Rule 4(k)(2). Moreover, aliens would be subject to the new subsection only when minimum contacts existed between them and the United States *but* did not exist between them and any state. William M. Richman, *Carnival Cruise Lines: Forum Selection Clauses in Adhesion Contracts*, 40 AM. J. OF COMP. L. 977, 977 n.1 (1992). For a survey of lower federal court decisions under Rule 4(k)(2), see Dora A. Corby, *Putting Personal Jurisdiction Within Reach: Just What Has Rule 4(k)(2) Done for the Personal Jurisdiction of Federal Courts?*, 30 MCGEORGE L. REV. 167 (1998). A particularly helpful approach can be found in *ISI Int'l, Inc. v. Borden Ladner Gervais LLP*, 256 F.3d 548, 552 (7th Cir. 2001). The court stated that "[a] defendant who wants to preclude use of Rule 4(k)(2) has only to name some other state in which the suit could proceed. Naming a more appropriate state would amount to a consent to personal jurisdiction there." The court added: "If,

PART A.
Received Traditions

The most significant modern developments in the law of territorial jurisdiction are those advancing (or limiting) the idea that nonresident, nonconsenting defendants who cannot be found and served within the forum can nonetheless be subject to the court's authority. We will treat Supreme Court cases that bear on this in parts B and C of this chapter. Important as these cases are, alone they are inadequate to explain the law of territorial jurisdiction. The Court has rested its major decisions in part on principles which it appears to assume the reader will grasp without much explanation. It is essential to understand this material, surveyed in Part A, both to learn about important aspects of current law untreated by the Court's recent decisions and to better understand the decisions themselves. We begin in § 3.02 with an introduction to the three categories of territorial jurisdiction that evolved by the beginning of this century. Section 3.03 focuses on the most significant of the three, personal jurisdiction, examining current means of obtaining personal jurisdiction that antedate modern theory. In § 3.04 we consider the timing of jurisdictional challenges, an important aspect of modern practice, which supplies additional context for the subjects presented in parts B and C.

§ 3.02 THREE CATEGORIES OF TERRITORIAL JURISDICTION

Historically, American courts have enjoyed three types of territorial juris-diction: *in personam*,[29] *in rem*,[30] and *quasi in rem*.[31] The United States Supreme Court once distinguished the three as follows:

> A judgment *in personam* imposes a personal liability or obligation on one person in favor of another. A judgment *in rem* affects the interests of all persons in designated property. A judgment *quasi in rem* affects the interests of particular persons in designated property. The relative significance of these categories has changed since the Court's obser-vation. But each has survived into contemporary law and the essential features of each remain unchanged.[32]

---

however, the defendant contends that he cannot be sued in the forum state and refuses to identify any other where suit is possible, then the federal court is entitled to use Rule 4(k)(2)."

[29] *See* Joseph J. Kalo, *Jurisdiction as an Evolutionary Process: The Development of Quasi In Rem and In Personam Principles*, 1978 Duke L.J. 1147; Philip B. Kurland, *The Supreme Court, the Due Process Clause and the In Personam Jurisdiction of State Courts — From Pennoyer to Denckla: A Review*, 25 U. Chi. L. Rev. 569 (1958).

[30] *See* Hans Smit, *The Enduring Utility of In Rem Rules: A Lasting Legacy of Pennoyer v. Neff*, 43 Brook. L. Rev. 600 (1977).

[31] *See Kalo*, note 29, *supra*; William R. Slomanson, *Real Property Unrelated to Claim: Due Process for Quasi In Rem Jurisdiction?*, 83 Dick. L. Rev. 51 (1978).

[32] *Hanson v. Denckla*, 357 U.S. 235, 246 n.12 (1958).

[1]   *In Personam* Jurisdiction

In personam jurisdiction, also called personal jurisdiction or jurisdiction over the person, provides courts with a basis for entirely determining controversies involving personal obligations (often tort or contract claims). Because the court's jurisdiction is over the person of the defendant, it can impose judgment indebtedness upon him to the full extent of the wrong done to the plaintiff. If an *in personam* judgment for damages cannot be fully satisfied where rendered,[33] plaintiff may collect the unsatisfied portion of the judgment in any other state or federal court.[34]

[2]   *In Rem* Jurisdiction

In rem jurisdiction focuses not on the person of the defendant but on some property located within the forum. Courts use this form of jurisdiction to adjudicate questions concerning the ownership and control of such property — to settle questions, it is sometimes said, against the whole world.[35] Theoretically, the function of *in rem* jurisdiction is to act upon the thing, or *res*, itself, rather than to act directly upon rights of individuals. This is an artificial distinction, since both types affect the rights of others to the property.

[3]   *Quasi in Rem* Jurisdiction

Like *in rem* jurisdiction, *quasi in rem* jurisdiction operates on property located within the forum and not directly against the person of individual defendants. Like an *in rem* judgment, a *quasi in rem* judgment binds the parties only with reference to their interests in the property (*res*) upon which jurisdiction is based.[36] Thus, the value of a *quasi in rem* judgment cannot exceed the value of the *res*.

---

[33] For the manner in which judgments are enforced, see § 15.02, *infra*.

[34] "The Full Faith and Credit Clause makes the valid *in personam* judgment of one State enforceable in all other States." *Shaffer v. Heitner*, 433 U.S. 186, 210 (1977). Federal statutory law requires that the same respect be given to state judgments in federal court and to federal judgments in either state or other federal courts. See § 15.10, *infra*.

[35] "Examples of such actions include suits to quiet title to real estate that purport to conclude all adverse claims, and in rem libels in admiralty." R. CASAD & R. RICHMAN, JURISDICTION IN CIVIL ACTIONS § 1-1[3] (3d ed. 1998).

[36] Thus, in contrast to *in personam* judgments (*see* note 3 and related text, *supra*), *in rem* and *quasi in rem* judgments usually have no effect elsewhere. A judgment *in rem* or *quasi in rem* only authorizes liquidation or alteration of the legal status of the *res* underpinning jurisdiction. In a few cases, courts limited to one of these two forms of jurisdiction have presumed to adjudicate the entire dollar amount of defendant's personal obligation to plaintiff. Courts elsewhere, however, are under no obligation to recognize such judgments. For example, in *Combs v. Combs*, 60 S.W.2d 368 (Ky. 1933), a Kentucky court refused to give effect to an Arkansas *in rem* judgment that not only adjudicated the status of Arkansas real estate, but also presumed to fix the entire sum defendant owed to plaintiff. But see *Harnischfeger Sales Corp. v. Sternberg Dredging Co.*, 191 So. 94 (Miss. 1939), where a Mississippi court noted that a prior Louisiana judgment was *in rem*, but gave it preclusive effect. However, "[t]here is scant judicial authority for this position." Richard W. Bourne, *The Demise of Foreign Attachment*, 21 CREIGHTON L. REV. 141, 151 n.84 (1987).

But, like *in personam* jurisdiction, *quasi in rem* jurisdiction can be used to adjudicate personal obligations.[37] *Harris v. Balk*,[38] perhaps the most famous *quasi in rem* case, provides an illustration. A Maryland plaintiff sued nonresident defendant Balk by serving one Harris to garnish[39] a debt owed by Harris to Balk. The *res* was the debt, deemed present wherever the debtor could be found. The plaintiff prevailed and recovered the *res* — the amount of Harris' debt. Thereafter, Balk sued Harris in North Carolina on the debt. Harris argued that he had discharged his obligation to Balk by paying the sum in the earlier case. Harris prevailed because the United States Supreme Court concluded that the Maryland court had properly exercised *quasi in rem* jurisdiction.[40]

Once the Supreme Court decided that exercises of *quasi in rem* jurisdiction must satisfy the same due process standards applicable to personal jurisdiction, the form of *quasi in rem* jurisdiction exemplified by *Harris* lost its special appeal.[41] Plaintiffs no longer obtain any jurisdictional advantage by attaching nonresident defendants' property and proceeding under a *quasi in rem* theory; they may just as well proceed directly and assert personal jurisdiction. Other forms of *quasi in rem* jurisdiction, however, continue to have application.[42]

§ 3.03 TRADITIONALLY ACCEPTED FORMS OF PERSONAL JURISDICTION

[1]   Suit in the Defendant's Home State

Courts of the defendant's home state traditionally have personal jurisdiction over the defendant in all cases.[43] The rule makes sense for several reasons.

---

[37] But, this use is now quite limited. *See* note 41 and related text, *infra*.

[38] 198 U.S. 215 (1905). For an illuminating discussion of this case, see WILLIAM M. RICHMAN & WILLIAM L. REYNOLDS, UNDERSTANDING CONFLICT OF LAWS § 42[b] (3d ed. 2002).

[39] *Garnishment* is the seizure of a debt by service of process on the debtor with a warning not to pay the debt pending litigation. *Attachment* is the actual or constructive seizure of real property using judicial process. Property may also be seized before judgment to provide security for an eventual judgment, rather than to confer territorial jurisdiction, or after judgment to execute upon the judgment. Pre-judgment seizures are subject to strict due process protection, *see* § 4.02[2], *infra*, while post-judgment seizures are typically subject to detailed local procedures, even in federal courts. *See generally* § 15.02 (enforcing money judgments), *infra*.

[40] For a further illustration of this form of *quasi in rem* jurisdiction, see the discussion of the *Seider* doctrine at § 3.08[2], *infra*.

[41] For discussion of these developments, see §§ 3.08[1] & [2], *infra*.

[42] For example, an action against named defendants to remove a cloud on the title to real estate. RICHMAN & REYNOLDS, note 38, *supra*, at § 41[b].

[43] "The notion that the plaintiff should sue the defendant at his home is of venerable age, and the rule permitting him to be sued there is universally accepted." Hans Smit, *Common and Civil Law Rules of In Personam Adjudicatory Authority: An Analysis of Underlying Policies*, 21 INT'L & COMP. L.Q. 335, 336 (1972). "[A] state has control over its citizens and over all persons domiciled within the state even when they have gone outside the state." Austin W. Scott, *Jurisdiction Over Nonresidents Doing Business Within A State*, 32 HARV. L. REV. 871, 875 (1919).

Amenability to suit can be seen as a fair exchange for the benefits and protection which the defendant enjoys from state citizenship. The United States Supreme Court so held in the landmark case, *Milliken v. Meyer*.[44] The Court ruled that a Wyoming court had personal jurisdiction over a defendant then living in the forum state. "Domicile in the state is alone sufficient to bring an absent defendant within the reach of the state's jurisdiction," said the Court.[45] "The state which accords [the defendant] privileges and affords protection to him and his property by virtue of his domicile may also exact reciprocal duties."[46] The Court added that "[o]ne such incident of domicile is amenability to suit within the state."[47] As a separate matter, there is much to be said for having one place where the plaintiff can file suit and be certain that personal jurisdiction exists over the defendant. Moreover, defendants frequently suffer the least expense and inconvenience when defending at home.[48]

[handwritten margin note: same reasoning in Shoe that led to purposeful availment in Hanson]

Which state is home for the defendant? The Supreme Court has never settled this, nor has it clearly identified the most appropriate terminology for resolving the question. In *Milliken*, it used the terms *residence, citizenship* and *domicile* to describe a party's relationship to the forum, without distinguishing among them. Courts often appear to use the terms more or less interchangeably.

For defendants who are individuals (natural persons), *domicile* might seem to provide the best standard. Domicile has a more consistent meaning than residence[49] and generally connotes a stronger nexus between an individual and the state.[50] A legally competent person acquires a domicile by being present there with the intention of making the place his home. Every person has a domicile, but never more than one.[51]

Yet domicile may not always provide the most helpful guide. An individual retains his old domicile until his actions and intentions coalesce to form a new one. He may be absent from his domicile for years before this occurs. In the interim, the different place where he resides may carry indicia more significant to personal jurisdiction. It may be where he receives the most protection and

---

[44] 311 U.S. 457 (1940).

[45] 311 U.S. at 462.

[46] 311 U.S. at 463.

[47] 311 U.S. at 464. *Cf.* Lea Brilmayer, *How Contacts Count: Due Process Limitations on State Court Jurisdiction*, 1980 SUP. CT. REV. 77, 85 ("[T]here can be no sovereignty objections to a State requiring its own citizens to appear and defend a suit brought in its courts.").

[48] "The defendant's interest is to be sued at home, since this will cause him the least inconvenience and permit him to litigate before a court of his own environs." Smit, note 43, *supra*, at 350. *Accord*, Rhonda Wasserman, *The Subpoena Power: Pennoyer's Last Vestige*, 74 *Minn. L. Rev.* 37, 62 (1989).

[49] *See* Willis L.M. Reese & Robert S. Green, *That Elusive Word, "Residence"*, 6 VAND. L. REV. 561 (1953).

[50] *See* David F. Cavers, *"Habitual Residence": A Useful Concept?*, 21 AM. U. L. REV. 475, 480 (1972).

[51] For an elaboration of these prerequisites, see RESTATEMENT (SECOND) OF CONFLICTS Ch. 2 (1971). *See also* § 5.05 (diversity of citizenship), *infra*.

benefits and where he could most conveniently defend. In such cases the more casual concept of residence would provide a better standard than domicile.[52]

Corporate defendants also may be sued at home. However, since corporations are legal creations rather than real persons, a different approach is necessary to determine what place or places serve as home for the corporation. Corporations have always been amenable to the jurisdiction of courts in the state in which they are incorporated.[53] Sometimes this will also be the state in which the corporation conducts its principal operations.[54] But when its principal operations are in a different state, it is likely that both will have personal jurisdiction over the corporation.[55] The matter becomes more complicated when the corporation has substantial white-collar and blue-collar resources and they are located in different states, or when the corporation's major activities of the same kind are divided between two or more such states. Federal courts have addressed the same factual problems in determining corporate citizenship for purposes of diversity subject matter jurisdiction.[56] It would be tempting to resolve personal jurisdiction issues by reference to this case law, but this is probably unwise. The due process law of personal jurisdiction and the law of federal subject matter jurisdiction are grounded on fundamentally different policies.[57] It may be best to apply the home-state principle of personal jurisdiction to corporations only where the forum is the place of incorporation or where the activities of the corporation are clearly concentrated.[58] Clear concentration of defendant's corporate activities in one state suggests that it is receiving extensive benefits there and that suit in that state would not be particularly inconvenient. It seems reasonable to require the corporation to defend against all suits filed there. Absent a clear concentration of corporate activity in the forum, it is better to examine each

---

[52] *See* Harold S. Lewis, Jr., *A Brave New World for Personal Jurisdiction: Flexible Tests Under Uniform Standards*, 37 VAND. L. REV. 1, 48–49 (1984). *See also* § 6.01[2] (discussing residence as a basis for venue), *infra*.

[53] Joseph J. Kalo, *Jurisdiction as an Evolutionary Process: The Development of Quasi In Rem and In Personam Principles*, 1978 DUKE L.J. 1147, 1166 (1978). *See also* Note, *Developments in the Law — State-Court Jurisdiction*, 73 HARV. L. REV. 909, 919 (1960) ("To the extent that jurisdiction was based upon power over the defendant, a charter state had power over the corporations it created and allowed to continue in existence."). Matters become more complicated, however, when the question becomes whether personal jurisdiction extends to the parent as well as the subsidiary corporation. For a study, see William A. Voxman, Comment, *Jurisdiction Over a Parent Corporation in Its Subsidiary's State of Incorporation*, 141 U. PA. L. REV. 327 (1992).

[54] This creates something of a parallel between corporate and individual defendants: "The community that chartered the corporation and in which it has its head office occupies a position somewhat analogous to that of the community of a natural person's domicile and habitual residence." von Mehren & Trautman, *supra* note 24, at, 1141-42.

[55] von Mehren & Trautman, note 24, *supra*, at 1141–42.

[56] *See, e.g.,* § 5.05, *infra*.

[57] The Supreme Court emphasized this point in *Insurance Corp. of Ireland, Ltd. v. Compagnie des Bauxites de Guinee*, 456 U.S. 694 (1982).

[58] *But see* von Mehren & Trautman, note 24, *supra*, suggesting that, when corporate white-collar activity is distributed evenly over two or more states, each should have jurisdiction.

case carefully to determine whether the corporation should be subject to the court's personal jurisdiction.[59]

[2]   Personal Jurisdiction Over Nonresidents Through Waiver or Express Consent

[a]   How Waiver Operates

State courts do not have the same authority to impose personal jurisdiction over nonresident defendants as they have over defendants who make their home in the forum state. But when the former have due process objections, they must take care to preserve them. The Supreme Court has observed that "[b]ecause the requirement of personal jurisdiction represents first of all an individual right, it can, like other such rights, be waived."[60]

Waiver need not be express. It is enough that a party act in a way which is incompatible with his argument that the forum lacks a basis for asserting personal jurisdiction over him. This is why nonresident plaintiffs waive due process objections to the court's jurisdiction by filing suit.[61] Note how the nonresident plaintiff's act of filing makes his relationship to the forum more intimate. He has now availed himself of the protection and benefits of the forum's judicial process. By setting up legal shop in the forum, plaintiff makes the forum a more convenient place not only to litigate his claim but to defend against such cross-claims or counterclaims as the forum might permit against him.[62]

Waiver of the right to challenge personal jurisdiction does not work quite so simply for nonresident *defendants*. Since it is unlikely that a court will respond to a defect in personal jurisdiction on its own initiative, defendant must move for dismissal. To say that the defendant waives his due process objection to personal jurisdiction by appearing in the case to press that objection as a ground for dismissal would create a confounding situation. Instead, procedural systems provide mechanisms for the defendant to appear and question the court's personal jurisdiction without curing plaintiff's problem in the process.

[b]   Special and Limited Appearances

Once, the standard way for defendant to protect himself was to file a *special appearance*. The special appearance permitted defendant to participate in the case without submitting to the court's personal jurisdiction. It was crucial, however, that defendant styled his entry into the suit as a special appearance

---

[59] For example, the question how extensive defendant's contacts with the forum must be when the facts of the controversy arose elsewhere is serious and unsettled under current law. *See* § 3.11 (general jurisdiction), *infra*.

[60] *Insurance Corp. of Ireland, Ltd. v. Compagnie des Bauxites de Guinee*, 456 U.S. 694, 703 (1982).

[61] *See* RESTATEMENT (SECOND) OF CONFLICTS Ch. 2, note 51, *supra*.

[62] RESTATEMENT (SECOND) OF CONFLICTS Ch. 2, note 51, *supra*. The Court upheld personal jurisdiction under such circumstances in *Adam v. Saenger*, 303 U.S. 59 (1938).

and that he was careful not to question anything but the court's personal jurisdiction. If the defendant used this opportunity to urge any other reason why the case should be dismissed or to dispute the merits of plaintiff's case, his entry took on the character of a *general appearance*,[63] which functioned as a submission to the court's jurisdiction.[64]

Today most state courts have followed the lead of federal courts and dispensed with special appearances.[65] This means that the defendant will not prejudice his motion to dismiss by joining with it other grounds for dismissal.[66] However, care must be taken even in courts that follow the federal model. Defendant will waive his challenge to personal jurisdiction if he either fails to include it in a motion to dismiss made on other grounds, or fails to raise the matter by motion or pleading.[67] Moreover, the Supreme Court held that defendant may also lose his personal jurisdiction challenge as a penalty for failure to comply with an order compelling discovery.[68]

Students sometimes confuse special appearances with *limited appearances*. Many jurisdictions permitted a defendant whose property was attached through *quasi in rem* jurisdiction to appear and resist a judgment on the merits against the property without, by so doing, submitting to the court's *in personam* jurisdiction. This was called a limited appearance. Recall that a *quasi in rem* judgment bound the defendant only with reference to his interest in the *res* upon which jurisdiction was based.[69] In contrast, an *in personam* judgment bound the defendant to the full measure of damages for his wrong to the plaintiff.[70]

Limited appearances thus differed from special appearances in that the former were not a means of raising the personal jurisdiction issue but were

---

63

> A general appearance is one where the defendant either enters an appearance in an action without limiting the purpose for which he appears or where he asks for relief which the court may give only if it has jurisdiction over him. An appearance which falls into either of these two categories is a general appearance even though the defendant protests at the same time that he does not submit himself to the jurisdiction of the court.

Restatement (Second) of Conflicts, note 51, *supra*, § 33 comment d. For discussion of the device in one jurisdiction, see Howard W. L'Enfant, *In Personam Jurisdiction — General Appearance*, 52 La. L. Rev. 519 (1992).

[64] Robert C. Casad & William B. Richman, Jurisdiction in Civil Actions § 3-1[5][a] (3rd ed. 1998).

[65] Casad & Richman, note 64, *supra*, at ¶ 3.01[5][b]. For one example of special appearance practice, see Newton & Wicker, *Personal Jurisdiction and the Appearance to Challenge Jurisdiction in Texas*, 38 Baylor L. Rev. 491 (1986).

[66] *See* Rule 12(g). A majority of states have adopted the Rule 12 model. *See generally* John B. Oakley & Arthur F. Coon, *The Federal Rules in State Courts: A Survey of State Court Systems of Civil Procedure*, 61 Wash. L. Rev. 1367 (1986).

[67] Rule 12(h)(1). *See generally* § 8.07[2][b] (waivable defenses), *infra*.

[68] *Insurance Corp. of Ireland, Ltd. v. Compagnie des Bauxites de Guinee*, 456 U.S. 694 (1982). Plaintiff sought discovery of facts supporting personal jurisdiction.

[69] *See* § 3.02 and related text, *supra*.

[70] *See* § 3.02 and related text, *supra*.

instead designed to permit the defendant a full opportunity to litigate the case on the merits, while minimizing the effects of an adverse judgment.

Limited appearances have lost much of their importance. As soon as the Supreme Court required that *quasi in rem* cases satisfy more rigorous standards previously associated only with *in personam* jurisdiction,[71] the popularity of *quasi in rem* jurisdiction (and, hence, the necessity for limited appearances) declined dramatically.

[c] Preserving the Jurisdictional Challenge in the Face of an Initial Adverse Ruling

If defendant's jurisdictional challenge succeeds, the court will order plaintiff's case dismissed. Absent a successful appeal, plaintiff will have to refile against defendant[72] in a forum where the jurisdictional climate may be more favorable. But what if the trial court rules against the defendant?

Many systems do not permit defendant to appeal immediately because denial of a motion to dismiss for lack of personal jurisdiction is an interlocutory (nonfinal) order, and such systems confine most appeals to those from final judgment.[73]

This could place the defendant in a dilemma. If his further participation in the case constitutes a submission to jurisdiction, defendant will lose his jurisdictional challenge by pressing other reasons for dismissal or disputing the merits of plaintiff's case. To preserve the jurisdictional issue for appeal, he would have to stop participating at the trial level once the court rejects his jurisdictional challenge. This would draw a default judgment on the merits for plaintiff, and defendant could renew his jurisdictional challenge by appealing that final judgment. The risk in this option is that defendant will be bound on the merits, should he lose the jurisdictional argument.[74]

Fortunately, most systems do not pose this hard choice. They permit the defendant to renew his objection to the court's personal jurisdiction on appeal of the final judgment, even though he has fully contested the case during the interim.[75]

---

[71] *See* § 3.08[1], *infra.*

[72] A dismissal for lack of personal jurisdiction has no preclusive effect on plaintiff's claim. *See* § 15.05, *infra.* It may, however, prejudice a subsequent attempt by plaintiff to refile the case in the same state. *See* § 15.06, *infra.*

[73] *See* § 13.03 (final judgment rule), *infra.*

[74] For further discussion of this dilemma, see CASAD & RICHMAN, note 64, *supra,* at § 3-1[5][a][i].

[75] Professor Casad offers representative cases from a number of states taking this view, and citations from three states (New Hampshire, Idaho and South Dakota) that do not. He observes that California also requires defendants to waive their jurisdictional challenge in order to contest the merits, but notes that defendants in California do have the option of interlocutory review of the jurisdictional question before they must proceed to the merits at trial. CASAD & RICHMAN, note 64, *supra,* at § 3-1[5][a][i]. Federal courts rarely permit interlocutory review but have long permitted defendants to renew their personal jurisdictional arguments on appeal, after fully litigating the case prior to final judgment. *Harkness v. Hyde,* 98 U.S. 476 (1879).

[d]   Jurisdiction by Consent

Under a rule similar to waiver, it has long been true that defendants could consent to a court's personal jurisdiction in advance of suit. Such consent, if expressly made, still functions to cure any jurisdictional defects which might otherwise exist.[76]

A leading express consent case is *National Equipment Rental v. Szukhent.* The Supreme Court upheld New York jurisdiction over Michigan defendants in a federal breach of contract suit. It did so on the ground that one of the clauses of the contract signed by the defendants named an individual in New York to receive service there on their behalf. "[I]t is settled," said the Court, "that parties to a contract may agree in advance to submit to the jurisdiction of a given court . . . ."[77] Of course, the contract must be valid and enforceable. The only line of escape in such cases may be for defendant to argue that the provision is deceptive, unconscionable or a contract of adhesion.[78]

A category of important consent cases consists of those where foreign corporations have filed with state authorities a consent to jurisdiction as a condition for doing business in the forum.[79] At the very least, such consent effectively confers personal jurisdiction over the corporation for the adjudication of all claims arising within the forum. Once it seemed equally clear that filing operated as consent to personal jurisdiction over claims arising elsewhere, if the sweep of the state consent statute was broad enough.[80] The position still seems to have wide acceptance,[81] but several courts have questioned whether this form of filing provides a basis for the adjudication of nonforum controversies against foreign corporations sufficient to satisfy due process.[82] Commentators have criticized the practice.[83]

---

[76] *Friedenthal, Kane & Miller* § 3.5. On the other hand, it is doubtful whether the fictitious concept of implied consent continues to provide a sufficient basis for personal jurisdiction. *See* E. Scoles & P. Hay, Conflict of Laws § 9.5 (2d ed. 1992).

[77] 375 U.S. 311, 315–16 (1964).

[78] Dissenting in *Szukhent,* Justice Black argued that the consent-to-jurisdiction portion of the contract was a "sham" and should be deemed unenforceable. 375 U.S. at 323–26.

[79]

> All states have statutes that require nonresident corporations that intend to conduct business in the state to comply with a registration procedure and to appoint a resident agent for the service of process. . . . Such statutes reach not only the in-state conduct of nonresident corporations, but potentially any claim — irrespective of its relationship with the . . . jurisdiction — pressed against a registered nonresident corporation.

Lee S. Taylor, *Registration Statutes, Personal Jurisdiction, and the Problem of Predictability*, 103 Colum. L. Rev. 1163, 1164–65 (2003).

[80] *Pennsylvania Fire Ins. Co. v. Gold Issue Mining & Milling Co.*, 243 U.S. 93 (1917) (opinion per Holmes, J.); *Smolik v. Philadelphia & Reading Coal & Iron Co.*, 222 F. 148 (1915) (opinion per L. Hand, J.). These decisions are criticized in William L. Walker, *Foreign Corporation Laws: A Current Account*, 47 N.C. L. Rev. 733, 735–37 (1969).

[81] *Restatement (Second) of Conflicts*, note 51, *supra*, § 44 & comment (c); Scoles & Hay, note 76, *supra*, at 455. *But see* Alfred Hill, *Choice of Law and Jurisdiction in the Supreme Court*, 81 Colum. L. Rev. 960, 981–82 (1981).

[82] *Wenche Siemer v. Learjet Acquisition Corp.*, 966 F.2d 179 (5th Cir. 1992); *In re Mid-Atlantic*

[e]   Prorogation (Exclusive Jurisdiction) Clauses

Some forum-selection provisions in contracts may include prorogation clauses.[84] That is, they not only consent to jurisdiction in a particular court, but also bar litigation in any other court. Unwilling to be ousted of what would otherwise be proper personal jurisdiction, some courts once refused to honor prorogation clauses. But the recent trend has been in favor of enforcing them. The Supreme Court stated in *M/S Bremen v. Zapata Off-Shore Co.*[85] that "such clauses are prima facie valid and should be enforced unless enforcement is shown by the resisting party to be 'unreasonable' under the circumstances."[86] Similarly, the American Law Institute's *Restatement (Second) of Conflicts* regards a prorogation agreement to be effective "unless it is unfair or unreasonable."[87] This now appears to be the standard in federal[88] and most state courts.[89]

Yet how do we determine when enforcement of the prorogation agreement would be unreasonable? *Bremen* appeared to offer a useful guide in that the case: "a private international prorogation agreement will be honored . . . [i]f the agreement was freely negotiated, unaffected by fraud, undue influence, or overweening bargaining power."[90] But later, in *Carnival Cruise Lines, Inc. v. Shute*, the Supreme Court upheld a prorogation clause appearing on the back of a passenger's steamship ticket[91] — circumstances many observers regarded to be unfair.[92] There was an "obvious distinction between the freely-negotiated

---

Toyota Antitrust Litig., 525 F. Supp. 1265 (D. Md. 1981); *Schreiber v. Allis-Chalmers Corp.*, 448 F. Supp. 1079 (D. Kan. 1978), *rev'd on other grounds*, 611 F.2d 790 (10th Cir. 1979); *Cedar Inv. Co. v. Canal Ins. Co.*, 262 F. Supp. 337 (E.D. Mo. 1966). In *Bendix Autolite Corp. v. Midwesco Enterprises, Inc.*, 486 U.S. 888 (1988), the Supreme Court limited the authority of states to require foreign corporations to submit to jurisdiction in controversies arising outside the forum. However, the Court's constitutional ruling rested on Commerce Clause rather than due process grounds.

[83]   *E.g.*, Mark Schuck, *Foreign Corporations and the Issue of Consent to Jurisdiction Through Registration to Do Business in Texas: Analysis and Proposal*, 40 Hou. L. Rev. 1455 (2004); Lee S. Taylor, *Registration Statutes, Personal Jurisdiction, and the Problem of Predictability*, 103 Colum. L. Rev. 1163 (2003).

[84]   *Moore* § 108.53[5][a].

[85]   407 U.S. 1 (1972).

[86]   407 U.S. at 10.

[87]   Section 80 (1971).

[88]   Casad & Richman, note 64 *supra*, at § 1-7. In all federal cases, federal (as opposed to state) law determines the enforcement of prorogation clauses. *Stewart Org., Inc. v. Ricoh Corp.*, 487 U.S. 22, 32 (1988).

[89]   "The state courts are free to adopt their own standards with respect to whether to honor a choice-of-forum clause, but it is fair to say that most state courts appear to have adopted something close to the *Zapata* standard." Linda J. Silberman, *The Impact of Jurisdictional Rules and Recognition Practice on International Business Transactions: The U.S. Regime*, 26 Houston J. of Int'l L. 327, 347 (2004).

[90]   Casad & Richman, note 64 *supra*, § 1-7.

[91]   499 U.S. 585 (1991).

[92]   *See, e.g.*, Mullenix, *Another Easy Case, Some More Bad Law: Carnival Cruise Lines and Contractual Personal Jurisdiction*, 27 Tex. Int'l L.J. 323 (1992).

commercial contract in *The Bremen* and the consumer adhesion contract in *Carnival Cruise Lines.*"[93]

[3]   Transient Jurisdiction

Transient jurisdiction is based on service within the forum of a nonresident defendant who happens to be in the state for a brief period. In one well-known case, defendant was served while an aircraft was flying over the forum state.[94] Transient jurisdiction is usually not available over those entering the the forum state "to participate in unrelated judicial procedings"[95] or over one induced into the forum state by fraud.[96] Once questioned, the validity of transient jurisdiction now seems fairly secure.[97] We will return to the topics of statutory consent and transient jurisdiction when considering recent due process developments.

§ 3.04   TIMING THE JURISDICTIONAL CHALLENGE

Two avenues have long been open to a defendant wishing to challenge the court's personal jurisdiction. First, defendant may use his challenge to keep the court from reaching the merits of the case. The defendant must participate in the lawsuit to use this option, called *direct attack*. Or the defendant may use his jurisdictional challenge later to argue that a judgment rendered against him is not entitled to enforcement. Defendant must avoid participating or making any kind of appearance in the case underlying judgment in order to use this option, called *collateral attack*.

[1]   Direct Attack

Federal and state courts make ample opportunities available for a nonresident defendant to question personal jurisdiction prior to trial. Moreover, if the defendant is careful to observe the niceties of the local procedural system, he usually will be able to join with his jurisdictional attack other reasons why plaintiff's suit should be dismissed[98] and (if necessary) to

---

[93] RICHMAN & REYNOLDS, note 38, *supra*, at § 30[2]. "[P]laintiff's right to a reasonable forum-. . . should not be so easily defeated by sharp drafting practices." *Id.*

[94] *Grace v. MacArthur*, 170 F. Supp. 442 (E.D. Ark. 1959).

[95] LINDA L. SILBERMAN, ALLAN R. STEIN & TOBIAS B. WOLFF, CIVIL PROCEDURE: THEORY AND PRACTICE 277 (Aspen 2d ed. 2006) ("Most commonly, immunity is granted to . . . witnesses, parties, and attorneys.").

[96]

> Sometimes, plaintiffs would lure the defendants into the [forum state] by fraudulent representations or by tricks or artifice. Even abduction was resorted to upon occasion. To remove the incentive for employing such devices, the courts developed a doctrine to avoid jurisdiction in cases where personal service on the defendant was obtained through force or fraud.

CASAD & RICHMAN, note 64, *supra*, at § 1-5.

[97] *Burnham v. Superior Court*, 495 U.S. 604 (1990).

[98] *See* § 3.03[2][b], *supra*. *See, e.g.*, Rule 12(b)(2).

resist the merits as well.[99] This is the great attraction of direct attack; it can be used with an array of other grounds for attacking plaintiff's case that are available in the initial forum.

The problem with direct attack is that it forces the defendant to give up part of the protection secured by due process.[100] He experiences the increased burden of defending in a distant and inconvenient forum as soon as he begins participating in the case. The difference in hardship between traveling to the forum in order to get the suit dismissed for lack of personal jurisdiction and remaining there to defend on the merits is one only of degree.

[2]   Collateral Attack

Due process therefore requires that defendant have the second option of collateral attack. Collateral attack is founded on the principle that, if plaintiff's choice of forum is so unfair as to violate defendant's right to due process, defendant's complete refusal to participate there should not preclude him from later questioning personal jurisdiction.[101] The United States Supreme Court has noted that: "[a] defendant is always free to ignore the judicial proceedings, risk a default judgment, and then challenge that judgment on jurisdictional grounds in a collateral proceeding."[102]

For an illustration of jurisdictional challenge by collateral attack, recall the example presented at the beginning of this chapter.[103] New Yorker B takes no part in A's Hawaii lawsuit. A obtains a default judgment for $100,000 against B. Since B has no assets in Hawaii to satisfy the judgment, A must sue on the judgment in a court of B's home state of New York.[104] B defends against the judgment in New York court on the ground that the Hawaii court lacked personal jurisdiction. B wins, the court ruling (as it must on these facts) that the Hawaii judgment is not entitled to enforcement. If A wishes a judgment against B enforceable in New York, A will have to sue B all over again in New York.

The problems with the collateral attack are that it is often unavailable and, when available, often risky to use. Courts will usually entertain collateral attack for lack of personal jurisdiction only if the defendant took no part whatsoever in the initial proceeding. If the defendant participated in the first case without questioning the court's personal jurisdiction, he cured any defect

---

[99] See § 3.03[2][c], *supra.*

[100] See § 3.01[2], *supra.*

[101] Under these circumstances, the "right to challenge jurisdiction makes" the defendant "an instrument for confining judicial authority to its prescribed limits." RESTATEMENT (SECOND) OF JUDGMENTS § 65 comment (b) (1982).

[102] *Insurance Corp. of Ireland, Ltd. v. Compagnie des Bauxites de Guinee*, 456 U.S. 694, 706 (1982). The position taken under American law is thus at variance with that of the European Community, where "jurisdictional challenges are not permitted in the State in which enforcement is sought, even with respect to default judgments." LINDA J. SILBERMAN, ALLAN R. STEIN & TOBIAS B. WOLFF, CIVIL PROCEDURE: THEORY AND PRACTICE 930 (Aspen 2d ed. 2006).

[103] § 3.01[1], *supra.*

[104] The process for suing on judgments is described in § 15.02, *infra.*

by waiver.[105] If the defendant did challenge the court's personal jurisdiction in the first case, he is precluded from relitigating the question in the judgment-enforcement proceeding. The Supreme Court's decision in *Baldwin v. Iowa State Traveling Men's Ass'n*[106] is a prominent example of the latter. Defendant appeared specially in the initial case and attacked the court's personal jurisdiction. When the trial court denied defendant's motion to dismiss, defendant withdrew from any further participation in the case and default judgment was thereafter entered against him. Defendant later attempted to relitigate his objection to personal jurisdiction by collaterally attacking the judgment. However, the Court refused to permit the challenge.

> The special appearance gives point to the fact that the respondent entered the Missouri court for the very purpose of litigating the question of jurisdiction over its person. It had the election not to appear at all . . . . It had also the right to appeal from the decision of the Missouri District Court . . . .[107]

The grounds upon which defendant can base a collateral attack are quite limited. Two which are clearly available — lack of notice[108] and the unenforceablity of the judgment where rendered[109] — require unusual supporting facts. Courts have occasionally permitted collateral attack on other grounds, but their availability in any given case is uncertain.[110] So, if defendant's collateral attack for lack of personal jurisdiction fails, there will usually be nothing to shield him from an obligation to pay the default judgment.[111]

---

[105] *See generally* § 3.03[2][a], *supra*.

[106] 283 U.S. 522 (1931).

[107] 283 U.S. at 525. *See also Underwriters Nat'l Assurance Co. v. North Carolina Life & Accident & Health Ins. Guar. Ass'n*, 455 U.S. 691 (1982); *Stoll v. Gottlieb*, 305 U.S. 165, 172 (1938).

[108] Defendants may assert denial of the notice and opportunity to be heard guaranteed by due process. RESTATEMENT (SECOND) OF JUDGMENTS, note 51, *supra*, Chapter 2 at 18. *See generally* § 4.01, *infra*.

[109] Defendants may invoke the sensible rule that a court need not enforce a foreign judgment if the rendering system would not. *See Ford v. Ford*, 371 U.S. 187 (1962) (full faith and credit does not obligate courts to give *greater* preclusive effect to a judgment than the rendering court). *See generally* § 15.11, *infra*.

[110] Cases like *Huntington v. Attrill*, 146 U.S. 657 (1892), raise the possibility that a judgment penal in character might be unenforceable, but "it is very possible that there is not much left of this penalty rule." Lawrence H. Averill, Jr., *Choice-of-Law Problems Raised by Sister-State Judgments and the Full-Faith-and-Credit Mandate*, 64 Nw. U. L. Rev. 686, 694 (1970). Similarly, the modern trend is away from permitting collateral attacks on subject matter jurisdiction grounds. *See generally* Karen N. Moore, *Collateral Attack on Subject Matter Jurisdiction: A Critique of the Restatement (Second) of Judgments*, 66 CORNELL L. REV. 534, 562 (1981).

[111] Default judgments are judgments on the merits (*see* § 15.05, *infra*), and it is axiomatic that collateral attack may not be used to question the merits underlying a judgment. *E.g., Fauntleroy v. Lum*, 210 U.S. 230 (1908); *Milliken v. Meyer*, 311 U.S. 457 (1940). The only questions left for the judgment enforcement proceeding are: is defendant in fact the person named in the judgment, and how soon can defendant pay? *See* § 15.02, *infra*.

[3]   Considerations Influencing the Choice Between Direct and Collateral Attack

As the preceding discussion indicates, the moment of defendant's irrevocable decision whether to raise his personal jurisdiction challenge by direct or collateral attack usually comes when he decides whether to participate in the initial proceeding. The choice defendant should make turns on tactical considerations and will vary with the circumstances of each case. Here are some things to keep in mind.

[a]   The Relative Advantages of Direct Attack

While the defendant does not reside in the forum, he may have substantial assets there. Not only may this enhance plaintiff's case for personal jurisdiction,[112] it means that plaintiff can levy a default judgment against defendant's assets without ever leaving the forum state. It would be a tactical error for defendant to default under these circumstances. He would then be faced with the choice of traveling to the forum and collaterally attacking the judgment in the enforcement proceeding or remaining at home and losing his property. If defendant must eventually travel to the forum to make his jurisdictional challenge anyway, he is better off doing it earlier by direct attack. That way he can challenge other aspects of plaintiff's case, too.

Direct attack may be the more attractive option even when defendant has no assets in the forum state. The greater the recovery sought by plaintiff, the more defendant may put at risk by electing to default and raise his jurisdictional challenge through the collateral attack option. Similarly, the weaker the plaintiff's case on the merits, the more problematical the collateral attack. Assume, for example, that the applicable statute of limitations has run on plaintiff's claim. For defendant to choose the option of collateral attack, his case against personal jurisdiction should be ironclad. Otherwise he should not imperil access to the statute of limitations defense by taking a default in the initial case.[113] Finally, if defendant's personal jurisdiction challenge is relatively weak, he should not hang a lot on it by opting for collateral attack.[114]

[b]   The Relative Advantages of Collateral Attack

Defendants often prefer to litigate at home.[115] There will be occasions when sound tactical considerations support this preference and defendant should opt for collateral rather than direct attack. One or more of the following may

---

[112] *See* § 3.12[1] (aggregating defendant's contacts with the forum both related and unrelated to the controversy in order to satisfy due process), *infra*.

[113] Similarly, defendant may not wish to imperil grounds for pretrial dismissal (*e.g.*, improper joinder) which seem strong in a particular case, when he could join them to his jurisdictional challenge under the option of direct attack.

[114] *Cf.* § 3.06[2][a] (describing defendant's unfortunate choice of collateral attack in *McGee v. International Life Ins. Co.*, 355 U.S. 220 (1957)), *infra*.

[115] Defendant's local attorney also might like to see the litigation unfold at home, since that is where the attorney can participate and collect a fee. It is, of course, unethical for the attorney to

apply. Damages sought by plaintiff may be too inconsequential to justify the added expense and inconvenience of defending away from home. Plaintiff's case as to both liability and amount of damages may be clearcut and very strong, suggesting little advantage from an opportunity to contest the merits. Or defendant's case against personal jurisdiction may be so strong that it seems very likely that his collateral attack will succeed and that plaintiff will be forced to recommence suit in defendant's home state.[116]

Although it is not easy to quantify, there is a another factor which may favor the option of collateral attack: the home court advantage. Theoretically, there should be no advantage. The defendant's home forum is obliged to evaluate the sufficiency of the distant forum's personal jurisdiction under precisely the same legal criteria — due process sufficiency and compliance with the distant forum's local law[117] — which the distant forum would have used if defendant had elected the option of direct attack. The federal due process issue is, of course, the same for either court. And defendant's forum may not substitute for the jurisdictional framework of the judgment-rendering state a more limited jurisdictional law of its own.[118]

For all that, it may be reasonable to assume that judges are at times influenced by sympathetic impulses toward local litigants.[119] Given the complicated and fact-variable nature of current due process doctrine,[120] there are many personal jurisdiction cases over which reasonable judges might disagree. The uncertainty of United States Supreme Court review when state courts take liberties with federal law short of blatant error[121] creates a climate conducive to state court resolution of close questions in favor of local litigants.[122]

---

permit this factor to influence his advice to defendant concerning where to defend. *See, e.g.,* American Bar Ass'n, *Model Rules of Professional Conduct,* Rule 1.7 comment [5] (1983).

[116] On the other hand, the extreme case may work the other way. If plaintiff selects a forum clearly incapable of exercising personal jurisdiction over the defendant, and that forum is either a federal court or a state court using as its rule a recent version of Rule 11, defendant might be able to recover the costs of having the suit dismissed. On Rule 11, see generally § 8.05[2], *infra.* For a case imposing Rule 11 sanctions on plaintiff for selecting a forum clearly without personal jurisdiction, see *Phoenix Airway Inn Assoc. v. Essex Financial Services, Inc.,* 741 F. Supp. 734 (N.D. Ill. 1990).

[117] *See* § 3.01[2][a], *supra.*

[118] *Adam v. Saenger,* 303 U.S. 59 (1938).

[119] Federal court diversity jurisdiction is built on this idea. Gene R. Shreve, *Pragmatism Without Politics — A Half Measure of Authority for Jurisdictional Common Law,* 1991 BYU. L. REV. 767, 787; Wythe Holt, *"To Establish Justice": Politics, the Judiciary Act of 1789, and the Invention of Federal Courts,* 1989 DUKE L.J. 1421, 1458. *See generally* § 5.04[1], *infra* (justification for diversity jurisdiction).

[120] *See* §§ 3.08–3.12, *infra.*

[121] *See* Preble Stolz, *Federal Review of State Court Decisions of Federal Questions: The Need for Additional Appellate Capacity,* 64 CALIF. L. REV. 943 (1976).

[122] Conversely, plaintiff's home state court may be more inclined to resolve a close case in favor of personal jurisdiction — another reason for the defendant to litigate the question at his home, if possible.

PART B.

Personal Jurisdiction Over Nonresident Defendants — *Pennoyer* and the Liberating Effects of *International Shoe*

§ 3.05 TERRITORIAL CONSTRAINTS ON PERSONAL JURISDICTION DURING THE *PENNOYER* ERA

[1]   Due Process Focused on Forum State Boundaries

In 1877, the constitutional framework for regulating personal jurisdiction of state courts was uncertain.[123] Then, in *Pennoyer v. Neff*,[124] the United States Supreme Court laid the groundwork for a due process analysis restricting the effect of judgments. Perhaps the most enduring contribution of *Pennoyer* was the manner in which the case identified and resolved the tension between respect for judgments required under the Full Faith and Credit Clause of the Constitution and countervailing policies secured by the Due Process Clause.[125]

---

[123] Albert A. Ehrenzweig, *The Transient Rule of Personal Jurisdiction: The "Power" Myth and Forum Conveniens*, 65 YALE L.J. 289, 303, 308 (1956). *See generally* the historical studies by Professors Weinstein, Kogan and Trangsrud, note 125, *infra*.

[124] 95 U.S. 714 (1878). Overviews of *Pennoyer*, its precursors, and developments after the case, include James Weinstein, *The Federal Common Law Origins of Judicial Jurisdiction: Implications for Modern Doctrine*, 90 VA. L. REV. 169 (2004); Patrick J. Borchers, *Jurisdictional Pragmatism: International Shoe's Half-Buried Legacy*, 28 U.C. DAVIS L. REV. 561 (1995); John B. Oakley, *The Pitfalls of "Hint and Run" History: A Critique of Professor Borchers's "Limited View" of Pennoyer v. Neff*, 28 U.C. DAVIS L. REV. 591 (1995); Patrick J. Borchers, *Pennoyer's Limited Legacy: A Reply to Professor Oakley*, 29 U.C. DAVIS L. REV. 115 (1995); Geoffrey C. Hazard, Jr., *A General Theory of State-Court Jurisdiction*, 1965 SUP. CT. REV. 241; Philip B. Kurland, *The Supreme Court, the Due Process Clause and the In Personam Jurisdiction of State Courts From Pennoyer to Denckla: A Review*, 25 U. CHI. L. REV. 569 (1958). For an account of the principals in the case, see Wendy C. Perdue, *Sin, Scandal, and Substantive Due Process: Personal Jurisdiction and Pennoyer Reconsidered*, 62 WASH. L. REV. 479 (1987).

[125]

> Since the adoption of the 14th Amendment to the Federal Constitution, the validity of such judgments may be directly questioned, and their enforcement in the State resisted, on the ground that proceedings in a court of justice to determine the personal rights and obligations of parties over whom the court has no jurisdiction, do not constitute due process of law.

95 U.S. at 733. Most see the *Pennoyer* case as a milestone, a view reflected in *Burnham v. Superior Court*, 495 U.S. 604 (1990).

There has been some interest in the legal history surrounding *Pennoyer*. Some contend that the requirement of in-state service on nonresident defendants existed well before *Pennoyer*. James Weinstein, *The Early American Origins of Territoriality in Judicial Jurisdiction*, 37 ST. LOUIS U. L.J. 1 (1992); Terry S. Kogan, *A Neo-Federalist Tale of Personal Jurisdiction*, 63 S. CAL. L. REV. 257 (1990). Another commentator has maintained that *Pennoyer* is best seen as a federal common law decision that later informed development of the due process test, accounting in large part for the persistence of territorial minimum contacts. Roger H. Trangsrud, *The Federal Common Law of Jurisdiction*, 57 GEO. WASH. L. REV. 849 (1989).

It was clear after *Pennoyer* that, while the Full Faith and Credit Clause compelled interstate enforcement of state judgments, it did not purge those judgments of any problems they might have under the Due Process Clause. Rather, the same federal due process grounds available to resist enforcement of a state judgment locally would also be available if enforcement was sought for that judgment in federal court or in the court of a sister state.

It remained for the Court to give content to its standard. The approach reflected in *Pennoyer* would dominate the law of personal jurisdiction for nearly seventy years. State courts could entertain suits against their citizens. They could also entertain suits against nonresidents so long as they consented or if they could be found and served within the forum state. But due process prevented suit against nonresident defendants who could only be found and served elsewhere.

Pennoyer involved two lawsuits. In the first, Mitchell obtained a default judgment in an Oregon state court against Neff for attorney's fees. Neff's Oregon property was seized and sold by the sheriff to Pennoyer in order to satisfy this judgment. In the second lawsuit, Neff sued Pennoyer in federal court for recovery of his property, and Pennoyer defended by claiming title under the sheriff's deed of sale.

Pennoyer's problem was that, when the Oregon court had entered a default judgment, Neff was neither a citizen of the forum nor had he been served there. Concluding that Oregon could not exercise personal jurisdiction over Neff, the United States Supreme Court invalidated the default judgment and resulting sheriff's sale. The Court held that if a state court attempts to exercise *in personam* jurisdiction over the defendant, that is, to adjudicate a case "that involves merely a determination of the personal liability of the defendant, he must be brought within its jurisdiction by service of process within the State, or his voluntary appearance."[126] The Court recognized that *quasi in rem* jurisdiction was an alternative when the defendant had property in the jurisdiction, but stressed that this form of territorial jurisdiction required a proper pre-judgment attachment of the property. Because Neff's property was first seized to enforce a judgment already obtained, *quasi in rem* jurisdiction was unavailable to save the Oregon judgment.

The boundaries of the forum state had transcendent importance in *Pennoyer*. "[E]very State possesses exclusive jurisdiction and sovereignty over persons and property within its territory,"[127] said the Court, but "no State can exercise direct jurisdiction and authority over persons or property without its territory."[128] The Court drove the point home. "Process from the tribunals of one State cannot run into another State, and summon parties there domiciled to leave its territory and respond to proceedings against them."[129]

---

[126] 95 U.S. at 733.

[127] 95 U.S. at 722.

[128] 95 U.S. at 722.

[129] 95 U.S. at 727.

The Court's approach in *Pennoyer* was in tune with the times. Justice Holmes was to observe somewhat later that "[t]he foundation of jurisdiction is physical power . . . ."[130] He was speaking of a court's physical power over the defendant. While it was no longer necessary for the defendant to be under the court's physical control,[131] the power concept remained. Writing for the Court in *Pennoyer*, Justice Field was greatly influenced by the theories of Joseph Story.[132] Story urged a strong relationship between territory and legal authority. One of the ideas he advanced was that the geographical origin of case facts determined when or if legal authority materialized. This notion grew in appeal in the second half of the nineteenth century. However, belief in detached legal principles then began to lose ground in American legal thought to "a growing perception that legal principles were in fact nothing more than doctrines found in . . . local law . . . ."[133]

[2]   Restlessness Under *Pennoyer*

Pennoyer's power rationale became outmoded over time. It was a formalistic doctrine and as such reflected a view of the law as a "static and closed logical system."[134] Increasingly, *Pennoyer*'s analysis seemed inadequate either to explain the Court's rule or — perhaps more importantly — to accommodate the needs of an era of increasing interstate activity. Two developments put particular strain on the *Pennoyer* doctrine: the growth of national corporate activity and the advent of the motorcar.

Pennoyer made some provision for personal jurisdiction over foreign corporations and others who did business in the forum state but could not be found and served there. The Court made clear that states could require them to appoint an in-state agent to receive court process. Moreover, when these

---

[130] *McDonald v. Mabee*, 243 U.S. 90, 91 (1917).

[131] In earlier times, "the power of a court to enter a judgment was dependent upon the actual physical presence of the defendant before the court." Joseph J. Kalo, *Jurisdiction as an Evolutionary Process: The Development of Quasi In Rem and In Personam Principles*, 1978 Duke L.J. 1147, 1148.

[132] Hazard, note 124, *supra*, at 262. *See generally* J. Story, Commentaries on the Conflict of Laws (1834).

[133] T. Freyer, Harmony & Dissonance: The *Swift* & *Erie* Cases in American Federalism 74 (1981). As Holmes said of the common law, it "is not a brooding omnipresence in the sky but the articulate voice of some sovereign . . . ." *Southern Pac. Co. v. Jensen*, 244 U.S. 205, 222 (1917) (Holmes, J., dissenting).

[134] Robert S. Summers, *Pragmatic Instrumentalism in Twentieth Century American Legal Thought — A Synthesis and Critique of Our Dominant General Theory About Law and its Use*, 66 Cornell L. Rev. 861, 867 n.4 (1981). *Cf.* Kenneth J. Vandevelde, *Ideology, Due Process and Civil Procedure*, 67 St. John's L. Rev. 265, 276 (1993) ("The law of personal jurisdiction articulated in *Pennoyer* . . . was consistent with the formalist ideology of the late nineteenth century conservatives."). Restlessness under *Pennoyer* represented only part of a larger movement away from procedural formalism and toward a functional or instrumental understanding of civil procedure. The trend, which continues, is described in Gene R. Shreve, *Pragmatism Without Politics — A Half Measure of Authority for Jurisdictional Common Law*, 1991 BYU L. Rev. 767, 793–96; Robert G. Bone, *Mapping the Boundaries of a Dispute: Conceptions of Ideal Lawsuit Structure From the Field Code to the Federal Rules*, 89 Colum. L. Rev. 1 (1989).

potential defendants refused to appoint someone, states appeared to have authority to designate a state official to accept service for them.[135]

Unfortunately, the Supreme Court was never able to develop an intelligible standard for determining when the forum involvement of the out-of-state defendant was sufficient to justify substituted service on a state officer. The Court invoked concepts of implied consent[136] and presence,[137] each leading to an inquiry about the amount of business done by the defendant in the forum state.[138] The results were arbitrary and unsatisfactory.[139] Ambiguity inherent in the nature of corporate identity compounded the problem. Legal confections, corporations did not literally exist anywhere. Thus, it was particularly difficult to subject them to *Pennoyer*'s legal metaphor based on geographical whereabouts and physical movement.[140]

Professor Hazard observed that *Pennoyer* "had a less secure place in particular application than it did in general theory."[141] The famous accident case, *Hess v. Pawloski*,[142] illustrates this point. Hess, a Pennsylvanian, struck and injured Pawloski while driving in Massachusetts. After Hess returned to Pennsylvania, Pawloski filed suit against him in a Massachusetts court. It was impossible to serve Hess personally in Massachusetts. Pawloski instead used a Massachusetts statute declaring that, by using Massachusetts highways, nonresident motorists constructively appointed a state officer to accept in-state service for them in Massachusetts accident cases. Hess challenged the appointment as fictitious, which, of course, it was. The Supreme Court nonetheless upheld personal jurisdiction.

The *Hess* Court acknowledged *Pennoyer*'s requirement that "actual service within the state" be made on the defendant "or upon someone authorized to accept service for him."[143] It also noted a previous case in which it had

---

[135] *Pennoyer*, 95 U.S. at 735. "States that had no statutes of this sort soon enacted them." Hazard, note 124, *supra*, at 272. This arrangement honored, at least technically, *Pennoyer*'s limitation that service of process be completed within the forum state. *See* note 129 and related text, *supra*.

[136] *E.g., Simon v. Southern Ry.*, 236 U.S. 115 (1915).

[137] *E.g., International Harvester Co. v. Kentucky*, 234 U.S. 579 (1914).

[138] *E.g., St. Louis Sw. Ry. v. Alexander*, 227 U.S. 218 (1913). *See* Kurland, note 124, *supra*, at 577–86; Austin W. Scott, *Jurisdiction Over Nonresidents Doing Business Within a State*, 32 HARV. L. REV. 871 (1919); Note, *Recent Interpretations of "Doing Business" Statutes*, 44 IOWA L. REV. 345 (1959).

[139] *See* Kurland, note 124, *supra*, at 584–86; *Developments in the Law-State-Court Jurisdiction*, 73 HARV. L. REV. 909, 919–23 (1960).

[140] *Developments*, note 139, *supra*, at 919. *See generally* William A. Holby, Note, *"Doing Business": Defining State Control Over Foreign Corporations*, 32 VAND. L. REV. 1105 (1979); Note, *Jurisdiction Over Foreign Corporations — An Analysis of Due Process*, 104 U. PA. L. REV. 381 (1955).

[141] Hazard, note 124, *supra*, at 272.

[142] 274 U.S. 352 (1927). *See generally* Austin W. Scott, *Jurisdiction Over Nonresident Motorists*, 39 HARV. L. REV. 563 (1926).

[143] 274 U.S. at 355.

invalidated as fictitious an analogous use of the concept of implied consent.[144] However, it upheld jurisdiction under the statute because of the strong interest Massachusetts had in highway safety:

> Motor vehicles are dangerous machines; and, even when skillfully and carefully operated, their use is attended by serious dangers to persons and property. In the public interest the State may make and enforce regulations reasonably calculated to promote care on the part of all, residents and non-residents alike, who use its highways. The measure in question operates to require a non-resident to answer for his conduct in the State where arise causes of action alleged against him, as well as to provide for a claimant a convenient method by which he may sue to enforce his rights.[145]

Most commentators would agree that the Court reached the best result in *Hess* and, in the language above, offered the best of reasons. It is impossible, however, to square this rationale for personal jurisdiction with *Pennoyer*. However desirable it might be for Massachusetts courts to have an opportunity to adjudicate Pawloski's claim, this has nothing to do with whether Hess was served there, or whether he may be regarded as having consented to suit through appointment of an in-state agent.

This dichotomy reveals the legal climate in which *Hess* was decided. Lower courts and the United States Supreme Court were growing disenchanted with an interpretation of due process which denied states the opportunity to address by judicial proceedings conduct occurring within their borders. The language from *Hess* quoted above says as much.[146] But there was little room in the approach of *Pennoyer* for this kind of sentiment. *Hess* reveals the schizophrenia eventually created in the law of personal jurisdiction by *Pennoyer*'s territorial limitations.

The weight upon the old rule eventually became intolerable. As a result, the Court quietly overthrew the restraints of *Pennoyer* in *International Shoe Co. v. Washington*.[147]

---

[144] 274 U.S. at 355 (*citing Flexner v. Farson*, 248 U.S. 289 (1919)).

[145] 274 U.S. at 356.

[146] *Henry L. Doherty & Co. v. Goodman*, 294 U.S. 623 (1935), provides another example. The Court permitted personal jurisdiction over a nonresident individual who had operated a securities business in the forum state. Plaintiff had invoked an implied consent statute which was about as tenuous as the one in *Hess*. As in *Hess*, the Court cited but refused to follow *Flexner*. *See* note 144 and related text, *supra*. The real reason for the decision in *Doherty* seems to be the Court's observation that "Iowa treats the business of dealing in corporate securities as exceptional, and subjects it to special regulation." 294 U.S. at 627. *See* Willis L. M. Reese & Nina M. Galston, *Doing an Act or Causing Consequences as Bases of Judicial Jurisdiction*, 44 Iowa L. Rev. 249 (1959).

[147] 326 U.S. 310 (1945).

§ 3.06   *INTERNATIONAL SHOE* AND THE BEGINNING OF THE MODERN ERA

[1]   *International Shoe Co. v. Washington*[148]

[a]   Due Process and the Reasonableness of Plaintiff's Forum Choice

The International Shoe Company was incorporated in Delaware and had its principal place of business in Missouri. International Shoe employed Washington residents to solicit orders there. They reported directly to the company's main office in St. Louis. Washington sued International Shoe to collect unemployment compensation tax upon salaries defendant had paid to its Washington employees. International Shoe challenged personal jurisdiction in Washington. The Washington Supreme Court ruled that personal jurisdiction existed over the defendant. It relied on United States Supreme Court doctrine[149] to conclude that International Shoe's Washington activities constituted a sufficient in-state presence to make it amenable to suit.

The United States Supreme Court affirmed, but on significantly different grounds. Noting that "the corporate personality is a fiction," the Court proceeded to divest corporate "presence" of its special significance:

> To say that the corporation is so far "present" [in a state] as to satisfy due process requirements . . . is to beg the question to be decided. For the terms "present" or "presence" are used merely to symbolize those activities of the corporation's agent within the state which courts will deem to be sufficient to satisfy the demands of due process. . . . Those demands may be met by such contacts of the corporation with the state of the forum as make it reasonable, in the context of our federal system of government, to require the corporation to defend the particular suit which is brought there.[150]

This language from the Court's opinion is illuminating in several respects. First, it reminds the reader why due process protection is necessary. Without it, plaintiff can "require" the defendant "to defend the particular suit" wherever plaintiff chooses to bring it. The guarantee of due process permits defendant to minimize the ordeal created by plaintiff's forum choice by giving defendant a means of attacking it directly at the outset of suit.[151] Due process also provides defendant an alternative by tempering the effect of full faith and credit, permitting defendant to ignore plaintiff's case altogether and to collaterally attack the resulting default judgment if plaintiff tries to enforce it in defen-

---

[148] 326 U.S. 310 (1945). *See generally, Symposium — Fifty Years of International Shoe: The Past and Future of Personal Jurisdiction*, 28 U. CAL. DAVIS L. REV. 513 (1995).

[149] For discussion of the doctrine and illustrative cases, see § 3.05, *supra*.

[150] 326 U.S. at 316–17.

[151] For a discussion of the dynamics of direct attack, see § 3.04[1], *supra*.

dant's home state.[152] Thus, plaintiff's power to require defendant to participate where plaintiff chooses is limited by the due process constraints on the scope of personal jurisdiction.[153]

Second, the above passage from *International Shoe* indicates that due process will limit plaintiff to "reasonable" choices and tells us that an important focus for determining jurisdiction will be on the "contacts" the corporate defendant has with the forum state. This is a pragmatic, fact-centered approach to setting limits on personal jurisdiction.[154] It differs from the formalistic approach of *Pennoyer* and lacks *Pennoyer*'s preoccupation with whether service of process has been completed within the territorial limits of the forum. Most important, the Supreme Court approved personal jurisdiction in *International Shoe* based upon service of process outside Washington's boundaries.[155]

For a nonresident defendant who cannot be found and served within the forum state, *Shoe* announced that good personal jurisdiction requires that the defendant "have certain *minimum contacts* with [the forum], such that the maintenance of the suit does not offend 'traditional notions of fair play and substantial justice.' "[156]

[b]   The Advent of Minimum Contacts

International Shoe's "minimum contacts" test has dominated the law of personal jurisdiction.[157] Absent consent, waiver, or suit in defendant's home state,[158] minimum contacts between the forum and the defendant are necessary to make plaintiff's choice a constitutional forum.[159] When plaintiff

---

[152] *E.g.*, *Hanson v. Denckla*, 357 U.S. 235, 255 (1958) ("Delaware is under no obligation to give full faith and credit to a Florida judgment invalid in Florida because offensive to the Due Process Clause of the Fourteenth Amendment"). For a discussion of collateral attack and of how direct and collateral attack options combine to secure due process protection, see § 3.04[2], *supra*.

[153] *See Ruhrgas AG v. Marathon Oil Co.*, 526 U.S. 574, 584 (1999).

[154] The Court notes this: "It is evident that the criteria by which we mark the boundary line between those activities which justify the subjection of a corporation to suit, and those which do not, cannot be simply mechanical or quantitative." *International Shoe*, 326 U.S. at 319.

[155] "In suggesting that service outside of the state without more would suffice, the opinion offered the states an opportunity to dispense with the cumbersome procedure of service on a state official plus extraterritorial notice, the method suggested in *Pennoyer* and utilized extensively by the states since." Philip B. Kurland, *The Supreme Court, the Due Process Clause and the In Personam Jurisdiction of State Courts From Pennoyer to Denckla: A Review*, 25 U. Chi. L. Rev. 569, 590 (1958). *See also* Peter Hay, *Refining Personal Jurisdiction in the United States*, 35 Int'l & Comp. L.Q. 32, 61 (1986) (observing that the case "freed American jurisdictional thinking from the territorial strait jacket of the historical requirement that the defendant be present in the forum at the time of service.").

[156] 326 U.S. at 316, *quoting Milliken v. Meyer*, 311 U.S. 457, 463 (1940) (emphasis added).

[157] *E.g.*, *Burger King, Inc. v. Rudzewicz*, 471 U.S. 462, 474 (1985) ("[T]he constitutional touchstone remains whether the defendant purposefully established 'minimum contacts' in the forum State" [*citing International Shoe*]). *International Shoe* also provides material for a due process hurdle beyond minimum contacts. *See* note 174 and accompanying text, *infra*.

[158] *See* § 3.03 (traditionally accepted forms of personal jurisdiction), *supra*.

[159] On how contacts function in the test, *see* § 3.09, *infra*.

selects defendant's home forum, the reasonableness of the choice will usually be so obvious as to gainsay the minimum contacts question.[160] But when and how is the minimum contacts test satisfied when plaintiff selects another forum?

For several reasons, *International Shoe* does not provide a complete answer to this question. To an extent, the problem is inherent in the approach announced by the case. Fairness is a vague concept. It is one thing to declare that due process permits jurisdiction over nonresident defendants when fair under the circumstances. It is another to sift the facts of cases in an effort to apply the standard.[161] Beyond that, the Court's analysis in *International Shoe* is blurred by reluctance to break sharply with prior decisions.[162] Finally, the facts of the case were not especially demanding. Washington state courts probably would have had personal jurisdiction over the case even under the Court's earlier, more restrictive case law.[163]

The broader jurisdictional implications of the minimum contacts test would become clear only in later cases. However, the Court's opinion did offer principles which were to provide much of the foundation for modern doctrine. To begin with, a geographical outlook concerning jurisdictional facts would be as important under *International Shoe* as it was under *Pennoyer*. The former simply attached clearer, more decisive importance to the location within the forum of facts about the controversy and about the defendant, and far less importance to whether service of process was completed there.[164]

International Shoe identified two types of contacts a nonresident defendant could have with the forum. Either, the case suggested, could support personal jurisdiction if sufficiently developed. The first type consisted of defendant's activity within the forum state related to the controversy. The second consisted of defendant's unrelated contacts.[165] The Court's recognition of the latter meant that, even when the facts of the controversy arose outside the forum, personal jurisdiction might be possible if a sufficient amount of the nonresident defendant's other activities occurred within the forum. "[T]here have been instances," observed the Court, "in which the continuous corporate

---

[160] *See* § 3.08[3][a] (a comparison of jurisdiction based on citizenship with jurisdiction over nonresident defendants supported by minimum contacts), *infra*.

[161] For discussion of how the fact-sensitive nature of the minimum contacts approach produces inherent uncertainties, see § 3.09[3], *infra*.

[162] "That the Supreme Court was cautious in developing the new approach and was unwilling to cut off precedent directly in *International Shoe* is not surprising. The history of jurisdiction has been one of gradual evolution, of new ideas growing out of old, until the new completely supplants the old." Joseph J. Kalo, *Jurisdiction as an Evolutionary Process: The Development of Quasi In Rem and In Personam Principles*, 1978 DUKE L.J. 1147, 1184 n.234.

[163] Kurland, note 155, *supra*, at 592.

[164] While the case established the principle that personal jurisdiction would not necessarily require service of process to be completed within the forum, it was silent concerning the converse — whether service on the defendant within the forum would invariably create good personal jurisdiction. For recent developments on this issue, see § 3.08[3][b], *infra*.

[165] In the subsequent refinement of minimum contacts doctrine, these were to provide support for *specific* and *general jurisdiction*, respectively. *See* § 3.09[2], *infra*.

operations within a state were thought so substantial and of such a nature as to justify suit against it on causes of action arising from dealings entirely distinct from those activities."[166] The Court did not clearly indicate when either type alone would be sufficient to provide minimum contacts. Both types may have been present in *International Shoe*. The company's general activities in the forum had been substantial, "systematic and continuous."[167] At the same time, "[t]he obligation . . . sued upon arose out of [the] very activities" of the defendant.[168]

[c]   Justifications for *Shoe*'s Extension of Personal Jurisdiction

The Supreme Court laid down three justifications for the Washington court's personal jurisdiction over International Shoe. Each provided a reason for attaching importance to defendant's contact with the forum; each would figure significantly in later cases.

First, the Court suggested that, given sufficient contacts, it would be reasonable to subject the defendant to suit as a fair exchange for the advantages it received from the forum.

> [T]o the extent that a corporation exercises the privilege of conducting activities within a state, it enjoys the benefits and protection of the laws of that state. The exercise of that privilege may give rise to obligations . . . .[169]

This suggests an analogy to forum citizenship as a basis for personal jurisdiction.[170] Granted, the nonresident defendant's enjoyment of forum benefits and protection is not likely to be as pervasive as that of a forum citizen, and thus the case for personal jurisdiction over the former may not be as easy to establish. However, the process of reasoning toward a conclusion of personal jurisdiction is much the same.[171] Under this rationale, a nonresident defendant's contacts

---

[166] 326 U.S. at 318.

[167] 326 U.S. at 320.

[168] 326 U.S. at 320.

[169] 326 U.S. at 319. This line of argument casts the nonresident defendant and the forum state into a relationship similar to that of contracting parties. Defendant thus bargains with the state by accepting benefits in return for consent to jurisdiction. "Consent is a seductive notion because it seems to explain obligations in terms of the obligated individual's voluntary choice." Lea Brilmayer, *Consent, Contract and Territory*, 74 MINN. L. REV. 1, 21 (1989). Note, however, that such jurisdiction does not require defendant's knowing and actual consent. Consent has less descriptive power in this context than where plaintiff has expressly contracted for defendant's consent to jurisdiction. This is why consent-to-jurisdiction clauses in contracts pose little analytic difficulty and are freely enforced. *See* § 3.03[2][d], *supra*.

[170] On forum citizenship as a basis for personal jurisdiction, see § 3.03[1], *supra*. It is significant that *International Shoe* describes its due process standard by quoting from *Milliken v. Meyer*, note 156 and related text, *supra*, an earlier case where the Supreme Court had confirmed a forum state's jurisdictional power over its own citizen.

[171] *Compare* the language from *International Shoe*, text accompanying note 169, *supra*, *with* the following from *Milliken v. Meyer*, 311 U.S. 457 (1940): "Domicile in the state is alone sufficient to bring an absent defendant within the reach of the state's jurisdiction . . . ." *Milliken*, 311 U.S.

with the forum (understood as advantages conferred by the forum state) could be so extensive as to support personal jurisdiction for causes of action arising elsewhere.[172]

Second, personal jurisdiction will be possible even when advantages conferred on a nonresident defendant by the forum are so small as to strain the idea of amenability to suit as a fair exchange, so long as defendant acted within the forum to cause the controversy. The forum is entitled to exercise jurisdiction in such cases in furtherance of a regulatory interest. The passage from *International Shoe* quoted above continues:

> . . . so far as those obligations arise out of or are connected with the activities within the state, a procedure which requires the corporation to respond to a suit brought to enforce them can, in most instances, hardly be said to be undue.[173]

Finally, the Court suggested another way of evaluating defendant's relationship with the forum. The burden in having to defend away from home will vary depending, among other things, on how unfamiliar or inconvenient the forum really is to the defendant. The Court thus observed that "[a]n estimate of the inconveniences which would result to the corporation from a trial away from its home or principal place of business is relevant" to an examination of defendant's contacts with the forum.[174] It may again be useful to make an analogy between personal jurisdiction over nonresidents and the same over forum citizens. A further reason supporting near automatic jurisdiction over the latter is that citizens usually experience the least disorientation and inconvenience when defending at home.[175] Significant contacts between the nonresident defendant and the forum may suggest that the place for suit selected by plaintiff bears at least some resemblance to defendant's home turf. This may be true even if defendant's contacts with the forum are unrelated to the controversy.[176]

---

at 462. "The state which accords him privileges and affords protection to him and his property by virtue of his domicile may also exact reciprocal duties." 311 U.S. at 463.

[172] The Supreme Court confirmed this possibility in *Perkins v. Benguet Consol. Mining Co.*, 342 U.S. 437 (1952), *discussed in* § 3.06[2][b], *infra.*

[173] 326 U.S. at 319. The Court gave this regulatory rationale greater attention later in *McGee v. International Life Ins. Co.*, 355 U.S. 220 (1957), *discussed in* § 3.06[2][a], *infra.* The rationale is of major contemporary significance. *See* § 3.10[1], *infra.*

[174] 326 U.S. at 317, *citing Hutchinson v. Chase & Gilbert*, 45 F.2d 139, 141 (2d Cir. 1930). This concern may now stand apart from the minimum contacts test. *Asahi Metal Ind. Co., Ltd., v. Superior Court*, 480 U.S. 102 (1987), indicates that a forum may have minimum contacts with a nonresident defendant yet be so inconvenient that due process prevents exercise of personal jurisdiction. Five Justices in *Asahi* suggested minimum contacts between the forum and the defendant may have existed. But they joined three other members of the Court to conclude that forcing a Japanese litigant to defend in California against a Taiwanese claimant would (in language drawn from *International Shoe*) violate "traditional notions of fair play and substantial justice." 480 U.S. at 113. On *Asahi*, see generally § 3.12[2], *infra.*

[175] *See* § 3.03[1], *supra.*

[176] "If the primary purpose of jurisdiction is to protect defendants from unfair litigation burdens, it is probably not oppressive for a defendant to be sued in a state where the defendant conducts highly regularized activities, even if those activities are unrelated to the plaintiff's

[2]   Jurisdictional Sufficiency Elaborated — Two Significant Early Cases

Two succeeding decisions in which the Supreme Court attempted to sort out the implications of the *International Shoe* test contributed enough to current law to merit discussion.

[a]   *McGee v. International Life Ins. Co.*[177]

The Court noted in *International Shoe* that a corporation's "single or isolated items of activities in a state . . . are not enough to subject it to suit on causes of action *unconnected* with the activities there."[178] At the same time, the case appeared to place a premium on the fact that there defendant's activities generating the controversy arose in the forum state.[179] What would happen if a foreign corporation's contacts with the forum state were "single or isolated," but the case arose out of those very contacts? The Supreme Court did not have to answer the question, because International Shoe's overall contacts with Washington were "systematic and continuous."[180] The Court subsequently answered the question in *McGee* and, in so doing, realized some of the more liberating implications of the minimum contacts approach.

McGee, as the beneficiary of her deceased son's life insurance policy, sued defendant International Life in California. Defendant was served by mail in Texas, its corporate home. International Life declined to appear in the case, and plaintiff obtained a default judgment. Plaintiff took the California judgment to Texas and attempted to enforce it. International Life collaterally attacked the judgment, arguing that California did not have personal jurisdiction. Texas courts agreed. The United States Supreme Court did not question defendant's right to argue that the California court lacked jurisdiction in an effort to resist the California judgment,[181] but found the argument without merit and reversed.

The facts revealed that defendant conducted virtually no business in California. Decedent's policy had been the only one in force there. It would be hard to imagine a clearer example of "single or isolated" corporate activity in

---

particular claim." Kathleen Waits, *Values, Intuitions, and Opinion Writing: The Judicial Process and State Court Jurisdiction*, 1983 U. Ill. L. Rev. 917, 940. *Accord*, R. Leflar, et al., American Conflicts Law § 22 (4th ed. 1986).

[177] 355 U.S. 220 (1957).

[178] 326 U.S. at 317 (emphasis added).

[179] *See* note 168 and related text, *supra.*

[180] *See* note 167 and related text, *supra.*

[181] Defendant was able to raise the personal jurisdiction issue only because it had not taken any part in the California proceeding. But, while defaulting in California preserved defendant's opportunity to litigate the personal jurisdiction question later in Texas, it also made everything turn on winning the issue. Because International Life lost, it was never able to present the substantial case it apparently had on the merits — that the policy was inapplicable because the insured died by suicide. 355 U.S. at 223. Such are the risks of favoring collateral over direct attack as a means of raising personal jurisdiction issues. For a discussion of direct and collateral attack on personal jurisdiction and considerations in choosing between the two, see § 3.04, *supra.*

the forum state. The Court nonetheless held that California had validly exercised jurisdiction over International Life, demonstrating that minimum contacts can be minimal indeed — so long as they are sufficiently related to the lawsuit:

> [W]e think it apparent that the Due Process Clause did not preclude the California court from entering a judgment binding on respondent. It is sufficient for purposes of due process that the suit was based on a contract which had substantial connection with that State. . . . The contract was delivered in California, the premiums were mailed from there and the insured was a resident of that State when he died.[182]

The Court explained why it mattered that defendant's forum contacts were related to the controversy. "It cannot be denied that California has a manifest interest in providing effective means of redress for its residents when their insurers refuse to pay claims."[183] "These residents would be at a severe disadvantage if they were forced to follow the insurance company to a distant State in order to hold it legally accountable."[184] And the Court suggested that, on the whole, California might have been the most logical place to try the case.[185] There might have been some inconvenience for International Life, "but certainly nothing which amounts to a denial of due process."[186]

The most enduring aspect of *McGee* is that it established beyond question the forum's authority to exercise jurisdiction over nonresident defendants in lawsuits resulting from their forum-directed activities.[187] On the other hand, it

---

[182] 355 U.S. at 223.

[183] 355 U.S. at 223.

[184] 355 U.S. at 223.

[185] "Often the crucial witnesses — as here on the company's defense of suicide — will be found in the insured's locality." 355 U.S. at 223.

[186] 355 U.S. at 224. *Travelers Health Ass'n v. Virginia*, 339 U.S. 643 (1950), foreshadowed the Supreme Court's approach in *McGee*. Defendant Travelers sold insurance in Virginia without registering as required by state law. Virginia sued for an order forbidding Travelers from doing business in the state. Travelers was served by mail in its home state of Nebraska. The corporation appeared specially to challenge jurisdiction over it in Virginia. Virginia's highest court upheld personal jurisdiction over Travelers, and the United States Supreme Court affirmed, holding the result to be "consistent with fair play and substantial justice," and "not offensive to the Due Process Clause." 339 U.S. at 649. In *Travelers*, the Court gave a clearer indication than it had in *International Shoe* of a policy supporting longer jurisdictional reach of courts: the legitimate need of a forum to regulate through judicial proceedings activities occurring within its borders. The "state has a legitimate interest," said the Court, "in all insurance policies protecting its residents against risks," 339 U.S. at 647, an interest sufficient to support personal jurisdiction even if the defendant cannot be found and served within the forum state. In addition, *Travelers* expanded upon *International Shoe*'s suggestion, note 174 and related text, *supra*, that courts address the actual degree of inconvenience to the defendant when evaluating minimum contacts in each case. The Court indicated that an examination of both sides of the convenience question might be in order, and that the inquiry might be expanded to take into account reasons why the present forum might be more convenient to plaintiff. 339 U.S. at 649.

[187] When, as in *McGee*, the cause of action arises entirely from activities of the defendant directed at the forum, it is universally accepted that due process does not prevent the forum from exercising jurisdiction. *Cf. RESTATEMENT (SECOND) OF CONFLICTS* § 35 comment e (1971) ("It is always reasonable for a State to exercise judicial jurisdiction over an individual as to causes of action

is difficult to say how much reliance can safely be placed on some of the more freewheeling arguments made by the Court in support of its conclusion. The Supreme Court has neither questioned *McGee*, nor been reluctant to cite the case. Yet it may be true that Supreme Court decisions on personal jurisdiction represent more a spectrum of opinion than a single point of view. If this is so, then *McGee* exists at one end of the spectrum.[188] As Professor Weintraub observed, the case "was the high-water mark of personal jurisdiction."[189]

[b] *Perkins v. Benguet Consolidated Mining Co.*[190]

International Shoe noted the possibility that "continuous corporate operations within a state" could be "so substantial and of such a nature as to justify suit against it on causes of action arising from dealings entirely distinct from those activities."[191] *Perkins* furnished an example five years later.

Benguet was a Philippine corporation whose operations there were disrupted by World War II. Benguet's president moved to an office in Ohio and transacted "a continuous and systematic, but limited, part of its general business" in Ohio.[192] Perkins sued Benguet in Ohio over corporate obligations arising outside the forum. Believing that due process prevented personal jurisdiction over Benguet, the Ohio courts refused to hear the case. The United States Supreme Court reversed.

The Court considered whether Ohio was under an obligation to provide Perkins with a forum for suit against Benguet and concluded that it was not. It also considered

> whether as a matter of federal due process, the business done in Ohio by the respondent mining company was sufficiently substantial and of such a nature as to *permit* Ohio to entertain a cause of action against a foreign corporation, where the cause of action arose from activities entirely distinct from its activities in Ohio.[193]

Invoking *International Shoe*, the Supreme Court set out to answer the question by examining Benguet's unrelated contacts with the forum. Noting that the corporate president "carried on in Ohio a continuous and systematic

---

arising from business done by him within its territory."). *See, e.g., Burger King Corp. v. Rudzewicz,* 471 U.S. 462, 473 (1985) (applying the principle and citing *McGee*). *See generally* § 3.10[3] (discussing *Burger King*), *infra.*

[188] *E.g.,* compare the *McGee* Court's recognition of the forum's interest in providing a means for its citizens to sue and of the significance of the forum as a generally convenient place for suit with the Court's rejection of the same concerns in *Hanson v. Denckla,* 357 U.S. 235 (1958). It may be possible to reconcile the results in the two cases, *see* § 3.07[2], *infra,* yet they do seem to reflect differences in philosophy.

[189] Russell J. Weintraub, *Due Process Limitations on the Personal Jurisdiction of State Courts: Time for Change,* 63 Or. L. Rev. 485, 489 (1984).

[190] 342 U.S. 437 (1952).

[191] 326 U.S. at 318.

[192] 342 U.S. at 438.

[193] 342 U.S. at 447 (emphasis in original).

supervision of the necessarily limited wartime activities of the company,"[194] the Court concluded that due process would permit Ohio courts to exercise personal jurisdiction over Perkins' claim.

Some commentators have read *Perkins* to suggest the possibility of personal jurisdiction wherever a corporation carries on activities capable of the "continuous and systematic" description.[195] Others argue a narrower reading of the case, pointing to exceptional circumstances which made Ohio the most feasible (perhaps the only) forum in which Perkins could have sued Benguet.[196] It is at least true that, like the facts of *International Shoe*, the facts of *Perkins* were so sympathetic to a finding of jurisdiction that the Court was not driven to explain what might satisfy due process in closer, more difficult cases.

At the same time, *Perkins* continues to figure importantly in the law of personal jurisdiction. It is one of only two cases in which the United States Supreme Court has applied *International Shoe* to chart the boundaries of personal jurisdiction when no contacts between the forum and the defendant could be funneled through the controversy. In the second case,[197] the Court was careful not to disturb *Perkins'* authority.

§ 3.07   PERSONAL JURISDICTION'S GREEN-LIGHT PERIOD — DEVELOPMENTS UNTIL 1977

Once state courts and legislatures were able to absorb the implications of *International Shoe* and succeeding cases, the results were dramatic. State legislatures greatly expanded the extraterritorial jurisdiction of their courts by equipping them with long-arm statutes.[198] Plaintiffs took advantage of the statutes to bring about a significant rise in interstate litigation.

Clearly, due process still imposed some limits on the extraterritorial jurisdiction of state courts. For over thirty years, however, the Supreme Court was relatively silent in declaring what those limits were. From the time of the

---

[194] 342 U.S. at 448.

> He kept there office files . . . carried on there correspondence . . . drew and distributed there salary checks maintained in Clermont County, Ohio, two active bank accounts carrying substantial balances of company funds. . . . Several directors' meetings were held at his office or home in Clermont County. From that office he supervised policies dealing with the rehabilitation of the corporation's properties in the Philippines and he dispatched funds to cover purchases of machinery for such rehabilitation.

342 U.S. at 448.

[195] *See* the authorities cited in note 176, *supra*.

[196] Arthur T. von Mehren & Donald T. Trautman, *Jurisdiction to Adjudicate: A Suggested Analysis*, 79 HARV. L. REV. 1121, 1144 (1966); Note, *Developments in the Law-State Court Jurisdiction*, 73 HARV. L. REV. 909, 932 (1960); RESTATEMENT (SECOND) OF JUDGMENTS introduction at 25 (1982).

[197] *Helicopteros Nacionales de Colombia, S.A. v. Hall*, 466 U.S. 408 (1984), *discussed in* § 3.11[1], *infra*.

[198] *See* § 3.07[1], *infra*.

Court's *International Shoe* decision until it decided *Shaffer v. Heitner*[199] in 1977, the Supreme Court handed down only one decision negating in general terms an attempted exercise of extraterritorial jurisdiction.

The case was *Hanson v. Denckla*.[200] *Hanson* was, however, a puzzling and rather unpopular decision. The Supreme Court all but abandoned it for twenty years. Meanwhile state and lower federal courts were left to grapple on their own with difficult questions in applying *International Shoe*. Some courts restrained themselves. Others did not. This was the great, freewheeling period of extraterritorial jurisdiction.

[1]   The Proliferation of State Long-Arm Statutes

International Shoe and succeeding cases[201] made clear that states could in appropriate cases exercise personal jurisdiction when service of process could not be completed in the forum state. But the Supreme Court's decisions alone did not give plaintiffs access to extraterritorial personal jurisdiction. States were under no obligation to endow their courts with such authority.[202] Even when they created extraterritorial jurisdiction, they were free to offer plaintiffs less than the full amount permitted by due process.[203]

Many rules of personal jurisdiction — for example, jurisdiction by domicile or actual consent[204] — had their origins in common law.[205] But personal jurisdiction in some types of cases was unknown under the common law. These were more likely to involve nonresident defendants, such as jurisdiction based on doing business in the forum[206] or on defendant's acts done or consequences caused in the forum.[207] Judicial authority in such cases traditionally derived from statutes.[208] Thus it was necessary for state legislatures to take the initiative if their courts were to capitalize on new opportunities for personal jurisdiction.[209]

---

[199] 433 U.S. 186 (1977).

[200] 357 U.S. 235 (1958). *See* § 3.07[2], *infra.*

[201] For a discussion of *International Shoe* and the Court's subsequent decisions in *McGee* and *Perkins*, see § 3.06, *supra.*

[202] *Perkins v. Consolidated Benguet Mining Co.*, 342 U.S. 437, 440 (1952).

[203] Eugene F. Scoles, Hay, Borchers & Symeonides, Conflict of Laws § 514 (4th ed. 2004); *Restatement (Second) of Judgments* § 4 comment (c) (1982).

[204] For a discussion of these grounds for jurisdiction, see § 3.03, *supra.*

[205] Graham C. Lilly, *Jurisdiction Over Domestic and Alien Defendants*, 69 Va. L. Rev. 85, 123 n.145 (1983).

[206] *See Restatement (Second) of Conflicts* § 35 comment (f) (1971).

[207] *See* Willis L.M. Reese & Nina M. Galston, *Doing an Act or Causing Consequences as Bases of Judicial Jurisdiction*, 44 Iowa L. Rev. 249, 265 (1959).

[208] *See Scoles & Hay*, note 203, *supra.*

[209] The response of state legislatures was rapid. Rhonda Wasserman, *The Subpoena Power: Pennoyer's Last Vestige*, 74 Minn. L. Rev. 37, 54–56 (1989). Today, "[a]ll states have statutes dealing with the exercise of jurisdiction in transactions having out-of-state elements. . . . Their shape has evolved in response to evolving Supreme Court interpretations of the Constitutional

They responded by enacting what have come to be called *long-arm statutes*.[210] These provide personal jurisdiction over nonresident defendants who cannot be found and served in the forum state. They have generally taken one of two forms. The first attempts to categorize factual situations which seem likely to satisfy the minimum contacts test of *International Shoe* and authorizes the court to exercise jurisdiction over nonresidents in such cases.[211] The second takes a blanket approach, conferring all jurisdiction permitted by state and federal constitutional law.[212]

Neither approach is ideal.[213] Implicit in the assumption of lawmaking authority by state legislatures is a judgment that they have a special function to perform in determining the appropriate reach of their court's personal jurisdiction.[214] They may be abdicating that responsibility when they enact blanket long-arm statutes. Moreover, in declining to be specific, the legislature withholds guidance from those wishing to learn in advance whether their in-state activities will expose them to personal jurisdiction.[215] On the other hand, legislatures enacting particularized long-arm statutes may unwittingly omit some legitimate factual category, impairing their courts' useful range of personal jurisdiction.[216]

Differences between the two approaches, however, have not turned out to be great in application. The state courts have tended to interpret their statutes to confer all of the jurisdiction permitted by due process, regardless of the statutes' language.[217]

---

limitations on state court jurisdiction." RESTATEMENT (SECOND) OF JUDGMENTS § 4 reporter's note (1981).

[210] Typically, long-arm provisions have been directly enacted by legislatures, but they can also emerge as court rules promulgated under legislative authority. *Lilly*, note 205, *supra*, at 205.

[211] *E.g.*, NEW YORK CIV. PRAC. LAW AND RULES § 302(a); 735 ILL. COMP. STAT. ANN. 512-209.

[212] *E.g.*, CAL. CIV. PROC. CODE § 410.10 (2006); N.J. COURT RULES 1969 R. 4:4-4(b)(1) (2006); R.I. GEN. LAWS ANN. § 9-5-33. For example, the California provision states: "A court of this state may exercise jurisdiction on any basis not inconsistent with the Constitution of this state or of the United States."

[213] For a review of the strengths and weaknesses of each approach, see Douglas D. McFarland, *Dictum Run Wild: How Long-Arm Statutes Extended to the Limits of Due Process*, 84 B.U. L. REV. 491, 531–36 (2004).

[214] *See* notes 208 and 209 and related text, *supra*.

[215] Two recent commentators argue against the blanket approach. McFarland, note 213, *supra*, at 536; Patrick J. Borchers, *Internet Libel: The Consequences of a Non-Rule Approach to Personal Jurisdiction*, 98 NW. U. L. REV. 473, 474 (2004).

[216] *See* R. WEINTRAUB, COMMENTARY ON THE CONFLICT OF LAWS 197 (4th ed. 2001).

[217] Robert H. Abrams & Paul R. Dimond, *Toward a Constitutional Framework for the Control of State Court Jurisdiction*, 69 MINN. L. REV. 75, 84 n.43 (1984). For one such example, see Carole L. Baab, Note, *Current Status of Personal and General Jurisdiction in Minnesota*, 16 WM. MITCHELL L. REV. 309, 334 (1990). *But cf.* M. GLANNON, CIVIL PROCEDURE 31 (6th ed. 2008) ("Unfortunately, courts have not always grasped [the] distinction between broad interpretation of . . . enumerated acts and absorbing the whole constitutional sphere.").

[2] *Hanson v. Denckla* — The Court's Isolated Warning

The facts of *Hanson v. Denckla*[218] were quite complicated.[219] Two factions fought over distribution of a $400,000 estate. The Denckla group claimed that the money passed to them through decedent's will. The Hanson group claimed that the funds were not affected by the will because they were the subject of a trust (with the Hanson group as beneficiaries) created by the decedent before her death. The Denckla group brought suit in Florida to have the trust declared invalid. The Florida Supreme Court eventually ruled that it was. It also ruled that personal jurisdiction existed over two Delaware trust companies, defendants in the case who had been appointed trustees for the disputed trust. On review, a narrowly divided Supreme Court disagreed, finding that the Florida courts lacked personal jurisdiction over the trustees.

First reaching the somewhat surprising conclusion that defendants properly within the Florida courts' jurisdiction could question jurisdiction over the absent trustees,[220] the Court proceeded to the due process issue. Clearly, the case for personal jurisdiction was weaker in *Hanson* than in previous cases decided by the Court after *International Shoe*. Unlike the defendant in *Perkins v. Benguet Mining Co.*,[221] the Delaware trust companies did not conduct "continuous and systematic" operations in the forum. Indeed, they had no offices in Florida and transacted no business there.[222] The controversy centered on the validity of the trust, and the trust was created in Delaware. Therefore, unlike the defendant in *McGee*,[223] the trustees directed little if any of their activities at the forum state.[224]

---

[218] 357 U.S. 235 (1958).

[219] For more detailed statements of the case, see Austin W. Scott, *Hanson v. Denckla*, 72 HARV. L. REV. 695 (1959); Philip B. Kurland, *The Supreme Court, the Due Process Clause and the In Personam Jurisdiction of State Courts From Pennoyer to Denckla: A Review*, 25 U. CHI. L. REV. 569, 610–23 (1958).

[220] Most of the Hanson-group defendants were Florida domiciliaries and were served there. However, the Delaware-trustee defendants were foreign corporations who maintained no office in Florida and had to be served out of state by mail. They refused to participate and ultimately defaulted. The challenge concerning Florida jurisdiction over the trustees was not raised by the trustees themselves, but by the Hanson group. Traditionally, the Court has been reluctant to permit litigants, whose own constitutional rights have not been injured, to object to the proceedings by raising the rights of others. The Court got around this in *Hanson* by reading Florida procedural law to make the Delaware trustees indispensable parties to the lawsuit. Thus, it reasoned, the case could not proceed if Florida was incapable of exercising jurisdiction over them. 357 U.S. at 254–55. *See* § 9.05[2] (compulsory joinder), *infra*. Dissenting, Justice Black questioned this interpretation of Florida law and argued that at the very least the case should be remanded to the Florida courts to give them an opportunity to pass on the indispensability question. 357 U.S. at 257–62. Professor Kurland called the Court's conclusion in *Hanson* that the due process issue was properly before it a "doubtful assumption." Kurland, note 219, *supra*, at 617.

[221] *See* § 3.06[2][b], *supra*.

[222] Scott, note 219, *supra*, at 702.

[223] *See* § 3.06[2][a], *supra*.

[224] On the other hand, Justice Black contended that the Delaware trustees were not altogether free of contact with Florida. The last time the decedent exercised her power under the trust

What divided the Court was that two theories, which previously combined to support personal jurisdiction, seemed in *Hanson* to pull in opposite directions. The first of these, a power theory, was refined in *International Shoe*[225] from earlier cases. Under this theory, submission to suit is a fair exchange for the benefits and protection a nonresident defendant receives from the forum state. The second, which received more glancing treatment in *Shoe*,[226] focused on the logic or convenience of plaintiff's forum choice. The burden on defendant from litigating there is a factor. Other factors are the degree of difficulty for plaintiff in suing elsewhere and possible interest the forum state might have in making its courts available to hear the case. The Court had utilized both theories in intervening cases.[227] Never before *Hanson* had they seemed at odds.

Dissenting from the Court's refusal to permit personal jurisdiction, Justice Black argued the convenience theory: that Florida would be a logical and convenient place to adjudicate the lawsuit.[228] The question of the trust's validity bore not only on the trust itself but also on the scope and effect of decedent's will. And the will was probated in Florida. Thus, contended Justice Black, "Florida was seriously concerned with winding up Mrs. Donner's estate and with finally determining what property was to be distributed under her will."[229]

However, the *Hanson* majority adopted the power theory. In so doing, the majority did not really dispute the relative convenience of Florida as a place for suit, or the interest of the plaintiffs and the State of Florida in a Florida adjudication. It simply concluded that, without minimum contacts between the nonresident defendants and the forum capable of supporting the power theory, these other considerations did not come into play.

First, the majority brushed aside the convenience of a Florida forum. The protections of due process, it said,

> are more than a guarantee of immunity from inconvenient or distant litigation. They are a consequence of territorial limitations on the power of the respective States. However minimal the burden of defending in a foreign tribunal, a defendant may not be called upon to

---

instrument to redirect the remainder, she did so from Florida. 357 U.S. at 258 (Black, J. dissenting). Presumably, this required the assistance of at least one of the trustees. Also, at least one of the trustees transmitted trust income to the decedent while she was living in Florida. 357 U.S. at 257. The latter contact would have been more significant if the case concerned whether the trustee had breached its duty under the trust instrument, instead of whether the trust itself was valid.

[225] *See* § 3.06, *supra.*

[226] *See* § 3.06, *supra.*

[227] The Court fleshed out the logic/convenience theory in *Traveler's Health Ass'n v. Virginia*, 339 U.S. 643 (1950) (*see* § 3.06[2][a], *supra*), and in *McGee v. International Life Ins. Co.*, 355 U.S. 220 (1957) (*see* § 3.06[2][a], *supra*). On the other hand, *Perkins v. Benguet Consol. Mining Co.*, 342 U.S. 437 (1952), *see* § 3.06[2][b], *supra*, seems to proceed on the power theory.

[228] "Florida, the home of the principal contenders for Mrs. Donner's largess, was a reasonably convenient forum for all." 357 U.S. at 259 (Black, J., dissenting).

[229] 357 U.S. at 259.

do so unless he has had the "minimal contacts" with that State that are a prerequisite to its exercise of power over him.[230]

The *Hanson* majority similarly discounted the significance of contacts between the plaintiffs and the forum, stating that the "unilateral activity of those who claim some relationship with a nonresident defendant cannot satisfy the requirement of contact with the forum State."[231] The Court also refused to attach importance to Florida's interest in adjudicating this kind of lawsuit.[232]

The majority left no doubt that (1) focus on the relationship between the forum and *defendant* was both central and indispensable to its minimum contacts inquiry, and (2) contacts would achieve the minimum only if they were sufficient to support the power theory:

> The application of that rule will vary with the quality and nature of the defendant's activity, but it is essential in each case that there be some act by which the defendant purposefully avails itself of the privilege of conducting activities within the forum State, thus invoking the benefits and protections of its laws.[233]

Hanson's history as precedent reflects a reversal of the usual pattern. The contemporary force of the case is far greater than were its immediate effects.[234] For a long time, *Hanson*'s chief importance seemed to lie in confirming *International Shoe*'s admonition that due process "does not contemplate that a state may make binding a judgment *in personam* against an individual or corporate defendant with which the state has no contacts, ties, or relations."[235] Perhaps this was significant in itself, providing "a stopping place . . . on what had been the road toward nationwide in personam jurisdiction for state courts."[236]

But the case left unanswered important questions concerning how the "quality and nature of defendant's activity" should be measured in order to

---

[230] 357 U.S. at 251 (citing *International Shoe*).

[231] 357 U.S. at 253.

[232] The *Hanson* Court entertained the possibility that the facts of the controversy might so involve Florida state interests as to justify application of Florida substantive law, but stated flatly: "The issue is personal jurisdiction, not choice of law." 357 U.S. at 254. Granted, there are situations where a court constitutionally capable of applying its own substantive law to a controversy may lack contacts with the defendant necessary for personal jurisdiction. *See* the example provided in Gene R. Shreve, *Interest Analysis as Constitutional Law*, 48 Ohio St. L.J. 51, 60 n.60 (1987). In *Hanson*, however, it might have been difficult for the Supreme Court to have upheld as constitutional the Florida court's rejection of Delaware trust law in favor of its own. Frederic L. Kirgis, Jr., *The Roles of Due Process and Full Faith and Credit in Choice of Law*, 62 Cornell L. Rev. 94, 144–46 (1976); Gene R. Shreve, *In Search of a Choice-of-Law Reviewing Standard — Reflections on Allstate Insurance Co. v. Hague*, 66 Minn. L. Rev. 327, 334 (1982). Because of its ruling of no personal jurisdiction, it was unnecessary for the Court to reach the choice-of-law question.

[233] 357 U.S. at 253 (*citing International Shoe*).

[234] The case was to underpin modern decisions regulating extraterritorial jurisdiction more stringently. *E.g., Shaffer v. Heitner*, 433 U.S. 186, 215–16 (1977); *World-Wide Volkswagen Corp. v. Woodson*, 444 U.S. 286, 294–99 (1980). *See generally* § 3.10, *infra*.

[235] *International Shoe Co. v. Washington*, 326 U.S. 310, 319 (1945).

[236] Kurland, note 219, *supra*, at 622.

determine whether minimum forum contacts existed. The Court's failure to address these questions in *Hanson*, or to return to them until 1977, left considerable ambiguity in its due process doctrine. Isolated, the authority of the *Hanson* case also suffered from its complicated and somewhat bizarre facts and from the Court's questionable judgment that there was a due process issue in the case at all.[237] "In the ensuing years many commentators and courts distinguished or effectively ignored it, while suggesting or taking a more expansive approach to jurisdiction. And there the Supreme Court let things lie for two decades."[238]

[3]   Lower Courts Do (or Do Not) Restrain Themselves

The Supreme Court's failure to give much guidance left state and lower federal courts with the task of sorting out the implications of *International Shoe*.[239] It is not surprising that some courts were more cautious in exercising personal jurisdiction than others. What most divided courts was determination of the point at which the quality and extent of the nonresident defendant's forum contacts satisfied the minimum required by due process.

Some courts read a good deal into the minimum contacts requirement. For example, in *Erlanger Mills, Inc. v. Cohoes Fibre Mills, Inc.*,[240] the court refused to hold a defendant New York corporation amenable to suit in North Carolina. Plaintiff's representative traveled to defendant's New York plant and contracted there for a shipment of synthetic yarn. Defendant shipped the yarn, FOB New York. The yarn arrived at plaintiff's North Carolina plant and plaintiff alleged it to be defective. Noting that the defendant had done no other business in North Carolina, the court found the transaction insufficient to provide minimum contacts between the defendant and the forum. The court feared grave consequences from finding personal jurisdiction in such cases: "It requires no flight of fancy to foresee the resulting maze of lawsuits adjudicating the interests of persons having only the faintest and most remote links with the State exercising authority."[241] Other decisions also reflect a relatively restrained view of the reach of personal jurisdiction permitted by the minimum contacts requirement.[242]

Some courts, however, were willing to entertain personal jurisdiction over nonresident defendants with less than extensive forum contacts. In one well-

---

[237] *See* note 220, *supra*.

[238] Kevin M. Clermont, *Restating Territorial Jurisdiction and Venue for State and Federal Courts*, 66 CORNELL L. REV. 411, 419 (1981).

[239] For discussion of some of the decisions during this period, see Michael H. Cardozo, *The Reach of the Legislature and the Grasp of Jurisdiction*, 43 CORNELL L.Q. 210 (1957); David P. Currie, *The Growth of the Long Arm: Eight Years of Extended Jurisdiction in Illinois*, 1963 U. ILL. L. REV. 533.

[240] 239 F.2d 502 (4th Cir. 1956).

[241] 239 F.2d at 509.

[242] *E.g.*, *O'Brien v. Comstock Foods, Inc.*, 194 A.2d 568 (Vt. 1963); *Putnam v. Triangle Publications*, 96 S.E.2d 445 (N.C. 1957).

known case, *Gray v. American Radiator & Standard Sanitary Corp.*,[243] for example, one of the defendants challenged personal jurisdiction in an Illinois suit for injuries from a water heater which had exploded there. Defendant had manufactured the safety valve on the exploding heater, but it did no business in Illinois. It manufactured the valve in question in Ohio and sold it to another defendant who assembled the water heater in Pennsylvania. The Illinois Supreme Court conceded that any wrongful behavior attributable to the valve company occurred outside the forum state, but nonetheless concluded that its courts had personal jurisdiction. The defendant, said the court, could have contemplated that products containing its valves would be used in the forum. And, "it has undoubtedly benefited, to a degree, from the protection which our law has given to the marketing of hot water heaters containing its valves."[244]

Similarly in *Buckeye Boiler Co. v. Superior Court*,[245] plaintiff sued for injuries when a boiler manufactured by defendant Buckeye, an Ohio corporation, exploded in California. Buckeye had not sold the boiler for use in California. It had apparently been resold by the original purchaser, although how the boiler reached California was unclear. Buckeye's only known California contacts were limited sales there of a different boiler model. Nonetheless, the California Supreme Court ruled that California courts could exercise personal jurisdiction over Buckeye. It reasoned that the unrelated business Buckeye conducted in California met the threshold requirement of contacts between the defendant and the forum. The California Supreme Court then justified its decision — notwithstanding *Hanson*'s requirement of "purposeful availment by defendant[246] — in part on plaintiff's interest in having a local forum and in California's interest in providing it.

The New York Court of Appeals used even less forum contact to justify personal jurisdiction over a nonresident defendant in *Bryant v. Finnish Nat'l Airline*.[247] Plaintiff alleged that her injuries at a Paris airport occurred as a consequence of defendant airline's negligent conduct there. She sued in New York state court. Defendant flew no aircraft in the United States. Finnair's only contact with the forum state was to employ a few persons in a small New York City office to take reservations for flights within Europe. Plaintiff had not used the office, nor was she a Finnair passenger when the accident occurred. Moreover, unlike *Buckeye* and *Gray*, no harm was inflicted upon plaintiff in the forum. Nevertheless, the court found personal jurisdiction.[248]

---

[243] 176 N.E.2d 761 (Ill. 1961). For an extensive recent discussion of *Gray*, see Diane S. Kaplan, *Paddling Up the Wrong Stream: Why Stream of Commerce Theory is Not Part of the Minimum Contacts Doctrine*, 55 Baylor L. Rev. 503 (2003).

[244] 176 N.E.2d at 766.

[245] 458 P.2d 57 (Cal. 1969).

[246] 357 U.S. 235 (1958). *See* notes 231 and 232 and related text, *supra*.

[247] 208 N.E.2d 439 (N.Y. 1965).

[248] It is at least arguable that the United States Supreme Court's decision in *Helicopteros Nacionales de Colombia, S.A. v. Hall*, 466 U.S. 408 (1984), had the effect of overruling *Bryant*. For discussion of *Helicopteros*, see § 3.11[1], *infra*.

PART C.
Territorial Jurisdiction in the Modern Era

§ 3.08   *INTERNATIONAL SHOE* GIVES BUT ALSO TAKES AWAY JURISDICTION — SPREAD OF THE MINIMUM CONTACTS STANDARD

International Shoe and the early cases following it were first and most easily seen as a force for expanding courts' personal jurisdiction. On another category of territorial jurisdiction, however, *Shoe* eventually exerted an opposite, restrictive effect. Supreme Court rulings in *Shaffer v. Heitner*[249] and *Rush v. Savchuk*[250] extended the minimum contacts standard to *quasi in rem* cases, stripping that jurisdictional category of much of its discrete significance and appeal to plaintiffs. These developments also make it useful to consider how remaining applications of territorial jurisdiction fare when subjected to *Shoe's* minimum contacts test.

[1]   Minimum Contacts and the Decline of *Quasi in Rem* Jurisdiction — *Shaffer v. Heitner*[251]

Plaintiff brought a shareholder derivative suit[252] against officers and directors of the Greyhound Corp. and its subsidiary, Greyhound, Inc. Plaintiff filed the suit in Delaware, alleging that the individual defendants had caused Greyhound and its subsidiary to incur substantial expenses from civil antitrust damages and a fine for criminal contempt. The defendants neither resided in Delaware nor received service there. Moreover, the alleged wrongful acts occurred outside Delaware. Delaware may have lacked minimum contacts necessary to support personal jurisdiction over the defendants.[253] Plaintiff attempted to avoid the problem, however, by proceeding upon a *quasi in rem* (rather than *in personam*) theory of jurisdiction.[254] There seems little question that plaintiff's case met traditional *quasi in rem* standards.[255] Each of the defendants held stock in Greyhound. Greyhound was a Delaware corporation, and plaintiff relied on a Delaware statute which conferred *quasi in rem* jurisdiction over stock issued by corporations chartered there. The Delaware state courts rejected defendant's jurisdictional attack.

---

[249]   433 U.S. 186 (1977).

[250]   444 U.S. 320 (1980).

[251]   A useful study of this case by Profesor Wendy Perdue appears in CIVIL PROCEDURE STORIES Ch. 3 (Kevin M. Clermont ed., Foundation 2d ed., 2008).

[252]   Shareholders bring this suit to assert rights of the corporation when its directors will not. *See* Rule 23.1. It is usually brought against the officers and directors of the corporation for fraud, breach of fiduciary duties and other mismanagement.

[253]   However, that was by no means clear. *See* note 256, *infra*.

[254]   For discussion of these two types of territorial jurisdiction and the third (*in rem*), see § 3.02 (classical categories of territorial jurisdiction), *supra*.

[255]   *See* § 3.02[3], *supra*.

Reversing, the United States Supreme Court set out two propositions. First, exercises of *quasi in rem* jurisdiction would henceforth satisfy due process only if they met *International Shoe*'s minimum contacts test. Second, *Shaffer* failed that test. The first of the two propositions was *Shaffer*'s lasting contribution. In contrast, the Court's conclusion that Delaware lacked minimum contacts with the defendants and the controversy is open to question.[256]

Concerning the first proposition, the Court flatly stated that "all assertions of state-court jurisdiction must be evaluated according to the standards set forth in *International Shoe* and its progeny."[257] This did not make *quasi in rem* jurisdiction unconstitutional per se. However, because the Court found defendant's in-state property to be "completely unrelated to the plaintiff's cause of action," it held that "the presence of the property alone would not support the State's jurisdiction."[258]

It is possible to overstate the impact of the Court's decision on prejudgment attachments. So long as minimum contacts exist, suits begun by attachment — whether called *in personam*[259] or *quasi in rem*[260] — survive *Shaffer*. In addition, the Court may have provided exceptions (albeit narrow) to its minimum contacts rule.[261]

The fact remains, however, that *Shaffer* divested *quasi in rem* jurisdiction of much of its special appeal. A great lure of *quasi in rem* for plaintiffs had been that it provided an end run around the minimum contacts requirements of personal jurisdiction. The availability of *quasi in rem* jurisdiction in courts incapable of exercising personal jurisdiction made them attract litigation, even though the scope of *quasi in rem* judgments cannot exceed the worth of forum

---

[256] Inasmuch as Greyhound was a Delaware corporation, the alleged dissipation of the worth of the corporation by the defendants was at least arguably forum-related. *See* Robert C. Casad, *Shaffer v. Heitner: An End to Ambivalence in Jurisdictional Theory*, 26 U. Kan. L. Rev. 61, 74 (1977); David H. Vernon, *Single-Factor Bases of In Personam Jurisdiction — A Speculation on the Impact of Shaffer v. Heitner*, 1978 Wash. U. L.Q. 273, 316. The Court's arguments to the contrary are somewhat clouded.

[257] 433 U.S. at 212. The Court's choice of words seemed calculated to make its rule as applicable to exercises of *in rem* jurisdiction as to the *quasi in rem* case at hand. Elsewhere in *Shaffer*, the Court made it clear that it was referring to "the minimum-contacts standard elucidated in *International Shoe*." 433 U.S. at 207. In *Rush v. Savchuk*, 444 U.S. 320, 327 (1980), the Court reiterated that its purpose in invoking *International Shoe* in *Shaffer* was to give across-the-board application to the minimum contacts test.

[258] 433 U.S. at 209. For discussion of the effect of this ruling on subsequent cases, see Michael B. Mushlin, *The New Quasi in Rem Jurisdiction: New York's Revival of a Doctrine Whose Time Has Passed*, 55 Brook. L. Rev. 1059 (1990).

[259] Courts exercising *in personam* jurisdiction may still under appropriate circumstances authorize security attachments to enhance the prospect of an enforceable judgment, should plaintiff prevail. *See* Linda J. Silberman, *Shaffer v. Heitner: The End of an Era*, 53 N.Y.U. L. Rev. 33, 54 (1978).

[260] A case may be capable of satisfying the minimum contacts test yet be beyond the amount of personal jurisdiction over nonresident defendants conferred by the state's long-arm statute. If the same state has a *quasi in rem* statute or common law rule which does apply, the court may continue to use it in such cases. *See Vernon*, note 256, *supra*, at 280–81.

[261] *See* § 3.08[3][d], *infra*.

property upon which jurisdiction is based.[262] Once the *Shaffer* principle was recognized,[263] however, it was evident that plaintiff had to make the same minimum contacts showing for *quasi in rem* (or *in rem*) jurisdiction that he did for personal jurisdiction. This means that plaintiff will usually have a case for personal jurisdiction if he has a jurisdictional case at all.[264] Given a choice, naturally plaintiff will invoke personal over *quasi in rem* jurisdiction in order to obtain a judgment compensating him for defendant's entire wrong.[265]

The Court's decision in *Shaffer* was overdue. Insulation of *quasi in rem* jurisdiction from *Shoe*'s minimum contacts test was indefensible. It was arbitrary to suggest that the concern for fairness to defendants explicit in *Shoe*'s approach provided a basis for restricting only personal jurisdiction. To so confine due process protection under *Shoe* was to engage in a kind of formalism and artificiality at odds with the Court's modern cases.[266]

[2]   Driving the Point Home — *Rush v. Savchuk*

Some of the most egregious exercises of *quasi in rem* jurisdiction prior to *Shaffer* occurred through application of the so-called *Seider* doctrine.[267] In *Harris v. Balk*,[268] the Court had earlier sanctioned *quasi in rem* jurisdiction based on the obligation of another to pay money to the defendant. A contemporary manifestation of this idea, the *Seider* doctrine permitted *quasi in rem* jurisdiction in accident cases where courts lacked minimum contacts with nonresident driver defendants. Courts reasoned that service within the forum on the nonresident driver's insurer[269] conferred *quasi in rem* jurisdiction. The property attached was the insurer's duty or "debt" under the policy to defend and indemnify the nonresident motorist.

Jurisdiction over nonresident drivers in these cases was unattainable under *International Shoe*'s minimum contacts test. So it should have been obvious after *Shaffer* that continued reliance on the *Seider* doctrine would run afoul of due process. However, several of the jurisdictions which had used the device

---

[262] This makes them less valuable than *in personam* judgments. *See* § 3.02, *supra*.

[263] *See* § 3.08[2], *infra*.

[264] In the event (now rare) that minimum contacts are present but no personal jurisdiction statute reaches the case, plaintiff might have access only to *quasi in rem* jurisdiction. *See* note 259, *supra*.

[265] *See* § 3.02[1], *supra*.

[266] Thus, reasoned the *Shaffer* Court, "if a direct assertion of personal jurisdiction over the defendant would violate the Constitution, it would seem that an indirect assertion of that jurisdiction should be equally impermissible." 433 U.S. at 209.

[267] The case giving name to the doctrine is *Seider v. Roth*, 216 N.E.2d 312 (N.Y. 1966). For other examples, see *Simpson v. Loehmann*, 234 N.E.2d 669 (N.Y. 1967); *Minichiello v. Rosenberg*, 410 F.2d 106 (2d Cir. 1968).

[268] 198 U.S. 215 (1905), *discussed in* § 3.02[3], *supra*.

[269] Usually the insurer did not issue the policy in question in the forum state, but was thought to have sufficient unrelated contacts by doing business there to support personal jurisdiction over the insurer. The sufficiency of personal jurisdiction under such circumstances may be more open to question today. *See* § 3.11 (developments in general jurisdiction), *infra*. With the demise of the *Seider* doctrine, however, the question became academic.

refused to give it up.[270] The Supreme Court responded by squarely rejecting the *Seider* doctrine in *Rush v. Savchuk*.[271]

Plaintiff in *Rush* was injured in an automobile accident in Indiana. Defendant was a resident of Indiana. Plaintiff was also an Indiana resident at the time of the accident, but later moved to Minnesota and sued the defendant there for his injuries. The Minnesota courts applied the *Seider* doctrine to reach the nonresident defendant through his insurer. Reversing, the Supreme Court held that jurisdiction over the defendant exceeded due process.

The Supreme Court applied the minimum contacts test. This meant that, "[i]n determining whether a particular exercise of state-court jurisdiction is consistent with due process, the inquiry must focus on the relationship among the defendant, the forum, and the litigation."[272] The Court concluded that defendant had no contact with the forum state, through the subject matter of the litigation or otherwise. The Court also rejected plaintiff's attempt to skirt the minimum contacts problem by arguing the existence of a "direct action" against the insurer.[273]

[3]   The Effect of Increased Due Process Requirements on Other Assertions of Territorial Jurisdiction

If the Court's language in *Shaffer* is to be taken seriously, the minimum contacts requirement transcends jurisdictional categories. "[A]ll assertions of state-court jurisdiction," said the Court, "must be evaluated according to the standards set forth in *International Shoe* and its progeny."[274] It referred particularly to *Shoe*'s minimum contacts test.[275] Most applications of territorial jurisdiction not before the Court in *Shaffer* seem able to satisfy the test.

---

[270] *See Baden v. Staples*, 383 N.E.2d 110 (N.Y. 1978); *O'Connor v. Lee-Hy Paving Corp.*, 579 F.2d 194, (2d Cir.), *cert. denied*, 439 U.S. 1034 (1978); *Savchuk v. Rush*, 272 N.W.2d 888 (Minn. 1978).

[271] 444 U.S. 320 (1980).

[272] 444 U.S. at 327 (*quoting from Shaffer*, 433 U.S. at 204).

[273] 444 U.S. at 330–31. *Seider* doctrine courts had frequently used "direct action" arguments to bolster their decisions. The argument proceeds from the assumption that governing substantive law makes the insurer directly liable for harm to the plaintiff caused by the insured. The court has good personal jurisdiction over the insurer, and, goes the argument, its jurisdiction over the nonresident driver is not a worry because the latter has nothing to lose. The *Rush* Court, however, felt that the insured would have something to lose, "if, for example, multiple plaintiffs sued in different States for an aggregate amount in excess of the policy limits, or if a successful claim would affect the policyholder's insurability." 444 U.S. at 331 n.20.

[274] 433 U.S. at 212. *See* note 247, *supra*. While *Shaffer* did not deal with an attempted exercise of *in rem* (as opposed to *quasi in rem*) jurisdiction, the categorical terms in which it extended *Shoe*'s reach clearly take in both *quasi in rem* and *in rem* jurisdiction.

[275] 433 U.S. at 207. On the present day significance of the minimum contacts test, see § 3.16[A], *infra*.

[a]   Old Forms of Territorial Jurisdiction Likely to Survive

Personal jurisdiction based on citizenship[276] seems capable of satisfying *International Shoe*'s minimum contacts test. The same is true concerning *quasi in rem* and *in rem* suits to determine the status of property permanently located within the forum. Finally, jurisdiction based on waiver or consent appears unaffected by *Shaffer*.

Jurisdiction by citizenship would appear to pose no problem. Recall that a nonresident defendant's contacts with the forum state are significant under *Shoe* when they suggest (1) that defendant has received sufficient benefits to make amenability to suit a fair exchange, and (2) that it would not be particularly inconvenient for defendant to defend there.[277] Given the pervasive relationship that usually exists between a citizen and his domicile, these justifications are likely to apply with at least as much force when a forum seeks to make its own citizens amenable to process.[278]

Prior to *Shaffer*, courts were free to adjudicate disputes over ownership of property (typically real estate) permanently located within the forum without worrying about *International Shoe*'s minimum contacts test. This was because jurisdiction in such cases was *quasi in rem*[279] not *in personam*. Concurring in *Shaffer*, Justices Powell and Stevens expressed concern that states would be left without authority to hear this important category of cases. Responding, the Court suggested that *Shoe*'s minimum contacts standard should not be difficult to satisfy in such cases:

> [W]hen claims to the property itself are the source of the underlying controversy between the plaintiff and the defendant, it would be unusual for the State where the property is located not to have jurisdiction. In such cases, the defendant's claim to property located in the State would normally indicate that he expected to benefit from the State's protection of his interest. The State's strong interests in assuring the marketability of property within its borders and in providing a procedure for peaceful resolution of disputes about the possession of that property would also support jurisdiction, as would the likelihood that important records and witnesses will be found in the State.[280]

---

[276] *See generally* § 3.03[1], *supra*.

[277] *See* § 3.06[1][c], *supra*.

[278] It is significant that *International Shoe* described its due process standard in part by quoting from *Milliken* v. *Meyer*, an earlier case where the Supreme Court upheld personal jurisdiction based on defendant's forum citizenship. *See* § 3.06, *supra*. *See also* § 3.03[1] (discussing *Milliken*), *supra*. Recognition of courts' authority to impose personal jurisdiction over forum citizens also promotes a measure of certainty. It "assures that there is one place in which defendant always may be sued." *Friedenthal, Kane & Miller* § 3.6.

[279] *See* § 3.02[3], *supra*.

[280] 433 U.S. at 207–08.

Justices Powell and Stevens had confined their concerns to the future of *quasi in rem* jurisdiction in such cases. The Court's response was broad enough, however, to suggest that both *quasi in rem* and *in rem* cases settling interests in property permanently located within the forum would be likely to satisfy the minimum contacts test.[281]

Nonresident plaintiffs who voluntarily chose the forum to assert their claims would seem to provide the forum with minimum contacts. The same is true for nonresident defendants who fail to preserve objections to personal jurisdiction, or who consent in advance to suit in the forum. However, it is probably more useful to view these situations apart from the minimum contacts principle of *International Shoe*. Parties may waive their due process objections to personal jurisdiction,[282] and the three situations may best be understood as species of waiver.[283] There may be no need then for the Supreme Court ever to bring these situations within minimum contacts analysis.[284]

[b]   The Triumph of Transient Jurisdiction — *Burnham v. Superior Court*

When *Shaffer* subjected all assertions of personal jurisdiction to minimum contacts scrutiny,[285] it seemed to cast a shadow over transient jurisdiction,[286] a form of personal jurisdiction under fire even before *Shaffer*. Transient jurisdiction occurs when a nonresident defendant is actually found and served within the forum state, but when defendant's presence there is (1) only intended to be brief and (2) is unrelated to the controversy raised by plaintiff's claim. In the well-known case of *Grace v. McArthur*[287] transient jurisdiction was found to exist when defendant was served on an aircraft flying over the airspace of the forum state.

---

[281] *See* 433 U.S. at 207 n.24. The difference between *quasi in rem* and *in rem* cases is whether plaintiff's suit is against particular defendants (*quasi in rem*) or against "the whole world" (*in rem*). In actions involving real property, it seems clear that *Shaffer* preserves both. RUSSELL J. WEINTRAUB, COMMENTARY ON THE CONFLICT OF LAWS 250–52 (4th ed. 2001). *Shaffer* also suggested the continued viability of jurisdiction to adjudicate status, such as marital status. The majority stressed in a footnote that "[w]e do not suggest that jurisdictional doctrines other than those discussed in text, such as the particularized rules governing adjudications of status, are inconsistent with the standard of fairness." 433 U.S. at 208 n.30.

[282] "Because the requirement of personal jurisdiction represents first of all an individual right, it can, like other such rights, be waived." *Insurance Corp. of Ireland Ltd. v. Compagnie Des Bauxites de Guinee*, 456 U.S. 694, 703 (1982).

[283] *See* § 3.03[2][a] (plaintiff's waiver through filing suit), *supra*; § 3.03[2][b] (defendant's waiver by acting other than to question personal jurisdiction), *supra*; § 3.03[2][d] (jurisdiction by consent, similar to waiver), *supra*.

[284] For another such situation, see *Phillips Petroleum Co. v. Shutts*, 472 U.S. 797 (1985) (Court refused to use the minimum contacts test to measure the relationship between the forum and unnamed members of plaintiff's class).

[285] *See* note 257 and related text, *supra*. On the application of the minimum contacts test to assertions of personal jurisdiction generally, see § 3.08[3][a], *supra*.

[286] *See* § 3.03[3], *supra*.

[287] 170 F. Supp. 442 (E.D. Ark. 1959). For further examples, *see* SCOLES, HAY, BORCHERS AND SYMEONIDES, CONFLICT OF LAWS § 6.2 (4th ed. 2004).

This means of bypassing minimum contacts was widely criticized, called by one commentator a "blot on American law."[288] Transient jurisdiction was valid prior to *International Shoe* because service was completed within the forum state.[289] So long as *Shoe* seemed only a means of adding to the jurisdictional reach of courts, transient jurisdiction was not in danger. Moreover, *Shoe* itself used language that implied that minimum contacts were required only if a defendant "be not present within the territory of the forum,"[290] thereby suggesting the continuing viability of transient jurisdiction. *Shaffer* demonstrated unequivocally, however, that due process doctrine emerging from *Shoe* and later cases was also capable of shortening the reach of courts. Transient jurisdiction seemed vulnerable to some commentators, because defendant's contacts with the forum were typically slight and unrelated to the controversy.

Worry over the continuing validity of transient jurisdiction lessened considerably, however, after the Supreme Court's decision in *Burnham v. Superior Court*.[291] Burnham was served as defendant in a California action for separation, child support, and spousal support during his brief visit there on business and to visit his children. The case seemed to present two basic questions. First, would applications of transient jurisdiction be subject to the standards of *International Shoe*? Second, if so, how would transient jurisdiction cases fare under *Shoe*?

All the Justices agreed in *Burnham* that California's attempt to exercise transient jurisdiction was permissible. They split, however, over the answer to the first question. Four Justices found it unnecessary to test the case under *International Shoe*. They were willing to uphold transient jurisdiction because it was satisfactory under the old *Pennoyer* doctrine.[292] Disagreeing, four other

---

[288] Albert A. Ehrenzweig, *From State Jurisdiction to Interstate Venue*, 50 OR. L. REV. 103, 108 (1971). In addition, *see* Vernon, note 256, *supra*, at 302–03; Joseph J. Kalo, *Jurisdiction as an Evolutionary Process: The Development of Quasi In Rem and In Personam Principles*, 1978 DUKE L.J. 1147, 1191.

[289] Prior to *Shoe*, the Supreme Court was preoccupied with completion of service within the forum. *See* § 3.05[1], *supra*.

[290] *International Shoe Co. v. Washington*, 326 U.S. 310, 316 (1945).

[291] 495 U.S. 604 (1990). The case prompted a good deal of commentary. *E.g.*, Patrick J. Borchers, *The Death of the Constitutional Law of Personal Jurisdiction: From Pennoyer to Burnham and Back Again*, 24 U.C. DAVIS L. REV. 19 (1990); Peter Hay, *Transient Jurisdiction, Especially Over International Defendants: Critical Comments on Burnham v. Superior Court*, 1990 U. ILL. L. REV. 593; Symposium, *The Future of Personal Jurisdiction: A Symposium on Burnham v. Superior Court*, 22 RUTGERS L.J. 559 (1991) (articles by Brilmayer, Silberman, Stein, Weintraub, Kogan, Twitchell, Redish, and Maltz); Phillip F. Cramer, *Constructing Alternative Avenues of Jurisdictional Protection: By Passing Burnham's Roadblock via Section 1404(a)*, 53 VAND. L. REV. 311 (2000).

For a variety of reasons, many of these writers are troubled by the manner in which *Burnham* gives free play to transient jurisdiction. Professor Earl Maltz, on the other hand, views matters more favorably. Earl M. Maltz, *Personal Jurisdiction and Constitutional Theory — A Comment on Burnham v. Superior Court*, 22 RUTGERS L.J. 689 (1991); Earl M. Maltz, *Sovereign Authority, Fairness, and Personal Jurisdiction: The Case for the Doctrine of Transient Jurisdiction*, 66 WASH. U. L.Q. 671 (1988).

[292] For discussion of the doctrine of *Pennoyer v. Neff*, *see* § 3.05[1], *supra*. Justice Scalia, in an

Justices applied _Shoe._ Yet the disagreement may not have been very significant. For the latter group posed a test under _Shoe_ that should in most cases be quite easy to satisfy.[293] Overall, the effect of the opinions in _Burnham_ was to give transient jurisdiction new life.[294]

[c]   Jurisdiction by Coerced Consent

Another traditional basis for personal jurisdiction may not fare as well. Jurisdiction over nonresident defendants is at times based on defendant's compliance with the forum's consent-to-service statute, even though the controversy arose outside the forum.[295] It now seems clear that a nonresident defendant's contacts with the forum must be more extensive if none are related to the controversy. Slight contacts will not suffice.[296] This raises a due process question, at least for statutes where such broad-ranging consent seems coerced.[297] The Supreme Court seems to have taken notice of this problem, although its response has been through the Commerce Clause of the

---

opinion joined by the Chief Justice and Justice Kennedy, gave transient jurisdiction a ringing endorsement under the _Pennoyer_ doctrine. Joining their opinion in part, Justice White left room for the theoretical possibility of an example of transient jurisdiction "so arbitrary and lacking in common sense" that a due process problem might arise. He added, however, that a due process problem is unlikely "where presence in the forum state is intentional." 495 U.S. at 638. He concluded: "Here, personal service in California, without more, is enough. . . . " 495 U.S. at 638

[293] In an opinion joined by Justices Marshall, Blackmun and O'Connor, Justice Brennan found jurisdiction sufficient under _International Shoe_ because Burnham had deliberately partaken (however briefly) of "significant benefits provided by the State." 495 U.S. at 637. Brennan left open the possibility of a different result under _Shoe_ when defendant's "presence in a State" is "involuntary or unknowing." 495 U.S. at 637 n. 11. For a possible example of the latter situation, see _Grace v. McArthur_, discussed _supra_, at note 287 and accompanying text.

[294] In contrast, transient jurisdiction is rejected as a basis for personal jurisdiction in European courts. _See_ Friedrich K. Juenger, _Traveling to the Hague in a Worn-Out Shoe_, 29 Pepperdine L. Rev. 7, 7 (2001); Linda J. Silberman & Andreas F. Lowenfeld, _A Different Challenge for the ALI: Herein of Foreign Country Judgments, an International Treaty, and an American Statute_, 75 Ind. L.J. 635, 641 (2000).

[295] For a discussion of this practice, see § 3.03, _supra_.

[296] "[I]t remains true that more substantial contacts must be shown if general jurisdiction is sought." Lea Brilmayer, _Related Contacts and Personal Jurisdiction_, 101 Harv. L. Rev. 1444 (1988). While precise lines are difficult to draw, it is clear that the amount of contact a nonresident defendant need have with the forum to satisfy minimum contacts is far less if the contact is related to the controversy. Compare defendant's limited but related contacts found sufficient in _McGee v. International Life Insurance Co._, 355 U.S. 220 (1957) (an example of specific jurisdiction discussed at § 3.06[2][a], _supra_), with defendant's limited and unrelated contacts found insufficient in _Helicopteros Nacionales de Colombia, S.A. v. Hall_, 466 U.S. 408 (1984) (an attempt at general jurisdiction discussed at § 3.11[1], _infra_).

[297] This assumes, of course, that nonresident defendants in this category have not waived their due process objections by registering under the statutes. On how waiver functions to cut short minimum contacts inquiry, _see_ note 283 and accompanying text, _supra_. When suit is wholly unrelated to defendant's forum activity, notions of waiver or consent to jurisdiction seem strained. The constitutionality after _International Shoe_ of such coerced consent is open to question. _See_ Lea Brilmayer, et al., _A General Look at General Jurisdiction_, 66 Tex. L. Rev. 721, 759–60 (1988); Alfred Hill, _Choice of Law and Jurisdiction in the Supreme Court_, 81 Colum. L. Rev. 960, 981–82 (1981).

Constitution.[298]

[d]   Applications of Territorial Jurisdiction Exempt From the Minimum Contacts Test

Despite the sweep of its rule extending *Shoe*'s minimum contacts test, the *Shaffer* Court may have exempted two situations from the test, and possibly a third.

First, the Court invoked another part of the Constitution to finesse the difficult question of whether a court enforcing a judgment obtained in another state must have minimum contacts with a nonresident defendant. "The Full Faith and Credit Clause, after all, makes the valid *in personam* judgment of one State enforceable in all other States."[299] Second, the court went further and approved attachment of defendant's property to secure payment of possible judgment in a case litigated in another forum (so-called "attachment for security"), so long as litigation in the latter could "be maintained consistently with *International Shoe*."[300]

These exemptions are significant. Granted, many attachments described in the two situations above would have passed *Shoe*'s minimum contacts test. Many of these cases undoubtedly are brought in defendant's home state, where defendant's citizenship provides the enforcement or attachment forum with sufficient material to satisfy the minimum contacts test.[301] In other cases, however, defendant may have property in, but only tangential contacts with, the forum. The latter were secure within the category of *quasi in rem* jurisdiction prior to *Shaffer*, and it seems the court did not wish to generate uncertainty about these cases by subjecting them to the rigors of *International Shoe.*

The Court entertained but stopped short of approving a third exemption for cases where the defendant has property in the forum and "no other forum is available to the plaintiff."[302] The scope of this exemption is unclear from *Shaffer*, and the Court has not really clarified it since.[303] It is reminiscent of

---

[298] The case, *Bendix Autolite Corp. v. Midwesco Enterprises*, 486 U.S. 888 (1988), found violative of the Commerce Clause Ohio law conditioning the availability of a favorable statute of limitations on consent to jurisdiction. For discussion of this case and criticism of the Court's failure to frame a due process issue, see Wendy C. Perdue, *Personal Jurisdiction and the Beetle in the Box*, 32 B.C. L. Rev. 529, 557–60 (1991).

[299] 433 U.S. at 210. Given parallel obligations imposed by federal statutes on federal courts to recognize state judgments and on state and other federal courts to recognize federal judgments (*see* § 15.10, *infra*) the passage in the accompanying text probably means that relief from the minimum contacts standard exists across the board in inter-system enforcement of judgments.

[300] 433 U.S. at 210. The attachments are for security, and not for obtaining territorial jurisdiction in order to litigate a claim.

[301] *See* note 278 and related text, *supra.*

[302] 433 U.S. at 211 n.37.

[303] For commentary on this point in *Shaffer*, see Peter Hay, *Refining Personal Jurisdiction in the United States*, 35 Int'l & Comp. L.Q. 32, 47–48 (1986).

the concept of "jurisdiction by necessity,"[304] which has largely failed to capture the imagination of the Court.[305]

§ 3.09   A CLOSER LOOK AT THE MINIMUM CONTACTS TEST — WHEN AND HOW CONTACTS COUNT

[1]   The Function of Contacts and the Special Importance of Defendant's Contacts With the Forum

In several later cases, the United States Supreme Court reaffirmed the requirement that assertions of personal jurisdiction over nonresident corporate and individual defendants[306] pass the minimum contacts test refined from *International Shoe*.[307] *Contacts* are geographical facts about the controversy or the parties — for example, where defendant allegedly committed the wrong. To understand the minimum contacts test, it is necessary to consider what types of contacts have significance and when forum contacts exist in sufficient quantity (when, in other words, sufficient geographical indicators point to the forum state) to satisfy the minimum requirements of due process. This section offers an overview of the process of ascertaining and weighing contacts which will be covered in greater detail in

---

[304] *See generally* George B. Fraser, Jr., *Jurisdiction by Necessity — An Analysis of the Mullane Case*, 100 U. Pa. L. Rev. 305 (1951).

[305] *See Helicopteros Nacionales de Colombia, S.A. v. Hall*, 466 U.S. 408, 419 n.13 (1984) ("We decline to consider adoption of a doctrine of jurisdiction by necessity — a potentially far-reaching modification of existing law — in the absence of a more complete record."). *But cf.* Geoffrey C. Hazard, Jr., *Interstate Venue*, 74 Nw. U. L. Rev. 711, 718 (1979) (finding support in *Western Union Tel. Co. v. Pennsylvania*, 368 U.S. 71 (1961), and several state cases for "the idea that a reasonably convenient state court has jurisdiction over all persons whose joinder is necessary to do consistent justice in a multiparty, multistate controversy.").

[306] Like *International Shoe*, many cases have involved nonresident corporate defendants. On the other hand, *Shoe* offered two cases involving individual defendants, *Milliken v. Meyer*, 311 U.S. 457 (1940), and *Hess v. Pawloski*, 274 U.S. 352 (1927), as background for its approach. There is some question whether due process protections afforded to nonresident individuals differ greatly, if at all, from those afforded to nonresident corporations. *See* David E. Seidelson, *Jurisdiction Over Nonresident Defendants: Beyond "Minimum Contacts" and the Long-Arm Statutes*, 6 Duq. L. Rev. 221, 225 n.28 (1967–68) (suggesting "the distinction between foreign corporations and nonresident natural persons for jurisdictional purposes probably has ceased to exist."). At the same time, jurisdictional issues can arise that are unique to the corporate defendant — e.g., the extent to which jurisdiction over a corporate subsidiary permits jurisdiction over the parent corporation. *See generally* William A. Voxman, Comment, *Jurisdiction Over a Parent Corporation in Its Subsidiary's State of Incorporation*, 141 U. Pa. L. Rev. 327 (1992).

[307] 326 U.S. 310 (1945). *E.g., World-Wide Volkswagen Corp. v. Woodson*, 444 U.S. 286, 291 (1980): "As has long been settled, and as we reaffirm today, a state court may exercise personal jurisdiction over a nonresident defendant only so long as there exist 'minimum contacts' between the defendant and the forum state." The Court later observed, also quoting *Shoe*, "the constitutional touchstone remains whether the defendant purposefully established 'minimum contacts' in the forum State." *Burger King Corp. v. Rudzewicz*, 471 U.S. 462, 474 (1985). "The modern foundation of United States jurisdiction lies in perhaps ten or so post-1945 Supreme Court decisions that extensively discuss the 'minimum contacts' test." Patrick J. Borchers, *Internet Libel: The Consequences of a Non-Rule Approach to Personal Jurisdiction*, 98 Nw. L. Rev. 473, 475 (2004).

succeeding sections. The relationship between the forum and the defendant is of overriding importance. Recall the context of the minimum contacts standard originally announced in *International Shoe*. Before forcing a nonresident defendant either to litigate (perhaps far from home) or accede to a default judgment,[308] it must be clear that the defendant has "certain minimum contacts" with the forum "such that the maintenance of the suit does not offend 'traditional notions of fair play and substantial justice.' "[309] So it follows that most due process inquiries about personal jurisdiction center on a minimum contacts test.[310]

[2]   Specific and General Jurisdiction[311]

We have already seen that a nonresident defendant may have contacts with the forum sufficient to support personal jurisdiction when those contacts are either related[312] or unrelated[313] to the controversy. Personal jurisdiction based on the first type of contacts is sometimes called *specific* jurisdiction.[314] Personal jurisdiction based on the second is called *general* jurisdiction.[315] The

---

[308] *See* § 3.06[1][a], *supra*.

[309] *International Shoe*, 326 U.S. at 316, *quoting Milliken v. Meyer*, 311 U.S. 457, 463 (1940). For an assessment of the minimum contacts test, see Kevin C. McMunigal, *Desert, Utility, and Minimum Contacts: Toward a Mixed Theory of Personal Jurisdiction*, 108 YALE L.J. 189 (1998).

[310] But not all. The Court has demonstrated that satisfaction of the minimum contacts test may not be enough. *Asahi Metal Ind. Co., Ltd. v. Superior Court*, 480 U.S. 102 (1987). Using a due process test which stood apart from minimum contacts, the Court refused to permit a California state court to exercise personal jurisdiction over a Japanese third-party defendant. Five members of the Court suggested minimum contacts might have existed between the forum and the defendant. But they joined three other Justices to conclude that forcing a Japanese litigant to defend in California against a Taiwanese claimant would (quoting *International Shoe*) violate "traditional notions of fair play and substantial justice." *Asahi Metal Ind. Co., Ltd.*, 480 U.S. at 113. The Court considered under this test the needs of other litigants for a California forum, California's interest in providing a forum, and the burden posed by a California forum on the party challenging jurisdiction.

How often will a court have minimum contacts with a nonresident defendant, yet lack personal jurisdiction because of *Asahi*'s additional due process test? The Court indicated that minimum contacts will often indicate satisfaction of the latter: "When minimum contacts have been established, often the interests of the plaintiff and the forum in the exercise of jurisdiction will justify even the serious burdens placed on the alien defendant." 480 U.S. at 114. The facts of *Asahi* did not bear this out because "the interests of the plaintiff and the forum in California's assertion of jurisdiction over Asahi [a third-party defendant] are slight." 480 U.S. at 114 For further discussion of the *Asahi* case, see § 3.12[2], *infra*.

[311] For studies explaining and comparing specific and general jurisdiction, see ROBERT C. CASAD & WILLIAM B. RICHMAN, JURISDICTION IN CIVIL ACTIONS § 2-5[2][b] (Lexis 3d ed. 1998); Charles W. Rhodes, *The Predictability Principle in Personal Jurisdiction: A Case Study on the Effects of a "Generally" Too Broad, But "Specifically" Too Narrow Approach to Minimum Contacts*, 57 BAYLOR L. REV. 135 (2005); Patrick J. Borchers, *The Problem with General Jurisdiction*, 2001 U. CHI. LEGAL F. 119.

[312] *See* the discussion of *McGee v. International Life Ins. Co.* at § 3.06[2][a], *supra*.

[313] *See* the discussion of *Perkins v. Benguet Consol. Mining Co.* at § 3.06[2][b], *supra*.

[314] For a discussion of the Supreme Court's more recent specific jurisdiction decisions, see §§ 3.10 & 3.12, *infra*.

[315] The Supreme Court used these terms in *Helicopteros Nacionales de Colombia v. Hall*, 466

Supreme Court has yet to indicate how extensive defendant's unrelated contacts need to be in order to support personal jurisdiction.[316] It is clear, however, that general jurisdiction requires far more extensive contact between the forum and the defendant than does specific jurisdiction.[317]

General jurisdiction proceeds from a relationship between the forum and defendant that is so extensive that defendant's submission to jurisdiction there is a fair exchange for the considerable privileges and protections that the forum state has extended to defendant. General jurisdiction is indifferent to where the controversy arose and its significance as a jurisdictional option comes in those cases where the controversy arose outside the forum.[318] Citizenship of defendant in the forum provides the strongest case for general jurisdiction,[319] so strong that jurisdiction of the forum over its own citizens is unquestioned.

The central question concerning general jurisdiction is: if a noncitizen defendant cannot be found and served within the forum, and if the cause of action arises entirely outside the forum, when do connections between the defendant and the forum (from purposeful acts by defendant taken in the forum or directed into the forum) become so extensive that the forum can exercise the same general jurisdiction that it does over its own citizens? United States Supreme Court decisions to date do not provide a great deal of help in drawing that line.

Specific jurisdiction proceeds from a relationship between the forum and the noncitizen defendant funneled through the facts of the controversy. When

---

U.S. 408, 414 nn.8–9 (1984), describing specific jurisdiction as that "in a suit arising out of or related to the defendant's contacts with the forum" and general jurisdiction as that "in a suit not arising out of or related to the defendant's contacts with the forum." *See* Mary Twitchell, *The Myth of General Jurisdiction*, 101 HARV. L. REV. 610, 680 (1988): "The Supreme Court's recent use of the general/specific terminology suggests that this typology will continue to play a central role in personal jurisdiction decisions." *See generally* Robert L. Theriot, Note, *Specific and General Jurisdiction — The Reshuffling of Minimum Contacts Analysis*, 59 TUL. L. REV. 826 (1985). To date, however, the Supreme Court has been far less informative about general jurisdiction. One writer has gone so far as to suggest: "The development of general jurisdiction analysis . . . seems to have atrophied at its 1945 level." B. Glenn George, *In Search of General Jurisdiction*, 64 TUL. L. REV. 1097, 1141 (1990).

[316] For a discussion of developments in this area, see § 3.11, *supra*.

[317] Compare defendant's limited but related contact found sufficient in *McGee v. International Life Ins. Co.*, 355 U.S. 220 (1957) (discussed at § 3.06[2][a], *supra*), with defendant's limited and unrelated contact found insufficient in *Helicopteros Nacionales de Colombia, S.A. v. Hall*, 466 U.S. 408 (1984). For a useful discussion of the relation between general and specific jurisdiction, see Linda S. Simard, *Hybrid Personal Jurisdiction: It's Not General Jurisdiction, or Specific Jurisdiction, But Is It Constitutional?*, 48 CASE W. RES. L. REV. 559 (1998).

[318] In contrast, European courts refuse to exercise personal jurisdiction under such circumstances. *See* Friedrich K. Juenger, *Traveling to the Hague in a Worn-Out Shoe*, 29 PEPERDINE L. REV. 7, 7 (2001); Linda J. Silberman & Andreas F. Lowenfeld, *A Different Challenge for the ALI: Herein of Foreign Country Judgments, an International Treaty, and an American Statute*, 75 IND. L.J. 635, 641 (2000).

[319] *Cf.* Patrick J. Borchers, *The Problem with General Jurisdiction*, 2001 U. CHI. LEGAL F. 119, 119–20 ("[A]ssertions of jurisdiction based upon . . . the defendant's domicile are assertions of general jurisdiction because they apply without regard to the nature of the dispute.").

plaintiff alleges that defendant has purposefully acted in the forum (or has directed acts there) to harm plaintiff, the sovereign is entitled to investigate. This theory focuses on local judicial power as an appendage of state regulatory or police power. When the controversy centers in the forum state (*e.g.*, an automobile accident there), applications of specific jurisdiction are as settled as are applications of general jurisdiction over the forum's own citizens.

Central questions concerning specific jurisdiction include: How related must defendant's forum acts be to the controversy? How purposeful must they be? Must they be such that defendant could foresee from his acts the possibility of being a defendant there? Again, the United States Supreme Court's decisions have not been terribly illuminating.

[3]   The Fact-Sensitive Nature of Minimum Contacts Inquiries

The search for contacts requires courts to sift facts. Because facts register and combine differently from case to case, uncertainties inhere in the minimum contacts test. The Court acknowledged as much in *International Shoe*: "It is evident that the criteria by which we mark the boundary line between those activities which justify the subjection of a corporation to suit, and those which do not, cannot be simply mechanical or quantitative."[320] The fact-sensitive nature of the approach has made it unpopular with some critics.[321] Few, however, would wish to return to the law of territorial jurisdiction that *Shoe* replaced.[322] It remains to be seen whether a different modern test would achieve more satisfactory results.[323]

---

[320] 326 U.S. at 319. For comments in a similar vein, see *Burger King Corp. v. Rudzewicz*, 471 U.S. 462, 485–86 & n.29 (1985); *Kulko v. Superior Court*, 436 U.S. 84, 92 (1978).

[321] *See, e.g.*, Geoffrey C. Hazard, Jr., *A General Theory of State-Court Jurisdiction*, 1965 SUP. CT. REV. 241, 283 ("the vagueness of the minimum-contacts general principle can make jurisdictional litigation uncertain at the trial level and frequent at the appellate level."); Russell J. Weintraub, *A Map Out of the Personal Jurisdiction Labyrinth*, 28 U.C. DAVIS L. REV. 531, 545 (1995) ("Courts cannot agree on how specific facts should influence the result.").

What has emerged recently as a due process test in addition to minimum contacts, see note 310, *supra*, seems in its way just as fact-sensitive. For a description of the new test, see Leslie W. Abramson, *Clarifying "Fair Play and Substantial Justice": How the Courts Apply the Supreme Court Standard for Personal Jurisdiction*, 18 HAST. CONST. L.Q. 441 (1991).

[322] For discussion of the rigidity of the rule of *Pennoyer v. Neff* and the fictions and lapses in enforcement which accompanied the rule, see § 3.05, *supra*. Looking back at the rejection of *Pennoyer*, the Supreme Court observed: "We have abandoned more formalistic tests that focused on a defendant's presence within a State in favor of a more flexible inquiry into whether a defendant's contacts with the forum made it reasonable, in the context of our federal system of government, to require it to defend the suit in that State." *Quill Corp. v. North Dakota*, 504 U.S. 298, 307 (1992).

[323] Proposals for replacement of the minimum contacts test with something else have been varied and extensive. *See, e.g.*, the list of articles in RUSSELL J. WEINTRAUB, COMMENTARY ON THE CONFLICT OF LAWS 144 n.135 (4th ed. 2001), and the arguments for reworking the relationship between personal jurisdiction and venue noted at § 6.03, *infra*.

§ 3.10   DEFENDANT'S FORUM CONTACTS RELATED TO THE CONTROVERSY (SPECIFIC JURISDICTION) — RECENT DEVELOPMENTS[324]

[1]   Jurisdiction in Cases Where Defendant Acts Elsewhere to Cause Harm in the Forum — An Introduction to the Problem

Specific jurisdiction exists when there is a connection between the forum and the acts of a nonresident defendant generating the controversy.[325] When defendant is alleged to have acted in the forum to wrong plaintiff, the court's authority to exercise personal jurisdiction is clear.[326] The same is usually true if defendant uses the mails or another mode of communication as a substitute for actually going to the forum,[327] or if the defendant sends another to the forum to act on his behalf.[328] The controversy may grow out of defendant's continuous and systematic forum activity.[329] However, the court also has jurisdiction when the controversy arises from defendant's forum-connected acts which are but a random or isolated aspect of defendant's activity as a whole.[330]

To grasp why connecting the defendant's controversy-generating activity to the forum is so significant, recall the regulatory rationale supporting

---

[324] On the distinction between specific and general jurisdiction, see § 3.09, *supra*. For further discussion of specific jurisdiction, see Robert C. Casad & William B. Richman, Jurisdiction in Civil Actions § 2-5[4 (Lexis 3d ed. 1998); Linda S. Simard, *Meeting Expectations: Two Profiles for Specific Jurisdiction*, 38 Ind. L. Rev. 343 (2005).

[325] Even under settled law, the process of classifying jurisdictional facts as related or unrelated to the controversy would sometimes be difficult. In addition, the area is troubled by some legal uncertainty and considerable debate whether facts supporting specific jurisdiction must "arise out of" the claim — be necessary somehow to proof of the claim — or can be more distantly related to the controversy. Much recent debate centers on the refusal of the Court to take seriously the possibility of specific jurisdiction in *Helicopteros Nacionales de Colombia v. Hall*, 466 U.S. 408 (1984). For discussion of this point in *Helicopteros* and a critique of the debate, see § 3.11, *infra*.

[326] "[I]t is most obviously fair and reasonable to attribute a related contact to the defendant where the event is an act performed within the forum by the defendant." Lea Brilmayer, *How Contacts Count: Due Process Limitations on State Court Jurisdiction*, 1980 Sup. Ct. Rev. 77, 90.

[327] "[I]f a foreign corporation purposefully avails itself of the benefits of an economic market in the forum State, it may subject itself to the State's in personam jurisdiction even if has no physical presence in the State." *Quill Corp. v. North Dakota*, 504 U.S. 298, 307 (1992). Additional applications of the principle appear in *Burger King Corp. v. Rudzewicz*, 471 U.S. 462, 476 (1985); *Travelers Health Ass'n v. Virginia*, 339 U.S. 643 (1950). *See generally* Willis L.M. Reese & Nina M. Galston, *Doing an Act or Causing Consequences as Bases of Judicial Jurisdiction*, 44 Iowa L. Rev. 249, 253 (1959).

[328] Brilmayer, note 326, *supra*, at 91.

[329] *International Shoe* was such a case. 326 U.S. at 320. For discussion of this category and further case examples, see Arthur T. von Mehren & Donald T. Trautman, *Jurisdiction to Adjudicate: A Suggested Analysis*, 79 Harv. L. Rev. 1121, 1147–48 (1966).

[330] *McGee v. International Life Ins. Co.*, discussed in § 3.06[2][a], *supra*, and *Hess v. Pawloski*, a precursor to *International Shoe*, discussed in § 3.05[2], *supra*, are examples. For discussion of *McGee* and *Hess* in this context, see von Mehren & Trautman, note 329, *supra*, at 1149–51.

International Shoe's expansion of personal jurisdiction beyond the limits set by *Pennoyer v. Neff*.[331] The forum has a legitimate interest in ascertaining through its judicial process whether wrongs have occurred there. "The most convincing justification" for imposition of jurisdiction over nonresident defendants "is the State's right to regulate activities occurring within the State."[332]

This principle explains why some cases involving random or isolated contacts definitely pass the minimum contacts test,[333] and why others definitely do not.[334] However, two important Supreme Court cases, addressed in this section, pose situations that seem closer to the line. In *World-Wide Volkswagen*, defendants did not know where the ultimate effects of their acts would occur. When such acts caused injury in the forum and the defendant had no other contacts there, the Court was called upon to decide whether the minimum contacts test had been satisfied. In *Burger King*, another minimum contacts case, defendants directed more of their controversy-related activity elsewhere than at the forum and appeared to have no forum contacts unrelated to the controversy.

[2]   Forum Injury Is Not Enough — *World-Wide Volkswagen v. Woodson*[335]

Plaintiffs purchased an Audi automobile from defendant retailer Seaway Volkswagen in New York. Seaway had obtained the car from defendant World-Wide Volkswagen, a regional distributor. Plaintiffs thereafter moved from New York, traveling in their Audi toward a destination in Arizona. The gas tank ignited in an Oklahoma collision, seriously injuring several members of the family. Plaintiffs brought suit in an Oklahoma state court against manufacturer Audi, importer Volkswagen of America, World-Wide Volkswagen and Seaway.

Plaintiffs made a substantial case for personal jurisdiction. Since product failure and injuries were alleged to have occurred in the forum, it seemed a

---

[331] *See* § 3.06 *supra.*

[332] Brilmayer, note 326, *supra*, at 86. Addressing the field of tort law, the American Law Institute observed: "A state has an especial interest in exercising judicial jurisdiction over those who commit torts within its territory. This is because torts involve wrongful conduct which a state seeks to deter, and against which it attempts to afford protection, by providing that a tortfeasor shall be liable for damages which are the proximate result of his tort." RESTATEMENT (SECOND) OF CONFLICTS § 36 comment (c) (1971). A state's interest in providing a judicial remedy may be most pronounced in tort cases, *see* Paul D. Carrington & James A. Martin, *Substantive Interests and the Jurisdiction of State Courts*, 66 MICH. L. REV. 227, 232 (1967), but it can occur in other settings. For example, in *Burger King Corp. v. Rudzewicz*, 471 U.S. 462, 472–73 (1985), the Supreme Court offered a regulatory rationale for extraterritorial jurisdiction in a contracts case.

[333] *See* note 330, *supra.*

[334] "[I]f a State is relying upon a regulatory justification for jurisdiction by claiming a right to regulate substantive occurrences within the State, imposition of legal burdens on the defendant is reasonable only if the defendant was somehow responsible for those occurrences." Brilmayer, note 326, *supra*, at 89.

[335] 444 U.S. 286 (1980).

natural place for plaintiff to bring suit. Moreover, the fact of injury in the forum appeared to provide Oklahoma with a regulatory interest in adjudicating the case. Nonetheless, the Supreme Court upheld the challenges of retailer Seaway and regional distributor World-Wide Volkswagen.[336] Noting that these "defendants' only connection with Oklahoma is the fact that an automobile sold in New York to New York residents became involved in an accident in Oklahoma,"[337] the Court held that Oklahoma courts were without minimum contacts necessary to assert personal jurisdiction.[338]

The problem to the Court was the lack of contacts between the defendants and the Oklahoma forum.[339] Granted, defendants could have foreseen that so mobile a product might reach Oklahoma highways, but " 'foreseeability' alone has never been a sufficient benchmark for personal jurisdiction under the Due Process Clause."[340] The Court did not wish to discard the concept of foreseeability.

---

[336] Audi does not appear to have challenged jurisdiction. Volkswagen of America dropped its jurisdictional objection prior to Supreme Court review. 444 U.S. at 288 n.3.

[337] 444 U.S. at 287.

[338] The Oklahoma court lacked jurisdiction,

> [e]ven if the defendant would suffer minimal or no inconvenience from being forced to litigate before the tribunals of another State; even if the forum State has a strong interest in applying its law to the controversy; even if the forum State is the most convenient location for litigation.

444 U.S. at 294.

The Court cited *Hanson v. Denckla*, 357 U.S. 235 (1958). Other modern cases, including *Shaffer v. Heitner*, 433 U.S. 186 (1977), discussed at § 3.08[1], *supra*, *Rush v. Savchuk*, 444 U.S. 320 (1980), discussed at § 3.08[2], *supra*, and *Kulko v. Superior Court*, 436 U.S. 84 (1978), also refurbished *Hanson*'s authority. *Kulko* involved a California custody and child support proceeding. The Supreme Court held that the fact that the New York father provided his daughter with a one-way ticket to California did not establish requisite minimum contacts between the defendant-father and the forum. California's interest in adjudicating the case was real, deriving from the presence there of the mother and two children. To the Court, however, the lack of contacts between California and the defendant made California's interest academic. Quoting *Hanson*, the Court stated:

> The unilateral activity of those who claim some relationship with a nonresident defendant cannot satisfy the requirement of contact with the forum State. . . . [I]t is essential in each case that there be some act by which the defendant purposefully avails [him]self of the privilege of conducting activities within the forum State.

436 U.S at 93–94. For more on personal jurisdiction in the domestic relations setting, see Rosemarie T. Ring, *Personal Jurisdiction and Child Support: Establishing the Parent-Child Relationship as Minimum Contacts*, 89 Cal. L. Rev. 1125 (2001); Rhonda Wasserman, *Parents, Partners, and Personal Jurisdiction*, 1995 U. Ill. L. Rev. 813.

The Supreme Court's refusal in *World-Wide Volkswagen* and *Kulko* to attach weight to forum convenience or forum interest in the absence of defendant's forum contacts is strongly reminiscent of the position it took in *Hanson*. For discussion of this and other aspects of *Hanson*, see § 3.07[2], *supra*.

[339] As it had in *Hanson*, the Court stressed that "the Due Process Clause does not contemplate that a state may make binding a judgment *in personam* against an individual or corporate defendant with which the state has no contacts, ties, or relations." 444 U.S. at 294 (*quoting* from *International Shoe Co. v. Washington*, 326 U.S. 310, 319 (1945)).

[340] 444 U.S. at 295. If it was, said the Court, failures in such products as tires, automobile jacks

But the foreseeability that is critical to due process analysis is not the mere likelihood that a product will find its way into the forum State. Rather, it is that the defendant's conduct and connection with the forum State are such that he should reasonably anticipate being haled into court there.[341]

The Court reasoned that the conduct of the retailer and wholesaler in *World-Wide Volkswagen* was not such as to cause them to anticipate being haled into court in Oklahoma. Neither sold cars, advertised, or carried on any other activity in the state.

World-Wide Volkswagen received a mixed reception.[342] Moreover, some lower court decisions continued to base personal jurisdiction over nonresident defendants on little more than the fact of injury in the forum.[343] The Court returned to the products liability area in *Asahi Metal Industry Co. v. Superior Court*.[344] Badly divided on the minimum contacts question, the *Asahi* Court used a different due process formula to restrain the personal jurisdiction of a California court.[345]

---

and soft drinks would expose local retailers to suit wherever plaintiff might transport the product. "Every seller of chattels would in effect appoint the chattel his agent for service of process. His amenability to suit would travel with the chattel." 444 U.S. at 296.

[341] 444 U.S. at 297. Then it is reasonable to impose personal jurisdiction because a corporation purposefully directing its activities at the forum

> has clear notice that it is subject to suit there, and can act to alleviate the risk of burdensome litigation by procuring insurance, passing the expected costs on to customers, or, if the risks are too great, severing its connection with the State.

444 U.S. at 297

[342] Professor Martin H. Redish wrote of the case that "[t]he Court appeared to take a major step backward in its search for a viable, coherent theory of personal jurisdiction." *Due Process, Federalism, and Personal Jurisdiction: a Theoretical Evaluation*, 75 Nw. U. L. Rev. 1112 (1981). For further criticism, see Harold J. Lewis, Jr., *A Brave New World for Personal Jurisdiction: Flexible Tests Under Uniform Standards*, 37 Vand. L. Rev. 1, 7–8 (1984). Some commentators generally approved of the case. Brilmayer, note 326, *supra*, at 92; Martin B. Louis, *The Grasp of Long Arm Jurisdiction Finally Exceeds Its Reach: A Comment on World-Wide Volkswagen Corp. v. Woodson and Rush v. Savchuk*, 58 N.C. L. Rev. 407, 426–27 (1980). Others had mixed reactions. David E. Seidelson, *Recasting World-Wide Volkswagen as a Source of Longer Jurisdictional Reach*, 19 Tulsa L.J. 1 (1983) (arguing that the rationale of the case could be reworked to expand rather than diminish jurisdiction); Arthur T. von Mehren, *Adjudicatory Jurisdiction: General Theories Compared and Evaluated*, 63 B.U. L. Rev. 279, 320 (1983) (approving the result in *World-Wide Volkswagen*, but suggesting that the Court should have written a different opinion).

[343] From his review of several such cases, Professor Russell J. Weintraub observed: "When a court sees blood on the ground, it is very likely to find jurisdiction over a nonresident seller of the product that caused the injury." *Due Process Limitations on the Personal Jurisdiction of State Courts: Time for a Change*, 63 Or. L. Rev. 485, 516 (1984).

[344] 480 U.S. 102 (1987).

[345] *See* § 3.12[2], *infra*.

[3]   All of Defendant's Contacts Related to the Controversy Need Not Be With the Forum — *Burger King Corp. v. Rudzewicz*[346]

World-Wide Volkswagen seemed to make clear that a nonresident defendant is not subject to specific personal jurisdiction unless he has directed acts toward the forum. However, a later case, *Burger King Corp. v. Rudzewicz*, demonstrated that not all of the defendant's contacts related to the controversy must be with the forum.

Through negotiation with Burger King's regional office in Michigan, Rudzewicz and another Michigan defendant obtained a franchise in that state. Defendants failed to make payments, and Burger King brought a federal diversity suit on the franchise agreement in Florida, its headquarters and place of incorporation. Rudzewicz appealed a judgment against him. Reversing, the Eleventh Circuit Court of Appeals held Rudzewicz to be beyond the constitutional reach of Florida's long-arm statute.[347] The Court of Appeals based its decision upon a determination that the bulk of the contacts giving rise to the controversy were with Michigan rather than Florida.[348]

Notwithstanding this, the United States Supreme Court concluded that personal jurisdiction over Rudzewicz was constitutional. Acknowledging the threshold importance of minimum contacts between defendant and the Florida forum, the Court held that there were enough Florida contacts related to the controversy to satisfy the test. Defendants at times dealt directly with Burger King's Miami headquarters; they contracted with Burger King to have Florida law govern the franchise agreement;[349] and they promised to send their franchise payments to Burger King's Florida address. Under the circumstances, the Court refused to attach importance to the fact that Rudzewicz had not been in the forum state.

> Although territorial presence frequently will enhance a potential defendant's affiliation with a State and reinforce the reasonable foreseeability of suit there, it is an inescapable fact of modern commercial life that a substantial amount of business is transacted solely by mail and wire communications across state lines, thus obviating the need for physical presence within a State in which business is conducted. So long as a commercial actor's efforts are

---

[346]   471 U.S. 462 (1985).

[347]   724 F.2d 1505 (11th Cir. 1984).

[348]   The two-judge majority stated that Rudzewicz had no office in Florida, nor did it appear that he had ever been there. Contract negotiations were conducted between Rudzewicz and Burger King's district representative entirely in Michigan. Anticipated profits from the franchise were to derive exclusively from Michigan food sales. Justice Stevens would later observe in his dissent: "Throughout the business relationship, appellee's principal contacts with appellant were with its Michigan office." 471 U.S. at 487.

[349]   This is not to be confused with contractual consent to jurisdiction. Had Rudzewicz consented to Florida jurisdiction, his only basis for resistance presumably would have been to argue that the clause was unconscionable, or represented a contract of adhesion, and hence was unenforceable. For discussion of this point, see § 3.03[2][d], *supra*.

"purposefully directed" toward residents of another State, we have consistently rejected the notion that an absence of physical contacts can defeat personal jurisdiction there.[350]

To save money and to place debtor-defendants at a financial and psychic disadvantage, a corporate creditor-plaintiff might prefer to file in its home state lawsuits arising from operations elsewhere. To read *Burger King* as a green light in such cases, so long as defendant directs some communications to the corporate home forum and accedes by contract to governance of the instrument by application of that forum's law, could lead to fundamentally unfair results.

Consider the following example. Maine consumer X reads a local advertisement placed by Y (a nationwide seller based in California) and orders a stereo by mail from Y. Y sends X an installment sales contract, which X signs and sends back to California. The stereo arrives and proves defective; therefore, X refuses to continue payments under the contract. Even with the contacts summarized in the preceding paragraph, California litigation by Y on the debt would be an unexpected and dislocating prospect for X — one seeming to lack fundamental fairness required by due process.[351] The *Burger King* Court may have anticipated this problem, stressing that Rudzewicz was commercially sophisticated and represented by an attorney throughout his negotiations with Burger King.[352]

On final analysis, *Burger King* may represent a realistic accommodation between the minimum contacts requirement of due process and the fact that controversy-related contacts are often spread over more than one state.[353] To recognize specific jurisdiction only in a place which is the exclusive or predominant source of related contacts would often deny forums the legitimate expression of their regulatory interests.[354]

---

[350] 471 U.S. at 476.

[351] *Cf.* von Mehren, note 342, *supra*, at 314 ("[A] party's economic and psychological ability to litigate in the other party's forum, as well as his expectations with respect to the possibility that he may have to do so, decrease as a direct function of the degree to which his normal activities are localized and have only local effects.").

[352] "We do not mean to suggest," the Court added, "that the jurisdictional outcome will always be the same in franchise cases. Some franchises may be primarily intrastate in character or involve different decision-making structures, such that a franchisee should not reasonably anticipate out-of-state litigation." 471 U.S. at 485 n.28.

[353] *See also Keeton v. Hustler Magazine*, 465 U.S. 770 (1984). The Court permitted jurisdiction under the New Hampshire long-arm statute in a defamation action, although only a small percentage of defendant's total circulation of the offending magazine issue occurred in the forum state. However, the facts of *Keeton* furnished added jurisdictional support not present in *Burger King*. Defendant had carried on continuous and systematic activity (albeit unrelated to the controversy) in New Hampshire. For discussion of *Keeton*, see § 3.12[1], *infra*. For further discussion of *Burger King*, see Rex R. Perschbacher, *Minimum Contacts Reapplied: Mr. Justice Brennan Has It His Way in Burger King Corp. v. Rudzewicz*, 1986 Ariz. St. L.J. 585; Martin B. Louis, *Jurisdiction Over Those Who Breach Their Contracts: The Lessons of Burger King*, 72 N.C. L. Rev. 55 (1993).

[354] On specific jurisdiction as an expression of the forum's regulatory interest, see § 3.10[1]. *supra*.

§ 3.11 DEFENDANT'S FORUM CONTACTS UNRELATED TO THE CONTROVERSY (GENERAL JURISDICTION)[355] — RECENT DEVELOPMENTS

General jurisdiction exists over a nonresident defendant when his contacts with the forum are so extensive that it is possible to overlook the fact that the cause of action arose elsewhere — that no contacts related to the controversy exist between the forum and the defendant.[356] The Court raised the possibility in *International Shoe*.[357] Five years later it provided an example, *Perkins v. Benguet Consolidated Mining Company*.[358] The Supreme Court eventually returned to the subject of general jurisdiction and threw some additional light on matters. However (as with *Perkins*), it selected a relatively easy case.

[1] *Helicopteros Nacionales de Colombia v. Hall*[359]

Respondents brought this Texas state wrongful death action as the result of the Peruvian crash of a helicopter operated by Helicopteros, a Colombian corporation. In their claims against Helicopteros, respondents alleged that pilot error caused the crash. Appearing specially, Helicopteros moved to dismiss for lack of personal jurisdiction. The trial court denied the motion, and respondents obtained a jury award in excess of one million dollars. The Texas Supreme Court eventually decided that the Texas court had personal jurisdiction over Helicopteros.[360] The United States Supreme Court reversed.

Helicopteros sent a representative to Texas to contract with a Texas helicopter manufacturer for the purchase and transport of most of its helicopter fleet, and for the training of its pilots, management and maintenance personnel.[361] Helicopteros also used a Texas bank account. The Supreme Court refused to consider whether these contacts provided a basis for specific jurisdiction because the plaintiffs apparently failed to argue this form of

---

[355] On the distinction between general and specific jurisdiction, see § 3.09, *supra*. For further commentary on general jurisdiction, see ROBERT C. CASAD & WILLIAM B. RICHMAN, JURISDICTION IN CIVIL ACTIONS § 2-5[3] (Lexis 3d ed. 1998); Charles W. Rhodes, *Clarifying General Jurisdiction*, 34 SETON HALL L. REV. 807 (2004); Friedrich K. Juenger, *The American Law of General Jurisdiction*, 2001 U. CHI. LEGAL F. 141.

[356] In other words, when there is no material for specific jurisdiction. For further discussion of the distinction between specific and general jurisdiction, see § 3.09, *supra*.

[357] The Court speculated that "continuous corporate operations within a state" could be "so substantial and of such a nature as to justify suit against it on causes of action arising from dealings entirely distinct from those activities." *International Shoe Co. v. Washington*, 326 U.S. 310, 318 (1945).

[358] 342 U.S. 437 (1952), *discussed in* § 3.06[2][b], *supra*.

[359] 466 U.S. 408 (1984).

[360] 638 S.W.2d 870 (Tex. 1982). For a detailed account of the Texas decisions in the case, see Dennis G. Terez, *The Misguided Helicopteros Case: Confusion in the Courts Over Contacts*, 37 BAYLOR L. REV. 913 (1985).

[361] The helicopter that crashed was manufactured in Texas and the pilot was trained there. 466 U.S. at 409–12.

jurisdiction.[362] It framed the issue instead as one of general jurisdiction: whether contacts between Helicopteros and the Texas forum were sufficient when seen as unrelated to the controversy. Invoking *International Shoe* and *Perkins*, the Court concluded that the case failed the minimum contacts test. Helicopteros lacked "the kind of continuous and systematic general business contacts" with Texas necessary to satisfy due process.[363] Since Helicopteros flew no commercial routes in Texas and kept no personnel there, the conclusion that no general jurisdiction existed was not difficult to reach.

[2]   The Future of General Jurisdiction

Clearly, minimum contacts necessary to support general jurisdiction are greater than those for specific jurisdiction.[364] But how much greater? *Helicopteros* may have the effect of overruling some of the most tenuous assertions of general jurisdiction among prior lower court decisions.[365] However, it left much unsettled.[366] Particularly troublesome is the question when or whether a national concern that regularly conducts some business in the forum has by so doing made itself amenable to process on a theory of

---

[362] "All parties to the present case," said the Court, "concede that respondents' claims against [Helicopteros] did not 'arise out of,' and are not related to, [Helicopteros'] activities within Texas." 466 U.S. at 415. See generally § 13.08 *infra*, on the necessity of preserving and presenting a question for appeal. Dissenting, Justice Brennan would have found the case properly within Texas's specific jurisdiction. Several commentators have agreed. Russell J. Weintraub, *Due Process Limitations on the Personal Jurisdiction of State Courts: Time for Change*, 63 OR. L. REV. 485, 530 (1984); Louise Weinberg, *The Helicopter Case and the Jurisprudence of Jurisdiction*, 58 S. CAL. L. REV. 913, 915 (1985); William J. Knudsen, Jr., *Keeton, Calder, Helicopteros and Burger King — International Shoe's Most Recent Progeny*, 39 U. MIAMI L. REV. 809, 832 (1985). For example, Professor Weintraub wrote: "The deaths in Peru 'arose out of' [Helicopteros'] Texas business contacts in the broadest 'but for' sense." Weintraub, *Due Process Limitations, supra*.

There may be problems, however, with so broad a conception of specific jurisdiction. Granted, Helicopteros' Texas contacts were not entirely isolated from the claims brought there. Yet a "but for" approach to specific jurisdiction seems capable of attaching significance to contacts which do not really provide the forum with regulatory concerns necessary to justify specific jurisdiction. See § 3.10[1], *supra*. In *Helicopteros*, "Texas probably has little interest in a wrongful death that occurred in Peru, especially when equipment manufactured and purchased in Texas was not at fault. . . . " Terez, note 360, *supra*, at 938. See generally Flavio Rose, *Related Contacts and Personal Jurisdiction: The "But For" Test*, 82 CALIF. L. REV. 1545 (1994).

[363] 466 U.S. at 416. Relying on an early case, *Rosenberg Bros. & Co. v. Curtis Brown Co.*, 260 U.S. 516 (1923), the Court added that the fact that the defendant purchased goods from the forum contributed little to respondent's case for jurisdiction. "[W]e hold that mere purchases, even if occurring at regular intervals, are not enough to warrant a State's assertion of *in personam* jurisdiction over a nonresident corporation in a cause of action not related to those purchase transactions." 466 U.S. at 418.

[364] See § 3.09[2], *supra*; Lea Brilmayer, *Related Contacts and Personal Jurisdiction*, 101 HARV. L. REV. 1444 (1988); Alfred Hill, *Choice of Law and Jurisdiction in the Supreme Court*, 81 COLUM. L. REV. 960, 980–81 (1981).

[365] See, e.g., *Bryant v. Finnish Nat'l Airline*, 208 N.E.2d 439 (N.Y. 1965), *discussed in* § 3.07[3], *supra, and criticized in* WILLIS L.M. REESE ET AL., CASES AND MATERIALS ON CONFLICT OF LAWS 114 (11th ed. 2000).

[366] It continues to be true that, "[b]eyond *Perkins* and *Helicopteros*, the Court has provided little guidance on the quality and quantity of contacts sufficient for general jurisdiction." ROBERT C. CASAD & WILLIAM B. RICHMAN, JURISDICTION IN CIVIL ACTIONS § 2-5[3][a] (Lexis 3d ed. 1998).

general jurisdiction. For example, is a car manufacturer or insurance company that routinely directs its product into many states within the general jurisdiction of the courts of each?

On one hand, it can be argued that all *International Shoe* and *Perkins* seem to require and all that should be required by the Due Process Clause is that the business carried on by the nonresident defendant in each forum be continuous, systematic and substantial. By this view, it is reasonable for many state courts to exercise general jurisdiction over a defendant operating on a large scale.[367] On the other hand, it has been argued that doctrine shaping general jurisdiction is not as susceptible to refined analysis as doctrine associated with specific jurisdiction,[368] and that it would be preferable to confine *Perkins* to its unusual facts and permit jurisdiction for causes of action arising elsewhere only where the defendant is a citizen of or has its principal place of business in the forum.[369] Between these opposing views on how much significance to attach to defendant's forum contacts unrelated to the claim, there may be a useful middle ground.

First, it is easier to justify general jurisdiction in a place neither the home nor the principal place of business of the defendant when the claim presented is similar to one which *could* have arisen from defendant's forum dealings. This might be a sensible way of limiting the *Helicopteros* ruling. Because Helicopteros neither solicited passengers nor flew routes in Texas, it could not "reasonably anticipate being haled into court there"[370] to defend against a claim based on pilot error. However, general jurisdiction over claims arising

---

367

    If a corporation conducts a major, or even a substantial, portion of its activities in a particular state, it is as fair for it to be sued there on causes of action arising elsewhere as it is for a corporation (or an individual) to be sued at its domicile on such causes of action. The substantial character of corporate activities in the state indicates that the corporation is reasonably equipped to defend lawsuits there.

Robert A. Leflar, American Conflicts Law 52 (3d ed. 1977). *Accord,* Kathleen Waits, *Values, Intuitions, and Opinion Writing: The Judicial Process and State Court Jurisdiction,* 1983 U. Ill. L. Rev. 917, 940.

368 Arthur T. von Mehren & Donald T. Trautman, *Jurisdiction to Adjudicate: A Suggested Analysis,* 79 Harv. L. Rev. 1121, 1144 (1966).

369 von Mehren & Trautman, note 368, *supra,* at 1141–42. *Accord, Developments in the Law — State-Court Jurisdiction,* 73 Harv. L. Rev. 909, 932 (1960).

370 *World-Wide Volkswagen v. Woodson,* 444 U.S. 286, 297 (1980). *World-Wide Volkswagen* dealt with attempted specific jurisdiction. But the point it made by the phrase quoted in the text — that it is reasonable to impose personal jurisdiction only if the defendant directed such activities toward the forum state to make the possibility of having to defend there reasonably foreseeable (*see* § 3.10[2][a], *supra*) — would also seem to bear on general jurisdiction. *Compare* David E. Seidelson, *Recasting World-Wide Volkswagen as a Source of Longer Jurisdictional Reach,* 19 Tulsa L.J. 1, 17–19 (1983) (developing this point), *with* Mary Twitchell, *The Myth of General Jurisdiction,* 101 Harv. L. Rev. 610, 680 (1988) (adopting a narrower view: "The court should exercise general jurisdiction only if it finds that the defendant's ties with the forum are so significant that the defendant should have expected to be answerable to most claims asserted against it within the forum.").

elsewhere is defensible when the lawsuit is "precisely the kind of action the defendant should have contemplated as a result of [forum] contacts."[371]

Second, in deciding whether the "continuous and systematic" standard is satisfied, the court should consider defendant's contacts as a whole for a reasonable period of time up until and including the date the suit was filed.[372] For example, in one case, the appellate court found that the district court had erred in limiting its jurisdictional inquiry to one year, and instead found the appropriate period to be six years in the circumstances of the case.[373]

Third, as we will examine in the following section, defendant's unrelated forum contacts may combine with some claim-related contacts between defendant and the forum to create jurisdiction when neither a theory of general nor specific jurisdiction alone would suffice.

§ 3.12   FURTHER DEVELOPMENTS

Two of the Supreme Court's more recent cases on the role of due process in regulating personal jurisdiction are discussed elsewhere.[374] We will review three more in this Section and discuss how each may have affected the shape of current law.

[1]   Combining Defendant's Related and Unrelated Forum Contacts — *Keeton v. Hustler Magazine*[375]

It is clear that sufficient claim-related contacts between the forum and a nonresident defendant make the defendant amenable to suit on a theory of specific jurisdiction,[376] and that sufficient contacts between the two which are unrelated to the controversy will produce the same result on a theory of general jurisdiction.[377] There will be cases, however, where the forum has both

---

[371] Seidelson, note 370, *supra*, at 18–19; Linda S. Simard, *Hybrid Personal Jurisdiction: It's Not General Jurisdiction, or Specific Jurisdiction, But Is It Constitutional?* 48 CASE W. RES. L. REV. 559, 590 (1998); B. Glenn George, *In Search of General Jurisdiction*, 64 TUL. L. REV. 1097, 1134–35 (1990). *See, e.g., Garfield v. Homowack Lodge, Inc.*, 378 A.2d 351 (Pa. Super. Ct. 1977) (upholding personal jurisdiction over a nonresident defendant regarding a tort claim arising outside the forum but comparable to claims which could have arisen from defendant's forum contacts).

[372] *See Metropolitan Life Ins. Co. v. Robertson-Ceco Corp.*, 84 F.3d 560, 569–71 (2d Cir. 1996).

[373] *Metropolitan Life Ins. Co.*, 84 F.3d at 570.

[374] In *Burger King Corp. v. Rudzewicz*, 471 U.S. 462 (1985), the Court permitted personal jurisdiction in Florida over a Michigan defendant — even though defendant had far more controversy-related contacts with Michigan than with Florida. The case is discussed at § 3.10[3], *supra*. In *Phillips Petroleum Co. v. Shutts*, 472 U.S. 797 (1985), the Court refused to invoke the minimum contacts test to measure the relationship between the forum and unnamed members of plaintiffs' class. The ruling permitted maintenance of nationwide, plaintiff class actions uncomplicated by *International Shoe*. *Shutts* is discussed at § 9.09[2][b], *infra*.

[375] 465 U.S. 770 (1984).

[376] *See* § 3.09[2] and the illustrations provided in § 3.10, *supra*.

[377] *See* § 3.06[2][b] and the illustrations provided in § 3.11, *supra*.

types of contacts with a nonresident defendant, but neither in sufficient quantity to alone support personal jurisdiction. May the forum satisfy due process in such cases by aggregating all of defendant's forum contacts?

The question once divided commentators[378] but now may be resolved in a way broadening opportunities for personal jurisdiction. Without endorsing general use of the technique, the Supreme Court appeared to combine related and unrelated contacts in holding that jurisdiction was proper in *Keeton v. Hustler Magazine.*

Plaintiff Keeton sued Hustler Magazine in New Hampshire federal court for libel. The First Circuit Court of Appeals upheld Hustler's objection to personal jurisdiction. It ruled that due process prevented New Hampshire's long-arm statute from reaching Hustler,[379] an Ohio corporation with its principal place of business in California. The Supreme Court reversed.

Hustler had some contacts with the New Hampshire forum both related and unrelated to the controversy. It had circulated in New Hampshire copies of the magazine alleged to have libeled plaintiff, and it had circulated other issues there in a continuous and systematic fashion. There is some indication, however, that neither defendant's related nor unrelated contacts would have alone been sufficient to support personal jurisdiction. The Court noted that the magnitude of the alleged libel was the total circulation of the offending issues and that "only a small portion" of that circulation occurred in New Hampshire.[380] Similarly, Hustler's activities in New Hampshire "may not" have been "so substantial as to support jurisdiction over a cause of action unrelated to those activities."[381] However, the combination of defendant's related and unrelated contacts with the forum proved enough. "[R]espondent is carrying on a 'part of its general business' in New Hampshire, and that is sufficient to support jurisdiction when the cause of action arises out of the very activity being conducted, in part, in New Hampshire."[382]

---

[378] *Compare, e.g.,* Harold S. Lewis, Jr., *A Brave New World for Personal Jurisdiction: Flexible Tests Under Uniform Standards,* 37 Vand. L. Rev. 1, 34 (1984) (arguing the possibility of establishing personal jurisdiction through "partial satisfaction of both versions of the contacts tests."), *with* Lea Brilmayer, *How Contacts Count: Due Process Limitations on State Court Jurisdiction,* 1980 Sup. Ct. Rev. 77, 88 ("These two bases are independent threshold tests, so that a greater quantum of unrelated activity does not compensate for attenuated related contacts."). For the latter view, see also K.A. Lambert, Comment, *De Reyes v. Marine Management & Consulting, Ltd.: The Abuse of General Jurisdiction,* 66 Tul. L. Rev. 2085, 2093 (1992) (criticizing a recent Louisiana case for "merging the two doctrines").

[379] *Keeton v. Hustler Magazine,* 682 F.2d 33 (1st Cir. 1982). On the significance of state long-arm statutes to the personal jurisdiction of federal courts, see § 3.01[2][b], *supra.*

[380] 465 U.S. at 775.

[381] 465 U.S. at 779.

[382] 465 U.S. at 780 (*quoting Perkins v. Benguet Mining Co.,* 342 U.S. 437, 438 (1952)). The Court added that, "Where, as in this case, respondent has continuously and deliberately exploited the New Hampshire market, it must reasonably anticipate being haled into court there in a libel action based on the contents of its magazine." 465 U.S. at 781. The Supreme Court had given earlier indication that related and unrelated contacts might have combined effect. For example, in *World-Wide Volkswagen Corp. v. Woodson,* 444 U.S. 286 (1980), the Court concluded that Oklahoma lacked jurisdiction only after finding that defendants' claim-related contacts with the

It may be that the Court is simply aggregating the contacts to reach a quantitative threshold in a case like *Keeton*, but, if so, it has backtracked from its disavowal in *International Shoe* of any "simply mechanical or quantitative" test.[383] A more plausible theory for "hybrid" cases (combining related with unrelated contacts to uphold personal jurisdiction) rests on the suggestion that general and specific jurisdiction are simply opposite ends of a sliding scale, by which the quantity and quality of the defendant's contacts and the relatedness of the contacts to the claim are inversely related.[384] The availability of unrelated contacts can therefore compensate for the paucity of related contacts, even though the case is "a near-miss"[385] on both — it does not reach either end of the scale.

An alternative theory is that the causally unrelated contacts with the forum state (distributing magazines other than the offending issue) are so like the causally related, though slight contact (distributing the particular offending issue of the magazine) that the defendant could reasonably foresee having to defend some libel action based on its magazines distributed there and that the state has a regulatory interest in the content of magazines distributed there. As one commentator has put it, "if . . . the defendant could have foreseen its forum contact resulting in factual circumstances similar to those that gave rise to the plaintiff's cause of action, then the defendant's contact should form the basis for asserting . . . jurisdiction in the forum."[386]

[2]   When Minimum Contacts Are Not Enough — *Asahi Metal Industry Co. v. Superior Court*[387]

Asahi was another product liability case.[388] Plaintiff sued in California over a serious accident there, allegedly caused by failure of the rear tire of plaintiff's motorcycle. Defendant Cheng Shin manufactured the tire in Taiwan. It attempted to bring Asahi, a Japanese concern and manufacturer of the tire's valve assembly, into the case on a theory of indemnification. Rejecting Asahi's

---

forum were slight *and* that defendants had no contacts unrelated to the controversy. *World-Wide Volkswagen Corp.*, 444 U.S. at 295.

[383] *International Shoe*, 326 U.S. at 319. *See RAR, Inc. v. Turner Diesel Ltd.*, 107 F.3d 1272, 1277 (7th Cir. 1997):

> We cannot simply aggregate all of a defendant's contacts with a state — no matter how dissimilar in terms of geography, time, or substance . . . . [W]hen doing business with a forum in one context, potential defendants should not have to wonder whether some aggregation of other past or future forum contacts will render them liable to suit there.

[384] *See* William M. Richman, *A Sliding Scale to Supplement the Distinction Between General and Specific Jurisdiction*, 72 CAL. L. REV. 1328 (1984).

[385] Richman, note 384, *supra*.

[386] Linda S. Simard, *Hybrid Personal Jurisdiction: It's Not General Jurisdiction, or Specific Jurisdiction, But Is It Constitutional?*, 48 CASE W. RES. L. REV. 559, 590 (1998).

[387] 480 U.S. 102 (1987).

[388] In an earlier product liability case, *World-Wide Volkswagen v. Woodson*, 444 U.S. 286 (1980), the Court found contacts between an Oklahoma court and certain nonresident defendants insufficient to support personal jurisdiction. *See generally* § 3.10[2], *supra*.

jurisdictional challenge, the California Supreme Court held that it could exercise personal jurisdiction over Asahi without violating the Due Process Clause.[389] The United States Supreme Court reversed.

Seven Justices joined in Justice O'Connor's conclusion that, whether or not minimum contacts existed between the forum and Asahi,[390] California's attempt to assert personal jurisdiction exceeded what the Court called a distinct "reasonableness" standard of due process. It drew the standard from language in *International Shoe* confining personal jurisdiction over nonresident defendants to "traditional notions of fair play and substantial justice."[391] The Court noted that

> the determination of the reasonableness of the exercise of jurisdiction in each case will depend on an evaluation of several factors. A court must consider the burden on the defendant, the interests of the forum state, and the plaintiff's interest in obtaining relief. It must also weigh in its determination "the interstate judicial system's interest in obtaining the most efficient resolution of controversies; and the shared interest of the several States in furthering fundamental substantive social policies."[392]

The Supreme Court found California's exercise of jurisdiction over Asahi to be unreasonable on balance. On one hand, "the interests of the plaintiff and the

---

[389] The California Supreme Court sought to neutralize *World-Wide Volkswagen* by finding in the case a "distinction between businesses that serve a local market and those that serve a broader market," deeming Asahi to be the latter. 39 Cal. 3d 35, 45, *rev'd*, 480 U.S. 102 (1987). In other words, while "a secondary distributor and retailer" was protected under *World-Wide Volkswagen*, "a manufacturer or primary distributor" was not. 39 Cal. 3d at 46. The United States Supreme Court's decision in *Asahi* makes clear that this categorical distinction does not work.

[390] Only the Chief Justice and Justices Powell and Scalia joined the portion of Justice O'Connor's opinion concluding the California forum lacked minimum contacts. Justice Brennan (joined by Justices White, Marshall and Blackmun) argued in a concurring opinion that the record in the case indicated minimum contacts. Justice Stevens (joined by Justices White and Blackmun) suggested in another concurring opinion that California may have had minimum contacts, but it was unnecessary for the Court to rule on the issue. For a comparison of approaches taken by members of the Court prior to *Asahi*, see John R. Leathers, *Supreme Court Voting Patterns Related to Jurisdictional Issues*, 62 WASH. L. REV. 631 (1987).

[391] *International Shoe Co. v. Washington*, 326 U.S. 310, 316 (1945), quoted in *Asahi*, 480 U.S. at 105.

[392] 480 U.S. at 113 (*quoting World-Wide Volkswagen*, 444 U.S. at 292). The Court confuses matters, however, by relying directly on *World-Wide Volkswagen* for its reasonableness test. When the Court raised the same concerns in *World-Wide Volkswagen*, it was discussing "the concept of minimum contacts." 444 U.S. at 291. The *Asahi* Court shifted these concerns into a separate, free-standing due process test. *World-Wide Volkswagen* did not portend this development, but the intervening *Burger King* case did: "Once it has been decided that a defendant purposefully established minimum contacts within the forum State, these contacts may be considered in light of other factors to determine whether the assertion of personal jurisdiction would comport with fair play and substantial justice." *Burger King Corp. v. Rudzewicz*, 471 U.S. 462, 476 (1985) (quoting *International Shoe*). For an attempt to sort out the new test, see Leslie W. Abramson, *Clarifying "Fair Play and Substantial Justice": How the Courts Apply the Supreme Court Standard for Personal Jurisdiction*, 18 HAST. CONST. L.Q. 441 (1991).

forum in California's assertion of jurisdiction over Asahi" were "slight." On the other hand, Asahi's burden from defending in California was "severe."[393]

Asahi's significance as a minimum contacts case is at best uncertain. No opinion on the issue commanded a majority,[394] and the suggestion of four Justices that minimum contacts were lacking has been roundly criticized.[395] However, the Court invalidated jurisdiction in a due process holding divorced from minimum contacts analysis — and that is significant. The result in *Asahi* confirmed that minimum contacts between the forum and a nonresident defendant do not guarantee that assertion of personal jurisdiction comports with due process. In addition to minimum contacts, the plaintiff must still show reasonableness of personal jurisdiction under the criteria listed in *Asahi*. Furthermore, some courts have held that minimum contacts and reasonableness are inversely related, such that a borderline showing of minimum contacts will require "an especially strong showing of reasonableness" to support jurisdiction.[396]

Asahi's ultimate importance may depend in part on how frequently the situation posed there recurs. How often will courts have minimum contacts over a nonresident defendant yet be unable to exercise personal jurisdiction without offending notions of "fair play and substantial justice"? Perhaps not very often.[397] It still remains to be seen whether *Asahi* stiffened due process

---

[393] 480 U.S. at 114.

> Asahi has been commanded not only to traverse the distance between Asahi's headquarters in Japan and the Superior Court of California but also to submit its dispute with Cheng Shin to a foreign nation's judicial system. The unique burdens placed upon one who must defend oneself in a foreign legal system should have significant weight in assessing the reasonableness of stretching the long arm of personal jurisdiction over national borders.

480 U.S. at 114.

[394] *See* note 390, *supra.*

[395] "The most ominous aspect of the *Asahi* opinion is that four Justices joined in the finding that Asahi did not have minimum contacts with California." Russell J. Weintraub, *Asahi Sends Personal Jurisdiction Down the Tubes*, 23 Tex. Int'l L.J. 55, 66 (1988). *Cf.* William M. Richman, *Understanding Personal Jurisdiction*, 25 Ariz. St. L. Rev. 599, 625 (1993) (the opinion poses an "ominous limitation" on the stream-of-commerce justification for personal jurisdiction); Christine M. Wiseman, *Reconstructing the Citadel: The Advent of Jurisdictional Privity*, 54 Ohio St. L.J. 403, 405–06 (1993) (criticizing the plurality for applying a "narrowly-defined jurisdictional privity" test). For discussion of Justice O'Connor's minimum contacts analysis and its possible effects on stream of commerce theory, see § 3.12[3], *infra.*

[396] *Ticketmaster-New York, Inc. v. Alioto*, 26 F.3d 201, 210 (1st Cir. 1994); *Ellicott Mach. Corp. v. John Holland Party, Ltd.*, 995 F.2d 474, 479 (4th Cir. 1993).

[397] The two tests — minimum contacts and reasonableness — may so overlap that usually to fail one will be to fail both. The *Asahi* Court seemed to suggest as much: "When minimum contacts have been established, often the interests of the plaintiff and the forum in the exercise of jurisdiction will justify even the serious burdens placed on the alien defendant." 480 U.S. at 114. To Justice Brennan, the fact that *Asahi* passed the minimum contacts test but failed the reasonableness test made it "one of those rare cases." 480 U.S. at 116. *Burger King*, where minimum contacts and reasonableness tests seem to provide the same answer, may be more indicative of future results under the two-test approach. On *Burger King* as a precursor for the Court's approach in *Asahi*, see note 392, *supra.*

doctrine appreciably or merely distributed between two categories consider-ations once clustered around minimum contacts.[398] Yet, at the very least, *Asahi* makes it necessary to frame some due process issues differently.

[3] Personal Jurisdiction in Product Liability Cases — Navigating the Elusive Stream of Commerce

Product liability cases can pose a special problem in applying personal jurisdiction's minimum contacts test — the measurement of defendant's activities purposefully (knowingly) directed into the forum state.[399] Recall the assumption of the Supreme Court and commentators that minimum contacts analysis can be divided into the subcategories of specific and general jurisdiction.[400] This has proved a useful discinction and accomodates most personal jurisdiction cases. But the distinction can be problematic when applied to product liability cases.[401]

The problem comes from the nature and scope of product laibility recovery. Liability for harm to consumers typically stems from from faulty product design or manufacture. Manufacturers of the completed product (along with producers of product ingredients or component parts involved in the failure) may therefore be liable. So may others responsible for moving the product along to the consumer (wholesalers, distributers, retailers). The points of origin for creation of the product, its component parts, or, ingredients may be distant from the point where a consumer purchases the product from a retailer. Those at the beginning of the chain may not have purposefully directed their product into the state where it failed inasmuch as they do not and could not purposefully direct any particular unit of the product anywhere.

Consider an example. A lawn mower injures consumer X in California, who bought it from retailer Y there. The cause is failure of a component part produced by Alabama company A and incorporated into the lawn mower by B, a large lawn mower manufacturer in New Jersey. Y and anyone in the distribution chain who purposefully moved the offending lawn mower into or through the California market will clearly be within the California court's

---

[398] *See* note 392, *supra*. For further discussion of the case, see Linda J. Silberman, *"Two Cheers" for International Shoe (and None for Asahi): An Essay on the Fiftieth Anniversary of International Shoe*, 28 U.C. Davis L. Rev. 755 (1995); R. Lawrence Dessem, *Personal Jurisdiction After Asahi: The Other (International) Shoe Drops*, 55 Tenn. L. Rev. 41 (1987); David E. Seidelson, *A Supreme Court Conclusion and Two Rationales that Defy Comprehension: Asahi Metal Indus. Co. Ltd. v. Superior Court of California*, 53 Brook. L. Rev. 563 (1987); Earl M. Maltz, *Unraveling the Conundrum of the Law of Personal Jurisdiction: A Comment on Asahi Metal Industry Co. v. Superior Court of California*, 1987 Duke L.J. 669.

[399] Extended discussion of the minimum contacts test appears in § 3.09, *supra*.

[400] *See* § 3.09[2].

[401] The chain-of-distribution problem and the response offered by the stream of commerce doctrine features most prominently in personal jurisdiction issues arising in product liability cases. However, the same situation may also arise in "tort, contract, domestic relations, fraud, antitrust, intellectual property, libel, defamation, unfair competition — to name a few." Diane S. Kaplan, *Paddling Up the Wrong Stream: Why the Stream of Commerce Theory Is Not Part of the Minimum Contacts Doctrine*, 55 Baylor L. Rev. 503, 506–07 (2003) (case citations omitted).

specific jurisdiction. But, while the particular products of A and B have failed in California so as to make them liable to X, neither can be said to have purposefully directed the particular lawn mower that failed into California. When that lawn mower left B's plant, it entered a nationwide distribution network, the details of which were beyond B's knowledge or control. B knew that its lawn mowers were in use in California, but A (and B) had no way of knowing which of A's lawn mowers would end up there.

Can a California court exercise personal jurisdiction over A and B? B did not knowingly direct the offending lawn mower into California. A and B have no purposefully-directed contacts with California related to the controversy, therefore nothing to support a theory of specific jurisdiction. Nor, we will assume, are B's California activities unrelated to the controversy so systematic, continuous and substantial as to provide a basis for general jurisdiction. All X has to work with to establish jurisdiction is the fact that A and B know that some of B's lawn mowers were ultimately sold and used in California. Until recently, personal jurisdiction for such product liability cases seemed relatively secure under law straddling the specific/general distinction: the so-called stream of commerce doctrine. The doctrine is often associated with landmark case, *Gray v. American Radiator & Standard Sanitary Corp.*[402] One of the defendants challenged personal jurisdiction in an Illinois suit for injuries from a water heater that had exploded there. Defendant had manufactured the safety valve on the exploding heater, but it did no business in Illinois. It manufactured the valve in question in Ohio and sold it to another defendant who assembled the water heater in Pennsylvania. The Illinois Supreme Court stated in *Gray* that, while the defendant may have been unaware that the valve that failed was destined for use in Illinois, "it is a reasonable inference that its commercial transactions, like those of other manufacturers, result in substantial use and consumption in this State."[403] Defendant did not purposefully direct the offending valve into Illinois, but the court found personal jusisdiction possible when "liability arises, as in this case, from the manufacture of products presumably sold in contemplation of use here."[404] Then, "it should not matter that the purchase was made from an independent middleman or that someone other than the defendant shipped the product into this State."[405] It was enough that defendant placed the defective valve into the stream of interstate commerce with the realization that some of its valves came to rest in the forum state.[406]

---

[402] 176 N.E.2d 761 (Ill. 1961).

[403] 176 N.E.2d at 766. "To the extent that its business may be directly affected by transactions occuring here it enjoys benefits from the laws of this State, and it has undoubtedly benefited, to a degree, from the protection which our law has given to the marketing of hot water heaters containing its valves." *Id.*

[404] 176 N.E.2d at 766.

[405] 176 N.E.2d at 766.

[406] "[I]t is not unreasonable, where a course of action arises from alleged defects in his product, to say that the use of such products in the ordinary course of commerce is sufficient contact with the State to justify a requirement that he defend there." 176 N.E.2d at 766.

The stream of commerce doctrine laid down in *Gray* had much to recommend it[407] and, for over twenty-five years, it received widespread if not unanimous[408] acceptance. As recently as 1980, the United States Supreme Court cited *Gray* with apparent approval, stating: "The forum state does not exceed its powers under the Due Process Clause if it asserts personal jurisdiction over a corporation that delivers its products into the stream of commerce with the expectation that they will be purchased by consumers in the forum State."[409]

Then the Supreme Court cast a shadow over the stream of commerce doctrine in *Asahi Metal Industry Co., Ltd. v. Superior Court.*[410] We reviewed the facts of this case earlier.[411] The question was whether a California court could exercise personal jurisdiction over a Japanese component parts manfacturer. The Court's minimum contacts ruling was not crucial to the outcome in *Asahi*, because eight Justices agreed that jurisdiction failed a separate due process "reasonableness" standard.[412] Yet all of the Justices expressed a view on minimum contacts and, in so doing, may have plunged the stream of commerce theory into a state of confusion.

Justice O'Connor and three other Justices maintained that minimum contacts did not exist. They did so by narrowing significantly the stream of commerce theory. It was not enough that the defendant placed the product in the stream of commerce and was aware that its products were in use in the forum state.[413] A stream of commerce basis for personal jurisdiction would be acceptable only if there were additional acts of the defendant directed into the forum state. Justice O'Connor offered as examples

---

[407] Like specific jurisdiction (*see* § 3.09[2], *supra*), stream of commerce theory enables the state to investigate through exercise of personal jurisdiction whether citizens have been harmed locally. And the latter has the incidental and salutary effect of permitting courts to adjudicate in one case the interests of more (perhaps all) defendants in the chain of distribution. A leading authority described stream of commerce as "a useful contribution to the developing law of jurisdiction; without it, an out-of-state enterprise could reap substantial rewards from goods sold in the forum, yet insulate itself from amenability by using middlemen." ROBERT C. CASAD & WILLIAM B. RICHMAN, JURISDICTION IN CIVIL ACTIONS § 2-5[4][b][v] (3d ed. 1998). *But see* Diane S. Kaplan, *Paddling Up the Wrong Stream: Why the Stream of Commerce Theory is Not Part of the Minimum Contacts Doctrine*, 55 BAYLOR L. REV. 503 (2003) (arguing forcefully and at length against the stream of commerce doctrine).

[408] A few courts found *Gray*'s stream of commerce approach too expansive. *E.g.*, *In-Flight Devices Corp. v. Van Dusen Air Inc.*, 466 F.2d 220 (6th Cir. 1972); *Beaty v. MS Steel Co.*, 276 F. Supp. 259 (D. Md. 1967).

[409] *World-Wide Volkswagen Corp. v. Woodson*, 444 U.S. 286, 297–98 (1980).

[410] 480 U.S. 102 (1987).

[411] § 3.12[2].

[412] 480 U.S. at 102.

[413] Justice O'Connor wrote: "The placement of a product into the stream of commerce, without more, is not an act of the defendant purposefully directed toward the forum State." 480 U.S. at 112. She added: "a defendant's awareness that the stream of commerce may or will sweep the product into the forum State does not convert the mere act of placing the product into the stream into an act purposefully directed toward the forum State." 480 U.S. at 112.

designing the product for the market in the forum State, advertising in the forum State, establishing channels for providing regular advice to customers in the forum State, or marketing the product through a distributor who has agreed to serve as the sales agent in the forum State.[414]

Strictly speaking, *Asahi* did not change the law concerning stream of commerce, since one can extrapolate from the opinions of the remaining five Justices the old view that placement of the product into the stream, when combined with defendant's realization that the product is purchased in the forum State, is enough. But, in the absence of subsequent clarification by the Court, *Asahi* has generated lower-court uncertainty about stream of commerce theory[415] — to the consequent dismay of many commentators.[416]

[4]   A Limited Role for Plaintiff's Forum Contacts — *Calder v. Jones*[417]

In Calder, a California plaintiff brought a libel suit there against a number of defendants concerning publication of a story about the plaintiff in a national tabloid. The defendant who wrote and the defendant who edited the story (both Floridians) attacked the California court's personal jurisdiction. The highest California court ruling on the matter concluded that jurisdiction over the defendants was valid, and the United States Supreme Court affirmed.

Keeton[418] had made clear that due process does not require minimum contacts between the *plaintiff* and the forum.[419] However, could the existence

---

[414] 480 U.S. at 112.

[415] *Compare, e.g., Luv n' Care, Ltd. v. Insta-Mix, Inc.*, 438 F.3d 465 (5th Cir. 2006); *Barone v. Rich Bros. Interstate Display Fireworks Co.*, 25 F.3d 610 (8th Cir. 1994) (following the pre-*Asahi* formula), *with Bridgeport Music, Inc. v. Still N The Water Publ'g*, 327 F.3d 472 (6th Cir. 2003); *Rodriguez v. Fullerton Tires Corp.*, 115 F.3d 81 (1st Cir. 1997) (imposing Justice O'Connor's added requirement).

[416] "The most ominous aspect of the *Asahi* opinion is that four Justices joined in the finding that Asahi did not have minimum contacts with California." Russell J. Weintraub, *Asahi Sends Personal Jurisdiction Down the Tubes*, 23 TEX. INT'L L.J. 55, 66 (1988). *Cf.* William M. Richman, *Understanding Personal Jurisdiction*, 25 ARIZ. ST. L.J. 599, 625 (1993) (the opinion poses an "ominous limitation" on the stream-of-commerce justification for personal jurisdiction); Christine M. Wiseman, *Reconstructing the Citadel: The Advent of Jurisdictional Privity*, 54 OHIO ST. L.J. 403, 405–06 (1993) (criticizing the plurality for applying a "narrowly-defined jurisdictional privity" test).

[417] 465 U.S. 783 (1984).

[418] *Keeton v. Hustler Magazine*, 465 U.S. 770 (1984), discussed at § 3.12[1], *supra*.

[419] Plaintiff Keeton was a New Yorker. The Court found the fact that her contacts with New Hampshire were "extremely limited" to be no obstacle to jurisdiction.

[W]e have not to date required a plaintiff to have "minimum contacts" with the forum State before permitting that State to assert personal jurisdiction over a nonresident defendant. On the contrary, we have upheld the assertion of jurisdiction where such contacts were entirely lacking.

465 U.S. at 779.

of such contacts enhance plaintiff's case for personal jurisdiction?[420] The Supreme Court's minimum contacts inquiry prior to *Calder* often seemed preoccupied with "the relationship among the defendant, the forum, and the litigation,"[421] a formula slighting plaintiff's forum contacts.[422] For a time at least, *Calder v. Jones* seemed to change that. The Court said there that plaintiff's contacts "may be so manifold as to permit jurisdiction when it would not exist in their absence."[423]

The Court needed to emphasize plaintiff's forum contacts to overcome added difficulties posed by personal jurisdiction over the individual defendants. *Keeton* suggested that jurisdiction over the tabloid itself would have been possible for plaintiff Jones in any state where the offending issue appeared as

---

[420] Plaintiff's contacts most often derive from forum citizenship. Just as defendants usually prefer to litigate at home (*see* § 3.04[2], *supra*), so do plaintiffs. The interest in litigating at home is most compelling for plaintiffs lacking the mobility, resources, or sophistication to sue nonresident defendants elsewhere. *See* Arthur T. von Mehren, *Adjudicatory Jurisdiction: General Theories Compared and Evaluated*, 63 B.U. L. Rev. 279, 311–14 (1983); Arthur T. von Mehren & Donald T. Trautman, *Jurisdiction to Adjudicate: A Suggested Analysis*, 79 Harv. L. Rev. 1121, 1150 (1966); Note, *Jurisdiction Over Foreign Corporations — An Analysis of Due Process*, 104 U. Pa. L. Rev. 381, 383 (1955).

Plaintiff's interest in obtaining a local judicial remedy coincides with the forum's interest in providing one to its citizens. Von Mehren, *Adjudicatory Jurisdiction, supra*, at 308. However, the forum state also may have interests in providing a place to sue which are unrelated to plaintiff's citizenship.

> It may be interested in creating a local forum so that its laws can be properly applied. It may be interested in controlling the actions of its [citizens]. It may be interested in creating a forum that is convenient for resident witnesses. It may have an interest in efficient administration of justice. And it may be interested in creating a local forum for the adjudication of disputes that have an impact on the economic and social life of the State.

Hans Smit, *Common and Civil Law Rules of In Personam Adjudicatory Authority: An Analysis of Underlying Policies*, 21 Int. & Comp. L.Q. 335, 351–52 (1972).

[421] *Shaffer v. Heitner*, 433 U.S. 186, 204 (1977); *Rush v. Savchuk*, 444 U.S. 320, 327 (1980). There are a few limited exceptions to this rule. *See* Arthur T. von Mehren & Donald T. Trautman, The Law of Multistate Problems 703–06 (1965). "The law in the United States has long been that the plaintiff's domicile [supports] specific jurisdiction with respect to certain aspects of the marriage relation." von Mehren & Trautman, *supra*, at 703.

[422] This is the accepted view. Von Mehren, *Adjudicatory Jurisdiction*, note 420, *supra*, at 310; Peter Hay, *Refining Personal Jurisdiction in the United States*, 35 Int'l & Comp. L.Q. 32, 36 (1986). *Rush v. Savchuk*, 444 U.S. 320 (1980), leaves little room for doubt. There, the Court rejected the argument that "plaintiff's contacts with the forum are decisive in determining whether the defendant's due process rights are violated," stating that "[s]uch an approach is forbidden by *International Shoe* and its progeny." *Rush*, 444 U.S. at 332. Whether this is fair to plaintiffs is a matter of debate. *Compare, e.g.*, Linda J. Silberman, *Shaffer v. Heitner: The End of an Era*, 53 N.Y.U. L. Rev. 33, 87 (1978) (criticizing what she sees as "a depreciated role in jurisdictional questions" for the factor of plaintiff's interest in selecting the particular forum), *and* Graham C. Lilly, *Jurisdiction Over Domestic and Alien Defendants*, 69 Va. L. Rev. 85, 108 (1983) ("The Court's fixation upon [defendant's forum contacts] has essentially destroyed the desirable balance among the interests of the plaintiff, the forum state, and the defendant."), *with* Brilmayer, note 378, *supra*, at 107 (questioning "why the legislative desire to provide a forum should be dispositive, or why residence of the plaintiff provides a basis for depriving this particular defendant of property.").

[423] 465 U.S. at 788.

part of the tabloid's regular circulation.[424] However, jurisdiction over the tabloid would not necessarily mean jurisdiction over individual staff members.[425] The Court justified jurisdiction over the latter by noting how plaintiff's relationship with the forum intensified the importance of defendants' forum contacts.[426]

However, Asahi[427] may require a narrower reading of Calder's holding concerning plaintiff's forum contacts.[428] Asahi suggested that plaintiff must pass two separate due process tests: minimum contacts and reasonableness. Since plaintiff's forum contacts are now a focal point in the reasonableness test,[429] can they still tilt the balance in a minimum contacts test? The Supreme Court has yet to confirm that, by creating a separate test for reasonableness concerns, it means to read the same concerns out of the minimum contacts test.[430] If that turns out to be true, however, Calder's significance as a plaintiff's-contacts case may be limited to the relatively few[431] cases surviving minimum contacts scrutiny where the outcome under the reasonableness test might be in doubt.

Of more lasting effect may be the holding in Calder that defendants could not as journalists use the First Amendment to the Constitution to bolster their case against California's personal jurisdiction. Prior to the decision, lower

---

[424] See § 3.12[1], supra.

[425] "Petitioners are correct that their contacts with California are not to be judged according to their employer's activities there. Each defendant's contacts with the forum State must be assessed individually." Calder, 465 U.S. at 790.

[426]

>   The allegedly libelous story concerned the California activities of a California resident. It impugned the professionalism of an entertainer whose television career was centered in California. The article was drawn from California sources, and the brunt of the harm, in terms both of the respondent's emotional distress and the injury to her professional reputation, was suffered in California. In sum, California is the focal point both of the story and of the harm suffered.

Calder, 465 U.S. at 788–89.

[427] Asahi Metal Indust. Co. v. Superior Court, 480 U.S. 102 (1987).

[428] See note 423 and accompanying text, supra.

[429] For discussion of these and other points in the case, see § 3.12[2], supra.

[430] Calder itself is not of much help here. As it had in World-Wide Volkswagen (see note 392, supra), the Calder Court attempted to fit its entire due process analysis under the heading of minimum contacts. Calder, 465 U.S. at 788. Asahi discarded this approach, administering concerns other than defendant's relationship to the forum under a separate reasonableness test. See § 3.12[2], supra. It is arguable that by doing so the Court eliminated these concerns from its minimum contacts test. On the other hand, Asahi does not expressly confirm this. A majority of the Court ruling on a minimum contacts issue in Burger King seemed to take an opposite view. The Court said of factors now in Asahi's reasonableness test: "These considerations sometimes serve to establish the reasonableness of jurisdiction upon a lesser showing of minimum contacts than would otherwise be required." Burger King Corp. v. Rudzewicz, 471 U.S. 462, 477 (1985) (citing, inter alia, Calder and Keeton).

[431] See note 397 and accompanying text, supra.

courts[432] and commentators[433] disagreed whether freedom-of-the-press concerns should make jurisdiction in libel cases more difficult to obtain. The response of the Court was simply to "reject the suggestion that First Amendment concerns enter into the jurisdictional analysis."[434]

[5]   Jurisdiction in Cyberspace

Increasingly, personal jurisdiction issues arise in controversies based entirely, or in significant part, on internet activity. The question in such cases is whether or how the rules and reference points of personal jurisdiction law can be made to work concerning defendant's cyberspace activity. One of the authors of this book posed the problem in this way:

> [P]ersonal jurisdiction retains a strong geographical dimension, typically resting on physical acts that were purposefully directed at a forum state. But cyberspace is structurally indifferent to geography. Internet addresses are logical addresses on the network, rather than geographic addresses in real space. Neither party to a transaction in cyberspace (by E-mail, Usenet post, or Worldwide Website) may know or care where the other is geographically located. If they transact in goods, their goods are likely to be digitized information products, not physical goods. And in many — if not most — cyberspace transactions, the remote party who is subsequently sued can hardly be said to have purposefully directed the information product or communication at a particular forum, except in the sense that she directed it at every forum.[435]

On the other hand, if cyberspace is indifferent to geography, "it does not and cannot change the fact that parties themselves exist in physical space."[436] This fact sounds a caution against any effort to jettison traditional personal jurisdiction law just because a suit arises out of a cyber transaction.

---

[432] *See* the decisions cited in Comment, *Long-arm Jurisdiction Over Publishers: To Chill a Mocking Word*, 67 COLUM. L. REV. 342 (1967).

[433] *Compare* Kevin M. Clermont, *Restating Territorial Jurisdiction and Venue for State and Federal Courts*, 66 CORNELL L. REV. 411, 451–52 (1981), *and* Paul D. Carrington & James A. Martin, *Substantive Interests and the Jurisdiction of State Courts*, 66 MICH. L. REV. 227, 240–41 (1967) (requirements for personal jurisdiction should be more demanding in libel cases), *with* Comment, *Long-Arm Jurisdiction Over Publishers*, note 432, *supra*, at 358, *and* Comment, *Constitutional Limitations to Long Arm Jurisdiction in Newspaper Libel Cases*, 34 U. CHI. L. REV. 436 (1967) (requirements should be the same).

[434] *Calder*, 465 U.S. at 790.

[435] P. Raven-Hansen, *Newsletter of the Section on Civil Procedure, Association of American Law Schools* at 2 (Fall, 1998). For a comprehensive study of commercial activity on the internet, see John Rothchild, *Protecting the Digital Consumer: The Limits of Cyberspace Utopianism*, 74 IND. L.J. 893 (1999).

[436] American Bar Association Jurisdiction in Cyberspace Project, *Achieving Legal and Business Order in Cyberspace: A Report on Global Jurisdiction Issues Created by the Internet* 8 (1999 draft) (hereinafter "ABA Cyberspace Report").

The subject of personal jurisdiction in cyberspace has produced extensive commentary.[437] The United States Supreme Court has not yet ruled in an internet jurisdiction case. But lower courts are grappling with the problem, and their decisions may offer some guidance. Many Courts have been influenced by the decision in *Zippo Manufacturing Co. v. Zippo Dot Com, Inc.*,[438] categorizing cyber contacts by whether they were passive, commercially transactional, or interactive.

For example, it appears that due process does not permit exercise of personal jurisdiction based just on the fact that defendant's website is passive — merely accessible to internet users in the forum state.[439] Refusing personal jurisdiction in such circumstances, the Ninth Circuit observed:

> So far as we are aware, no court has ever held that an Internet advertisement alone is sufficient to subject the advertiser to jurisdiction in the plaintiff's home state. . . . Rather [in the internet cases permitting jurisdiction], there has been "something more" to indicate that the defendant purposefully (albeit electronically) directed his activity in a substantial way to the forum state.[440]

Any other rule would subject the sponsor of a passive website to personal jurisdiction the world over, because its website can be accessed by connected computers anywhere. The website's passive presence is ubiquitous and beyond its control.[441]

But when, as in the case of *CompuServe Inc. v. Patterson*,[442] the defendant directs particular internet activity into the forum state that is related to the

---

[437] *E.g.*, *ABA Cyberspace Report*, note 436, *supra*; A. Benjamin Spencer, *Jurisdiction and the Internet: Returning to Traditional Principles to Analyze Network-Mediated Contacts*, 2006 U. ILL. L. REV. 71; Joel R. Reidenberg, *Technology and Internet Jurisdiction*, 153 U. PA. L. REV. 1951 (2005); Symposium, *Personal Jurisdiction in the Internet Age*, 98 NW. U. L. REV. 409 (2004); Note, *A "Category-Specific" Legislative Approach to the Internet Personal Jurisdiction Problem in U.S. Law*, 117 HARV. L. REV. 1617 (2004); Jack L. Goldsmith, *Against Cyberanarchy*, 65 U. CHI. L. REV. 1199 (1998); Dan L. Burk, *Federalism in Cyberspace*, 28 CONN. L. REV. 1095 (1996); Mark S. Kende, *Lost in Cyberspace: The Judiciary's Distracted Application of Free Speech and Personal Jurisdiction Doctrines to the Internet*, 77 OR. L. REV. 1125 (1998); Christine E. Mayewski, *The Presence of a Web Site as a Constitutionally Permissible Basis for Personal Jurisdiction*, 73 IND. L.J. 297 (1997).

[438] 952 F. Supp. 1119 (W.D. Pa. 1997). "*Zippo* has earned a place in history as one of the most-cited district court opinions ever." Patrick J. Borchers, *Internet Libel: The Consequences of a Non-Rule Approach to Personal Jurisdiction*, 98 NW. U. L. REV. 473, 478 (2004). For extensive discussion of *Zippo* and cases following it, see A. Benjamin Spencer, *Jurisdiction and the Internet: Returning to Traditional Principles to Analyze Network-Mediated Contacts*, 2006 U. ILL. L. REV. 71, 78–85.

[439] *See e.g.*, *Bensusan Restaurant Corp. v. King*, 937 F. Supp. 295 (S.D.N.Y. 1996), *aff'd*, 126 F.3d 25 (2d Cir. 1997); *Cybersell, Inc. v. Cybersell*, Inc., 130 F.3d 414 (9th Cir. 1997); *Weber v. Jolly Hotels*, 977 F. Supp. 327 (D.N.J. 1997). *See also ABA Cyberspace Report*, note 436, *supra*, at 18 ("Personal or prescriptive jurisdiction should not be asserted based solely on the accessibility in the state of a passive web site that does not target the state").

[440] *Cybersell*, 130 F.3d at 418.

[441] *ABA Cyberspace Report*, note 436, *supra*, at 59.

[442] 89 F.3d 1257 (6th Cir. 1996). The case is featured in Bryce A. Lenox, *Personal Jurisdiction*

controversy, the forum acquires specific jurisdiction.[443] The Sixth Circuit in *CompuServe* ruled that defendant's contacts with the Ohio forum, while "almost entirely electronic in nature," [444] were sufficient to support personal jurisdiction. The court noted that defendant

> was on notice that he had made contracts, to be governed by Ohio law, with an Ohio-based company. Then, he repeatedly sent his computer software, via electronic links, to the CompuServe system in Ohio, and he advertised that software on the CompuServe system. Moreover, he initiated the events that led to the filing of this suit by making demands of CompuServe via electronic and regular mail messages.[445]

The court was therefore able to conclude that defendant "purposefully availed himself of CompuServe's Ohio-based services."[446] This will generally be true of commercially transactional websites, through which the sponsor directs a product to a specified forum in exchange for payment by a purchaser in the forum.

The *Zippo* categorization is less helpful for the category in between these cases: the interactive website. How much interaction is required for jurisdiction and why? An American Bar Association report on jurisdiction and cyberspace offers this explanation:

> Jurisdiction is about chosen contacts between the defendant and the forum. . . . [T]he sponsor of a passive web site has no way to control which fora she is "connected to" by the site. On the other hand, the site sponsor who does business electronically knows or can take reasonable steps to discover the location of the party with whom she is interacting. The provision of the interactive site, alone, may express the sponsor's willingness to become connected to all fora in which the site is accessible (assuming it does not contain any disclaimers, etc.) but it does not constitute that connection. Nor, of course, does the mere accessing of the site by forum residents. . . .
>
> Reliance, then, on the nature of the web site alone is misplaced. If an interactive site is not targeted to a specific forum, courts should focus on how the site is actually used. Knowing and willing use of it by a nonpresent party to enter into dealings with persons or business in the

---

in Cyberspace: Teaching the Stream of Commerce Dog New Internet Tricks: CompuServe, Inc. v. Patterson, 22 U. Dayton L. Rev. 331 (1997); Daniel V. Logue, *If the International Shoe Fits, Wear It: Applying Traditional Personal Jurisdiction Analysis to Cyberspace in CompuServe, Inc. v. Patterson*, 42 Vill. L. Rev. 1213 (1997); Aaron A. VanderLaan, *CompuServe, Inc. v. Patterson: Civil Procedure Enters the Cyberage*, 41 St. Louis U. L.J. 1399 (1997); David D. Tyler, *Personal Jurisdiction via E-mail: Has Personal Jurisdiction Changed in the Wake of CompuServe v. Patterson?*, 51 Ark. L. Rev. 429 (1998).

[443] For a discussion of specific jurisdiction as a subcategory of personal jurisdiction, see § 3.09[2].

[444] 89 F.3d at 1262.

[445] 89 F.3d at 1264.

[446] 89 F.3d at 1264. For a similar case, see *Panavision Int'l v. Toeppen*, 141 F.3d 1316 (9th Cir. 1998).

forum demonstrates a chosen contact with the forum, provides the forum with an interest in the relationships thus created, and makes it less likely that multiple fora with different applicable laws will attempt to regulate the site and assert jurisdiction over its sponsor.[447]

This analysis suggests that *Zippo*'s categorization is superficial, or, at least, just the beginning of the inquiry.[448] The real inquiry ought to be how the website is used, whether it targets the forum, and the defendant's intent or willingness to contact forum users — in a word (or, more accurately, two words): "purposeful availment." It remains to be seen, however, whether the courts will probe beyond *Zippo*'s categories to stay abreast of new developments in internet technology.[449]

[6]   Global Perspectives

The assorted human affairs giving rise to civil litigation are becoming increasingly global in character. This affects personal jurisdiction as well as other civil procedure topics.[450]

The law of personal jursdiction in American courts is outwardly unaffected by whether the defendant is a citizen of a sister state or of a foreign country. That law is shaped by the Due Process Clause, which protects *all* defendants. At the same time, problems arising under personal jurisdiction law may become more acute when the defendant is abroad. For example, "the remoteness of a foreign defendant makes the motion to dismiss for lack of personal jurisdiction an extremely powerful tool in the context of transnational litigation."[451] And the international character of internet activity can accentuate problems of determining jurisdiction in cyberspace.[452]

---

[447] *ABA Cyberspace Report*, note 436, *supra*, at 60–61.

[448] For recent criticisms of *Zippo*, see A. Benjamin Spencer, *Jurisdiction and the Internet: Returning to Traditional Principles to Analyze Network-Mediated Contacts*, 2006 U. ILL. L. REV. 71, 87–88; Allan R. Stein, *Personal Jurisdiction and the Internet: Seeing Due Process Through the Lens of Regulatory Precision*, 98 NW. U. L. REV. 411, 430–32 (2004); Patrick J. Borchers, *Internet Libel: The Consequences of a Non-Rule Approach to Personal Jurisdiction*, 98 NW. U. L. REV. 473, 479–80 (2004). More sympathetic treatment of *Zippo* appears in Note, *A "Category-Specific" Legislative Approach to the Internet Personal Jurisdiction Problem in U.S. Law*, 117 HARV. L. REV. 1617, 1619–24 (2004).

[449] For example, a recent commentator suggests that advances in information technology permit targeting of the forum producing an "interactivity [giving] the victim's state a greater nexus with offending acts and [providing] a direct relationship with the offender for purposes of personal jurisdiction." Joel R. Reidenberg, *Technology and Internet Jurisdiction*, 153 U. PA. L. REV. 1951, 1953 (2005). *Accord*, A. Benjamin Spencer, *Jurisdiction and the Internet: Returning to Traditional Principles to Analyze Network-Mediated Contacts*, 2006 U. ILL. L. REV. 71.

[450] These are surveyed in § 15.12, *infra*.

[451] THOMAS MAIN, GLOBAL ISSUES IN CIVIL PROCEDURE 63 (2006). "Indeed, unlike a purely domestic litigation matter where plaintiff must refile in another *state* when the court lacks personal jurisdiction over the defendant, the plaintiff must commence litigation in another *country*. Dreading the inconvenience or fearing the unfamiliar, that case may simply never be pursued elsewhere once the action is dismissed in the United States." *Id.*

[452] *See* § 13.12[5], *supra*. In international litigation, "assertions of national authority have raised many . . . legal conundrums regarding nation-state sovereignty, territorial borders, and legal

The United States is not a party to any international treaty on personal jurisdiction.[453] The absence of a treaty leaves American courts considerable latitude to refuse to enforce the judgments of foreign courts and vice versa. United States courts have on the whole been willing to enforce foreign judgments, but foreign courts have often been reluctant to enforce U.S. judgments.[454] Among the numerous idiosyncrasies of American civil procedure[455] that account for what one writer has called "the nasty aroma American litigation seems to elicit in much of the rest of the world,"[456] differences over personal jurisdiction are prominent. Some applications of personal jurisdiction accepted in the U.S. are rejected elsewhere as invalid.[457] More generally, tension arises from differences between the common law and civil law approaches to the subject.[458]

---

jurisdiction." Paul Schiff Berman, *The Globalization of Jurisdiction*, 151 U. Pa. L. Rev. 311, 317 (2002).

[453] Kevin M. Clermont, *A Global Law of Jurisdiction and Judgments: Views from the United States and Japan*, 37 Corn. Int'l L.J. 1, 2 (2004).

[454] "[C]ompanies often do not sue in the United States when the assets are elsewhere because they fear the uncertainty of subsequent enforcement of a United States judgment overseas." Louise Ellen Teitz, *The Hague Choice of Court Convention: Validating Party Autonomy and Providing an Alternative to Arbitration*, 53 Am. J. Comp. L. 543, 548 (2005).

[455] Richard L. Marcus, *Putting American Procedural Exceptionalism into a Globalized Context*, 53 Am. J. Comp. L. 709, 709–10 (2005).

[456] *Id.* at 710.

[457] Thus, "United States courts' assertions of 'general jurisdiction' on grounds of 'tag' and 'doing business' are often viewed as excessive and exorbitant by other countries." Linda J. Silberman & Andreas F. Lowenfeld, *A Different Challenge for the ALI: Herein of Foreign Country Judgments, an International Treaty, and an American Statute*, 75 Ind. L.J. 635, 639 n. 22 (2000).

[458] Teitz, *supra* n. 454, at 549, noting "theoretical divisions between common law and civil law approaches to jurisdiction. The civil law's rejection of broad discretion in the exercise of jurisdiction lends itself to detailed provisions covering all contingencies which will easily produce inconsistencies and hinder compromise."

Chapter 4

NOTICE AND OPPORTUNITY TO BE HEARD

§ 4.01 THE DUE PROCESS GUARANTEE OF NOTICE AND THE OPPORTUNITY TO BE HEARD

Federal and state adjudications are binding only when they satisfy the Due Process Clauses of the United States Constitution.[1] Having seen how the clauses impose limits on courts' territorial jurisdiction,[2] we will now consider how they deny effect to adjudications unless those to be bound were given prior notice and an opportunity to participate.[3]

Notice is tied to the procedure for service of process. The United States Supreme Court has reemphasized the importance of service of process, stating that "[s]ervice of process, under longstanding tradition in our system of justice, is fundamental to any procedural imposition on a named defendant."[4] As the Court observed in another case, "the core function of service is to supply notice of the pendency of a legal action, in a manner and at a time that affords the defendant a fair opportunity to answer the complaint and present defenses and objections."[5]

Process usually consists of a summons, directing defendant to respond or appear in court on penalty of default, and a copy of the complaint. *Service* is the formal means by which process is delivered to a defendant. Assurance of a quality of notice sufficient to satisfy due process is an important function of each system's service procedure.[6] We shall see that actual notice is not an invariable due process requirement. That is, it is possible under the right circumstances for defendant to be bound by an adjudication although he neither participated

---

[1] Restricting federal and state courts respectively, the Fifth and Fourteenth amendments protect against deprivation of "life, liberty or property, without due process of law." A cause of action is "property" within the meaning of the amendments and cannot be forfeited through proceedings lacking in due process. Due process similarly protects litigants who are claimed against. For elaboration of these points, see § 3.01[2] (law limiting the court's reach), *supra*.

[2] Chapter 3, *supra*.

[3] These two branches of due process doctrine are explained and compared in *Phillips Petroleum Co. v. Shutts*, 472 U.S. 797 (1985). See § 3.01, *supra*. For restatement of the due process principle of notice and the opportunity to be heard, see *Nelson v. Adams USA, Inc.*, 529 U.S. 460, 466 (2000) (voiding a judgment without requisite prior notice). On the contemporary importance of the principle, see Patrick Woolley, *Rethinking the Adequacy of Adequate Representation*, 75 Tex. L. Rev. 571 (1997).

[4] *Murphy Bros., Inc. v. Michetti Pipe Stringing, Inc.*, 526 U.S. 344, 350 (1999).

[5] *Henderson v. United States*, 517 U.S. 654, 672 (1996).

[6] *E.g.*, *Jones v. Flowers*, 547 U.S. 220 (2006).

in it nor made an informed decision to forgo participation.[7] At the same time, due process places a heavy burden of justification on attempts to bind those who have not received actual notice.

The Court laid down the modern standard in *Mullane v. Central Hanover Bank & Trust Co.*[8]

> An elementary and fundamental requirement of due process in any proceeding which is to be accorded finality is notice reasonably calculated, under all the circumstances, to apprise interested parties of the pendency of the action and afford them an opportunity to present their objections . . . . The notice must be of such nature as reasonably to convey the required information . . . , and it must afford a reasonable time for those interested to make their appearance . . . . But if with due regard for the practicalities and peculiarities of the case these conditions are reasonably met, the constitutional requirements are satisfied.[9]

Mullane involved adjudication by a New York state court of the interests of trust beneficiaries. The beneficiaries fell into three categories: (1) those whose names and addresses were known; (2) those who were unknowable; (3) and those whose names and addresses could be ascertained at considerable expense. The Court refused to permit notice by publication to the first category, "because under the circumstances it is not reasonably calculated to reach those who could easily be informed by other means at hand."[10] When addresses were known, "the reasons disappear for resort to means less likely than the mails to apprise them of [the] pendency [of the proceeding]."[11] Since a substantial number of beneficiaries would thus have actual (individual) notice, the Court was willing to dispense with a requirement of individualized notice for beneficiaries in categories two and three.

> This type of trust presupposes a large number of small interests. The individual interest does not stand alone but is identical with that of a class. The rights of each in the integrity of the fund and the fidelity of the trustee are shared by many other beneficiaries. Therefore notice reasonably certain to reach most of those interested in objecting is likely to safeguard the interest of all, since any objection sustained would inure to the benefit of all. We think that under such circumstances reasonable risks that notice might not actually reach every beneficiary are justifiable.[12]

---

[7] *E.g., Dusenbery v. United States*, 534 U.S. 161 (2002).

[8] 339 U.S. 306 (1950).

[9] 339 U.S. at 314–15.

[10] 339 U.S. at 319.

[11] 339 U.S. at 318.

[12] 339 U.S. at 319.

Accordingly, the Court approved constructive notice by publication to the beneficiaries for whom individualized notice was impractical.[13]

Mullane and its progeny "radically modified" the historical notice requirement.[14] *Mullane* curtailed notice by publication, holding that it could not substitute for individual notice when the latter was practicable.[15] On the other hand, *Mullane* authorized service by the best alternative means, possibly publication,[16] in some situations where individual notice was impracticable. The Court did not offer a comprehensive list of these situations and has not since. However, the manner in which the Court reacted to the circumstances in *Mullane* suggests that something less than individual notice is most likely to satisfy due process when proof of the impracticability of individual notice is accompanied by proof that (1) the suit is in the interest of the absentees, (2) they will be adequately represented by one before the court, and (3) the value of their individual interests is not too great.

The Supreme Court has subsequently adhered to the *Mullane* reasonableness-under-the-circumstances approach to notice. In *Greene v. Lindsey*,[17] it rejected a Kentucky state service of process scheme permitting notice of eviction proceedings to be left at the homes of defendants under circumstances where there was substantial possibility that passers-by would remove the notices before defendants knew of them. In *Greene* and in the subsequent case of *Mennonite Board of Missions v. Adams*,[18] the Court seemed to suggest that constitutional defects in service could have been cured through the additional step of mailing a copy of court process to the due process

---

[13] Similarly, the Supreme Court recently observed that "the Due Process Clause does not require . . . heroic efforts" to give defendant actual notice. *Dusenbery v. United States*, 534 U.S. 161, 170 (2002). Discussions of the case appear in David F. Benson, *United States v. Dusenbery: Supreme Court Silence and the Lingering Echo of Due Process Violations in Civil Forfeiture Actions*, 78 Chi.-Kent L. Rev. 409 (2003); W. Alexander Burnett, *Dusenbery v. United States: Setting the Standard for Adequate Notice*, 37 U. Rich. L. Rev. 613 (2003).

[14] Restatement (Second) of Judgments 27 (introductory note to Ch. 2) (1982).

[15] 339 U.S. at 318.

[16] "The rule in *Mullane* recognizes that persons can be bound even if they cannot be found through reasonably diligent search. Assuming that such a search has been made, the fiction is indulged that publication notifies the absentee." Restatement (Second) of Judgments, note 11, *supra*, § 2 comment g. "Publication of notice creates an additional possibility of bringing the proceeding to the absentee's attention. Perhaps more important, however, publication of notice is a ceremony whose performance assures that the termination of the absentee's rights is not done in secret." Restatement (Second) of Judgments, note 14, *supra*, § 2 comment g.

[17] 456 U.S. 444 (1982). For a discussion of *Greene*, see Arthur F. Greenbaum, *The Postman Never Rings Twice: The Constitutionality of Service of Process by Posting After Greene v. Lindsey*, 33 Am. U. L. Rev. 601–41 (1984).

[18] 462 U.S. 791 (1983). The case is examined in Linda S. Akchin, Note, *Mennonite Board of Missions v. Adams: Expansion of the Due Process Notice Requirements*, 46 La. L. Rev. 311 (1985). Later, in *Tulsa Professional Collection Services, Inc. v. Pope*, 485 U.S. 478 (1988), the Supreme Court again found circumstances requiring actual notice. Attention has turned to the constitutionality of internet service. *See* Matthew R. Schreck, *How Service of Process By E-Mail Does Not Meet Constitutional Procedural Due Process Requirements*, 38 J. Marshall L. Rev. 1121 (2005); Jeremy A. Colby, *The Modern Trend Towards Universal Electronic Service of Process*, 51 Buff. L. Rev. 337 (2003); Rachel Cantor, *Internet Service of Process: A Constitutionally Adequate Alternative?* 66 U. Chi. L. Rev. 943 (1999).

claimant.[19] Similarly, the Court recently held in *Jones v. Flowers*[20] that, when notice by certified mail was returned to defendant as undelivered, due process required defendant to take other practical steps to attempt to notify plaintiff of the case.[21]

§ 4.02 SPECIAL DUE PROCESS CONCERNS ARISING FROM CLASS ACTIONS AND PREJUDGMENT ATTACHMENTS

[1]   Class Actions

While class actions and special due process considerations pertaining to them are discussed elsewhere,[22] it is useful to make a few observations here. The special contribution of the class action device is to conclude simultaneously the interests of a far greater number of persons than could actively participate in the case. Those who do not actively participate but are nonetheless bound by the adjudication of class issues are called *passive* members of the class.

Due process does not (and, for class actions to exist, could not) require the active participation of each person to be bound in a civil action. The Supreme Court's classic standard for applying the Due Process Clauses to class actions is "that there has been a failure of due process only in those cases where it cannot be said that the procedure adopted, fairly insures the protection of the interests of absent parties who are to be bound by it."[23] Read broadly, this might suggest that the due process touchstone for class actions is adequate representation, rather than actual notice. However, since class actions are fully subject to *Mullane*'s due process requirement of best notice practicable,[24] so broad a reading would be unwise. Actual notice is clearly the best notice, and due process requires it to be given to class members whenever practicable.[25]

---

[19] It seems desirable to permit the party initiating service to cure through informal mailing a constitutional insufficiency in the formal scheme. However, in *Wuchter v. Pizzutti*, 276 U.S. 13 (1928), the Court struck down a judgment on due process notice grounds because the statute failed to require service on the defendant, even though the defendant in the case had in fact received actual notice. The Supreme Court has not expressly overruled *Wuchter*, but the continuing authority of the case is in some doubt. *See* Scoles, Hay, Borchers & Symeonides, Conflict of Laws § 12.3 (4th ed. 2004). "The more discerning cases have recognized that the requirement is adequate notice and that it is fulfilled by actual notice whose tenor indicates it ought to be taken seriously." Restatement (Second) of Judgments, note 14, *supra*, § 2 comment d.

[20] 547 U.S. 220 (2006).

[21] Defendant could "resend the notice by regular mail, so that a signature was not required." 547 U.S. at 234. "Other reasonable followup measures . . . would have been to post notice on the front door, or to address otherwise undeliverable mail to 'occupant.' " 547 U.S. at 235.

[22] *See* § 9.09, *infra*.

[23] *Hansberry v. Lee*, 311 U.S. 32, 42 (1940) (citation omitted).

[24] For discussion of *Mullane*'s requirements, see § 4.01, *supra*. The Supreme Court has consistently applied *Mullane* to class actions. *E.g., Phillips Petroleum Co. v. Shutts*, 472 U.S. 797 (1985).

[25] In addition, federal class action Rule 23 and the rules of many states require actual notice to class members in some situations whether or not actual notice would be required by due process.

[2]   Prejudgment Attachments

In theory, post-judgment attachment of the real or personal property of one against whom judgment is rendered (the judgment debtor) helps the judgment creditor to realize all or part of the value of the judgment.[26] The procedure is worthless, however, when the judgment debtor has little or nothing of value to attach. Pre-judgment attachment provides some hedge against this possibility because it "prevent[s] the defendant from disposing of or otherwise impairing the value of property that might be used to satisfy the judgment in an action."[27] Absent settlement, property remains frozen by prejudgment attachment until the plaintiff wins on the merits and is able to enforce his judgment against the property, or until defendant recaptures the property by having the attachment dissolved, posting surety, or winning on the merits.

At first glance, the due process law of notice[28] seems to restrain prejudgment attachments less than it does judicial proceedings generally. Current due process doctrine permits some decisions authorizing prejudgment attachments to be made after *ex parte* proceedings — proceedings conducted without notice to or participation by the defendant.[29] Defendant in such cases usually learns of the existence of suit only when prejudgment attachment separates him from his property. Earlier notice would make it possible for defendant to appear and contest plaintiff's application before the court decides to issue the attachment order. Since defendants in such cases typically are easy to find and notify prior to the attachment proceeding,[30] earlier notice might seem practicable in the *Mullane* sense and hence required by due process.[31]

Given the purpose of prejudgment attachments, however, requiring plaintiff to give notice to defendant before the fact of attachment might be impracticable in a different sense. Recall that prejudgment attachments exist to secure defendant's property to which plaintiff can look if he prevails on the merits. Alerting defendant to the attachment proceedings (or even to the existence of suit) may defeat this purpose. Defendant may transfer his interest

---

See § 9.09[2][a], *infra.* Neither the rule, nor due process, requires notice in some class actions when it is impracticable. *See* § 9.09[2][c], *infra.*

[26] *See* § 15.02 (enforcement of judgments), *infra.*

[27] Friedenthal, Kane & Miller § 15.2. Garnishment, another so-called provisional remedy, functions the same way. Sometimes the latter term is favored to describe seizure of defendant's liquid assets, including wages and debts owed him by others. *See, e.g., Sniadach v. Family Fin. Corp.*, 395 U.S. 337 (1969). For discussion of a different provisional remedy, the temporary injunction, see § 14.02[2], *infra.*

[28] When prejudgment attachment cases proceed on a theory of *quasi in rem* jurisdiction, a second branch of due process doctrine (regulating the exercise of territorial jurisdiction over nonresident defendants) may also be a factor. *See* § 3.08[1], *supra.*

[29] The Court upheld such a procedure in *Mitchell v. W.T. Grant Co.*, 416 U.S. 600 (1974).

[30] Indeed, plaintiff will probably be required to notify defendant quite soon *after* the attachment.

[31] *See* § 4.01 (notice), *supra.*

in property to another, remove it from the jurisdiction, hide it, or otherwise diminish its value,[32] leaving little to attach.

It is unwise to ban *ex parte* attachments altogether for the reasons noted above. On the other hand, any use of the judicial process depriving one of notice and property in so calculated a fashion must be subjected to careful scrutiny. The Supreme Court has struggled in four decisions to strike the proper balance. Whether these decisions, *North Georgia Finishing, Inc. v. Di-Chem, Inc.*,[33] *Mitchell v. W.T. Grant Co.*,[34] *Fuentes v. Shevin*,[35] and *Sniadach v. Family Finance Corp.*,[36] are entirely compatible is an open question.[37] The approach in each, however, centers on two inquiries.

First, what is the nature of the *ex parte* proceeding? The Supreme Court has made clear that the fact that only the plaintiff participates should not decide the outcome. Rather, procedures for deciding an *ex parte* application for attachment should take into account the interests of the defendant *in absentia* and carry the possibility that the application would be refused in appropriate cases. When the Court struck down prejudgment attachment procedures in *Fuentes* and *Di-Chem*, therefore, it gave considerable weight to the fact that the applications required of plaintiffs were undemanding in form and content,[38] and that issuance of attachment was left to clerical employees. The Court noted that circumstances were different in *Grant*. A sworn and factually detailed showing was necessary under Louisiana law. Moreover, the decision to issue the writ was made by a judge — an official more used to saying "no" to attorneys. Overall, the Court was able to conclude in *Grant* that "[t]he system protects the debtor's interest in every conceivable way, except allowing him to have the property to start with . . . ."[39]

The second inquiry is: how long is defendant likely to be separated from custody or control of the property? Even systems invalidated in *Fuentes* and *Di-Chem* provided some procedure for defendant to recapture the property prior to the conclusion of the case. The problem was that the procedures were insufficiently prompt and accessible. *Grant* noted that the procedure available

---

[32] Not only is there a possibility of transfer or malicious waste of the property, but also decline in value through ordinary continued use by the defendant during the pendency of the case. This may be of special concern to plaintiff when it holds a security interest in the property, a factor noted in *Mitchell v. W.T. Grant Co.*, 416 U.S. 600, 608 (1974).

[33] 419 U.S. 601 (1975).

[34] 416 U.S. 600 (1974).

[35] 407 U.S. 67 (1972).

[36] 395 U.S. 337 (1969).

[37] *See* Robert S. Catz & Edmund H. Robinson, *Due Process and Creditor's Remedies: From Sniadach and Fuentes to Mitchell, North Georgia and Beyond*, 28 Rutgers L. Rev. 541 (1975); Comment, *A Confusing Course Made More Confusing: The Supreme Court, Due Process, and Summary Creditor Remedies*, 70 Nw. U. L. Rev. 331 (1975). In *Lugar v. Edmondson Oil Co., Inc.*, 457 U.S. 922, 927 (1982), the Court said that the four decisions could be read together as due process law governing prejudgment attachments.

[38] For example, Florida law in *Fuentes* required merely "the bare assertion of the party seeking the writ that he is entitled to one." 407 U.S. at 74.

[39] 416 U.S. at 618.

to defendants in *Fuentes* was too obscure, leaving them "in limbo to await a hearing that might or might not 'eventually' occur. . . . "[40] The scheme upheld in *Grant* did not suffer from this problem. "Louisiana law," the Court stated, "expressly provides for an immediate hearing and dissolution of the writ 'unless the plaintiff proves the grounds upon which the writ was issued.' "[41]

The Supreme Court's message continues to be that state legislatures must beef up defendant's side of the formal adversary process. In *Grant*, the quality of procedure before and after the attachment was clearly superior to that in *Sniadach, Fuentes*, and *Di-Chem*. Returning to the subject in 1991, the Court in *Connecticut v. Doehr* faulted a Connecticut statute for failing to reach the standard set in *Grant*. Instead, the statute permitted issuance of an *ex parte* attachment on "only a skeletal affidavit" constituting "one-sided, self-serving, and conclusory submissions."[42]

Yet, while the procedural scheme was best for the defendant in *Grant*, the question remains: was the defendant there treated fairly enough to satisfy what should be the requirements of due process? Greater protection before and after issuance of the *ex parte* order is a procedural advantage theoretically available to all defendants facing attachment. But will low-income debtors such as the defendant in *Grant* be as likely as other debtors to exploit the advantage?[43]

---

[40] 416 U.S. at 618. "Nor was it apparent in *Sniadach* with what speed the debtor could challenge the validity of the garnishment." 416 U.S. at 614.

[41] 416 U.S. at 618 (*quoting* state statute).

[42] 501 U.S. 1, 14 (1991). Plaintiff in *Doehr* sought a real estate attachment against defendant pursuant to his claim for assault and battery. The fact that plaintiff wanted to attach real estate rather than movables of the defendant appeared to work against plaintiff. The Court noted that the "[p]laintiff had no existing interest in Doehr's real estate when he sought the attachment" and that "there was no allegation that Doehr was about to transfer or encumber his real estate. . . . " The Court concluded that "plaintiff's interest in attaching the property does not justify the burdening of Doehr's ownership rights without a hearing to determine the likelihood of recovery." 501 U.S. at 16. An illuminating study of this case by Professor Robert G. Bone appears in Civil Procedure Stories Ch. 4 (Kevin M. Clermont ed. Foundation 2d ed., 2008).

[43] For an argument that the United States Supreme Court relies unduly on adversary formalities in its attempt to secure due process objectives, see Jerry L. Mashaw, *The Management Side of Due Process: Some Theoretical and Litigation Notes on the Assurance of Accuracy, Fairness, and Timeliness in the Adjudication of Social Welfare Claims*, 59 Cornell L. Rev. 772 (1974). In prejudgment attachment and other legal contexts, equality in theory may not be equality in fact.

§ 4.03   RULES REGULATING SERVICE OF PROCESS

[1]   The Interplay of Constitutional Law and Rules or Statutes; Diversity of Local Approaches

We have seen that the Constitution does no more than set a pragmatic general standard for the quality of service of process.[44] Important as due process doctrine is, it does not create the particular structure and detail necessary for service-of-process rules or statutes. Because constitutional notice can take different forms, and because nothing stops legislatures from creating service requirements more demanding than those required by due process, approaches to service vary.[45]

The legal consequences attached to service also vary. Some states use *service* to define commencement of civil suit for statute of limitations and other purposes. Other states use *filing* to define commencement, as do federal courts under Rule 3. When a state uses service to define commencement for limitations purposes, however, federal courts in diversity cases must follow the state law in determining whether state law claims are time-barred.[46]

[2]   The Federal Rule Model

Federal court service is said to have "changed drastically"[47] with the 1983 amendments to Rule 4. The process leading to this development was unusual in itself. A year earlier, the Supreme Court proposed to Congress extensive changes in Rule 4.[48] Congress did not follow its usual practice of remaining silent, thereby permitting the Court's recommendation to become law.[49] Instead, Congress first postponed the effective date of the Court's rule, then amended it by statute.[50]

---

[44] *See* § 4.01 (due process guarantee of notice), *supra*.

[45] *See, e.g.*, the comparison between Massachusetts law (requiring service in hand) and Rule 4(d)(1) (permitting process to be left at defendant's home under certain circumstances) as interpreted by the Supreme Court in *Hanna v. Plumer*, 380 U.S. 460 (1965).

[46] *Compare Walker v. Armco Steel Corp.*, 446 U.S. 740 (1980) (Rule 3 gave way to Oklahoma's service-based definition of commencement), *with Schiavone v. Fortune*, 477 U.S. 21 (1986) (Rule 3 followed when New Jersey law also used a filing-based definition of commencement). For more on the interplay of state law and the Federal Rules of Civil Procedure, see § 7.04, *infra*.

[47] WRIGHT § 64. *See generally* Kent Sinclair, *Service of Process: Rethinking the Theory and Procedure of Serving Process Under Federal Rule 4(c)*, 73 VA. L. REV. 1183 (1987).

[48] The Chief Justice's letter appears at 456 U.S. 1014 (1982). The Advisory Committee note intended to explain the Court's revision of Rule 4 appears at 93 F.R.D. 255, 262–63 (1982).

[49] The Rules Enabling Act, 28 U.S.C. § 2072, contemplates (but does not require) a passive role for Congress. Congress usually remains silent, but has shown a greater tendency to become actively involved in recent years. *Cf.* John H. Ely, *The Irrepressible Myth of Erie*, 87 HARV. L. REV. 693, 693–94 (1974) (describing congressional resistance to the Court's proposed Federal Rules of Evidence). For a general description of the federal procedural rule-making process, see § 1.02 (sources of civil procedure), *supra*.

[50] The Federal Rules of Civil Procedure Amendments Act of 1982, Public Law 97-462, 96 Stat. 2527 (Jan. 12, 1983). Since Congress discarded the work of the Advisory Committee, no Advisory Committee notes accompany this amendment to Rule 4. However, the legislative history for Public

The 1983 amendment to Rule 4 attempted to make two fundamental changes urged by the Supreme Court in its unsuccessful proposal.[51] The first was to give plaintiff (or plaintiff's attorney) control over service of process. The second was to permit service by mail as a form of federal service.

Prior to the 1983 amendment, federal marshals had usually been responsible for service of plaintiff's summons and complaint. "The principal purpose of the amendments adopted in 1983 was to end this."[52] Responsibility was placed "squarely on the plaintiff."[53]

The change made sense. Federal marshals and their deputies have always had many responsibilities involving both civil and criminal litigation. Even with provision in the prior rule for special appointment of process servers, backlogs in summons and complaint service were common prior to 1983. It is usually in plaintiff's best interest to move the case along. Plaintiff's attorney can therefore be expected to handle responsibilities under Rule 4 quickly and correctly. To provide for cases which do not bear out this assumption, the rule gives the plaintiff 120 days from filing the complaint to serve the summons and complaint on defendant or (absent "good cause" for delay) suffer dismissal without prejudice.[54]

The 1983 provision for mail service was less successful than its proponents had hoped. The procedure for return of the acknowledgment form confused plaintiffs and defendants alike, and its applicability outside the forum state was unclear.[55] Moreover, defendants had little incentive to cooperate in the 1983 mail service because the only sanction for failure to return the acknowledgment form was the payment of usually insignificant costs of alternative service, and because the expense of collecting these costs discouraged enforcement of even this modest sanction.[56]

Law 97-462 offers some help in interpreting the amendment and is reprinted in David D. Siegel, *Practice Commentary on Amendment of Federal Rule 4 (Eff. Feb. 26, 1983) With Special Statute of Limitations Precautions*, 96 F.R.D. 88, 116–30 (1983) [hereinafter *1983 Commentary*]. For discussion of subsequent practice under Rule 4, *see* David D. Siegel, 28 U.S.C.A. Fed. R. Civ. P. 4, practice commentaries (1992) [hereinafter *1992 Commentary*].

[51] *See generally* Rachel Cantor, *Internet Service of Process: A Constitutionally Adequate Alternative?*, 66 U. CHI. L. REV. 943 (1999); Linda S. Mullenix, *The New Federal Express: Mail Service of Process Under Amended Rule 4*, 4 REV. LITIG. 299 (1985); Note, *Service of Process by First-Class Mail Under Rule 4 of the Federal Rules of Civil Procedure*, 15 RUTGERS L.J. 993 (1984).

[52] WRIGHT § 64.

[53] MOORE, 1987 Rules Part 1, at 44. *Cf.* Siegel, *1983 Commentary*, note 50, *supra*, at 94 ("The main purpose of the 1983 revision was to take the marshals out of the summons serving business almost entirely."). In a limited number of situations stated in Rule 4, the marshal retains authority to make service of the summons and complaint when requested by the party wishing service.

[54] Rule 4(m).

[55] Rule 4 advisory committee's notes (1993).

[56] Rule 4 advisory committee's notes (1993). *See generally* David S. Welkowitz, *The Trouble with Service by Mail*, 67 NEB. L. REV. 289 (1988); Mullenix, note 51, *supra*; Note, *Service of Process*, note 51, *supra*; *Report of the Committee on Federal Courts of the New York State Bar Association on Service of Process by Mail Pursuant to Rule 4(c)(2)(C)(ii) of the Federal Rules of Civil Procedure*, 116 F.R.D. 169 (1987).

The 1993 rule amendment addressed all of these shortcomings. First, it substituted the language of waiver for acknowledgment, making its operation and effect clearer to all parties.[57] Plaintiff or plaintiff's attorney may now mail the complaint, a request for waiver of formal service, and a form explaining the consequences of waiver to the defendant by first class mail. Second, the new procedure was clearly made applicable to service outside the state.[58] Third, it imposed on the defendant "a duty to avoid unnecessary expenses of serving the summons" and provided new incentives to defendant to discharge that duty. The defendant who returns a waiver of service form gets 60 days after the request for waiver was sent to answer the complaint instead of the usual 20. The defendant who does not is made liable not only for the costs of alternative service, but also for attorney's fees incurred in any motion to collect the costs of service.[59]

Changes in Rule 4 brought about by the 1993 amendment extend well beyond service by mail. The rule was almost completely rewritten. Much of the pre-1993 substance was preserved, but the amendment rearranged the sequence of matters discussed and worked a number of changes. These include authorization to use the service procedures of the state in which service is made as well as those of the forum state,[60] nationwide service of process in some cases founded on federal question jurisdiction,[61] and express reference to the Hague Convention.[62]

[3]   Service Abroad; The Hague Convention

Rule 4(f) offers means for effecting service of process in foreign countries. However, it does not in itself eliminate the risk that a federal court judgment might be denied enforcement abroad. This matters most in cases where assets sufficient to satisfy a judgment exist only in the foreign defendant's home country. Then it is essential that service on the defendant there comport with

---

[57] Rule 4(d)(2).

[58] Rule 4(k)(1) ("filing a waiver of service establishes personal jurisdiction" over defendant who could be subjected to jurisdiction of forum state courts).

[59] Rule 4(d)(1), (2) & (3). Prior to the 1993 amendment to Rule 4, courts disagreed concerning the availability of attorney's fees necessitated by additional service arrangements. *E.g., compare Premier Bank v. Ward*, 129 F.R.D. 500 (D. La. 1990) (attorney's fees available), *with McCarthy v. Wolfeboro Res. Serv.*, 132 F.R.D. 613 (D. Mass. 1990) (attorney's fees unavailable). Much turned on this. "Without attorney's fees, costs awards will usually be paltry, depriving defendants of incentive to acknowledge mail service voluntarily." Siegel, *1992 Commentary*, note 50, *supra*.

[60] Rule 4(e)(1).

[61] Rule 4(k)(2) states:

For a claim that arises under federal law, serving a summons or filing a waiver of service establishes personal jurisdiction over a defendant if: (A) the defendant is not subject to jurisdiction in any state's courts of general jurisdiction; and (B) exercising jurisdiction is consistent with the United States Constitution and laws.

For discussion of the rather limited effect of this new subsection on the personal jurisdiction, see § 3.01[2][b], *supra*.

[62] Rule 4(f)(1).

that foreign country's service requirements. Otherwise, the courts there may refuse for that reason to enforce the judgment.

For cases to which it applies, the Hague Convention[63] may offer a means of stabilizing international service of process from American courts. For example, each signatory to the Convention designates a "Central Authority" to process service in that country,[64] and the treaty makes some provision for service by mail.[65]

At the same time, the treaty does not completely cure problems in international service of process. Not all countries are signatories to the Hague Convention. Moreover, those that have joined have often attached conditions to their participation.[66] It is useful, then, to note alternatives to the Hague Convention.[67] First, there may be means of effecting service abroad apart from that treaty.[68] Second, it will be possible in some cases to establish jurisdiction over foreign nationals without resorting to service of process abroad.

The availability of the second option was greatly enhanced by the Supreme Court's decision in *Volkswagenwerk v. Schlunk.*[69] The Court suggested the

---

[63] Hague Convention on Service Abroad of Judicial and Extrajudicial Documents in Civil and Commercial Matters, 20 U.S.T. 361; T.I.A.S. 6638. *See generally* SCOLES, HAY, BORCHERS & SYMEONIDES, CONFLICT OF LAWS § 12.7 (4th ed. 2004); Pamela M. Parmalee, Note, *International Service of Process: A Guide to Serving Process Abroad Under the Hague Convention*, 39 OKLA. L. REV. 287 (1986); Robert M. Hamilton, *An Interpretation of the Hague Convention on the Service of Process Abroad of Judicial and Extrajudicial Documents Concerning Personal Service in Japan*, 6 LOY. L.A. INT'L & COMP. L.J. 143 (1983).

The United States has also joined the Inter-American Convention on Letters Rogatory. 14 INT'L LEG. MAT. 339 (1975); 18 INT'L LEG. MAT. 1238 (1979). *See generally* Anne-Marie Kim, *The Inter-American Convention and Additional Protocol on Letters Rogatory: The Hague Service Conventions "Country Cousins"?*, 36 COLUM. J. TRANSNAT'L L. 687 (1998); Lucinda A. Low, *International Judicial Assistance Among the American States — The Inter-American Conventions*, 18 INT'L LAW 705 (1984).

[64] Art. 2.

[65] Art. 10(a). Federal decisions are divided over whether 10(a) authorizes direct service abroad by mail without using the foreign country's central authority or diplomatic channels. *Compare Ackermann v. Levine*, 788 F.2d 830 (2d Cir. 1986) (yes); *Eli Lilly & Co. v. Roussel Corp.*, 23 F. Supp. 2d 460 (D.N.J. 1998) (yes) *with Bankston v. Toyota Motor Corp.*, 889 F.2d 172 (8th Cir. 1989) (no); *Knapp v. Yamaha Motor Corp.*, 60 F. Supp. 2d 566 (S.D. W. Va. 1999) (no).

[66] These reservations, called declarations, are used by countries to modify or negate obligations set out in the treaty. For examples, *see* DAVID BORN & GARY B. WESTIN, INTERNATIONAL CIVIL LITIGATION IN THE UNITED STATES 1100–05 (3d ed. 1996).

[67] *See generally* THOMAS O. MAIN, GLOBAL ISSUES IN PROCEDURE 124–47 (Thomson/West 2006).

[68] "The Convention is not, as has occasionally been supposed, automatically preemptive of all methods that may be used for service abroad." Siegel, *1992 Commentary*, note 50, *supra*. Professor Siegel adds: "As long as the nation concerned has not, in its ratification or in any other part of its law, imposed any limits on other methods, these others remain available and the Convention and its local implementing materials serve as supplements." Siegel, *1992 Commentary*, note 50, *supra*.

[69] 486 U.S. 694 (1988). The decision is discussed in Kenneth M. Minesinger, Note, *The Supreme Court Interprets the Hague Service Convention*, 23 GEO. WASH. J. INT'L L. & ECON. 769 (1990); Brenda L. White, Note, *Service of Process: Application of the Hague Service Convention in the United States*, 30 HARV. INT'L L.J. 277 (1989).

Hague Convention does not require jurisdiction to be established through service of process abroad when the facts of the case support a local theory of personal jurisdiction. That is, whenever the joint due process requirements of minimum contacts and of reasonableness are satisfied, jurisdiction exists in state (or federal) courts over foreign nationals — just as it does over Americans residing outside the forum in sister states. The Court held in *Schlunk* that service upon a German corporation was permissible under the Illinois long-arm statute. State law permitted substituted service on the defendant's subsidiary located in the United States. State law and federal due process provided the appropriate tests, and those tests were satisfied.[70]

---

[70] "Where service on a domestic agent is valid and complete under both state law and the Due Process Clause, our inquiry ends and the Convention has no further implications." 486 U.S. at 707. *But see* Stephen R. Burbank, *The United States' Approach to International Civil Litigation: Recent Developments in Forum Selection*, 19 U. PA. J. INT'L ECON. L. 1, 5–8 (1998) (endorsing recent lower court opinions requiring compliance with Hague Convention even after service was made in-state on foreign agent).

Chapter 5

A COURT WITH JURISDICTION OVER THE SUBJECT

§ 5.01 INTRODUCTION

[1] Subject Matter Jurisdiction Generally

Subject matter jurisdiction refers to a court's power or "competence" to decide a particular kind of controversy. To render a binding decision, the court must be "competent by its constitution — that is, by the law of its creation — to pass upon the subject-matter of the suit."[1] Typically, that law will include the organic law (the constitution) of the sovereign, any implementing jurisdictional legislation, and the common law gloss placed on such legislation by the courts. Because the constitutions and jurisdictional statutes of the states and the federal government differ, so does the subject matter jurisdiction of their respective courts.

Subject matter jurisdiction can, however, be described by certain generic terms. All states have courts of *limited, special, or inferior jurisdiction*, which are vested with the power only to hear cases of a particular kind. Small claims courts or traffic courts are courts of limited jurisdiction, the former limited to cases of a particular amount in controversy and the latter obviously limited to traffic violation cases. Virtually every state has at least one court of *general jurisdiction*, which is vested with a comprehensive residual subject matter jurisdiction to hear all cases not exclusively allocated to courts of limited jurisdiction. Such general jurisdiction courts, frequently established at the county level, are the workhorses of the state judicial systems, hearing the majority of significant civil and criminal cases.

Another generic distinction is between *original* and *appellate jurisdiction*. Those courts in which suits are first filed have original jurisdiction; the cases originate there. Courts that review cases that originate elsewhere, either in lower courts or in administrative agencies, are vested with appellate jurisdiction, usually but not always requiring some degree of deference to the original decision and hence a limited intensity of review.[2]

Finally, subject matter jurisdiction can be *concurrent* — shared between several different kinds of courts — or *exclusive*, restricted to a particular kind of court. State courts of general jurisdiction and federal district courts, for example, have concurrent jurisdiction of most cases involving questions of federal constitutional or statutory law, but the latter are vested with exclusive

---

[1] *Pennoyer v. Neff*, 95 U.S. 714, 733 (1878).

[2] *See* § 13.10 (intensity of review on appeal), *infra*.

jurisdiction over *some* topics, including admiralty, maritime, patent, plant variety protection, copyright,[3] and certain cases in which the United States is a defendant.[4]

It is more difficult to generalize about the timing and mode of challenging subject matter jurisdiction. These procedural incidents often differ depending upon whether the jurisdiction is general or limited. Strict rules for challenging subject matter jurisdiction have developed in federal courts because they are courts of limited jurisdiction. Subject matter jurisdiction implicates the distribution of federal judicial power and the separation of powers between the branches, rather than the personal rights of the parties to a litigation. Consequently, the parties cannot enlarge a federal court's subject matter jurisdiction by consent or waiver.[5] Any other rule would effectively enable the parties by their acts to amend Article III of the Constitution or federal jurisdictional statutes. Parties may therefore challenge a federal court's subject matter jurisdiction at any point in the litigation,[6] including appeal.[7] Moreover, a federal court is required on its own motion (*sua sponte*) to consider whether it has subject matter jurisdiction when the litigants have not raised the question.[8] Finally, in courts of limited jurisdiction the burden of

---

[3] 28 U.S.C. §§ 1333, 1338.

[4] 28 U.S.C. § 1346(f).

[5] Nor may a federal rule, because Congress has not given the rulemakers authority to extend or restrict the subject matter jurisdiction conferred by statute. *See Willy v. Coastal Corp.*, 503 U.S. 131 (1992). Rule 82 acknowledges this fact expressly.

[6] However, a subject matter jurisdiction challenge does not necessarily take precedence over a challenge to personal jurisdiction; "there is no unyielding jurisdictional hierarchy." *Ruhrgas AG v. Marathon Oil Co.*, 526 U.S. 574, 578 (1999). In *Ruhrgas*, a unanimous Court held that a federal court has discretion to decide personal ahead of subject matter jurisdiction when the former question is more easily and readily resolved. This discretion helps the courts avoid unnecessary determination of complex and novel questions of subject matter jurisdiction. In contrast, the Court has emphasized that a court must decide subject matter jurisdiction before ruling on the merits. *Steel Co. v. Citizens for a Better Environment*, 523 U.S. 83 (1998). *See generally* Jack H. Friedenthal, *The Crack in the Steel Case*, 68 GEO. WASH. L. REV. 258 (2000) (comparing *Steel* and *Ruhrgas*).

[7] In *Capron v. Van Noorden*, 6 U.S. (2 Cranch) 126 (1804), for example, the plaintiff lost at trial and then successfully appealed the judgment on the grounds that the court that *he* had selected lacked subject matter jurisdiction over his claim. However, collateral attacks on subject matter jurisdiction — challenges made not at trial or on direct appeal but in a separate litigation, such as one brought to enforce a prior judgment — are not allowed except in extraordinary circumstances, given the strong public interest in the finality of judgments. *Des Moines Navigation & R.R. Co. v. Iowa Homestead Co.*, 123 U.S. 552 (1887). *See generally* Robert J. Martineau, *Subject Matter Jurisdiction as a New Issue on Appeal: Reining in an Unruly Horse*, 1988 B.Y.U. L. REV. 1 (1988); Karen Nelson Moore, *Collateral Attack on Subject Matter Jurisdiction: A Critique of the Restatement (Second) of Judgments*, 66 CORNELL L. REV. 534 (1981); Dan B. Dobbs, *Beyond Bootstrap: Foreclosing the Issue of Subject Matter Jurisdiction Before Final Judgment*, 51 MINN. L. REV. 491 (1967). *The Restatement (Second) of Judgments* would permit collateral attacks for lack of subject matter jurisdiction, just as they are permitted for lack of personal jurisdiction, but it acknowledges that few courts have agreed. *Compare* RESTATEMENT (SECOND) OF JUDGMENTS § 65 (1982) *with* RESTATEMENT (SECOND) OF JUDGMENTS § 12 cmt. f.

[8] "If the court determines at any time that it lacks subject-matter jurisdiction, the court must dismiss the action." Rule 12(h)(3). The parties can assert the defense by a motion to dismiss for lack

pleading and proving jurisdiction rests on the party who invokes jurisdiction.[9] Disputes about facts that are relevant to deciding subject matter jurisdiction — issues of "jurisdictional fact" — are ordinarily for the judge to decide, looking to the pleadings, any record evidence, affidavits, deposition testimony, and even live evidence.[10]

While some states apply similar rules, many have more relaxed attitudes towards subject matter jurisdiction. Some treat the objection to subject matter jurisdiction as waivable,[11] and most place the burden of raising the issue of subject matter jurisdiction on the party who challenges it.[12]

[2] Subject Matter Jurisdiction of the Federal Courts

The United States Constitution sets out the permissible scope of the judicial power of federal courts in Article III, § 2. It lists the following types (sometimes called "heads") of federal subject matter jurisdiction:

- cases "arising under this Constitution, the Laws of the United States, and Treaties made . . . under their Authority," popularly known as *federal question* jurisdiction;
- cases affecting ambassadors and other official representatives of foreign sovereigns;
- admiralty and maritime cases;
- controversies to which the United States is a party;
- controversies between states and between a state and citizens of another state;
- cases between citizens of different states, popularly known as *diversity* jurisdiction;
- cases between citizens of the same state claiming lands under grants of different states;
- and cases between a state or its citizens and foreign states and their citizens or subjects, sometimes known as *alienage* jurisdiction.[13]

Article III directly vests the Supreme Court with original jurisdiction of cases affecting ambassadors and other foreign officials and those to which a state is a party, and such appellate jurisdiction as Congress may create. In contrast, Article III vests no jurisdiction directly in lower federal courts; in other words, it is not self-executing. Instead, it authorizes Congress to create and endow them with subject matter jurisdiction.[14] Congress therefore has the

---

of jurisdiction over the subject matter. Rule 12(b)(1). *See* § 8.07[2][c] (challenging pleadings on the basis of non-waivable defenses), *infra*.

[9] Rule 8(a) & Form 7.

[10] *See* MOORE § 12.30[3]. *See, e.g., Valentin v. Hospital Bella Vista,* 254 F.3d 358, 362–65 (1st Cir. 2001) (court may, but is not required to, order discovery, consider extrinsic evidence, and hold evidentiary hearing to determine its own jurisdiction).

[11] *See* Dobbs, note 7, *supra,* at 504.

[12] *See* JAMES, HAZARD, & LEUBSDORF § 2.22.

[13] U.S. CONST. art. III, § 2.

[14] "The judicial power of the United States, shall be vested . . . in such inferior Courts as the

constitutional authority to decide by legislation how much of the federal subject matter jurisdiction available under Article III shall be vested in the lower federal courts.[15]

While it established lower federal courts in the very first jurisdictional legislation, Congress has never vested them with as much subject matter jurisdiction as Article III permits. Except for the short-lived "Midnight Judges Act" in 1801,[16] the lower federal courts were not given general federal question jurisdiction until 1875.[17] They have never been given the whole of Article III diversity jurisdiction, as Congress has always limited this head of jurisdiction to cases that involve a specified amount in controversy. In other words, while Article III authorizes federal jurisdiction over *any* claim between citizens of different states, Congress has also set some dollar floor on such claims, apparently reasoning that some are too small to be worth federal court time.[18] Today, the main heads of federal jurisdiction are federal question jurisdiction and diversity jurisdiction, usually concurrent with state court jurisdiction, giving plaintiffs the choice in most cases of whether to file in federal or state courts.[19]

Congress *may* from time to time ordain and establish." U.S. CONST. art. III, § 1 (emphasis added).

[15] How little federal subject matter jurisdiction can be vested in the lower federal courts is a hotly debated question that arises from time to time in connection with proposed jurisdiction-stripping legislation. *See, e.g.*, Lawrence Gene Sager, *The Supreme Court 1980 Term, Foreword: Constitutional Limitations on Congress' Authority to Regulate the Jurisdiction of the Federal Courts*, 95 HARV. L. REV. 17 (1981); Ronald D. Rotunda, *Congressional Power to Restrict the Jurisdiction of the Lower Federal Courts and the Problem of School Busing*, 64 GEO. L.J. 839, 842–43 (1976); Martin H. Redish & Curtis E. Woods, *Congressional Power to Control the Jurisdiction of the Lower Federal Courts: A Critical Review and a New Synthesis*, 124 U. PA. L. REV. 45, 52–55 (1975); Theodore Eisenberg, *Congressional Authority to Restrict Lower Federal Court Jurisdiction*, 83 YALE L.J. 498 (1974).

[16] Act of Feb. 13, 1801, 2 Stat. 89, *repealed by* Act of March 8, 1802, 2 Stat. 132.

[17] Act of March 3, 1875, ch. 137, 18 Stat. 470. *See generally* FELIX FRANKFURTER & JAMES M. LANDIS, THE BUSINESS OF THE SUPREME COURT (1928) (history of federal judicial system).

[18] *See* 28 U.S.C. §§ 1332(a) (more than $75,000) & 1335(a) (disputed money or property of a value greater than $500 in interpleader actions). *See* § 9.07 (interpleader), *infra*.

[19] Federal diversity jurisdiction is always concurrent. Federal subject matter jurisdiction is presumptively concurrent unless it is expressly made exclusive by statute or impliedly "by incompatibility in its exercise arising from the nature of the particular case." *Claflin v. Houseman*, 93 U.S. 130, 136 (1876); *see also Tafflin v. Levitt*, 493 U.S. 455, 459 (1990); *Charles Dowd Box Co. v. Courtney*, 368 U.S. 502 (1962). For examples of exclusive federal jurisdiction, see 28 U.S.C. §§ 1333 (admiralty, maritime, and prize cases), 1337 (antitrust; exclusive by implication), & 1338(a) (patent, plant variety protection, and copyright). *See generally* ERWIN CHEMERINSKY, FEDERAL JURISDICTION § 5.2 (5th ed. 2007); Michael E. Solimine, *Rethinking Exclusive Federal Jurisdiction*, 52 U. PITT. L. REV. 383 (1991).

PART A.
Federal Question Jurisdiction

§ 5.02 CONSTITUTIONAL SCOPE

The most important federal subject matter jurisdiction today is federal question jurisdiction. This head of jurisdiction is premised on the belief that federal courts should have the authority to interpret and apply federal law because of their expertise in that law, their relative insulation from local and majoritarian pressures (and correspondingly more protective attitude toward federal rights), and their ability to give federal law more uniform application than state courts.[20] In *Osborn v. Bank of the United States*,[21] Chief Justice Marshall suggested in dicta the outer constitutional limits of federal question jurisdiction. He reasoned that Article III federal question jurisdiction extends not only to the federal question in a lawsuit, but "to a whole case" and all the questions in it.[22]

> [W]hen a question to which the judicial power of the Union is extended by the constitution, forms an ingredient of the original cause, it is in the power of Congress to give the Circuit Courts [which were trial courts at the time] jurisdiction of that cause, although other questions of fact or of law may be involved in it.[23]

That is, Marshall suggested that Congress could authorize a court, that has before it a case involving some federal question, to decide other questions and claims in the same case, even if they were not themselves federal. Marshall did not define what he meant by "ingredient," but suggested that it is at least sufficient that the right or title asserted by a party may be defeated by one construction of federal law and sustained by the opposite.[24]

He went on to suggest that it did not matter whether federal questions were actually put forth by the parties, as long as they were potentially available in

---

[20] *See* Burt Neuborne, *The Myth of Parity*, 90 Harv. L. Rev. 1105 (1977). These premises have not gone unchallenged. *See, e.g.*, Paul M. Bator, *The State Courts and Federal Constitutional Litigation*, 22 Wm. & Mary L. Rev. 605 (1981) (noting practical inevitability of state court decision of federal law and resulting need to expand experience of state judges with federal law). For reviews of factors that are or should be considered in the allocation of business between federal and state courts, see Martin H. Redish, *Reassessing the Allocation of Judicial Business Between State and Federal Courts: Federal Jurisdiction and "The Martian Chronicles,"* 78 Va. L. Rev. 1769 (1992); Barry Friedman, *Under the Law of Federal Jurisdiction: Allocating Cases Between Federal and State Courts*, 104 Colum. L. Rev. 1211 (2004).

[21] 22 U.S. (9 Wheat.) 738, 822 (1824).

[22] By this reasoning, Marshall helped lay the groundwork for the subsequent development of the judicial doctrines of pendent and ancillary jurisdiction and the codification of supplemental jurisdiction over non-federal claims and parties in cases that also present federal questions. *See* § 5.08 (overview of supplemental jurisdiction and its antecedents), *infra*.

[23] *Osborn*, 22 U.S. at 823.

[24] 22 U.S. at 823.

the action.[25] Justice Frankfurter later explained that by this theory, federal question jurisdiction would be extended "whenever there exists in the background some federal proposition that might be challenged, despite the remoteness of the likelihood of actual presentation of such a federal question."[26]

Finally, Marshall extended his logic even to federal questions that had already been definitively answered by prior cases. Reasoning that the federal character of a legal question is not transformed by its having been answered, and that an answered federal question might well be renewed, he concluded that it is still an ingredient of the case sufficient to confer *constitutional* federal question jurisdiction.[27]

The Supreme Court has not again explored the reach of Article III's federal question jurisdiction as fully as Chief Justice Marshall did in *Osborn*. But in 1983, it endorsed *Osborn* as "[t]he controlling decision" on the scope of that jurisdiction.[28] The most frequently debated questions remaining involve less the theoretical scope of that jurisdiction than how much of it Congress has actually vested in the federal courts.

§ 5.03 STATUTORY SCOPE[29]

Although Congress approximated the language of Article III in vesting statutory federal question jurisdiction in the lower federal courts,[30] the courts have been reluctant, in light of the limited character of the federal judicial power in general, to construe their own authority expansively. They have therefore given a narrower scope to statutory federal question jurisdiction than Chief Justice Marshall gave constitutional federal question jurisdiction in *Osborn*. Congress, after all, could "correct" what it finds to be too narrow a

---

[25] 22 U.S. at 825. *See Pacific R.R. Removal Cases*, 115 U.S. 1 (1885) (federal question jurisdiction upheld over purely state law claims asserted by federally chartered railroads because federal questions concerning their charter could potentially arise).

[26] *Textile Workers Union of America v. Lincoln Mills*, 353 U.S. 448, 471 (1957) (Frankfurter, J., dissenting).

[27] *Osborn*, 22 U.S. at 825.

[28] *Verlinden B.V. v. Central Bank of Nigeria*, 461 U.S. 480, 492 (1983).

[29] *See generally* Alan D. Hornstein, *Federalism, Judicial Power and the "Arising Under" Jurisdiction of the Federal Courts: A Hierarchical Analysis*, 56 IND. L.J. 563 (1981); William Cohen, *The Broken Compass: The Requirement That A Case Arise "Directly" Under Federal Law*, 115 U. PA. L. REV. 890 (1967); Paul J. Mishkin, *The Federal "Question" In The District Courts*, 53 COLUM. L. REV. 157 (1953); Ray Forrester, *The Nature Of A "Federal Question,"* 16 TUL. L. REV. 362 (1942).

[30] "The district courts shall have original jurisdiction of all civil actions arising under the Constitution, laws, or treaties of the United States." 28 U.S.C. § 1331. Similar language is also employed in 28 U.S.C. §§ 1337 and 1338(a) and they are usually given the same interpretation as § 1331. *See Carlson v. Coca-Cola Co.*, 483 F.2d 279 (9th Cir. 1973). *But see T.B. Harms Co. v. Eliscu*, 339 F.2d 823, 828 (2d Cir. 1964), *cert. denied*, 381 U.S. 915 (1965) (arguing that exclusivity of § 1338(a) jurisdiction justifies narrower construction). *See generally* Amy B. Cohen, *"Arising Under" Jurisdiction and the Copyright Laws*, 44 HASTINGS L.J. 337 (1993). At least one commentator has argued that the drafters of the 1875 federal question statute intended to vest the full constitutional federal question jurisdiction in the lower federal courts. *See, e.g.*, Forrester, note 29, *supra*, at 374–75.

judicial construction of statutory jurisdiction by amending a jurisdictional statute; it obviously has no equivalent power to amend a narrow construction of Article III.

There is no "single, precise definition" of the statutory jurisdiction.[31] Many federal courts today cite Justice Cardozo's reformulation of Chief Justice Marshall's suggestion in *Osborn*:

> [A] right or immunity created by the Constitution or laws of the United States must be an element, and an essential one, of the plaintiff's cause of action. The right or immunity must be such that it will be supported if the Constitution or laws of the United States are given one construction or effect, and defeated if they receive another.[32]

But their recitation of this test or other language from prior cases is often formulaic, "a substitute for analysis of the case that is actually before them."[33]

Still, the cases together suggest three statutory filters for federal question jurisdiction. First, all federal courts are agreed that the federal question must be "substantial" in the sense that it is not frivolous, that the basis for jurisdiction set out in the complaint is colorable — the "substantial question" filter. Second, a federal question must be part of a "well-pleaded" complaint (one shorn of anticipated defenses and other allegations not necessary to state a claim) — the "well-pleaded complaint" filter. Finally, the federal question must implicate a sufficiently significant federal interest to warrant a federal forum — the "significance" filter. In other words, the substantial question filter tests whether the federal question is too frivolous to serve as a basis for federal jurisdiction; the well-pleaded complaint filter tests whether the federal question is properly found in the complaint; and the significance filter tests whether the question is "federal enough" to justify the federal forum.[34]

[1]   The Substantial Question Filter

A "substantial" federal question is one that is not "so attenuated and insubstantial as to be absolutely devoid of merit," "wholly insubstantial," "obviously frivolous," "plainly insubstantial," or "unsound[] . . . [because] previous decisions . . . foreclose the subject and leave no room for the inference that the questions sought to be raised can be the subject of controversy."[35] This filter for federal question jurisdiction is uncontroversial and understandable: a litigant should not be permitted to invoke federal jurisdiction and consume a federal court's valuable resources with a wholly contrived and plainly phoney federal question. Nevertheless, the substantiality

---

[31] *Franchise Tax Bd. v. Construction Laborers Vacation Trust*, 463 U.S. 1, 8 (1983).

[32] *Gully v. First Nat'l Bank*, 299 U.S. 109, 112 (1936) (citations omitted). Professor Mishkin's formulation is also popular: whether plaintiff asserts a "substantial claim founded 'directly' upon federal law." Mishkin, note 29, *supra*, at 1268.

[33] 13B *Wright & Miller* § 3562.

[34] *See* Richard D. Freer, *Of Rules and Standards: Reconciling Statutory Limitations on "Arising Under" Jurisdiction*, 82 IND. L. REV. 309, 317, 320–21 (2007).

[35] *Hagans v. Lavine*, 415 U.S. 528, 536–38 (1974) (quoting cases; citations omitted).

requirement can be confusing because it may seem that if the court deems a federal claim to be frivolous, it should dismiss on the merits for failure to state a claim. Nevertheless, the rule is well established: if the basis for federal jurisdiction is "insubstantial" — frivolous — then the dismissal is for want of jurisdiction. If not — if there is a colorable basis for federal jurisdiction — then the decision must go to the merits, whether on a Rule 12(b)(6) motion to dismiss for failure to state a claim, a Rule 56 motion for summary judgment, or by trial. A court could therefore deny a motion to dismiss for want of subject matter jurisdiction, yet grant a motion to dismiss for failure to state a claim. Jurisdiction would not disappear just because the court ultimately decides that a federal claim is without merit.[36] Thus, the Supreme Court explained in *Bell v. Hood*,[37]

> Jurisdiction . . . is not defeated as respondents seem to contend, by the possibility that the averments might fail to state a cause of action on which petitioners could actually recover. For it is well settled that the failure to state a proper cause of action calls for a judgment on the merits and not for a dismissal for want of jurisdiction. Whether the complaint states a cause of action on which relief could be granted is a question of law and just as issues of fact it must be decided after and not before the court has assumed jurisdiction over the controversy. If the court does later exercise its jurisdiction to determine that the allegations in the complaint do not state a ground for relief, then dismissal of the case would be on the merits, not for want of jurisdiction.

[2]   The Well-Pleaded Complaint Filter[38]

Although we have seen that in *Osborn*, Chief Justice Marshall suggested that constitutional federal question jurisdiction extended even to potential or anticipated federal questions,[39] the federal courts have rejected the proposition that the mere potentiality of a federal question will suffice for statutory jurisdiction. It is not enough that there is a *potential* federal question in a case to satisfy the jurisdictional statute; it must appear in plaintiff's complaint. A plaintiff cannot invoke the original jurisdiction of the federal courts either by anticipating a federal defense or otherwise importing a federal question into his complaint that is not essential to his case, and the federal court will examine only so much of the complaint as is "well-pleaded"

---

[36] 13B *Wright & Miller* § 3564.

[37] 327 U.S. 678, 682 (1946).

[38] *See generally* Arthur R. Miller, *Artful Pleading: A Doctrine in Search of Definition*, 76 Tex. L. Rev. 1781 (1998); Robert A. Ragazzo, *Reconsidering the Artful Pleading Doctrine*, 44 Hastings L.J. 273, 317–27 (1993); Donald L. Doernberg, *There's No Reason for It; It's Just Our Policy: Why the Well-Pleaded Complaint Rule Sabotages the Purposes of Federal Question Jurisdiction*, 38 Hastings L.J. 597 (1987).

[39] *See* § 5.02 (constitutional scope), *supra*.

— confined to the essential elements — to decide its federal question jurisdiction.[40]

Operation of the well-pleaded complaint filter is illustrated by *Louisville & Nashville Railroad Co. v. Mottley*.[41] In 1871, the Mottleys settled a claim against the railroad in exchange for free lifetime passes. But in 1907, the railroad declined to renew the passes, citing a new federal statute allegedly prohibiting free passes. The Mottleys then sued in federal court for specific performance of the settlement agreement, alleging alternatively that the federal statute did not prohibit free passes or that, if it did, it offended the Fifth Amendment.

Neither party raised the issue of subject matter jurisdiction, but when the case reached the Supreme Court, the Court considered the issue on its own motion. Although the federal statute presented a potential and even likely federal defense by the railroad, "[i]t is not enough that the plaintiff alleges some anticipated defense to his cause of action and asserts that the defense is invalidated by . . . the Constitution."[42] Well-pleaded, *i.e.*, shorn of the anticipated federal defense, the Mottley complaint merely stated a state common law claim for specific performance of the settlement agreement and therefore presented no federal question.

The "well-pleaded complaint rule" has its advantages. Because subject matter challenges go to the heart of federal judicial competence, they must be addressed promptly. The rule facilitates this, relieving the court of the burden of speculating what federal questions might later enter into the case. It also assures that a federal court will not waste its time and effort on a case that it is ultimately without jurisdiction to decide because the potential federal question fails to materialize. Consider, for example, the outcome if a federal court had taken jurisdiction of the Mottleys' complaint, only to find that the railroad never asserted the federal statute defense. The well-pleaded complaint rule also promotes federalism by leaving to state courts those cases that turn entirely or predominantly on state law. Finally, it reduces, if crudely, the federal question caseload burden on the federal courts by excluding cases in which the federal question is posed as a defense.

These advantages have been achieved at some cost, however. First, the rule substantially delays eventual federal decision of a federal defense or other post-complaint federal question. Such delay may seriously prejudice federal rights. In *Mottley*, for example, the railroad did assert the federal statute defense to the Mottleys' lawsuit in state court after the Supreme Court decision, and the case ultimately came back to the Supreme Court for review,[43]

---

[40] The Supreme court has endorsed this rule repeatedly. *See, e.g., Franchise Tax Bd. v. Construction Laborers Vacation Trust*, 463 U.S. 1 (1983).

[41] 211 U.S. 149 (1908).

[42] 211 U.S. at 152.

[43] If the plaintiff is confined to state court, any resulting judgment may thereafter have preclusive effect in federal court — that is, the federal court will treat the state court judgment as binding and the parties will not be permitted to relitigate it. *See* § 15.10[2], *infra*. This limits the prospect of federal adjudication when the plaintiff is confined to state court to United States

resulting in a ruling for the railroad.[44] Application of the well-pleaded complaint rule thus only delayed for four years a federal court decision of the federal question.

Second, the rule can place a premium on pleading technicalities and distinctions between forms of action[45] that otherwise have no place in federal courts.[46] For example, it results in federal jurisdiction over an action to remove a specific cloud over title, but not over an action to quiet title, when defendant claims adversely under federal law. The difference is that in an action to remove a cloud, the plaintiff is required to plead facts showing the invalidity of the adverse claim that is dependent on federal law. But in an action to quiet title, the source and nature of the adverse claim is not an essential element of plaintiff's cause of action. Hence, the well-pleaded claim to quiet title has no federal ingredient.[47]

These consequences of the well-pleaded complaint rule[48] could be mitigated by allowing a party to "remove" (effectively, to transfer)[49] to federal court any state court action in which a federal defense or other post-complaint federal question is actually presented.[50] Presently, however, the removal statute restricts removal to those cases that could have been brought in federal court originally, *i.e.*, those presenting federal questions in the well-pleaded complaint.[51]

Supreme Court review of the state court's decision — a possibility in some cases, but by no means a certainty. *See* Preble Stoltz, *Federal Review of State Decisions of Federal Questions*, 64 CALIF. L. REV. 943 (1976).

[44] *Louisville & Nashville R.R. Co. v. Mottley*, 219 U.S. 467 (1911).

[45] *See* § 8.02[1] (common law pleading), *infra*.

[46] *See* Rule 8(e)(1) ("No technical form [of pleading] is required."); § 8.04 (modern notice pleading), *infra*.

[47] *See* MOORE § 2.03[1]. *See also Additive Controls & Measurements Sys., Inc. v. Flowdata, Inc.*, 986 F.2d 476, 478–79 (Fed. Cir. 1993) (deciding federal question jurisdiction by whether the state allocates burden of pleading truth or falsity of assertions of federal patent infringement to plaintiff or defendant in state-created business disparagement suit).

[48] *See* Doernberg, note 38, *supra*, for fuller discussion of negative consequences.

[49] *See* § 5.07 (removal jurisdiction).

[50] In its study of federal jurisdiction, the American Law Institute (ALI) recommended that the law be changed to permit removal of these cases. Criticizing the well-pleaded complaint rule, the ALI observed that "[t]he alignment of parties to a lawsuit is often quite fortuitous," and that "[t]he dangers against which jurisdiction guards are as likely to be met when federal law is relied on defensively as when it is relied on offensively." ALI, STUDY OF THE DIVISION OF JURISDICTION BETWEEN STATE AND FEDERAL COURTS 189 (1969). *See also* Mary P. Twitchell, *Characterizing Federal Claims: Preemption, Removal, and the Arising-Under Jurisdiction of the Federal Courts*, 54 GEO. WASH. L. REV. 812 (1986); Michael G. Collins, *The Unhappy History of Federal Question Removal*, 71 IOWA L. REV. 717 (1986).

[51] *See* § 5.07[1] (removal), *infra*. *See generally* Ragazzo, note 38, *supra*; Note, *Artful Pleading and Removal Jurisdiction: Ferreting Out the True Nature of a Claim*, 35 UCLA L. REV. 315 (1987). The well-pleaded complaint rule has also substantially diminished the remedial scope of declaratory judgments. The federal Declaratory Judgment Act, 28 U.S.C. § 2201, was intended to help parties like the railroad in *Mottley*, which had no way to test its belief that federal law prohibited its renewal of the Mottleys' free pass other than to refuse renewal and invite suit by the Mottleys for breach of contract. Instead of waiting for that suit, under the Declaratory Judgment

The undesirable consequences of the well-pleaded complaint rule can also be avoided by looking beyond a pleading in which the plaintiff has attempted to defeat removal to federal court by artfully leaving out a substantial federal question. The Supreme Court has used the "artful pleading doctrine" to look past such a pleading "when federal legislation reveals an intent by Congress to preempt a field completely, which means that regardless of what the plaintiffs plead, a federal claim — by definition raising a substantial federal question — has been raised."[52] Thus, the formalism of the well-pleaded complaint rule can sometimes be softened by the artful pleading doctrine to enable federal courts to take jurisdiction of real but omitted federal questions.

[3]   The Significance Filter

That a substantial federal question appears in the well-pleaded complaint is not enough to justify statutory federal question jurisdiction unless it is "federal enough"[53] to require the expert and sympathetic attention of a federal forum. The courts have used both the "creation test" and the "embedded federal question test" for deciding the significance of the federal question.

[a]   The Creation Test

A question is presumptively federal enough when federal law actually creates the plaintiff's right to sue. Justice Holmes so concluded in *American Well Works Co. v. Layne & Bowler Co.*,[54] applying what has since become known as the "creation test" for federal question jurisdiction. There the Court was asked to decide whether federal jurisdiction was available for a claim that defendants had libeled and slandered plaintiff by falsely stating that plaintiff's pump infringed the defendants' federally granted patent. Justice Holmes reasoned that "[a] suit arises under the law that creates the cause of action," and therefore found federal jurisdiction lacking, since libel and slander are state-created causes of action.[55] By this reasoning, causes of action created

---

Act, the railroad could have obtained a declaration of its rights from a federal court by suing there for a "declaratory judgment." In *Skelly Oil Co. v. Phillips Petroleum Co.*, 339 U.S. 667 (1950), however, the Supreme Court reasoned that because the Declaratory Judgment Act did not alter the federal courts' jurisdiction, it should not be construed to allow jurisdiction over a suit like the railroad's if, applying the well-pleaded complaint rule, there would be no jurisdiction over the coercive suit that would have been brought by the Mottley's had declaratory relief been unavailable. The Court has since extended *Skelly* to state declaratory judgment complaints that defendants attempt to remove to federal court, explaining that at this late date it is for Congress, not the courts, to change the rule. *Franchise Tax Bd. v. Construction Laborers Vacation Trust*, 463 U.S. 1 (1983). *See generally* TEPLY & WHITTEN Ch. 2, § C(5).

[52] *See* Miller, note 38, *supra*, at 1818. The Court has explained that "Congress may so completely pre-empt a particular area that any civil complaint raising this select group of claims is necessarily federal in character." *Metropolitan Life Ins. Co. v. Taylor*, 481 U.S. 58, 63–64 (1987). It reaffirmed the vitality of this branch of the artful pleading doctrine in *Rivet v. Regions Bank*, 522 U.S. 470, 476 (1998) (dictum).

[53] The term is Freer's. *See* Freer, note 34, *supra* at 320.

[54] 241 U.S. 257 (1916).

[55] 241 U.S. at 260.

expressly[56] or "impliedly" under a federal statute[57] or "impliedly" under the Constitution[58] are presumptively within the statutory federal question jurisdiction of the federal courts. If federal law created the right to sue, it is reasonable to presume that there is a sufficient federal interest to justify a federal forum. This is true whether or not the defendant challenges the existence of the cause of action by filing a Rule 12(b)(6) motion — whether or not the complaint states a cognizable claim. "The question whether a cause of action exists," the Court has said, "is not a question of jurisdiction, and therefore may be assumed without being decided."[59] The creation test works well for the majority of federal question cases.

[b]   The Embedded Federal Question Test

However, the creation test is not conclusive. Even a state-created claim could turn on a question that may, in rare cases, be significant enough — "federal enough" — to "justify resort to the experience, solicitude, and hope of uniformity that a federal forum offers."[60] Just five years after *American Well Works*, the Court decided *Smith v. Kansas City Title & Trust Co.*[61] The plaintiff sought to enjoin the defendant trust company from investing its funds in federal farm loan bonds on the grounds that their issuance was unconstitutional. The cause of action clearly arose under state law, which prohibited the company's directors from making any investment not authorized by a valid law. Nevertheless, citing *Osborn*, the Court declared that "where it appears . . . that the right to relief depends upon the construction or application of [federal law] . . . , the District Court has jurisdiction."[62] Because the plaintiff shareholders would prevail if the federal law authorizing the bonds was found unconstitutional and lose on the opposite construction, the district court had jurisdiction of the case; the federal question embedded in plaintiff's state law claim was pivotal to that claim. The *embedded federal question test* applied in the *Smith* case reached beyond Holmes' *creation test*, which has since appropriately been described as "more useful for inclusion than for the exclusion for which it was intended."[63] In other words, a claim that passes the creation test presumptively qualifies for federal question

---

[56] *E.g.*, 42 U.S.C. § 1983 (civil rights actions).

[57] *E.g.*, *Cannon v. University of Chicago*, 441 U.S. 677 (1979) (citing legislative intent to approve an implied cause of action for damages under federal statute).

[58] *E.g.*, *Bivens v. Six Unnamed Agents of Federal Bureau of Narcotics*, 403 U.S. 388 (1971) (approving an implied cause of action for damages as a necessary remedy for violation of plaintiff's Fourth Amendment rights).

[59] *Burks v. Lasker*, 441 U.S. 471, 476 n.5 (1979). *See also Bell v. Hood*, 327 U.S. 678 (1946). Rule 12 (identifying defenses that may be asserted by motion to dismiss) thus distinguishes between the defense of lack of subject matter jurisdiction (12(b)(1)) and the defense of failure to state a claim (12(b)(6)). *See* § 5.03[1], *supra*.

[60] *Grable & Sons Metal Prods. v. Darue Eng'g & Mfg.*, 545 U.S. 308, 312 (2005).

[61] 255 U.S. 180 (1921).

[62] 255 U.S. at 199. *See also Franchise Tax Bd. v. Construction Laborers Vacation Trust*, 463 U.S. 1, 13 (1983) (federal question jurisdiction appropriate when "it appears that some substantial, disputed question of federal law is a necessary element of one of the well-pleaded state claims").

[63] *T.B. Harms Co.*, 339 F.2d at 827 (2d Cir. 1964), *cert. denied*, 381 U.S. 915 (1965).

jurisdiction, but a claim that does not pass the creation test is not necessarily disqualified for such jurisdiction because it may still contain a qualifying pivotal federal question.

At the same time, the Court has cautioned that the mere presence of a federal issue in a state-created cause of action — even one that is pivotal to the claim — does not automatically confer federal question jurisdiction. Its availability depends in part on "an evaluation of the nature of the federal interest at stake":[64] whether it is sufficiently significant to require a federal trial forum. Unfortunately, the Court has been less than clear about how a district court is to evaluate the nature of the federal interest.

In *Merrell Dow Pharmaceuticals, Inc. v. Thompson*,[65] the plaintiffs sued the defendant on a state claim of negligence, among others. They alleged also that the defendant had "misbranded" its products in violation of federal law, creating a rebuttable presumption of negligence under state law. The Supreme Court found that the federal issue thus incorporated into state law was "insufficiently substantial"[66] to confer federal question jurisdiction,[67] a conclusion suggested in part — if not compelled, according to the majority — by the fact that Congress had created no private cause of action for violations of the federal law at issue.[68]

Merrell Dow usefully focused on the significance of the federal question, but its terminology was confusing and its logic questionable. The *Merrell Dow* majority appeared to conflate the question whether Congress intended to create a private right of action with the question of whether plaintiff's state law claim included a pivotal federal question. Yet it hardly followed from Congress' intention to leave a statute's enforcement to public authorities that, when a federal statutory question arises as part of a state-created right of action, Congress also intended to leave the question to state court interpretation (subject only to the statistically remote possibility of Supreme Court review).

---

[64] *Merrell Dow Pharm., Inc. v. Thompson*, 478 U.S. 804, 804–15 n.12 (1986) (endorsing this characterization by commentators of the Supreme Court's cases regarding federal question jurisdiction).

[65] 478 U.S. 804.

[66] 478 U.S. at 814. The Court's choice of the word "substantial" in *Merrell Dow* was unfortunate because, as we have seen, the word is already used in the law of subject matter jurisdiction to mean not "wholly insubstantial and frivolous" or "patently without merit." *Bell v. Hood*, 327 U.S. 678, 682–83 (1946). *See infra* § 5.03[1], *supra*. But in the context of the *Merrell Dow* decision, the Supreme Court's use of "substantial" was clearly intended to suggest the significance of the federal interest.

[67] *See also Moore v. Chesapeake & Ohio Ry. Co.*, 291 U.S. 205 (1934). In fact, the Court has sometimes denied jurisdiction over even federally-created causes of action "because of an overwhelming predominance of state-law issues." *Merrell Dow*, 478 U.S. at 814–15 n.12, *citing Shulthis v. McDougal*, 225 U.S. 561, 569–70 (1912); *Shoshone Mining Co. v. Rutter*, 177 U.S. 505, 507 (1900) (both involving federally-created causes of action to vindicate property claims under state law). This is why we said that federally-created claims only "presumptively" invoke federal jurisdiction under the creation test.

[68] *Merrell Dow*, 478 U.S. at 810–12, 817. Insofar as such federal questions may eventually need federal appellate review, they are still subject to such review on appeal of the highest state court decision to the United States Supreme Court. 478 U.S. at 816 n.14, *citing Moore*, 291 U.S. at 214–15.

On this score, the dissent may have had the better argument. Congress' intent to rely on public enforcement "reflects congressional concern with obtaining more accurate implementation and more coordinated enforcement of a regulatory scheme." These are concerns which, if anything, strengthen the argument for federal jurisdiction over the embedded question of compliance with federal product regulations.[69]

More recently, the Court tried to clarify the significance filter for embedded federal questions. In *Grable & Sons Metal Products, Inc. v. Darue Engineering & Manufacturing*,[70] Grable sued Darue in state court on a state-created claim to quiet title. The Internal Revenue Service (IRS) had seized Grable's land for its failure to pay taxes, sent Grable notice of the seizure by mail, and then sold the seized land to Darue. Grable argued that the sale was invalid because federal law did not permit service by mail.

Darue removed the case to federal court on federal question grounds. As we discuss below,[71] to invoke federal jurisdiction by removal Darue had to show that Grable's case could have been brought originally in federal court — that there was federal question jurisdiction over Grable's claim. Darue argued that although state law created the right to sue, the state law claim of invalidity turned on the answer to a federal question: whether federal law permitted service by mail. The lower courts and the Supreme Court agreed, finding jurisdiction.

But how was *Grable* different from *Merrell Dow*? The Court explained that "even when the state action discloses a contested and substantial federal question, the exercise of federal jurisdiction is subject to a possible veto . . . [f]or the federal issue will ultimately qualify for a federal forum only if federal jurisdiction is consistent with congressional judgment about the sound division of labor between state and federal courts . . . ."[72] This "federalism veto" did not apply to *Grable*, because the narrow issue of mail notice that it posed was unlikely to arise as part of state law claims very often, yet cried out for a uniform answer to facilitate IRS tax-enforcement administration. The rarity with which it arose in state claims suggested that "federal jurisdiction to resolve genuine disagreement over federal tax title provisions will portend only a microscopic effect on the federal-state division of labor."[73] In contrast, the federalism veto applied to prevent jurisdiction in *Merrell Dow* because allowing jurisdiction there for the federal question embedded in the plaintiff's state-created negligence per se claim would open the federal courthouse doors to thousands of similar routine state tort claims, a result that would distort the traditional allocation of tort business between

---

[69] 478 U.S. at 832. *See generally* Patti Alleva, *Prerogative Lost: The Trouble with Statutory Federal Question Doctrine After Merrell Dow*, 52 OHIO ST. L.J. 1477 (1991); Note, *The Supreme Court, 1985 Term*, 100 HARV. L. REV. 100, 230–40 (1986).

[70] 545 U.S. 308 (2005).

[71] *See* § 5.07, *infra*.

[72] 545 U.S. at 313.

[73] 545 U.S. at 315.

state and federal courts, and one that Congress surely never intended.[74]

Grable thus adds a further layer to the significance filter. In evaluating the nature of the federal interest presented by an embedded federal question, a court must decide not only the significance of the federal question to the parties (whether it is pivotal to a claim) and to federal interests, but also whether taking jurisdiction would distort the allocation of business between state and federal courts and thus invoke the "federalism veto." Whether this nuance clarifies analysis is debatable,[75] and it seems unlikely that this will be the Court's last word.

PART B.
Diversity Jurisdiction

§ 5.04 IN GENERAL

[1] Rationale and the Modern Critique

The traditional justification for diversity jurisdiction[76] is that it protects out-of-state litigants from local bias.[77] With the passage of time and the decline in the intensity of state allegiances, many have criticized the continued availability of diversity jurisdiction.[78] First, they argue that local bias is no

---

[74] 545 U.S. at 318 ("[I]f the federal labeling standard without a federal cause of action could get a state claim into federal court, so could any other federal standard without a federal cause of action. And that would have meant a tremendous number of cases.").

[75] *Compare* Freer, note 34, *supra* at 344 (yes; its "sensible balancing" puts the statutory test for federal question jurisdiction "in better shape now than it has been in a generation"), *and* Rory Ryan, *No Welcome Mat, No Problem?: Federal-Question Jurisdiction After Grable*, 80 St. John's L. Rev. 621 (2006) (yes; *Grable* established a four-pronged test: (1) necessity; (2) actually disputed; (3) substantiality; and (4) disruptiveness), *with* Douglas D. McFarland, *The True Compass: No Federal Question in a State Claim*, 55 U. Kan. L. Rev. 1 (2006) (no; courts should exclusively use the creation test for the clarity it provides).

[76] 28 U.S.C. § 1332(a) confers jurisdiction *inter alia* over all civil actions between "citizens of different States" when the matter in controversy exceeds $75,000.

[77] Neither the records of the Constitutional Convention nor the records of the First Congress, which vested the federal courts with diversity jurisdiction of cases involving more than $400, describe this or any other justification in any detail. The historical reasons for the jurisdiction must therefore be gleaned from ratification debates and contemporary judicial opinions. *See, e.g.*, Henry J. Friendly, *The Historic Basis of Diversity Jurisdiction*, 41 Harv. L. Rev. 483 (1928). Chief Justice Marshall explained that "the constitution itself either entertains apprehensions" about the impartiality of state courts towards non-resident litigants, "or views with . . . indulgence thei[r] possible fears and apprehensions." *Bank of the United States v. Deveaux*, 9 U.S. (5 Cranch) 61, 87 (1809). Subsequently the Court opined that the protection of diversity jurisdiction was intended principally to "give security to all contracts [and] stability to credit" by protecting out-of-state creditors from the bias of local courts. *Ogden v. Saunders*, 25 U.S. (12 Wheat.) 213, 237 (1827).

[78] The arguments for and against diversity jurisdiction have been rehearsed in a succession of congressional hearings and sundry articles. A typical collection of statements, from which the arguments in the text are drawn, may be found in *Diversity of Citizenship Jurisdiction 1982: Hearings on H.R. 6691 Before the Subcomm. on Courts, Civil Liberties and the Administration of*

longer a serious concern in most cases. They add that even if it were, existing diversity jurisdiction is too broad in affording the choice of federal court even to a plaintiff who sues an out-of-state citizen in plaintiff's home state.[79] Advocates of diversity jurisdiction respond that some bias still exists, often exacerbated by the selection of state juries from a single county as opposed to district or state-wide jury pools. They add that, in any event, out-of-state litigants still need the protection of federal courts to avoid the prejudice inherent in their lack of familiarity with local judicial procedures.

Second, critics of diversity cite the caseload burden it imposes on the federal courts, interfering with their primary role in construing and protecting federal rights. Diversity cases consistently account for about 20% of the federal district court civil caseload. Moreover, they remain on the dockets longer, require more pretrial proceedings, go to trial more often, and require jury trials more frequently than other civil cases in the federal courts.[80] Diversity proponents respond that abolition of diversity jurisdiction would only shift the burden to equally taxed state courts.[81] They contend that the solution to the federal caseload is instead to create more federal judges and magistrates and to reform federal pretrial process.

Third, critics of diversity jurisdiction emphasize the hopelessly complex procedural, jurisdictional, and choice-of-law problems that it creates. Courts must now spend substantial time analyzing and applying elaborate, abstract, and often quite arbitrary rules in determining citizenship, aggregating claims for purposes of computing the amount in controversy, properly aligning parties, determining the effect of joinder and intervention in diversity cases, judging the propriety of separate and independent claim removal, and unmasking prohibited devices to manufacture diversity, all of which would be largely unnecessary were diversity to be eliminated.[82] Perhaps more significantly, the *Erie* doctrine requires federal courts sitting in diversity to apply state law as rules of decision, a task easier for their state court brethren to perform.[83]

Justice of the House Comm. on Judiciary, 97th Cong., 2d Sess. (1982) (hereinafter cited as *1982 Diversity Hearings*).

[79] Even Chief Justice Rehnquist urged abolition of at least this much of diversity jurisdiction. William H. Rehnquist, *Remarks of the Chief Justice*, 21 St. Mary's L.J. 5, 7–9 (1989).

[80] *1982 Diversity Hearings* at 10 (statement of J. Rose, Assistant Attorney General). This may be explained in part by the fact that nearly one-half of diversity cases are personal injury lawsuits in which the plaintiff expects to obtain a larger award from a jury than from the court. Report of the Proceedings of the Judicial Conference of the United States 136, Table C-2 (1999).

[81] Indeed, a statistical study conducted by the National Center for State Courts found that the abolition of just in-state plaintiff diversity jurisdiction, as urged by Chief Justice Rehnquist, *see* note 79, *supra*, "would have a surprisingly burdensome effect on state court caseloads . . . nearly as much . . . as would . . . total abolition of diversity jurisdiction." Victor E. Flango & Craig Boersema, *Changes in Federal Diversity Jurisdiction: Effects on State Court Caseloads*, 15 U. Dayton L. Rev. 405, 455 (1990).

[82] *See* Thomas D. Rowe, *Abolishing Diversity Jurisdiction: Positive Side Effects and Potential for Further Reforms*, 92 Harv. L. Rev. 963, 980–81 (1979). For a discussion of some of these rules, see §§ 5.04[2]–[3], 5.05, 5.06, *infra*.

[83] *See* § 7.02[3] (ascertaining the content of state law), *infra*.

Diversity advocates respond that much of the complexity could be avoided by the elimination of the statutory requirement of *complete diversity*[84] in favor of minimal diversity,[85] and argue that the *Erie* problem is exaggerated. Moreover, they contend that diversity jurisdiction results in "cross-pollination" of state and federal courts to the lasting benefit of both.

At a time when federal caseloads are excessive and federal question cases must compete for scarce judicial resources with diversity cases, the critics of diversity appear to have the better of the arguments. It is both most efficient and most faithful to a federal scheme of dual judicial systems that the subject matter of litigation be allocated according to the systems' comparative advantages and the sovereigns' primary interests and responsibilities. Federal courts are best at and have a special protective interest in determining and applying federal law. The continuation of broad diversity jurisdiction diverts them from their primary mission to no better end, in most cases today, than assuring some litigants a tactical choice of forum. Yet, as long as more members of Congress come from the ranks of practicing lawyers who value that choice[86] than from the academy or the bench, it appears unlikely that diversity will be abolished.[87]

[2] Diversity Between Whom?

While Congress has not yet acted to eliminate general diversity, the federal courts have often taken the matter into their own hands by construing diversity legislation narrowly.

> The policy of the [diversity] statute calls for its strict construction. The power reserved to the states, under the Constitution, to provide for the determination of controversies in their courts may be restricted only by the action of Congress in conformity to [Article III]. Due regard for the rightful independence of state governments, which should actuate federal courts, requires that they scrupulously confine their own jurisdiction to the precise limits which the statute has defined.[88]

---

[84] Complete diversity refers to the statutory requirement that every plaintiff be diverse from every defendant. *See* § 5.04[2], *infra*.

[85] *Minimal diversity* refers to the constitutional requirement that at least one plaintiff and one defendant be of diverse citizenship. *See* § 5.04[2], *infra*.

[86] *See* Victor E. Flango, *Attorneys' Perspectives on Choice of Forum in Diversity Cases*, 25 AKRON L. REV. 41, 56, 105 (1991) (finding that fear of bias against non-resident clients was a significant factor in choice of forum for more than 60% of attorneys surveyed).

[87] Of course, it will never be wholly abolished. All agree that *alienage diversity*, jurisdiction over suits between citizens and foreign nationals, must remain in the federal courts. It is likely, too, that diversity jurisdiction will be continued over multi-party lawsuits that could otherwise not be brought in any single state court. *See* REPORT OF THE FEDERAL COURTS STUDY COMM. 38–42 (1990); *1982 Diversity Hearings*, note 78, *supra*, at 263 (multidistrict mass tort litigation consolidated under 28 U.S.C. § 1407); 28 U.S.C. § 1397 (interpleader).

[88] *Healy v. Ratta*, 292 U.S. 263, 270 (1934).

This is most apparent in the requirement for complete diversity. Although the Supreme Court has held that Article III requires only minimal diversity[89] (that at least one party be a citizen of a different state from at least one opposing party), in *Strawbridge v. Curtiss*[90] it construed the general diversity *statute* to require complete diversity (that no party may share citizenship with any opposing party).[91] In modern multi-party litigation, the statutory requirement for complete diversity is in theory quite restrictive; it defeats jurisdiction whenever any plaintiff is a citizen of the same state as any defendant.

The courts have further narrowed the availability of diversity jurisdiction by looking behind the pleadings in some disputes and "realigning" the parties according to their real interests. Assume, for example, that a mortgagee sues its mortgagor and a city with whom the mortgagor has a contract for specific performance of a contract. Since the mortgagee and mortgagor have the same interest in specific performance, they should be aligned together, which will destroy complete diversity if the mortgagor and the city are citizens of the same state.[92] Realignment is more difficult when interests are shared on some issues and divided on others. But in such cases, the court will look to the "principal purpose of the suit" and the "primary and controlling matter in dispute" for purposes of alignment.[93]

[3]   Further Limitations on Diversity Jurisdiction

Deferring to state courts, federal courts have traditionally declined to exercise jurisdiction in certain *in rem* (regarding title to property),[94] probate cases, and domestic relations cases, even when the parties satisfy the

---

[89] *State Farm Fire & Casualty Co. v. Tashire*, 386 U.S. 523 (1967) (upholding constitutionality of federal interpleader statute, 28 U.S.C. § 1397, which requires only minimal diversity).

[90] 7 U.S. (3 Cranch) 267 (1806). *See* Howard P. Fink, *Supplemental Jurisdiction — Take It to the Limit!*, 74 IND. L.J. 161 (1998) (calling for elimination of rule of complete diversity); David P. Currie, *The Federal Courts and the American Law Institute*, 36 U. CHI. L. REV. 1, 18–21 (1968) (criticizing the complete diversity rule).

[91] Although Congress has not overridden the Supreme Court's construction of the general diversity statute, 28 U.S.C. § 1332(a), to require complete diversity, it has adopted minimal diversity for some claims. *See, e.g.*, 28 U.S.C. §§ 1332(d)(2) (authorizing federal jurisdiction for class action claims where "any member of a class of plaintiffs is a citizen of a State different from any defendant" and aggregate amount in controversy exceeds $5,000,000); 1335(a)(1) (providing federal jurisdiction for interpleader claims when "[t]wo or more adverse claimants [are] of diverse citizenship" and amount at stake is $500 or more).

[92] *See Dawson v. Columbia Trust Co.*, 197 U.S. 178 (1905).

[93] *See, e.g., Indianapolis v. Chase Nat'l Bank*, 314 U.S. 63, 69 (1941), *citing East Tennessee, V. & G. R.R. v. Grayson*, 119 U.S. 240, 244 (1886), *and Merchants' Cotton Press & Storage Co. v. Insurance Co.*, 151 U.S. 368, 385 (1894). In *Chase Nat'l Bank*, the Court dismissed several secondary issues on which the mortgagor and mortgagee were divided as mere "window-dressing designed to satisfy the requirements of diversity jurisdiction." 314 U.S. at 72. In a case which presents multiple issues of equal importance, it is arguable that a court should not realign parties who are truly divided on any one of the issues, but the case law is divided on this point. *See* WRIGHT § 30.

[94] *See* § 3.02[2] (*in rem* jurisdiction), *supra*.

requirements for diversity jurisdiction. In addition, they are also obliged by statute to deny jurisdiction which has been "improperly or collusively made."[95]

Considerations of respect owed state courts and of reciprocity — which courts lump under the phrase "comity" — have motivated federal courts to decline jurisdiction over diversity suits in which, in order to give effect to their judgments, they must take control of property that is already in the custody of a state court of competent jurisdiction. Such suits may include "suits . . . brought to marshal assets, administer trusts, or liquidate estates."[96] In part, similar considerations have supported the "probate exception."

> The probate exception reserves to state probate courts the probate or annulment of a will and the administration of a decedent's estate; it also precludes federal courts from endeavoring to dispose of property that is in the custody of a state probate court.[97]

A time-honored but possibly erroneous construction of the diversity statute, as well as recognition that the "whole subject of the domestic relations of husband and wife, parent and child, belongs to the laws of the States," account for the long-standing exclusion of domestic relations actions from diversity jurisdiction.[98] In *Ankenbrandt v. Richards*,[99] the Supreme Court traced the domestic relations exception to the historical assumption that alimony and divorce lay outside the jurisdiction of the chancery courts in England and therefore outside the diversity jurisdiction "in suits of a civil nature at common law or in equity" conferred by the Judiciary Act of 1789. Without confirming this assumption, the Court deferred to "Congress' apparent acceptance of this construction of the [early] diversity jurisdictional provisions" and its subsequent reenactment of diversity jurisdiction without substantive change.[100] This statutory conclusion has modern-day appeal. State courts are more closely associated with state and local governmental units dedicated to monitoring compliance with domestic relations decrees, and federal judges understandably lack enthusiasm for burdensome, fact-bound, and often protracted domestic relations disputes.[101]

---

[95] 28 U.S.C. § 1359.

[96] *Princess Lida v. Thompson*, 305 U.S. 456, 466 (1939).

[97] *Marshall v. Marshall*, 547 U.S. 293 (2006).

[98] *In re Burrus*, 136 U.S. 586, 593–94 (1890) (dictum). In a full account of the history of the "domestic relations" exception, Judge Friendly has also traced it and the exception for probate actions to the belief that such cases were not "suits of a civil nature in law and equity" within the language of the first diversity jurisdiction statute because they were historically within the jurisdiction of ecclesiastical courts. *See Phillips, Nizer, Benjamin, Krim & Ballon v. Rosenstiel*, 490 F.2d 509, 513 (2d Cir. 1973).

[99] 504 U.S. 689 (1992).

[100] 504 U.S. at 700.

[101] 504 U.S. at 703 (noting sound policy considerations supporting the exception); *Rosenstiel*, 490 F.2d at 516 n.8 (Friendly, J.) (candidly opining that taking jurisdiction would be a "waste" of scarce federal judicial resources).

On the other hand, the *Ankenbrandt* Court stressed the relatively narrow scope of the domestic relations exception. It divests the federal courts of the power to issue divorce, alimony, and child custody decrees. It does not encompass other intra-family legal claims, including ordinary tort or contract claims.[102]

Finally, the courts are barred by statute from asserting jurisdiction when a party contrives to create diversity. Assignments of claims between non-diverse parties to diverse parties for purposes of manufacturing diversity were outlawed in the very first Judiciary Act, but poor drafting invited evasion.[103] Today the statute prohibits this by denying jurisdiction when a party "by assignment or otherwise, has been improperly or collusively made or joined to invoke the jurisdiction of such court."[104] Appointment of out-of-state administrators to represent infants, incompetents, or the estates of decedents was also a popular device to create diversity. Since 1988, the diversity statute defeats this device by deeming the citizenship of a legal representative to be that of the infant, incompetent, or decedent.[105]

§ 5.05   CITIZENSHIP

In deciding diversity jurisdiction, the courts look to the citizenship of the parties at the time of filing of the complaint. As the Supreme Court has said,

> This time-of-filing rule is hornbook law (quite literally) taught to first-year law students in any basic course on federal civil procedure. It measures all challenges to subject-matter jurisdiction premised upon diversity of citizenship against the state of facts that existed at the time of filing — whether the challenge be brought shortly after filing, after the trial, or even for the first time on appeal.[106]

This measuring point provides precision because the clerk time-stamps and dockets the complaint on filing, and stability, because the existence of diversity jurisdiction is unaffected by the vicissitudes of the subsequent litigation. Post-commencement changes in citizenship of the parties can neither create jurisdiction where none existed at commencement, nor divest the court of jurisdiction that was proper at commencement. However, realignment of the parties during the litigation[107] may show that diversity was or was not present at commencement of the suit. In addition, the Court has long recognized an exception to the time-of-filing rule by which incomplete diversity at filing can be

---

[102] *See, e.g., Ankenbrandt*, 504 U.S. at 704 (finding that diversity jurisdiction exists over physical and sexual abuse claims by children against a parent).

[103] *See generally* WRIGHT § 31.

[104] 28 U.S.C. § 1359. The statutory bar on collusive or improperly made diversity jurisdiction literally only applies to devices to "invoke" jurisdiction. The courts, however, are increasingly refusing to give effect to comparable devices to *defeat* diversity jurisdiction, typically arising in response to attempted removals of actions from state to federal court. WRIGHT § 31.

[105] 28 U.S.C. § 1332(c)(2).

[106] *Grupo Dataflux v. Atlas Global Group, L.P.*, 541 U.S. 567, 570–71 (2004).

[107] *See* § 5.04[2] (diversity between whom), *supra*.

cured by dropping the non-diverse parties during the litigation pursuant to Rule 21,[108] if they are dispensable.[109]

Citizenship for diversity purposes requires a party to be a citizen of both the United States and of a state. United States citizenship ordinarily poses no analytic difficulties, since it is usually conferred by birth to citizen parents or birth on United States soil, but state citizenship can be more problematic. The courts have equated the state citizenship of natural persons with *domicile* in a state. Domicile itself, however, is a legal fiction imposed on persons in order to simplify legal determinations, unlike *residence*, which has a practical meaning outside the law. "The very meaning of domicile is the technically pre-eminent headquarters that every person is compelled to have in order that certain rights and duties that have been attached to it by the law may be determined."[110]

Domicile is created by the concurrent establishment of physical residence in a state and an intent to remain there indefinitely[111] — that is, we look to residence and intent at the same point in time. Although a person can have more than one residence at one time, he can by definition only form the requisite intent with respect to a single state at one time, and therefore can have only one domicile at a time.[112] Neither residence nor intent alone will suffice to establish domicile; both must be established concurrently. Accordingly, once established, domicile continues until a person has concurrently changed both her state of residence and her intent to remain. A mere change of residence without a concurrent formation of an intent to remain indefinitely in the state of new residence, or the mere formation of an intent to go elsewhere unaccompanied by a change in residence, will not alter a previously established domicile. Indeed, although the burden of pleading and proving citizenship is on the party invoking diversity jurisdiction, she enjoys a presumption in favor of her last-established domicile which must be rebutted by the party alleging a change in domicile.[113]

Because the requisite intent is a state of mind, it can only be shown circumstantially. Sundry affiliating circumstances may be offered in evidence of that intent: place of employment, voter or vehicle registration, driver's license, current residence, presence of other property or intangible interests, bank accounts, club memberships, mailing address, etc.[114] The courts once shortcut

---

[108] *Grupo Dataflux*, 541 U.S. at 572–73. Defective allegations of jurisdiction can also be amended during the litigation, provided that jurisdiction in fact existed at commencement. *See* 28 U.S.C. § 1653.

[109] *See* Rule 19, discussed at § 9.05[2], *infra*.

[110] *Williamson v. Osenton*, 232 U.S. 619, 625 (1914) (Holmes, J.).

[111] The requisite intent has also been characterized as the intent to return to the residence when one is absent, WRIGHT § 26, and the absence of any present intention to live elsewhere. *Williamson*, 232 U.S. at 623.

[112] 232 U.S. at 623. Thus, it is not usually sufficient for a plaintiff to allege mere residence of the parties in order to allege citizenship for diversity purposes. *See, e.g., Rosenquist v. Gustafson*, 803 F. Supp. 1325 (N.D. Ill. 1992). *See* Form 7.

[113] *Bank One, Texas, N.A. v. Montle*, 964 F.2d 48, 50 (1st Cir. 1992); *Janzen v. Goos*, 302 F.2d 421 (8th Cir. 1962).

[114] *See, e.g., Tanzymore v. Bethlehem Steel Corp.*, 457 F.2d 1320 (3d Cir. 1972) (affirming

such proof in some instances, however, by adopting the "now vanishing fiction of identity of person,"[115] by which the domicile of the husband was attributed to the wife and domicile of parent attributed to child. Modern courts have been increasingly willing to discard this fiction when appropriate and to determine the domicile of each of the parties on his or her individual facts.

This trend and many of the foregoing principles are well-illustrated by *Mas v. Perry*.[116] Mr. and Mrs. Mas, graduate students studying at Louisiana State University, sued their landlord, a Louisiana citizen, in federal court for damages resulting from his spying on their bedroom through a two-way mirror. The landlord challenged diversity jurisdiction. The challenge was clearly unsound as to Mr. Mas; he was a French national whose suit fell within alienage jurisdiction as it then existed.[117] By the fiction of identity of person, however, diversity was arguably lacking as to Mrs. Mas, as she would be assigned the French domicile of her husband but, as a United States citizen, would not qualify for alienage jurisdiction.

Instead, the court discarded the fiction and traced her last established domicile to Mississippi, where she had lived with her parents before her marriage. Neither her establishment of a Louisiana residence as a student, nor her candid admission that she did not intend to return to Mississippi, changed her Mississippi domicile because she had not yet formed an intent to remain indefinitely in Louisiana or any other state. Moreover, the Mas' change of residence to Illinois *after* commencement of the action was immaterial to jurisdiction. Not only had they formed no intent to remain indefinitely in Illinois, but Mrs. Mas' domicile at commencement of the action remained Mississippi. Thus, there was diversity at commencement of the action, and the landlord's challenge failed.

Two legal fictions, domicile and the corporate entity, complicate the process of determining citizenship for corporations. But the amendment of the diversity statute to deem a corporation to be the citizen of "any State by which it has been incorporated *and* of the state where it has its principal place of business"[118] has simplified matters greatly. Because corporations often have dual citizenship under the statute, the party invoking diversity must plead not only its citizenship by incorporation, but also its citizenship by principal place of business.[119]

---

dismissal for lack of diversity, when deposition of plaintiff showed none of these affiliating circumstances); *Simmons v. Skyway of Ocala*, 592 F. Supp. 356, 360 (S.D. Ga. 1984) ("grab-bag of indicia having to do with everyday life" established Florida domicile).

[115] *Williamson*, 232 U.S. at 625.

[116] 489 F.2d 1396 (5th Cir. 1974).

[117] 28 U.S.C. § 1332(a)(2). However, a permanent resident alien is now deemed a citizen of the state where she is domiciled. 28 U.S.C. § 1332(a).

[118] 28 U.S.C. § 1332(c)(1) (emphasis added). Some unnecessary ambiguity may have been perpetuated by the amendment's use of "any state" instead of "every state," but most courts and commentators are agreed that the latter is the intended meaning of the amendment. *See* WRIGHT § 27.

[119] *Canton v. Angelina Casualty Co.*, 279 F.2d 553 (5th Cir. 1960). *See* Form 7 (plaintiff is [a

Incorporation is a definite and ascertainable legal act, but determining the "principal place of business" can become difficult when a corporation conducts business in multiple states. The statute contemplates a single principal place of business; how should a pleader and the court choose among them? The test courts have used most looks to the locus of the bulk of the corporation's activities, measured by corporate assets, sales or other physical measures.[120] Alternatively, instead of this place-of-operations, bulk-of-the-assets, or "muscle" test, many courts apply the home office — or "nerve center" — test, looking to the locus of the corporation's operating headquarters.[121]

Lurie Co. v. Loew's San Francisco Hotel Corp.[122] illustrates the application and offers one possible reconciliation of the two tests. The corporation's officers and chief legal and financial advisers were located in New York, which was thus its nerve center where overall policy was formulated. The corporation's only asset, however, was located in California, the locus also of 95% of its employees, 93% of its operating expenses and all of its revenue. The court concluded that "these factors clearly establish California as the 'place of operations' or place of 'day-to-day activities,' " and therefore the principal place of business, reasoning that the nerve center test was only applicable when no single state could be identified as the locus of such activities because of the far-flung nature of a corporation's business.[123] Some courts, instead of prioritizing the tests in this fashion, have simply concluded that "the ultimate question is not which test to apply, but rather what consideration, on the basis of the totality of the facts, predominates."[124]

Finally, the federal courts have traditionally held that unincorporated associations, such as partnerships and labor unions, take the citizenship of each of their members.[125] This rule reflects the historical assumption that such organizations are not juridical persons and therefore must be disregarded for citizenship purposes. In 1990, the Court reaffirmed this view and distinguished an apparently contrary decision as going to the question whether parties who were natural persons were real parties to the controversy, not whether an artificial entity is a citizen.[126] However, the rule has not been applied to class

---

citizen of State A] and "defendant is [a corporation incorporated under the laws of State [B with its principal place of business in State B].").

[120] *See, e.g., Anniston Soil Pipe Co. v. Central Foundry Co.,* 329 F.2d 313 (5th Cir. 1964) (locus of plant and production facilities rather than of executive offices); *Kelly v. United States Steel Corp.,* 284 F.2d 850 (3d Cir. 1960) (locus of largest number of executive officers and corporate operating committee, as well as of largest percentage of employees and assets); *United States Fid. & Guar. Co. v. DiMassa,* 561 F. Supp. 348 (E.D. Pa. 1983) (locus of corporate operations as well as main computer).

[121] *See, e.g., Scot Typewriter Co. v. Underwood Corp.,* 170 F. Supp. 862 (S.D.N.Y. 1959).

[122] 315 F. Supp. 405 (N.D. Cal. 1970).

[123] 315 F. Supp. at 416.

[124] *J.A. Olson Co. v. City of Winona, Miss.,* 818 F.2d 401 (5th Cir. 1987) (calling this the "total activity test").

[125] *See, e.g., Carden v. Arkoma Assocs.,* 494 U.S. 185 (1990); *United Steelworkers v. R.H. Bouligny, Inc.,* 382 U.S. 145, 150–51 (1965).

[126] *Carden,* 494 U.S. 185 (distinguishing *Navarro Sav. Ass'n v. Lee,* 446 U.S. 458 (1980)).

actions; diversity is determined by the citizenship of the representative parties, without regard to the absent class members.[127]

§ 5.06   AMOUNT IN CONTROVERSY

[1]   The "Legal Certainty Test" and the Single Claim

Since the First Judiciary Act, Congress has imposed a monetary limitation on diversity jurisdiction.[128] The present amount in controversy is $75,000, exclusive of interest and costs.[129] The purpose of the limitation has always been to ration federal judicial resources by screening out penny-ante cases. The device has never really proven effective to this end, however, since litigants have often been able to adjust their pleadings as necessary to invoke jurisdiction. Moreover, the amount in controversy requirement has probably itself wasted federal judicial resources in uselessly complex disputes about the jurisdictional amount. Arguably, then, little would be lost in terms of caseload control, and much gained in saved time and energy, were the jurisdictional amount in diversity cases eliminated.

Like citizenship, jurisdictional amount must be pled and (if challenged) proven by the plaintiff, and is determined as of the time of commencement of the action.[130] The Supreme Court stated the proper test for amount in controversy in the leading case of *St. Paul Mercury Indemnity Co. v. Red Cab Co.*:[131]

> [T]he sum claimed by the plaintiff controls if the claim is apparently made in good faith. It must appear to a legal certainty that the claim is really for less than the jurisdictional amount to justify dismissal. The inability of plaintiff to recover an amount adequate to give the court jurisdiction does not show his bad faith or oust the jurisdiction. Nor

---

[127] *Supreme Tribe of Ben-Hur v. Cauble*, 255 U.S. 356 (1921). Unincorporated associations or other entities that may be unable to satisfy diversity requirements due to the citizenship of their members may therefore be able to avoid diversity problems by suing through representative members in class actions. *See* Rule 23.2 (permitting such suits if representative parties will fairly and adequately protect the interests of the association and its members). *See generally* § 9.09 (class actions), *infra*.

[128] Until 1980, Congress also imposed a monetary limitation on general federal question jurisdiction. However, dissatisfaction with its application to constitutional claims of incalculable monetary value and resulting relaxed applications of the requirement in many federal question cases led to the abandonment of the requirement. Act of Dec. 1, 1980, Pub. L. No. 96-486, 94 Stat. 2369. Nevertheless, many of the old federal question cases are still relevant authority for ascertaining amount in controversy in diversity cases.

[129] 28 U.S.C. § 1332(a).

[130] It is the direct effect of the immediate lawsuit that is relevant for ascertaining the jurisdictional amount, not its collateral effects or importance to strangers or society at large. *See, e.g., Healy v. Ratta*, 292 U.S. 263, 267 (1934) (collateral effect via *stare decisis* may not be considered). *See generally* MOORE § 102.106.

[131] 303 U.S. 283 (1938).

does the fact that the complaint discloses the existence of a valid defense to the claim.[132]

Jurisdictional amount is thus ordinarily computed from the plaintiff's viewpoint without regard to possible defenses, and plaintiff's good faith pleading controls unless the court concludes to "a legal certainty" that he cannot recover the pleaded amount.

When plaintiff seeks only liquidated — arithmetically ascertainable — damages, the amount is easily determined. Suits seeking unliquidated damages, equitable relief, or inherently unquantifiable relief have proven more difficult.

In suits seeking unliquidated damages, *legal certainty in law*[133] is established by the legal unavailability of relief necessary to reach the jurisdictional amount. For example, if the applicable law requires aggravating circumstances before punitive damages can be recovered in a contract action, and the plaintiff has not and cannot in good faith allege such circumstances, his prayer for punitive damages must be disregarded as a matter of law.[134] Similarly, the applicable law may place a statutory ceiling on the recovery[135] or may limit special damages to interest on property in a suit to recover personal property.[136] As the Supreme Court put it as early as 1798,[137] "where the law gives the rule, the legal cause of action, and not the Plaintiff's demand, must be regarded."

Legal certainty in fact is much more difficult to find, because it requires a court to appraise the evidentiary basis for plaintiff's claim. The court must chart a course

> between a rule on the one hand that allows some cases involving inflated claims for relief to be brought in a federal forum in order to insure access to that forum for all those cases that properly may be brought there, and, on the other hand, a rule that closes the doors to the federal forum in the face of some claims that properly could be brought there in order to insure the denial of the forum to cases involving inflated claims.[138]

The cases divide between the two approaches.

Some courts give presumptive effect to plaintiff's claim of amount in controversy, no matter how unlikely it is that she will prevail on the facts at

---

[132] 303 U.S. at 288–89 (footnotes omitted). However, if plaintiff fails at the end to recover the jurisdictional amount, the court has the discretion to reverse the usual award of costs. 28 U.S.C. § 1332(b).

[133] *Kahal v. J.W. Wilson Assocs. Inc.*, 673 F.2d 547, 548 (D.C. Cir. 1982) (distinguishing between legal certainty in law and in fact).

[134] *Kahal*, 673 F.2d at 549 (dismissing contract claim in which compensatory damages were below the jurisdictional amount).

[135] *See, e.g., Ringsby Truck Lines, Inc. v. Beardsley*, 331 F.2d 14 (8th Cir. 1964).

[136] *See Vance v. W.A. Vandercook Co.*, 170 U.S. 468 (1898).

[137] *Wilson v. Daniel*, 3 U.S. (Dall.) 401, 408 (1798).

[138] *Deutsch v. Hewes St. Realty Corp.*, 359 F.2d 96, 100 (2d Cir. 1966).

trial.[139] These courts reason that any other approach would run the risk of depriving the plaintiff of her right to a jury trial by converting the jurisdictional inquiry into a mini-trial of the merits.

Other courts test plaintiff's claim of amount in controversy for reasonableness in light of the evidence adduced in an evidentiary hearing on the motion to dismiss for lack of jurisdiction.[140] These courts assert that the focus on plaintiff's right to a jury trial begs the question whether she *has* a right to come into the federal court room to try her claim. Since judges may, through their power to set aside excessive verdicts,[141] place upper limits on jury awards, they should not be timid in relating that upper limit to the jurisdictional floor for purposes of deciding diversity jurisdiction.[142]

Actions for equitable relief pose special problems. In *Mississippi & Mo. R.R Co. v. Ward*,[143] a suit by a steamboat owner to abate the nuisance posed by a bridge over the Mississippi River, the Supreme Court declared that "removal of the obstruction is the matter of controversy, and the value of the object must govern." This rule focuses on the value of the object of the equitable relief, but value to whom? The value to plaintiff of having the obstruction removed will rarely be the same as the cost to defendant of having to remove it. A majority of courts have looked at the cost to the plaintiff if relief is not afforded,[144] while a minority have considered the greater of "the pecuniary result[s] to *either* party which the judgment would directly produce."[145] The minority rule seems preferable because otherwise a suit in which plaintiff seeks an injunction to remove a 50-story office building encroaching on a few inches of his land would fall outside the diversity jurisdiction of the federal courts despite the enormous expense to the defendant. Since "[t]he purpose of an amount in controversy requirement is to ensure the substantiality of the suit itself, not solely the amount which the plaintiff stands to recover," a federal court should look to the

---

[139] *See, e.g.*, Deutsch v. Hewes St. Realty Corp., 359 F.2d 96, 100 (2d Cir. 1966).

[140] *See, e.g.*, Nelson v. Keefer, 451 F.2d 289, 293 (3d Cir. 1971).

[141] *See* § 12.09[2][b] (new trials), *infra*.

[142] *Nelson*, 451 F.2d 289. *See also Jimenez Puig v. Avis Rent-A-Car Sys.*, 574 F.2d 37 (1st Cir. 1978) ("brief embarrassment" of having defendant's agent erroneously seize and destroy plaintiff's credit card for non-payment will not factually support punitive damages claim necessary to satisfy jurisdictional amount); *Sierra v. Lidchi*, 651 F. Supp. 1019 (D.P.R. 1986) (counterclaim for defamation based on hearsay allegation that plaintiff called defendant a thief will not support jurisdictional amount).

[143] 67 U.S. 485, 492 (1863).

[144] *See, e.g.*, City of Milwaukee v. Saxbe, 546 F.2d 693, 702 (7th Cir. 1976); *cf. Glenwood Light & Water Co. v. Mutual Light, Heat & Power Co.*, 239 U.S. 121, 125 (1915) (measuring amount by harm to plaintiff's business rather than by defendant's cost of removal, without, however, expressly endorsing "plaintiff viewpoint" as the only test). The "plaintiff viewpoint" rule does not avail a defendant who seeks removal of a case brought in state court when the plaintiff's injury is below the jurisdictional amount. A few courts have therefore suggested that jurisdictional amount be measured from the viewpoint of the party who invokes federal jurisdiction. *See* Moore § 102.109[5].

[145] *Ronzio v. Denver & R.G.W.R. Co.*, 116 F.2d 604, 606 (10th Cir. 1940) (emphasis supplied). *See also McCarty v. Amoco Pipeline Co.*, 595 F.2d 389 (7th Cir. 1979) (discussing four tests for amounts in controversy in equitable actions); Moore § 0.91[1].

largest effect on either party and take jurisdiction of such a suit, according to the minority view.[146]

Finally, the courts have found some claims involving inherently unquantifiable relief to fall outside monetarily limited jurisdiction grants. An early Supreme Court decision suggested that amount in controversy could be satisfied only "where the rights of property are concerned, and where the matter in dispute has a known and certain value, which can be proved and calculated, in the ordinary mode of a business transaction."[147] While the Court has since rejected any distinction between personal and property rights for jurisdictional purposes,[148] some courts still insist on susceptibility of the claim to ready pecuniary appraisal. In a suit by the Senate Watergate Committee to compel President Nixon to give up the Watergate tapes, for example, the court refused to place any monetary value on the interference with the Committee's constitutional obligations and therefore denied jurisdiction.[149] Courts have reached the same result in suits to compel inspection of a corporation's books and records, to prohibit divulging of telephone intercepts, to adjudicate lunacy, and to declare marital status.[150]

[2]   Aggregating Multiple Claims

The discussion of amount in controversy to this point has assumed that plaintiff asserts a single claim against a single defendant. But liberal modern joinder rules encourage multiple claims, posing the question whether the amounts in controversy on such claims can be aggregated to satisfy the jurisdictional amount.[151] Unfortunately, the judge-made aggregation rules do not track the joinder rules and do not follow transactional or any other apparent logic. Consequently, "it is not altogether easy to say what the law is in this area, and it is quite hard to say why it is as it seems to be."[152] Consider three joinder situations: the plaintiff joins multiple claims against a single defendant; multiple parties, whether plaintiffs or defendants or both, are joined on one or more claims; defendant counterclaims against plaintiff.

It is well-established that a plaintiff may aggregate all the claims he asserts against a single defendant, whether or not they are transactionally related and whether or not any of them alone satisfies the jurisdictional amount.[153] Thus,

---

[146] *See* MOORE § 102.109[4].

[147] *Barry v. Mercein*, 46 U.S. (5 How.) 103, 120 (1847).

[148] *Lynch v. Household Fin. Corp.*, 405 U.S. 538 (1972).

[149] *Senate Select Comm. on Presidential Campaign Activities v. Nixon*, 366 F. Supp. 51, 59 (D.D.C. 1973). The amount in controversy requirement has since been abolished in general federal question cases. *See* note 128, *supra*.

[150] See cases cited in J. MOORE, MOORE'S FEDERAL PRACTICE ¶ 0.92[5] (2d. ed.).

[151] *See generally* WRIGHT § 36; Note, *The Federal Jurisdictional Amount and Rule 20 Joinder of Parties: Aggregation of Claims*, 53 MINN. L. REV. 94 (1968).

[152] WRIGHT § 36, at 209. *But see* Jeffrey L. Rosenberger, *The Amount in Controversy: Understanding the Rules of Aggregation*, 26 ARIZ. ST. L.J. 925 (1994) (asserting that aggregation rules are more firmly rooted in policy than commentators have supposed).

[153] *MOORE* § 102.108[1].

in this joinder situation, aggregation is co-extensive with joinder under Rule 18.[154]

The rule is different, however, when plaintiff joins several defendants to the same claim or several plaintiffs join in the same claim against one or more defendants pursuant to Rule 20.[155] Aggregation is possible if several parties have a common undivided interest or title, but not if they have separate and independent interests.[156] For example, when multiple plaintiffs sue on the basis of common title, or multiple defendants assert common title as a defense to a suit to recover land, the matter in controversy is the entire tract of land, not just its several parts. Aggregation is therefore permitted.[157] On the other hand, the necessary common and undivided interest is not established merely because claims derive from a single instrument or because multiple parties share a community of interest.[158] Nor will the fact that defendants are joint tortfeasors justify aggregation; plaintiff's claim against each tortfeasor is ordinarily separate and distinct and must therefore stand alone for purposes of satisfying the jurisdictional amount.[159] The aggregation rules are thus more restrictive than Rule 20, governing joinder of parties, and are essentially artifacts of a bygone era before the liberalization of joinder in federal courts.

Finally, the logic of computing the amount in controversy from plaintiff's complaint alone and the separate and distinct nature of original claims and counterclaims suggest that their aggregation should not be permitted.[160] But

---

[154] *See* § 9.02 (claim joinder), *infra*.

[155] *See* § 9.05[1] (permissive party joinder), *infra*.

[156] WRIGHT §§ 36, 102.108[2]–[3]. The circuit courts are divided about whether punitive damages among plaintiff class members can be aggregated on the theory that they share a common and undivided interest in punishing the defendant and deterring the offending conduct. *See* Christopher J. Willis, *Aggregation of Punitive Damages in Diversity Class Actions: Will the Real Amount in Controversy Please Stand Up*, 30 LOY. L.A. L. REV. 775 (1997). The answer is important in consumer class actions where the class members' individualized compensatory damages fall below $75,000 and there is no federal question jurisdiction.

[157] *Cornell v. Mabe*, 206 F.2d 514, 516 (5th Cir. 1953).

[158] WRIGHT § 36.

[159] These rules applied to class actions as well and therefore required that each class member satisfy the jurisdictional amount when their claims are separate and distinct. *Zahn v. International Paper Co.*, 414 U.S. 291 (1973); *Snyder v. Harris*, 394 U.S. 332 (1969). However, the Supreme Court has now ruled that if a representative class member satisfies the amount in controversy, the court can exercise "supplemental jurisdiction" under 28 U.S.C. § 1367 over the below-amount claims of other class members. *See* § 5.11, *infra* (discussing impact of supplemental jurisdiction on the no-aggregation rule). In addition, in the Class Action Fairness Act of 2005, codified at 28 U.S.C. § 1332(d), Congress provided that an aggregate total of claims exceeding $5,000,000 would suffice for federal jurisdiction in certain class actions in which any member of the class is diverse from any defendant, thus superseding the usual requirement for such actions that all members, and even the requirement for supplemental jurisdiction that at least one class member assert a claim exceeding $75,000.

[160] On the other hand, a no-aggregation rule interacts with the removal provisions to permit a party with a small claim to force his adversary to litigate his much larger counterclaim in state court, provided that the former wins the race to the courthouse. WRIGHT § 37. It also risks a wasteful minuet whereby a plaintiff's complaint is dismissed despite a compulsory counterclaim that satisfies the jurisdictional amount, and then is reinstated as a compulsory counterclaim, now within the

in *Horton v. Liberty Mutual Insurance Co.*,[161] the Court held 5-4 that the then-$10,000 jurisdictional amount was satisfied when the plaintiff insurer alleged that defendant would counterclaim for $14,035, even though the insurer actually sued to set aside a workmen's compensation award of only $1050. Under Texas law, however, the insurer's suit reopened the entire compensation claim below regardless of the award and might therefore be viewed as an action for a judgment declaring the insurer's non-liability as to the entire $14,035 workmen's compensation claim. Most federal decisions have read the case as involving a quirk of Texas law and confined it to its facts.[162] But until the Supreme Court distinguishes or overrules *Horton* it leaves uncertain the question whether (and when) claims and counterclaims can be aggregated to satisfy the amount in controversy.

PART C.
Removal and Supplemental Jurisdiction

§ 5.07 REMOVAL JURISDICTION

[1] In General

Removal jurisdiction is an exception to the usual rule that plaintiff chooses the court.[163] Although the Constitution makes no express provision for removal, it is now well-established that a defendant may, pursuant to statute,[164] remove a civil action from a state court. The state court has to have neither subject matter jurisdiction[165] nor personal jurisdiction[166] in order for defendant to remove the case to federal court, although she is free to challenge personal jurisdiction when she gets there. The purpose of removal is to make the option of suit in federal court as available to defendants (except for resident defendants in a diversity-only case) as it is to plaintiffs.[167] This

---

court's supplemental jurisdiction, to the defendant's now independently standing claim. 1 J. MOORE, MOORE'S FEDERAL PRACTICE ¶ 0.98[1] (2d ed.). This minuet, however, does serve to give the original defendant the choice whether to stay in the federal forum, which he would be denied by a rule of aggregation. 1 J. MOORE, MOORE'S FEDERAL PRACTICE ¶ 0.98[1] (2d ed.).

[161] 367 U.S. 348 (1961).

[162] *See* WRIGHT § 37.

[163] *See* Chapter 2, *supra.*

[164] The general removal statute is 28 U.S.C. § 1441, which is discussed in this section. Congress has also provided for removal of specific civil actions not discussed here. *See, e.g.*, 28 U.S.C. § 1442 (suits against federal officers); 28 U.S.C. § 1442a (suits against members of the armed forces); 28 U.S.C. § 1443 (suits in which civil rights are denied); 28 U.S.C. § 2679(d) (suits against federal employees arising out of motor vehicle accidents within the scope of employment). In addition, Congress has guaranteed plaintiffs their choice of forum by prohibiting removal in certain cases. *See, e.g.*, 28 U.S.C. § 1445(a) (Federal Employers' Liability Act suits); 28 U.S.C. § 1445(c) (workmen's compensation suits); 46 U.S.C. § 30104 (Jones Act suits).

[165] 28 U.S.C. § 1441(e).

[166] *See Lambert Run Coal Co. v. Baltimore & Ohio R.R. Co.*, 258 U.S. 377 (1922).

[167] *See* Neal Miller, *An Empirical Study of Forum Choices in Removal Cases Under Diversity*

purpose has been given effect in several ways by the provisions of the general removal statute and by the judicial gloss upon them.

First, because removal is a protective option for defendants, only defendants may invoke it.[168] The courts have read this limitation strictly, prohibiting a plaintiff who is sued upon a federal counterclaim from removing on that account.[169] Moreover, they have added the gloss that all defendants must join in the notice of removal save in cases of removal of "separate and independent" claims under 28 U.S.C. § 1441(c), in which case all defendants to such a claim must join in the notice.[170]

Second, because removal is intended just to make existing federal jurisdiction available to defendants, only civil actions "of which the district courts . . . have original jurisdiction . . . may be removed."[171] Removal jurisdiction is therefore keyed to original jurisdiction, and all the rules and principles previously discussed concerning federal question and diversity jurisdiction apply. That is, the court decides on the facts as they existed at the time the notice of removal was filed whether the action would have satisfied the requirements for federal jurisdiction had it originally been filed in federal court.[172] A court, however, may consider post-removal evidence of what those facts were at the time of filing.[173] Furthermore, the plaintiff may cure problems in a case nonremovable when filed by amending to increase the amount in controversy or to add a removable claim or by dismissing a non-diverse defendant, because removal jurisdiction is measured at the filing of the notice of removal, not the complaint.[174]

---

and Federal Question Jurisdiction, 41 AM. U. L. REV. 369 (1992) (finding that fear of local bias against out-of-state litigants is a significant factor in removal).

[168] 28 U.S.C. § 1441(a) (civil actions "may be removed by the defendant or the defendants").

[169] *See Shamrock Oil & Gas Corp. v. Sheets*, 313 U.S. 100 (1941). Realignment of the parties may affect designation of the "defendant." *See* § 5.04[2] (diversity between whom), *supra*.

[170] *See, e.g., Chicago, R.I. & Pac. Ry. Co. v. Martin*, 178 U.S. 245 (1900); WRIGHT § 40.

[171] 28 U.S.C. § 1441(a).

[172] Ordinarily, therefore, the court does not have jurisdiction if it is only *after* removal that facts necessary to establish jurisdiction come into existence (for example, that the parties become diverse). In *Caterpillar Inc. v. Lewis*, 519 U.S. 61 (1996), however, the Supreme Court held that when incomplete diversity at the filing of the notice of removal was cured by dismissal of the non-diverse party before final judgment, that judgment could stand. It explained that once a case has been tried, "considerations of finality, efficiency, and economy become overwhelming." *Caterpillar Inc.*, 519 U.S. at 75. Setting aside a judgment entered when there was complete diversity would waste the federal resources expended in reaching the judgment and possibly impose the costs of retrying the case on state courts.

Subsequently, the Court explained that *Caterpillar* made only a limited exception for perfection of jurisdiction by dismissal of the non-diverse party and therefore "did not augur a new approach to deciding whether a jurisdictional defect has been cured." *Grupo Dataflux v. Atlas Global Group, L.P.*, 541 U.S. 567, 572 (2004). The exception, it asserted, is authorized by Rule 21, permitting dismissal of the jurisdiction-destroying party by motion or by the court *sua sponte*. *Grupo Dataflux*, 541 U.S. at 572–73.

[173] *See e.g., Sierminski v. Transouth Fin. Corp.*, 216 F.3d 945 (11th Cir. 2000).

[174] MOORE § 107.14[2][h]. As noted above, the removing party may also move to drop a jurisdiction-defeating party under Rule 21 even after removal, under a limited exception to the usual time-of-filing-notice rule. *See* n.172, *supra*.

The interaction of the time-of-filing-notice rule with the well-pleaded complaint rule[175] creates an anomaly (some might say, perversity) of removal law: that a defendant who asserts a federal defense or counterclaim to a non-diverse plaintiff's state claim cannot remove (unless federal law has completely preempted state law in this area), inasmuch as a federal court would not have had original jurisdiction over the plaintiff's claim. The anomaly is that some important federal questions — those arising by way of defense — are stuck in state court, without rescue by removal.[176] On the other hand, the Court has repeatedly held that a plaintiff cannot defeat removal by artfully failing to plead potentially preemptive federal law.[177] "If the only remedy available to plaintiff is federal, because of preemption or otherwise, and the state court necessarily must look to federal law in passing on the claim, the case is removable regardless of what is in the pleading."[178]

Third, because the protective rationale for removal is inapplicable to a defendant sued upon state law claims in his own state court, diversity cases are removable "only if none of the parties in interest properly joined and served as defendants is a citizen of the State in which such action is brought."[179] Thus, a citizen of Virginia sued in a Virginia state court by a citizen of Maryland may not remove the case to federal court — he does not need protection from his own state's court. In this respect, removal jurisdiction is narrower than original jurisdiction.

The procedure for removal is clearly laid out by statute.[180] Within thirty days after receipt of the pleading or other paper affording grounds for removal,[181] defendant must file a notice of removal in the federal court for the district "embracing" the place where the state court action is pending,[182] setting forth a short and plain statement of the grounds for removal, together

---

[175] See § 5.03[2], *supra*.

[176] See, e.g., *Oklahoma Tax Comm'n v. Graham*, 489 U.S. 838 (1989) (holding the case not removable despite the federal defense of tribal immunity to state tax claims). The Supreme Court has acknowledged that a rational jurisdictional system might well discard the equation of original and removal jurisdiction in these circumstances, since "the defendant's petition for removal could furnish the necessary guarantee that the case necessarily presented a substantial question of federal law." *Franchise Tax Bd.*, 463 U.S. at 11 n.9. But the Supreme Court also has noted that removal is statutory and that reform must therefore come from the Congress. 463 U.S. at 10–11.

[177] See, e.g., *Avco Corp. v. Aero Lodge No. 735*, 390 U.S. 557 (1958); § 5.03[2], *supra*.

[178] WRIGHT & MILLER § 3722 (2d ed.). See generally Arthur R. Miller, *Artful Pleading: A Doctrine in Search of Definition*, 76 TEX. L. REV. 1781 (1998); Robert A. Ragazzo, *Reconsidering the Artful Pleading Doctrine*, 44 HASTINGS L.J. 273 (1993). The courts, however, have increasingly distinguished "ordinary preemption" cases, which often fall outside federal question jurisdiction when plaintiff chooses to frame his claim purely in terms of state law, from "complete preemption" cases, in which the federal law is so controlling that it necessarily substitutes a federally created cause of action for the state claim, however the latter is framed. *WRIGHT & MILLER* § 3722.1.

[179] 28 U.S.C. § 1441(b).

[180] 28 U.S.C. §§ 1446–50.

[181] 28 U.S.C. § 1446(b). In addition, actions removed on grounds of diversity must be removed no more than one year after they were commenced in state court.

[182] 28 U.S.C. § 1441(a). This provision thus provides venue for the removed action, superseding the other federal venue statutes. *Polizzi v. Cowles Magazines, Inc.*, 345 U.S. 663, 665–66 (1953).

with all filings from the state court action. Filing of a copy of the notice with the state court perfects removal and ousts that court of all further jurisdiction; no permission of either court is required. The federal court thereafter proceeds under the Federal Rules of Civil Procedure[183] as if the case had been filed with it originally, without regard to the usual venue requirements.[184] Plaintiff may oppose the removal by a motion to remand, or the court will decide its jurisdiction *sua sponte*. If there is any doubt of removability, the court should *remand* — send the case back to state court — in accord with the rule of strict construction of jurisdictional statutes.[185] A decision to remand the case is unreviewable, except for remands in civil rights cases removed under a special statute.[186] Denial of a motion to remand is, of course, reviewable on appeal of the final judgment by the federal court.

Finally, removal is one-way, from state to federal court. While an improperly removed case can be sent back to state court by remand, there is no procedure for moving a case originally filed in federal court to state court. If for any reason, the federal court lacks jurisdiction, it can only dismiss the case, not send it to state court. (Nor, as we will see in Chapter 6, can it transfer the case to state court. *Transfer* is a term of art for changing the *venue* within a court system — for moving a case from a court within a state to another court within the same state, or from one federal district court to another federal district court, for reasons of convenience. There is no transfer *between* states, between the state and federal courts, or between U.S. and foreign courts.)

Congress, of course, can change the foregoing restrictions on removal and did in the Class Action Fairness Act of 2005.[187] In response to alleged abuses of class action rules in state courts, Congress made removal of such actions to federal court easier by abolishing the restriction against removal by in-state defendants, the requirement that all defendants join in the notice of removal, the one-year time limit on removal, and the bar on appellate review of decisions to remand. Instead, it carved out some exceptions for local and for certain other controversies, and gave the court discretion to refuse removal in certain other circumstances.[188]

---

[183] *See* Rule 81(c).

[184] *See* WRIGHT & MILLER § 3726.

[185] *See* WRIGHT § 41.

[186] 28 U.S.C. § 1447(d) (exempting remand of civil rights cases removed under 28 U.S.C. § 1443 from the bar on appeal). A remand for other reasons may be reviewed for abuse of discretion. *Thermtron Prods., Inc. v. Hermansdorfer*, 423 U.S. 336 (1976). Commentators have criticized the statutory bar on appeal as anachronistic and destructive of federal rights. *See* Rhonda Wasserman, *Rethinking Review of Remands: Proposed Amendments to the Federal Statute*, 43 EMORY L.J. 83 (1994).

[187] Codified at 28 U.S.C. § 1332(d).

[188] *See generally* WILLIAM B. RUBENSTEIN, UNDERSTANDING THE CLASS ACTION FAIRNESS ACT OF 2005, *available at* http://www.classactionprofessor.com/cafa-analysis.pdf. For further discussion of the impact of the Act on class action litigation, see § 9.09, *infra*.

[2]   Removal of Separate and Independent Claims

Suppose that P, a citizen of Virginia, joins a state law claim to a federal question claim against D, also a citizen of Virginia. Should we allow D only to remove the latter to federal court? Although this partial removal would put each claim in its "own" court system, the result is problematic. If partial removal is not allowed, plaintiffs will have an incentive to join non-removable claims to removable claims in state court in order to defeat removal of the case. On the other hand, if partial removal is allowed, it could promote inefficiently duplicative litigation. Congress originally responded by authorizing removal of "the entire case" containing one or more "separate and independent claim[s] or cause[s] of action which would be removable if sued upon alone," vesting discretion in the federal judge to retain the entire case or to remand the independently non-removable claims. "Separate and independent" was originally given a restrictive interpretation by the Supreme Court in a diversity case,[189] and the lower court case law is complex and often inconsistent. Today it can perhaps best be generalized as construing the requirement to mean "factually unrelated."[190]

In 1990, Congress restricted separate and independent claim removal to cases in which the independently removable claim poses a federal question. Congress authorized the federal court, in the judge's discretion, to retain the whole removed case or to remand "all matters in which State law predominates."[191] However, Congress may have largely mooted this branch of removal jurisdiction by enacting supplemental jurisdiction at the same time.[192] If the otherwise non-removable state law claim is part of the same constitutional case or controversy as the federal question claim (essentially, arising from the same transaction, as we discuss below), then the state law claim falls within the supplemental jurisdiction of the court[193] and can be removed pursuant to sections 1441(a) & (b) of the statute.

If the state law claim does not fall within the same constitutional case or controversy as the federal question claim (that is, it arises from a different transaction), then the removal of the state law claim to federal court may present a serious constitutional question: whether Article III permits jurisdiction absent diversity among the parties.[194] If this is true, it leaves only

---

[189] *American Fire & Cas. Co. v. Finn*, 341 U.S. 6 (1951) (claims arising from a "single wrong" are not separate and independent).

[190] *See* Moore §§ 107.14[6][d] (discussing cases which appear to apply this interpretation) & 107.14[6][f].

[191] 28 U.S.C. § 1441(c).

[192] David D. Siegel, 28 U.S.C.A. § 1441 commentary (1990).

[193] *See* § 5.11 *infra*.

[194] *See* Teply & Whitten, Chap. 2, § C(5); William Cohen, *Problems in the Removal of a Separate and Independent Claim or Cause of Action*, 46 Minn. L. Rev. 1, 20–25 (1961). *But see* Joan Steinman, *Supplemental Jurisdiction in § 1441 Removed Cases: An Unsurveyed Frontier of Congress' Handiwork*, 35 Ariz. L. Rev. 305 (1993). In *Twentieth Century-Fox Film Corp. v. Taylor*, 239 F. Supp. 913 (S.D.N.Y. 1965), the court suggested that the prior version of § 1441(c) gave it removal jurisdiction over the independent claims and was a valid exercise of Congress' authority

a small category of separate federal claims made unremovable by particular statutes, or separate state claims that satisfy minimal but not complete diversity requirements,[195] which a federal court could constitutionally hear by removal under § 1441(c). Presumably, most of the latter would then be remanded anyway because of the predominance of state law.[196] It may be hard, therefore, to escape the conclusion that "with the slim pickings the subdivision has in [federal question cases], it may have to grope for some gainful employment."[197]

§ 5.08   OVERVIEW OF SUPPLEMENTAL JURISDICTION AND ITS ANTECEDENTS

All cases that fall within the subject matter jurisdiction of the federal courts must begin with the allegation of at least one claim capable of invoking a statutory grant of federal subject matter jurisdiction. Many federal cases are made up entirely of these claims. But sometimes a federal court will use its statutory subject matter jurisdiction over one such predicate or "anchor" claim to justify its adjudication of one or more related claims that would not independently satisfy subject matter jurisdictional requirements. Such extended jurisdiction[198] historically evolved under the separate labels of *pendent* and *ancillary* jurisdiction, although the courts' terminology was often inconsistent.[199] In 1990, Congress codified much of the prior law of pendent and ancillary jurisdiction as *supplemental jurisdiction*.[200] After introducing the terminology in this section, in succeeding sections we explore pendent, ancillary and supplemental jurisdiction in greater detail.

As used here, *pendent jurisdiction* refers to the courts' extension of jurisdiction from a claim that independently falls within federal (usually federal question) jurisdiction — the anchor claim —[201] to an otherwise jurisdictionally

---

under the Necessary and Proper Clause. The Supreme Court has yet to rule on the question.

[195] *See* § 5.04[2], *supra. See* Edward Hartnett, *A New Trick from an Old and Abused Dog: Section 1441(c) Lives and Now Permits the Remand of Federal Question Cases*, 63 FORDHAM L. REV. 1099, 1150–54 (1995).

[196] Siegel, note 192, *supra.*

[197] Siegel, note 192, *supra.*

[198] *See, e.g.*, Richard D. Freer, *A Principled Statutory Approach to Supplemental Jurisdiction*, 1987 DUKE L.J. 34; Richard A. Matasar, *Rediscovering "One Constitutional Case": Procedural Rules and the Rejection of the Gibbs Test for Supplemental Jurisdiction*, 71 CAL. L. REV. 1399, 1402 n.3 (1983) ("supplemental jurisdiction . . . suggests an extension of power over claims normally outside federal jurisdiction in order to serve important federal interests that supplement the purposes underlying the decision of the original federal claims"); Note, *A Closer Look at Pendent and Ancillary Jurisdiction: Toward a Theory of Incidental Jurisdiction*, 95 HARV. L. REV. 1935 (1982) [hereinafter cited as *Incidental Jurisdiction*].

[199] *See, e.g.*, *County of Oakland v. City of Berkley*, 742 F.2d 289, 296 (6th Cir. 1984) (court expresses uncertainty whether lower court exercised pendent or ancillary jurisdiction); *By-Prod Corp. v. Armen-Berry Co.*, 668 F.2d 956, 962 (7th Cir. 1982) (discussing ancillary jurisdiction over defendant's counterclaim as "pendent jurisdiction").

[200] 28 U.S.C. § 1367.

[201] *See generally* § 5.03 (statutory scope), *supra.* Various federal jurisdictional grants will

insufficient (usually state law) claim by a plaintiff or plaintiffs. Since the latter thus depends on the anchor claim for jurisdiction, it is commonly called the *pendent claim*. Pendent jurisdiction applied, for example, to a state claim for unauthorized use of a play that plaintiff joins with an anchor federal claim for copyright violation against a non-diverse defendant. Commentators also coined the phrase *pendent party jurisdiction* to describe jurisdiction extended from the anchor claim to a pendent claim against a new party that would not independently fall within the court's subject matter jurisdiction.

A rationale of convenience supported pendent jurisdiction.[202] It avoided piecemeal lawsuits and the unnecessary decision of federal questions in federal courts by allowing them to hear and decide related state law questions. It also avoided duplicative litigation in state courts that might otherwise have resulted from the plaintiff's splitting of related federal and state law claims between the two court systems. But convenience was not the sole rationale for pendent jurisdiction. It also promoted the protective purposes of federal jurisdiction by giving the plaintiff with related federal and state claims unimpeded access to the federal forum.[203] Without pendent jurisdiction, plaintiff would have to (1) split her claims between federal and state courts, running the risk that a state court judgment would preclude her from relitigating common issues in the federal action; (2) forgo one of her claims in favor of litigating just the other in one forum; or (3) pursue both claims in state court, when the federal claim is not within the exclusive jurisdiction of the federal court, thereby forgoing the protection of federal court jurisdiction.[204]

In contrast, *ancillary jurisdiction* extended jurisdiction from the anchor (often diversity) claim to an otherwise jurisdictionally insufficient claim by the defendant(s) or similarly situated parties such as intervenors as of right,[205] who, as a practical matter, did not choose the forum. The latter was often called the *ancillary claim*. In a diversity action, for example, ancillary jurisdiction supported a compulsory counterclaim or cross-claim for less than the jurisdictional amount or an impleader of a non-diverse party. The rationale was one of fairness and necessity. Ancillary jurisdiction permitted the federal courts to give full and effective relief by hearing claims and deciding rights that might be lost or compromised if forced into another forum.[206] This is particularly necessary as a matter of fairness to parties who are involuntarily in the federal

---

support the anchor claim, including admiralty jurisdiction. *See, e.g., Leather's Best, Inc. v. S.S. Mormaclynx,* 451 F.2d 800 (2d Cir. 1971) (admiralty). At least one court has held that even diversity jurisdiction will support the anchor. *See Seybold v. Francis P. Dean, Inc.,* 628 F. Supp. 912 (W.D. Pa. 1986) (diversity, where pendent claim was jurisdictionally insufficient federal claim).

[202] *See, e.g.,* Richard A. Matasar, *A Pendent and Ancillary Jurisdiction Primer: The Scope and Limits of Supplemental Jurisdiction,* 17 U.C. Davis L. Rev. 103, 152 (1983); Note, *Unraveling the "Pendent Party" Controversy: A Revisionist Approach to Pendent and Ancillary Jurisdiction,* 64 B.U. L. Rev. 895, 900, 927 n.170 (1985) [hereinafter cited as *Revisionist Approach*].

[203] Matasar, note 202, *supra,* at 1402 n.3, 1404–07 n.6; Friedenthal, Kane & Miller § 2.12.

[204] Matasar, note 202, *supra,* at 1402 n.3, 1404–07 n.6.

[205] *See* § 9.08[1], *infra.*

[206] *Revisionist Approach,* note 202, *supra,* at 900; Matasar, note 202, *supra,* 17 U.C. Davis L. Rev. at 151–52.

forum and who assert essentially defensive claims.[207]

Whether a court could exercise either pendent or ancillary jurisdiction was initially a question of constitutional power. Article III sets the constitutional boundaries on federal subject matter jurisdiction and appears to confine it to the nine listed heads of jurisdiction.[208] Yet Article III speaks to judicial power over "cases" arising under federal law and "controversies" between diverse citizens, not over questions or issues. Thus, provided that a civil action has within it at least one jurisdictionally sufficient anchor claim, a federal court arguably has the constitutional power to hear any otherwise jurisdictionally insufficient claims which are part of the same constitutional case.[209] The trick is to define the parameters of a constitutional case: to determine what relationship is required between the anchor claim and the jurisdictionally dependent claims for them to be considered part of the same case. The focal point of analysis is therefore the particular relationship between the anchor claim,[210] which is jurisdictionally self-sufficient, and the dependent (pendent or ancillary) claim, which is not.

Even if a court has constitutional power to extend its jurisdiction, it must still satisfy itself that it has statutory power and that it should exercise its power in the circumstances. If so, then it may hear and decide additional claims without regard to venue over them.[211] Personal jurisdiction over each of the parties is also still required, but is often obtained for pendent or ancillary claims by plaintiff's reliance on the 100-mile bulge rule,[212] federal statutory provision for nationwide service of process on the federal claims,[213] or defendants' waiver of personal jurisdiction.

§ 5.09 PENDENT JURISDICTION

[1]   Pendent Claim Jurisdiction

The leading case of pendent jurisdiction is *United Mine Workers v. Gibbs*.[214] Gibbs sued the non-diverse United Mine Workers in federal court for violations of the federal Labor Management Relations Act and of the common

---

[207] *See, e.g., Incidental Jurisdiction*, note 198, *supra*, at 1937.

[208] *See* § 5.01[2] (federal subject matter jurisdiction), *supra*.

[209] *United Mine Workers v. Gibbs*, 383 U.S. 715, 725 (1966). *See also Osborn*, 22 U.S. at 821, discussed in § 5.02, *supra*.

[210] The cases and commentators regularly refer to the anchor claim as a "federal" claim, and the dependent claim as the "nonfederal claim." *See, e.g., Owen Equip. & Erection Co. v. Kroger*, 437 U.S. 365, 372 n.11 (1978). Because the anchor claim can be an admiralty or a state claim within diversity jurisdiction, this usage is somewhat confusing and is therefore not followed here.

[211] WRIGHT §§ 9 & 19.

[212] Rule 4(k) (allowing service within 100 miles of courthouse). *See generally* §§ 4.03[2] (service), *supra*, 9.05[2][b] (compulsory joinder) & 9.06 (impleader), *infra*.

[213] WRIGHT § 9 (noting split of authority concerning whether availability of nationwide service confers ancillary jurisdiction over jurisdictionally insufficient claims).

[214] 383 U.S. 715 (1966).

law of Tennessee as a result of its interference with his hauling contract during a labor dispute. After the jury decided for Gibbs on both claims, the trial court set aside the verdict on the federal claim, reasoning that the union interference was not cognizable under federal law, but entered judgment on the state law claim. The Court of Appeals affirmed, and the Supreme Court was presented the question whether the federal courts had jurisdiction over the pendent state claim in the absence of diversity. The Court held that constitutional power exists to decide the pendent claim whenever it is so related to the federal claim that they comprise "but one constitutional 'case.' "[215] It suggested a three-part test for *constitutional case.*

First, to anchor such a case, plaintiff must assert a federal claim that has "substance sufficient to confer subject matter jurisdiction on the court."[216] Gibbs's anchor claim met the requirements for federal question jurisdiction,[217] asserting a right to relief created by the federal Labor Management Relations Act. That is, he presented a substantial federal question in a well-pleaded complaint that passed the creation test for federal question jurisdiction.

Second, the anchor and pendent claims "must derive from a common nucleus of operative fact."[218] In so ruling, the Court discarded as "unnecessarily grudging" a "cause of action" test for constitutional case which confined the term *case* to alternative federal and nonfederal grounds for the same cause of action.[219] Since Gibbs' federal anchor and pendent state law claims involved overlapping facts concerning the union's actions, the common nucleus requirement was satisfied. But it would also be consistent with an expansive exposition of Article III power over "cases" to find the requirement satisfied by less than substantial overlap, even just a common origin in the same-transaction-or-occurrence or simply a logical relationship between the claims, like that required for several forms of joinder under the federal rules of civil procedure.[220] Most courts have opted for this definition of common nucleus.[221]

---

[215] 383 U.S. at 725.

[216] 383 U.S. at 725.

[217] *See* § 5.03[2], *infra.*

[218] *Gibbs*, 383 U.S. at 725.

[219] The cause of action test was set forth in the pre-rules case of *Hurn v. Oursler*, 289 U.S. 238 (1933). But the concept of "cause of action" has presented serious ambiguities in all of its applications, *see, e.g.*, § 15.03 (res judicata), *infra*, causing the drafters of the rules to reject it in favor of "civil action." Rule 2. The *Gibbs* court noted this history in discarding *Hurn*. *Gibbs*, 383 U.S. at 722–25.

[220] Joinder under Rules 13(a) (compulsory counterclaims), 13(g) (cross-claims), and 20 (permissive joinder of parties) requires that the joined claim arise out of the same transaction or occurrence that is the subject matter of existing claims. Most modern courts have interpreted this transactional nexus to mean simply a "logical relationship" between the claims. *See, e.g.*, *Great Lakes Rubber Corp. v. Herbert Cooper Co.*, 286 F.2d 631 (3d Cir. 1961). *See generally* §§ 9.02–9.05 (simple joinder), *infra.*

Professor Matasar illustrates the difference between factual overlap and logical relationship by positing an action by a welfare recipient from whom a social worker has gathered confidential information and then disclosed the same to third persons. *See* Matasar, note 202, *supra*, at 129–32. If the federal claim is that the information was gathered in violation of federal regulations, and the

Third, *Gibbs* seemed also to require that the federal and nonfederal claims be such that the plaintiff "would ordinarily be expected to try them all in one judicial proceeding."[222] This apparently referred to a plaintiff's anticipation of the possible claim-preclusive effects of a federal judgment on the anchor claim in subsequent state court suits asserting the jurisdictionally insufficient claims. Under the modern law of claim preclusion or res judicata,[223] a plaintiff is expected to try all transactionally-related claims together, in that he is precluded by a final judgment on any of them from subsequently trying the others. The expected-to-try part of the *Gibbs* test for constitutional case was therefore perhaps best viewed as a restatement of the common nucleus requirement rather than an independent requirement.[224]

Constitutional power to exercise pendent jurisdiction was decided on the pleadings. But *Gibbs* also held that the "power need not be exercised in every case in which it is found to exist."[225] "Needless decisions of state law should be avoided" to assure both comity and "surer-footed reading" of state law.[226] In addition, justification for pendent jurisdiction lay "in considerations of judicial economy, convenience and fairness to litigants," which differ from case to case and from one stage of a single case to another. Whether a court should exercise its power of pendent jurisdiction was therefore a question of discretion open throughout the case.

The factors that guided the exercise of discretion reflected these considerations and comity concerns. Timing of the disposition of the anchor claim was a key factor. Ordinarily if the anchor claim was resolved early in the

---

state claim is that it was disclosed in violation of state privacy law, there is neither factual identity nor overlap between the claims. They arguably arise out of the same transaction and are logically related, however, which would permit pendent jurisdiction under the broadest interpretation of "common nucleus of operative fact." Matasar, at 132; *cf. Reyes v. Edmunds*, 416 F. Supp. 649 (D. Minn. 1976). *But cf. Mason v. Richmond Motor Co., Inc.*, 625 F. Supp. 883 (E.D. Va. 1986) (rejecting "[m]ere commonality of facts" in favor of a stricter test).

[221] At least one court has suggested that the "common nucleus of operative fact" test is broader than the "transaction or occurrence" test of the federal rules. *See Ambromovage v. United Mine Workers*, 726 F.2d 972, 990 (3d Cir. 1984). The Supreme Court has also implied that the constitutional case may include factually unrelated claims whose resolution is necessary and proper to give full effect to a federal court's federal subject matter jurisdiction. *See* § 5.10, *infra*.

[222] *Gibbs*, 383 U.S. at 725.

[223] *See* §§ 15.02–15.05, *infra*. The older law of claim preclusion gave preclusive effect only to those claims which were part of the same "cause of action," § 15.03[4][a], *infra*, precisely the test that *Gibbs* expressly rejected in adopting the common nucleus test.

[224] Matasar, note 202, *supra*, at 138. *But see* WRIGHT & MILLER § 3567.1 (requirements are cumulative).

[225] 383 U.S. at 726.

[226] 383 U.S. at 726. Federal court decision of unsettled state law questions poses at least two serious federalism concerns. There is no mechanism by which federal errors of state law can be corrected on appeal by state courts, and state courts may be reluctant in later cases to reject even "lead-footed" federal decisions of state law because of intervening public reliance on the latter. *See Financial Gen. Bankshares, Inc. v. Metzger*, 680 F.2d 768, 772–75 (D.C. Cir. 1982) (explaining why trial court abused its discretion in exercising jurisdiction over pendent claim involving unsettled state law after pretrial disposition of federal claims). On the difficulty of ascertaining the meaning of state law, see generally § 7.06, *infra*.

litigation, refusing jurisdiction over pendent state claims would not result in wasteful duplication of effort and could well yield a "surer-footed" decision of state law from the state court in which the refused claims would then have to be brought. In fact, dictum in *Gibbs* stated that state claims "[c]ertainly . . . should be dismissed" without prejudice if the federal claims were dismissed before trial.[227] The Court subsequently backed away from its dictum,[228] however, and most lower courts recognized that the timing of dismissal was only a surrogate for a more basic factor: the likelihood of wasteful duplication of effort should pendent jurisdiction be refused.[229]

Predominance of state claims — in terms of proof, scope or remedy — was also a factor weighing against pendent jurisdiction. Exercising pendent jurisdiction when the state claims predominate and the federal claims drop out of the case before trial "smacks of the tail wagging the dog."[230]

The possibility of jury confusion was another factor, since the possible cure of ordering separate trials on the anchor and pendent claims[231] could sacrifice the judicial economy that in part justified pendent jurisdiction.

On the other hand, these factors could be outweighed by a close connection between the state claims and federal policy. For example, in *Gibbs* itself there was a substantial question whether the state law claim was preempted by federal labor law, which "afforded a special reason for the exercise of pendent jurisdiction."[232]

[2] Pendent Party Jurisdiction[233]

Gibbs presented the classic case of pendent jurisdiction, in which the plaintiff appended state law claims to an anchor federal law claim against the same defendant. But *Gibbs* also acknowledged that "[u]nder the [federal] [r]ules, the impulse is toward entertaining the broadest possible scope of action consistent with fairness to the parties; joinder of claims, *parties* and remedies is strongly encouraged."[234] Accordingly, some plaintiffs invoked *pendent party jurisdiction* to assert claims against new parties over whom independent federal subject matter jurisdiction was unavailable.

Such jurisdiction, for example, was invoked in diversity cases to add a defendant on a claim for less than the jurisdictional amount in controversy.[235]

---

[227] 383 U.S. at 726.

[228] *See Rosado v. Wyman*, 397 U.S. 397 (1970) (approving pendent jurisdiction after federal claims became moot before trial, where substantial time and energy had been expended on case).

[229] *See, e.g., Financial Gen. Bankshares, Inc.*, 680 F.2d at 773–74 (and cases there cited).

[230] *McFaddin Express, Inc. v. Adley Corp.*, 346 F.2d 424, 427 (2d Cir. 1965), *cert. denied*, 382 U.S. 1026 (1966).

[231] *See* Rule 42(a) (separate trials).

[232] 383 U.S. at 729.

[233] *See generally* David P. Currie, *Pendent Parties*, 45 U. Chi. L. Rev. 753 (1978.

[234] 383 U.S. at 724 (emphasis added).

[235] *See, e.g., F.C. Stiles Contracting Co. v. Home Ins. Co.*, 431 F.2d 917 (6th Cir. 1970).

This form of pendent party jurisdiction, however, offends the rule against aggregating claims for amount in controversy in diversity cases.[236] In *Zahn v. International Paper Co.*,[237] the Court applied the rule forbidding aggregation of the plaintiffs' claims against different defendants (absent suit upon a joint and undivided interest) to deny pendent party jurisdiction in a class action in which the parties did not all meet the amount in controversy requirement. *Zahn* thus suggested, though it did not decide, that pendent party jurisdiction generally could not be used to avoid the rule against aggregation.[238]

Pendent party jurisdiction was also invoked in federal question cases to add non-diverse parties to state law claims. In *Aldinger v. Howard*,[239] however, the Court cast doubt over this form of extended jurisdiction. Plaintiff had brought a civil rights action against the county treasurer and then appended a transactionally-related state law claim against the county and its commissioners. The Court refused jurisdiction over the state claim despite its factual overlap with the federal claims. It explained first that there is a difference between simply adding a state law claim against a defendant already in court on a jurisdictionally sufficient federal question and adding a new defendant on a pendent claim. Arguably the latter is a further, and often more burdensome, extension of jurisdiction than the former. The Court then noted that jurisdiction over the county was, in any event, expressly negated by a fair reading of the Civil Rights Act.[240]

At the same time, the Court in *Aldinger* was careful not to rule out pendent party jurisdiction altogether. "Other statutory grants and other alignments of parties and claims might call for a different result."[241] For example, the Court suggested[242] that if an anchor claim was within the exclusive jurisdiction of the federal courts, then *only* in federal court can all the claims be heard together. Allowing pendent party jurisdiction in this case would arguably effectuate the special protective purpose of exclusive federal jurisdiction. Consequently, *Aldinger* may still have held open the door of the federal court to pendent party jurisdiction when the anchor and pendent claims share a common nucleus of operative fact, and when jurisdiction, given the alignment of the parties, was not expressly or impliedly negated by the anchoring jurisdictional statute.[243]

---

[236] *See* § 5.06[2] (aggregating multiple claims), *supra.*

[237] 414 U.S. 291 (1973).

[238] *See* Darell D. Bratton, *Pendent Jurisdiction in Diversity Cases — Some Doubts*, 11 SAN DIEGO L. REV. 296, 322–23 (1974).

[239] 427 U.S. 1 (1976).

[240] 427 U.S. at 16. It later changed its mind about the Act. *Monell v. New York City Dep't of Social Servs.*, 436 U.S. 658 (1978). The Court also denied pendent party jurisdiction in a diversity case in which plaintiff tried to assert a state law claim against a non-diverse third party defendant. The statutory requirement of complete diversity negated the existence of pendent party jurisdiction in such circumstances. *Kroger*, 437 U.S. at 365. *See* § 5.10, *infra*, for further discussion of *Kroger* as an ancillary jurisdiction case; § 9.06, *infra*, for further discussion of third-party practice.

[241] 427 U.S. at 18.

[242] 427 U.S. at 18.

[243] Every circuit but the Ninth upheld exercises of pendent party jurisdiction after *Aldinger*.

To the general surprise of commentators, however, the Court slammed that door shut in *Finley v. United States*.[244] *Finley* presented precisely the case about which the *Aldinger* Court had speculated: plaintiff asserted an anchor claim within the exclusive jurisdiction of the federal courts[245] and sought to join transactionally-related state law claims against non-diverse defendants. Absent pendent party jurisdiction, plaintiff would be forced to forgo her state law claims against the non-diverse parties or to bring separate actions in federal and state court. The Court acknowledged the inefficiency and inconvenience of this result, yet denied pendent party jurisdiction because the underlying jurisdictional statute contained no "affirmative grant of pendent-party jurisdiction."[246] The Court thus turned the *Aldinger* search for implied congressional negation of pendent jurisdiction into a requirement for congressional affirmation of such jurisdiction.[247] Because Section 1331 (general federal question jurisdiction) and most other federal jurisdictional statutes are silent about pendent jurisdiction, the logic of *Aldinger* imperiled all pendent (and all ancillary) jurisdiction,[248] notwithstanding the Court's disclaimer of any "intent to limit or impair" the *Gibbs* line of cases.[249]

§ 5.10   ANCILLARY JURISDICTION

Ancillary jurisdiction originally developed independently of pendent jurisdiction. In *Freeman v. Howe*,[250] a United States marshal had seized certain railroad cars under a writ of attachment issued by a federal court sitting in diversity. The railroad's mortgagees sought replevin (return of property) against the marshal in state court, but were ultimately rebuffed when the Supreme Court held that the state court was powerless to interfere with property under federal judicial control. They were therefore left without a forum in which to pursue their claims to the property unless they could get into federal court. Despite their lack of diversity to the marshal and the absence of

---

See *Feigler v. Tidex, Inc.*, 826 F.2d 1435, 1438 (5th Cir. 1987) (so noting). See generally Samuel Hoar, Note, *Unraveling the "Pendent Party" Controversy: A Revisionist Approach to Pendent and Ancillary Jurisdiction*, 64 B.U. L. REV. 895, 938 (1985) (suggesting the test whether fairness in the circumstances compels a statutory interpretation that would allow jurisdiction); Matasar, note 202, *supra*, at 163–65 (expressing doubt that there is a practical difference between a claim and a party in light of possible net efficiency to judicial system of joining the latter).

[244] 490 U.S. 545 (1989).

[245] 28 U.S.C. § 1346(b) (conferring exclusive jurisdiction of "civil actions on claims against the United States").

[246] 490 U.S. at 553.

[247] *See, e.g.*, Richard D. Freer, *Compounding Confusion and Hampering Diversity: Life After Finley and the Supplemental Jurisdiction Statute*, 40 EMORY L.J. 445, 465–66 (1991) ("In *Finley*, the presumption [of congressional authorization for pendent jurisdiction] is turned 180 degrees.").

[248] Some courts read *Finley* "as sounding the death knell" for at least pendent party jurisdiction, *see, e.g.*, *Sarmiento v. Texas Bd. of Veterinary Med. Exam'rs*, 939 F.2d 1242, 1247 (5th Cir. 1991), and the commentators went further. *See, e.g.*, Thomas M. Mengler, *The Demise of Pendent and Ancillary Jurisdiction*, 1990 BYU L. REV. 247 (1990); Wendy Collins Perdue, *Finley v. United States: Unstringing Pendent Jurisdiction*, 76 VA. L. REV. 539 (1990).

[249] 490 U.S. at 556.

[250] 65 U.S. (24 How.) 450 (1860).

any federal question, the Court said that they could have asserted their claims in federal court on the theory that their claim was "ancillary and dependent, supplementary merely to the original suit, out of which it had arisen."[251] The justification for this extension of jurisdiction was clearly fairness — necessity from the perspective of the mortgagees — in that they were otherwise unable to assert their rights to the property in any forum.

Subsequently in *Moore v. New York Cotton Exchange*,[252] the Court extended ancillary jurisdiction in a federal antitrust action to a transactionally-related state law counterclaim, emphasizing the close, mirror-image relationship between the claims.[253] The necessity or fairness to a defendant of having such a counterclaim heard in federal court was not comparable to the necessity presented by the mortgagees in *Freeman*. Presumably the convenience of litigating the claims at the same time supported ancillary jurisdiction in this setting, although the Court did not elaborate or even characterize the jurisdiction as ancillary. But by premising the extension of jurisdiction on the close factual relationship between the claims, *Moore* led the eventual expansion of ancillary jurisdiction to transactionally-related joinders of claims and parties under the Federal Rules of Civil Procedure.

The expansion was summarized, and perhaps slowed, by the 1978 decision in *Owen Equipment & Erection Co. v. Kroger*.[254] There the Court found two broad requirements for ancillary jurisdiction in diversity cases.

First, ancillary jurisdiction, like pendent jurisdiction, required constitutional power to hear the jurisdictionally insufficient claims. The Court "assume[d] without deciding" that the *Gibbs* common nucleus requirement delineates the outer constitutional boundaries of federal diversity as well as federal question jurisdiction.[255]

Second, ancillary jurisdiction required a court to determine that Congress had neither expressly nor impliedly negated the exercise of jurisdiction, a determination based upon "the posture in which the nonfederal claim is

---

[251] 65 U.S. (24 How.) at 460.

[252] 270 U.S. 593 (1926).

[253] 270 U.S. at 610 ("[I]t only needs the failure of the [antitrust claim] to establish a foundation for the [counterclaim].").

[254] 437 U.S. 365 (1978).

[255] 437 U.S. at 372. The Court wisely declined to decide the question because its own prior cases suggest that a common nucleus of operative fact is only a sufficient and not a necessary predicate for constitutional power. *Freeman* itself allowed apparently unrelated claims to be asserted against the property under the court's ancillary jurisdiction, 65 U.S. (24 How.) 450, and the Court has approved ancillary jurisdiction over unrelated claims by a receiver to collect a debtor's assets and by and against trustees in bankruptcy. *See* cases cited in Richard A. Matasar, *Rediscovering "One Constitutional Case": Procedural Rules and the Rejection of the Gibbs Test for Supplemental Jurisdiction*, 71 CAL. L. REV. 1401, 1465–74 (1983). If these claims fall within the concept of constitutional case, it must be because they are either necessary and proper to give full effect to a particular subject matter jurisdiction or, more doubtfully in light of Rule 82, because the constitutional case extends as far as the scope of permissible joinder under the rules. Matasar, 71 CAL. L. REV. at 1477–90 (proposing the latter solution).

asserted" and an examination of the anchoring jurisdictional statute.[256] In *Kroger*, the plaintiff was attempting to assert a state law claim against a non-diverse third-party defendant in a diversity case. Unlike the defendant who had brought the third-party defendant into the case, however, the plaintiff had voluntarily chosen the federal forum. "By contrast, ancillary jurisdiction typically involves claims by a defending party haled into court against his will, or by another person whose rights might be irretrievably lost unless he could assert them in an ongoing action in a federal court."[257] Thus, the posture in which the dependent claim was asserted did not suggest such unfairness to plaintiff from denying ancillary jurisdiction as to overcome the usual statutory requirement of complete diversity.[258] On the other hand, the Court's analysis would presumably have supported a transactionally-related claim by the involuntary third-party defendant against the plaintiff, and, once such a claim is entertained, perhaps any claim by the plaintiff in the nature of a transactionally-related counterclaim, since such a claim would then be asserted defensively.[259]

The Court's analysis of ancillary jurisdiction explains the doctrine's extension to at least impleader under Rule 14,[260] presented by *Kroger* itself, cross-claims under Rule 13(g), compulsory counterclaims under Rule 13(a), parties added under Rule 13(h) to cross-claims and compulsory counterclaims, and sometimes intervention as of right under Rule 24(a).[261] Each of these kinds of joinder requires a transactional nexus under the rules between the joined and the anchor claim (thus presumptively satisfying the common nucleus requirement), and each is invoked defensively by a defendant or another party who has no practical choice of forum. Conversely, ancillary jurisdiction was not extended to permissive counterclaims under Rule 13(b),[262] permissive joinder of parties under Rule 20 or permissive intervention under Rule 24(a). These kinds of joinder either involve transactionally-unrelated claims and/or are invoked by parties who voluntarily chose the forum, and thus fail the *Kroger* test.

Once a court satisfied itself of constitutional power to assert ancillary jurisdiction, and that Congress had not negated such jurisdiction, there

---

[256] *Kroger*, 437 U.S. at 373 (*citing Aldinger v. Howard*, 427 U.S. 1 (1976), discussed in § 5.09[2], *supra*).

[257] 437 U.S. at 366.

[258] *See* § 5.04[2] (diversity between whom), *supra*.

[259] FRIEDENTHAL, KANE & MILLER § 2.12 (suggesting that a majority of courts have found ancillary jurisdiction for these claims and citing cases).

[260] For detailed analysis of joinder under Rule 14 and the other rules mentioned in the text, *see* §§ 9.02–9.08 (joinder), *infra*.

[261] *Kroger*, 437 U.S. at 375 n.18. The overlap between Rules 19 and Rule 24(a) led to an anomaly in ancillary jurisdiction. Because it is not available for necessary parties under Rule 19, *see* § 9.05[2], *infra*, the courts reasoned that it must also be unavailable when such a party tries to intervene as of right under Rule 24(a). *See generally* WRIGHT & MILLER § 1610; John E. Kennedy, *Let's All Join In: Intervention Under Federal Rule 24*, 57 KY. L.J. 329, 362–63 (1969).

[262] *But see* Matasar, note 255, *supra*, at 1474–75 (noting that it has sometimes been extended to setoffs for liquidated claims). *See* § 9.03 note 27, *infra* (defining set-offs).

remained the question whether it *should* assert it as a matter of discretion. Some commentators and courts, stressing the historical roots of ancillary jurisdiction in "necessity," treated the doctrine as mandatory once power was found.[263] But as the rationale for ancillary jurisdiction evolved from strict necessity to a mixture of fairness and convenience, the better view was that a court had the discretion to decide whether to exercise ancillary jurisdiction.[264] The factors that the courts should consider were those identified in *Gibbs*,[265] except that there was ordinarily no federal policy interest in a diversity case. "Necessity," or related considerations of fairness and convenience of involuntary parties, meant only that the discretionary part of the analysis should less often result in denial of ancillary jurisdiction, not that this jurisdiction was mandatory.

So the law stood when *Finley v. United States*[266] was decided. As we noted in the prior section, *Finley*'s insistence on affirmative evidence of congressional approval for pendent jurisdiction logically extended to ancillary jurisdiction as well. Some lower federal courts therefore began to restrict ancillary jurisdiction. Some even disallowed ancillary jurisdiction over third-party (impleader) claims[267] by defendants, despite the Supreme Court's endorsement of that application of ancillary jurisdiction in *Kroger*.[268] Other lower courts, however, confined *Finley* to its context — plaintiff's invocation of pendent party jurisdiction — and continued to uphold ancillary jurisdiction in other contexts. A few courts continued to uphold pendent party jurisdiction under different statutes.[269]

§ 5.11 STATUTORY SUPPLEMENTAL JURISDICTION[270]

The Court ended its opinion in *Finley* with the reminder that "[w]hatever we say regarding the scope of jurisdiction conferred by a particular statute can of course be changed by Congress."[271] Congress accepted the Court's invitation in

---

[263] *See, e.g.*, Note, note 202, *supra*, at 929. ("ancillary jurisdiction is an implied command to promote fairness"); Matasar, note 202, *supra*, at 184 (it is unclear whether discretionary factors apply at all and few courts have considered the question); Arthur R. Miller, *Ancillary and Pendent Jurisdiction*, 26 S. Tex. L.J. 1, 7 (1985) (noting that the issue "has never been seriously adjudicated" and that there is an inconsistency between jurisdictional discretion and lack of discretion in the court in permitting compulsory counterclaims under Rule 13(a)).

[264] *See, e.g.*, Matasar, note 202, *supra*, at 187–88; Friedenthal, Kane & Miller § 2.12; Wright § 76. Since the Court found no statutory power in *Kroger*, it never reached the question of discretion. Justices White and Brennan, dissenting, assumed that the trial court had discretion, as it would in a case of pendent jurisdiction. *Kroger*, 437 U.S. at 382 n.4 (White, J., dissenting).

[265] *See* § 5.09[1] (pendent claims), *supra*.

[266] 490 U.S. 545 (1989).

[267] *See* § 9.06 (impleader), *infra*.

[268] *See, e.g.*, Aetna Cas. & Sur. Co. v. Spartan Mech. Corp., 738 F. Supp. 664, 675 (E.D.N.Y. 1990) (finding that a defendant's third-party claim against a non-diverse defendant "comes under the prohibition of *Finley*" because the diversity statute does not affirmatively grant jurisdiction).

[269] *See* Freer, note 247, *supra*, at 467–69 (finding that most courts were reading *Finley* narrowly).

[270] For a thorough review of the initial commentary about and issues posed by statutory

1990 by enacting the supplemental jurisdiction statute.[272] The House Report accompanying the statute explained that it "would authorize jurisdiction in a case like *Finley*, as well as essentially restore the pre-*Finley* understandings of the authorization for and limits on other forms of supplemental jurisdiction."[273] The law professors who helped write the bill added that the measure was intended "to repair *Finley*'s damage in a noncontroversial manner without expanding the scope of diversity jurisdiction" and "was therefore framed to restore and regularize jurisdiction, not to revamp it."[274] Whether Congress accomplished all it set out to do remains to be seen, but it definitely did not avoid controversy. Here we first consider what the supplemental jurisdiction statute has accomplished and how it works, and then consider several apparent problems it poses.

[1]   The Three-Part Test for Supplemental Jurisdiction

Section 1367's subsections suggest three stages of inquiry in deciding the availability of supplemental jurisdiction over a claim for which there is no independent jurisdiction. The first is whether the claim qualifies for supplemental jurisdiction under § 1367(a) by falling within the same constitutional case or controversy as the anchor claim that enjoys independent jurisdiction.[275] If § 1367(a) is satisfied, but the anchor claim is based only on diversity, the second stage of inquiry is whether the supplemental claim is disqualified for supplemental jurisdiction by § 1367(b). If not, the third stage of inquiry is whether the court should nonetheless decline to exercise supplemental discretion for any of the reasons listed in § 1367(c).

[a]   Qualifying Under Section 1367(a)

Subsection 1367(a) codifies the authority for the extension of jurisdiction that *Finley* found lacking. Subsection 1367(a) overrules *Finley* by expressly providing that "supplemental jurisdiction shall include claims that involve joinder or intervention of parties," thereby authorizing jurisdiction over what

---

supplemental jurisdiction, see Denis F. McLaughlin, *The Federal Supplemental Jurisdiction Statute — A Constitutional and Statutory Analysis*, 24 Ariz. St. L.J. 849 (1992). The statute engendered a heated debate between its first critics and the three law professors who helped to draft it, published in the articles cited by McLaughlin, 24 Ariz. St. L.J. at 854 n.6. For a later reappraisal, see articles collected in *Symposium: A Reappraisal of the Supplemental Jurisdiction Statute: Title 28 U.S.C. § 1367*, 74 Ind. L.J. 1–250 (1998) (hereinafter "*Reappraisal*").

[271] 490 U.S. 545, 556 (1989).

[272] 28 U.S.C. § 1367.

[273] Federal Courts Study Committee Implementation Act of 1990, H.R. Rep. No. 101-734, 101st Cong., 2d Sess. 28 (1990) [hereinafter *H.R. Rep.*].

[274] Thomas M. Mengler et al., *Congress Accepts Supreme Court's Invitation to Codify Supplemental Jurisdiction*, 74 Judicature 213, 214–15 (1991).

[275] We continue to call the "anchor claim" a claim that would be jurisdictionally viable by itself. *See* § 5.08, *supra*. Jurisdictional support for such a claim may come from one of several federal statutes. *E.g.*, 28 U.S.C. § 1331 (federal question jurisdiction). In contrast, a claim for which jurisdiction is sought under § 1367 is never viable alone. Rather, jurisdiction over such a claim depends upon whether it relates to an anchor claim in a way that satisfies § 1367. We therefore call such a claim the "supplemental" claim.

were formerly called pendent party claims. Authority for supplemental jurisdiction is extended to any claim satisfying this subsection, unless it is one of the claims in diversity-only cases for which supplemental jurisdiction is withdrawn by subsection 1367(b), or jurisdiction is expressly negated by another federal statute.

Moreover, the new statutory jurisdiction "go[es to] the constitutional limit."[276] Despite legislative history suggesting that Congress intended to codify only the familiar transaction-or-occurrence test for extending jurisdiction,[277] subsection 1367(a) expressly extends federal jurisdiction from anchor claims within the original jurisdiction of the federal court to supplemental claims that are "so related [to the anchor claims] . . . that they form part of the same case or controversy under Article III of the United States Constitution." Whatever Congress's intent, its plain words refrain from creating yet another gap between statutory and constitutional jurisdiction. Assuming that the constitutional case is broader than same-transaction-or-occurrence, subsection 1367(a) apparently leaves scope for the exercise of supplemental jurisdiction over transactionally unrelated but logically related claims in the rare case where it may be appropriate.[278]

Despite Congress's adoption of the vague "same case or controversy" test for supplemental jurisdiction instead of the familiar "same transaction or occurrence" test which appeared in earlier legislative drafts of section 1367(a), the latter should still suffice for deciding to *include* a supplemental claim. Thus, most courts have found that claims which satisfy the same transaction or occurrence standard for joinder under Rules 13(a) (compulsory counterclaim),[279] 13(g) (crossclaim), or 20 (joinder of parties) also qualify for supplemental jurisdiction. As one court explained in deciding ancillary jurisdiction before section 1367 was enacted, "[t]he tests are the same because Rule 13(a) and the doctrine of ancillary jurisdiction are designed to abolish the same evil, viz., piecemeal litigation in the federal courts."[280]

But a claim which does not meet the same transaction test is not necessarily *excluded* from supplemental jurisdiction. A court may properly take a narrower view of "transaction or occurrence" in the counterclaim context,

---

[276] David S. Siegel, 28 U.S.C.A. § 1367 practice commentary (1990).

[277] *See* TEPLY & WHITTEN, Chap. 2, § C(4)(d) (arguing for this intent by tracing § 1367(a) to Federal Courts Study Committee Report, but conceding that "Congress may have inadvertently exercised" the full Article III power).

[278] *See* § 5.10 note 255, *supra* (citing cases); MOORE §§ 106.24[1][2] (noting division in courts about logical-relation test for supplemental jurisdiction and rejection of mere "but for" relationship); TEPLY & WHITTEN Chap. 2, § C(4)(d) (asserting that the "better approach" to deciding the scope of a constitutional case would be "to examine every grant of authority over factually unrelated federal and nonfederal claims to determine whether Congress has sound reasons, grounded in the fair and efficient operation of federal subject-matter jurisdiction grants, for providing such authority"). Teply and Whitten, however, opt for a narrow transaction-or-occurrence construction of section 1367(a) to avoid "'inconvenient' effects." TEPLY & WHITTEN Chap. 2, § C(4)(d).

[279] *See* § 9.03, *infra*.

[280] *Great Lakes Rubber Corp. v. Herbert Cooper Co.*, 286 F.2d 631, 633 (3d Cir. 1961).

because of the harsh result of finding that a previously unasserted claim was compulsory (it cannot be asserted later), than in the supplemental jurisdiction context, where the results are less draconian (the claim can still be heard in state court).[281] Thus, for example, one court has said that even if a supplemental counterclaim does not arise from the same transaction or occurrence as plaintiff's anchor original claim (so that it is a permissive, not a compulsory counterclaim), it can still qualify for supplemental jurisdiction if it bears even a loose factual relationship to the anchor claim.[282]

[b]   Disqualifying Under § 1367(b)

Subsection 1367(b) provides that in diversity-only cases, the courts do not have supplemental jurisdiction over claims by plaintiffs against persons made parties by Rules 14, 19, 20 or 24, when exercising such jurisdiction "would be inconsistent with the jurisdictional requirements of subsection 1332." The House Report explains that the "net effect of subsection (b) is to implement the principal rationale of *Owen Equipment & Erection Co. v. Kroger.*"[283]

The subsection would thus deny supplemental jurisdiction for the Rule 14(a) claim that plaintiff Kroger asserted against the non-diverse third-party defendant, as well as other claims that a plaintiff might add to evade the complete diversity requirement of § 1332. As the House Report explains,

> [i]n diversity-only actions the district courts may not hear plaintiffs' supplemental claims when exercising supplemental jurisdiction would encourage plaintiffs to evade the jurisdictional requirement of 28 U.S.C. § 1332 by the simple expedient of naming initially only those defendants whose joinder satisfies § 1332's requirements and later adding claims not within original federal jurisdiction against other defendants who have intervened or been joined on a supplemental basis.[284]

A good case can be made for overruling *Kroger*, or, conversely, for mooting it by eliminating diversity altogether.[285] However, if it is to be left largely intact, the statute is generally faithful to the task,[286] although it suffers from several

---

[281] *See* Moore § 106.25 (arguing that different purposes of test for joinder and test for supplemental jurisdiction justify different applications, but acknowledging that "courts have generally continued to equate the factual identity for supplemental jurisdiction with that required for the presence of a compulsory counterclaim"); Mary Kay Kane, *Original Sin and the Transaction in Federal Civil Procedure*, 76 Tex. L. Rev. 1723, 1730–33 (1998) (noting different policy purposes animating use of transaction test in different settings).

[282] *Polaris Pool Sys. v. Letro Prods., Inc.*, 161 F.R.D. 422, 425 (C.D. Cal. 1995). *See also Channell v. Citicorp Nat'l Servs., Inc.*, 89 F.3d 379, 385–86 (7th Cir. 1996) (endorsing loose factual connection as sufficient for supplemental jurisdiction).

[283] *H.R. Rep.*, note 273, *supra*, at 29 n.16. For discussion of *Kroger*, see § 5.10, *supra*.

[284] *H.R. Rep.*, note 273, *supra*, at 29.

[285] *See* § 5.04[1] (reviewing the arguments for and against diversity jurisdiction), *supra*.

[286] Subsection 1367(b) makes what the House Report characterizes as "one small change" in *Kroger* and pre-*Finley* practice. *H.R. Rep.*, note 273, *supra*, at 29. *Kroger* noted that ancillary jurisdiction had been extended to Rule 24(a) intervenors as of right, 437 U.S. at 375 n.18, subject

problems discussed below.[287]

[c]   Discretion Under § 1367(c)

Subsection 1367(c) codifies a discretionary step in what was pendent jurisdiction analysis. Although the subsection includes only some of the factors identified in the pendent jurisdiction cases, it invites courts, "in exceptional circumstances," to consider "other compelling reasons for declining jurisdiction."[288] Subsection 1367(c) thus serves as a counterweight to subsection 1367(a). It gives courts discretion to refuse jurisdiction within the outer limits of their power, when dismissal of the anchor claim on other than jurisdictional grounds,[289] the novelty or predominance of state law issues in federal question cases, or other good reasons suggest that the supplemental claims would more appropriately be decided by state courts. The Supreme Court has indicated that the statute reflects the understanding that a federal court " 'should consider and weigh in each case, and at every stage of the litigation, the values of judicial economy, convenience, fairness, and comity.' "[290]

On the other hand, the mandatory "shall" in § 1367(a) and § 1367(c)'s reference to "exceptional circumstances" and "compelling reasons" for declining supplemental jurisdiction has led some courts to conclude that § 1367(c) gives less discretion to decline jurisdiction than courts enjoyed under *Gibbs*. By this view, § 1367(a) effectively *requires* the court to exercise supplemental jurisdiction *unless* the court finds one of the listed grounds, or other *exceptional* circumstances, to be a *compelling* reason to decline.[291] A court could not therefore decline to exercise jurisdiction for an unlisted reason just because it promotes "economy, convenience, fairness, and comity," absent especially compelling circumstances. Another way of stating this view is that qualification for supplemental jurisdiction creates a presumption in favor of its exercise which can only be rebutted by one of the "compelling" reasons listed in § 1367(c).

---

to the anomaly that jurisdiction was denied intervenors as of right who also qualified as necessary parties under Rule 19. *See* § 5.10 n.261. Subsection 1367(b) "cures" the anomaly by denying supplemental jurisdiction to *all* plaintiff-intervenors. Critics have charged that this cure runs the wrong way and is worse than the anomaly, cutting off access to federal court for intervenors whose interest forces them into the federal forum without any intent to evade complete diversity. *See, e.g.,* McLaughlin, note 270, *supra,* at 960–70; Freer, note 247, *supra,* at 476–78.

[287] *See* § 5.11[2], *infra.*

[288] *See* McLaughlin, note 270, *supra,* at 975–76.

[289] Dismissal of the putative anchor claim for lack of subject matter jurisdiction deprives the court of supplemental jurisdiction because it eliminates the constitutional case or controversy. Dismissal of the anchor claim for other reasons leaves the court the power to hear the supplemental claims at its discretion under subsection 1367(c)(3). *See* McLaughlin, note 270, *supra,* at 979 (citing cases).

[290] *City of Chicago v. International Coll. of Surgeons,* 522 U.S. 156, 173 (1997) (quoting *Carnegie-Mellon Univ. v. Cohill,* 484 U.S. 343, 350 (1988)).

[291] *MOORE* §§ 106.60–106.61. *See, e.g., Executive Software N. Am., Inc. v. United States Dist. Court,* 24 F.3d 1545 (9th Cir. 1994) ("declining jurisdiction outside of subsection (c)(1)–(3) should be the exception, rather than the rule").

[2]   Problems With Subsection 1367(b)

It is chiefly what the statute did not say that generated much initial criticism. We identify only some of its alleged omissions here.

[a]   Overinclusiveness?

We noted in § 5.10 that *Kroger's* focus on the posture in which the supplemental claim is asserted did not necessarily foreclose the assertion in a diversity-only case of jurisdiction over a plaintiff's essentially defensive claims (*e.g.*, compulsory counterclaims or cross-claims against non-diverse parties), and some courts so held.[292] Does subsection 1367(b)'s restriction now prohibit even defensive claims by plaintiffs? That would require plaintiffs to bring separate state court actions for indemnification or contribution from non-diverse defendants, with the possibility that their transactionally-related federal claims could be precluded by state court judgments.[293]

One solution is to read subsection 1367(b) to reach only plaintiff's original claims, not counterclaims, cross-claims, or third-party claims added after the original complaint.[294] This facile reading, however, is hard to square with subsection 1367(a)'s use of the generic "claims." Arguably, it is also unnecessary. Subsection 1367(b)'s restriction on claims by the plaintiff is not absolute. It applies only "when exercising supplemental jurisdiction over such claims would be inconsistent with the jurisdictional requirements of section 1332." The plaintiff who asserts a defensive claim against a non-diverse party is typically not attempting to evade the complete diversity requirement; therefore, exercising supplemental jurisdiction over that claim would not be inconsistent with the requirements of diversity as they were articulated in *Kroger.* So federal courts reasoned before enactment of supplemental jurisdiction, and the qualifying clause in subsection 1367(b) permits that precedent to continue undisturbed, although courts have not observed this nuance.[295]

[b]   Underinclusiveness?

A second troublesome omission in subsection 1367(b) concerned the joinder of claims by persons made parties by Rule 23, the class action rule.[296] We noted in subsection 5.09[2] that the Supreme Court had denied pendent party

---

[292] *See* § 5.10 note 259, *supra*; Freer, note 247, *supra*, at 463 & n.103 (citing cases).

[293] *See* Freer, note 247, *supra*, at 482–83.

[294] Richard Freer, in *Reappraisal*, note 270, *supra*, at 5, 12–15; Siegel, note 276, *supra*; Mengler, et al., note 274, *supra*, at 215 n.17. A comparable solution is to read "plaintiff" in subsection 1367(b) to mean only a party who files an aggressive pleading rather than a defensive pleading. The rules themselves do not use "plaintiffs" this way, however. When they are intended to apply more generally, they use "parties asserting a claim" or "opposing parties." *Compare* Rule 20(a) *with* Rules 13 & 18.

[295] *See generally* Peter Raven-Hansen, *The Forgotten Provison of § 1367(b) (And Why We Forgot)*, in *Reappraisal*, note 270, *supra*, at 197.

[296] *See* § 9.09 (class actions), *infra.*

jurisdiction in plaintiff class actions over claims by class members that did not individually satisfy the amount in controversy.[297] Subsection 1367(b), however, omits joinder of such claims from its qualified restriction on supplemental jurisdiction. The inference is that supplemental jurisdiction is available pursuant to the general grant in subsection 1367(a). This inference contradicts the indications of congressional intent found in the statute's legislative history. Commentators and some courts have therefore favored the intent over the letter of the statute.[298] It is at least arguable that resort to the legislative history is warranted by subsection 1367(b)'s silence about Rule 23 joinder.

On the other hand, the principle of *expressio unius est exclusio alterius* (the expression of one thing is the exclusion of another) could be applied to uphold supplemental jurisdiction over supplemental plaintiff class action claims. Moreover, upholding such jurisdiction makes sense. In effect, the Supreme Court now allows supplemental jurisdiction over non-diverse class members in plaintiff class actions.[299] A plain language reading of subsection 1367(b) to allow supplemental jurisdiction over class members' monetarily insufficient claims would be perfectly consistent with the treatment of the diversity requirement in plaintiff class actions.[300]

In *Exxon Mobil Corp. v. Allapattah Services, Inc.*,[301] the Supreme Court adopted the plain language reading to find supplemental jurisdiction over monetarily insufficient class claims as long as there was at least one monetarily sufficient anchor class claim. In *Allapattah*, plaintiffs filed a class action complaint[302] against Exxon on behalf of 10,000 Exxon dealers, alleging that Exxon had employed a scheme to overcharge them for fuel. Although at least one of the representative class members had a claim exceeding the amount in controversy for diversity jurisdiction, many did not. The district court held, and the Court of Appeals affirmed, that it had supplemental jurisdiction over the monetarily insufficient claims, thus finding that the supplemental jurisdiction statute had overruled *Zahn*, notwithstanding the inconsistent legislative history. The Supreme Court agreed.

> When the well-pleaded complaint contains at least one claim that satisfies the amount-in-controversy requirement, and there are no other relevant jurisdictional defects, the district court, beyond all question, has original jurisdiction over that claim. The presence of other claims in the complaint, over which the district court may lack original jurisdiction, is of no moment. If the court has original

---

[297] *Zahn v. International Paper Co.*, 414 U.S. 291 (1973) (denying aggregation of amounts to satisfy jurisdictional requirement).

[298] *See* McLaughlin, note 270, *supra*, 972–74 (citing *H.R. Rep.*, note 273, *supra*, at 29); *cf. Griffin v. Dana Point Condo. Ass'n*, 768 F. Supp. 1299, 1301–02 (N.D. Ill. 1991) (refusing to exercise supplemental jurisdiction over co-plaintiffs' jurisdictionally insufficient claims).

[299] *See Supreme Tribe of Ben-Hur v. Cauble*, 255 U.S. 356 (1921) (counting only the citizenship of the representative class action plaintiffs for purposes of diversity).

[300] *See* § 9.09[2][b] (discussing problems of federal class actions after *Zahn*), *infra*.

[301] 545 U.S. 546 (2005).

[302] *See* Rule 23; § 9.09, *infra*.

jurisdiction over a single claim in the complaint, it has original jurisdiction over a "civil action" within the meaning of § 1367(a), even if the civil action over which it has jurisdiction comprises fewer claims than were included in the complaint. Once the court determines it has original jurisdiction over the civil action, it can turn to the question whether it has a constitutional and statutory basis for exercising supplemental jurisdiction over the other claims in the action.[303]

Because at least one of the class action representative's claims exceeded the amount in controversy required for diversity jurisdiction, and thus qualified, standing alone, for diversity jurisdiction, the federal courts had original jurisdiction over the civil action of which that claim was a part. It therefore had a basis for exercising supplemental jurisdiction over the monetarily insufficient dealers' claims in the same action (clearly based on the same fuel sale transaction). The Supreme Court found no ambiguity in the plain language of section 1367 that would justify resort to some legislative history eschewing a congressional intent to overrule *Zahn*.[304]

The same reasoning resolved another problem in section 1367(b) caused by the absence of any reference in it to Rule 20 joinder of plaintiffs. While the subsection denies jurisdiction for supplemental claims made *against* persons made parties under Rule 20 in diversity-only cases, it does *not* deny supplemental jurisdiction over joinder of non-diverse or below-amount claims *by* persons who join as plaintiffs under Rule 20. In a companion case decided with *Allapattah, Ortega v. Star-Kist Foods, Inc.*,[305] a nine-year old plaintiff had invoked diversity jurisdiction for serious injuries suffered when she cut her finger severely on a tunafish can, and her family members had joined as co-plaintiffs[306] with monetarily insufficient claims for emotional distress and medical expenses. The court of appeals ruled that there was no supplemental jurisdiction over the joined claims, reasoning that section 1367 did not overrule the long-standing rules against aggregation notwithstanding its language. The Court disagreed. Because the nine-year-old plaintiff's claims satisfied the amount-in-controversy requirements for diversity jurisdiction, the district court had jurisdiction over the entire case (civil action) of which they were part, and section 1367(b) did not withdraw supplemental jurisdiction over her family's joined claims (obviously arising from the same tuna can accident).

What then of supplemental jurisdiction for claims by *non-diverse* plaintiffs who join under Rule 20? Suppose, for example, that although the nine-year-old plaintiff was diverse from defendant, one of the joined family members was not. Now, reading the plain words of section 1367(b) to allow supplemental

---

[303] 545 U.S. at 559. Note that this analysis still requires an anchor claim exceeding the jurisdictional amount. If no claim does so, then the amount requirement cannot be met by aggregating the claims. *Allapattah* did not abolish the no-aggregation rule, and on these facts, there is no anchor for the supplemental claims.

[304] 545 U.S. at 567–71. It added that the legislative history, in any event, was "far murkier than selective quotation" from a single report would indicate. 545 U.S. at 569.

[305] 545 U.S. 546 (2005).

[306] *See* Rule 20.

jurisdiction would destroy the hoary *Strawbridge v. Curtiss* rule of complete diversity,[307] a statutory interpretation that Congress has been content to leave undisturbed for more than 200 years. The answer, the Court said, is that complete diversity is necessary to confer the original jurisdiction that section 1367(a) requires before you even get to section 1367(b).

> In order for a federal court to invoke supplemental jurisdiction under *Gibbs*, it must first have original jurisdiction over at least one claim in the action. Incomplete diversity destroys original jurisdiction with respect to all claims, so there is nothing to which supplemental jurisdiction can adhere.

> In contrast to the diversity requirement, most of the other statutory prerequisites for federal jurisdiction, including the federal-question and amount-in-controversy requirements, can be analyzed claim by claim.[308]

The Court's analysis can be defended as a matter of plain language construction. Whether it comports in both cases with what Congress thought it was doing by enacting the supplemental jurisdiction statute is less clear (assuming that we can divine what "Congress" thought it was doing). In any event, the flaws of section 1367 should not be allowed to obscure its virtues. The statute did *most* of what it set out to do from the start, and the Supreme Court's construction in *Allapattah* has clarified two of its central ambiguities. The result is both a firmer basis for extended jurisdiction and greater clarity in its most common applications.

---

[307] *See* § 5.04[2], *supra.*

[308] 545 U.S. at 554.

Chapter 6

A CONVENIENT COURT

§ 6.01 TRADITIONAL BASES FOR VENUE

[1] In General

The law of venue is founded on the realization that a court with subject matter and territorial jurisdiction can still be an inefficient, inconvenient location for litigation. Justice Scalia has observed that

> [v]enue is often a vitally important matter, as is shown by the frequency with which parties contractually provide for and litigate the issue. Suit might well not be pursued, or might not be as successful, in a significantly less convenient forum. Transfer to such a less desirable forum is, therefore, of sufficient import that plaintiffs will base their decisions on the likelihood of that eventuality when they are choosing whether to sue in state or federal court.[1]

Rules of *venue* are rules of convenience for allocating cases territorially, usually among state courts (usually by county) *within* a state's judicial system or among federal judicial districts and their divisions within the federal judicial system. That is, venue involves the choice of court within a state or federal judicial system, not among them.

Venue differs from subject matter jurisdiction in several ways. Objection to improper venue is waived if not promptly asserted.[2] Similarly, a court is not obliged to question venue on its own initiative, and parties can stipulate or contract to an otherwise improper venue. While courts typically entertain objections to subject matter jurisdiction throughout the lawsuit, venue questions are likely to be resolved at the outset. Jurisdictional defects usually require dismissal of a lawsuit, but improper venue can frequently be cured by transfer of the action to another court within the same judicial system. Finally, unlike some jurisdictional defects, improper venue does not subject a judgment to collateral attack.

Venue also differs from personal jurisdiction in several respects. Unlike personal jurisdiction, venue applies chiefly to original claims (the general

---

[1] *Stewart Org., Inc. v. Ricoh Corp.*, 487 U.S. 22, 39–40 (1988) (Scalia, J., dissenting).

[2] *See, e.g.*, Rule 12(h)(1). Note, however, that Rule 12 only governs the defense of "improper venue." Motions to transfer venue from one proper venue to another that is better — more convenient — may be made at any time. WRIGHT § 44.

federal venue statute speaks of where an "action . . . may . . . be brought"),[3] and not to claims added later.[4] The original parties, already present and litigating, are unlikely to be inconvenienced by litigating additional claims. Claims against additional parties usually enjoy what might be termed "ancillary," "pendent,"[5] or "derivative" venue[6] if those claims are sufficiently related to the original claims. Finally, defendant must plead the defenses of improper venue and lack of personal jurisdiction. But improper venue is treated like an affirmative defense which the defendant must prove, while personal jurisdiction must be demonstrated by the party invoking it.

As statutory rules, venue requirements differ from judicial system to system, but similarities predominate. Subsection 2 describes the usual statutory bases for venue, using the general federal venue statute to illustrate some of them. Subsection 3 then discusses several judge-made exceptions to venue requirements.

[2] Bases for Venue

To promote party and forum convenience, most venue statutes are based on some logical relationship between the parties or subject matter of the lawsuit and the place of trial. A comprehensive survey of typical venue statutes identified the following kinds of relationships as typical:

(1) the locus of the *res* (property) or event that is the subject of the lawsuit;
(2) where the claim arose;
(3) where the defendant resides, does business, or retains an agent;
(4) where the plaintiff resides; or,
(5) in suits by or against government parties, where the seat of government is located.[7]

"The most common provision," the survey concluded, "and the basic one, appears to be venue based upon the residence of the defendant."[8] But venue provisions are also based on other criteria, usually designed to facilitate suit, such as where the defendant is served or may be found.[9]

---

[3] 28 U.S.C. §§ 1391(a) & (b).

[4] MOORE § 110.06. *See, e.g., United States v. Acord,* 209 F.2d 709, 713–14 (10th Cir. 1954). However, if the plaintiff amends its complaint, the amended complaint is treated as a new action for venue purposes. The plaintiff could otherwise avoid venue requirements by artful pleading.

[5] WRIGHT & MILLER § 3808. *See, e.g., Garrel v. NYLCare Health Plans, Inc.,* 1999 U.S. Dist. LEXIS 9778, *8 (S.D.N.Y. June 24, 1999) ("The doctrine of pendent venue is ordinarily employed where venue is lacking for a state law claim that arises from the same nucleus of operative facts as a 'properly venued' federal claim"). If separate venue statutes govern each claim, then the problem may be more complicated. *Garrel,* 1999 U.S. Dist. LEXIS 9778 at *12.

[6] William D. Underwood, *Reconsidering Derivative-Venue in Cases Involving Multiple Parties and Multiple Claims,* 56 BAYLOR L. REV. 579 (2004).

[7] *See* George Neff Stevens, *Venue Statutes: Diagnosis and Proposed Cure,* 49 MICH. L. REV. 307, 331–32 (1951).

[8] Stevens, note 7, *supra,* at 315.

[9] *See* Stevens, note 7, *supra,* at 332.

The general federal venue provision[10] illustrates some of the common criteria.[11] It provides two general alternatives for venue and a fallback provision keyed to the limits of personal jurisdiction.

First, it lays venue literally at the doorstep of a single defendant, or multiple defendants who reside in the same state, by allowing suit to be brought in the judicial district where any of them reside.[12] Courts are split on whether residence for venue purposes should be equated with domicile or citizenship as these terms are used for deciding diversity jurisdiction (the majority rule), or given an independent definition.[13] The practical difference lies in the number of proper venues; an individual can only have one domicile or state citizenship at a time,[14] while she may maintain several residences. An 1892 Supreme Court dictum is authority for equating residence and citizenship.[15] Most courts have since equated residence with domicile for venue purposes.[16] But giving residence an independent and natural meaning may be more consistent with the convenience rationale of the general federal venue statute, because it will often expand the number of possible venues.

Section 1391(c) of the general federal venue statute[17] was intended to resolve another interpretative issue by defining the residence of a defendant corporation to be "any judicial district in which it is subject to personal jurisdiction at the time the action is commenced." In using the general phrase "personal jurisdiction," the subsection appears to subsume both specific and general jurisdiction.[18] The courts have divided about whether to measure personal jurisdiction under section 1391(c) by the constitutional minimum contacts test alone, by the forum state's long arm statute, or by other jurisdictional provisions as well. Because section 1391 venue is a question of federal law, the better view is that it is the former alone which controls.[19] In multi-district states in which the corporation is subject to personal jurisdiction,

---

[10] 28 U.S.C. § 1391. In addition to 28 U.S.C. § 1391, there are numerous special federal venue statutes. *See* 28 U.S.C. §§ 1394–1403, 1407–1410. For discussion of 28 U.S.C. § 1407, authorizing venue consolidation for multidistrict litigation, see § 9.10[1][b] (multidistrict litigation), *supra.*

[11] *See generally* Christian E. Mammen, Note, *Here Today, Gone Tomorrow: The Timing of Contacts for Jurisdiction and Venue Under 28 U.S.C. § 1391,* 78 CORNELL L. REV. 707 (1993); David D. Siegel, 28 U.S.C.A. § 1391 Commentary on 1990 Revision of Subdivisions (a), (b), and (e).

[12] 28 U.S.C. §§ 1391(a)(1) & 1391(b)(1).

[13] WRIGHT § 42. *Compare Rosenfeld v. S.F.C. Corp.,* 702 F.2d 282, 283 (1st Cir. 1983) (treating "citizenship" and "residence" as synonymous), *with Townsend v. Bucyrus-Erie Co.,* 144 F.2d 106, 108 (10th Cir. 1944) (treating them as "related or cognate terms" but also asserting that they "are not necessarily one and the same thing").

[14] *See* § 5.05 (citizenship), *supra.*

[15] *Shaw v. Quincy Mining Co.,* 145 U.S. 444, 447 (1892).

[16] *MOORE* § 110.03[1]. *See, e.g., Manley v. Engram,* 755 F.2d 1463, 1466 n.3 (11th Cir. 1985) ("It is well settled that an individual's mere residence in a state is not enough for purposes of establishing the propriety of venue there. Rather, it is an individual's 'permanent' residence — i.e., his domicile — that is the benchmark for determining proper venue.").

[17] 28 U.S.C. § 1391.

[18] *See* § 3.09[2] (specific and general jurisdiction), *supra.*

[19] *See MOORE* § 110.03[4][c].

the corporation is deemed to reside in any district "within which its contacts would be sufficient to subject it to personal jurisdiction if that district were a separate State," or, if there is none, "in the district within which it has the most significant contacts."[20] This provision is designed to provide some additional venue protection to the corporation that does business only in one district of the state, although it is doubtful that the benefit it affords is worth the costs of re-targeting the contacts analysis.

Second, a plaintiff may lay venue in "a judicial district in which a substantial part of the events or omissions giving rise to the claim occurred, or a substantial part of property that is the subject of the action is situated."[21] Under a prior version of the statute, this venue alternative depended, like many state venue statutes, on the district where "the claim arose."[22] But identifying the single district in which the claim arose would be problematic for many cases in which the facts giving rise to the claim occurred in two or more districts.[23] By substituting "a" for "the" district, and looking to "a substantial part" of the events or omissions giving rise to the claim, the new subsection eases the problem by enlarging the number of permissible venues. For example, in a civil racketeering suit against a California-based defendant who phoned a party in Kansas and sent mail there, the court held these contacts substantial enough under subsection 1391(b)(2) to make the District of Kansas a proper venue, even though defendant's activities in California "might have been more substantial, or the most substantial."[24] "Events or omissions giving rise to the claim" has been given a common sense construction. Courts have looked at where a contract was made, executed, or to be performed, where breach occurred, where tortious acts took place, where the harms were felt, and where communications were transmitted or received, among many other factors.[25]

Finally, if neither of these venue alternatives is available (and *only* then), the plaintiff has a fallback venue. In diversity-only cases, he may sue in "a judicial district in which any defendant is subject to personal jurisdiction at the time the action is commenced . . . ."[26] In other cases, he may sue in a judicial district "in which any defendant may be found . . . ."[27] The legislative history of section 1391 indicates that the purpose of the fallback provisions was to provide a venue "safety net" in cases "in which no substantial part of the events happened in the United States and in which all the defendants do not

---

[20] 28 U.S.C. § 1391(c).

[21] 28 U.S.C. §§ 1391(a)(2) & (b)(2).

[22] Act of Nov. 2, 1966, Pub. L. No. 89-714, 80 Stat. 1111, *amending* 28 U.S.C. §§ 1391(a) & (b). *See* WRIGHT & MILLER § 3806.

[23] *See, e.g., Leroy v. Great W. United Corp.*, 443 U.S. 173 (1979) (involving claims arising out of public tender offer by Delaware-incorporated and Texas-based corporation trying to take over publicly-listed Washington-incorporated corporation with executive offices and assets in Idaho and business in New York and Maryland).

[24] *Merchants Nat'l Bank v. Safrabank*, 776 F. Supp. 538, 541 (D. Kan. 1991).

[25] WRIGHT & MILLER § 3806.1

[26] 28 U.S.C. § 1391(a)(3).

[27] 28 U.S.C. § 1391(b)(3).

reside in the same state."[28] The difference between "subject to personal jurisdiction" in subsection 1391(a)(3) and "may be found" in subsection 1391(b)(3) is probably unintended. The may-be-found formula could literally refer only to jurisdiction based on presence at the time of service (transient jurisdiction),[29] to the exclusion of long-arm jurisdiction based only on contacts.[30] Yet such a restrictive reading may conflict with the legislative history, which seems to use the may-be-found formula interchangeably with "subject to personal jurisdiction."[31]

Instead of a statutory venue, parties may select a venue by including a forum selection clause in their contract. In *Bremen v. Zapata*,[32] the Supreme Court held that federal courts sitting in admiralty should enforce such clauses absent a showing that doing so "would be unreasonable and unjust, or that the clause was invalid for such reasons as fraud or overreaching."[33] It has since enforced even non-negotiable forum selection clauses.[34]

The applicability of this law to forum selection clauses in the Internet era is illustrated by *Caspi v. The Microsoft Network, L.L.C.*[35] There, a state appellate court upheld enforcement of such a clause in an online subscriber agreement because it found that the plaintiffs had validly assented to it by a mouse click. Notwithstanding disparity in size between the plaintiff class and Microsoft, the court found that the on-line computer service industry offered plaintiffs competitive choices, and that they were free to scroll through computer screens presenting the terms of the bargain before clicking their assent. Finally, it dismissed the plaintiffs' lack-of-notice argument. It concluded that nothing in the content, size, or placement of the clause in the online subscriber agreement was unusual or obfuscatory. Since the vast majority of web surfers click assent indiscriminately without reading the terms of online subscriber agreements, the court's analysis makes it clear that it is the *opportunity* to notice, comprehend, and reject the agreement containing the forum selection clause that counts.

[3]　Judge-Made Exceptions

Courts have carved several exceptions out of the usual venue statutes. They have held that actions properly removed to federal courts need not satisfy federal venue requirements because the removal statute itself specifies the

---

[28] H.R. Rep. No. 101-734, 101st Cong., 2d Sess. 23 (1990).

[29] *See* § 3.08[3][b], *supra*.

[30] Courts interpreting the same phrase in other venue statutes are divided on this issue. *See* WRIGHT & MILLER § 3802.1.

[31] Unfortunately, the legislative history is itself confused and marred by what may be typographical errors. *See* Siegel, note 11, *supra*.

[32] 407 U.S. 1 (1972).

[33] 407 U.S. at 15.

[34] *See Carnival Cruise Lines, Inc. v. Shute*, 499 U.S. 585 (1991). A more extended discussion of forum selection clauses appears in § 3.03[2][d], *supra*.

[35] 732 A.2d 528 (N.J. Super.), *cert. denied*, 743 A.2d 851 (N.J. 1999).

district to which the case must be removed.[36] As we noted above, courts usually have not applied federal venue requirements to supplemental claims when venue was proper on the anchor claim, partly on the theory that convenience was already taken into account in the jurisdictional analysis in such cases.[37]

A broader exception, made by most state courts as well as federal courts, is for real property-based actions. Under the common law *local action rule*, the only proper venue for such an action is the locus of the property which is the subject of the action. This exception is an artifact of history, tracing its origin to an era in which juries were selected for their knowledge of the case. When an action involved real property, the only proper venue was necessarily where the property was located because only juries from that location knew enough about the property to decide the facts.[38] In contrast, all other actions — called *transitory actions* — can be heard wherever they arise. Distinguishing local from transitory actions, however, was no easy task. At English common law, the former included not only *in rem* and real actions for possession, ejectment, partition, foreclosure and quieting title, but also certain actions for trespass, and the states differ in their incorporation of this law.[39] Nevertheless, most courts continue to make this exception to the statutory venue requirements, and the federal venue statute, among others, makes passing reference to it,[40] which may help account for its continued vitality in the federal system.

§ 6.02 CHANGE OF VENUE

[1] Dismissal and Forum Non Conveniens[41]

Objection to improper venue is ordinarily made by a preliminary motion to dismiss, and the indicated remedy is, therefore, dismissal of the action without prejudice. If, however, the statute of limitations has since expired,[42] a

---

[36] WRIGHT & MILLER § 3804. On removal, see generally § 5.07, supra. Once the case has been removed, however, any party may seek a transfer of venue in accord with 28 U.S.C. § 1404. See § 6.02[2] (transfer), infra.

[37] MOORE § 110.06.

[38] See, e.g., WRIGHT § 42. The local action exception was also historically based on judicial reluctance, for reasons of sovereignty and ability, to decide disputes concerning foreign property. See Reasor-Hill Corp. v. Harrison, 249 S.W.2d 994 (Ark. 1952) (questioning application of this reasoning to interstate disputes about property, in rejecting the "majority [local action] rule").

[39] See, e.g., Livingston v. Jefferson, 15 F. Cas. 660 (C.C.D. Va. 1811) (No. 8,411) (applying local action rule to dismiss suit in Virginia federal court against former President Jefferson for trespass to property in Louisiana Territory).

[40] See 28 U.S.C. § 1392 (venue for civil actions "of a local nature" involving property located in different districts within the same state). See generally Note, Local Actions in the Federal Courts, 70 HARV. L. REV. 708 (1957). Subsections 1391(a)(2) & (b)(2) may now supplant the local action rule in federal court rendering it unnecessary.

[41] See generally David W. Robertson & Paula K. Speck, Access to State Courts in Transnational Personal Injury Cases: Forum Non Conveniens and Antisuit Injunctions, 68 TEX. L. REV. 937 (1990); Allan R. Stein, Forum Non Conveniens and the Redundancy of Court-Access Doctrine,

dismissal effectively extinguishes the plaintiff's right of action without reaching the merits. To avoid this harsh result, the plaintiff will usually seek the transfer of the action to a proper venue within the same judicial system as an alternative to dismissal. Most venue laws permit such transfers in the alternative.

In the federal system, for example, a court in which venue has improperly been laid may dismiss, "or if it be in the interest of justice, transfer [the] case to any district or division in which it could have been brought."[43] As federal courts have interpreted this provision, a court with subject matter jurisdiction, whether or not it has personal jurisdiction over the parties,[44] may transfer a case laying improper venue to any federal forum which, without defendant's consent, would have had personal jurisdiction over the defendant and would have been a proper venue initially.[45] Almost all states have similar or less restrictive provisions for transfer in lieu of dismissal, if there is a proper alternative venue within the state judicial system.

Suppose, however, that the alternative forum is outside the state's judicial system or even outside the United States. State courts have no power to transfer cases to the courts of other states, and neither state nor federal courts have the power to transfer cases to the courts of foreign countries.[46] In such cases, most judicial systems permit dismissal of suits under the doctrine of *forum non conveniens*, in anticipation that the plaintiff will recommence the suit in the alternative foreign venue.[47] The Supreme Court has characterized the doctrine as "a supervening venue provision, permitting displacement of the ordinary rules of venue when, in light of certain conditions, the trial court

---

133 U. Pa. L. Rev. 781 (1985); Margaret G. Stewart, *Forum Non Conveniens: A Doctrine in Search of a Role*, 74 Cal. L. Rev. 1259 (1986).

[42] Under some statutes, the pendency of the lawsuit — even in an improper venue — tolls the statute. *See generally* § 8.08[2][b] (limitations defense), *infra*.

[43] 28 U.S.C. § 1406(a).

[44] *Goldlawr, Inc. v. Heiman*, 369 U.S. 463 (1962).

[45] *Cf. Hoffman v. Blaski*, 363 U.S. 335 (1960) (rejecting argument under federal venue transfer provision, 28 U.S.C. § 1404, that a forum in which a case "might have been brought" includes an otherwise improper venue to which defendants consent, and, by implication, rejecting same "consent" argument for a forum that otherwise lacks personal jurisdiction over defendants). *Hoffman*'s analysis should apply with even greater force to transfers in lieu of dismissal under 28 U.S.C. § 1406, since that provision speaks of districts where the action "could have been brought." *See generally* Wright § 44.

[46] Nor can federal courts transfer cases onto the dockets of state courts. However, there is less need for transfer in this setting. A state court in the state where the federal court is sitting usually will not be appreciably more convenient than the federal court there. The court of a second state might be more convenient, but so too would a federal court in the second state. The federal court where suit originated can affect intra-system transfer to the latter under 28 U.S.C. § 1404. *See* § 6.02[2] (transfer of venue), *infra*.

[47] The federal courts have asserted an inherent common law power to dismiss on *forum non conveniens* grounds. *But see* Elizabeth T. Lear, *Congress, the Federal Courts, and Forum Non Conveniens: Friction on the Frontier of the Inherent Power*, 91 Iowa L. Rev. 1147 (2006) (arguing that courts' assumption of inherent *forum non conveniens* power to dismiss cases satisfying statutory venue requirements is unconstitutional).

thinks that jurisdiction ought to be declined."[48] To obtain a *forum non conveniens* dismissal, defendant must satisfy two requirements.

First, he must show that an adequate alternative forum is available.[49] Since *forum non conveniens* presupposes a proper original venue, it would be unfair to plaintiff who correctly chose it and would frustrate the purposes of venue law to dismiss a case for which there was no adequate alternative forum. In *Piper Aircraft Co. v. Reyno*,[50] plaintiff argued that his case should not be dismissed from a proper federal venue under the doctrine of *forum non conveniens* when the alternative Scottish forum would apply less favorable substantive law. The Supreme Court held that the mere possibility of an unfavorable change in the applicable law does not bar a *forum non conveniens* dismissal, unless the change makes the remedy "so clearly inadequate or unsatisfactory that it is no remedy at all."[51] In another case, a federal district court ruled that alleged defects and disadvantages of the Indian legal system, including prohibitive filing fees of up to 5% of total damages sought, serious case backlogs occasioned in part by unlimited interlocutory appeals, and underdeveloped tort laws,[52] did not render an Indian forum inadequate in the litigation spawned by the catastrophic Bhopal pesticide leak.[53] On the other hand, a lack of subject matter jurisdiction in the alternative forum clearly renders it inadequate for *forum non conveniens* purposes.[54]

Second, the defendant must show that considerations of party and forum convenience override the plaintiff's choice of forum and justify dismissal.

---

[48] *American Dredging Co. v. Miller*, 510 U.S. 443, 453 (1994).

[49] *Gulf Oil Corp. v. Gilbert*, 330 U.S. 501, 506–07 (1947). *See generally* Megan Waples, Note, *The Adequate Alternative Forum Analysis in Forum Non Conveniens: A Case for Reform*, 36 CONN. L. REV. 1475 (2004); Annotation, *Forum Non Conveniens in State Court as Affected by Availability of Alternative Forum*, 57 A.L.R.4TH 973 (1987); Ann Alexander, Note, *Forum Non Conveniens in the Absence of an Alternative Forum*, 86 COLUM. L. REV. 1000 (1986). A few courts have treated the availability of an adequate alternative forum as just one factor to weigh in a *forum non conveniens* decision, rather than a prerequisite to such a decision. *E.g., Islamic Republic of Iran v. Pahlavi*, 467 N.E.2d 245 (N.Y. 1984).

[50] 454 U.S. 235 (1981).

[51] 454 U.S. at 254.

[52] *See generally* Marc Galanter, *Legal Torpor: Why So Little Has Happened in India After the Bhopal Tragedy*, 20 TEX. INT'L L.J. 273 (1985); James Stewart, *Why Suits for Damages Such as Bhopal Claims Are Very Rare in India*, WALL ST. J., Jan. 23, 1985, at 1.

[53] *In re Union Carbide Corp. Gas Plant Disaster at Bhopal, India*, 634 F. Supp. 842 (S.D.N.Y. 1986), *aff'd as modified*, 809 F.2d 195 (2d Cir. 1987) (hereinafter cited as Bhopal Litigation). On the Bhopal Litigation generally, see Tim Covell, *The Bhopal Disaster Litigation: It's Not Over Yet*, 16 N.C. J. INT'L L. & COM. REG. 279 (1991); Stephen J. Darmody, *An Economic Approach to Forum Non Conveniens Dismissals Requested by U.S. Multinational Corporations — The Bhopal Case*, 22 GEO. WASH. J. INT'L L. & ECON. 215 (1988); Ved P. Nanda, *For Whom the Bell Tolls in the Aftermath of the Bhopal Tragedy: Reflections on Forum Non Conveniens and Alternative Methods of Resolving the Bhopal Dispute*, 15 DENV. J. INT'L L. & POL'Y 235 (1987); Richard Schwadron, Note, *The Bhopal Incident: How the Courts Have Faced Complex International Litigation*, 5 B.U. INT'L L.J. 445 (1987).

[54] *Piper Aircraft*, 454 U.S. at 254 n.22 (ordinarily amenability of defendants to suit in the alternative forum evidences its adequacy, while lack of subject matter jurisdiction in the alternative forum makes it inadequate).

Typical party or "private" considerations include relative ease of access to proof, availability of compulsory process for attendance of witnesses, the cost of obtaining their attendance, the possibility of obtaining a jury view of the scene of the accident or property which is the subject of the action, and the enforceability of any eventual judgment in the original forum.[55] Ordinarily the plaintiff's choice of forum enjoys a strong presumption of convenience. When these factors indicate that the alternative forum would be more convenient for the parties, however, then the plaintiff's choice was presumably tactical, or even harassing, and may therefore be disturbed. This is more likely to be true when the plaintiff is a foreign party than when he is someone suing on his "home turf."

Forum or "public" considerations reflect the relative burdens and benefits of imposing the litigation on the contending forums, including effect on judicial calendars, imposition of jury duty on the forum community, local interest in the controversy, and the choice of law.[56] Clearly, forum convenience — the public interest — is best served by localizing the litigation and assigning it to the forum most familiar with the applicable law.

The *forum non conveniens* determination is committed to the sound discretion of the trial court,[57] and, as such, is largely immune from effective appellate review.[58] The Supreme Court has held, moreover, that where the normally predicate issues of subject matter or personal jurisdiction are difficult (or require extensive discovery), and convenience points to an adequate foreign forum, a district court may by-pass them and take the "less burdensome course" of dismissing on *forum non conveniens* grounds.[59] Included within the court's discretion is the power to condition dismissal on a defendant's satisfaction of various conditions that will ensure the adequacy of the alternative forum (such as agreement to waive a limitations defense to a refiled suit or to submit to the personal jurisdiction of the alternative forum)[60] or conditions that will enhance the party convenience of that forum (such as defendant's agreement to provide certain discovery).[61]

---

[55] *See, e.g.*, 454 U.S. at 257–58; *Gulf Oil*, 330 U.S. at 508. In some states, a resident plaintiff's interest in having his case heard by his own courts trumps all other private and public considerations and bars dismissal. *See, e.g., Ferreira v. Ferreira*, 512 P.2d 304 (Cal. 1973); *Iacouzze v. Iacouzze*, 672 P.2d 949 (Ariz. Ct. App. 1983). *See generally* Peter G. McAllen, *Deference to the Plaintiff in Forum Non Conveniens*, 13 S. ILL. sU. L.J. 191 (1989).

[56] *Piper Aircraft*, 454 U.S. at 259–61; *Gulf Oil*, 330 U.S. at 508–09.

[57] *Piper Aircraft*, 454 U.S. at 257.

[58] *See* Stein, note 41, *supra*, at 831–32; Christina Melady Morin, Note, *Review and Appeal of Forum Non Conveniens and Venue Transfer Orders*, 59 GEO. WASH. L. REV. 715 (1991); § 13.04[2] (noting unavailability of statutory interlocutory appeal under 28 U.S.C. § 1292(b) for review of venue transfer decisions), *infra*.

[59] *Sinochem Int'l Co. Ltd. v. Malaysia Int'l Shipping Corp.*, 127 S. Ct. 1184, 1194 (2007).

[60] *Bhopal Litigation*, 809 F.2d at 203, 204 (conditioning dismissal in part on defendant's consent to personal jurisdiction of Indian courts and waiver of limitations defenses).

[61] *See Piper Aircraft*, 454 U.S. at 257 n.25. *See generally* John Bies, *Conditioning Forum Non Conveniens*, 67 U. CHI. L. REV. 489 (2000).

[2]   Transfer of Venue

In § 2.02 we discussed factors influencing the choice of court. But defendants also forum shop by moving to transfer venue. Indeed, one commentator alleges that "the transfer motion has become a common, almost reflexive defendant response to a lawsuit."[62] Because courts lack the power to transfer cases outside their own judicial system, the doctrine of *forum non conveniens* is still used as a substitute for inter-system "transfer" from state or federal courts to state or foreign courts.[63] For intra-system transfers, however, relaxed versions of the doctrine have been codified in many jurisdictions.

The statutory provision for transfer of venue within the federal system[64] is probably typical. Unlike the common law *forum non conveniens* doctrine, the statute provides for transfer to a district where the case might have been brought,[65] instead of dismissal. Section 1404's "might have been brought," like section 1406's "could have been brought," has been interpreted to mean a district with venue and personal jurisdiction, although there is no requirement for either in the transferor court.[66] Because the statute provides this milder remedy of transfer, it is available upon a lesser showing[67] than required for *forum non conveniens* dismissal. The relaxed showing is phrased generally and unhelpfully as "the convenience of parties and witnesses, [or] in the interest of justice."[68] The parties' contractual choice of forum is not dispositive in this showing, but certainly an important factor to be considered.[69] Moreover, unlike *forum non conveniens* dismissals, transfers of venue between federal courts are available to plaintiffs and defendants alike.[70]

---

[62] Stowell R.R. Kelner, Note, *"Adrift on an Uncharted Sea": A Survey of Section 1404(a) Transfer in the Federal System*, 67 N.Y.U. L. Rev. 612, 615 (1992).

[63] *See* note 46 and accompanying text, *supra*. It is not the only inter-system venue device, however. Some courts will stay proceedings before them until the plaintiff has refiled and defendant has submitted in a better foreign venue, and others will entertain actions by parties who are defendants in an inconvenient foreign venue to enjoin the plaintiff from prosecuting her action there. *See generally* Robertson & Speck, note 41, *supra*; Comment, *Forum non Conveniens, Injunctions Against Suit and Full Faith and Credit*, 29 U. Chi. L. Rev. 740, 741 (1962).

[64] 28 U.S.C. § 1404. *See generally* Maryellen Corna, Note, *Confusion and Dissension Surrounding the Venue Transfer Statutes*, 53 Ohio St. L.J. 319 (1992); Kelner, note 62, *supra*; David E. Steinberg, *The Motion to Transfer and the Interests of Justice*, 66 Notre Dame L. Rev. 443 (1990).

[65] 28 U.S.C. § 1404(a).

[66] *See supra* note 45. If the transferor lacks venue, the transfer is made under section 1406, not section 1404.

[67] *Piper Aircraft*, 454 U.S. at 253; *Norwood v. Kirkpatrick*, 349 U.S. 29, 29–33 (1955) (Section 1404 is not merely a codification of *forum non conveniens*, but adopts a more relaxed test for transfer in the federal system).

[68] 28 U.S.C. § 1404(a).

[69] *See Stewart Org., Inc. v. Ricoh Corp.*, 487 U.S. 22 (1988). *See generally* Leandra Lederman, Note, *Viva Zapata! Toward a Rational System of Forum-Selection Clause Enforcement in Diversity Cases*, 66 N.Y.U. L. Rev. 422, 450–64 (1991).

[70] *See Ferens v. John Deere Co.*, 494 U.S. 516 (1990) (discussing choice of law after plaintiff-initiated transfer).

The effect of a transfer is also different from the effect of a dismissal. Statutory transfer is intended only to change the place of trial and not the applicable law or the availability of limitations defenses. Accordingly, the Supreme Court has held that a federal transferee court must apply the law that would have been applied in the transferor court, whether the movant was the plaintiff or the defendant.[71] But courts have applied this holding only to section 1404 transfers, and not section 1406 transfers for improper venue,[72] for otherwise it would be too easy for a plaintiff to shop for favorable law by intentionally filing in an improper venue.

The law the transferor court would have applied includes choice of law rules. Thus, if a federal court in the Northern District of California transfers a diversity action asserting a tort claim arising from an accident in Ohio to the Middle District of Pennsylvania, the latter must ordinarily apply California's choice of law rules. If those rules apply the law of the place where the accident took place to such a tort claim, then the federal court for the Middle District of Pennsylvania must apply the tort law of Ohio, just as the transferor court would have. In short, the transferor law rule does not automatically mean that the transferee court will end up applying the substantive law of the transferor forum; it must first apply the transferor's choice of law rules. Only in this way do the courts assure that the transfer changes only the place of trial, not the applicable law.

After the transfer, the transferee court takes up the litigation where the transferor court left it, and no recommencement of the action is necessary, which preserves to plaintiff the date of the original commencement of the lawsuit for purposes of satisfying the statute of limitations.

The interaction of liberal federal venue, relaxed federal transfer standards, the uncertain effects of the parties' contractual choice of forum, and the general absence of effective appellate supervision of transfer decisions has bred substantial confusion in the case law and new opportunities to forum shop.[73] Whether a given court will transfer is unpredictable. The rule applying the law that the transferor court would apply lets plaintiffs forum-shop for the statute of limitations in some cases; less obviously, the willingness of at least some transferee courts to overrule the law of the case (that is, re-decide interlocutory decisions by the transferor court)[74] lets defendants forum-shop for reconsideration of adverse interlocutory decisions.[75] Critics of the current

---

[71] *Ferens*, 494 U.S. at 516 (plaintiff's transfer under 28 U.S.C. § 1404); *Van Dusen v. Barrack*, 376 U.S. 612, 639 (1964) (defendant's transfer under 28 U.S.C. § 1404). *See generally* § 7.05[3] (*Klaxon* and § 1404(a)), *infra*. It is unclear whether the rule applies when a federal court transfers under circumstances in which a forum state court would have dismissed under the doctrine of *forum non conveniens*. *See* Wright § 44; John D. Currivan, Note, *Choice of Law in Federal Court After Transfer of Venue*, 63 Cornell L. Rev. 149 (1977).

[72] *See* Moore § 111.38[1].

[73] *See, e.g.*, Kimberly Jade Norwood, *Double Forum Shopping and the Extension of Ferens to Federal Claims that Borrow State Limitation Periods*, 44 Emory L.J. 501 (1995); Corna, note 64, *supra*; Kelner, note 62, *supra*.

[74] *See* § 15.14 (law of the case), *infra*.

[75] *See* Kelner, note 62, *supra*, at 636–42; Joan Steinman, *Law of the Case: A Judicial Puzzle in*

system, however, are undecided whether closer appellate supervision or statutory reform is the better solution.

§ 6.03 PROPOSALS REGARDING THE RELATIONSHIP OF PERSONAL JURISDICTION AND VENUE

A careful reader of Chapters 3 and 6 cannot help but note the similarities between personal jurisdiction and venue. Both address in part the reasonableness of the forum from defendant's perspective and the forum interests in the locus of suit. More generally, these doctrines of court access share common historical roots and purposes and have similar analytic structures.[76] Little wonder that students and lawyers alike occasionally have difficulty understanding how a court that may "reasonably" exercise personal jurisdiction over a defendant can be too inconvenient to the defendant to serve as an appropriate venue.

Critics have attempted to reformulate these court-access doctrines to eliminate or explain their overlap within a judicial system. One approach is capsulized in the prediction, "jurisdiction must become venue."[77] Proponents of this reformulation urge a system of nationwide service of federal process, under which the venue rules alone carry the full burden of assuring a reasonably convenient forum.[78]

"Venue must become jurisdiction" summarizes another alternative. Its approach is to abolish federal venue requirements and look solely to a federal long-arm statute to ensure a reasonably convenient forum.[79] Long-arm jurisdiction would be available in any district where a substantial part of the events giving rise to suit occurred or where defendant resides. To a significant degree, the 1990 amendments to the general federal venue statute moved in this direction, by laying venue in the district in which significant contacts occur, or, for corporate defendants, where they are subject to personal jurisdiction, or, when these venues are unavailable, in the district in which the defendants are subject to personal jurisdiction.[80]

Alternatively, and more modestly, the *forum non conveniens* doctrine alone could be eliminated from venue law in favor of an expanded jurisdictional inquiry that expressly takes into account the private and public interests now

---

Consolidated and Transferred Cases and in Multidistrict Litigation, 135 U. Pa. L. Rev. 595 (1987).

[76] *See* Kevin M. Clermont, *Restating Territorial Jurisdiction and Venue for State and Federal Courts*, 66 Cornell L. Rev. 411, 430–34 (1981).

[77] Albert A. Ehrenzweig, *From State Jurisdiction to Interstate Venue*, 50 Or. L. Rev. 103, 113 (1971).

[78] *See* Edward L. Barrett, Jr., *Venue and Service of Process in the Federal Courts — Suggestions for Reform*, 7 Vand. L. Rev. 608, 627–35 (1954); David E. Seidelson, *Jurisdiction of Federal Courts Hearing Federal Cases: An Examination of the Propriety of the Limitations Imposed by Venue Restrictions*, 37 Geo. Wash. L. Rev. 82, 84 (1968).

[79] *See* David P. Currie, *The Federal Courts and the American Law Institute* (pt. 2), 36 U. Chi. L. Rev. 268, 299–311 (1969).

[80] *See* 28 U.S.C. § 1391, discussed in § 6.02, *supra*.

canvassed under that doctrine.[81] Courts in Texas, for example, have taken this approach, finding themselves prohibited by statute from entertaining *forum non conveniens* motions and therefore importing *forum non conveniens* considerations into the law of personal jurisdiction.[82]

Another approach is to retain an assortment of access doctrines, but redefine their content to minimize overlap. This approach proposes a three-part inquiry: power (requiring only some contact with the forum), reasonableness (a constitutional due process requirement), and subconstitutional convenience (all other restrictions on geographic choice of forum, including the local action rule).[83] No system has yet adopted these approaches, and it remains to be seen whether any would respond more effectively to concerns treated by current law.

---

[81] Stein, note 41, *supra*, at 844–45.

[82] *See generally* Alex Wilson Albright, *In Personam Jurisdiction: A Confused and Inappropriate Substitute for Forum Non Conveniens*, 71 TEX. L. REV. 351 (1992).

[83] Clermont, note 76, *supra*, at 437–43.

Chapter 7

ASCERTAINING THE APPLICABLE LAW

§ 7.01 OVERVIEW

This chapter explores the duty of federal courts to ascertain and apply state law when deciding cases within their diversity jurisdiction.[1] The source of the obligation is the *Erie* doctrine,[2] which reads the federal Rules of Decision Act[3] to require use of state law when the difference between state and federal law might substantially affect the outcome of the case.

Section 7.02 of this chapter examines the origins of the *Erie* doctrine and the policies responsible for its creation that have contemporary significance. Section 7.03 considers subsequent developments in the doctrine and offers some suggestions for understanding and applying the various tests that have emerged from United States Supreme Court decisions. Section 7.04 looks at how federal courts have used the *Erie* doctrine to resolve tensions between the federal rules of procedure and state law.

To decide that *Erie* requires a federal diversity court to look to state rather than federal law may be only the first step toward decision. Difficult questions can also arise concerning which of the conflicting laws of two or more states should govern the case and concerning the content of state law. These questions are discussed in Sections 7.05 and 7.06, respectively.

Erie eliminated general federal common law, but left specific federal common law undisturbed in federal question cases. Section 7.07 examines when that law applies and how it is determined.

---

[1] General diversity jurisdiction exists for federal courts under 28 U.S.C. § 1332. For a discussion of federal diversity jurisdiction, see § 5.04, *supra*.

[2] *See Erie R.R. Co. v. Tompkins*, 304 U.S. 64 (1938), and its progeny, discussed *infra*.

[3] 28 U.S.C. § 1652:

> The laws of the several states, except where the Constitution or treaties of the United States or Acts of Congress otherwise require or provide, shall be regarded as rules of decision in civil actions in the courts of the United States, in cases where they apply.

§ 7.02   THE EVOLUTION FROM *SWIFT* TO *ERIE*[4]

[1]   *Swift v. Tyson*

The Supreme Court held in *Swift v. Tyson*,[5] a federal diversity case, that the Rules of Decision Act[6] did not require it to follow New York state judicial decisions concerning the law of negotiable instruments. Writing for the Court, Justice Story stated that, at least with regard to "contracts and other instruments of a commercial nature," federal diversity courts were free to follow their own best understanding of the "general principles and doctrines of commercial jurisprudence."[7] In such cases, said Justice Story, state judicial decisions to the contrary were not part of the "laws of the several states," as that term was used in the Rules of Decision Act. The Act's mandate that state laws be followed "as rules of decision" did not apply because the *Swift* Court regarded its application to be limited

> to state laws strictly *local*, that is to say, to the positive statutes of the state, and the construction thereof adopted by the local tribunals, and to rights and titles to things having a permanent locality . . . . It never has been supposed by us, that the section did apply, or was designed to apply, to questions of a more *general* nature.[8]

[2]   The Controversial Reign of the *Swift* Doctrine

Swift and the succeeding cases that made up the *Swift* doctrine permitted federal judges to displace state with federal common law simply because the federal court's diversity jurisdiction had been invoked. Law that federal judges made and applied under these circumstances came to be called *federal general common law*. At the time *Swift* was decided, assertion of this lawmaking authority does not seem to have been questioned.[9] During nearly a century when the *Swift* doctrine was in force, attitudes toward it changed and the doctrine became increasingly controversial. Two developments help explain this.

First, federal general common law expanded to rival state common law in a growing number of fields. The "general" and local categories created in *Swift* left many points of law unaccounted for, and usually it was the general law category into which the new problems were placed. Moreover, the Supreme

---

[4] For an extended version of this Section, see Gene R. Shreve, *From Swift to Erie: An Historical Perspective*, 82 MICH. L. REV. 869 (1984).

[5]   41 U.S. (16 Pet.) 1 (1842).

[6]   The statute was enacted as § 34 of the Judiciary Act of 1789. It has been amended in respects which do not bear on this discussion and now appears as 28 U.S.C. § 1652. Section 1652 is reproduced in § 7.01, *supra*.

[7]   41 U.S. at 19.

[8]   41 U.S. at 18 (emphasis added).

[9]   *See* TONY FREYER, HARMONY & DISSONANCE: THE *SWIFT* AND *ERIE* CASES IN AMERICAN FEDERALISM 36 (1981); GRANT GILMORE, THE AGES OF AMERICAN LAW 33–34 (1977).

Court increasingly tended to displace state law even within the sanctuary of "local" matters originally defined in *Swift*.[10]

Second, it became relatively easy for corporate litigants to gain access to a federal court by invoking its diversity jurisdiction. Corporations had grown enormously as a class of litigants since the time of *Swift*. They frequently found federal general common law more congenial than state common law.[11] Through tactical selection of the place of incorporation, a corporation was often able to forum shop — to ensure that suits by or against it would be litigated in a federal diversity court — which gave it the benefit of federal general common law. This was especially true after Congress enlarged the scope of general diversity jurisdiction and removal in 1875.[12]

The *Swift* doctrine was never without its champions, who hoped it would promote uniformity among state and federal courts. By the twentieth century, however, it drew strong criticism from the legal community. Many saw federal diversity courts as protectors of the monied, corporate interests. But at the heart of the problem was the more basic issue of federalism. Which sovereign should have authority to create rules of decision to govern federal diversity cases? Forceful arguments were made in Supreme Court dissents that only states had such authority.[13]

[3] *Erie R.R. Co. v. Tompkins*

The reign of *Swift* was finally brought to an end in 1938 by the Supreme Court's decision in *Erie Railroad Co. v. Tompkins*.[14] Plaintiff there sought to recover for injuries he received when struck by an object protruding from defendant's passing train. Plaintiff was on a path adjacent to the tracks at the time of the accident. The defendant railroad argued that the common law of Pennsylvania regarded the plaintiff as a trespasser under such circumstances and therefore imposed upon the defendant railroad only the duty to refrain from acts of wanton negligence. Plaintiff countered that the federal diversity court was free under *Swift* to disregard Pennsylvania judicial precedents and

---

[10] The most significant example was the withdrawal of state cases interpreting state statutes or constitutions from the preserve of "local" law created by *Swift*. *See Rowan v. Runnels*, 46 U.S. (5 How.) 134 (1847); *Watson v. Tarpley*, 59 U.S. (18 How.) 517 (1855); *Gelpcke v. City of Dubuque*, 68 U.S. (1 Wall) 175 (1863); *Burgess v. Seligman*, 107 U.S. 20 (1882). These cases are discussed in Robert H. Jackson, *The Rise and Fall of Swift v. Tyson*, 24 A.B.A.J. 609, 611–13 (1938).

[11] *See* James Willard Hurst, The Growth of American Law — The Law Makers 190 (1950); Alfred B. Teton, *The Story of Swift v. Tyson*, 35 Ill. L. Rev. 519, 529–30 (1941).

[12] Freyer, note 9, *supra*, at 55–56.

[13] *See, e.g., Black & White Taxicab & Transfer Co. v. Brown & Yellow Taxicab & Transfer Co.*, 276 U.S. 518 (1928) (dissenting opinion of Justices Holmes, Brandeis and Stone). For a survey of other attacks on the *Swift* doctrine by Supreme Court dissenters, *see* William R. Casto, *The Erie Doctrine and the Structure of Constitutional Revolutions*, 62 Tul. L. Rev. 907, 914–27 (1988); Shreve, note 4, *supra*, at 875 n.41.

[14] 304 U.S. 64. For an illuminating discussions of the facts and procedural history of *Erie*, see Irving Younger, *What Happened in Erie*, 56 Tex. L. Rev. 1011 (1978); and Edward A. Purcell, Jr., *Governing Law — The Story of Erie: How Litigants, Lawyers, Judges, Politics, and Social Change Reshape the Law, in* Civil Procedure Stories, Ch. 1 (Kevin M. Clermont ed., 2d ed. 2008).

to regard plaintiff as an invitee to whom defendant owed a duty of ordinary care under federal general common law.

When the case finally reached the United States Supreme Court, the Court ruled in favor of the defendant and, in so doing, overruled *Swift*'s interpretation of the Rules of Decision Act. Writing for the Court, Justice Brandeis stated:

> Except in matters governed by the Federal Constitution or by Acts of Congress, the law to be applied in any case is the law of the State. And whether the law of the State shall be declared by its Legislature in a statute or by its highest court in a decision is not a matter of federal concern. There is no federal general common law.[15]

Brandeis noted that the uniformity of law sought by the advocates of the *Swift* doctrine had not materialized. State courts continued to make and adhere to their own precedents, while federal diversity courts were free to disregard them. Moreover, Brandeis observed that *Swift* had actually produced three undesirable results. First, the inability of courts to draw a clear line between local and general law had led to considerable confusion. Second, *Swift* worked mischief by providing non-citizens the forum-shopping advantage of invoking diversity jurisdiction to evade state common law rules, when plaintiffs who shared the citizenship of their defendants could not.[16] Third and most important, *Swift* had eroded the states' legitimate authority to regulate their own affairs.[17]

---

[15] 304 U.S. at 78. Of course, Justice Brandeis did not suggest that federal courts should entirely give up making common law. "[T]he same justice the same day in another case pointed out that there may be questions of 'federal common law' upon which state statutes and decisions cannot be conclusive, such as the apportionment between two states of the water of an interstate stream." Charles E. Clark, *State Law in the Federal Courts: The Brooding Omnipresence of Erie v. Tompkins*, 55 YALE L.J. 267, 273 (1946) (*citing Hinderlider v. La Plata River and Cherry Creek Ditch Co.*, 304 U.S. 92, 110 (1938)). Federal common law is discussed in § 7.07, *infra*.

[16] In overruling *Swift*, *Erie* deprived litigants of their greatest gain from manipulating federal diversity jurisdiction — access to federal general common law. But *Erie* did not actually restrict the manipulation itself. Congress has since addressed the problem by barring the exercise of diversity jurisdiction when a party "has been improperly or collusively made or joined to invoke the jurisdiction of such court," 28 U.S.C.§ 1359, and by rendering jurisdictional manipulation through incorporation, *see* note 12 and accompanying text *supra*, more difficult by extending the citizenship of a corporation to the additional state, if any, "where it has its principal place of business." 28 U.S.C. § 1332(c). On developments in federal diversity jurisdiction generally, *see* § 5.04, *supra. See also* § 5.05 (corporate citizenship), *supra*.

[17] Brandeis suggested that *Swift* was simply wrong in reading the Rules of Decision Act to permit federal diversity courts to disregard state common law. He based this part of his attack on *Swift* upon Professor Charles Warren's research and argument that Justice Story had misconstrued the original purpose of the Rules of Decision Act. Charles Warren, *New Light on the History of the Federal Judiciary Act of 1789*, 37 HARV. L. REV. 49, 51–52, 81–88, 108 (1923). Brandeis's reliance upon this article was to cast a slight shadow over *Erie*, since Warren's methods and conclusions were, in time, roundly attacked. *See* the authorities cited in WRIGHT § 54; FREYER, note 9, *supra*, at 178 n.21. *Erie*'s authority was undamaged, however, because the principle of state lawmaking autonomy it vindicated rested upon a foundation broader than Warren's work. The principle was extended in decisions beginning with *Guaranty Trust Co. v. York*, 326 U.S. 99 (1945).

Erie was a momentous decision for several reasons. *Erie* not only overruled *Swift* and the long line of Supreme Court decisions adhering to it, it also invalidated hundreds — perhaps thousands — of federal general common law precedents in torts, commercial law and many other fields. In so doing, *Erie* repudiated the Court's prior settled interpretation of an act of Congress — something the Court does only with great reluctance.[18] This may explain why, despite the strong policy arguments for the result in *Erie* previously discussed, the Court found it necessary to further justify its decision by suggesting that the *Swift* doctrine was constitutionally suspect.[19] Finally, *Erie* worked a lasting change in the judicial arrangements of federalism. The case "announces no technical doctrine of procedure or jurisdiction but goes to the heart of the relations between the federal government and the states and returns to the states a power that had for nearly a century been exercised by the federal government."[20]

---

[18] *See, e.g.*, EDWARD H. LEVI, AN INTRODUCTION TO LEGAL REASONING 32 (1948).

[19] Writing of the *Swift* doctrine, Justice Brandeis stated: "If only a question of statutory construction were involved, we should not be prepared to abandon a doctrine so widely applied throughout nearly a century. But the unconstitutionality of the course pursued has now been made clear and compels us to do so." *Erie*, 304 U.S. at 77–78. Concurring separately, Justice Reed saw no need to raise a constitutional question in order to overrule *Swift*. 304 U.S. at 9092. The Supreme Court has not chosen since to clarify or refine *Erie*'s constitutional dimension beyond the cryptic observation that *Erie* "indicated that Congress does not have the constitutional authority to make the law that is applicable to controversies in diversity of citizenship cases." *Bernhardt v. Polygraphic Co. of Am., Inc.*, 350 U.S. 198, 202 (1956). *See generally* Bradford R. Clark, *Erie's Constitutional Source*, 95 CALIF. L. REV. 1289 (2007).

The matter has been much debated in the literature. A number of commentators have endorsed the suggestion in *Erie* that the Constitution required the result there. *See, e.g.*, Paul J. Mishkin, *Some Further Last Words on Erie — The Thread*, 87 HARV. L. REV. 1682 (1974); Henry J. Friendly, *In Praise of Erie — and of the New Common Law* 39 N.Y.U. L. REV. 383, 392–98 (1964); Henry M. Hart, Jr., *The Relations Between State and Federal Law*, 54 COLUM. L. REV. 489, 509–10 (1954); Herbert Wechsler, *Federal Jurisdiction and the Revision of the Judicial Code*, 13 LAW AND CONTEMP. PROBS. 216, 239 n.121 (1948); Note, *The Competence of Federal Courts to Formulate Rules of Decision*, 77 HARV. L. REV. 1084, 1086 (1964). *But see, e.g.*, Charles E. Clark, *State Law in the Federal Courts: The Brooding Omnipresence of Erie v. Tompkins*, 55 YALE L.J. 267, 278–79 (1946); Philip B. Kurland, *Mr. Justice Frankfurter, The Supreme Court and the Erie Doctrine in Diversity Cases*, 67 YALE L.J. 187, 197 (1957); *cf.* John H. Ely, *The Irrepressible Myth of Erie*, 87 HARV. L. REV. 693 (1974) (suggesting a less restrictive role for the Constitution and a commensurately greater range of options for Congress); American Law Institute, Study of the Division of Jurisdiction Between State and Federal Courts 442 (1969) ("[I]t does not necessarily follow that the *Erie* holding was constitutionally compelled in the technical sense of being legally imposed by the fundamental instrument.").

[20] WRIGHT § 55. This is part of a broader principle. "Today, in our post-*Erie* world, . . . law in American courts must be positivistically attributable to a relevant sovereign, a sovereign with a legitimate interest in governing the particular issue presented in the particular circumstances." Louise Weinberg, *Back to the Future: The New General Common Law*, 35 J. MAR. L. & COM. 523, 526 (2004).

Most commentators have supported *Erie*, but not all. *See, e.g.*, John B. Corr, *Thoughts on the Vitality of Erie*, 41 AM. U. L. REV. 1087 (1992) (suggesting that *Swift* was preferable to *Erie*). *Cf.* Patrick J. Borchers, *The Origins of Diversity Jurisdiction, The Rise of Legal Positivism, and a Brave New World for Erie and Klaxon*, 72 TEX. L. REV. 79 (1993) (questioning the continued desirability of *Erie*).

Some of the implications of this power shift are still being worked out by the courts, and the resulting *Erie* doctrine questions will be the subject of the sections that follow.

§ 7.03 TESTS FOR APPLYING *ERIE*

[1]   The Substance-Versus-Procedure Test and Its Criticism in *York*

The choice between state and federal common law in *Erie* involved competing standards of duty in tort law — what was then and is now understood to be substantive law.[21] It was never doubted that substantive law was most directly and obviously contemplated by the term "rules of decision" in the Rules of Decision Act. Therefore, once the Supreme Court reached the conclusion that the Act extended to state common law, *Erie* was easy to decide.

Subsequent litigants, however, were not content to confine their state law arguments under *Erie* to matters of torts or contracts. They argued that conflicting federal law must give way to local state law not only to determine the content of rights, but also to decide how and under what circumstances rights would be vindicated. These questions, which concern the processes by which the claims of rights are examined, are resolved according to a body of law often regarded as *procedural* rather than substantive in character.[22]

Those wishing to check the expansion of *Erie* attempted to use the distinction between substance and procedure as a dividing line. Under a substance-versus-procedure test, matters characterized as substantive would be governed by state law, and those characterized as procedural would be governed by federal law.[23] With the Supreme Court's decision in *Guaranty Trust Co. v. York*,[24] however, it became clear that this test would not be adequate to resolve all issues arising under the Rules of Decision Act.

Plaintiff in *York* brought a class action alleging that defendant breached its fiduciary duty as trustee in a corporate financing transaction. *Erie* left no doubt that the scope of defendant's fiduciary duty to plaintiff was to be

---

[21] *Swift* and virtually all intervening cases had, in the same sense, also involved substantive law. *See, e.g., Black & White Taxicab & Transfer Co. v. Brown & Yellow Taxicab & Transfer Co.*, 276 U.S. 518 (1928) (a federal diversity action in which a contract, unenforceable under Kentucky state common law, was enforced under federal general common law).

[22] *See* § 1.01[2] (substance and procedure), *supra*.

[23] Concurring in *Erie*, Justice Reed had said, "[n]o one doubts federal power over procedure." 304 U.S. at 92. The institution most obviously empowered to make federal procedural law is Congress. *Cf.* Riyaz A. Kanji, Note, *The Proper Scope of Pendent Appellate Jurisdiction in the Collateral Order Context*, 100 YALE L.J. 511, 522 (1990) ("Congress' Article III power to create the lower federal courts enables it to organize their operations as it sees fit."). When no statute interferes with their power to do so, federal courts may also make federal procedural law. For examples, see *Byrd v. Blue Ridge Rural Elec. Coop., Inc.*, 356 U.S. 525 (1958); *Chambers v. NASCO, Inc.*, 501 U.S. 32 (1991).

[24] 326 U.S. 99 (1945). For extended discussion of *York*, see Philip B. Kurland, *Mr. Justice Frankfurter, the Supreme Court and the Erie Doctrine in Diversity Cases*, 67 YALE L.J. 187 (1957).

determined under New York state law. Defendant urged, however, that *Erie* also required application of the state statute of limitations, which barred the action.[25] Plaintiff countered that the limitations question was instead governed by federal law. The Court sided with the defendant and, in a majority opinion written by Justice Frankfurter, held *Erie* to be fully applicable. Justice Frankfurter did not, however, adopt the defendant's argument that *Erie* was applicable because the limitations issue in *York* was substantive in character. He found the substance-versus-procedure test inadequate to explain the result in the case, observing that " 'substance' and 'procedure' are the same key-words to very different problems . . . . Each implies different variables depending upon the particular problem for which it is used."[26]

[2]   The Outcome-Determination Test

In *York*, Justice Frankfurter read *Erie* to provide a different test. He wrote:

> In essence, the intent of that decision was to insure that, in all cases where a federal court is exercising jurisdiction solely because of the diversity of citizenship of the parties, the outcome of the litigation in the federal court should be substantially the same, so far as legal rules determine the outcome of a litigation, as it would be if tried in a State court.[27]

This came to be regarded as the *outcome-determination* test. Under it, state rules controlled if the choice between state or federal law could be outcome-determinative in the case.

Clearly, the *York* decision carried the rule of *Erie* well beyond the facts of the *Erie* case. But just how far? One commentator observed that "to such a principle there is no apparent stopping place."[28] In three cases decided after *York*, the Supreme Court indeed seemed unable to find a stopping place in applying the outcome-determination test. These cases seemed to suggest that federal law could not be employed to decide questions of *procedure*[29] in diversity cases if state law conflicted and the choice could possibly affect the outcome. Some lower federal courts so applied the outcome-determination test during the nine years before the Supreme Court again addressed the subject. Then, in *Byrd v. Blue Ridge Rural Electric Cooperative, Inc.*,[30] the Supreme Court relaxed the test.

---

[25] On statutes of limitation generally, see § 8.08[2][b], *infra*.

[26] 326 U.S. at 108.

[27] 326 U.S. at 109.

[28] *Wright* § 59.

[29] *Ragan v. Merchants Transfer & Warehouse Co.*, 337 U.S. 530 (1949) (time of commencement for purpose of tolling limitations); *Cohen v. Beneficial Indus. Loan Corp.*, 337 U.S. 541 (1949) (whether plaintiff must post security-for-expenses bond); *Woods v. Interstate Realty Co.*, 337 U.S. 535 (1949) (whether corporate plaintiff must meet state business qualification requirement in order to sue). *Ragan* and *Cohen* are discussed in § 7.04, *infra*.

[30] 356 U.S. 525 (1958).

[3]   *Byrd* and the Assessment of State and Federal Interests

The plaintiff in *Byrd* brought a federal diversity action for negligence, alleging injury while working on defendant's power line. The defendant argued that the work undertaken by plaintiff was the same as that done by defendant's own employees; therefore, plaintiff's only remedy was under the South Carolina worker's compensation act. Plaintiff contended that his work was not sufficiently like that of defendant's employees to satisfy the statute and sought a jury trial of this and other factual issues. Had plaintiff sued in South Carolina state court, a jury trial would not have been available on the statutory coverage issue. The defendant argued that the *Erie* doctrine operated to bar a federal jury trial as well.

The Supreme Court held that the plaintiff was entitled to a jury trial, notwithstanding the possibility "that in the instant personal-injury case the outcome would be substantially affected by whether the issue . . . is decided by a judge or a jury."[31] The Court did not repudiate the outcome-determination test, but made clear that outcome determination would not settle the *Erie* question in all cases.

Byrd added a new mode of analysis: an assessment of governmental interests behind the rules contending for application. The Court concluded that important policies supporting the federal jury rule would be sacrificed if plaintiff could not claim a jury in *Byrd*, but that it was far from clear that policies accounting for the South Carolina rule would be offended if plaintiff got his jury trial. Thus, it might be said that only the federal government was demonstrably interested in the application of its rule.

Byrd is the most perplexing of the *Erie* doctrine cases, in part because of the innate difficulty of interest-balancing analysis[32] and in part because portions of the Court's opinion in *Byrd* are not altogether clear. To begin with, the Court did not say that plaintiff had a constitutional right to a federal jury trial under the Seventh Amendment.[33] Rather, it favored plaintiff because neither the outcome-determination implication of the case nor the policy force behind South Carolina's rule against jury trials was sufficient to displace "[a]n essential characteristic of the [federal court system:] . . . the manner in which . . . it distributes trial functions between judge and jury . . . ."[34] Given the Supreme Court's approach in *Byrd*, the result might have been

---

[31] 356 U.S. at 537.

[32] *See* Joseph P. Bauer, *The Erie Doctrine Revisited: How a Conflicts Perspective Can Aid the Analysis*, 74 NOTRE DAME L. REV. 1235, 1281–99 (1999) (suggesting refinements in interest balancing).

[33] "Our conclusion makes unnecessary the consideration of — and we intimate no view upon — the constitutional question whether the right of jury trial protected in federal courts by the Seventh Amendment embraces the factual issue . . . here . . . ." 356 U.S. at 537 n.10. If the Court had found that plaintiff had a Seventh Amendment right to a jury trial, the *Erie* issue would not have arisen because the Constitution would control. For a discussion of the Seventh Amendment right to jury trials in federal court, see § 12.07[1], *infra*.

[34] 356 U.S. at 537.

different if the policy interests of the federal courts had been weaker, or those of South Carolina stronger.[35] *Byrd* shortened the reach of *York*'s outcome-determination test. At least in close cases, *Erie* questions were to be answered by assessing the state and federal interests behind the laws vying for application.

[4] *Hanna* and the Modified Outcome-Determination Test

The Supreme Court completed its modification of the outcome-determination test in *Hanna v. Plumer*.[36] The plaintiff there suffered personal injuries in an automobile accident and brought a federal diversity action against the estate of the alleged wrongdoer. The administrator of the estate was served by leaving a copy of the papers at his home in compliance with what was then federal Rule (4)(d)(1). The defendant-administrator argued, however, that the action could not be maintained because he had not been personally served as required by Massachusetts law. The Supreme Court rejected this argument and held service under Rule 4(d)(1) adequate.

The *Hanna* Court dismissed defendant's outcome-determination argument as too literal-minded. Granted, once the lawsuit was filed, plaintiff would lose if the state rule applied, while the litigation would continue if the federal rule applied. "[I]n this sense," observed the Court, "*every* procedural variation is 'outcome determinative.' "[37] The Court made clear, however, that such differences alone were insignificant. The real question was

> whether application of the [state] rule would make so important a difference to the character or result of the litigation that failure to enforce it would unfairly discriminate against citizens of the forum state, or whether application of the rule would have so important an effect upon the fortunes of one or both of the litigants that failure to enforce it would be likely to cause a plaintiff to choose the federal court.[38]

Applying this more subdued version of the outcome determination test, the *Hanna* Court found the difference between the state and federal rules to be too insubstantial to raise the danger of inequitable administration of law posed in *Erie*.

---

[35] The Court indicated in *Byrd* that no strong state policy would be sacrificed by refusal to follow the South Carolina rule in a federal diversity case. *Id.* at 535–36.

[36] 380 U.S. 460 (1965).

[37] 380 U.S. at 468 (emphasis in original).

[38] 380 U.S. at 468 n.9. The Court reiterated these points in *Chambers v. NASCO, Inc.*, 501 U.S. 32, 52 (1991). Note, however, that the *Erie* doctrine will require choice of the state rule in some cases where plaintiff does not appear to have shopped for the federal rule. The Court subsequently held a federal diversity court to a state law definition of "commencement" of suit, even though there was "no indication that when petitioner filed his suit in federal court he had any reason to believe that he would be unable to comply with the service requirements of Oklahoma law or that he chose to sue in federal court in an attempt to avoid those service requirements." *Walker v. Armco Steel Corp.*, 446 U.S. 740, 753 n.15 (1980). *Walker* is discussed more fully in § 7.04, *infra*.

[5]   Later *Erie* Issues

A subsequent issue involving *Erie* has been whether federal diversity courts will enforce state statutory requirements that certain claims must be submitted in the first instance to state administrative tribunals. After some initial resistance,[39] several federal courts have concluded that *Erie* requires the enforcement of such provisions.

Typical of these cases is the First Circuit's decision in *Feinstein v. Massachusetts General Hospital.*[40] The plaintiff sued defendant hospital for medical malpractice, invoking the federal court's diversity jurisdiction. Defendant moved to refer plaintiff's claim to a medical malpractice panel appointed under a Massachusetts statute. The purpose of the panel was to screen malpractice claims, reviewing plaintiff's proof by a standard similar to that used for directed verdicts.[41] If the panel found for defendant, plaintiff was to post a bond payable to defendant in the event plaintiff did not prevail at trial. The plaintiff conceded that the statute would have applied had he filed his malpractice case in Massachusetts state court, but argued that it was without effect in federal proceedings.

The First Circuit, however, agreed with defendant that *Erie* required that the Massachusetts statute be followed. The Court observed that "[t]he statute's referral procedure and associated provisions were designed to serve . . . substantive policy objectives . . . ."[42]

The approach taken in *Feinstein* has been viewed sympathetically.[43] At least part of the motivation for state creation of administrative panel prerequisites is to reduce the size and incidence of recoveries obtained through either trial or settlement, and some plaintiffs may have shopped for a federal forum in order to avoid this consequence. State statutes establishing administrative prerequisites to suit are somewhat analogous to state "door-closing" rules which operate to prevent certain types of cases from being heard altogether. The *Feinstein* approach thus may draw support from the fact that the Supreme Court has interpreted the *Erie* doctrine to mean that state door-closing doctrine bars federal diversity litigation.[44]

---

[39] *See Wheeler v. Shoemaker*, 78 F.R.D. 218 (D.R.I. 1978) (denying defendant's motion to refer plaintiff's claim to a state malpractice panel).

[40] 643 F.2d 880 (1st Cir. 1981). *See also DiAntonio v. Northampton-Accomack Mem'l Hosp.*, 628 F.2d 287 (4th Cir. 1980); *Hines v. Elkhart Gen. Hosp.*, 603 F.2d 646 (7th Cir. 1979).

[41] *See generally* § 12.09[1] (directed verdicts and judgments n.o.v.), *infra*.

[42] *Feinstein*, 643 F.2d at 885. The Court described the objectives as "providing for a prompt determination of the likely merits of a claim and requiring that a plaintiff who is unsuccessful before the malpractice tribunal post a bond" if he wishes to continue suit. Therefore, stated the Court, "[i]n the absence of any overriding federal interest in not applying the statute . . . we conclude that the Rules of Decision Act requires that federal courts to apply the state rules at issue here." 643 F.2d at 885.

[43] Vincent C. Alexander, *State Medical Malpractice Screening Panels in Federal Diversity Actions*, 21 Ariz. L. Rev. 959 (1979).

[44] *Angel v. Bullington*, 330 U.S. 183 (1947). "[D]iversity jurisdiction must follow State law and policy. A federal court in North Carolina, when invoked on grounds of diversity of citizenship,

At the same time, to graft administrative referrals (or other satellite procedures contemplated by state litigation) onto federal cases creates "significant burdens on the parties and on the federal courts" in diversity litigation "of a sort inconsistent with the concept of those courts as an independently functioning judicial system."[45] Until federal courts are willing to view this concern as overriding, however, *Byrd*'s interest assessment test is unlikely to lead to a refusal to honor state administrative law in medical malpractice cases.

In *Gasperini v. Center for Humanities, Inc.*,[46] the United States Supreme Court invoked the Rules of Decision Act to require use of a state-law standard to determine whether a verdict was so excessive as to warrant a new federal trial under Rule 59(a)(1).[47] That provision authorizes a new trial "for any reason for which a new trial has heretofore been granted in an action at law in federal court." The Rule does not offer a test for determining when new trial orders (or conditional new trial orders)[48] are warranted in response to excessive jury verdicts, and federal courts have often applied a "shocks the conscience" test.[49] But defendant in *Gasperini* invoked the more favorable New York state law standard permitting court intervention whenever the verdict "deviates materially from what would be reasonable compensation."[50]

---

cannot give that which North Carolina has withheld." *Angel*, 330 U.S. at 192. Despite the breadth of this language, the reach of Angel is limited in at least two respects. First, the constitutionality of a state closing its doors to particular litigation may be open to question. RUSSELL J WEINTRAUB, COMMENTARY ON THE CONFLICT OF LAWS § 10.6B (4th ed. 2001). Naturally, if a state court could not constitutionally close its doors to a lawsuit, *Erie* cannot require a federal diversity court to do so. Second, the door-closing rule must reflect state substantive rather than procedural policies. If, for example, the state door-closing rule rests on a concern of *forum non conveniens, see* § 6.02[1], *supra, Erie* should impose no obligation on a federal diversity court to follow it. WEINTRAUB, at 576. *Stewart Org., Inc. v. Ricoh Corp.*, 810 F.2d 1066 (11th Cir. 1987), *aff'd* 487 U.S. 22 (1988), presents the converse situation where Alabama law opens its courts to suit, notwithstanding an agreement between the parties to confine suit to New York. The Eleventh Circuit invokes a federal law principle to honor the agreement.

[45] PAUL M. BATOR, PAUL J. MISHKIN, DAVID L. SHAPIRO, & HERBERT WECHSLER, THE FEDERAL COURTS AND THE FEDERAL SYSTEM 171 (2d ed. 1981 supplement).

A similar issue is whether a federal diversity judge must defer to a state arbitration award when a state court would have been required to do so. *See Towey v. Catling*, 743 F. Supp. 738, 740 (D. Hawaii 1990) (following state law to enforce an arbitration award, because that law was "an integral, substantive part of state policy . . . "). *Towey* is featured in John S. Mackey, Note, *Enforcement of State Annexed-arbitration Rules in Federal Courts with Diversity Jurisdiction*, 1991 J. DISP. RESOL. 397.

[46] 518 U.S. 415 (1996).

[47] *See* § 12.09, *infra* (new trial motions).

[48] That is, when the trial judge grants the motion for new trial unless the opposing party agrees to a reduction (remittitur) of the verdict. *See* § 12.09(2)(b), *infra*.

[49] *E.g., Abrams v. Lightolier*, 841 F. Supp. 584 (D.N.J. 1994). For additional cases, see WRIGHT & MILLER § 2807 n.7.

[50] N.Y. CIV. PRAC. L. & R. § 5501(c).

Once it ruled that Rule 59 did not govern the issue,[51] the Supreme Court was able to turn to the question whether application of the state court "deviates materially" standard was required by the Rules of Decision Act. The Court concluded that it was, because New York's "objective is manifestly substantive."[52] Apart from this observation, the majority's opinion in *Gasperini* is not terribly clear. One commentator has observed: "It is possible that *Gasperini* employs an overarching RDA [Rules of Decision Act] approach similar to that embraced in *Byrd*. But such an interpretation is more the result of the reader's speculation than the Court's explanation."[53]

[6]   Analytical Summary: Three Contemporary Tests Under the *Erie* Doctrine

Byrd's interest-dominated inquiry is analytic labor of the most demanding sort. It requires a determination of the nature and force of state and federal policies that might be implicated in the case. Often, only the policy (or policies) supporting one of the two rules will actually be at stake in the outcome. Then only the source (federal or state) providing that rule is really interested in having its law applied. This level of interest analysis may be sufficient to account for most or all of the Court's actual work under the *Byrd* branch of the *Erie* doctrine.[54] There is, however, the specter of cases even more taxing, those where *both* a state and the federal government would be interested in having their conflicting rules applied.[55]

---

[51] Had Rule 59 itself provided the federal-law standard, any conflicting state law would have given way as a result of Rules Enabling Act analysis. *See* § 7.04, *infra*.

[52] 518 U.S. at 429.

[53] Richard D. Freer, *Some Thoughts on The State of Erie After Gasperini*, 76 Tex. L. Rev. 1637, 1641 (1998). *See also* Thomas D. Rowe, Jr., *Not Bad for Government Work: Does Anyone Else Think the Supreme Court is Doing a Halfway Decent Job in its Erie-Hanna Jurisprudence?*, 73 Notre Dame L. Rev. 963 (1998); C. Douglas Floyd, *Erie Awry: A Comment on Gasperini v. Center for Humanities, Inc*, 1997 BYU L. Rev. 267. A recent appraisal of *Gasperini* and other *Erie* doctrine cases appears in Earl C. Dudley, Jr. & George Rutherglen, *Deforming the Federal Rules: An Essay on What's Wrong With the Recent Erie Decisions*, 92 Va. L. Rev. 707 (2006).

[54] The opposing results in two cases illustrate the point. The Supreme Court seemed to question in *Byrd* whether South Carolina was much if at all interested in application of its no-jury rule. Since the interests behind the federal jury rule were strongly implicated by the case (*see* § 7.03[3], note 13 and related text, *supra*), *Byrd* directed choice of the federal rule. In *Walker v. Armco Steel Corp.*, 446 U.S. 740 (1980), the situation was reversed and the Supreme Court therefore applied state law. Policies behind the Oklahoma state statute of limitations were at stake in the case and no federal interest supported a refusal to treat the action as time-barred. The Court concluded:

> There is simply no reason why . . . an action based on state law which concededly would be barred in the state courts by the state statute of limitations should proceed through litigation to judgment in federal court solely because of the fortuity that there is diversity of citizenship between litigants. The policies underlying diversity jurisdiction do not support such a distinction between state and federal plaintiffs, and *Erie* and its progeny do not permit it.

Walker, 446 U.S. at 753.

[55] Difficulties in determining whether law sources are interested and, if two or more are, which law to choose, are also at the center of modern choice-of-law analysis. Gene R. Shreve, *Conflicts Law – State or Federal?*, 68 Ind. L.J. 907 (1993); Eugene F. Scoles, Peter Hay, Patrick J. Borchers

Yet it would exaggerate the difficulty of the *Erie* doctrine to assume that the *Byrd* test need be applied in every case. Actually, all three tests that we have considered — substance-versus-procedure, modified outcome-determination, and the assessment of state and federal interests — have some role in contemporary analysis. It is only those cases that cannot be decided by one of the first two tests that require resort to *Byrd*-type interest assessment.

The substance-versus-procedure test serves as a first-stage screening device in modern *Erie* analysis. It is true that the words of the test still carry a stigma from their unsympathetic reception in *York*.[56] It is also true that the closer the *Erie* question, the more unreliable the substance-versus-procedure distinction becomes. For all that, however, the difference between substance and procedure, between the body of "rules which define legal rights" and rules "structuring and regulating the judicial process"[57] retains importance under the Rules of Decision Act.[58] In many cases, application of the distinction is all that will be necessary to resolve the *Erie* issue.[59]

Some cases eluding treatment under a substance-versus-procedure test will be appropriate for decision under the modified outcome-determination test. This test will suffice for statute of limitations problems, as in *York*, where the state law is not grounded entirely on substantive or procedural policies but instead derives from both.[60] Absent compelling circumstances for applying the federal rule, the modified outcome-determination test should advance state law when that law serves substantive interests at least in part. The *Byrd* interest assessment test is available as a last resort, when state substantive policies become more difficult to discern, or when policies supporting federal law approach overriding importance.

& SYMEON C. SYMEONIDES, CONFLICT OF LAWS ch. 3 (4th ed. 2004); Gene R. Shreve, *Teaching Conflicts, Improving the Odds*, 90 MICH. L. REV. 1672, 1673–75 (1992). The main difference between mainstream choice-of-law cases and those under the *Erie* doctrine is that sovereigns providing conflicting laws in the former are roughly co-equal, *e.g.*, a conflict between New York and Colorado. Yet the parallel is stronger than one might think. A federal diversity judge using *Byrd*'s interest analysis might give federal law the nod when both federal and state sources are interested; similarly, state judges are free under the Constitution to favor their own law over that of a sister state when both states are interested. *See* Louise Weinberg, *Choice of Law and Minimal Scrutiny*, 49 U. CHI. L. REV. 440 (1982); Gene R. Shreve, *Interest Analysis as Constitutional Law*, 48 OHIO ST. L.J. 51 (1987).

[56] *See* § 7.03[1], *supra*.

[57] Note, *The Law Applied in Diversity Cases: The Rules of Decision Act and the Erie Doctrine*, 85 YALE L.J. 678, 696 (1976).

[58] The substance-procedure distinction continues to command attention in commentary on the *Erie* doctrine. *E.g.*, Allan R. Stein, *Erie and Court Access*, 100 YALE L.J. 1935, 1942–46 (1991); Richard D. Freer, *Erie's Mid-Life Crisis*, 63 TUL. L.REV. 1087, 1131–34 (1989); Gregory Gelfand & Howard B. Abrams, *Putting Erie on the Right Track*, 49 U. PITT. L. REV. 937, 958–64 (1988).

[59] For example, in *Stineman v. Fontbonne College*, 664 F.2d 1082 (8th Cir. 1981), the Eighth Circuit held that a federal diversity judge was required to follow state law to decide whether damages in a tort action were excessive, but was not required to follow state law requiring that instructions be given to the jury in writing. The first issue was clearly substantive, and the second clearly procedural.

[60] *Cf. Walker v. Armco Steel Corp.*, 446 U.S. 740, 751 (1980) (referring to Oklahoma law defining its statute of limitation as "a statement of a substantive decision by that State").

Functionally, the three tests can be linked as follows. Substance-versus-procedure marked the initial boundaries of the *Erie* doctrine and remains an easy and useful means for demonstrating why law made possible through exercise of federal diversity jurisdiction cannot displace state law created to advance substantive interests. The modified outcome-determination test recognizes that a state law which is both substantive and procedural in purpose should be honored under *Erie* whenever possible because of its substantive dimension. *Byrd*'s interest assessment test requires more precise calibration of the substantive state interests and the procedural federal interests underlying the competing rules. It can lead (as in *Byrd*) to nullification of the result of the outcome-determination test and application of federal law.

It is useful to remember that, for all their quirks, the cases making up the *Erie* doctrine have never strayed far from the notions of reason and justice central to *Erie* itself. When a federal diversity judge makes victory possible for a plaintiff who could not have won in state court, that judge must be saying to the defendant: "You lost because you and the plaintiff live in different states." That is an unacceptable reason for choosing winners and losers in our legal system. It is unacceptable because it is substantively grotesque to use the accident of diversity to shrink or swell rights, because it blocks the legitimate efforts of states to regulate local conduct through substantive laws, and because forum shopping would exacerbate these evils and hold federal courts up to ridicule.

§ 7.04   STATE LAW VERSUS THE FEDERAL RULES OF CIVIL PROCEDURE — THE IMPORTANCE OF THE RULES ENABLING ACT

[1]   Early Uncertainty

The Federal Rules of Civil Procedure were promulgated in 1938, the same year in which *Erie* was decided. The new rules promised sweeping reforms.[61] The emerging *Erie* doctrine, however, was to cast a shadow over their operation in diversity cases.

York and the outcome-determination cases which followed it appeared to suggest that state law controlled whenever the outcome of a diversity case might conceivably be affected by the choice of state, as opposed to federal law.[62] In two post-*York* cases, the Supreme Court invoked the outcome-determination test in refusing to apply a Federal Rule of Civil Procedure. In

---

[61] On the effect of the Federal Rules of Civil Procedure on existing practice, see WRIGHT § 62; Robert G. Bone, *Mapping the Boundaries of a Dispute: Conceptions of Ideal Lawsuit Structure From the Field Code to the Federal Rules*, 89 COLUM. L. REV. 1 (1989); Stephen N. Subrin, *How Equity Conquered Common Law: The Federal Rules of Civil Procedure in Historical Perspective*, 135 U. PA. L. REV. 909 (1987). For contemporary assessments of the Rules, see Symposium, *The 50th Anniversary of the Federal Rules of Civil Procedure, 1938–1988*, 137 U. PA. L. REV. 1874 (1989); Symposium, *The Fiftieth Anniversary of the Federal Rules of Civil Procedure*, 63 NOTRE DAME L. REV. 597 (1988).

[62] *See* § 7.03[2], *supra*.

Ragan v. Merchants Transfer & Warehouse Co.,[63] the Court used the Kansas rule that suit commenced with service of process to conclude that plaintiff failed to sue within the time permitted by Kansas' statute of limitations. Plaintiff unsuccessfully argued that the definition of commencement contained in Federal Rule 3 should govern.[64] In *Cohen v. Beneficial Indus. Loan Corp.*,[65] the Supreme Court imposed a New Jersey requirement that plaintiff in a stockholder's derivative suit must post a bond. The Court rejected plaintiff's argument that federal Rule 23.1, which did not require a bond, should govern.

These cases led many observers to fear that the Federal Rules of Civil Procedure would be thwarted in diversity cases, unless they coincided with state law. The Supreme Court eventually put these fears to rest in *Hanna v. Plumer*.[66]

[2] *Hanna, Walker* and *Woods*: The Resilience of Federal Rules of Procedure

Hanna seems to rest on alternative holdings. We have already seen how the first holding, that *Erie* did not require the application of state law, was notable because it softened the outcome-determination test.[67]

The second holding, that *Erie* did not even apply, bolstered the authority of the Federal Rules of Civil Procedure in diversity cases. The Supreme Court called "incorrect" the "assumption that the rule of *Erie* constitutes the appropriate test of the validity and therefore the applicability of a Federal Rule of Civil Procedure."[68] The *Hanna* Court found what was then Rule 4(d)(1) to be valid because it "neither exceeded the congressional mandate embodied in the Rules Enabling Act[69] nor transgressed constitutional bounds."[70] Since the rule answered the service question in *Hanna*, Massachusetts state law had to give way.

The majority did not fully explain its reasoning, but the message conveyed by the Court's opinion in *Hanna* was clear. When challenged under *Erie*, federal rules of procedure were to receive different and more protective treatment than that given to federal doctrine. The Court stated that the constitutional authority to make a federal court system, augmented by the Necessary and Proper Clause of the United States Constitution,

---

[63] 337 U.S. 530 (1949).

[64] Rule 3 states that "[a] civil action is commenced by filing a complaint with the court." Plaintiff filed his action within the applicable limitations period, but served the complaint after it had run. Regarding statutes of limitations generally, see § 8.02[2][b], *infra*.

[65] 337 U.S. 541 (1949).

[66] 380 U.S. 460 (1965). *See generally* John C. McCoid, II, *Hanna v. Plumer: The Erie Doctrine Changes Shape*, 51 VA. L. REV. 884 (1965).

[67] *See* § 7.03[4], *supra*.

[68] 380 U.S. at 469–70.

[69] 28 U.S.C. § 2072. On the process of rule creation and revision under the Rules Enabling Act, see note 104, *infra*, and § 1.02, *supra*.

[70] 380 U.S. at 464.

carries with it congressional power to make rules governing the practice and pleading in those courts, which in turn includes a power to regulate matters which, though falling within the uncertain area between substance and procedure, are rationally capable of classification as either.[71]

Compared to the "relatively unguided *Erie* choice"[72] used when neither a federal statute nor rule of procedure is involved, the approach of the majority in *Hanna* seemed simple and direct. So long as it is constitutional and complies with the Rules Enabling Act, the Federal Rule of Civil Procedure controls.[73]

In 1980, the Supreme Court again considered whether state law or a Federal Rule of Civil Procedure should apply in a diversity case, this time deciding in favor of state law. In *Walker v. Armco Steel Corp.*,[74] plaintiff sued for injuries he received while using defendant's product. Relying on the definition of commencement found in federal Rule 3, plaintiff argued that he had filed suit within the Oklahoma statute of limitations. The defendant argued that *Erie* required the court to follow the Oklahoma law defining commencement as service of process, and that service of process had not been made within the limitations period. The defendant relied on the Court's decision in *Ragan v. Merchant's Transfer & Warehouse Co.*[75] While *Ragan* appeared indistinguishable, plaintiff's argument proceeded on the assumption — shared by many observers — that *Ragan* had been weakened, if not overruled, by *Hanna v. Plumer.*

The Supreme Court did not agree. It refused to apply the Rules Enabling Act approach it announced in *Hanna* because it found "no direct conflict between the Federal Rule and the state law."[76] For there to be a conflict, refusal to apply Rule 3 would have to thwart some purpose the federal rule was intended to achieve. This did not happen in *Walker*, since "Rule 3 governs the date from which various timing requirements of the Federal Rules begin to run,[77] but does not affect state statutes of limitations."[78]

Walker is a useful reminder that favored treatment for federal procedural rules under the Rules Enabling Act is only appropriate *when the rules apply*. Because Rule 3 did not bear on the case, "the *Hanna* analysis does not apply.

---

[71] 380 U.S. at 472.

[72] 380 U.S. at 471.

[73] 28 U.S.C. § 2072. For extended discussion of developments under the Act, see Karen N. Moore, *The Supreme Court's Role in Interpreting the Federal Rules of Civil Procedure*, 44 Hast. L.J. 1039, 1041–53 (1993); Stephen B. Burbank, *The Rules Enabling Act of 1934*, 130 U. Pa. L. Rev. 1015 (1982).

[74] 446 U.S. 740 (1980).

[75] *See* note 63 and accompanying text, *supra*.

[76] *Walker*, 446 U.S. at 752. But Rule 3 probably would be used to measure commencement within the running of the statute of limitations had the case rested on the court's federal question jurisdiction. *See Henderson v. United States*, 517 U.S. 654, 657 (1990).

[77] The Court presumably had in mind the use of Rule 3's definition of commencement for timing requirements contained in such rules as 13(a), 14(a), 30(a), 31(a) and 33(a).

[78] *Walker*, 446 U.S. at 751.

Instead, the policies behind *Erie* . . . control the issue . . . ."[79] This permitted the substantive purpose behind Oklahoma's definition of commencement to become more of a factor in the decision.[80] The choice of Oklahoma law became clear once *Erie* and the Rules of Decision Act came into play.[81]

> There is simply no reason why, in the absence of a controlling
> federal rule, an action based on state law which concededly would be
> barred in the state courts by the state statute of limitations should
> proceed through litigation to judgment in federal court solely because
> of the fortuity that there is diversity of citizenship between the
> litigants.[82]

The case settled the question whether Rule 3 has any effect on state statute of limitations questions.[83]

Although *Walker* applied state law, it accepted the principle announced in *Hanna* that validly enacted and properly applied Federal Rules of Civil Procedure control. This raises the possibility that, no matter how substantive applicable state law may be in such cases, the *Erie* doctrine offers it no protection.

The Supreme Court did nothing to negate this suggestion in a later decision, *Burlington Northern Railroad v. Woods*.[84] *Woods* presented the Court with a choice between Federal Rule of Appellate Procedure 38 (giving federal courts of appeal discretion to award damages for frivolous appeals) and Alabama state law (making damages in such cases mandatory). Unlike *Walker*, the Court found the federal rule applicable. Faced with a "direct collision" between the federal and state rules, the *Woods* Court returned to the two-part test it used in *Hanna*. Because the issue before the court was within the scope of Federal Rule 38, that rule "must . . . be applied if it represents a valid exercise of

---

[79]　446 U.S. at 752.

[80]　The Court noted that "the Oklahoma statute is a statement of a substantive decision by that State that actual service on, and accordingly actual notice by, the defendant is an integral part of the several policies served by the statute of limitations." *Id.* at 751. It read Oklahoma law to have substantially the same statute-of-limitations effect as Kansas law did in *Ragan*; therefore, *Walker* followed *Ragan* in holding plaintiff's claim to be time-barred.

[81]　For more on the relationship between the Rules of Decision Act and the Rules Enabling Act, see § 7.04[3][b], *infra*.

[82]　446 U.S. at 753.

[83]　*See, e.g., Cambridge Mut. Fire Ins. Co. v. City of Claxton*, 720 F.2d 1230 (11th Cir. 1983) (use of Rule 3 to enlarge the Georgia statute of limitations refused upon the authority of *Walker*). Applications of the *Walker* case are confined to exercises of federal diversity jurisdiction. When plaintiff's claim is based on federal law, "the action is not barred if it has been 'commenced' in compliance with Rule 3 within the . . . [limitations] period." *West v. CONRAIL*, 481 U.S. 35, 39 (1987).

[84]　480 U.S. 1 (1987). For discussions of the case, see Ralph U. Whitten, *Erie and the Federal Rules: A Review and Reappraisal After Burlington Northern Railroad v. Woods*, 21 Creighton L. Rev. 1 (1987); Kurt M. Saunders, *Plying the Erie Waters: Choice of Law in the Deterrence of Frivolous Appeals*, 21 Ga. L. Rev. 653 (1987).

Congress' rule-making authority, which originates in the Constitution and has been bestowed on this Court by the Rules Enabling Act . . . ."[85]

Beginning with the constitutional phase of its test, the Court noted that "constitutional constraints on the exercise of this rulemaking authority define a test of reasonableness . . . ," and that "[r]ules regulating matters indisputably procedural are *a priori* constitutional."[86] The Court seemed to see no constitutional problem in the fact that damage to state substantive interests might occur in the process. Quoting *Hanna*, it observed, "Rules regulating matters which, though falling within the uncertain area between substance and procedure, are rationally capable of classification as either, also satisfy this constitutional standard."[87]

Turning to the Rules Enabling Act, it interpreted the Act's limitation that federal rules "shall not abridge, enlarge or modify any substantive right . . . ."

> The cardinal purpose of Congress in authorizing the development of a uniform and consistent system of rules governing federal practice and procedure suggests that *rules which incidentally* affect litigants' substantive rights do not violate this provision if reasonably necessary to maintain the integrity of that system of rules.[88]

Note that the key word in this test is "incidental" — not "insignificant." This suggests that any impact upon state substantive interests (no matter how serious) is tolerable, so long it is a byproduct of (incidental to) advancement of a federal procedural policy. Thus, at both the constitutional and Rules Enabling Act levels, the *Woods* Court seems to accept disruption of state substantive interests, so long as application of federal law would advance clear procedural interests.

[3] Modern Analysis

[a] Matters "Procedural" Within the Meaning of the Rules Enabling Act

Rules validated as properly procedural in *Hanna* (service of process) and in *Woods* (regulation of frivolous appeals) are but some of those protected by the Rules Enabling Act.[89] Recall the Court's description in *Woods* of congressional intent in the Rules Enabling Act to create "a uniform and consistent system of

---

[85] 480 U.S. at 5.

[86] 480 U.S. at 5.

[87] 480 U.S. at 5.

[88] 480 U.S. at 5. (emphasis added). *Cf. Business Guides v. Chromatic Commc'ns Ent.*, 498 U.S 533, 552 (1991) ("There is little doubt that Rule 11 is reasonably necessary to maintain the integrity of the system of federal practice and procedure, and that any effect on substantive rights is incidental.").

[89] The Supreme Court recently has invoked *Woods* and *Hanna* to give broad application to Rule 11. *Business Guides v. Chromatic Commc'ns Ent.*, 498 U.S. 533 (1991). In *Business Guides*, a diversity case, the Court read Rule 11 to impose a form of liability on represented parties that did not exist under state law.

rules governing federal practice and procedure." Consider the purpose of the Federal Rules of Civil Procedure: "to secure the just, speedy, and inexpensive determination of every action and proceeding."[90] The breadth of such mandates suggests that a rule regulating any aspect of judicial administration is probably procedural within the meaning of the Rules Enabling Act.

To illustrate, note that the Supreme Court's refusal to follow a federal rule in *Walker* was based on the conclusion that the particular federal rule had no application concerning statutes of limitation.[91] *Walker* did not say that a Federal Rule of Civil Procedure was incapable of nullifying a state statute of limitations in diversity cases. Rule 15(c) in fact does just that, allowing plaintiff under certain circumstances to amend her complaint by claiming against a new defendant, even though the statute of limitations[92] has run since the suit was originally filed.[93] This "relation-back" feature of Federal Rule 15[94] reflects a strong procedural policy favoring liberal pleading.[95] State law in direct collision with Rule 15(c) has thus given way in diversity cases.[96]

[b] The Relationship Between the Rules Enabling Act and the Rules of Decision Act

Subsequent cases have confirmed Professor Ely's distinction:

> [W]here there is no relevant Federal Rule of Civil Procedure or other Rule promulgated pursuant to the Enabling Act and the federal rule in issue is therefore wholly judge-made, whether state or federal law should be applied is controlled by the Rules of Decision Act, the statute construed in *Erie* and *York*. Where the matter in issue is covered by a

---

[90] Rule 1.

[91] *See* § 7.04[2], *supra.*

[92] On statutes of limitations generally, see § 8.08[2][b], *infra.*

[93] *See generally* § 8.10[3][b] (relation back of amendments changing parties), *infra.*

[94] *See* § 8.10[3], *infra.*

[95] *See* § 8.10[3], *infra.*

[96] "Application of Rule 15(c) will mean in some instances that the action can go forward against the new defendant even though in state court that party would have a good defense of limitations. In this situation the courts have uniformly held . . . that Rule 15(c) can be applied and that to do so does not violate the substantive rights' proviso of the Enabling Act." WRIGHT § 59. *Cf. Freund v. Nycomed Amersham*, 347 F.3d 752 (9th Cir. 2003) (imposing the requirement under FED. R. CIV. P. 50 that a prior motion for directed verdict was a prerequisite for moving for judgment notwithstanding the verdict, even though California state law would impose no such prerequisite for testing punitive damage awards, and even though the court found California law rooted in public policy).

But see Douglas v. NCNB Texas Nat'l Bank, 979 F.2d 1128 (5th Cir. 1992). Invoking the substantive abridgement clause of § 2072, *Douglas* refused to give effect to the compulsory counterclaim requirement of Rule 13(a). Texas state law made clear that a secured lender's opportunity to recover could not be cut off through preclusion by rule. "Application of rule 13(a)", stated the court, "would abridge the lender's substantive rights and enlarge the debtor's substantive rights." *Id.* at 1130. While the case involves a different federal rule, the position on § 2072 taken in *Douglas* is difficult to reconcile with the Rule 15(c) cases surveyed by Professor Wright.

Federal Rule, however, the Enabling Act — and not the Rules of Decision Act itself or the line of cases construing it — constitutes the relevant standard.[97]

This distinction can alter the choice between state and federal law. For example, consider what would happen if the relation-back principle was not embedded in Rule 15(c), as discussed above,[98] but instead derived from federal judicial doctrine. Because the Rules Enabling Act would then be inapplicable, it would not insulate federal law from scrutiny under the Rules of Decision Act. Enforcement of the Rules of Decision Act through the *Erie* doctrine would likely lead to the choice of state over federal law.[99]

State substantive interests clearly receive less respect under the Rules Enabling Act approach of *Hanna* and *Woods* than they would under the *Erie* doctrine and the Rules of Decision Act. Some have questioned this discrepancy, suggesting a role for *Erie* and the Rules of Decision Act even when federal diversity courts are presented with applicable and valid rules of procedure.[100] More basically, the language of the Rules Enabling Act simply fails to support the conclusion that federal rules of procedure fare better against state law than does judge-made federal law. On the contrary, the provision in the Act denying federal rules authority to "abridge . . . any substantive right . . . ." would seem to vindicate substantive state interests even at the sacrifice of federal procedural objectives.[101] Nevertheless, the Supreme Court reads the Act differently, vindicating federal procedural objectives even at the sacrifice of state substantive interests.[102] The position taken by the Court is not altogether surprising. It is natural for the Court to be concerned about the resilience of

---

[97] John H. Ely, *The Irrepressible Myth of Erie*, 87 Harv. L. Rev. 693, 698 (1974).

[98] *See* § 7.04[3][a], *supra* (state statutes of limitation yield to the relation-back principle in Rule 15(c)).

[99] Defendant need merely demonstrate that the state statute of limitations functions at least in part to secure substantive policies. The Court in *Walker* enforced a state statute of limitations upon such a showing, once it concluded that the federal rules did not require the result sought by plaintiff.

[100] *See, e.g.*, Justice Harlan's concurrence in *Hanna*, entertaining the possibility that "*Erie* and the Constitution" might "require that the state rule prevail, even in the face of a conflicting federal rule." 380 U.S. at 475; Martin H. Redish & Carter G. Phillips, *Erie and the Rules of Decision Act: In Search of the Appropriate Dilemma*, 91 Harv. L. Rev. 356 (1977) (advocating an interest-weighing approach for *Hanna*).

[101] Despite its apparent clarity, this passage of the Rules Enabling Act "has been a source of substantial controversy in the courts and among commentators over the years." Moore, note 73, *supra*, at 1042. Thus, while there is much support in the literature for the view that "Congress' concern in formulating the procedure/substance dichotomy was the preservation of an enclave of state law in diversity cases," Burbank, note 73, *supra*, at 1110, Burbank himself disagrees. He argues that the purpose of the dichotomy was to protect laws made by Congress from abridgment through court-generated rulemaking. Burbank, note 73, *supra*, at 1122–23. For more on substantive-abridgement provision of the Rules Enabling Act, see Leslie M. Kelleher, *Taking "Substantial Rights" (in the Rules Enabling Act) More Seriously*, 74 Notre Dame L. Rev. 47 (1998); Paul D. Carrington, *Substance and Procedure in the Rules Enabling Act*, 1989 Duke L.J. 281 (1989).

[102] *See* note 88 and related text, *supra*.

procedural law governing federal litigation.[103] Moreover, the Rules Enabling Act assigns to the Supreme Court a major role in the creation of most rules. The Court must give serious thought — albeit in the abstract — to the constitutionality and Rules Enabling Act validity of rules before it transmits them to Congress for final approval.[104] All this may explain why the Supreme Court has never invoked the abridging-substance limitation of the Act to deny effect to a Federal Rule of Civil Procedure.[105]

§ 7.05 WHICH STATE'S LAW?

[1] The Conflict-of-Laws Problem

When the parties come from different states or when facts creating the controversy occur in more than one state, the source of governing law may become one of the issues in the case. This happens when laws of different states appear to produce contradictory results. For example, the same facts may make defendant liable to plaintiff under the law of New York but not under the law of California.

The variety of approaches courts use to resolve conflicts can lead to differences in the law chosen.[106] It thus becomes important to determine which body of choice-of-law rules apply to resolve a given conflict. State courts

---

[103] To give as much play to state substantive interests as the language of the Act suggests would create considerable uncertainty over application of federal rules of procedure in diversity cases. *Cf.* Ely, note 97, *supra*, at 698 ("The Court has correctly sensed that [the Enabling Act] cannot be construed to protect state prerogatives as strenuously as the Rules of Decision Act protects them in the absence of a Federal Rule."). *But see* Whitten, note 84, *supra*, at 42 (criticizing the approach of Court and concluding: "the one constant in the Court's decisions dealing with Federal Rules-state law conflicts . . . has been its refusal to provide significant content to the Act's substantive rights restriction."); Leslie M. Kelleher, *Amenability to Jurisdiction as a "Substantive Right": The Invalidity of Rule 4(k) Under the Rules Enabling Act*, 75 IND. L.J. 1191 (2000) (similar conclusion).

[104] "[T]he recommendations of the [Judicial] Conference pass to the Court; any rule changes finally adopted by the Court are laid on the tables of Congress in accordance with the Rules Enabling Act." Benjamin Kaplan, *Amendments of the Federal Rules of Civil Procedure, 1961–63 (I)*, 77 HARV. L. REV. 601, 602 (1964). *See generally* § 1.02 (the federal rulemaking process), *supra*.

[105] As the Court observed, one challenging a federal rule under the Rules Enabling Act "has a large hurdle to get over." *Business Guides v. Chromatic Commc'ns Ent.*, 498 U.S. 533, 552 (1991). That hurdle has proven insurmountable in cases before the United States Supreme Court. Perhaps the closest a challenge came to succeeding was in *Sibbach v. Wilson & Co., Inc.*, 312 U.S. 1 (1941). The Court ruled 5 to 4 there that (notwithstanding the substantive-abridgment provision of the Rules Enabling Act) state law protecting litigants from physical examinations had to yield to federal discovery Rule 35. Three justices who dissented in *Business Guides* raised the substantive-abridgment provision to argue for a narrower interpretation of Rule 11, but they reserved opinion "[w]hether or not Rule 11 as construed by the majority exceeds our rule-making authority . . . ." 498 U.S. at 568.

[106] For surveys of approaches currently in use, see SCOLES, ET AL., CONFLICT OF LAWS, note 55 *supra*, at §§ 2.18–2.25 ; Hermer H. Kay, *Theory into Practice: Choice of Law in the Courts*, 34 MERCER L. REV. 521 (1983); Gene R. Shreve, *In Search of a Choice-of-Law Reviewing Standard-Reflections on Allstate Insurance Co. v. Hague*, 66 MINN. L. REV. 327, 341–44 (1982). *See also* § 7.03[6], *supra* (comparing the choice-of-law process with certain applications of the *Erie* doctrine).

usually apply their own common law of conflicts. Federal courts apply their own conflicts law in federal question cases.[107] Prior to *Erie*, federal conflicts doctrine governed in diversity cases as well. That changed with *Klaxon Co. v. Stentor Electric Manufacturing*,[108] where the Supreme Court extended the *Erie* principle to choice of law.

[2]   The *Klaxon* Rule

Klaxon ended brief uncertainty whether federal conflicts doctrine was still available to federal courts sitting in diversity or was part of the federal general common law that *Erie* invalidated.[109] Ruling it to be the latter, *Klaxon* required federal diversity courts to administer the conflicts law of the states in which they were sitting ("forum states"). Reasoning from *Erie*, *Klaxon* held that a plaintiff should not be permitted to use federal diversity jurisdiction to obtain a more favorable conflicts law.

The *Klaxon* rule has been both criticized and defended.[110] Critics note that it forces federal judges to use a kind of state law (conflicts doctrine) that is particularly difficult to fathom[111] and that it imported local state bias into federal court decision-making.[112] Nonetheless, conflicts rules do determine the content of *substantive* law governing the case. It would therefore seem outcome-determinative[113] in the clearest, forum-shopping sense for federal diversity courts to be able to declare a different winner by choosing different law. The Supreme Court has since reaffirmed the *Klaxon* rule in *Day & Zimmerman, Inc. v. Challoner*.[114]

---

[107] *E.g., United States v. Little Lake Misere Land Co.*, 412 U.S. 580 (1973); *Siegelman v. Cunard White Star, Ltd.*, 221 F.2d 189 (2d Cir. 1955).

[108] 313 U.S. 487 (1941).

[109] *See* § 7.02[2], *supra.*

[110] *Compare* RANDALL BRIDWELL & RALPH V. WHITTEN, THE CONSTITUTION AND THE COMMON LAW: THE DECLINE OF THE DOCTRINES OF SEPARATION OF POWERS AND FEDERALISM 135 (1977), and the authorities appearing in WRIGHT § 57 (attacking *Klaxon*), *with* David F. Cavers, *The Changing Choice-of-Law Process and the Federal Courts*, 28 LAW & CONTEMP. PROBS. 732 (1963); American Law Institute, Study of the Division of Jurisdiction of State and Federal Courts 379 n.7 (1969) (defending *Klaxon*). *Cf.* Earl M. Maltz, *Choice of Forum and Choice of Law in the Federal Courts: A Reconsideration of Erie Principles*, 79 KY. L.J. 231 (1990–91) (*Klaxon* defensible when decided but incompatible with modern conflicts doctrine).

[111] Ascertaining state law when the same is "confused or nonexistent" is a chronic problem in administering the *Erie* doctrine. Charles E. Clark, *State Law in the Federal Courts: The Brooding Omnipresence of Erie v. Tompkins*, 55 YALE L.J. 267, 290 (1946). *See generally* § 7.06, *infra.* The problem is especially great in ascertaining state conflicts law under *Klaxon*, due in part to the innate difficulty of conflicts doctrine. *Cf.* Max Rheinstein, *How to Review a Festschrift*, 11 AM. J. COMP. L. 632, 655 (1962) (calling conflicts the "most difficult and most confused of all branches of the law").

[112] "At bottom, the argument that federal courts should always apply their own conflict rules assumes that federal courts, being by nature less parochial than the courts of the state in which they are sitting, are more likely to evolve better choice-of-law rules . . . ." RUSSELL J. WEINTRAUB, COMMENTARY ON CONFLICT OF LAWS § 10.5A (4th ed. 2001).

[113] On the contemporary use of the outcome-determination test, see § 7.03[6], *supra.*

[114] 423 U.S. 3 (1975).

[3]   *Klaxon* and § 1404(a)

We will consider the interplay of *Klaxon* and federal change-of-venue law with the aid of an example. A New York plaintiff files a federal diversity action in New York against a California defendant. The case is transferred under § 1404(a)[115] to a federal diversity court in California. Assume that applicable tort laws from New York and California conflict. Assume further that New York conflicts doctrine would require application of New York tort law, while California conflicts doctrine would require California tort law. Does the state conflicts law of the transferor forum (New York) or that of the transferee forum (California) govern? Current law reads *Erie, Klaxon,* and § 1404(a) to require the governing state conflicts doctrine to be that of the transferor forum (New York). As the Supreme Court stated in a leading case, *Van Dusen v. Barrack,*

> . . . the transferee district court must be obligated to apply the state law that would have been applied if there had been no change of venue. A change of venue under § 1404(a) generally should be, with respect to state law, but a change of courtrooms.[116]

Van Dusen left open the question whether the same rule applied to actions which, if originally filed in state court, would have been dismissed there[117] on *forum non conveniens* grounds.[118] Some lower federal courts have applied the rule in such cases.[119] Yet to do so may actually frustrate *Erie* by permitting plaintiffs to use federal diversity jurisdiction to shop for favorable substantive law. Two points explain this.

First, it is useful to understand why plaintiff might want to shop for conflicts doctrine. Return to the example. Assume that the New York plaintiff wants New York tort law applied because it is easier to recover under that law. The plaintiff also wants New York's own state conflicts doctrine to be used because that doctrine happens to use litigant citizenship as a tool for choosing law and would permit plaintiff to use his New York citizenship to obtain application of New York tort law.[120]

---

[115] For a discussion of the federal change-of-venue statute, 28 U.S.C. § 1404(a), see § 6.02[2] *supra.* The focus here will be on § 1404(a) transfers in diversity cases, although the statute governs transfer of cases under other forms of federal subject matter jurisdiction.

[116] 376 U.S. 612, 639 (1964). The Court applied the rule to " 'ensure that the accident' of federal diversity jurisdiction does not enable a party to utilize a transfer to achieve a result in federal court which could not have been achieved in the courts of the State where the action was filed." *Id.* at 638 (quoting *York*). The Supreme Court reiterated the *Van Dusen* rule and rationale in *Ferens v. John Deere Co.,* 494 U.S. 516 (1990).

[117] *Van Dusen,* 376 U.S at 640.

[118] On the doctrine generally, see § 6.02[1], *supra.*

[119] *See, e.g., In re Korean Air Lines Disaster of September 1, 1983,* 664 F. Supp. 1478 (D.D.C. 1986); *In re Air Crash Disaster at Boston, Mass.,* 399 F. Supp. 1106 (D. Mass. 1975).

[120] For an illustrative New York case, *see Tooker v. Lopez,* 249 N.E.2d 394 (N.Y. 1969). The practice has been criticized, John H. Ely, *Choice of Law and the State's Interest in Protecting Its Own,* 23 Wm. & Mary L. Rev. 173 (1981). But it is constitutional (and common) for a state to advance through its conflicts law the object that its citizens be compensated. For discussion how and why

Second, the *Erie* problem arises if our plaintiff is unable to obtain application of New York conflicts doctrine (and hence favorable New York substantive law) in any state court but is able to obtain New York conflicts doctrine in a federal diversity case originating in New York and transferred to California. To understand how state *forum non conveniens* doctrine can bring this about, note that our plaintiff can file his case in one of four courts: (1) a state or (2) federal diversity court in New York, or (3) a state or (4) federal diversity court in California.

Assume that plaintiff begins with option (1). New York state courts lack authority to transfer cases to the docket of another court system; therefore, if plaintiff runs afoul of New York state *forum non conveniens* doctrine, his New York state case would simply be dismissed without prejudice. Naturally, plaintiff in this situation would not last long enough in New York state court to benefit from favorable New York tort law.

If plaintiff files (or refiles) the same case in California state court, the suit would be governed by California conflicts law. California conflicts law will also govern if plaintiff files (or refiles) in California federal district court — this time under *Klaxon's* directive.

Only through strategic use of the *Van Dusen* rule could our plaintiff sidestep the application of California conflicts doctrine. Plaintiff's route would be to begin with a federal diversity action in New York, and then either finesse defendant into seeking a § 1404(a) transfer or move for one himself.[121] In short, rigid application of *Van Dusen's* requirement that conflicts law of the transferor forum governs would permit plaintiff to exploit the availability of diversity jurisdiction in New York to alter eventual decision on the merits in California.

Commentators have urged more sensitivity in determining whether transferor or transferee law should be applied regarding § 1404(a) transfers.[122] Federal courts should at least have flexibility to choose transferee over transferor law in situations where plaintiff uses federal diversity jurisdiction to orchestrate a choice-of-law result. The Supreme Court's decision in *Ferens v. John Deere Co.*,[123] however, does not support a flexible approach. Plaintiffs there filed in a federal forum (Mississippi) where apparently they never intended to litigate. Rather, plaintiffs moved successfully under § 1404(a) for transfer to a Pennsylvania federal court and sought to use Mississippi

---

this controversial principle dominates modern conflicts doctrine, see Gene R. Shreve, *Conflicts Law — State or Federal?*, 68 IND. L.J. 907 (1993).

[121] In *Ferens v. John Deere Co.*, 494 U.S. 516 (1990), the Supreme Court required application of the conflicts law of the transferor forum even though plaintiff initiated the transfer. Thus, "the legal system allowed the plaintiffs to shop for Mississippi law . . . ." George D. Brown, *The Ideologies of Forum Shopping — Why Doesn't A Conservative Court Protect Defendants?*, 71 N.C. L. REV. 649, 655 (1993).

[122] Michael B. Rodden, Comment, *Is 28 U.S.C. § 1404(a) a Federal Forum-Shopping Statute?*, 66 WASH. L. REV. 851 (1991); Ursula M. Henninger, Comment, *The Plaintiff's Forum Shopping Gold Card: Choice of Law in Federal Courts After Transfer of Venue Under § 1404(a) — Ferens v. John Deere Co.*, 26 WAKE FOREST L. REV. 809 (1991); SCOLES & HAY, note 106, *supra*, at § 3.46; Maltz, note 110, *supra*.

[123] 494 U.S. 516 (1990).

(transferor) law to maintain an action barred under Pennsylvania (transferee) law. The Supreme Court followed its *Van Dusen* rule and rewarded plaintiffs with Mississippi law. The dissent observed,

> one must be blind to reality to say that it is the *Mississippi* federal court in which these plaintiffs have chosen to sue. That was merely a way station in route to suit in the Pennsylvania federal court. The plaintiffs were seeking to achieve exactly what Klaxon was designed to prevent: the use of a Pennsylvania federal court instead of a Pennsylvania state court in order to obtain application of a different substantive law.[124]

§ 7.06   ASCERTAINING THE CONTENT OF STATE LAW

[1]   The Elusive Model of the Highest State Court

State law controlling in federal court under *Erie*[125] must be determined and applied as it would have been if the case had, instead, been adjudicated by the highest state court whose law is being applied. This rule reflects the fact that the ultimate authority on the meaning of state law is the state's highest court,[126] just as the United States Supreme Court is the ultimate authority on the meaning of federal law.

The problem is that a federal diversity court may not know how a state high court would rule on the case at hand because it is often impossible or impracticable for federal judges to certify state law questions to state courts in order to find out.[127] This leaves federal courts in an awkward position, particularly when state law is unsettled. No federal court can give genuinely

---

[124]   494 U.S. at 535.

[125]   The process for determining state law discussed in this section also applies in federal court searches for the meaning of state laws that are not required under *Erie*. For examples, see § 7.07, *infra*.

[126]   The principle is well-established. *E.g., Exxon Corp. v. Eagerton*, 462 U.S. 176, 181 n.3 (1983); *Commissioner v. Estate of Bosch*, 387 U.S. 456, 465 (1967). *See generally* Paul L. Caron, *The Role of State Court Decisions in Federal Tax Litigation: Bosch, Erie, and Beyond*, 71 OR. L. REV. 781 (1992). *Cf. City of Chi. v. Morales*, 527 U.S. 41, 61 (1999) ("We have no authority to construe the language of a state statute more narrowly than the instruction given by that State's highest court.").

[127]   "Except in those few jurisdictions permitting a federal court to certify an unsettled question of state law to the state's highest court, a federal court's decision on state law cannot be corrected, for the benefit of the litigants in the particular case, by the state's authoritative tribunal." *Factors Etc., Inc. v. Pro Arts, Inc.*, 652 F.2d 278, 282 (2d Cir. 1981), *cert. denied*, 456 U.S. 927 (1982).

The Supreme Court gave guarded approval to the technique of certification in *Salve Regina College v. Russell*, 499 U.S. 225, 237 (1991). *See generally* Deborah J. Challner, *Distinguishing Certification From Abstention in Diversity Cases, Postponement Versus Abdication of the Duty of Exercise Jurisdiction*, 38 RUTGERS L.J. 847 (2007); Geri J. Yonover, *A Kinder, Gentler Erie: Reining in the Use of Certification*, 47 ARK. L. REV. 305 (1994); Richard M. Chase, *A State Court's Refusal to Answer Certified Questions: Are Inferences Permitted?*, 66 ST. JOHN'S L. REV. 407 (1992); John B. Corr & Ira P. Robbins, *Interjurisdictional Certification and Choice of Law*, 41 VAND. L. REV. 411 (1988); CARROLL SERON, CERTIFYING QUESTIONS OF STATE LAW: EXPERIENCE OF FEDERAL JUDGES (Federal Judicial Center 1983).

authoritative meaning to state law.[128] Yet federal courts usually cannot avoid the ambiguities of state law by declining jurisdiction.[129] Instead, they must "vicariously"[130] create enough state law to decide the case at hand by attempting to "forecast" the state's law "as it would be expressed by its highest court."[131]

[2] Data to Be Used in Forecasting State Law

The most authoritative indication of how the state's high court would rule on the same case frequently will be found in that court's opinions. In keeping with the principle of *stare decisis*, a court usually can be expected to adhere to its own precedents.[132] If the precedent of the state's highest court is indistinguishable, a federal diversity court usually will have no choice but to follow it.[133] Since, however, all appellate courts overrule some of their own precedents over time, the requirement that federal diversity courts follow apposite state high court cases is not ironclad. Federal diversity courts have refused to follow state high court precedents when they are convinced that the state high court would not follow them either.[134] At least by negative implication, the Supreme Court lent support to this view in *Bernhardt v. Polygraphic Co. of America*.[135] It was aided in part in reaching its decision to follow a 40-year old Vermont Supreme Court precedent by the fact that

---

For examples where certification was workable, see *Reyes-Cardona v. J.C. Penney Co.*, 694 F.2d 894 (1st Cir. 1982); *Strange v. Krebs*, 658 F.2d 268 (5th Cir. 1981).

[128] At times, a federal decision on the meaning of state law has been followed by a subsequent federal court. *E.g.*, *Factors Etc., Inc. v. Pro Arts, Inc.*, 652 F.2d 278, 282 (2d Cir. 1981), *cert. denied*, 456 U.S. 927 (1982). But it is clear that the courts of the state are free to disregard all federal court pronouncements — even those of the Supreme Court — concerning the meaning of state law. The Supreme Court has acknowledged on numerous occasions the need to look to state courts for "an authoritative construction" of state law. *See, e.g., Babbitt v. United Farm Workers Nat'l Union*, 442 U.S. 289, 308 (1979).

[129] *Meredith v. City of Winter Haven*, 320 U.S. 228 (1943). For instances where extraordinary circumstances required federal diversity courts to abstain from decision, see *Burford v. Sun Oil Co.*, 319 U.S. 315 (1943); *Louisiana Power & Light Co. v. City of Thibodaux*, 360 U.S. 25 (1959).

[130] The term is from WRIGHT & MILLER § 4507.

[131] *McKenna v. Ortho Pharm. Corp.*, 622 F.2d 657, 662 (3d Cir.), *cert. denied*, 449 U.S. 976 (1980).

[132] On stare decisis generally, see § 15.13, *infra*.

[133] "[T]he duty rests upon federal courts to apply state law under the Rules of Decision statute in accordance with the then controlling decision of the highest state court." *Vandenbark v. Owens-Illinois Glass Co.*, 311 U.S. 538, 543 (1941). *Vandenbark* held that a federal circuit court was not free to disregard an apposite decision handed down by the Ohio Supreme Court while the federal case was on appeal.

[134] *See Rock Island Improvement Co. v. Helmerich & Payne, Inc.*, 698 F.2d 1075 (10th Cir.), *cert. denied*, 461 U.S. 944 (1983) (refusing to follow an Oklahoma Supreme Court case because of an intervening declaration of policy by the Oklahoma legislature); *Mason v. American Emery Wheel Works*, 241 F.2d 906 (1st Cir.), *cert. denied*, 355 U.S. 815 (1957) (refusing to follow a thirty-year-old Mississippi Supreme Court case, noting that the liability limitation imposed by the case had been discredited in other state jurisdictions and reasoning that the Mississippi Supreme Court would overrule it).

[135] 350 U.S. 198 (1956).

there appears to be no confusion in the Vermont decisions, no developing line of authorities that casts a shadow over the established ones, no dicta, doubts or ambiguities in the opinions of Vermont judges on the question, no legislative development that promises to undermine the judicial rule.[136]

When no decision of the highest state court is on point, federal courts must base their forecasts on other material. Decisions of intermediate state appellate courts carry considerable weight in such situations. The rule was once that federal diversity courts "must follow the decisions of intermediate state courts in the absence of convincing evidence that the highest court of the state would decide differently."[137] While some federal circuit courts have restated the rule,[138] the Supreme Court appeared to relax it in *Commissioner v. Estate of Bosch*.[139] The Court noted that "under some conditions, federal authority may not be bound by an intermediate state appellate court ruling."[140] An influential circuit court opinion has read *Bosch* to permit a wide-ranging examination of legal sources in order to forecast the Ohio Supreme Court's position when none of its decisions were on point:

> The primary source that must be analyzed, of course, is the decisional law of the Ohio Supreme Court. In the absence of authority directly on point, decisions by that court in analogous cases provide useful indications of the court's probable disposition of a particular question of law . . . . Considered dicta by the state's highest court may also provide a federal court with reliable indicia of how the state tribunal might rule on a particular question . . . . Of somewhat less importance to a prognostication of what the highest state court will do are decisions of lower state courts and other federal courts. Such decisions should be accorded "proper regard" of course, but not conclusive effect . . . . Additionally, federal courts may consider scholarly treatises, the Restatement of Law, and germane law review articles . . . .[141]

---

[136] 350 U.S. at 205.

[137] *Stoner v. New York Life Ins. Co.*, 311 U.S. 464, 467 (1940).

[138] *E.g.*, *Silverberg v. Paine, Webber, Jackson & Curtis, Inc.*, 710 F.2d 678, 690 (11th Cir. 1983); *Delano v. Kitch*, 663 F.2d 990, 996 (10th Cir. 1981), *cert. denied*, 456 U.S. 946 (1982).

[139] 387 U.S. 456 (1967).

[140] 387 U.S. at 465. Citing *Bernhardt*, the Court went on to observe, "If there be no decision by [the state's highest court] then federal authorities must apply what they find to be the state law after giving 'proper regard' to relevant rulings of other courts of the State." 387 U.S. at 465.

[141] *McKenna v. Ortho Pharm. Corp.*, 622 F.2d 657, 662 (3d Cir.) (*quoting Bosch*, 387 U.S. at 471), *cert. denied*, 449 U.S. 976. For discussion of the uses and limitations of state high-court dicta in forecasting state law, see MOORE § 124.22[3]. Federal diversity courts also may be influenced by broad trends in the development of a substantive field of law. *See, e.g.*, *Michelin Tires Ltd. v. First Nat'l Bank of Boston*, 666 F.2d 673, 682 (1st Cir. 1981); *Mason v. American Emery Wheel Works*, 241 F.2d 906, 908 (1st Cir.), *cert. denied*, 355 U.S. 815 (1957). On sources for determining state law, see Jed I. Bergman, *Putting Precedent in Its Place: Stare Decisis and Federal Predictions of State Law*, 96 COLUM. L. REV. 969 (1996); Note, *Federal Interpretation of State Law — An Argument for Expanded Scope of Inquiry*, 53 MINN. L. REV. 806 (1969).

[3]   How Much Freedom Do Federal Judges Have in Handling State Law?

The inability of federal courts to make truly authoritative pronouncements of state law and the constraints of the *Erie* doctrine make it impossible to reduce the process of forecasting state law to a simple formula. Federal judges use state law in a way that is not comparable to how either trial or appellate judges use it within the state judicial system.

On one hand, federal judges — whether trial or appellate[142] — require greater freedom than state trial judges in handling state precedents. State trial judges are controlled by precedents created by their superiors in the state judicial hierarchy.[143] Federal courts similarly constrained would not really be applying state law as state courts would, since state adjudication carries the possibility of review by a state appellate court powerful enough to overrule the state precedent.

On the other hand, federal courts cannot have as much freedom to react to state precedents as the state appellate courts which created them. All courts have the power to repudiate their own precedents at any time, although the doctrine of *stare decisis* usually restrains them.[144] However, forecasts whether or when a state appellate court will overrule its own precedent are likely to be speculative.[145] Moreover, guesses by federal diversity judges that state precedents would be overruled are likely to be colored by their own convictions about what the law ought to be. This kind of forecasting is dangerously akin to the federal general common law approach banned by *Erie*.[146]

All this explains why, in discharging the obligation to apply state law, federal diversity judges do not function as exact equivalents of either state lower or high court judges. They exercise instead a degree of authority somewhere between the two. When required to forecast whether the highest state court would overrule its own cases, federal courts should — and usually do — proceed with caution.[147] They have more latitude in resolving state law

---

[142] In *Salve Regina College v. Russell*, 499 U.S. 225 (1991), the Supreme Court ruled that determinations by federal trial judges of the meaning of state law are to receive no special weight. Rather, state law issues are reviewable *de novo* in federal courts of appeals.

Salve seems correctly decided. As we argued in the first edition of this book, the distinction between federal trial and federal appellate judges is unimportant in this context. Both address the same issue: how would the highest state court rule? *See* note 126 and accompanying text, *supra*. A federal appellate court may reverse because it disagrees with the federal district court's answer to this question, but both are alike in their inability to give authoritative meaning to state law. *See* note 128, *supra*.

[143] *See* § 15.13, *infra*.

[144] *Id.*

[145] The lines of the doctrine of *stare decisis* are indistinct and departures from it are episodic and frequently controversial. *See, e.g.*, Chief Justice Bell's vigorous dissent to the Pennsylvania Supreme Court's overruling of its decisions which had limited recovery for negligently inflicted emotional distress. *Niederman v. Brodsky*, 261 A.2d 84, 90 (Pa. 1970).

[146] *See* § 7.02, *supra*.

[147] *See* § 7.06[2], *supra*.

questions of first impression.[148] Even then, however, federal courts should weigh matters carefully before vicariously creating new state law. A noted circuit decision reflects this view.

> Like many other plaintiffs in diversity cases filed in federal courts, the appellant here is asking that we anticipate the birth of a state law doctrine in the womb of time, but whose birth is distant. We have been asked to deliver prematurely a new doctrine of Pennsylvania tort law, and as a federal court we are unwilling to do so.[149]

When particularly close questions arise over the content of state law, there is something to be said for resolving them against the litigant invoking federal diversity jurisdiction.[150] This seems fair since, by directing the case to federal rather than state court, that litigant has effectively avoided authoritative state court decision in favor of what will be at best an informed federal court guess how the highest state court would rule.[151] This approach is also in keeping with the *Erie* doctrine's objective of keeping litigants from obtaining a substantive law advantage simply because they are capable of invoking federal diversity jurisdiction.[152]

§ 7.07 FEDERAL COMMON LAW[153]

The same day that Justice Brandeis declared in *Erie R.R. v. Tompkins*[154] that "[t]here is no federal general common law,"[155] he wrote that "whether the water of an interstate stream must be apportioned between the States is a question of 'federal common law' upon which neither the statutes nor the decisions of either State can be conclusive."[156] Justice Jackson subsequently explained this apparent inconsistency:

> The federal courts have no *general* common law, as in a sense they have no general or comprehensive jurisprudence of any kind, because

---

[148] *Cf. Moore* § 124.22[3].

[149] *Vargus v. Pitman Mfg. Co.*, 675 F.2d 73, 76 (3d Cir. 1982).

[150] The litigant may be either a plaintiff who has invoked the federal court's original diversity jurisdiction under 28 U.S.C. § 1332, *see* §§ 5.04–5.06, *supra*, or a defendant who has removed the case on federal diversity grounds under 28 U.S.C. § 1441. *See* § 5.07, *supra*.

[151] There are some cases, however, where uncertainty over the meaning of state law will be as perplexing for state judges. In conflict-of-laws situations, a state court may be called upon to ascertain the meaning of the law of another state. *See* § 7.05[1], *supra*. In grappling with the law of another state, state judges face essentially the same analytic difficulties as federal judges do in administering the *Erie* doctrine. *See* Corr & Robbins, note 127, *supra*.

[152] *See* § 7.02 (evolution from *Swift* to *Erie*), *supra*.

[153] *See generally Federal Courts Symposium*, 12 PACE L. REV. 227–357 (1992); Martha A. Field, *Sources of Law: The Scope of Federal Common Law*, 99 HARV. L. REV. 881 (1986); Thomas W. Merrill, *The Common Law Powers of Federal Courts*, 52 U. CHI. L. REV. 1 (1985); Martin H. Redish, *The Power of the Federal Courts to Fashion Federal Common Law*, in FEDERAL JURISDICTION: TENSIONS IN THE ALLOCATION OF JUDICIAL POWER 119 (2d ed. 1990).

[154] 304 U.S. 64 (1938), discussed in § 7.02[3], *supra*.

[155] 304 U.S. at 78.

[156] *Hinderlider v. La Plata River & Cherry Creek Ditch Co.*, 304 U.S. 92, 110 (1938).

many subjects of private law which bulk large in the traditional common law are ordinarily within the province of the states and not of the federal government. But this is not to say that wherever we have occasion to decide a federal question which cannot be answered from federal statutes alone we may not resort to all of the source materials of the common law, or that when we have fashioned an answer it does not become a part of the federal non-statutory or common law.[157]

Whenever a federal court is free to decide for itself what rule of decision to apply, it is making or applying federal common law.[158] Federal common law has been applied to interstate water disputes,[159] as Justice Brandeis noted, other interstate disputes,[160] questions regarding the proprietary (commercial) interests of the United States,[161] foreign relations questions,[162] maritime and admiralty questions,[163] questions regarding the defenses available to federal officials sued in private actions,[164] statute of limitations questions when relevant federal statutes are silent,[165] and the question whether a plaintiff has an implied cause of action under a federal statute[166] or constitutional provision.[167] Despite this range of subjects, the Supreme Court has said that applications of federal common law are "few and restricted."[168] Once it applies, however, it is controlling under the Supremacy Clause of the Constitution,[169] whether the forum is state or federal,[170] and whether the federal jurisdiction is diversity or federal question,[171] until and unless Congress overrides it by

---

[157] *D'Oench, Duhme & Co. v. FDIC*, 315 U.S. 447, 469 (1942) (Jackson, J., concurring) (emphasis in original).

[158] WRIGHT § 60. *See generally* Jay Tidmarsh & Brian J. Murry, *A Theory of Federal Common Law*, 100 Nw. U. L. Rev. 585 (2006).

[159] Including questions of interstate pollution. *See Illinois v. City of Milwaukee*, 406 U.S. 91 (1972).

[160] *See, e.g., Texas v. New Jersey*, 379 U.S. 674 (1965).

[161] *See, e.g., United States v. Kimbell Foods, Inc.*, 440 U.S. 715 (1979) (priority of federal lien over private liens); *Clearfield Trust Co. v. United States*, 318 U.S. 363 (1943) (effect of late notice of forgery on U.S. rights as drawee to recover on guaranty of endorsements on check).

[162] *See, e.g., Banco Nacional de Cuba v. Sabbatino*, 376 U.S. 398 (1964) (effect of act of state doctrine on private litigation).

[163] *See, e.g., Edmonds v. Compagnie Generale Transatlantique*, 443 U.S. 256 (1979).

[164] *See, e.g., Howard v. Lyons*, 360 U.S. 593 (1959) (availability of privilege as defense to libel action).

[165] *See, e.g., Johnson v. Railway Express Agency, Inc.*, 421 U.S. 454, 462–66 (1975). *See generally* Note, *Limitation Borrowing in Federal Courts*, 77 MICH. L. REV. 1127 (1979) [hereinafter called *Limitation Borrowing*]; § 8.08[2][b] (the affirmative defense of limitations), *infra*.

[166] *See Cort v. Ash*, 422 U.S. 66, 78 (1975); § 5.03[1] (creation test for federal question jurisdiction), *supra*.

[167] *See Bivens v. Six Unknown Named Agents of Fed. Bureau of Narcotics*, 403 U.S. 388 (1971).

[168] *City of Milwaukee v. Illinois*, 451 U.S. 304, 313 (1981) *citing Wheeldin v. Wheeler*, 373 U.S. 647, 651 (1963). *See also* Redish, note 153, *supra*, at 80; Field, note 153, *supra*, at 885 (federal common law is usually said to be the exception, not the rule).

[169] U.S. Const. art. VI.

[170] Field, note 153, *supra*, at 897.

[171] *See, e.g., Banco Nacional de Cuba*, 376 U.S. at 421; *Howard*, 360 U.S. 593.

legislation.[172]

Beyond these generalizations, there is little clarity. Federal common law can be viewed as posing three questions, although they are not distinct in practice: (1) whether a federal court may make common law, (2) when it should make such law, and (3) what law it should make?

The threshold problem is that there is no general authority for federal common lawmaking. The federal government, unlike the state governments, is a government of limited powers. Its limitations are reflected in the Rules of Decision Act, which provides that the laws of the states shall be regarded as rules of decision in cases where they apply, "except where the Constitution or treaties of the United States or Acts of Congress otherwise require or provide."[173] The most common rationale for federal common lawmaking is that it is interstitial; it "implements the federal Constitution and statutes, and is conditioned by them," by filling gaps in such law.[174] These positive laws can be read as "requiring" such common lawmaking in the sense of the Rules of Decision Act because the gaps must be filled to decide cases. Another rationale for federal common lawmaking is that Congress or the Constitution has delegated lawmaking for particular subjects to the courts.[175] The positive laws can be read as "providing" for delegated judicial lawmaking in the sense of the Rules of Decision Act.

Whether a bare jurisdictional grant can alone serve as a delegation of lawmaking authority is unclear. Article III's grant of original jurisdiction to the Supreme Court to decide interstate disputes, and its authorization of lower court jurisdiction over admiralty and maritime cases and over controversies to which the United States is a party are sometimes cited as authority for federal common lawmaking in these areas.[176] Yet the analogous theory of delegated authority under the grant of diversity jurisdiction was rejected in *Erie*.[177] Arguably something more than just the jurisdictional grant is required, whether it is a practical necessity created by the absence of any logically applicable state law (to decide, for example, foreign relations questions or

---

[172] Redish, note 153, *supra*, at 97. *See, e.g., City of Milwaukee*, 451 U.S. at 313 (acknowledging "paramount authority of Congress" to override federal common law announced just one year earlier).

[173] 28 U.S.C. § 1652.

[174] *D'Oench, Duhme*, 315 U.S. at 471–72 (Jackson, J., concurring). *See generally* Kevin R. Johnson, *Bridging the Gap: Some Thoughts About Interstitial Lawmaking and the Federal Securities Laws*, 48 WASH. & LEE L. REV. 879 (1991). One commentator has characterized the process as "preemptive lawmaking," by which a court "finds that some federal policy specifically intended by an enacting body 'preempts' the application of state law to some collateral or subsidiary point about which the enacting body has been silent." Merrill, note 153, *supra*, at 36. *See generally* Henry M. Hart, Jr., *The Relations Between State and Federal Law*, 54 COLUM. L. REV. 489 (1954).

[175] *See, e.g., Textile Workers Union of Am. v. Lincoln Mills*, 353 U.S. 448, 451 (1957) (§ 301(a) of the Labor Management Relations Act of 1947, 29 U.S.C. § 185, "authorizes federal courts to fashion a body of federal law for the enforcement of . . . collective bargaining agreements").

[176] *See* Field, note 153, *supra*, at 916, 953–54 n.309 (citing authorities); Redish, note 153, *supra*, at 81–82.

[177] *See* § 184, *supra*; Field, note 153, *supra*, at 916.

interstate boundary disputes), or "a bit of legislative history" consistent with federal common lawmaking.[178]

When a court *should* make federal common law is also unclear. The predicate for making it appears to be a showing that the choice of the substantive legal rule will significantly affect an "identifiable federal policy or interest."[179] More recently, the Court has endorsed the description of the predicate or "precondition" for making federal common law as "a significant conflict between some federal policy or interest and the use of state law."[180] In the leading case of *Clearfield Trust Co. v. United States*,[181] for example, the issue was whether late notice by the United States of a forged signature on its check kept it from recovering against guarantor Clearfield Trust. Under state law, prejudice to Clearfield from the late notice was presumed and recovery by the United States barred, while under pre-*Erie* federal commercial law Clearfield had the burden of proving prejudice. A web of federal statutes and regulations governed the rights and duties of the United States on commercial paper, but none addressed the precise issue in the case. Citing these laws to demonstrate the federal interest in the subject, the Supreme Court held that in the absence of an applicable statute, "it is for the federal courts to fashion the governing rule of law according to their own standards."[182] Clearly, here the federal interest in recovering from the guarantor absent prejudice from late notice was in conflict with the state's presumption of prejudice.

In contrast, the Court held in *Bank of America National Trust & Savings Ass'n. v. Parnell*[183] that state law rather than federal common law set the burden of proof on the issue of good faith in the purchase of bearer bonds guaranteed by the United States. The suit involved only private parties and the Court saw no significant federal interest at stake. *Parnell* demonstrated that analysis of the federal interest must proceed on an issue-by-issue basis, for the Court upheld application of federal common law to the collateral issue of

---

[178] Henry J. Friendly, *In Praise of Erie — and of the New Federal Common Law*, 39 N.Y.U. L. Rev. 383, 413 (1964) (suggesting that for federal common lawmaking it is sufficient that there is a "grant of federal jurisdiction . . . adorned with a bit of legislative history").

[179] *See Wallis v. Pan Am Petroleum Corp.*, 384 U.S. 63, 68 (1966). *See* Redish, note 153, *supra*, at 80. Some scholars have attempted to refine these interests in order to escape the "enclave approach" to federal common law, which simply lists subjects to which it applies. One such effort suggests that federal common law should only be made when the transactions to which it will apply fall beyond the legislative competence of the states, and when making federal law promotes a constitutional structure or relationship such as the separation of powers (e.g., the "exclusive" foreign relations authority of the political branches) or the constitutional equality of the states (e.g., interstate disputes). *See* Bradford R. Clark, *Federal Common Law: A Structural Reinterpretation*, 144 U. Pa. L. Rev. 1245, 1251–52 (1996).

[180] *Atherton v. FDIC*, 519 U.S. 213 (1997) (*quoting O'Melveny & Myers v. FDIC*, 512 U.S. 79, 87 (1994)).

[181] 318 U.S. 363 (1943).

[182] 318 U.S. at 367. Whether the background federal statutes and regulations truly declared any identifiable policy or interest has been questioned. *See* Note, *Clearfield: Clouded Field of Federal Common Law*, 53 Colum. L. Rev. 991, 1002–05 (1953).

[183] 352 U.S. 29 (1956).

overdueness of the bonds.[184]

Finally, when the federal common lawmaking authority is exercised, the question of the content of the law remains. In fact, the phrase federal common law is somewhat misleading. It is more accurately called the "law of independent federal judicial decision,"[185] because once a court is satisfied that it should exercise lawmaking power, it is free to choose state law, fashion distinct federal law, or create some hybrid of the two.[186] Because states do not make their laws with federal interests in mind, the choice of state law as the content of federal common law would sometimes frustrate federal policy. But if a court finds as a threshold matter that the choice of state law would not frustrate federal policy, it may then consider such additional factors as the need for uniformity, the strength of a state's interest in having its own rules govern, the availability of developed state law, and the feasibility of judicially fashioning a substitute.[187] For example, this analysis has generally led the federal courts to "borrow" state limitations periods in federal causes of action for which Congress has not expressly provided limitations, and at the same time caused them to fashion distinct federal equitable tolling rules[188] in order to give effect to federal interests in the underlying cause of action.[189] Similarly, the Court concluded there was no federal interest in a uniform rule for determining the res judicata effect of a federal diversity judgment and therefore chose, as the applicable federal common law, the res judicata rule that would be applied by the forum state's courts.[190] At the same time, it was careful to note "the federal reference to state law will not obtain, of course, in situations in which the state law is incompatible with federal interests," such as a state law which would deny res judicata effect to a federal court dismissal for wilful violation of discovery orders.[191]

Of course, state law borrowed to supply the content of federal common law does not apply of its own force or by force of the Rules of Decision Act. It applies only because the federal court chose it. By the same token, the authority of state law as such is unaffected by its adoption (or later displacement) as federal common law.[192]

---

[184]   352 U.S. at 34.

[185]   *United States v. Standard Oil Co.*, 332 U.S. 301, 308 (1947).

[186]   *United States v. Kimbell Foods, Inc.*, 440 U.S. 715, 728 (1979). The Supreme Court has described federal common law "in the strictest sense" as a "rule of decision that amounts, not simply to an interpretation of a federal statute or a properly promulgated administrative rule, but, rather, to a judicial 'creation' of a specific federal rule of decision." *Atherton*, 519 U.S. at 218.

[187]   *See Wallis*, 384 U.S. at 68–69. *See generally* Field, note 153, at 953–62, *supra*. The borrowing court applies federal law to decide which state's law it will borrow. *De Sylva v. Ballentine*, 351 U.S. 570 (1956).

[188]   Equitable tolling rules stop the running of the statute limitations because of the defendant's conduct. *See* § 8.08[2][b] (the affirmative defense of limitations), *infra*.

[189]   *See generally Limitation Borrowing*, note 165, *supra*.

[190]   *Semtek Int'l Inc.v. Lockheed Martin Corp.*, 531 U.S. 497, 508 (2001).

[191]   *Semtek Int'l Inc.*, 531 U.S. at 508.

[192]   Field, note 153, *supra*, at 887.

Chapter 8

SIMPLE PLEADING AND PRACTICE

§ 8.01 OVERVIEW: THE FUNCTIONS AND HISTORY OF PLEADING

Pleading is the exchange of written allegations to ascertain the subject for decision in a civil action. The pleadings are documents containing statements (averments) or denials of facts: the complaint, the answer and, where permitted, the reply, as well as statements of claims or defenses.[1] Legal objections to pleadings are made by *demurrer* (in some state courts) or a *motion to dismiss* the pleading — requests for action by the court against the pleading[2] — while arguments about the law or how it applies to the facts are presented by memoranda of law called *briefs*. This chapter introduces the basics of pleading in the simple case of a single claim by a single plaintiff against a single defendant. Chapter 9 treats the more common and complex case in which multiple parties or claims are *joined* in the litigation.

To understand fully the requirements of pleading and their evolution, it is necessary to understand the functions of pleading. First, pleading can *give notice* to the parties of the nature of claims and defenses, helping them prepare their case. Second, pleading can help to *eliminate sham or insufficient claims or defenses*, conserving scarce judicial resources and protecting litigants against harassing litigation. Third, pleading can help to *narrow the issues*, streamlining a case for trial and efficiently focusing the attention of the decisionmakers. Fourth, pleading can *guide the parties and the court in the conduct of the case*, helping them to define the scope of pretrial factual preparation and of evidentiary relevance at trial. Finally, pleading can *supply a record* for judgment, permitting the eventual application of the law of *res judicata* to preclude relitigation of once-decided claims and issues.[3]

The priority assigned these systemic functions of pleading determines the rules of pleading. Historically in Anglo-American law, the most important function of pleading was issue identification and narrowing. *Common law pleading* and practice developed elaborate and arcane judge-made rules to this end, until it grew so technical and arbitrary that it was discarded by most states in favor of simplified rules of procedure codified in pleading codes. The primary functions of *code pleading* were notice and guidance. To these ends, it emphasized the pleading of facts constituting a *cause of action*, but it eventually

---

[1] *See* Rule 7(a); §§ 8.06 & 8.08–8.09, *infra*.

[2] *See* Rule 7(b); § 8.07, *infra*.

[3] *See generally* Chapter 15, *infra*.

also bogged down in disputation about the required specificity of fact pleading and the meaning of the term "cause of action."

In 1938, the Federal Rules of Civil Procedure abolished fact pleading and the concept of cause of action in favor of what some courts and commentators (though not the rules themselves) originally called *notice pleading*. As this term suggested, modern federal pleading — since copied in whole or part by a majority of states[4] — serves primarily the function of giving notice to the opposing party. Other procedural devices such as discovery (fact-gathering), summary judgment (pretrial disposition on the law when the material facts are undisputed), and pretrial conferences serve the remaining functions.

No American jurisdiction requires pure common law pleading today, and a declining number follow code pleading. Yet exposure to these systems of pleading aids the understanding of modern pleading for several reasons. Much of the terminology of modern pleading is inherited from common law or code pleading. Many of the rules of modern pleading are best understood as attempts to cure problems that dogged common law or code pleading. Moreover, the focus of both common law and code pleading on the pleader's legal theory is still important. Finally, as the father of the federal rules observed, "by a kind of Gresham's Law, the bad or harsh procedural decisions drive out the good, so that in time a rule becomes entirely obscured by its interpretive barnacles."[5] To the extent that some of the barnacles on modern pleading are of ancient lineage, it is worth tracing that lineage at least in outline.

Accordingly, sections 8.02 and 8.03 sketch some of the essential elements of common law/equity and code pleading, respectively. Section 8.04 then introduces and briefly traces the evolution of modern federal pleading, and section 8.05 discusses the candor and care requirements of modern pleading. The remaining sections trace the course of modern pleading and practice chronologically from complaint to amendment.

§ 8.02   PRE-CODE PLEADING AND PRACTICE

[1]   Common Law Issue Pleading and Practice[6]

Pleading in early English history consisted of oral exchanges before feudal and communal courts. The difficulty of remembering long oral presentations probably compelled pleaders to exchange short allegations until they had

---

[4] John B. Oakley & Arthur F. Coon, *The Federal Rules in State Courts: A Survey of State Court Systems of Civil Procedure*, 61 WASH. L. REV. 1367, 1369 (1986).

[5] Charles E. Clark, *Special Problems in Drafting and Interpreting Procedural Codes and Rules*, 3 VAND. L. REV. 493, 498 (1950).

[6] The outline of historical pleading requirements and practices given in this section is drawn largely from JOSEPH H. KOFFLER & ALISON REPPY, HANDBOOK OF COMMON LAW PLEADING (1969), and BENJAMIN J. SHIPMAN, HANDBOOK OF COMMON-LAW PLEADING (H. Ballantine 3d ed. 1923), except as otherwise noted.

reduced the dispute to a specific issue that the decider and the pleaders could easily keep in mind.[7]

Two developments transpired over a period of centuries to mature this system. In the 14th century, written pleadings were introduced, permitting the elaboration of pleading allegations and the formalization of the oral practice of "pleading to the issue." The necessity for pleading to a single issue became the driving force of an increasingly formalistic common law pleading system.

In addition, jurisdictional turf-building by the royal courts led to the development of entire modes or *forms of action*. A plaintiff in the royal courts began his action by obtaining a *writ* from the king's representative ordering a sheriff to compel the defendant to satisfy the plaintiff's claim or to appear in court to defend himself. As long as feudal and communal courts still heard the major share of the judicial business, such writs were limited to a small number of claims on which the king could give relief. The writ, in effect, conferred a limited jurisdiction on and between the several royal courts, and the plaintiff's claim had to fall within the writ — the particular royal court's jurisdiction — or it would fail. The royal courts gradually expanded their jurisdiction by issuing new writs or by stretching the limits of existing writs through legal fictions.

Eventually, each permitted writ became associated with its own substantive legal theory and developed its own procedural incidents. As a result, a *form of action* came to embrace not only the appropriate writ, court, and substantive law,[8] but also the forms of pleas, modes of trial, and forms of judgment.[9] At the same time, the language of the plaintiff's pleading was increasingly divorced from reality, as it was used largely to justify a particular writ under the formulary system rather than to describe the actual case. "The primary question before the [common law] courts has not been the general one whether the plaintiff's statement of his case showed a right in him and a violation by the defendant; it has rather been whether the case presented facts which constituted a 'cause of action' in 'trespass,' 'assumpsit,' or other particular form attempted to be used."[10] Once the writ was issued, the plaintiff would begin the pleading process by filing a *declaration*, describing his case in the formalistic and often fictitious language held necessary under the particular writ and associated with the attendant form of action. Consistent with the objective of reducing the case to a single issue, no hypothetical (if, then) or alternative (either/or) pleading was permitted. From the outset, the plaintiff had to elect a particular set of facts, and by virtue of the formulary system, a particular legal theory. Any deviation between the writ selected and the declaration, or between the declaration and eventual proof at trial, was termed a *variance* and

---

[7] JAMES STEPHEN, THE PRINCIPLES OF PLEADING IN CIVIL ACTIONS 37, 147–50 (Tyler ed. 1882).

[8] The forms of action evolved gradually. They included, at different points in time, trespass, trespass on the case (encompassing various indirect injuries and non-physical torts), trover (for the return of property), ejectment, detinue (return of property and damages for its wrongful detention), replevin, debt, and special assumpsit. See KOFFLER & REPPY, note 6, *supra*, Chs. 7–13, 16.

[9] *See generally* FREDERIC WILLIAM MAITLAND, EQUITY, ALSO THE FORMS OF ACTION AT COMMON LAW (1909); CECIL HERBERT STUART FIFOOT, HISTORY AND SOURCES OF THE COMMON LAW — TORT AND CONTRACT (1949).

[10] SHIPMAN, note 6, *supra*, § 27.

forbidden.[11] Any pleading *departure* from the previously pleaded facts or legal theory was fatal to the pleading, because it was inconsistent with narrowing the issues.[12] Relief was limited to that sought in the declaration upon the facts and legal theory there asserted. The harshness of these principles is illustrated by a decision reversing a judgment for plaintiff because he had pleaded a debt of $2,579.57, but proved a debt of $2,579.57 1/2![13]

The drive toward a single issue was also reflected in the requirements for further pleading. There were three possible responses to a claim.

First, a party could *demur*, asserting that, even if true, the claimant's allegations state no legal claim. The demurrer had to attack a pleading on its face; so-called *speaking demurrers*, which relied on additional matter beyond the four corners of the pleading, were prohibited. At first, the demurrer did not specify the defect in the pleading that it attacked. This left the pleader in the dark as to whether his legal theory was deficient, he had omitted some necessary ritualistic language, or he had simply committed some other minor and easily corrected error of form. After a 16th century reform, however, defects of form had to be attacked by *special demurrer* specifying the defect or they were waived. The *general demurrer* was reserved for substantive legal defects.

Second, a party could respond with a *dilatory plea*, asserting some legal reason, incidental to the merits, why the court could not hear the case.[14] *Pleas to the court's jurisdiction* challenged the court's subject matter jurisdiction and, if sustained, required dismissal of the case. *Pleas in suspension* sought to suspend the action until some problem, such as the plaintiff's legal disability through outlawry, had been removed. *Pleas in abatement* challenged defects in the pleading itself, going to the capacity of the pleader, misjoinder of claims or parties, etc.

Third, the party could respond on the merits with a *plea in bar*, also called a *peremptory plea*, asserting a defense that could bar recovery. By asserting the plea in bar called the *traverse*, the pleader denied the allegations of the claim against him, creating a factual issue for trial. To assure singleness of issue, however, treacherous rules evolved concerning the precise form of denials in a traverse. The traps which these rules set for the unwary eventually made a different form of traverse popular — the *general issue*, essentially the civil version of a "not guilty" plea. By filing the general issue, a defendant could contest liability and even assert various affirmative defenses without having to specify which allegations of the complaint he denied or which of the affirmative defenses he would assert at trial.[15] The plea of the general issue neither gave

---

[11] KOFFLER & REPPY, note 6, §§ 26–27; SHIPMAN, note 6, *supra*, § 82.

[12] SHIPMAN, note 6, *supra*, §§ 217–229.

[13] *Spangler v. Pugh*, 21 Ill. 85 (1859).

[14] Most such pleas asserted curable preliminary defects or problems and would only delay rather than permanently bar an action by a persistent plaintiff — hence the generic term, *dilatory pleas*. KOFFLER & REPPY, note 6, *supra*, § 203.

[15] *See* KOFFLER & REPPY, note 6, *supra*, § 224.

notice nor helped to reduce the case to a single issue, but its "popularity . . . with the common law pleaders may be in part explained on the theory that it was a practical method of simplifying a system of pleading which had grown too technical for successful application."[16] Finally, an alternative plea in bar was the *plea in confession and avoidance*. It required defendant to admit (confess) plaintiff's claim and to plead an excuse: new matter that avoided the claim.

Both the demurrer and the dilatory plea created legal issues, while the traverse created a factual issue. Additional pleading was necessary to raise an issue on the plea of confession and avoidance, since no issue was created by the confession of plaintiff's claim. To achieve singleness in pleading, the demurrer, traverse and plea in confession and avoidance were mutually exclusive; combining pleas or otherwise raising more than one issue in a pleading was prohibited as *duplicity*.[17]

Once the defendant had answered, it was the plaintiff's turn to respond by filing a *replication*, asserting one of the three possible analytic responses described above. If the issue was still not joined, the defendant then filed a *rejoinder*. Additional rounds of pleading by way of *surrejoinder, rebutter, surrebutter* and theoretically beyond were also possible until issues had been joined. At the conclusion of this usually protracted and procedurally land-mined pleading process, trial with fact-finding by a jury was often "something of an afterthought."[18]

Complicated as this outline sounds, it does not begin to portray the true technicality of the common law pleading system in its heyday, or to illustrate the extent of the legal fictions which permeated the forms of action. Professor Charles Alan Wright pronounced a just and fitting verdict on the system: "This system was wonderfully scientific. It was also wonderfully slow, expensive and unworkable. The system was better calculated to vindicate scientific rules of pleading than it was to dispense justice."[19]

---

[16] Charles Liebert Crum, *Scope of the General Denial*, 27 N.D. L. Rev. 11, 14 (1951).

[17] Koffler & Reppy, note 6, *supra*, §§ 234–35.

[18] Richard L. Marcus, *The Revival of Fact Pleading Under the Federal Rules of Civil Procedure*, 86 Colum. L. Rev. 433, 437 (1986) (citations omitted).

[19] Wright § 68.

[2]   Equity Pleading and Practice[20]

For dispensation of justice frustrated by the scientific complexities of the common law system or by the unavailability of a suitable writ or of adequate law relief in the traditional form of damages,[21] plaintiffs petitioned the king directly. He sent them to his chief minister, the chancellor, and by the 16th century, a *court of chancery* had developed to hear such petitions or *bills of complaint.*[22] The predicate for seeking equity in the chancery court was a showing of inadequate remedy at law. The remedy at equity was a decree ordering the respondent personally and directly to do or not to do something, *i.e.*, a decree of specific performance or an injunction.[23]

As an alternative to the common law system, equity developed its own procedures. First, the bill of complaint consisted of a repetitive narrative of evidentiary facts culminating in *interrogatories* to respondent. The bill of complaint, framed partly to force disclosure of the defendant's case by his sworn answer and partly to serve as evidence in lieu of oral testimony at trial to the chancellor,[24] thus served as an early form of discovery of evidence from the adversary, unknown at common law. Eventually it gave rise to a *bill of discovery*, which could be brought in equity in aid of an action or defense at law.

Second, in order to do full justice, equity permitted the joinder of parties who could not be joined in a common law suit. *Cross-bills* in equity permitted claims between co-defendants, by defendant against the plaintiff, and against some third parties, while *interpleaders* and *derivative suits* permitted even more sophisticated forms of joinder. Equity procedures, then, were the forerunners of modern complex joinder devices.[25]

Third, equity did not ordinarily use the jury as a fact-finder. The trial was instead to the chancellor on the pleadings, answers to interrogatories, depositions (written examinations of witnesses under oath) and documentary evidence rather than on oral testimony. The role of the chancellor as fact-finder led eventually to a different degree of appellate deference to his findings than to jury findings, which is today reflected in the federal standards of appellate review.[26]

---

[20] *See generally* FREDERIC WILLIAM MAITLAND, EQUITY (2d rev. ed. 1936); JOHN NORTON POMEROY, CODE REMEDIES (5th ed. 1929). The following outline is drawn primarily from these sources, except as otherwise noted.

[21] Actually the law courts granted relief by declaring a legal relationship between plaintiff and defendant, usually that plaintiff was entitled to a sum of money ("damages") from the defendant. *See generally* § 14.01 (damages remedies), *infra*.

[22] Some scholars date the development of equity as a separate system to the 14th century. *See, e.g.*, Harold Dexter Hazeltine, *The Early History of English Equity, in* ESSAYS IN LEGAL HISTORY 261–85 (P. Vinogradoff ed. 1913).

[23] *See generally* § 14.02 (equitable relief), *infra*.

[24] MAITLAND, note 20, *supra*, Lecture 1, at 5.

[25] *See generally* Chapter 9 (complex pleading and practice), *infra*.

[26] *See* § 13.10[2][b] (clearly erroneous standard of review), *infra*.

Despite equity's origins as a flexible alternative to the rigidities of common law practice and procedure, it became encrusted with its own procedural barnacles. One study of equity practice concluded that equity actions were frequently interminable and that even in those which came to a successful conclusion, "the honest suitor emerged from the ordeal victorious rather than triumphant, for too often he had been ruined by the way."[27]

§ 8.03   CODE FACT PLEADING AND PROCEDURE[28]

[1]   In General

Neither common law nor equity pleading was imported in all its technical glory to the colonies. But enough was adopted to prompt reform by the mid-19th century. New York led the way in 1848 with the adoption of the *Field Code of Civil Procedure*. It became a model for pleading reforms in more than half the states, and the code pleading which it introduced is still retained in a few.[29]

The *Field Code* abolished the forms of action and the distinction between law and equity actions in favor of "one form of action, denominated a civil action."[30] It also discarded all existing pleading rules that were inconsistent with its provisions. The hallmark of the code was *fact pleading*: the requirement that the complaint state "facts constituting a cause of action, in ordinary and concise language."[31] Issue-narrowing was no longer the primary function of pleading. Its objective, instead, was "three-fold: to present the facts on which the court is to pronounce the law; to present them in such a manner, as that the precise points in dispute shall be perceived, to which the proofs may be directed; and to preserve the record of the rights determined."[32] Since pleading no longer had to generate a single issue, pleadings were confined to a complaint, answer and reply, which were all to be liberally construed.[33]

The adoption of code pleading brought with it two major problems: what constituted a cause of action, and how specifically did plaintiff have to plead

---

[27] Baron Bowen, *Progress in the Administration of Justice During the Victorian Period, in* 1 SELECT ESSAYS IN ANGLO-AMERICAN LEGAL HISTORY 516, 526–27 (E. Freund et al. eds. 1907).

[28] *See generally* CHARLES E. CLARK, HANDBOOK OF THE LAW OF CODE PLEADING (2d ed. 1947), by any measure the leading authority on the subject, from which the following outline is drawn, except as otherwise noted.

[29] For example, California, Oklahoma, South Carolina, and Virginia have retained fact pleading requirements among other code pleading rules at the same time that they have adapted discovery, amendment and sometimes summary judgment provisions from the Federal Rules of Civil Procedure. *FRIEDENTHAL, KANE & MILLER*, § 5.1. *See, e.g.*, Va. Code Ann. §§ 8.01 (2000); *see generally* Ian Wilson & William Payne, Note, *The Specificity of Pleading in Modern Civil Practice*, 25 U. RICH. L. REV. 135 (1990) (discussing Virginia fact pleading).

[30] N.Y. Code Civ. Proc. § 69 (1848) (hereinafter *Field Code*).

[31] *Field Code* § 142(2).

[32] FIRST REPORT OF THE COMMISSIONERS ON PRACTICE AND PLEADINGS, 123–24, 137–38, 140–41, 144 (1848) (report which led to promulgation of the Field Code).

[33] *Field Code* §§ 156 & 159.

facts constituting a cause of action? These are explored in the discussion which follows.

[2]   The Cause of Action and the Theory of the Pleadings

The code drafters agreed that "[i]n some manner it is necessary to state the limits to which relief for a number of grievances or one severe and long-continued grievance may be accorded in a *single* suit."[34] The common law, of course, established narrow and seemingly precise limits through the forms of action and the attendant pleading niceties. But the abolition of the forms and old pleading rules made it unnecessary and arguably improper to plead the discarded common law allegations in order to set forth facts constituting a cause of action. On the other hand, conclusory pleading would not do either, in view of the code's emphasis on facts.

Between these extremes, at least two approaches to limiting the suit developed. The first equated a cause of action with a right of action or the legal or primary right suggested by the facts relied upon by the plaintiff.[35] The second looked to the "aggregate of operative facts," "limited as a lay onlooker would to a single occurrence or affair, without particular reference to the resulting legal right or rights."[36] The latter pragmatically anticipated the unit of facts that would most naturally and conveniently be presented at trial. But it was ahead of its time. Its very flexibility appeared to threaten the objective of notice by leaving unclear which legal rights arose from the aggregate of operative facts and therefore what law applied.

Consequently, most observers agreed on the need for some sort of legal right as the measuring stick for the plaintiff's pleading.[37] The result was a *theory-of-pleadings* approach to defining a cause of action in many, though not all, code states, which unfortunately helped perpetuate much of the rigidity of formulary pleading and its corresponding rules against variance and departure. In *Jones v. Winsor*,[38] for example, the plaintiffs sued for return of money deposited with their attorney, alleging in part that his fee was unjust, unlawful and fraudulent. But the complaint failed to state a cause of action for conversion because of plaintiffs' omission of allegations of ownership or possession of the money entrusted to the attorney. On the other hand, if the cause of action was taken to be a contractual one for money had and received, the complaint would have been sufficient, and the allegations of fraudulent conversion were just surplusage. The court upheld a demurrer, reasoning that

---

[34] CLARK, note 28, *supra*, § 19, at 128 (emphasis in original). Because such limits are also necessary to define the scope of a final judgment for purposes of the law of claim preclusion, detailed discussion of them is deferred until Chapter 15. See § 15.03 (claim preclusion), *infra*.

[35] *See* CLARK, note 28, *supra*, § 19; JOHN NORTON POMEROY, 1 EQUITY JURISPRUDENCE § 347 (5th ed. 1941).

[36] CLARK, note 28, *supra*, § 19 at 130, 137.

[37] Clark, note 28, *supra*, § 19 at 130, 137.

[38] 118 N.W. 716 (S.D. 1908). *See also Mescall v. Tully*, 91 Ind. 96, 99 (1883).

[a] complaint should be framed upon the theory that it is either a complaint in tort or one *ex contractu*, and the two theories cannot be combined in one action; neither can an action at law and an action in equity be combined in one count in the same action . . . . "On demurrer to a complaint, or any count thereof, the court must determine what cause of action such complaint or count is designed to state, and then whether it states facts sufficient to constitute such a cause of action; and, if not, the demurrer must be sustained, though facts may be stated sufficient to show that plaintiff has a cause of action of a different character."[39]

Similarly, other courts held that if a complaint stated a cause of action on one legal theory, the action would fail if that legal theory was not proven at trial, even though allegations in the complaint and proof at trial would have supported a cause of action on a different legal theory.[40] Plaintiff had, in effect, made a fatal departure or variance from the legal theory articulated by his complaint; he should have elected the successful legal theory before trial. Other courts rejected such harsh applications of the theory-of-the-pleadings approach by considering whether defendants were adequately apprised of the theory plaintiff ultimately argued at trial or whether they were surprised — considerations more in keeping with the objectives of fact pleading under the codes. Yet even these courts gave defendants the option of moving before trial to strike surplusage from the complaint and "to compel the plaintiff to make it more definite, or to elect in regard to the *form of action*."[41] As the language of this "progressive" ruling reveals, in many states the forms of action still ruled code pleading from the grave.

[3]   The Specificity of Fact Pleading Under the Codes

In reaction to the often fictitious quality of common law pleading, the codes required the pleading of only "dry, naked, actual facts,"[42] to which the court would apply the substantive law. Plaintiff was therefore obliged to avoid pleading a conclusory legal evaluation of his facts. At the same time, he was charged with pleading concisely. In short, he could plead neither too little nor too much, but just the so-called *ultimate facts* from which an appropriate cause of action could be inferred.

Pleading too little — bare conclusions of law — subjected the complaint to demurrer. But the dividing line between improper conclusions of law and proper ultimate facts proved evanescent. Typically nettlesome allegations included the following: plaintiff and defendant mutually agreed; plaintiff is the owner of property; defendant's servant was acting within the scope of his

---

[39] *Jones v. Winsor*, 118 N.W. at 718 (*quoting Supervisors of Kewaunee County v. Decker*, 30 Wis. 624 (1872)).

[40] *See Ross v. Mather*, 51 N.Y. 108 (1872).

[41] *Conaughty v. Nichols*, 42 N.Y. 83, 88 (1870) (emphasis supplied) (permitting plaintiff to amend his complaint after trial by striking language of conversion, in order to recover on a contractual theory). *Contra, Jones*, 118 N.W. 716.

[42] *WRIGHT* § 68 (quoting JOHN NORTON POMEROY, CODE REMEDIES 640 (1929)).

employment; defendant was in charge of the construction. Sometimes the allegations as a group were held conclusory. In *Gillespie v. Goodyear Service Stores*,[43] plaintiff alleged that

> [o]n or about May 5, 1959, and May 6, 1959, the defendants, *without cause or just excuse and maliciously* came upon and trespassed upon the premises occupied by the plaintiff as a residence, and by the use of harsh and threatening language and physical force directed against the plaintiff assaulted the plaintiff and placed her in great fear, and humiliated and embarrassed her by subjecting her to public scorn and ridicule, and caused her to be seized and exhibited to the public as a prisoner, and to be confined in a public jail.[44]

The appellate court affirmed dismissal of the complaint on a demurrer, reasoning that it stated no facts upon which the italicized "legal conclusions" could be predicated.[45] "Plaintiff's allegations do not disclose *what* occurred, *when* it occurred, *where* it occurred, *who did what*, the relationships between defendants and plaintiff or of defendants *inter se*, or any other factual data that might identify the occasion or describe the circumstances."[46]

The plaintiff who sought to avoid such a result by pleading detailed *evidentiary facts*, however, risked pleading too much. Although this vice was rarely fatal, because the court could usually still draw the necessary legal inferences from the collective evidentiary facts, the plaintiff could never be sure that the consequences would not be more serious. In *McCaughey v. Schuette*,[47] the appellate court actually reversed a judgment for plaintiff because his complaint seeking possession of property contained only "a statement of evidentiary facts, which, if proven at the trial, would authorize the court in finding the ultimate fact of ownership and right to possession in the plaintiff."[48]

The codes attempted to distinguish among legal conclusions, ultimate facts, and evidentiary facts, that was "one of degree only," not of kind.[49] Even frequent appellate treatments of the distinction furnished no guidance to the trial courts because they were inescapably ad hoc. When the issue was essentially whether the pleader had pleaded too little or too much, most precedents were distinguishable, most pleadings were fair game, and form was again elevated over substance as it had been under the common law.

---

[43] 128 S.E.2d 762 (N.C. 1963).

[44] 128 S.E.2d at 763 (emphasis supplied).

[45] 128 S.E.2d at 766.

[46] 128 S.E.2d at 766

[47] 48 P. 1088 (Cal. 1897) (*per curiam*).

[48] 46 P. 666, 666 (Cal. 1896).

[49] CLARK, note 28, *supra*, § 38.

§ 8.04   MODERN FEDERAL PLEADING

The drafters of the Federal Rules of Civil Procedure attempted to adopt the successes and avoid the failures of code pleading. In prescribing the basic federal pleading requirement, they therefore rejected both the phrases "facts" and "cause of action" in favor of the rule that a pleading contain "a short and plain statement of the claim showing that the pleader is entitled to relief."[50] Under the federal rules, issue-narrowing, fact development and guidance, and screening of sham or insufficient claims or defenses are accomplished by devices other than pleading. The chief remaining function of modern pleading is to give notice of claims or defenses. "The real importance of the Rules dealing with pleadings is that they make pleadings, in and of themselves, relatively unimportant. Cases are to be decided on their merits."[51]

We will examine four questions surrounding "notice pleading." First, how specific must the pleading be? Second, has the theory-of-the-pleadings doctrine been finally abandoned? Third, what form must notice pleading take? Finally, what specific pleading rules have survived and why?

[1]   The Specificity of Federal Pleading

The required specificity of federal pleading has evolved over time. From the rhetoric (if not always the reality) of "notice pleading," it evolved in many courts to a more demanding "elements pleading" standard and in a few to a quite demanding "heightened pleading" standard, before the Supreme Court seemed to call halt. More recently, however, the Court has sown renewed confusion by seeming to endorse a "plausible pleading" standard for at least some cases.

[a]   Notice Pleading

The phrase "notice pleading" suggests more the spirit than the letter of a sufficient pleading and was disavowed by the federal rulemakers themselves.[52] But Rule 8(a)(2)'s requirement of a "short and plain statement of the claim showing that the pleader is entitled to relief" is hardly more helpful. On one hand, it could mean that a sufficient pleading could inform defendant of little more than that she has been sued. On the other hand, it could contemplate a detailed statement of facts making out each and every element of a claim.

The Supreme Court lent some support to the first view in *Conley v. Gibson*[53] by endorsing what it called "simplified 'notice pleading'" and "the accepted rule that a complaint should not be dismissed for failure to state a claim unless it appears beyond doubt that the plaintiff can prove no set of facts

---

[50] Rule 8(a)(2).

[51] James William Moore, Moore's Federal Practice § 8.02 (2d ed.)

[52] *See* Charles E. Clark, *Two Decades of the Federal Civil Rules*, 58 Colum. L. Rev. 435, 450–51 (1958).

[53] 355 U.S. 41 (1957).

in support of his claim which would entitle him to relief."[54] *Dioguardi v. Durning*,[55] cited with approval in *Conley* and penned by the chief drafter of the federal rules, appeared to set a very modest standard for the statement of such matter and illustrates the leniency of the *Conley* statement. Plaintiff's "obviously home drawn" complaint against the Collector of Customs alleged cryptically that certain "medicinal extracts" imported by plaintiff had disappeared and that others had been given to a third party "with my betting [bidding?] price of $110: and not their price of $120."[56] Judge Clark reversed the dismissal of the action for failure to state a claim, concluding that the plaintiff had stated claims against the collector for conversion and improper public sale, "however inartistically."[57]

Read together, *Conley* and *Dioguardi* appeared to embrace a liberal view of notice pleading whereby no complaint will be held insufficient for failure to state a claim unless "the pleader makes allegations that show on the face of the complaint some insuperable bar to relief."[58] By this view, a plaintiff does not have to allege all the facts necessary to prove its claim.[59] This is consistent with a theory of pleading that emphasizes notice and notice alone as the essential function of pleadings.

[b]   **Elements Pleading**

While *Conley* gave the most oft-quoted rule, it could hardly be taken literally, or (as the Supreme Court later critically commented), "a wholly conclusory statement of claim would survive a motion to dismiss whenever the pleadings left open the possibility that a plaintiff might later establish some 'set of [undisclosed] facts' to support recovery."[60] Read literally, *Conley*'s no-set-of-facts standard would permit plaintiff to allege nothing but that defendant was liable to plaintiff and pass muster. The allegations in *Conley* itself went well beyond this, and the form complaints accompanying the federal rules and declared to "suffice" thereunder by Rule 84 also supply some specific factual matter in addition to the conclusory statements that "defendant owes plaintiff money" or that "defendant negligently drove a motor vehicle against plaintiff."[61] In other words, they imply that the complaint should state the

---

[54] 355 U.S. at 45–46, 48.

[55] 139 F.2d 774 (2d Cir. 1944).

[56] 139 F.2d at 775 (bracketed material in original). The full amended complaint is reproduced in JOHN J. COUND, JACK H. FRIEDENTHAL, ARTHUR R. MILLER & JOHN E. SEXTON, CIVIL PROCEDURE: CASES AND MATERIALS 502–03 n.1 (7th ed. 1997).

[57] *Dioguardi*, 139 F.2d at 775.

[58] WRIGHT § 68 (citations omitted).

[59] *See, e.g., Sparrow v. United Air Lines, Inc.*, 216 F.3d 1111 (D.C. Cir. 2000).

[60] *Bell Atlantic Corp. v. Twombly*, 127 S. Ct. 1955, 1968 (U.S. 2007), discussed in § 8.04[1][d], *infra*. Many prior courts and commentators had made the same observation. *See Car Carriers, Inc. v. Ford Motor Co.*, 745 F.2d 1101, 1106 (7th Cir. 1984), *cert. denied*, 470 U.S. 1054 (1985); Richard L. Marcus, *The Revival of Fact Pleading Under the Federal Rules of Civil Procedure*, 86 COLUM. L. REV. 433, 434 (1986) ("Taken literally, it might have precluded dismissal in any case where the plaintiff invoked a valid legal theory.").

[61] Forms10–15.

circumstances, occurrences, and events that give rise to the claim, even though they can be stated quite generally.[62]

The inclusion of such factual matter in both the case and the forms provided support for the view that screening sham or legally insufficient complaints is still a proper secondary function. As Judge Richard Posner put it, the purpose of the federal pleading rule under this view is less to give defendant information with which to prepare his defense "than to allow the court to determine at the outset . . . whether the plaintiff has any tenable theory or basis of suit, so that if he does not the case can be got rid of immediately without clogging the court's docket and imposing needless expense on the defendant."[63]

Taking this view of modern pleading, some courts have required that "a complaint must . . . contain either direct or inferential allegations respecting all the material elements necessary to sustain a recovery under *some* viable legal theory."[64] Bare notice is insufficient; the pleader must at least allege sufficient factual detail to set out all the elements necessary to establish a claim — usually duty, breach, injury, and causation.[65] Such a complaint is said to state a *prima facie* claim. The Supreme Court, however, seemed to reject the idea that a complaint had to plead facts corresponding to all the elements of a claim, asserting that a *prima facie* case is an evidentiary standard, not a pleading standard.[66]

Still, although a plaintiff may not be required to plead facts "in support of every arcane element of his claim," he should not omit those facts that "would clearly dominate the case," or else the court may fairly assume that they do not exist.[67] It may even be fair to require that a sufficient pleading allege facts establishing a civil analogue to probable cause in criminal proceedings — probable cause to believe in the existence of a claim entitling plaintiff to relief.[68] This view of pleading leaves most of the work of discovery, preparation guidance, and merits dispositions to other procedural devices under the rules, but still affords appropriately limited scope for merits dispositions on the pleadings to screen undeserving cases.

Moreover, whether or not the relevant circuit requires so much, in fact most competent lawyers try, as a matter of good practice, to plead factual allegations corresponding to all the elements of each of their claims. Furthermore,

---

[62] WRIGHT § 68 (citations omitted).

[63] *Ryan v. Mary Immaculate Queen Ctr.*, 188 F.3d 857, 860 (7th Cir. 1999).

[64] *In re Plywood Antitrust Litigation*, 655 F.2d 627, 641 (5th Cir. 1981) (emphasis in original), *cert. denied*, 462 U.S. 1125 (1983). *See Car Carriers, Inc. v. Ford Motor Co.*, 745 F.2d 1101 (7th Cir. 1984), *cert. denied*, 470 U.S. 1054 (1985). *See generally* Marcus, note 60, *supra*, at 459–65.

[65] *See* § 8.06[2], *infra*.

[66] *Swierkiewicz v. Sorema N.A.*, 534 U.S. 506, 510–12 (2002). *See* MOORE § 8.04[1a] (3d ed. 2007).

[67] *O'Brien v. Di Grazia*, 544 F.2d 543, 545 n.3 (1st Cir. 1976). *See also Daves v. Hawaiian Dredging Co.*, 114 F. Supp. 643, 645 (D. Haw. 1953); WRIGHT & MILLER § 1216. This proposition is reinforced by the care and candor requirements of Rule 11. *See* § 8.05[2] (certification), *infra*.

[68] *See* JAMES, HAZARD & LEUBSDORF § 3.6.

an attorney setting out the client's cause in writing for the first time may not want the simplest statement of the claim possible. This pleader may well desire to impress the client, the opponent, the opponent's insurance adjuster, the opponent's counsel, and, in appropriate cases, the public. Pleaders want pleadings to make a statement that draws attention to the claim and impresses with its seriousness; and pleaders may resort to unnecessary legal theorizing or statements of impressive but unnecessary evidentiary facts to make the desired impression.[69]

"Elements pleading" is therefore arguably the de facto federal pleading standard, whether or not it is required as a matter of rule interpretation.

[c]   **Heightened Pleading**

Until at least 1993, however, some circuits went beyond even elements pleading and selectively used an especially demanding version of this approach to dispose of disfavored actions on the pleadings. Typically these actions were disfavored because of the heavy burden they placed on the courts relative to their apparent rate of success. The *heightened pleading* standard was essentially a revival of fact pleading[70] as the courts insisted on very specific factual pleading of the elements in disfavored actions. It was thus applied to prisoners' complaints, partly because incarcerated plaintiffs are uninhibited by the usual practical and ethical restraints on frivolous suits against governmental officials.[71] Some circuits also applied it to other civil rights actions,[72] citing the volume of such cases, the number that are frivolous, and a consequential "public policy to weed out the [latter] at an early stage in the litigation."[73] Less systematically, courts applied the heightened pleading standard to securities fraud and antitrust complaints[74] and complaints against government action.[75]

From the start, this trend raised problems that had been associated with fact pleading under the codes.[76] Imposing special fact pleading requirements on disfavored actions introduces the same ad hoc differences of degree in

---

[69] Moore § 8.04[7a].

[70] See Marcus, note 60, *supra*, at 433.

[71] See James Dickson Phillips, Jr., *Foreword*, 39 Wash. & Lee L. Rev. 425, 428 (1982).

[72] See Douglas A. Blaze, *Presumed Frivolous: Application of Stringent Pleading Requirements in Civil Rights Litigation*, 31 Wm. & Mary L. Rev. 935 (1990); Keith Wingate, *A Special Pleading Rule for Civil Rights Complaints: A Step Forward or a Step Back?*, 49 Mo. L. Rev. 677 (1984); Marcus, note 60, *supra*, at 449–50.

[73] *Rotolo v. Borough of Charleroi*, 532 F.2d 920, 922 (3d Cir. 1976) (quoting *Valley v. Maule*, 297 F. Supp. 958 (D. Conn. 1968)).

[74] Marcus, note 60, *supra*, at 447–49.

[75] Marcus, note 60, *supra*, at 447–49. (noting use of special "fact" pleading rules to resolve questions of standing in such challenges). *See, e.g., Lujan v. National Wildlife Fed'n*, 497 U.S. 871 (1990) (finding that individualized injury was not pled with sufficient specificity to establish standing to challenge government action).

[76] See § 8.03[3], *supra*, discussing *Gillispie v. Goodyear Serv. Stores*, 128 S.E.2d 762 (N.C. 1963).

pleading that created such uncertainty under the codes,[77] and thus invites a sufficiency attack on the complaint in every disfavored action. Selective application of heightened pleading requirements also may reflect hidden judicial value preferences about the rights being asserted.[78] Not only are such preferences often contrary to those reflected by the congressional grant of federal jurisdiction to hear the judicially disfavored actions, but they may also be based on erroneous assumptions about the number of claims that are frivolous.[79] It is arguably for the legislature and the rulemakers to articulate and implement such preferences, not the courts.[80] Furthermore, more affluent (hence well-counseled) litigants can almost always meet a special pleading requirement whereas the pro se litigant often cannot. The difference will not necessarily reflect differences between the merits of their claims.

The Supreme Court's decision in *Leatherman v. Tarrant County Narcotics Intelligence and Coordination Unit*[81] finally slowed — though it did not halt — the trend towards applying heightened pleading. There, the district court had applied the Fifth Circuit's heightened pleading standard to dismiss two civil rights complaints alleging municipal liability. In a brief opinion, the Court unanimously found it "impossible to square the 'heightened pleading standard' . . . with the liberal system of 'notice pleading' set up by the Federal Rules."[82] Rule 9(b) *does* impose specific pleading requirements in certain listed instances, but its very existence precludes applying them to other instances. This reasoning applies with equal force to other applications of the heightened pleading standard and therefore may hasten its demise.

This is not to conclude that bare notice should always be sufficient under modern pleading rules. Scholars have, in fact, remarked on "the puzzling persistence of pleading practice" into the next millennium, concluding that, in a small but significant number of cases, heightened pleading and its enforcement by Rule 12 motion practice help to implement substantive law and dispose of unsupportable claims.[83]

---

[77] *See Rotolo*, 532 F.2d at 924–25 (Gibbons, J., dissenting) (faulting majority for introducing "puzzling" standard of pleading sufficiency that evidently contemplates the pleading of evidence "beyond any prior holding of this court").

[78] *Rotolo*, 532 F.2d at 927 ("The explanation . . . for the imposition of a fact pleading requirement in [civil rights] cases . . . must be found in the attitude of the court toward the rights being asserted.").

[79] 532 F.2d at 927. *See, e.g.*, Eisenstadt, *Section 1983: Doctrinal Foundations and an Empirical Study*, 67 Cornell L. Rev. 482, 537 (1982) ("The vast majority of nonprisoner section 1983 cases involve classic rights of obvious importance; the trivial claims are a sideshow.").

[80] The federal rulemakers have already set out a few special pleading requirements in Rule 9. *See* § 8.04[4], *infra*. Arguably, the omission of other special pleading requirements was intentional and should be cured by the rulemakers, subject to congressional disapproval, *see* § 1.02 (the rulemaking process), *supra*, rather than by the courts.

[81] 507 U.S. 163 (1993).

[82] 507 U.S. at 168.

[83] Richard L. Marcus, *The Puzzling Persistence of Pleading Practice*, 76 Tex. L. Rev. 1749 (1998).

[d]   Plausible Pleading

The Supreme Court muddied the pleading waters in 2007 with its decision in *Bell Atlantic Corp. v. Twombly*.[84] In *Twombly*, plaintiffs brought an antitrust claim under the Sherman Act charging that a group of regional telephone companies ("Baby Bells") had conspired to restrain competition. They alleged that the Baby Bells had conspired to engage in parallel conduct to inhibit the growth of certain upstart local companies and to refrain from competing with one another in contiguous markets. Except for "a few stray statements [that] speak directly of agreement,"[85] plaintiffs relied on an inference of agreement from their allegations of defendants' conscious parallel conduct. The lower court granted a motion to dismiss for failure to state a claim, observing that defendants' parallel conduct could equally be explained by their lawful self-interests. The Court of Appeals reversed, asserting that it could not conclude that "there is no set of facts that would permit a plaintiff to demonstrate that the particular parallelism asserted was the product of collusion rather than coincidence,"[86] a seemingly straightforward application of the *Conley v. Gibson* no-set-of-facts notice pleading formula.

The Supreme Court reversed. Stressing that Rule 8(a) itself requires a "showing," rather than just a blanket assertion, of entitlement to relief, it held that "stating . . . a [Sherman Act § 1] claim requires a complaint with enough factual matter (taken as true) to suggest that an agreement was made" — "plausible grounds to infer an agreement . . . ."[87] It acknowledged that the *Conley* no-set-of-facts formula seemed to set a lower pleading standard, but found that such a standard, literally read, would permit the survival of claims on the basis of the mere possibility that a plaintiff might later find facts to support them. In part to avoid the massive discovery costs that this reading could unleash, the Court reasoned that a plaintiff in federal court must plead more than mere possibility, if less than probability. She must plead "enough facts to state a claim to relief that is plausible on its face," that crosses the "line from conceivable to plausible . . . ."[88]

Applying this "plausibility standard" to the complaint, the Court found that the parallel conduct alleged was perfectly consistent with natural, lawful economic conduct of the defendants. Observing that mere conscious parallelism can be "consistent with conspiracy, but just as much in line with a wide swath of rational and competitive business strategy unilaterally prompted

---

[84] 127 S. Ct. 1955 (U.S. 2007). *See generally* Saritha Komatireddy Tice, *A "Plausible" Explanation of Pleading Standards: Bell Atlantic Corp. v. Twombly*, 31 HARV. J.L. & PUB. POL'Y 827 (2008); Benjamin Spencer, *Plausibility Pleading*, 49 *B.C. L. Rev.* 431 (2008); Keith Bradley, *Pleading Standards Should Not Change After Bell Atlantic v. Twombly*, 102 NW. U. L. REV. COLLOQUY 117 (2007); Amy J. Wildermuth, *What Twombly and Mead Have in Common*, 102 NW. U. L. REV. COLLOQUY at 276.

[85] 127 S. Ct. at 1971.

[86] 425 F.3d 99, 114 (2d Cir. 2005).

[87] 127 S. Ct. at 1965.

[88] 127 S. Ct. at 1974.

by common perceptions of the market,"[89] the Court concluded that the complaint plausibly asserted no more. It therefore was properly dismissed.

Was *Twombly* merely an application of the pre-existing federal notice standards? Or, just the opposite, did it announce a new higher, possibly "heightened," federal pleading standard? Or did it do something in between, raising the bar for conspiracy claims in antitrust suits and possibly for similarly inferential and circumstantial claims in other cases as well?

The first alternative — that *Twombly* changed nothing[90] — is hard to square with its language. Not only did it expressly reject the *Conley* no-set-of-facts standard, but it also called into question two venerable corollaries. First, it dismissed plaintiffs' scattered allegations of actual agreement as "merely legal conclusions."[91] But the federal rules had been thought to have discarded the no-legal-conclusion rule of code pleading (*see* Form 11), as long the pleading also showed some facts entitling relief. Second, it seemingly refused to draw a plaintiff-favoring inference from allegations that supported both conspiracy and coincidental parallel conduct. Most importantly, the majority used "plausible" or variations on it fifteen times. "[I]t is difficult to see how [the allegation in Form 11 that defendant "negligently drove a motor vehicle against the plaintiff] . . . would enable a court to decide whether the negligence claims so asserted are 'plausible,'" even with the additional (minimal) factual allegations of time and place. *Twombly* seems to require something more.[92]

On the other hand, the opposite conclusion — that *Twombly* introduced a new, *generally* applicable higher standard[93] — may also be hard to square with its language and antitrust context. The Court went out of its way twice to stress that it was not requiring "any 'heightened' pleading standard" or "heightened fact pleading of specifics," and added that it was not seeking to broaden the scope of Rule 9 either. In disavowing *Conley*'s no-set-of-facts language, the Court left untouched the rest of *Conley* and other court formulae consistent with federal notice pleading. Indeed, just two weeks later, the Court stated that a complaint need only "'give the defendant fair notice of what

---

[89] 127 S. Ct. at 1964.

[90] *See, e.g., Equal Employment Opportunity Comm'n v. Concentra Health Servs., Inc.*, 496 F.3d 773, 779, 783 n.4 (7th Cir. 2007) (asserting, after *Twombly*, that "Rule 8(a)(2)'s 'short and plain statement of the claim' must contain a minimal level of factual detail, although that level is indeed very minimal"); Bradley, note 84, *supra* (arguing that "plausibility" is "antitrust jargon" and *Twombly* must be read in the context of antitrust law).

[91] 127 S. Ct. at 1970.

[92] *MOORE* § 8.04 [1][a] (2008).

[93] *See, e.g.,* Tice, note 84, *supra,* at 832 ("*Twombly* seems to have created a more stringent pleading standard"); Scott Dodson, *Pleading Standards after Bell Atlantic Corp. v. Twombly,* 93 VA. L. REV. IN BRIEF 135, 138 (2007), www.virginialawreview.org/inbrief/2007/07/09/dodson.pdf (link) ("The best reading of *Bell Atlantic* is that the new standard is absolute, that mere notice pleading is dead for all cases and causes of action"); Spencer, note 84, *supra* at 447 ("the Court's plausibility pleading is a new, more stringent pleading standard that deprives plaintiffs the benefits of inferences in their favor when the pleaded facts are consistent with alternate explanations that do not involve wrongdoing").

the . . . claim is and the grounds upon which it rests,'" quoting *Conley*, as quoted in *Twombly*, without ever mentioning "plausibility."[94]

With the dry understatement that "these conflicting signals create some uncertainty as to the intended scope of the Court's decision," the Second Circuit Court of Appeals has charted the third course, somewhere in between.[95] "[W]e believe the Court is not requiring a universal standard of heightened fact pleading, but is instead requiring a flexible 'plausibility standard,' which obligates a pleader to amplify a claim with some factual allegations in those contexts where such amplification is needed to render the claim *plausible*."[96] This alternative sounds like a plausible (no pun intended) interpretation of *Twombly*, but it introduces its own uncertainty: how to identify "contexts where such amplification is needed."[97] Conspiracy allegations in antitrust claims are clearly one. The *Iqbal* court declined to find that substantive and procedural due process claims in a civil rights suit were another, although it urged tight case management to give effect to the defendants' possible defense of qualified immunity. Other circuits have not helped to resolve this uncertainty. They have applied *Twombly* to Title VII violations, cruel and unusual punishment, age discrimination, privacy, intentional infliction of emotional distress, and free speech claims, among many others, showing no distinctive common characteristics that your authors can discern.[98]

However, the conspiracy allegation in *Twombly* may suggest a few. The allegation was made in stating a complex antitrust claim, as opposed to a simple negligence claim. It described events equally susceptible to a lawful as to an unlawful explanation. Finally, if the complaint was sustained on a bare, merely possible allegation of conspiracy, it risked opening the door to vastly expensive and protracted antitrust discovery, with resulting *in terrorem* pressure for settlement.[99] It remains to be seen whether courts that follow *Iqbal*'s lead will refine the test for "contexts where . . . amplification is needed."

Yet *Twombly* produced two certainties and a prediction. One is that every defendant's lawyer worth her salt will surely invoke it to attack complaints in

---

[94] *Erickson v. Pardus*, 127 S. Ct. 2197, 2200 (U.S. 2007), quoting *Twombly*, 127 S. Ct. at 1973 n. 14 (citing *Leatherman* and authority quoting it). *Erickson* was a pro se complaint, for which pleading rules have traditionally been relaxed, but the Court stated the "fair notice" pleading standard before turning to relaxed pleading for pro se litigants.

[95] *Iqbal v. Hasty*, 490 F.3d 143, 157 (2d Cir. 2007), *cert. granted*, 128 S. Ct. 2931 (U.S. 2008).

[96] *Iqbal*, 490 F.3d at 158. Some commentators call this a "notice-plus" pleading standard for certain types of cases. *See* Dodson, note 93, *supra*, at 138.

[97] *See* Amanda Sue Nichols, *Alien Tort Statute Accomplice Liability Cases: Should Courts Apply the Plausibility Pleading Standard of Bell Atlantic v. Twombly?*, 76 Fordham L. Rev. 2177, 2222 (2008) (urging yes to question in title, citing large and complex corporate character of defendants, costs of litigation, and other factors). *See generally* Moore § 8.04 (2008) (urging application of plausibility pleading standard to complex but not to simple claims).

[98] *See* cases cited in Wright & Miller § 1216 n.32.17 (2008 Pocket Part).

[99] *See Iqbal*, 490 F.3d at 157 (plausibility pleading standard may be "limited to cases where massive discovery is likely to create unacceptable settlement pressures").

federal court. The other is that every plaintiff's lawyer worth his salt will anticipate the attack by pleading more facts than he would have thought required before *Twombly*. We predict that judges, now slightly better armed to weed out weak cases, will grant incrementally more motions to dismiss for failure to state a claim, citing *Twombly*.[100]

[2]   Consistency and the Theory of the Pleadings in Modern Pleading

Whatever view is taken of the basic requirement of notice pleading, the de-emphasis of pleading under modern notice pleading has substantially eliminated the theory-of-the-pleadings approach[101] and the related concepts of variance and election of remedies. "It is not necessary to set out the legal theory on which the claim is based,"[102] so long as there exists some theory that would entitle the claimant to relief. The test for the sufficiency of a pleading is whether the pleader has stated a claim under *any* legal theory, not just under *his* asserted theory of the pleadings. Rule 8(d) expressly permits the pleading of alternative or hypothetical claims and defenses and as many claims or defenses as a party has "regardless of consistency," and Rule 8(a) permits demands for alternative types of relief. The rulemakers recognized that a party often does not know enough to elect a legal theory at the start of the litigation and that a compelled election by the pleadings would either encourage needlessly verbose pleading, defeating the objective of short and plain statements, or entrap the uninformed.

If the pleadings are of reduced significance before trial, after trial they "lose such little significance as they had before, and judgment is to be in accordance with the evidence."[103] Rule 15(b) permits amendment of the pleadings to conform to the evidence at trial, and indeed provides for constructive amendment when the parties have consented to any variance from the pleadings.[104] As discussed in more detail below,[105] the focus of the rule on amendment is properly now on possible prejudice to the opposing parties, rather than on the initial intent of the pleader in electing his legal theory. Moreover, Rule 54(c) provides that "[e]very . . . final judgment should grant the relief to which each party is entitled, even if the party has not demanded that relief in its pleadings."[106]

---

[100] Wildermuth, note 84, *supra*, at 276 (cited in 5000 cases by April 2008, less than a year after opinion was announced).

[101] *See* § 8.03[2] (cause of action and theory of pleadings in code pleading), *supra*.

[102] *Siegelman v. Cunard White Star, Ltd.*, 221 F.2d 189, 196 (2d Cir. 1955) (Harlan, J.).

[103] WRIGHT § 68.

[104] *See* § 8.10[2] (amendment during and after trial), *infra*.

[105] *See* § 8.10, *infra*.

[106] *See, e.g., Webb v. Arresting Officers*, 749 F.2d 500 (8th Cir. 1984) (plaintiff was entitled to judgment on his post-trial theory that defendants had a duty to intervene for his protection, as long as it was tried and proven, even though this theory was never alleged in the pleadings and his pleaded theory of unnecessary force was not proven).

For several reasons, however, the theory of the pleadings doctrine is not wholly dead. First, the substantive law may require a party to elect his remedies. Thus a party that started by seeking one remedy or asserting one theory may be estopped from switching in mid-stream to another when defendant has reasonably relied in some fashion on the initial election.[107] But the election is not compelled as a matter of pleading form in such a case; it is rooted in the substantive law of estoppel.[108]

Second, the theory of the pleadings may determine which statute of limitations is applicable to the action[109] and whether the pleader is entitled to a jury trial as a matter of right.[110] Limitations periods vary by type of action, and constitutional and some statutory guarantees of jury trial are often tied to historical forms of action or other particular kinds of suit.[111]

Third, federal judges are authorized by Rule 16 to frame pretrial orders that may require the parties to exchange pretrial briefs in which they commit to particular legal theories.[112] Such orders are binding unless modified, and the last pretrial order may be modified "only to prevent manifest injustice."[113]

Fourth, obligations of candor and care may also restrict a pleader's freedom to plead inconsistently, change his legal theory, or introduce new lines of proof. "[A]lternative pleading is not permitted when in the nature of things the pleader must know which of the inconsistent averments is true and which is false."[114]

[3]   The Form of Notice Pleading

Modern notice pleading requires no "technical form" of pleading.[115] While sufficient under the rules, the form pleadings that accompany the federal rules are only examples.[116] A pleading need only include a caption, numbered paragraphs containing averments "limited as far as practicable to a statement of a single set of circumstances," and separate counts for different claims or defenses ("whenever a separation facilitates the clear presentation of the matters set forth").[117] Averments may be incorporated by reference and by

---

[107] *See generally* Charles E. Clark, Handbook of the Law of Code Pleading § 77 (2d ed. 1947).

[108] *Id.*

[109] *See generally* § 8.08[2][b] (the statute of limitations), *infra.*

[110] *See* § 12.07[1] (right to jury trial), *infra.*

[111] For example, the Seventh Amendment provides that "[i]n suits at common law, where the value in controversy shall exceed twenty dollars, the right of trial by jury shall be preserved." U.S. Const. amend. VII. It thus ties the right to a jury trial to actions that originated in the common law or are analogous to common law actions and is inapplicable to equitable actions. *See* § 12.07[1] (right to a jury trial), *infra.*

[112] *See* § 12.03[3] (pretrial orders), *infra.*

[113] Rule 16(e).

[114] *Church v. Adler,* 113 N.E.2d 327, 332 (Ill. App. Ct. 1953). *See* § 8.05[2] (certification), *infra.*

[115] Rule 8(e)(1).

[116] Rule 84.

[117] Rule 10(a) & (b).

documents attached to the pleading.[118] None of these requirements is strictly enforced because "[a]ll pleadings shall be so construed as to do substantial justice."[119]

[4]   Special Pleading Rules in Modern Pleading

Notice pleading is the norm. Yet most modern pleading jurisdictions retain a few idiosyncratic special pleading rules, in addition to judge-made special pleading requirements for disfavored litigation. Special pleading rules are adopted for practical reasons which are reflected in Rule 9. They may be enforced by motions to strike or dismiss or for more definite statements.[120]

Some special pleading rules were adopted to discourage disfavored litigation. Fraud suits, for example, are disfavored because of the injury they may do to reputations and their potential to intimidate.[121] Claims of mistake are also disfavored because they upset the normal business expectations underlying contract law. As a result, Rule 9(b) requires that a party "state with particularity the circumstances constituting fraud or mistake." It must be harmonized, however, with the general pleading directives of Rule 8; Rule 9(b) "does not require nor make legitimate the pleading of detailed evidentiary matter."[122] The Supreme Court has also reminded us to harmonize Rule 9(b) with "the flexibility provided by Rule 11(b)(3),"[123] which allows anticipatory pleading: pleading of contentions "likely [to] have evidentiary support after a reasonable opportunity for further investigation or discovery."[124]

What this kind of specific pleading requirement really achieves is only a marginal increase in the trial court's discretion to use the pleadings to screen disfavored litigation, usually without much lasting effect.[125]

Legislatures are free, of course, to impose special pleading requirements by statute to discourage disfavored litigation. An example is the 1995 Private Securities Litigation Reform Act,[126] which was passed to curb alleged abuses in federal securities litigation. The Act requires the plaintiff to "state with particularity facts giving rise to a strong inference that the defendant acted

---

[118]   Rule 10(c).

[119]   Rule 8(f).

[120]   *See* § 8.07[2][a] (challenging defects of form), *infra*.

[121]   *See, e.g., Ross v. A. H. Robins Co.*, 607 F.2d 545 (2d Cir. 1979), *cert. denied*, 446 U.S. 946 (1980) (citing importance of fair notice, of protecting defendants from harm to reputation and goodwill, and of reducing possibility that plaintiffs will pursue largely groundless fraud claims for their *in terrorem* settlement value).

[122]   *Ross*, 607 F.2d at 557 n.20.

[123]   *Rotella v. Wood*, 528 U.S. 549, 560 (2000).

[124]   *See* § 8.05[2][b], *infra*.

[125]   *See generally* William M. Richman et al., *The Pleading of Fraud: Rhymes Without Reason*, 60 S. Cal. L. Rev. 959 (1987); William C. Baskin III, Note, *Using Rule 9(b) to Reduce Nuisance Securities Litigation*, 99 Yale L.J. 1591 (1990).

[126]   Pub. L. 104-52, 109 Stat. 737 (codified in scattered sections of 15 U.S.C. (Supp. I 1995)).

with the required state of mind" for liability.[127] It also requires specific pleading for alleging false or misleading statements. The Act appears not to have had a dramatic effect on pleading practice, but it certainly encourages courts to take a closer look at securities fraud complaints.[128]

Other special pleading rules promote pleading efficiency and convenience. Under the law of contract, the plaintiff usually must have performed all conditions precedent to defendant's contractual obligations before he may complain of a breach. But in the typical case in which defendant does not dispute performance of such conditions precedent, it would be wasteful to require plaintiff to plead them compendiously. Rule 9(c) therefore permits plaintiff to aver generally the performance of all conditions precedent and requires defendant to deny performance "with particularity."[129] The same rationale accounts for the requirement in Rule 9(a) that defendant specifically challenge the legal existence or capacity of a party to sue.

Special pleading is sometimes required to avoid surprise. The averment of injury or breach of contract puts defendant fairly on notice that the kinds of damages usually associated with injury (pain and suffering) or with breach (lost profits on the contract) will be claimed. No special pleading of such *general damages* is required. But general pleading is insufficient to put defendant on notice of unusual or unanticipated damages of a sort not ordinarily associated with the alleged injury or breach. Rule 9(g) therefore requires that items of *special damage* "be specifically stated." For example, the failure specifically to plead damages for higher blood pressure said to have been caused by an automobile collision prevented their recovery in *Ziervogel v. Royal Packing Co.*,[130] because this kind of damage, unlike damages for back or neck injuries, is not a normal and expected consequence of such an accident.

Finally, special pleading may reflect the requirements of the substantive law.[131] The usual rule of contract law, for example, is that plaintiff may only recover those damages within the contemplation of the parties at the time that the contract was made.[132] The pleading of "specials" in a contract case is therefore required to state the plaintiff's *prima facie* case. Similarly, the law's solicitude for free expression and competition, and its suspicion of intangible injuries to reputation, are reflected in the common substantive requirement that a plaintiff suing for defamation, slander, libel or disparagement show special damages and their proximate causation by the tort.[133] A pleading that

---

[127] Pub. L. 104-52, 109 Stat. 737.

[128] Marcus, note 83, *supra*, at 1765–67.

[129] *See generally* § 8.06[2], *infra*, for discussion of the allocation of pleading burdens.

[130] 225 S.W.2d 798 (Mo. Ct. App. 1949). Other special damages include medical expenses; unusual injuries such as induced abortion, epilepsy and insanity; expenses incurred in mitigation; and losses of use and income. *See Restatement (Second) of Torts* § 904, cmt. b (1979).

[131] *See* Jeffrey A. Parness et al., *The Substantive Elements in the New Special Pleading Laws*, 78 NEB. L. REV. 412 (1999).

[132] *See, e.g., Hadley v. Baxendale*, 156 Eng. Rep. 145 (1854).

[133] *See, e.g., Fairyland Amusement Co. v. Metromedia, Inc.*, 413 F. Supp. 1290 (W.D. Mo. 1976) (defamation, slander and libel complaint dismissed for plaintiff's failure to plead specifically its loss

omits such specific allegations not only offends special pleading rules, but fails to state a claim for relief.

§ 8.05 CANDOR AND CARE REQUIREMENTS IN MODERN PLEADING

The simplicity and flexibility of modern notice pleading has expanded opportunity for the careless or sharp practitioner to abuse pleading to bluff, bargain, delay, or harass. Motion practice[134] has been the most effective tool for coping with such abuses. However, most jurisdictions have also imposed candor or care standards on litigants and/or their attorneys, requiring *verification or certification* of pleadings.[135]

[1] Verification

Verification of a pleading attests under oath to the truth of its contents, effectively transforming it into an affidavit usable as evidence at trial when the averments are made on the pleader's personal knowledge. Jurisdictions that still require verification reserve it for pleadings in actions that turn uniquely on allegations whose truth or falsity are known only to the parties, such as domestic relations actions. Verification is not generally required of federal pleadings[136] because it would defeat the intentions of the federal rulemakers by either preventing the unsure plaintiff from filing at all or forcing her into a premature election of facts. Moreover, the requirement that *parties* verify their pleadings is ineffective to encourage good faith and reasonable inquiry by their *attorneys*, whom many regard as the principal source of procedural abuse in modern litigation.

[2] Certification and Rule 11

A certification requirement suffers neither of these defects. Instead of verifying the allegations of the pleading, the signatory — usually the attorney of record or pro se litigant — certifies only to proper purpose and reasonable care in filing the pleading. Rule 11 is an example of a particularly strong certification requirement. Many states have modeled their own certification requirements on some version of the federal rule.[137]

---

of patronage as a result of the false publication).

[134] *See* § 8.07 (motion practice), *infra.*

[135] In addition, federal courts have both statutory and inherent power to punish attorney and litigant misconduct. *See* § 8.05[2][e] (sanctions), *infra.*

[136] *But see* Rule 23.1; *cf.* Rules 27, 65 & 68. *See Surowitz v. Hilton Hotels Corp.*, 383 U.S. 363 (1966) (purpose of verification for shareholder derivative suits under Rule 23.1 is to discourage "strike suits," filed to coerce settlement regardless of their truth).

[137] Gerald F. Hess, *Rule 11 Practice in Federal and State Court: An Empirical, Comparative Study*, 75 MARQ. L. REV. 313, 315 n.8, 316 n.9 (1992); *Report of the Special Committee to Consider Sanctions for Frivolous Litigation in New York State Courts*, 18 FORDHAM URB. L.J. 3, 32–33 (1990) (comparing state approaches to abusive litigation).

[a]   Rule 11 in General[138]

Prior to 1983, Rule 11 provided that by signing a pleading, motion or other paper, an attorney or party certified that he had read the pleading, that "to the best of his knowledge, information, and belief" there was "good ground to support it," and that it was "not interposed for delay." The rule authorized but did not mandate unspecified "disciplinary action" for "*wilful* violation[s]."[139] The implied prerequisite of subjective intent and the absence of any required sanctions, however, rendered the pre-1983 rule of little use in federal courts. Only 19 cases involving Rule 11 motions were reported between 1938 and 1983.[140]

Concluding that "[e]xperience shows that in practice Rule 11 has not been effective in deterring abuses,"[141] the Advisory Committee on Civil Rules completely revised the rule in 1983. The 1983 revision provided that by signing a pleading or other paper, the attorney or party certified that, "to the best of his knowledge, information, and belief formed after reasonable inquiry it is well-grounded in fact and warranted by existing law or a good faith argument for the extension, modification, or reversal of existing law, and that it is not interposed for any improper purpose." Under the 1983 rule, it was not only what an attorney actually believed (subjective good faith) that mattered, but what he should have believed as a competent attorney after reasonable pre-filing inquiry (objective reasonableness).[142] The substitution of an objective for

---

[138] Probably more has been written about Rule 11 since 1983 than about any other civil procedure topic. *See generally* GEORGENE VAIRO, RULE 11 SANCTIONS: CASE LAW PERSPECTIVES AND PREVENTIVE MEASURES APP. F (2d ed. 1995 Supp.) (listing law review articles). The rule has spawned its own looseleaf service, *id.*, its own newsletter, *see Attorney Sanctions Newsletter* (Shepard's), several book-length analyses, *see, e.g.*, SECTION OF LITIG., AMERICAN BAR ASS'N, SANCTIONS: RULE 11 & OTHER POWERS (M. Nelken, ed.) (3d ed. 1992); GREGORY P. JOSEPH, SANCTIONS: THE FEDERAL LAW OF LITIGATION ABUSE (1989), and a host of empirical studies. *See, e.g.*, Lawrence C. Marshall et al., *The Use and Impact of Rule 11*, 86 Nw. U. L. REV. 943 (1992); FEDERAL JUDICIAL CENTER, RULE 11: FINAL REPORT TO THE ADVISORY COMM. ON CIVIL RULES OF THE JUD. CONF. OF THE U.S. (undated), *summarized in* Elizabeth Wiggins et al., *The Federal Judicial Center's Study of Rule 11*, 2 FJC DIRECTIONS (1991); STEPHEN B. BURBANK, AMERICAN JUDICATURE SOC'Y, RULE 11 IN TRANSITION: THE REPORT OF THE THIRD CIRCUIT TASK FORCE ON FEDERAL RULE OF CIVIL PROCEDURE 11 (1989).

[139] *WRIGHT & MILLER* § 1331 (emphasis added).

[140] D. Michael Risinger, *Honesty in Pleading and Its Enforcement: Some "Striking" Problems With Federal Rule of Civil Procedure 11*, 61 MINN. L. REV. 1, 35–37 (1976). Of course, one would expect that most Rule 11 motions are unreported. *See* Wiggins, note 138, *supra*, at (finding that only 6.6% of district court cases involving Rule 11 activity were reported, and that reporting practices were highly variable); BURBANK, note 138, *supra*, at 59 (only 9% of dispositions involving Rule 11 were reported in Third Circuit sample; only 33% were available on Lexis). But even if ten times as many cases were decided as were reported prior to 1983, the reported case data would indicate fewer than 200 Rule 11 cases over forty-five years.

[141] Rule 11 advisory committee's notes (1983).

[142] *See* Rule 11 advisory committee's notes (1983). Although the text of the 1983 rule contained both objective and subjective components, the rulemakers clearly intended to eliminate the necessity for a finding of subjective bad faith as a predicate for sanctions, in a deliberate departure from prior case law. *See, e.g.*, *Eastway Constr. Co. v. City of New York*, 762 F.2d 243, 253 (2d Cir. 1985). The no-improper-purpose requirement also prohibited, for example, the filing of tactical pleadings or motions to upset settlement negotiations in order to obtain fee-related concessions from defendant in other litigation, *In re Itel Sec. Litig.*, 596 F. Supp. 226 (N.D. Cal. 1984), *aff'd*, 791

a subjective standard made it easier for courts to find violations, and the mandatory sanction provision of the 1983 rule appeared to require them to punish such violations.

Practice under the 1983 rule, however, suggested to some that the pendulum had swung too far. Between 1983 and 1993, there were 6000 reported Rule 11 cases.[143] Eighty-one percent of the federal judges surveyed in one study thought that the 1983 rule had a positive effect,[144] and the actual percentage of cases in which Rule 11 activity occurred was reported at only 2–3%.[145] Yet critics charged that enforcement was inconsistent and unpredictable; that the rule was enforced disproportionately against plaintiffs in general (and civil rights plaintiffs in particular) with chilling effects on novel plaintiffs' litigation; that courts relied almost exclusively on fee-shifting and compensation as sanctions, effectively modifying the American rule against fee-shifting; that sanctions were often imposed without fair procedure; and that Rule 11 motion practice had generated a Kafkaesque nightmare of satellite litigation (including Rule 11 motions against Rule 11 motions).[146] These criticisms were not always supported by the empirical data, and some may have been premature (reflecting transitional problems in judicial applications of the 1983 rule revisions), but enough persisted to prompt another rule revision in 1993.

As discussed in subsections [b] and [c] below, the 1993 rule equalized the burdens imposed by the rule on plaintiffs and defendants. As discussed in subsection [d] below, it abolished mandatory sanctions in favor of discretionary non-monetary sanctions. It also made several other significant changes, several of which are noted in the remainder of this subsection.

First, Rule 11(b) expanded the scope of certification from a pleading or other paper to individual "claims, defenses, and other legal contentions" and "allegations and other factual contentions." It thus rejected the pleading-as-a-whole approach to Rule 11 taken by some courts, by which they found a violation only when the pleading as a whole (and not just some part of it)

F.2d 672 (9th Cir. 1986); motions to disqualify opposing counsel for the purpose of harassing the other side and increasing the costs of litigation, *Wold v. Minerals Eng'g Co.*, 575 F. Supp. 166 (D. Colo. 1983) (imposing attorney's fees on party who made the motion for these purposes); or attempts to continue the "economic and political warfare" of labor negotiations by using litigation to intimidate. *WSB Elec. Co. v. Rank and File Comm. to Stop 2-WSB Elec. Co. v. Rank and File Comm. to Stop 2-Gate Sys.*, 103 F.R.D. 417, 421 (N.D. Cal. 1984).

[143] Mark Spiegel, *The Rule 11 Studies and Civil Rights Cases: An Inquiry Into the Neutrality of Procedural Rules*, 32 Conn. L. Rev. 155, 157 (2000). This number of *reported* cases indicates that there may have been as many as 17,000 Rule 11 cases altogether in this decade. *See* Mark Spiegel, *The Rule 11 Studies and Civil Rights Cases: An Inquiry Into the Neutrality of Procedural Rules*, 32 Conn. L. Rev. 155, 157 (1999).

[144] Wiggins, note 138, *supra*, at 34.

[145] Wiggins, note 138, *supra*, at 6.

[146] *See, e.g.*, Wright & Miller § 1332; Burbank, note 138, *supra*, at 57, 65; Melissa L. Nelken, *Has the Chancellor Shot Himself in the Foot? Looking for a Middle Ground on Rule 11 Sanctions*, 41 Hastings L.J. 383 (1990); William W. Schwarzer, *Rule 11 Revisited*, 101 Harv. L. Rev. 1013 (1988).

violated the good grounds and proper purposes requirements.[147] Still, the 1983 Advisory Committee cautioned that Rule 11 motions "should not be made or threatened for minor, inconsequential violations." Inclusion of a minor ungrounded allegation or argument in an otherwise well-grounded paper thus should not be treated as a violation. Furthermore, the relative importance in the paper of the offending section may still be considered in deciding the severity of any sanction, as we discuss below in section [d].

Second, the 1993 rule amendments compromised on the issue whether of litigants have a continuing duty to correct or even withdraw papers in light of post-filing events. Most courts under the 1983 rule had rejected the concept of continuing duty in favor of a "snapshot rule." This focused only on whether a paper complied with the rule in "the instant when a picture is taken — when the signature is placed on the document."[148] These courts rejected the concept of continuing duty both because of the phrasing of the 1983 rule and the updating burden that such a duty would impose. In contrast, a few courts had imposed such a duty to effectuate the purpose of the rule.[149] The 1993 amendments provided that the rule is violated by "signing, filing, submitting, *or later advocating*" a paper when the litigant knows that it is no longer well-grounded.[150] Thus a lawyer who during a pretrial conference presses a claim or defense would be subject to the rule's obligations "measured as of that time" — not only as of the time she signed the paper containing the claim or defense.[151] On the other hand, the 1993 rule amendments did not saddle a litigant with the burden of curing pleadings by formal amendments to correct or withdraw such claims or defenses.[152]

Nevertheless, a litigant may formally withdraw such a claim or defense to bring itself into the rule's "safe harbor." Rule 11(c)(2) grants a litigant 21 days between service and filing of a Rule 11 motion[153] to correct or withdraw the

---

[147] *See, e.g.*, Carl Tobias, *Civil Rights Plaintiffs and the Proposed Revision of Rule 11*, 77 Iowa L. Rev. 1775, 1780 (1992). The majority of courts that had considered the issue had rejected the pleadings-as-a-whole approach. *See* Section of Litig., note 138, *supra*, at 3.

[148] *See, e.g., Thomas v. Capital Sec. Servs., Inc.*, 836 F.2d 866, 874 (5th Cir. 1988).

[149] *See cases cited in* Neal Klausner, Note, *The Dynamics of Rule 11: Preventing Frivolous Litigation by Demanding Professional Responsibility*, 61 N.Y.U. L. Rev. 300, 325–26 n.195 (1986).

[150] Rule 11(b) (emphasis added).

[151] Rule 11(b) advisory committee's notes (1993). The 1993 amendments thus make it clear that Rule 11 applies to the complaint in a case that has been removed from state to federal court once the plaintiff "advocates" the claims in that complaint in federal court.

[152] *See* James R. Simpson, Note, *Why Change Rule 11? Ramifications of the 1992 Amendment Proposal*, 29 Cal. W. L. Rev. 495, 508 (1993).

[153] The safe harbor is available only against Rule 11 motions and does not apply to show cause orders issued at the court's own initiative. Rule 11(c)(3). The 1993 Advisory Committee reasoned that show cause orders will ordinarily only be issued in extreme situations akin to contempt of court, which do not deserve any safe harbor. Rule 11 advisory committee's notes (1993). Relying on this language, the Second Circuit Court of Appeals reasoned that a court should apply a "bad faith" standard when it *sua sponte* sanctions a lawyer for a paper long after the offender has had an opportunity to correct or withdraw it, despite the absence of any bad faith requirement in the rule. *In re Pennie & Edmonds LLP*, 323 F.3d 86 (2d Cir. 2003). *Contra Jenkins v. Methodist Hospitals of Dallas, Inc.*, 478 F.3d 255 (5th Cir. 2007).

offending paper. This provision is intended to reduce the amount of satellite litigation under the rule by letting rule offenders moot Rule 11 motions before they are filed in court. It may only codify what some lawyers are doing already. On the other hand, some critics view this informal practice of "threat and retreat" as "problematic," concluding that its codification will accentuate "one of [the former] Rule's worst features . . . ."[154] Justice Scalia also objected to the safe-harbor provision on the ground that it will encourage abusers, because they "will be able to file thoughtless, reckless, and harassing pleadings, secure in the knowledge that they have nothing to lose . . . ."[155]

[b]   Evidentiary Support

Rule 11(b)(3) and (4) require litigants to certify that their factual allegations or denials of factual allegations "have evidentiary support or, if specifically so identified, will likely have evidentiary support after a reasonable opportunity for further investigation or discovery." This provision clarifies and expands the 1983 rule in several respects.

Because it extends to *denials* of factual allegations, the 1993 rule has helped equalize the burden imposed on plaintiffs and defendants. By insisting just on *evidentiary support*, the rule makes clear that the litigant is not required to certify that its factual contentions will prevail.[156] Moreover, by authorizing certification of allegations that "likely" will have such support, the rule gives plaintiffs the same option of "information-and-belief" pleading now afforded defendants by Rule 8(c). This also lessens the rule's previously disproportionate impact on plaintiffs. The provision slightly relaxes the former rule's ban on "file now, check later" practice, by affording "a reasonable [post-filing] opportunity for further investigation" of specifically identified information-and-belief contentions, so long as the litigant has done its best before filing.[157] If that investigation turns up no evidentiary support for such contentions, then the litigant may not continue to advocate them.

At the same time, tolerance of anticipatory, "likely-to-have-support" pleading poses a dilemma for the pleader. On one hand, the pleader is not expressly required to have that support at the time of the pleading, provided he specifically identifies the "likely-to-have-support" contentions as such. On the other hand, the Advisory Committee warned that this tolerance "is not a license to join parties, make claims, or present defenses without any factual basis or justification."[158] What must the pleader do to engage in such anticipatory pleading without running afoul of the rule? The Advisory Committee's notes, coupled with the rule, suggest an answer.[159] First, he must still conduct a prefiling inquiry which is reasonable in the circumstances.

---

[154] Carl Tobias, *Reconsidering Rule 11*, 46 U. Miami L. Rev. 855, 877 (1992).

[155] Dissenting statement of Justice Scalia on Amendments to the Federal Rules of Civil Procedure, 113 S. Ct. CCCVI, CCCVII (1993).

[156] Rule 11(b) & (c) advisory committee's notes (1993).

[157] Rule 11(b) & (c) advisory committee's notes (1993).

[158] Rule 11(b) & (c) advisory committee's notes (1993).

[159] *See* Lisa Pondrom, Comment, *Predicting the Unpredictable Under Rule 11(b)(3): When Are*

Second, he must have some "factual basis" for his contentions, even if it is not yet in evidentiary form. Third, he must, if challenged, be able to demonstrate that there was a need and reasonable opportunity for further discovery, by showing that circumstances beyond his control — such as time constraints or his adversary's or a third party's control of the information — prevented him from obtaining evidentiary support before filing.

Reasonableness of the required inquiry both before and after filing takes into account the litigant's access to necessary factual information and time available in which to make inquiry. Since the litigant's state of mind is not controlling, reasonableness is open to empirical verification. The focus is upon the facts of the pre-filing investigation, although the 1983 Advisory Committee expressly cautioned the courts against using hindsight in making that examination.[160]

The cases suggest that the requisite pre-filing factual investigation must at least include a thorough interview with the client and the key witnesses, if they are available.[161]

> To decide if the attorney may rely solely on his client, he should determine if his knowledge is direct or hearsay and check closely the plausibility of the client's account. When an attorney must rely on his client, he should question him thoroughly, not accepting the client's version on faith alone. However, "if all the attorney has is his client's assurance that facts exist or do not exist, when a reasonable inquiry would reveal otherwise, he has not satisfied his obligation."[162]

It follows that when an attorney can obtain factual information from public sources, he must do so and cannot rely solely on his client.[163] On the other hand, if the necessary information is primarily within the control of the prospective defendants, reliance on the client is reasonable under the rule.[164]

[c] Legal Support

Reasonable inquiry into the law is what any competent attorney would make into the standard legal research sources. She must determine that any legal position asserted in a filing is warranted by existing law. Alternatively, in order not to chill advocacy for change in the law, Rule 11(b) shelters

---

Allegations "Likely" to Have Evidentiary Support?, 43 UCLA L. REV. 1393 (1996) (suggesting the answer in the text).

[160] Rule 11 advisory committee's notes (1983).

[161] *See Wold v. Minerals Eng'g Co.*, 575 F. Supp. 166, 167 (D. Colo. 1983); *Rhinehart v. Stauffer*, 638 F.2d 1169, 1171 (9th Cir. 1979) (decision under pre-1983 Rule 11).

[162] *Nassau-Suffolk Ice Cream, Inc. v. Integrated Res., Inc.*, 114 F.R.D. 684, 689 (S.D.N.Y. 1987) (quoting *Coburn Optical Indus., Inc. v. Cilco, Inc.*, 610 F. Supp. 656, 659 (M.D.N.C. 1985); other citations omitted). *See generally* James E. Ward IV, Note, *Rule 11 and Factually Frivolous Claims — The Goal of Cost Minimization and the Client's Duty to Investigate*, 44 VAND. L. REV. 1165 (1991).

[163] *Kendrick v. Zanides*, 609 F. Supp. 1162, 1172–73 (N.D. Cal. 1985); *Mohammed v. Union Carbide Corp.*, 606 F. Supp. 252 (E.D. Mich. 1985).

[164] *See, e.g., Kamen v. American Telephone & Telegraph Co.*, 791 F.2d 1006 (2d Cir. 1986).

"nonfrivolous argument for extending, modifying, or reversing existing law . . . ."[165] Critics argued that this shelter was insufficient for civil rights plaintiffs, who often advocate the recognition of new rights.[166] The 1993 amendments to the rule therefore added "[arguments for the] . . . establishment of new law" to the shelter.

Must such plaintiffs flag such claims as novel to alert the court and the opposing parties? Some courts concluded that they must, but the 1993 Advisory Committee said that "arguments for a change of law are not required to be specifically so identified, [although] a contention that is so identified should be viewed with greater tolerance under the rule."[167]

Does the duty of legally-warranted argument imposed by Rule 11(b)(2) carry with it a corollary duty of candor, for example, to disclose contrary legal authority in the papers? Assuming *arguendo* that the uncited authority was directly contrary, the Ninth Circuit Court of Appeals nevertheless concluded that

> neither Rule 11 nor any other rule imposes a requirement that the lawyer, in addition to advocating the cause of his client, step first into the shoes of opposing counsel to find all potentially contrary authority, and finally into the robes of the judge to decide whether the authority is indeed contrary or whether it is distinguishable.[168]

The court acknowledged that the ethical rules proposed by the American Bar Association prohibit an attorney from knowingly failing to disclose "legal authority in the controlling jurisdiction known to the lawyer to be directly adverse to the position of the client and not disclosed by opposing counsel."[169] But it concluded that Rule 11 should not be used for broad-spectrum enforcement of ethical obligations.[170]

Arguably, the court of appeals ignored both the language and the history of the Rule.[171] Focusing only on the requirement that a filing be warranted by existing law, the court disregarded the independent requirement that it not be

---

[165] For examples of frivolous legal claims, *see, e.g., Heimbaugh v. City and County of San Francisco*, 591 F. Supp. 1573 (N.D. Cal. 1984) (complaint alleged that city's ban on playing softball on field reserved for hardball violated First Amendment right to advocate democracy in sports); *Blair v. Shenandoah Women's Ctr., Inc.*, 757 F.2d 1435 (4th Cir. 1985) (attorney for a man who filed suit against a women's shelter in which his wife sought refuge from his abuse was properly assessed attorney's fees in view of the complaint's scandalous accusations and frivolous legal positions).

[166] See critics cited and analyzed in Mark Spiegel, *The Rule 11 Studies and Civil Rights Cases: An Inquiry in the Neutrality of Procedural Rules*, 32 Conn. L. Rev. 155, 158 n.12 (1999).

[167] Rule 11(b) & (c) advisory committee's notes (1993).

[168] *Golden Eagle Distrib. Corp. v. Burroughs Corp.*, 801 F.2d 1531, 1542 (9th Cir. 1986).

[169] *Burroughs Corp.*, 801 F.2d at 1539 (citing American Bar Ass'n, *Model Rules of Professional Conduct* R. 3.3(a)(3) (1983)).

[170] 801 F.2d at 1542. *But see* Daisy Hurst Floyd, *Candor Versus Advocacy: Courts' Use of Sanctions to Enforce the Duty of Candor Toward the Tribunal*, 29 Ga. L. Rev. 1035 (1995) (endorsing such use of Rule 11).

[171] *See Golden Eagle*, 809 F.2d at 586 (9th Cir. 1987) (Noonan, Sneed, Anderson, & Kozinski, JJ., dissenting from denial of reh'g *en banc*).

interposed for *any* improper purpose.[172] A knowing omission of directly contrary authority within the controlling jurisdiction evidences an intent to mislead the court. Filing with that intent is surely filing with an improper purpose. Moreover, a filing would appear to be unwarranted when it is directly contrary to the legal authority within the controlling jurisdiction. Courts have therefore divided over the duty of candor that was rejected by the Ninth Circuit.[173]

Does a court's eventual rejection of a legal argument necessarily suggest that its proponent violated Rule 11? The rule's express embrace of the word "nonfrivolous" suggests the contrary; nonfrivolous is not the same as correct. On the other hand, the same phrase focuses more judicial attention on the quality of a litigant's legal argument than on its pre-filing inquiry. Indeed, one judge has suggested that "the submissions of the parties are to be marked on a scale of 'A' through 'F.' Anything falling on the far side of 'C' merits not only loss of one's case but loss of one's shirt as well."[174] This kind of standard invites rulings that are based on product rather than on conduct, and rulings that risk conflating the merits of claims and defenses with the care with which they are asserted.[175] The Advisory Committee acknowledges this risk and tries to guard against it by directing a court to take into account a litigant's pre-filing conduct: "the extent to which a litigant has researched the issues and found some support for its theories even in minority opinions, in law review articles, or through consultation with other lawyers . . . ."[176]

[d] Improper Purpose

The converse question has divided the courts — whether a court's acceptance of a legal argument or, more broadly, finding that a paper is well-founded, necessarily suggests that Rule 11 was *not* violated. The Seventh Circuit may have rejected this proposition by asserting that it may be necessary to explore the filer's subjective intent even if the paper was objectively well-founded.[177] Several other appellate courts have taken the opposite view, holding that the filing of a well-founded complaint is not ordinarily sanctionable under the improper purpose standard (at least absent

---

[172] *See* § 8.05[d], *infra.*

[173] *See, e.g.*, cases cited in Klausner, note 149, *supra*, at 321 n.164; *De Sisto College, Inc. v. Line*, 888 F.2d 755, 766 (11th Cir. 1989) (rule imposes duty of candor); *Cousin v. District of Columbia*, 142 F.R.D. 574, 577 (D.D.C. 1992) (imposing sanctions for failing to disclose and discuss adverse authority).

[174] *Szabo Food Serv., Inc. v. Canteen Corp.*, 823 F.2d 1073, 1085 (7th Cir. 1987) (Cudahy, J., concurring in part and dissenting in part). *See* Samuel J. Levine, *Seeking a Common Language for the Application of Rule 11 Sanctions: What Is "Frivolous"?*, 78 NEB. L. REV. 677, 679–85 (1999) (criticizing inconsistency of courts' interpretation of frivolous legal arguments and urging a graduated standard instead).

[175] *See generally* BURBANK, note 138, *supra*, at 10–13; Stephen B. Burbank, *The Transformation of American Civil Procedure: The Example of Rule 11*, 137 U. PA. L. REV. 1925, 1933–34 (1989).

[176] Rule 11(b) & (c) advisory committee's notes (1993).

[177] *Szabo Food Serv., Inc. v. Canteen Corp.*, 823 F.2d 1073, 1083 (7th Cir. 1987), *cert. dismissed*, 485 U.S. 901 (1988).

unusual circumstances, such as multiple filings amounting to harassment).[178]

The latter holdings reflect several problems in finding a violation of Rule 11's improper purpose provision. The first is that the rule generally tests papers by objective, reasonable lawyer standards, rather than by the signer's subjective intent. The Ninth Circuit has concluded that "because of the objective standard applicable to Rule 11 analysis, a complaint that is found well-grounded in fact and law cannot be sanctioned as harassing regardless of the attorney's subjective intent."[179] Second, even if subjective intent may be appropriately considered in deciding whether a filing has an improper purpose, its proof is circumstantial and problematic. It must necessarily be inferred from the paper itself, as well as from the consequences of filing. When the paper is well-founded, the circumstantial evidence is in conflict even if the consequences are delay or expense to opponents. Finally, sanctioning colorable claims may raise constitutional questions by deterring the presentation of grievances to the courts.[180] The Second Circuit has also suggested that filing to generate adverse publicity for the defendants may be constitutionally protected under the First Amendment. "It is not the role of Rule 11 to safeguard a defendant from public criticism that may result from the assertion of nonfrivolous claims."[181] On the other hand, assertion of an *unfounded* claim to use the judicial forum for a public protest has been held sanctionable by the D.C. Circuit.[182] Clearly, it is easier to infer improper purpose from an unfounded paper.

But if improper purpose can only be inferred from unfounded filings, the improper purpose provision of the rule would be superfluous. Such papers already violate the warranted-by-law and evidentiary-support provisions of the rule. For the improper purpose standard to play any independent role, it must be applicable to even well-founded papers in unusual circumstances which circumstantially prove an improper intent. The most common circumstances involve multiple filings and a pattern of harassment. Courts have also inferred improper purposes from the timing of filing when it results in strategic delays.[183]

[e]   Sanctions

Rule 11 formerly provided that, after finding a violation, a court "shall impose appropriate sanctions," including reasonable attorney's fees. Although it also authorized nonmonetary sanctions, 95% of all sanctions imposed under

---

[178] *Moore* § 11.11[8][d] (citing 2d, 5th and 9th Circuits).

[179] *Hudson v. Moore Bus. Forms, Inc.*, 836 F.2d 1156, 1159 (9th Cir. 1987).

[180] *Moore* § 11.11[8][d].

[181] *Sussman v. Bank of Israel*, 56 F.3d 450, 459 (2d Cir.), *cert. denied sub nom. Bank of Isr. v. Lewin*, 516 U.S. 916 (1995).

[182] *Saltany v. Reagan*, 886 F.2d 438 (D.C. Cir. 1989).

[183] *See, e.g., Aetna Life Ins. Co. v. Alla Med. Servs., Inc.*, 855 F.2d 1470, 1476 (9th Cir. 1988) (emphasizing pattern of abusive litigation and successive papers in approving sanctions, even when papers were nonfrivolous); cases cited in *Moore* § 11.11[8][a].

the rule were monetary, including some very substantial fee awards.[184] Courts under the former sanctions regime appeared to have lost sight of the fact that Rule 11's purpose is deterrence rather than compensation.[185] Rule 11(c)(4) attempts to correct this by making sanctions discretionary and by expressly reminding the court of the availability of nonmonetary sanctions, including orders to pay penalties into court. The 1993 Advisory Committee presented examples of orders striking the offending paper; admonishing, reprimanding, or censuring the offender; requiring the offender to participate in educational programs; or referring the matter to disciplinary authorities. Courts have imaginatively developed others. (Our personal favorite: an order that the offending attorney take and pass a law school course on federal jurisdiction, remanded for further consideration because it might impose too great a burden *on the law school!*)[186] Moreover, when the court on motion does impose a monetary sanction, the sanction is limited to the reasonable attorney's fees and other expenses "incurred as a direct result of the violation" and may not be awarded against a represented party for violations of Rule 11(b)(2) — the warranted-by-the-law certification requirement.

The court's discretion in awarding sanctions is limited. Although the 1993 Advisory Committee apparently rejected a least-severe sanction standard,[187] it did provide in Rule 11(c)(4) that sanctions "must be limited to what suffices to deter repetition of [the violative conduct] or comparable conduct by others similarly situated." It suggested that the factors that should inform discretion include

> [w]hether the improper conduct was willful, or negligent; whether it was part of a pattern of activity, or an isolated event; whether it infected the entire pleading, or only one particular count or defense; whether the person has engaged in similar conduct in other litigation; whether it was intended to injure; what effect it had on the litigation process in time or expense; whether the responsible person is trained in the law; what amount, given the financial resources of the responsible person, is needed to deter that person from repetition in the same case; [and] what amount is needed to deter similar activity by other litigants . . . .[188]

The 1993 amendment also assures a minimum of procedural fairness in the sanctioning process. All motions for sanctions may be made only "after notice and a reasonable opportunity to respond," and a court may impose sanctions on its own initiative only after issuing an order directing a party to show cause why

---

[184] *See, e.g., Avirgan v. Hull*, 932 F.2d 1572 (11th Cir. 1991) (over $1 million); *Brandt v. Schal Assocs., Inc.*, 131 F.R.D. 485 (N.D. Ill. 1990) (over $350,000).

[185] Rule 11 advisory committee's notes (1983) (noting that "the word 'sanctions' in the [rule] caption . . . stresses a deterrent orientation in dealing with improper pleadings, motions or other papers").

[186] *See Willhite v. Collins*, 459 F.3d 866, 869–71 (8th Cir. 2006) (trial court should consider requiring continuing legal education instead).

[187] *See* Tobias, note 154, *supra*, at 881.

[188] Rule 11(c) advisory committee's notes (1993).

the party has not violated the rule.[189] In addition, Rule 11(c)(6) requires the court in a sanctions order to describe the offending conduct and "to explain the basis for the sanction imposed." This provision assures an adequate basis for appellate review, which was not always provided under the former Rule 11 practice.[190]

Finally, the advisory committee's notes to the 1993 amendment reaffirm that Rule 11 is not the exclusive source of sanctioning authority in federal court. Congress has by statute authorized courts to assess costs, including attorney's fees, against an attorney who "multiplies the proceedings in any case unreasonably and vexatiously."[191] This statute differs significantly from Rule 11. It is broader because it applies to the whole course of counsel's litigation conduct (not just filing papers) and imposes a continuing duty to avoid dilatory tactics. But it is also narrower because it requires subjective bad faith by counsel and does not apply to clients.[192] The Supreme Court has also held that federal courts retain inherent power to discipline attorneys and parties who appear before them.[193] Although Rule 11's procedures ordinarily supersede the courts' inherent powers in cases to which the rule applies, these powers may be used to punish in-court conduct and inappropriate oral remarks beyond the reach of the rule.

[f]   Assessment

In the first edition of this book, we suggested that vigorous enforcement of Rule 11 could make kitchen-sink pleadings and mechanical Rule 12 motions[194] endangered species, while over-zealous enforcement of Rule 11 risked a return to the problems of unfairness and inefficiency that plagued code pleading. In the second edition, we predicted that the 1993 amendments made both outcomes less likely, because, first, the de-emphasis of monetary sanctions would diminish incentives to file Rule 11 motions, and, second, the authorization of information-and-belief pleading, coupled with the safe harbor provision, would give litigants more leeway in pleading.

Assessments of the amendment's effect appear to be consistent with these predictions. Commentators have noted a "marked decline in formal Rule 11 activity" and in corresponding satellite litigation, as well as an amelioration of the rule's chilling effect on novel claims and arguments.[195] A 1995 survey of

---

[189] Rule 11(c)(1) & (3). Previously, courts had not always afforded fair notice and an opportunity to be heard when they imposed sanctions *sua sponte. See* Wiggins, note 138, *supra,* at 17.

[190] *See, e.g., Brown v. Federation of State Med. Bds.,* 830 F.2d 1429, 1438–40 (7th Cir. 1987).

[191] 28 U.S.C. § 1927.

[192] *See United States v. International Bhd. of Teamsters,* 948 F.2d 1338, 1344 (2d Cir. 1991). The statute also lacks Rule 11's safe harbor and separate motion provisions.

[193] *See Chambers v. NASCO, Inc.* 501 U.S. 32 (1991).

[194] *See* § 8.07 (motions practice), *infra.*

[195] *See, e.g.,* Georgene Vairo, *Rule 11 and the Profession,* 67 Ford. L. Rev. 589, 626, 643 (1998); *cf.* Theodore C. Hirt, *A Second Look at Amended Rule 11,* 48 Am. U. L. Rev. 1007 (1999) (noting "anecdotal evidence" of these effects but concluding that it may be premature to declare complete success).

judges and lawyers provided lukewarm support for these assessments.[196] While most thought "groundless litigation" a "small" problem which had not changed much since the amendments, 14% of the judges and 11–13% of the lawyers thought it had declined. Substantial majorities supported the safe harbor provision and more than one-third of the judges thought it had reduced Rule 11 activity on their dockets, a conclusion which individual courts have stated in their reported opinions.[197] These assessments shows that Justice Scalia's fear that the 1993 amendments would "gut[]" the rule[198] has not materialized.

On the other hand, a majority of judges and lawyers in the 1995 survey supported changing the rule to make compensation, as well as deterrence, a purpose of sanctions. Perhaps, the more rigorous pre-filing inquiry is intercepting *negligently* prepared papers, or the safe harbor is being used to correct or withdraw them, with the result that the unsupported papers that remain are the kind that intentionally violate the rule? If so, they are papers for which non-monetary sanctions seem inadequate to lawyers who incur uncompensated expenses in opposing them. This conclusion is consistent with the claim that other, less circumscribed sanctions, such as those afforded by 28 U.S.C. § 1927 or the courts' inherent power,[199] are being used with increasing frequency since the 1993 amendments.[200]

Finally, the 1993 amendments do not fully address a serious problem of certification: its tendency to focus judicial sanctioning attention on a litigant's product rather than her conduct. It has proven impossible to draw a bright line between unsuccessful or merely inept papers and factually unwarranted or frivolous papers. But, as one critic puts it, Rule 11 was never intended as "an open-ended charter for upgrading the legal profession."[201] The proper focus of a certification rule is on a litigant's conduct in investigating the facts and researching the law before filing; other motions are available to test the merits and other devices (such as continuing legal education) to improve the bar's competency.

---

[196] JOHN SHAPARD ET AL. (FEDERAL JUDICIAL CENTER), REPORT OF A SURVEY CONCERNING RULE 11, FEDERAL RULES OF CIVIL PROCEDURE (1995).

[197] *See* cases cited by Hirt, note 195 *supra*, at 1030–31. Whether the safe harbor also has revived professional collegiality and civility by making lawyers talk to each other, as some had hoped, is more doubtful. *See* Hirt, note 195 at 1031, 1041 (citing judicial opinions expressing this hope); Vairo, note 195, *supra*, at 643–47 (raising doubts).

[198] Dissenting statement of Justice Scalia on amendments to the Federal Rules of Civil Procedure, 113 S. Ct. CCCVI, CCCVIX (1993).

[199] *See* § 8.05[2][e], *supra*.

[200] Vairo, note 195, *supra*, at 643.

[201] BURBANK, note 138, *supra*, at 13.

§ 8.06   THE COMPLAINT

In most modern pleading systems, the complaint (and any other pleading that sets out a claim for relief) should contain a statement of jurisdiction when necessary, a statement of the claim, and a demand for relief.[202] The federal complaint is illustrative.

[1]   Statement of Jurisdiction

Rule 8(a) requires the claimant to include a statement of the "grounds upon which the court's jurisdiction depends" unless the court already has jurisdiction and the claim needs no independent grounds. This requirement reflects the limited jurisdiction of the federal courts,[203] and similar requirements apply to state courts of limited jurisdiction as well. Because the chief workhorses of state judicial systems are usually courts of general jurisdiction, no such jurisdictional statement is required for claims filed there, unless a jurisdictional requirement is built into the substantive claim itself.

The content of the jurisdictional statement depends upon how the court's subject matter jurisdiction is defined.[204] In federal courts, jurisdictional allegations that track the language of Form 7 are sufficient. Technical forms of pleading are no more necessary to plead jurisdiction than to plead a claim. Even with respect to jurisdictional allegations, pleadings should be construed liberally to do substantial justice. The court should search not just the pleading, but the whole record, to see if it will support subject matter jurisdiction.[205] By statute, defects in the pleading of jurisdiction can also be cured through amendment in the trial court or on appeal.[206] Note, however, that these rules apply only to the cure of defects in the *allegation* of jurisdiction; they cannot be invoked to supply jurisdiction that was not present at the commencement of the action.[207]

[2]   Statement of Claim and the Burden of Pleading

Matters of form and detail in modern claim pleading were discussed in section 8.04. Here we will consider what elements must be pleaded and by whom. The substantive law from which the claim arises provides an answer to the first question. Special pleading rules like Rules 8(c) and 9 or precedent generally supply an answer to the second question. "Precedent as such," however, "does nothing for the inquiring mind."[208] Thus it is useful to consider

---

[202] *See* Rule 8(a).

[203] *See* § 5.01[2] (federal subject matter jurisdiction), *supra*.

[204] *See* §§ 5.03 (federal question jurisdiction) & 5.04–5.06 (diversity), *supra*.

[205] Wright § 69 (citations omitted).

[206] 28 U.S.C. § 1653.

[207] *See* § 5.01[1] (subject matter jurisdiction generally), *supra*.

[208] Edward W. Cleary, *Presuming and Pleading: An Essay on Juristic Immaturity*, 12 Stan. L. Rev. 5, 10 (1959).

the logic of allocating burdens in pleading (if any). We start with the burden of producing evidence at trial, which the burden of pleading usually follows.

A plaintiff has the burden of producing evidence at trial that would enable a rational trier of fact to find for him (1) *if* he also carries his burden of persuasion, *i.e.*, persuades the trier of fact that it is more probable than not that he is correct, and (2) *unless* defendant in turn carries *her* burden of producing evidence that would enable the trier of fact to find that she has a defense.[209] When the plaintiff does not carry his initial burden of production at trial, the court can dismiss the action and enter judgment as a matter of law for the defendant.[210]

To the plaintiff typically (though not invariably) goes the burden of pleading matters for which he has the initial burden of production at trial: the *prima facie* case.[211] One reason is that the plaintiff is challenging the status quo and may fairly be asked to demonstrate why. Another is the assumption that if he is unable with due candor and care to plead such matters, he will probably also be unable to satisfy his burden of production at trial. If his case would be dismissed at trial, it would be wasteful to let it get that far. Requiring the plaintiff to plead those elements as to which he would have the burden of production at trial forces him to expose any basic infirmity in the case at the pleading stage, permitting its dismissal at the front of the litigation.

The defendant has the burden of pleading the elements as to which she carries the burden of production at trial. This allocation is efficient because it relieves the plaintiff of the task of pleading the negative of every possible defense, including many on which the defendant might never rely. It also forces the defendant to identify the specific defenses on which she will rely, information that would be withheld from plaintiff and the court until trial were the burden of pleading the nonexistence of all possible defenses placed on plaintiff.

Whether a jurisdiction classifies a particular element as part of the plaintiff's *prima facie* case or as part of a defense depends upon a highly variable mix of policy, fairness, convenience and probability considerations, as well as history and accident.[212] *Gomez v. Toledo*[213] illustrates the interplay of some of these. Gomez sued a public official for violating his civil rights. The Supreme Court had held that such officials are entitled to a qualified immunity from liability for acts performed in the reasonable belief that they were lawful. *Gomez* posed the question whether a civil rights plaintiff has the burden of pleading the defendant's bad faith and unreasonable belief as part of his *prima*

---

[209] Edward W. Cleary, *Presuming and Pleading: An Essay on Juristic Immaturity*, 12 STAN. L. REV. at 15–16 (1959). "Burden of proof" is often used as a shorthand reference for the burdens of production and persuasion together. *See generally* § 12.04 (burdens and standards of proof), *infra*.

[210] *See* Rules 41(b) & 50(a), and §§ 11.04[2] & 12.09[1], *infra* respectively.

[211] *See* § 8.04[1] (notice pleading), *supra*.

[212] *See generally* Cleary, note 208, *supra*. Some of these we have already considered in analyzing special pleading rules. *See* § 8.04[4], *supra*.

[213] 446 U.S. 635 (1980).

facie case, or whether the defendant has the burden of pleading good faith and reasonable belief as part of his defense. The Court placed the burden on the defendant, reasoning in part that "whether such immunity has been established depends on facts peculiarly within the knowledge and control of the defendant."[214] Not only would it therefore be more convenient for defendant to assume the burden, but it would be unfair to ask the plaintiff to plead a state of mind that turns on factors "which [he] cannot reasonably be expected to know."[215] In a later case, the Supreme Court placed the burden of pleading a claimant's failure to exhaust his administrative remedies on the defendant, in part because the statute containing the exhaustion requirement was "not a source of a [claimant's] claim," suggesting another factor in allocating burdens of pleading.[216] It added that "[t]he argument that screening [complaints] would be more effective if exhaustion had to be shown in the complaint proves too much; the same could be said with respect to any affirmative defense."[217]

[3] Demand for Relief

The demand for relief has lost much of the significance it held at common law because most modern pleading systems frequently authorize the court to "grant the relief to which [the prevailing] party is entitled, even if the party has not demanded such relief in its pleadings."[218] Any other rule would be a reversion to the discarded doctrines of the theory of the pleadings and election of remedies.[219]

Nevertheless, the demand for relief is useful even under modern notice pleading. When the court's subject matter jurisdiction is limited by an amount in controversy,[220] the demand for monetary relief, or *ad damnum*, may determine the grounds for jurisdiction. The type of relief demanded also has jurisdictional significance in those systems that have maintained the division between law and equity. It can bear on the availability of a jury trial, which is often tied to particular kinds of actions.[221]

Finally, the prayer for relief may set a ceiling on the plaintiff's recovery in the event of default — an adverse judgment against defendant resulting from his failure to appear or otherwise defend.[222] Default, after all, is sometimes strategic, reflecting defendant's cost-benefit analysis of defending an action. To perform that analysis, defendant must know the maximum cost of not defending, information that is conveyed by the demand for judgment contained

---

[214] 446 U.S. at 641.

[215] 446 U.S. at 641.

[216] *Jones v. Bock*, 549 U.S. 199 (2007).

[217] *Bock*, 549 U.S. at 215.

[218] Rule 54(c). *See, e.g., Bail v. Cunningham Bros., Inc.*, 452 F.2d 182 (7th Cir. 1971).

[219] *See* § 8.04[2] (consistency and the theory of the pleadings in modern pleading), *supra*.

[220] *See* § 5.06 (amount in controversy), *supra*.

[221] *See* § 12.07[1] (right to a jury), *infra*.

[222] *See* § 11.02 (default), *infra*.

in the complaint. If, after defendant's default, the judgment could exceed the demand in the complaint, this cost-benefit analysis would be impossible to perform reliably, and default would cease to be a viable strategic option. Rule 54(c) therefore provides that "[a] default judgment must not differ in kind from, or exceed in amount, what is demanded in the pleadings."

§ 8.07 CHALLENGING PLEADINGS: MOTION PRACTICE

[1] Motion Practice in General

One of the principal reforms carried forward from code pleading to the federal rules was the reduction of the many responsive pleadings at common law[223] to just three responses: motion, answer, and (when permitted) reply.[224] A *motion* is an application to the court for an order. It must state with particularity the grounds upon which it relies. A supporting memorandum of authorities (brief) and a proposed form of order often accompany a motion.[225] Like pleadings, motions are subject to the candor and care requirements of Rule 11 and do not require any technical forms.[226]

The federal rules and many state rules in notice pleading jurisdictions permit the defendant to file a motion attacking the complaint in lieu of an answer. Federal Rule 12(g) requires the movant to join in any pre-answer motion all the Rule 12(b) defenses and Rule 12 motions then available to him. This rule eliminates the undesirable practice of successive pre-answer motions in favor of a single, omnibus pre-answer motion in federal courts.

The pre-answer motion may be used to present what the common law called dilatory defenses, including matters in abatement and challenges to jurisdiction.[227] In some jurisdictions, some of these defenses can only be presented by motion; in federal court, all the Rule 12(b) defenses can be asserted by motion or in a responsive pleading. Such attacks do not go to the merits, or, ordinarily, to the sufficiency of the pleading alone. Therefore, a motion presenting them may be decided on the basis of materials submitted by the parties, as well as on the pleadings.

In contrast, a pre-answer motion that presents the defense of failure to state a claim (Rule 12(b)(6)) or defense (Rule 12(f)) attacks the substantive content of a pleading and must usually be decided upon the face of the pleading alone — that is, on the basis of the allegations in the pleading, and not any

---

[223] *See* § 8.02[1] (common law pleading), *supra.*

[224] *See* § 8.09 (the reply), *infra.*

[225] *See* Rule 7(b)(1) & Form 40. Motions are usually written, but can be made orally in the course of a recorded hearing. Rule 7(b)(1) is often implemented by more detailed local rules, promulgated under the authority of Rule 83. *See, e.g.,* Local Civil Rule 7 of the United States District Court for the District of Columbia (establishing page limits and requirements for included matter).

[226] *See* Rules 11 & 8(d)(1).

[227] *See* § 8.02[1] (common law practice), supra.

additional factual matter from "outside the four corners of the pleading," in the common parlance. However, the court may take judicial notice of the law, other pleadings, its own records, and universally undisputed facts.[228] Moreover, in federal courts, the submission of materials outside the pleadings in support of or opposition to a Rule 12(b)(6) motion is not forbidden. It simply converts the Rule 12(b)(6) motion into a motion for summary judgment subject to the usual procedural safeguards of Rule 56.[229] Thus, the common law rule against "speaking demurrers"[230] has been discarded by the federal rules.

After the pleadings have closed in federal court, either side may seek judgment on the pleadings under Rule 12(c). This motion goes to the merits insofar as they appear from the pleadings. Whereas the scope of a Rule 12(b)(6) motion is confined to the face of the complaint, a Rule 12(c) motion takes in all the pleadings on file. Submission of materials outside the pleadings converts the Rule 12(c) motion to a motion for summary judgment. In fact, Rule 12(c) motions have been largely superseded by motions for summary judgment and are today "little more than . . . relic[s] of the common law and code eras."[231]

Some have suggested that the de-emphasis of pleading in modern civil practice has made Rule 12(b)(6) motions relics as well, infrequently made and rarely dispositive.[232] Data from selected district courts in 1975 and 1988 indicate that Rule 12(b)(6) motions were made in 13–15% of the sampled cases, granted in 8–12% of the sampled cases (*e.g.*, 52–65% of the time), and dispositive in 3–6% of the sampled cases (*e.g.*, 51–72% of the granted cases).[233] These data support the assertion that Rule 12(b)(6) motions are rarely dispositive, although they apparently dispose of approximately as many cases as does trial.

But it does not follow that they are useless relics. Even if a motion does not finally dispose of a case, it may eliminate some marginal claims and parties, or at the very least signal the defendant's determination to litigate with immeasurable but real effect on settlement dynamics. A Rule 12(b)(6) motion

---

[228] This is an over-simplification of the nuances of judicial notice. *See* Fed. R. Evid. 201.

[229] *See* § 11.03[2] (procedure for summary judgment), *infra*. Submission of such materials in support of a Rule 12 motion asserting defenses 12(b)(1)–(5) or (7) does not convert it into a summary judgment motion. These defenses "only challenge the propriety of the court adjudicating the claim before it and do not reach the validity of the claim itself." WRIGHT & MILLER § 1366. *See. e.g., Weidner Commc'ns, Inc. v. H.R.H. Prince Bandar Al Faisal*, 859 F.2d 1302, 1306 n.6 (7th Cir. 1988) (noting that Rule 12(b)(2) motion cannot be converted into summary judgment motion); *Haase v. Sessions*, 835 F.2d 902, 905–07 (D.C. Cir. 1987) (holding that Rule 12(b)(1) motion cannot be converted to summary judgment motion, although defendant may challenge standing by formally moving for summary judgment).

[230] *See* § 8.02[1] (common law practice), *supra*.

[231] WRIGHT & MILLER § 1369.

[232] WRIGHT § 66; ARTHUR R. MILLER, THE AUGUST 1983 AMENDMENTS TO THE FEDERAL RULES OF CIVIL PROCEDURE: PROMOTING EFFECTIVE CASE MANAGEMENT AND LAWYER RESPONSIBILITY 7–8 (1984).

[233] THOMAS E. WILLGING, USE OF RULE 12(B)(6) IN TWO FEDERAL DISTRICT COURTS 6–8 (Federal Judicial Center 1989). These data are inflated by the inclusion of prisoners' cases, which are probably more vulnerable to 12(b)(6) dismissal than other cases. *Id.* at 7 & Table 2, 8 n.19.

"that whittles a complaint with twenty claims down to two viable claims has not been a failure in terms of merits dispositions."[234] Moreover, if heightened pleading requirements survive the Supreme Court's decision in *Leatherman v. Tarrant County Narcotics Intelligence and Coordination Unit*,[235] Rule 12(b)(6) motions may be effective in the sub-set of cases to which such standards are applied. Finally, if *Twombly*'s "plausible pleading" standard is widely applied,[236] it may incrementally revitalize Rule 12(b)(6) practice.

[2]   Bases for Motions

[a]   Defects of Form

Because modern notice pleading does not require technical forms of pleading, attacks on pleadings for defects of form are virtually extinct in modern pleading jurisdictions. Under the federal rules, the only defects of form that can be challenged are that the complaint is unintelligible or that it contains "redundant, immaterial, impertinent, or scandalous matter."[237]

A complaint that is too vague, ambiguous or confused to enable the defendant to respond may be attacked by a Rule 12(e) motion for more definite statement in the federal courts, or by a special demurrer in states that retain this nomenclature.[238] In a notice pleading jurisdiction, however, discovery, and not pleading, is the device intended to obtain information about an adversary's case. Accordingly, a Rule 12(e) motion should not be granted just because the movant wants to know more than enough to prepare some response. In light of the leeway afforded by the rules to formulate responses,[239] few litigants are able to make the necessary showing.[240]

Rule 12(f) motions to strike (delete) any of the various kinds of improper matter from a pleading are even less likely to be granted than Rule 12(e) motions. As long as pleadings are not shown to the jury, quibbling about how immaterial, nasty, or gratuitous they are is a waste of everyone's time unless their availability in the public record is likely to prejudice the movant. Rule

---

[234] Richard L. Marcus, *The Puzzling Persistence of Pleading Practice*, 76 Tex. L. Rev. 1749, 1756 (1998). Such a whittling effort may also encourage settlement.

[235] 507 U.S. 163 (1993). *See* § 8.04[1] (specificity of modern pleadings), *supra*.

[236] *See* § 8.04[1][d].

[237] Rule 12(f).

[238] *See, e.g.*, Cal. Civ. Proc. Code § 430.10(f) (1992).

[239] *See, e.g.*, *Hodgson v. Virginia Baptist Hosp., Inc.*, 482 F.2d 821 (4th Cir. 1973) (denying Rule 12(e) motion because Rule 8(b) permitted the response that defendant lacks knowledge or information sufficient to form a belief as to the truth of an averment in complaint). *See generally* § 8.08[1] (denials), *infra*.

[240] Rule 12(e) motions have been used in two other limited settings. They have been invoked to enforce Rule 9(b) requirements for special pleading of fraud and mistake. *See* Moore § 12.36; Wright & Miller § 1300; *see generally* § 8.04[4], *supra*. This use of the motion makes a reasonable accommodation between these requirements and Rule 8(a)'s requirement for a "short and plain statement," without requiring dismissal of a complaint. Rule 12(e) motions are also sometimes used to uncover threshold defenses such as the statute of limitations or fraud. *See* Wright & Miller § 1376.

12(f) motions to strike improper matter are therefore universally disfavored. Usually the allegations that have been stricken were obviously prejudicial: describing a car as a "death trap," or plaintiff's co-conspirators as "strong arm men" and "racketeers."[241]

[b]   Waivable Preliminary Defenses

Lack of personal jurisdiction,[242] improper venue,[243] insufficiency of process (the papers served on the parties),[244] and insufficiency of service (the means of service)[245] are typical defenses that can or must be asserted by pre-answer motion. They are personal to the defendants, and their availability is usually clear from the outset of litigation. In almost all jurisdictions, therefore, defendants are required, on penalty of waiver,[246] to raise them preliminarily, before the court and the parties invest much time in the litigation or reach the merits. Federal Rules 12(g) and 12(h)(1) provide that these defenses are waived unless they are asserted in a single pre-answer motion, or, if none is filed, in an answer or reply or any amendment thereto permitted as a matter of course.

Rule 12's treatment of waivable defenses suggests a simple rule of thumb in federal court: a party should assert them in her first defensive paper. The same applies in many state courts as well. In some states, all of these defenses except improper venue can be asserted by *motions to quash* service. In a few, the assertion of defenses to the complaint constitutes a general appearance, submitting to the jurisdiction of the court. It is therefore necessary to *appear specially* to assert the defense of lack of personal jurisdiction.[247] Rule 12(b) effectively eliminates the need for special appearances in federal court by expressly providing that "[n]o defense or objection is waived by joining it" with any other in a responsive pleading or motion.

---

[241] *See* Stephen C. Yeazell, Civil Procedure 453 n.7 (4th ed. 1996) (citing cases). *Cf. Theriault v. Silber*, 574 F.2d 197 (5th Cir. 1978) (striking "vile and insulting" references to trial judge in appellant's notice of appeal). Rule 12(f) may also be used to attack the substantive sufficiency of an answer or reply, *see* § 8.07[2][c] (failure to state defense), *infra*, and, in a few courts, to strike averments of fraud or mistake that violate Rule 9(b). *See* Wright & Miller § 1300.

[242] Rule 12(b)(2). *See* Chapter 3, *supra*.

[243] Rule 12(b)(3). *See* Chapter 6, *supra*.

[244] Rule 12(b)(4). *See* § 4.03, *supra*.

[245] Rule 12(b)(5). *See* § 4.03, *supra*.

[246] *See* § 3.03[2] (waiver of personal jurisdiction defense), *supra*.

[247] For more extensive discussion of opportunities in state and federal court to question personal jurisdiction, see § 3.03[2][b] (special and general appearances), *supra*.

[c]   Failure to State a Claim (or Defense), and Other Nonwaivable Defenses

The defenses of failure to state a claim or defense, lack of subject matter jurisdiction, and, in federal courts, failure to join a party under Rule 19[248] are not waived by their omission from a pre-answer motion.[249] Rule 12(h)(3), in fact, provides that the defense of lack of subject matter jurisdiction may be raised at any time, while Rule 12(h)(2) states that the other nonwaivable defenses may be asserted in any pleading, by motion for judgment on the pleadings, or even "at trial."[250] Were the rule otherwise, judgments could be recovered on claims or defenses unrecognized by the law, and courts would be unable to protect absent parties whose indispensability to the litigation first becomes evident as it progresses.

The most common nonwaivable defense is the failure to state a claim. It is asserted by a Rule 12(b)(6) motion in federal court and by general demurrer in many state courts. The test for disposition of the motion depends on the jurisdiction's requirement for stating a claim or cause of action.[251] All well-pleaded facts (*e.g.*, not legal conclusions, rank opinion, or speculation) in the challenged pleading are taken as true for purposes of the motion or demurrer, and all reasonable inferences are drawn in favor of the pleader.[252] The province of Rule 12(b)(6) motions and demurrers is to question the availability of a legal formula justifying relief on the alleged facts, not to test or determine the facts themselves. On the other hand, "courts are not . . . required to speculate that factual propositions unmentioned, or evidentiary links unrevealed, are among the facts plaintiff intends to prove at trial."[253]

In some code pleading states, a demurrer was overruled unless the entire pleading was defective.[254] This is no longer true in most jurisdictions, and a

---

[248] *See* § 9.05[2] (compulsory joinder), *infra*.

[249] Rule 12(h)(2) & (3).

[250] A failure to state a claim is usually raised at trial by a motion for dismissal (or judgment as a matter of law in federal courts) in a trial to the court, Rule 52(c), *see* §§ 11.04[2] & 12.10, *infra*; and by a motion for a directed verdict (or for judgment as a matter of law in federal courts) in a trial to a jury. Rule 50(a). *See* § 12.09[1] (directed verdicts), *infra*. The phrasing of Rule 12(h)(2) suggests that a post-answer 12(b)(6) motion is not a proper vehicle for asserting the defense.

[251] *See generally* Yoichiro Hamabe, *Functions of Rule 12(b)(6) in the Federal Rules of Civil Procedure: A Categorization Approach*, 15 CAMPBELL L. REV. 119 (1993); §§ 8.03 (code pleading), 8.04[1] (modern notice pleading), & 8.06[2] (statement of claim), *supra*.

[252] *See* MOORE § 12.34. The same standards are applied in the determination of Rule 12(c) motions for judgment on the pleadings. MOORE § 12.38. *Cf.* § 12.09[3][c] (comparing these with motions for directed verdict), *infra*. As noted in Section 8.04[1][d], in *Twombly*, 127 S. Ct. 1955 (U.S. 2007), the Supreme Court appeared unwilling to draw an inference of collusion from allegations of conscious parallel conduct by the defendant corporations, when the inference of independently motivated conduct was equally reasonable. It seems improbable that the Court meant to reject the plaintiff-favoring rule generally, however.

[253] *ACLU Found. S. Cal. v. Barr*, 952 F.2d 457, 472 (D.C. Cir. 1991) (stating also that "[a] court must take care not to put words into counsel's mouth by reading into a complaint factual allegations not fairly comprehended within what is actually asserted.").

[254] *See* CHARLES E. CLARK, HANDBOOK OF THE LAW OF CODE PLEADING § 79 (2d ed. 1947).

litigant can attack part of the complaint, usually a count, for failure to state a claim. Technically, perhaps, a Rule 12(f) motion to strike the defective count or claim is the correct vehicle under the federal rules.[255] However, since Rule 8(d)(1) abolished technical forms of motions, a Rule 12(b)(6) motion should be equally effective.

The phrasing of the latter ("failure to state a *claim* upon which relief can be granted"), suggests its unsuitability for attacking the legal insufficiency of a *defense*. Instead, a Rule 12(f) motion to strike is used for this purpose. The test for striking a defense for insufficiency is analogous to that used in deciding a Rule 12(b)(6) motion for failure to state a claim.[256]

[3]   Consequences of Challenging a Pleading

[a]   Successful Challenge

One reason why Rule 12(b)(6) motions appear so ineffective is that a plaintiff will often moot a strong pre-answer motion by amending his defective complaint. Rule 15(a) allows a party to amend his pleading once "as a matter of course" at any time before a responsive pleading is filed, and a pre-answer *motion* is not a responsive *pleading*.[257] Depending upon the federal circuit, amendment as of right or by permission is available even *after* a motion to dismiss has been granted, unless the court indicates that no curative amendment is possible.[258]

If plaintiff opts to amend, he runs the risk of waiving his argument that the original complaint was sufficient. Both state and federal courts are divided on this question of waiver. The better federal rule appears to be that such a plaintiff waives his objection to the court's dismissal order only insofar as it applies to technical defects in the original complaint. He may still argue, on appeal of an unfavorable final judgment after trial of the amended complaint, that the erroneous grant of the Rule 12(b)(6) motion against his original complaint "struck a vital blow" to a substantial portion of his case.[259]

If the plaintiff stands on his original complaint and takes a successful appeal from its dismissal, the complaint will be reinstated and the defendant will have to file a responsive pleading. If the appellate court affirms the dismissal,

---

[255] *See, e.g., Mills v. Fox*, 421 F. Supp. 519 (E.D.N.Y. 1976) (striking punitive damages not recoverable under state law); *Fry v. Lamb Rental Tools, Inc.*, 275 F. Supp. 283 (W.D. La. 1967) (striking demand for damages for losses not recoverable under state law).

[256] *See, e.g., Donovan v. Robbins*, 99 F.R.D. 593 (N.D. Ill. 1983). *But see generally* Robert D. Loomis, *Motion to Strike Affirmative Defenses — The Equivalent of Partial Summary Judgment*, 13 Am. J. Trial Advocacy 645 (1989) (asserting that the no-genuine-issue standard for summary judgment (*see* § 11.03[3], *infra*) is different, but used by some courts to decide Rule 12(f) motions to strike affirmative defenses, even though the rule does not provide for converting such motions to summary judgment).

[257] Rule 7(a). *See generally* § 8.10[1] (amendment before trial), *infra*.

[258] *See* § 8.10[1] (amendment before trial), *infra*, noting split in the circuits.

[259] *See, e.g., Wilson v. First Houston Inv. Corp.*, 566 F.2d 1235, 1238 (5th Cir. 1978), *vacated on other grounds*, 444 U.S. 959 (1979); *Blazer v. Black*, 196 F.2d 139, 143–44 (10th Cir. 1952) (dictum).

however, the plaintiff will have forfeited his opportunity to amend[260] unless the appellate mandate preserves it.[261]

[b]   Unsuccessful Challenge

The options posed by denial of defendant's motion to dismiss are simpler. She may, of course, file an answer, although in federal court she cannot include the waivable defenses if they were omitted from her motion.[262] By answering, she forgoes the opportunity to obtain immediate appellate review of the denial of her motion, unless the jurisdiction permits interlocutory appeals, because there is no final judgment from which to take an appeal.[263]

Depending upon the jurisdiction, she may also waive her preliminary defenses by going forward. But she can preserve the defense that the complaint fails to state a claim by raising it by motion at trial for dismissal, directed verdict, or, in federal courts, for judgment as a matter of law, and after trial, for judgment notwithstanding the verdict, and by appropriate evidentiary objections at trial. It will thereby be preserved on appeal of an eventual final judgment. In federal courts, it is preserved by the original Rule 12 motion.[264]

Alternatively, the defendant may elect to stand on her motion and refuse to answer. This course will result in the entry of a default judgment[265] against her, from which she can appeal. If the appellate court agrees with her, it should remand with leave for plaintiff to amend. But if the court affirms, defendant may lose the opportunity to defend on the merits.

§ 8.08   THE ANSWER

The answer may contain three kinds of responses: denials controverting the pleader's allegations, defenses, and claims by the defendant.[266]

[1]   Denials

In all jurisdictions, the defendant must in her answer admit or deny all the well-pleaded allegations of the complaint. An admission takes the issue from the fact-finder and is conclusive at trial. The old common law plea of the general issue theoretically survives as a *general denial* of each and every

---

[260] Some appellate courts have taken the view that the plaintiff-appellant also waives the right to argue any alternative legal theories that might have formed the basis of an amended complaint. *See Mitchell v. Archibald & Kendall, Inc.*, 573 F.2d 429, 433 (7th Cir. 1978) ("By appealing, the plaintiffs-appellants elected to stand on their original complaint and thereby relinquished the legal theory they now assert.").

[261] Federal appellate courts have broad remedial powers. *See* 28 U.S.C. § 2106.

[262] *See* § 8.07[2][b] (waivable preliminary defenses), *supra*.

[263] *See* § 13.03 (final judgment rule), *infra*.

[264] Rule 46.

[265] *See* § 11.02 (default), *infra*.

[266] *See* Form 30.

allegation of the complaint,[267] but it will almost always be impossible to square with candor and care requirements like those of Rule 11.[268] Instead, most defendants *specifically deny* particular paragraphs or sentences of the complaint. In fact, Rule 8(b) commands that a "denial must fairly respond to the substance of the allegation . . . . A party that does not intend to deny all the allegations must either specifically deny designated allegations or generally deny all except those specifically admitted." Failure to deny an allegation in a required responsive pleading, other than an allegation of the amount of damages, is deemed an admission.[269] But answers do not require technical forms and are construed, like all pleadings, to do substantial justice.

A well-known case, *Zielinski v. Philadelphia Piers, Inc.*,[270] illustrates some of these principles. In a personal injury suit, defendant generally denied a paragraph in the complaint that alleged that a forklift "owned, operated and controlled" by it and its employees was negligently driven so that it hit and injured the plaintiff. In fact, unknown to plaintiff, defendant had sold its business and transferred its employees to a third party prior to the accident, retaining only ownership of the forklift. By the time that plaintiff learned of these facts, it was too late under the applicable statute of limitations to sue the third party. Plaintiff therefore argued that the defendant's denial was ineffective and should be treated as an admission for purposes of the action.

The court ruled that defendant's failure to deny specifically the "operated and controlled" allegations in the quoted paragraph deprived plaintiff of warning that he had sued the wrong defendant. Although defendant's denial was literally true,[271] it did not "fairly meet the substance of the averments denied."[272] Moreover, not only should defendant have admitted ownership, but it should also have admitted that the forklift hit and injured the plaintiff, which was known to it from an accident report. Although a defective denial should not automatically be deemed an admission under the federal rules, the circumstances (compounded by a misleading and inaccurate answer to interrogatories during discovery) justified finding the defendant equitably estopped from denying ownership and agency for purposes of the action.

When a defendant neither knows nor can learn whether an averment in the complaint is true or false, most jurisdictions permit him to say so in the answer

---

[267] *See* Rule 8(b)(3) (expressly authorizing general denial).

[268] *See, e.g., Williamson v. Clapper*, 199 P.2d 337, 339 (Cal. Ct. App. 1948) ("[L]oose practice of pleading [the general denial] which results in the incorporation in the answer of known false denials is to be condemned."). Rule 8(b) takes some pains to warn counsel of the danger of such "known false denials" by reminding him that a general denial controverts even routine jurisdictional allegations in the complaint. That is, it asks, "Can you really deny your client's your name or address consistently with Rule 11?"

[269] Rule 8(b)(6). *See Lipton Indus., Inc. v. Ralston Purina Co.*, 670 F.2d 1024, 1030 (C.C.P.A. 1982).

[270] 139 F. Supp. 408 (E.D. Pa. 1956).

[271] Because plaintiff used conjunctions to connect different averments, the entire paragraph was true literally only if all of its conjoined averments were true.

[272] *Zielinski*, 139 F. Supp. at 411–12 (quoting Fed. R. Civ. P. 8(b) (1993)).

with the effect of a denial.[273] But he cannot blind himself to what he should know, and facts presumptively within the control or knowledge of the defendant may be deemed admitted if he responds with an empty-headed denial of knowledge or information.[274] Moreover, Rule 11(b)(4) imposes a duty of reasonable inquiry on defendant by which he may obtain the necessary knowledge or information and explicitly applies to "denials of factual contentions."

[2]   Other Defenses

[a]   Preliminary, Nonwaivable and Affirmative Defenses

Besides denials, an answer should contain "in short and plain terms" other defenses to each claim in the complaint. Unless they have been waived by their omission from a pre-answer motion, some or all of the preliminary defenses may be asserted by an answer or, when permitted, a reply.[275] The nonwaivable defenses may also be asserted.

A defendant should also plead his *affirmative defenses*, if any. An affirmative defense is the lineal descendant of the common law plea in confession and avoidance[276] — in effect, an excuse or justification for his action that would avoid plaintiff's claim, even if that claim is proven at trial. It differs from its ancestor in that confession is no longer a predicate for avoidance, because a defendant may combine denials and affirmative defenses in his answer under modern pleading rules.[277] It differs from a counterclaim in that an affirmative defense makes no claim against any party and seeks no relief other than the defeat of plaintiff's claim.[278] Finally, it differs from a denial in that it does not tend to controvert the plaintiff's *prima facie* case, but instead affirmatively asserts new matter outside that case and beyond the plaintiff's claim.

Because such matter is new, it is not put in issue by a defendant's general or specific denials of the plaintiff's allegations. Affirmative defenses must be pleaded "as a condition to the admissibility of such evidence at the trial."[279] When defendant has failed to plead an affirmative defense, the admissibility of some tendered evidence will depend upon whether it goes to the plaintiff's

---

[273] Rule 8(b)(5) (defendant "lacks knowledge or information sufficient to form a belief about the truth").

[274] *See, e.g., Mesirow v. Duggan*, 240 F.2d 751, 756 (8th Cir. 1957); *Oliver v. Swiss Club Tell*, 35 Cal. Rptr. 324 (Cal. Ct. App. 1963).

[275] Rule 12(b); Form 30.

[276] *See* § 8.02[1] (common law pleading), *supra*.

[277] *See, e.g.*, Rule 8(d)(2).

[278] In any event, the federal rules are merciful to the defendant who confuses an affirmative defense and a counterclaim in his pleading, requiring the court to treat the pleading "as though it were correctly designated." Rule 8(c)(2).

[279] *Layman v. Southwestern Bell Tel. Co.*, 554 S.W.2d 477, 480 (Mo. Ct. App. 1977).

prima facie case or whether it is truly new matter. If the latter, it may not come in unless the opposing party fails to object or the court permits amendment of the pleadings during trial.[280] One traditional test for deciding this question — and thus for identifying affirmative defenses — is whether the tendered evidence "tend[s] *to destroy* rather than *avoid* the cause of action as alleged by the complaint."[281] Another formulation is whether it arises by logical inference from the allegations of plaintiff's complaint.[282]

For example, when the complaint is for trespass and alleges plaintiff's ownership of the property and defendant's entry, evidence of defendant's title by adverse possession is logically related to ownership and tends to destroy an essential allegation of plaintiff's complaint. It is therefore admissible under a general denial, and the defendant need not plead an affirmative defense of adverse possession.[283] On the other hand, evidence of an easement is not admissible in defense of a trespass action unless defendant has pleaded an easement as an affirmative defense. Such evidence does not controvert ownership, but only goes to show justification for disturbing it.[284]

The distinction between evidence supporting defendant's denials and evidence that is admissible only in support of a pled affirmative defense, however, is not always easy to follow. This only reflects the fact that the underlying question is simply one of allocating pleading burdens. It is therefore decided less often by logic or formula than by precedent, itself based upon idiosyncratic considerations that vary from jurisdiction to jurisdiction.[285] For this same reason, however, the problem is today more theoretical than real. Most state jurisdictions have identified affirmative defenses by precedent, rule, or statute. The picture is not as clear in federal court. Rule 8(c) lists many of the affirmative defenses available there. But federal courts also borrow from the forum state's laws or rules to identify affirmative defenses not listed in Rule 8(c).[286]

The risk that the evidence will be excluded or that amendment will be denied dictates pleading an issue as an affirmative defense when in doubt.[287] In a few jurisdictions, the danger of this strategy is that by pleading an issue as an affirmative defense, defendant may be considered to have assumed the burden of proof, even if it would otherwise rest on the plaintiff.[288] This result

---

[280] *See* § 8.10[2], *infra.*

[281] *Denham v. Cuddeback*, 311 P.2d 1014, 1016 (Or. 1957) (emphasis in original).

[282] Charles E. Clark, Handbook of the Law of Code Pleading § 96 (2d ed. 1947).

[283] *Denham*, 311 P.2d at 1017.

[284] *Layman*, 554 S.W.2d 477.

[285] *See* § 8.06[2] (statement of claim and burden of pleading), *supra.*

[286] Such local law is not binding because, under the *Erie* doctrine, the allocation of the burden of pleading is a procedural matter to be decided as a matter of federal law. *See Palmer v. Hoffman,* 318 U.S. 109, 117 (1943) (implying that burden of pleading is controlled by Rule 8(c), though burden of proof is a question of local law in diversity cases) (dictum). *See generally* Wright & Miller § 1272; § 7.04, *supra.* On the nature and effect of the *Erie* doctrine generally, *see* Chapter 7, *supra.*

[287] *See* Wright & Miller § 1278 (footnote omitted).

[288] *See* James, Hazard & Leubsdorf § 4.7.

is unsound because it elevates the form of pleading over the often substantive policy underlying the allocation of the burden of proof.[289] It will often be wise even in such jurisdictions for defendant to plead the matter as an affirmative defense. Otherwise, he risks exclusion of the relevant evidence altogether.[290]

Most modern pleading jurisdictions do not permit a reply to defenses asserted by answer unless the court orders one.[291] Absent a reply, allegations supporting a defense are simply taken as denied by plaintiff.[292] Challenges to the legal sufficiency of defenses are made by a Rule 12(f) motion to strike in federal courts or by demurrer in states that retain the device.[293]

[b]   A Note on the Affirmative Defense of the Statute of Limitations

This common affirmative defense merits further discussion because of its significance to procedure. Statutes of limitation require claimants to file their claims within a given time period or lose them. They reflect a conviction that, after the passage of the limitations period, realization of the substantive goals underpinning the claim is less important than protecting opposing parties from the frustrations of coping with stale claims. Chief among these frustrations are the loss from delay of evidence that might have defeated the claim and the emotional stress and financial uncertainty generated by the specter of future litigation.[294] The availability of statutes of limitations defenses depends upon three factors.

The first factor is when the claim *accrued* or came into existence. In most jurisdictions, tort actions accrue at the time of the injury[295] and contract actions accrue at the time of the breach,[296] but there are many nuances in the law governing accrual of actions. In particular, many courts have adopted a discovery/diligence rule of accrual for some torts (especially medical malpractice), by which the action accrues when the plaintiff should, by exercise of reasonable diligence, have discovered his injury (and, some courts add, its connection to defendant).[297] Using this rule of accrual protects a patient who is injured from some medical instrument or sponge misplaced during surgery, the presence of which she does not discover until years later when another doctor accurately diagnoses her stomach pain.

---

[289] *See* Moore § 8.07.

[290] There will usually be no reason why defendant cannot raise the matter in his answer *both* by specific denial and by affirmative defense.

[291] *See, e.g.*, Rule 7(a).

[292] Rule 8(b)(6).

[293] *See* § 8.07[2][c], *supra*.

[294] *See, e.g., Elkins v. Derby*, 525 P.2d 81 (Cal. 1974). *See generally* 51 Am. Jur. 2d *Limitation of Actions* §§ 17–18 (1970 & Supp. 1999).

[295] *See, e.g., Roberts v. Richard & Sons, Inc.*, 304 A.2d 364 (N.H. 1973); 51 Am. Jur. 2d *Limitation of Actions* § 135 (1970 & Supp. 1999).

[296] *See, e.g., Struthers Wells-Gulfport, Inc. v. Bradford*, 304 So. 2d 645 (Miss. 1974); 51 Am. Jur. 2d *Limitation of Actions* § 126 (1970 & Supp. 1999).

[297] 51 Am. Jur. 2d *Limitation of Actions* § 167 (2000).

The second factor is the *period of limitation*. This also varies enormously from jurisdiction to jurisdiction, although short (one year) periods are commonly associated with intentional torts and disfavored actions like defamation,[298] intermediate (two or three year) periods with negligence and oral contract claims,[299] and longer periods (five or six years) with actions involving written contracts and instruments.[300] The longest periods are associated with claims to enforce previously awarded judgments.[301]

The last factor is when the period *tolls* or stops running. In most statutes, the period is tolled by the commencement of an action in court, but the rules defining commencement vary. Some statutes define commencement as filing plus service on the defendant. Others state that the period is tolled by filing, if service on defendant is accomplished within some additional short period — "service tail" — after filing.[302] Because of the potentially harsh application of a statute of limitations, many jurisdictions have statutory exceptions[303] or *equitable tolling* doctrines, whereby defendant's fraudulent concealment of his wrongdoing or other good reason is said to toll the period until plaintiff knew or should have known of her injury or that she had an action against defendant.[304] By statute, periods are also often tolled during the legal incapacity of a plaintiff to sue as a result of her minority or incompetency.[305]

State statutes of limitations are regarded as substantive law for *Erie* purposes, and therefore control in federal diversity actions.[306] Because there is no federal statute of limitations for many federal claims, courts often borrow state statutes of limitations in federal question cases,[307] if they are not inconsistent with the purpose of the federal law.[308] Federal equitable tolling doctrines are still applied to borrowed periods, creating an often confusing hybrid law of limitations in federal courts.[309]

When the ground for a limitations defense is obvious from the face of the complaint, it can be raised by a Rule 12(b)(6) motion, or in some state courts,

---

[298] *See, e.g.*, Md. Cts. & Jud. Proc. Code Ann. § 5-105 (1984) (assault, slander, libel).

[299] *E.g.*, Md. Cts. & Jud. Proc. Code Ann. at § 5-101 (contracts).

[300] *E.g.*, Md. Cts. & Jud. Proc. Code Ann. at § 5-102(a) (1) (twelve years for instruments under seal).

[301] *See, e.g.*, N.Y. Civ. Prac. L. & R. 211 (McKinney 2000) (twenty years).

[302] *See, e.g.*, Okla. Stat. tit. 12, § 97 (repealed 1984), analyzed in *Walker v. Armco Steel Corp.*, 446 U.S. 740, 751–52 (1980) and § 7.04[2], *supra*.

[303] *See, e.g.*, N.Y. Civ. Prac. L. & R. 213(8) (McKinney 2000).

[304] 51 Am. Jur. 2d *Limitation of Actions* §§ 146–69 (1970 & Supp. 1999).

[305] *See, e.g.*, N.Y. Civ. Prac. L. & R. 208 (McKinney 2000) (infancy and insanity toll the statute).

[306] *See* § 7.03[1] (analyzing the *York* decision), *supra*.

[307] *See* § 5.03 (statutory scope of federal question jurisdiction), *supra*.

[308] *See, e.g.*, *Banks v. Chesapeake & Potomac Tel. Co.*, 802 F.2d 1416 (D.C. Cir. 1986). *See generally* Note, *Limitation Borrowing in Federal Courts*, 77 Mich. L. Rev. 1078 (1979); § 7.07 (federal common law), *supra*.

[309] *See Banks*, 802 F.2d at 1420. *See also Holmberg v. Armbrecht*, 327 U.S. 392 (1946) (fraudulent concealment tolls borrowed state statute of limitations).

by demurrer.[310] This procedure is disfavored by many courts, however, because it complicates plaintiff's offer of factual matter in avoidance of the defense, such as fraudulent concealment under the doctrine of equitable tolling.[311] Even when the defense appears on the face of the complaint, therefore, these courts have urged that it be raised by answer (which presents plaintiff the opportunity to seek leave to reply) and that it be presented for decision by motion for summary judgment.[312]

[3] Claims by Way of Answer

A defendant may also respond to the complaint by asserting claims against the plaintiff, other defendants or third parties.[313] Claims against existing parties are usually asserted in the answer.[314]

§ 8.09 THE REPLY AND OTHER PLEADINGS

Under the federal rules, further pleading is necessary after an answer only if the latter introduces a claim. Such a claim is tantamount to a complaint. Rule 7(a) therefore requires a reply to a counterclaim[315] denominated as such and answers to all other claims[316] included in the original answer. No other pleadings are allowed as of right, and all averments in the last required pleading are deemed denied or avoided.[317] The abandonment of issue-identification as the primary function of pleading accounts for this early cut-off; the complaint, answer, and reply suffice to give fair notice.

On rare occasions, the defendant may want the plaintiff to respond to an answer in order to ascertain what issues plaintiff will contest at trial. More rarely, the plaintiff herself may wish to respond affirmatively to new matter pleaded as an affirmative defense in the answer, by, for example, pleading facts showing fraud in response to the affirmative defense of release. Replies in these circumstances are not required or permitted as of right. Rule 7(a) does,

---

[310] *See* Comment, *Raising Defense of Statute of Limitations by Demurrer, Equivalent Motion to Dismiss, or by Motion for Judgment on Pleadings*, 61 A.L.R.2D 300 (1999).

[311] *See* Richard L. Marcus, *Fraudulent Concealment in Federal Court: Toward a More Disparate Standard?*, 71 GEO. L.J. 829, 902–04 (1983).

[312] *See, e.g., Richards v. Mileski*, 662 F.2d 65, 73 (D.C. Cir. 1981). *See generally* Rhynette Northcross Hurd, *The Propriety of Permitting Affirmative Defenses to Be Raised by Motions to Dismiss*, 20 MEMPHIS ST. U. L. REV. 411 (1990). The Supreme Court has permitted a trial court to dismiss a case on limitation grounds *sua sponte*, even where the defendant (respondent) failed to raise the affirmative defense, explaining that the trial judge could just have brought the oversight to the defendant's attention and invited an amendment of its answer, but also cautioning that before it dismisses, the court must give the plaintiff (petitioner) fair notice and an opportunity to be heard. *Day v. McDonough*, 547 U.S. 198 (2006).

[313] *See generally* §§ 9.04 (cross-claims), 9.05 (permissive and compulsory party joinder), & 9.06 (impleader), *infra*.

[314] *See, e.g.*, Rules 13 (counterclaims and cross-claims) and 22 (interpleader); Form 30.

[315] *See* § 9.03, *infra*.

[316] *See* §§ 9.04 (cross-claims), 9.05[1] (permissive party joinder), & 9.06, (impleader), *infra*.

[317] Rule 8(b)(6).

however, give courts discretion to allow a reply, and on rare occasions they do so.[318] Although some states once mandated a reply to affirmative defenses,[319] today the pleading rules in most modern pleading jurisdictions do not require replies.

The only other pleading contemplated under federal and many state rules is a supplemental pleading "setting out any transaction, occurrence, or event that happened after the date of the pleading to be supplemented."[320] Such pleadings are most commonly used to allege new damages,[321] or affirmative defenses that have accrued since filing of the complaint, such as discharge in bankruptcy, release or *res judicata*. Before a supplemental pleading may be filed, the court must grant leave and may set conditions designed to minimize its complicating or prejudicial impact on the pending litigation.[322] To the same ends, no responsive pleading is required or permitted to a supplemental pleading unless the court so orders.[323]

§ 8.10   AMENDMENT OF PLEADINGS

One key to the de-emphasis of the pleadings in modern procedure is liberal amendment. Accordingly, many modern pleading jurisdictions allow amendment without permission early in litigation, and almost all provide liberal opportunities for amendment by permission later. The remaining constraints on amendment are functional rather than formalistic, imposed by concerns for efficient judicial administration, prejudice to opposing parties, and, where applicable, the policy of the statute of limitations. Widely copied in the states, Rule 15 accommodates these concerns and is therefore the focus of this section.

[1]   Amendment Before Trial

The earlier an amendment is made, the less likely it is to disrupt judicial administration or prejudice opposing parties. Rule 15(a) therefore provides that a party may amend "once as a matter of course" (without permission from the court or consent of other parties) before a responsive pleading is served, or within twenty days of service if no responsive pleading is required. Because a Rule 12(b) motion to dismiss is not a responsive pleading within the definition

---

[318] "[O]ccasions when this power should be or has been exercised are extremely rare." WRIGHT § 66. "The theory is that by the complaint and the answer each of the parties will have indicated the general position he is taking in the litigation, and that further pleading is not worth the trouble." WRIGHT § 66.

[319] *See* WRIGHT § 66.

[320] Rule 15(d). Amendment, in contrast, deals with events that occurred *prior* to the date of the pleading sought to be amended. *See generally* § 8.10 (amendment), *infra*.

[321] *See, e.g., Fritz v. Standard Sec. Life Ins. Co. of N.Y.*, 676 F.2d 1356, 1358 & nn.3 & 4 (11th Cir. 1982) (supplemental complaint for insurance payments that accrued after filing of complaint); *McHenry v. Ford Motor Co.*, 269 F.2d 18 (6th Cir. 1959) (complaint to enjoin flooding of plaintiff's land; supplemental pleading to recover for new damage to plaintiff's house).

[322] The relevant factors are comparable to those considered in granting leave to amend. *See* § 8.10[1] (amendment before trial), *infra*.

[323] Rule 15(d).

of Rule 7, Rule 15(a)'s language permits one amendment as of right to cure defects raised by such a motion, without the necessity of any hearing or ruling on the motion. Such an amendment promotes efficient judicial administration and ordinarily works no prejudice against other parties who have not yet invested resources in responsive pleadings and who are typically given ample time to respond[324] to the amended pleading.[325]

Once issues have been joined by the filing of a responsive pleading, amendment would usually moot that pleading, and necessitate preparation and filing of a new responsive pleading. In light of this inefficiency and the possible prejudice to the adverse parties, leave of court is required to amend.[326] Rule 15(a) provides, however, that "[t]he court should freely give leave when justice so requires." Provided that amendment will promote disposition of the action on the merits, there is a virtual presumption favoring it. This presumption is only rebutted by a showing that the amendment is unreasonably dilatory, futile (e.g., amendment cannot cure the problem) or in bad faith, or that the opposing party will be unduly prejudiced.[327]

Beeck v. Aquaslide 'N' Dive Corp.[328] illustrates this standard. In its answer to a complaint for personal injury, the defendant admitted design and manufacture of the water slide alleged to have caused the injury. Subsequently, after the statute of limitations on plaintiff's personal injury claim had expired, defendant sought to amend its answer because it belatedly discovered that it had not manufactured the defective slide. The trial court granted defendant leave to amend its answer in order to deny design and manufacture. Plaintiff appealed from a judgment on an eventual verdict for defendant, asserting that the grant of leave to amend was error. The appellate court affirmed.

---

[324] Rule 15(a)(3) provides that a response shall be made within the original time remaining for response or ten days after service of the amended pleading, whichever is longer.

[325] After a motion to dismiss has been granted, some of this efficiency is lost because the court has already ruled. The Second Circuit therefore holds that the right to amend without permission terminates unless the court, in ruling on the motion, explicitly grants leave to amend. *See Elfenbein v. Gulf & Western Indus., Inc.*, 590 F.2d 445, 448 & n.1 (2d Cir. 1978). In contrast, some circuits distinguish dismissal of the complaint from dismissal of the action, and read Rule 15(a) literally to allow a plaintiff to amend once as of right after dismissal of the complaint pursuant to a pre-answer motion. *See Ruby v. Secretary of Navy*, 365 F.2d 385, 387 (9th Cir. 1966), *cert. denied*, 386 U.S. 1011 (1967); *222 East Chestnut Street Corp. v. Lakefront Realty Corp.*, 256 F.2d 513 (7th Cir. 1958), *cert. denied*, 358 U.S. 907 (1958). The Eleventh Circuit has taken the intermediate position that plaintiff may amend with leave of court after dismissal, unless the court either holds that no amendment is possible or that dismissal of the complaint also constitutes dismissal of the action. *See Czeremcha v. International Ass'n of Machinists and Aerospace Workers, AFL-CIO*, 724 F.2d 1552 (11th Cir. 1984).

[326] Leave is requested by filing a motion to amend accompanied by the proposed amendment. WRIGHT & MILLER § 1485.

[327] *See Foman v. Davis*, 371 U.S. 178, 182 (1962); *Espey v. Wainwright*, 734 F.2d 748, 750 (11th Cir. 1984) ("This policy of Rule 15(a) in liberally permitting amendments to facilitate determination of claims on the merits circumscribes the exercise of the trial court's discretion; thus, '[u]nless there is a substantial reason to deny leave to amend, the discretion of the district court is not broad enough to permit denial.'") (citations omitted).

[328] 562 F.2d 537 (8th Cir. 1977).

The amendment was not futile, for it presented what proved to be a winning defense, and it permitted the parties to litigate a material factual issue on the merits. In addition, there was no evidence of bad faith or unreasonable delay. Defendant had relied on the conclusions of three different insurance companies in preparing its initial answer and had promptly sought amendment upon discovering their error in identifying the slide's manufacturer.

Plaintiffs were unable to show undue prejudice sufficient to overcome these justifications for the amendment. They were, of course, disadvantaged on the merits by the amendment, which interjected a new and difficult fact issue into the litigation. But this kind of prejudice cannot be undue because it is inherent in every amendment; otherwise, the movant would not seek amendment. Instead, undue prejudice ordinarily consists of "preparation prejudice" flowing from delay in offering the amendment — a substantial litigation disadvantage that the party opposing the amendment would not have faced had the amended pleading been filed originally. In *Beeck*, plaintiffs might well have made this showing by persuading the court that the amendment came too late for them to sue other parties (including the real manufacturer of the slide) under the applicable statute of limitations. But the trial court found that causes of action in fraud or contract might still be available against other parties, and that such parties might be equitably estopped[329] from asserting a limitations defense.[330] On this record, the appellate court saw no abuse of discretion and affirmed the judgment for defendants.

Even when a proposed amendment may prejudice opposing parties, the court may impose conditions upon the amendment that mitigate the prejudice. For example, allowance of the amendment may be accompanied by a grant to the party opposing it of additional discovery, continuances, or time extensions. Financial prejudice may be controlled by conditioning amendment upon payment of costs.[331]

[2]　　Amendment During and After Trial

At common law, evidence offered outside the issues framed by the pleadings was inadmissible because *variance* from the pleadings was forbidden.[332] Rule 15(b), in deliberate contrast, anticipates such variance and authorizes curing amendments by consent and over objection, during trial and even after judgment, "to conform [the pleadings] to the evidence."[333]

---

[329] *See* § 8.08[2][b] (the statute of limitations defense), *supra*.

[330] 67 F.R.D. 411, 415 (S.D. Iowa 1975).

[331] *See* WRIGHT & MILLER § 1486.

[332] *See* § 8.02[1] (common law practice), *supra*.

[333] A more functional version of the doctrines of variance and of the theory of the pleadings, *see* § 8.04[2], *supra*, is now embodied in the provision for binding pretrial orders. *See* Rule 16(e); § 12.03[3] (binding effect of pretrial orders), *infra*.

[a]   Conforming Amendment by Consent

The parties may always expressly consent to the trial of issues outside the pleadings. Rule 15(b) provides that the issues will then be treated as if they had been raised in the pleadings. Unpleaded issues may also be tried by implied consent of the parties. In either case, a party may move at any time, even after judgment, to amend the pleadings to conform to the evidence, although amendment is not necessary.

Implied consent presupposes both knowledge that an unpleaded issue has been injected into the litigation and a meaningful opportunity to litigate the issue.[334] Usually the offer of evidence bearing upon an unpleaded issue gives the requisite notice, and a failure to object signifies implied consent. This basis for inferring consent fails, however, when the evidence is also applicable to pleaded issues.

In *Moore v. Moore*,[335] for example, after trial of a husband's complaint for child custody, the trial court granted the wife's motion to amend her answer to include counterclaims for custody, child support, separate maintenance, and attorney's fees. On appeal, the appellate court reasoned that the complaint for custody necessarily raised the issues of which parent was entitled to custody and of support for that custody, putting the husband on notice of these claims. The court also concluded that the husband had impliedly consented to trial of these issues by introducing evidence on them and failing to object to the wife's offer of evidence of the child's financial needs. However, the issue of separate maintenance, involving the marital relationship, is not normally litigated in a suit focused on child custody.

> While evidence of [the wife's] financial needs was admitted without objection relatively late in the proceedings, we cannot conclude that this evidence was so uniquely pertinent to her support alone, in contrast with the custody or the child support issues, that it justifies our concluding that appellant had adequate, timely notice of, and an opportunity to contest, a claim by his wife for her own support.[336]

The appellate court therefore ruled that the trial court abused its discretion in granting the amendment to add the separate maintenance claim.

A failure to object to evidence that is apposite to both pleaded and unpleaded issues may evidence consent when combined with other indicia. The test for implied consent searches the entire record and considers a party's conduct in all the circumstances. In *Nielson v. Armstrong Rubber Co.*,[337] the plaintiff moved at the close of the evidence to amend his simple negligence complaint to include a claim of strict products liability. While the defendant had not objected at trial

---

[334] *See Moore v. Moore*, 391 A.2d 762, 768 (D.C. 1978).

[335] *Moore*, 391 A.2d 762, 768 (D.C. 1978).

[336] 391 A.2d at 770. *See also DCPB, Inc. v. City of Lebanon*, 957 F.2d 913, 917 (1st Cir. 1992) ("The introduction of evidence directly relevant to a pleaded issue cannot be the basis for a founded claim that the opposing party should have realized that a new issue was infiltrating the case.").

[337] 570 F.2d 272 (8th Cir. 1978).

to evidence of dangerousness and of failure to include a warning, he argued that this evidence applied to the negligence claim as well as the unpleaded claim of strict products liability. Yet the defendant had received plaintiff's pretrial memorandum citing the law of products liability, introduced evidence to rebut a strict liability claim, and been present when the trial court said, "it seems to me that we have now amended our pleadings."[338] On the whole record, defendant clearly had notice and an opportunity to litigate the unpleaded issue, and the amendment to conform to the evidence was proper.

[b]   Conforming Amendment Over Objection

The functional approach to amendment is most dramatically reflected by the provision for conforming amendment over the objection that evidence is outside the issues framed by the pleadings. Rule 15(b) encourages the federal courts to grant such amendments "freely . . . when doing so will aid in presenting the merits" and the objecting party fails to make a showing of prejudice in maintaining his action or defense upon the merits. This provision offers further proof of the sympathetic climate for amendment generally.[339]

Nevertheless, the presumption favoring amendment is slightly weakened once trial has begun, given the lateness of the amendment and its effect on the on-going trial.[340] To the extent that the objecting party complains that he needs more preparation time to litigate the unpleaded issue, Rule 15(b) expressly authorizes continuances. In jury cases, however, a mid-trial continuance may not be a realistic option.

[c]   The Objecting Party's Tactical Dilemma

When evidence apposite to an unpleaded issue is introduced at trial, the adverse party may feel, under Rule 15(b), that he is damned if he objects and damned if he does not. By objection, he invites a motion for a conforming amendment, which the court will often grant under the liberal standard embodied in the rule. The most an objecting party usually stands to gain is a continuance to prepare to meet the new evidence and/or conditions on amendment, such as the payment of costs.

On the other hand, if he fails to object, he runs a substantial risk that his muteness will be taken as implied consent to the interjection of the new issue. Moreover, by this tactic, he waives his opportunity to litigate the merits of the new issue, since the introduction of rebuttal evidence and other defensive conduct might be taken as further indicia of consent.

The safe course in these circumstances is to object and defend. This is also the course most in keeping with the purposes of modern pleading, because it subserves presentation and decision on the merits and rejects sandbagging and pretense as litigation tactics.

---

[338] 570 F.2d at 275.

[339] *See* § 8.10[1] (amendment before trial), *supra.*

[340] These same considerations account for the restrictive "only-to-prevent-manifest-injustice" test for amending final pretrial orders. *See* Rule 16(e), discussed in § 12.03[3], *infra.*

[3] Amendment and the Statute of Limitations

[a] Relation Back of Amendments Amending Claims Against the Same Parties

When the applicable statute of limitations expires between the date of an original pleading and the date of a proposed amendment to it, is the amendment time-barred or does it take (*relate back* to) the date of the original pleading? In federal and most state courts, the answer to this question depends on the nature of the amendment. Under Rule 15(c)(1)(A), an amendment amending claims relates back if relation back is permitted by the state or federal law that provides the applicable statute of limitations.

It also relates back if it is allowed by Rule 15(c)(1)(B). When the amendment presents a claim that is completely new and factually unrelated to the original claims, it operates, in effect, as an independent original action brought after the applicable limitations period has expired. Allowing it to relate back would offend the policy of limitations — to protect against stale claims and assure repose[341] — no less than would an original action brought beyond the limitations period. But when the amendment presents a matter that is closely related to a timely-filed original pleading, allowing it to relate back would not offend the policy of limitations. In that case, the filing of the original pleading gives defendant notice to start gathering evidence before it grows stale and to plan for the possibility of liability under any closely related pleading. Almost all jurisdictions therefore today permit relation back in these circumstances. This policy, which is implicit in Rule 15(c)(1)(B) and (C) is made explicit by the corresponding North Carolina rule: a claim added by amendment "is deemed to have been interposed at the time the claim in the original pleading was interposed, unless the original pleading does not give notice of the transactions, occurrences, or series of transactions or occurrences, to be proved pursuant to the amended pleading."[342]

The problem is to determine how close the relationship between the original pleading and its amendment must be before the jurisdiction will allow relation back of the latter. In code pleading jurisdictions, the solution was to allow relation back of amendments as long as they did not change the cause of action originally pleaded.[343] When cause of action is defined narrowly in terms of legal right or a particular legal theory, this approach to relation back is correspondingly restrictive. For example, some courts deny relation back to an amendment in a malpractice action adding a claim of failure to obtain informed consent to an original complaint sounding only in negligence.[344]

---

[341] *See* § 8.08[2][b] (the affirmative defense of limitations), *supra*.

[342] N.C. R. Civ. P. 15(c).

[343] *See* § 8.03[2] (the cause of action in code pleading), *supra*.

[344] *See, e.g., Keenan v. Yale New Haven Hosp.*, 355 A.2d 253 (Conn. 1974).

Rule 15(c)(1)(B) rejects the cause of action concept[345] and instead premises relation back on a transactional relationship between the original pleading and the amendment. It allows relation back, *inter alia*, when "the amendment asserts a claim or defense that arose out of the conduct, transaction, or occurrence set forth — or attempted to be set forth — in the original pleading."[346] In a modern notice pleading jurisdiction, a complaint gives the defendant notice "that the whole transaction described in it will be fully sifted, by amendment if need be,"[347] and that liability for claims arising out of the transaction may be premised not only on the legal theory articulated in the complaint, but also on any other legal theory that the transaction might support.[348] The wise defendant therefore gathers evidence concerning and prepares to defend the transaction and not just against the theory of recovery articulated in the complaint.

The transactional relationship test clearly permits relation back of amendments that merely change the legal theory on which plaintiff seeks relief for the identical transaction. An example is an amendment adding a strict products liability claim to a complaint that originally asserted a simple negligence claim arising out of injuries received in the use of a product, or an amendment adding a claim for failure to obtain informed consent to a malpractice claim.[349]

On the other hand, Rule 15(c)'s concern with fairness and notice to the party opposing the pleading informs the liberality with which courts should apply the transactional standard. *McGregor v. Louisiana State University Board of Supervisors*,[350] supplies a good illustration. A handicapped law student sued the school and its officials for violating the Rehabilitation Act of 1973 by denying him advancement to his second year. His original, timely complaint asserted that the school discriminated against him by insisting that he take a full-time schedule, have in-class exams, and attain a certain GPA before he advanced. After the statute of limitations had run, he sought to amend his complaint by adding due process claims on the ground that the school had provided no written procedure concerning his right to appeal denial of his petitions to the school. Although an expansive reading of Rule 15(c) might view this claim as arising from the same transaction as his original claim (his failure to advance), the appellate court agreed with the district court that the original

---

[345] *See* § 8.04[2] (theory of pleadings in modern pleadings), *supra.*

[346] Rule 15(c)(1)(B). Transactional relationship is also the nexus for many joinder provisions of the federal rules, *see* §§ 9.03–9.08[1], *infra,* one possible test for identifying a constitutional "case or controversy" for purposes of supplemental jurisdiction, *see* §§ 5.08 & 5.11, *supra,* and the modern test for the scope of claim preclusion. *See* § 16.03[2], *infra. But see* Mary Kay Kane, *Original Sin and the Transaction in Federal Civil Procedure,* 76 TEX. L. REV. 1723 (1998) (arguing that different purposes of these provisions and doctrines call for different interpretations of "same transaction").

[347] *Barthel v. Stamm,* 145 F.2d 487, 491 (5th Cir. 1944), *cert. denied,* 324 U.S. 878 (1945).

[348] *See* §§ 8.04[1] & [2] (modern notice pleading), *supra.*

[349] *See, e.g., Neeriemer v. Superior Court,* 477 P.2d 746 (Ariz. Ct. App. 1970). *See also De Malherbe v. International Union of Elevator Constructors,* 449 F. Supp. 1335 (N.D. Cal. 1978) (adding constitutional claim to statutory discrimination claim).

[350] 3 F.3d 850, 863–64 (5th Cir. 1993).

complaint had not put defendant on notice of the due process claim. That complaint made no mention whatever of any appeals procedures or policy, and therefore, the court concluded, the amendment "set forth new and distinct conduct, transactions, or occurrences not found in the original complaint."[351] The court clearly applied the transaction standard "with an eye toward what legitimately should have been known or recognized within the scope of the litigation as a result of the initial pleadings."[352]

[b]   **Relation Back of Amendments Amending Parties**

Amendments seeking to change parties beyond the applicable period of limitations are more problematic because the original pleading did not formally put the new party on notice. As a stranger to the original lawsuit, he was not served. When the new party is a defendant, relation back is far more likely to be prejudicial than relation back of a new claim against an original defendant.[353] As a general rule, then, such amendments are disallowed in many jurisdictions. Exceptions are made to the general rule when the amendment arises out of the same transaction as the original pleading and the new party had some form of timely notice of the original pleading. In federal court, again, an amendment changing parties relates back if relation back is permitted by the state or federal law that provides the applicable statute of limitations, or if it is permitted by Rule 15(c)(3).[354] Thus, relation back is determined under the most forgiving of the applicable laws.

Many jurisdictions permit relation back of an amendment which simply corrects a *misnomer* — a reasonable mistake in the name of the party intended to be sued.[355] In such a case, the party intended to be sued received notice of the action from the original complaint. No real change in parties is made and no offense is done the policy of limitations by what is in effect a typographical correction to the pleadings.

---

[351] 3 F.3d at 864.

[352] Kane, note 346, *supra*, 76 TEX. L. REV. at 1728.

[353] Relation back of amendments substituting new plaintiffs may not present comparable problems because a substitution will often cause no prejudice to the defendant. *See e.g., Staggers v. Otto Gerdau Co.*, 359 F.2d 292, 297 (2d Cir. 1966). The relation back of additional plaintiffs, however, may in some cases allow tardy plaintiffs to increase geometrically defendant's potential liability and the tactical complexity of their defenses long after the statute of limitations has run. *See Leachman v. Beech Aircraft Corp.*, 694 F.2d 1301, 1309 (D.C. Cir. 1982). In these cases, the courts have imposed requirements for relation back approximating those of Rule 15(c)(1)(C). *See, e.g., Andujar v. Rogowski*, 113 F.R.D. 151 (S.D.N.Y. 1986).

[354] *But see Arroyo v. Pleasant Garden Apartments*, 14 F. Supp. 2d 696 (D.N.J. 1998) (finding that state law forbidding relation back of amendment adding parties is controlling under *Erie* (*see* § 7.04, *supra*), despite Rule 15(c)(1)(C). Because this rule is "arguably procedural," commentators have argued that it should prevail over inconsistent state law and most courts have so ruled. *See* MOORE § 15.20[2] (citing cases). On the other hand, its effect on the state's substantive law of limitations might be thought sufficient to raise a question whether it runs afoul of the Rules Enabling Act.

[355] *See, e.g., Grooms v. Greyhound Corp.*, 287 F.2d 95 (6th Cir. 1961) (amendment to change name from "Pennsylvania Greyhound Lines, Inc." to "The Greyhound Corporation"); *Clark v. Southern Ry. Co.*, 87 F.R.D. 356 (N.D. Ill. 1980) (amendment to change name from "Southern Railway Systems" to "Southern Railway Company").

Relation back is also permitted in some jurisdictions when there is sufficient *identity of interests* between the party originally sued and the new party that notice to the former can be imputed to the latter. In *Stauffer v. Isaly Dairy Co.*,[356] for example, the plaintiff timely sued the Isaly Dairy Company of Pittsburgh, a corporation maintaining the same address as the proper defendant, the Isaly Dairy Company, and served a common officer of both corporations. The court held that an amendment to name the proper defendant related back because the intermingling of the corporations gave the impression that they were one and the same. The rationale is both imputed notice and equitable estoppel.[357]

Rule 15(c)(3) takes an approach in some respects broader and in some respects narrower than that suggested by these exceptions. Under the rule, an amendment changing the parties relates back if (1) it asserts a claim arising out of the same conduct, transaction, or occurrence set out in the original pleading, and (2) within the 120-day period provided by Rule 4(m) for service of process,[358] the party added by amendment (3) received such notice of the institution of the action that he would not be prejudiced in defending on the merits and (4) knew or should have known that the action would originally have been brought against him, but for a mistake in identity of the proper party.

The first requirement is the core transactional relationship requirement for any relation back, and the third and fourth requirements encompass most misnomer and identity of interests cases, although they are not confined to them. The second requirement was revised in 1991 to change the result reached by the Supreme Court in *Schiavone v. Fortune*.[359] Under the prior version of Rule 15(c), the party added by amendment had to receive the requisite notice "within the period provided by law." *Schiavone* posed the question whether the "period provided by law" referred literally only to the applicable limitations period or whether it included any reasonable period tacked on for service of the complaint as well.[360] The Court ruled that it referred only to the limitations period, even though the original complaint was filed within the limitations period and the amended party had received the notice of the filing within the 120-day period provided by Rule 4 for service of process. The 1991 amendment to Rule 15(c) clearly changes this result by

---

[356] 211 N.E.2d 72 (Ohio Ct. App. 1965).

[357] The estoppel theory extends beyond the identity of interests case to any case in which the proper defendant has lulled plaintiff into suing the wrong defendant. *See Zielinski v. Philadelphia Piers, Inc.*, 139 F. Supp. 408 (E.D. Pa. 1956), *discussed in* § 8.08[1] (denials) *supra. See generally* WRIGHT & MILLER § 1500.

[358] *See* § 4.03[2], *supra.*

[359] 477 U.S. 21 (1986).

[360] *See* § 8.08[2][b] (statute of limitations), *supra.* The question arose under statutes that provide that the limitations period is tolled by filing of the complaint, provided that service is perfected within some additional number of days or "tail period" after filing. *See Ingram v. Kumar*, 585 F.2d 566 (2d Cir. 1978), *cert. denied*, 440 U.S. 940 (1979) (relation back permitted when service is accomplished within a reasonable time allowed under the federal rules for service of process but after the period has run).

expressly including that 120-day period as part of perthe period within which the amended party must receive the requisite notice of the institution of the original action.[361]

What constitutes a "mistake concerning the proper party's identity" is unclear. "The classic example of mistake is misnomer,"[362] when plaintiff misnames a defendant (using trade name instead of corporate name, or naming subsidiary instead of parent). In such cases, the "correct" defendant is actually served and should know that, but for plaintiff's mistake, the action would have been brought against it, so it suffers no prejudice from relation back. In other cases, it's not so easy. For example, in *Singletary v. Pennsylvania Dept. of Corrections*,[363] the plaintiff had sued certain "John Doe" defendants, and then sought to replace them with real names when he learned them after the limitations period had run. The court of appeals held that his amendment substituting the real names related back, even though his failure to name them in the original complaint stemmed from lack of knowledge, not a mistake. The court acknowledged case law denying relation back in similar "John Doe" situations,[364] but reasoned that allowing it was consistent with the policy of the rule, as long as the named defendant also received the notice required by the rule.

As the court's later reasoning also suggests, the rule rests on the theory that the new party received timely notice of the original suit curing any prejudice from the late amendment, but this poses the additional question of what kind of "notice" satisfies the rule. The Advisory Committee's notes to the rule state that notice "need not be formal."[365] Yet more may be needed than just notice of the litigation-provoking transaction because Rule 15(c)(3) itself speaks of "notice of the action."[366] A mere demand letter threatening to sue has also been held insufficient.[367] In contrast, a letter from the mistakenly named defendant to the proper one advising of the pendency of the lawsuit, and warning of the possibility that the latter might be drawn into the lawsuit, was held sufficient.[368] The court in *Singletary* also noted that sometimes notice is imputed through a shared attorney, and sometimes through shared (identity of) interests, though it found neither in that case.[369]

---

[361] *See, e.g., Worthington v. Wilson*, 790 F. Supp. 829 (C.D. Ill. 1992).

[362] Moore § 15.19[3][d].

[363] 266 F.3d 186 (3d Cir. 2001).

[364] *See* Moore § 15.19[3][d] (noting that most courts have held that plaintiff's lack of knowledge of identity of defendant does not constitute mistake).

[365] Rule 15(c) advisory committee's notes (1966).

[366] *But see* Wright & Miller § 1498.

[367] *See Schrader v. Royal Caribbean Cruise Line, Inc.*, 952 F.2d 1008, 1012–13 (8th Cir. 1991).

[368] *Loveall v. Employer Health Servs., Inc.*, 196 F.R.D. 399 (D. Kan. 2000).

[369] 266 F.3d at 196–200.

[c]   Responding to Amendment

The Supreme Court has reminded us that the propriety of amendment depends not only on "the state of affairs prior to amendment" — presumably including the reasons for and timing of the amendment — "but also on what happens afterwards."[370] Because amendment may change the claims or defenses asserted against a party, the rule directs that she be given an at least ten days to respond.[371] This can apply even to amendments after trial. In *Nelson v. Adams, USA, Inc.*,[372] the district court amended a judgment to add a new (though closely affiliated) party without giving him an opportunity to respond and the court of appeals affirmed, finding no prejudice. The Supreme Court reversed, holding that the new party was entitled to be served with the amendment and to respond, unless he had consented to the amendment. In dictum, it added that the same is true for amendments which relate back.

§ 8.11   A CONCLUDING NOTE ON COMMON SENSE IN PLEADING

Professor Moore once said that "what was a good pleading before [the federal rules] continues to be good pleading" today.[373] By this assertion, he was stating more than the uninteresting truism that the federal rules are no more demanding than code pleading or the common law. He was also emphasizing that good pleading, as distinguished from technically sufficient pleading, obeys the rules of common sense and good practice, as well as the formal procedural rules of the jurisdiction.

For example, despite the rejection of the doctrine of the theory of the pleadings in modern jurisdictions, no competent attorney files a pleading without having formulated a primary legal theory of recovery or defense.[374] Ordinarily, the attorney formulates that theory after preliminary factual investigation of her client's story and initial legal research into alternative legal theories available in the jurisdiction. She then drafts her pleadings to reflect at least the primary theory of recovery or defense. She may also include alternative theories as well, as a precaution against dismissal and factual surprises during discovery.

Moreover, she ordinarily will plead each and every element of her legal theories. Less might suffice, but the complaint is intended not only to give minimal notice that would survive motions to dismiss, but also to create impressions in the minds of the defendant and the judge. A full complaint helps educate the defendant about his potential exposure in the litigation and to prepare him for settlement negotiations. It also helps justify the judge's investment of time in the action. Furthermore, a full complaint can provide the

---

[370] *Nelson v. Adams, USA, Inc.*, 529 U.S. 460, 466 (2000).

[371] Rule 15(a)(3).

[372] 529 U.S. 460 (2000).

[373] James W. Moore, *Moore's Federal Practice* § 8.02. (2d ed.)

[374] *See* Wright & Miller § 1219.

plaintiff's first discovery; "a plaintiff who includes rifle-shot allegations may be rewarded with precise admissions and denials that advance the case."[375]

Common sense also cautions against pleading or motion practice aimed at trapping, surprising, or delaying your opponent. The pleader who seeks to divert the parties and the court from the merits more often than not succeeds only in alienating them, and in encouraging satellite litigation culminating in sanctions under amended Rule 11 or its state counterpart. The pay-off from deploying modern pleading rules in service of functions for which they were not intended is rarely worth the effort. Real pay-offs lie in marrying the persuasive power of careful pleading with effective discovery, well-researched and analyzed legal theories, and a thorough practical understanding of the parties' willingness and ability to litigate the merits.

The rules of pleading — like all rules of procedure — are never a substitute for common sense. They are just a framework within which it must be applied.

---

[375] Richard L. Marcus, *The Puzzling Persistence of Pleading Practice*, 76 Tex. L. Rev. 1749, 1768 (1998).

Chapter 9

COMPLEX PLEADING AND PRACTICE

§ 9.01   OVERVIEW

[1]   Definitions of Complex Litigation

The simplest case consists of one claim brought by a single plaintiff against a single defendant. Any expansion of the number of claims (and possibly the number of parties) beyond this minimal configuration represents a form of complex litigation.

It is most useful to approach complex litigation by focusing on claims rather than parties. It is possible to increase the number of claims adjudicated in a case without necessarily increasing the number of parties.[1] The case is complicated by expansion of a claim *and* a party whenever the added claim requires for its binding adjudication the presence of an additional party before the court.[2]

Most of this chapter treats complex litigation in this traditional sense. The term has also taken on a second meaning: to describe litigation scattered over many states (often in both state and federal courts) that arises from a common event or wrong.[3] The wrong might stem from an air crash or from a disease attributed to a substance like asbestos. We conclude the chapter with a review of recent developments in this area.

[2]   Reasons for Complex Litigation

Complicating civil litigation with multiple claims, multiple claimants, or multiple parties claimed against, carries inevitable risks. Possibilities for delay and confusion arise when multiple claims compete for attention. This is even more likely to be true when multiple plaintiffs or defendants separately exercise their litigation prerogatives through discovery, pretrial motions and trial of the case.[4] Complex litigation thus bears a burden of justification. It

---

[1] Claim joinder, counterclaim and crossclaim rules perform this function and are the subject of Part A of this chapter, *infra*.

[2] Claim expansion which also requires party expansion occurs through permissive and compulsory joinder, impleader, interpleader, intervention, and class actions — treated in Part B of this chapter, *infra*.

[3] American Law Institute, Complex Litigation: Statutory Recommendations and Analysis, Chapter 2 (1994).

[4] "Additional parties always take additional time. Even if they have no witnesses of their own, they are the source of additional questions, objections, briefs, arguments, motions and the like

satisfies the burden in two ways.

[a]   Judicial Efficiency

Delayed and laborious as complex litigation may be in the short run, a multiple-claim or multiple-party lawsuit is usually preferable to multiple lawsuits. When it averts multiple lawsuits, complex litigation becomes the lesser of two evils, expediting resolution of the entire controversy and avoiding the drain on party and judicial resources caused by inefficient, often redundant litigation.[5]

The wisdom of this objective is most evident when the lawsuit averted would have gone over much of the same ground. Many procedural devices for joining additional claims or parties thus require a nexus between the subject matter of successive claims.[6] Even where claims are unrelated, however, litigating both in one case may promote more efficient use of judicial resources.[7]

[b]   Avoiding Prejudice to a Party or Absentee

The substantive rights of either an absentee or a party may be prejudiced if the absentee is not made an additional party in the case. Prejudice in this sense is different from the prejudice of added expense and delay of protracted litigation. For example, substantive prejudice is a concern when an absentee runs the risk of being adversely affected by the outcome in a case without an opportunity to influence that outcome as only parties can.[8] Another example occurs when an existing party suffers from the court's failure to have before it all those involved in the controversy, creating for that party the prospect of conflicting judgments and multiple liability.[9] In both examples, justifications for adding a party go beyond mere judicial efficiency.

[3]   How the Federal Rules of Civil Procedure Facilitate Expansion of Claims and Parties

Like other aspects of civil procedure, the law of claim and party joinder has undergone substantial change. The courts of the United States, the fifty states, and the District of Columbia each administer their own law in the field. For our

---

which tend to make the proceeding a Donnybrook Fair." *Crosby Steam Gage & Valve Co. v. Manning, Maxwell & Moore Inc.*, 51 F. Supp. 972, 973 (D. Mass. 1943).

[5] Courts are motivated by the same concerns in giving preclusive effect to their judgments. The trend is toward giving judgments greater preclusive effect, penalizing piecemeal litigation and delay. *See generally* Chapter 15, *infra*.

[6] *See* for example, discussion of compulsory counterclaims, crossclaims, and necessary and indispensable parties in §§ 9.03, 9.04 & 9.05[2], *infra*.

[7] This is the assumption underlying claim joinder and permissive counterclaims. *See* §§ 9.08[1], 9.02 & 9.03, *infra*.

[8] This problem is addressed by Rule 24(a), governing intervention of right. *See* § 62[A], *infra*.

[9] A problem addressed, for example, by Rule 19(a), governing joinder of required parties. *See* § 9.05[2], *infra*.

primary model when discussing complex litigation, we will use the Federal Rules of Civil Procedure.

The approach of the federal rules is typical of approaches taken elsewhere.[10] The objective is to combine received traditions[11] with an appreciation of the practical necessities of modern civil litigation into a more or less cohesive body of rules. These rules seek to sort, authorize and limit structural devices which enlarge litigation from the minimum configuration of one plaintiff, one defendant and one claim. However, the rules alone cannot alter the jurisdiction of federal courts or venue of federal actions.[12]

In this chapter, we will examine claim and party expansion situations usually taken up by rules.[13] We will consider the functional effect of each rule, justification for its use and limitation, and special problems or issues.

PART A.
Adding Claims Without Adding Parties

In this Part we will consider multiclaim procedure: rules governing claim joinder, counterclaims, and crossclaims. These procedural devices add claims to the litigation, but do not, by themselves, authorize the addition of parties.[14] Each of the multiclaim rules we will consider has the purpose of reducing delay, needless repetition, and expense in civil litigation by reducing the possibility of multiple lawsuits. The function of multiclaim rules, then, is to promote the adjudication of as many claims as possible in the first instance.

---

[10] Most state procedural systems use the approach and often a good deal of the language of the Federal Rules of Civil Procedure. *See generally* John B. Oakley & Arthur F. Coon, *The Federal Rules in State Court: A Survey of State Court Systems of Civil Procedure*, 61 WASH. L. REV. 1367 (1986); § 2 n.4 and accompanying text, *supra*.

[11] Multiclaim and multiparty rules have their antecedents in English law, often in equity practice. For one example, see Geoffrey C. Hazard, Jr., *Indispensable Party: The Historical Origin of a Procedural Phantom*, 61 COLUM. L. REV. 1254 (1961).

[12] Rule 82. Until recently, the federal courts extended the reach of federal subject matter jurisdiction and venue through common law. *See* §§ 9.03, 9.04 & 9.05[2], *infra*. Much of that law has now been codified. *See generally* § 5.08, *supra*.

[13] Beyond the federal rules of civil procedure, statutes governing interpleader and multidistrict consolidation of pretrial proceedings are of sufficient general importance to be covered in this chapter. *See* §§ 9.07 & 9.10[2], *infra*.

[14] Thus, while Rule 13(h) indicates that one may join a party in order to make a counterclaim or crossclaim, the provision makes clear that such expansion must separately satisfy rules pertaining to party joinder (one of the multiparty rules discussed in Part B, *infra*). Of course, once an additional party has been brought into the litigation on the authority of one of the multiparty rules, the extent to which he may thereafter claim or be claimed against is usually governed by the multiclaim rules discussed in this Part. *Cf.* WRIGHT & MILLER § 1655 ("If the requirements for joinder of parties [under Rule 20] have been satisfied . . . Rule 18 [claim joinder] may be invoked independently to permit plaintiff to join as many other claims as the plaintiff has against the multiple defendants . . . .").

§ 9.02   CLAIM JOINDER[15]

Rule 18 governs claim joinder, the process by which one who has made a claim may join further claims with it against the same opponent.[16] Rules of civil procedure treating aspects of complex litigation are usually two-sided in their effect. They authorize, but also limit, claim or party expansion.[17] Rule 18 is an exception. It authorizes claim joinder without limitation.[18] Rule 18(a) states that "[a] party asserting a claim" of any kind "may join as independent or alternate claims, as many claims as it has against an opposing party."[19] A claimant wishing to assert entirely unrelated claims against the same party finds no obstacle in Rule 18. For two reasons, however, possibilities for multiple claim adjudication in federal court are not as great as the bare language of Rule 18 might suggest.

First, Rule 18 does not insulate claims from difficulties unrelated to the joinder rules. A federal rule of civil procedure cannot "extend or limit the jurisdiction of the district courts or the venue of actions in those courts."[20] Consider the following example. Federal plaintiff A wishes to make two unrelated claims against defendant B. The first falls within the court's general federal question jurisdiction.[21] The second is based on state law. Absent either diversity of citizenship between A and B or the requisite jurisdictional amount,[22] there is no original federal subject matter jurisdiction over the second claim. Supplemental jurisdiction requires a close relationship between the subject matter of the two claims.[23] Rule 18 may appear to authorize both

---

[15] *See generally* MOORE §§ 18.01–18.23; WRIGHT & MILLER §§ 1581–1594; Benjamin Kaplan, *Continuing Work of the Civil Committee: 1966 Amendments of the Federal Rules of Civil Procedure (II)*, 81 HARV. L. REV. 591, 591–98 (1968); William W. Blume, *A Rational Theory for Joinder of Causes of Action and Defences, and for the Use of Counterclaims*, 26 MICH. L. REV. 1 (1927).

[16] Rule 18 authorizes claim but not party joinder. Rule 20 governs the latter, and permits party joinder only when at least one claim arising out of the same transaction or occurrence is applicable to the joined parties and a question of law or fact is common. For further discussion of the requirements of Rule 20, *see* § 9.05[1], *infra*.

[17] See for example, limitations placed on party joinder discussed in the preceding note or on the availability of crossclaims discussed in § 9.04, *infra*.

[18] *Cf.* Arthur F. Greenbaum, *Jacks or Better to Open: Procedural Limitations on Co-Party and Third-Party Claims*, 74 MINN. L. REV. 507, 532 (1990) (noting acceptance of the view that Rule 18 enables one to "raise any claim against another party after raising a qualifying claim."). Rule 13 similarly permits counterclaims without limitation. *See* § 9.03, *infra*.

[19] Elements of a "claim" are defined in Rule 8(a). For discussion of claim pleading under the federal rules, *see* §§ 8.04 & 8.06[2], *supra*. Most state procedural systems employ the same approach and much of the same language as federal Rule 18. *E.g.*, ALA. CODE R. CIV. P. 18; DEL. CODE ANN. R. CIV. P. 18; KY. REV. STAT. ANN. R. CIV. P. 18.01.

[20] Rule 82. The reference is to federal subject matter jurisdiction. *Cf. Snyder v. Harris*, 394 U.S. 332, 337 (1969) (even if expansion of federal diversity jurisdiction might otherwise be implied from an amendment making class actions more available under Rule 23, such expansion was prohibited under Rule 82).

[21] 28 U.S.C. § 1331, *discussed in* § 5.03, *supra*.

[22] The prerequisites for general diversity jurisdiction under 28 U.S.C. § 1332, discussed in §§ 5.04–5.06, *supra*.

[23] 28 U.S.C. § 1367, *discussed in* § 5.11, *supra*.

claims, but it will not save the second from dismissal for lack of subject matter jurisdiction.

Second, Rule 18 merely allows parties to plead claim joinder. It does not guarantee that the claims will be tried together. "The Rule addresses pleadings, not trials. The district judge may order separate trials of claims or issues."[24]

The availability of other means for regulating the entry and trial of multiple claims explains in part why Rule 18 contains no limitation on claim joinder. A further reason can be found in the fact that prior attempts to distinguish between permissibly and impermissibly joined claims proved unsatisfactory. Common law and code distinctions were often difficult to administer,[25] generating unproductive litigation. The original Rule 18 attacked the problem by largely eliminating the possibility of impermissible claims. The process was completed with amendment of paragraph (a) of the rule in 1966.[26]

§ 9.03 COMPULSORY AND PERMISSIVE COUNTERCLAIMS[27]

When a party claims against one who previously claimed against him, the claim back is called a counterclaim.[28] Rule 13 divides these into *compulsory counterclaims* under paragraph (a) and *permissive counterclaims* under paragraph (b).[29]

---

[24] *MOORE* § 18.02[6]. "The district court has broad authority to proceed with separate trials for a variety of reasons, including the prevention of embarrassment, delay, prejudice or expense." *MOORE* § 18.02[6]. *See, e.g., Long & Foster Real Estate, Inc. v. NRT Mid-Atlantic, Inc.*, 357 F. Supp. 2d 911 (E.D. Va. 2005).

[25] *WRIGHT & MILLER* § 1581.

[26] Prior to the amendment, the language of the rule "led some courts to conclude that the rules regulating joinder of parties were intended to be superimposed on Rule 18(a) and encouraged them to apply special restrictions to the joinder of claims in multiparty situations." *WRIGHT & MILLER* § 1583.

[27] *See generally MOORE* §§ 13.01–13.50; *WRIGHT & MILLER* §§ 1401–1430; Kevin M. Clermont, *Common-Law Compulsory Counterclaim Rule: Creating Effective and Elegant Res Judicata Doctrine*, 79 NOTRE DAME L. REV. 1745 (2004); Michael D. Conway, Comment, *Narrowing the Scope of Rule 13(a)*, 60 U. CHI. L. REV. 141, 141–42 (1993); John E. Kennedy, *Counterclaims Under Federal Rule 13*, 11 HOUS. L. REV. 255 (1974); Charles A. Wright, *Estoppel By Rule: The Compulsory Counterclaim Under Modern Pleading*, 38 MINN. L. REV. 423 (1954).

[28] Counterclaims evolved from the common law claims of *recoupment* and *set-off*. CHARLES E. CLARK, HANDBOOK OF THE LAW OF CODE PLEADING 633–36 (2d ed. 1947). By recoupment, defendant was entitled to defeat or reduce the plaintiff's recovery by pleading a claim against him arising out of the same transaction as the plaintiff's claim. By set-off, defendant was permitted to plead a transactionally unrelated claim against the plaintiff, provided that it was a claim for a liquidated sum. *See generally* JOSEPH H. KOFFLER & ALLISON REPPY, HANDBOOK OF COMMON LAW PLEADING § 278 (1969); BENJAMIN J. SHIPMAN, HANDBOOK OF COMMON-LAW PLEADING §§ 209–10 (3d ed. 1923).

[29] Many state procedural systems also maintain the distinction (*e.g.*, FLA. R. CIV. P. 1.170(a) & (b); IND. CODE ANN. CT. R. TRIAL 13(A) & (B); N.M. STAT. ANN. R. CIV. P. DIST. CT. 1-013(A) & (B)), but some do not. New York is an example of the latter. *See* David Siegel, Practice Commentary to N.Y. CPLR 3019, McKinney's Consolidated Laws of New York, vol. 7B (2006) ("All counterclaims are permissive in New York: D can use his claim as a counterclaim or save it and sue on it

Important consequences can turn on this distinction, as we shall see. However, the status of a counterclaim as compulsory or permissive has nothing to do with its availability to a party under the joinder rules. The scope for counterclaims under Rule 13 is unlimited,[30] like that for claim joinder under Rule 18.[31] But Rule 13 is also like Rule 18 in that satisfaction of the rule offers no guarantee that the counterclaim will be adjudicated at the same time as the preceding claim, or at all. The counterclaim must conform to the requirements of venue and federal subject matter jurisdiction,[32] and the court presented with the counterclaim is free "to order separate trial of a particular issue if this is in fact more convenient or desirable."[33]

The difference between compulsory and permissive counterclaims is important. The status of a claim as permissive may confer an advantage in the realm of preclusion law. Compulsory counterclaims take their name from the fact that parties having them must either plead or forfeit them.[34] In contrast, one may plead a permissive counterclaim or reserve it for future litigation.[35] At the same time, permissive counterclaims are more likely to encounter jurisdictional obstacles. A counterclaim beyond original federal court jurisdiction cannot be brought within the language of the supplemental jurisdiction statute[36] unless it is so related in subject matter to plaintiff's claim that it would also meet the test for compulsory counterclaims.[37] Merely permissive counterclaims thus are often ineligible for supplemental jurisdiction.

Counterclaims are permissive unless they meet the compulsory-counterclaim test of Rule 13(a). The test involves several prerequisites.[38]

---

separately."); DAVID SIEGEL, NEW YORK PRACTICE § 224 (4th ed. 2004).

[30] "It is immaterial whether the counterclaim is legal or equitable, in contract or in tort, or even whether it has any connection with plaintiff's claim." WRIGHT § 79, at 564.

[31] See § 9.02, supra.

[32] Compulsory counterclaims fare better here. See note 58, infra.

[33] WRIGHT § 79.

[34] This is sometimes called preclusion by rule and is discussed in § 15.03[3], infra.

[35] "The defendant or party who did not choose the forum or control the litigation, although bound on those matters actually litigated, should not be bound on those claims that, under the law of the first forum, he was not compelled to litigate." Eugene F. Scoles, Interstate Preclusion by Prior Litigation, 74 Nw. U. L. REV. 742, 754 (1979).

[36] 28 U.S.C. § 1367, discussed in § 5.11, supra.

[37] Prior to enactment of the statute in 1990, the same distinction limited the availability of ancillary jurisdiction. The doctrine of ancillary jurisdiction tracked compulsory counterclaim, crossclaim and impleader definitions found in the Federal Rules of Civil Procedure. Owen Equip. & Erection Co. v. Kroger, 437 U.S. 365, 375 & n.18 (1978). It appears that these applications of ancillary jurisdiction have been preserved and codified under § 1367. See §§ 5.08–5.11, supra.

[38]

> In an action in personam, a claim defendant has against plaintiff is a compulsory counterclaim if it meets four conditions. It must: (1) arise "out of the transaction or occurrence that is the subject matter of the opposing party's claim;" (2) be matured and owned by the pleader at the time the pleading is served; (3) not require for its adjudication the presence of third parties of whom the court cannot acquire personal jurisdiction; and (4) not have been, at the time the original action was commenced, the subject matter of another pending action.

However, just one, "that the claim arise out of the transaction or occurrence that is the subject of the opposing party's claim," has posed problems.[39] At least four different definitions of the required transactional nexus have been suggested in the cases.[40] The "same-issue" test suffers a timing problem, since it is hard to know what the issues of law and fact are before the plaintiff has replied to the counterclaim. The "*res judicata*" test asks whether a judgment in the case would bar a subsequent suit on a reserved counterclaim. But "[t]his is no test at all," Professor Wright notes, because, absent a compulsory counterclaim rule, counterclaims can be sued upon independently.[41] The "same-evidence" test is more useful because it assures that compulsory joinder of the counterclaim will produce real economies by preventing duplicative discovery and trial of the same evidence in successive lawsuits. Yet it fails to reach counterclaims which are logically part of the existing controversy between the parties, but which require different proof. In addition, both the same-issue and same-evidence tests are ambiguous because they do not indicate how close to identical the issues or evidence need be.

Most federal courts therefore have adopted a fourth, more generous transactional test: whether the counterclaim is logically related to the existing claim against the prospective counterclaimant.[42] For example, plaintiff debtor sued her lender on a truth-in-lending cause of action in *Plant v. Blazer Financial Services, Inc.*[43] The lender counterclaimed with a state law cause of action on the debt. Because the parties were not diverse, the counterclaim could only be heard if it was compulsory and therefore within the court's supplemental (then termed, ancillary) jurisdiction. Although a truth-in-lending claim and a debt counterclaim pose different issues of law and fact and involve substantially different evidence,[44] the court of appeals applied the logical relationship test to affirm the judgment on the counterclaim. "Applying the logical relationship test literally to the counterclaim in this case clearly suggests its compulsory character," reasoned the court, "because a single aggregate of operative facts, the loan transaction, gave rise to both plaintiff's and defendant's claim."[45]

WRIGHT § 79 (footnotes omitted). *See, e.g., Critical-Vac Filtration Corp. v. Minuteman Int'l Inc.*, 233 F.3d 697, 702 (2d Cir. 2000); *Sparrow v. Mazda Am. Credit*, 385 F. Supp. 2d 1063, 1068 (E.D. Cal. 2005).

[39] WRIGHT § 79. *Cf.* Michael D. Conway, Comment, *Narrowing the Scope of Rule 13(a)*, 60 U. CHI. L. REV. 141, 141–42 (1993) (different interpretations of the requirement persist).

[40] *See* WRIGHT § 79.

[41] WRIGHT § 79. *See generally* § 15.03[3] (preclusion by rule), *infra*.

[42] WRIGHT & MILLER § 1410. *See, e.g., Eon Labs, Inc. v. SmithKline Beecham Corp.*, 298 F. Supp. 2d 175, 179 (D. Mass. 2003).

[43] 598 F.2d 1357 (5th Cir. 1979).

[44] *See, e.g., Whigham v. Beneficial Fin. Co.*, 599 F.2d 1322, 1323–24 (4th Cir. 1979) (noting these differences in holding the debt counterclaim not compulsory).

[45] *Plant*, 598 F.2d at 1361. *Cf. Moore v. New York Cotton Exch.*, 270 U.S. 593, 610 (1926) ("[The transaction] is the one circumstance without which neither party would have found it necessary to seek relief."). The *Plant* court noted a split in the courts on the issue whether a counterclaim on the debt is compulsory in truth-in-lending suits, but also attributed it primarily to judicial concern about the chilling effect of such counterclaims on private enforcement of federal truth-in-lending

"The hallmark of [the logical relationship] approach is its flexibility."[46] In this respect and in its ultimate reach, the logical relationship test for compulsory counterclaims is very similar to the "transactional relationship" test for modern claim preclusion.[47] This is not surprising. The ultimate concern of both compulsory counterclaim rules and the law of claim preclusion is the appropriate scope of a lawsuit.

§ 9.04 CROSSCLAIMS[48]

When a party claims against a co-party (rather than an opposing party) the claim is called a crossclaim. Crossclaims in federal court are governed by Rule 13(g), which states:

> A pleading may state as a crossclaim any claim by one party against a coparty if the claim arises out of the transaction or occurrence that is the subject matter either of the original action or of a counterclaim, of if the claim relates to any property that is the subject matter of the original action.[49]

Most federal courts have interpreted the "transaction-or-occurrence" requirement to mean that there must be a logical relationship[50] between the crossclaim and either the original action or a counterclaim.[51]

The scope for crossclaims is less than the scope for permissive counterclaims in Rule 13(b),[52] and slightly larger than that created for compulsory counterclaims under 13(a).[53] Like compulsory counterclaims, crossclaims are generally within federal courts' supplemental jurisdiction.[54] They differ, however, in an important respect. While the holder of a compulsory counterclaim must plead or forfeit it, one may either plead a crossclaim or reserve it for further

---

policy. *But see Peterson v. United Accounts, Inc.*, 638 F.2d 1134 (8th Cir. 1981) (despite some overlap of issues, there is no logical relationship between collection claim and truth-in-lending counterclaim).

[46] WRIGHT & MILLER § 1410.

[47] *See* § 15.03[2] (discussing the emergence of § 24 of the *Restatement (Second) of Judgments*), *infra.*

[48] *See generally* MOORE §§ 13.60–13.80; WRIGHT & MILLER §§ 1431–3143; John D. Bessler, Note, *Defining "Co-Party" Within Federal Rule of Civil Procedure 13(g): Are CrossClaims Between Original Defendants and Third-Party Defendants Allowable?*, 66 IND. L.J. 549 (1991).

[49] Many state systems have adopted this approach. *E.g.*, ALA. CODE R. CIV. P. 13(G); MINN. STAT. ANN. R. CIV. P. DIST. CT. 13.07; N.C. GEN. STAT. § 1A-1, R. 13(g).

[50] *See* the discussion of the role of the logical relationship test in determining compulsory counterclaims at § 9.03, notes 44–47 and accompanying text, *supra.*

[51] WRIGHT & MILLER § 1431.

[52] "It is immaterial whether the [permissive] counterclaim is legal or equitable, in contract or in tort, or even whether it has any connection with plaintiff's claim." WRIGHT § 79.

[53] That the scope of crossclaims is somewhat greater than that of compulsory counterclaims may be suggested from Rule 13(g)'s inclusion of contingent as well as ripened claims. *See* WRIGHT & MILLER § 1431. Nonetheless, "most courts have held that the standards developed for dealing with compulsory counterclaims also apply to crossclaims under Rule 13(g)." WRIGHT & MILLER § 1432.

[54] *See* § 5.11, *supra.*

litigation; crossclaims are never compulsory under Rule 13(g).[55]

A crossclaim arguably makes co-parties opposing parties. This means that, should the target of a crossclaim wish to direct a claim back against the crossclaimant, this claim back would be a counterclaim.[56] For Rule 13 to treat this last claim as a counterclaim rather than as a crossclaim may mean that the claimant will lose it if it is compulsory and he fails to plead it.

Consider the following illustration. A, B, C and D enter into various construction and material supply contracts related to a large public works project. A sues B, C and D for breach of one of the contracts.[57] B counterclaims against A for breach of the same contract and pleads a claim against C for breach of a different but related contract. So long as it is sufficiently related to the subject matter of the original claim or counterclaim, B's claim against C is a good crossclaim.[58] If C has a claim against B sufficiently related to B's crossclaim, C must plead it back against B as a compulsory counterclaim. If C has any other claim against B, he has the option of pleading it as a permissive counterclaim.

Rule 13(g) also permits crossclaims against a party on the theory that he "is or may be liable to the crossclaimant for all or part of a claim asserted in the action against the cross-claimant." The rule thus provides a joinder mechanism for contingent or derivative claims.[59]

PART B.
Adding Claims by Adding Parties

§ 9.05   PERMISSIVE AND COMPULSORY JOINDER[60]

[1]   Permissive Joinder

Federal Rule 20 authorizes the permissive[61] joinder of claims by multiple plaintiffs or against multiple defendants. In either case, the rule permits the assertion of "any right to relief" held "jointly, severally, or in the alternative,"

---

[55] *Moore* § 13.70[1]. Crossclaims are in this sense like permissive counterclaims. *See* § 59.03 *supra. See, e.g., Pouliot v. Paul Arpin Van Lines, Inc.*, 303 F. Supp. 2d 135, 138 (D. Conn. 2004).

[56] *See* Moore § 13.71[1]. The shift follows the language of Rule 13. Both paragraph (a) (compulsory counterclaims) and (b) (permissive counterclaims) describe the claimant's target as the "opposing party." *Cf.* Arthur F. Greenbaum, *Jacks or Better to Open: Procedural Limitations on Co-Party and Third-Party Claims*, 74 Minn. L. Rev. 507, 520–21 (1990) ("[M]ost courts and commentators read the Rules to incorporate a shifting status based on the actual posture of the parties. Thus, if B brings a crossclaim against C, B then becomes an opposing party to C because they now are formally opposing each other on a claim.").

[57] The procedure permitting A to join B, C and D as multiple defendants is discussed in § 9.05, *infra.*

[58] In a well-known case, the Sixth Circuit ruled on facts like these that the two contracts were sufficiently related to the same construction project to bring the crossclaim within the "transaction

so long as claims joined to bring multiple parties into the lawsuit are "with respect to or arising out of the same transaction, occurrence, or series of transactions or occurrences and . . . any question of law or fact common to all plaintiffs will arise in the action." The object of Rule 20 "is to promote trial convenience and expedite the final determination of disputes, thereby preventing multiple lawsuits."[62] To achieve this purpose, it authorizes party joinder to a substantially greater extent than was possible under common law or code systems.[63]

Common law and code systems generally permitted parties plaintiff to join their claims only with reference to rights held in common (jointly). The distinction between rights held jointly and rights held individually (severally) was often difficult for courts to draw. This restricted and complicated joinder practice.[64] Rule 20 clarified matters and increased judicial efficiency by extending party joinder to both categories of claims.[65] It expanded joinder of

---

or occurrence" test of Rule 13(g). *See Lasa Per L'Industria Del Marmo Societa Per Azioni of Lasa v. Alexander*, 414 F.2d 143 (6th Cir. 1969).

[59] The comparable joinder device for such claims against outsiders is impleader. *See* § 9.06, *infra*.

[60] *See generally*, MOORE §§ 19.01–19.09, 20.01–20.09; *Wright & Miller* §§ 1601–6160; John B. Oakley, *Joinder and Jurisdiction in the Federal District Courts: The State of the Union of Rules and Statutes*, 69 TENN. L. REV. 35 (2001); Joan Steinman, *Postremoval Changes in the Party Structure of Diversity Cases: The Old Law, the New Law, and Rule 19*, 38 U. KAN. L. REV. 863, 908–27 (1990); Carl Tobias, *Rule 19 and the Public Rights Exception to Party Joinder*, 65 N.C. L. REV. 745 (1987); Richard D. Freer, *Rethinking Compulsory Joinder: A Proposal to Restructure Federal Rule 19*, 60 N.Y.U. L. REV. 1061 (1985); John C. McCoid, *A Single Package for Multiparty Disputes*, 28 STAN. L. REV. 707 (1976); Benjamin Kaplan, *Continuing Work of the Civil Committee: 1966 Amendments of the Federal Rules of Civil Procedure (I)*, 81 HARV. L. REV. 356, 358–75 (1967); *Developments in the Law — Multiparty Litigation in the Federal Courts*, 71 HARV. L. REV. 874, 879–97 (1958).

[61] Rule 20 permits but does not require party joinder. In contrast, Rule 19 mandates party joinder whenever feasible. *See* § 9.05[2], *infra*. The distinction created between federal Rules 19 and 20 has its counterpart in many state procedural systems. *E.g.*, DEL. CODE ANN. R. CIV. P. 19–20; KY. REV. STAT. ANN. R. CIV. P. 19.01–20.01; MINN. STAT. ANN. R. CIV. P. DIST. CT. 19.01–20.01.

[62] *WRIGHT & MILLER* § 1652. *Accord*, MOORE § 20.02[1][a]. *See, e.g., John S. Clark Co. v. Travelers Indem. Co.*, 359 F. Supp. 2d 429, 438 (M.D.N.C. 2004); *DirecTV, Inc. v. Barrett*, 220 F.R.D. 630, 631 (D. Kan. 2004).

[63] *FRIEDENTHAL, KANE & MILLER* § 6.4. The scheme set out in Rule 20 corresponds more closely to English practice. *See* MOORE § 20.03.

[64] *Ryder v. Jefferson Hotel Co.*, 113 S.E. 474 (S.C. 1922), is as an example frequently cited. Plaintiffs, who were husband and wife, alleged that they suffered humiliation and financial loss when ousted from their hotel room by defendant. South Carolina procedure permitted plaintiffs to join their claims only with reference to jointly held interests. A majority of the South Carolina Supreme Court concluded that the Ryder's interests were several, likening them to those of two railroad passengers suing for injuries from a train wreck. The dissent argued that the injury alleged in the case was to a jointly held interest, likening plaintiffs to a partnership.

[65] "Illustratively, suppose a bus collides with an automobile. All of the bus passengers who suffered personal injuries or property damage may join as plaintiffs in a single action against defendant under Rule 20(a), even though their respective claims are several rather than joint." *WRIGHT & MILLER* § 1654.

parties defendant by permitting joinder of multiple defendants claimed against alternatively.[66]

The test for party joinder under Rule 20 is two-fold. The claims supporting party joinder must (1) arise from the same transaction or occurrence and (2) have in common a question of law or fact. The common question requirement is easier to satisfy, since only one common question of law or fact need exist to connect the claims.[67] The transaction or occurrence requirement of Rule 20(a) also appears in paragraphs (a) and (g) of Rule 13, governing compulsory counterclaims and crossclaims respectively.[68] The prevailing interpretation of the requirement in all three settings appears to be the same: a logical relationship between claims.[69] This flexible interpretation of the requirement[70] facilitates joinder.[71]

Should the prerequisites for permissive joinder of parties be as accommodating as those for compulsory counterclaims and crossclaims? While all have the common purpose of promoting judicial efficiency, it is at least arguable that Rule 20 should have more limited application because it encumbers the suit with an additional party as well as an additional claim.[72]

On the other hand, Rule 20 only operates at the pleading level. It does not guarantee that multiparty claims joined will be tried at the same time, or that all will be tried in federal court. The limitations of subject matter jurisdiction and venue may pose problems.[73] The burdensome presence of an added party can be avoided, moreover, even when proper jurisdiction and venue exist. "[T]he convenience of the parties and the court can be protected fully, though

---

[66] "The need for alternative joinder of defendants typically arises when the substance of plaintiff's claim indicates that the plaintiff is entitled to relief from someone, but the plaintiff does not know which of two or more defendants is liable under the circumstances set forth in the complaint." WRIGHT & MILLER § 1654

[67] WRIGHT & MILLER § 1653. *See, e.g., Jamison v. Purdue Pharma Co.*, 251 F. Supp. 2d 1315, 1322-23 (D. Miss. 2003).

[68] *See* §§ 9.03 & 9.04, *supra.*

[69] "Usually, a court applies the transaction-or-occurrence requirement in a particular case by asking whether there is a logical relationship between the claim involving the party to be joined and the rest of the case." FRIEDENTHAL, KANE & MILLER § 6.4. This is also how the requirement is read concerning compulsory counterclaims and crossclaims. *See* §§ 9.03 & 9.04, *supra.* For discussions of alternative tests for transaction or occurrence, see § 9.03, notes 44–47, *supra.*

[70] At the same time, the language of the transaction or occurrence requirement in Rule 20 should at least prevent joinder of claims evolving from entirely different facts, even if identical in type. Most federal courts have so read the rule. *See, e.g., Scott v. Fairbanks Capital Corp.*, 284 F. Supp. 2d 880, 888 (S.D. Ohio 2003); *Saval v. BL, Ltd.*, 710 F.2d 1027 (4th Cir. 1983). "[C]ourts properly refuse joinder when claims, while legally similar, are factually distinct." MOORE § 20.05[3].

[71] Professor Wright notes that "it seems practically desirable to give the broadest possible reading to the permissive language of Rule 20(a)." WRIGHT § 71.

[72] *See* § 9.01, *supra.*

[73] MOORE §§ 20.07–20.08; John B. Oakley, *Joinder and Jurisdiction in the Federal District Courts: The State of the Union of Rules and Statutes*, 69 TENN. L. REV. 35 (2001). In contrast, compulsory counterclaims and crossclaims are sheltered by the supplemental jurisdiction statue, *see* § 9.03, *supra*, and pose no serious venue problems.

joinder is allowed, by separate trials, pursuant to Rules 20(b) and 42(b) . . . ."[74]

[2]   Compulsory Joinder

Compulsory joinder has its origin in equity practice. Rule 19 governs compulsory joinder in federal court. We have seen that Rule 20 is not compulsory, that it merely determines how much freedom exists under the rules for joinder of parties plaintiff or defendant. In contrast, Rule 19 treats situations where the quality of the adjudication will suffer without the absentee. Rule 19(a) provides a framework for determining whether the absentee is a necessary party: one whose relation to the case is such that he must be joined if he can be. When joinder of a person falling under Rule 19(a) is not feasible, Rule 19(b) provides a framework for determining whether the person's absence is so problematic to the case that it cannot go on without him. Cases under this rule may be subject to as many as three inquiries: (1) *requirement* of joinder of the absentee, (2) *feasibility* of joinder; and (3) whether the case should go on when required joinder is not feasible.

[a]   Required Parties Under Rule 19(a) — When Must Joinable Persons Be Brought In?

The object of rules facilitating expansion of claims and parties in civil litigation is either to reduce delay, needless repetition and expense in civil litigation, or to avoid prejudice to a party or absentee.[75] The multiclaim rules considered earlier share the first objective with Rule 20. Compulsory joinder under Rule 19 also fosters judicial efficiency, but it is most concerned with the second objective. Absentees falling within Rule 19(a) are called by the subdivision *required parties*. Paragraph (a) sets up three separate categories of required parties, stating that each "must be joined as a party" when joinder is feasible. The three categories are couched in flexible, pragmatic terms.

One is required according to Rule 19(a)(1)(A) if "in that person's absence, the court cannot accord complete relief among existing parties." Emphasis here is on "the desirability of joining those persons in whose absence the court would be obliged to grant partial or hollow rather than complete relief to the parties before the court."[76]

In close cases, it may be necessary to determine whether the absence of a person makes likely further lawsuits among those already parties or, whether, instead, "meaningful relief can be granted without the absentee."[77]

One is also a required party when, according to Rule 19(a)(1)(B)(i), "the person claims an interest relating to the subject of the action and is so situated that disposing of the action in the person's absence may . . . as a practical

---

[74] *Wright* § 71.

[75] *See* § 7.04, *supra*.

[76] Rule 19, advisory committee's notes (1966).

[77] *Moore* § 19.03[2][d]. *See, e.g., Wilbur v. Locke*, 423 F.3d 1101, 1112 (9th Cir. 2005).

matter impair or impede the person's ability to protect the interest . . . ." Here the rule "recognizes the importance of protecting the person whose joinder is in question against the practical prejudice to him which may arise through a disposition of the action in his absence."[78] Emphasis on practical impairment means that it is not necessary for the absentee to risk the possibility of being bound by the case in a formal sense.[79] What is necessary is a prospect of detriment to the absentee from the case serious enough to entitle him to an opportunity to influence the outcome in ways only a litigant can.[80] At the same time, one whose interests may be thus impaired by the litigation probably has a right to intervene in the case.[81] An absentee's opportunity to intervene thus may be taken into account in determining prejudice to the absentee in the absence of joinder.[82]

Finally, one who "claims an interest relating to the subject of the action" is a required party according to Rule 19(a)(1)(B)(ii) when "disposing of the action in the person's absence may . . . leave an existing party subject to a substantial risk of incurring double, multiple, or otherwise inconsistent obligations because the interest."[83] The strongest case for Rule 19(a)(1)(B)(ii) joinder is where a party, usually a defendant, risks either double liability or inconsistent judgments.

Consider occasions for Rule 19(a)(1)(B)(ii) joinder through the following illustration. Plaintiff A sues a bank to recover funds. An adjudication that A is entitled to the funds will bind the bank defendant to A but will not bind absentee B, who intends to bring suit against the bank claiming the same funds. The bank thus runs the risk of having to pay two judgments, or twice the value of the obligation. If, instead, B was joined with A in the initial suit, the court would determine which of the two was entitled to recover. That single adjudication would bind the bank in favor of the winning claimant, but it would also bind the losing claimant in favor of the bank. A single lawsuit would remove the risk to the bank of double liability.[84]

---

[78] Rule 19, advisory committee's notes (1966).

[79] Indeed, the constitutional law of due process will usually prevent that from happening. *See* § 15.08[1], *infra*.

[80] Party prerogatives include setting boundaries of materiality through pleadings, developing the facts by discovery, creating parts of the factual record, and appeal.

[81] Intervention of right is usually governed by Rule 24(a)(2), discussed more fully in § 9.08[1], *infra*. The language used in Rules 19(a)(1)(B)(i) and 24(a)(2) to describe practical impairment to interests of the absentee is almost identical. The opportunity of absentees described in Rule 19(a)(1)(B)(i) for timely intervention under Rule 24(a)(2) is limited only when their interests are adequately represented by one already a party, or when their joinder would have defeated diversity jurisdiction.

[82] It would be difficult to reach any other conclusion. When the absentee could intervene but chooses not to, any practical impairment from the litigation seems almost self-inflicted. Unfortunately, the availability of intervention makes it harder to identify a discrete role for Rule 19(a)(1)(B)(i).

[83] A party prejudiced in the manner described in Rule 19(a)(1)(B)(ii) will sometimes be able to resort to interpleader to force all competing claimants to make their claims against him in one proceeding. On interpleader, see generally § 9.07, *infra*.

[84] In a case corresponding to this illustration, the court invoked Rule 19. *See Rapoport v. Banco*

The bank in our illustration may urge B's joinder by also arguing that, even if successive suits do not lead to double liability, they may produce inconsistent judgments. Suppose the bank prevails in A's suit through favorable determination of an issue broad enough to defeat B's claim as well. If B is not made a party to the initial case, B will be entitled to relitigate the issue, resulting in the possibility of inconsistent judgments.[85] In addition, the bank can argue that B's joinder should be required simply to spare the bank the vexation and expense of litigating in two lawsuits rather than one. On the other hand, plaintiff can counter that he should be allowed to pick his defendants.[86]

So long as joinder is feasible, a person required according to Rule 19(a) must be joined in order for the lawsuit to continue.[87] If the person will not enter the lawsuit voluntarily, he will in most cases be brought in under the rule as a defendant.[88] This is true whether the person joined is a claimant or one claimed against.[89] If the absentee is a claimant, however, the court may realign an involuntarily joined claimant to determine jurisdiction in diversity cases.[90] In addition, Rule 19(a)(2) provides that an absentee claimant may be made "in a proper case, an involuntary plaintiff." Relatively few absentees, however, are subject to involuntary plaintiff treatment.[91]

Mexicano Somex, S.A., 668 F.2d 667 (2d Cir. 1982).

[85] This is not double liability, since the bank will be liable only to B. Yet it seems no more than fair for the bank to have an opportunity to bind both A and B to a determination favorable to the bank in the initial suit. This is especially true since B might have been able subsequently to use offensive non-mutual issue preclusion had the issue in an initial suit between the bank and A alone come out in B's favor. *See* § 15.08[2], *infra*. The prospect of inconsistent judgments has been used to require joinder. *E.g., Lopez v. Martin Luther King, Jr. Hosp.*, 97 F.R.D. 24 (C.D. Cal. 1983).

[86] Every application of joinder under Rule 19(a)(1)(B)(ii) would by definition seem to avert multiplicity of litigation. This feature has been stressed in some cases. *E.g., Walsh v. Centeio*, 692 F.2d 1239 (9th Cir. 1982). It is uncertain, however, how much play this factor will or should have in cases where defendant cannot persuasively argue risk of multiple liability or inconsistent judgments. At some point, what has been called the " 'plaintiff autonomy' premise," JAMES, HAZARD & LEUBSDORF § 10.12, becomes a potent counterforce to claimant joinder. There is considerable tradition and sentiment behind the notion that plaintiffs are entitled to sue whomever they want. This notion explains why, under federal procedure and that of many states, joint tortfeasors are not considered necessary [required] parties by reason of their tortfeasor relationship alone. *E.g., Temple v. Synthes Corp.*, 498 U.S. 5, 7 (1990) ("It has long been the rule that it is not necessary for all joint tortfeasors to be named as defendants in a single lawsuit.").

[87] *See, e.g., Dubay v. Wells*, 437 F. Supp. 2d 656, 659 (E.D. Mich. 2006); *Temple Univ. Hosp., Inc. v. Group Health, Inc.*, 413 F. Supp. 2d 420, 425 (E.D. Pa. 2005). The court "will usually give the plaintiff an opportunity to add the absentee. If the plaintiff fails to do so, the court may dismiss the action because of plaintiff's noncompliance." MOORE § 19.04[4][a].

[88] MOORE § 19.04[4][b]. *See, e.g., EEOC v. Peabody W. Coal Co.*, 400 F.3d 774, 782 (9th Cir. 2005), *cert. denied*, 546 U.S. 1150 (2006).

[89] Rule 19(a)(2) states that "[a] person who refuses to join as a plaintiff may be made a . . . defendant."

[90] *See, e.g., Keith v. Volpe*, 858 F.2d 467, 476 (9th Cir. 1988). *See generally* § 5.04[2] (diversity between whom?), *supra*.

[91] There must be "a relationship between the plaintiff and the absentee such that the absentee must allow the use of its name as plaintiff to enable the extant plaintiff to secure relief. Courts have found such relationships in cases involving exclusive licensees of patents and beneficial owners of copyrights." MOORE § 19.04[4][b] (footnote omitted).

[b]   Rule 19(a) — When is Joinder of a Required Party Feasible?

However important a person might be to the lawsuit, his joinder may be infeasible for one of three reasons. Rule 19(a) makes clear that the person can only be joined when "subject to service of process" (personal jurisdiction) and when his joinder "will not deprive the court of subject-matter jurisdiction . . . ." Moreover, it also excuses an involuntarily joined party from the case if he "objects to venue and the joinder . . . would make venue improper . . . ."

Insurmountable difficulties may arise when it is necessary to serve process beyond the borders of the state where the federal court is sitting. We saw earlier that Congress has limited the personal-jurisdiction authority of federal courts in most cases to that enjoyed by local state courts.[92] Rule 4 relaxes this constraint to a degree regarding joinder of parties required under Rule 19, authorizing process against them (and therefore personal jurisdiction) up to a distance of 100 miles from the federal courthouse. Although useful "in major metropolitan areas that span more than one state," the so-called 100-mile bulge "is of limited importance given the general expansion in availability of extraterritorial service under state long-arm statutes."[93]

Even if Rule 19 had made no reference to the topics, it would have been clear that the rule alone could not create subject matter jurisdiction or venue. A federal rule of civil procedure cannot "extend or limit the jurisdiction of the district courts or the venue of actions in those courts."[94] What is more, express requirements in Rule 19 for subject matter jurisdiction and venue forestalled applications of ancillary jurisdiction and ancillary venue[95] that were possible in certain other multiclaim and multiparty settings before the enactment of supplemental jurisdiction.[96] Problems therefore arise from attempts to join one who would destroy diversity jurisdiction[97] or who properly objects to venue.[98]

---

[92] See § 3.01[2][b], supra.

[93] MOORE § 19.04[2].

[94] Rule 82. The reference is to federal subject matter jurisdiction. Cf. Snyder v. Harris, 394 U.S. 332, 337 (1969) (even if expansion of federal diversity jurisdiction might otherwise be implied from an amendment making class actions more available under Rule 23, the same was prohibited under Rule 82).

[95] But see George B. Fraser, Ancillary Jurisdiction of Federal Courts of Persons Whose Interest May Be Impaired If Not Joined, 62 F.R.D. 483 (1967) (arguing that the objectives of ancillary jurisdiction would be well served by giving play to the doctrine in Rule 19 joinder situations). Now, under the supplemental jurisdiction statute, federal subject matter jurisdiction is unavailable for most applications of Rule 19. For discussion of the statute, see §§ 5.08–5.11, supra.

[96] For an explanation of prior doctrines of ancillary jurisdiction in complex litigation, see § 9.03, supra.

[97] Provident Tradesmen's Bank & Trust Co. v. Patterson, 390 U.S. 102 (1968).

[98] See WRIGHT & MILLER § 1610.

[c]   **Rule 19(b) — When Is the Absence of a Person Who Cannot Be Joined So Problematic that the Case Must Be Dismissed?**

Rule 19(b) states that when one required under paragraph (a) "cannot be joined,[99] the court must determine whether, in equity and good conscience, the action should proceed among the existing parties, or should be dismissed."[100] Rule 19(b) then sets out four factors to be weighed in each case before the court decides whether the case should go on without the absentee. In presenting these considerations, the approach taken in the rule is somewhat unusual. Criteria listed in the rules may be serial[101] or cumulative,[102] but they usually line up in support of a common conclusion. Rule 19(b) instead lists factors supporting opposite results.

The first factor is "the extent to which a judgment rendered in the person's absence might prejudice that person the existing parties . . . ." This is the same concern expressed earlier in subclauses (i) and (ii) of Rule 19(a)(1)(B).[103] Tempering the effect of the first factor is the second factor, "the extent to which any prejudice could be lessened or avoided by . . . protective provisions in the judgment . . . shaping the relief; . . . or other measures . . . ." The third factor, "whether a judgment rendered in the person's absence would be adequate," is the same concern expressed earlier in Rule 19(a)(1).[104] It is counterbalanced by the fourth factor, "whether the plaintiff would have an adequate remedy if the action were dismissed for nonjoinder."

This list of factors offers no reasons for concern about the absence of a party beyond those previously raised in Rule 19(a). It is evident from the manner in which the factors are juxtaposed, however, that reasons for treating an absentee as a required party under Rule 19(a) will not invariably support a decision to dismiss the case when joinder is infeasible. The Supreme Court's decision in *Provident Tradesmen's Bank & Trust Co. v. Patterson*[105] bears this out.

The *Provident* case resulted from a motor vehicle accident which caused multiple deaths and serious injury. Various tort claimants sued the indigent

---

[99] Technically, the venue hurdle created in Rule 19(a) comes after the absentee has been joined. Joinder in such cases (although temporary and unavailing) is feasible in a narrow sense. Yet it is better to read Rule 19(b) to apply to joinder problems including "limitations on service of process, subject matter jurisdiction, *and venue*." Rule 19, advisory committee's notes (1966) (emphasis added). On feasibility of joinder, see generally § 9.05[2][b], *supra*.

[100] A 19(b) motion to dismiss may be made at the outset of the case under Rule 12(b)(7), or it may be made later in accordance with Rule 12(h)(2).

[101] For example, satisfaction of any of the three categories in Rule 19(a) makes an absentee a required party. *See* § 9.05[2][a], *supra*.

[102] For example, satisfaction of all of the four categories of Rule 23(a) is necessary for a class action. *See* § 9.09, *infra*.

[103] For discussion of this concern as manifested in Rules 19(a)(1)(B)(i) & (ii), see § 9.05[2][a], *supra*.

[104] For discussion of this concern as manifested in Rule 19(a)(1), see § 9.05[2][a], *supra*.

[105] 390 U.S. 102 (1968).

estate of one driver (Cionci) and an insurance company for a declaratory judgment that Cionci was driving the car of one Dutcher with Dutcher's permission. If the car was driven with Dutcher's permission, then Cionci's estate shared with Dutcher coverage on Dutcher's liability insurance policy. That policy had been issued by the insurance company defendant.

The Court concluded that Dutcher's relationship to the lawsuit was such that Rule 19(a) required him to be joined, if joinder was feasible. It was not. Dutcher's citizenship would have destroyed diversity of the parties upon which the lower court's jurisdiction depended. That brought the Court to Rule 19(b). The Court concluded that suit should go on without Dutcher. The case suggests some of the circumstances in which it is possible to continue suit in the absence of one deemed required under Rule 19(a).

First, plaintiffs had fully litigated their case at the trial level without Dutcher (defendants having made no Rule 19 challenge there). Stressing the fourth factor in Rule 19(b), the Court noted the unfairness of forcing plaintiffs to start from scratch in state court. The Court declined to speculate whether a Rule 19 dismissal of plaintiffs' case before trial would have afforded them an "adequate remedy" in state court. "After trial, however, the adequacy of this hypothetical alternative, from the plaintiffs' point of view, was obviously greatly diminished."[106]

Second, plaintiffs undercut perhaps the strongest argument in favor of a Rule 19(b) dismissal by agreeing to limit all of their claims to the amount of the insurance policy issued by the defendant insurance company.[107] The insurer otherwise would have faced the risk of paying twice on the same policy,[108] a form of prejudice from proceeding without Dutcher that would be entitled to considerable weight under the first factor in Rule 19(b).[109]

It is impossible to lay down hard and fast rules about the application of the four factors of Rule 19(b). The United States Supreme Court observed recently in *Republic of Philippines v. Pimentel*[110] that "the issue of joinder

---

[106] 390 U.S. at 112. Continuing, the Court observed: "Their interest in preserving a fully litigated judgment should be overborne only by rather greater opposing considerations than would be required at an earlier stage when the plaintiffs' only concern was for a federal rather than a state forum." 390 U.S. at 112. It is conceivable that the Supreme Court would have been presented with a fully litigated judgment even if defendants had sought dismissal of the suit on Rule 19(b) grounds prior to trial. This is because denial of the motion to dismiss probably would not have been reviewable prior to trial. *See* § 13.04 (limited authority of federal appellate courts to hear interlocutory appeals), *infra*. It is unclear whether plaintiff's "interest in preserving a fully litigated judgment" would be as strong under this scenario.

[107] 390 U.S. at 116.

[108] Had plaintiffs preserved the option of suing Dutcher in a subsequent lawsuit, Dutcher would have claimed sole protection under the policy and probably would have been able to relitigate the permission issue. 390 U.S. at 115. If successful, Dutcher would prevent the insurer from subtracting from its liability coverage amounts paid out to cover Cionci.

[109] This corresponds to a party's risk of double liability, identified in Rule 19(a)(1)(B)(ii) and discussed in § 9.05[2][a], *supra*.

[110] 128 S. Ct. 2180, 2188 (2008). The Court was careful to follow the approach laid out in *Provident*. It concluded, largely on international sovereign immunity grounds, that the case could

can be complex, and determinations are case specific."[111]

§ 9.06   IMPLEADER[112]

Impleader reduces the possibility of duplicative litigation. It addresses situations where one outside the litigation may either share or be legally responsible for defendant's liability to plaintiff.[113] Defendant under such circumstances is often able to bring in (implead) the outsider and thereby settle all legal questions in the initial case.

Consider the following situation — first, without impleader. Customer sues retailer on a product liability claim. The facts of the case are that, if retailer is held liable, he will have a strong argument that the manufacturer should *indemnify* or reimburse him for all or part of that liability.[114] However, the consumer does not join the manufacturer as a co-defendant,[115] nor does the manufacturer seek to intervene.[116]

If the consumer obtains a judgment against the retailer, retailer must thereafter bring a separate lawsuit against the manufacturer for indemnification. Moreover, because the manufacturer was not a party to the consumer's lawsuit, the manufacturer is free to relitigate issues determined there which underlie the consumer's judgment against the retailer.[117]

On the other hand, impleader would permit the retailer to join the manufacturer in the initial suit. As a party to the case, the manufacturer will then be bound along with the retailer to an adjudication of issues establishing the consumer's right to recover against the retailer. In addition, the retailer may obtain an adjudication of its indemnification claim in the same lawsuit. Permitting impleader in such cases "will avoid circuity of action and eliminate duplication of suits based on closely related matters."[118]

---

not proceed in the absence of the Philippine government and of a special Philippine commission. The two parties were required under Rule 19(a) but could not be joined. The court ruled that Rule 19(b) required the case to be dismissed.

[111] 128 S. Ct. at 2188. "[T]o a substantial degree the effective operation of the rule depends on the careful exercise of discretion by the district court." WRIGHT & MILLER § 1608. A survey of cases interpreting the factors appears, *id.*, and in MOORE § 19.05[1][a]. *See, e.g., Erline Co. S.A. v. Johnson*, 440 F.3d 648, 652 (4th Cir. 2006).

[112] *See generally* MOORE §§ 14.01–14.42; WRIGHT & MILLER §§ 1441–1465; Arthur F. Greenbaum, *Jacks or Better to Open: Procedural Limitations on Co-Party and Third-Party Claims*, 74 MINN. L. REV. 507, 525–31 (1990); John C. Feirich, *Third Party Practice*, 1967 ILL. L.F. 236; *Developments in the Law — Multiparty Litigation in the Federal Courts*, 71 HARV. L. REV. 874, 906–13 (1958).

[113] When a co-defendant is in this position, the proper device for asserting this legal responsibility in federal court is a crossclaim. *See* § 9.04 (discussing Rule 13(g)), *supra.*

[114] *See generally* Symposium, *Products Liability: Economic Analysis and the Law*, 38 U. CHI. L. REV. 1 (1970).

[115] For discussion of joinder under Rule 20, see § 9.05[1], *supra.*

[116] For discussion of intervention under Rule 24, see § 9.08, *infra.*

[117] The manufacturer would be a stranger to the first suit and therefore could not be bound by issue preclusion. *See* § 15.08, *infra.*

[118] WRIGHT & MILLER § 1443. *See, e.g., Irwin v. Mascott*, 94 F. Supp. 2d 1052, 1056 (N.D. Cal.

Impleader enjoys widespread use in federal and many state courts.[119] Rule 14 authorizes it in the former. Within ten days after service of the defendant's answer, Rule 14 permits defendant to serve a *third-party complaint* on the outsider.[120] In this capacity, defendant becomes a *third-party plaintiff*, the outsider a *third-party defendant*. The third-party defendant or any other party to the suit may move to strike defendant's impleader, either by arguing that it is beyond the scope of Rule 14, or that the court should use its discretion to refuse impleader even if the rule appears satisfied.[121]

The rule requires that the nature of the third-party claim be such that the third-party defendant "is or may be liable" to the third-party plaintiff "for all or part of the claim against it." For impleader to work, it is often necessary to bring in the third-party defendant before the third-party plaintiff's liability to plaintiff can be established. Rule 14 thus authorizes impleader against one who "*may be* liable."[122] An eventual judgment for the original plaintiff binds not only the defendant/third-party plaintiff, but also precludes the third party defendant from relitigating issues underlying the third-party plaintiff's liability to the original plaintiff.[123]

The heart of impleader is the requirement that the claim supporting it be based on secondary or derivative liability. That is, the third-party plaintiff must seek reimbursement from the third-party defendant for all or part of the former's liability to plaintiff.[124] It is not enough that the impleader claim arose out of the same transaction or occurrence as the original plaintiff's claim; the impleader must, in addition, be contingent or derivative.[125]

2000). FRIEDENTHAL, KANE & MILLER § 6.9, note that "[t]he availability of impleader saves the time and cost of duplicating evidence in two proceedings, avoids inconsistent results on related claims based on identical or similar evidence, and eliminates the serious prejudice to the original defendant that might result from a time lag between the plaintiff's judgment against him and a judgment in the defendant's favor against the third-party defendant."

[119] FRIEDENTHAL, KANE & MILLER § 6.9.

[120] Rule 14(a) requires court approval for service of the third-party complaint after the ten-day period.

[121] *See* text accompanying notes 132–136, *infra*.

[122] Emphasis added. This language in the rule has long been interpreted to permit impleader even when the claim against the third-party defendant is not yet ripe for suit under applicable substantive law because the third-party plaintiff's liability has yet to be determined. See, e.g., the well-known case, *Jeub v. B/G Foods, Inc.*, 2 F.R.D. 238 (D. Minn. 1942).

[123] Rule 14(a) confers litigant status on the third-party defendant in the case, thereby creating an opportunity for the third-party defendant to join with the third-party plaintiff in attempting to defeat plaintiff's claim. Rule 14(a)(2)(C) states that "[t]he third-party defendant may assert against the plaintiff any defenses that the third-party plaintiff has to the plaintiff's claim."

[124] "The secondary or derivative liability notion is central and it is irrelevant whether the basis of the third-party claim is indemnity, subrogation, contribution, express or implied warranty, or some other theory." WRIGHT & MILLER § 1446 (citing illustrative cases). Thus, except for admiralty and maritime claims treated separately in Rule 14(c), the rule does not permit defendant to implead an outsider on the theory that the outsider should be liable to plaintiff *instead* of the defendant. WRIGHT & MILLER § 1444; FRIEDENTHAL, KANE & MILLER § 6.9.

[125] *See, e.g., Lewis v. Cimarron Valley R.R.*, 162 F. Supp. 2d 1220, 1227 (D. Kan. 2001); *National Bank of Can. v. Artex Indus., Inc.*, 627 F. Supp. 610, 613 (S.D.N.Y. 1986). *See generally* WRIGHT & MILLER § 1446.

While the third-party plaintiff's liability is established by a judgment for plaintiff against the third-party plaintiff, the existence of the contingent or derivative liability is a separate question. The answer to it is not supplied by Rule 14, which merely provides the procedure by which such a duty is asserted as an impleader claim.[126] Instead, the answer must be found in the applicable substantive law. Four common theories of contingent or derivative liability are indemnity, subrogation, contribution and warranty. Their precise elements vary somewhat from jurisdiction to jurisdiction.

A right to *indemnification* either arises out of an express contractual provision whereby one party agrees to indemnify (or "hold harmless") another for certain liabilities, or by implication.[127] A right to indemnification will be implied when a person without fault is held legally liable for damages caused by the fault of another.[128]

Subrogation is the succession of one person to the rights of another.[129] "Subrogees are generally joint tortfeasors or innocent insurers who have compensated the insured for an injury resulting from the negligence of a third-party."[130] An insurer sued by its insured on an insurance policy may therefore implead the negligent third party on a subrogation theory to the extent that the insurer is or may be liable to its insured on the policy.

The right of *contribution* typically arises among joint tortfeasors, two or more persons who are jointly or severally liable in tort for the same injury.[131]

Finally, a *warranty*, in the impleader context, is an express or implied statement or representation typically made by a seller to a buyer or others in the chain of product distribution regarding the character of or title to the product.

Thus, in our hypothetical product liability suit, the retailer may in most jurisdictions implead the manufacturer either on the basis of an express indemnification clause in a sales contract or on the implied indemnity theory that the retailer is or may be liable to the consumer for defects in the product which are the fault of the manufacturer. Alternately, he may base his impleader on a theory of contribution, if he and the manufacturer are jointly or severally

---

[126] *See, e.g., Assicurazioni Generali S.p.A. v. Terranova,* 40 Fed. R. Serv. 2d (Callaghan) 850, 852 (S.D.N.Y. 1984) ("Rule 14 provides only a procedural means of adding a [third-party] defendant; it does not confer any substantive rights on the [third-party] plaintiff.").

[127] *See, e.g., Terranova,* 40 Fed. R. Serv. 2d at 852 (*construing* New York law); *Anderson v. Dreibelbis,* 104 F.R.D. 415 (E.D. Pa. 1984) (*construing* Pennsylvania law), *aff'd,* 787 F.2d 580 (3d Cir. 1986).

[128] *Terranova,* 40 Fed. R. Serv. 2d at 852; *Anderson,* 104 F.R.D. at 416–17.

[129] *See, e.g., Terranova,* 40 Fed. R. Serv.2d at 853. "[S]ubrogation is of two kinds, 'legal' and 'conventional.' The former is grounded in equity and arises by operation of law, which gives to a third person who has been compelled to pay a remedy against one who, in justice, ought to pay. 'Conventional' subrogation is grounded upon contract, express or implied." *Insurance Co. of N. Am. v. Medical Protective Co.,* 768 F.2d 315, 320 (10th Cir. 1985).

[130] *Terranova,* 40 Fed. R. Serv. 2d at 853 (*construing* New York law).

[131] 40 Fed. R. Serv. 2d at 852–53 (*construing* New York law); *Anderson,* 104 F.R.D. at 416 (*construing* Pennsylvania law).

liable for causing the consumer's injury. Finally, he may invoke warranty, on the theory that the manufacturer expressly or impliedly warranted the product to be free of defects and should therefore reimburse the retailer for any liability arising from a product defect.

Since Rule 14 focuses on an easily defined and demonstrable source of judicial inefficiency, it is not surprising that federal courts have usually given it a sympathetic reading. At the same time, the rule is permissive rather than compulsory. Parties claimed against are not obliged to implead an outsider, and whether particular applications of the rule should be permitted when impleader is sought is a matter best left to the sound discretion of the court.[132] In exercising its discretion, a federal court will balance potential savings of time and resources through impleader[133] against any problems posed by addition of the third-party defendant. In some cases these problems will be sufficient to defeat impleader.

For example, the court should not permit impleader when it seems reasonably clear that defendant will defeat plaintiff, with or without the added presence of a third-party defendant. From the court's case-management perspective, impleader would simply burden the case with a gratuitous party. In addition, subjecting the third-party defendant to the angst and expense of participation under these circumstances seems unfair.

There are also circumstances where the federal court should use its discretion to refuse impleader even though plaintiff may prevail and thus prompt a further lawsuit between defendant and the outsider. For example, the added presence of a third-party defendant may unduly delay trial for plaintiff.[134] Or the employer-defendant to a *respondeat superior* claim of negligence could prejudice the plaintiff by impleading a shallow-pocket employee whose presence might prompt a sympathetic jury to return a smaller verdict on the underlying claim against the deep-pocket employer.[135] There may also be "a lack of similarity between the issues and evidence required to prove the main and third-party claims . . . ."[136] Many of these problems, however, can be cured without disallowing the impleader by ordering separate trials under Rule

---

[132] WRIGHT & MILLER § 1443. *See, e.g., Dishong v. Peabody Corp.*, 219 F.R.D. 382, 385 (E.D. Va. 2003).

[133] Prejudice to the defendant from proceeding in the absence of the outsider does not seem to play a very large role in justifying impleader. Yet the possibility of prejudice can be quite real. Recall the possibility for the retailer of conflicting judgments in the hypothetical opening this section. However, the appropriate response in such cases may be for defendant to argue compulsory joinder of the outsider under Rule 19(a), or dismissal of the case under 19(b) if joinder is not feasible. *See* § 9.05[2], *supra*.

[134] For discussion of this point and illustrative cases, see WRIGHT & MILLER § 1443. *See, e.g., Riccitelli v. Water Pik Technologies, Inc.*, 203 F.R.D. 62, 63 (D.N.H. 2001).

[135] *See, e.g., Goodhart v. United States Lines Co.*, 26 F.R.D. 163 (S.D.N.Y. 1960) (impleader of employee is denied when it could serve only to suggest to the jury that the employee will pay the judgment or to threaten the employee with bankruptcy unless he testifies favorably to the employer). For further discussion of this point and illustrative cases, see WRIGHT & MILLER § 1443.

[136] WRIGHT & MILLER § 1443. *See, e.g., Dishong v. Peabody Corp.*, 219 F.R.D. 382, 385 (E.D. Va. 2003).

42, should the prejudice be a factor come trial.[137]

Rule 14 authorizes inclusion of third-party defendants without confronting extrinsic difficulties of personal jurisdiction, subject matter jurisdiction and venue which could actually prevent the third-party defendants from entering the suit. A federal court usually enjoys only as much personal jurisdiction as the courts of the forum state.[138] Rule 4(k)(1)(b) supplements this for process under Rules 14 and 19 with the so-called 100-mile bulge — an added reach of 100 miles from the federal courthouse[139] — which may be inadequate to reach a prospective third-party defendant. The picture is brighter for federal subject matter jurisdiction and venue, however. Impleader claims that would not be within the original subject matter jurisdiction of federal courts now appear covered by the supplemental jurisdiction statute.[140] Similarly, venue does not appear to pose much of a problem in the impleader setting.[141]

§ 9.07   INTERPLEADER[142]

"Interpleader is a form of joinder open to one who does not know to which of several claimants he or she is liable, if liable at all."[143] Interpleader resembles impleader[144] in that it protects one claimed against from multiple and possibly inconsistent lawsuits,[145] and it resembles permissive joinder[146] in

---

[137]

> [T]he court always must remain flexible in its approach to an attempted impleader and should bear in mind that means other than dismissal may be available to prevent prejudice or confusion. Thus, if it appears that the action may become unduly complex because unrelated issues or evidence are present, or if knowledge of the identity or existence of a third party may cause prejudice to any litigant, the proper remedy is for the court to permit impleader and then to order separate trials pursuant to Rule 42 if any of these concerns becomes a reality.

WRIGHT & MILLER § 1443.

[138] See § 3.01[2][b], supra.

[139] A more detailed explanation appears at § 9.05[2][b], supra.

[140] See § 9.03, supra.

[141] "The prevailing interpretation of the federal venue rule is that if venue is properly established for the original action, the third-party defendant cannot object that venue would have been improper if the action had originally included him or her as a defendant." JAMES, HAZARD & LEUBSDORF § 10.18. Recent statutory developments in federal venue have, if anything, made the possibility of venue for impleader claims more secure. See § 6.01, supra.

[142] See generally MOORE §§ 22.01–22.04; WRIGHT & MILLER §§ 1701–21; Paula J. McDermott, Comment, Can Statutory Interpleader Be Used As a Remedy By the Tortfeasor in Mass Tort Litigation?, 90 DICK. L. REV. 439 (1985); Mark W. Smith, Comment, Deference to State Courts in Federal Interpleader Actions, 47 U. CHI. L. REV. 824 (1980); Geoffrey C. Hazard, Jr., & Myron Moskovitz, An Historical and Critical Analysis of Interpleader, 52 CAL. L. REV. 706 (1964); Developments in the Law — Multiparty Litigation in the Federal Courts, 71 HARV. L. REV. 874, 913–28 (1958).

[143] WRIGHT § 74. It "is a procedural device which enables a person holding money or property, in the typical case conceded to belong in whole or in part to another, to join in a single suit two or more persons asserting mutually exclusive claims to the fund." MOORE § 22.02[1].

[144] See § 9.06 (Rule 14), supra.

[145] JAMES, HAZARD & LEUBSDORF § 10.19.

that it permits a party to sort out its legal relationships with a number of opposing parties simultaneously.[147]

Absent interpleader, the party claimed against might have to defend against competing claimants in different courts, perhaps in different parts of the country. This might lead to multiple liability, inconsistent judgments,[148] or (at the very least) the vexation of multiple lawsuits.[149] Interpleader permits one (called a stakeholder) to avoid this by forcing all claimants to proceed against him in one lawsuit.[150]

Although many states authorize interpleader, interpleader in federal court is often preferable, at least in cases where the party claimed against faces the prospect of litigation spread across more than one state. This is not because of any advantage offered by the Federal Rules of Civil Procedure. Federal Rule 22, covering interpleader, provides little not already afforded by the rules of a majority of state courts.[151] Rather, it is because Rule 22 is usually overshadowed by an additional procedural remedy available only in federal court: statutory interpleader.[152] Congress created a special enclave of subject matter jurisdiction within the interpleader statute,[153] complemented the arrangement with a statute creating special venue possibilities,[154] and (most significant in creating an advantage over interpleader actions in state court) liberalized

---

[146] See § 9.05[1] (Rule 20(a)), supra.

[147] Interpleader is most like the part of Rule 20(a) "allowing the joinder of plaintiffs in the alternative when they are uncertain which of them has the right to relief and the joinder of defendants in the alternative when it is uncertain which of them is liable." WRIGHT & MILLER § 1702.

[148] Multiple liability and inconsistent judgments, the most troublesome byproducts of an excessive number of lawsuits, are described at § 9.05[2][a], supra.

[149] Professor Wright suggested that the possibility of vexatious multiple lawsuits can alone be sufficient to justify interpleader. WRIGHT § 74. Treinies v. Sunshine Mining Co., 308 U.S. 66 (1939), is a famous example of interpleader as a response to the concerns listed in the text. Two factions claimed right of ownership to the same block of mining company stock. One claimed on the strength of a Washington court judgment, the other on an Idaho judgment. Uncertain which judgment to honor, the mining company cleared the air by interpleading both claimants in a single action in federal court.

[150] See, e.g., Estate of Ellington v. EMI Music Publ'g, 282 F. Supp. 2d 192 (S.D.N.Y. 2003); Aon Corp. Accidental Death & Dismemberment Plan v. Hohlweck, 223 F. Supp. 2d 510, 513-14 (S.D.N.Y. 2002). Interpleader is most frequently used as a basis for commencing suit, but it can be initiated in ongoing litigation through a counterclaim, crossclaim or third party claim. See generally WRIGHT & MILLER § 1708.

[151] The language of the state rules is often nearly identical. E.g., FLA. R. CIV. P. 1.240; N.M. STAT. ANN. R. CIV. P. DIST. CT. 1-022; WIS. STAT. ANN. § 803.07.

[152] See 28 U.S.C. § 1335.

[153] Section 1335 requires diversity of citizenship between only two or more of the adverse claimants (called minimal diversity) see § 5.04[2], supra and, at least $500 in controversy, measured by the value of the stake. In contrast, a federal interpleader action brought solely under Rule 22 would have to qualify either under the general diversity statute, 28 U.S.C. § 1332, requiring complete diversity of citizenship between the stakeholder and all of the claimants, and more than $75,000 in controversy, or under some federal question jurisdictional grant. See WRIGHT § 74.

[154] Statutory interpleader has its own venue statute, 28 U.S.C. § 1397, permitting suit in any district where a claimant resides.

service of process and, therefore, personal jurisdiction.[155]

Whether proceeding by statute or Rule 22, the stakeholder deposits with the court the stake (fund) — property or money[156] — which is the target of the competing claims against the stakeholder. The stakeholder may then seek interlocutory relief, enjoining maintenance of other suits against him with respect to the fund during the federal interpleader action.[157] There are two stages to federal interpleader adjudications.

> In the "first stage," the court determines whether interpleader is appropriate on the facts of the case. If so, in the "second stage," the court adjudicates the adverse claims and distributes the stake.[158]

The stakeholder may be either disinterested or interested. If disinterested, he takes the position that one of the claimants is entitled to the fund — stage two of the interpleader action will determine which. A disinterested stakeholder participates only in stage one. After a hearing, the court decides if the stakeholder is entitled to an interpleader remedy. If he is, he is excused from further involvement in the case, leaving the fund with the court to be fought over by rival claimants.[159] However, the stakeholder's lack of interest in the stake is no longer a prerequisite for interpleader. An interested stakeholder may remain to participate in stage two of the interpleader action, claiming that he is obligated to no one and, in effect, competing with the rival claimants for the fund.

State Farm Fire & Casualty Co. v. Tashire[160] offers a good illustration of the scope of federal interpleader. Stakeholder State Farm filed an interpleader action in Oregon federal court based on both the statute and Rule 22, in response to claims made on a $20,000 insurance policy. Its insured had been operating a truck when he collided with a bus in California. The accident resulted in two deaths, injuries to many people, and lawsuits seeking more than $1,000,000 in damages from the insured and the bus company, among others. The federal district court directed claimants to make all of their claims against the stakeholder, its insured, the bus company, and the bus driver in the interpleader action. Reversing, the federal court of appeals viewed the case as altogether inappropriate for interpleader. The Supreme Court reversed in turn, holding that statutory interpleader was available to State Farm to confine to one lawsuit all claims made on the $20,000 policy. The Court refused, however,

---

[155] 28 U.S.C. § 2361 authorizes service of process on all competing claimants in any judicial district of the United States. "Thus, in statutory interpleader actions, only those claimants who cannot be found or who reside outside of the United States are beyond the reach of the statute." FRIEDENTHAL, KANE & MILLER § 16.12.

[156] The stakeholder will usually be permitted to give a bond in lieu of money. MOORE § 22.03[1][b].

[157] See, e.g., Star Ins. Co. v. Cedar Valley Express, LLC, 273 F. Supp. 2d 38 (D.D.C. 2002). Injunctive authority in statutory interpleader cases is explicit in 28 U.S.C. § 2361. WRIGHT & MILLER § 1717.

[158] MOORE § 22.03[1][a] (footnote omitted).

[159] See MOORE § 22.03[2][a].

[160] 386 U.S. 523 (1967).

to resurrect interpleader on the scale attempted by the district court. It noted that "State Farm's interest in this case, which is the fulcrum of the interpleader procedure, is confined to its $20,000 fund."[161] The insurer

> should not be allowed to determine that dozens of tort plaintiffs must be compelled to press their claims — even those claims which are not against the insured and which in no event could be satisfied out of the meager insurance fund — in a single forum of the insurance company's choosing. There is nothing in the statutory scheme, and very little in the judicial and academic commentary upon that scheme, which requires that the tail be allowed to wag the dog in this fashion.[162]

§ 9.08 INTERVENTION[163]

The party joinder devices we have examined so far are available only to one already a party in the case. Intervention differs in that it provides a means for outsiders to make themselves parties. Federal court interventions usually are governed by Rule 24, which has its counterpart in most state procedural systems.[164] The rule contemplates both intervention of right under 24(a) and permissive intervention under 24(b).

[1] Intervention of Right

Rule 24(a) states that

> on timely motion, the court must permit anyone to intervene who: (1) is given an unconditional right to intervene by a federal statute; or (2) claims an interest relating to the property or transaction that is the subject of the action, and is so situated that disposing of the action may as a practical matter impair or impede the movant's ability to protect its interest, unless existing parties adequately represent that interest.

Most applications for intervention of right are made under Rule 24(a)(2).[165] To qualify, the applicant must satisfy three requirements.

---

[161] 386 U.S. at 535.

[162] 386 U.S. at 535. "We recognize," added the *Tashire* Court, "that our view of interpleader means that it cannot be used to solve all the vexing problems of multiparty litigation arising out of a mass tort. But interpleader was never intended to perform such a function, to be an all-purpose bill of peace." 386 U.S. at 535.

[163] *See generally* Moore §§ 24.01–24.24; Wright & Miller §§ 1901–1923; Amy M. Gardner, *An Attempt to Intervene in the Confusion: Standing Requirements for Rule 24 Intervenors*, 69 U. Chi. L. Rev. 681 (2002); Carl Tobias, *Standing to Intervene*, 1991 Wis. L. Rev. 415; Gene R. Shreve, *Questioning Intervention of Right — Toward a New Methodology of Decisionmaking*, 74 Nw. U. L. Rev. 894 (1980); Symposium, *Problems of Intervention in Public Law Litigation*, 13 U.C. Davis L. Rev. 211 (1980); Edward J. Brunet, *A Study in the Allocation of Scarce Judicial Resources: The Efficiency of Federal Intervention Criteria*, 12 Ga. L. Rev. 701 (1978); David C. Shapiro, *Some Thoughts on Intervention Before Courts, Agencies, and Arbitrators*, 81 Harv. L. Rev. 721 (1968).

[164] *E.g.*, Ind. Code Ann. Ct. R. Trial 24; N.C. Gen. Stat. § 1A-1 T. 24; Minn. Stat. Ann. R. Civ. P. Dist. Ct. 24.

[165] The function of subdivision (1) of Rule 24(a) is to note provisions for intervention of right

First, the applicant must demonstrate that the lawsuit carries a possibility of detriment to him serious enough to entitle him to an opportunity to influence the outcome in ways that only a litigant can.[166] It is no longer necessary for the applicant to demonstrate that the lawsuit is capable of binding him in a formal sense.[167] Rule 24(a)(2) contemplates merely "practical" impairment. The Supreme Court has noted that the applicant need only have a "significantly protectable interest."[168] However, the scope of absentee interests protected through intervention of right has proven difficult to define precisely.[169]

Second, the applicant must demonstrate a substantial possibility that none of the present parties will adequately represent his interest. A successful applicant will thereafter make or defend against a claim,[170] generally aligning himself with one already a party. The adequacy question thus boils down to whether the existing party can be expected to represent the applicant's interests adequately in the course of representing his own. If so, the applicant has no right to intervene under Rule 24(a)(2). When the applicant's stake in the outcome is no greater than that of an existing party with whom the applicant would be aligned, and when that existing party is not in collusion with an opposing party, incompetent, or hostile toward the applicant, representation by the existing party often will be deemed adequate and intervention of right will be denied.[171]

---

appearing elsewhere in federal statutes. For examples, *see Moore* § 24.02. Absent acknowledgement in Rule 24 of the existence of prior federal statutes governing intervention, the latter might have been extinguished by the rule because the Rules Enabling Act, 28 U.S.C. § 2072, states that "[a]ll laws in conflict" with the federal rules "shall be of no further force or effect after such rules have taken effect."

[166] Party prerogatives include setting boundaries of relevancy through pleadings, developing facts by discovery and creating parts of the factual record, and appealing adverse judgments.

[167] The Supreme Court had given this narrow reading to an earlier version of Rule 24 in *Sam Fox Publishing Co. v. United States*, 366 U.S. 683 (1961), prompting amendment of the rule in 1966.

[168] *Diamond v. Charles*, 476 U.S. 54, 68 (1986).

[169] Professor Shapiro noted that "[t]he range of possible interests may defy adequate classification, spreading over a spectrum that is extremely hard to chart." Note 162, *supra*, at 740. Examples include the possible *stare decisis* impact of the case on the applicant, *e.g., Atlantis Dev. Corp. v. United States*, 379 F.2d 818, 822 (5th Cir. 1967), and possible frustration of the applicant's opportunity to obtain future injunctive relief. *E.g., Stallworth v. Monsanto Co.*, 558 F.2d 257, 268 (5th Cir. 1977).

[170] Rule 24(c) requires the applicant's motion to intervene to "be accompanied by a pleading that sets out the claim or defense for which intervention is sought."

[171] *See, e.g., United States v. City of Miami*, 278 F.3d 1174, 1178-79 (11th Cir. 2002); *Delaware Valley Citizens' Council for Clean Air v. Pennsylvania*, 674 F.2d 970 (3d Cir. 1982). In some cases, the argument for inadequate representation will be that the interest of the applicant in the outcome is, upon careful examination, more focused or more intense than that of the existing party with whom the applicant would be aligned. Consider, for example, the facts of a well-known intervention case, *Ford Motor Co. v. Bisanz Bros., Inc.*, 249 F.2d 22 (8th Cir. 1957). Plaintiffs sued to shut down a railroad spur as a private nuisance. Ford sought to intervene on the side of the railroad defendant on the ground that it could not continue to operate one of its plants if it could not use the spur. The court ruled that Ford was entitled to intervention as of right. Ford had far more to lose from elimination of the spur than did the railroad. Therefore, while there was no suggestion that the railroad would be less than diligent in protecting *its* interests, the railroad's stake in the outcome did not give it the same incentive that Ford had to litigate vigorously.

Third, the application must be timely. Rule 24 sets no deadline for interventions. Absentees may move to intervene after trial of the case and even on appeal. Since, however, the intervener takes the case as he finds it,[172] the later he intervenes the fewer opportunities he will have to influence the outcome. Moreover, it is generally true that interventions become increasingly difficult to justify as the case unfolds.[173] Two questions recur when the timeliness of the application is an issue: whether the court and those already parties will suffer from the fact the application did not come earlier,[174] and whether the applicant can be faulted for applying as late as he did.[175] The latter point can be resolved in favor of intervention when, for example, applicant's earlier motion would have failed because representation by an existing party then seemed adequate.[176]

[2]   Permissive Intervention

Rule 24(b) states in part that "[o]n timely motion, the court may permit anyone to intervene who . . . has a claim or defense that shares with the main action a common question of law or fact." [177] The present-day function of Rule 24(b)(1)(B) seems confined to promoting judicial economy. Therefore, permissive intervention is warranted only when savings of party and judicial resources from avoiding an extra lawsuit outweigh costs from the added presence of the intervener.[178] Concern over the latter is clear from Rule

---

[172] *Cf. Arizona v. California*, 460 U.S. 605, 615 (1983) ("Of course, permission to intervene does not carry with it the right to relitigate matters already determined in the case, unless those matters would otherwise be subject to reconsideration.").

[173] Thus, "[t]here is considerable reluctance on the part of the courts to allow intervention after the action has gone to judgment and a strong showing will be required of the applicant." WRIGHT & MILLER § 1916.

[174] For a survey of federal decisions on this point, see *id. See also Doe #1 v. Glickman*, 256 F.3d 371, 376 (5th Cir. 2001).

[175] For a survey of federal decisions on this point, see WRIGHT & MILLER § 1916. *See, e.g., Long Island Trucking, Inc. v. Brooks Pharmacy*, 219 F.R.D. 53, 55 (E.D.N.Y. 2003).

[176] *Smuck v. Hobson*, 408 F.2d 175 (D.C. Cir. 1969), is a noted example. Applicants' interests were at least arguably represented by the defendant until defendant decided not to appeal an adverse ruling by the federal district court. The court of appeals granted intervention, thus avoiding a Catch-22 interplay of the adequacy-of-representation and timeliness concerns which would have shut off the possibility of intervention altogether.

[177] Rule 24(b)(1)(A) recognizes the possibility of a statutory "conditional right to intervene." The functional relationship between (b)(1)(A) and (b)(1)(B) is thus the same as that between (a)(1) and (a)(2) described at note 165, *supra*.

[178] *See* Shreve, note 163, *supra*, at 908–09:

A grant of intervention may adversely affect the original parties in a number of ways. Intervention forces the nominal co-party to relinquish partial management of the case. Moreover, the intervener may complicate the original parties' preparation and litigation of the case by maintaining a separate position on existing issues or by adding new claims, parties, or witnesses. Thus, the existing parties' expectations of an expeditious adjudication and an orderly resolution of their claims . . . may be defeated by the delays and complications accompanying intervention. In addition, the complications resulting from intervention may so strain the resources of the original parties that their continued ability to participate is jeopardized, and the forum becomes correspondingly less accessible.

24(b)(3): "In exercising its discretion, the court must consider whether the intervention will unduly delay or prejudice the adjudication of the original parties' rights."[179]

Rule 24 does not require applicants to confine their motion to intervene to either paragraph (a) or (b). Applicants frequently seek both in the alternative. Since intervention of right is narrower in scope, adding a request for permissive intervention provides the applicant with a fall-back position.

[3] Comparing Intervention of Right and Permissive Intervention

If an application for intervention falls within Rule 24(a), the paragraph provides that it "must" be granted. If the applicant merely satisfies 24(b), intervention "may" (or may not) be granted. The reason for different treatment can be found in the interests of the applicant in intervening that are reflected in each paragraph. Intervention of right under Rule 24 (a) secures participation in the case for one whose substantive interests may be compromised.[180] Permissive intervention under Rule 24(b) rarely does more than advance the interest of the applicant and possibly the court in more cost-efficient litigation.[181]

The impact of the distinction on an applicant's chances for successful intervention is two-fold. First, the greater premium Rule 24(a) places on interventions is likely to influence the federal district court as initial decisionmaker. Second, while a decision denying permissive intervention is insulated from review by the trial court's discretion,[182] the decision that the

---

In times of crowded dockets, the court may also have a concern in keeping the case from becoming too burdensome and, in the interests of justice, seeing that the reasonable concerns of existing parties are protected. Related are the interests of the original parties and the court in settling cases, and the concern that an intervener might effectively block settlement.

Reprinted by special permission of the Northwestern University Law Review, © 1980 by Northwestern University School of Law, volume 74.

[179] Quoting this passage, the Supreme Court observed: "Particularly in a complex case . . . , a district judge's decision on how best to balance the rights of the parties against the need to keep the litigation from becoming unmanageable is entitled to great deference." *Stringfellow v. Concerned Neighbors in Action*, 480 U.S. 370, 380 (1987).

[180] Minus reference to the possibility of inadequate representation, the relationship of the absentee to the lawsuit is the same as that described in Rule 19(a)(1)(B) of one who must be joined if feasible. *See* § 9.05[2][a], *supra*.

[181] It is thus comparable to permissive party joinder under Rule 20. *See* § 9.05[1], *supra*.

[182] *E.g., Reid v. Illinois State Bd. of Educ.*, 289 F.3d 1009, 1020 (7th Cir. 2002); *County of Orange v. Air Cal.*, 799 F.2d 535 (9th Cir. 1986) ("If there is no right to intervene under Rule 24(a), it is wholly discretionary with the court whether to allow intervention under Rule 24(b) and even though there is a common question of law or fact, or the requirements of Rule 24(b) are otherwise satisfied, the court may refuse to allow intervention."). *See* WRIGHT & MILLER § 1913 (citing numerous examples).

applicant is not entitled to intervene of right is open to a considerable measure of appellate redecision.[183]

The distinction may in addition affect the court's willingness to attach conditions when it grants a motion to intervene. Limitations on the nature and degree of the applicant's participation are not uncommon in permissive interventions under Rule 24(b), but the propriety of similarly limiting 24(a) interveners of right is open to question.[184]

§ 9.09 CLASS ACTIONS[185]

Parties brought in through the joinder devices we have considered so far share active participation with all other parties in the case. Modern rules of procedure, consolidated litigation,[186] even specially constructed courtrooms,[187] may enable courts to accommodate many active participants in a single case.

---

[183] *See, e.g., Trans. Chem. Ltd. v. China Nat'l Mach. Imp. & Exp. Corp.*, 332 F.3d 815, 822 (5th Cir. 2003). Most federal courts of appeal have regarded the Rule 24(a)(2) questions of whether the applicant risks practical impairment from the outcome of the case and whether applicant's interests are adequately represented by an existing party to be open to reexamination on appeal. "[T]he appellate court can substitute its judgment for that of the trial court if it regards the urgency as great enough to warrant a determination that intervention should be allowed as of right." JAMES, HAZARD & LEUBSDORF § 10.17. *But see United States v. Hooker Chems. & Plastics*, 749 F.2d 968, 990 (2d Cir. 1984) (noting the traditional distinction between reviewing standards for (a) and (b) intervention denials but stating, "it is now the rule in this circuit that denials of motions to intervene as of right under Rule 24(a)(2) also are to be reviewed under an abuse of discretion standard.").

Refusals to grant intervention based on untimeliness are regarded as discretionary, whether the application is grounded on (a) or (b) of Rule 24. Therefore, a finding that an application to intervene of right is untimely "will be reviewed only for an abuse of discretion." WRIGHT & MILLER § 1916.

[184] *See* Shapiro, note 162, *supra*, at 759. Courts refused to limit Rule 24(a) interventions in *Spangler v. United States*, 415 F.2d 1242 (9th Cir. 1969), and *Exchange Nat'l Bank of Chi. v. Abramson*, 45 F.R.D. 97 (D. Minn. 1968). *But see Harris v. General Coach Works*, 37 F.R.D. 343 (E. D. Mich. 1964) (appearing to limit a Rule 24(a) intervener).

[185] The literature on class actions is voluminous. *See, e.g.,* MOORE §§ 23.01–23.87; WRIGHT & MILLER §§ 1751–1820; HERBERT B. NEWBERG, NEWBERG ON CLASS ACTIONS (4th ed. 2002); Tobias B. Wolff, *Preclusion in Class Action Litigation*, 105 COLUM. L. REV. 717 (2005); Elizabeth J. Cabraser, *The Class Action Counterrefformation*, 57 STAN. L. REV. 1475 (2005); Theodore Eisenberg & Geoffrey Miller, *The Role of Opt-Outs and Objectors in Class Action Litigation: Theoretical and Empirical Issues*, 57 VAND. L. REV. 1529 (2004); John C. Coffee, Jr., *Class Action Accountability: Reconciling Exit, Voice, and Loyalty in Representative Litigation*, 100 COLUM. L. REV. 370 (2000); Rhonda Wasserman, *Dueling Class Actions*, 80 B.U. L. REV. 461 (2000); Linda Silberman, *The Vicissitudes of the American Class Action — With a Comparative Eye*, 7 TUL. J. OF INT'L & COMP. L. 201 (1999); Geoffrey C. Hazard, Jr., John L. Gedud & Stephen Sowle, *An Historical Analysis of the Binding Effect of Class Suits*, 146 U. PA. L. REV. 1849 (1998); David C. Shapiro, *Class Actions: The Class as Party and Client*, 73 NOTRE DAME L. REV. 913 (1998); Symposium, *The Institute of Judicial Administration Research Conference on Class Actions*, 71 N.Y.U. L. REV. 1 (1996); John C. Coffee, Jr., *Class Wars: The Dilemma of the Mass Tort Class Action*, 95 COLUM. L. REV. 1343 (1995).

[186] *See* § 9.10, *infra*.

[187] *See Megacourtroom*, TIME, March 18, 1985 at 67 (discussing the construction of a "mega-courtroom" for Manville Corp. asbestos litigation).

There are limits, however. Exercise of the prerogatives of party participation[188] is time-consuming. A distinguished federal trial judge once observed: "Additional parties always take additional time. Even if they have no witnesses of their own, they are the source of additional questions, objections, briefs, arguments, motions and the like which tend to make the proceeding a Donnybrook Fair."[189] Procedural safeguards offered for dividing cases or trials that have grown too large[190] or for staggering the adjudication of claims within a case[191] provide only limited protection. Courts must draw the line somewhere,[192] protecting those already parties and themselves from congestion which would overwhelm the case.

The special contribution of the class action device is to facilitate adjudication of additional claims without enlarging the number of active parties. This usually works by designating a party (or parties)[193] to litigate not only for himself but also as a representative for a group (the class). At least where class representation has been adequate,[194] class members will be bound by the outcome of the case.[195] That is, they will fare on issues common to the class as does their class representative. However, only their class representative will be an active litigant. They will remain passive, unless they exclude themselves from the lawsuit (*opt out*)[196] or appear in the litigation to litigate actively along with the

---

[188] *See* § 9.08, *supra.*

[189] *Crosby Steam Gage & Valve Co. v. Manning, Maxwell & Moore, Inc.*, 51 F. Supp. 972, 973 (D. Mass. 1943) (Wyzanski, J.).

[190] *See* § 9.02, *supra.*

[191] Federal Rule 54(b) provides, "[w]hen an action presents more than one claim for relief . . . , or when multiple parties are involved, the court may direct entry of a final judgment as to one or more, but fewer than all, claims or parties . . . ." *See* § 13.03[2] (finality in multi-party and multi-claim cases), *infra.* Many state procedural systems have similar provisions allowing partial adjudication. *E.g.*, IND. CODE ANN. CT. R. TRIAL 54(B); KY. REV. STAT. ANN. R. CIV. P. 54.02; MINN. STAT. ANN. R. CIV. P. DIST. CT. 54.02.

[192] *See* for example, discussion of concerns weighing against permissive intervention at § 9.08, *supra.*

[193] There can be and often is more than one class representative. For convenience, however, we will use the singular form.

[194] *See* Susan P. Koniak, *How Like a Winter? The Plight of Absent Class Members Denied Adequate Representation*, 79 NOTRE DAME L. REV. 1787 (2004); Linda S. Mullenix, *Taking Adequacy Seriously: The Inadequate Assessment of Adequacy in Litigation and Settlement Classes*, 57 VAND. L. REV. 1687 (2004); Patrick Woolley, *The Availability of Collateral Attack for Inadequate Representation in Class Suits*, 79 TEX. L. REV. 383 (2000).

[195] *See* Tobias B. Wolff, *Preclusion in Class Action Litigation*, 105 COLUM. L. REV. 717 (2005); Samuel Issacharoff, *Preclusion, Due Process, and the Right to Opt Out of Class Actions*, 77 NOTRE DAME L. REV. 1057 (2002).

[196] Federal Rule 23 and the class action provisions of most states have a mechanism for class members with discrete claims to exclude themselves from class actions, avoiding preclusive effects of a judgment later in the case. The process is often called "opting out." For critique and illustration of current practice, *see* Theodore Eisenberg & Geoffrey Miller, *The Role of Opt-Outs and Objectors in Class Action Litigation: Theoretical and Empirical Issues*, 57 VAND. L. REV. 1529 (2004); Steve Baughman, Note, *Class Actions in the Asbestos Context: Balancing the Due Process Considerations Implicated by the Right to Opt Out*, 70 TEX. L. REV. 211 (1991); Mark W. Friedman, Note, *Constrained Individualism in Group Litigation: Requiring Class Members to Make a Good Cause Showing Before Opting Out of a Federal Class Action*, 100 YALE L.J. 745 (1990).

class representative.[197]

[1]　Class Actions Under Rule 23

Most federal court class actions are governed by Rule 23.[198] Plaintiff usually is the class representative. He pleads an individual claim, but also pleads the existence of a class and a claim or claims on their behalf.[199] Rule 23(c)(1) provides for certification of the case as a class action, stating that, "[a]t an early practicable time after a person sues or is sued as a class representative, the court must determine by order whether to certify the action as a class action." Filing a complaint alleging the existence of the class and pleading class claims will usually toll the applicable statute of limitations against members of the putative class.[200]

The burden is on plaintiff to demonstrate that the requirements of Rule 23 have been met. To succeed under the rule, a case must (1) conform to the four requirements of paragraph (a); (2) satisfy two further requirements not expressly stated in the rule;[201] and (3) fit into one of the categories in Rule 23(b).

Rule 23(a) states:

A class member who opts out probably will be unable to exploit through nonmutual offensive issue preclusion a judgment thereafter rendered in favor of the class. WRIGHT & MILLER § 1789. This is because, by opting out of the class, the party knowingly foregoes an earlier opportunity to litigate the issue. See § 15.08[2][b], *infra.*

[197] Federal Rule 23(d)(1)(B)(iii) raises possibilities that class members might either appear or intervene in the action. The rule does not explain how the two differ. Professors Wright and Miller suggest that courts may be reluctant to complicate class actions by permitting extensive use of either device. WRIGHT & MILLER § 1799. *But cf. Devlin v. Scardelletti*, 536 U.S. 1 (2002) (holding that an unnamed class member may appeal approval of a class action settlement without intervening).

[198] Prior to its 1966 amendment, Rule 23 also governed actions now treated by Rules 23.1 and 23.2. Rule 23.1 deals with shareholder derivative actions. Rule 23.2 "enables a representative suit to be brought by or against the association itself." MOORE § 23.2.02.

[199] Much less frequently, plaintiff sues against rather than on behalf of a class. Defendant-class actions are, as one commentator put it, "as rare as unicorns." John C. Coffee, Jr., *Class Action Accountability: Reconciling Exit, Voice, and Loyalty in Representative Litigation*, 100 COLUM. L. REV. 370, 388 (2000). *See also* John Bronsteen & Owen Fiss, *The Class Action Rule*, 78 NOTRE DAME L. REV. 1419, 1422 (2003).

[200] Usually, the statute of limitations will either resume running or begin running anew if certification is eventually denied, depending on the statute. *See, e.g., Chardon v. Fumero Soto*, 462 U.S. 650 (1983) (the statute of limitations began running anew after class certification was denied). *See generally* Rhonda Wasserman, *Tolling: The American Pipe Tolling Rule and Successive Class Actions*, 58 FLA. L. REV. 803, 813-33 (2006).

[201] The class must be capable of definition. It must describe a group that genuinely exists, and it must do so with sufficient clarity to inform the court and the party opposing the class of the stakes in the litigation. *See* MANUAL FOR COMPLEX LITIGATION (Fourth) § 21.222 (2004). The representative must also be a member of the class. *Wright & Miller* § 1761. *Cf. General Tel. Co. of the Sw. v. Falcon*, 457 U.S. 147, 156 (1982) ("We have repeatedly held that a class representative must be part of the class.") (quoting *East Texas Motor Freight Sys. v. Rodriguez*, 431 U.S. 395, 403 (1977)). This also satisfies the requirement under Article III of the United States Constitution that the class representative have standing. *Ortiz v. Fibreboard Corp.*, 527 U.S. 815 (1999).

One or more members of a class may sue or be sued as representative parties on behalf of all members only if (1) the class is so numerous that joinder of all members is impracticable; (2) there are questions of law or fact common to the class; (3) the claims or defenses of the representative parties are typical of the claims or defenses of the class; and (4) the representative parties will fairly and adequately protect the interests of the class.

Subdivisions (1) and (2) pose rudimentary questions about the appropriateness of the case as a class action. The first is sometimes called the "numerosity" requirement.[202] If the group offered as a class is so small that active participation of each member is feasible, there is no need for the class action device.[203] The second is sometimes called the "commonality" requirement.[204] If the group does not share issues in common, there is no material in the case for a class-wide adjudication.[205]

The purpose of subdivision (3) (the "typicality" requirement) and subdivision (4) of Rule 23(a) is to assure that representation of the passive class members' interests will be good enough[206] to make it fair to bind them by the result in the case.[207] If subdivisions (3) and (4) had been omitted from Rule 23(a), the constitutional law of due process doubtless would have required federal courts to supplement the rule with these requirements.[208] As it is, Rule 23 not only reflects due process requirements, but secures a greater measure of protection for class members by advancing nonconstitutional policies of procedural fairness.[209] This is evident from the "stricter rules for the appointment of class

---

[202] E.g., General Tel. Co. of the Sw. v. Falcon, 457 U.S. 147, 156 (1982).

[203] "The question of what constitutes impracticability . . . depends on the particular facts of each case and no arbitrary rules regarding the size of classes have been established by the courts." WRIGHT & MILLER § 1762.

[204] E.g., General Tel. Co. of the Sw. v. Falcon, 457 U.S. 147, 156 (1982).

[205] See, e.g., Trevizo v. Adams, 455 F.3d 1155, 1163 (10th Cir. 2006). "It is important to note that this provision does not require that all the questions of law and fact raised by the dispute be common . . . . All that can be divined from the rule itself is that the use of the plural 'questions' suggests that more than one issue of law or fact must be common to members of the class." WRIGHT & MILLER § 1763.

[206] See, e.g., Steinberg v. Nationwide Mut. Ins. Co., 224 F.R.D. 67, 75 (E.D.N.Y. 2004). "Quality of representation embraces both the competence of the legal counsel of the representatives and the stature and interest of the named parties themselves." WRIGHT & MILLER § 1766.

[207] Of the two, subsection (4) reflects this purpose most clearly. Subsection (3) does not appear to add much, although it "assures that the claims of the named parties are similar enough to the claims of the class so that the representative will adequately represent them." WRIGHT & MILLER § 1764.

[208] This is evident from the Supreme Court's opinions in Hansberry and Mullane, discussed in § 9.09[2][c], infra. Cf. WRIGHT & MILLER § 1765 ("The binding effect of all class action decrees raises substantial due process questions that are directly relevant to Rule 23(a)(4).").

[209] It is difficult and (from the standpoint of administering Rule 23) unnecessary to determine precisely where constitutional requirements end and prudential, rule-based requirements begin. For discussion of the adequate representation requirement in class actions, see Ronan E. Degnan, Foreward: Adequacy of Representation in Class Actions, 60 CAL. L. REV. 705 (1972); Daneil J. Steininger, Note, Class Actions: Defining the Typical and Representative Plaintiff Under Subsections (a)(3) and (4) of Federal Rule 23, 53 B.U. L. REV. 406 (1973).

attorneys, awarding attorney's fees, and approving settlements"[210] adopted in the 2003 amendments to Rule 23.[211]

A class action brought under Rule 23 must also fall within one of the four categories contained in paragraph (b) of the rule.[212] The first two categories exist in Rule 23(b)(1) which "permits a class action when this is necessary to avoid possible adverse effects on the opponents of the class or on absent members of the class."[213] The justification for class actions under (b)(1) is generally understood to be narrower than that of merely promoting judicial economy. Thus, "subdivision (b)(1)(A) is applicable when practical necessity forces the opposing party to act in the same manner toward the individual class members and thereby makes inconsistent adjudications in separate actions unworkable or intolerable."[214]

The third category is in Rule 23(b)(2), authorizing a class action when "the party opposing the class has acted or refused to act on grounds that apply generally to the class, so that final injunctive relief or corresponding declaratory relief is appropriate respecting the class as a whole . . . ." Rule 23(b)(2) has figured prominently in federal suits directed against state or local officials, where relief sought often is declaratory[215] or injunctive. While (b)(2) was created "essentially as a tool for facilitating civil rights actions,"[216] it is not limited to such cases.[217]

---

[210] Edward F. Sherman, *Class Actions After the Class Action Fairness Act of 2005*, 80 Tul. L. Rev. 1593, 1595 n.8 (2006).

[211] Federal Rule 23(d)-(h). Of particular note is paragraph (e) regulating settlement. This, along with 28 U.S.C. §§1711-1715 (part of the Class Action Fairness Act of 2005) were intended to address prior unfair settlements "that resulted in large fees to attorneys with little benefit to class members." Sherman, *supra*, note 210 at 1594-95. Problems associated with class action settlements have evoked considerable commentary. *See* John Bronsteen, *Class Action Settlements: An Opt-In Proposal*, 2005 U. Ill. L. Rev. 903 (205); Howard M. Erichson, *A Typology of Aggregate Settlements*, 80 Notre Dame L. Rev. 1769 (2005); Lisa M. Mezzetti & Whitney R. Case, *The Coupon Can Be the Ticket: The Use of "Coupon" and Other Non-Monetary Redress in Class Action Settlements*, 18 Geo. J. Legal Ethics 1431 (2005); Allan Kanner & Tibor Nagy, *Exploding the Blackmail Myth: A New Perspective on Class Action Settlements*, 57 Baylor L. Rev. 681 (2005).

[212] For a useful explanation and critique of the various categories in paragraph (b), see John Bronsteen & Owen Fiss, *The Class Action Rule*, 78 Notre Dame L. Rev. 1419, 1427-39 (2003).

[213] Wright § 72. Class actions under Rule 23(b)(1)(A) are designed to avert prejudice to the party opposing the class "if inconsistent results in individual adjudications establish incompatible standards of conduct to which he must adhere, as in a suit by taxpayers to invalidate municipal action or in a suit involving the rights and duties of riparian owners." Wright § 72. Class actions under Rule 23(b)(1)(B) protect absent class members from the relative disadvantage of pursuing their interests in individual lawsuits, "as in a suit to compel reorganization of a fraternal association or a suit by stockholders to compel declaration of a dividend." Wright § 72. The latter category also includes actions presenting multiple claims against a common limited pool of assets.

[214] Wright & Miller § 1773. For discussion of the scope and application of Rule 23(b)(1), see *Ortiz v. Fibreboard Corp.*, 527 U.S. 815 (1999).

[215] *See* Andrew Brandt, *"Much to Gain and Nothing to Lose": Implications of the History of the Declaratory Judgment for the (b)(2) Class Action*, 58 Ark. L. Rev. 767 (2006).

[216] Moore § 23.43[1][b].

[217] *See* Advisory Committee Note to the 1966 amendment to Rule 23.

The accepted reading of Rule 23(b)(2) is that "[t]he subdivision does not extend to cases in which the appropriate final relief relates exclusively or predominantly to money damages."[218] Note that this standard does not necessarily exclude from (b)(2) cases seeking damages as well as declaratory or injunctive relief.[219] The question is whether the damages portion of the remedial package predominates. One study concluded that "cases involving claims for both money damages and injunctive or declaratory relief present significant difficulties of classification" under Rule 23.[220]

Rule 23(b)(3) creates a final, significant category of class actions.[221] It authorizes the device when, in the language of (b)(3), "the court finds that the questions of law or fact common to class members predominate over any questions affecting only individual members, and that a class action is superior to other available methods for fairly and efficiently adjudicating the controversy."[222]

Subdivision (b)(3) has greater scope than (b)(1) or (2) in one respect and less in another. While (b)(1) and (2) demand a closer relationship among class interests than the requirement in Rule 23(a)(3) that there be predominant common questions of law or fact,[223] predominance is enough for (b)(3). On the other hand, the court may certify (b)(1) and (2) classes without the finding required under (b)(3) that the class action is superior to other forms of adjudication.

Despite these differences in description, the categories created in Rule 23(b) are not mutually exclusive. Some class actions appropriate to (b)(1) or (2) also appear to fit within (b)(3).[224] In such cases, certification under (b)(1) or (b)(2) can offer advantages over certification under (b)(3). This is because Rule

---

[218] Rule 23 advisory committee's notes (1966). On distinctions between damages, injunctions and declaratory judgments, see Chapter 14, *infra*.

[219] Thus, "certification under Rule 23(b)(2) may be allowed in actions involving some damages as long as they are incidental, such as back pay claims in employment-discrimination suits seeking to end certain practices of the employer." WRIGHT & MILLER § 1775. *See, e.g., Parker v. Time Warner Entm't Co., L.P.*, 331 F.3d 13, 18 (2d Cir. 2003).

[220] ABA Section of Litigation, *Report and Recommendations of the Special Committee on Class Action Improvements* (1986), at 197. The Committee went on to note that "an artful pleader can endeavor to make the declaratory or injunctive relief appear to 'predominate.'" *Id.*

[221] "The great bulk of reported cases in which class actions have been allowed under the revised rule have been (b)(3) actions." WRIGHT § 72.

[222] To aid in resolving these issues, Rule 23(b)(3) identifies four considerations:

> (A) the class members' interests in individually controlling the prosecution or defense of separate actions; (B) the extent and nature of any litigation concerning the controversy already begun by or against class members; (C) the desirability or undesirability of concentrating the litigation of the claims in the particular forum; and (D) the likely difficulties in managing a class action.

[223] Members of a 23(b)(2) class must be united in their request for an injunction or declaratory judgment. Satisfaction of (b)(1) will only be possible when the interests of individual class members, although discrete, resemble one another to a large degree.

[224] *See, e.g.,* WRIGHT & MILLER § 1772 (raising the possibility of "an action . . . under both Rule 23(b)(1) and Rule 23(b)(3).").

23(c)(2) requires notice to be sent to members of a (b)(3) class and gives them the opportunity to request exclusion from ("opt out of") the class.[225]

It is now clear that the requirements posed by subdivisions (a) and (b) of Rule 23 apply also to classes certified solely for purposes of settlement.[226]

[2] Reconciling Judicial Economy and Public Law Enforcement (b)(3) Class Actions

A major goal in drafting Rule 23(b)(3) was one we have encountered previously in this chapter — judicial economy.[227] If only judicial economy was involved, the arguments for and against Rule 23(b)(3) certifications would follow a familiar pattern. The argument for certification would be that efficiency would result from simultaneous adjudication of elements of individual claims common to the class, while the counter-argument would be that maintenance of a class action would confuse and delay the case in ways counterproductive to judicial economy and prejudicial to interests of those opposing the class.[228]

The picture for (b)(3) class actions is complicated, however, by the recurrent suggestion that they perform a function apart from promoting judicial economy — that of providing a means for private citizens to sue in the public interest. Thus viewed, Rule 23(b)(3) should be given maximum play when class representatives can, as private attorneys general, protect members of the public who are unable to protect themselves.[229] But it is possible to argue that,

---

[225] See WRIGHT & MILLER § 1772. On notice in (b)(3) actions, see § 9.09[2][c], *infra*. On opt-out procedure, see note 196, *supra*.

[226] *Ortiz v. Fibreboard*, 527 U.S. 815 (1999); *Amchem Prods. v. Windsor*, 521 U.S. 591 (1997).

[227] "Subdivision (b)(3) encompasses those cases in which a class action would achieve economies of time, effort, and expense, and promote uniformity of decision as to persons similarly situated, without sacrificing procedural fairness or bringing about other undesirable results." Rule 23 advisory committee's notes (1966).

[228] The same pattern would be followed, for example, in arguments for and against permissive intervention. *See* § 9.08[2], *supra*.

[229] Government lawyers litigate to protect the public, but they labor with limited resources and limited authority to obtain compensation for those who have been wronged by violation of federal law. Seeking damages for himself and a group of people similarly wronged, the class representative supplements the role of government lawyers. He becomes a kind of private attorney general, blurring the line between public and private litigation. The Supreme Court noted with apparent approval this use of (b)(3):

> "The policy at the very core of the class action mechanism is to overcome the problem that small recoveries do not provide the incentive for any individual to bring a solo action prosecuting his or her rights. A class action solves this problem by aggregating the relatively paltry potential recoveries into something worth someone's (usually an attorney's) labor."

Alchem Products, Inc. v. Windsor, 521 U.S. 591, 617 (1997) (quoting *Mace v. Van Ru Credit Corp.*, 109 F.3d 338, 344 (1997). *Accord Phillips Petroleum Co. v. Shutts*, 472 U.S. 797, 809 (1985); *Deposit Guar. Nat'l Bank v. Roper*, 445 U.S. 326, 339 (1980).

For discussion of private-attorney-general interpretations of paragraph (b)(3), see Howard M. Erichson, *Mississippi Class Actions and the Inevitability of Mass Aggregate Litigation*, 24 MISS.

since the private attorney-general theory has greatest application when class members' damage claims are too small to be viable as individual lawsuits,[230] use of the idea to justify (b)(3) class actions stands the rule on its head. That is, assuming that (b)(3) was intended to promote judicial economy,[231] it would seem to have the opposite effect when used to facilitate litigation which could not exist otherwise.[232]

One way to resolve the conflict between judicial economy and public law enforcement would be to place in Rule 23(b)(3) a provision expressly recognizing the latter.[233] While Supreme Court rulings on Rule 23 and on other aspects of federal procedure have restricted the private attorney-general theory of class actions in federal court,[234] the concept has enjoyed greater application in class action practice in some state courts.[235]

C.L. REV. 285 (2005); William B. Rubenstein, *On What a "Private Attorney General" Is — And Why It Matters*, 57 VAND. L. REV. 2129 (2004); Daniel J. Meltzer, *Deterring Constitutional Violations by Law Enforcement Officials: Plaintiffs and Defendants as Private Attorneys General*, 88 COLUM. L. REV. 247 (1988); Carl Cheng, *Important Rights and the Private Attorney General Doctrine*, 73 CAL. L. REV. 1929 (1985).

[230] Rule 23(b)(3) class actions in federal court "have been especially popular in antitrust and securities fraud cases, when individual persons allegedly injured are in a poor position to seek redress, either because they do not know enough or because the cost of suit is disproportionate to each individual claim." WRIGHT § 72. It is certainly true that many claims of class members or even class representatives in such cases would not support the cost of a separate lawsuit. For example, the individual damage claim of Mort Eisen, class representative in the multimillion dollar case, *Eisen v. Carlisle & Jacquelin*, 417 U.S. 156 (1974), was for $70.

[231] *See* Rule 23(b)(3) advisory committee's notes (1966).

[232] One commentator wrote of the private-attorney-general argument, "this purpose is enunciated nowhere in Rule 23. Furthermore, in practice such a principle — if embodied within (b)(3) — would produce a direct conflict with the professed purpose of economy of time, expense and effort." Thomas J. Weithers, *Amended Rule 23: A Defendant's Point of View*, 10 B.C. IND. & COM. L. REV. 515, 518 (1969); *cf. Eisen v. Carlisle & Jacquelin*, 391 F.2d 555, 572 (2d Cir. 1968) (Lumbard, C.J., dissenting) ("The appropriate action for this Court is to affirm the district court and put an end to this Frankenstein monster posing as a class action."). *But see* Tom Ford, *Federal Rule 23: A Device for Aiding the Small Claimant*, 10 B.C. IND. & COM. L. REV. 501, 504 (1969) (one of the purposes of revised Rule 23 is "taking care of the smaller guy") (quoting Professor Kaplan, Reporter for the Advisory Committee).

[233] This was proposed by the *Report and Recommendations of the Special Committee on Class Action Improvements*, note 220, *supra*, and by the Office for Improvements in the Administration of Justice (OIAJ) of the United States Department of Justice. The OIAJ proposal is discussed in Stephen Berry, *Ending Substance's Indenture to Procedure: The Imperative for Comprehensive Revision of the Class Damage Action*, 80 COLUM. L. REV. 299 (1980); Patricia L. Wells, Note, *Reforming Federal Class Action Procedure: An Analysis of the Justice Department Proposal*, 16 HARV. J. ON LEGIS. 543 (1979).

[234] *See* § 9.09[2], *supra*.

[235] § 9.09[2], *supra*.

[3]   Small-Claim, Large-Class Actions

[a]   Comparative Availability of Federal and State Class Actions

Procedural opportunities for one filing suit in state court often are about the same as they would be in federal court. A federal forum offers a clear advantage in a few situations.[236] However, a suit brought on behalf of a nationwide class — especially when individual class claims are small — may fare better in the courts of some states than in federal court.[237]

First, states seem less inclined to follow the federal rules model when treating class actions,[238] and several have promulgated class rules more accommodating than Federal Rule 23.[239] Second, even state courts presented with language in their class action rules identical to Rule 23 are not bound by federal court interpretations of the latter,[240] and are in any event free from the

---

[236] See for example, the discussion of statutory interpleader in § 9.07, *supra.*

[237] At the same time, class actions can succeed under Federal Rule 23(b)(3), particularly when a governmental entity is willing to litigate on behalf of the class, or when the size of individual class claims increases. Multistate class actions are at times easier to maintain in federal court because the courts of some states are still reluctant to take them on. Moreover, antitrust and certain other federal claims can be heard only in federal court. See § 5.01[2], *supra.* States, however, may take jurisdiction over class actions based on state antitrust law. *See generally* Herbert Hovenkamp, *State Antitrust in the Federal Scheme*, 58 Ind. L.J. 375 (1983).

[238] According to a leading study, "only a minority of states have embraced the system and philosophy of the Federal Rules wholeheartedly enough to permit classification as true federal replicas." John B. Oakley & Arthur F. Coon, *The Federal Rules in State Courts: A Survey of State Court Systems of Civil Procedure*, 61 Wash. L. Rev. 1367, 1369 (1986). A number of states pick and choose models among the federal rules, adopting some (perhaps most), but not all. In this regard, Rule 23 appears to be among those most frequently passed over. For example North Carolina and Wisconsin modeled their intervention rules closely upon Federal Rule 24, but ignored Federal Rule 23. For more on how states approach the subject, see Robert A. Skirnick & Patricia I. Avery, *The State Court Class Action — A Potpourri of Differences*, 20 Forum 750 (1985).

[239] Florida amended its class action law "to eliminate problems in the federal rule through court decisions." Fla. R. Civ. P. 1.240 committee's note (1980). Like Florida, New York also rejected the federal approach and adopted more liberal class action law. N.Y. Civ. Prac. L. & R. Art. 9.

[240] The meaning of even identical language in a state rule raises a question of state rather than federal law. Under such circumstances, federal court interpretations of the federal rules (even those by the United States Supreme Court) are no more than persuasive precedent. The best and final authority on the meaning of all state law is the highest state court. See § 7.06[1], *supra.* At the same time, federal rule decisions can be quite persuasive when a state court is looking at the same language in its own rule. The following response of an Indiana court may be typical.

> Indiana . . . Rule 23 is the general rule governing class actions. With two exceptions it follows the federal rule, F.R.C.P. 23, verbatim. In addition, our civil code study commission comments direct the bar, with approval, to the note of the Advisory Committee to the federal rule.

> For these reasons, and because this is an area of complex litigation where the bench and bar are greatly benefited by a broad body of interpretative law, we will, as far as possible, adopt the federal interpretation of the language of the rule.

Bowen v. Sonnenburg, 411 N.E.2d 390, 396–97 (Ind. Ct. App. 1980); *accord Wal-Mart Stores, Inc. v. Rhodus*, 808 N.E.2d 1198, 1207-08 (Ind. Ct. App. 2004).

constraints of subject matter jurisdiction which further limit federal class actions.

[b] Problems Small-Claim, Large-Class Actions Pose in Federal Court

The Supreme Court's decision in *Eisen v. Carlisle & Jacquelin*[241] sharply curtailed Rule 23(b)(3) litigation involving small claims in federal court. The Court read Rule 23(c)(2) to require individual notice of the action at the representative's expense to each member of a (b)(3) class whose name and address was available to the class representative, and to prevent shifting any of the cost of notice to the party opposing the clases. Later, in *Oppenheimer Fund, Inc. v. Sanders*,[242] the Supreme Court ruled that the class representative was also required to pay the party opposing the class the latter's expenses in compiling the names and addresses of the class for the representative. Resulting expense dampened the private-attorney-general movement in federal court.[243] However, since *Eisen* and *Oppenheimer* were not constitutional law decisions, they do not control class actions in state courts. States are free to adopt class rules philosophically opposed to *Eisen*.[244]

The availability of class actions under Federal Rule 23(b)(3) is also limited by the reluctance of many federal courts to certify class actions if the process of distributing damages to individual class members seems too complicated or the prospect of actual reimbursement to class members uncertain. Federal courts must take these factors into account,[245] and obstacles to class certification increase when classes become larger and the size of individual claims smaller. Yet certification may be warranted even in such cases, when it is possible to determine (without examining individual class claims) both the liability of the opposing party to the entire class[246] and the total amount of damages inflicted upon the class.[247] Certification in this setting may turn on

---

[241] 417 U.S. 156 (1974).

[242] 437 U.S. 340 (1978).

[243] Costs generated by *Eisen* and *Oppenheimer* will be beyond the means of most class representatives and are in any event greatly disproportionate to the value of the representative's personal claim.

[244] *See e.g.*, N.Y. Civ. Prac. L. & R., Art. 9.

[245] The interests of members of Rule 23(b)(1) and (2) classes tend to be closely tied. "But in an action under Rule 23(b)(3) the members are loosely bound together by common questions of law or fact and considerations of convenience. Even the damages they seek generally are individual in character and disparate in amount." *Wright & Miller* § 1784. The requirement in Rule 23(b)(3) that class issues predominate in the case and concern in (b)(3)(D) over "difficulties likely to be encountered in the management of a class action" make the rule sensitive to possible difficulties in distributing damage awards to individual members of the class. *Wright & Miller* § 1784.

[246] The feasibility of proving defendants wrong class-wide will depend on the facts and plaintiff's theory of liability. Antitrust cases are frequently susceptible to such proof. *See* note 247, *infra*. On the other hand, proof of class-wide fraud under § 10(b) of the Securities Exchange Act of 1934 may be more problematic. *See generally* Note, *The Impact of Class Actions on Rule 10b-5*, 38 U. Chi. L. Rev. 337 (1971).

[247] For example, consider the antitrust case where plaintiff's class is the public with whom the defendants transacted business during a given period. Whether plaintiff's class has been wronged

the legitimacy of so-called fluid recovery.

Fluid recovery is a means of disposing of the portion of class-wide damages which goes unclaimed by class members by directing that it be spent in the public interest in a way at least generally responsive to concerns raised in the case.[248] Small-claim, large-class actions may proceed from adjudication of defendant's liability to the class to class-wide assessment of damages and the creation of a fund.[249] After attorney's fees and expenses for litigation and for administering the fund are deducted, the balance of the fund theoretically goes to class members in proportion to the value of their individual claims. But most small-claim, large-class actions offer the likelihood that a substantial portion of the class fund will go unclaimed. This may be because many members of the class are unknown and may not learn of the existence of a class award or because the sum involved may be so small that some class members will not bother to apply for their individual recoveries. Most lower federal courts have refused to administer class actions offering the prospect of substantial unclaimed recovery, "unless it is part of a distribution arising out of a settlement."[250] In contrast, some state courts have been more willing to employ fluid recovery.[251]

The actual notice requirement of Rule 23(c)(2) and the reluctance of federal judges to employ fluid recovery combine to restrict the availability of small-

---

as a matter of antitrust law, and, if so, in what amount, are not simple questions. At the procedural level, however, these issues are often quite susceptible to class-wide resolution, *e.g.*, resolution without the necessity of examining a single individual class claim. Common issues would include whether defendants engaged in price-fixing and, if so, the amount of their total charges to the class during the relevant period, and the differential between those charges and the charges defendants would have made in the absence of price-fixing.

[248] On the topic of fluid recovery, see *Developments*, note 184, *supra* at 1516–23; Michael Malina, *Fluid Class Recovery as a Consumer Remedy in Antitrust Cases*, 47 N.Y.U. L. REV. 477 (1972). Cases utilizing the device include *Gordon v. Boden*, 586 N.E.2d 461 (Ill. App. Ct. 1991) (damages from sale of adulterated orange juice products available either to fund a charitable project to benefit class or to reduce the price of future product sales); *Bruno v. Superior Court*, 179 Cal. Rptr. 342 (Cal. Ct. App. 1981) (profits from illegal milk prices applied to lower the price of milk in the future); *Market St. Ry. v. Railroad Comm'n*, 171 P.2d 875 (Cal. 1946) (profits from illegal train fares directed to upgrade train facilities). These cases share features common to most fluid recovery cases: (1) the fund is fluidly distributed only after an attempt is made to reach and compensate class members directly for their actual harm; and (2) the means chosen to dispose of the fund is calculated to provide some advantage to members of the class who were not individually compensated. That is, those wronged through past purchase of milk or train tickets are among those most likely to share in the advantage of reduced prices in the future. Of course, the process is inexact. Reduced prices in the future will be a windfall for those members of the class who did make individual claims against the fund and for members of the public not wronged in the past. Iowa, North Dakota and New Jersey have codified their law of fluid recovery. *See* NEWBERG, note 185, *supra*, § 13.49.

[249] "Devising a plan to distribute a lump sum recovery is beneficial because it may eliminate the need for separate trials on damage issues. In a case involving an extremely large plaintiff class whose members only have small individual claims, the savings in time and expense for all will be considerable." WRIGHT & MILLER § 1784.

[250] WRIGHT & MILLER § 1784. A well-known example of the latter is *West Virginia v. Chas. Pfizer & Co.*, 440 F.2d 1079 (2d Cir. 1971), *cert. denied*, 404 U.S. 871 (1971), an antitrust case in which the court administered a settlement fund of $100,000,000.

[251] See the discussion of state decisions in note 240, *supra*.

claim, large-class actions in federal court. This led to more careful consideration of possible advantages from filing a class action in state rather than federal court. Several state courts have willingly provided a sanctuary for nation-wide class actions that are difficult or impossible to bring in federal court.[252] The viability of such cases in state court improved after the Supreme Court's decision in *Phillips Petroleum Company v. Shutts*.[253]

Prior to *Shutts*, it was unclear whether a state court could exercise personal jurisdiction over passive members[254] of a plaintiff class when their contact with the forum was so tenuous that the constitutional law of due process would have prevented jurisdiction over the same persons as defendants.[255] Some state courts refused to entertain nationwide class actions because of what they perceived to be the lack of minimum contacts[256] between the forum and nonresident members of the plaintiff class.[257] *Shutts* gave state courts the green light by ruling that the relationship between the forum and members of the plaintiff class did not have to meet the stringent due process requirements applied to the relationship between a forum and defendants. The minimum contacts test did not apply.[258]

---

[252] "[R]ecent United States Supreme Court cases restricting access to the federal courts in class actions suits have made it necessary for state courts to hear nation-wide class actions." *Shutts v. Phillips Petroleum Co.*, 679 P.2d 1159, 1169 (Kan. 1984), *rev'd on other grounds*, *Phillips Petroleum Co. v. Shutts*, 472 U.S. 797 (1985). *See also Miner v. Gillette Co.*, 428 N.E.2d 478 (Ill. 1981); *Schlosser v. Allis-Chalmers Corp.*, 271 N.W.2d 879 (Wis. 1978); *Anthony v. General Motors Corp.*, 109 Cal. Rptr. 254 (Cal. Ct. App. 1973); *Paley v. Coca Cola Co.*, 209 N.W.2d 232 (Mich. 1973). *Cf.* G. ALAN TARR & MARY CORNELIA PORTER, STATE SUPREME COURTS IN STATE AND NATION 45 (1988) (noting that a number of states, "either through legislation or court decisions, have developed guidelines on class actions that are considerably more liberal than those prevailing in the federal courts.").

[253] 472 U.S. 797 (1985).

[254] Passive members are those remaining in the class who neither serve as class representatives nor surface by appearance or intervention. *See* notes 196-197 and accompanying text (the distinction between active and passive class members), *supra*.

[255] *See* Barbara A. Winters, Note, *Jurisdiction Over Unnamed Plaintiffs in Multistate Class Actions*, 73 CAL. L. REV. 181 (1985); Comment, *Jurisdiction and Notice in Class Actions: "Playing Fair" with National Classes*, 132 U. PA. L. REV. 1487 (1984).

[256] On the function of the minimum contacts test in regulating personal jurisdiction, see § 3.09[1], *supra*.

[257] *E.g.*, *Feldman v. Bates Mfg. Co.*, 362 A.2d 1177 (N.J. Sup. Ct. 1976); *Klemow v. Time*, 352 A.2d 12 (Pa.), *cert. denied*, 429 U.S. 828 (1976).

[258] The Court stated that "[b]ecause States place fewer burdens upon absent class plaintiffs than they do upon absent defendants in nonclass suits, the Due Process Clause need not and does not afford the former as much protection from state-court jurisdiction as it does the latter." 472 U.S. at 811. All that due process required of plaintiffs' class actions was adequate representation by the class representative accompanied by notice to class members that was reasonable under the circumstances of the case. *See* note 270 & accompanying text, *infra*. On the significance of *Shutts* state class actions, see Kurt A. Schwarz, Note, *Due Process and Equitable Relief in State Multistate Class Actions After Phillips Petroleum Co. v. Shutts*, 68 TEX. L. REV. 415 (1989); Diane P. Wood, *Adjudicatory Jurisdiction and Class Actions*, 62 IND. L.J. 597 (1987); Arthur R. Miller & David Crump, *Jurisdiction and Choice of Law in Multistate Class Actions After Phillips Petroleum Co. v. Shutts*, 96 YALE L.J. 1 (1986); John E. Kennedy, *The Supreme Court Meets the Bride of Frankenstein: Phillips Petroleum Co. v. Shutts and the Multistate Class Action*, 34 KAN. L. REV. 255 (1985). The Supreme Court subsequently questioned whether its *Shutts* ruling should

On the other hand, prospects for state-court class actions dimmed when Congress enacted the Class Action Fairness Act of 2005[259] ("CAFA"). Class action authority Edward Sherman explained that

> the main thrust of CAFA was . . . alleged forum shopping. In recent years, federal courts had been perceived by both plaintiff and defendant lawyers as less sympathetic to class actions and to plaintiff's cases that certain state courts. As federal court judges became more critical of class actions, class action attorneys increasingly filed in state courts. Businesses especially complained that an undue proportion of class actions were filed in certain "magnet venue" state courts . . . where judges, usually elected, were more likely to certify a class action and the juries were likely to be more pro-plaintiff. In addition, corporations that do business in multiple states complained that they were subjected to national or multistate class actions in state courts that could thereby establish legal standards that would govern their activities throughout the country. These kinds of concerns let to focusing the legislation on expanding federal court "diversity jurisdiction" and defendants' right to remove state class actions to federal court.[260]

[4]   Due Process Requirements Common to Federal and State Class Actions

One source of law limits federal and state class actions alike: the constitutional law of due process. The function of the modern class action in federal and most state courts is to bind the class members by the outcome as though they were active parties in the case.[261] This raises due process considerations, since one cannot be bound without participating in a judicial proceeding unless his interests are adequately represented.

---

apply in class actions where members did not receive notice or a clear opportunity to opt out of the class. *Ortiz v. Fibreboard Corp.*, 527 U.S. 815, 847–48 (1999). The minimum contacts requirement may reappear in such cases.

[259] The Act created 28 U.S.C. §§ 1453 & 1711-1715 and amended 28 U.S.C. §§ 1332, 1335, and 1603. For analyses of the CAFA, see Richard L. Marcus, *Assessing CAFA's Stated Jurisdictional Policy*, 156 U. Pa. L. Rev. 1765 (2008); Adam N. Steinman, *"Less" is "More"? Textualism, Intentionalism, and a Better Solution to the Class Action Fairness Act's Appellate Deadline Riddle*, 92 Iowa L. Rev. 1183 (2007); Edward F. Sherman, *Class Actions After the Class Action Fairness Act of 2005*, 80 Tul. L. Rev. 1593 (2006); Anna Andreeva, *Class Action Fairness Act of 2005: The Eight-Year Saga is Finally Over*, 59 U. Miami L. Rev. 385 (2005).

[260] Edward F. Sherman, *Class Actions After the Class Action Fairness Act of 2005*, 80 Tul. L. Rev. 1593, 1595 (2006) (citations omitted). *Cf.* Linda J. Silberman, Allan R. Stein & Tobias B. Wolff, Civil Procedure Theory and Practice 1047 (2d ed. 2006) (describing the "basic spirit animating the Act" as "hostility toward the perceived abuses of class-action proceedings, particularly in the state courts"). For an explaination of the enlargements of diversity and removal jurisdiction noted in the accompanying text, see Chapter 5, *supra*.

[261] "Class actions rest on a relatively simple proposition: self-selected class representatives and their lawyers, properly supervised by the court, can represent class members as a group sufficiently well to overcome members' individual rights to be heard." Bryant G. Garth, *Studying Civil Litigation Through the Class Action*, 62 Ind. L.J. 497, 497 (1987). "The fascination of foreign scholars with class actions is fairly easy to explain: this principle of representation remains unacceptable to almost the entire legal world outside of the United States." *Id.*

Hansberry v. Lee[262] continues to be of central importance in elaborating the constitutional standard. Hansberry established a principle essential for true class actions, that (under the right circumstances) class action judgments could bind passive class members.[263] Yet the due process ruling in *Hansberry* also imposed important limits on class actions. The Court stated that it was "justified in saying that there has been a failure of due process only in those cases where it cannot be said that the procedure adopted, fairly insures the protection of the interests of absent parties who are to be bound by it."[264] Thus, "members of a class not present as parties to the litigation may be bound by the judgment where they are in fact adequately represented by parties who are present . . . ."[265]

When is an absent class member "adequately represented?" In answering this question, due process doctrine places greatest reliance on the opinion held prior to the proceeding by the person to be bound. A passive class member may be thought to express his own favorable opinion on adequacy of representation when he knowingly permits the class representative to act for him. He likely will be bound by the class judgment in such cases — even if the representation of the class representative turns out to be lackluster.[266] But, even if the work of the class representative will be superlative, the class member is entitled whenever possible to decide before the fact whether he wants to entrust his interests to that person. Naturally, the class member is only able to control how his interests will be represented if made aware of the case prior to adjudication. That is why in due process doctrine the concept of adequate representation is closely tied to that of notice.

The classic statement on the extent of notice required for binding adjudications appears in *Mullane v. Central Hanover Bank & Trust Co.*[267]

> An elementary and fundamental requirement of due process in any proceeding which is to be accorded finality is notice reasonably calculated, under all the circumstances, to apprise interested parties of the pendency of the action and afford them an opportunity to present their objections. The notice must be of such nature as reasonably to convey the required information, and it must afford a reasonable time for those interested to make their appearance. But if with due regard for the practicalities and peculiarities of the case these conditions are

---

[262] 311 U.S. 32 (1940). For useful analysis and background, see Jay Tidmarsh, *The Story of Hansberry: The Rise of the Modern Class Action, in* CIVIL PROCEDURE STORIES, Ch. 6 (Kevin Clermont, ed., 2d ed. 2008).

[263] "[T]here is scope within the framework of the Constitution for holding in appropriate cases that a judgment rendered in a class suit is *res judicata* as to members of the class who are not formal parties to the suit." 311 U.S. at 42.

[264] 311 U.S. at 42.

[265] 311 U.S. at 42–43.

[266] 311 U.S. at 43 (class members are bound "where they actually participate in the conduct of the litigation in which members of the class are present as parties.").

[267] 339 U.S. 306 (1950). On *Mullane* and this topic generally, see § 4.02[1] (special due process concerns arising from class actions), *supra*.

reasonably met, the constitutional requirements are satisfied.[268]

This is a pragmatic approach to notice. *Mullane* holds that actual notice to those to be bound by the litigation is always required where practicable.[269] Furthermore, *Mullane* indicates that those for whom individual notice is impracticable may only be bound under special circumstances. That is, notice to them must be attempted by the best alternative means (possibly publication), and there must be a strong showing that they will be adequately represented by one before the court.[270]

The interplay of due process and rule requirements for class actions varies within federal Rule 23. Subdivision (c)(2) of Rule 23 governs (b)(3) actions. The first part of Rule 23(c)(2)[271] appears to have been written under *Mullane*'s influence. Unfortunately, (c)(2) thereafter loses much of its *Mullane*-like flexibility, mandating individual notice to all class members whose names and addresses are known — without reference to practicability.[272] Once it read (c)(2) to require notice in the manner indicated above,[273] the Supreme Court found it unnecessary to reach the question whether due process required such notice as well.[274] Federal class actions under Rule 23(b)(1) and (2) are not subject to (c)(2), but only to the general limitations of due process,[275] as are state class actions.[276]

---

[268] 339 U.S. at 314–15 (citations omitted).

[269] 339 U.S. at 318.

[270] Because the Court required mail notice to trust beneficiaries whose addresses were known, it was comfortable excusing such personal notice for beneficiaries whose addresses were not known or were ascertainable only at considerable expense. It reasoned that

> [t]his type of trust presupposes a large number of small interests. The individual interest does not stand alone but is identical with that of a class. The rights of each in the integrity of the fund and the fidelity of the trustee are shared by many other beneficiaries. Therefore notice reasonably certain to reach most of those interested in objecting is likely to safeguard the interest of all since any objection sustained would inure to the benefit of all. We think that under such circumstances reasonable risks that notice might not actually reach every beneficiary are justifiable.

339 U.S. at 319.

[271] "In any class action maintained under subdivision (b)(3), the court shall direct to the members of the class the best notice practicable under the circumstances."

[272] At the same time, Rule 23(c)(2) does not reduce notice flexibility under *Mullane* for (b)(3) class members whose names and addresses cannot be ascertained. Concerning this group, "it should be remembered that Rule 23(c)(2) only directs the court to give 'the best notice practicable under the circumstances.'" WRIGHT & MILLER § 1786. When some class members are individually notified, notice by publication to those whose whereabouts are unknown will often suffice. WRIGHT & MILLER § 1786.

[273] *Eisen v. Carlisle & Jacquelin,* 417 U.S. 156 (1974), discussed at note 241 and accompanying text, *supra.*

[274] *See* Adolf Homburger, *State Class Actions and the Federal Rule,* 71 COLUM. L. REV. 609, 646 (1971) (arguing "there is nothing in *Hansberry* or *Mullane* to suggest a constitutional prohibition against dispensation with notice in any kind of class suit if procedural fairness and adequacy of representation are safeguarded in other ways.").

[275] *Newberg,* note 184, *supra,* § 8.05.

[276] *See Phillips Petroleum Co. v. Shutts,* 472 U.S. 797, 811–12 (1985).

[5]   Class Actions in Global Perspective[277]

The diminishing importance of national boundaries has affected civil procedure[278] as it has other subjects. Class actions are beginning to obtain global dimensions. Special problems arise for U.S. courts in such cases. These include concerns over the proper administration of class actions under Federal Rule 23 regarding international notice, the wish of foreign members of the class to be included or excluded, global settlement, and the enforcement of class judgments abroad. Such actions can also raise special questions about personal jurisdiction and federal subject matter jurisdiction.

§ 9.10   CONSOLIDATING CASES — CURRENT LAW AND POSSIBILITIES FOR THE FUTURE

[1]   Intradistrict Consolidation — Rule 42(a)[279]

Federal Rule 42(a) authorizes the court to "join for hearing or trial" cases pending within the same judicial district that "involve a common question of law or fact." A number of states have essentially the same rule.[280]

The object of Rule 42(a) is to promote judicial economy.[281] Judicial economy has been a recurrent theme in this chapter. Yet Rule 42(a) functions in relative isolation. It does not appear in the pleading or parties sections of the federal rules, as do the other rules we have considered. It has also been suggested that

---

[277] Aspects of the subject have interested commentators. *See, e.g.*, Hannah L. Buxbaum, *Multinational Class Actions Under Federal Securities Law: Managing Jurisdictional Conflict*, 46 COLUM. J. TRANSNAT'L L. 14 (2007); Note, *Actualizing the Trope of Internationalism in Class Action Theory*, 118 HARV. L. REV. 2914 (2005); Ilana T. Buschkin, *The Viability of Class Action Lawsuits in a Global Economy — Permitting Foreign Claimants to be Members of Class Action Lawsuits in the U.S. Federal Courts*, 90 CORNELL L. REV. 1563 (2005); Edward F. Sherman, *American Class Actions: Significant Features and Developing Alternatives in Foreign Legal Systems*, 215 F.R.D. 130 (2003); Debra Lyn Bassett, *U.S. Class Actions Go Global: Transnational Class Actions and Personal Jurisdiction*, 72 FORDHAM L. REV. 41 (2003).

[278] *See* Gene R. Shreve, *Civil Procedure: Other Disciplines, Globalization, and Simple Gifts*, 92 MICH. L. REV. 1401 (1994).

[279] *See generally* MOORE §§ 42.10–42.15; Elizabeth J. Cabraser. *The Class Action Counterreformation*, 57 STAN. L. REV. 1475, 1493-99 (2005); Joan Steinman, *The Effects of Case Consolidation on the Procedural Rights of Litigants: What They Are, They Might Be Part I: Justiciability and Jurisdiction (Original and Appellate)*, 42 UCLA L. REV. 717 (1995); Joan Steinman, . . . *Part II: Non-Jurisdictional Matters*, 42 UCLA L. REV. 967 (1995); Richard L. Marcus, *Confronting the Consolidation Conundrum*, 1995 BYU L. REV. 879; WRIGHT & MILLER §§ 2382–86; MANUAL FOR COMPLEX LITIGATION (THIRD) § 31.11 (1995); Gaylord A. Virden, *Consolidation Under Rule 42 of the Federal Rules of Civil Procedure*, 141 F.R.D. 169 (1992). *Cf.* Theodore Goldberg & Tybe A. Brett, *Consolidation of Individual Plaintiff Personal Injury-Toxic Tort Actions*, 11 J.L. & COM. 59 (1991) (discussing applications of Rule 42(a) in asbestos injury litigation); Charles Silver, *Comparing Class Actions and Consolidations*, 10 REV. LITIG. 495 (1991) (comparing Rules 23 and 42(a)).

[280] *E.g.*, DEL. CODE ANN. R. CIV. P. 42; MINN. STAT. ANN. R. CIV. P. DIST. CT. R. 42.01; N.M. STAT. ANN. R. CIV. P. DIST. CT. 1-042.

[281] "The obvious virtue of consolidation is that it increases the productivity of the judicial system by arranging for simultaneous resolution of issues or entire actions." *FRIEDENTHAL, KANE & MILLER* § 6.2.

"it would be a mistake to assume that the standard for consolidation is the same as that governing original joinder of parties or claims."[282]

Therefore, one cannot simply assume that Rule 42(a) provides a means of reconstructing litigation along lines possible under federal joinder rules before the cases were filed. The availability of consolidation is in one respect more restricted than joinder, since "in a suit between a single plaintiff and a single defendant, plaintiff may join all of his claims, no matter how unrelated they may be, against the defendant. If the plaintiff brings separate actions, however, only those actions having a common question of law or fact may be consolidated."[283] In another respect, consolidation is less restricted.

> [M]ore than one party can be joined on a side under Rule 20(a) only if there is asserted on behalf of or against all of them one or more claims for relief arising out of the same transaction or occurrence or series of transactions or occurrences. This is in addition to the requirement that there be some question of law or fact common to all the parties. But the common question by itself is enough to permit consolidation, even if the claims arise out of independent transactions.[284]

Orders granting or denying Rule 42(a) motions to consolidate are interlocutory and hence difficult to appeal.[285] The federal court's authority to consolidate exists only when two or more cases present a common issue of law or fact. Presence of a common issue empowers the court to order consolidation but does not require it to do so. This is an area where considerable discretion should and does exist. "[I]t is for the court to weigh the saving of time and effort that consolidation would produce against any inconvenience, delay or expense that it would cause."[286]

A federal trial judge has authority under Rule 42(a) to consolidate only cases pending within her judicial district. She may not use the rule to consolidate cases pending in more than one district.[287] The Judicial Panel on Multidistrict Litigation may order consolidation of such cases for pretrial purposes,[288] however, and a trial judge may weigh the possibility of consolidation in deciding whether to transfer a case to another district.[289]

---

[282] *Wright & Miller* § 2382.

[283] *Wright & Miller* § 2382.

[284] *Wright & Miller* § 2382.

[285] *Moore* § 42.12[1]. *See generally* § 13.03 (final judgment rule), *infra*.

[286] *Wright & Miller* § 2383. Weighing against consolidation are possibilities of juror confusion, delay, administrative difficulties and prejudice to a party. *Moore* § 42.10[5]. *See, e.g., Solvent Chem. Co. v. E.I. Dupont De Nemours & Co.*, 242 F. Supp. 2d 196, 221 (W.D.N.Y. 2002).

[287] *Moore* § 42.11[1]. *See In re Penn Cent. Commercial Paper Litig.*, 62 F.R.D. 341 (S.D.N.Y. 1974), *aff'd*, 515 F.2d 505 (2d Cir. 1975).

[288] 28 U.S.C. § 1407. *See* § 9.10[2], *infra*.

[289] 28 U.S.C. § 1404. *See generally* § 6.02[2] (venue transfer), *supra*.

[2]   Federal Multidistrict Litigation Under Section 1407[290]

Section 1407(a) of Title 28 reads in part: "When civil actions involving one or more common questions of fact are pending in different districts, such actions may be transferred to any district for coordinated or consolidated pretrial proceedings." By authorizing multidistrict consolidation, Section 1407 exceeds Rule 42(a) in scope. However, it is more narrow than Rule 42(a) in two respects. Section 1407 applies literally only to pretrial proceedings[291] and only to cases having common questions of fact.[292] Moreover, it authorizes transfers only when they "will be for the convenience of the parties and witnesses and will promote the just and efficient conduct of such actions."[293]

Congress enacted Section 1407 in response to the confusion and repetition generated by multiple antitrust suits in the electronics industry in the 1960s.[294]

Section 1407 creates a "judicial panel on multidistrict litigation"[295] which decides when cases should be consolidated for pretrial proceedings and to which judge they should be transferred. The section has been invoked most frequently in antitrust cases and "common disaster (air crash) actions, patent and trademark suits, products liability actions and securities law violation actions."[296]

Section 1407 has been quite useful in expediting and reducing the expense of discovery. The section also permits judges to whom cases have been transferred (*transferee* courts) to consider a variety of pretrial motions,

---

[290] *See generally* WRIGHT & MILLER §§ 3861–3867; MANUAL, note 201, *supra*, § 20.13; Richard L. Marcus, *Cure-All For an Era of Dispersed Litigation? Toward a Maximalist Use of the Multidistrict Litigation Panel's Transfer Power*, 82 TULANE L. REV. 2245 (2008); Symposium, *Multidistrict Litigation and Aggregation Alternatives*, 31 SETON HALL L. REV. 877 (2001).

[291] Rule 42(a) contemplates joint hearing or trial and has been read to cover pretrial as well as trial proceedings. "If one of the purposes of consolidation for trial be to expedite the proceedings and avoid needless time and expense to the litigants and to the court, such objectives are as desirable and as attainable in the period utilized in preparing for trial." MANUAL, note 201, *supra*, § 31.11 (*quoting MacAlister v. Guterma*, 263 F.2d 65, 68 (2d Cir. 1958)).

[292] Rule 42(a) encompasses actions that "involve a common question of *law* or fact" (emphasis added).

[293] 28 U.S.C. § 1407(a). For additional discussion comparing Rule 42(a) with § 1407, see Diana E. Murphy, *Unified and Consolidated Complaints in Multidistrict Litigation*, 132 F.R.D. 597 (1991); Gregory R. Harris, Note, *Consolidation and Transfer in the Federal Courts: 28 U.S.C. Section 1407 Viewed in Light of Rule 42(a) and 28 U.S.C. Section 1404(a)*, 22 HASTINGS L.J. 1289 (1971).

[294] Comment, *The Judicial Panel on Multidistrict Litigation: Time for Rethinking*, 140 U. PA L. REV. 711, 1001 (1991).

[295] The panel "shall consist of seven circuit and district judges . . . no two of whom shall be from the same circuit." 28 U.S.C. § 1407(d).

[296] WRIGHT & MILLER § 3862 (*quoting* from the legislative history of § 1407). *See also* C. Clyde Atkins, *An Apologia for Transfer of Aviation Disaster Cases Under Section 1407* 38 J. AIR L. & COM. 205 (1972). *See, e.g., Allen v. Bayer Corp.*, 460 F.3d 1217, 1230 (9th Cir. 2006).

including motions capable of terminating all or part of the consolidated litigation.[297]

Section 1407(a) requires return to the courts of origin (*transferor* courts) of transferred cases which are still alive when multidistrict proceedings are over.[298] In practice, however, transferee courts had frequently retained the cases for consolidated trial. "Federal courts had achieved this result either by securing the consent of the parties or by invoking Section 1404(a), the general transfer provision"[299] to effect a "self-assignment" of the case for trial. In *Lexecon v. Milberg Weiss*,[300] however, the Supreme Court put an end to the practice, holding that self-assignment by a § 1407 transferee court is prohibited by the plain language of § 1407.[301]

---

[297] "Although the transferee judge has no jurisdiction to conduct a trial in the transferred cases, the judge may terminate actions by ruling on motions to dismiss, for summary judgment, or pursuant to settlement, and may enter consent decrees." MANUAL, note 201, *supra*, § 20.132.

[298] "Each action so transferred shall be remanded by the panel at or before the conclusion of such pretrial proceedings to the district from which it was transferred unless it shall have been previously terminated . . . ." 28 U.S.C. § 1407(a).

[299] WRIGHT & MILLER § 3862. On § 1404 transfer, see § 6.02[2], *supra*. On the whole, "the great majority of cases transferred by the Panel under section 1407 have been disposed of by transferee courts and not remanded to their original districts." *The Judicial Panel*, note 294, *supra*, at 1001–02. The Federal Courts Study Committee has recommended that § 1407 be amended to expressly authorize "consolidated trial as well as pretrial proceedings . . . ." REPORT OF THE FEDERAL COURTS STUDY COMMITTEE 45 (1990).

[300] 523 U.S. 26 (1998).

[301] *See* text quoted in note 298, *supra* (which uses the mandatory "shall").

Chapter 10

DISCOVERY

§ 10.01 OVERVIEW

Before filing a complaint, most plaintiffs and their lawyers make some effort to gather facts about the events that gave rise to suit. The lawyer ordinarily will interview the client and obtain information from the client's agents. He may also interview witnesses. But this kind of self-help can only advance the fact-gathering so far for several reasons. Many of the most important facts are often within the knowledge and control of the prospective defendant. A wary prospective defendant may stonewall the lawyer who tries to interview him. Ex parte (without the presence of the other party's lawyer) interviews also require the lawyer to walk a tight ethical line. Ethical rules in many jurisdictions prohibit the lawyer from stating or implying that he is disinterested, misstating the facts, engaging in conduct to embarrass, delay or burden a third person, or, in a few jurisdictions, giving advice or secretly taping the interview.[1] After the complaint has been filed, these rules prohibit him from communicating at all about the subject of suit with a party represented by a lawyer without that lawyer's consent (unless authorized by law).[2] This prohibition poses especially difficult problems of interpretation when the party is an organization and the witness is a present or former employee.[3]

Formal discovery of facts under court rules picks up where self-help leaves off and avoids most of these problems. Liberalization of such discovery was the most dramatic procedural reform brought by the Federal Rules of Civil Procedure in 1938.

> No longer can the time-honored cry of "fishing expedition" serve to preclude a party from inquiring into the facts underlying his opponent's case. Mutual knowledge of all relevant facts gathered by both parties is essential to proper litigation. To that end, either party may compel the other to disgorge whatever facts he has in his possession.[4]

---

[1] *See generally* Model Rules of Professional Conduct Rule 3.1 cmt. 1, Rules 4.1, 4.3, & 4.4 (2007) (hereinafter ABA Model Rules); Donald J. Farage, *Ex Parte Interrogation: Invasive Self-Help Discovery*, 94 Dick. L. Rev. 1 (1989).

[2] ABA Model Rules, note 1, *supra*, Rule 4.2.

[3] *See, e.g.*, Susan J. Becker, *Conducting Informal Discovery of a Party's Former Employees: Legal and Ethical Concerns and Constraints*, 51 Md. L. Rev. 239 (1992); Eugene P. Gurr, *Ethics of Conducting Ex Parte Interviews*, 3 St. John's J. Legal Comment. 234 (1988); John E. Iole & John D. Goetz, *Ethics or Procedure? A Discovery-Based Approach to Ex Parte Contacts with Former Employees of a Corporate Adversary*, 68 Notre Dame L. Rev. 81 (1992).

[4] *Hickman v. Taylor*, 329 U.S. 495, 507 (1947) (citation omitted).

Liberal discovery permitted the deemphasis of pleading and more liberal amendment. It made trial preparation more effective. Along with liberal joinder and broadened preclusion, liberal discovery was intended to promote judicial efficiency by making it easier to dispose of the entire controversy in one lawsuit.[5] The federal discovery rules proved so useful that a majority of states adopted them,[6] including some that have otherwise retained their own procedural rules.[7]

We therefore use the federal discovery rules as a model for the discussion of formal discovery. Part A explores *what* information can be discovered under the federal rules (the scope of discovery). Part B considers *how* such information can be discovered and used at trial (the mechanics of discovery). After discussing required disclosures, we survey the principal discovery methods, including depositions (oral or written examinations of live witnesses), interrogatories (written questions answered in writing), requests for production of documents and things or for entry upon land, and physical or mental examinations.[8] Finally, Part C considers the judicial *control* of discovery and discovery abuse.

The reported, visible law of discovery is relatively straightforward. Problems arise almost exclusively in its application, usually out of sight of the national reporters and law services.[9] Discovery rulings are often by magistrates rather than judges and rarely generate extensive trial (much less appellate) opinions.[10] As a result, lower court decisions should often be viewed as fact-bound rulings rather than as legal precedents. Moreover, litigants often negotiate discovery disputes outside the court, as they are encouraged and authorized to do by Rule 29. "The very existence of the rules encourages lawyers to use more efficient and economical means to exchange information [including] [b]ilateral trading of documents, cooperative bartering of information, [and] mutual alteration of procedures . . . ."[11]

Litigants use discovery for overlapping purposes. The most significant is to prepare for trial and to avert surprise. Discovery permits a plaintiff who has commenced suit on the barest of facts to flesh out and, with liberal amendment,

---

[5] On the interrelation of pleading, complex litigation, discovery and preclusion in modern civil procedure, see JAMES, HAZARD & LEUBSDORF § 11.16; Gene R. Shreve, *Preclusion and Federal Choice of Law*, 64 TEX. L. REV. 1209, 1215 (1986).

[6] *See* FRIEDENTHAL, KANE & MILLER § 7.1.

[7] *See, e.g.*, VA. RULES ANN. 4:1–4:12 (2000) (adopting federal discovery rules almost verbatim, while otherwise retaining vestiges of code and common law pleading); FLA. R. CIV. P. 1.280–1.380 (patterned on federal discovery provisions as amended in 1970).

[8] Requests for admission are an additional discovery method, but are primarily used at the close of discovery as a pretrial device. They are therefore discussed as such in § 12.02, *infra*.

[9] "Thankfully, most of the mountainous volume of the District Courts' pre-trial activity never reaches the pages of a reporter or the files of a computer." *Union City Barge Line, Inc. v. Union Carbide Corp.*, 823 F.2d 129, 134 n.10 (5th Cir. 1987).

[10] This is in part because of the general federal rule against interlocutory appellate review. *See* §§ 13.02 & 13.03, *infra*.

[11] ROGER S. HAYDOCK & DAVID F. HERR, DISCOVERY PRACTICE § 1.1 (4th ed. 2002).

even alter his case for trial.[12] It also affords parties opposing claims the same opportunity to prepare for trial. In addition, discovery helps to streamline the trial itself by permitting pretrial authentication of documents, "nailing down" the likely testimony of witnesses, and creating a storehouse of recollection-refreshing and impeaching material.[13]

On the other hand, the removal of all surprise at trial is not necessarily beneficial. Judge Aldrich observed:

> Not merely may too many rehearsals, in the form of too much discovery, take the bloom off the opening night, but this absence of freshness may make the performance sterile. A certain amount of surprise is often the catalyst which precipitates the truth. Alternatively it may serve as a medium by which the court or jury may gauge the accuracy of the account.[14]

Realizing this, the experienced litigator seeks both to prepare as thoroughly as possible for trial and to preserve as much surprise as possible in her case. These dual purposes coexist uneasily and often strain the discovery rules.

A second purpose of discovery is to preserve evidence for trial. When witnesses are likely to be unavailable for trial, due to age, illness or location beyond the reach of the trial court, their testimony can be preserved by deposition. The discoverer with this purpose cannot simply fish for information. She must be concerned about the content and admissibility of the elicited testimony at trial because she has no second chance at the witness.[15]

Third, discovery can be used to narrow or eliminate issues. By ascertaining whether and which issues are genuinely disputed, discovery can set up Rule 12(b) dismissals, summary judgment, and issue-narrowing or eliminating pretrial orders that can substantially simplify trial.[16] Perhaps even more important in light of litigation statistics, this use of discovery may even encourage settlement.[17] The discoverer with this objective may, contrary to the usual practice, *invite* discovery of the strengths of her case.

But the sheer burden of discovery can also extort settlement, particularly when the resources of the parties are unequal.[18] Discovery thus can have a

---

[12] At the same time, liberal discovery, pleading, and amendment rules can combine to invite frivolous litigation by making it easier for plaintiff's counsel to file first and closely examine the claim later. Attorney certification requirements and sanctions for improper certification offer some protection against this. *See* Rule 11 (certification for pleadings and motion papers) discussed in § 8.05[2], *supra*, and Rule 26(g) (certification of discovery requests, responses and objections), discussed in § 10.13[1], *infra*.

[13] *See, e.g.*, HAYDOCK & HERR, note 11, *supra*, § 1.1; JAMES, HAZARD, & LEUBSDORF § 5.2.

[14] *Margeson v. Boston & Me. R.R.*, 16 F.R.D. 200, 201 (D. Mass. 1954).

[15] *See* HAYDOCK & HERR, note 11, *supra*, § 3.4.2.

[16] HAYDOCK & HERR, note 11, *supra*, § 1.1.

[17] *But cf. MOORE* § 26.02 (noting that discovery may discourage settlement and that settlement pressures may encourage withholding of unfavorable matter in discovery).

[18] *See MOORE* § 26.02.

fourth (and illicit) purpose: harassment, delay and attrition.[19] The Supreme
Court has noted that

> to the extent that . . . [discovery] permits a plaintiff with a largely
> groundless claim to simply take up the time of a number of other
> people, with the right to do so representing an *in terrorem* increment
> of settlement value, rather than a reasonably founded hope that the
> process will reveal relevant evidence, it is a social cost rather than a
> benefit.[20]

Considerable uncertainty remains over the prevalence of the problem and the
most effective cure.[21]

The discoverer's mix of purposes determines the scope, frequency, and
methods of the discovery she will pursue. We shall see that most discovery goes
on without court involvement. When a party does ask for judicial intervention
(either to block or coerce discovery), a comparison of the benefits of proper
discovery with the costs of improper or excessive discovery suggests how much
and what kind of control a court should impose. Read the remaining sections of
this chapter with this comparison in mind.

PART A.
Scope of Discovery

§ 10.02   IN GENERAL

Rule 26(b) describes what may be discovered under the federal rules[22] and
effectively erects a presumption of discoverability.[23] A party may discover any
matter that is (1) "relevant to any party's claim or defense" and reasonably
calculated to lead to discovery of admissible evidence, and neither (2) privileged
nor (3) prepared or acquired in anticipation of litigation or for trial, unless (4)
discovery has been otherwise limited by a protective order of the court. A
special showing is required for discovery of *work product* prepared or acquired
in anticipation of litigation or for trial. Sections 10.03 to 10.06 successively treat
each of these aspects of the scope of discovery, except that the discussion of

---

[19] *See Herbert v. Lando*, 441 U.S. 153, 202 (1979) (Marshall, J., dissenting) (libel case in which
defendant's editor was deposed intermittently for one year, yielding 3000 pages of testimony and
240 exhibits in 26 volumes of transcript).

[20] *Blue Chip Stamps v. Manor Drug Stores*, 421 U.S. 723, 741 (1975).

[21] *See* § 10.12 (abuse of discovery), *infra*.

[22] What *must* be discovered (required disclosures) is discussed in Part B, section 10.07, together
with other general aspects of the mechanics of discovery. Limitations on the permissible scope of
discovery apply to required disclosures.

[23] Disputes concerning the scope of discovery are usually resolved in favor of allowing discovery.
This outcome reflects in part judges' and magistrates' awareness that orders allowing discovery are
far less likely to be reversed on an eventual appeal than orders limiting or prohibiting it. HAYDOCK
& HERR, note 11, *supra*, § 1.4.

protective orders has been deferred to § 10.13[3] in Part C on the control of discovery.

§ 10.03 THE FADING FEDERAL PRESUMPTION OF DISCOVERABILITY

[1]   Relevant to the Claim or Defense of Any Party

Rule 26(b)(1) originally fixed the scope of discovery as "relevant to the subject matter." One appellate court paraphrased it as "any matter that bears on, or reasonably could lead to other matter that could bear on, any issue that is or may be in the case, . . . not limited to issues raised by the pleadings . . . [or] to [the] merits of the case . . . ."[24] In antitrust or business tort litigation, for example, virtually any matter involving the industry of which the parties are part arguably satisfied that standard. In securities fraud litigation, theoretically any factor that may affect the market for the stock at issue would satisfy that standard. In light of the generality with which discovery requests can be framed under the rules, some questioned whether the original relevant-to-the-subject-matter standard imposed any practical limit on federal discovery.

Heeding these doubts, the rulemakers changed the relevancy standard in 2000 by differentiating party-controlled discovery from court-authorized discovery. For the former, the standard was changed to "relevant to the claim or defense of any party."[25] This standard is narrower than the original standard because it is tied to the pleadings (which assert the claims or defenses of the parties), but also arguably broader than the alternative standard "relevant to the issues," which had initially been adopted by some states[26] and urged by some critics of the original rule. At the same time, the rulemakers authorized the court, on good cause shown, to allow discovery under the original "relevant-to-the-subject-matter" discovery standard.[27]

Whether the change in the relevancy standard for party-controlled discovery has made much difference, standing alone, is questionable. The Advisory Committee itself admitted that the dividing line between the standards "cannot be defined with precision." It then proceeded to suggest that in a negligence or product liability suit arising from one incident, other "incidents of the same type, or involving the same product, could be properly discovered under the revised standard."[28] Ironically, however, it was precisely in products liability suits that some defense lawyers said that the old standard was abused to cast a dragnet for remotely relevant information about other

---

[24] *Oppenheimer Fund, Inc. v. Sanders*, 437 U.S. 340, 351 & n.12 (1978) (citations omitted). *Compare Kelly v. Nationwide Mut. Ins. Co.*, 188 N.E.2d 445 (Ohio C.P. 1963) (applying relevancy-to-the-issues standard under former Ohio rules).

[25] Rule 26(b)(1).

[26] *E.g.*, Ohio. *See Kelly*, 188 N.E.2d 445 (discussing old and new Ohio rules).

[27] Rule 26(b)(1).

[28] Rule 26(b)(1) advisory committee's note (2000).

incidents and the same type of products. The Advisory Committee's own explanations, therefore, lend some credence to the prediction that this "semantic change [is] unlikely to have much salutary effect on the conduct of discovery in the hurly-burly world of litigation."[29] A survey of the cases agrees; "[t]he amendment does not effect a dramatic change in the scope of discovery."[30]

On the other hand, the change in the relevancy standard for party-controlled discovery should not be viewed in isolation from the authorization for court-controlled discovery under the old relevancy standard. Responding to the common complaint of litigators that courts have failed to intervene in discovery disputes early or often enough, the Advisory Committee explained that the latter part of the amendment "is designed to involve the court more actively in regulating the breadth of sweeping or contentious discovery."[31] Courts may incrementally enforce the "claim or defense" standard more often, given the safety valve of broader discovery for good cause shown, and thus sometimes play a more active role in managing more sweeping discovery. Considering both of these effects of the rule amendment, at least one commentator has concluded that it reversed the presumption of discoverability:

> Instead of assuming that any matter relevant to the subject matter is discoverable, with the burden on the party opposing discovery to show non-relevance, burden, or privilege, the presumption is that information beyond "claims or defenses" is *not* discoverable. The burden is newly placed on the party seeking discovery either to convince the judge that the information sought falls within the core definition of relevance or to make an undefined and "flexible" showing that there is good cause to allow further discovery.[32]

Finally, as a corollary of the amendment's effect on discovery, some commentators predicted that it would impact pleading. They speculated that the "claim or defense" standard would cause plaintiffs to draft more particu-larized allegations in order to obtain needed discovery, threatening abandon-ment of notice pleading and a return to "fact pleading"[33] with all of its problems[34] and attendant motion practice.[35] Any such impact of the amend-

---

[29] John S. Beckerman, *Confronting Civil Discovery's Fatal Flaws*, 84 MINN. L. REV. 505, 510–11 (2000).

[30] WRIGHT & MILLER § 2008 (2008 Pocket Part).

[31] Rule 26(b)(1) advisory committee's notes (2000).

[32] Elizabeth G. Thornburg, *Giving the "Haves" a Little More: Considering the 1998 Discovery Proposals*, 52 SMU L. REV. 229, 251–52 (1999) (emphasis in original) (commenting on relevancy standard in 1998 proposal identical to that adopted in 2000). *See also* Jeffrey W. Stempel, *Politics and Sociology in Civil Rulemaking: Errors of Scope*, 52 ALA. L. REV. 529, 584–86 (2001) (agreeing that rule change shifts "burden of uncertainty" from those opposing discovery to those seeking it, and finding change "misguided" for this and other reasons).

[33] *See, e.g.*, Beckerman, note 29, *supra*, at 541; Carl Tobias, *Congress and the 2000 Federal Civil Rules Amendments*, 22 CARDOZO L. REV. 75, 83 (2000).

[34] *See* § 8.03[3] (discussing the specificity of fact pleading).

ment will presumably only be reinforced by the Supreme Court's ambiguous endorsement of the plausibility standard of pleading in *Bell Atlantic Corp. v. Twombly*.[36]

Skepticism about the semantic precision of the amendment may be beside the point. The change was really intended as a signal to the parties to try to confine discovery to the pleadings and to the court to watch closely if more is sought. Even if the change failed to supply a bright line for changing the scope of discovery in individual cases, it probably succeeded on the Advisory Committee's terms if it caused a change in the mind set of litigators and the courts which reduces the breadth of discovery at the margins.[37]

A better answer may be to limit directly the amount of discovery, or to emphasize and expand the courts' discretionary powers to control discovery on an ad hoc basis. The rulemakers have done both. In 1993 and again in 2000, they amended the discovery rules to impose quantitative limits on depositions and interrogatories, as we discuss in Part B. They also authorized courts to limit discovery pursuant to Rule 26(b)(2) when "the burden or expense of the proposed discovery outweighs its likely benefit." The rule had previously been amended in 1983 to give the courts the power to control "the frequency or extent of use" of discovery.[38]

[2]   Reasonably Calculated to Lead to the Discovery of Admissible Evidence

Rule 26(b)(1) provides that "[r]elevant information need not be admissible at the trial if the discovery appears reasonably calculated to lead to the discovery of admissible evidence." What a witness has heard about the issues in the case, for example, is usually hearsay which may be inadmissible at trial unless it falls within an exception to the evidentiary rule against hearsay or constitutes an admission by a party. It is still discoverable, however, because it may lead to the discovery of the identity of fact witnesses (witnesses to the incident giving rise to the claim and others with personal knowledge of relevant facts)[39] or other facts that might themselves be admissible. Similarly,

---

[35] Gregory P. Joseph, *Civil Rules II*, Nat'l L.J., April 24, 2000, A17 ("It would be reasonable to anticipate more Rule 12 motion practice, including Rule 12(f) motions to strike . . . which now may have a discernible impact on the scope of discovery.").

[36] 550 U.S. 544 (2007). *See* § 8.04[1][d], *supra*.

[37] *See generally* Christopher C. Frost, *The Sound and the Fury or the Sound of Silence: Evaluating the Pre-Amendment Predictions and Post-Amendment Effects of the Discovery Scope-Narrowing Language in the 2000 Amendments to Federal Rule of Civil Procedure 26(b)(1)*, 37 Ga. L. Rev. 1039 (2003).

[38] *See* § 10.13[2] (managerial orders), *infra*.

[39] Rule 26(a)(1) requires initial disclosure of the identity of fact witnesses, and Rule 26(a)(3) requires pretrial disclosure of the identity of trial witnesses (persons who will be called to testify). Prior to the 1993 amendment mandating such disclosures, some courts ruled that a party is not entitled to discover the identity of trial witnesses. They reasoned that the discoveree often does not know her trial witnesses until the eve of trial, or that the identity of such witnesses should be protected as work product under Rule 26(b)(3). Some state courts still follow this reasoning, although many require the mutual identification of trial witnesses in connection with a final pretrial

information about a subsequent repair may be inadmissible at trial to prove negligence because of the public policy to encourage such repairs.[40] Nevertheless, it is discoverable as relevant to a claim in a negligence action.[41]

[3]   Examples and Problem Areas

[a]   Information Already in the Discoverer's Possession

Even when the discoverer already knows or possesses certain information, he is entitled to discover it from his adversary. A party is entitled to discover what the other parties know and contend, in order to facilitate his own preparation and possible settlement. Moreover, knowledge is not the same thing as proof, which is what will be required at trial. A party is entitled to whatever jury impact he can get from proving the facts through evidence produced by his adversary. A court always retains the power, however, to intervene in particular cases when discovery becomes "*unreasonably cumulative or duplicative* . . . [or] the party seeking discovery has had ample opportunity to obtain the information by discovery in the action . . . ."[42] If the opposing party has already admitted a fact, for example, a court might conclude that discovery of the fact is "unreasonably cumulative," or that the burden or expense of such discovery outweighs its likely benefit.[43]

[b]   Impeachment Material

Except for required disclosures under Rule 26(a)(1)-(3)[44] discovery is not limited to direct substantive evidence, but includes material that may impeach an opponent's witnesses. Discovery of material that may impeach the discoverer's own witnesses has been more troublesome to the courts. Some have held that discovery is ordinarily not proper "where the only purpose . . . is to prevent effective cross-examination."[45]

Discovery of surveillance evidence, often movies made by defendant's representatives of plaintiff at work or play after the accident in a personal injury case, furnishes a good example. Many courts reason that surveillance movies, created after commencement of the litigation, have nothing to do with the merits, contain information already intimately and better known to the discoverer, and serve as a possible check on a "fertile field for fraud and

---

conference. *See, e.g., Ladner v. Ladner*, 436 So. 2d 1366, 1372 (Miss. 1983) (construing state discovery rule modeled on Rule 26(b)). *See generally* § 12.03 (pretrial conference), *infra*.

[40] FED. R. EVID. 407 advisory committee's note.

[41] *See, e.g., Culligan v. Yamaha Motor Corp., U.S.A.*, 110 F.R.D. 122, 124 (S.D.N.Y. 1986).

[42] Rule 26(b)(2)(C)(i) & (ii) (emphasis supplied). *See* § 10.13[2] (managerial orders), *infra*.

[43] *See* Rule 26(b)(2)(C)(i) & (iii). *But see Cornet Stores v. Superior Court*, 492 P.2d 1191 (Ariz. 1972) (stipulation that plaintiff was highest paid manager will not foreclose discovery of pay of other managers in wrongful discharge action).

[44] *See* § 10.07, *infra*.

[45] *Stone v. Marine Transp. Lines, Inc.*, 23 F.R.D. 222, 226 (D. Md. 1959).

magnification."[46] Moreover, impeachment material is gathered or developed in preparation for trial, and thus may fall within the spirit, if not always the letter, of Rule 26(b)(3)'s protection for work product.[47]

The trend in the modern cases, however, is to require discovery of even impeachment material. One important reason is that the assumption that matter useful for impeachment has nothing to do with the merits is not always reliable. The same matter can be used to advance a party's substantive position and to impeach.[48]

A second and more commonly articulated reason is that impeachment material poses its own risk of fraud and magnification. In *Boldt v. Sanders*,[49] for example, one of the plaintiffs in a personal injury action denied having suffered any prior accidents or personal injuries and sought discovery from defendant of any information that would contradict that denial. Defendant's objection rested on "the premise that defendant's evidence which plaintiffs seek to elicit constitutes the unblemished truth which, if prematurely disclosed, will prevent defendant from revealing to the jury the sham and perjury inherent in plaintiffs' claims."[50] The court rejected this premise, posing the equally plausible hypothetical of the defendant who "has resorted to fraud and perjury in fabricating pictures of what purport to be plaintiff's physical activities subsequent to the accident, and has manufactured evidence to prove that plaintiff sustained his injuries in prior accidents."[51] Absent a principled basis for choosing between these possibilities, the court fell back on the general rule of mutual discoverability.[52]

[c]   Opinions and Contentions

Discovery is not limited to facts, but may also include opinions held by non-experts[53] and contentions regarding the facts or the application of law to the facts. This scope of discovery is expressly set out in Rule 33(b) concerning interrogatories and Rule 36(a) concerning requests for admissions, because they are most often used to probe opinions or contentions. But it is also implicit in Rule 26(b)(1)'s generic statement of the scope of discovery.[54] The only limitation is that the discoveree may defer responding until he has completed

---

[46] *Zimmerman v. Superior Court*, 402 P.2d 212, 219 (Ariz. 1965) (Struckmeyer, J., dissenting).

[47] *See DiMichel v. South Buffalo Ry. Co.*, 604 N.E.2d 63 (N.Y. 1992), *cert. denied sub nom Poole v. Consolidated Rail Corp.*, 510 U.S. 816 (1993). *See generally* § 10.05 (work product), *infra*.

[48] *See* WRIGHT § 81.

[49] 111 N.W.2d 225 (Minn. 1961).

[50] 111 N.W.2d at 227.

[51] 111 N.W.2d at 227.

[52] Many courts have qualified that rule with regard to impeachment material, however, by giving the discoveree the opportunity to depose the discoverer first before having to disclose the impeachment material. *See, e.g., Daniels v. National R.R. Passenger Corp.*, 110 F.R.D. 160, 161 (S.D.N.Y. 1986).

[53] For discussion of the discovery of opinions held by experts, see § 10.06, *infra*.

[54] *See* MOORE §§ 26.41, 26.43.

discovery of his own and thus had an opportunity to form informed opinions and contentions.[55]

The discoverer, however, may not ask what the law is, because the parties' legal conclusions are considered irrelevant. Only the court can say what the law is.[56] Similarly, the discoverer is not entitled to the discoveree's rank speculation on hypothetical facts, unrelated to the facts or to the application of the law to the facts in the case.[57] Relevancy is probably also at the bottom of this restriction because untrammeled speculation by a witness or a party is arguably not relevant to anything.

[d]   Insurance and Other Information About Financial Assets

Rule 26(a)(1) expressly requires disclosure of insurance agreements available to satisfy any or all of any eventual judgment, even though they remain inadmissible at trial. Prior to the 1970 amendment to the rule, some federal courts had denied discovery on relevancy grounds, and many states still do.[58] But the existence of insurance can be relevant to the issue of ownership. More important, it almost always bears significantly on settlement negotiations. It was chiefly to advance the social policy of encouraging settlement that the 1970 amendment made insurance agreements expressly discoverable.

Other information concerning the discoveree's financial position might also be useful in settlement negotiations, but is far less open to discovery. In support of the 1970 amendment, the Advisory Committee observed that insurance is an asset created specifically to satisfy claims, the insurer often controls the lawsuit, the information is usually available only from the insured or the insurer, and no privacy concerns are implicated by its discoverability.[59] None of these considerations in allowing discovery of insurance agreements applies to routine discovery of other financial assets. A party's general assets are obviously not created for the express purpose of satisfying a legal claim and are usually invested with significant privacy interests.

Accordingly, unless the amount of a party's assets is itself a relevant issue in the case, as it would be in an action to enforce a money judgment or in an action for punitive damages measured by the amount of the assets,[60] discovery of assets other than insurance, and of related information such as tax returns

---

[55] *See* Rules 33(b) & 36(a).

[56] *See, e.g., O'Brien v. International Bhd. of Elec. Workers*, 443 F. Supp. 1182 (N.D. Ga. 1977) (an interrogatory requesting an explanation as to why provisions of a union constitution are not deprived of effect by a federal statute seeks purely legal conclusions).

[57] Moore § 26.41.

[58] *See* James, Hazard, & Leubsdorf § 5.8 (noting arguments against relevancy in an action against the insured); Annotation, *Pretrial Examination or Discovery to Ascertain from Defendant in Action for Injury, Death, or Damages, Existence and Amount of Liability Insurance and Insurer's Identity*, 13 A.L.R.3d 822 (1967 & 2000 Supp.).

[59] Rule 26(b)(2) advisory committee's note (1970).

[60] *See, e.g., Renshaw v. Ravert*, 82 F.R.D. 361, 363 (E.D. Pa. 1979) (punitive damages).

and bank statements, is sometimes denied. Even when assets are relevant and discoverable, privacy concerns may warrant postponing discovery until the discoveree has had an opportunity to contest the claim to which the assets are relevant.[61]

[e]   Electronic Information[62]

Rule 34 was originally called "Discovery and Production of Documents and Things for Inspection, Copying, or Photographing." While "documents" could be (and was) construed to include various kinds of electronically stored information, it was not ideally suited to the task. Neither were the rules themselves, as they understandably reflected the paper-based mind set of the original rulemakers. Technology has long since overtaken that mind set. Information that was maintained and communicated by paper is now maintained in electronic files that often are never printed out, spreadsheets, emails, websites, and text messages, stored on floppy discs, CD-ROMs, laser discs, thumb drives, zip drives, and DVDs, at the office and at home, on local and on distant servers, on networked computers and stand-alone laptops, and on PDAs, and MP3 players. Even hard copies are now scanned and digitized (and often destroyed once thus electronically preserved).[63] The electronically stored information include metadata (data about the data embedded in the file, containing markers that may show changes, author identity, and creation and modification dates) that is not usually reflected in a printout of the data and of which the naïve author may therefore be unaware, other hidden data (comments, highlights, etc.), residual deleted data (data that has been "deleted" but resides on the computer until overwritten by a new file),[64] "backup tapes" maintained for archival or data-recovery purposes, and "legacy data" (data that can be used only by superseded computer systems or software).[65] In 2005, it was reported that "more than 90% of all corporate information . . . is electronic; North American businesses exchange over 2.5 trillion e-mails per day; . . . less than 1% of all communication will ever appear in paper form; and, on average, a 1000-person corporation will generate nearly 2 million e-mails annually."[66] In 2008 and beyond, these figures are conservative.

---

[61] *See, e.g., Larriva v. Montiel*, 691 P.2d 735, 737–38 (Ariz. Ct. App. 1984) (discoverer must first make *prima facie* showing that he will be entitled to present punitive damages claim to jury).

[62] *See, e.g.,* Michael Arkfeld, Arkfeld on Electronic Discovery and Evidence (2d ed. 2008); John K. Rabiej, *Discovery of Electronically Stored Information*, Moore ch. 37A; Shira A. Scheindlin, E-Discovery: The Newly Amended Federal Rules of Civil Procedure (2006); The Sedona Principles: Best Practices, Recommendations & Principles for Addressing Electronic Document Discovery (The Sedona Conference Working Group Series, July 2005 ver.), available generally at http://www.thesedonaconference.org.

[63] *See generally* Moore § 37A.02[1]–[4].

[64] Moore § 37A.03[1]–[3].

[65] Fed. R. Civ. P. 34 advisory committee's note (2006).

[66] Harvey L. Kaplan, *Electronic Discovery in the 21st Century: Is Help on the Way?*, 733 PLI/Lit 65, 67 (2005) (citations omitted).

This explosion of electronically stored information causes a raft of discovery problems. First, although it usually dramatically lowered *search costs*,[67] the sheer volume of electronically stored information coupled with problems of formatting often make *production costs* much higher, raising new and thorny questions of discovery cost allocation. Thus, one court commented on a discovery demand for backup tapes that

> [i]t must be recalled that ordering the producing party to restore backup tapes upon a showing of likelihood that they will contain relevant information in every case gives the plaintiff a gigantic club with which to beat his opponent into settlement. No corporate president in her right mind would fail to settle a lawsuit for $100,000 if the restoration of backup tapes would cost $300,000. While that scenario might warm the cockles of certain lawyers' hearts, no one would accuse it of being just.[68]

Second, the variety of electronically stored information — even versions of the same data (PDF image of the word processing document, or electronic file with metadata?) poses questions of the form of disclosure. Third, data retention policies test traditional understandings about data preservation — so-called "litigation holds" to preserve documents during the pendency of suit. Fourth, the costs of privilege review (reviewing documents before disclosure to cull out and withhold privileged documents) and risks of inadvertent disclosure are magnified by electronically stored information. Of course, lawyers can still send their most junior associates to the computer screen (just as they once sent them to dusty storage rooms) to review the data for privileged matter before making disclosures, but

> [w]ith electronically stored information, . . . difficulties [of wasteful privilege review] may become more acute due to volume of such material and the informality that attends the use of some forms of electronic communication such as e-mail. In addition, the possibility that computer programs may retain draft language, marginal notes and other items not apparent to the reader introduces further complexities for the privilege-review process.[69]

Some of these problems — and some solutions — were illustrated in an early landmark case, *Zubulake v. UBS Warburg LLC*.[70] In *Zubulake*, the plaintiff sued for gender discrimination and sought discovery of emails among defendant's employees. Their relevancy was undisputed; plaintiff had already obtained a potential "smoking gun" email "suggesting that she be fired 'ASAP'

---

[67] The Supreme Court foresaw this impact as early as 1978. *See Oppenheimer Fund, Inc. v. Sanders*, 437 U.S. 340, 362 (1978) ("[A]lthough it may be expensive to retrieve information stored in computers when no program yet exists for the particular job, there is no reason to think that the same information could be extracted any less expensively if the records were kept in less modern forms. Indeed, one might expect the reverse to be true, for otherwise computers would not have gained such widespread use in the storing and handling of information.").

[68] *McPeek v. Ashcroft*, 202 F.R.D. 31, 34 (D.D.C. 2001).

[69] WRIGHT & MILLER § 2051.1.

[70] 217 F.R.D. 309 (S.D.N.Y. 2003).

after her EEOC charge was filed, in part so that she would not be eligible for year-end bonuses."[71] Defendant produced 350 pages of documents, including hundreds of emails, but balked at producing emails from backup tapes at an alleged cost of $300,000. Certain emails were preserved on backup tapes that took periodic "snapshots" of email traffic, thus preserving some that were later deleted by users, but also missing some that were created and deleted between backups. Another set of emails from certain regulated employees were preserved on optical disks. Search costs varied by medium. A software program permitted rapid word searches of the optical disks, but the backup disks took five days to restore, after which their emails had to be imported into a common email application and then reviewed one at a time.

The court rejected the argument that costs should be shifted to the responding party in every E-discovery dispute. "'The presumption is that the responding party must bear the expense of complying with discovery requests . . . ,'" the court asserted, and there is no exception for E-discovery.[72] Cost-shifting, however, could be considered when electronic discovery places an undue burden on the responding party. In an E-discovery dispute, the cost of production depends primarily on whether the data is kept in an accessible or inaccessible format[73] which, in turn, depends largely on the media on which it is stored. The court then found that active email files and those stored on easily searched optical disks were reasonably accessible, but those on the backup tapes were not.

It was therefore appropriate for the court to consider cost-shifting to the plaintiff, taking into account a variety of factors, most of them suggested by what is now Rule 26(b)(2)(C).[74] They included the specificity of the discovery request; the availability of such information from other sources; the total cost of production, compared to the amount in controversy and the resources of each party; the relative ability of each party to control costs and its incentive to do so; the importance of the issues at stake in the litigation; and the relative benefits to the parties of obtaining the information. The court then ordered defendant to produce the accessible emails and emails at its expense from five sample backup tapes chosen by plaintiff. Based on the costs of accessing the sample, the court would then revisit the cost allocation issue for any remaining backup tapes on which plaintiff insisted.

---

[71] 217 F.R.D. at 312 n.8.

[72] 217 F.R.D. at 317, quoting *Oppenheimer Fund*, 437 U.S. at 358.

[73] "Examples of inaccessible paper documents could include (a) documents in storage in a difficult to reach place; (b) documents converted to microfiche and not easily readable; or (c) documents kept haphazardly, with no indexing system, in quantities that make page-by-page searches impracticable. But in the world of electronic data, thanks to search engines, any data that is retained in a machine readable format is typically accessible." 217 F.R.D. at 318 (citation omitted).

[74] The 2006 rule amendments have subsequently added a cost-benefit rule tailored to E-discovery disputes, modeled in part on the court's analysis in *Zubulake*. *See* Rule 26(b)(2)(B). *See* Henry S. Noyes, *Good Cause Is Bad Medicine for the New E-Discovery Rules*, 21 Harv. J. L. & Tech. 50 (2007).

In the last edition of this hornbook, we said that the issues posed by discovery of electronically stored information "appear to be sufficiently serious as to call for an overhaul of Rule 34, if not other anachronistically document-oriented discovery rules, in the near future." The rulemakers undertook that overhaul in 2006. But those who look to the rule changes for "E-discovery" for detailed guidance in particular cases will be disappointed. Instead, the rulemakers mainly empowered the courts and the parties to develop detailed solutions themselves, in light of the what *Zubulake* identifies as the predicate for resolving E-discovery disputes: "understanding the responding party's computer system, both with respect to active and stored data."

§ 10.04 THE NON-DISCOVERABILITY OF PRIVILEGED MATTER

Discovery in every jurisdiction extends only to unprivileged matters.[75] *Privilege* is a legal term of art. It refers to the protection from disclosure that the common law, statute, or rule[76] affords particular communications in order to promote relationships to which confidential communication is essential. Although their elements vary, most privileges require the communications for which the privilege is sought (1) to have been made with an expectation of confidentiality, that is (2) essential to a socially approved relationship or purpose and (3) has not been waived by disclosure of the contents of the communications to persons outside the relationship.[77] The attorney-client, doctor-patient, priest-penitent, spousal privilege, and the privilege against self-incrimination are commonly recognized privileges.[78] A privilege that will bar evidence at trial will also prevent disclosure of the same evidence in discovery. This is because violation of the confidence compromises the relationship in either event.

Privileges are narrowly construed in order to minimize their effect on liberal disclosure.[79] The proponent of a privilege has the burden of establishing its existence. This ordinarily requires him to lay a foundation for the existence of the privilege by supplying enough information about the circumstances of the communication to show that it is privileged — a "privilege log." This foundation requirement is codified in Rule 26(b)(5). The 1993 Advisory Committee cautions that a party's failure to supply this information will not only subject it to sanctions under Rule 37, but may also waive the privilege.[80]

---

[75] *See, e.g.*, Rule 26(b)(1).

[76] *See, e.g.*, FED. R. EVID. 501 (incorporating federal common law).

[77] *See, e.g.*, HAYDOCK & HERR, note 11, *supra*, § 2.1.

[78] Litigants, and occasionally courts, loosely and inaccurately describe as "privileges" the protection accorded to trial preparation materials, which are discoverable upon the proper special showing, *see* §§ 10.05 & 10.06, *infra*, or to materials like trade secrets or membership lists, which are discoverable but often subject to discovery limitations established by a court order to protect their confidentiality. *See* § 10.13[3], *infra*.

[79] *Moore* § 26.47[1].

[80] Because preparing the privilege log can itself be burdensome, and because waiver is a harsh sanction, some courts have reserved the sanction for unjustifiably delayed, boilerplate privilege logs

Although detailed discussion of particular privileges belongs to the law of evidence rather than to civil procedure, it is useful to develop the attorney-client privilege as an example. Probably the classic judicial statement of the privilege is found in *United States v. United Shoe Machinery Corp.*:[81]

> The privilege applies only if (1) the asserted holder of the privilege is or sought to become a client; (2) the person to whom the communication was made (a) is a member of the bar of a court, or his subordinate and (b) in connection with this communication is acting as a lawyer; (3) the communication relates to a fact of which the attorney was informed (a) by his client (b) without the presence of strangers (c) for the purpose of securing primarily either (i) an opinion on law or (ii) legal services or (iii) assistance in some legal proceeding, and not (d) for the purpose of committing a crime or tort; and (4) the privilege has been (a) claimed and (b) not waived by the client.

It is the communication itself, not the underlying facts, that is privileged.[82] Thus a client cannot cloak evidence with the privilege simply by telling it to his lawyer. The privilege is unavailable if third parties were present at the communication, destroying its confidentiality, or if the client has waived it by subsequent disclosure.[83] Finally, the privilege is not available to protect communications made for improper purposes.[84]

The possibility of waiver always haunts lawyers in the discovery process and usually prompts tedious privilege reviews of documents before disclosures are made, as well as the mandated preparation of a privilege log for the withheld documents. Nevertheless, mistakes are made and privileged material may be inadvertently disclosed. Rule 26(b)(5) now provides that the producing party may notify the recipient of the claim of privilege after an inadvertent disclosure. The recipient must then return the putatively privileged matter, sequester, or destroy it, and may not use or disclose it until any dispute about the availability of the privilege is resolved. The law of waiver is unchanged,[85] but the rule now provides a more orderly process for applying it after an inadvertent disclosure.

---

and have endorsed a "holistic reasonableness analysis" for other inadequacies in the log. *See Burlington N. & Santa Fe Ry. Co. v. United States Dist. Court for the Dist. of Mont.*, 408 F.3d 1142, 1149 (9th Cir.) (rejecting a per se waiver rule, but upholding waiver where boilerplate privilege log was filed five months late), *cert. denied*, 546 U.S. 939 (2005).

[81] 89 F. Supp. 357, 358–59 (D. Mass. 1950). *See generally* EDNA S. EPSTEIN, THE ATTORNEY-CLIENT PRIVILEGE AND THE WORK PRODUCT DOCTRINE (5th ed. 2007); JOHN W. GERGACZ, ATTORNEY-CORPORATE CLIENT PRIVILEGE (3d ed. 2000); PAUL R. RICE ET AL., ATTORNEY-CLIENT PRIVILEGE IN THE UNITED STATES (2d ed. 1999).

[82] *See, e.g., Upjohn Co. v. United States*, 449 U.S. 383, 395–96 (1981).

[83] Indeed, one court has even held the privilege waived by the clients' discarding of privileged documents in a trash dumpster from which they were removed by an enterprising if pungent third party. *Suburban Sew 'N Sweep, Inc. v. Swiss-Bernina, Inc.*, 91 F.R.D. 254 (N.D. Ill. 1981).

[84] *See generally* RICE, note 81, *supra*, §§ 8.2–8.15.

[85] That law, and the ethical considerations it implicates, is changing in response to disclosures of metadata (see § 10.03[e], *supra*). State bar associations are developing different rules about the consequences of disclosures of metadata and the recipients' obligations not to use and to return such data. *See generally* Courtney Ingraffic Barton, *E-Discovery Ethics — Highlights from 2007*, 76 U.S.L.W. 2387 (Jan. 8, 2008). As a general rule, the burden is on the sender to remove metadata.

§ 10.05   WORK PRODUCT[86]

Work product can be defined preliminarily as information prepared or obtained in anticipation of litigation or preparation for trial. In the landmark case of *Hickman v. Taylor*,[87] the Supreme Court recognized a common law qualified immunity of work product from discovery. The rulings in this case were subsequently codified and enlarged by Rule 26(b)(3). Subdivision 1 of this section discusses *Hickman*; Subdivision 2 defines work product more thoroughly in terms of Rule 26(b)(3); Subdivision 3 discusses how the immunity is asserted during discovery; and Subdivision 4 discusses how it is overcome.

[1]   *Hickman v. Taylor* and Work Product Immunity

Originally, the federal rules of civil procedure contained no provisions regarding discovery of work product. A few lower federal courts recognized a federal common law[88] protection for such materials. In 1947, the Supreme Court endorsed and explained this common law protection in *Hickman v. Taylor*.

Hickman arose out of the accidental sinking of a tugboat and the resulting death of five crew members. Three days after the sinking, the tug owners and their underwriters employed attorney Fortenbaugh and his firm to defend them against potential suits by the decedents' representatives and to sue a third party for damages to the tug. After a public hearing before the United States Steamboat Inspectors at which the surviving crew members testified, Fortenbaugh privately took written statements from the survivors. He also interviewed other fact witnesses and made memoranda of the interviews.

A decedent's representative ultimately sued the tug owners and filed interrogatories directed to them. One interrogatory asked whether statements of the surviving crew members had been taken and required any written statements to be attached to the answers[89] and any oral statements to be set forth in detail.[90] Additional interrogatories sought the identity and content of any other oral or written statements, memoranda or reports made concerning the subject matter of the suit.

The tug owners admitted in answers prepared by Fortenbaugh that statements had been taken, but declined to set forth the answers' contents in part on the ground that they were "privileged matter obtained in preparation

---

[86] *See generally* Epstein, note 81, *supra*; Elizabeth G. Thornburg, *Rethinking Work Product*, 77 Va. L. Rev. 1515 (1991); Jeff A. Anderson et al., *The Work Product Doctrine*, 68 Cornell L. Rev. 760 (1983); Annotation, *Development, Since Hickman v. Taylor, of Attorneys Work Product" Doctrine*, 35 A.L.R.3d 412 (1971 & 1993 Supp.).

[87] 329 U.S. 495 (1947).

[88] For discussion of specific federal common law, see § 7.07, *supra*.

[89] Technically, this part of the plaintiff's discovery request was improper. Document production from a party is ordinarily obtained by filing a request for production of documents pursuant to Rule 34. *See* § 10.10[1] (procedures for production requests), *infra*.

[90] *Hickman*, 329 U.S. at 499.

for litigation."[91] The district court ruled that the written witness statements taken by Fortenbaugh were not privileged and ordered Fortenbaugh to produce them.[92] When he refused, he was ordered imprisoned for contempt. The Court of Appeals reversed, ruling that the information was "work product" and as such privileged from discovery. The Supreme Court affirmed on somewhat different reasoning.

The Court first rejected Fortenbaugh's claim of privilege. It noted that the attorney-client privilege extends neither to information obtained from third parties outside the attorney-client relationship nor to all material prepared by counsel for his own use in prosecuting his client's case.[93] The purpose of the attorney-client privilege is to encourage full disclosure of information between an attorney and her client by protecting the confidentiality of their communications.[94] That purpose did not apply to the materials Fortenbaugh had prepared.

This conclusion, however, did not answer the discovery question presented by the case. The Court held that discovery of attorney Fortenbaugh's work product "contravenes the public policy underlying the orderly prosecution and defense of legal claims," absent any showing of necessity beyond mere relevance or any claim that denial of discovery would cause undue prejudice.[95]

> In performing his various duties, however, it is essential that a lawyer work with a certain degree of privacy, free from unnecessary intrusion by opposing parties and their counsel. Proper preparation of a client's case demands that he assemble information, sift what he considers to be the relevant from the irrelevant facts, prepare his legal theories and plan his strategy without undue and needless interference. . . . This work is reflected, of course, in interviews, statements, memoranda, correspondence, briefs, mental impressions, personal beliefs, and countless other tangible and intangible ways — aptly though roughly termed by the Circuit Court of Appeals in this case as the "work product of the lawyer." Were such materials open to opposing counsel on mere demand, much of what is now put down in writing would remain unwritten.[96]

---

[91] 329 U.S. at 499.

[92] This order was also improper. Interrogatories and requests for production of documents could only be directed at parties, and Fortenbaugh was not a party. The only proper procedure for obtaining documents from a non-party was to take her deposition and, in that connection, to serve her with a *subpoena duces tecum*. 329 U.S. at 499. The Supreme Court noted this but it did not figure in the Court's holding. 329 U.S. at 504–05.

[93] 329 U.S. at 508.

[94] *See* § 10.04 (privilege), *supra*. *See generally* Moore § 26.70[8] (comparing the attorney-client privilege and the protection of attorney work product).

[95] *Hickman*, 329 U.S. at 509–10. It follows that the work product protection is broader than the attorney-client privilege. Wright & Miller § 2023 (2008 Pocket Part).

[96] 329 U.S. at 510. *But see* Thornburg, note 86, *supra*, at 1526–32 (arguing that the adversary system itself provides sufficient inducement for thorough, written preparation, without the need for work product immunity).

The Court made clear, however, that the immunity accorded work product is qualified. When the discoverer goes beyond a bare demand, and shows that production is "essential to the preparation" of his case and that denial of discovery would cause hardship because "witnesses are no longer available or can be reached only with difficulty," production of "relevant and non-privileged facts . . . in an attorney's file" should be allowed.[97] The plaintiff in *Hickman* had made no such showing. On the contrary, his counsel admitted that he wanted the witness statements "only to help prepare himself to examine witnesses and to make sure that he [had] overlooked nothing."[98] He had ready access to the surviving crew members' prior public testimony before the Steamboat Inspectors and apparently to the witnesses themselves. Moreover, the Court emphasized, he could employ interrogatories to the tug owners to obtain any relevant and non-privileged facts known to them, including any facts learned by their attorney.[99]

Finally, the Court implied that although a showing of necessity and hardship would be sufficient to require production of the written witness statements, it might not be enough to require production of oral witness statements taken by Fortenbaugh, "whether presently in the form of his mental impressions or memoranda."[100] It reasoned that in addition to the previously discussed policy arguments for protection, there is special concern about making the attorney a witness, by forcing him to testify to the contents of oral witness statements he has taken. As Justice Jackson noted in his concurring opinion,

> [t]he lawyer who delivers such statements often would find himself branded a deceiver afraid to take the stand to support his own version of the witness's conversation with him, or else he will have to go on the stand to defend his own credibility — perhaps against that of his chief witness or possibly even his client.[101]

Discoverability of such statements could thus transform the attorney from officer of the court into ordinary witness, contrary to the standards of the profession.[102]

Hickman stood as the common law foundation for the qualified immunity of attorney work product for twenty-three years. Finally, the 1970 amendments to the federal rules codified and enlarged much of the common law doctrine.

---

[97] *Hickman*, 329 U.S. at 511.

[98] 329 U.S. at 513.

[99] 329 U.S. at 513.

[100] 329 U.S. at 512.

[101] 329 U.S. at 517.

[102] *ABA Model Rules*, note 1, *supra*, Rule 3.7. *But see* Thornburg, note 86, *supra*, at 1540–44 (arguing that the problem is more imaginary than real because attorneys can have others interview witnesses, tape-record the interview, or simply depose the witnesses).

[2]　Defining Work Product

Rule 26(b)(3) enlarges the common law protection from attorney work product to "documents and tangible things . . . prepared in anticipation of litigation or for trial by or for another party or . . . [his] representative." Where the rule applies, it supplants the common law doctrine of *Hickman*. But *Hickman* still controls the discovery of intangible materials that literally fall outside the rule,[103] and its spirit animates the rule.

[a]　Documents and Tangible Things

The Court in *Hickman* emphasized that although the written witness statements and Fortenbaugh's memoranda were not discoverable on a bare demand, the discoverer was free to obtain the facts gleaned by Fortenbaugh by putting interrogatories — written questions — to his clients. Rule 26(b)(3) rather crudely reflects this distinction between the documents assembled by the client or his representatives, and the underlying facts themselves, by protecting only "documents and tangible things." The qualified immunity for work product does not protect against discovery of facts contained in the work product, including the identity of fact witnesses or the existence of the protected documents and things, "if a litigant can figure out the right question to ask."[104]

In application, however, the distinction is not so clean. Since the rule could be easily circumvented if a discoverer could require the discoveree to describe in detail the contents of protected documents, courts deny such discovery on the theory that it is "the equivalent to discovery of the documents themselves" and therefore prohibited by the rule,[105] or that it violates the broader common law rule of *Hickman*.[106] The distinction is subtle; you may obtain the facts in the document, but may not require the discoveree to recreate the document for you. It is also logical. By its organization and fact selection, the written presentation of the facts often reflects tactical or strategic emphases and priorities that are at the heart of the immunity, even though the bare facts themselves are not. The same reasoning is sometimes given for the denial of discovery of what questions an attorney privately put to a witness.[107]

A similar concern for circumvention of the rule is leading some courts to restrict discovery of even the facts themselves when that discovery is sought

---

[103] The rule expressly extends protection only to tangible work product. *See* MOORE § 26.70[2]. But the courts interpret *Hickman* to require work product protection for both tangible and intangible work product. *See In re Cendant Corp. Sec. Litig.*, 343 F.3d 658, 662 (3d Cir. 2003).

[104] Thornburg, note 86, *supra*, at 1520. *See generally* WRIGHT § 82.

[105] *See, e.g., Peterson v. United States*, 52 F.R.D. 317, 322 (S.D. Ill. 1971).

[106] *Cf. Gilhuly v. Johns-Manville Corp.*, 100 F.R.D. 752 (D. Conn. 1983); *Bercow v. Kidder, Peabody & Co.*, 39 F.R.D. 357 (S.D.N.Y. 1965).

[107] *See, e.g., Ford v. Philips Elecs. Instruments Co.*, 82 F.R.D. 359, 360 (E.D. Pa. 1979) (discovery denied "[i]nsofar as defendant's question attempted to elicit from the witness the specific questions that plaintiff's counsel posed to him, or even the area of the case to which he directed the majority of his questions," but not "insofar as it was directed to the substance of the witness' knowledge of relevant facts").

from the parties' attorneys, rather than from their clients or other witnesses. Not only does the deposition of an opposing attorney unnecessarily make a witness of the attorney (contrary to *Hickman*'s admonition), but it inevitably targets the attorney's mental impressions and legal theories by forcing her to reveal what she thought important enough to remember. Accordingly, the Court of Appeals for the Eighth Circuit upheld an attorney's refusal during her deposition to acknowledge even the existence of trial preparation materials.[108] It reasoned that

> [i]n cases that involve reams of documents and extensive document discovery, the selection and compilation of documents is often more crucial than legal research. We believe [that the attorney's] selective review of [her client's] numerous documents was based upon her professional judgment of the issues and defenses involved in this case. . . . Moreover, . . . any recollection [she] may have of the existence of documents in [her client's] possession likely would be limited to those documents she has selected as important to her legal theories concerning this case.[109]

In addition, the court more generally disapproved of the increasingly popular device of deposing opposing counsel and emphasized that henceforth it should be limited to cases in which the discoverer can make the kind of showing of substantial need and undue hardship required by Rule 26(b)(3) for discovery of tangible trial work product.[110]

In short, although Rule 26(b)(3) expressly only protects tangible work product, in the form of documents and other tangible things, the common law declared by *Hickman* extends such protection to some intangible work product as well when it would advance the policies articulated in *Hickman*. Some commentators have urged a distinction between "direct" intangible work product, such as a lawyers testimony about her trial strategy, and "indirect" intangible work product, such as a lawyers selection of documents to use at a deposition (from which strategy could at best be inferred circumstantially[111]), arguing that only the former ordinarily deserves protection, but the courts have yet to adopt this distinction or any other consistent framework for treating intangible work product.[112]

---

[108] *Shelton v. American Motors Corp.*, 805 F.2d 1323 (8th Cir. 1986). *See generally* Kathleen Waits, *Opinion Work Product: A Critical Analysis of Current Law and a New Analytical Framework*, 73 ORE. L. REV. 385 (1994) (criticizing *Shelton*); Brian R. Pioske, Comment, *Suppose You Want to Depose Opposing Counsel: Shelton v. American Motors Corp.*, 73 MINN. L. REV. 1116 (1989) (arguing that courts should only limit and not prohibit depositions of opposing counsel).

[109] *Shelton*, 805 F.2d at 1329 (citations omitted).

[110] 805 F.2d at 1327. *See generally* Steven W. Simmons, Note, *Deposing Opposing Counsel Under the Federal Rules: Time for a Unified Approach*, 38 WAYNE L. REV. 1959 (1992).

[111] *See* James Holmes, *The Disruption of Mandatory Disclosure with the Work Product Doctrine: An Analysis of a Potential Problem and a Proposed Solution*, 73 TEX. L. REV. 177, 188 (1994).

[112] Waits, note 108, *supra*. *See* § 10.05[4][c] (discussing opinion work product), *infra*.

[b]   Prepared in Anticipation of Litigation or for Trial[113]

Because qualified work product immunity is designed to promote "the public policy underlying the orderly prosecution and defense of legal claims,"[114] the immunity is limited by Rule 26(b)(3) to materials "prepared in anticipation of litigation or for trial." Litigation need not be pending, but a mere contingency is insufficient. One court has asserted that "the lawyer must at least have had a subjective belief that litigation was a real possibility, and that belief must have been objectively reasonable."[115] Most courts add that the primary purpose of preparing the documents must have been to assist in such litigation.[116] Thus, documents prepared for ordinary business purposes (*e.g.*, a routine accident report), public regulatory requirements (*e.g.*, statutorily-required report to police of automobile accidents involving injuries), or other nonlitigation purposes (*e.g.*, self-evaluation) are not protected.[117]

Purpose alone, however, is often unhelpful as a test for the applicability of the immunity. For example, because it is the ordinary course of business for an insurer to investigate claims in anticipation of litigation, the purpose test alone is unavailing to classify claims investigation materials. Instead, the court must also consider all the circumstances of preparation, including who prepared the materials and precisely when they were prepared in relation to anticipated litigation.[118] A few courts have therefore rejected the primary purpose standard as too narrow in favor of the formulation "prepared because of" the prospect of litigation, which encompasses some business documents not intended to assist in the litigation.[119] A memorandum prepared to assess the effects of possible litigation on the desirability of a merger would qualify as work product under this standard, for example, even though it was not prepared primarily to assist in litigation.

Carver v. Allstate Insurance Co. [120] is illustrative. In an action to recover proceeds under a fire insurance policy and statutory penalties for the insurer's bad faith refusal to pay, the insured sought discovery of daily investigative

---

[113] *See generally* Sherman L. Cohn, *The Work Product Doctrine: Protection Not Privilege*, 71 Geo. L.J. 917, 925–29 (1985); Robert H. Oberbillig, *Work Product Discovery: A Multifactor Approach to the Anticipation of Litigation Requirement of Federal Rule of Civil Procedure 26(b)(3)*, 66 Iowa L. Rev. 1277 (1981).

[114] *Hickman*, 329 U.S. at 509.

[115] *In re Sealed Case*, 146 F.3d 881, 884 (D.C. Cir. 1998).

[116] *See, e.g., Janicker v. George Wash. Univ.*, 94 F.R.D. 648 (D.D.C. 1982).

[117] *See generally* Rule 26(b)(3) advisory committee's note (1970); Thomas Wilson, Note, *The Work Product Doctrine: Why Have an Ordinary Course of Business Exception?*, 1988 Colum. Bus. L. Rev. 587.

[118] *See* Wright § 82.

[119] *United States v. Adlman*, 134 F.3d 1194 (2d Cir. 1998). *See, e.g.*, Eric C. McNamara, *Business Planning as It Should Be: Why Adlman Should Be the Standard When Interpreting the Work Product Doctrine*, 34 Val. U. L. Rev. 201 (1999); Charles M. Yablon & Steven S. Sparling, *United States v. Adlman: Protection for Corporate Work Product?*, 64 Brook. L. Rev. 627 (1998).

[120] 94 F.R.D. 131 (S.D. Ga. 1982).

reports or "diary sheets" prepared by the insurer's claims adjusters. The court allowed discovery of the diary sheets prepared by the initial claims adjuster during the first two months after the fire. It reasoned that such reports are not primarily prepared for the contingency of litigation but rather for the routine business purpose of deciding whether to pay or resist the claim.

However, the court denied discovery of the diary sheets of a second claims adjuster to whom the claim was assigned after the first claims adjuster determined that the claim would be substantial and that the origins of the fire were suspicious. At that point, all the circumstances indicated that the insurer's activities shifted from "mere claims evaluation to a strong anticipation of litigation."[121] The court acknowledged that although an insurer always works in anticipation of litigation, at some point the probability of litigation becomes substantial and imminent, triggering the qualified immunity for materials prepared thereafter.

[c] By a Party or His Representative

Although *Hickman* dealt just with materials prepared by an attorney, preparation of materials in anticipation of litigation or for trial routinely and necessarily requires the assistance of non-attorneys, as well the parties themselves. Rule 26(b)(3) thus expressly extends the qualified immunity to materials prepared by a party or a party's representative, "including [his] attorney, consultant, surety, indemnitor, insurer, or agent."[122] This enlargement of the literal original common law rule accounts in part for Rule 26(b)(3)'s abandonment of the phrase "attorney work product" in favor of "trial preparation materials."

[3] Asserting the Qualified Immunity

While the burden rests on the discoverer to overcome a properly asserted qualified immunity for work product,[123] the discoveree must first lay a proper foundation for the immunity. As previously noted in connection with claims of privilege,[124] this requirement is codified in Rule 26(b)(5). Disregarding the requirement risks sanctions as well as waiver of the immunity. The rule does not specify what information must be provided. "Details concerning time, persons, general subject matter, etc., may be appropriate if only a few items are withheld, but may be unduly burdensome when voluminous documents are claimed to be privileged or protected, particularly if the items can be described by categories."[125] This advice of the Advisory Committee must be taken cautiously because the case law is hostile to blanket claims of privilege.[126]

---

[121] 94 F.R.D. at 134.

[122] Materials prepared by a party's expert are covered by Rule 26(a)(2) (testimonial expert's written report) or Rule 26(b)(4) (other experts). *See* § 10.06, *infra*.

[123] *See* § 10.05[4], *infra*.

[124] *See* § 10.04 (non-discoverability of privileged matters), *supra*.

[125] Rule 26(b)(5) advisory committee's note (1993).

[126] *See, e.g., Eureka Fin. Corp. v. Hartford Accident & Indem. Co.*, 136 F.R.D. 179, 182 (E.D.

[4]   Overcoming the Qualified Immunity

Once qualified work product immunity has been properly asserted, the burden of overcoming it shifts to the discoverer and depends upon whether the work product consists of *witness statements* requested by the witness, other *factual work product*, or *opinion work product*.

[a]   Witness Statements Requested by the Witness

Although witness statements qualify as work product, Rule 26(b)(3)(C) expressly provides that a party or witness may on demand obtain a copy of his own substantially verbatim statement[127] concerning the subject matter of the action. The 1970 Advisory Committee gave a partial explanation of this exception to qualified immunity in terms of the importance of a person's statement, which is admissible against him at trial as an admission. Since a person who gives a statement without insisting on a copy often does so without benefit of counsel, in ignorance of its legal consequences, and "at a time when he functions at a disadvantage," the Committee reasoned that its discoverability would increase fairness.[128]

[b]   Factual Work Product

The immunity for factual work product can be overcome only upon a showing by the discoverer of "substantial need for the materials to prepare [its] case" and that it "cannot without undue hardship, obtain their substantial equivalent by other means."[129] Although the cases do not always sharply distinguish these requirements, they are logically discrete.

Substantial need refers to the importance of the materials to the discoverer's case. *Hickman* itself demonstrates that substantial need means more than that the materials will help the discoverer make sure that he has overlooked nothing, because the Court rejected that showing. Such need, the "natural desire to learn the details of his adversary's preparations for trial," is present in every case and cannot be the substantial need required to overcome the immunity.[130] Nor, obviously, will mere relevance to a claim or defense suffice, or else substantial need would be redundant with the generic scope of discovery.[131] But the stronger the relevance and importance to the

---

Cal. 1991). A court may also disregard an untimely establishment of foundation for the immunity. *Peat, Marwick, Mitchell & Co. v. West*, 748 F.2d 540, 541–42 (10th Cir. 1984), *cert. dismissed*, 469 U.S. 1199 (1985).

[127] *See* Kathleen Waits, *Work Product Protection for Witness Statements: Time for Abolition*, 1985 WIS. L. REV. 305 (criticizing applicability of this provision only to a witness's own statement).

[128] Rule 26(b)(3) advisory committee's notes (1970). *See generally* § 10.03[3][b] (discoverability of impeachment material), *supra*.

[129] Rule 26(b)(3).

[130] *Alltmont v. United States*, 177 F.2d 971, 978 (3d Cir. 1949), *cert. denied*, 339 U.S. 967 (1950) (pre-rule decision).

[131] *See* § 10.03[1] (relevancy), *supra*.

discoverer's claim or defense-in-chief, the more likely a court is to find this requirement satisfied.[132]

Hickman also demonstrates that *undue hardship* from denial of discovery cannot exist when a party has other reasonable access to the information. There the discoverer had access to contemporaneous sworn testimony and to the witnesses themselves. When matter is unavailable to the discoverer because the witnesses have died, moved beyond the reach of compulsory process, lost their memories, deviated from their prior testimony, or refused to cooperate, undue hardship can be established.[133] Similarly, the physical disappearance or alteration of evidence reflected in work product, such as photographs of skid marks or conditions at the scene of an accident, may establish undue hardship — indeed, impossibility — in obtaining the substantial equivalent by other means.[134] More generally, any time that important facts are exclusively in the control of the discoveree, the undue hardship requirement should be satisfied.[135]

[c]   Opinion Work Product[136]

Hickman implied that special protection was due an attorney's mental impressions and legal theories — what might be termed *opinion work product*. Rule 26(b)(3)(B) gave expression to this implication by providing that in ordering discovery of work product after the required showing has been made, the court "must protect against disclosure of the mental impressions, conclusions, opinions, or legal theories of a party's attorney or other representative concerning the litigation."

Many courts and commentators have read this clause to confer an absolute protection on opinion work product, citing the mandatory verb "shall" in the original rule (now a "must").[137] When factual and opinion work product are intermixed, a court can often protect the latter by inspecting the materials *in camera* (out of the presence of counsel seeking discovery) and ordering

---

[132] *See, e.g., Wheeling-Pittsburgh Steel Corp. v. Underwriters Laboratories, Inc.*, 81 F.R.D. 8 (N.D. Ill. 1978) (statistical data on damages could not be properly analyzed without discovery of work product consisting of methodology used in computing damages). *See generally* WRIGHT & MILLER § 2025.

[133] Rule 26(b)(3) advisory committee's note (1970). *See In re Int'l Sys. & Controls Corp. Sec. Litig.*, 693 F.2d 1235 (5th Cir. 1982) (noting memory loss and cost of obtaining information elsewhere as appropriate particularized showings to make out undue hardship). *See generally* Missy K. Atwood, Comment, *Rule 166b: The Discovery of Work Product Based on Substantial Need and Undue Hardship*, 42 BAYLOR L. REV. 573, 579–87 (1990) (surveying federal cases).

[134] *See, e.g., Rackers v. Siegfried*, 54 F.R.D. 24 (W.D. Mo. 1971) (ordering discovery of insurance adjuster's measurements of skid marks).

[135] *See* MOORE § 26.70[5].

[136] Waits, note 127, *supra*; Warren H. Smith, Comment, *The Potential for Discovery of Opinion Work Product Under Rule 26(b)(3)*, 64 IOWA L. REV. 103 (1978); Note, *Protection of Opinion Work Product Under the Federal Rules of Civil Procedure*, 64 VA. L. REV. 333 (1978).

[137] *See, e.g., Duplan Corp. v. Moulinage et Retorderie de Chavanoz*, 509 F.2d 730 (4th Cir. 1974), *cert. denied*, 420 U.S. 997 (1975); *United States v. Chatham City Corp.*, 72 F.R.D. 640, 643 n.3 (S.D. Ga. 1976). *See generally* WRIGHT § 82.

disclosure only of segregable factual materials.

Arguably, however, Rule 26(b)(3) does not expressly prohibit disclosure of opinion work product; it only commands the courts to "protect against disclosure." In *Upjohn Co. v. United States*,[138] the Supreme Court suggested that opinion materials merit "special protection" and cited Rule 26(b)(3) and *Hickman* for the proposition that such materials cannot be disclosed "simply" on the usual showing of substantial need and undue hardship.[139] The Court did not reach the question of what further showing might suffice. Lower federal courts have on rare occasions allowed discovery of even opinion work product when attorneys or other representatives are charged with coercion, malpractice, fraud, or crime, or when their opinions and impressions are pivotal to bad faith, limitations, laches, or estoppel issues in the lawsuit.[140] The additional showing that these cases apparently have in common is that the attorney's or other representative's opinions are themselves an issue in the lawsuit, for which evidence is unavailable by other means.

§ 10.06 EXPERTS[141]

[1] In General

In *Hickman*, Justice Jackson observed that "[d]iscovery was hardly intended to enable a learned profession to perform its functions . . . on wits borrowed from the adversary."[142] Nor was discovery intended to enable attorneys to prepare for trial with experts borrowed from their adversaries. Indeed, the concern about freeloading discovery is especially acute in the case of experts retained in anticipation of litigation because of the substantial fees experts often demand. On the other hand, the complexity and importance of expert testimony at trial also presents a very real risk of surprise to opposing parties who have not had discovery of the expert.

The rules balance these concerns by differentiating between, on one hand, experts expected to testify at trial (*testifying experts*) and, on the other hand, those merely retained or specially employed in anticipation of trial who are

---

[138] 449 U.S. 383 (1981).

[139] 449 U.S. at 401.

[140] *See, e.g., Holmgren v. State Farm Mut. Auto. Ins. Co.*, 976 F.2d 573 (9th Cir. 1992) (bad faith denial of insurance claim); *In re Sealed Case*, 676 F.2d 793, 807 (D.C. Cir. 1982) (crime/fraud); *Byers v. Burleson*, 100 F.R.D. 436, 439 (D.D.C. 1983) (limitations); *Donovan v. Fitzsimmons*, 90 F.R.D. 583 (N.D. Ill. 1981) (reliance on advice-of-counsel defense); *Bird v. Penn Cent. Co.*, 61 F.R.D. 43, 47 (E.D. Pa. 1973) (laches). *See generally* G. Michael Halfenger, Comment, *The Attorney Misconduct Exception to the Work Product Doctrine*, 58 U. Chi. L. Rev. 1079 (1991).

[141] *See generally* Kathleen M. Brennan, *Must the Show Go On? Defining When One Party May Call or Compel an Opposing Party's Consultative Expert to Testify*, 78 Minn. L. Rev. 1191 (1994); Michael H. Graham, *Expert Witness Testimony and the Federal Rules of Evidence: Insuring Adequate Assurance of Trustworthiness*, 1986 U. Ill. L. Rev. 43; Michael H. Graham, *Discovery of Experts Under Rule 26(b)(4) of the Federal Rules of Civil Procedure: Parts I & II*, 1976 U. Ill. L.F. 895, 1977 U. Ill. L.F. 169.

[142] 329 U.S. at 516 (Jackson, J., concurring).

not, however, expected to testify (*non-testifying experts*). Rule 26(a)(2) requires disclosure of the identity and expected testimony of the testifying experts and Rule 26(b)(4)(A) permits their depositions.[143] Rule 26(b)(4) conditionally protects the non-testifying experts from discovery absent a special showing.

Neither part of the rule, however, protects against discovery of an expert who acquires his information as an actor or viewer in the transactions or occurrences that give rise to the lawsuit.[144] Thus, the police officer who responds to the accident scene, the doctor who attends in the emergency room, and the mechanic who services the car whose brakes failed, are all just ordinary fact witnesses, subject to orthodox discovery under the rules, even though they may also be experts.[145]

Rule 26 does not address per se the issue of discovery of experts who have been consulted in anticipation of litigation but not retained or specially employed.[146] The 1970 Advisory Committee's notes suggest that the omission was intentional, and that discovery of such experts, or even of their identity, is precluded.[147] The omission of any provision for discovery of generally employed non-testifying experts arguably creates the same inference. Some courts, however, have rejected that inference for such a "party-expert" on the grounds that he is more partisan than professionally objective.[148] If such an expert learned facts and acquired opinions in anticipation of litigation, however, any materials that he has generated reflecting those facts and opinions would presumably be independently protected from discovery by ordinary work product immunity.[149]

---

[143] Discovery of reports of physical or mental examinations conducted pursuant to Rule 35 is governed separately by its provisions. *See* § 10.11 (procedure for taking physical and mental examinations), *infra*.

[144] Rule 26(b)(4) advisory committee's note (1970).

[145] *See, e.g., Nelco Corp. v. Slater Elec., Inc.*, 80 F.R.D. 411 (E.D.N.Y. 1978) (expert may be deposed as an "actor" in the events that are the subject of the litigation). Of course, the rule shields only the facts and opinions held by the expert. " 'It does not . . . excuse the party from disgorging what facts he may have in his possession' " or allow him to insulate those facts from discovery by giving them to an expert. *Marine Petroleum Co. v. Champlin Petroleum Co.*, 641 F.2d 984, 994 (D.C. Cir. 1980) (*quoting* J. MOORE, MOORE'S FEDERAL PRACTICE ¶ 26.66[2] (2d ed.)).

[146] *See* Brennan, note 141, *supra*.

[147] The 1970 Advisory Committee said that the rule "precludes discovery against experts who were informally consulted in preparation for trial, but not retained or specially employed. As an ancillary procedure, a party may on a proper showing require the other party to name experts retained or specially employed, but not those formally consulted."

[148] *See, e.g., Kansas-Nebraska Natural Gas Co. v. Marathon Oil Co.*, 109 F.R.D. 12, 15–16 (D. Neb. 1985). For an especially thoughtful discussion of the issue, see also *Virginia Elec. & Power Co. v. Sun Shipbuilding & Dry Dock Co.*, 68 F.R.D. 397, 406–10 (E.D. Va. 1975). *See generally* James R. Pielemeier, *Discovery of Non-Testifying "In-House" Experts Under Federal Rule of Civil Procedure 26*, 58 IND. L.J. 597, 625 (1983) (arguing that "discovery of in-house experts should be treated in the same manner as discovery of 'retained or specially employed' experts" under Rule 26(b)(4)).

[149] *See* § 10.05 (work product), *supra*.

A 1991 amendment to Rule 45 may have modified this law by acknowledging the possibility of discovery of "unretained experts,"[150] subject to motions to quash or modify discovery or trial subpoenas. Prior to the amendment, some courts treated unretained and unconsulted experts as ordinary witnesses who are not exempt from the citizen's duty to give evidence. But the problem of freeloading noted above applies to such experts with special force. "[C]ompulsion to give evidence may threaten the intellectual property of [such] experts denied the opportunity to bargain for the value of their services," noted the 1991 Advisory Committee. Rule 45(c), therefore, now allows for motions to quash or modify any subpoena that requires "disclosing an unretained expert's opinion or information that does not describe specific occurrences in dispute and results from the expert's study that was not requested by a party" unless the requesting party can show substantial need for such testimony and undue hardship and assures that she will reasonably compensate the expert.

[2] Testifying Experts

The 1970 Advisory Committee concluded that any prohibition of discovery from the testifying expert "produces in acute form the very evils that discovery has been created to prevent." The complexity of expert testimony and frequent prior experience of the testifying expert with the rigors of cross-examination require particularly careful preparation by the cross-examiner.[151] If a discovery bar handicaps that preparation, the careful lawyer will often compensate by going slow, over-preparing expert rebuttal testimony, or seeking a continuance to prepare in mid-trial, all in derogation of Rule 1's goal of a "just, speedy and inexpensive determination of every action and proceeding."

Rule 26 originally accommodated these concerns by allowing limited discovery of the testifying expert by interrogatories, with a possibility of discovery by deposition on court order. Because lawyers usually draft the answers to interrogatories, however,[152] this mode of discovery was often insufficient to prepare for the examination of expert witnesses. On the other hand, parties often overcame this problem by agreeing to reciprocal deposition discovery of their expert witnesses.

The 1993 amendment solved the problem by rule, and the solution has been preserved in subsequent amendments. Rule 26(a)(2) requires parties at least ninety days before trial (or at times directed by the court) to disclose the identity and report the expected testimony of their testifying experts. The required report must include a complete statement of the expert's opinion, as well as the basis and reasons for the opinion, any underlying data and

---

[150] Rule 45(c).

[151] These characteristics of expert testimony are aggravated in federal court by Federal Rule of Evidence 702, which permits an expert to give his opinion without prior disclosure of the underlying facts, contrary to the common law procedure. The opposing party may therefore have to bring out the factual predicate on cross-examination, a procedure with traps for the unprepared.

[152] *See* Rule 26(a)(2) advisory committee's note (1993); § 10.09[2], *infra*.

supporting exhibits, the expert's qualifications and publications within the preceding ten years, the expert's compensation, and a listing of other cases in which the expert has testified in the preceding four years. The report, then, is intended to be the functional equivalent of the expert witness' testimony. It also includes precisely the kinds of information needed to cross-examine the witness effectively at trial. Rule 26(b)(4) also allows a party to depose a testifying expert without leave of court after the report is provided. These two discovery devices are expected to work together; a complete report may obviate or at least shorten the deposition of the expert witness.

[3] Retained or Specially Employed Non-Testifying Experts

There is less need for discovering facts known and opinions held by an expert who is not expected to testify at trial, at least when a party can reasonably consult or retain a comparable expert. Rule 26(b)(4) therefore permits discovery by interrogatories or deposition of "retained or specially employed" non-testifying experts only "on showing exceptional circumstances under which it is impracticable for the party to obtain facts or opinions on the same subject by other means." The discoverer can meet this burden by showing that the expert had a unique and irreplicable opportunity to view the scene or to conduct tests relevant to the subject matter,[153] or, more rarely, that the expert is one of a kind. The mere fact that no other expert will hold precisely the same opinion is insufficient, if comparable experts are practically available to the discoverer.[154] Any court-ordered discovery of such a non-testifying expert is ordinarily conditioned on fee-sharing.[155]

PART B.
Mechanics of Discovery

§ 10.07 REQUIRED DISCLOSURES AND OTHER GENERAL MECHANICS

Each of the federal modes of discovery has distinctive characteristics, explored in the succeeding sections. But most discovery also shares several common features, unless exempted by local rule, court order, or party stipulation under Rule 29. The parties (1) must begin the discovery process with a mandatory planning conference, (2) make certain disclosures thereafter without being asked in most cases, and (3) supplement the required disclosures and specified discovery responses at appropriate intervals.

---

[153] *See, e.g., Delcastor, Inc. v. Vail Assocs., Inc.*, 108 F.R.D. 405 (D. Colo. 1985) (expert's opinion concerning cause of mudslide is discoverable where he was the only expert to have examined mudslide area immediately following the slide).

[154] *Marine Petroleum Co.*, 641 F.2d at 996 (the rule's reference to the "same subject" is not to the particular expert's testimony itself, but rather to its subject matter).

[155] Rule 26(b)(4)(C).

[1] Mandatory Discovery Conference and Discovery Plans

Rule 29 has long permitted the parties to stipulate to the mechanics of most discovery, partly in the (often forlorn) hope that discovery could proceed cooperatively without a need for judicial intervention. In 1993, Rule 26(f) was amended to require the parties to confer as soon as practicable[156] to discuss the case and possibilities for settlement, to arrange for required disclosures, to discuss E-discovery issues (including "litigation holds" on data storage), and to develop a discovery plan incorporating these and other agreements for subsequent discovery. Rule 26(d) forbids them from taking any discovery prior to this conference.[157]

Within fourteen days after the conference, the parties must submit a report of their plan to the court. The rules anticipate that the plan will be incorporated into the scheduling order that the court is required by Rule 16(b) to issue within 120 days after the complaint has been served.

The mandatory conference requirement is clearly intended to require cooperative discovery and thereby reduce the need for subsequent judicial intervention into the discovery process. But in many cases the parties will have to confer while Rule 12 motions to dismiss the complaint are still pending and before any answers have been filed. It is unclear how much a conference in such cases can accomplish toward identifying disputed facts, promoting settlement, or even determining the amount and timing of discovery.

[2] Required Disclosures[158]

The 1993 rule amendments adopted provisions for self-executing discovery of three kinds: initial disclosures of basic information, disclosures of expert testimony (discussed above in section 10.06[2]), and pretrial disclosures of trial

---

[156] Tracing the amended rule's circumlocutory statement of timing requirements suggests that parties will ordinarily have to meet within 69 days of the appearance of a defendant or 99 days after the complaint has been served. *See* Rules 16(b) (mandating issuance of discovery scheduling order within ninety days after the appearance of "a" defendant or 120 days after the complaint was served on "a" defendant) and 26(f) (mandating planning conference at least 21 days before a scheduling order is due).

[157] Rule 27, however, permits discovery by deposition even before litigation commences in order to *perpetuate* (preserve) testimony regarding "any matter cognizable in" (within the subject matter jurisdiction of) a United States court. A person seeking such pre-complaint discovery must establish that the matter would be within the subject matter jurisdiction of a federal court, that he is presently unable for good cause to bring an action in any court, and that there is a substantial danger that the testimony sought would become unavailable before a complaint can be filed. *See, e.g., In re Boland,* 79 F.R.D. 665 (D.D.C. 1978). Generally it is not sufficient reason that he does not know whether a claim exists; pre-action discovery is not intended to be a fishing expedition for a claim. *Id.* at 668 n.3. Rule 27(a) also requires the discoverer to describe the subject matter of the intended action, the facts he seeks to establish and why, and the identities of prospective adverse parties who are entitled to notice of pre-action depositions.

[158] *See generally* Griffin B. Bell et al., *Automatic Disclosure in Discovery — The Rush to Reform,* 27 GA. L. REV. 1 (1992); Kuo-Chang Huang, *Mandatory Disclosure: A Controversial Device with No Effects,* 21 PACE L. REV. 203 (2000); Samuel Issacharof & George Loewenstein,

evidence. The provisions for required disclosures have teeth: a party who without substantial justification fails to disclose material subject to required disclosure is precluded under Rule 37(c)(1) from using that material as evidence at trial.

[a]   Initial Disclosures

Rule 26(a)(1) requires initial disclosure (within fourteen days after the Rule 26(f) discovery conference) of the basic information needed in most cases to prepare for trial or to assess settlement, except in eight categories of cases which historically involve little or no discovery.[159] This basic information is usually targeted anyway by discovery requests (if discovery is taken at all). The requirement is intended merely to "accelerate the exchange of basic information" and "eliminate the paper work involved in requesting" it, according to the 1993 Advisory Committee.

Basic information covered by Rule 26(a)(1) includes the identity of possible fact witnesses, and identification of documents and reasonably accessible electronically stored information[160] in the possession, custody or control of a party, "that the disclosing party may use to support its claim or defenses, unless the use would be solely for impeachment." Parties need not actually produce these documents; the purpose of initial disclosure is only to identify them to help the parties refine subsequent discovery requests. Moreover, voluminous documents may be identified by category. In short, initial disclosures under Rule 26(a)(1)(A)(I) and (ii) are the functional equivalent of responses to interrogatories asking a party to identify witnesses and documents or other tangible things relevant to allegations in the pleadings.[161] Rule 26(a)(1)(A)(iii) and (iv) require parties also to disclose computations of damages and to produce underlying documents and other evidence, as well as insurance agreements that may be used to satisfy all or part of a judgment which may be entered in the action.

The "use-to-support" relevancy standard for initial disclosures was added by amendment in 2000 to replace the more problematical original standard: "relevant to disputed facts alleged with particularity in the pleadings." The original standard was always somewhat at odds with the liberal "notice

---

Unintended Consequences of Mandatory Disclosure, 73 TEX. L. REV. 753 (1995); Thomas M. Mengler, *Eliminating Abusive Discovery Through Disclosure: Is It Again Time for Reform?*, 138 F.R.D. 155 (1991); Linda S. Mullenix, *Hope Over Experience: Mandatory Informal Discovery and the Politics of Rulemaking*, 69 N.C. L. REV. 795 (1991); William W. Schwarzer, *The Federal Rules, the Adversary Process, and Discovery Reform*, 50 U. PITT. L. REV. 703, 721–23 (1989); Ralph K. Winter, *Foreword: In Defense of Discovery Reform*, 58 BROOK. L. REV. 263 (1992).

[159] Rule 26(a)(1)(B) (including, for example, petitions for habeas corpus, actions to quash administrative subpoenas, and actions by the United States to recover benefit payments or collect student loans).

[160] The 2006 E-discovery amendments expressly provide that a party need not provide discovery of electronically data "from sources the party identifies as not reasonably accessible because of undue burden or cost." Rule 26(b)(2)(B). *See* § 10.03[e] (using pre-amendment decision in *Zubulake* as an example).

[161] Rule 26(a)(1) advisory committee's note (1993).

pleading" requirements of Rule 8,[162] and also with the usual chronology of litigation, in which it is the answer (often coming after initial disclosures are due) which places pleaded facts in dispute. Moreover, the original standard was also criticized for placing lawyers in an awkward conflict by forcing them to disclose unfavorable information to their adversaries.[163] The new standard alleviates these concerns. The amended rule specifically addresses the timing problem by providing that a party may object that initial disclosures are "not appropriate in [the] action" and then await the court's ruling before making the disclosures. A party is no longer required to disclose to an adversary unfavorable information that it does not intend to use.[164] This not only reduces any alleged conflict for the disclosing lawyer, it also substantially narrows the scope[165] — and therefore burden — of the initial disclosures.

[b]   Pretrial Disclosures

In addition to the required disclosure of expert witness testimony (discussed in section 10.06[2]), the parties must exchange lists of trial witnesses and trial exhibits at least thirty days before trial. This disclosure includes not only witnesses and exhibits that a party expects to present at trial, but also those that the party may use if the need arises (other than any held in reserve solely for impeachment purposes). Fourteen days after the required exchange, the parties must serve and file any evidentiary objections they have to the materials that have been listed by the opposing parties. Objections not made (other than objections under Federal Rules of Evidence 402 (relevancy) and 403 (prejudice)) are waived.

These exchanges are not really discovery at all; they are more accurately viewed as part of the trial process. Indeed, before the 1993 amendment, many courts required such exchanges in connection with the final pretrial conference.[166] Such exchanges not only facilitate trial preparation, but also permit *in limine* (at the threshold of trial) rulings on the evidence that help streamline trial.

[c]   An Assessment of Required Disclosure

The promulgation in 1993 of provisions for required disclosures of expert witness testimony and of trial witnesses and trial evidence in essence just codified what many federal courts were already doing. These provisions were generally uncontroversial. The requirement for initial disclosures of basic information, however, was new and very controversial. Indeed, Justice Scalia

---

[162] Rule 9 identifies only a few categories of allegations which must be pled with particularity. *See* § 8.04[4] (discussing special pleading requirements).

[163] *See, e.g.*, Bell, note 158, *supra*, at 46 n.175.

[164] Rule 26(a)(1) advisory committee notes (2000). "Use" is not limited to trial; it includes any use at pretrial conferences or to support a motion. Bell, note 158, *supra*, at 46 n.175.

[165] Carl Tobias, *Congress and the 2000 Federal Civil Rules Amendments*, 22 Cardozo L. Rev. 75, 79 (2000).

[166] *See* § 12.03[2] (procedures for pretrial conferences), *infra*.

objected to it as "potentially disastrous and certainly premature."[167] Critics argued that it was potentially disastrous for several reasons.

First, they raised the specter of satellite litigation.[168] This objection chiefly reflected the rule's original requirement of disclosure of information "relevant to disputed facts alleged with particularity in the pleadings," and the fear that this peculiar wording would encourage a return to discredited fact pleading. The subsequent amendment of the rule in 2000 to tie the disclosure requirement instead to information a party "may use to support its claims or defenses" substantially met this objection.

Another critique was that the burden of required disclosure fell unfairly on one side. Some early critics alleged that required disclosure unfairly burdened the plaintiff to the advantage of product liability defendants and other defendants.[169] But many product liability, toxic tort, and securities fraud plaintiffs start litigation on relatively little information beyond the facts of their own injury. The burden of initial disclosure on them may be slight, while "the potential scope of document disclosure that may be required [of a corporate defendant] under such an amorphous standard is virtually unlimited."[170]

Third, critics argued that the initial disclosure rule would increase discovery costs, by imposing initial disclosures in cases that would otherwise have little or no discovery, and by adding another costly layer of discovery to cases in which well-heeled parties would pursue specific discovery anyway after such disclosures.[171] But the 2000 rule amendments, however, categorically exempted certain kinds of cases in which discovery is usually slight, and the parties are always free to stipulate to forgo initial disclosures.

Empirical studies of experience with initial disclosures through 1997 refute much of what remains of the first critique. The rule generated surprisingly little satellite litigation.[172] A majority of defendants' and plaintiffs' lawyers

---

[167] *Amendments to the Federal Rules of Civil Procedure*, 113 S. Ct. CCC, CCCIX (dissenting statement of J. Scalia), 146 F.R.D. 401, 410 (1993).

[168] *See generally* Paul R. Sugarman & Marc G. Perlin, *Proposed Changes to Discovery Rules in Aid of "Tort Reform": Has the Case Been Made?*, 42 Am. U. L. Rev. 1465 (1993); Bell, note 158, *supra*, at 43–45.

[169] Sugarman & Perlin, note 168, *supra*, at 1495; Mengler, note 158, *supra*, at 159, 162.

[170] Bell, note 158, *supra*, at 39; Colleen McMahon & Jordana G. Schwartz, Analysis of Amendments to the Federal Rules of Civil Procedure as Approved by the Judicial Conference and Forwarded to the Supreme Court 15 (ALI-ABA 1993).

[171] *See, e.g.*, Bell, note 158, *supra*, at 40, 45; 113 S. Ct. at CCCIX (dissenting statement of J. Scalia). Some critics add that the frontloading of discovery costs may actually impede settlement by giving the parties too great an investment in continuing the litigation. *See* Issacharoff & Loewenstein, note 158, *supra*, at 786; Carol C. Cure, *Practical Issues Concerning Arizona's New Rules of Civil Procedure: A Defense Perspective*, 25 Ariz. St. L.J. 55, 57 (1993).

[172] James S. Kakalik et al., Rand Institute for Civil Justice, *Discovery Management: Further Analysis of the Civil Justice Reform Act Evaluation Data*, 39 B.C. L. Rev. 613, 658 (1998) (hereinafter "Rand Report"); Thomas E. Willging et al., Federal Judicial Center, *An Empirical Study of Discovery and Disclosure Practice Under the 1993 Federal Rule Amendments*, 39 B.C. L. Rev. 525, 535 (1998) (hereinafter "*FJC Survey*").

alike also reported that the rule had no perceived effect on the length of cases, fairness of outcome, or prospects for settlement.[173] Their shared perceptions do not support the critique that initial disclosures would favor one side or the other. Moreover, the empirical evidence suggests that initial disclosures had little or no effect on costs or time spent in litigation.[174] On the other hand, one study did report that in 89% of the cases in which initial disclosure was made, further discovery took place — "disclosure infrequently replace[d] discovery entirely."[175] Thus, although initial disclosure apparently did not increase discovery costs, it did not reduce them either or avoid later, discretionary discovery.

If these findings are accurate, they raise the question why the rulemakers did not just drop initial disclosures in 2000, instead of refining them. One commentator has suggested that the Advisory Committee acknowledged the rule's minimal effect, "but . . . evinced reluctance to abandon the mechanism altogether and attempted to maintain a vestige of the notion."[176] A better answer may be that even if only a minority of lawyers (39%) reported that initial disclosures decreased overall expenses,[177] this result was enough to justify retaining the rule, especially if its costs are reduced by categorically exempting certain proceedings which usually lack discovery, and by narrowing the scope of disclosure to materials which will be used to support a claim or defense. Unless the latter change fosters satellite litigation, in short, the amended Rule 26(a)(1) may reduce discovery costs in a minority of cases while doing no harm in most of the rest.

[3] Supplementation of Discovery

The typical litigator has several cases pending at the same time. In each there may be substantial discovery. The burden of continuously reviewing old discovery responses for accuracy and updating them whenever new information becomes available would be great. On the other hand, a failure to supplement an incorrect, misleading or obsolete discovery response may give rise to the very surprise at trial that discovery was intended partly to avoid.

Rule 26(e) originally struck a compromise between these two concerns by imposing a quite limited duty of supplementation on party-discoverees. That compromise was partly undone by the 1993 rule amendments, which require a party to correct or complete its required disclosures (as well as any deposition given by its expert witness), if the additional or corrective information has not already been made known to other parties. This expanded duty to supplement

---

[173] *FJC Survey*, note 172, *supra*, at 563.

[174] *Rand Report*, note 172, *supra*, at 658–61; *FJC Survey*, note 172, *supra*, at 563; Huang, *supra*, note 158, at 263. The *FJC Survey* did find that of the minority of lawyers who reported that initial disclosures had affected litigation, most thought the effects were positive. *See FJC Survey*, note 172, at 237 (explaining FJC data).

[175] *FJC Survey*, note 172, *supra*, at 559.

[176] Tobias, note 165, *supra*, at 82.

[177] *FJC Survey*, note 172, *supra* at 563.

is as broad as the scope of required disclosures. It obligates a lawyer to keep track of all information that might make previous disclosures incomplete or incorrect in any respect.

Rule 26(e) extends the same duty to prior responses to an interrogatory, request for production, or request for admission. The lawyer must therefore also monitor the completeness and correctness of such responses throughout the lawsuit. Only responses given in deposition (except depositions by expert witnesses) are exempted, presumably on the theory that these are often given by non-party witnesses and that monitoring them would be extremely burdensome, if not impossible.

Ordinarily, only incurably prejudicial breaches of the rule will support sanctions or constitute grounds for relief from judgment.[178] A common sanction for breach of the duty to supplement is exclusion at trial of evidence withheld by the discoveree.[179] This sanction is inappropriate, however, if a continuance and opportunity for mid-trial discovery can enable the discoverer to overcome his surprise and prepare effective cross-examination and rebuttal.[180]

§ 10.08 DEPOSITIONS

[1]   Procedure for Taking

A deposition is the recorded examination of a live witness under oath by oral or written questions before a qualified oath administrator,[181] who is usually a court reporter.[182] The deposition may be recorded by sound, sound-and-visual, or stenographic means at the expense of the taker. In a Rule 30 deposition upon oral questions, an attorney asks the questions and the deponent answers spontaneously, like an examination of a witness at trial. In a Rule 31(a) deposition upon written questions, the discoverer serves his direct questions

---

[178] *See, e.g., Johnson v. H. K. Webster, Inc.*, 775 F.2d 1, 7–8 (1st Cir. 1985). For discussion of the rule of prejudicial error, see § 13.09[1], *infra*.

[179] *See, e.g., Scott & Fetzer Co. v. Dile*, 643 F.2d 670 (9th Cir. 1981) (failure to list 20 of 23 trial witnesses and 26 of 51 exhibits in response to interrogatories prejudicially denied the discoverer the right to prepare effective cross-examination and rebuttal and requires their exclusion, especially where the undisclosed witnesses included an expert witness and were used to support a previously undisclosed theory of the case).

[180] *See, e.g., Moore v. Boating Indus. Ass'ns*, 754 F.2d 698 (7th Cir. 1985); *Lewis Refrigeration Co. v. Sawyer Fruit, Vegetable & Cold Storage Co.*, 709 F.2d 427 (6th Cir. 1983); *Gebhard v. Niedzwiecki*, 122 N.W.2d 110, 115 (Minn. 1963) (suggesting that preclusion is proper when the violation is willful and the discoveree seeks to benefit from it "at a time when the harm cannot be undone").

[181] *See* Rule 28 (persons before whom depositions may be taken).

[182] Depositions traditionally have been recorded by a court reporter. Rule amendments eventually liberalized the requirements for taking of depositions by non-stenographic means. *See* Rules 30(b)(3)–(4). The parties no longer need to agree to non-stenographic means or obtain a court order; such means are available *unless* the court orders otherwise. Parties must still stipulate to or obtain a court order for taking depositions by telephone or other remote electronic means. *See* Rule 30(b)(4).

on the deponent and the other parties in advance, after which any cross, redirect or recross questions[183] are served. The oath administrator reads the written questions to the deponent, who answers them live, if not quite spontaneously (given the prior opportunity to rehearse the answers). Interrogatories differ from the deposition upon written questions partly in that answers to interrogatories are written and often prepared by a party's attorney.[184]

A party does not ordinarily need leave of court to take a deposition unless the deposition would exceed the seven-hour durational limit set by Rule 30(d)(1) or the ten-deposition numerical limit established by Rule 30(a)(2)(A)(I). The procedure for orally deposing a party under Rule 30 is simply to serve the deponent and parties with reasonable written notice of the time and place of the deposition and identity of the deponent,[185] as well as a Rule 34 request for production of documents when documents are sought in connection with the deposition.[186] A party must comply with the notice or seek a protective order[187] because, by the initial service of process on her, she has already been subjected to the personal jurisdiction of the court and therefore brought within the reach of properly invoked procedural rules.

This is not true of a non-party witness, however. To compel the attendance at deposition of a non-party witness, the discoverer must first procure the issuance of a *subpoena*[188] from the court for the district in which the deposition will be taken.[189] The non-party witness may ask the court to quash or modify the subpoena if it allows insufficient time for compliance, necessitates excessive travel, requires disclosure of protected or confidential information, or subjects the witness to undue burden.[190]

Under Rule 30(b)(6), a party may name as a deponent in his notice and subpoena a corporation, agency, partnership or other legal entity and describe the matters on which examination is requested. The entity must then designate one or more officers, directors, managing agents, or other persons with relevant knowledge to testify on its behalf. As noted below[191] the

---

[183] Direct examination is a party's questioning of his own witness. Cross-examination is questioning of a witness called by an opposing party. Redirect is direct examination of a witness after cross-examination. Recross is cross-examination of a witness after redirect. *See generally* McCORMICK ON EVIDENCE § 4 (J. Strong, 4th ed. 1992).

[184] *See* § 10.09 (interrogatories), *infra.*

[185] Rule 30(b)(1). The notice must be accompanied by the direct questions in the case of a deposition upon written questions. Rule 31(a).

[186] Rule 30(b)(2).

[187] *See* § 10.13[3] (protective orders), *infra.*

[188] *See* Rule 45. A *subpoena duces tecum* must be used if document production is sought in connection with the deposition.

[189] Rules 30(a) & 45. Many states provide for the issuance of subpoenas for depositions to be used in proceedings pending in other states. *See e.g.*, ARIZ. R. CIV. PROC. 30(h) (2001); ME. R. CIV. PROC. 30(h) (2001).

[190] Rule 45(c)(3).

[191] *See* § 10.08[2] (use and value of depositions), *infra.*

deposition of a person so designated may be offered at trial as direct evidence against the designating entity. Rule 30(b)(6)'s legislative history suggests that it was intended simply as a device to facilitate the discovery of appropriate witnesses who could provide further discovery regarding an institutional litigant, in order "to defeat a shield of obfuscation and inefficiency that could be thrown up by . . . [such a] litigant."[192] Instead, it has sometimes been misused to force such litigants to create a witness who can give a "grand synthesis" of evidence to bind the litigant.[193] On the other hand, courts have held that the designating party has a duty to prepare its designee to answer questions on the described matters — you can't just designate a stone.[194]

The chief difference between the conduct of a deposition upon oral questions and examination of a witness at trial is the absence of the trial judge. Consequently, objections to the competency of the witness or to the competency, relevancy, or materiality of testimony are preserved until trial, when the judge can rule upon them. Rule 32(d)(3)(A) expressly states that they are not waived by a failure to make them at the deposition. In contrast, objections to errors which "might have been corrected at that time" are waived if not seasonably made before or during the deposition.[195] These include objections to the qualifications of the presiding officer; to errors and irregularities in the notice; to the manner of taking the deposition; oath or affirmation; to the conduct of the parties; or to the form of the questions. For example, "when did you stop beating your wife [or husband]?" is objectionable as to form, for it assumes a predicate. But the objection could be obviated by reforming the question as several separate questions: "Did you beat your wife [husband]?; [if yes] did you stop?; [if yes] when?"[196] If the objecting party could defer the objection to this question until the deposition is offered at trial, it could deprive the examiner of an opportunity to reform the question. Consequently, if no objection is made to the form of the question, the objection is waived and lost should the resulting testimony be offered at trial.

Despite the preservation of most objections until the proffer of deposition testimony as evidence at trial, some lawyers make them anyway, not only to create a technically unnecessary record, but sometimes also to educate the witness or obstruct the examination. Indeed, some lawyers instruct the witness not to answer questions that do not call for privileged information, in effect daring the examiner to halt the deposition to seek judicial assistance. Amendments to Rule 30 now discourage both tactics by requiring objections to be made concisely and in a "nonargumentative and nonsuggestive manner," and by forbidding instructions not to answer except when necessary to preserve a privilege, comply with a court order, or to present a motion to limit

---

[192] Kent Sinclair & Roger P. Fendrich, *Discovering Corporate Knowledge and Contentions: Rethinking Rule 30(b)(6) and Alternative Mechanisms*, 50 ALA. L. REV. 651, 749 (1999).

[193] *Id.*

[194] *See International Ass'n of Machinists & Aerospace Workers v. Werner-Matsuda Corp.*, 390 F. Supp. 2d 479 (D. Md. 2005); WRIGHT & MILLER § 2103 (2008 Pocket Part).

[195] Rules 32(d)(3)(A) & (B).

[196] *See generally* McCORMICK ON EVIDENCE, note 183, *supra*, at § 5-7.

or terminate the deposition.[197] Rule 30(d)(3) authorizes a court to grant such a motion upon a showing that the examination is being conducted oppressively or in bad faith.[198]

The amended rule does not deal directly with a similar deposition tactic: mid-deposition coaching of deponents in private lawyer-client discussions. Some courts, however, are inferring authority from the rules to combat this tactic.[199] Complaining that "[t]he witness comes to the deposition to testify, not to indulge in a parody of Charlie McCarthy [the puppet used by famous ventriloquist, Edgar Bergen], with lawyers coaching or bending the witness's words to mold a convenient record," one court has prohibited private lawyer-client discussions during depositions and deposition recesses, except for the limited purpose of deciding whether to assert a privilege.[200] This court's order, like amended Rule 30(c)(2), reflects the proposition that "[i]n general, counsel should not engage in any conduct during a deposition that would not be allowed in the presence of a judicial officer."[201]

At the completion of the deposition, a transcript of the recorded examination may be prepared by a court reporter or by any party, according to Rule 30(e). On request by the deponent or a party, the transcript is submitted to the deponent for correction and signature. The presiding officer is then responsible for sealing the deposition with her certificate and filing it in the court in which the action is pending or sending it to the lawyer who noticed the deposition, along with the originals or copies of any documents marked for identification during the deposition.[202]

[2] Use and Value of Depositions

Under Rule 32(a) any or all of a deposition may be used at trial, as if the witness were then present and testifying, against any party who had notice of the deposition and a reasonable opportunity to obtain counsel or to move for a protective order. The proponent of the deposition testimony may offer it in

---

[197] Rule 30(c)(2).

[198] Indeed, some courts have held that the Rule 30(d) procedure is the exclusive remedy and censured a lawyer who directed his client not to answer obnoxious questions when that direction was not necessary to preserve any privilege. *See Redwood v. Dobson*, 476 F.3d 462, 469 (7th Cir. 2007) ("instructions not to respond that neither shielded a privilege nor supplied time to apply for a protective order were unprofessional and violated the Federal Rules of Civil Procedure as well as the ethical rules that govern legal practice.").

[199] On deposition ethics generally, see A. Darby Dickerson, *The Law and Ethics of Civil Depositions*, 57 Md. L. Rev. 273 (1998); Janeen Kerper & Gary L. Stuart, *Rambo Bites the Dust: Current Trends in Deposition Ethics*, 22 J. Legal Prof. 103 (1997–1998); Jean M. Cary, *Rambo Depositions: Controlling an Ethical Cancer in Civil Litigation*, 25 Hofstra L. Rev. 561 (1996). Some jurisdictions have adopted voluntary "civility codes" to deal with this and related problems of "Rambo" tactics in civil litigation, *see, e.g.,* D.C. Bar Voluntary Standards for Civility in Professional Conduct (1997), but there is yet little evidence that they have changed the adversarial dynamics which seem to breed such tactics.

[200] *Hall v. Clifton Precision*, 150 F.R.D. 525, 528 (E.D. Pa. 1993).

[201] Rule 30(d) advisory committee's note (1993).

[202] Rule 30(f).

stenographic form, or in nonstenographic form if he also provides the court and the parties with a transcript. Indeed, Rule 32(c) allows any party to a jury trial to demand that deposition testimony offered as substantive evidence be presented in nonstenographic form, when it is available. When a party offers only part of a deposition in evidence, she designates the relevant part and submits it to the judge in a bench trial or causes it to be read or played to the jury in a jury trial. Under Rule 32(a)(6), an adverse party may require the proponent to introduce additional parts "that in fairness should be considered with the part introduced."

Hearsay is an out-of-court statement offered in evidence to prove the truth of the matter stated.[203] The rule against the admissibility of hearsay would thus appear to prohibit the offer of deposition testimony at trial unless it falls within one of the rule's many exceptions. By providing that the deposition is to be tested for admissibility as if it were given live, however, Rule 32(a) is itself an exception to the rule against hearsay.[204] The rule echoes the Federal Rules of Evidence by permitting the use of deposition testimony to impeach or contradict the deponent as a witness,[205] or as an admission of a adverse party or officer, director, managing agent or designated deponent of an adverse party.[206] In addition, Rule 32(a) permits the use of deposition testimony at trial when the deponent is unavailable because of death, illness, age, imprisonment or is beyond the reach of process.

However, Rule 32 only overcomes the initial hearsay hurdle to the use of a deposition. The rules of evidence still apply to admission of its contents.

> Speaking metaphorically, a deposition is like a box that contains certain evidence. The court must make two determinations. The first is a procedural one: whether to admit the box itself into the trial. In making this assessment, the court applies . . . [Rule 32 or its state equivalent]. Once the court has decided that the deposition meets these procedural requirements, the court then must address the ancillary evidentiary issues such as whether the contents of the box qualifies as admissible evidence. This step is akin to opening the box, assessing its content and then ruling on its admissibility.[207]

The availability of a deposition in lieu of live testimony helps to make it the most valuable method of discovery. So does its flexibility. The contemporaneity of the examination upon oral questions permits the discoverer to frame

---

[203] FED. R. EVID. 801(c).

[204] WRIGHT § 84.

[205] *Compare* Rule 32(a)(2) *with* FED. R. EVID. 801(d)(1) (prior inconsistent statement is not hearsay).

[206] *Compare* Rule 32(a)(3) *with* Fed. R. Evid. 801(d)(2) (admission by party-opponent is not hearsay). Who is a managing agent for purposes of this provision is decided pragmatically, depending on the scope of the deponent's job responsibilities, assigned discretion and identification with an employer's interests. *See generally* HAYDOCK & HERR, note 11, *supra*, § 3.10.1; *cf.* M. Minnette Massey, *Depositions of Corporations: Problems and Solutions — Fed. R. Civ. P. 30(b)(6)*, 1986 ARIZ. ST. L.J. 81.

[207] *Shives v. Furst*, 521 A.2d 332, 335–36 (Md. Ct. Spec. App. 1987). *See* WRIGHT & MILLER § 2142.

follow-up questions, pursue new and unanticipated leads, observe demeanor, and pin down witnesses in order to foreclose factual arguments or at least lay a foundation for later impeachment.[208] Finally, the deposition usually is the only method of discovery available against non-party witnesses to elicit testimonial evidence.[209]

On the other hand, the chief drawback of depositions is their expense. Not only do they consume enormous amounts of attorney time in preparation, travel and taking, but court reporter fees and travel expenses can also mount quickly, putting extensive deposition discovery beyond the reach of many litigants. In addition, a deposition can educate the deponent, provide a useful rehearsal of examination at trial for the deponent and opposing parties, and of course, elicit and perpetuate unhelpful testimony.[210] On balance, however, almost all practitioners would agree that these drawbacks of deposition discovery are outweighed by its advantages.

§ 10.09 INTERROGATORIES

[1]   Procedure for Asking

Interrogatories are written questions directed to a party, who must answer them in writing and under oath, or (by his attorney) object with particularity. Although the client often supplies all or part of the underlying facts, his attorney usually prepares both the answers and the objections. If the objection is to the entire set of interrogatories on grounds of undue burden, it can also be made by a motion for a protective order under Rule 26(c).[211]

Interrogatories target not just what is known by the discoveree, but also what is reasonably obtainable by him — "the collective knowledge" of the recipient.[212] A party is charged with knowledge of what his agents know, or what is in records available to him, or even, for purposes of Rule 33, what others have told him on which he intends to rely in his suit.[213] Even if a duty of reasonable inquiry was not already implicit in Rule 33, it is now explicit in Rule 26(g)'s certification requirement for discovery responses and objections.[214]

---

[208] *See generally* HAYDOCK & HERR, note 11, *supra*, § 3.1.1; *Hall v. Clifton Precision*, 150 F.R.D. 525, 528 (E.D. Pa. 1993) (noting that depositions serve the purpose of "the memorialization, the freezing, of a witness's testimony at an early stage of the proceedings").

[209] A subpoena can be used to require a non-party witness to produce documents for inspection. *See* Rule 45.

[210] *See generally* HAYDOCK & HERR, note 11, *supra*, § 3.1.2.

[211] *MOORE* § 33.175.

[212] HAYDOCK & HERR, note 11, *supra*, § 4.6.1.

[213] *WRIGHT* § 86. *See, e.g., Brunswick Corp. v. Suzuki Motor Co.*, 38 Fed. R. Serv. 2d (Callaghan) 1246, 1248 (E.D. Wis. 1983); *Riley v. United Air Lines, Inc.*, 32 F.R.D. 230, 233 (S.D.N.Y. 1962). Rule 26(b)'s limits on the scope of discovery still apply, including the qualified immunity for work product. *See* § 10.05, *supra*.

[214] *See* § 10.13[1] (certification), *infra*.

On the other hand, interrogatories do not require the discoveree to do the discoverer's work for him by undertaking elaborate investigations, discovery and data compilation.[215] The standard is reasonableness under the circumstances. Moreover, when the answer to an interrogatory can be ascertained from the discoveree's business records (including electronically stored data) as easily by the discoverer as by the discoveree, the latter has the option under Rule 33(c) of specifying the relevant records and making them available in lieu of answer. The specification requirement precludes the tactic of referring the discoverer to an undifferentiated haystack of records in which the needle may be buried.

There are no special limitations on the form or subject of interrogatories apart from the generic limitations of Rule 26(b). But under Rule 33(b) a court may postpone the time for answering *contention interrogatories*[216] which require the discoveree to apply the law to the facts (e.g., "Do you contend that the plaintiff assumed the risk of the collision?"), because he may not know what his contentions will be until completion of discovery or a late pre-trial conference.[217] Were the rule otherwise, the discoveree might be forced into a premature statement of what his legal contentions *will be*, evoking shades of the now-discarded theory of the pleadings.[218] In contrast, requiring the party after discovery and on the eve of trial to state what his contentions *are* is not only fairer but conducive to issue-narrowing and surprise-avoidance at trial. Indeed, the parties are sometimes required to exchange their contentions in pre-trial briefs anyway,[219] whether or not contention interrogatories are pending.

The 1970 Advisory Committee concluded that interrogatories had generated a greater percentage of objections and motions than any other discovery method. Probably the most common objection is that they are *unduly burdensome*. The reason for the frequency of this objection is obvious. The discoveree is ordinarily inclined to read interrogatories narrowly and against their drafter. Knowing this, and not sure what information is out there, the discoverer drafts numerous and sweeping interrogatories to defeat narrow constructions. As a result, just the sheer number of interrogatories can create an undue burden on the discoveree. That burden may be aggravated by indiscriminate use of *pattern* or *form interrogatories* — standardized, form-book interrogatories for particular kinds of cases[220] — and by multiplication of interrogatories by means of elaborate definitions. Overbreadth is also a

---

[215] *See, e.g., La Chemise Lacoste v. Alligator Co.*, 60 F.R.D. 164 (D. Del. 1973).

[216] *See In re Convergent Techs. Sec. Litig.*, 108 F.R.D. 328, 332 (N.D. Cal. 1985) (defining different kinds of contention interrogatories).

[217] *In re Convergent Techs.*, 108 F.R.D. at 333–34.

[218] *See* § 8.03[2] (theory of pleadings), *supra*.

[219] *See* § 12.03[1] (pretrial), *infra*.

[220] *See, e.g., Robbins v. Camden City Bd. of Educ.*, 105 F.R.D. 49 (D.N.J. 1985) (259 interrogatories were repetitious and objectionable as a result of discoverer's nonspecific use of several sets of pattern interrogatories); *Blank v. Ronson Corp.*, 97 F.R.D. 744, 745 (S.D.N.Y. 1983) (sanctions may be appropriate when interrogatories have been produced by "some word-processing machine's memory of prior litigation"). There is nothing wrong with the discriminating use of

common ground for an undue burden objection. Yet a litany of terms like "overly broad, burdensome, oppressive and irrelevant" does not satisfy Rule 33(b)(4)'s requirement that the grounds for the objection be stated with specificity. The discoveree should specify by affidavit his claim of undue burden.[221]

The 1993 amendments to the discovery rules were intended to reduce the need for and abuse of interrogatory practice. "Because Rule 26(a)(1)–(3) requires disclosure of much of the information previously obtained by [interrogatories]," the 1993 Advisory Committee reasoned, "there should be less occasion to use [them]." In addition, a party may now ask no more than twenty-five interrogatories (including all discrete subparts) without leave of court.[222] Finally, Rule 33(b) now requires a party not only to state the grounds for objections with specificity, but to answer "to the extent [the interrogatory] is not objected to . . . ."

[2] Use and Value of Interrogatories

Rule 33(c) provides that answers to interrogatories may be used to the extent permitted by the rules of evidence. They can therefore usually be used *against* the discoveree as a party admission, but not *by* him as substantive evidence. They do not ordinarily bind or limit proof by the discoveree, who may depart from them, modify them, or attempt to explain them away at trial.[223] But in the exceptional case of the discoverer's reasonable and detrimental reliance on the answers, the courts have used concepts of estoppel or preclusion to give greater effect to interrogatory answers.[224]

The chief appeal of discovery by interrogatories is that they are a cheap way to access the collective knowledge of a party. Some have called them the poor man's deposition. For two reasons, however, this tag is unwarranted. First, their economy is one-sided and therefore often only temporary. It is cheap for the discoverer to prepare a set of interrogatories, but can be time-consuming and thus expensive for the attorney for the discoveree to draft answers to them. Once reciprocal discovery by interrogatories is initiated, these costs are reversed. Second, the attorney will often find some colorable objection to the

---

pattern interrogatories as long as they are tailored to the facts of the particular case. *See* HAYDOCK & HERR, note 11, *supra*, § 4.4.4.

[221] *See, e.g., Roesberg v. Johns-Manville Corp.*, 28 Fed. R. Serv. 2d (Callaghan) 1170 (E.D. Pa. 1980); *In re Folding Carton Antitrust Litig.*, 83 F.R.D. 260, 264 (N.D. Ill. 1979).

[222] Rule 33(a). How much this numerical limitation will reduce litigation about interrogatories is unclear. In the past such numerical limits have generated arid controversies about how multi-part interrogatories should count towards the limit. The Advisory Committee tried to anticipate this problem by noting that "a question asking about communications of a particular type should be treated as a single interrogatory even though it requests that the time, place, persons present, and contents be stated separately for each such communication."

[223] Rule 33(b) advisory committee's note (1970).

[224] *See generally* MOORE § 37.96. *Cf., e.g., Zielinski v. Philadelphia Piers, Inc.*, 139 F. Supp. 408 (E.D. Pa. 1956) (relying on estoppel-type theory to preclude defendant from introducing evidence on an issue as to which plaintiff was misled by defendant's interrogatory answers), discussed in § 8.08[1], *supra*.

most difficult interrogatories or draft answers that are as unhelpful as he can make them. Consequently, a federal judge has described interrogatories as "useless because any lawyer who can't answer interrogatories without giving [an] opponent useful information is not worth his salt."[225]

This critique is exaggerated. The attorney's role in drafting answers will usually make interrogatories ineffective to discover subjective and interpretative information, including state of mind, or complex information that will require explanation.[226] On the other hand, well-drafted interrogatories can be effectively used to pinpoint the existence and location of witnesses and evidence not already disclosed pursuant to Rule 26(a), to make more specific the factual basis for pleading allegations, and (towards the end of the discovery period) to narrow the issues.

§ 10.10 PRODUCTION AND ENTRY REQUESTS

[1] Procedure for Making

Rule 34(a) authorizes the discoverer to request that a party produce and permit the inspection and copying of documents or electronically stored data, or the copying, testing, or sampling of things, or entry upon land. A request must designate the documents, things or land with reasonable particularity and specify the time, place and manner of production or entry.[227] At the specified time and place, the discoveree must either permit inspection or entry, or object by item, specifying her grounds. A mere "litany of . . . boilerplate objections," however, is insufficient because it fails to show specifically how a discovery request is burdensome or oppressive by affidavit or other evidence substantiating the objections.[228] An objection to a requested form for producing electronically stored data is expressly allowed.[229]

A Rule 34 production request embraces not only that which is in the possession of the discoveree but also documents and property within her custody or control.[230] *Control* means that the discoveree has a legal right to the document or thing or to enter upon the land.[231] The discoveree cannot avoid production by giving possession of a document or thing to an agent, such

---

[225] Quoted in Brazil, *View from the Front Line: Observations by Chicago Lawyers About the System of Civil Discovery*, 1980 A.B.A. FOUND. RES. J. 217, 233. *See also In re Convergent Techs.*, 108 F.R.D. at 338.

[226] HAYDOCK & HERR, note 11, *supra*, § 4.6.

[227] *See* Official Form 50.

[228] *See, e.g., St. Paul Reinsurance Co., Ltd. v. Commercial Fin. Corp.*, 198 F.R.D. 508, 514 (N.D. Iowa 2000) (imposing Rule 26(g) sanction for such objections, by requiring objecting lawyer to write and submit for publication an article explaining why they were improper).

[229] Rule 34(b)(2)(D).

[230] *See, e.g., Weck v. Cross*, 88 F.R.D. 325 (N.D. Ill. 1980). *See generally* Note, *Meaning of "Control" in Federal Rules of Civil Procedure 34 Defined to Protect Policy Underlying Trading with Enemy Act*, 107 U. PA. L. REV. 103 (1958).

[231] *See Searock v. Stripling*, 736 F.2d 650, 653–54 (11th Cir. 1984).

as her attorney. The rule thus embraces items in the actual or constructive possession of the discoveree, whether or not she owns them.

The requested documents or things must be described with sufficient clarity for a party of ordinary intelligence to understand what is meant and for the court to determine whether the items have been produced.[232] This task is made substantially easier by the disclosures required by Rule 26(a).[233] The 1993 Advisory Committee reasoned that these required disclosures will enable parties to "frame their document requests in a manner likely to avoid squabbles resulting from the wording of the requests." Rule 34(b) also expressly permits designation of items by category.

The practice is to arrange categories by subject matter and to cross-reference all documents identified by required disclosures or in answers to any prior interrogatories. The discoveree should ordinarily produce or object in kind, by item or category, but the practice is often to produce documents *en masse*. The 1980 amendment to Rule 34(b) prohibited the deliberate burial of potentially useful documents among the undifferentiated mass by requiring the discoveree to produce documents "as they are kept in the usual course of business" or by the categories of the request.

This requirement, however, had uncertain application to electronically stored data. Did it mean "native forms," including metadata, or the form in which the responding party itself used the data? Did it include the code for interpreting that data, if one is needed? Rule 34's reference to "translation . . . by the responding party into a reasonably usable form" suggests an affirmative answer, but production of codes may raise trade secret issues calling for protective orders from the court. Can the producing party simply produce the electronically stored information in hard copy form, denying the requesting party the ability to manipulate the data without, at least, incurring the burden of manually inputting the hard copy data back into electronic form?

Rule 34(b)(2)(E) now attempts to answer these questions by providing that if the requesting party does not specify a form of production, "a party must produce it in a form or forms in which it is ordinarily maintained or in a reasonably usable form or forms," but need not produce it in more than one form.[234]

That helps, but it is unlikely to resolve the infinite number of permutations that evolving electronically stored information will throw up. Here again, the

---

[232] *See In re Hunter Outdoor Prods., Inc.*, 21 Bankr. 188 (Bankr. D. Mass. 1982) (specification inadequate when it requires discoveree to form subjective opinion in order to determine what is requested). *See generally* HAYDOCK & HERR, note 11, *supra*, § 5.8.

[233] *See* § 10.07[2], *supra*.

[234] *See generally* WRIGHT & MILLER § 2219 (2008 Pocket Part). For example, in *Autotech Technologies Ltd. P'ship v. AutomationDirect.com, Inc.*, 248 F.R.D. 556 (N.D. Ill. 2008), the defendant had not specified the form of the data, and plaintiff responded by producing it in PDF and paper format. Realizing belatedly that this format deprived it of the metadata, defendant moved to compel production of an electronic copy in "native format" — with the metadata. Citing the new rule, the court denied the motion.

rules look primarily to the court and the parties themselves, in discovery conference, to work out the answers.

Production requests and requests for entry upon land may be directed only to parties. But Rule 45 allows the issuance of subpoenas for document production by non-parties. Prior to the amendment of this rule in 1991, the primary method of obtaining documents from non-parties was deposing the custodian of the documents. This cumbersome technique is no longer necessary; a subpoena to compel production of documents by a non-party independent of any deposition is now essentially the equivalent of a Rule 34 request for production of documents by a party. The chief differences lie in the geographic reach of such subpoenas (limited to places within the district of the issuing court, within 100 miles of the place of production or inspection therein, or a place allowed by relevant state or federal statute or state court rule)[235] and in the procedure for objecting to a subpoena (motions to quash or modify).[236]

[2] Use and Value of Production and Entry Requests

The fruits of production and entry requests can be used at trial subject to the rules of evidence. The practice is often to procure the discoveree's agreement at the time of production to the use of copies in lieu of the originals at trial, obviating one evidentiary objection.

The document production request is the most frequently used discovery device, as well as one which generates a high percentage of discovery problems.[237] Production requests are widely used as a step in discovery prior to depositions. They can be highly productive relative to their cost, although, like interrogatories, they generate a large number of undue burden objections. In addition, document production requests frequently provoke objections of attorney-client privilege and work product immunity, leading to motions to compel and attendant hearings with occasional *in camera* inspection of the disputed documents by a judge or magistrate.

§ 10.11 PHYSICAL AND MENTAL EXAMINATIONS

[1] Procedure for Taking

When the physical or mental condition of a party (or person in the custody or legal control of a party) is in controversy, a court may on motion and for good cause shown order her to undergo a physical or mental examination under Rule 35. Together with Rule 27 (prelitigation deposition), discovery that

---

[235] Rule 45(b) & (c)(3)(B)(iii).

[236] Rule 45(c). Of course, a person responding to a subpoena may withhold a document on a claim of privilege or work product, provided that the claim is made expressly and with sufficient foundation to enable the discoverer to contest the claim. Rule 45(d)(2).

[237] *FJC Survey*, note 172, *supra*, at 554 (reporting that higher percentage of lawyers reported problems in document discovery than in initial disclosures, expert disclosure, or depositions).

exceeds the numerical limits on depositions or interrogatories, and discovery of matters going beyond claims or defenses, this discovery method requires a court order and a showing of good cause. These requirements and the limitation of examinations to conditions in controversy reflect the strong privacy interest counterbalancing this form of discovery.[238] The same privacy interest is reflected in Rule 37(b)(2)(A)(vii), which makes contempt of court available for disobedience of any discovery order *except* a Rule 35 order. Similar concerns have created considerable variety among the states in their rules for discovery by physical or mental examination.[239]

Rule 35(a) limits those who are subject to discovery by examination to parties or persons in their *custody or legal control*.[240] In light of the privacy concern, the legal control limitation of Rule 35(a) has been read much more narrowly than the roughly comparable provision of Rule 34 for requests for production and entry. Minor children are in the custody of their parents for purposes of examination when the parents sue for injuries to their children.[241] It is less clear whether a wife is within the legal control of her husband when he sues for injuries to her.[242] But a party's agent, such as a driver/employee in a personal injury action arising from a traffic accident, is usually not within the party's legal control.[243]

The showing that the condition is in controversy must establish more than relevancy. The condition is usually put in controversy by the pleadings. A complaint to recover for personal injuries is the classic illustration, putting in controversy the related condition of the plaintiff. But the requisite controversy is also shown when the condition contributes to the accident, bears on performance of a contract or other obligation, is the subject of an alleged libel to which truth is asserted as a defense, or is asserted as a defense of incompetency.[244]

The Supreme Court decision in *Schlagenhauf v. Holder* [245] illustrates the in-controversy requirement and how it is satisfied. In a complicated personal

---

[238] The Supreme Court has ruled that these interests do not make Rule 35 "substantive" for purposes of compliance with the Rules Enabling Act. *Sibbach v. Wilson & Co.*, 312 U.S. 1 (1941). *See* §§ 7.04[2]–[3] (state law and federal rules of civil procedure), *supra*.

[239] *See, e.g.*, CAL. CIV. PROC. CODE § 2032 (2001) (expressly includes agents of a party, unlike Rule 35); Md. R. Civ. Proc. R. 2-423 (1993) (providing that court order may regulate filing and distribution of examination findings and examiner's testimony at trial instead of federal rule of reciprocity discussed *infra*).

[240] When the examinee is a non-party in the custody or legal control of a party, the order actually issues to the party, who is merely obligated to use good faith efforts to produce the attendance of the examinee at the examination. Rule 35(a) advisory committee's note (1970).

[241] *See* WRIGHT & MILLER § 2233.

[242] WRIGHT & MILLER § 2233 (concluding that she is).

[243] Although some commentators have argued the contrary, see HAYDOCK & HERR, note 11, *supra*, § 6.2.1, the legislative history of Rule 35 suggests that agents are not within its scope. *See Schlagenhauf v. Holder*, 379 U.S. 104, 115 n.12 (1964). In many cases involving agents, however, the discoverer can avail himself of the rule by naming the agent as a defendant.

[244] *See, e.g.*, cases cited in MOORE § 35.03; WRIGHT & MILLER § 2232.

[245] 379 U.S. 104 (1964).

injury litigation arising out of a bus and truck collision, the defendant truck owners cross-claimed against the defendant bus company and its driver. The truck owner alleged that the bus company knew that its driver's eyes and vision were impaired. The truck owner's attorney filed an affidavit stating that the bus driver had seen red lights for ten to fifteen seconds before the accident and had been involved in a prior accident. On these allegations, the district court ordered a battery of physical, visual, and mental examinations. The court of appeals denied a petition for a writ of mandamus[246] against the trial judge.

On *certiorari*, the Supreme Court emphasized that the requirements of Rule 35(a) "are not met by mere conclusory allegations of the pleadings . . . but require an affirmative showing by the movant."[247] Applying this principle, the Court found that nothing in the pleadings or the affidavit showed that the bus driver's general physical or mental condition was in controversy.[248] The Court suggested that the allegation in the cross-claim that the bus driver's eyes and vision were impaired, in conjunction with the affidavit, might have supported the eye examination had one been ordered alone. But it nevertheless vacated the eye examination order, too, in light of the necessity for remanding the case anyway for reconsideration of the other orders.

Weighing the in-controversy and good cause requirements, the Court noted that "[t]he ability of the movant to obtain the desired information by other means is also relevant."[249] Accordingly, courts have analogized *good cause* to the undue hardship requirement for overcoming the qualified immunity of work product under Rule 26(b)(3), and thus measured it by the reasonable availability of the information from other sources.[250] In *Crider v. Sneider*,[251] for example, a defendant's loss of recollection due to traumatic amnesia did not establish good cause for a physical examination under a state discovery rule like Rule 35 because information about the accident could be discovered from other sources.

An order to submit to examination should specify the conditions and scope of the examination. One of the reasons for vacating the orders for multiple examinations in *Schlagenhauf* was that they were framed too generally, possibly leaving the internal medicine examination open to blood tests, cardiograms, or X-ray examinations — some of which were irrelevant under any theory of the case.[252] In specifying the condition and scope of the

---

[246] *See* § 13.04[3] (mandamus), *infra.*

[247] 379 U.S. at 118.

[248] Justice Black dissented with a characteristically pithy argument that when a bus driver has had a prior accident, it is fair to ask, "What is the matter with the driver? Is he blind or crazy?" 379 U.S. at 123 (Black, J., concurring in part and dissenting in part).

[249] 379 U.S. at 118.

[250] *Compare Anson v. Fickel*, 110 F.R.D. 184 (N.D. Ind. 1986) (good cause found where discoverer had already tried to obtain information by other means), *with Marroni v. Matey*, 82 F.R.D. 371 (E.D. Pa. 1979) (good cause lacking where no such showing made).

[251] 256 S.E.2d 335 (Ga. 1979).

[252] *Schlagenhauf*, 379 U.S. at 121 n.16.

examination, a court must balance the discoverer's needs against the privacy interest and safety of the examinee.[253]

Rule 35(b) establishes a rule of reciprocity for the exchange of examination reports. The examinee is entitled to the report of the examination upon request. In exchange, she must produce any prior reports of examinations of the same condition, and she waives any privilege she has regarding the testimony of anyone who has or will examine her concerning that condition.

The actual practice under Rule 35 and comparable state provisions is less formal. Usually the parties stipulate to physical and mental examinations and the exchange of relevant examination reports without seeking any court order.[254]

[2]   Use and Value of Physical and Mental Examinations

Examination results may be used at trial subject to the rules of evidence. In most cases, the physician-patient privilege is waived voluntarily by a party-examinee's proffer of evidence, or, in some states, by statute. The examining doctor typically qualifies as an expert, and other experts may also testify on the basis of the examination when it is the kind upon which experts in the field reasonably rely.[255]

A physical or mental examination is an expensive form of discovery because the discoverer must pay the fees of the examining doctor. Yet it is often essential. No one has raised doubts of the value of Rule 35, although some have argued for its extension to non-parties, such as agents and spouses, in particular cases.[256]

PART C.
Control of Discovery

§ 10.12   THE ABUSE OF DISCOVERY[257]

Discovery abuse is a chronic complaint of litigators. It is also the rallying cry of rule reformers and a major justification for periodic amendments to the discovery rules. Yet there is no corresponding consensus about what discovery

---

[253] WRIGHT § 88.

[254] WRIGHT § 88.

[255] *See generally* FED. R. EVID. 702–705. Use of such trial experts is subject to the required disclosure requirements of Rule 26(a)(2). *See* § 10.07[2], *supra.*

[256] *See* JAMES, HAZARD & LEUBSDORF § 5.6.

[257] *See generally* Beckerman, note 29, *supra;* Wayne D. Brazil, *Civil Discovery: How Bad Are the Problems?,* 67 A.B.A.J. 450 (1981); PAUL CONNOLLY, EDITH HOLLEMAN & MICHAEL KUHLMAN, JUDICIAL CONTROLS AND THE CIVIL LITIGATIVE PROCESS: DISCOVERY (Federal Judicial Center 1978); Julius B. Levine, *"Abuse" of Discovery: Or Hard Work Makes Good Law,* 67 A.B.A.J. 565 (1981); Randy L. Agnew, Note, *Recent Changes in the Federal Rules of Civil Procedure: Prescriptions to*

abuse is or how often it occurs, let alone what should be done about it. Litigators are likely to describe it, "quite simply, [as] what your opponent is doing to you."[258] The 1983 Advisory Committee identified the problems as over-discovery and evasion.[259]

Over-discovery (or runaway discovery) can be redundant discovery. It can also be discovery that is disproportionate to the individual lawsuit as measured by its nature and complexity, the amount in controversy, the social significance of the issues, and the relative resources of the parties.[260] *Evasion* consists of conduct calculated to prevent, distort, or stall disclosure of information legitimately sought through discovery.[261]

The 1983 Advisory Committee did not address the prevalence of these problems. However, other studies have suggested that, while they are common in large and complex cases, they do not permeate the majority of federal filings.[262] A 1997 survey of lawyers by the Federal Judicial Center indicated that 61% of the lawyers in complex cases reported discovery problems, compared to 50% of lawyers in "somewhat complex cases" and 33% in non-complex cases.[263] It also found that lawyers in high-stakes cases were twice as likely to report multiple discovery problems as lawyers in low-stakes cases.[264] Lawyers hired for complex high-stakes cases probably view discovery as simply another tool for conflict.

The line separating over-discovery and evasion from vigorous advocacy is therefore difficult to draw. Some of what may be portrayed as the former may be inherent in an open-ended and party-regulated discovery scheme. Judge Easterbrook has observed that:

> Lawyers cannot limit their search for information in discovery, because they do not know what they are looking for. They do not know when to stop, because they never know when they have enough . . . . When the stakes are high — and often the stakes for corporations are many times the ad damnum of the complaint — it is worthwhile to invest the legal resources needed to produce even a small change in the probable outcome. Lawyers practicing in good faith, therefore, engage

---

Ease the Pain?, 15 TEX. TECH. L. REV. 887 (1984) (hereinafter *Recent Changes*).

[258] ARTHUR R. MILLER, THE AUGUST 1983 AMENDMENTS TO THE FEDERAL RULES OF CIVIL PROCEDURE: PROMOTING EFFECTIVE CASE MANAGEMENT AND LAWYER RESPONSIBILITY 31 (1984).

[259] Rule 26(b) advisory committee's note (1983).

[260] *See* text accompanying § 10.03[1] n.5 (noting that over-discovery involves both discovery breadth and depth), *supra*.

[261] *See* Brazil, note 257, *supra*, at 451; *Recent Changes*, note 257, *supra*, at 909.

[262] *See, e.g.*, Brazil, note 257, *supra*, at 452; CONNOLLY et al., note 257, *supra*, at xi; Levine, note 257, *supra*, at 567 (ascribing perception of widespread abuse to anecdotal evidence from large and complex cases).

[263] *FJC Survey*, note 172, *supra*, at 554–55. *See also* Robert L. Nelson, *The Discovery Process as a Circle of Blame: Institutional, Professional, and Socio-Economic Factors That Contribute to Unreasonable, Inefficient, and Amoral Behavior in Corporate Litigation*, 67 FORDHAM L. REV. 773 (1998) (explaining discovery abuse in high-stakes corporate litigation).

[264] *FJC Survey*, note 172, *supra*, at 555.

in extensive discovery; anything less is foolish.[265]

If the client can afford it, a lawyer may heed the ethical admonition to represent clients with "zeal in advocacy"[266] by pursuing discovery with a vengeance. The adversary process also encourages the aggressive lawyer to pursue remote but possible discovery targets or to assert every colorable ambiguity or objection in response to discovery requests. Reciprocity and cooperation are, after all, not hallmarks of the hotly contested lawsuit; the litigation process has been described as "inherently partisan and contentious," which makes the expectation of cooperation in discovery "a striking anomaly."[267] And, regrettably, there is a greater tendency for over-discovery and evasion when lawyers are compensated by the hour.[268]

On the other hand, over-discovery and evasion may also result from premeditated abuse. *Predatory discovery*[269] is intended less to uncover information than to delay, harass, embarrass, or financially burden the discoveree. Evasion for the same purposes becomes *obstruction* of discovery. Predatory discovery and obstruction are correctly viewed as the abuse of discovery, often characterized by rule violations and by unethical conduct.[270]

While there is no bright line separating systemically caused over-discovery and evasion from improperly motivated predatory discovery and obstruction, the distinction may still be worth drawing because these problems suggest somewhat different solutions. The systemic origins of over-discovery and evasion suggest systemic solutions: changes in attitudes and economic incentives of the bar, generic limitations on discovery, and managerial controls by the courts, at least in large and complex cases. Most of these limitations and controls would be applied at the start of and during discovery to avoid over-discovery and evasion. This was the approach of the 1993 discovery rule reforms although they were not limited to large and complex cases. In contrast, predatory discovery and obstruction are less open to cure from front-end limitations and controls. Given their improper purposes and bad faith, they may require more and tougher sanctions for discovery rule violations.

§ 10.13   FRONT-END CONTROLS: PREVENTING THE ABUSE OF DISCOVERY

The federal rules take three approaches to preventing discovery abuse. First, they require parties or their attorneys to certify to the reasonable basis, proper purpose, and proportionality of discovery requests and responses.

---

[265] Frank H. Easterbrook, *Discovery as Abuse*, 69 B.U. L. Rev. 635, 641 (1989) (footnote omitted).

[266] *ABA Model Rules*, note 1, *supra*, Rule 1.3 comment.

[267] Beckerman, note 29, *supra*, at 521.

[268] *See generally Recent Changes*, note 257, *supra*, at 909–11.

[269] The phrase is from *Marrese v. American Academy of Orthopaedic Surgeons*, 726 F.2d 1150, 1162 (7th Cir. 1984).

[270] *Cf.* ABA Model Rules, note 1, *supra*, Rules 3.2–3.4. *See generally* Robert E. Sarazen, Note, *An Ethical Approach to Discovery Abuse*, 4 Geo. J. Legal Ethics 459 (1990).

Second, they permit and encourage judicial management of discovery by pretrial conferences and managerial orders regulating discovery. Finally, they authorize the issuance of protective orders against specific hardships from discovery.

[1]   Certification Requirements

Rule 26(g) imposes two different kinds of certification requirements on discovery initiatives. It requires an attorney or unrepresented party to certify that to the best of the signer's knowledge, information or belief, formed after reasonable inquiry, the disclosure under Rule 26(a)(1) or (3) is "complete and correct as of the time it is made." The 1993 Advisory Committee cautioned, however, that the rule does not require exhaustive inquiry so early in the case. Instead, the type of investigation that is required in connection with Rule 26(a) disclosures will depend upon

> the number and complexity of the issues; the location, nature, number, and availability of potentially relevant witnesses and documents; the extent of past working relationships between the attorney and the client, particularly in handling related or similar litigation [e.g., is client a repeat player?]; and of course how long the party has to conduct an investigation, either before or after the filing of the case.[271]

In addition, Rule 26(g) imposes a certification requirement for discovery requests, responses and objections paralleling that of Rule 11. The purpose of this certification requirement is to deter over-discovery and evasion by making "each attorney . . . stop and think about the legitimacy of a discovery request, a response thereto, or an objection."[272] By signing such a request or response, the attorney certifies that "to the best of [his] knowledge, information and belief formed after a reasonable inquiry," the discovery paper is (if a disclosure), "complete and correct as of the time it is made," "consistent with these rules and warranted" by law, "not interposed for any improper purpose," and not disproportionate to the needs of the case.[273]

The reasonable basis-in-law and proper-purpose certifications generally track those required by Rule 11.[274] An attorney is not required, however, to certify to the truthfulness of her client's factual responses to a discovery request.[275]

It is doubtful whether these certification requirements had really added much to the deterrence of predatory discovery or obstruction of discovery,[276] since the discovery rules have always implicitly prohibited such conduct. But the additional certification that discovery is not disproportionate to "the needs

---

[271] Rule 26(g) advisory committee's note (1993).

[272] Rule 26(g) advisory committee's note (1983).

[273] Rule 26(g).

[274] *See* § 8.05[2] (certification), *supra*.

[275] Rule 26(g) advisory committee's note (1983).

[276] *See* § 10.12 (discovery abuse), *supra*.

of the case, the discovery already had . . . , the amount in controversy, and the importance of the issues . . . ," may awaken some attorneys to the impropriety of over-discovery. According to one authority,

> [i]t is no longer sufficient, as a precondition for conducting discovery, to show that the information sought "appears reasonably calculated to lead to the discovery of admissible evidence." After satisfying this threshold requirement counsel *also must* make a common sense determination, taking into account all the circumstances, that the information sought is of sufficient potential significance to justify the burden the discovery probe would impose, that the discovery tool selected is the most efficacious of the means that might be used to acquire the desired information (taking into account cost effectiveness and the nature of the information being sought), and that the timing of the probe is sensible, *i.e.*, that there is no other juncture in the pretrial period when there would be a clearly happier balance between the benefit derived from and the burdens imposed by the particular discovery effort.[277]

This certification requirement incorporates this common sense determination into discovery even in the absence of appropriate managerial orders by the court under Rule 26(b)(1).[278]

Rule 26(g) mandates appropriate sanctions against the person who certifies in violation of the rule, the party on whose behalf the corresponding disclosure, request, or response was made, or both.[279] In practice, violations of Rule 26(g) will usually be accompanied by violations of other discovery rules subject to sanction under Rule 37, and Rule 26(g) sanctions can be decided simultaneously with Rule 37 sanctions.[280] The 1993 Advisory Committee emphasized, however, that Rule 11 no longer applies to such violations.

[2]   Managerial Orders

Section 10.12 suggests that one reason for over-discovery and evasion is that discovery is an open-ended party-regulated adversarial process. One obvious response is more judicial regulation. The 1980 and 1983 amendments to the rules provided this by authorizing and encouraging early judicial intervention by pretrial conference, and by empowering the court, as educated by such conferences, to issue managerial discovery orders.[281] The 1993

---

[277] *In re Convergent Techs. Sec. Litig.*, 108 F.R.D. 328, 331 (N.D. Cal. 1985) (Brazil, Mag.) (emphasis in original).

[278] *See* § 10.13[2] (managerial orders), *infra*.

[279] *See, e.g., Appeal of Licht & Semonoff*, 796 F.2d 564 (1st Cir. 1986) (dismissing, for lack of jurisdiction, appeal of unreported decision that Rule 26(g) was violated by use of depositions to harass opponents in proxy contest and to gain information for that contest, rather than to advance the lawsuit).

[280] *See, e.g., Perkinson v. Houlihan's/D.C., Inc.*, 108 F.R.D. 667 (D.D.C. 1985); *Tise v. Kule*, 37 Fed. R. Serv. 2d (Callaghan) 846 (S.D.N.Y. 1983). *See generally* § 10.14[2] (nature and incidence of sanctions), *infra*.

[281] *See Stillman v. Nickel Odeon, S.A.*, 102 F.R.D. 286, 287 (S.D.N.Y. 1984) (the amendments

amendments strengthened the courts' managerial powers because the Advisory Committee believed that "there [was] a greater need for early judicial involvement to consider the scope and timing of the disclosure requirements of Rule 26(a) and the presumptive limits on discovery imposed" by the rules. The 2000 amendments reinforced the court's powers, by making it the gatekeeper for discovery of matters beyond the claims or defenses in the case, yet relevant to the subject matter.[282] Some states have accomplished the same ends more indirectly by fixing discovery time limits by rule for civil actions,[283] often categorized by their complexity or amount in controversy.

The courts have long had the power under Rule 16 to hold pretrial conferences and issue orders which encompass discovery, and Rule 16(b) contemplates that the court may hold a discovery conference after the parties have conferred and submitted a discovery plan.[284] Whether or not a discovery conference is held by the court, it "shall" enter an order identifying issues for discovery purposes, limiting and scheduling discovery (including required disclosures), determining other matters incidental to discovery, such as cost allocation, and limiting the time by which the parties must complete discovery.[285]

Against reduction of over-discovery and evasion that such rules might provide must be balanced the risk that they will prompt over-management, especially in routine and relatively simple litigation. Rule 16(b) thus provides that local rules may exempt categories of inappropriate cases. Whether this will be sufficient to prevent unwarranted application of the rule's requirements remains to be seen.

If Rules 26(g) and 16(b) supply the occasion for managerial intervention by the courts into discovery, Rule 26(b)(1) supplies the tools "to enable the court to keep tighter rein on the extent of discovery," according to the 1993 Advisory Committee. Rules 30 and 33 presumptively limit the number of depositions and interrogatories, and Rule 26(b)(2) allows courts by local rule or order to alter these limits, as well to limit the length of depositions or the number of requests for admissions. Perhaps more important, Rule 26(b)(2)(C) also provides that the "court must limit the frequency or extent of discovery" if it determines that the discovery sought is excessive for any of three overlapping reasons.

Rule 26(b)(2)(C)(I) requires the court to limit discovery which is unreasonably cumulative or duplicative or is obtainable from a less burdensome and expensive source. Under this provision, courts have

---

encourage courts to take a "strong supervisory role in discovery and to consider innovative cost-shifting concepts").

[282] *See* § 10.03[1], *supra*.

[283] *See, e.g.*, D.C. SUPER. CT. R. 26(d).

[284] Rule 26(f) formerly required such a conference on motion by a party. The 1993 amendment deleted the requirement, apparently on the assumption that the mandatory planning conference of the parties would substitute for it and generate a discovery plan on which the court can base the still-required discovery scheduling order. *See* § 10.07[1], *supra*.

[285] *See generally* § 12.03 (pretrial conference), *infra*.

prohibited discovery by interrogatories when the discoverer has already obtained the same information from the subject by depositions.[286]

Rule 26(b)(2)(C)(ii) requires the court to limit discovery when the discoverer has had ample prior opportunity to discover the information sought. This rule has been used to justify court-imposed time limits on discovery.[287]

Finally, Rule 26(b)(2)(C)(iii) requires the court to limit discovery when "the burden or expense of the proposed discovery outweighs its likely benefit, considering the needs of the case, the amount in controversy, the parties' resources, the importance of the issues at stake in the litigation, and the importance of the discovery in resolving the issues." The rule thus gives a federal court the power to "limit unnecessarily expensive discovery."[288] When this limitation should be imposed depends on the facts of the case. In *TIE/Communications, Inc. v. Bumper Products Corp.*,[289] the discoverer sought to re-depose a corporate employee after having failed to inquire into a subject during the first deposition "due to inadvertence." Refusing to block the deposition, the court considered that the subject involved $100,000, 30% of the damages claimed, that the parties would have to get together anyway for other employee depositions, and that the party opposing discovery had shown no special hardship.

The cases reported to date suggest that the courts have not yet made much use of the managerial power that Rule 26(b)(2)(C)(i)–(iii) requires them to exercise. Stressing the difficulty trial courts face balancing discovery benefits against burdens, one appellate judge has predicted that unless the imbalance is dramatic, "past habit is likely to cause the court to permit it."[290] But the 2000 amendment to the rule expressly cross-references the Rule 26(b)(2) managerial power in Rule 26(b)(1) to remind the courts of their authority and obligation, and the Supreme Court has itself emphasized that what is now Rule 26(b)(2)(C)(iii) "vests the trial court with broad discretion to tailor discovery narrowly and to dictate the sequence of discovery."[291] Perhaps such pointed reminders will yet overcome "past habit."

Finally, the 2006 rule amendments separately authorized similar cost-benefit analysis for the production of electronically stored information that is not reasonably accessible because of undue burden or cost. If the responding party shows this kind of inaccessibility, the requesting party must show good

---

[286] *See, e.g., Continental Ill. Nat'l Bank & Trust Co. v. WH Venture*, 1986 U.S. Dist. LEXIS 28237 (E.D. Pa. March 13, 1986) (magistrate's decision) (stating that ordinarily "a motion to compel answers to subsequent interrogatories seeking to elicit the same information as obtained by way of the earlier depositions should be denied," but allowing interrogatory discovery to enable discoverer to close gaps in deponents' answers).

[287] *See, e.g., Slomiak v. Bear Stearns & Co.*, 597 F. Supp. 676 (S.D.N.Y. 1984).

[288] *Brock v. Frank V. Panzarino, Inc.*, 109 F.R.D. 157, 160 (E.D.N.Y. 1986) (properly rejecting this argument as a way around Rule 26(b)(3)'s protection of witness statements).

[289] 1987 U.S. Dist. LEXIS 10037 (E.D. Pa. Nov. 6, 1987).

[290] Winter, note 158, *supra*, at 265.

[291] *Crawford-El v. Britton*, 523 U.S. 574, 598 (1998).

cause for discovery using the cost-benefit formula of Rule 26(b)(2)(C). If the court grants discovery, it may specify conditions for the discovery, which may include cost-shifting.[292]

[3]   Protective Orders Against Specific Hardship[293]

Upon motion and for good cause shown, almost all jurisdictions authorize the entry of orders protecting against burdensome or oppressive discovery. Rule 26(c), for example, authorizes the federal courts to issue *protective orders* on motion and the movant's certification that she has conferred in good faith with other parties to resolve the dispute. Protective orders are not materially different from what we have termed *managerial orders*,[294] but protective orders have traditionally been issued to protect against specific hardships from discovery[295] rather than to manage and control over-discovery. In deciding a motion for a protective order, the court must balance hardship to the discoveree if discovery is allowed as sought against the hardship to the discoverer if discovery is denied or restricted.[296] Most commonly, parties seek protective orders against unduly burdensome or invasive discovery.

Discovery can be unduly burdensome because of the location or condition of the discoveree. For example, because there are no geographic limitations on the location of opposing-party depositions, they are sometimes noticed for locations distant from the residence of the party-deponent. A protective order changing the location of the deposition or conditioning it on payment of travel expenses may be appropriate.[297] Or the age or health of a deponent may make a scheduled all-day deposition unduly burdensome and present good cause for shortening it, spacing it, or preventing it in favor of a less burdensome discovery method such as interrogatories.[298]

Discovery may be unduly invasive when it probes matter that, though unprivileged, is confidential. Predatory discovery, in fact, probes such matter more to embarrass and harass the discoveree than to obtain information.[299] As a result, parties often argue confidentiality when they seek a protective

---

[292] *See* § 10.03[e] (discussing *Zubulake* and factors it suggested for deciding cost-shifting for discovery of electronically stored information that is not reasonably accessible).

[293] *See generally* Jacqueline S. Guenego, Note, *Trends in Protective Orders Under Federal Rule of Civil Procedure 26(c): Why Some Cases Fumble While Others Score*, 60 FORDHAM L. REV. 541 (1991); Richard L. Marcus, *Myth and Reality in Protective Order Litigation*, 69 CORNELL L. REV. 1 (1983).

[294] *See* § 10.13[2], *supra.*

[295] *See Cipollone v. Liggett Group, Inc.*, 785 F.2d 1108, 1121 (3d Cir. 1986) (stressing burden on movant to show particular need for protection).

[296] *See Marrese v. American Acad. of Orthopaedic Surgeons*, 726 F.2d 1150, 1159 (7th Cir. 1984) (*en banc*).

[297] *See, e.g., Haviland & Co. v. Montgomery Ward & Co.*, 31 F.R.D. 578, 580 (S.D.N.Y. 1962).

[298] *Haviland & Co. v. Montgomery Ward & Co.*, 31 F.R.D. 578, 580 (S.D.N.Y. 1962) *See generally* A. Darby Dickerson, *Deposition Dilemmas: Vexatious Scheduling and Errata Sheets*, 12 GEO. J. LEGAL ETHICS 1 (1998) (discussing protective orders and other responses to vexatious deposition scheduling).

[299] *See, e.g., Seattle Times Co. v. Rhinehart*, 467 U.S. 20 (1984) (noting that such discovery

order.[300] In commercial litigation, for example, confidentiality is often invoked to protect trade secrets or customer lists from competitors.[301] It has also been invoked to protect against unconditional discovery of financial information, group membership information, peer review information in connection with tenure, promotion and other personnel decisions, and institutional self-critiques.[302] However, the courts have been vigilant in requiring a specific showing of hardship from discovery of confidential matters and have rejected conclusory assertions by the discoveree of embarrassment or unfairness.[303]

Prohibition of discovery is just one of eight different types of protective orders that Rule 26(c) describes. This mix reflects the rule's strong preference for orders restricting discovery rather than denying it altogether. A court may impose conditions on the location, method, scope, and sequence of discovery, or on any other incident of discovery as required to give sufficient protection to the movant. When the asserted hardship is invasion of confidentiality, for example, the court may restrict disclosure to particular parties or their attorneys and prohibit dissemination of the discovered information. In commercial litigation, *umbrella protective orders* are commonplace, extending protection against dissemination to any document that the discoveree designates confidential without any individualized review by the court.[304]

In *Seattle Times Co. v. Rhinehart*,[305] the Supreme Court rejected a First Amendment challenge to the entry of a protective order restricting dissemination of information obtained by discovery. There, the defendant newspaper in a defamation action sought discovery of the plaintiff religious group's membership and donor lists, candidly acknowledging that such information might be disseminated in newspaper articles. The Court first emphasized that litigants have no First Amendment right of access to information made available only for purposes of trying a suit and that such discovery is not a traditionally public source of information.[306] It then found

---

implicates not only privacy interests but also litigants' interests in unimpeded access to the courts if they are forced to forgo pursuit of their claims rather than give up their privacy); *Marrese*, 726 F.2d at 1162 (finding a "hint of predatory discovery" in plaintiff's request for membership information as a basis for deposing members who voted against his application).

[300] *See* Laurie K. Dore, *Secrecy by Consent: The Use and Limits of Confidentiality in the Pursuit of Settlement*, 74 Notre Dame L. Rev. 283 (1999).

[301] *See* James R. McKown, *Discovery of Trade Secrets*, 10 Santa Clara Computer & High Tech. L.J. 35 (1994).

[302] *See generally* Moore §§ 12.101, 26.104, 26.105 (listing cases). *Cf. Granger v. National R.R. Passenger Corp.*, 116 F.R.D. 507, 508 (E.D. Pa. 1987) (applying "critical self-analysis doctrine" to protect recommendations in railroad's accident analysis).

[303] *See, e.g., Cipollone*, 649 F. Supp. 664 (rejecting as unspecific cigarette manufacturers' sweeping claims that discovery of information regarding their knowledge of the health risks of smoking might prove embarrassing, detrimental to the market price of their stock, and helpful to their competitors or other plaintiffs).

[304] *See, e.g.,* Dore, note 300, *supra*; Richard L. Marcus, *The Discovery Confidentiality Controversy*, 1991 U. Ill. L. Rev. 457 (1991); Marcus, note 293, *supra*, at 9; Arthur R. Miller, *Confidentiality, Protective Orders, and Public Access to the Courts*, 105 Harv. L. Rev. 427 (1991).

[305] 467 U.S. 20 (1984).

[306] 467 U.S. at 32.

that "the prevention of abuse that can attend the coerced production of information under a state's discovery rule is sufficient justification for the authorizing of protective orders."[307]

On the other hand, the Supreme Court has long acknowledged the public's common law right of access to judicial proceedings and judicial records.[308] If documents under a protective order are actually filed in court or submitted into evidence, the strong presumption of access must be balanced against competing interests to determine whether disclosure will be made. Moreover, even in *Seattle Times*, the Court emphasized that the particular protective order for discovery materials was limited in nature and did not restrict the dissemination of information gained outside the discovery process. Other courts have noted that First Amendment interests of discoverers and the public can sometimes be accommodated by properly limited protective orders, requiring, for example, *in camera* inspection of the information by the trial judge, *redaction* (deletion) of names or other especially private information prior to disclosure, or postponement of discovery of private matter until the discoveree has had the opportunity to test the discoverer's *prima facie* claims or defenses.[309] One court has tried to craft a compromise between protection and public access, by holding that material filed with discovery motions under an umbrella protection order is "not subject to the common-law right of access, whereas discovery material filed in connection with pretrial motions that require judicial resolution of the merits is subject to the common-law right."[310]

§ 10.14 BACK-END CONTROLS: SANCTIONS

[1] The Predicate for Sanctions

All procedural systems authorize sanctions against parties and attorneys who violate the discovery rules or discovery orders. Governing law in federal court includes Rules 37 and 26(g), a statute,[311] and common law.[312] Under Rule 37, no party may move for an order compelling discovery or for sanctions without certifying that it has tried in good faith to resolve the discovery dispute with other parties without court action.[313] Sanctions most commonly result from a party's defiance of a prior discovery order. Accordingly, Rule 37(b) authorizes sanctions for a failure to comply with an order to compel

---

[307] 467 U.S. at 35–36.

[308] *Nixon v. Warner Commc'ns, Inc.*, 435 U.S. 589 (1978).

[309] *See, e.g., Marrese*, 726 F.2d at 1160.

[310] *Chicago Tribune Co. v. Bridgestone/Firestone, Inc.*, 263 F.3d 1304 (2001) (per curiam). *See generally* Richard L. Marcus, *A Modest Proposal: Recognizing (at Last) That the Federal Rules Do Not Declare That Discovery Is Presumptively Public*, 81 CHI.-KENT L. REV. 331 (2006).

[311] 28 U.S.C. § 1927.

[312] *See Roadway Express, Inc. v. Piper*, 447 U.S. 752, 764–67 (1980).

[313] Rule 37(e) now provides that no sanctions will lie for a failure to provide electronically stored information "lost as a result of routine, good-faith operation of an electronic information system." This rule thus reinforces the importance of an early discovery conference in which the parties discuss a "litigation hold" on relevant electronic information.

discovery or equivalent discovery order.[314] Rules 26(g), 37(c) and 37(d), however, permit the imposition of sanctions without an intervening discovery order in some circumstances. When a discovery order has been violated, or the facts warrant bypassing the usual predicate of a discovery order, the court may impose sanctions tailored to the offense.

The discoverer may move under Rule 37(a)[315] for an order compelling discovery either when the discoveree objects to discovery or responds evasively or incompletely. In the former circumstances, this motion tests any objections that the discoveree has interposed to the requested discovery.[316] If the motion to compel is granted, Rule 37(a)(5) requires the court to award the movant attorney's fees and other expenses incurred in making the motion unless it finds that opposition to the motion was "substantially justified."[317] If the motion is denied, then the discoveree has a similar opportunity for reimbursement and the court may issue a protective order in his favor. "The great operative principle of Rule 37(a)(4) is that the loser pays."[318]

Violation of an order compelling discovery or of an equivalent discovery order, whether or not willful,[319] is the predicate for discovery sanctions under Rule 37(b). Evincing a general hesitancy about imposing discovery sanctions,[320] the courts have been strict in rejecting arguments that general managerial or pretrial orders not expressly compelling discovery can satisfy Rule 37(b)'s predicate of a discovery order.[321]

When the discoveree simply refuses to respond — fails to appear at all for her deposition, or to serve any response to interrogatories or production requests — the predicate of a discovery order is eliminated. Rule 37(d) then permits the discoverer to move directly for sanctions short of contempt and for all expenses caused by the failure of discovery, not just those incurred in making the Rule 37(d) motion. Efficiency is the rationale for this shortcut to sanctions. Requiring a court order to compel a response, followed in all likelihood by a second motion to test objections made in the compelled

---

[314] Equivalent discovery orders include Rule 35 orders providing for physical or mental examinations and arguably Rule 16(b) scheduling orders, although they are not mentioned in Rule 37(b).

[315] A motion seeking an order against a party must be filed in the court where the action is pending. Motions against non-parties must be filed in the court for the district where the discovery is being, or is to be, taken. Rule 37(a)(1).

[316] *See* Rule 33(a).

[317] "Making a motion, or opposing a motion, is 'substantially justified' if the motion raised an issue about which reasonable people could genuinely differ on whether a party was bound to comply with a discovery rule." WRIGHT & MILLER § 2288.

[318] WRIGHT & MILLER § 2288

[319] *See Societe Internationale Pour Participations Industrielles et Commerciales, S.A. v. Rogers,* 357 U.S. 197 (1958). The violator's *scienter* — state of mind — does go to the severity of sanctions, however. *See* § 10.14[2] (nature and incidence of sanctions), *infra*.

[320] *See* § 10.14[2] (incidence of sanctions), *infra*.

[321] *See, e.g., Salahuddin v. Harris,* 782 F.2d 1127 (2d Cir. 1986) (neither Rule 30(a) order *allowing* deposition nor "implied orders" provide the predicate for Rule 37(b) sanctions).

response, would intolerably delay discovery in many cases and invite abuse.[322] Rule 37(d) therefore, provides that a failure to respond is not excused upon the ground that the discovery is objectionable, unless the discoveree has applied for a protective order. The proper way to object to discovery is to apply for such an order under Rule 26(c) or to make the objections in a written response or at the deposition.

An order compelling discovery is not a prerequisite for sanctions in some additional situations. Rule 37(e) provides for the award of expenses against an attorney who fails to participate in good faith in the framing of a discovery plan under Rule 26(f). Rule 37(c) provides a self-executing sanction for a party's prejudicial failure to disclose information required to be disclosed by Rule 26(a), by precluding that party from using the information as evidence at trial. More importantly, Rule 26(g) requires appropriate sanctions against an attorney or party for violation of its certification requirement.[323] Because most violations of the discovery rules can also be construed as violations of the certification requirement, Rule 26(g) may encourage federal courts to impose discovery sanctions more often without an intervening order compelling discovery.[324]

Rule 26(g) also supplies the sole authority under the rules for imposing sanctions for over-discovery. A limiting order under Rule 26(b)(2)(C)(i)–(iii) or 26(c) need not precede these sanctions,[325] although it is likely that some courts will infer the necessity of one due to the novelty of the offense[326] and their accustomed sanctions practice.

[2]   The Nature and Incidence of Sanctions

Courts have long had discretion to impose discovery sanctions under rules like Rule 37(b) and 37(d).[327] Often, however, they have been reluctant to exercise that discretion. This created a climate conducive to discovery abuse.

> The typical pattern of sanctioning that emerges from the reported cases is one in which the delay, obfuscation, contumacy, and lame excuses on the part of litigants and their attorneys are tolerated without any measured remedial action until the court is provoked

---

[322] *Moore* § 37.90. "Rule 37(d) deals, then, with failure to make the initial response required by the Rules, while subdivisions (a) and (b) provide a method of resolving differences between the parties and enforcing the court's determinations." *Salahuddin v. Harris*, 782 F.2d 1127 (2d Cir. 1986).

[323] *See also* § 12.02[1] (requests for admissions), *infra*, discussing sanction of expenses for unjustified refusals to admit under Rule 36.

[324] *See, e.g., St. Paul Reinsurance Co., Ltd. v. Commercial Fin. Corp.*, 198 F.R.D. 508 (N.D. Iowa 2000) (imposing Rule 26(g) sanction *sua sponte*, without prior order compelling discovery, on discoveree for making boilerplate and frivolous objections).

[325] *See, e.g., Hayes v. National Gypsum Co.*, 38 Fed. R. Serv. 2d (Callaghan) 645 (E.D. Pa. 1984) (awarding expenses incurred by discoveree because of duplicative discovery, despite the absence of any court-ordered limit on same).

[326] *See* § 10.13[2] (managerial orders), *supra*.

[327] Both of these subprovisions provide that the court "may" issue an order for sanctions.

beyond endurance. At that point the court punishes one side or the other with a swift and final termination of the lawsuit by dismissal or default. This "all or nothing" approach to sanctions results in considerable laxity in the day-to-day application of the rules. Attorneys are well aware that sanctions will be imposed only in the most flagrant situations.[328]

For two reasons, this historical reluctance may be abating. First, the Supreme Court has taken notice of it and reminded the trial courts that the purpose of sanctions is to deter as well as to punish.[329] Second, Rule 26(g) imposes mandatory sanctions for violation of the discovery certification requirements.[330] Since virtually any discovery abuse or discovery rule violation can be construed as a violation of the certification requirement, Rule 26(g)'s mandate may carry well beyond its literal boundaries into Rule 37.

At the same time, courts retain discretion to decide the severity of the sanction even under Rule 26(g). Limited only by the due process requirement that the sanction be proportionate to the offense,[331] or that the same be "just" and "appropriate" in the language of the Rules, federal courts may choose from a range of Rule 37(b) sanctions varying in severity.[332] The court may award discovery expenses against the violator, deem established facts that were the object of discovery,[333] prevent the violator from presenting certain evidence or supporting or opposing certain claims or defenses, strike all or part of the pleadings, hold the violator of a discovery order (other than one for a physical or mental examination) in contempt,[334] dismiss the action, or render judgment by default.

The latter sanctions of dismissal or default are the most severe,[335] presupposing correspondingly severe abuse of discovery. Accordingly, the courts have suggested that "willfulness, bad faith, or . . . fault" must be found before

---

[328] ROBERT E. RODES, JR., KENNETH F. RIPPLE & CAROL MOONEY, SANCTIONS IMPOSABLE FOR VIOLATIONS OF THE FEDERAL RULES OF CIVIL PROCEDURE 85 (Fed. Jud. Ctr. 1981). Copyright © 1981 by the Federal Judicial Center. Reprinted with permission. *See also* Brazil, note 277, *supra*, at 456 (noting that attorneys believe that courts fail miserably in imposing sanctions).

[329] *National Hockey League v. Metropolitan Hockey Club, Inc.*, 427 U.S. 639 (1976) (*per curiam*). *See also Roadway Express, Inc. v. Piper*, 447 U.S. 752 (1980).

[330] Rule 26(g) advisory committee's note (1983).

[331] *See Insurance Corp. of Ireland, Ltd. v. Compagnie des Bauxites de Guinee*, 456 U.S. 694 (1982).

[332] *See generally* Joel Slawotsky, *Rule 37 Discovery Sanctions — The Need for Supreme Court Ordered National Uniformity*, 104 DICK. L. REV. 471 (2000) (surveying sanction practice and finding that relatively unguided discretion has led to disuniformity).

[333] *Id.* (jurisdictional facts).

[334] *See* Greg Neibarger, *Chipping Away at the Stone Wall: Allowing Federal Courts to Impose Non-Compensatory Monetary Sanctions Upon Errant Attorneys Without a Finding of Contempt*, 33 IND. L. REV. 1045 (2000) (proposing other non-monetary sanctions in addition to contempt for discovery abuse).

[335] *See, e.g., Trans World Airlines, Inc. v. Hughes*, 449 F.2d 51 (2d Cir. 1971) (default judgment for $145 million against Howard Hughes for his failure to comply with order to appear for deposition), *rev'd on other grounds sub nom., Hughes Tool Co. v. TWA*, 409 U.S. 363 (1973).

dismissal or entry of default is appropriate, even though no such scienter requirement attaches to the underlying finding that a discovery rule or order has been violated.[336]

The question whether these severe sanctions are appropriate is further complicated when they are levied for transgressions by the attorney rather than the party. The courts have always been reluctant to penalize parties on the merits for the acts of their attorneys, at least absent the client's knowledge or complicity.[337] For example, before the drastic sanction of dismissal is imposed for discovery misconduct of an attorney, the Court of Appeals for the Third Circuit has required the trial court to consider whether the party is responsible for the conduct, the degree of the party's responsibility, the resulting prejudice to the opposing party, whether the attorney has had a history of dilatory discovery tactics, whether the conduct was wilful or in bad faith, whether other effective sanctions short of dismissal are viable, and whether the party's claim or defense is "meritorious."[338]

---

[336] *Societe Internationale*, 357 U.S. at 212. *See also Cine Forty-Second St. Theatre Corp. v. Allied Artists Pictures Corp.*, 602 F.2d 1062, 1065 (2d Cir. 1979).

[337] *See generally* Charles B. Renfrew, *Discovery Sanctions: A Judicial Perspective*, 67 CAL. L. REV. 264, 273–74 (1979). *But see Link v. Wabash R.R. Co.*, 370 U.S. 626, 633 (1962) (a litigant chooses counsel at his peril).

[338] *Poulis v. State Farm Fire & Cas. Co.*, 747 F.2d 863, 868–70 (3d Cir. 1984). *See also Scarborough v. Eubanks*, 747 F.2d 871 (3d Cir. 1984). In these companion cases (ironically involving the same attorney) the court, respectively, affirmed dismissal for a pattern of dilatory conduct which prejudiced the opposing party, but reversed dismissal for a failure to abide court-ordered deadlines, when no prejudice resulted and the opposing party also missed them. *See also Bluitt v. Arco Chem. Co.*, 777 F.2d 188, 190–91 (5th Cir. 1985).

Chapter 11

DISPOSITION WITHOUT TRIAL

§ 11.01 OVERVIEW

All procedural systems provide a variety of alternatives for obtaining judgment before trial. If a defendant fails to respond to a pleading within the time designated for response, he is in *default* and subject to entry of a *default judgment*, discussed in section 11.02. If defendant responds by successfully attacking the pleading, it may be dismissed, as previously discussed in section 8.07. When materials outside the pleadings are submitted in support of some motions attacking the pleadings, the motions are converted to motions for *summary judgment*, discussed in section 11.03. Summary judgment is also available to either party whenever it can show that there is no genuinely triable issue of material fact and that it is entitled to judgment as a matter of law. Finally, when the plaintiff elects to withdraw his action before a final judgment on the merits, he may seek a *voluntary dismissal* or *nonsuit*. Alternatively, if he simply abandons the action by failing to prosecute or disobeys court orders or rules, he is subject to *involuntary dismissal* or *compulsory nonsuit*. Dismissals and nonsuits are discussed in Section 11.04.[1]

§ 11.02 DEFAULT

Our procedural systems rely principally on the parties to move cases along. A party's complete failure to respond to a pleading exposes an adversary to costly delay and uncertainty. Almost all systems therefore make *default judgments* available as a protection for the rights of the claimant. At the same time, all procedural systems prefer dispositions on the merits to default judgments.[2] Rule 55 is quite typical in reconciling these concerns by assuring that the unresponsive party is aware of the risk of such a judgment. The usual pattern under the rule begins when the default is formally noted in some fashion, as by a clerk's entry on the docket sheet. Only after entry of default may the court, in its discretion and often pursuant to notice to the defaulting party and sometimes a hearing on damages, enter a default judgment. In short,

---

[1] Motions to dismiss a complaint under Rule 12 are discussed in § 8.07, *supra*.

[2] *See, e.g., Varnes v. Glass Bottle Blowers Ass'n*, 674 F.2d 1365 (11th Cir. 1982); *Ellingsworth v. Chrysler*, 665 F.2d 180 (7th Cir. 1981). Default judgments are common, nevertheless. In the general trial courts of Maine and Delaware, for example, approximately 3% and 15% of civil cases, respectively, ended in default judgments. STATE OF MAINE, ADMINISTRATIVE OFFICE OF THE COURTS, 1987 ANNUAL REPORT 90 (1988) and ADMINISTRATIVE OFFICE OF THE COURTS, 1982 ANNUAL REPORT OF THE DELAWARE JUDICIARY 79 (1983), cited in Hillard M. Sterling & Philip G. Schrag, *Default Judgments Against Consumers: Has the System Failed?*, 67 DENVER U. L. REV. 357 (1990).

be careful to distinguish default from a default judgment.

[1]   Default and Its Entry

A party is in default and subject to the rules governing default judgments when he has "failed to plead or otherwise defend," as, for example, by filing motions to attack the adversary's pleadings.[3] Default is a corollary to the strict time limits most systems impose for responding to pleadings.[4] When a party has responded within the time limit by pleading or attacking the complaint, his subsequent failure to appear for trial does not, without more, place him in default. By pleading, he places the case at issue, obligating his adversary to present his proof in order to recover a judgment.[5]

Rule 55 authorizes the clerk to enter a default when it appears from the docket or is shown by affidavit of the claimant. *Entry of default* is simply a notation of the fact of default and an interlocutory — interim — step towards the entry of a default judgment. It cuts off the defaulting party's right to further notice, unless he has appeared in the litigation.[6]

Rule 55(c) authorizes the court in its discretion to set aside a docket entry of default upon good cause shown. The court may consider the defaulting party's willfulness, prejudice to the adversary should the default be set aside, and the existence of any meritorious defense to the claim.[7] The courts' preference for merits dispositions, however, usually makes them lenient towards the defaulting party on motions to set aside the entry of default where he evinces a desire to correct the default.[8]

[2]   Entry of Default Judgment

Judgment may follow entry of default in two ways. Clerks have authority under Rule 55(b)(1) to enter default judgments, but only if the defaulting party is not an unrepresented minor or incompetent, that party has not appeared in the action, and the claimant shows by affidavit that the relief sought is a liquidated (arithmetically ascertainable) sum. Only the court may enter

---

[3] *See, e.g.,* Rule 55(a). *See generally* Carl B. Schultz, *Sanctioning Defendants' Non-Willful Delay: The Failure of Rule 55 and a Proposal for Its Reform,* 23 U. Rich. L. Rev. 203, 204 (1989).

[4] *See, e.g.,* Rule 12(a) (requiring a party against whom a claim is pled to answer, reply or move against the pleading under Rule 12 within 20 days after service).

[5] *See, e.g., Coulas v. Smith,* 395 P.2d 527 (Ariz. 1964) (rules governing default judgments are inapplicable to judgment entered against a defendant who answered the complaint and a crossclaim, but then failed to appear at trial). *See generally Bass v. Hoagland,* 172 F.2d 205 (5th Cir.), *cert. denied,* 338 U.S. 816 (1949). Most courts are also empowered by rule, statute, or inherent power to enter penalty default judgments against parties who violate rules or orders of the court. *See, e.g.,* Rules 11, 16, 26(g), and 37.

[6] Moore § 55.12[1]. *See* § 11.02[2] (defining appearance), *infra.*

[7] Moore § 55.50[1].

[8] Moore § 55.50[1].; Wright & Miller § 2692.

judgment in all other cases. When the defaulting party has appeared, notice and possibly a hearing will be necessary.[9]

An *appearance* is any action that demonstrates sufficient interest by the defaulting party in the litigation to suggest that he might contest the award of relief by default judgment, and therefore could benefit from notice of application for such a judgment. A party usually appears formally by filing a *praecipe* or notice of appearance by his attorney, or by making other submissions to the court during the lawsuit. In part to encourage settlement efforts by parties, the courts have also found the necessary appearance from participation in protracted settlement negotiations, correspondence, or other communications inconsistent with the complete abandonment of the litigation and disregard for judicial process.[10]

After any required notice, Rule 55(b)(2) authorizes the court to conduct a hearing on the proper measure of relief. The judicial hearing is not a trial in most systems, and there is no right to a jury. Some states, however, entitle the non-defaulting party who previously claimed a jury to a jury trial on damages.[11] The default establishes all well-pleaded facts as true and forecloses any offer of proof by the defaulting party as to liability. However, the defaulting party does not admit conclusions of law and in many jurisdictions may still argue that his adversary's pleading states no claim.[12] Defendant also may offer evidence on the measure of relief. Courts use their discretion to determine whether to enter a default judgment at all, what proof to allow, and how much and what kind of relief they will grant.[13]

Like other final judgments, default judgments are subject to timely post-judgment attack under Rule 60(b).[14] Courts are particularly apt to grant a motion to vacate a default judgment when the defaulting party was served constructively rather than in person,[15] or was denied notice of the application for judgment to which his prior appearance entitled him. Relevant factors are otherwise the same as those considered on a motion to set aside entry of

---

[9] Rule 55(b)(2).

[10] *See generally* MOORE § 55.21[2]. If, however, during informal communications, the defaulting party was clearly informed of his adversary's intent to seek a default judgment, then the court will usually not find an appearance entitling the defaulting party to notice under Rule 55(b)(2). *Compare Wilson v. Moore & Associates, Inc.*, 564 F.2d 366 (9th Cir. 1977) (plaintiff's counsel warned defendant by letter that failure to answer would place him in default; no appearance), *with Lutomski v. Panther Valley Coin Exch.*, 653 F.2d 270 (6th Cir. 1981) (informal contacts regarding proper amount of damage constituted an appearance).

[11] *See, e.g.*, VA. SUP. CT. R. 3:19 (West, Westlaw through Mar. 2007 amendments).

[12] *See, e.g.*, *Caruso v. Krieger*, 698 S.W.2d 760 (Tex. Ct. App. 3d Dist. 1985); MOORE § 55.12[1].

[13] The last is subject to Rule 54(c)'s limitation of the relief to the kind or amount sought in the pleaded demand for relief. *See* § 8.06[3] (demand for relief), *supra*.

[14] *See* § 12.11[2][b] (motions to vacate judgment within one year), *infra*. The Supreme Court has held that due process forbids states from conditioning such relief on the existence of a meritorious defense, if the default was entered without proper notice to defendant. *Peralta v. Heights Medical Ctr., Inc.*, 485 U.S. 80 (1988).

[15] *See, e.g.*, N.Y. CIV. PRAC. L. & R. § 317 (McKinney, Westlaw through 2007 legislation); VA. CODE ANN. § 8.01-322 (LEXIS through 2007 Reg. Sess.).

default, with one important difference. The systemic interest in finality of judgments[16] enters into the equation as a counterweight to leniency. Doubts are still resolved in favor of the defaulting party,[17] but the courts are less lenient than they are in finding good cause to set aside interlocutory entries of default.[18]

§ 11.03　SUMMARY JUDGMENT

[1]　Purposes

Once pleadings were only open to facial attack (an attack on the sufficiency of allegations appearing on the face of the pleading).[19] The truth and sufficiency of facts supporting a pleading could be tested only at trial.[20] Summary judgment evolved to intercept before trial factually insufficient claims or defenses — those which would probably suffer a motion for a directed verdict (now termed judgment as a matter of law in federal courts)[21] at trial. The Supreme Court, in fact, has characterized summary judgments as pretrial equivalents of directed verdicts.[22] The summary judgment motion permits a party to go beyond the allegations in the pleadings to the evidence to show that there is no genuine dispute of material fact that would necessitate or justify the expense of trial, and to argue that the court should enter judgment for him on some or all claims and defenses as a matter of law. Like the motion for directed verdict, it is consistent with the right to jury trial because it tests whether there is any genuine factual dispute for the jury to resolve. "Summary judgment distinguishes the merely formal existence of a dispute as framed in the pleading from the actual substantive existence of a controversy requiring trial."[23]

By forcing the parties to preview their trial evidence and to relate it to their legal theories, a motion for summary judgment may result in what is effectively a form of discovery. This is because the risk of judgment posed by

---

[16] *See* § 13.01 (overview of appeal), *infra*.

[17] *Hritz v. Woma Corp.*, 732 F.2d 1178, 1185 (3d Cir. 1984). *See generally* Schultz, note 3, *supra*, at 213–14, 216–20 (finding that courts frequently reject default as an inappropriate sanction for non-willful delay).

[18] Wright & Miller § 2692. *See generally* Mary Kay Kane, *Relief from Federal Judgments: A Morass Unrelieved By a Rule*, 30 Hastings L.J. 41 (1978) (urging amendment to Rule 55(c) to make explicit that the standard for relief from entry of default is more lenient than the standard for relief from default judgment).

[19] *See* § 8.07[1] (motion practice in general), *supra*.

[20] *See* Charles E. Clark, Code Pleading § 80 (2d ed. 1947); John A. Bauman, *Evolution of the Summary Judgment Procedure*, 31 Ind. L.J. 329 (1956).

[21] *See* § 12.09[1] (directed verdicts), *infra*.

[22] *See Anderson v. Liberty Lobby, Inc.*, 477 U.S. 242, 250 (1986) (the standard governing summary judgment "mirrors the standard for a directed verdict . . . "); *cf.* § 12.09[3][c] (discussing how motions for summary judgment and directed verdict bear a functional resemblance to motions to dismiss for failure to state a claim, for judgment on the pleadings, and for judgment notwithstanding the verdict).

[23] Moore § 56.02.

a motion for summary judgment may force the parties to sift the typically undifferentiated mass of evidence produced by normal discovery methods to identify their material evidence in opposition to the motion. "The very intimation of mortality when summary judgment is at issue assures us that the motion will be rebutted with every factual and legal argument available."[24]

A related (but probably insufficient) purpose of summary judgment is educating the parties and the court about the case. Often a motion for summary judgment presents the first occasion for the parties to pull the case together, set priorities in their claims and defenses, relate the facts unearthed by discovery to their legal theories, and assess overall strengths and weaknesses. Even when existence of a factual dispute causes it to fail, the motion may promote settlement by alerting the nonmovant and the court to the weakness of the nonmovant's case.[25] Alternatively, the motion may at least simplify eventual trial by illuminating the genuine issues.

On the other hand, until recently at least, the movant often paid a price for such education by having to preview his *own* evidence. Thus, commentators cautioned that

> the decision to make a summary judgment motion involves a balancing of the possible damage to the movant's case by educating the opponent through supporting documents against the possible benefit of termination of the case through a favorable ruling on the motion and the possible advantage of learning more about the opponent's case through his supporting affidavits.[26]

In addition, an unsuccessful summary judgment motion may evoke a legal ruling that will haunt the movant later in the case.[27]

A trio of decisions by the Supreme Court in 1986, however, changed the price of summary judgment for some movants. Today a defendant who would not have the burden of persuasion at trial may be able to move for summary judgment on little more than a bare motion, placing almost the entire cost of summary judgment on the plaintiff.[28] This possibility invites abuse of the motion as a tool for discovery, or worse, harassment. One appellate court has commented that the motion "has often been used improperly: as a discovery device; to educate the trial judge; in the hope, however faint, of quick victory;

---

[24] *Georgia S. & Fla. Ry. Co. v. Atlantic Coast Line R.R. Co.*, 373 F.2d 493, 498 (5th Cir.), *cert. denied*, 389 U.S. 851 (1967). *See also* CLARK, note 20, *supra*, § 13.02.

[25] *See* William P. McLauchlan, *An Empirical Study of the Federal Summary Judgment Rule*, 6 J. LEGAL STUD. 427, 458 (1977); *cf.* WILLIAM W. SCHWARZER ET AL., THE ANALYSIS AND DECISION OF SUMMARY JUDGMENT MOTIONS 69 (1991).

[26] ROBERT McC. FIGG, RALPH C. McCULLOUGH & JAMES L. UNDERWOOD, CIVIL TRIAL MANUAL 2 526 (ALI-ABA student 2d ed. 1980). Copyright © 1980 by the American Law Institute. Reprinted with permission of the American Law Institute — American Bar Association Committee on Continuing Professional Education. *See also* John E. Kennedy, *Federal Summary Judgment: Reconciling Celotex v. Catrett with Adickes v. Kress and the Evidentiary Problem Under Rule 56*, 6 REV. LITIG. 227, 253 (1987).

[27] *See* § 15.14 (law of the case), *infra*.

[28] *See* § 11.03[3][b] (relationship to trial burdens), *infra*.

and in the expectation, frequently realized, of retarding the progress of a suit and making litigation more expensive."[29] Rule 11[30] (or its state procedural equivalent) acts as a control on such abuse in theory, but it is unclear how effective for this purpose it is in practice.

[2]   Procedure

[a]   Initial Motion

A motion for summary judgment may be filed by any party, although it is in practice primarily a defendant's device.[31] The motion asserts that there is no triable or "genuine" issue of material fact and that the moving party is entitled to judgment as a matter of law.[32]

While it is customary for the movant to support the motion with affidavits and other materials, Rule 56 expressly authorizes the motion "with or without supporting affidavits."[33] However, many federal courts have adopted local rules requiring the movant to accompany his motion with a statement of undisputed material facts, citing to supporting materials or the record.[34] Some states have also taken this approach.[35]

The movant may support the motion with "the pleadings, the discovery and disclosure materials on file . . . ,"[36] and any other materials that present facts

---

[29] *Professional Managers, Inc. v. Fawer, Brian, Hardy & Zatzkis*, 799 F.2d 218, 221–22 (5th Cir. 1986).

[30] *See* § 8.05[2], *supra*; Beverly Dyer, *A Genuine Ground in Summary Judgment for Rule 11*, 99 YALE L.J. 411 (1989).

[31] McLauchlan, note 25, *supra*, at 441. Defendant may usually move at any time. Plaintiff must wait a period of time after serving the complaint to enable the defendant to obtain counsel and materials beyond the pleadings with which to respond to the motion. *See, e.g.*, Rule 56(a) (20 days unless adverse party has served a motion for summary judgment).

[32] *See, e.g.*, Rule 56(c); CAL. CIV. PROC. CODE § 437c(c) (West, Westlaw through 2007). *See* § 11.03[3] (the standard for summary judgment), *infra*.

[33] *See Celotex Corp. v. Catrett*, 477 U.S. 317, 323 (1986).

[34] Note, *Court Examination of the Discovery File on a Motion for Summary Judgment*, 79 MICH. L. REV. 321, 325 n.19 (1980) (listing 28 district courts that have adopted such rules) (hereinafter cited as *Court Examination*). While such local rules are probably consistent with Rule 56 (*see* § 1.02, *supra*, and Rule 83), a local "procedure" adopted by individual judges requiring advance screening of summary judgment motions was found inconsistent and therefore invalid in *Brown v. Crawford County*, 960 F.2d 1002 (11th Cir. 1992). The Court of Appeals there noted that a survey had identified no fewer than thirty federal courts with local rules that conflict with Rule 56. *Brown*, 960 F.2d at 1009 n.10, *citing Local Rules Project* 140 (1989)

A recent study of summary judgment motion practice in a sampling of federal courts revealed very few differences between courts that had adopted such rules and those that had not. JOE CECIL & GEORGE CORT, REPORT ON SUMMARY JUDGMENT PRACTICE ACROSS DISTRICTS WITH VARIATIONS IN LOCAL RULES at 1 (FEDERAL JUDICIAL CENTER, AUG. 13, 2008).

[35] *See, e.g.*, CAL. CIV. PROC. CODE § 437c(b) (West, Westlaw through 2007 Reg. Sess.).

[36] Rule 56(c). *See generally* Edward Brunet, *Summary Judgment Materials*,147 F.R.D. 647 (1993).

that would be admissible at trial.[37] The summary judgment motion looks prospectively to what can be proven at trial;[38] the admissibility limitation ensures that "trial would [not be] futile on account of lack of competent evidence."[39] For example, material grounded in rumor and hearsay will not support summary judgment.[40] Evidentiary defects in supporting materials are waived if not challenged, just as they would be at trial.[41]

While oral evidence has supported the motion in rare cases, and Rule 43(c) authorizes the court to hear such evidence, its routine acceptance would convert summary judgment procedure into a trial.[42] Rule 56 and all but one state therefore permit the use of affidavits (sworn written statements) to support summary judgment motions. Affidavits must be made on personal knowledge by someone competent to testify.[43] Like all supporting materials, they must "set out facts that would be admissible in evidence."[44] Hearsay, speculation, conclusions of law, conclusory ultimate facts, and promises that the necessary evidence will be offered at trial therefore cannot support a motion for summary judgment, even when presented by an otherwise proper affidavit.[45]

When admissible material is offered in support of a Rule 12(b)(6) motion to dismiss for failure to state a claim or a Rule 12(c) motion for judgment on the pleadings, these federal rules provide that the motion shall be treated as a summary judgment motion. In addition, when evidentiary material in the record suggests the availability of summary judgment, a federal court may grant summary judgment *sua sponte* (on its own, without motion).[46] Fair

---

[37] *See, e.g., Duplantis v. Shell Offshore, Inc.*, 948 F.2d 187 (5th Cir. 1991); *Canada v. Blain's Helicopters, Inc.*, 831 F.2d 920, 925 (9th Cir. 1987); *Aguilera v. Cook County Police & Corr. Merit Bd.*, 760 F.2d 844, 849 (7th Cir.), *cert. denied*, 474 U.S. 907 (1985); *Brown v. Trans World Airlines, Inc.*, 746 F.2d 1354, 1358–59 (8th Cir. 1984). *But cf.* Kennedy, note 26, *supra*, at 256 (rule is ambiguous). *See generally* Brunet, note 36, *supra*, at 653–55.

[38] *See* James J. Duane, *The Four Greatest Myths About Summary Judgment*, 52 WASH. & LEE L. REV. 1523, 1535–41 (1996).

[39] *Kern v. Tri-State Ins. Co.*, 386 F.2d 754, 756 (8th Cir. 1967); *See* William W. Schwarzer, *Summary Judgment: A Proposed Revision of Rule 56*, 110 F.R.D. 213, 220 (1987).

[40] *See, e.g.*, Schwarzer, note 39, *supra*.

[41] *See, e.g., Catrett v. Johns-Manville Sales Corp.*, 826 F.2d 33, 37 (D.C. Cir. 1987), *cert. denied, Celotex Corp. v. Catrett*, 484 U.S. 1066 (1988); McCORMICK'S HANDBOOK OF THE LAW OF EVIDENCE § 4, at 140 (J. Strong 4th ed. 1992). *But see* SCHWARZER, note 25, *supra*, at 51 (criticizing the waiver rule).

[42] *See Stewart v. RCA Corp.*, 790 F.2d 624 (7th Cir. 1986) (asserting that although what is now Rule 43(c) gives judges full menu of methods for gathering evidence to resolve disputes, Rule 56 is not intended to resolve disputes).

[43] Kent Sinclair & Patrick Hanes, *Summary Judgment: A Proposal for Procedural Reform in the Core Motion Context*, 36 WM. & MARY L. REV. 1633, app. B (1995).

[44] Rule 56(e). *See, e.g., Sitts v. United States*, 811 F.2d 736 (2d Cir. 1987).

[45] *See, e.g., Leonard v. Dixie Well Service & Supply, Inc.*, 828 F.2d 291 (5th Cir. 1987) (bare statement that plaintiff was a "[s]eaman" when that is the issue will not suffice); *Campbell v. Fort Worth Bank & Trust*, 705 S.W.2d 400 (Tex. Ct. App. Dist. 2 1986, *writ ref'd n.r.e.*) (averments "to the best of my knowledge" do not represent the required personal knowledge). *See generally* Brunet, note 36, *supra*, at 658–59.

[46] *See United States v. Grayson*, 879 F.2d 620 (9th Cir. 1989) (approving *sua sponte* summary

notice to the opposing party and an opportunity to respond are prerequisites for either the conversion of a Rule 12 motion to a summary judgment motion or *sua sponte* action by the court.

[b] Responses to the Motion

Within a reasonable period of time set by Rule 56(c),[47] the non-movant may respond to a summary judgment motion in three ways and may also cross-move for summary judgment.

First, he may present an affidavit under Rule 56(f) stating why he cannot now present facts in opposition to summary judgment.[48] Because most jurisdictions permit defendants to file summary judgment motions at any time, a rule like Rule 56(f) is necessary to give the plaintiff time to undertake discovery.[49] When plaintiff files such an affidavit, the court may either deny the motion for summary judgment or grant a continuance so plaintiff can later respond with affidavits in opposition to summary judgment. The reasonableness of plaintiff's request for time is a crucial factor in the exercise of the court's discretion.[50] It is an abuse of discretion for a court to grant summary judgment without affording the opposing party a reasonable opportunity to take discovery pertinent to the motion, even when that party has not filed a Rule 56(f) affidavit.[51] "If the documents or other discovery sought would be relevant to the issues presented by the motion for summary judgment," one appellate court has said, "the opposing party should be allowed

---

judgment, even without notice to losing party, when that party has "full and fair opportunity to ventilate the issues"); *Portsmouth Square, Inc. v. Shareholders Protective Comm.*, 770 F.2d 866 (9th Cir. 1985) (affirming trial court's *sua sponte* summary judgment based on plaintiff's inability to establish genuine dispute of material fact in pretrial brief and supporting evidentiary materials). *See generally Celotex Corp.*, 477 U.S. at 326 ("[d]istrict courts are widely acknowledged to possess the power to enter summary judgments *sua sponte*, so long as the losing party was on notice . . . .") (dictum). When courts are reluctant to assert this power, they can usually accomplish the same ends by inviting the parties to file for summary judgment.

[47] Rule 56(c) assures a party opposing summary judgment at least ten days before hearing on the motion in which to respond. Many state rules provide an even longer response time in recognition of the time which a party may need to gather materials in opposition to summary judgment. *See, e.g.*, CAL. CIV. PROC. CODE § 437c(a) (West, Westlaw through 2007 Reg. Sess.) (75 days). A court may properly disregard untimely submissions. *See Lujan v. National Wildlife Fed'n*, 497 U.S. 871, 894–97 (1990).

[48] *See generally* JOHN F. BRUNET, SUMMARY JUDGMENT: FEDERAL LAW & PRACTICE § 7.02 (3d ed. 2006); John F. Lapham, Note, *Summary Judgment Before the Completion of Discovery: A Proposed Revision of Federal Rule of Civil Procedure 56(f)*, 24 U. MICH. J.L. REFORM 253, 267–81 (1990).

[49] *See, e.g.*, CAL. CIV. PROC. CODE § 437c(h) (West, Westlaw through 2007 Reg. Sess.); N.Y. CIV. PRAC. L. & R. § 3212(f) (McKinney, Westlaw through 2007 legislation).

[50] *Compare Littlejohn v. Shell Oil Co.*, 483 F.2d 1140 (5th Cir.) (*en banc*), *cert. denied*, 414 U.S. 1116 (1973) (abuse of discretion in the district court's refusal of a continuance pursuant to Rule 56(f), when the 56(f) affidavit demonstrated that the evidence was in the control of the movants and there were complicating factors regarding agreements between counsel about the timing of discovery), *with Walters v. City of Ocean Springs*, 626 F.2d 1317 (5th Cir. 1980) (grant of summary judgment affirmed when the opposing party had ample time to discover allegedly essential non-party witnesses).

[51] *See, e.g.*, *Snook v. Trust Co. of Georgia Bank*, 859 F.2d 865 (11th Cir. 1988).

the opportunity to utilize the discovery process to gain access to the requested materials."[52]

Second, even when a party could file materials in opposition to the motion, he may do nothing. Rule 56(e)(2) expressly requires a response with supporting materials only "[w]hen a motion for summary judgment is properly made and supported." The federal rule therefore casts a burden of production upon the movant to make a *prima facie* showing that there is no genuine dispute of material fact. This must be satisfied before the burden shifts to the opposing party.[53] "A right to judgment as a matter of law is not established merely because the opposing party fails to respond."[54] In *Adickes v. S.H. Kress & Co.*,[55] for example, the Supreme Court reversed a summary judgment in favor of the defendant restaurant in a civil rights action despite plaintiff's failure to oppose the motion with admissible materials. The case arose from the plaintiff's arrest for vagrancy. Although the defendant properly denied a conspiracy, evidence in the record that the arresting policeman had been in defendant's restaurant permitted the inference that he and the defendant had conspired to deny the plaintiff service, creating a genuine dispute of material fact.

If, on the other hand, the movant meets her burden of production and the opposing party does nothing, then Rule 56(e)(2) expressly provides that "summary judgment should be entered against that party." To avoid summary judgment in such a case, the opposing party may not rely merely on allegations or denials of his pleading, but his response, "by affidavits or as otherwise provided in this rule," must "set out *specific facts* showing a genuine issue for trial."[56] The reason for the exclusion of mere pleadings is clear; the very purpose of summary judgment is "to separate what is formal or pretended in denial or averment from what is genuine and substantial, so that only the latter may subject a suitor to the burden of a trial."[57] Thus, the nonmovant — no less than the movant — must present materials that would be admissible in evidence. But the Supreme Court has said in dictum that "[w]e do not mean that the nonmoving party must produce evidence in a form that would be

---

[52] *Snook*, 859 F.2d at 870.

[53] *See Celotex Corp.*, 477 U.S. at 330–31 (Brennan, J., dissenting). *See generally* § 11.03[3][b] (relation of summary judgment standard to trial burdens), *infra*; Linda S. Mullenix, *Summary Judgment: Taming the Beast of Burdens*, 10 AM. J. TRIAL ADVOC. 433, 441 (1987). Of course, the nonmoving party will rarely take the risk of not responding.

[54] *MOORE* § 56.10[3][b].

[55] 398 U.S. 144 (1970). *Adickes* also suggested that the moving party had to "foreclose the possibility" that the nonmovant might prevail at trial. 398 U.S. at 157. *See* Samuel Issacharoff & George Loewenstein, *Second Thoughts About Summary Judgment*, 100 YALE L.J. 73, 80 & n.39 (1990) (citing cases). The Court subsequently rejected this implication. *See Celotex Corp.*, 477 U.S. 317; § 11.03[3][b], *infra*.

[56] Rule 56(e)(2) (emphasis supplied).

[57] *Richard v. Credit Suisse*, 152 N.E. 110, 111 (N.Y. 1926) (Cardozo, J.). Verified pleadings, *see* § 8.05[1] (verification), *supra*, however, are sworn statements which may be treated as affidavits, if they are made upon personal knowledge by a competent affiant and present admissible facts. *See, e.g., Forts v. Malcolm*, 426 F. Supp. 464, 466 (S.D.N.Y. 1977).

admissible at trial in order to avoid summary judgment."[58] A few courts have read this dictum in isolation to permit the nonmoving party to oppose a summary judgment motion with unauthenticated or otherwise inadmissible evidence.[59] A more faithful reading is that the Court merely meant that depositions were not required and that evidence could be presented in any of the forms approved by the rule, not that the evidence itself could be inadmissible.[60]

The Supreme Court has applied the specific-fact requirement rigorously, emphasizing that a court may not infer specific facts from conclusory affidavits. "Rather, the purpose of Rule 56 is to enable a party who believes there is no genuine dispute as to a specific fact essential to the other side's case to demand at least one sworn averment of that fact before the lengthy process of litigation continues."[61] When local rules require the movant to file a statement of undisputed material facts, the opposing party is usually required to deny specifically those facts that he contends are genuinely disputed and to file a counter-statement, or the court may accept movant's statement as admitted.[62]

Finally, the opposing party is free to make a cross-motion for summary judgment. He does not concede the absence of genuine issues on the initial motion by doing so. The filing of cross-motions does not require the court to grant either; it may deny both. Each stands on its own bottom.[63]

[c]　　Disposition and Appeal

To grant summary judgment, a court must conclude that the movant has met its burden of showing that the material facts are undisputed and that it is entitled to judgment as a matter of law.[64] An evidentiary hearing will not usually attend this determination, although the court may hear oral arguments on the motion. Some federal cases suggest that "the court is obliged to take account of the entire setting of the case and must consider all papers of record

---

[58] *Celotex Corp.*, 477 U.S. at 324.

[59] *See, e.g., Offshore Aviation v. Transcon Lines, Inc.*, 831 F.2d 1013, 1015 n.1 (11th Cir. 1987); *Bushman v. Halm*, 798 F.2d 651, 654 n.5 (3d Cir. 1986). *See generally* Melissa J. Nelken, *One Step Forward, Two Steps Back: Summary Judgment After Celotex*, 40 Hastings L.J. 53, 56, 60–62 (1988) (noting that majority's statements in *Celotex* regarding formal requirements for evidence on summary judgment invited lower court confusion).

[60] *See, e.g., Duplantis v. Shell Offshore, Inc.*, 948 F.2d 187 (5th Cir. 1991). *See generally* Brunet, note 36, *supra*, at 656–57; Schwarzer, note 25, *supra*, at 50.

[61] *Lujan*, 497 U.S. at 888. *See generally* Brunet, note 36, *supra*, at 661–63. The specific-fact requirement may preclude reliance on an expert's affidavit if the affiant fails to state specifically the factual basis on which it rests. *Compare Mid-State Fertilizer Co. v. Exchange Nat'l Bank*, 877 F.2d 1333, 1339 (7th Cir. 1989) (so ruling), *with Bulthuis v. Rexall Corp.*, 777 F.2d 1353, 1356 (9th Cir. 1985) (allowing consideration of such an affidavit, subject to moving party's right to request disclosure of underlying facts), *amended on other grounds*, 789 F.2d 1315 (9th Cir. 1985). *See generally* Schwarzer, note 25, *supra*, at 52–57; Edward Brunet, *The Use and Misuse of Expert Testimony in Summary Judgment*, 22 U.C. Davis L. Rev. 93 (1988).

[62] *See, e.g., Wienco, Inc. v. Katahn Assocs., Inc.*, 965 F.2d 565 (7th Cir. 1992).

[63] *See* Schwarzer, note 25, *supra*, at 73.

[64] *See* § 11.03[3][b] (relation of standard for summary judgment to trial burdens), *infra*.

as well as any materials prepared for the motion."[65]

This obligation may be qualified, however, by local rules requiring submission of statements of undisputed facts and of counter-statements.[66] When a party fails to identify relevant parts of the record and material facts, these rules deem admitted the adverse party's statements. This makes the disposition of summary judgment more efficient.

One commentator has persuasively argued that the dramatic expansion of discovery since the enactment of the federal rules would make a record-searching obligation on the court inconsistent with Rule 1's admonition that the rules be administered to "secure the just, speedy, and inexpensive determination of every action and proceeding."[67] Reflecting this view, several circuit courts have held that a court ruling on summary judgment is not required to consider what the parties fail to point out.[68]

If the court finds that the movant has met his burden, it may enter judgment on a claim or defense. It may enter judgment on the issue of liability alone, even though the amount of damages remains for trial.[69] A federal judge need not make findings of fact or conclusions of law in granting summary judgment,[70] but the Supreme Court has pointedly reminded the lower federal courts that such "findings are extremely helpful to a reviewing court."[71]

If the ruling does not obviate trial, Rule 56(d) requires the court "to the extent practicable, [to] determine what material facts are not genuinely at issue." The purpose of this provision "is to salvage constructive results of the court's denial of a properly-brought but unsuccessful summary judgment motion."[72] The key words, however, are "to the extent practicable." The

---

[65] *Celotex Corp.*, 477 U.S. at 331 n.2 (Brennan, J., dissenting) (citing cases).

[66] *See* note 34, *supra*. In *Stepanischen v. Merchants Despatch Transp. Corp.*, 722 F.2d 922, 931 (1st Cir. 1983), the court of appeals, acknowledging that the whole-record obligation posed "the specter of district court judges being unfairly sandbagged by unadvertised factual issues," endorsed adoption of such local rules.

[67] *Court Examination*, note 34, *supra*, at 322. *See also* SCHWARZER, note 25, *supra*, at 49 (arguing that record-searching often poses "an unmanageable burden" on the trial judge).

[68] *Skotak v. Tenneco Resins, Inc.*, 953 F.2d 909, 915 n.7 (5th Cir.) ("Rule 56 does not impose upon the district court a duty to sift through the record . . . ."), *reh'g en banc denied, op. withdrawn, in part*, 1992 U.S. App. LEXIS 5388 (5th Cir. Mar. 26, 1992), *cert. denied*, 506 U.S. 832 (1992); *Downes v. Beach*, 587 F.2d 469 (10th Cir. 1978).

[69] Rule 56(a) & (c). *See, e.g., Leasing Serv. Corp. v. Graham*, 646 F. Supp. 1410 (S.D.N.Y. 1986); *see generally* SCHWARZER, note 25, *supra*, at 71 (noting possibility that such partial judgments may encourage settlement).

[70] Rule 52(a)(3). *See Anderson*, 477 U.S. at 250.

[71] *Anderson*, 477 U.S. at 250 n.6.

[72] *SFM Corp. v. Sundstrand Corp.*, 102 F.R.D. 555, 558 (N.D. Ill. 1984). "There is no such thing as a Rule 56(d) motion"; 56(d) orders are the residual of properly-brought summary judgment motions, not proper ends by themselves. *SFM Corp.*, 102 F.R.D. 555, 558 (N.D. Ill. 1984) (citing cases). *See generally* WRIGHT & MILLER § 2737. Because a Rule 56(d) order does not dispose of any claims or defenses, it is more appropriately called a partial summary adjudication (*see* WRIGHT & MILLER § 2737) or partial summary determination (*see* JAMES, HAZARD & LEUBSDORF § 4.11) than summary *judgment*.

salvage operation usually fails because of the trial courts' reluctance to hazard Rule 56(d) orders in cases that will be tried anyway.

While summary judgments address the merits, they may not be immediately appealable. Summary judgment as to liability alone is interlocutory in character and identified as such under Rule 56(d)(2). Therefore it is not ordinarily appealable in the federal system.[73] Similarly, summary judgment with respect to fewer than all the claims or parties is also not (without more) considered final for purposes of federal appeal, although a court may direct entry of a final judgment in such cases in conformity with Rule 54(b).[74]

When summary judgment is appealable, the appellate court decides for itself (*de novo*) whether the record, when viewed most favorably to the loser,[75] reveals any genuine issue of material fact and whether the prevailing party was entitled to judgment as a matter of law.[76]

[3] The Standard for Summary Judgment

[a] In General

Rule 56(c) codifies the traditional summary judgment standard, stating that judgment shall be rendered if the movant carries his burden of showing "that there is no genuine issue as to any material fact and that . . . [he] is entitled to judgment as a matter of law." Most state rules phrase the standard similarly or identically.[77] Because the primary purpose of summary judgment is to avoid an unnecessary trial, the court searches for a genuine issue the determination of which at trial might affect the outcome of the lawsuit. If it finds such an issue, its inquiry is at an end and summary judgment must be denied. The court's function is to determine whether there is such an issue, not to resolve it. A party is entitled to *try* the genuinely disputed issues of material fact and cannot be deprived of the protections of the trial process by summary determination of disputed facts, even by a judge in a case where no jury has been requested. That is, a party is entitled to *try* factual disputes, whether the fact-finder is judge or jury.

Issues of material fact are those "that might affect the outcome of the suit under the governing law."[78] A *material* fact is an essential element of claim or defense for purposes of summary judgment.[79] In a creditor's action on a

---

[73] *See* § 13.03[1] (the final judgment rule in general), *infra*.

[74] *See* § 13.03[2] (finality in multi-claim and multi-party cases), *infra*.

[75] *See, e.g., Walters*, 626 F.2d at 1322.

[76] *See* SCHWARZER, note 25, *supra*, at 79; § 13.10[2][a] (*de novo* review standard), *infra*.

[77] *See, e.g.*, CAL. CIVIL PROC. CODE § 437c(c) (West, Westlaw through 2007 Reg. Sess.) ("there is no triable issue as to any material fact and that the moving party is entitled to judgment as a matter of law").

[78] *Anderson*, 477 U.S. at 248. SCHWARZER, note 25, *supra*, at 43–44. Whether something is a fact is often a difficult question in itself. *Id.* at 13–37; § 13.10[2][a], *infra*.

[79] Martin B. Louis, *Federal Summary Judgment Doctrine: A Critical Analysis*, 83 YALE L.J.

guaranty, for example, whether the debtor has complied with the underlying agreement by submitting timely financial reports is clearly a material fact because the answer to it can decide the lawsuit.[80] In contrast, the issue whether the parties had reached an oral agreement is immaterial to summary judgment when such an agreement would be unenforceable under the statute of frauds. Whether there was such an agreement or there was not does not matter to the outcome, because it is unenforceable in any case.[81]

A *genuine dispute* is one which a reasonable jury could resolve against the movant.[82] The Supreme Court has declared that the standard for summary judgment mirrors the standard for directed verdict (now judgment as a matter of law in federal courts), "which is that the trial judge must direct a verdict if, under the governing law, there can be but one reasonable conclusion as to the verdict."[83] Thus, summary judgment should be granted if the evidence is such that it would require a directed verdict (or judgment as a matter of law) for the movant at trial.[84]

Summary judgment decisions regularly repeat the formula that the judge should not herself weigh the evidence and determine the truth of the matter, but should only determine whether there is a genuine issue for trial. After paying lip service to this formula, the Supreme Court in *Anderson v. Liberty Lobby, Inc.* [85] implicitly recognized that some weighing of the evidence is unavoidable because the judge decides whether the dispute is one that a jury could *reasonably* resolve against the movant. The *Anderson* Court restated the inquiry as "whether the evidence presents a sufficient disagreement to require submission to a jury or whether it is so one-sided that one party must prevail as a matter of law."[86] The Court added that the standard for summary judgment "necessarily implicates the substantive evidentiary standard of proof that would apply at the trial on the merits."[87] In the normal civil case, the judge must therefore determine whether a reasonable jury could resolve the issue for the non-movant by a preponderance of the evidence.[88]

745, 747 (1974). *Cf.* § 8.06[2] (the burden of pleading a claim), *supra*.

[80] *United Brands Co. v. Intermediate Credit Corp.*, 426 F. Supp. 856 (S.D.N.Y. 1977).

[81] *Soar v. National Football League Players Ass'n*, 438 F. Supp. 337 (D.R.I. 1975), *aff'd*, 550 F.2d 1287 (1st Cir. 1977).

[82] *Anderson*, 477 U.S. at 248.

[83] *Anderson*, 477 U.S. at 250. *See also* Rule 50(a).

[84] *Anderson*, 477 U.S. at 250 (citation omitted). *But see* Kennedy, note 26, *supra*, at 232–34 (arguing differences between the standards); Mullenix, note 53, *supra*, at 467–68 (same); § 11.03[3][d], *infra*.

[85] 477 U.S. 242 (1986).

[86] 477 U.S. at 251–52.

[87] 477 U.S. at 252.

[88] *See* § 12.04 (burdens of proof), *infra*. Accordingly, *Anderson* ultimately held that when the more rare clear and convincing standard of proof, 477 U.S. at 252, applies to the issue of actual malice in a defamation case, the proper inquiry on a motion for summary judgment is "whether the evidence presented is such that a reasonable jury might find that actual malice had been shown with convincing clarity." *Anderson*, 477 U.S. at 257.

As one district judge has explained, "a directed verdict analysis necessarily involves a qualitative evaluation of the evidence, and a decision as to whether a rational factfinder could find in the nonmovant's favor. Such an analysis necessarily calls for a decision of fact, and places the judge in the factfinder's shoes."[89] After *Anderson*, this analysis applies not only to directed verdict, but to summary judgment.

Whether *Anderson* did more than restate the old cliches about summary judgment is unclear. Federal courts still pay lipservice to the following laundry list of considerations assembled by the Court of Appeals for the Fourth Circuit:

> [The non-movant] is . . . entitled, as on a motion for a directed verdict, to have the credibility of his evidence as forecast assumed, his version of all that is in dispute accepted, all internal conflicts in it resolved favorably to him, the most favorable of possible alternative inferences from it drawn in his behalf; and finally, to be given the benefit of all favorable legal theories invoked by the evidence so considered.[90]

Anderson did not purport to invalidate these considerations; it only added the valuative component of reasonableness to each of them. The non-movant still benefits from doubts about the material facts, but only from the reasonable, and not just from the "slightest doubts."[91] Yet, in a companion summary judgment decision, *Matsushita Electric Industrial Co. v. Zenith Radio Corp.*,[92] the Court implied that summary judgment is proper even when there are equally plausible competing inferences. This may be technically correct. Yet some courts may take it as an invitation to invade the factfinder's province when the court finds one inference more plausible than another.

Once the trial judge determines that there is no genuine issue of material fact, he has still to decide whether the movant is entitled to judgment as a matter of governing law. Modern pleading jurisdictions usually have dispensed with the doctrine that a party is bound by the legal theory presented in his pleadings,[93] and the court will decide the legal question by any available theory

---

[89] Charles R. Richey, *Thoughts on Summary Judgment in Employment Discrimination Cases*, 1 FED. JURIST 4 (1989) (emphasis in original). Judge Richey decided *Celotex* in the trial court.

[90] *Charbonnages de France v. Smith*, 597 F.2d 406, 414 (4th Cir. 1979).

[91] Courts have occasionally embraced the "slightest doubt" test for summary judgment, to the nearly universal opprobrium of academic commentators. *See, e.g.,* WRIGHT § 99; WRIGHT & MILLER § 2727; Louis, note 79, *supra*, at 760–62. This gloss on Rule 56(c) should not survive *Anderson*. *See* Alan Steven Childress, *A New Era for Summary Judgments: Recent Shifts at the Supreme Court*, 6 REV. LITIG. 263, 280 (1987).

[92] 475 U.S. 574, 596–97 (1986). *See generally* SCHWARZER, note 25, *supra*, at 64–68; Marcy J. Levine, Comment, *Summary Judgment: The Majority View Undergoes a Complete Reversal in the 1986 Supreme Court*, 37 EMORY L.J. 171, 196 (1988); Jack H. Friedenthal, *Cases on Summary Judgment: Has There Been a Material Change in Standards?*, 63 NOTRE DAME L. REV. 770, 784–87 (1988).

[93] *See* §§ 8.03[2] (theory of pleadings under the codes) & 8.04[2] (under modern pleading), *supra*.

— whether or not pleaded.[94] Mere difficulty of the legal question is not grounds for postponing its decision if the record is sufficiently complete.[95] It is not, after all, a genuine dispute about the law that is reserved for trial, but only a genuine dispute about the material facts. Yet novel or constitutionally sensitive questions of law are often best decided upon the fuller record made at trial. Courts thus have discretion to deny summary judgment "where there is reason to believe that the better course would be to proceed to a full trial."[96]

Although we have been using the jury case as our model, the rules of summary judgment theoretically apply to nonjury cases with equal force. A party is entitled to *try* genuinely disputed facts, whether before a judge (bench trial) or a jury (jury trial). Some commentators and courts, however, argue a party can be deprived of a bench trial by summary judgment "when the question for decision concerns drawing inferences from undisputed evidence, or interpreting and evaluating evidence to derive legal conclusions, [because] a trial *may* not add to the judge's ability to decide."[97] They even urge summary judgment in such cases when the judge needs a fuller record, because she can then simply hold "a limited evidentiary hearing" under Rule 43(c) "to develop the record."[98] This argument either assumes that the opportunity to hear all the evidence in context adds nothing to the accuracy of the fact-finding, or that the nonmoving party may be obliged to make the full record in advance of trial. Both assumptions are controversial,[99] and the latter, coupled with a Rule 43(c) evidentiary hearing, converts the summary judgment hearing into trial-before-trial.[100] And the argument ignores or at least blurs the Advisory Committee's distinction between a Rule 52(c) judgment on partial findings in bench trials and summary judgment. These judgments are subject to different standards of appellate review.[101]

---

[94] *See* WRIGHT & MILLER § 2725.

[95] WRIGHT & MILLER § 2725.

[96] *Anderson*, 477 U.S. at 255 (*citing Kennedy v. Silas Mason Co.*, 334 U.S. 249 (1948)). *See generally* WRIGHT & MILLER § 2725.

[97] SCHWARZER, note 25, *supra*, at 39 (emphasis added). *Accord, Nunez v. Superior Oil Co.*, 572 F.2d 1119, 1123–24 (5th Cir. 1978).

[98] SCHWARZER, note 25, *supra*, at 39. *See also* Richey, note 89, *supra*, at 7.

[99] *See* Jeffrey W. Stempel, *A Distorted Mirror: The Supreme Court's Shimmering View of Summary Judgment, Directed Verdict, and the Adjudication Process*, 49 OHIO ST. L.J. 95, 99, 177–78 (1988) (context of full trial improves accuracy of fact-finding); § 13.10[2][b] (suggesting same rationale for deference to trial court fact-finding).

[100] *See Stewart v. RCA Corp.*, 790 F.2d 624, 628 (7th Cir. 1986) ("If [a judge could make a factual finding at a Rule 43(e) hearing], it would be the end of the difference between summary judgment and trial . . . ."); WRIGHT & MILLER § 2416 ("The purpose of summary judgment in giving a speedy adjudication in cases that present no genuine issue is defeated if the hearing on the motion becomes a preliminary trial."); Brunet, note 36, *supra*, at 649–52.

[101] Judgment entered under Rule 52(c) differs from a summary judgment under Rule 56 in the nature of the evaluation made by the court. A judgment on partial findings is made after the court has heard *all the evidence bearing on a crucial issue of fact*, and the finding is reversible only if the appellate court finds it to be "clearly erroneous." A summary judgment, in contrast, is made on the basis of facts established on account of the absence of contrary evidence or presumptions; such establishments of fact are rulings on questions of law as provided in Rule 56(a) and are not shielded by the "clear error" standard of review. *See* Rule 52(c) advisory committee's notes (1991); § 12.10

[b]   Relationship to Trial Burdens

The analogy of summary judgment to directed verdict (or judgment as a matter of law at trial) works well when the movant is the party with the burden of persuasion[102] at trial. His burden on summary judgment is then aligned with his trial burden: to show that there is no genuine dispute concerning all the material factual elements of his claim or affirmative defense.[103] This kind of summary judgment motion can be called a *proof-of-the-elements* motion for summary judgment, made by a claimant for judgment on her claim or, probably more often, by defendant for judgment on an affirmative defense (for which a defendant bears the burden of proof at trial).

Lundeen v. Cordner[104] is a well-known example. The suit involved competing claims for proceeds of a life insurance policy. An intervenor claimed that the decedent had intended to change the beneficiaries in intervenor's favor. Governing law did not require the change to be written into the policy in order to be effective, so long as the insured's intent was proven. The intervenor supported her motion for summary judgment with an affidavit of a neutral witness attesting to decedent's stated intent to change the beneficiaries and to the contents of the change, and with other supporting documentation. The opposing party could point to no specific facts in rebuttal. The court granted summary judgment because the movant, on whom the burden of persuasion would fall at trial, established that there was no genuine dispute concerning all of the essential elements of her claim.

The analogy between summary judgment and directed verdict (or judgment as a matter of law at trial) breaks down, however, when the movant would not have the burden of persuasion at trial. Were the case to go to trial, the motion for directed verdict would there come after the non-movant has put on its case, and the movant could simply argue deficiencies in that case. But before trial, the non-movant attacked by summary judgment has yet to put on a case. How can the movant then satisfy his burden of production?

If the analogy to directed verdict (or judgment as a matter of law at trial) held, the movant in these circumstances could satisfy his burden by a naked motion putting the opposing party to her proof.[105] We might call this a *no-*

(bench trials), *infra. But see* SCHWARZER, note 25, *supra*, at 79–81 (suggesting clearly-erroneous review for finding of "ultimate facts" by summary judgment).

[102] *See* § 12.04 (burdens of proof), *infra*.

[103] *See generally* Louis, note 79, *supra*, at 747; SCHWARZER, note 25, *supra*, at 45–46.

[104] 354 F.2d 401 (8th Cir. 1966).

[105] *See* David P. Currie, *Thoughts on Directed Verdicts and Summary Judgments*, 45 U. CHI. L. REV. 72, 79 (1977) (urging this construction of movant's burden in order to accomplish summary judgment's purpose of determining whether there is sufficient evidence to justify trial). Texas has expressly authorized a "no-evidence motion" for summary judgment in its summary judgment rule:

> No-Evidence Motion. After adequate time for discovery, a party without presenting summary judgment evidence may move for summary judgment on the ground that there is no evidence of one or more essential elements of a claim or defense on which an adverse party would have the burden of proof at trial. The motion must state the elements as to which there is no evidence. The court must grant the motion unless the respondent produces summary judgment evidence raising a genuine issue of material

evidence motion for summary judgment. However, permitting such a motion would invite use of summary judgment as a tool of harassment. The movant would be able to force a preview of the opposing party's evidence without paying the price of previewing his own.[106]

An alternative is to require the movant to support the motion with evidence completely negating the existence of an essential element of the opposing party's case. We might call this a *disproof-of-an-element* motion for summary judgment. In the oft-cited case of *Dyer v. MacDougall*,[107] the defendant to a defamation claim won summary judgment by presenting affidavits of all the persons present at the alleged slander, denying that it took place. This alternative, however, shifts the burden of persuasion from the opposing party (who would have it at trial) to the movant. It may thwart the primary purpose of summary judgment by letting a party who has no evidence that would survive a motion for directed verdict or judgment as a matter of law at trial remain in the shadows, while a summary judgment movant struggles to prove a negative. For this reason, some commentators have proposed that a summary judgment movant who would not have the burden of persuasion at trial need show only enough evidence to permit — not require — the jury to find in his favor.[108]

The Supreme Court addressed but did not clearly resolve this issue in *Celotex Corporation v. Catrett*.[109] Celotex was defendant in a products liability suit brought by a survivor of a victim of asbestosis. It moved for summary judgment on the ground that plaintiff had failed to produce any evidence that Celotex's products were the cause of the asbestosis — a no-evidence motion for summary judgment. The trial court granted summary judgment, and the court of appeals reversed on the grounds that the movant had failed to adduce any affirmative evidence in support of its motion. The Supreme Court reversed and remanded.

Eight Justices rejected the first alternative discussed above, agreeing that, even if a party would not have the burden of production at trial, its case for summary judgment must consist of more than the naked no-evidence motion. They agreed that such a movant must at least identify those portions of the

---

fact.

Tex. R. Civ. P. 166(a)(i). *See generally* Charles T. Frazier Jr. et al., *Celotex Comes to Texas: No-Evidence Summary Judgments and Other Recent Developments in Summary Judgment Practice*, 32 Tex. Tech. L. Rev. 111 (2000).

[106] *See* § 11.03[1], *supra*, regarding this built-in control on summary judgment. Rule 11's certification requirements might deter some harassment, *cf.* Stuart R. Pollak, *Liberalizing Summary Adjudication: A Proposal*, 36 Hastings L.J. 419, 428–29 (1985) (urging the adoption of certification requirements in California summary judgment practice in order to reduce the likelihood of such harassment), but summary judgment practice might still be substantially unbalanced.

[107] 201 F.2d 265 (2d Cir. 1952).

[108] *See* Louis, note 79, *supra*, at 748, 753–59.

[109] 477 U.S. 317 (1986). *See generally* Adam N. Steinman, *The Irrepressible Myth of Celotex: Reconsidering Summary Judgment Burdens Twenty Years After the Trilogy*, 63 Wash. & Lee L. Rev. 81 (2006).

discovery record at summary judgment that demonstrate the absence of a genuine issue of material fact.[110] At least seven Justices also appeared to reject the alternative at the other extreme: that such a movant can only satisfy his summary judgment burden by submitting a disproof-of-an-element motion, with affirmative evidence negating an essential element of the non-movant's case.[111]

The Supreme Court exhibited less certainty over application of these principles, disagreeing about whether Celotex had identified portions of the record showing an absence of a genuine issue of material fact on causation. Moreover, the case left unclear how much beyond a naked no-evidence motion for summary judgment was required of a movant who would not have the burden of persuasion at trial. Celotex had supported its motion for summary judgment by noting that the plaintiff had failed in answers to interrogatories to identify any witnesses who could testify about the decedent's exposure to Celotex's asbestos products. Four Justices thought this enough to satisfy Celotex's burden of production on summary judgment and remanded for the Court of Appeals to decide whether plaintiff's opposing evidence was admissible.[112] Three Justices thought that plaintiff's identification elsewhere in the record of a possible witness on the issue of exposure obligated Celotex to attack the adequacy of the witness's evidence, despite the plaintiff's failure to supply it by affidavit or otherwise.[113] Justice White voted to remand for the Court of Appeals to address this point.[114]

One commentator has suggested a means for reconciling the apparently divergent views of the Justices in *Celotex* regarding application of the *Celotex* principles. She suggests that if, during discovery prior to a summary judgment motion, the nonmoving party has identified sources of evidence for elements of its case, then the movant is obliged to track down that evidence by its own discovery before seeking summary judgment. Thus, had the plaintiff in *Celotex* identified during discovery the two possible witnesses who could support her case, the defendant would have been obliged to depose them or take other additional discovery prior to making its motion for summary judgment. This solution seeks to avoid the problem of forcing a nonmoving party to depose her own witnesses in order to avoid no-evidence summary judgment, without relaxing the requirement for admissible evidence.[115]

---

[110] 477 U.S. at 324 (Rehnquist, C.J., writing for the Court), 327 (White, J.), 331 (Brennan, Blackmun, and Burger, JJ., dissenting).

[111] 477 U.S. at 324 (Rehnquist, C.J., writing for the Court), 337 (Brennan, Blackmun, and Burger, JJ., dissenting).

[112] 477 U.S. at 328.

[113] 477 U.S. at 336–39.

[114] 477 U.S. at 328–29. On remand, the Court of Appeals again held that summary judgment was inappropriate. It found that Celotex waived its objections to admissibility of the plaintiff's evidence by failing to make timely objection below, and then concluded that the evidence raised a genuine issue of material fact concerning causation. *Catrett v. Johns-Manville Sales Corp.*, 826 F.2d 33 (D.C. Cir. 1987), *cert. denied*, 484 U.S. 1066 (1988).

[115] *See generally* Nelken, note 59, *supra*, at 75–76.

[c]   Particular Issues: Credibility and State of Mind

Numerous courts have said that summary judgment is inappropriate in cases involving issues of credibility and state of mind.[116] They offer different reasons for this view, emphasizing that demeanor is crucial in such cases and uniquely for the fact-finder to assess; that the facts are in the control of the movant where his credibility or state of mind is relevant; that self-interest infuses the statements of the parties and alone raises a triable issue of fact; and that parties opposing summary judgment in such cases are entitled to the incentive to truth provided by the formality of trial.[117]

These points may be valid in particular cases. Nonetheless, summary judgment cases are sufficiently varied to elude this kind of treatment by formula.[118] The better approach is to examine credibility and state of mind objections critically on a case-by-case basis. As Professor Moore has said, "[h]ere, on last analysis, a problem of judging is involved."[119]

Lundeen[120] again provides an illustration. Movant there offered two affidavits by an employee of the company for whom the insured had worked before his death, attesting to the insured's stated intent to change the beneficiaries of an insurance policy purchased by the company. In opposition, the adverse party argued that the employee-affiant's story was so vital that the case should proceed to trial where his demeanor could be observed during his testimony and where he could be cross-examined.

Affirming the grant of summary judgment for the movant, the appellate court reasoned that the same argument could be leveled at any affidavit offered in support of summary judgment. "[I]f plaintiff's position is correct that an affiant's credibility is always an issue for the trial court, then the granting of a summary judgment would be virtually impossible when it is based in any way upon an affidavit."[121] The court's reasoning is persuasive. To accept plaintiff's bald argument would negate the role contemplated for affidavits in Rule 56 and unduly restrict the availability of summary judgments.

---

[116] J. Palmer Lockard, *Summary Judgment in Pennsylvania: Time for Another Look at Credibility Issues*, 35 Duq. L. Rev. 625 (1997) (criticizing Pennsylvania rule restricting summary judgment where supporting evidence is testimonial). *See generally* David A. Sonenshein, *State of Mind and Credibility in the Summary Judgment Context: A Better Approach*, 78 Nw. U. L. Rev. 774, 780 (1983) (citing illustrative cases); Daniel P. Collins, Note, *Summary Judgment and Circumstantial Evidence*, 40 Stan. L. Rev. 491 (1988).

[117] For example, in the oft-cited case of *Poller v. Columbia Broadcasting System, Inc.*, 368 U.S. 464, 473 (1962), the Supreme Court cautioned that summary judgment "should be used sparingly in complex antitrust litigation where motive and intent play leading roles, the proof is largely in the hands of the alleged conspirators, and hostile witnesses thicken the plot."

[118] *See First Nat'l Bank of Ariz. v. Cities Serv. Co.*, 391 U.S. 253 (1968). *See* Wright & Miller § 2725.

[119] J. Moore, Moore's Federal Practice ¶ 56.15[1.-0] (2d ed. 1994).

[120] 354 F.2d 401, discussed in § 11.03[3][b], *supra*.

[121] 354 F.2d at 409.

Instead, credibility should be put at issue by a showing of "specific facts"[122] raising a genuine issue. While the opposing party in *Lundeen* apparently did not attempt such a showing, the appellate court approved summary judgment only after conducting an unsuccessful search of the record for a genuine issue of credibility. It noted that the employee-affiant was competent and in a position to observe the facts related in his affidavits. He appeared to be an unbiased witness without personal or financial interest in the litigation. His affidavits were "positive, internally consistent, unequivocal, and in full accord with the documentary exhibits."[123] There was therefore not the slightest indication that he might be impeached by cross-examination or might supply useful information for the opposing party. Finally, that party had made no effort to secure his deposition, which suggested that even she believed there was little to gain from cross-examination.[124]

To block summary judgment, matters of credibility and state of mind should be placed specifically at issue by the traditional modes of impeachment: "bias, interest, prejudice, corruption, defects in testimonial capacity, prior bad acts bearing on veracity, prior convictions, poor character for veracity, and prior inconsistent statements."[125] The interest of a party-affiant or deponent does not invariably raise an issue of credibility; nor is the control of relevant information by the movant always a sufficient reason for the inability of the opposing party to specify facts suggesting impeachment. Interest and lack of access together may in particular cases establish a genuine issue.[126]

The allocation of the burden of persuasion at trial is also relevant to credibility issues. When the non-movant would have the burden of persuasion at trial, she may not defeat summary judgment simply by raising an issue of the credibility of the movant's denials of material facts. The reason is that she is not by that showing relieved of her own burden of showing evidence from which a reasonable jury could find in her favor.

It is axiomatic that a party is not permitted to prove a positive proposition by first offering a witness who refutes the proposition, and then impeaching that witness. The jury cannot on this basis find that

---

[122] Rule 56(e)(2).

[123] *Lundeen*, 354 F.2d at 408.

[124] The affiant was overseas and a deposition upon oral questions would have imposed a substantial expense on the opposing party that would otherwise fall on the movant, who would have had to call the affiant as her witness or offer his deposition at trial to meet her burden of persuasion. Such considerations of relative cost and convenience may fairly be considered in ruling on a summary judgment motion in the circumstances, but it is incumbent on the opposing party to make them known by a Rule 56(f) affidavit. In any event, the opposing party in *Lundeen* did not avail itself of even less expensive discovery options, like a deposition upon written questions. *See* § 10.08[1] (procedure for taking depositions), *supra*.

[125] Sonenshein, note 116, *supra*, at 798-01. This obligation is, of course, subject to any reasonable explanation by an opposing party for its inability to present the necessary facts to establish a genuine issue. *See* Rule 56(f).

[126] *See, e.g., Wilmington Trust Co. v. Manufacturers Life Ins. Co.*, 624 F.2d 707 (5th Cir. 1980) (reversing summary judgment for insurer with burden of proof, when it rested on subjective testimony of the insurer's own employee and when the facts were within the insurer's exclusive knowledge).

the positive proposition is a proven fact . . . . [A] contrary rule would permit the jury to *find* a fact . . . despite the absence of any affirmative evidence of that fact in the record.[127]

On the other hand, when the movant would also have the burden of persuasion at trial, specifically established issues of credibility should be enough to defeat summary judgment.[128]

[d]　Assessment

A study of summary judgment from 1975 to 2000 in six federal district courts showed that the rate at which summary judgment motions are filed was about 21% at the conclusion of the period, while the rate of cases with motions granted in whole or in part, and the rate at which cases are terminated by summary judgment, was about 12 percent and 8 percent, respectively, at that point.[129]

To assess summary judgment, we need to consider what the courts do, what they say, and what effect their actions and rhetoric have on the "just, speedy and inexpensive determination of every action and proceeding."[130]

Prior to the Supreme Court's *Anderson-Celotex-Matsushita* trilogy of summary judgment opinions in 1986, the traditional view was that summary judgment was rarely granted and that grants were often reversed.[131] Open judicial hostility to summary judgment was not uncommon.[132] But in each of the trilogy cases, the Supreme Court ruled in support of summary judgment, and in *Celotex*, the Court sang its praises:

> Summary judgment procedure is properly regarded not as a disfavored procedural shortcut, but rather as an integral part of the Federal Rules as a whole, which are designed "to secure the just, speedy and inexpensive determination of every action." Fed. Rule Civ. Proc. 1. . . . Rule 56 must be construed with due regard not only for the rights of persons asserting claims and defenses that are adequately based in fact to have those claims and defenses tried to a jury, but also

---

[127] Sonenshein, note 116, *supra*, at 789. Reprinted by special permission of the Northwestern University Law Review, © 1983 by Northwestern University School of Law, vol. 78. *See Anderson*, 477 U.S. at 256–57.

[128] *See, e.g., Wilmington Trust Co.*, 624 F.2d 707.

[129] Joe S. Cecil et al., *A Quarter-Century of Summary Judgment Practices in Six District Courts*, 4 J. EMPIRICAL LEGAL STUD. 861, 896 (2007).

[130] Rule 1.

[131] *See, e.g.,* McLauchlan, note 25, *supra*, at 449 (reporting 49% reversal rate in sample of federal courts); Sonenshein, note 116, *supra*, at 775 n.5 (50% in California; 81.2% in Florida; 50% in Fifth Circuit; 70% of cases that reached Texas Supreme Court) (citations omitted); Kennedy, note 25, *supra*, at 254 n.112.

[132] *See, e.g., Wells v. Oppenheimer & Co.*, 101 F.R.D. 358, 359 (S.D.N.Y. 1984) (Knapp, J.) ("motions for summary judgment in this Circuit [2d] were usually a waste of time and should be discouraged"), *vacated*, 106 F.R.D. 258 (S.D.N.Y. 1985). One district judge in New Orleans acknowledged the Fifth Circuit's hostility by posting the sign, "No Spitting, No Summary Judgments!" Childress, note 91, *supra*, at 264.

for the rights of persons opposing such claims and defenses to demonstrate in the manner provided by the Rule, prior to trial, that the claims and defenses have no factual basis.[133]

Depending on their affection for trial, commentators heralded or bemoaned the dawn of a new era in summary judgment. They predicted, and some found in the short term, a surge in the filing and success of summary judgment motions, especially motions by defendants.[134]

These predictions have not come to pass in the long term. A survey of summary judgment practice from 1975–2000 shows that the likelihood of a case containing one or more summary judgment motions increased from 12 percent in 1975 to 17 percent in 1986 — the year of the trilogy — and remained fairly steady at about 19 percent since then.[135] Although this is was a 40% increase in filings, most of it occurred *before* the trilogy, and it reflects, in part, the increase in filings of civil rights cases that have always experienced a high rate of summary judgment practice. Moreover, there was no statistically significant difference in outcomes between plaintiffs' and defendants' motions.[136]

These findings at first seem inconsistent with a reported substantial shift in federal case dispositions from disposition by trial to disposition by summary judgment. One report found that in 1973, there were an average of 14 summary judgment dispositions per volume of the *Federal Reporter* compared to an average of 52 trial dispositions, while the comparable numbers for 1997–98 (eleven years after the trilogy) had changed to 47 summary judgment dispositions compared to 20 trial dispositions.[137] Reporting on "summary judgment at 60" in the D.C. Circuit, Judge Wald also noted that 22% of case terminations in that circuit in 1996–97 were by summary judgment compared to about 3% by trial, leading her to speculate that "summary judgment may in fact be the more

---

[133] 477 U.S. 317, 327 (1986) (citation omitted).

[134] *See, e.g.*, Issacharoff & Lowenstein, note 55, *supra*, at 88–89; Stempel, note 99, *supra*, at 99 (stating that the trilogy "effected major changes in summary judgment doctrine and practice"); Gregory A. Gordillo, Note, *Summary Judgment and Problems in Applying the Celotex Trilogy Standard*, 42 CLEV. ST. L. REV. 263 (1994); John J.P. Howley, Note, *Summary Judgment in Federal Court: New Maxims for a Familiar Rule*, 34 N.Y.L. SCH. L. REV. 201, 203 (1989) (asserting that new doctrine announced in trilogy "has virtually eliminated trial in certain types of cases").

[135] Cecil, note 129, *supra*, at 861. These findings cast some doubt on the long-term significance of reported spikes in summary judgment filings in product liability, antitrust, libel, and civil rights (particularly employment discrimination) cases after the trilogy. *See* Ann C. McGinley, *Credulous Courts and the Tortured Trilogy: The Improper Use of Summary Judgment in Title VII and ADEA Cases*, 34 B.C. L. REV. 203 (1993); Patricia M. Wald, *Summary Judgment at Sixty*, 76 TEX. L. REV. 1897, 1938 (1998) (noting that employment discrimination lawyers widely report more frequent grant of summary judgment in employment discrimination cases than in others); Howley, note 134, *supra*, at 213–14 n.99, 218–19 n.125. *See also* Theresa M. Beiner, *The Misuse of Summary Judgment in Hostile Environment Cases*, 34 WAKE FOREST L. REV. 71 (1999) (finding excessive use of summary judgment in sexual harassment cases).

[136] Cecil, note 129, *supra*, at 861.

[137] Paul W. Mollica, *Federal Summary Judgment at High Tide*, 84 MARQ. L. REV. 141, 144, 218–19 (2000). *See also* Martin H. Redish, *Summary Judgment and the Vanishing Trial: Implications of the Litigation Matrix*, 57 STAN. L. REV. 1329, 1330 (2005) ("Changes in the law of summary judgment quite probably explain at least a large part of the dramatic reduction in federal trials.").

commonly used mode of disposition on the merits, outnumbering settlement by court-annexed arbitration, mediation, early neutral evaluation, and other settlement techniques," as well as trial.[138] It is not clear, however, whether such statistics reflect significant increases in the rate of summary judgment or just a decline in the trial rate, due as much to settlement (and attendant dismissal) as summary judgment. "Summary judgment is but one of several dispositive motions that may result in the drop in the trial rate."[139]

If summary judgment has not increased by as much (or at all) after the trilogy as most scholars and commentators had predicted, should it have? Advocates of summary judgment certainly tout it as an efficient tool for clearing dockets and avoiding trial costs.[140] But this accounting is incomplete. It omits the cost of preparing and, more significantly, of opposing the summary judgment motion itself, including some costs (especially to plaintiff) that would not be incurred in trial (*e.g.*, deposing your own witnesses). It also omits the costs of denied motions.[141]

It may also be that the costs of the so-called new summary judgment may not be evenly distributed. *Celotex* seemed to lower the price of summary judgment for defendant-movants who would not have the burden of proof at trial.

> Something close to a one page form motion by defendant can throw on the plaintiff the responsibility to dredge, structure, collate and cross-reference all materials in the file to make them available to the judge before trial. Because the material must be reduced to a coherently structured written form, this task can sometimes take as long or longer than actually trying the case.[142]

The low cost to defendant-movants of making a "put-up-or-shut-up" motion (usually a no-evidence motion) and the corresponding high price to plaintiffs could alter the balance of power, and, some have suggested, discourage settlement.[143] On the other hand, this result may simply compensate for unfair

---

[138] Wald, note 135, *supra* at 1915. Because of the number of cases to which the federal government is party, and the possibility that statutory issues are more significant in such cases than in private cases, the D.C. Circuit's experience may not be typical.

[139] Cecil et al., *supra* note 129, at 906. In any case, assessments based on reported dispositions are unreliable, because many dispositions are not published, especially denials. *Id.* at 4.

[140] *Id.* (implying that summary judgment eases docket pressures). *But see* McLauchlan, note 25, *supra*, at 456–58 (finding little time-saving in summary judgment). Federal judges also report that prompt rulings on motions for summary judgment are among the two most effective methods for controlling groundless litigation. Elizabeth C. Wiggins et al., *The Federal Judicial Center's Study of Rule 11*, 2 FJC DIRECTIONS 31 (1991).

[141] Richard L. Marcus, *Completing Equity's Conquest? Reflections on the Future of Trial Under the Federal Rules of Civil Procedure*, 50 U. PITT. L. REV. 725, 774–75 (1989); Stempel, note 99, *supra*, at 171, 191 & n.449.

[142] D. Michael Risinger, *Another Step in the Counter-Revolution: A Summary Judgement on the Supreme Court's New Approach to Summary Judgment*, 54 BROOKLYN L. REV. 35, 41 (1988).

[143] *See, e.g.*, Risinger, note 142, *supra*, at 39; Issacharoff & Lowenstein, note 55, *supra*, at 75; Stempel, note 99, *supra*, at 161–62, 180–81. *See generally* John Bronsteen, *Against Summary Judgment*, 75 GEO. WASH. L. REV. 522 (2007) (asserting that summary judgment imposes extra costs

advantages plaintiffs enjoyed with notice pleading and essentially unlimited discovery.

The question remains whether any "new" summary judgment even at the reported rates intrudes seriously on trial by converting once "summary" proceedings into a full dress trial rehearsal. The possible costs of downgrading trial[144] include diminished accuracy from the loss of demeanor evidence, spontaneity, and whatever comprehensibility oral testimony affords; loss of participant satisfaction; loss of public interest and access; and loss of confidence in the reliability of judgment because of the substitution of unaccountable federal judges for juries of peers. Some commentators also suggest that litigants pay a price in constitutional rights to try their factual disputes.[145]

These critiques all suggest that Supreme Court rhetoric should not be allowed to obscure the fact that summary judgment and directed verdict are not, after all, the same. "The crucial difference between summary judgment and the directed verdict, . . . is that before trial *all* the evidence is not available to the judge for consideration. The directed verdict standard requires that the judge assess what a reasonable jury could find on *all* the evidence, which is not the case at summary judgment."[146] Directed verdict rests on a known record; summary judgment on a predicted record.[147] As Judge Wald put it, summary judgment in her circuit is "something more like a gestalt verdict based on an early snapshot of the case,"[148] "applying legal principles to incomplete, often anemic, factual scenarios."[149]

The reliability of factfinding, and often even of law-deciding, is greater the larger the data base.[150] One commentator notes that "the largest increase in the data base and its reliability occurs between summary judgment and directed verdict at the close of the plaintiff's case."[151] To the extent that the new summary judgment, by so emphatically equating summary judgment and directed verdict, "permits courts to conclude a case as though they did so upon a much richer data base than actually possessed," it may be "bad science and probability theory, as well as bad law."[152]

---

by discouraging settlement and creates a pro-defendant bias).

[144] *See generally* Marcus, note 141, *supra*, at 757–83; Stempel, note 99, *supra*, at 171–73, 191.

[145] Mollica, note 137, *supra* at 181–205 (arguing that many applications of summary judgment "press against tolerable constitutional limits" established by due process as well as the Seventh Amendment). *See also* Suja A. Thomas, *Why Summary Judgment Is Unconstitutional*, 93 VA. L. REV. 139 (2007).

[146] Mullenix, note 53, *supra*, at 474.

[147] Risinger, note 142, *supra*, at 37–38.

[148] Wald, note 135, *supra*, at 1917.

[149] Wald, note 135, *supra*, at 1944.

[150] *See* Stempel, note 99, *supra*, at 176–77 (analogizing from statistics).

[151] Stempel, note 99, *supra*, at 177.

[152] Stempel, note 99, *supra*, at 177.

§ 11.04   DISMISSAL OR NONSUIT

[1]   Voluntary Dismissal or Nonsuit

There are times when plaintiff would like to withdraw suit. This happens whenever plaintiff's case seems likely to lead to a binding adjudication that will defeat or compromise his claim and when it seems reasonable to expect a more favorable result from suit brought at a different time or place.[153] If such a plaintiff can obtain dismissal *without prejudice* to his opportunity to litigate the same claim later,[154] he will voluntarily dismiss his claim.

The common law treated plaintiff as master of his case and therefore permitted him to dismiss or take a *nonsuit* without prejudice at any time before verdict.[155] Today plaintiff's right to dismiss is balanced against the investment of resources made by the other parties and by the court in the lawsuit. Consequently, most systems confine plaintiff's unilateral right to break off the case to the early stages of litigation: prior to the substantial investment of resources in trial,[156] or even prior to the point at which issues are joined. Federal Rule 41(a)(1) adopts the latter point of no return, providing that plaintiff may dismiss once without leave of court by filing notice of dismissal before an answer or motion for summary judgment is served upon him. Thus, a Rule 12(b) motion to dismiss the complaint does not cut off plaintiff's right to such *notice dismissal* unless the motion is converted into a summary judgment motion by the offer of supporting materials outside the pleadings.[157]

After an issue is joined by the service of an answer or motion for summary judgment, plaintiff may voluntarily dismiss only by stipulation of the parties or

---

[153] For example, when a defendant has asserted a limitations defense that appears to be good in the forum, *see generally* Susan Clark Taylor, Note, *Rule 41(a)(2) Dismissals: Forum Shopping for a Statute of Limitations*, 20 Mem. St. U. L. Rev. 629 (1990), or a troublesome party has intervened or been impleaded, or the court or the jury is likely to rule against the plaintiff.

[154] *See* Chapter 15 (respect for final judgments), *infra*.

[155] *See* Benjamin J. Shipman, Common Law Pleading §§ 328–329 (3d ed. 1923). In some states, the right to dismiss is still essentially absolute until trial. *See* James T. Ferrini & Richard R. Winter, *Voluntary Dismissals — From Shield to Sword by the Convergence of Improvident Actions*, 21 J. Marshall L. Rev. 549 (1988) (so characterizing Illinois law).

[156] *See generally* Annotation, *Time When Voluntary Nonsuit or Dismissal May Be Taken as of Right Under Statute So Authorizing at Any Time Before "Trial," "Commencement of Trial," "Trial of the Facts," or the Like*, 1 A.L.R.3d 711 (1965) (discussing rules that permit voluntary dismissal as of right prior to trial or "commencement of trial").

[157] *See* Rules 12(b) & (d). *See generally* §§ 8.07[1] discussing conversion of Rule 12(b)(6) and 12(c) motions to Rule 56 motions) & 11.03[2] (procedure for summary judgment), *supra*. Rule 41(a)(1) is usually (but not always) applied strictly. *See, e.g., American Soccer Co. v. Score First Enters.*, 187 F.3d 1108 (9th Cir. 1999) (even when court treats a hearing as one for summary judgment, the "point of no return" is not reached unless formal motion is filed); *Santiago v. Victim Services Agency*, 753 F.2d 219 (2d Cir. 1985) (motion for a preliminary injunction does not cut off plaintiff's right to notice dismissal). The Supreme Court has held, however, that even a voluntary dismissal as of right does not deprive a court of power to impose Rule 11 sanctions on the plaintiff for filing the dismissed action. *Cooter & Gell v. Hartmarx Corp.*, 496 U.S. 384 (1990).

by order of the court upon such terms and conditions as it deems proper.[158] However, trial courts usually allow such dismissals unless doing so would unavoidably inflict plain legal prejudice on other parties.[159] Prejudice to defendant must ordinarily consist of more than "the mere prospect of a second law suit,"[160] since that prospect is generally present when a plaintiff seeks voluntary dismissal. Furthermore, the court can often alleviate or remove prejudice to other parties by conditioning voluntary dismissal on plaintiff's reimbursement of the parties' costs, production of discovery materials, or fulfillment of other terms.[161] The Supreme Court has asserted that the parties could make their compliance with a settlement agreement one of the judicially-enforceable conditions of voluntary dismissal.[162]

Unless the court specifies otherwise, an initial voluntary dismissal is without prejudice to plaintiff's reinstitution of the action. It leaves the parties in the same position they were in prior to suit, but for the passage of time.[163] Federal courts are empowered by Rule 41(d)(1), however, to require a plaintiff who reinstitutes his action to reimburse the parties for the costs of the previously dismissed action.

Most jurisdictions follow a two-dismissal rule, by which a second voluntary dismissal is *with prejudice* to reinstitution.[164] The second thus operates as an adjudication upon the merits with whatever preclusive effect is given judgments by the law of the rendering jurisdiction.[165]

---

[158] Rule 41(a)(2).

[159] *See, e.g., Paulucci v. City of Duluth*, 826 F.2d 780 (8th Cir. 1987) (denying dismissal, citing absence of explanation for it and prejudice from continuing uncertainty over title to land). *See generally* Lawrence Mentz, Note, *Voluntary Dismissal by Order of Court — Federal Rule of Civil Procedure 41(a)(2) and Judicial Discretion*, 48 Notre Dame Law. 446 (1972); Moore § 41.40[5].

[160] *See, e.g., Phillips v. Illinois Cent. Gulf R.R.*, 874 F.2d 984, 987 (5th Cir. 1989); *see generally* Moore § 41.40[5][c]. *Compare* § 8.10[1] (making same observation with respect to amendment), *supra*. Courts are divided, however, about whether the loss of a good limitations defense is clear legal prejudice to defendant. Some balance the equities when this prejudice is present by considering also plaintiff's diligence and conduct in seeking dismissal and defendant's expenditure of time and money. *See generally* Taylor, note 153, *supra*, at 638–54.

[161] *See, e.g., Radiant Tech. Corp. v. Electrovert USA Corp.*, 122 F.R.D. 201 (N.D. Tex. 1988) (identifying factors to be considered in allowing conditional dismissal, as well as in denying dismissal); *see generally* Moore § 41.40[10].

[162] *Kokkonen v. Guardian Life Ins. Co. of Am.*, 511 U.S. 375, 381 (1994) (dictum).

[163] Of course, the passage of time is sometimes significant because it may raise the bar of limitations to reinstitution of the action. Some jurisdictions therefore provide by statute for the tolling of the statute of limitations during the pendency of the dismissed or nonsuited action, provided that it is reinstituted within a stated period after the dismissal. *See, e.g.,* Va. Code Ann. § 8.01-229(E) (LEXIS through 2007 Reg. Sess.).

[164] *See, e.g.,* Rule 41(a)(1)(B).

[165] *See generally* Chapter 15 (respect for final judgments), *infra*.

[2] Involuntary Dismissal or Compulsory Nonsuit

We have noted that a default judgment is available in most jurisdictions for the defendant's failure to respond to claims against him or as a penalty for his disobedience of various procedural rules.[166] *Involuntary dismissal or compulsory nonsuit* is an analogous remedy for the defendant when the plaintiff fails to prosecute her claims[167] or to obey court rules or orders.[168]

Rule 41(b) does not define a failure to prosecute, but rules locally adopted by federal courts often do.[169] Disobedience that would justify dismissal also often consists of litigation delays, or of failures to appear, respond, or take other required action.[170] Because these matters threaten the trial court's control over its docket, it follows that it may draw on its inherent powers to dismiss plaintiff's action *sua sponte* (on its own initiative).[171]

Involuntary dismissal is a harsh sanction. In exercising discretion to dismiss a claim for want of prosecution or for plaintiff's disobedience of a court rule or order, courts should consider the degree of plaintiff's personal responsibility for the inaction or disobedience, the actual prejudice to defendant, and the availability of lesser sanctions.[172] While Rule 41(b) does not require notice and hearing, they are desirable prior to an order of involuntary dismissal.

Rule 41(b) involuntary dismissals also formerly provided a means for federal courts to decide cases midway through bench (nonjury) trials. Now this purpose is served by motions for judgment as a matter of law under Rule 52(c).[173] In states that have not followed this federal rule change, however, a motion to dismiss at the close of plaintiff's case is still used to put the question whether on the facts and the law plaintiff has met his burden of persuasion.[174] This kind of motion differs from its cousin, the motion for directed verdict in jury cases, because the latter only tests whether plaintiff's evidence could

---

[166] *See* § 11.02, *supra.*

[167] *See Ad West Marketing, Inc. v. Hayes,* 745 F.2d 980 (5th Cir. 1984) (failure of attorney representing the plaintiff corporation and two of the cross-defendants to appear for trial justified involuntary dismissal of plaintiff's claims and default judgment against cross-defendants). *See generally* Russell G. Vineyard, Note, *Dismissal with Prejudice for Failure to Prosecute: Visiting the Sins of the Attorney Upon the Client,* 22 GA. L. REV. 195 (1987).

[168] The Supreme Court has excepted the disobedience of discovery rules and orders from operation of Rule 41(b), however, on the theory that discovery sanctions are governed by Rule 37. *Societe Internationale Pour Participations Industrielles et Commerciales v. Rogers,* 357 U.S. 197, 207 (1958).

[169] *See* MOORE § 41.51[1] (listing federal cases based on locally adopted rules). State rules or statutes also treat this. *See, e.g.,* D.C. SUPER. CT. R. 41(b); FLA. R. CIV. P. 1.420(e) (LEXIS through 2007) (inaction for one year).

[170] *See generally* MOORE § 41.52 (citing examples).

[171] *See, e.g., Link v. Wabash R.R. Co.,* 370 U.S. 626, 629 (1962); *Boudwin v. Graystone Ins. Co.,* 756 F.2d 399 (5th Cir. 1985).

[172] *See, e.g., Boudwin,* 756 F.2d 399; *Scarborough v. Eubanks,* 747 F.2d 871 (3d Cir. 1984). *See generally* Vineyard, note 167, *supra,* at 206–14.

[173] *See* § 12.10 (bench trials), *infra.*

[174] *See* § 12.04[3] (trial burdens), *infra.*

reasonably lead to a favorable verdict.[175] The greater demand placed on plaintiff by a motion for involuntary dismissal reflects the added fact-finding power judges assume in bench trials. Judges may resolve close questions of fact (including issues of credibility) against the plaintiff at the close of his case-in-chief that would otherwise go to juries in a jury case.[176] Involuntary dismissals simply save time by permitting judges to cut bench trials short when an outcome adverse to the plaintiff has become clear.

Involuntary dismissals and compulsory nonsuits are with prejudice to reinstitution of the action in the same court, unless otherwise provided or unless grounded on failure of a precondition to suit.[177] Rule 41(b) expressly identifies jurisdiction, proper venue, or joinder of a party under Rule 19, as such preconditions. Dismissals based on plaintiff's failure to satisfy these conditions do not operate as adjudications upon the merits. In this regard, "jurisdiction" is sometimes expansively construed to include dismissals based on the failure of other preconditions, such as posting of security bonds or filing of good cause certificates in certain immigration proceedings.[178]

§ 11.05　ALTERNATIVE DISPUTE RESOLUTION

Parties can also resolve their disputes without trial by alternative dispute resolution (ADR). Alternative dispute resolution is as old as formal adjudication, since parties to civil litigation have always had the option of agreeing to *settle* the case. Growing concern, however, about the time and expense of formal adjudication has led to greater interest in dispute resolution by other means. Among the ADR devices now used in addition to traditional settlement negotiation are *mediation, arbitration,* and *summary jury trials.*

Congress has required all federal courts to offer some ADR procedures.[179] Many states allow courts to order mandatory ADR for particular kinds of cases.[180] But probably the most common source of ADR is the parties themselves, who contract to use a specified ADR method to resolve disputes under the contract, who agree ad hoc to try an ADR technique before the

---

[175] *See* § 12.09[1] (directed verdicts), *infra.*

[176] The judge's view of the facts in a jury trial is comparatively insignificant. When the evidence is rationally capable of supporting a verdict for either side, the jury's conclusion is largely immune from court interference. *See* § 12.09, *infra.*

[177] *See Semtek Int'l Inc. v. Lockheed Martin Corp.*, 531 U.S. 497, 505 (2001) (holding that R. 41(b) dismissal without prejudice bars refiling in same court).

[178] *See generally* MOORE § 41.50[7]. *Cf. Saylor v. Lindsley*, 391 F.2d 965 (2d Cir. 1968) (dismissal for failure to post bond for security for costs does not operate as adjudication upon the merits despite Rule 41(b)'s express language).

[179] Alternative Dispute Resolution Act of 1998, 28 U.S.C. §§ 651–658 (2007). ("Each United States district court shall authorize, by local rule adopted under section 2071(a), the use of alternative dispute resolution processes in all civil actions, including adversary proceedings in bankruptcy, in accordance with this chapter, except that the use of arbitration may be authorized only as provided in section 654.")

[180] *See, e.g.,* ALASKA STAT. § 25.20.080 (2007) (for child custody matters); MICH. COMP. LAWS § 600.4951 (2006) (for civil actions based on tort); MONT. CODE ANN. § 39-71-2401(2005) (for workers' compensation benefit disputes).

matter gets to court, or who simply try to negotiate settlement after a suit is filed.

[1]   Settlement

Law students often assume that the object of litigation is to win at trial. If so, most litigators are dismal failures, as fewer than 5% of all civil cases are ever tried, and not all of these actually result in a judgment.[181] One reason for these surprisingly low numbers is that cases settle short of trial, or even at or just after trial, before judgment. This facts suggests the true purpose of most litigation: to resolve the dispute as favorably as possible for your client. Litigation ending in a court judgment is just one means of achieving this purpose, and not always the most efficient.[182] The appeal of settlement is that it can avoid the costs of trial, it can take into account a broader array of interests that can the often rigid law, and it permits a broader range of outcomes (win/win) than the usually bipolar alternatives (win/lose) at trial. It not only may yield a resolution more satisfying to the parties, but also one that better preserves an ongoing relationship.

A settlement is a contract negotiated among the parties. It usual results in payment of some sum of money by the defendant in return for a *release* of claims by the plaintiff. Because of ethical restrictions on contacting represented parties directly,[183] as well as the parties' emotional baggage in some cases, the negotiations are typically conducted by the lawyers. They can start even before the lawsuit, sometimes in response to a demand letter or a "courtesy copy" of the proposed complaint. More commonly, they commence after initial motions to dismiss are decided, significant discovery has occurred, summary judgment is denied, at the final pretrial conference, on the eve of trial, or, as noted, during trial in response to the evidence. At each of these points in the chronology of a civil lawsuit, the estimated value of a claim changes, in response to court action, discovery, evidence at trial, or simply the accumulating costs of prosecution and defense. Indeed, one of the uses of civil procedure is to influence these costs and thus the settlement potential of a claim.

Settlement discussions are typically held privately and in confidence. Although the court can be instrumental in encouraging settlement,[184] and may even ask the parties' lawyers for general progress reports on settlement discussions, the initiative lies with the parties and the details are typically left to their negotiations. The Federal Rules of Evidence protect the negotiations by making inadmissible offers to compromise as well as most "conduct and statements in compromise negotiations."[185] The court's approval of a

---

[181] *See* § 1.01[4], *supra.*

[182] *See, e.g.*, Samuel R. Gross & Kent D. Syverud, *Don't Try: Civil Jury Verdicts in a System Geared to Settlement*, 44 UCLA L. Rev. 1 (1996); David M. Trubek et al., *The Costs of Ordinary Litigation*, 31 UCLA L. Rev. 72 (1983).

[183] *See* § 10.01 (citing ethical rules), *supra.*

[184] *See* § 12.03[1][b], *infra.*

[185] Fed. R. Evid. 408.

settlement is usually not required except in class actions,[186] and the terms of the settlement are often confidential,[187] although some courts have held that the common law right of access trumps the private interest in confidentiality.[188] Because a settlement agreement is a contract, a party may ask a court to enforce the contract or to award damages from a breach.

[2]   Mediation

Mediation has been defined as "a dispute resolution process in which disputants are assisted by a neutral third person (the mediator) to come to a mutually satisfying, self-determined solution."[189] One crucial difference between mediation and adjudication procedures like arbitration or litigation is that the parties maintain control and ultimately decide for themselves the final outcome of the mediation.

In other words, mediation is nothing more than settlement negotiation facilitated by an outsider. Mediation is most likely to succeed in settings where opposing parties have good reason to agree but are hostile, alienated or distrustful. The mediator performs a facilitative function by serving as a buffer and medium of communication for settlement. She may also perform an evaluative function in clarifying for each party their own best interests, although some mediators studiously refrain from doing so.[190]

Parties tend to be more directly involved in mediation because the mediator insists on their presence. Mediation therefore often gives the parties an opportunity to tell their stories more freely than they can in traditional litigation. The flexibility afforded by mediation allows parties to reach individualized and creative solutions, rather than the standardized remedies imposed by the litigation system. Finally, mediation can help promote a sense of accomplishment and community that litigation is not as likely to foster.[191]

---

[186] *See* Rule 23(e).

[187] *See* Laurie Kratky Doré, *Secrecy By Consent: The Use and Limits of Confidentiality in the Pursuit of Settlement*, 74 Notre Dame L. Rev. 283 (1999).

[188] *See Bank of America Nat'l Trust & Sav. Ass'n v. Hotel Rittenhouse Assocs.*, 800 F.2d 339 (3d Cir. 1986); Cynthia A. Deiters, Note, *A Setback for the Public Policy of Encouraging Settlements*, 1988 J. Disp. Resol. 219.

[189] National Center for State Courts, Alternative Dispute Resolution (ADR) (2001). Discussion of developments in mediation practice and theory appear in *Symposium*, 2000 J. of Disp. Resol. 245; and *Symposium on the Structure of Court-Connected Mediation Programs*, 14 Ohio St. J. on Disp. Resol. 711 (1999).

[190] For a critique of the evaluative and facilitative functions of mediation, see Jeffrey W. Stempel, *The Inevitability of the Eclectic: Liberating ADR from Ideology*, 2000 J. Disp. Resol. 247.

[191] *See* Carrie Menkel-Meadow, Lela P. Love, Andrea K. Schneider & Jean R. Sternlight, Dispute Resolution: Beyond the Adversarial Model 268–71 (2005).

[3] Arbitration

Arbitration is closer in form to litigation itself, inasmuch as the neutral third person (the arbitrator) actually considers the case and designates a winner.[192] The appeal of arbitration is a faster and usually less costly decision than one obtained by trial. The arbitration often applies streamlined hearing procedures and allows at best limited discovery. The arbitrator typically does not issue a lengthy opinion explaining her decision, as it is not published and has no precedential value outside (or sometimes within) the arbitration.

Whether parties are required to submit to arbitration and, if so, whether the arbitrator's result is binding, usually depends on the nature of the agreement or prior consent of the parties. Thus, if the parties have contracted to submit their disputes to arbitration, they usually must do so before commencing judicial proceedings.[193] Similarly, if the parties have contracted that the arbitrator's decision is binding, it will usually be given preclusive effect in any subsequent case.[194]

The arbitration can be administered by a person or a group. The case administrator helps select the arbitrator who will hear the case, arrange the location where the arbitration will be held, and exchange documents before the hearing. Courts and government agencies typically administer nonbinding arbitration, while specialized organizations typically administer binding arbitrations under their own rules.[195]

The Uniform Arbitration Act (UAA) was developed to help states provide uniform rules and procedures for arbitration. Thirty-two states and the District of Columbia have adopted the UAA. In 2000, the National Conference of Commissioners on Uniform State Laws created the Revised Uniform Arbitration Act (RUAA). The RUAA gives more power to arbitrators and attempts to resolve ambiguities in the previous version of the model act. Eight states have adopted the RUAA, and the act is endorsed by the American Arbitration Association, which is one of the nation's oldest and most influential arbitration providers.[196]

Commentators have suggested that the modern trend toward enforcement of contractual arbitration clauses is problematic for several reasons. First, in

---

[192] *See* JACQUELINE M. NOLAN-HALEY, ALTERNATIVE DISPUTE RESOLUTION IN A NUTSHELL, Ch. 4 (1992).

[193] *See* The Federal Arbitration Act, 9 U.S.C. § 2 (making contractual arbitration agreements "valid, irrevocable, and enforceable, save upon such grounds as exist at law or in equity for the revocation of any contract."). Section 2 is enforceable in state as well as federal court. *Southland Corp. v. Keating*, 465 U.S. 1 (1984). State laws give similar effect to arbitration agreements. *See, e.g.*, CALIF. CODE OF CIV. PROC. § 1281; Art. 75, N.Y. CIV. PRAC. L. & R. § 7501; TEX. CIV. PRAC. & REM. § 171.001.

[194] AMERICAN LAW INSTITUTE, RESTATEMENT (SECOND) OF JUDGMENTS § 84 (1982). "It is well-settled that the doctrines of res judicata and collateral estoppel apply to arbitration awards." NOLAN-HALEY, note 192, *supra* at 162.

[195] *See* MENKEL-MEADOW ET AL., note 191, *supra* at 449.

[196] *See* Robert E. Wells, Jr., *Alternative Dispute Resolution — What is it? Where is it now?*, 28 S. ILL. U. L.J. 651, 660 (2004).

some cases of boilerplate arbitration provisions, it effectively denies a judicial remedy to those in inferior bargaining positions, like employees,[197] securities investors,[198] or internet consumers.[199] On the other hand, a judicial remedy may be more illusory than real, given the costs of litigation. For many of those in inferior bargaining positions, it may be arbitration or nothing.

Second, arbitration allows important decisions to be made privately, which deprives the public of any benefit from the precedential value those decisions would have carried had they been announced by courts.[200]

[4]   Summary Jury Trials[201]

Summary jury trials are a supplement to normal litigation that can provide the parties with a kind of crystal ball, suggesting the outcome of the case before the labor and expense of formal adjudication is actually undertaken. The parties summarize the evidence gathered in discovery, usually taking less than a day to present the case in the summary jury trial. The parties can also use testimony and argument, but cannot call live witnesses.[202]

The evidence is presented to a small test jury, drawn from the normal jury pool. They hear the evidence and argument by both sides, and reach a consensus non-binding verdict. The verdict is then disclosed to both sides, giving them a sense of how a real jury will evaluate the case and thereby facilitating settlement.[203] The parties even have the opportunity to talk to the jurors to find out more about the reasoning behind the verdict.

However, the summary jury trial has also been criticized for several reasons. First, the mandated use of summary jury trials for unwilling parties might be an unauthorized use of judicial power. Circuits have split on whether courts can mandate participation in summary jury trials.[204]

---

[197] Jean R. Sternlight, *Rethinking the Constitutionality of the Supreme Court's Preference for Binding Arbitration: A Fresh Assessment of Jury Trial, Separation of Powers, and Due Process Concerns*, 72 Tul. L. Rev. 1, 7 (1997).

[198] *Id.* at 7–8.

[199] Elizabeth G. Thornburg, *Going Private: Technology, Due Process, and Internet Dispute Resolution*, 34 U.C. Davis L. Rev. 151, 184 (2000).

[200] *See* Laurie Kratky Dore, *Public Courts Versus Private Justice: It's Time to Let Some Sun Shine in on Alternative Dispute Resolution*, 81 Chi.-Kent L. Rev. 463 (2006) (arguing that because arbitration is more like litigation than like settlement, it requires more transparency and access than settlement negotiations).

[201] *See* § 12.03[1][b], *infra*.

[202] *See* Richard Posner, *The Summary Jury Trial and Other Methods of Alternative Dispute Resolution: Some Cautionary Observations*, 53 U. Chi. L. Rev. 366, 369 (1986).

[203] *See* Menkel-Meadow et al., note 191, *supra*, at 647.

[204] *Compare Cincinnati Gas & Elec. Co. v. General Elec. Co.*, 854 F.2d 900, 904 n.4 (6th Cir. 1988) (noting that courts do "have the power to conduct summary jury trials under either Fed. R. Civ. P. 16 or as a matter of the court's inherent power to manage its cases"), *with Strandell v. Jackson County*, 838 F.2d 884 (7th Cir. 1987) (holding that Fed. R. Civ. P. 16 does not permit courts to force unwilling parties to participate in settlement negotiations through summary jury trials). *See* § 12.03[1][b], *infra*.

Second, jurors usually do not know that their verdict will be advisory rather than binding, leading to ethical questions about how, when, and, if these jurors should be informed about the truth.[205]

Third, some have questioned whether we should be using public courtrooms and resources to encourage private settlements.[206] Given the rate of settlement and the much reduced role of trial in modern civil litigation, however, this objection may seem quaint.

---

[205] *See* Posner, note 202, *supra* at 386–87 (1986) (arguing that while telling jurors in advance that their verdict is non-binding might make them less serious about the case at hand, a practice of deceiving jurors might lead to jurors in other cases taking their important role less seriously).

[206] *See* MENKEL-MEADOW ET AL., note 191, *supra*.

Chapter 12

TRIAL AND POST-TRIAL MOTIONS

§ 12.01 OVERVIEW: THE TRIAL PROCESS

The incidents of civil trial are similar in most jurisdictions,[1] reflecting the common historical origins of the trial process and the influence of unwritten custom. While federal and most state courts have rules of evidence regulating proof of facts at trial,[2] rules of civil procedure usually give little attention to the trial process. The Federal Rules of Civil Procedure are typical in their preoccupation with matters before and (to a lesser extent) after trial.

The trial process itself is best introduced chronologically.

[1]   Setting the Case For Trial

This initial step in the trial process should in theory await completion of the pretrial process, particularly discovery. However, as Samuel Johnson once said of the prospect of hanging, an early trial date "wonderfully concentrates the mind." Because it forces the pace of litigation, it is increasingly common for courts to set the trial date early as a reckoning point for setting deadlines, such as the cut-off of discovery and the completion of pretrial motion practice.[3] Some jurisdictions set the trial date as soon as issues in the case are joined by completion of the pleadings. Commonly the parties advise the court by memorandum that the case is at issue, after which the court places the case on its trial calendar.

[2]   Final Pretrial Conference[4]

The use of final pretrial conferences has increased for complex litigation in federal and many state courts. Rule 16 establishes procedure for the former. Parties often exchange briefs (memoranda) at the final pretrial conference, identifying their witnesses and other evidence and delineating their factual and legal contentions. These briefs help the court gauge the time required for trial, streamline the trial itself by flushing out potential evidentiary problems for resolution *in limine* (at the threshold of trial), and may facilitate settlement by

---

[1] *See generally* J. Alexander Tanford, *An Introduction to Trial Law*, 51 Mo. L. Rev. 623 (1986).

[2] *See* § 12.08[2], *infra*.

[3] Rule 16(b)(3)(B)(v) permits but does not require the inclusion of the trial date in the initial pretrial scheduling order.

[4] *See generally* § 12.03 (pretrial conference), *infra*.

previewing the real strength of the parties' trial positions. They may also present an occasion for summary judgment on some or all of the claims.[5]

Information presented in the parties' briefs and further agreements reached during the final pretrial conference provide material for the court's order. The order functions as a kind of program for trial. Often it shrinks the bounds of relevancy set by the pleadings alone.[6] It may also restrict the availability of even relevant evidence at trial by limiting sources of proof to those identified in the order.[7] Parties thereafter seeking enlargement of the final pretrial order bear a considerable burden of justification. Rule 16(e) permits modification of the order "only to prevent manifest injustice."

[3]   Jury Selection[8]

The jury is selected on the first day of trial after motions *in limine* and other housekeeping matters have been resolved. Jury selection is a two-step process. The first — assembling the *venire* from which the jury panel of twelve or fewer (plus alternates) is selected — is performed by the clerk's office according to statutory criteria and procedures.[9] The second — questioning (*voir dire*) of the potential jurors (*veniremen*) to select the panel — is performed by counsel, or by the judge with the aid of *voir dire* questions suggested by counsel.

The *voir dire* is intended to expose biases or interests of veniremen that would disqualify them for cause. Usually parties are given unlimited *challenges for cause* and a limited number of *peremptory* challenges. The latter permit counsel to keep persons off the jury without offering a reason, although the Supreme Court has ruled that civil litigants may not use their peremptory challenges to exclude jurors on account of their race or gender.[10]

While twelve jurors is the traditional number, use of juries of six has grown among federal and many state courts for civil jury trials.

---

[5] This may happen when the parties have narrowed the issues by requests for admissions (discussed in § 12.02, *infra*) or the court orders them to admit or deny factual assertions in each other's pretrial briefs at the pretrial conference. *See* § 12.03[3], *infra*.

[6] *See* § 12.03[3] (pretrial order and its effect), *infra*; WRIGHT & MILLER § 1527 (noting that the court "might preclude a party from introducing evidence on a claim or defense that is not revealed" at the final pretrial conference).

[7] *See* WRIGHT & MILLER § 1527 (noting that "the court may refuse to allow witnesses not named at the pretrial conference to testify at the trial.").

[8] *See generally* AMER. BAR ASS'N, JURIES AND JURY TRIALS (2005). On jury trials, *see* §§ 12.06 (the tactical decision whether to claim a jury), 12.07 (obtaining jury trial), 12.08 (judge-jury interaction), & 12.09 (taking the case from the jury), *infra*.

[9] *See, e.g.*, 28 U.S.C. §§ 1861–1869.

[10] *See Edmonson v. Leesville Concrete Co.*, 500 U.S. 614 (1991) (race); *J.E.B. v. Alabama*, 511 U.S. 127 (1994) (gender). Three peremptory challenges are permitted in federal courts. 28 U.S.C. § 1870.

[4]   Opening Statements

Once the jury has been empaneled, the plaintiff usually gives the first opening statement. Defendant may go first in rare cases where he concedes plaintiff's case-in-chief and has the burden of producing evidence concerning an affirmative defense. In non-jury cases, the judge often dispenses with the formality of opening statements because he or she has already become familiar with the case from presiding over pretrial hearings or from perusing the pleadings.

A well-organized and persuasive opening can go far to influence a fresh and attentive jury.[11] The function of an opening statement is not merely to preview the evidence but to tell the jury the story of a party's case. This is necessary because the presentation of testimony and tangible evidence during the trial is often piecemeal and anachronistic (e.g., out of chronological order). Plaintiff's opening statement thus gives the jury a road map to follow through trial.

For these same reasons, the defendant usually gives her opening statement after the plaintiff. In many jurisdictions, however, the defendant has the option to wait until plaintiff has presented his evidence. A defendant who has waited until then to open can take plaintiff's evidence into account.[12]

[5]   Presentation of Plaintiff's Case-in-Chief

After opening statements, the parties proceed with their proof. Testimonial evidence enters by direct examination of a witness by the plaintiff's counsel, followed by cross-examination by the defendant's counsel, and then re-direct and re-cross as necessary. Documents and other tangible exhibits are first marked for identification. Once counsel establishes ("lays") a foundation for such an exhibit with prior evidence or the foundation was conceded by pretrial admission, the exhibit may be offered for admission.

[6]   Mid-Trial Motion for Directed Verdict, Involuntary Dismissal or Judgment as a Matter of Law

After the plaintiff completes the presentation of his case-in-chief, the defendant may test that case by motion. In a jury trial, defendant moves for a directed verdict or, in federal court, for judgment as a matter of law.[13] The motion tests whether plaintiff has met his burden of production by presenting sufficient evidence to enable a reasonable jury to find for him.[14] When plaintiff's failure to satisfy this burden is sufficiently clear, there is no point in submitting the case to the jury because the judge would have to set aside a verdict for plaintiff on a proper motion for judgment notwithstanding the

---

[11] One commentator asserts that opening statements determine the outcome in 50–85% of the cases. Weyman I. Lundquist, *Advocacy in Opening Statements*, 8 Litig. 23 (1982).

[12] *See* Salvatore F. Stramondo & Andrew R. Goodspeed, Note, *Defendant's Presentation*, 57 Mass. L.Q. 179 (1972).

[13] *See* § 12.09[1], *infra.*

[14] § 12.09[1], *infra*; § 12.04[2], *infra.*

verdict or, in federal court, for judgment as a matter of law. But if plaintiff has met his burden or if the question is a close one, defendant's motion should be denied[15] without prejudice to defendant's case.

In a non-jury trial, the defendant tests plaintiff's case by a motion for involuntary dismissal or, in federal court, for judgment as a matter of law.[16] Because the trial judge sits as the trier of facts in a non-jury case, this motion tests the sufficiency *and* weight of the evidence. The judge thus may determine the facts and enter judgment against the plaintiff. On the other hand, because defendant has not yet had the opportunity to put on her evidence, the judge who denies defendant's mid-trial motion in a non-jury case will not ordinarily enter judgment against her at this stage.

[7]   Presentation of Additional Evidence

If defendant's mid-trial motion is denied, she puts on her evidence on the issues assigned her. Following her evidence, plaintiff may present rebuttal evidence. Defendant, in turn, may present its rebuttal evidence.

[8]   Motions at the Close of All the Evidence

At the close of all the evidence in a jury trial, either party may make a motion for a directed verdict or, in federal court, for judgment as a matter of law. This motion again tests the sufficiency of the opponent's evidence to support a jury verdict.

[9]   Closing Argument

Most jurisdictions permit closing arguments in three parts, with the plaintiff going first and last. Closing argument affords each party an opportunity to put evidence admitted in the case in the best possible light. Counsel may and usually do offer the jury conflicting interpretations of the evidence in their closing arguments, but they may not offer conflicting interpretations of law, or supplement the record by alluding to facts outside it. The court is the only source of guidance on legal standards by which the jury is to weigh the evidence. Therefore, counsels' closing arguments must be entirely consistent with the court's jury instructions,[17] which usually come later. When they do, the best and most widespread practice is for the court to indicate to counsel prior to closing arguments how it will be instructing the jury.[18]

---

[15] *See* § 12.09[3][b] (discussing the importance of reserving close questions for treatment by judgment n.o.v.), *infra*

[16] *See* §§ 11.04[2], *supra*, & 12.10, *infra*.

[17] *Cf.* Tanford, note 1, *supra*, at 692 (noting that it is improper in closing argument for counsel "to discuss law that is not part of the instructions . . . .").

[18] Thus Rule 51(b)(1) states that "must inform the parties of its proposed instructions and proposed action on the requests before instructing the jury and before final jury arguments."

Unfortunately, some attorneys see in closing argument an opportunity to grandstand, emote, go beyond the evidence, or prey on perceived prejudices of the jury.[19] This behavior can backfire, seeding the trial record with reversible error.

In non-jury cases, post-trial briefs often take the place of closing arguments.

[10]   Instructions to the Jury

In most jurisdictions, the judge instructs the jury after closing arguments, although federal judges have the option to instruct "the jury before or after the argument, or both."[20] Usually counsel submit proposed jury instructions, sometimes as early as the final pretrial conference, and the judge advises them of which instructions she will give. Almost all jurisdictions require counsel to object to errors in the instructions before the jury retires. This prevents sandbagging and permits cure of flawed instructions before the jury begins deliberations.

[11]   Jury Deliberation and Verdict

After the jury is instructed, it is placed in the custody of a bailiff. It then deliberates privately and, infrequently, may be *sequestered* (isolated) until it reaches a verdict. At the jury's request and upon notice to the parties, the judge may reread some or all of the instructions or permit the jury to re-examine record evidence or rehear testimony. Jurisdictions and individual judges differ in their tolerance for jury possession of written instructions or trial transcripts in the jury room.

At common law, a twelve-person jury had to reach a unanimous verdict. While unanimity is still required of federal juries, the Supreme Court has approved the use of fewer than twelve jurors. States differ widely in both the number of jurors and the degree of required agreement. However, all are subject to the requirements of due process under the Fourteenth Amendment. The Supreme Court has invoked the Due Process Clause to prohibit six-person, non-unanimous juries in criminal cases.[21] It has yet to define the outer limits of due process in civil state jury cases.

The jury's verdict may take several forms, depending upon the judge's instructions and the jurisdiction. In federal courts, the jury may deliver a traditional *general verdict* finding for or against each party, a *special verdict* answering factual interrogatories framed by the judge, or a combination of these verdicts.[22]

---

[19] Tanford, note 1, *supra*, at 685–93.

[20] Rule 51. *See generally* § 12.08[3] (instructing the jury), *infra*.

[21] *Burch v. Louisiana*, 441 U.S. 130 (1979); *Ballew v. Georgia*, 435 U.S. 223 (1978).

[22] Jury verdicts are discussed in greater detail in § 12.08[4], *infra*.

[12]   Challenges to Verdict and the Entry of Judgment

After the jury delivers its verdict, the judge may direct entry of judgment upon it. Most jurisdictions, however, authorize motions for judgment notwithstanding the verdict (judgment n.o.v.).[23] Parties in federal court have until ten days after the court's entry of judgment on a verdict to move for judgment as a matter of law, or, alternatively, for new trial.

In non-jury trials, the court finds the facts and enters judgment accordingly. There is no analogue to a motion for judgment n.o.v., although the parties usually can move for reconsideration or amendment of the judgment[24] within a fixed period of time.

[13]   Other Post-Trial Motions

In addition to the post-verdict and post-judgment motions noted above, courts permit motions for new trial.[25] Historically, new trials have been granted because of prejudicial conduct by jurors or attorneys, judicial errors, or because the verdict was against the weight of the evidence. New trial orders wipe out the jury verdict, but they do not give movant victory on the merits. The trial judge therefore is given greater power to grant new trials than to grant judgments n.o.v.[26]

After time for moving for judgment n.o.v., judgment as a matter of law, new trial, reconsideration, or amendment has passed, trial-level attack on the judgment becomes difficult. What remains for the party aggrieved by the judgment is the limited prospect of extraordinary relief. Most jurisdictions permit post-trial motions to set aside judgments. Federal procedure is typical in providing relief because of clerical error[27] or because circumstances suggest that it would be unfair to enforce the judgment.[28] Extraordinary relief provides a fairly reliable means for correcting clerical errors. To a lesser extent, it functions to vacate default judgments. Beyond that, extraordinary relief is usually unavailable, confined, as the term suggests, to *extraordinary* cases. This is consistent with society's interest in the finality of judgments.[29]

---

[23] "N.O.V." is an abbreviation of the Latin phrase *non obstante veredicto*, which means notwithstanding the verdict. See generally § 12.09, *infra*, for extensive discussion of motions for judgment notwithstanding the verdict and their relation to motions for directed verdicts made earlier in the case (now all called *motions for judgment as a matter of law* in federal court) and to motions for new trial.

[24] *See* § 12.11[2][c], *infra*.

[25] *See* § 12.09[2] (new trials), *infra*.

[26] On the relationship between judgments n.o.v. (and judgments as a matter of law) and orders for new trial, see §§ 12.09[2][b] & 12.09[3][d], *infra*.

[27] Rule 60(a).

[28] Rule 60(b).

[29] For more extended discussion of Rule 60 and extraordinary relief from judgments, see § 12.11[2][b], *infra*.

PART A.
Narrowing Issues and Allocating Burdens

§ 12.02   REQUESTS FOR ADMISSIONS[30]

[1]   Procedure for Requesting Admissions

Many jurisdictions provide a procedure like Federal Rule 36 by which a party may request his adversary to admit the truth of any matters within the scope of discovery. Unless amended or withdrawn by leave of court, admissions are binding at trial[31] and thus relieve their proponent of the time and expense of proving the admitted matter. Although the request for admissions is usually classified as a discovery procedure,[32] it presupposes that the requesting party already has sufficient information about the case to formulate the requested admissions, and it is usually filed at the close of discovery. It is therefore more accurately regarded as a pretrial, issue-narrowing procedure and is so treated here.[33]

The requested admissions must take a declaratory form that is susceptible to the bare response "admit" or "deny." Federal Form 25 offers the following examples: "That each of the following documents, exhibited with this request, is genuine," and "That each of the following statements is true." Under the federal rules, admissions are subject only to the generic limitations of Rule 26(b).[34] They may embrace disputed issues, ultimate issues (negligence, breach, etc.) as well as evidentiary facts, and the application of law to fact, but not pure legal conclusions.[35] A few courts still disapprove of requests concerning ultimate issues in the case. They do so either on the ground that ultimate issues involve legal conclusions or on the ground that probable denial, followed by a request for expenses under Rule 37(c) should the denying party lose at trial, would circumvent the American rule against awarding attorney's

---

[30] *See generally* Jeffrey S. Kinsler, *Requests for Admission in Wisconsin Procedures: Civil Litigation's Double-Edged Sword*, 78 Marq. L. Rev. 625 (1995); Ted Finman, *The Request for Admissions in Federal Civil Procedure*, 71 Yale L.J. 371 (1962).

[31] *See, e.g.*, Rule 36(b).

[32] Rule 36, for example, appears at Part V of the federal rules, entitled "Depositions and Discovery."

[33] *See James, Hazard & Leubsdorf* § 5.7 ("[i]n some ways, . . . a pleading device that narrows the issues to be tried rather than a discovery device to obtain evidence"); *Wright* § 89 (not, strictly speaking, a discovery device at all); Roger S. Haydock & David F. Herr, Discovery: Theory, Practice, and Problems § 5.2 (1983) ("more of a trial practice rule").

[34] *See* § 10.03 (scope of federal discovery), *supra*.

[35] *Wright* § 89. *See, e.g., Williams v. Krieger*, 61 F.R.D. 142 (S.D.N.Y. 1973) (request for admission of pure legal conclusion is improper). *See also* Russell G. Donaldson, Annotation, *Permissible Scope, Respecting Nature of Inquiry, of Demand for Admissions Under Modern State Civil Rules of Procedure*, 42 A.L.R.4th 489; § 10.03[3][c] (discoverability of contentions), *supra*; § 10.09[1] (contention interrogatories), *supra*.

fees to the prevailing party.[36] This reasoning is largely specious, since Rule 37(c) itself exempts a denying party from sanctions for failing to admit when he had "reasonable ground to believe that he might prevail on the matter." There is usually such reasonable ground on the ultimate issues of liability in the ordinary lawsuit.[37]

To ignore requests for admission is unwise, since Rule 36(a) deems failure to reply an admission. If in reasonable doubt of the truth of a requested admission, a party may simply deny. Alternatively, he may object on the ground that the request exceeds the permissible scope of discovery, seek a protective order for any of the reasons listed in Rule 26(c),[38] admit part and deny the balance, qualify his admissions and denials as necessary, or state that after reasonable inquiry the information available to him is insufficient to enable him to admit or deny.[39] To be entitled to the last response, a party may not rely just on his immediate personal knowledge. He must make reasonable inquiry.[40]

Prior to the 1970 amendment to Rule 36, it was unclear whether a defective response to a request for admission relieved the requesting party of the burden of proving the matter at trial.[41] The amended rule permits that party to move before trial to test the sufficiency of answers or objections to requests in order to remove this uncertainty.

An admission obtained under Rule 36, like one appearing in a pleading or by stipulation, takes the admitted matter from the fact-finder and "conclusively establishe[s]" it for purposes of the pending action.[42] No evidence need be proffered to establish the matter admitted, and none will be admitted to refute it, although it is still subject to objections to admissibility.[43] In this respect, admissions are different from the product of the discovery procedures such as answers to interrogatories, which are only evidentiary and therefore subject both to proffer and to rebuttal at trial.

Admissions may be withdrawn or amended with leave of court pursuant to Rule 36(b), however, if it will subserve the presentation of the merits and if the party who requested the admission is unable to show prejudice from the

---

[36] *See, e.g., Naxon Telesign Corp. v. GTE Info. Sys., Inc.,* 89 F.R.D. 333 (N.D. Ill. 1980). On the American rule generally, see § 14.01[2], *infra.*

[37] *See generally* David L. Shapiro, *Some Problems of Discovery in an Adversary System,* 63 Minn. L. Rev. 1055, 1078–92 (1979) (arguing that a party may deny if he reasonably doubts, on the basis of all the admissible evidence known to him, that the requester could prevail at trial).

[38] *See* § 10.13[3] (protective orders against specific hardships), *supra.*

[39] *Compare* Rule 36(a) with Rule 8(b). *Cf.* § 8.08[1] (specific denials), *supra.*

[40] *See, e.g., Al-Jundi v. Rockefeller,* 91 F.R.D. 590, 593–94 (W.D.N.Y. 1981) (blanket assertion that the necessary information is in the knowledge of third persons is insufficient without reasonable inquiry of them). The duty of inquiry is underscored by the certification requirement of Rule 26(g). *See* § 10.13[1] (discovery certification requirement), *supra.*

[41] Rule 36 advisory committee's notes (1970).

[42] Rule 36(b). It supersedes the pleadings *pro tanto.* Friedenthal Kane & Miller § 7.10.

[43] *See* Wright & Miller § 2264.

amendment.[44] "Although an admission should ordinarily be binding on the party who made it," observes one authority, "there must be room in rare cases for a different result, as when an admission no longer is true because of changed circumstances or through honest error a party has made an improvident admission."[45] Prejudice in this context means more than that the party obtaining the request will now have to convince the fact-finder of the truth. It means preparation prejudice — any difficulty posed for the requesting party in obtaining and making proof beyond that which would have occurred if no admission had been made.[46]

[2]   Use and Value of Requests for Admissions

The chief purpose of requests for admissions is not to discover new information, but rather to expedite trial and to reduce the costs of proof.[47] But the leeway afforded by Rule 36 to deny the important issues and the weak sanction provisions of Rule 37(c) have rendered requests for admissions among the least used, most abused, and often disappointing procedural tools.[48] Requests to admit the authenticity of documentary evidence attached to the request are an exception. Because they are easy to frame and hard to evade, these requests are an effective means of avoiding the time and cost of authentication testimony at trial.

§ 12.03   PRETRIAL CONFERENCE[49]

[1]   Purposes

In a pretrial conference, lawyers (and sometimes the parties) meet with judge, magistrate[50] or master before trial. Unknown at common law, the pretrial conference was authorized for the federal courts by Rule 16. It is said to be the most popular federal rule and has stimulated widespread adoption of

---

[44] *See, e.g., Reyes v. Vantage S.S. Co.*, 672 F.2d 556 (5th Cir. 1982) (admission was based on a faulty assumption).

[45] WRIGHT & MILLER § 2264.

[46] *See Brook Vill. N. Assocs. v. General Elec. Co.*, 686 F.2d 66, 70–71 (1st Cir. 1982). *Compare* § 8.10[1] (amendments in general and the prejudice requirement), *supra*.

[47] WRIGHT § 89.

[48] *See, e.g.*, Helen H. Stern Cutner, *Discovery — Civil Litigation's Fading Light: A Lawyer Looks at the Federal Discovery Rules After Forty Years of Use*, 52 TEMP. L.Q. 933, 981 (1979); Shapiro, note 37, *supra*, at 1078. *But see* WRIGHT & MILLER § 2253 (for their purposes, requests are more effective than other discovery).

[49] *See generally* Wayne D. Brazil, *Improving Judicial Controls Over the Pretrial Development of Civil Actions: Model Rules for Case Management and Sanctions*, 1981 AM. B. FOUND. RES. J. 873; David L. Shapiro, *Federal Rule 16: A Look at the Theory and Practice of Rulemaking*, 137 U. PA. L. REV. 1969 (1989); MAURICE ROSENBERG, THE PRETRIAL CONFERENCE AND EFFECTIVE JUSTICE (1964).

[50] *See* 28 U.S.C. §§ 631, 636 (authorizing participation of magistrates in pretrial proceedings), *construed in Mathews v. Weber*, 423 U.S. 261 (1976). *See generally* Arthur L. Sr. Burnett, *Practical, Innovative and Progressive Utilization of United States Magistrates to Improve the Administration of Justice in United States District Courts*, 28 HOW. L.J. 293 (1985).

similar rules in the states.[51]

A primary purpose of pretrial conferences has always been to simplify, shorten, and possibly avoid trial.[52] The 1983 amendments to Rule 16 added another managerial purpose: to control, expedite and reduce the waste of pretrial litigation generally.[53] In addition, pretrial conferences continue to have the secondary purpose of facilitating settlement. The 1993 amendments reinforced all of these purposes.

[a]   **Managerial Purposes**

Pretrial conferences alleviate some of the uncertainty inherent in liberalized pleading, joinder, and discovery.

Modern pleading gives notice to the parties of what the case *may* include; pretrial conferences and orders help to define what the issues *are* on the eve of trial.[54] The order emerging from the final pretrial conference supersedes the sketchy descriptions of the case allowed in notice pleading jurisdictions.[55] That conference comes after the pleader has had the opportunity to develop his case by discovery. It provides a useful occasion for informing the parties and the judge more precisely about the case, lessening surprise at trial.

There is a significant relationship between pretrial conferences and the discovery process. The 1993 amendments to Rule 16 emphasize that "a major objective of pretrial conferences should be to consider appropriate controls on the extent and timing of discovery."[56] Moreover, broad discovery is permissible today in part because the undifferentiated mass of admissible and inadmissible evidence that it produces can be culled at the pretrial conference. The court can require the parties to specify their factual contentions[57] and their evidence for trial, and it can rule on its admissibility *in limine* (at the threshold of trial).[58]

The pretrial conference also complements liberal joinder of claims and parties by providing for on-going and anticipatory control of the resulting complexity.[59] It permits courts to schedule or divide cases when necessary, order early presentation of evidence regarding potentially dispositive issues, limit the time allowed for presenting evidence at trial, and address other

---

[51] WRIGHT § 91.

[52] WRIGHT § 16.03[1].

[53] *See* Rule 16 advisory committee's notes (1983); MOORE § 16.03[1].

[54] *Cf.* JAMES, HAZARD, & LEUBSDORF § 5.19.

[55] *See* §§ 8.01 (history and functions of pleading) & 8.04 (modern notice pleading), *supra*.

[56] Rule 16(c) advisory committee's notes (1993).

[57] *See* Rules 33(b) and 36(a) (permitting postponement until pretrial conference of discovery of contentions regarding application of law to the facts).

[58] *See* Robert E. Bacharach, *Motions in Limine in Oklahoma State and Federal Courts*, 24 OKLA. CITY U. L. REV. 113 (1999).

[59] *See generally* Chapter 9 (joinder), *supra*.

managerial problems arising in complex litigation.[60]

[b] Facilitating Settlement

Settlement has been a natural by-product of the pretrial conference in many cases because the exchange of contentions, admissions, and evidentiary specifications, and the prospect of an actual trial soon after the conference, make the parties and their lawyers reassess their cases. Some judges have gone further and affirmatively used the pretrial conference to promote settlement. They see judicial initiatives as necessary to compensate for the frequent hesitation of the parties to display weakness by initiating settlement negotiations.[61] On the other hand, outright coercion of settlement is reversible error,[62] and some judges studiously refrain from becoming involved in settlement. The 1993 amendments to Rule 16 apparently endorse the former view by addressing, though not fully resolving, two issues of settlement that have arisen under the rule.

The first is whether a federal judge may order a represented party to attend a settlement conference. Although the former rule only compelled an attorney who will conduct the trial or an unrepresented party to attend the final pretrial conference, a sharply divided Seventh Circuit Court of Appeals sitting *en banc* ruled in *G. Heileman Brewing Co., Inc. v. Joseph Oat Corp.*,[63] that a federal court had inherent authority to compel a represented party to attend a pretrial conference in order to promote settlement. The dissenters argued that the plain language of Rule 16(d) was exclusive,[64] and that compelling parties to attend was tantamount to compelling them to negotiate, which was an abuse of judicial managerial authority.[65] A 1993 amendment to Rule 16 cautiously sides with the *Heileman* majority by explicitly providing that a court may require a party or its representative to be present or reasonably available by telephone to consider possible settlement.[66]

One federal judge, confronted with particularly contentious counsel, is reported to have said, "I cannot order a duel, and thus achieve a salubrious reduction in the number of counsel to put up with. However, a summary jury

---

[60] *See generally* THE MANUAL FOR COMPLEX LITIGATION (4th ed. 2004) (recommending at least four pretrial conferences in such cases).

[61] *See generally* Robert R. Merhige & Alvin B. Rubin, *The Role of the Judge in the Settlement Process*, 75 F.R.D. 203, 205 (1978); Walter E. Craig & Gordon E. Christenson, *The Settlement Process*, 59 F.R.D. 252, 253–55 (1973).

[62] *See, e.g.*, *Kothe v. Smith*, 771 F.2d 667 (2d Cir. 1985); Rule 16 advisory committee's note (1983). *See generally* Carrie Menkel-Meadow, *For and Against Settlement: Uses and Abuses of the Mandatory Settlement Conference*, 33 UCLA L. REV. 485 (1985).

[63] 871 F.2d 648 (7th Cir. 1989).

[64] 871 F.2d at 658 (Coffey, J., dissenting), at 666 (Manion, J., dissenting).

[65] 871 F.2d at 665 (Easterbrook, J., dissenting).

[66] Rule 16(c). The 1993 advisory committee's notes add that this explicit authorization "is not intended to limit the reasonable exercise of the court's inherent powers," citing *Heileman*. *See also* Civil Justice Reform Act of 1990, 28 U.S.C. § 473(b)(5) (providing that locally adopted plans for reduction of expense and delay may include compulsory attendance requirements).

trial is so ordered."[67] His order presents a second settlement-related issue under Rule 16: whether it authorizes a federal judge to direct a summary jury trial in order to promote settlement. The summary jury trial is an alternative dispute resolution device by which parties summarize their evidence to a small test jury that then reports a consensus verdict.[68]

Courts that ordered such summary jury trials before the 1993 amendments to Rule 16 relied in part on the rule's inclusion of "the possibility of settlement or the use of extrajudicial procedures to resolve the dispute" among the permissible subjects of conference, as well as the rule's limited compulsory attendance provision.[69] In *Strandell v. Jackson County*,[70] however, the Seventh Circuit Court of Appeals disagreed, ruling that these provisions of old Rule 16 did not authorize *mandatory* summary jury trial. The 1993 amendments to Rule 16 sidestep this issue by explicitly including as a permissible subject of pretrial conference "using special procedures to assist in resolving the dispute *when authorized by statute or local rule.*"[71] The underscored qualifier leaves open the issue of a court's inherent authority to mandate summary jury trial.

The foregoing issues, and the rules' caution in approaching them, indicate that there is still no consensus about whether a judge can take the initiative in settlement during pretrial, and still display the neutrality and detachment that has been traditional in our judicial systems,[72] and whether court-ordered alternative dispute resolution is consistent with fair[73] and public[74] process.

---

[67] *Choose Your Weapons*, 78 A.B.A.J. 44 (1992).

[68] *See, e.g.,* § 11.05[4], *supra*; Ann E. Woodley, *Strengthening the Summary Jury Trial: A Proposal to Increase Its Effectiveness and Encourage Uniformity in Its Use*, 12 Ohio St. J. on Disp. Resol. 541 (1997); Shirley A. Wiegand, *A New Light Bulb or the Work of the Devil? A Current Assessment of Summary Jury Trials*, 69 Or. L. Rev. 87 (1990); Charles F. Webber, *Mandatory Summary Jury Trial: Playing by the Rules?*, 56 U. Chi. L. Rev. 1495 (1989); Richard A. Posner, *The Summary Jury Trial and Other Methods of Alternative Dispute Resolution: Some Cautionary Observations*, 53 U. Chi. L. Rev. 366 (1986).

[69] *See, e.g., McKay v. Ashland Oil, Inc.*, 120 F.R.D. 43 (E.D. Ky. 1988); *Arabian American Oil Co. v. Scarfone*, 119 F.R.D. 448 (M.D. Fla. 1988).

[70] 838 F.2d 884 (7th Cir. 1987).

[71] Rule 16(c)(2)(L) (emphasis added). Such other "special procedures" include mini-trials, mediation, neutral evaluation, and nonbinding arbitration. Rule 16(c)(2)(L) advisory committee's notes (1993).

[72] *See generally* Stephen McG. Bundy, *The Policy in Favor of Settlement in an Adversary System*, 44 Hastings L.J. 1 (1992); Judith Resnik, *Managerial Judges*, 96 Harv. L. Rev. 374 (1982); Steven Flanders, *Blind Umpires — A Response to Professor Resnik*, 35 Hastings L.J. 505, 507 (1984); Marla Moore, Note, *Mandatory Summary Jury Trials: Too Hasty a Solution to the Growing Problem of Judicial Inefficiency?*, 14 Rev. Litig. 495 (1995). For views by federal judges, see Charles E. Clark, *Objectives of Pretrial Procedure*, 17 Ohio St. L.J. 163, 167 (1956) ("Pre-trial used as a club to force settlements will destroy its utility as a stage of the trial process itself."); J. Skelly Wright, *The Pretrial Conference*, 28 F.R.D. 141, 145–47 (1960) ("we try to take the load off . . . the lawyer's back by telling them what we think the case should settle at . . . .").

[73] *See generally* Thomas B. Metzloff, *Reconfiguring the Summary Jury Trial*, 41 Duke L.J. 806 (1992); Jennifer O'Hearne, *Compelled Participation in Innovative Pretrial Proceedings*, 84 Nw. U. L. Rev. 290 (1989); Note, *Mandatory Mediation and Summary Jury Trial Guidelines for Ensuring Fair and Effective Processes*, 103 Harv. L. Rev. 1086 (1990).

Even if judicial neutrality can be achieved by assigning different judges to accomplish the managerial and settlement-facilitating purposes of pretrial conferences, the process issues remain, assuring that the settlement-related provisions of Rule 16 will themselves continue to generate litigation.

[c]   Assessment

Whether pretrial conferences have successfully accomplished the foregoing purposes is unclear. The evidence that pretrial has shortened trial and reduced congestion is weak, but there is stronger evidence that it has improved the quality of trials by facilitating better presentation of cases and reducing surprise.[75] There is some evidence that it has facilitated settlement, although it is unclear how much of this is a by-product of neutral managerial uses of pretrial and how much the result of more aggressive judicial settlement initiatives.[76] What is clear is that Rule 16 may be changing the adversary system. Instead of leaving its control to the parties by their lawyers, "it directs the sharing of power in handling the processing of a lawsuit."[77] Whether this change is for the better, or whether it is "redefining *sub silentio* our standards of what constitutes rational, fair, and impartial adjudication" in favor of an inquisitorial model of dispute resolution,[78] is an open question.

[2]   Procedures for Pretrial Conferences[79]

Rule 16(a) and most state rules make the holding of pretrial conferences discretionary with the trial judge. The advisory committee in 1983 found that mandatory rules result in the over-regulation of some cases and under-regulation of others.[80] Some jurisdictions accordingly make the conference mandatory only in particular categories of cases.

When only one pretrial conference is held, it is usually scheduled after the completion of discovery, shortly before trial.[81] At that point it is reasonable to

---

[74] *See Cincinnati Gas & Elec. Co. v. General Elec. Co.*, 854 F.2d 900 (6th Cir. 1988) (affirming order closing summary jury trial to public), *cert. denied*, 489 U.S. 1033 (1989). *See generally* Angela Wade, Note, *Summary Jury Trials: A "Settlement Technique" That Places a Shroud of Secrecy on Our Courtrooms?*, 23 IND. L. REV. 949 (1990).

[75] *See generally* STEVEN FLANDERS, CASE MANAGEMENT AND COURT MANAGEMENT IN UNITED STATES DISTRICT COURTS 18–19, 35–37 (1977); ROSENBERG, note 49, *supra*, at 29–42.

[76] *See generally* ROSENBERG, note 49, *supra*, at 49–50; Robert J. Plourde, *Pretrial in Maine Under New Rule 16: Settlement, Sanctions, and Sayonara*, 34 ME. L. REV. 111, 126 (1982) (suggesting that the dichotomy is false and that settlement is a co-product of management).

[77] Arthur R. Miller & Diana G. Culp, *The New Rules of Civil Procedure: Managing Cases, Limiting Discovery*, NAT'L L.J., Dec. 5, 1983, at 23–25.

[78] *See* Resnik, note 72, *supra*, at 380. *See also* Todd D. Peterson, *Restoring Structural Checks on Judicial Power in the Era of Managerial Judging*, 29 U.C. DAVIS L. REV. 41 (1995).

[79] *See generally* JUDICIAL CONF. OF UNITED STATES, HANDBOOK FOR EFFECTIVE PRETRIAL PROCEDURE (1964), *reprinted in* 37 F.R.D. 255; Robert F. Peckham, *The Federal Judge as a Case Manager: The New Role in Guiding a Case From Filing to Disposition*, 69 CAL. L. REV. 770 (1981).

[80] Rule 16 advisory committee's notes (1983).

[81] *See* Rule 16(e) (providing that the final pretrial conference shall be held as close to the time of trial as reasonable under the circumstances).

make the parties specify issues and evidence and to amend the pleadings. Most rules, like Rule 16, also authorize multiple pretrial conferences in the judge's discretion.

Rule 16(b) also requires the judge to enter a scheduling order within 90 days after the appearance of a defendant or 120 days after the complaint is served, setting time limits for joinder and amendment, motion practice, and completion of discovery, and (optionally) setting the dates for mandatory discovery, pretrial conferences, and trial, subject to modification for good cause.[82] This initial order helps accomplish the stated purpose of "establishing early and continuing control" of the lawsuit.[83]

In addition to now authorizing a court to require the attendance or availability by phone of a party or its representative, Rule 16 requires attorneys to prepare for and attend every pretrial conference and requires at least one of the attorneys who will conduct the trial to attend the final pretrial conference.[84] Backed by sanctions under Rule 16(f),[85] these provisions are aimed at preventing the sabotage of effective pretrial by indifferent preparation or the dodge that the attorney is unauthorized to stipulate or enter into other agreements that might be made at pretrial.

Rule 16(c) supplies a non-exhaustive list of the subjects that may be considered in pretrial.[86] Usually the parties will be asked to submit pretrial briefs.[87] These may state the undisputed facts, identify the disputed facts (often with citation to the discovery record), summarize legal contentions, and list trial witnesses and exhibits. The parties may also be required to make authenticity objections to proposed trial exhibits and are invited to raise other evidentiary objections that could be ruled upon before trial.[88] Now some of these functions of pretrial briefs are fulfilled instead by Rule 26(a)(3), requiring identification at least thirty days before trial of trial witnesses, exhibits, and other evidence, and objections within fourteen days thereafter (at the risk of waiver). Even with this required pretrial disclosure, however, courts may continue to require the parties to propose findings of fact in their pretrial briefs and to admit or deny each other's proposed findings, as a way of clarifying the issues for trial.[89] Furthermore, to expedite the trial, the court

---

[82] The rule provides that courts may exempt categories of cases from this requirement. Rule 16(b). The Advisory Committee gave social security benefits, *habeas corpus*, and some administrative law cases as examples. Rule 16 advisory committee notes (1983).

[83] Rule 16(a)(2).

[84] Rule 16(c) & (e).

[85] *See also Link v. Wabash R.R. Co.*, 370 U.S. 626 (1962) (affirming dismissal under court's inherent power to punish failure to attend pretrial conferences and other misconduct). *See generally* § 12.03[3] (the pretrial order and its effect), *infra*.

[86] *See generally* MOORE §§ 16.30–16.36; WRIGHT & MILLER § 1525.

[87] WRIGHT & MILLER § 1524.

[88] *See* Edna S. Epstein, *Motions in Limine — A Primer, in* THE LITIGATION MANUAL 642 (American Bar Ass'n 1999).

[89] Larry Lempert, *AT&T Case May Become Complex Litigation Model,* LEGAL TIMES OF WASHINGTON, Feb. 4, 1980, at 1.

may order early presentation of evidence on a potentially dispositive issue, as noted above, and, more controversially, set reasonable limits on the time allowed for presenting evidence.[90]

By their pretrial briefs, or by formal motion under Rule 15(a), parties often amend their pleadings at pretrial. The imminence of trial creates an incentive to drop borderline claims or defenses for which there was little support from discovery and to sharpen or add others suggested by discovery, eliminating the need to accomplish the same end through disruptive mid-trial amendments. Moreover, it is well-established that the court may itself redefine or even terminate the lawsuit by entering summary judgment on particular claims and defenses, should the pretrial briefs establish the absence of genuine factual dispute.[91]

The pretrial conference, however, is no substitute for discovery or for trial. Although the 1993 amendments authorize inclusion of " controlling and scheduling discovery" as a pretrial conference subject,[92] perhaps impliedly settling the previously unresolved issue of the courts' authority to order discovery pursuant to a pretrial conference,[93] the conference is still not intended as a discovery tool for the parties. It is surely not a device for deciding disputed issues of material fact; it confers no greater power on the court than it already has under the summary judgment rule.[94]

[3]   The Pretrial Order and Its Effect

Rule 16(d) requires the court to enter an order after a pretrial conference to preserve the work done there. The order is often prepared by counsel for the approval of the court.[95] Its content varies with the work of the conference. A 1962 study reported that in one-third of federal pretrial conferences, the trial judge failed to file a pretrial order,[96] although that figure has probably declined since the 1983 amendments to Rule 16. In those cases, however, the parties' pretrial memoranda were often given the same effect as a pretrial order.[97]

Rule 16(d) provides that the pretrial order "controls the course of action unless the court modifies it," and that the final pretrial order shall be modified

---

[90] Rule 16(c)(2)(N) & (O).

[91] *See, e.g., Portsmouth Square, Inc. v. S'holders Protective Comm.*, 770 F.2d 866 (9th Cir. 1985) ("The court need not await a formal motion, . . . [as long as] the party against whom judgment was entered had a full and fair opportunity to develop and present facts and legal arguments in support of its position." (citation omitted)). *See also* Rule 16(c) advisory committee's notes (1983).

[92] Rule 16(c)(2)(F).

[93] *See* MOORE § 16.13[2].

[94] *See* § 11.03[1] (summary judgment at court's initiative), *supra*.

[95] WRIGHT & MILLER § 1526. The Advisory Committee for the 1983 amendments to Rule 16 were content to leave the question of how a pretrial order should be prepared to the discretion of the presiding judges. Rule 16 advisory committee's notes (1983).

[96] *See* REPORT OF PROCEEDINGS OF THE JUDICIAL CONFERENCE OF THE UNITED STATES 79–80 (1962).

[97] *See Price v. Inland Oil Co.*, 646 F.2d 90, 96 (3d Cir. 1981).

"only to prevent manifest injustice." The final pretrial order supersedes the pleadings. Objections to the pleadings, claims and defenses, or issues not incorporated in the order are waived.[98]

> [A] party need offer no proof at trial as to matters agreed to in the order, nor may a party evidence or advance theories at trial that are not included in the order or which contradict its terms. Disregard of these principles would bring back the days of trial by ambush and discourage timely preparation by the parties for trial.[99]

The binding effect given the pretrial order thus affords the parties a measure of certainty concerning the real issues for trial and their evidentiary burden.

This contrast between the pretrial order and modern pleading merits emphasis. Modern federal pleading is intended only to give notice to the adversary of the events giving rise to a claim or defense. The pleader is not held to any single theory of the pleadings.[100] This system is based on the presumption that pleaders at the outset often lack sufficient information to articulate details and all possible claims or defenses. Modern pleading assumes that parties will be able to ascertain that information by discovery. However, the presumption runs the other way as the parties near the end of the lawsuit. Fairness and trial efficiency then require a higher degree of certainty about what is and what is not at issue.[101]

Exclusion is the typical trial sanction for enlargement of the issues or evidence beyond the pretrial order. Rule 16(f) also authorizes the court to punish disobedience of the pretrial order by striking claims or defenses, dismissing the action, entering a default judgment, or holding the disobedient party in contempt. Thus, the court may refuse to admit into evidence documents that the proponent failed to list in the pretrial order or brief,[102] and it may exclude witnesses that were omitted from final witness lists at

---

[98] *See, e.g., Simcox v. San Juan Shipyard, Inc.*, 754 F.2d 430, 440 (1st Cir. 1985) (Rule 9(b) objection that complaint did not plead fraud with particularity was waived by failure to object to incorporation of fraud claim in pretrial order); *Syrie v. Knoll Int'l*, 748 F.2d 304, 308 (5th Cir. 1984) (incorporation of unpleaded claim into pretrial order amends the pleadings *pro tanto*).

[99] *United States v. First Nat'l Bank of Circle*, 652 F.2d 882, 886 (9th Cir. 1981).

[100] *See* § 8.04 (modern notice pleading), *supra*.

[101] This is true even though a pretrial order is generally given a liberal construction to include "any of the possible legal or factual theories that might be embraced by its language." WRIGHT & MILLER § 1527. *See, e.g., Miller v. Safeco Title Ins. Co.*, 758 F.2d 364 (9th Cir. 1985) (pretrial order statement of issue as whether a debt was secured by a trust deed construed to include issue whether deed was in the nature of a performance bond). *But see Flannery v. Carroll*, 676 F.2d 126, 129 (5th Cir. 1982) ("District courts are encouraged to construe pre-trial orders narrowly without fear of reversal.").

[102] *See, e.g., Smith v. Rowe*, 761 F.2d 360 (7th Cir. 1985); *United States v. Rayco, Inc.*, 616 F.2d 462 (10th Cir. 1980).

pretrial.[103] Similarly, the court may bar a party from asserting a new claim or theory of recovery, if it was omitted from the pretrial order or memorandum.[104]

While final pretrial orders are not ironclad, Rule 16(e) authorizes their modification "only to prevent manifest injustice."[105] In making that determination, the court should consider the comparative prejudice to the parties from modifying or failing to modify the order, the impact of modification on the orderly and efficient conduct of the litigation, and any degree of wilfulness, bad faith or inexcusable neglect by the proponent of the modification.[106] For example, modification has been allowed to permit evidence of which the opponent had eleven months' notice despite its omission from the pretrial order,[107] when the opponent mitigated any prejudice to it by effective cross-examination of a previously omitted witness,[108] and when the evidence was newly discovered since the entry of the pretrial order.[109] Modification has been denied when the opponent was lulled into withholding a possible defense by the omission from the pretrial order of an alternative theory of recovery.[110] Of course, when there is no objection to the offer of evidence or claims outside the pretrial order, the court should ordinarily allow it.[111]

Matters pursued at trial that are outside the final pretrial order may also be outside the pleadings. The objecting party actually has two grounds in this situation: Rule 16(e) and the evidentiary grounds of irrelevance or immateriality. The latter are not a very significant addition, however, because Rule 16(e) poses a standard more favorable to the objecting party.[112]

Matters outside the final pretrial order may also be objectionable at trial because they are inconsistent with admissions under Rule 36. Again, Rule 16(e) seems to give more weight to the objection than Rule 36.[113]

---

[103] *See, e.g., Spray-Rite Serv. Corp. v. Monsanto Co.*, 684 F.2d 1226 (7th Cir. 1982), *aff'd on other grounds*, 465 U.S. 752 (1984); *Keyes v. Lauga*, 635 F.2d 330 (5th Cir. 1981).

[104] *See, e.g., Allen v. United States Steel Corp.*, 665 F.2d 689 (5th Cir. 1982); *Price v. Inland Oil Co.*, 646 F.2d 90, 96 (2d Cir. 1981).

[105] A court commits reversible error by amending a pretrial order at trial over objection unless it finds that it is necessary to prevent manifest injustice. *See Hale v. Firestone Tire & Rubber Co.*, 756 F.2d 1322 (8th Cir. 1985).

[106] *See First Nat'l Bank of Circle*, 652 F.2d at 887 (citations omitted).

[107] *See Joubert v. Travelers Indem. Co.*, 736 F.2d 191, 194 (5th Cir. 1984).

[108] *Syvock v. Milwaukee Boiler Mfg. Co.*, 665 F.2d 149 (7th Cir. 1981).

[109] *See* MOORE § 16.78[4].

[110] *See Flannery*, 676 F.2d 126.

[111] *See, e.g., Gorby v. Schneider Tank Lines, Inc.*, 741 F.2d 1015 (7th Cir. 1984); *Mechmetals Corp. v. Telex Computer Prods., Inc.*, 709 F.2d 1287 (9th Cir. 1983). *Compare* § 8.10[2][a] (conforming amendments by consent at trial), *supra*.

[112] Compare the standard for mid-trial amendment of pleadings in Rule 15(b) (amendments need only subserve the merits and inflict no prejudice on the opposing party) with the presumption against modifying final pretrial orders in Rule 16(e) (they can be modified "only to prevent manifest injustice"). On mid-trial amendments generally, see § 8.10[2], *supra*.

[113] Rule 16(e) seems more stringent, although this time the difference is not as great. Compare the provision in Rule 36(b) for relieving a party of the effects of his admissions (it is "conclusively established unless the court, on motion, permits the admission to be withdrawn or amended") with

In short, because of greater risk of inefficiency and prejudice, requests for modification or amendment of final pretrial orders will usually receive a less generous reception than earlier requests to amend pleadings or admissions.

§ 12.04 BURDEN OF PROOF

[1] In General[114]

Plaintiff sues defendant for negligence. If at trial plaintiff fails to produce any evidence of injury, the court should find for defendant. The result is the same whether the issue is tried to the court or the jury; there is nothing for the jury to decide regarding injury. Suppose, however, that the evidence appears to support the positions of plaintiff and defendant to about the same degree. In that event, too, the court in a bench trial should find for defendant. In a jury trial, the issue would be submitted to a jury. But the court could still influence the jury's deliberations by instructing it that if it finds evidence on a critical point evenly balanced, it should return a verdict for defendant.[115]

Loss in either event stems from plaintiff's failure to meet his *burden of proof*. Evidence scholars[116] have modified the term in some settings by substituting more refined (if not always consistent) terminology to describe what is happening in the foregoing hypothetical. The plaintiff who fails to produce evidence on an essential element of his claim has failed the *burden of production* or *burden of going forward*. In a jury case, he has failed to produce sufficient evidence to reach the jury, and the court should grant a directed verdict or, in federal court, judgment as a matter of law against him. By contrast, the plaintiff who fails to convince the trier of fact to some pre-established degree of certainty or by a pre-established *standard* of proof of the facts necessary to his claim has failed his *burden of persuasion* or assumed the *risk of nonpersuasion*.[117] In most civil cases, the required standard of proof is a *preponderance of the evidence*: that the facts are more likely than not as the plaintiff contends.

Many of the traditional maxims offered to explain how parties acquire burdens of production and persuasion are of little use. It is said that the burden rests on the party who seeks to disturb the status quo or for whom a particular issue is essential. However, these explanations are only "facile

---

the presumption against modifying final pretrial orders in Rule 16(e) (they can be modified "only to prevent manifest injustice"). On the effect of Rule 36 admissions generally, see § 12.02, *supra*.

[114] *See generally* Bruce L. Hay, *Allocating the Burden of Proof*, 72 IND. L.J. 651 (1997); MCCORMICK ON EVIDENCE ch. 36 (K. Brown ed., 6th ed. 2006); JOHN MACARTHUR MAGUIRE, EVIDENCE: COMMON SENSE AND COMMON LAW (1947); John T. McNaughton, *Burden of Production of Evidence: A Function of a Burden of Persuasion*, 68 HARV. L. REV. 1382 (1955); WRIGHT & MILLER § 5122.

[115] WRIGHT & MILLER § 5122.

[116] *See, e.g.*, JAMES BRADLEY THAYER, PRELIMINARY TREATISE ON EVIDENCE 355 (1898).

[117] Some state evidence codes have also adopted such terminology. *See, e.g.*, OR. REV. STAT. §§ 40.105–40.115, rules 305 & 307 (1999). Federal Rule of Evidence 301 uses "burden of going forward" in juxtaposition to "burden of proof in the sense of the risk of nonpersuasion."

form[s] of statement of the result."[118] It is often defendant who disturbed the status quo outside court; affirmatives can be restated as negatives; and to designate issues as essential begs the question. The explanation that the burden of proof follows the burden of pleading[119] is so often contradicted by practice[120] as to be unreliable. Yet, at least initially, the same party usually does assume the burdens of pleading, production, and persuasion. That is because each burden is shaped by the same factors, called by one treatise "the Three P's: Policy, Probability, and Possession of [access to] Proof."[121] We will consider the burdens of production and persuasion in greater detail in the subsections which follow.[122]

[2]   The Burden of Production

The plaintiff has the initial burden of production regarding at least some issues. Collectively, they may be called plaintiff's *prima facie* case.[123] Plaintiff must produce sufficient evidence on those issues to enable a reasonable jury, or the judge in a nonjury trial, to find for him absent rebuttal evidence by defendant. If plaintiff does so in a jury trial, the court must deny defendant's motion for a directed verdict or judgment as a matter of law.[124] On the other hand, even if defendant fails to produce any evidence in rebuttal, plaintiff ordinarily would not be entitled to a directed verdict or judgment as a matter of law in *his* favor. Instead the jury usually will be asked to decide whether to accept or reject plaintiff's evidence, at least where acceptance turns on credibility and inference.

It is possible, however, for plaintiff to produce so much evidence that — on the strength of it alone — no reasonable jury could decide against him. In such a case, the burden of production shifts from plaintiff to defendant. It is then defendant who must produce sufficient evidence to meet plaintiff's evidence, or he will suffer a directed verdict. If defendant, in turn, produces so much

---

[118] Edmund M. Morgan, *Some Observations Concerning Presumptions*, 44 HARV. L. REV. 906, 910–11 (1931). *See also* Edward W. Cleary, *Presuming and Pleading: An Essay on Juristic Immaturity*, 12 STAN. L. REV. 5 (1959).

[119] *See* Ronald J. Allen, *Presumptions in Civil Actions Reconsidered*, 66 IOWA L. REV. 843, 849 (1981).

[120] *See, e.g., Palmer v. Hoffman*, 318 U.S. 109, 117 (1943) (federal rules control burden of pleading, but state law in diversity case controls burden of proof); *Knowles v. Gilchrist Co.*, 289 N.E.2d 879 (Mass. 1972) (bailor has burden of pleading negligent bailment, but once bailor has produced evidence establishing bailment and loss of or damage to bailed good, bailee has burden of proof of due care).

[121] WRIGHT & MILLER § 5122. *See generally* MCCORMICK, note 114, *supra*, § 337 (noting natural tendency to place burdens on party desiring change, special policy concerns such as those disfavoring certain defenses, convenience, fairness, and the judicial estimate of the probabilities as illustrative factors); Cleary, note 118, *supra*, at 8–14.

[122] On the burden of pleading, *see* § 8.06[2] (using *Gomez v. Toledo*, 446 U.S. 635 (1980), to illustrate significance of possession of proof to allocation of burden of pleading), *supra*; § 8.08[2][a] (the burden and affirmative defenses), *supra*.

[123] *See Texas Dep't of Cmty. Affairs v. Burdine*, 450 U.S. 248, 250 (1981).

[124] *See* § 12.09[1] (directed verdict and judgment as a matter of law in general), *infra*.

evidence that no reasonable jury could find against him, the burden of production shifts once again to plaintiff.

This process is depicted in Figure 12-1, a variation on the well-known diagram originally proposed by Professor Wigmore.[125]

Figure 12-1

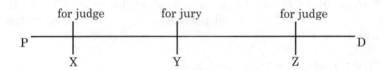

If P has the burden of production on an issue, he must produce sufficient evidence to get past X or he will suffer a directed verdict. If he gets past X into the XZ range, the issue will go to the jury. If, however, he produces so much evidence that he passes Z, then the burden of production shifts to D. Unless D now produces enough evidence to pass Z, he will suffer a directed verdict or judgment as a matter of law. Should he produce enough evidence to cross X, then the burden of production shifts back to plaintiff.[126]

The process is essentially similar in a bench (non-jury) trial, as the Supreme Court explained in *Texas Department of Community Affairs v. Burdine.*[127] *Burdine* was a Title VII employment discrimination case.[128] The court of appeals had held that once plaintiff produced evidence establishing a *prima facie* case of discrimination — that plaintiff applied for a position for which she was qualified and was rejected for reasons which gave rise to an inference of discrimination — the defendant had the burden of proving by a preponderance of the evidence the existence of legitimate, non-discriminatory reasons for its employment action. The Supreme Court reversed. It noted that *"prima facie case . . .* may be used by courts to describe the plaintiff's burden of producing enough evidence to permit the trier of fact to infer the fact at issue."[129] Once plaintiff meets her burden, however, it is not the burden of persuasion that shifts to defendant, but only the burden of producing evidence establishing nondiscriminatory reasons for the defendant's employment action.

> The plaintiff retains the burden of persuasion. [If defendant meets its burden, plaintiff] . . . now must have the opportunity to demonstrate that the proffered reason was not the true reason for the employment decision. This burden now merges with the ultimate

---

[125] *See* 9 JOHN HENRY WIGMORE, EVIDENCE § 2487 (3d ed. 1940).

[126] To visualize the burden of persuasion, see § 12.04[3], *infra*, explaining line Y in Figure 86-1.

[127] 450 U.S. 248 (1981).

[128] *See generally* Robert Belton, *Burdens of Pleading and Proof in Discrimination Cases: Toward a Theory of Procedural Justice*, 34 VAND. L. REV. 1205 (1981).

[129] 450 U.S. at 254 n.7 (citation omitted). If the judge believes plaintiff's evidence, and defendant produces none, the judge is required to enter judgment for the plaintiff. 450 U.S. at 254.

burden of persuading the court that she had been the victim of intentional discrimination.[130]

[3] The Burden of Persuasion

The burden of persuasion is the requirement that a party convince the trier of fact of the truth of an issue to a predetermined level of certainty.[131] The function of that level or standard of proof is to "instruct the fact-finder concerning the degree of confidence our society thinks he [or they] should have in the correctness of factual conclusions for a particular type of adjudication."[132] In most civil cases, society is only minimally concerned with outcome, and the level of certainty is usually expressed as a preponderance of the evidence, sometimes also characterized as the *greater weight of the evidence*.[133] The burden of persuasion by a preponderance of the evidence is harder to visualize accurately by diagram, but inserting a Y through the middle of Figure 12-1 may help. To carry his burden of persuasion by a preponderance of the evidence, P must present evidence that will get past Y. If he presents less, or if the evidence is in equipoise at Y, the jury should find against him.

Diagraming the burden in this way can be misleading, however. It suggests a quantitative standard, as does the phrase *greater weight of the evidence*. The preponderance standard refers not to the quantity of evidence — the greater number of witnesses or exhibits — but rather to its convincing force. Weight or movement on the diagramed scale therefore represents the degree of persuasiveness or certainty in the fact-trier's mind that the evidence will produce.

In criminal cases and some civil cases society's greater concern in the outcome increases the burden of persuasion. Society's interest in avoiding erroneous criminal convictions accounts for the requirement that the prosecution must prove guilt *beyond a reasonable doubt*.[134] This demanding standard would move the Y on Figure 12-1 to the right, indicating a much heavier burden for P — the government in a criminal case. The Supreme Court has also required plaintiffs to persuade by *clear and convincing evidence* in some civil cases where interests more significant than money are at stake.[135] This standard falls between preponderance of the evidence and proof

---

[130] 450 U.S. at 256.

[131] Ronald J. Allen, *Presumptions, Inferences, Burden of Proof in Federal Civil Actions — An Anatomy of an Unnecessary Ambiguity and a Proposal for Reform*, 76 Nw. U. L. Rev. 892, 908 (1982).

[132] *In re Winship*, 397 U.S. 358, 370 (1970) (Harlan, J., concurring).

[133] *See generally* McCormick, note 114, *supra*, § 339; Neil Orloff & Jery Stedinger, *A Framework for Evaluating the Preponderance-of-the-Evidence Standard*, 131 U. Pa. L. Rev. 1159 (1983).

[134] *See Santosky v. Kramer*, 455 U.S. 745, 755 (1982).

[135] *Addington v. Texas*, 441 U.S. 418, 424 (1979) (civil commitment). *See also Santosky*, 455 U.S. at 745 (termination of parental rights); *Woodby v. Immigration & Naturalization Serv.*, 385 U.S. 276, 285 (1966) (deportation). At common law in many jurisdictions, fraud and mistake must also be

beyond a reasonable doubt.[136] Thus, the Y in the figure would not be moved quite as far to the right as it would be in a criminal case. It is uncertain whether juries can differentiate such standards, or whether they apply any of them instead of simply deciding "who is right."[137]

[4]   Presumptions[138]

The subject of presumptions has been aptly described as "one of the most complex topics in the law of evidence" and "a sea of technicality which defies logical analysis."[139] Extended discussion of presumptions is better left to writers of evidence texts. We will confine our attention here to introductory terminology. The term *presumption* is used to describe at least four different concepts.

First, the presumption of innocence is said to apply in criminal trials. This is not really a presumption at all, but a way of saying that the prosecution has the burden of proof and of suggesting that the standard of proof is beyond a reasonable doubt. It would be more accurate to term it an *assumption* than a presumption.

Second, presumption is used generally to refer to a logical inference from the evidence. For example, circumstantial evidence was once treated in the evidence books under the heading "presumptive evidence."[140] Triers of fact draw such inferences all the time. The process does not necessarily relate to burdens of proof.

Third, a presumption may reflect the idea in substantive law that proof of one fact establishes beyond argument the truth of another. Many states, for example, presume the legitimacy of children from proof that they were born to a wife cohabiting with her husband. Such a presumption may or may not be logical, but, in any event, it is not subject to rebuttal, even by evidence of the biological impossibility of paternity.[141] Such *conclusive* or *legal presumptions* are best regarded as part of the substantive law, rather than the law of evidence or procedure.

---

proven by clear and convincing evidence. *See, e.g., Hofmann v. Hofmann*, 446 N.E.2d 499, 506 (Ill. 1983).

[136] One scholar suggested that if preponderance means that a proposition is more probably true than false, clear and convincing means only that it is much more probably true than false. Edmund M. Morgan, *Instructing the Jury Upon Presumptions and Burden of Proof*, 47 HARV. L. REV. 59, 67 (1933).

[137] *See, e.g.*, Kathleen F. O'Reilly, *Why Some Juries Fail*, 41 D.C.B.J. 69 (1974); Ralph K. Winter, *The Jury and the Risk of Non-Persuasion*, 5 LAW & SOC'Y REV. 335 (1971); MORGAN, note 136, *supra*, at 66–67.

[138] *See generally* JAMES, HAZARD & LEUBSDORF § 7.17; Allen, note 119, *supra*; Charles Nesson, *Rationality, Presumptions and Judicial Comment: A Response to Professor Allen*, 54 HARV. L. REV. 1574 (1981); McCORMICK, note 114, *supra*, §§ 342–45.

[139] WRIGHT & MILLER § 5122.

[140] WRIGHT & MILLER § 5122.

[141] *See, e.g., Estate of Cornelious*, 674 P.2d 245 (Cal. 1984).

Finally, the term is used to refer to *rebuttable presumptions* that affect the burden of production and sometimes of persuasion. This happens when plaintiff in establishing one fact is deemed to have established a second, *unless* the defendant offers evidence rebutting the second fact at trial. For example, evidence that a letter has been properly posted creates a rebuttable presumption of delivery to the addressee. The rebuttable presumption thus operates to satisfy the proponent's burden of production, and a court cannot grant a motion for a directed verdict or judgment as a matter of law grounded on non-delivery once posting has been shown, absent rebuttal evidence.[142]

What happens when the opposing party puts on rebuttal evidence is much more controversial. The two leading alternative theories are illustrated by *Legille v. Dann*.[143] To challenge the presumed fact of delivery, defendant offered proof of its routine mail-handling practices. Calling it the majority view, the court adopted the "bursting bubble theory" whereby the production of rebuttal evidence causes the original presumption to "burst" and be without further effect in the case. Thus limited, the effect of the presumption

> is merely to invoke a rule of law compelling the [trier of fact] to reach a conclusion in the absence of evidence to the contrary from the opponent. If the opponent does offer evidence to the contrary (sufficient to satisfy the judge's requirement of some evidence), the presumption disappears as a rule of law, and the case is in the [factfinder's] hands free from any rule.[144]

In short, the presumption affects the production burden only. The majority in *Legille* therefore reversed a grant of summary judgment for the party invoking the presumption of delivery and remanded for trial.[145]

The dissenting judge argued in contrast that the rebuttal evidence was not sufficient to overcome the "strong presumption" of delivery.[146] He would have given the delivery presumption continuing effect, even after some rebuttal evidence was produced. This is consistent with the theory that proof of the basic fact shifts the burden of proof (*i.e.*, burdens of both production and persuasion) to the party against whom the presumption operates.[147] Proponents of this

---

[142] *See* McCORMICK, note 114, *supra*, § 343 (illustrative rebuttable presumptions).

[143] 544 F.2d 1 (D.C. Cir. 1976).

[144] 544 F.2d at 5-6, *quoting* 9 JOHN HENRY WIGMORE, EVIDENCE § 2491 (3d ed. 1940).

[145] The majority noted that the presumption of delivery and the presumption of procedural regularity

> both . . . have a common origin in regularity of action. We see nothing suggesting that the methodology buttressing the one is any more or less foolproof than that underpinning the other. We are mindful that some presumptions are founded in part upon exceptionally strong and visible policies, which have been said to persist despite proof rebutting the factual basis for the presumption. The answer here is that from aught that appears the policy reflections are in equilibrium.

544 F.2d at 7 n.39.

[146] 544 F.2d at 11 (Fahey, J., dissenting).

[147] *See* MORGAN, note 136, *supra*, at 83 ("in situations where a presumption owes its origin to an important social policy, it should operate to fix the burden of persuasion").

approach criticized the bursting bubble theory for subverting substantive policies underpinning presumptions, giving them too "slight and evanescent" an effect.[148]

There are other theories as well.[149] Moreover, statutes may define the effect of presumptions and thus displace judicial doctrine. The same factors that determine the allocation of burdens of production and persuasion ultimately determine the availability of presumptions.[150]

PART B.
Trial and Judgment

§ 12.05   OVERVIEW

Most civil cases filed never come to trial. Usually they are settled, voluntarily withdrawn, or decided on the merits prior to trial.[151] Yet many cases do require trial. As a more basic matter, the idea and prospect of trial strongly influence the shape of procedure for all civil cases. Pleadings and pretrial proceedings set bounds of inquiry for trial; discovery and less formal means of investigation prepare the parties for trial; and trial can be either a specter that facilitates or an enticement that blocks settlement.[152]

The function of the trial is two-fold: (1) to sift from a controverted factual record the true story — or, at least, the story most likely upon the evidence to be true — and (2) to attach legal significance to that story. The first function culminates in a verdict if performed by a jury or in findings of fact if performed by the judge. The judge always performs the second function, but the manner in which she performs it depends on whether the case is tried with or without a jury. In this Part we will consider some of the ways in which civil procedure is complicated by the fact that some cases are tried through judge-jury collaboration while others are tried by judges alone.

§ 12.06   THE TACTICAL DECISION WHETHER TO DEMAND A JURY TRIAL

The desirability of the jury as a social institution rests on several assumptions: that collective judgment is superior to individual judgment, that an anonymous collective judgment is more easily accepted by the loser than a

---

[148] Edmund M. Morgan & John MacArthur MaGuire, *Looking Backward and Forward at Evidence*, 50 Harv. L. Rev. 909, 913 (1937).

[149] *See, e.g.*, Edmund M. Morgan, Basic Problems of State and Federal Evidence 28–30 (J. Weinstein, 5th ed. 1976) (listing eight).

[150] *See* McCormick, note 114, *supra* at § 343.

[151] *See* Chapter 11 (pretrial judgments), *supra*.

[152] *See* Samuel R. Gross & Kent D. Syverud, *Don't Try: Civil Jury Verdicts in a System Geared to Settlement*, 44 UCLA L. Rev. 1 (1996) (using empirical evidence to conclude that "[t]he main function of trials is not to resolve disputes but to deter other trials").

personalized individual judgment, and that judgment by one's peers is preferable to judgment by non-peers.[153] While these assumptions have come under attack,[154] the public may still have a mild preference for trial by jury.[155]

However, such concerns are unlikely to figure greatly if at all in a particular decision whether to demand a jury trial. Nor is that decision usually made in the first instance by a client. Instead, lawyers decide based upon their personal experiences, subjective and intuitive assessments of the probabilities of success, and highly pragmatic considerations of calendar, cost, and settlement leverage. To place the procedures for obtaining a jury trial in context, it is useful to identify a few of these necessarily ad hoc factors.

One is counsel's assessment of the need for "jury legislation": jury modification (or even nullification) of the letter of the law. While jury research indicates that judges and juries agree in 75% of all cases, much of their disagreement is due not only to differing assessments of the evidence, but also to the jury's recognition of "values which fall outside the official rules."[156] Juries thus have relaxed the letter of the law by substituting their own notions of comparative negligence for the rule of contributory negligence, or by "improperly" taking into account insurance, collateral benefits, mitigation and ability to pay.[157] Similarly, juries have refused to make findings supporting "technical defenses" based on statutes of frauds or limitations, or on releases or waivers obtained in unequal bargaining situations.[158]

Counsel's subjective and intuitive assessment of the role of sentiment and expertise is another crucial factor in the decision whether to demand a jury trial. When the witnesses for one side are credible, expert, or likely to provoke sympathy, the fact may dictate a strong preference for trial by jury. On the other hand, counsel will often favor a non-jury trial when the evidence and the theory of recovery are complex and technical.[159]

---

[153] For more extended discussion of these considerations, see § 12.08[1], *infra*. The literature on the nature and significance of jury trials is extensive. *See, e.g.*, Symposium, *Jury Reform: Making Juries Work*, 32 U. Mich. J.L. Reform 213 (1999); Symposium, *The American Civil Jury: Illusion and Reality*, 48 DePaul L. Rev. 197 (1998); Valerie P. Hans & Neil Vidmar, Judging the Jury (1986); Ronald C. Wolf, *Trial By Jury: A Sociological Analysis*, 1966 Wis. L. Rev. 820 (1966); Paula DiPerna, Juries on Trial (1984); Jerome Frank, Courts on Trial (1949).

[154] *See, e.g.*, Frank, note 153, *supra*; Fleming James, Jr., *Trial By Jury and the New Federal Rules of Civil Procedure*, 45 Yale L.J. 1022 (1936).

[155] Wolf, note 153, *supra*, at 826 n.14. *But see* Kenneth S. Klein, *Unpacking the Jury Box*, 47 Hastings L.J. 1325 (1996) (noting growing distrust of juries, partly in response to their growing diversity).

[156] Howard S. Erlanger, *Jury Research in America*, 4 Law & Soc. Rev. 345, 349 (1970).

[157] *Id.* at 350–51. *See generally* Arie M. Rubenstein, *Verdicts of Conscience: Nullification and the Modern Jury Trial*, 106 Colum. L. Rev. 959 (2006); Alan W. Scheflin & Jon M. Van Dyke, *Merciful Juries: The Resilience of Jury Nullification*, 48 Wash. & Lee L. Rev. 165 (1991).

[158] *See* Leighton Bledsoe, *Jury or Non-Jury Trial — A Defense Viewpoint*, 5 Am. Jur. Trials 123, 135 (1966).

[159] *But see* Kevin M. Clermont & Theodore Eisenberg, *Trial by Jury or Judge: Transcending Empiricism*, 77 Cornell L. Rev. 1124 (1992) (raising doubts about the conventional intuition).

Another factor is the nature of the evidence at the margin, evidence arguably inadmissible. When such evidence is damaging to a party, he would ordinarily prefer a jury trial from which that evidence will be excluded to a non-jury trial in which the marginal evidence will be taken for what it is worth.[160]

Additional factors include calendar and cost. Jury-tried cases take, on average, 40% longer than judge-tried cases.[161] As a result jury trials are harder to schedule and more costly than non-jury trials. The party who seeks a quick result, due to financial need or fear that evidence might be lost, will ordinarily prefer a non-jury trial. Because it is often an injured plaintiff who is in this posture, the demand for a jury trial can work to the defendant's benefit in such circumstances. Even the defendant who is not anxious to go before a jury may consider demanding a jury trial in order to obtain bargaining leverage for a pretrial settlement.

Other factors which may also encourage defendants to demand a jury trial include the requirement for unanimous verdicts and the greater likelihood of reversible errors during jury trials. Where unanimity is required, defendant has but to convince one juror to find for him in order to prevail, a task which may often look more promising than convincing the judge.[162] A defendant anticipating tactical advantages from appeal may also prefer the jury trial because of the opportunities for reversible error in the admission of evidence, instruction of the jury, and jury deliberations,[163] although such reckoning is tempered by awareness of the universal rule of greater deference on appeal to jury verdicts than to findings of fact by the judge.[164]

§ 12.07 OBTAINING JURY TRIAL

[1] The Right to Trial by Jury: The Federal Model

Federal courts and all of their state counterparts give litigants the right in some cases to have the facts tried before a jury.[165] The scope of the right varies from system to system. The United States Constitution does not confer

---

[160] "This practice is based on the theory that the judge, with his knowledge of the rules of evidence, can separate the wheat from the chaff and pay no attention to evidence otherwise inadmissible . . . ." Bledsoe, note 158, *supra*, at 137.

[161] HANS ZEISEL, HARRY KALVEN & BERNARD BUCHHOLZ, DELAY IN THE COURT 71–81 (1959). Of course, the proper comparison is not just between trial times, but between the time elapsed from commencement of trial to decision. Jury trials have the virtue of rendering a decision at the close of the trial itself; judges will often delay for months after trial before they render their decisions. Bledsoe, note 158, *supra*, at 141–42. Moreover, part of this delay may result from extensive, and therefore expensive, post-trial briefing by the parties.

[162] Bledsoe, note 158, *supra*, at 141.

[163] Bledsoe, note 158, *supra*, at 133.

[164] *See* §§ 13.10[2][b] & [c] (federal standards of review for findings by the court and by the jury), *infra*.

[165] In the broadest sense, jury right also takes in the right of persons to be jurors. "Jury duty is both a civic responsibility and an obligation of all qualified citizens. It is also a constitutional right of citizens recognized by the Supreme Court. *Powers v. Ohio*, 499 U.S. 400 (1991)." AMEIRCAN BAR

a right to jury trial in *state* civil cases.[166] The courts of each state honor the right to the extent it is created in their constitutions or local statutes.[167] Federal courts rely on the United States Constitution and federal statutes.

Federal litigants enjoy under the Seventh Amendment a right to trial by jury "[i]n suits at common law, where the value in controversy shall exceed twenty dollars . . . ."[168] In one sense, the Amendment does not *create* a right to jury trial.[169] It merely states that "the right to trial by jury shall be preserved . . . ." The significance of this distinction is that the process of determining which issues[170] entitle a litigant to claim a jury has turned more on history than logic. The reckoning point is English common law in 1791, the year the Amendment was ratified.[171]

The right to a jury trial had been enjoyed to a greater or lesser extent in the colonies,[172] but the right preserved in the Seventh Amendment was that which existed under English law. In a long line of decisions,[173] the Supreme Court has read "common law" in the Seventh Amendment to refer to the jurisdiction of English common-law courts in 1791. These courts dispensed remedies "at law," including damage awards. Litigants in these courts enjoyed extensive rights to trial by jury. England administered at the same time a separate system of chancery or "equity"[174] courts, dispensing equitable remedies, including injunctions.[175] Juries were unavailable in equity proceedings.

The law-equity distinction has been central in determining the scope of the Seventh Amendment.[176] The distinction was significantly blurred, however, by

---

ASSOCIATION, PRINCIPLES FOR JURIES AND JURY TRIALS 10 (2005).

[166] *City of Monterey v. Del Monte Dunes at Monterey, Ltd.*, 526 U.S. 687, 719 (1999). In contrast, the Supreme Court has read the Sixth and Fourteenth Amendments to confer a right to jury trial in serious state *criminal* cases. *See, e.g., Duncan v. Louisiana*, 391 U.S. 145 (1968); *Blanton v. City of N. Las Vegas*, 489 U.S. 538 (1989).

[167] *Cf. FRIEDENTHAL, KANE & MILLER* § 11.7 ("almost all states have . . . constitutional guarantees.").

[168] There is no federal court right to jury trial, however, when the defendant is the United States. *City of Monterey v. Del Monte Dunes at Monterey, Ltd.*, 526 U.S. 687, 719 (1999).

[169] *See MOORE* § 38.10[1].

[170] "[T]he basic decisional unit in determining the existence of a right to jury trial is not the case. It is the particular issue within a case on which jury trial is demanded." *WRIGHT & MILLER* § 2302.

[171] Not all agree. *See* AKHIL R. AMAR, THE BILL OF RIGHTS: CREATION AND RECONSTRUCTION 89 (1998) (asserting that reckoning point is forum state law); Stanton D. Krauss, *The Original Understanding of the Seventh Amendment Right to Jury Trial*, 33 U. RICH. L. REV. 407, 479–80 (1999) (arguing that reckoning point is in the discretion of Congress).

[172] "Each of the thirteen colonies, as might be expected, had developed an individual style and emphasis, in part because each had begun borrowing from a slightly different state of the English historical development." Edith G. Henderson, *The Background of the Seventh Amendment*, 80 HARV. L. REV. 289, 299 (1966).

[173] *See* the cases cited in *MOORE* § 38.10[2]. *See also Agfa Corp. v. Creo Prods.*, 451 F.3d 1366, 1373 (Fed. Cir. 2006); *Millsap v. McDonnell Douglas Corp.*, 368 F.3d 1246, 1252 n.4 (10th Cir. 2004).

[174] *See* § 8.02[2] (equity pleading and practice), *supra*.

[175] On the modern-day significance of damage and injunctive remedies, see Chapter 14, *infra*.

[176] *See, e.g., City of Monterey v. Del Monte Dunes at Monterey, Ltd.*, 526 U.S. 687 (1999). Juries

the merger of law and equity proceedings brought about by the adoption of the Federal Rules of Civil Procedure.[177] The merger posed several serious questions about the right to jury trial in federal court. The Court answered three of them in a series of Seventh Amendment decisions establishing the modern trend favoring jury trials.[178]

The first question was whether there is a right to jury trial when the plaintiff brings an equitable claim, and defendant brings a legal counterclaim, or vice versa. The Court answered this question in *Beacon Theatres, Inc. v. Westover*.[179] Plaintiff in *Beacon* sued for equitable relief. Defendant counterclaimed for damages on antitrust grounds, demanding a jury trial. The Supreme Court held that, because the law and equity claims had issues in common, the trial court could not first try the equity portion without a jury. To permit this would "compel Beacon to split its antitrust case, trying part to a judge and part to a jury."[180] The Court apparently assumed that, because common factual issues resolved in the initial equity phase of the case would not be open to relitigation in the later jury phase, a jury trial on them would be lost to the defendant altogether.[181]

A second question was whether there was a right to jury trial in an action in which the plaintiff joins legal and equitable claims,[182] and the equitable claims

---

were also unavailable in English admiralty proceedings. In the broadest sense, then, "those actions that are analogous to 18th-century cases tried in courts of equity or admiralty do not require a jury trial." *Tull v. United States*, 481 U.S. 412, 417 (1987). Recent developments in the Supreme Court's Seventh Amendment jurisprudence suggest continued emphasis on the law-equity distinction, but less attention to the particulars of 18th century English practice. *See* note 198, *infra*.

[177] Rule 2 states: "There is one form of action — the civil action." The situation prior to adoption of the Federal Rules has been described as follows:

> Unlike some state systems, there have never been separate law and equity courts in the federal judicial system. But the first Process Act of 1789 introduced separate procedures for actions at law and suits in equity; and two distinct procedures for these civil actions — one applicable on the law side, the other on the equity side of the same court — continued down to 1938 when the Federal Rules became effective.

Moore, 1999 *Rules Pamphlet Part 1*, ¶ 2.3.

[178] *Cf.* WRIGHT § 92 ("The Supreme Court has been zealous to safeguard, perhaps even to enlarge, the function of the jury.").

[179] 359 U.S. 500 (1959). *See generally* John C. McCoid, II, *Procedural Reform and the Right to Jury Trial: A Study of Beacon Theatres, Inc. v. Westover*, 116 U. PA. L. REV. 1 (1967).

[180] 359 U.S. at 508.

[181] 359 U.S. at 508 & n.10. This assumption of *Beacon* has been tied to the law of prior adjudications. FRIEDENTHAL, KANE & MILLER § 11.5. *Accord, Lytle v. Household Mfg., Inc.*, 494 U.S. 545 (1990). Since, however, the effect of the issue determination in the equity phase of the case is felt prior to judgment, it may be more accurate to attribute any prejudicial effect to the law-of-the-case doctrine. *See generally* § 15.14, *infra*. For discussion of relatively rare instances where that doctrine has been applied to settled issues of fact (rather than law), see WRIGHT & MILLER § 4478.

Since *Beacon*, the Court has ruled that a party may be precluded from relitigating facts before a jury in a legal action that were decided against him in a separate and prior equitable action. *Parklane Hosiery Co. v. Shore*, 439 U.S. 322 (1979).

[182] Rule 18 expressly permits the joinder of legal and equitable claims. *See generally* § 9.02, *supra*.

predominate. The Court addressed this question in *Dairy Queen, Inc. v. Wood*.[183] Plaintiff sued over defendant's alleged failure to make payments due under a trademark licensing contract, seeking an injunction against defendant's continued use of the trademark and an accounting for the sum defendant owed. The Court looked behind plaintiff's labels and concluded that "insofar as the complaint requests a money judgment it presents a claim which is unquestionably legal."[184] The Seventh Amendment "right to trial by jury," said the Court, "cannot be made to depend upon the choice of words used in the pleadings."[185] Moreover, the right applies "whether the trial judge chooses to characterize the legal issues presented as 'incidental' to the equitable issues or not."[186]

A third question posed by the merger of law and equity was whether jury trial was available for claims asserted by an historically equitable procedure, such as interpleader, a class action, or a derivative action. All these had been adopted by the Federal Rules of Civil Procedure.[187] The Court answered this question in *Ross v. Bernhard*.[188] Plaintiffs brought a shareholder's derivative action under Rule 23.1. The Court of Appeals held that the action was equitable and that none of it could be tried before a jury. Again the Supreme Court reversed. The shareholder derivative device was a creature of equity, and equitable principles still explain why shareholders in such suits can sue on behalf of the corporation. Yet the Court held that "the right to jury trial attaches to those issues in derivative actions as to which the corporation, if it had been suing in its own right, would have been entitled to a jury."[189] The Court added: "[A]s our cases indicate, the 'legal' nature of an issue is determined by considering, first, the pre-merger custom with reference to such questions; second, the remedy sought; and third, the practical abilities and limitations of juries . . . ."[190]

---

[183] 369 U.S. 469 (1962).

[184] 369 U.S. at 476. Viewing the plaintiff's "accounting" demand "[a]s an action on a debt allegedly due under a contract, it would be difficult to conceive of an action of a more traditionally legal character." 369 U.S. at 477 (footnote omitted). In fact, an accounting does trace its origins to equity, but the range of remedies now available under the federal rules, including the appointment of a special master under Rule 53(b) to assist the jury in complicated monetary computations, must be considered in characterizing a claim for purposes of deciding the Seventh Amendment question. *See* McCoid, note 179, *supra*, at 8–9.

[185] 369 U.S. at 477–78.

[186] 369 U.S. at 473. *Accord Tull v. United States*, 481 U.S. 412, 424–25 (1987). Thus, *Beacon* and *Dairy Queen* together stand for the proposition that if, disregarding the parties' labels, there is any claim or defense in the case — incidental or otherwise — that would be characterized as legal at English common law, it must be tried first to a jury upon timely demand.

[187] *See* Rules 22, 23 & 23.1 respectively.

[188] 396 U.S. 531 (1970). *See generally* Note, *Ross v. Bernhard: The Uncertain Future of the Seventh Amendment*, 81 YALE L.J. 112 (1971); John G. Gibbons, Comment, *From Beacon Theatres to Dairy Queen to Ross: The Seventh Amendment, The Federal Rules, and a Receding Law-Equity Dichotomy*, 48 J. URBAN L. 459 (1971).

[189] 396 U.S. at 532–33.

[190] 396 U.S. at 538 n.10. The Supreme Court recently extended its holding in *Ross* to the general class action rule, Rule 23. *Ortiz v. Fibreboard Corp.*, 527 U.S. 815, 846 (1999).

Congress has created many causes of action which were unknown to English jurisprudence in 1791. Nothing limits the authority of Congress to supplement the Seventh Amendment by creating a right to trial by jury in federal court whenever it wishes to.[191] But, in determining whether a *constitutional* right to jury trial exists for a statutory cause of action in which Congress has not expressly created a right to jury trial, federal courts have been required to determine whether the issue at hand most closely resembles something adjudicated on the law side or on the equity side of the line in 1791.[192] The Supreme Court's decision in *Tull v. United States*[193] provides an example.

The United States brought suit in *Tull* against a developer for violation of the Clean Water Act. The district court denied defendant's demand for a jury trial. After a bench trial (trial before the judge), the court found that defendant acted in violation of the Act and imposed numerous fines. The Court of Appeals affirmed. The Supreme Court reversed on Seventh Amendment grounds. "Prior to the enactment of the Seventh Amendment," it noted, "English courts had held that a civil penalty suit was a particular species of an action in debt that was within the jurisdiction of the courts of law."[194] The case was thus "clearly analogous to the 18th-century action in debt, and federal courts have rightly assumed that the Seventh Amendment required a jury trial."[195]

Many commentators find the historical approach to defining the scope of the Seventh Amendment troublesome. Even if the content of old English law was clear, analogizing new issues to it would at times be perplexing.[196] Matters are worse because the line between law and equity at that time was not terribly clear.[197] Moreover, sorting cases by historical category obscures useful thought about policies which should shape the contemporary roles of judge and jury. In line with these concerns, the Supreme Court in 1990 appeared reluctant to overstate the importance of specific investigations of 18th-century English practice in resolving jury questions under the Seventh Amendment.

---

[191] For examples, see MOORE § 38.44[3]. *See also Blackmon v. American Home Prods. Corp.*, 328 F. Supp. 2d 647, 657-58 (S.D. Tex. 2004).

[192] *See* notes 172–76 and related text, *supra*. Congress has also created many administrative enforcement schemes and specialized (Article I or legislative) courts in which it has failed to provide for jury trials. In addition to looking for historical analogies to decide the Seventh Amendment question in such cases, the Supreme Court has suggested that "public rights" can constitutionally be enforced in special non-jury proceedings. *See, e.g., Atlas Roofing Co. v. Occupational Safety & Health Review Comm'n*, 430 U.S. 442, 458 (1977). This formulation leaves the question of how one identifies such rights.

[193] 481 U.S. 412 (1987).

[194] 481 U.S. at 418.

[195] 481 U.S. at 418. Using a similar approach later, in *Feltner v. Columbia Pictures Television*, 523 U.S. 340 (1998), the Supreme Court saw a historic jury analog to the determination of statutory damages under the Copyright Act of 1976 and ruled that a right to jury trial existed under the Seventh Amendment.

[196] Declaratory judgments, for example, posed difficulties of classification. For discussion of developments, see FRIEDENTHAL, KANE & MILLER § 11.5.

[197] JAMES, HAZARD & LEUBSDORF § 8.2.

Rather, they are "only preliminary" to a more functional question whether the remedy sought is legal or equitable.[198]

On another front, the growing controversy over the role of juries in complex litigation has created additional pressure on the Supreme Court to address the right to jury trial problem in a manner which takes the demands of contemporary litigation more directly into account. Juries in complex cases may be required to listen to more than a year of testimony and to consider reams of documentary evidence. Jury suffering aside, the situation offers the disagreeable prospect of jury members so overwhelmed that they are incapable of rational decision. Perhaps the Seventh Amendment should not be read to require a jury in such cases.[199] Supreme Court dicta may leave room for this conclusion.[200] Perhaps jury deliberation under such circumstances would produce deliberative incoherence raising countervailing constitutional due process concerns.[201]

On the other hand, the language of the Seventh Amendment may not be broad or general enough to accommodate this policy concern. Nor, for that matter, can we assume that judges as factfinders would necessarily be superior in unraveling complications.[202] The Ninth Circuit noted, in rejecting a complexity exception to the Seventh Amendment, that

> [j]urors, if properly instructed and treated with deserved respect, bring collective intelligence, wisdom, and dedication to their tasks,

---

[198] *Chauffeurs, Teamsters and Helpers Local No. 391 v. Terry*, 494 U.S. 558, 569 (1990). Thus, while historical analysis accounting for the law-equity dividing line is likely to remain central to Seventh Amendment decisions, obsession with historical details of 18th century English practice is waning. Writing separately in *Terry*, Justice Brennan urged a complete break. He wrote that "our insistence that the jury trial right hinges in part on a comparison of the substantive right at issue to forms of action used in English courts 200 years ago needlessly convolutes our Seventh Amendment jurisprudence." *Local No. 391*, 494 U.S. at 575. "I would decide Seventh Amendment questions on the basis of the relief sought. If the relief is legal in nature, *i.e.*, if it is the kind of relief that historically was available from courts of law, I would hold that the parties have a constitutional right to a trial by jury . . . ." *Local No. 391*, 494 U.S. at 575.

[199] *See Cotten v. Witco Chem. Corp.*, 651 F.2d 274, 276 (5th Cir. 1981) (reversing grant of motion to strike jury demand and stating that *if* "complexity exception" to Seventh Amendment exists it is only for cases so complex that jury could not render rational decision based upon reasonable understanding of evidence), *cert. denied*, 455 U.S. 909 (1982).

[200] The Court held out the possibility in *Beacon* that there might be "imperative circumstances" that would justify trying common issues in a nonjury trial, 359 U.S. at 510–11, and in *Dairy Queen* that there might be "a rare case" in which matters "are of such a 'complicated nature' that only a court of equity can satisfactorily unravel them." 369 U.S. at 478. Its refined historical test from *Ross* also directs the courts to take into account the "practical abilities and limitations of juries" when deciding the Seventh Amendment question. 396 U.S. at 538 n.10. But in *Terry*, the Court reminded courts that it had "never relied on [consideration of a jury's competency] 'as an independent basis for extending the right to a jury trial under the Seventh Amendment.'" *Terry*, 494 U.S. at 565 (quoting *Tull*, 481 U.S. at 418 n.4).

[201] *But see SRI Int'l v. Matsushita Elec. Corp.*, 775 F.2d 1107, 1128 (Fed. Cir. 1985) (dictum) (the due process argument "confuses the route with the destination, for 'due process' is just that, a process . . . . It is not a result.").

[202] Nor can we even assume that all factual controversies are capable of rational resolution. *See* § 12.08[1] (the institutional role of juries in difficult cases), *infra*.

which is rarely equaled in other areas of public service . . . . We do not accept [the view] "that a single judge is brighter than the jurors, collectively functioning together."[203]

As a result, the complexity exception has met a mixed reception in the appellate courts.[204] The Third Circuit has hinted at one,[205] the Ninth has rejected it,[206] and the Second[207] and Fifth Circuits[208] have refused to apply it using language raising doubt whether it exists. The debate rages on,[209] awaiting Supreme Court resolution.

[2]   Claiming a Jury Trial

State and federal court litigants are free to waive their right to jury trials. Most systems find waiver in the failure of a party to demand a jury within a requisite period of time.[210] Federal Rule 38 provides an illustration.

Rule 38(a) recites that rights to jury trial created under the Seventh Amendment or by congressional enactment "is preserved to the parties inviolate." Rule 38(b) describes the procedure for demanding a jury:

On any issue triable of right by a jury, a party may demand a jury trial by: (1) serving the other parties with a written demand — which may be included in a pleading — no later than 10 days after the last pleading directed to the issue is served . . . .[211]

Under Rule 38(d), the failure of a party to make an effective jury demand within the time allowed "waives by jury trial." Waiver occurs whether the right to trial by jury would have been conferred by the Seventh Amendment or by

---

[203] *In re U.S. Financial Sec. Litig.*, 609 F.2d 411, 430–31 (9th Cir. 1979) (*quoting* Patrick E. Higginbotham, *Continuing The Dialogue: Civil Juries and the Allocation of Judicial Power*, 56 Tex. L. Rev. 47, 53 (1977)), *cert. denied*, 446 U.S. 929 (1980).

[204] *See* George K. Chamberlin, *Complexity of Civil Action as Affecting Seventh Amendment Right to Trial By Jury*, 54 A.L.R. Fed. 733 (1981 and 1999 Supp.).

[205] *In re Japanese Elec. Prods. Antitrust Litig.*, 631 F.2d 1069 (3d Cir. 1980).

[206] *In re U.S. Financial Sec. Litig.*, 609 F.2d 411 (9th Cir. 1979).

[207] *City of New York v. Pullman, Inc.*, 662 F.2d 910, 919 (2d Cir. 1981).

[208] *Cotten v. Witco Chem. Corp.*, 651 F.2d 274, 276 (5th Cir. 1981), *cert. denied*, 455 U.S. 909 (1982).

[209] "Much has been written on every side of this argument." Wright § 92. *See generally* Graham C. Lilly, *The Decline of the American Jury*, 72 U. Colo. L. Rev. 53 (2001); Joseph Sanders, *Scientifically Complex Cases, Trial by Jury, and the Erosion of Adversarial Processes*, 48 DePaul L. Rev. 355 (1998); Stephen I. Friedland, *The Competency and Responsibility of Jurors in Deciding Cases*, 85 Nw. U. L. Rev. 190 (1990); Patrick Devlin, *Equity, Due Process and the Seventh Amendment*, 81 Mich. L. Rev. 1571 (1983).

[210] James, Hazard & Leubsdorf § 8.5.

[211] Once a party makes an effective jury demand, he may not withdraw it without the consent of the other parties in the case. Rule 38(d).

congressional enactment.[212] This contrasts with the traditional reluctance of the Supreme Court to infer waiver of constitutional rights.[213]

There is a ray of hope for a party neglecting to demand a jury trial, in that the trial court has discretion to order one anyway.[214] However, "district judges have been extremely reluctant to exercise this discretion."[215] A party may also amend its pleading to inject a legal issue and start the ten-day clock running again under Rule 39(a), but the courts look askance at amendments made just to recover a previously waived jury right.[216]

§ 12.08   JUDGE-JURY INTERACTION; VERDICTS

[1]   Allocating Issues Between Judge and Jury — An Overview

Unsettled questions about the truth (what did or did not happen) place the case within the sacred preserve of the jury. Jury verdicts should and usually do govern cases where a rational response to the evidence could be a verdict for *either* plaintiff or defendant.

There are at least two arguments for giving juries the last word in such cases.[217] The first is that a group of people (the jury) will be better able to reach the right decision than a single person (judge or juror). The Supreme Court observed:

> Twelve men of the average of the community, comprising men of education and men of little education, men of learning and men whose learning consists only in what they have themselves seen and heard, the merchant, the mechanic, the farmer, the laborer; these sit together, consult, apply their separate experience of the affairs of life to the facts proven, and draw a unanimous conclusion. This average judgment thus given it is the great effort of law to obtain. It is assumed that twelve men know more of the common affairs of life than does one man, that they can draw wiser and safer conclusions from admitted facts thus occurring than can a single judge.[218]

---

[212] A party need not claim a jury to protect his right to jury trial if another party in the case has already claimed one. "[A]ll of the parties to the action who are interested in the issues for which jury trial has been demanded may rely on that demand . . . ." *Wright & Miller* § 2318.

[213] *See, e.g., Johnson v. Zerbst*, 304 U.S. 458, 464 (1938)).

[214] Rule 39(b) states: "the court may, on motion, order a jury trial on any issue for which a jury might have been demanded."

[215] *Wright & Miller* § 2321.

[216] *See, e.g., American Home Prods. Corp. v. Johnson & Johnson, McNeilab, Inc.*, 5 Fed. R. Serv. 3d (Callaghan) 581, 584–89 (S.D.N.Y. 1986).

[217] *See* § 12.06, *supra.*

[218] *Sioux City & Pacific Railroad Co. v. Stout*, 84 U.S. 657, 664 (1874). Today, this rationale is least likely to hold up in exceedingly complex cases, where even the Seventh Amendment right to jury trial is under fire. *See* § 12.07[1], *supra.*

The second argument reaches a conclusion of jury autonomy from the opposite direction. When the evidence provides reasonable bases for conflicting results, perhaps there is no right result.[219] Yet the need for decision remains, and what the judicial process in such cases lacks in precision it can try to make up for in pageantry. Trial before and decision by a jury gives the loser his "day in court" in the fullest popular sense. It seasons resolution of controversies which the law is powerless to decide[220] with a measure of public opinion.

However, there is a serious limitation on jury power. Matters of law are the exclusive concern of the judge.[221] The law-fact distinction pervades law delineating the trial roles of judge and jury, often circumscribing the latter. The judge's function as guardian of the law authorizes him to decide what facts are worthy of the jury's consideration,[222] how the jury should consider them,[223] and whether, in appropriate cases, the jury's verdict should be erased[224] or even turned around.[225]

[2]   Evidentiary Controls

The first opportunity to examine the evidence goes not to the jury but to the judge. When called upon to do so by timely objection, the trial court considers whether the evidence should go to the jury (be admitted). The law of evidence is quite extensive and the subject of a major law school course usually taken after civil procedure.

In setting the scope of discovery,[226] civil procedure gives a less stringent meaning to the term *relevance* than does the law of evidence.[227] Yet relevance

---

[219] *See* Jerome Michael, *The Basic Rules of Pleading*, 5 RECORD OF N.Y.C.B.A. 175, 199–200 (1950).

[220] The fact that none of the motions for deciding the merits (beginning with demurrer/Rule 12(b)(6) and ending with judgment n.o.v. or judgment as a matter of law) works in such cases means that decision as a pure matter of law never materializes. For a survey and comparison of motions deciding the merits, see § 12.09[3][c], *infra*.

[221] The law-fact distinction is not always easy to draw. *See generally* Mark S. Brodin, *Accuracy, Efficiency, and Accountability in the Litigation Process — The Case for the Fact Verdict*, 59 U. CINN. L. REV. 15 (1990). And, as is generally true with the technique of characterization in legal analysis, it is open to abuse. *Cf.* Joseph Morse, *Characterization: Shadow or Substance*, 49 COLUM. L. REV. 1027 (1949) (noting frailties of characterization associated with conflict of laws). *See* § 13.09[2][a] (fact-law distinction on appeal), *infra*.

[222] *See* § 12.08[2] (evidentiary controls), *infra*. He also decides facts underlying preliminary defenses. *See* §§ 8.07[2][b] & [c], *supra*.

[223] *See* § 12.08[3] (jury instructions), *infra*.

[224] *See* § 12.09[2] (new trials), *infra*.

[225] *See* § 12.09[1][b] (judgments notwithstanding the verdict), *infra*.

[226] Rule 26(b)(1), generally limiting discovery, states that "[r]elevant information need not be admissible at the trial if the discovery appears reasonably calculated to lead to the discovery of admissible evidence." *See* § 10.03 (the federal presumption of discoverability), *supra*.

[227] When evidence offered at trial cannot support any rule of law applicable to the case, to admit it would at best clutter the case with inconsequential fact and at worst induce the jury to render a verdict unsupported by law. The court will exclude such evidence as irrelevant or immaterial. The court may also exclude evidence if it is unreliable (if there is a sufficient possibility that it is not what

(materiality) in the law of evidence is rooted in civil procedure. The boundaries of relevance at trial are set by the pleadings. These boundaries may narrow as a result of motion practice prior to trial[228] or pretrial orders.[229] Or they may be enlarged by amendment conforming the pleadings to evidence admitted at trial.[230]

In federal courts, the law of evidence is codified in the Federal Rules of Evidence. Although these were originally proposed in the same manner as the Federal Rules of Civil Procedure, under authority of the Rules Enabling Act,[231] congressional concern about the displacement of state laws of privilege[232] led to the revision and enactment of the rules as statutory law.[233]

[3]   Instructing the Jury

In nonjury cases, the judge is both the law enforcer and the trier of fact. Since both functions are performed by the same person, fine distinctions separating the two will usually be unnecessary.

Matters are quite different, however, in jury trials. Jurors use the evidence to answer factual questions.[234] But they may not resolve issues about the meaning or application of law. Only the judge does that.[235] Not only is the judge an authority on all legal questions, she must also see to it that the law is enforced. One way in which the judge must maintain legal control is in the way she instructs (charges) the jury.

> Simple, vague instructions allow the jury to decide the case with little guidance . . . . If a judge gives detailed and comprehensive jury instructions relating to the substantive law to be applied by the jury (as opposed to "housekeeping" instructions), the judge is staking out a relatively large perimeter surrounding the "legal" issues that the jury must not cross. Detailed instructions correspondingly diminish the jury's remaining function, finding the "facts" of the case. The more

---

it is offered to be) or if it is prejudicial (it is likely to inflame or prejudice the jury). *See generally* McCormick on Evidence ch. 16 (Kenneth S. Brown ed., 6th ed. 2006).

[228] For example, from the award of partial summary judgment. On summary judgments, see generally § 11.03, *supra*.

[229] On pretrial orders, *see* § 12.03[3], *supra*.

[230] *See* § 8.10[2], *supra*.

[231] *See* § 1.02 (explaining procedure for creating federal rules of civil procedure), *supra*.

[232] *Cf.* § 7.04 (discussing relation of federal procedural law and state law), *supra*.

[233] After the Supreme Court transmitted the proposed Federal Rules of Evidence to Congress, Congress deferred their effective date until such time as they were enacted into law. Pub. L. No. 93-12; 87 Stat. 9 (March 30, 1973). The proposed rules, as modified by Congress, were subsequently enacted into law. Pub. L. No. 93-595, 88 Stat. 1926 (Jan. 2, 1975).

[234] In federal and many state courts, the judge has the right to comment on the evidence as an aid to the jury. Moore § 51.10[3]. She may not distort it or add to it, of course, *see Quercia v. United States*, 289 U.S. 466 (1933), and the jury is typically reminded that, as the sole trier of fact, it has the right to disagree with her. *See, e.g., Trezza v. Dame*, 370 F.2d 1006, 1009 (5th Cir. 1967).

[235] The point is explored at greater length in the discussion of directed verdicts, judgments notwithstanding the verdict, and judgments as a matter of law in § 12.09, *infra*.

detailed and comprehensive the instructions, the less discretion the jury enjoys to "make law" by applying its own notions as to what the statute really says, or as to what elementary fairness requires.[236]

Consider an illustration. At trial in an automobile accident case, the jury is presented with conflicting evidence on the question whether plaintiff's own carelessness was a contributing cause of the accident. The jury, not the judge, must weigh the evidence and answer the question. However, only the judge can determine what the answer to the question means to the outcome of the case.[237] Thus, the judge must not only decide what tort law principle applies but limit the work of the jury to the confines of that principle. Assume that the judge concludes that the governing principle is that contributory negligence is an absolute bar to recovery. She might impose this on the jury by saying in her instructions: "Members of the jury, if you find that plaintiff's carelessness was a contributing cause of the accident, you *must* return a verdict for defendant."

In many jurisdictions, *pattern jury instructions* have been prepared for use in civil cases.[238] The authority of such standardized instructions lies somewhere between the authority of appendix of forms to the Federal Rules of Civil Procedure[239] and form pleadings and interrogatories,[240] depending upon how they were assembled. But even when they were assembled by a committee appointed by the courts, they must be used with caution.

> They may not be swallowed whole. They are intended as an aid to the preparation of appropriate instruction in a particular case. Each case has its own peculiar facts, and formalized instructions must be tailored to the requirements of the facts and the issues.[241]

The parties have the right to propose appropriate jury instructions. Rule 51 treats the manner in which jury instructions are to be prepared and given in federal court. Parties may file written requests for jury instructions and "[t]he court must inform the parties of its proposed instructions and proposed action on the requests before instructing the jury and before final jury arguments." A federal court may instruct the jury before or after argument or both.

---

[236] Ronald W. Eades, *The Problem of Jury Instructions in Civil Cases*, 27 CUMB. L. REV. 1017, 1018 (1997) (citation omitted).

[237] *But cf.* WRIGHT & MILLER § 2503 ("Some of the most famous students of the judicial process have argued that one of the purposes of the jury system is to permit the jury to temper strict rules of law by the demands and necessities of substantial justice, thereby adding a much needed element of flexibility."). *See also* § 12.06, *supra*.

[238] *See, e.g.,* EDWARD DEVITT, CHARLES B. BLACKMAR & MICHAEL A. WOLFF, FEDERAL JURY PRACTICE AND INSTRUCTIONS (4th ed. 1987 and 1992), which is widely used in federal courts. *See generally* Eades, note 236, *supra*, at 1020–23; ROBERT G. NIELAND, PATTERN JURY INSTRUCTIONS: A CRITICAL LOOK AT A MODERN MOVEMENT TO IMPROVE THE JURY SYSTEM (1979).

[239] *See* Rule 84 (forms "suffice under [the] rules").

[240] *See* §§ 1.02 (sources of civil procedure) & 10.09[2] (interrogatories), *supra*.

[241] DEVITT & BLACKMAR, note 238, *supra*, § 8.03. *See generally* Walter W. Steele, Jr. & Elizabeth G. Thornburg, *Jury Instructions: A Persistent Failure to Communicate*, 67 N.C. L. REV. 77 (1988).

Whether or not the parties request instructions, a judge has the duty in most jurisdictions to instruct the jury on the applicable law.[242] However, the failure to request specific instructions may operate as a waiver; the judge is charged only with instructing on "the broad general fundamental rules of law."[243] Moreover, Rule 51 is typical in providing that a party may challenge instructions on appeal only if he objected "on the record, stating distinctly the matter objected to and the grounds for the objection." Failure to object usually puts an end to the matter, subject only to a narrow common law power in the appellate courts to correct *plain errors* — errors so egregious that the trial courts should have known them when they saw them.[244]

Errors of law in jury instructions are among the most common grounds for new trials.[245] The appellate courts decide the correctness of the instructions *de novo* (anew).[246] But they view the instructions as a whole, including any curative instructions,[247] and reverse only for prejudicial error.[248]

[4]   Verdicts

In the usual civil jury trial, the jury is charged with returning a *general verdict*, that is, a verdict for one side or another supplying no explanation why the jury decided as it did. Such verdicts are in extensive use and can work well in relatively simple cases. Their weakness is that they fail to illuminate the jurors' decision-making process. It is fairly easy for jurors to ignore constraints and admonitions in the charge when they can hide behind a general verdict. It is also difficult to preserve the work of the jury if problems arise with the case on appeal of a general verdict.[249]

The *special verdict* is an alternative intended to address these shortcomings. Jury instructions designed to elicit a special verdict contain a

---

[242] *See, e.g., Turner Constr. Co. v. Houlihan*, 240 F.2d 435, 439 (1st Cir. 1957). *But see Ouille v. Saliba*, 149 So. 2d 468, 469 (Miss. 1963) (in absence of request for instructions on counterclaim, judge "cannot instruct the jury on his own motion").

[243] *Turner Constr. Co.*, 240 F.2d at 439.

[244] "Actual reversals on the basis of plain error are rare, though they have become more numerous in recent years." WRIGHT & MILLER § 2558. *See* § 13.08[2] (preservation of error below as predicate for review), *infra*.

[245] *See* § 12.09[2][c] (new trials), *infra*.

[246] *See* § 13.10[2][a] (the *de novo* standard of review), *infra*.

[247] *See, e.g., Ayoub v. Spencer*, 550 F.2d 164, 167 (3d Cir.), *cert. denied*, 432 U.S. 907 (1977) ("Our function is to determine whether the charge, taken as a whole and viewed in the light of the evidence, fairly and adequately submits the issues in the case to the jury.").

[248] Rule 61. *See generally* § 13.09[1] (prejudicial effect as predicate for review), *infra*.

[249] "For example, if a prevailing plaintiff asserts several possible theories of recovery, and the appellate court finds the evidence for one of those theories to have been admitted erroneously, a new trial on all issues will be required because there is no way of discovering which theory the jury relied on in reaching the verdict." FRIEDENTHAL, KANE & MILLER § 12.1. In summing up the deficiencies of the general verdict, a recent commentator described it as "the ultimate in 'black box decision-making.' . . . This product of jury deliberations comes into court . . . with no indication whether it is based upon particular findings of fact, or particular interpretation of law, or both, or neither." Brodin, *supra*, note 219, at 34.

series of short-answer fact questions.[250] The jurors answer the questions instead of designating a winner. From all the answers, the judge constructs the equivalent of a general verdict. If the answers appear inconsistent, the judge is obliged to "attempt to reconcile the jury's findings, by exegesis if necessary, . . . " before either resubmitting them or ordering a new trial.[251]

Parties to complex cases may prefer a special verdict because of the guidance it gives the jury in fact-finding.[252] However, they have no right to have the jury return a special verdict in federal courts. They can only request one.[253] Many trial judges have been reluctant to use the device. Some reluctance may stem from the fact that judges are unfamiliar with it. Some apparently comes from a fear of encroaching upon the independence of the jury.[254] Compared to general verdicts at least, special verdicts do impose tighter controls and may therefore reflect a more suspicious attitude toward juries.[255] Finally, some hesitation to use special verdicts stems from concern about the possibility of inconsistent findings.[256]

Some courts seem receptive to a compromise: a general verdict accompanied with answers to written interrogatories. Federal Rule 49(b) provides this option, again, at the discretion of the court. This verdict form permits jurors to declare a winner but requires them to show their work. However, it is even more vulnerable to inconsistencies than the special verdict, since the jury's answers may be inconsistent not only with each other, but also with the general verdict. Subdivision (b) proposes different solutions for this problem, none of them entirely reassuring.

---

[250] Rule 49(a), governing special verdicts in federal court, refers to "written questions susceptible of a categorical or other brief answer . . . ." On the uses and contributions of special verdicts in federal litigation, see *Brodin, supra*, note 221, at 62–84.

[251] *Gallick v. Baltimore & Ohio R.R. Co.*, 372 U.S. 108, 119 (1963). *See generally* Donald Olander, Note, *Resolving Inconsistencies in Federal Special Verdicts*, 53 FORDHAM L. REV. 1089 (1984).

[252] *See* Elizabeth A. Faulkner, *Using the Special Verdict to Manage Complex Cases and Avoid Compromise Verdicts*, 21 ARIZ. ST. L.J. 297 (1989). Another, less common reason for requesting a special verdict may be to isolate particular facts. For example, a public figure who brings a libel action may be as interested in having a jury find that the libel was false as he is in recovering, and more likely to obtain the former, too, given the heavy burden of proving actual malice.

[253] Rule 49(a) "is permissive, not mandatory. Whether a special or general verdict is to be returned (by the jury) rests in the sound discretion of the trial court." WRIGHT & MILLER § 2505.

[254] FRIEDENTHAL, KANE & MILLER § 12.1.

[255] A special verdict "puts psychological pressure on the jurors to adhere to their legally prescribed functions and to prevent them from deciding cases on grounds they are instructed to ignore." JAMES, HAZARD & LEUBSDORF § 7.23.

[256] *See generally* Shaun P. Martin, *Rationalizing the Irrational: The Treatment of Untenable Federal Civil Jury Verdicts*, 28 CREIGHTON L. REV. 683 (1995). Of course, general verdicts, too, can be inconsistent. Shaun P. Martin, *Rationalizing the Irrational: The Treatment of Untenable Federal Civil Jury Verdicts*, 28 CREIGHTON L. REV. 683 (1995) Motions for j.n.o.v. (judgment as a matter of law in federal courts) or new trial can be used to control the jury in such cases. *See* § 12.09, *infra*.

§ 12.09   TAKING THE CASE FROM THE JURY: MOTIONS FOR JUDGMENT AS A MATTER OF LAW AND FOR NEW TRIAL

[1]   Directed Verdicts and Judgments N.O.V. Rephrased as Judgments as a Matter of Law

After trial has begun, a party may by motion request the court either to render judgment without letting the case go to a jury verdict, or (if a verdict has been entered) to render judgment opposed to that indicated by the verdict. Traditional terminology for the first such order is *directed verdict* and, for the orders of the second type, *judgment n.o.v.* (or judgment notwithstanding the verdict).

A 1991 amendment to Rule 50 of the Federal Rules of Civil Procedure discarded the two terms in favor of the single phrase, *judgment as a matter of law*. This development must be noted. Yet, for several reasons, it may not be terribly important. First, the amendment will work little if any change in decisionmaking,[257] since the test for a judgment as a matter of law appears to be the same as the test previously applied to both directed verdicts and judgments n.o.v. Second, many state courts will continue for the foreseeable future to be governed by procedural law employing the two older terms. Third, even federal courts may continue to employ them, since directed verdict and judgment n.o.v. are useful to differentiate the two subspecies of the topic covered by the more generic term, judgment as a matter of law.

By whatever name, separate procedural devices for taking the jury out of the picture before or after a verdict still function in all American courts. It continues to be important to grasp their similarities and differences and, for convenience and clarity of discussion, it will be useful to refer to them by their traditional titles, directed verdict and judgment n.o.v.

Motions for directed verdict and for judgment notwithstanding the verdict have much in common. Each is governed by the same legal standard. They can and often do address the same factual record. Appellate courts freely reexamine decisions on both. For all that, we shall see that each makes a discrete contribution as part of a series of motions screening the merits of the case.

---

[257] The Advisory Committee note to the 1991 amendment makes this clear, stating that the new terminology "effects no change in the existing standard. That existing standard was not expressed in the former rule, but was articulated in long-standing case law." For a dissenting view, that the outcome in some cases may be affected by the amendment, see Michael J. Waggoner, *New Rule 50 May End Directed Verdicts for Plaintiffs*, 22 Sw. U. L. Rev. 389 (1993).

The Advisory Committee also stated that the change in terminology was merely a technicality. "If a motion is denominated a motion for directed verdict or for judgment notwithstanding the verdict, the party's error is merely formal. Such a motion should be treated as a motion for judgment as a matter of law in accordance with this rule."

[a] The Theoretical Justification for Court Intervention in Jury Cases

Recall that the function of the jury is to deliberate, to weigh the evidence in choosing between a result favorable to plaintiff or to defendant. Juries derive their autonomy from the character of the evidence in the case. So long as evidence creates a genuine and substantial controversy over who should win, juries should and do have the last word. Judges have the last word, however, when the evidence supports only one side.[258]

The jury's verdict could coincide with the only right result in such cases. Once, however, the jury loses authority to choose between conflicting results, its presence becomes incidental.

The conclusion that the evidence supports only one result in the case can be as evident to the court before the jury deliberates as after. The first opportunity to end the case thus comes by means of a motion for directed verdict, whereby the court can interpose its decision on the evidence and keep the jury from ever considering the case. The second opportunity comes by means of a motion for judgment n.o.v.[259] (judgment notwithstanding the verdict), whereby the court can reverse a jury verdict unsupported by evidence.

[b] The Legal Standard Governing Directed Verdicts and Judgments N.O.V.

Each system applies a single legal standard to decide both directed verdicts and judgments n.o.v.[260] Systems have varied, however, in how stringent that standard should be. At one extreme, the judge may not interfere if there is any evidence — even just a "scintilla" — supporting a verdict against the moving party.[261] At the other extreme, a party supported by evidence reasonably

---

[258] That is, they have the authority to resolve the merits of the case in favor of the only litigant whose position is supported by the evidence. "Whether the evidence presented at trial is sufficient to create an issue of fact for the jury or will permit the court to enter judgment as a matter of law is solely a question of law to be determined by the trial court." WRIGHT & MILLER § 2524. In other situations, the judge may not have the last word in this sense but does have the authority to undo the work of the jury by ordering a new trial. See § 12.09[2], *infra*. New trial decisions based on an evaluation of the evidence are governed by a different legal standard from the one governing directed verdicts and judgments n.o.v. discussed in this subsection. WRIGHT & MILLER § 2524.

[259] From the Latin phrase *non obstante veredicto*.

[260] Thus, in federal court, the "standard . . . is the same whether it arises in the procedural context of a motion for judgment as a matter of law prior to the submission of the case to the jury or in the context of a renewed motion for judgment as a matter of law after the jury has returned a verdict." WRIGHT & MILLER § 2524. That standard has been express in Rule 50 since 1991. After technical revisions made by amendment in 2007, Rule 50(a) states that a judgment as a matter of law may be entered "[i]f a party has been fully heard on an issue during a jury trial and the court finds that a reasonable jury would not have a legally sufficient evidentiary basis to find for the party on that issue . . . ."

[261] This is called the "scintilla" rule from the Latin term referring to a mere particle. For discussion of the rule and citation of illustrative Alabama state decisions, see FRIEDENTHAL, KANE & MILLER § 12.3.

capable of supporting a jury verdict could fall prey to one of the motions.[262]

Federal and most state courts steer a middle course. "The court should review the record as a whole," the Supreme Court has said, but "it must disregard all evidence favorable to the moving party that the jury is not required to believe. That is, the court should give credence to the evidence favoring the nonmovant as well as that 'evidence supporting the moving party that is uncontradicted and unimpeached, at least to the extent that that evidence comes from disinterested witnesses.' "[263] On the other hand, the existence of just *any* favorable evidence (no matter how meager) will not protect federal litigants from directed verdicts or judgments n.o.v. The test federal courts usually administer has often been called the *substantial evidence* test. Evidence is substantial in this sense when it is capable of providing a reasonable basis for a juror to find for the party opposing the directed verdict or judgment n.o.v. motion. Or, as one federal circuit court put it, the test

> is whether the evidence is such that, without weighing the credibility of the witnesses or otherwise considering the weight of the evidence, there can be but one conclusion as to the verdict that reasonable men [or women] could have reached.[264]

To call this the substantial evidence test has always been somewhat misleading.[265] It suggests that the motion tests the quality or weight of the evidence, when it really tests whether there is *sufficient* evidence from which a reasonable jury could find against the movant. It is more useful to describe it as a "reasonable juror" test, and the 1991 amendment to Rule 50(a) should encourage this shift in thinking by expressly referring to a "reasonable jury" standard.

[2]   New Trial Motions

[a]   In General

The most widely used form of judicial control of juries is the order granting a new trial on all or some part of the issues. The power to set aside verdicts and grant new trials was well-established in 1791 and is therefore consistent with the constitutional guarantee of jury trial.[266] All jurisdictions permit this control and confer broad (in some circumstances, practically unreviewable)

---

[262] WRIGHT & MILLER § 2538.

[263] *Reeves v. Sanderson Plumbing Prods., Inc.*, 530 U.S. 133, 151 (2000) (quoting WRIGHT & MILLER § 2529).

[264] *Simblest v. Maynard*, 427 F.2d 1, 4 (2d Cir. 1970). The United States Supreme Court has observed that "the standard for a directed verdict under Federal Rule of Civil Procedure 50(a) . . . is that the trial judge must direct a verdict if, under the governing law, there can be but one reasonable conclusion as to the verdict . . . . If reasonable minds could differ as to the import of the evidence, however, a verdict should not be directed." *Anderson v. Liberty Lobby, Inc.*, 477 U.S. 242, 250 (1986).

[265] *See* note 264, *supra.*

[266] *Capital Traction Co. v. Hof*, 174 U.S. 1, 13–14 (1899):

discretion on the trial judge to deploy it. But all also sharply restrict its availability to a short period — ten days in federal courts[267] — after the verdict is returned or judgment is entered.

The grounds for new trial are as numerous as the sources of possible error in the trial. Some states rules list the grounds,[268] but Federal Rule 59(a)(1) and many state rules simply authorize new trial for "any reason for which a new trial has heretofore been granted in an action at law in federal court." Most grounds for new trial, however, fall into two categories. The first and most troublesome category consists of errors in the jury's evaluation of the evidence. The second consists of errors in the trial process, including errors in the law applied.[269]

[b] Evaluative Errors: Verdicts That Are Excessive, Inadequate, or Otherwise Against the Weight of the Evidence

When the trial judge concludes that the verdict is excessive, inadequate, or otherwise against the weight of the evidence, she is second-guessing the jury in its evaluation of the evidence.[270] Yet, unlike directed verdict, judgment n.o.v., or judgment as a matter of law, an order for a new trial on the grounds that the verdict is against the weight of the evidence does not deprive the verdict-winner of jury trial. It only forces him to submit his evidence to a new jury. His problem is that he gets "too much jury trial, not too little."[271]

This explains why the test for granting new trial is less restrictive than the test for directed verdict/judgment n.o.v.[272] On the other hand, for the judge to set aside the verdict and order a new trial just because she would have decided the case differently would undercut the jury as fact-finder.[273]

"Trial by jury," in the primary and usual sense of the term at common law and in the American constitutions . . . is a trial by a jury of twelve men in the presence and under the superintendence of a judge empowered to instruct them on law and to advise them on the facts, and . . . to set aside their verdict if, in his opinion, it is against the law or the evidence.

---

[267] Rule 59(b).

[268] *See, e.g.*, MINN. R. CIV. P. 59.01.

[269] Another, less important category consists of newly discovered evidence that could not, with reasonable diligence, have been discovered and produced at trial. Since such evidence is rarely discovered within the customarily short time periods for seeking new trial, it is probably more commonly advanced in support of a motion for relief from judgment. *See* Rule 60(b)(2), discussed at § 12.11[2][b], *infra*.

[270] Of course, the verdict may be excessive because it exceeds statutory limits. The error is then not evaluative, but an error of law.

[271] FRIEDENTHAL, KANE & MILLER § 12.4.

[272] Indeed, were it the same, no new trial should be granted because the court could enter judgment as a matter of law. WRIGHT § 95. As a result, only a minority of states have adopted a new trial standard that is the same as the reasonable jury standard usually used for directed verdict/judgment n.o.v. *See* JAMES, HAZARD & LEUBSDORF § 7.28.

[273] Although some states have adopted this "thirteenth juror" test for new trial, *see* JAMES,

The test for federal and most state courts lies somewhere in between. We say "somewhere" because the test is necessarily approximate. One of the most frequently quoted formulas was stated in *Aetna Casualty & Surety Co. v. Yeats*:[274]

> On such a motion it is the duty of the judge to set aside the verdict and grant a new trial, if he is of opinion that the verdict is against the clear weight of the evidence, or is based upon evidence which is false, or will result in a miscarriage of justice, even though there may be substantial evidence which would prevent direction of a verdict.

This formulation makes it clear that the court may grant a new trial even if it finds "substantial evidence" to support the verdict, because on new trial, unlike directed verdict or j.n.o.v, the court *does* weigh the evidence, not just test it for sufficiency. Another common formula is that the judge must be left with a definite and firm conviction that a mistake has been committed.[275]

In application, this test must take into account the deliberative skill of the jury in the circumstances of the case. The verdict in "a trial that is long and complicated and deals with a subject matter not lying within the ordinary knowledge of jurors . . . should be scrutinized more closely" than the verdict in a simple trial dealing with familiar subject matter.[276] Certainly, the trial judge should be most hesitant to set aside the verdict and order new trial on evidentiary grounds when the key issue in the case was credibility, a matter classically for the jury.

Another kind of evaluative error is that the verdict is excessive or inadequate as a matter of fact.[277] This is logically no different from a weight of the evidence claim. Yet the determination of unliquidated and punitive damages is often so speculative to begin with that judicial intervention on a new trial motion may seem especially problematical. The conditional grant of new trial has often provided a way out, however. The trial judge grants the motion unless the opposing party agrees to a reduction (*remittitur*) or increase (*additur*) of the verdict.[278] In federal courts, the court may order a remittitur if the verdict is so excessive that it "shocks the conscience."[279] The party who consents to such a remittitur waives any right to appellate review of it.[280] The Supreme Court has upheld remittitur against Seventh Amendment attack, relying on historical

---

HAZARD, & LEUBSDORF § 7.28, it is doubtful that their judges actually exercise as much discretion as the test seems to confer.

[274] 122 F.2d 350, 352–53 (4th Cir. 1941).

[275] *See* WRIGHT § 95.

[276] *Lind v. Schenley Indus., Inc.*, 278 F.2d 79, 90–91 (3d Cir. 1960).

[277] As opposed to excessive as a matter of law. *See* note 270, *supra*.

[278] He must give the opposing party the option, however, and may not simply fix the proper level of damages himself. *McKinnon v. City of Berwyn*, 750 F.2d 1383, 1389 (7th Cir. 1984). Federal courts are divided on what the proper level should be: the highest reasonable amount, a reasonable amount, or the lowest reasonable amount. *See, e.g., Gorsalitz v. Olin Mathieson Chem. Corp.*, 429 F.2d 1033, 1047 (5th Cir. 1970).

[279] MOORE § 59.13[2][g][iii][B].

[280] *Donovan v. Penn Shipping Co.*, 429 U.S. 648 (1977).

grounds and some dubious logic, but has condemned additur as unconstitutional.[281]

In *Gasperini v. Center for Humanities, Inc.*,[282] the Supreme Court added a further wrinkle to remittitur practice in federal diversity cases. There state law authorized trial courts to set aside as excessive any verdict which "deviates materially from what would be reasonable compensation." This is a broader standard than the federal miscarriage-of-justice or "shocks the conscience" standard.[283] The Supreme Court held that the state standard served substantive purposes and therefore controlled in a federal diversity case.

The grant of partial new trial limited to the issue of damages is another possibility when the amount of the verdict has been attacked. In federal court, partial new trial "may not be resorted to unless it clearly appears that the issue to be retried is so distinct and separate from the others that a trial of it alone may be had without injustice."[284] Such orders must be made cautiously, however. A jury that has evaluated damages improperly may well also have evaluated liability improperly. In particular, an inadequate verdict may be a compromise verdict which cannot fairly be set aside only in part.

New trial determinations differ from directed verdicts and judgments n.o.v. not just in availability. Decisions granting or denying directed verdicts or judgments n.o.v. are open to reconsideration on review.[285] In contrast, it is quite difficult to obtain reversal of the court's decision granting or refusing to grant a motion for new trial. In the first place, the grant of a new trial motion — standing alone — is interlocutory. It is not appealable until a final judgment is rendered after a new trial,[286] assuming that the judgment is unfavorable to the party who resisted the new trial.[287] Even then, it is reviewable only for abuse of discretion.[288] When the new trial determination is based on evidentiary grounds, the standard of appellate review for abuse of discretion is extremely narrow.[289]

---

[281] *Compare Dimick v. Schiedt*, 293 U.S. 474, 486 (1935) ("what remains is included in the verdict along with the unlawful excess — in that sense it has been found by the jury — and the remittitur has the effect of merely lopping off an excrescence"), *with Jehl v. Southern Pacific Co.*, 427 P.2d 988 (Cal. 1967) (allowing additur in state court). *See* Sann, *Remittiturs (and Additurs) in Federal Courts: An Evaluation With Suggested Alternatives*, 38 Case W. Res. L. Rev. 157 (1988) (urging elimination of remittitur in federal courts to eliminate inconsistency and inefficiency).

[282] 518 U.S. 415, 422 (1996).

[283] 518 U.S. at 424.

[284] *Gasoline Prods. Co. v. Champlin Ref. Co.*, 283 U.S. 494, 500 (1931).

[285] *See* § 12.09[3][b], *infra*.

[286] *Allied Chem. Corp. v. Daiflon, Inc.*, 449 U.S. 33, 34, 36 (1980).

[287] *See* § 12.09[3][a], *infra*.

[288] 518 U.S. at 436.

[289] For a discussion of the standard and its application to new trial determinations, see § 13.09[2][d], infra.

[c]　Process Errors

There are a variety of errors that may taint the trial process. These include judicial errors in instructing the jury or admitting or commenting on the evidence, and misconduct by parties, counsel, witnesses or jurors, as well as prejudicial happenstance.[290] The judge has discretion to grant a new trial for such errors.[291] This is subject, however, to the possibility that the error may be deemed harmless.[292] No verdict may be set aside and new trial granted unless the error adversely affected the substantial rights of the complaining party. The trial judge's superior ability to assess the prejudicial effect of errors on the trial process explains why he generally enjoys such discretion on ruling on motions for new trial.

Of the sundry errors of trial process which may justify a new trial, jury misconduct merits further discussion. The historic rule at common law was that a juror may not impeach his own verdict.[293] The rule was intended partly to protect the candor of secret jury deliberations and perhaps to protect the institution of jury fact-finding itself from embarrassing disclosure of its imprecision.[294] Since juries typically deliberate in secret, the rule made it extremely difficult to prove jury misconduct in many cases.

Today, most jurisdictions have struck a compromise between the desire to protect candid jury deliberation and the need to control jury misconduct. Almost all jurisdictions use an exclusionary evidentiary rule to protect the mental processes of jurors from disclosure.[295] But "the permissibility of juror testimony hinges upon the purpose for which it is offered."[296] Jurors are often permitted to testify about extraneous information or outside influence that may have tainted the jury's deliberations.[297]

In re Beverly Hills Fire Litigation[298] supplies a good illustration of the modern rule and suggests one test for jury misconduct. There, one of the jurors reported to the jury the results of his home experiment with electrical wiring, in contradiction of expert testimony during the trial. On appeal, the court considered the jurors' testimony about this extraneous information and rejected the verdict winners' arguments that the experimenting juror was only relying on his own general knowledge and common experience. Instead, it found that the juror's actions "went beyond mere general knowledge and was

---

[290]　*See generally* MOORE § 59.13.

[291]　In theory, there is no discretion in deciding new trial motions based on judicial errors, since they present questions of law. In practice, the assessment of their prejudicial effect invokes a discretion which is entitled to substantial respect on appeal. *See* JAMES, HAZARD & LEUBSDORF § 7.25. Regarding the appellate review of discretionary orders generally, see § 13.09[2][d], *infra*.

[292]　*See* Rule 61.

[293]　*See* Comment, *Impeachment of Jury Verdicts*, 25 U. CHI. L. REV. 360 (1958).

[294]　*See generally* JAMES, HAZARD & LEUBSDORF § 7.27.

[295]　FRIEDENTHAL, KANE & MILLER § 12.5.

[296]　*Attridge v. Cencorp Div. of Dover Techs. Int'l, Inc.*, 836 F.2d 113, 117 (2d Cir. 1987).

[297]　*See, e.g.*, Fed. R. Evid. 606(b). *See generally* MOORE § 59.13[2][e][iii][D].

[298]　695 F.2d 207, 214 (6th Cir. 1982).

instead a response to the case at hand," prejudicially supplementing the record. It reversed and remanded for a new trial.

In contrast, a closely divided Supreme Court in *United States v. Tanner*[299] held that what the dissenters characterized as "profoundly disturbing" evidence of extensive juror drug and alcohol intoxication *during* deliberations went to the mental processes of the jury and was therefore inadmissible to impeach the verdict. The majority thus aggressively enforced the federal version of the exclusionary evidentiary rule, notwithstanding a strong argument that drug and alcohol consumption are extraneous and antecedent to the jury's deliberative process.

[3] The Interplay of Directed Verdicts and Judgments N.O.V. With Other Procedural Law

[a] The Consistency of Directed Verdicts and Judgments N.O.V. With the Right to Jury Trial

There is no logical difficulty in squaring directed verdicts and judgments n.o.v. with the right in federal court to trial by jury.[300] Such dispositions are unavailable unless the jury could reasonably find only for the moving party. The only function for the jury to perform in such cases would be the ceremonial one of announcing the sole possible result.[301] Since, however, the Seventh Amendment right to jury trial at times represents a triumph of history over logic,[302] the matter requires further discussion.

Directed verdicts have not posed much of a problem. Early on, the United States Supreme Court appeared to regard the authority of courts to direct verdicts as well-established in common law.[303] By 1943, the Supreme Court observed that Seventh Amendment challenges to federal directed verdicts were "foreclosed by repeated decisions made here consistently for nearly a century."[304] The Supreme Court did read the Seventh Amendment to block judgment n.o.v. in one famous pre-rule decision.[305] However, the Court altered

---

[299] 483 U.S. 107 (1987). For a trenchant criticism of the case and an analysis of Fed. R. Evid. 606, *see* Edward T. Swaine, Note, *Pre-Deliberations Juror Misconduct, Evidential Incompetence, and Juror Responsibility*, 98 YALE L.J. 187 (1990).

[300] For discussion of the latter, see § 12.07[1], *supra.*

[301] "This internally inconsistent practice" was rendered unnecessary by the 1963 amendment of Rule 50(a). MOORE § 50 App. 102. The rule now states that "[t]he order of the court granting a motion for a directed verdict is effective without any assent of the jury."

[302] *See* § 12.07[1], *supra.*

[303] In *Parks v. Ross*, 52 U.S. 362, 373 (1851), the Court noted that "[i]t is undoubtedly the peculiar province of the jury to find all matters of fact, and of the court to decide all questions of law arising thereon. But a jury has no right to assume the truth of any material fact, without some evidence legally sufficient to establish it." That directed verdicts differ "in some major respects" from "the historic jury control devices — the demurrer to the evidence, nonsuit, and a motion for new trial . . .," FRIEDENTHAL, KANE & MILLER § 12.3, has not troubled the Supreme Court.

[304] *Galloway v. United States*, 319 U.S. 372, 389 (1943).

[305] *Slocum v. New York Life Ins. Co.*, 228 U.S. 364 (1913).

its position in later cases,[306] using the well-accepted rule that directed verdicts were permissible to create something of a legal fiction. A federal judge reserving decision on a motion for directed verdict could later turn around a verdict unsupported by evidence on the theory that he was reviving consideration of the motion for directed verdict.[307] Rule 50(b) codifies this fiction by making judgments n.o.v. available only to the party who has made "a motion for a judgment as a matter of law . . . under Rule 50(a)" specifying the grounds on which the motion is based.[308] The court need not expressly reserve decision on the motion; the rule provides that "the court is considered to have submitted the action to the jury subject to the court's later deciding the legal questions raised by the motion." The later determination may also be by an appellate court, reversing the trial court's denial of judgment n.o.v.[309] Indeed, the Supreme Court has held that a court of appeals may even direct entry of judgment as a matter of law (instead of remanding) when, after it has excised evidence which was erroneously admitted by the trial court, there is insufficient evidence left to support the jury verdict.[310]

[b]   How Directed Verdicts and Judgments N.O.V. Complement Each Other

Since the same legal standard governs both directed verdicts and judgments n.o.v.,[311] and since they often address the same factual record, it is natural to ask why both are necessary.

The principal contribution of judgments n.o.v. is that they make it possible for trial judges to conserve court and party resources. They do this by permitting trial courts to defer acting on the conclusion that the evidence permits only one result until the jury has deliberated and returned its verdict. For two reasons, this is one of the few instances in civil procedure where delay ultimately serves judicial efficiency. First, if the jury eventually finds for the movant, the trial court is spared from making a ruling that is more vulnerable on appeal than a judgment on a jury verdict. Second, deferring a ruling until a motion for judgment n.o.v. reduces the necessity for retrial of the case if appeal is successfully taken,[312] by allowing the jury to return a verdict that can

---

[306]   *E.g., Baltimore & Carolina Line, Inc. v. Redman*, 295 U.S. 654 (1935).

[307]   *Redman*, 295 U.S. at 658–59.

[308]   Federal courts usually apply the limitation strictly, and the specification requirement added in 1991 effectively rejected earlier cases holding that something less than a formal motion for directed verdict was sufficient to preserve a party's right to move for judgment n.o.v. *See* Moore § 50.40[3]; Rule 50(a) advisory committee's note (1991 amendment). Since Seventh Amendment concerns are local to federal courts, states — even those which typically adopt language of the Federal Rules of Civil Procedure — are free to dispense with the directed verdict prerequisite in their judgment n.o.v. rules. *See, e.g.,* Ind. R. of Trial Proc., Trial Rule 50.

[309]   *Cf. Neely v. Martin K. Eby Constr. Co.*, 386 U.S. 317, 322 (1967) ("there is no greater restriction on the province of the jury when an appellate court enters judgment *n.o.v.* than when a trial court does . . . .").

[310]   *Weisgram v. Marley Co.*, 528 U.S. 440 (2000).

[311]   *See* § 12.09[1][b], *supra.*

[312]   *Cf.* Friedenthal, Kane & Miller § 12.3 ("By waiting, the judge avoids disputes about the

be reinstated on remand.

Consider an example. Defendant moves for a directed verdict in a federal case. The judge concludes that plaintiff has fallen just short of submitting enough evidence to meet the substantial evidence standard.[313] However, he denies defendant's motion. By delaying decision until the jury has returned a verdict, the judge creates the strong possibility that the jury will return a verdict in favor of defendant. If this happens, the court will never have to pass on the highly reviewable question (whether a reasonable jury could find for plaintiff) posed earlier by defendant's motion for directed verdict.[314] Defendant will be content with the jury verdict. Since there will be substantial evidence supporting the verdict, plaintiff cannot successfully attack it. The case is over.[315]

Let us change one element of our hypothetical case. Assume that the jury returns a verdict for plaintiff. Now the judge must act upon his conviction that plaintiff's case is unsupported by substantial evidence by granting defendant's motion for judgment n.o.v. The judgment n.o.v. option also conserves time and effort in this setting. The trial judge's decision to grant defendant's motion for judgment n.o.v. may be affirmed on appeal. But a new trial should not be necessary even if he is reversed. The appellate court can merely reinstate the jury verdict. If, on the other hand, the trial court had granted defendant's motion for a directed verdict, reversal would have required an entirely new trial.[316]

A further justification for the added opportunity for decision provided by judgments n.o.v. may be that the quality of decisions will improve if the court has more time to decide. The court really cannot long delay sending the case to the jury in order to mull over a difficult directed verdict question. The prospect of a motion for judgment n.o.v. permits the court to consider the question for a substantially longer period of time.[317]

---

propriety of a directed verdict, as well as appeals from its grant, and also defers to the jury.").

[313] Or concludes that an unsettled question of law makes the decision whether to grant a directed verdict close, even if the evidence is clear. For example, when the legal definition of a particular claim is unsettled, evidence in the case may clearly support the claim as plaintiff defines it and fail with equal clarity to support the claim as defined by defendant.

[314] Appellate courts freely substitute their judgment for that of trial courts when reviewing directed verdicts. Like trial courts, they must draw all reasonable inferences favorable to the party opposed to the motion. MOORE § 50.92[1].

[315] Cf. WRIGHT & MILLER § 2533 ("If the jury agrees with the court's appraisal of the evidence, and returns a verdict for the party who moved for judgment as a matter of law, the case is at an end.").

[316] "For this reason the appellate courts have repeatedly said that it is usually desirable to take a verdict, and then pass on the sufficiency of the evidence on a post-verdict motion." WRIGHT & MILLER § 2533.

[317] The directed verdict motion flags the question for the court. The motion for judgment n.o.v. in federal court may come as late as 10 days after judgment. Rule 50(b). The trial court may not unduly delay decision on a motion for judgment n.o.v., but has more time to consider it than was practically available to consider the motion for a directed verdict.

Directed verdicts also make a discrete and important contribution. First, judgments n.o.v. would often be impossible if the judicial system did not also recognize the possibility of a directed verdict. A constitutional right to jury trial prevents grant of judgment n.o.v. by either the trial or the appellate court absent an earlier motion for directed verdict in federal courts and in the courts of some states.[318] Second, not all cases profit from delaying decision until after the jury has returned a verdict. Directed verdicts make it possible to terminate trial as soon as it becomes clear that the evidence fails to offer a legally permissible choice to the jury. This may be as soon as all the evidence is submitted, when plaintiff has submitted all of his evidence, or, in rare cases, even immediately after plaintiff gives his opening statement.[319]

[c] The Relationship of Directed Verdicts and Motions for Judgments N.O.V. to Earlier Motions for Deciding Cases in Lieu of Trial

Directed verdicts and judgments n.o.v. are the last in a series of five motions used to decide civil cases on the merits and thereby interrupt the ordinary trial process. The first such motion in federal court is a motion to dismiss for failure to state a claim upon which relief can be granted.[320] Motions for judgment on the pleadings[321] and for summary judgment[322] follow.

Apart from the recent amendment in Rule 50 consolidating directed verdicts and judgments n.o.v. into the single term, *judgment as a matter of law*, there are only a few attempts in the federal rules to inform the reader of the interrelationship of these motions.[323] Yet decisions, commentary and language in the rules support the conclusion that all pose the same test: *Do the established facts support a legal rule which should be applied to decide all or part of the case?*[324]

---

[318] On how the Seventh Amendment requires directed verdict motions as predicates for judgments n.o.v. in federal court, see § 12.09[3][a], *supra*. There is a constitutional right to jury trial in the courts of most states closely patterned on the Seventh Amendment. *See* Friedenthal, Kane & Miller § 11.7.

[319] In spite of the failure of Rule 50 to contemplate the last option, federal "courts continued to hold that they have power to direct a verdict on the opening statement but that the power should not be exercised if there is any doubt about the facts." Wright & Miller § 2533.

[320] Rule 12(b)(6), *discussed in* § 8.07[2][c], *supra*.

[321] Rule 12(c), *discussed in* § 8.07[1], *supra*.

[322] Rule 56, *discussed in* § 11.03, *supra*.

[323] For example, Rule 12(d) states that when "matters outside the pleadings are presented to and not excluded by the court, the [12(b)(6)] motion shall be treated as one for summary judgment . . . ."

[324] Rule 56(c) governing summary judgments makes explicit reference to the test, stating summary judgment "should be rendered" when affidavits or other types of materials deemed appropriate "show that there is no genuine issue as to any material fact and that the movant is entitled to a judgment as a matter of law." After recent amendments, Rule 50(2)(1) makes what was formerly termed directed verdict and judgment available upon a showing that "a reasonable jury would not have a legally sufficient evidentiary basis" to resolve the case differently; and that the movant is therefore entitled to "judgment as a matter of law." *See also* Rule 12(d) (consideration of matters outside the complaint converts a 12(b)(6) motion to one for summary judgment) & Rule

This is the same question posed by trial itself. We could thus administer this test without motions by sending every case to trial and treating every jury verdict as settled fact. If that was our system, however, it would have two major drawbacks. The facts in some cases are established long before trial. To require them to be tried would needlessly burden the party who holds what should be the winning cards and waste judicial resources. Therefore, the first three motions available permit termination of the case before trial begins. Second, treating jury verdicts as established fact may sometimes deny parties substantive justice. The last two motions offer protection here.

To better understand when and why it is appropriate to decide cases by motion rather than by the ordinary trial process, it is useful to examine our subject in larger perspective. Civil adjudication has two essential functions. One might be called a *law* function. The law function is to attach the proper legal significance to settled facts. The process of research, argument and deliberation making up the law function is indifferent to how or when facts are settled. Courts conclude civil adjudication by performing the law function and may do so as soon as they deem established those facts supporting a case-ending rule. The other essential in civil adjudication might be called the *fact* function. The fact function is to resolve factual controversies. The fact function often consumes a far larger amount of party and judicial resources than the law function.

The first three motions available to decide the merits (dismissal for failure to state a claim, judgment on the pleadings, and summary judgment) serve to reduce the cost of the fact function of civil adjudication. They do this by creating opportunities for courts to deem facts established as early as possible. The existence of three such motions reflects the realization that the point of the pretrial phase at which facts are established varies from case to case.[325] Substantially less time and effort will be saved by granting a directed verdict, none by granting judgment n.o.v.[326] The rationale for these motions derives instead from the need to preserve rights of the parties under substantive law. Jurors do not consider substantive law as such, but it determines the freedom they are given by the court's instructions to weigh the evidence in reaching a verdict.[327] When the evidence is such that jurors could find for a party only by exceeding that freedom, then a verdict for that party would do violence to the substantive rights of the opposing party.[328] The same concern does not arise in nonjury cases, since legal guardian and fact-finder are one. That explains why

---

12(c) (consideration of matters outside the pleadings converts a motion for judgment on the pleadings to one for summary judgment).

[325] In a Rule 12(b)(6) motion, defendant challenges plaintiff's legal theory by using as established fact plaintiff's own allegations. When completed pleadings create established fact, either party may move for judgment on the pleadings. When established facts necessary to decision can only be presented from sources outside the pleadings, either party may move for summary judgment.

[326] *Cf.* Robert J. Gregory, *One Too Many Rivers to Cross: Rule 50 Practice in the Modern Era of Summary judgment*, 23 Fla. St. U. L. Rev. 689 (1996) (arguing that relaxation of standards for summary judgment should diminish use of Rule 50 procedures).

[327] *See* § 12.08[3], *supra.*

[328] *See, e.g., Freund v. Nycomed Amersham*, 347 F.3d 752, 761 (9th Cir. 2003). *C.f. Wright &*

directed verdicts and judgments n.o.v. have no real counterpart in bench trials.[329] Motions for deciding cases without (or notwithstanding) trial reflect the procedural judgment that it is not always necessary or desirable to reach the merits through the ordinary process of trial. Trials are indispensable only in those cases where the facts never become established prior to trial, and juries have the last word only where the evidence provides reasonable support for either plaintiff or defendant's conflicting versions of the facts.

[d]   The Interrelationship of Post-Trial Motion Practice and Dispositions on Appeal

In most jurisdictions, the party against whom a verdict is returned may seek judgment n.o.v. or a new trial in the alternative.[330] The verdict-winner in federal court also may move for a new trial ten days after judgment n.o.v. (judgment as a matter of law) is granted against him.[331] In handling alternative motions, the trial court has a complete range of options. It may grant judgment n.o.v. and a new trial, deny both motions, or grant either motion while denying the other.[332] Each response carries its own implications for appellate review.[333]

When the district court denies judgment n.o.v., but grants new trial, its order is not immediately appealable in the federal system because there is no final judgment.[334] The party may raise the question of the validity of the new trial order only on appeal from an eventual final judgment after the second trial.[335]

When the district court denies judgment n.o.v. and new trial, both decisions are appealable in the normal course. On appeal, the party who prevailed on the

---

MILLER § 2522 (declaring Rule 50 to be "essential to the preservation and proper application of the applicable substantive law.").

[329] A federal litigant may move under Rule 41(b) for involuntary dismissal, but the motion is of relatively minor significance. See § 11.04 (involuntary dismissals), *supra*, § 912.10 (bench trials), *infra*.

[330] Rule 50(b). He need not await entry of judgment on the verdict in federal court. Rules 50(b) and 59(b) both require only that the motions be filed no later than ten days after entry of the judgment.

[331] Rule 50(c)(2).

[332] In rare cases, the court may deny judgment n.o.v. and order a new trial, when only a motion for judgment n.o.v. is before the court. The language of Rule 50(b) seems to provide for this. Yet the practice should be limited to cases where grounds for judgment n.o.v. exist but the court "believes that the defect in the proof might be remedied on a second trial, or if needed evidence was ruled out by some error of the court." WRIGHT & MILLER § 2538.

[333] For a more extended discussion of this process, see WRIGHT & MILLER § 2540; Note, *Post-Verdict Motions Under 50: Protecting the Verdict-Winner*, 53 MINN. L. REV. 358 (1968). On the limitation on federal interlocutory review, *see* § 13.04, *infra*.

[334] *See* § 13.03 (the final judgment rule), *infra. Cf. Allied Chem. Corp. v. Daiflon, Inc.*, 449 U.S. 33, 34 (1980) (emphasizing unavailability also of *mandamus* to review grant of new trial). An increasing number of state systems, however, do confer appellate jurisdiction over orders granting new trials. See FRIEDENTHAL, KANE & MILLER § 12.4; Rabinowitz, *Appellate Review of Trial Court Orders Granting New Trials*, 8 RUTGERS L. REV. 465 (1954).

[335] *Allied Chem.*, 449 U.S. at 34.

motion may argue grounds for a new trial in the event that the appellate court finds error in the denial of the motion for judgment n.o.v.[336] The appellate court may then enter judgment n.o.v., award a new trial, or remand for the trial court to make the new trial determination.[337]

When the district court grants the motion for judgment n.o.v., Rule 50(c) requires it also to rule conditionally on the new trial motion in anticipation of a possible reversal of the judgment n.o.v. on appeal. On appeal, the appellate court will either affirm judgment n.o.v. and end the matter, or reverse. In the event of reversal, when the district court has denied the motion for new trial, the appellate court may order entry of judgment on the verdict, reverse the denial of the motion for new trial and order a new trial, or remand the case to the trial court for reconsideration of the motion for new trial.[338]

When the district court grants the motion for judgment n.o.v. and conditionally grants new trial as well, there is a final judgment from which to appeal. Although the conditional grant of new trial is still technically nonfinal, it is practical to permit the appellate court to review the new trial order because the case is already before it on appeal of the judgment n.o.v. and it has already become familiar with much of the evidence in the case in ruling on that judgment. Rule 50(c)(1) therefore assumes that the appellate court may reach the new trial order if it reverses the judgment n.o.v.[339] In this event, the appellate court may remand the case to the trial court for new trial,[340] reverse the grant of the motion for new trial and order entry of judgment on the verdict, or remand the case to the trial court for reconsideration of the motion for new trial.[341]

§ 12.10 BENCH TRIALS (NON-JURY CASES)

Some cases are triable only before judges.[342] Others must be tried before a judge because the parties waive their jury claims.[343] Non-jury (bench) trials make up a significant portion of trial litigation.[344] Not only is the bench trial in

---

[336] Rule 50(d). *See Neely v. Martin K. Eby Constr. Co.*, 386 U.S. 317 (1967).

[337] Rule 50(d). On the authority of the court of appeals to enter a judgment as a matter of law directly, see *Weisgram v. Marley Co.*, 528 U.S. 440, 447–49 (2000).

[338] *Moore* § 50.94.

[339] However, use of any federal rule of civil or appellate procedure as authority for relaxing the finality requirement arguably exceeds the strictures of Federal Rule of Civil Procedure 82 and Federal Rule of Appellate Procedure 1(b) that the rules not be construed to expand jurisdiction.

[340] *Montgomery Ward & Co. v. Duncan*, 311 U.S. 243, 254 (1940) ("If the judgment were reversed, the case, on remand, would be governed by the trial judge's award of a new trial.").

[341] *Moore* § 50.94[2]. As noted earlier, trial courts enjoy considerable discretion in ordering new trials. *See* § 12.09[2], *supra*. However, perhaps because Rule 50(c)(1) explicitly entertains the possibility of reversal, conditional orders granting new trials appear somewhat more vulnerable. *See, e.g.*, the cases cited in *Wright & Miller* § 2540.

[342] The right to a jury trial is protected by constitutional or statutory law, *see* § 12.07[1], *supra*, and "no similar requirement protects trial by the court . . . ." *Beacon Theatres, Inc. v. Westover*, 359 U.S. 500, 510 (1959).

[343] *See* § 12.07[2], *supra*. At the same time, a "court may, if it wishes, submit an issue to an

extensive use, but "it raises . . . fewer procedural problems than does trial to a jury."[345]

The judge in a bench trial is both law enforcer *and* trier of fact. Since these functions are performed by the same person, distinctions between the two do not matter as they do in jury trials. Consequently, directed verdicts and judgments n.o.v., which protect against lawless jury verdicts, have no real counterpart in bench trials. A defendant in a bench trial may move for dismissal, or, in a federal court, for judgment as a matter of law, at the close of plaintiff's submission of evidence,[346] but unlike the motion for directed verdict, this motion is not to avert mischief by the fact-finder. The person ruling on the motion *is* the fact finder. In fact, under Rule 52(c), either party in a bench trial may move for judgment as a matter of law whenever his opponent has been fully heard with respect to a potentially dispositive issue of fact, and the court may (but need not) enter "judgment on partial findings" at any time it can appropriately make a finding of fact on that issue.[347]

Nor do new trial motions in jury trials have precise counterparts in bench trials. Most errors prompting new trial orders[348] occur only in jury trials.[349] When an error does arise in a bench trial, the court often simply rehears part of the case or reconsiders its decision.[350] Yet bench trials are not easier than jury trials in all respects. They can put quite a strain on judges who must rule on the admissibility of evidence and consider its weight if admitted, at roughly the same time.[351]

Federal Rule 52(a) requires the court to make findings of fact in non-jury cases or when the jury is used only in an advisory capacity. Often the trial court will direct the prevailing party to prepare proposed findings of fact and the

---

advisory jury on its own initiative, but the verdict of such a jury is advisory only, and the ultimate responsibility for finding the facts remains with the court." WRIGHT & MILLER § 92. Professor Wright adds: "In an action not triable to a jury as of right, the court may, with the consent of both parties, order a trial with a jury whose verdict has the same effect as if trial by jury had been a matter of right." WRIGHT & MILLER § 92.

[344] *Beacon Theatres, Inc.*, 359 U.S. 500 (reporting that more federal cases are tried before judges than before juries).

[345] *Beacon Theatres, Inc.*, 359 U.S. at 644.

[346] *See* Rule 52(c).

[347] Rule 52(c) advisory committee's notes (1991).

[348] *See* § 12.09[2][a], *supra*.

[349] "Although theoretically new trial motions may be granted in judge as well as jury trials, . . . the type of errors meriting a new trial typically arise only in jury trials. For example, even if the court erroneously receives certain evidence in a nonjury trial, the judge simply may disregard that evidence when rendering judgment, avoiding the need for a new trial." FRIEDENTHAL, KANE & MILLER § 12.4.

[350] Thus, motions for rehearing or for reconsideration are probably more common than motions for new trial in bench trials. Indeed, Rule 59 authorizes new trial in bench trials "for any reason for which rehearing has heretofore been granted in a suit in equity . . . ."

[351] For an examination of bench trials from the perspective of the trial judge, see Roger S. Haydock & John Sonsteng, *Court Trial Empirical Survey: Interview Responses From Trial Judges Explaining Their Experiences and Views Regarding the Trial of Non-jury Cases*, 11 WM. MITCHELL L. REV. 775 (1985).

loser to object, as appropriate, and then craft its own findings from the submissions. The appellate courts have sharply chastised the trial courts which do this uncritically, citing the "potential for overreaching and exaggeration on the part of attorneys preparing findings of fact when they have already been informed that the judge has decided in their favor."[352] When, however, the trial court provides a framework for the proposed findings by its bench ruling, the loser takes the opportunity to respond to them, and the court does not simply adopt the findings verbatim, the Supreme Court has approved the process.[353]

Rule 52 states that, on appeal, "[f]indings of fact, whether based on oral or other evidence, must not be set aside unless clearly erroneous, and the reviewing court must give due regard to the trial court to judge the witnesses' credibility." Thus, judgment in a bench trial differs from summary judgment in that the judge's fact findings in a bench trial are reversible only if clearly erroneous; summary judgment is not similarly shielded on review by the clearly erroneous standard because it is based on the judge's determination, *as a matter of law*, that the material facts are without genuine dispute.[354] Section 13.09[2][b], *infra*, discusses standards of appellate review.

§ 12.11 JUDGMENTS

[1] The Nature and Force of Judgments

Defining the term in a broad sense, Federal Rule 54(a) states that "Judgment . . . includes a decree and any order from which an appeal lies." The rule thus ties judgments to final orders and a small class of interlocutory orders appealable in federal court.[355]

This definition fails to capture the functional significance judgments have in completing the case. In federal court, judgment follows decision. *Decision* describes determinations of fact made by the judge's findings or by jury verdict. *Judgment* "is the pronouncement of that decision and the act that gives it legal effect."[356] The judgment is filed by delivery to the district court clerk and entered through recording by the clerk.[357] While the act of entry is not performed by the court, it is nonetheless important to the force and effect of the judgment.[358]

---

[352] *Anderson v. Bessemer City*, 470 U.S. 564, 572 (1985); *Ramey Constr. Co. v. Apache Tribe of Mescalero Reservation*, 616 F.2d 464, 466–68 (10th Cir. 1980) (emphasizing also the effect of judicial origination of findings on the quality of decision-making). *See* Kristen Fjeldstad, *Just the Facts, Ma'am — A Review of the Practice of the Verbatim Adoption of Findings of Fact and Conclusions of Law*, 44 St. Louis U. L.J. 197 (2000).

[353] *Anderson*, 470 U.S. at 572.

[354] Rule 52(c) advisory committee's notes (1991 amendment).

[355] *See* §§ 13.03–13.05, *supra*.

[356] Wright & Miller § 2651.

[357] Rule 58.

[358] "[I]t is crucial to the effectiveness of the judgment and for measuring the time periods for appeal and the filing of various post-trial motions." Wright & Miller § 2651.

The significance of a judgment can be twofold. First, judgment either for damages[359] or an injunction[360] gives the judgment-holder leverage over the person against whom the judgment was rendered. The money-judgment-holder has access to special procedures to expedite payment of the award.[361] One ordered to behave a certain way by an injunction must do so or suffer civil and possibly criminal contempt.[362] Second, judgments final and on the merits preclude parties in the future from relitigating issues and whole claims which might otherwise consume time, money and scarce judicial resources.[363]

[2] Resisting the Preclusive Effect of Final Judgments

Parties disadvantaged by judgments must consider what if anything they can do to improve their lot when the judgment has become final — that is to say, when appeal has been unsuccessful or the time for taking an appeal has elapsed. Three approaches are considered below. One can prevail upon a subsequent court presented with the judgment to declare it unenforceable because it is defective (collateral attack), one can try to be excused from the judgment (extraordinary relief), or one can try to make the judgment more agreeable (amendment).

[a] Collateral Attack[364]

So strong is the need to resolve controversies and such is the force of preclusion doctrine that parties are not free to relitigate a prior judgment just because it was wrong on the merits.[365]

There are only a few paths of escape, known as points of collateral attack. The most important are the guarantee of notice and the constraint on territorial jurisdiction which is part of the law of constitutional due process. The likelihood that these or the few other grounds for collaterally attacking judgments[366] will be available in a given case is remote.

[b] Extraordinary Relief

When the time for direct attack on the judgment by motion for judgment n.o.v. or for new trial or by appeal has expired, many jurisdictions provide limited extraordinary relief from the judgment by further motion in the trial

---

[359] On damages, see generally § 14.01. *infra.*

[360] On injunctions, see generally § 14.02, *infra.*

[361] On the nature of money-judgment enforcement proceedings, see § 15.02, *infra.*

[362] On the prerequisites for civil and criminal contempt, see § 14.02[2], *infra.*

[363] On the prerequisite to claim preclusion that judgments be final and on the merits, see § 15.05, *infra.*

[364] On the meaning of collateral attack and how it differs from direct attack, see § 3.04, *supra.*

[365] *See, e.g., Milliken v. Meyer,* 311 U.S. 457, 462 (1940); *Federated Dep't Stores, Inc. v. Moitie,* 452 U.S. 394, 398 (1981) (stating that the "*res judicata* consequences of a final, unappealed judgment [are not] altered by the fact that the judgment may have been wrong . . . .").

[366] They are discussed in § 3.04[2], *supra.*

court. Federal Rule 60 is typical. Rule 60 sorts problems into serious and not-so-serious categories.

Subdivision (a) addresses the second category, correction by the district court of "'clerical' mistakes — mistakes that cause a judgment, order, or other part of the record to reflect something other than what was actually decided or what actually transpired."[367] Subdivision (b) addresses the first category:

> (1) mistake, inadvertence, surprise, or excusable neglect; (2) newly discovered evidence that, with reasonable diligence, could not have been discovered in time to move for a new trial under Rule 59(b); (3) fraud (whether previously called intrinsic or extrinsic), misrepresentation, or misconduct of an opposing party; (4) the judgment is void; (5) the judgment has been satisfied, released, or discharged; it is based on an earlier judgment that has been reversed or vacated; or applying it prospectively is no longer equitable; or (6) any other reason that justifies relief.

Subdivision (c) states that grounds (1)–(3) must be offered no later than a year from judgment.

It is not easy to obtain relief from a judgment under this provision, but easier certainly than it is to attack collaterally the legal sufficiency of the judgment offered for enforcement in a later lawsuit.[368] Space permits only a few specific comments on the grounds listed in Rule 60(b).[369]

Ground (1) is especially suited to relief from default judgments.[370] Rule 55 treats entry of a default and entry of judgment on the default as separate stages. "The court may set aside an entry of default for good cause" when it is unaccompanied by judgment.[371] The void-judgment category of ground (4) is limited to a judgment "void only on grounds of lack of jurisdiction or for some failure of due process in the original proceeding."[372] Finally, despite the open-ended phrasing of ground (6), courts have evinced understandable hesitation in using it. It seems to exist for "unusual cases" and "not for the

---

[367] MOORE § 60.02[1]. *See generally* Theodore A. Donahue, Jr., *A History and Interpretation of Rule 60(a) of the Federal Rules of Civil Procedure*, 42 DRAKE L. REV. 461 (1993).

[368] See the discussion of collateral attack, § 12.11[2][a], *supra*.

[369] The United States Supreme Court reaffirmed the limitation of Rule 60(b) to extraordinary cases in *United States v. Beggerly*, 524 U.S. 38, 47 (1998) ("under the Rule, an independent action should be available only to prevent a grave miscarriage of justice."). For extended discussion of the grounds, see WRIGHT & MILLER §§ 2846–2864.

[370] *See* FRIEDENTHAL, KANE & MILLER § 12.6, (noting it "most frequently is invoked successfully in the default setting or when the plaintiff's suit was dismissed for failure to prosecute and judgment was entered by mistake since the party fully intended actively to litigate the dispute."). *See generally* Peter H. Bresnan & James P. Cornelio, Note, *Relief From Default Judgments Under Rule 60(b) — A Study of Federal Case Law*, 49 FORDHAM L. REV. 956 (1981). To succeed in having a default judgment vacated, one may have to demonstrate the existence of a "meritorious defense," WRIGHT & MILLER § 2862, unless the judgment was procured without notice. *See Peralta v. Heights Medical Center, Inc.*, 485 U.S. 80 (1988).

[371] Rule 55(c). *See generally* § 11.02 (default judgments), *supra*.

[372] FRIEDENTHAL, KANE & MILLER § 12.6.

purpose of relieving a party from free, calculated, and deliberate choices he has made."[373]

[c] Amendment

Rule 59(e) gives parties in federal court a brief opportunity to seek amendment of judgment. Rule 59(e) motions resemble in purpose those filed under Rule 60(a).[374] The purpose of each is to give true effect to the judgment by eliminating unwitting error.[375]

However, the motions differ in several respects. Rule 59(e) motions must be filed within ten days from entry of judgment. Timely filing keeps the judgment from becoming final for purposes of appeal. A Rule 60(a) motion can be made at any time without affecting the time for appeal.[376] Moreover, while the focus of Rule 60(a) is on clerical mistakes, Rule 59(e) contemplates mistakes by the court.[377]

---

[373] WRIGHT & MILLER § 2864. "A party remains under a duty to take legal steps to protect his own interests. In particular, it ordinarily is not permissible to use this motion to remedy a failure to take an appeal." *Id. See, e.g., Primus Auto Fin. Servs. v. Otto-Wal, Inc.*, 284 F. Supp. 2d 845, 847-48 (N.D. Ohio 2003).

[374] *Discussed in* § 12.11[2][b], *supra*.

[375] Parties cannot use Rule 59(e) or Rule 60(a) to alter the intended effect of a judgment. These motions are confined "to clerical errors or matters of clear oversight, not questions involving the right to additional recovery, or a reduction in an award." *FRIEDENTHAL, KANE & MILLER* § 12.6. Such substantial changes require a motion for new trial made no later than ten days after entry of judgment, or a motion for relief from the judgment, which may or may not be subject to a one-year time limit depending on the ground for relief used. *See* § 12.11[2][b], *supra*.

[376] *MOORE* § 60.12.

[377] *Boaz v. Mutual Life Insurance Co. of New York*, 146 F.2d 321 (8th Cir. 1944), is frequently offered as an illustration. There the trial court corrected its error, granting defendant's motion to amend the judgment from dismissal of plaintiff's case without prejudice to dismissal with prejudice. The present version of Rule 59(e) codifies this authority. *WRIGHT & MILLER* § 2810.1. *See, e.g., Venegas-Hernandez v. Sonolux Records*, 370 F.3d 183, 189 (1st Cir. 2004); *United States v. $23,000 in United States Currency*, 356 F.3d 157, 165 n.9 (1st Cir. 2004).

Chapter 13

APPEAL

§ 13.01 OVERVIEW

Appeal is the submission of a lower court's disposition of a matter to the review of a higher court.[1] One purpose of appeal is to *ensure the correctness* of lower court dispositions.[2] This purpose is reflected by the availability in most judicial systems of at least one layer of obligatory review — appeal as of right. Another purpose of appeal is *institutional review* to assure uniformity in the application of law and to furnish guidance to the lower courts. In many judicial systems, this systemic purpose is served by the availability of some form of discretionary appeal — appeal by permission — to the system's highest court, which allows it to pick and choose its cases for optimal institutional benefit.[3] Both of these purposes of appeal may be at odds with two other objectives of procedural systems: *efficiency* and *finality*. These objectives call for technical (some would say grudging) application of many procedures for appeal, lest the proceedings of the lower courts be disrupted or their judgments devalued by too ready appeal. Consequently, the law of appeal can be viewed as a fine balance of concern for correctness and uniformity of disposition on one hand,

---

[1] *Rehearing* serves the same purposes as appeal but submits the disposition to review by the same court, although sometimes a different or fuller panel. *See generally* David W. Louisell & Ronan E. Degnan, *Rehearing in American Appellate Courts*, 44 CAL. L. REV. 627 (1956). A federal *habeas corpus* action effectively submits the state court system's disposition of a criminal case to the review of a federal district court, but that review is only to test the constitutional validity of state detention after the normal course of state appeals and not to test the accuracy of the state courts' judgments. *See* 28 U.S.C. §§ 2241–2255. *Removal* is a procedure for withdrawing the case from the jurisdiction of one court and lodging it with another before any disposition, and therefore is not a form of appeal. *De novo* review may be and is here considered an appeal, but it is a do-over, not a review; the appeals court decides the matter anew without regard to the prior disposition by the lower court.

[2] *See generally* Steven Shavell, *The Appeals Process as a Means of Error Correction*, 24 J. LEGAL STUD. 379 (1995).

[3]

> No litigant is entitled to more than two chances, namely, to the original trial and to a review, and the intermediate courts of review are provided for that purpose. When a case goes beyond that, it is not primarily to preserve the rights of the litigants. The Supreme Court's function is for the purpose of expounding and stabilizing principles of law for the benefit of the people of the country, passing upon constitutional questions and other important questions of law for the public benefit. It is to preserve the uniformity of decision among the intermediate courts of appeal.

Testimony by Chief Justice Taft regarding the "Judges' Bill," *quoted in Dick v. New York Life Ins. Co.*, 359 U.S. 437, 448 (1959) (Frankfurter, J., dissenting). *See generally* Craig M. Bradley, *The Uncertainty Principle in the Supreme Court*, 1986 DUKE L.J. 1.

and efficiency and finality on the other.

Appeal poses five questions: when, where, how, what, and how much? *When* is the question of appealability, discussed in Part A. *Where* and *how* are questions of perfecting the appeal, discussed in Part B. *What* and *how much* are questions of the scope and intensity of review, discussed in Part C.

PART A.
When? Appealability

§ 13.02 APPEALABILITY IN GENERAL

Appealability poses a choice between appeal of the final judgment at the end of the litigation and one or more *interlocutory* appeals during its course. These alternatives can be compared using the following formula:

> The costs of allowing interlocutory appeals are the costs of an unnecessary extra appeal if the trial judge turns out to have been correct. (The appeal is an extra one because an appeal will still be allowed at the end.) The costs of not allowing interlocutory appeals are those of an unnecessary or an unnecessarily long trial if the trial judge turns out to have been wrong. If we assume that the costs of an unnecessary extra appeal are approximately the same as the costs of the unnecessary or unnecessarily long trial, the overall costs are proportional to the number of times the trial judge is right versus the number of times he is wrong. If trial judges are right more often than they are wrong (measured by eventual reversal when appeal finally occurs), then the general policy should disfavor interlocutory appeals.[4]

In fact, most trial court rulings are affirmed,[5] and the general policy in the federal system and in most states disfavors interlocutory appeals. On the other hand, a few states assess the costs and benefits differently and allow routine interlocutory appeal.[6] Section 13.03, *infra*, uses the federal system to discuss

---

[4] STEPHEN C. YEAZELL, CIVIL PROCEDURE 848 (6th ed. 2004). Copyright © by Aspen Law & Business. Reprinted with permission. *See also Richardson-Merrell, Inc. v. Koller*, 472 U.S. 424, 434 (1985) (performing cost-benefit analysis to deny interlocutory appeal of order disqualifying counsel); *Reise v. Board of Regents of Univ. of Wis.*, 957 F.2d 293, 295 (7th Cir. 1992), *cert. denied*, 510 U.S. 892 (1993):

> Because almost all interlocutory appeals from discovery orders would end in affirmance (the district court possesses discretion, and review is deferential), the costs of delay via appeal, and the costs to the judicial system of entertaining these appeals, exceed in the aggregate the costs of the few erroneous discovery orders that might be corrected were appeals available.

[5] WRIGHT & MILLER § 3907. For the twelve months ended Sept. 30, 2007, only 8.3% of the appeals terminated on the merits in federal appellate courts were reversals; over 86% were affirmances or dismissals. 2007 JUD. BUS. OF THE U.S. CTS. ANN. REP. OF THE DIRECTOR, Table B-5, at 113.

[6] *See, e.g.*, N.Y. CIV. PRAC. L. & R. 5701(a)(2)(iv) & (v) (McKinney, through Leg. Sess. 2000) (allowing interlocutory appeal of any order which "involves some part of the merits" or which

the general policy against interlocutory appeal.

Even in the majority of jurisdictions that disfavor interlocutory appeals, there are exceptions. These include cases in which the costs of error are particularly large and irreversible, the alleged errors involve unresolved questions of law increasing the likelihood of error by the trial judge, or where issues are presented that, as a practical matter, will be lost to a party before appeal from a final judgment can be taken. Interlocutory appeal can have important benefits, as the Supreme Court has explained.

> In certain cases, it may avoid injustice by quickly correcting a trial court's error. It can simplify, or more appropriately direct, the future course of litigation. And, it can thereby reduce the burdens of future proceedings, perhaps freeing a party from those burdens entirely.[7]

Sections 13.04 and 13.05, *infra*, use the federal system to illustrate typical statutory and judge-made exceptions to the general policy against interlocutory appeal.

§ 13.03 FINAL JUDGMENT RULE

[1] In General

In most jurisdictions, statute or decisional law has made an entry of final judgment a jurisdictional prerequisite to appeal.[8] The court of appeals must satisfy itself that a final judgment was entered below or dismiss the appeal, whether or not the parties raise this issue.[9] The final judgment rule, or rule against piecemeal appeals, is that the parties can only appeal from a final judgment on all claims in the action, whether the alleged errors are in that judgment or in the pretrial or trial procedures leading to it. The rule thus does not go to *whether* such errors may be appealed, but only *when*. It serves simply "to combine in one review all stages of the proceeding that effectively may be reviewed and corrected if and when final judgment results."[10]

The cost analysis that underlies all questions of appealability suggests that a primary purpose of the final judgment rule[11] is to avoid extra and

---

"affects a substantial right"). *See generally* Harold L. Korn, *Civil Jurisdiction of the New York Court of Appeals and Appellate Division*, 16 Buffalo L. Rev. 307 (1967).

[7] *Johnson v. Jones*, 515 U.S. 304, 309–10 (1995).

[8] *See, e.g.*, 28 U.S.C. § 1291 (granting federal courts of appeals jurisdiction of appeals "from all final decisions" of the district courts). Congress has given the Supreme Court power to define when a district court ruling is final for purposes of appeal under section 1291. 28 U.S.C. § 2072(c). *See generally* Robert J. Martineau, *Defining Finality and Appealability by Court Rule: Right Problem, Wrong Solution*, 54 U. Pitt. L. Rev. 717 (1993).

[9] *Brown Shoe Co. v. United States*, 370 U.S. 294, 305 (1962).

[10] *Cohen v. Beneficial Indus. Loan Corp.*, 337 U.S. 541, 546 (1949).

[11] On this and other purposes of the rule, see generally Elizabeth G. Thornburg, *Interlocutory Review of Discovery Orders: An Idea Whose Time Has Come*, 44 Sw. L.J. 1045, 1047–49 (1990); Note, *Appealability in the Federal Courts*, 75 Harv. L. Rev. 351, 351–52 (1961); Wright & Miller § 3907.

unnecessary appeals: interlocutory appeals that might be mooted by the further course of litigation should the trial judge change her interlocutory decision or the interlocutory appellant ultimately prevail. The rule also promotes consolidation of alleged errors in a single appeal, permitting appellate review of each of them in the context of the whole and on the fullest trial court record.[12] At the same time, the rule helps to expedite the proceedings in the trial court by protecting them from appellate interruption. This promotes efficiency and also comity — the institutional goal of "maintaining the appropriate relationship" between the trial and appellate courts[13] and respect for trial court decisions. Finally, the rule guards against tactical abuse of appeal to harass and delay.

Rule 58 makes it easy to identify when a judgment has been entered by requiring judgments to be set forth on a separate document. But whether the judgment is also final has proven a more elusive question. The Supreme Court has declared that a final judgment "ends the litigation on the merits and leaves nothing for the court to do but execute the judgment."[14] Thus, a trial court decision of liability, but not of all damages, is interlocutory. On the other hand, a decision to grant a permanent injunction is final if no other remedy is sought, even though the court nominally retains jurisdiction to ensure compliance. Other applications of the concept are more problematic.[15] Uncertainty exists because the courts have sensibly taken a "pragmatic approach to the question of finality" that precludes the formulation of any precise verbal formula for deciding it.[16]

Federal courts carried pragmatism too far in according finality to refusals to certify suits as class actions. The argument was that such decisions sounded a "death knell" for the litigation because the plaintiffs found it economically imprudent to pursue their claims individually without the incentive of a possible group recovery.[17] Rejecting this view, the Supreme Court noted in *Coopers & Lybrand v. Livesay*[18] that this logic would apply with equal force to

---

[12] Indeed, one scholar has traced the final judgment rule at common law to the need for a full record below. *See* Carleton M. Crick, *The Final Judgment as Basis for Appeal*, 41 YALE L.J. 539, 542–43 (1932).

[13] *Coopers & Lybrand v. Livesay*, 437 U.S. 463, 476 (1978), *quoting Parkinson v. April Indus. Inc.*, 520 F.2d 650, 654 (2d Cir. 1975).

[14] *Catlin v. United States*, 324 U.S. 229, 233 (1945). Requests for attorney's fees are not part of the merits and their pendency does not affect the finality of a decision on the merits. *Budinich v. Becton Dickinson & Co.*, 486 U.S. 196 (1988).

[15] *Compare Catlin*, 324 U.S. at 232–33 (decree of title in condemnation case is not final decision, when question of compensation is still open), *with Brown Shoe Co. v. United States*, 370 U.S. 294, 305 (1962) (order of divestiture in antitrust case is final decision, even though question how divestiture is to be accomplished is still open).

[16] *Brown Shoe*, 370 U.S. at 306. Professor Wright suggests that the saving grace of the courts' approach is that "in almost all situations it is entirely clear" from the nature of the order or the decisional law that the order is or is not final. WRIGHT § 101.

[17] Typically, the prospective individual recovery was insufficient incentive in light of plaintiffs' liability for their own attorney's fees, which might otherwise come out of a class recovery. *See* § 9.09 (class actions), *supra*.

[18] 437 U.S. 463 (1978).

many interlocutory orders in ordinary litigation, from venue to discovery and summary judgment, "that may have such tactical economic significance that a defeat is tantamount to a 'death knell' for the entire case."[19] Moreover, whether such orders did sound the death knell would turn on the courts' perception of their impact on the parties in particular cases. The Court concluded that the death-knell doctrine undermined efficient judicial administration by eroding the final judgment rule, while requiring "individualized jurisdictional inquiry" into the financial stamina of the would-be class representatives from case to case.[20]

The *Coopers & Lybrand* Court therefore held "that the fact that an interlocutory order may induce a party to abandon his claim before final judgment is not a sufficient reason for considering it a 'final decision' within the meaning of [28 U.S.C.] § 1291."[21] Interestingly, the rules were amended in 1998 to give appellate courts the discretion to permit an interlocutory appeal from an order granting or denying class-action certification.[22] But *Coopers & Lybrand* may well have sounded the death knell for other applications of this kind of pragmatic approach to appellate jurisdiction.[23]

[2]   Finality in Multi-Claim and Multi-Party Cases

Literal application of the final judgment rule in cases involving multiple claims or parties would prohibit appeal of decisions on individual claims until all have been decided. The result could often be to delay for years review and execution of early-decided claims. On the other hand, if immediate appeal of such decisions were allowed, they would have to be clearly identified as final or parties would be uncertain when to appeal to protect their rights. Rule 54(b) provides the solution in the federal system, authorizing the trial court in multi-claim actions to make "direct entry of a final judgment" on fewer than all of the claims or parties upon "if the court expressly determines that there is no just cause for delay."[24] Rule 54(b) is not an exception to the final judgment rule, but only a statutory standard for its application in multi-claim and multi-party cases.[25] It applies to trial court decisions that would have been appealable final judgments standing alone but for the liberal joinder permitted by the federal rules.

---

[19] 437 U.S. at 470.

[20] 437 U.S. at 473.

[21] 437 U.S. at 477 (footnote omitted).

[22] Rule 23(f). *See* Aimee G. Mackay, *Appealability of Class Certification Orders Under Federal Rule of Civil Procedure 23(f): Towards a Principled Approach*, 96 Nw. U.L. Rev. 755 (2002).

[23] *But see* Wright & Miller § 3912.

[24] Of course, a party with multiple claims could also "manufacture" a final judgment by voluntarily dismissing (*see* § 11.04[1], *supra*) other claims after a court has ruled on the one it wishes to appeal. *See* Rebecca A. Cochran, *Gaining Appellate Review by "Manufacturing" a Final Judgment Through Voluntary Dismissal of Peripheral Claims*, 48 Mercer L. Rev. 979 (1997).

[25] *Sears, Roebuck & Co. v. Mackey*, 351 U.S. 427, 435 (1956). The courts are divided on Rule 54(b)'s application in cases that have been consolidated under Rule 42(a). *See* Jacqueline Gerson, Note, *The Appealability of Partial Judgments in Consolidated Cases*, 57 U. Chi. L. Rev. 169 (1990).

A threshold issue on appeal is whether the trial court has finally disposed of an individual *claim* in a multi-claim or multi-party case or merely one of several legal *theories* or alternative *requests for relief* on a single claim. The trial court's determination is not controlling; the appeals court must decide for itself. In *Liberty Mutual Insurance Co. v. Wetzel*,[26] for example, the plaintiff alleged employment discrimination and sought injunctive relief, damages, and attorney's fees. The trial court granted plaintiffs' motion for partial summary judgment and then purported to direct entry of final judgment pursuant to Rule 54(b) on the issue of liability. Defendant appealed.

The Supreme Court ruled that, notwithstanding entry of judgment under Rule 54(b), the trial court had not finally adjudicated a separate claim for purposes of appeal. Treatment of the liability determination as a declaratory judgment[27] would not alter this since Rule 54(b) is *claim* rather than relief-focused. The Court held that a "complaint asserting only one legal right, even if seeking multiple remedies for the alleged violation of that right, states a single claim for relief."[28] Since plaintiffs advanced "but one legal theory" (employment discrimination in violation of federal law) applicable to only one set of facts, and since the ruling on liability left open questions of injunctive relief and damages, Rule 54(b) was inapplicable.[29]

The Court expressly refrained from resolving definitively what constitutes a claim for relief under the rules, but its analysis is reminiscent of the tests for deciding a cause of action for purposes of *res judicata* or claim preclusion.[30] In the same vein, the Second Circuit Court of Appeals has suggested using the test of whether the action involves theories of recovery that could be separately enforced.[31] The Seventh and D.C. Circuit Courts of Appeals noted the affinity to preclusion, holding that when alleged "claims [are] so closely related that they would fall afoul of the rule against splitting claims [under the law of claim preclusion] if brought separately," they do not qualify as separate claims within the meaning of Rule 54(b).[32]

To understand these tests, consider a suit for personal injuries in which the plaintiff alleges several different bases for relief — simple negligence, gross negligence, breach of implied warranty, and breach of express warranty. Summary judgment on any one such basis would not be appealable as judgment on a separate claim under Rule 54(b) because each is an alternative legal theory applicable to the same basic set of facts, and they all assert but one legal right to freedom from personal injury. If plaintiff pursued an action

---

[26] 424 U.S. 737 (1976).

[27] *See* § 14.03 (declaratory relief), *infra*.

[28] *Wetzel*, 424 U.S. at 743 n.4.

[29] 424 U.S. at 743.

[30] *See* § 15.03, *infra*.

[31] *Rieser v. Baltimore & Ohio R.R.*, 224 F.2d 198, 199 (2d Cir. 1955) (Clark, J.), *cert. denied*, 350 U.S. 1006 (1956).

[32] *Local P-171, Amalgamated Meat Cutters & Butcher Workmen v. Thompson Farms*, 642 F.2d 1065, 1070–71 (7th Cir. 1981) (adding as another "rule[] of thumb" the test whether separate recovery is possible on each claim); *Tolson v. United States*, 732 F.2d 998 (D.C. Cir. 1984).

to judgment on any one of these theories, he would be precluded in most jurisdictions from suing separately upon the rest under the doctrine of claim preclusion; separating the action by theories would be splitting a cause of action. Allowing a litigant, even with the assent of the trial court under Rule 54(b), to define a claim as any one such theory while others remain for decision would permit evasion of the final judgment rule.

If Rule 54(b) applies, the trial judge must additionally determine that "there is no just reason for delay" in entering final judgment. In part, this involves consideration whether the claims are so interrelated (though separate) that efficient appeal requires review only as a single unit.[33] By this reasoning, for example, there may be just reason for delay when the remaining claims include a possible set-off to the separate claim and therefore ought to be considered together, or when they will inevitably present the same issues on appeal as are presented by the separate claim.[34] Determination of "no just reason for delay" also involves consideration of the equities in the litigation, such as a disparity between the statutory and market rates of interest that would cause a claimant to lose money from any delay in execution on a separate claim.[35]

Since the trial judge can best assess the relevant considerations, both determinations are reviewable only for abuse of discretion.[36] An abuse of discretion occurs, for example, when the trial court finds "no just cause for delay" simply because early appellate review of its ruling on the sufficiency of the evidence might avoid possible retrial of the entire case. The Second Circuit Court of Appeals has held that

> absent any special circumstances indicating that adherence to the normal and federally preferred practice of postponing appeal until after a final judgment has been entered, disposing of all the claims of all the parties, will cause an unusual hardship or work an injustice, the district court's preference to have pretrial appellate review of its assessment of the sufficiency of the evidence to support a given claim is an improper basis for entry of an immediate partial final judgment.[37]

§ 13.04 STATUTORY INTERLOCUTORY APPEAL

[1] Statutory Interlocutory Appeal as of Right

Justification for immediate review of interlocutory orders is greatest when they have immediate and irreparable consequences. Then the cost of possible error outweighs the cost of an extra appeal, and there can be no effective later appeal at final judgment. Many jurisdictions allow interlocutory appeal of such orders by statute. As exceptions to the final judgment rule, such provisions are

---

[33] *See Curtiss-Wright Corp. v. General Elec. Co.*, 446 U.S. 1, 10 (1980).

[34] *See Curtiss-Wright Corp.*, 446 U.S. at 8.

[35] 446 U.S. at 11.

[36] *See* § 13.10[2][d], *infra*.

[37] *Hogan v. Consolidated Rail Corp.*, 961 F.2d 1021, 1026 (2d Cir. 1992).

strictly construed, and the scope of appeal is typically limited to issues involving only the interlocutory order.[38] The federal interlocutory appeal provisions are illustrative.

Section 1292(a)(1) authorizes appeal of interlocutory orders granting, modifying, refusing, or otherwise affecting injunctions.[39] Orders granting or denying an interlocutory injunction can be as important to the parties as the court's eventual decision whether to grant a permanent injunction.[40] The court's decision has immediate effect, either requiring a party to take or refrain from action or permitting an allegedly harmful action or condition to continue. Costs of error under the circumstances are sufficiently great to justify immediate appellate review.

Section 1292(a)(1) extends to orders addressing motions for preliminary injunctions. Because of the wording of the statute, however, some doubt exists concerning its applicability to temporary restraining orders.[41] Rule 65 provides for both types of interlocutory injunction.[42] Once it seemed settled that temporary restraining orders were not appealable under the statute. But "[t]he cases seem to be edging slowly toward a principle that rulings with respect to temporary restraining orders are appealable on a sufficiently strong showing of potential irreparable injury."[43]

Because the justification for immediate appellate review is practical, the federal courts look to the practical effect of trial court rulings and not to whether they expressly address injunctive relief. Yet "a litigant must show more than that the order has the practical effect of refusing [or granting] an injunction"; he must also show that it might have "serious, perhaps, irreparable, consequence," and that it can be " 'effectually challenged' only by immediate appeal."[44] The Supreme Court has thus held that the denial of summary judgment in an action for a permanent injunction did not qualify for immediate appeal, because appellants failed to show that it would cause them irreparable harm during the lawsuit, and because permanent injunctive relief might have been obtained after trial.[45] The Court also concluded that denial of class certification in a sex discrimination suit seeking permanent injunctive

---

[38] *See, e.g.,* WRIGHT § 102 (discussing 28 U.S.C. § 1292(a)(1)). Congress has given the Supreme Court rulemaking power to provide for interlocutory appeals not otherwise provided for by the interlocutory appeal statute. 28 U.S.C. § 1292(e). *See generally* Martineau, note 8, *supra.*

[39] 28 U.S.C. § 1292(a). Similar provisions are common in state law as well. *See, e.g.,* MD. CODE ANN., CTS. & JUD. PRO. CODE ANN. § 12-303 (LEXIS through 2007 Reg. Sess.). On injunctions generally, see § 14.02, *infra.*

[40] *See generally* Susan H. Black, *A New Look at Preliminary Injunctions,* 36 ALA. L. REV. 1 (1984); John Leubsdorf, *The Standard for Preliminary Injunctions,* 91 HARV. L. REV. 525 (1978).

[41] On distinctions between preliminary injunctions and temporary restraining orders generally, see § 14.02[2], *infra*; Bernard J. Nussbaum, *Temporary Restraining Orders and Preliminary Injunctions — The Federal Practice,* 26 SW. L.J. 265 (1972).

[42] *See* § 14.02[2] (provisional equitable relief), *infra.*

[43] WRIGHT § 102. *But see* WRIGHT & MILLER § 2962.

[44] *Carson v. American Brands, Inc.,* 450 U.S. 79, 85 (1981), *quoting Baltimore Contractors, Inc. v. Bodinger,* 348 U.S. 176, 181 (1955).

[45] *Switzerland Cheese Ass'n, Inc. v. E. Horne's Market, Inc.,* 385 U.S. 23 (1966).

relief was not immediately appealable; appellant had not sought preliminary injunctive relief nor made any showing of direct and irreparable consequences from the order.[46] In contrast, one federal circuit court has held that an order refusing to enter a consent decree, though not phrased in terms of injunctive relief, was immediately appealable. The order had the effect of denying an injunction directing defendants to restructure their transfer and promotion policies as provided in the proposed consent order, and it imposed irreparable costs by denying the parties the benefits of their negotiated settlement and exposing them to the burden and uncertainties of litigation.[47] The federal statute also makes immediately appealable orders appointing receivers, or refusing to wind up receiverships or to direct sales or other disposals of property.[48] The possible immediate and irreversible effect of such orders on property transfers justifies the exception to the final judgment rule. Many states make similar exceptions and expand them to a broader category of judicial orders effecting the transfer or attachment of property and changes in title or custody.[49]

[2]   Statutory Interlocutory Appeal by Permission

Many jurisdictions also allow discretionary interlocutory appeal, in part to serve the systemic purposes of uniformity and guidance, and in part to accommodate unusual cases in which the likelihood of error is so great that a cost analysis supports immediate appeal. Section 1292(b), the federal provision for discretionary interlocutory appeal, is perhaps more onerous than the typical state provision, but still provides a useful illustration.

Section 1292(b) poses three requirements. First, the trial court must have issued an order from which appeal is taken. Section 1292(b) is not a provision for certifying questions to obtain advisory opinions.[50] Second, the trial court must exercise its discretion to certify that the order (a) "involves a controlling question of law as to which there is substantial ground for difference of opinion" and (b) "that an immediate appeal from the order may materially advance the ultimate termination of the litigation."[51] Finally, the court of appeals must also agree in its discretion to allow the appeal.[52]

---

[46] *Gardner v. Westinghouse Broad. Co.*, 437 U.S. 478 (1978).

[47] *Carson*, 450 U.S. at 83.

[48] 28 U.S.C. § 1292(a)(2).

[49] *See, e.g.*, MINN. STAT. ANN. R. 103.03(c), (f) (West, WESTLAW through Jan. 15, 2008); VA. CODE ANN. § 8.01-670 (LEXIS 2007).

[50] *See, e.g., Nickert v. Puget Sound Tug & Barge Co.*, 480 F.2d 1039, 1041 (9th Cir. 1973). A little-used federal statute authorizes certification of particular questions of law from the courts of appeals to the Supreme Court, 28 U.S.C. § 1254(2), and such provisions are fairly common at the state level.

[51] 28 U.S.C. § 1292(b). If the district court refuses to cooperate, that will usually put an end to the matter. In rare cases, appellant can proceed in the face of the district court's refusal to certify under § 1292(b) by seeking a writ of prohibition or mandamus from the court of appeals. *See* § 13.04[3] (mandamus and prohibition), *infra*.

[52] 28 U.S.C. § 1292(b)

A section 1292(b) interlocutory appeal differs from an appeal of a Rule 54(b) judgment in two respects: it does not contemplate or require a final judgment on any separate claim in the trial court, and it vests the courts of appeals with complete discretion to take the appeal of a certified question, not just a power of review of the propriety of the trial court certification.

The requirement that the trial court certify a controlling question of law helps to confine discretionary interlocutory appeal to those cases in which the likelihood of trial court error is greatest. For example, when the trial court changes its mind three times on the sufficiency of a novel and potentially absolute defense, there is self-evidently substantial ground for difference of opinion within the meaning of section 1292(b).[53] In contrast, interlocutory orders that lie in the discretion of a trial judge are usually unsuitable for interlocutory review because they do not as clearly pose questions of law, and because their discretionary component makes likelihood of reversible error much smaller.[54] Thus, several circuit courts of appeals have suggested that challenges to trial court discretion in granting or denying federal venue transfers[55] are unsuitable for interlocutory appeal.[56]

Certification that interlocutory appeal will materially advance the litigation speaks to its effect on trial. This varies from case to case, explaining why determinations are discretionary. Section 1292(b) exists only for exceptional cases. Litigation will rarely be advanced by allowing immediate review of orders regarding the sufficiency of pleadings, in light of the ease of amendment, or of any case that is likely to go to trial regardless of the correctness of the interlocutory ruling.[57]

The narrow construction federal courts have given section 1292(b) has severely limited its availability.[58] But the discretion that district courts enjoy as a result may be preferable to greater use of judge-made interlocutory appeal and has the added virtue of statutory legitimation. There is an argument for revitalizing statutory interlocutory appeal "based primarily upon the need to clarify the law on issues which typically do not reach appellate courts, and upon a recognition that the vast majority of cases terminate before appeal via settlements or otherwise."[59] Alternatively, the Supreme Court may use its rulemaking power to the same end.[60]

---

[53] *See, e.g., SEC v. National Student Mktg. Corp.*, 68 F.R.D. 157 (D.D.C. 1975), *aff'd*, 538 F.2d 404 (D.C. Cir. 1976), *cert. denied*, 429 U.S. 1073 (1977).

[54] *See* § 13.10[2][d] (describing deferential appellate review of exercises of discretion), *infra*.

[55] On venue transfers, see § 6.02[2], *supra*.

[56] *See, e.g., Garner v. Wolfinbarger*, 433 F.2d 117 (5th Cir. 1970).

[57] WRIGHT § 102.

[58] *See* Michael E. Solimine, *Revitalizing Interlocutory Appeals in Federal Courts*, 58 GEO. WASH. L. REV. 1165, 1171–74, 1193–1201 (1991).

[59] Solimine, note 58, *supra*, at 1213.

[60] *See* 28 U.S.C. § 1292(e); Martineau, note 8, *supra*.

[3]   Extraordinary Statutory Review: Mandamus and Prohibition

A few trial court errors may be so costly, either to the parties or to the integrity of the judicial system, that a cost analysis favors immediate appeal even without irreparable harm. Most jurisdictions historically provided interlocutory appeal in these rare cases by petition for a *writ of mandamus* — ordering the trial judge to issue an order or fulfill a mandatory duty — or a *writ of prohibition* — forbidding the trial judge from acting in excess of her jurisdiction. Historical distinctions between the two have faded over time, and in the federal system mandamus is used for both purposes,[61] serving as an extraordinary allowance of statutory[62] review of the propriety of actions in the trial court. It is extraordinary because it is not a substitute for appeal[63] and is therefore only available when there is "no other adequate means to attain" the desired relief from circumstances amounting to "a judicial 'usurpation of power . . . .' "[64]

What circumstances or errors amount to judicial usurpation is neither clear nor uniform across judicial systems. The historical rule was that mandamus extended to "jurisdictional errors," and, indeed, many states authorize it for interlocutory challenges to assertions of subject matter or personal jurisdiction.[65] Another common generalization is that mandamus is in aid of appellate jurisdiction.[66] This explains the availability of mandamus for an order transferring venue out of one federal circuit to another,[67] but is no more helpful as an explanation for mandamus than is "jurisdictional error" in most cases.

Cases in which the Supreme Court has approved of mandamus[68] suggest two categories. One is breach by the trial judge of a clear legal duty. The Court has approved mandamus on this basis when a trial court, on the grounds that it was too busy, abdicated its duty to try a case by referring it to a special master,[69] and when a trial court denied a party its constitutional right to a jury

---

[61] *See In re Simons*, 247 U.S. 231, 239 (1918).

[62] 28 U.S.C. § 1651.

[63] *Roche v. Evaporated Milk Ass'n*, 319 U.S. 21, 26 (1943).

[64] *Kerr v. U.S. District Court*, 426 U.S. 394, 402–03 (1976) (citing *Roche*, 319 U.S. at 26).

[65] *See, e.g, World-Wide Volkswagen Corp. v. Woodson*, 585 P.2d 351 (Okla. 1978), *rev'd*, 444 U.S. 286 (1980) (writ of prohibition against exercise of personal jurisdiction over foreign defendants); CAL. CIV. PROC. CODE § 418.10 (West, WESTLAW through 2007).

[66] *United States v. Beatty*, 232 U.S. 463, 467 (1914).

[67] *In re Fireman's Fund Ins. Cos. v. Pennington*, 588 F.2d 93 (5th Cir. 1979).

[68] *See generally* Annotation, *Mandamus as an Appropriate Remedy to Control Action of Federal Court in Civil Case — Supreme Court Cases*, 57 L. Ed. 2d 1203 (1979).

[69] *La Buy v. Howes Leather Co.*, 352 U.S. 249 (1957). Rule 53(a)(1)(B)(i) now expressly states that a court may appoint a master "to hold trial proceedings and make or recommend findings of fact on issues to be decided without a jury if appointment is warranted by some exceptional condition . . . ," but nothing in the rule or its history authorizes referrals merely because of calendar congestion.

trial.[70] In contrast, the grant of a new trial, even if error, does not occasion mandamus, there being no clearcut and mandatory standard for granting new trials.[71]

Errors for which appellate review may carry broad precedential significance for judicial administration make up the second category. Thus, while routine discovery orders will almost never qualify for review by mandamus,[72] an interlocutory order presenting a question of first impression about the federal discovery rules may justify a kind of *supervisory mandamus*, on the theory that appellate precedent in such a case can generally improve the administration of justice.[73] Reflecting these categories, the courts of appeals have enunciated their own tests for deciding whether mandamus relief is warranted. The Court of Appeals for the Ninth Circuit, for example, considers whether the petitioner has other adequate means to obtain relief and will be irreparably damaged or prejudiced without mandamus relief, as well as whether the district court order was clearly erroneous as a matter of law, was an oft-repeated error or manifests a persistent disregard of the rules, or raises new and important issues of first impression.[74]

Mandamus makes the trial judge a litigant by directing the writ at her in form, but the parties conduct the appeal in substance. Considerations of comity between the trial and appellate courts reinforce the policy against piecemeal appeals and the exacting standards for the issuance of the writ to make it truly extraordinary relief.[75] Courts of appeals often strain to avoid censuring a trial judge by issuing a writ of mandamus. Instead, even when the error below calls for correction, an appellate court will typically deny the writ with an opinion expressing confidence that the trial judge will do what the appellate court describes as the right thing,[76] or, at worst, will delay issuance of the writ to allow her time to do so.

---

[70] *Beacon Theatres, Inc. v. Westover*, 359 U.S. 500 (1959). *See* Nathan A. Forrester, Comment, *Mandamus as a Remedy for the Denial of Jury Trial*, 58 U. Chi. L. Rev. 769 (1991).

[71] *Allied Chem. Corp. v. Daiflon, Inc.*, 449 U.S. 33 (1980). *See generally* § 12.09[2] (new trial), *supra*. A minority of states expressly authorize interlocutory review of new trial rulings. *See, e.g.*, N.Y. Civ. Prac. L. & R. 5602(b)(2)(iii) (McKinney, WESTLAW through L. 2008); Minn. Stat. Ann. R. 103.03(d) (1993).

[72] *See Kerr*, 426 U.S. 394. *But see* Thornburg, note 11, *supra* (surveying use of mandamus in Texas to review discovery orders and urging interlocutory review of such orders in other courts).

[73] *See, e.g.*, *Schlagenhauf v. Holder*, 379 U.S. 104 (1964) (the appropriate scope of Rule 35); *Colonial Times, Inc. v. Gasch*, 509 F.2d 517 (D.C. Cir. 1975) (question of first impression concerning scope of Rule 30(b)(4)).

[74] *United States v. Fei Ye*, 436 F.3d 1117, 1121–1124 (9th Cir. 2006). A petitioner need not establish all of these factors.

[75] *See Kerr*, 426 U.S. at 403.

[76] *See, e.g.*, 426 U.S. at 406; *Colonial Times, Inc. v. Gasch*, 509 F.2d 517 (D.C. Cir. 1975). As an appellate judge has admitted, "[t]his is but a delicate way of issuing the writ, for the trial court would not lightly ignore this court's 'suggestion.'" *United States v. Harrod*, 428 A.2d 30, 35 n.1 (D.C. 1981) (Ferren, J., concurring, in an opinion in which JJ. Kelly and Mack join). *See generally* Robert S. Berger, *The Mandamus Power of the United States Courts of Appeals: A Complex and Confused Means of Appellate Control*, 31 Buffalo L. Rev. 37, 86–87 (1982).

§ 13.05   JUDGE-MADE EXCEPTIONS TO THE FINAL JUDGMENT RULE

[1]   Collateral Order Doctrine[77]

The most important judge-made exception to the final judgment rule in federal courts is for interlocutory orders that are incidental — *collateral* — to the merits and that cannot be effectively preserved for review on appeal from a final judgment. Since they pose no risk of repetitive appellate review, a cost analysis favors interlocutory review.

The leading federal case is *Cohen v. Beneficial Industrial Loan Corp.*[78] The trial court had denied a corporation's motion that the plaintiff be required, pursuant to state statute, to post security for defendant's reasonable expenses in defending a shareholder's derivative action.[79] Acknowledging that the final judgment rule would preclude appeal, the Supreme Court nevertheless reasoned that its purposes would not be served by refusing appeal in the circumstances. The trial court's ruling was final as to the subject it addressed, did not touch on the merits of the case, and would therefore not be merged into the final judgment. The Court noted that final judgment would be too late in any event to review the ruling, because the statutory rights would then have been lost, probably irretrievably.[80] The Court, therefore, held that the

> decision appears to fall in that small class which finally determine claims of right separable from, and collateral to, rights asserted in the action, too important to be denied review and too independent of the cause itself to require that appellate consideration be deferred until the whole case is adjudicated.[81]

The Supreme Court maintains that *Cohen* did not amend the final judgment rule, but only "continued a tradition of giving [it] a 'practical rather than a technical construction.' "[82]

The Court has since refined *Cohen* to impose three strict requirements for invocation of the collateral order doctrine.[83] First, the order must finally and

---

[77] *See* Lloyd C. Anderson, *The Collateral Order Doctrine: A "Serbonian Bog" and Four Proposals for Reform*, 46 DRAKE L. REV. 539 (1998).

[78] 337 U.S. 541 (1949).

[79] *See* Rule 23.1.

[80] *Cohen v. Beneficial Indus. Loan Corp.*, 337 U.S. at 546–47. The purpose of the security requirement was to discourage frivolous derivative actions, known as "strike suits," and assure reimbursement to the corporation of the reasonable expenses of a successful defense. Appellate correction of the trial court's error after a final judgment would obviously come too late to accomplish the deterrent effect of the security requirement, and in all likelihood too late to assure the corporation of funds from which to collect its expenses.

[81] *Cohen*, 337 U.S. at 546.

[82] *Firestone Tire & Rubber Co. v. Risjord*, 449 U.S. 368, 375 (1981).

[83] *Coopers & Lybrand*, 437 U.S. at 468. The Supreme Court has disapproved a purported exercise of pendent appellate jurisdiction to hear otherwise non-appealable issues in connection with a collateral order appeal, although it did not rule out such jurisdiction in all cases. *Swint v.*

conclusively determine the disputed question. In *Cohen*, the court's denial of defendant's motion conclusively disposed of the question of security; that question could only arise at the front of the case. By contrast, a ruling on class certification is expressly subject under Rule 23(c)(1) to revision before final judgment and therefore "inherently tentative"[84] and unsuitable for interlocutory appeal as a collateral order. An order refusing to disqualify counsel is similarly subject to revision (should conflicts of interest materialize later in the litigation) and is therefore not immediately appealable.[85]

Second, the order must resolve an important issue completely collateral to the merits. It must be collateral, because if enmeshed in the merits, it is likely that it can only be fairly assessed after trial.[86] It must be important in terms of the difficulty of resolution it poses and its effect both upon and beyond the litigation.[87] This requirement prevents appeal of interlocutory decisions that, precisely because they are collateral to the merits, are also insignificant. The order regarding security in *Cohen* met this requirement because it did not touch on the merits and presented a "serious and unsettled question."[88] In contrast, an order refusing to certify a class was not completely collateral, since Rule 23's certification provisions expressly require the court to identify common questions of law or fact and make other determinations that inevitably touch on the merits.[89]

Finally, the order must be effectively unreviewable on appeal from the final judgment, so that the "opportunity for meaningful review will perish unless immediate appeal is permitted."[90] Like the order denying security in *Cohen*, this was true of orders denying summary judgment on the defenses of absolute immunity[91] and double jeopardy,[92] both designed to spare a defendant the rigors of trial, a protection that would obviously be irretrievably lost unless immediate appeal is allowed. On the other hand, the Court has held that an

---

Chambers County Comm'n, 514 U.S. 35 (1995). *See generally* Joan Steinman, *The Scope of Appellate Jurisdiction: Pendent Appellate Jurisdiction Before and After Swint*, 49 HASTINGS L.J. 1337 (1998).

[84] *Coopers & Lybrand*, 437 U.S. at 469 n.11.

[85] *Firestone*, 449 U.S. at 377.

[86] 449 U.S. at 377, 378.

[87] *See Will v. Hallock*, 546 U.S. 345, 352 (2006) (stressing significance of importance factor). *See In re Ford Motor Co.*, 110 F.3d 954 (3d Cir. 1997) (discussing importance factor). *But see Under Seal v. Under Seal*, 326 F.3d 479, 480–85 (4th Cir. 2003) (declining to apply the importance factor based on inconsistent treatment of factor in both circuit and Supreme Court precedent).

[88] *Cohen*, 337 U.S. at 546–47.

[89] *Coopers & Lybrand*, 437 U.S. at 468 & n.12. *See also Van Cauwenberghe v. Biard*, 486 U.S. 517 (1988) (denying collateral order appeal of *forum non conveniens* dismissal because it is not completely separate from the merits); *Richardson-Merrell, Inc. v. Koller*, 472 U.S. 424 (1985) (denying collateral order appeal of order to disqualify counsel for conflict because it is based on the possibility that a conflict will infect the proceedings and is therefore intertwined with the merits).

[90] *Firestone*, 449 U.S. at 377–78.

[91] *Helstoski v. Meanor*, 442 U.S. 500, 506–08 (1979). *See also P.R. Aqueduct & Sewer Auth. v. Metcalf & Eddy, Inc.*, 506 U.S. 139 (1993) (authorizing collateral order review of 11th Amendment immunity claims).

[92] *Abney v. United States*, 431 U.S. 651, 660–62 (1977).

order compelling discovery as against a claim of privilege is not immediately appealable. Its theory was that the party may defy the order and then challenge it on direct appeal of a resulting contempt citation.[93]

From time to time, courts have intimated that the importance requirement is a distinct fourth requirement for collateral order appeals,[94] a view for which Justice Scalia has expressed support.[95] Without deciding whether it is, the Supreme Court has nevertheless emphasized that it is not an alternative or dispensable requirement, whose absence can be overcome if the other requirements are satisfied. "To the contrary," the Court has declared, "a third *Cohen* question, whether a right is 'adequately vindicable' or 'effectively reviewable,' simply cannot be answered without a judgment about the value of the interests that would be lost through rigorous application of a final judgment requirement."[96]

In short, the collateral order appellant must satisfy all requirements, including the importance requirement. Furthermore, the Supreme Court has repeatedly emphasized that the collateral order doctrine "is a narrow one, and the courts have applied it stringently to assure that it does not swallow the general rule."[97]

[2]   Other Judge-Made Exceptions

The federal courts have made several other exceptions to the final judgment rule. They have permitted immediate appeal of criminal contempt orders because of their serious consequences and practical finality.[98] Courting criminal contempt, however, is a risky way to obtain interlocutory appeal since a wrong guess leaves the appellant with a fine or imprisonment. The courts have also allowed non-parties to appeal civil contempt orders on the theory that they have no standing to appeal from an eventual final judgment.[99] Parties, in contrast, must await the final judgment in pending cases.

The Supreme Court suggested in *Gillespie v. United States Steel Corp.*[100] that it might allow interlocutory appeal when it would save time in the circumstances and was in the spirit of the federal discretionary appeal statute, although the trial court had never certified the question under it. Taken for all it is worth, this reasoning does violence to the statutory scheme and is

---

[93] *Cobbledick v. United States*, 309 U.S. 323, 327 (1940). See § 13.05[2], *infra*.

[94] *See, e.g.*, WRIGHT & MILLER § 3911.

[95] *Gulfstream Aerospace Corp. v. Mayacamas Corp.*, 485 U.S. 271, 291–92 (1988) (Scalia, J., concurring).

[96] *Digital Equip. Corp. v. Desktop Direct, Inc.*, 511 U.S. 863, 878–79 (1994). *Accord Will v. Hallock*, 546 U.S. 345 (2006).

[97] MOORE § 202.07[1] (citing cases).

[98] *See generally* WRIGHT & MILLER § 3917; MOORE § 26.07[2][g].

[99] MOORE § 202.11[9]; WRIGHT & MILLER § 3917. *See generally Shillitani v. United States*, 384 U.S. 364, 369–70 (1966) (explaining that criminal contempt is intended to punish, while civil contempt is intended merely to coerce).

[100] 379 U.S. 148 (1964).

inconsistent with the federal policy disfavoring piecemeal review. It is not surprising that it has met with little approval.[101] The Court has since acknowledged that "[i]f *Gillespie* were extended beyond the unique facts of that case, section 1291 would be stripped of all significance."[102] *Gillespie* may not have much continuing force.

Finally, an early Supreme Court decision adopted a hardship test, allowing interlocutory appeal of an order that would cause "irreparable injury" before final judgment.[103] While the Court itself has not consistently applied this test in its subsequent decisions, the practical construction it has given the requirement for finality — to the point of rationalizing the collateral order doctrine as a mere application of the statutory requirement — points in the direction of such a test.[104]

PART B.
Where and How? Perfecting Appeal

§ 13.06   APPELLATE SYSTEMS

Where an appellant takes an appeal is typically determined by statute or constitutional provision. Systems vary widely from jurisdiction to jurisdiction. A four-tier court system is common, however.

Appeal from the bottom tier, courts of limited jurisdiction, is usually to courts of general jurisdiction which re-try the matter *de novo* (anew). Little or no deference is paid the lower court decision because of the restrictions on its jurisdiction and, in many cases, on its procedures.[105]

Appeal from a court of general jurisdiction is to a true appellate court. This was traditionally to the highest court in many states, but a growing number have created intermediate appellate courts to ease the workload on the highest courts and free them for review on a discretionary basis. Appeal to an intermediate appellate court is usually as of right,[106] as it is in the federal

---

[101] *But see* Wright & Miller §§ 3905, 3913 (approving "pragmatic approach" of *Gillespie* to allow disposition on the merits of appeals mistakenly taken from non-final decisions).

[102] *Coopers & Lybrand*, 437 U.S. at 477 n.30.

[103] *Forgay v. Conrad*, 47 U.S. (6 How.) 201, 205–06 (1848) (review of an order to transfer property).

[104] *See* Wright § 101, *quoting United States v. Wood*, 295 F.2d 772, 778 (5th Cir. 1961), *cert. denied*, 369 U.S. 850 (1962), to same effect. The irreparable injury test has also been endorsed as part of a balancing approach urged by some commentators. *See* Martin Redish, *The Pragmatic Approach to Appealability in the Federal Courts*, 75 Colum. L. Rev. 89 (1975).

[105] In the Virginia system, for example, the jurisdiction of the district court is limited by amount in controversy, and the district court rules do not permit full discovery or jury trials. Va. Code Ann. §§ 16.1-77, 16.1-113 (2007 Reg. Sess.). Some courts of general jurisdiction, however, may give great weight to findings of such inferior courts. *See* 5 Am. Jur.2d *Appeal and Error* § 822 (1962 & 1993 Supp.) (listing cases).

[106] *See, e.g.*, Md. Code Ann., Cts. & Jud. Proc. § 12-301 (2007).

system to the circuit courts of appeals.[107] In some jurisdictions, the decision of the intermediate appellate court is final for the most fact-bound and routine kinds of cases, such as domestic relations and non-capital criminal cases, subject perhaps to discretionary appeal for constitutional questions.

Appeal from the intermediate appellate court to the highest court is predominantly by permission, with exceptions for a small number of important cases selected by the legislatures, such as administrative law cases involving governmental parties or capital criminal cases.[108] Some systems limit the appellate jurisdiction of the highest court by amounts in controversy or subject; most empower the highest court to select, by *certiorari* or other permission, cases posing serious constitutional issues, conflicts in the lower courts, or other special needs for appellate guidance.[109]

The United States Supreme Court's rules, for example, list the following factors as relevant in granting *certiorari*: inter-circuit conflicts, conflicts between the courts of appeals and state courts of last resort, interstate conflicts on federal questions, conflicts with Supreme Court decisions on federal questions, important and unsettled federal questions, and other federal rulings calling for the exercise of the Supreme Court's power of supervision.[110] The Supreme Court's *certiorari* jurisdiction is thus highly discretionary,[111] so discretionary that the Court has repeatedly stressed that its refusal to grant review by *certiorari* connotes little if anything about the correctness of the decision below.[112]

In addition, the Supreme Court exercises mandatory appellate jurisdiction in a few very limited circumstances.[113]

---

[107] 28 U.S.C. § 1291. The mounting workload of the federal appellate courts has prompted some calls for making appeal to them discretionary. *See* Ronald M. Parker & Ron Chapman, Jr., *Accepting Reality: The Time for Adopting Discretionary Review in the Court of Appeals Has Arrived*, 50 SMU L. Rev. 573 (1997). Other options include splitting the workload in some circuits by splitting the circuit, *see* Commission on Structural Alternatives for Federal Courts of Appeals, Final Report (1998), *discussed in* Carl Tobias, *The Federal Appeals Courts at Century's End*, 34 U.C. Davis L. Rev. 549 (2000), and truncating appellate procedures (including oral argument) as well as the decisionmaking process itself. *See* William M. Richman & William L. Reynolds, *Elitism, Expediency, and the New Cetiorari: Requiem for the Learned Hand Tradition*, 81 Cornell L. Rev. 273 (1996) (criticizing this trend and endorsing increase in number of appellate judges as a remedy); Federal Judicial Center, Stalking the Increase in the Rate of Federal Civil Appeals 18 (1995) (noting truncated procedures as response to caseload).

[108] *See, e.g.*, Va. Code Ann. § 8.01-670 (2007 Reg. Sess.).

[109] *See, e.g.*, Md. Code Ann., Cts. & Proc. Code Ann. § 12-301-305 (2007).

[110] Sup. Ct. R. 10.

[111] *See generally* Robert L. Stern, Eugene Gressman & Stephen Shapiro, Supreme Court Practice §§ 4.1–4.26 (8th ed. 2002).

[112] *See, e.g.*, *Maryland v. Baltimore Radio Show*, 338 U.S. 912 (1950) (Frankfurter, J.). *See generally* Stern, Gressman & E. Shapiro, note 111, *supra*, at §§ 5–7; Peter Linzer, *The Meaning of Certiorari Denials*, 79 Colum. L. Rev. 1227 (1979).

[113] 28 U.S.C. § 1253 (authorizing direct appeal from orders granting or denying interlocutory or permanent injunctions by three-judge courts).

§ 13.07   PROCEDURAL STEPS IN PERFECTING APPEAL

In most jurisdictions the procedures for perfecting an appeal appear in detail in statutes or rules.[114] Consequently, only the broad general outlines of the typical steps are presented in this section, with illustrative citation to the federal rules of appellate procedure.[115]

The first and (in many jurisdictions) only crucial step in taking an appeal as of right is timely filing of notice of appeal.[116] The appellate court usually has discretion to excuse errors or lateness respecting the taking of all subsequent steps, but not respecting the filing of notice of appeal. This step is therefore said to be jurisdictional — a predicate to the exercise of appellate power in most systems.[117] Appellant usually must file notice with the court rendering the judgment, not the higher court, and must state clearly what party is appealing from what parts of the judgment.[118] Appellant usually must pay a filing fee at that time, post a bond for costs on appeal, and (because the pendency of appeal does not alone automatically stay the enforcement of a judgment) either post a *supersedeas* bond to suspend the enforcement of a money judgment or seek a stay from the lower court of other granted relief.[119] In the federal system, the notice of appeal must be filed within 30 days of the entry of judgment or the date of an order deciding any timely filed post-trial ten-day motion[120] in civil actions between private parties.[121]

Second, other parties must file notices of cross-appeal. Timely filing is necessary to preserve any cross-appeal, but the rule is usually framed to allow filing of defensive cross-appeals within a reasonable time after the initial notice

---

[114] Such rules include local rules of appellate courts, which have been proliferating in the federal system. *See* Gregory C. Sisk, *The Balkanization of Appellate Justice: The Proliferation of Local Rules in Federal Circuits*, 68 U. Colo. L. Rev. 1 (1997).

[115] For more detailed description of appellate procedure generally, see Paul D. Carrington et al., Justice on Appeal (1976); Robert L. Stern, Appellate Practice in the United States (1981); of federal appellate procedure in particular, see Wright § 104.

[116] When the appeal is discretionary, the appellant must file a petition for permission to appeal with the appellate court, instead of notice of appeal in the trial court.

[117] *But see* Marie A. Hall, *The Jurisdictional Nature of the Time to Appeal*, 21 Ga. L. Rev. 399 (1986) (arguing that appeal periods should be subject to waiver).

[118] *See* Fed. R. App. P. 3.

[119] *See* Fed. R. App. P. 7 & 8.

[120] *See* Fed. R. App. P. 4(a)(4); § 12.09[1] (directed verdicts, judgments n.o.v., and new trial), *supra*. Rule 60 motions for relief from judgment do not toll the 30-day time period for filing notice of appeal. *See* § 12.11[2][b], *supra*.

[121] *See* Fed. R. App. P.4(a)(4). An untimely post-trial motion does not postpone the time in which to take appeal, *see, e.g., Hulson v. Atchison, Topeka & Santa Fe Ry. Co.*, 289 F.2d 726 (7th Cir. 1961), although the district court may for "excusable neglect or good cause" grant an extension of time up to thirty days. Fed. R. App. P. 4(a)(5). The circuits are split on the question whether improper district court permission to file a post-trial motion out of time can ever postpone the time for filing notice of appeal. The arguments for and against are discussed in *Bailey v. Sharp*, 782 F.2d 1366, 1369–74 (7th Cir. 1986) (Easterbrook, J., concurring).

of appeal.[122]

Third, the appellant must prepare and transmit the record. The record may comprise the transcript, exhibits, and docket from the trial court,[123] but there is substantial variation in what an appellant actually must transmit to the appellate court. Most jurisdictions allow him to designate and appellee to cross-designate parts of the record. As an alternative procedure, some provide for appellant's preparation of a narrative summary of the record, subject to appellee's objections and trial court certification.[124]

Fourth, the parties brief the issues. Usually the appellant and appellee file briefs in succession, and appellant is permitted a shorter reply.[125] In some jurisdictions, the parties support their briefs with a joint appendix of key excerpts from the record.[126]

Finally, the parties may be heard in oral argument some time after submission of their briefs.[127] Summary disposition, with little (*e.g.*, fifteen minutes) or no argument, is an increasingly common response of appellate courts to burgeoning caseloads. Few jurisdictions grant oral argument as of right.

PART C.
What and How Much?
The Scope and Intensity of Review

The appealability of a judgment or interlocutory order does not determine whether or how intensively a particular claim of error will be reviewed. Section 13.09 treats whether an error is within the scope of review (reviewability). Section 13.10 discusses the intensity (standard) of review.

§ 13.08   SCOPE OF REVIEW — REVIEWABILITY

Whether a particular claim of error is reviewable on appeal turns on its *prejudicial effect, preservation below*, and *presentation above*. Questions of uniformity and systemic guidance aside, appeal is primarily intended to correct improper dispositions by the lower courts when necessary to protect adversely affected parties. The scope of review is therefore restricted to prejudicial errors appealed by aggrieved parties. The systemic goal of efficiency dictates giving the trial court opportunity to correct its own errors and to create a clear record

---

[122] *See* FED. R. APP. P. 4(a)(3) (within 14 days of notice of appeal by any other party or time provided for original notice, whichever is longer).

[123] *See* FED. R. APP. P. 10(a).

[124] *See* VA. SUP. CT. R. 5:11(c) & (d). *See also* FED. R. APP. P. 10(c) (authorizing statement of the evidence in limited circumstances); 10(d) (authorizing agreed statement of facts in lieu of the record).

[125] *See* FED. R. APP. P. 28.

[126] *See* FED. R. APP. P. 30.

[127] *See* FED. R. APP. P. 34.

for appeal. The scope of review is therefore further restricted ordinarily to errors that are preserved in the record below. Last, efficiency also requires that the appellant present the error to the appellate court, in order to relieve it of the tedious and wasteful task of searching the record.

[1]   Prejudicial Effect

The term *prejudicial effect* is used here to embrace two principles of reviewability. First, the appeal must be taken by an aggrieved party.[128] An aggrieved party is one who did not receive the full disposition he requested. Appeal is to correct an improper disposition below, not to make trials error-free nor to make clearer the grounds for initial disposition. Appeal will not usually lie to substitute some other ground for a judgment below or to correct findings unnecessary to the judgment,[129] since they are unlikely to be preclusive[130] and so cannot legally aggrieve a party to the judgment. What findings are necessary to a judgment depends on the substantive law.[131]

These principles are not always easy to apply. Even in damage cases, "amount is not the sole measure of relief to which a party may be entitled."[132] Thus one court has held that a party who recovers a judgment in the amount prayed, but on a theory of indemnification rather than of fraud, may appeal the court's ruling on the fraud theory when that ruling may have collateral effects in subsequent proceedings.[133] The Supreme Court has also allowed an alleged patent infringer to appeal a decree in his favor, when the decree literally incorporated an otherwise immaterial finding that the patent was valid.[134] What these decisions may have in common is a concern for the judgment's possible preclusive effects against the appellant.[135]

---

[128] *Deposit Guar. Nat'l Bank v. Roper*, 445 U.S. 326, 333 (1980). *See generally* MOORE § 205.04[1]; WRIGHT & MILLER § 3902. The party is ordinarily party to the judgment, but proper interveners may also appeal if they are aggrieved. *See, e.g., Smuck v. Hobson*, 408 F.2d 175 (D.C. Cir. 1969). Non-parties may argue on appeal as *amicus curiae* by permission only. *See generally* Note, *The Amicus Curiae*, 55 Nw. U. L. REV. 469 (1960).

[129] *Electrical Fittings Corp. v. Thomas & Betts Co.*, 307 U.S. 241, 242 (1939) ("A party may not appeal from a judgment or decree in his favor, for the purpose of obtaining a review of findings he deems erroneous which are not necessary to support the decree.").

[130] *See* § 15.07[3] (adjudication of the issue must have been necessary to judgment), *infra*.

[131] The same question of necessity to the judgment is treated under the law of collateral estoppel or issue preclusion. *See* § 15.07[3], *infra*.

[132] *Aetna Cas. & Sur. Co. v. Cunningham*, 224 F.2d 478, 480 (5th Cir. 1955). *Cf.* Rule 54(c) (". . . every . . . final judgment should grant the relief to which each party is entitled, even if the party has not demanded that relief in the pleadings").

[133] *Aetna Casualty*, 224 F.2d 478.

[134] *Electrical Fittings*, 307 U.S. 241.

[135] The concern in *Aetna* would have been that the finding of no fraud might preclude use of that theory to avoid a later bankruptcy discharge by the judgment debtor, and in *Electrical Fittings* that the finding of patent validity might preclude the judgment winner from asserting a defense to future suits by the patent holder. However, these concerns may be redundant with protections already built into the law of preclusion, which does not usually permit preclusion by judgments that are unreviewable on appeal or by findings that are unnecessary to the judgment. *See* § 15.07[3], *infra*. Commentators have accordingly noted the circularity between the "aggrieved by the

Second, the errors alleged must have been harmful to the appellant in the sense that they may have materially contributed to the adverse part of the judgment. Congress has given expression to this concept by providing that appellate courts should disregard any errors that "do not affect the substantial rights of the parties."[136] Errors in the exclusion or admission of evidence are frequently rendered harmless by the cumulative weight of other, properly admitted evidence; error at one stage of an action can often be neutralized by curative action at a later stage.

Yet some errors are so central to the integrity of the fact-finding process, or so unsusceptible to proof of actual prejudice, that harm must be presumed. For example, many cases hold that the taint of the jury by exposure to extraneous evidence outside the record falls into this category.[137] Although the proper standard of harmlessness remains an open question, some courts have suggested that a "more probable than not" standard is most appropriate to civil cases in line with the usual preponderance burden of proof.[138]

[2]   Preservation Below[139]

Ordinarily, only errors appearing in the record made below are reviewable. Failure to make timely objection is tantamount to a waiver for purposes of reviewability on appeal. This limitation is necessary to give the trial court the opportunity to correct its own errors and thereby moot an appeal; to guard against sandbagging by the parties below (holding claims of error in reserve in case they lose); and to develop and clarify the record on appeal, which may include the trial court's analysis of the point.[140] In the federal system, objection need not take the form of formal exception. It is sufficient that a

---

judgment" rule and preclusion law. *See, e.g.,* WRIGHT & MILLER § 3902. Perhaps the Court believed in *Electrical Fittings* that incorporation of the finding in the decree would dignify it sufficiently to give it issue-preclusive effect, and therefore justified appellate reformation of the decree.

[136] 28 U.S.C. § 2111. *See also* Rule 61.

[137] *See, e.g., In re Beverly Hills Fire Litig.,* 695 F.2d 207 (6th Cir. 1982) (juror told jury the results of his own, unsupervised experiment); *Gertz v. Bass,* 208 N.E.2d 113 (Ill. App. Ct. 1965) (bailiff gave jurors a dictionary that defined key terms differently from jury instructions). However, the Supreme Court has held that a juror's mistaken answer to *voir dire* questions, *see generally* § 12.01[3] (selecting a jury), *supra,* is not presumptively harmful absent a showing that the juror answered dishonestly and that an honest answer would have provided a valid basis for a challenge for cause. *McDonough Power Equip., Inc. v. Greenwood,* 464 U.S. 548, 556 (1984).

[138] *See, e.g., Haddad v. Lockheed Calif. Corp.,* 720 F.2d 1454, 1459 (9th Cir. 1983). Professors Wright and Miller endorse the discussion by the Supreme Court in *Kotteakos v. United States,* 328 U.S. 750, 765 (1946) (" . . . if one cannot say, with fair assurance, after pondering all that happened without stripping the erroneous action from the whole, that the judgment was not substantially swayed by the error, it is impossible to conclude that substantial rights were not affected."). WRIGHT & MILLER § 2883. *See generally* ROGER J. TRAYNOR, THE RIDDLE OF HARMLESS ERROR (1970).

[139] *See generally* Robert J. Martineau, *Considering New Issues on Appeal: The General Rule and the Gorilla Rule,* 40 VAND. L. REV. 1023 (1987); Rhett R. Dennerline, Note, *Pushing Aside the General Rule in Order to Raise New Issues on Appeal,* 64 IND. L.J. 985 (1989).

[140] *See Pfeifer v. Jones & Laughlin Steel Corp.,* 678 F.2d 453, 456 (3d Cir. 1982), *vacated and remanded,* 462 U.S. 523 (1983). *See generally* Ferdinand Fairfax Stone, *Scope of Review and Record on Appeal,* 2 F.R.D. 317 (1943).

party makes known to the trial court what action he desires the court to take or the general grounds for his objection.[141] However, creation of a strong record for appeal frequently requires more than cursory objection. In this as in other matters of procedure, a lawyer must be guided by tactical common sense and not just the minimum required by the rules.

Some courts have relaxed their rules for so-called *plain errors*.[142] They reason that "[a] litigant surely has the right to assume that a . . . trial judge knows the elementary substantive legal rules, long established by the precedents and . . . will act accordingly, without prompting by the litigant's lawyer."[143] Although the lay litigant may reasonably make the same assumption of his own attorney, concerns for the appearance of justice and the integrity of the legal system make ignorance in the trial judge less tolerable than ignorance in counsel. Yet what errors are plain enough to overcome the normal requirement for objection, not to mention the explicit requirement of Rule 51(c) for objection to jury instructions, is unclear.[144] For example, the Ninth Circuit Court of Appeals has declined to invoke plain error to reach errors in jury instructions in the absence of objection below.[145]

The preservation-below requirement usually applies also to any legal arguments made to *challenge* a judgment. One federal court has explained:

> By requiring parties to present all their legal issues to the district court as well, we preserve the hierarchical nature of the federal courts and encourage ultimate settlement before appeal. It also prevents surprise on appeal and gives the appellate court the benefit of the legal analysis of the trial court.[146]

The same rule is not strictly applied to arguments for *affirmance* of a judgment, even though they may also attack the reasoning of the lower court. Instead, any

---

[141] Rule 46. *But see* Catherine Murr Young, Comment, *Should a Motion in Limine or Similar Preliminary Motion Made in the Federal Court System Preserve Error on Appeal Without a Contemporaneous Objection*, 79 Ky. L.J. 177 (1990–1991) (noting that at least three federal circuits require contemporaneous objection at trial to evidence that objector unsuccessfully sought to exclude by motion *in limine*). The requirement for objection to proposed jury instructions may be slightly more exacting, because the rule is stated separately from the general rule regarding objection and requires objections to be stated "distinctly." Rule 51. Of course, the lack of objection is excused when there is no opportunity to make one. Rule 46.

[142] *See* Fed. R. Evid. 103(d) (nothing in rule requiring objection to evidence precludes "taking notice of plain errors affecting substantial rights although they were not brought to the attention of the court").

[143] *Troupe v. Chicago, Duluth & Georgian Bay Transit Co.*, 234 F.2d 253, 261 (2d Cir. 1956) (Frank, J., concurring).

[144] As a result, one commentator has criticized the plain error rule as an unpredictable and *ad hoc* "Gorilla Rule." *See* Martineau, note 139, *supra*. He proposes a standard for the review of a new issue on appeal that would be analogous to the standard for Rule 60 motions. *See* Martineau, note 139, *supra*, at 1059–61; § 12.11[2][b], *supra*.

[145] *Moore v. Telfon Commc'ns Corp.*, 589 F.2d 959, 966 (9th Cir. 1978).

[146] *Patterson v. Cuyler*, 729 F.2d 925, 929 (3d Cir. 1984). Courts have made an exception to this requirement when the legal argument first becomes available on appeal as a result of an unanticipated change in the law and is supported by the record. *See, e.g., Carson Prods. Co. v. Califano*, 594 F.2d 453 (5th Cir. 1979).

legal argument that is fairly supported by the record may be made in support of the judgment.[147]

For example, after an appellate court rejected the fraud theory of recovery that plaintiff advanced below to recover a money judgment, it permitted plaintiff/appellee to argue for the first time on appeal a theory of quasi-contract in support of the judgment. It was enough that the new theory "did not contemplate any factual situation different from that established by the evidence in the trial court."[148]

The different treatment on appeal of arguments attacking and supporting the judgment stems from considerations of economy and finality. Entertaining new arguments to attack the judgment *detracts* from finality by increasing the likelihood of reversal, while entertaining new arguments to support it *promotes* finality and avoids an inefficient remand for the trial court to re-enter the same judgment on an alternative ground.[149]

Arguments in support of the judgment, however, must be distinguished from arguments to enlarge or diminish it.[150] The latter place their proponent in the position of appellant and subject him to the usual requirement of presentation below, as well as the procedural necessity for taking a timely cross-appeal.[151] In *Standard Accident Insurance Co. v. Roberts*,[152] for example, the plaintiffs recovered a judgment against an insurer on an estoppel theory, although the trial court also found no coverage under the insurance contract. On appeal by the insurer, the plaintiffs/appellees argued that the insurer was estopped, that they were covered under the policy, that the contract should have been reformed to cover them, and that they were entitled to reasonable attorneys fees and a statutory penalty. Only the first two arguments were properly made without cross-appeal. Both had been presented below and were, in any event, merely alternative grounds to support the judgment, while the latter two arguments would have modified and expanded the judgment.

---

[147] *Schweiker v. Hogan*, 457 U.S. 569, 585 n.24 (1982); *United States v. American Ry. Express Co.*, 265 U.S. 425, 435 (1924). "Fairly supported in the record" means not just that the record is sufficient, but that it is in "the same basic posture as it would have been" had the argument been made below. FRIEDENTHAL, KANE, & MILLER § 13.4.

[148] *Ward v. Taggart*, 336 P.2d 534, 537–38 (Cal. 1959).

[149] *See, e.g.*, *Southard v. Southard*, 305 F.2d 730, 732 (2d Cir. 1962) (justifying hearing new argument on appeal by inevitability of trial court judgment on that argument and desirability of expediting termination of litigation).

[150] *See, e.g.*, *American Ry. Express Co.*, 265 U.S. at 435.

[151] *See* § 13.07 (procedural steps in appeal), *supra*. *See generally* William H. Baughman, Jr., *Federal Cross-Appeals — A Guide and a Proposal*, 42 OHIO ST. L.J. 505 (1981); Robert L. Stern, *When to Cross-Appeal or Cross-Petition — Certainty or Confusion?*, 87 HARV. L. REV. 763 (1974); Annotation, *Effect of Party's Failure to Cross-Appeal on Scope of Appellate Review as to Contentions of a Party Relating to Judgment Below — Supreme Court Cases*, 63 L. Ed. 2d 911 (1981).

[152] 132 F.2d 794 (8th Cir. 1942).

[3]   Presentation Above

Without more, preservation of the objection or argument in the record below is not sufficient to make it reviewable. Apart from questions of subject matter jurisdiction, which an appellate court must raise at its own initiative,[153] the court will not search the record for error. Instead, the appellant must identify and present the issue in his brief. This requirement obviously promotes efficiency on appeal by sparing the appellate court the rigors of a complete search and by encouraging well-prepared briefs.[154] It also minimizes the likelihood of surprise. In interlocutory appeals, it serves the additional purpose of discouraging a party from injecting "a sham issue as the vehicle to . . . [appeal] at the interlocutory stage for a declaration on an order not otherwise reviewable."[155] When review is restricted to just that issue, there is little to be gained by this tactic except delay.

In the Supreme Court, the presentation-above rule is codified as Sup. Ct. R. 14.1(a). It provides that "[o]nly the questions set forth in the petition [for *certiorari*], or fairly included therein, will be considered by the Court." This rule serves two purposes, the Court has explained. It provides respondent with notice of the grounds upon which a petitioner seeks *certiorari* and thus enables the respondent "to sharpen the arguments as to why *certiorari* should not be granted."[156] It also, of course, helps the Court select the cases in which *certiorari* will be granted, an important consideration for a court that faces over 5000 petitions for *certiorari* each term.

Like its companions in the law of reviewability, the presentation-above rule is flexible. Many appellate courts assert the power to reach any issue that is sufficiently illuminated to permit decision without further development below — what a disapproving court has described as "a sort of ad hoc pendent jurisdiction."[157] The Tenth Circuit Court of Appeals, for example, has set out criteria for what it unabashedly calls "pendent appellate jurisdiction." These are the sufficiency of the legal and factual development of the pendent issue for review, the overlap between the appealable and the pendent issues, and "whether judicial economy will be better served by resolving the otherwise nonappealable issue, notwithstanding the federal policy against piecemeal appeals."[158] While pendent appellate jurisdiction may promote efficiency in otherwise proper appeals from final judgments, it is more problematic on interlocutory appeals that are justified on issue-specific grounds.[159] Finally,

---

[153] This is a particular concern of federal appellate courts. *See* § 5.01[2] (federal subject matter jurisdiction in general), *supra*.

[154] *Cf. Hospital Corp. of Am. v. FTC*, 807 F.2d 1381, 1392 (3d Cir. 1986) (four out of eighty-five pages in a brief is insufficient to present constitutional argument; "[b]revity may be the soul of wit, but seismic constitutional change is no laughing matter").

[155] *See Garner v. Wolfinbarger*, 433 F.2d 117, 120 (5th Cir. 1970).

[156] *Yee v. City of Escondido*, 503 U.S. 519, 536 (1992).

[157] *Garner*, 433 F.2d at 120. *See generally* Steinman, note 83, *supra*.

[158] *Colorado v. Idarado Mining Co.*, 916 F.2d 1486, 1491 (10th Cir. 1990), *cert. denied*, 499 U.S. 960 (1991).

[159] *Compare, e.g., Energy Action Educ. Found. v. Andrus*, 654 F.2d 735, 745 n.54 (D.C. Cir.

another exception is for a limited category of plain errors that the appellate courts uncover at their own initiative.[160]

§ 13.09 INTENSITY OF REVIEW

[1] In General

Intensity of review refers to how much an appellate court should defer to or substitute judgment for a decision made below. Intensity of review is issue-specific. It is sometimes said that it depends on whether the issue is fact or law, but this is an oversimplification. Fact-law distinctions merely reflect the subtle interaction of the objectives of correctness, finality, and efficiency in shaping intensity of review.

Correctness is best served by adjusting the intensity of review to relative competency. The trial court has all the advantages of being there; it hears all evidence as it comes in, observes the demeanor of witnesses, and experiences nuance and context that are at best imperfectly conveyed by the cold record considered by the appellate court.[161] Hence the trial court, and the jury when it is the fact finder, have a comparative advantage in fact finding that justifies substantial appellate deference to findings of fact made below. In addition, the trial court is experienced in making managerial decisions regarding scheduling, managerial limitations on discovery, continuances, and new trial that are not susceptible to precise rules of decision. Best left to the discretion of the trial judge, such decisions should also be reviewed deferentially. In contrast, the appellate court may be superior to the trial court in researching, interpreting and applying the law, due to its specialization in deciding law questions, its customarily greater library and law clerk resources, and its habit of collegial decision-making. Along with the need for uniformity, these considerations justify appellate substitution of judgment for conclusions of law and, arguably, of mixed law and fact.

But these observations are tempered by consideration of the systemic procedural objectives of finality and efficiency. At least when the trial and appellate courts are equally competent, these objectives support limiting review, in order to increase respect for lower court judgments and to discourage the number and individual burden of appeals.

> The judicial process is at best a less than scientific method of determining the facts. . . . All that can be expected is the opportunity to present to a neutral *factfinder* the parties' respective versions, under

---

1980) (promotes efficiency), *with* Riyaz A. Kanji, Note, *The Proper Scope of Appellate Jurisdiction in the Collateral Order Context*, 100 YALE L.J. 511 (1990) (urging narrow scope of pendent appellate jurisdiction in collateral order appeals).

[160] *See generally* Allan D. Vestal, *Sua Sponte Consideration in Appellate Review*, 27 FORDHAM L. REV. 477 (1959) (also describing other exceptions, including questions of the interpretation of written instruments, important public policy issues, and when justice otherwise demands appellate consideration of an issue in the record).

[161] *See* Maurice Rosenberg, *Judicial Discretion of the Trial Court, Viewed from Above*, 22 SYRACUSE L. REV. 635, 660–65 (1971).

rules designed to assure a measure of fairness, and to let that *factfinder* draw inferences. Since certainty is impossible no matter how often the process is repeated, society's interest emphasizes finality at that point.[162]

Unfortunately many courts have approached the problem of intensity of review with conclusory labels or *standards of review* ("*de novo*," "clearly erroneous," "abuse of discretion"). Students of appellate opinions thus may begin to distrust the standards of review and to conclude that the intensity of review is wholly result-oriented. Indeed, some courts themselves are expressing skepticism. Thus, one circuit reports a split in its ranks

> over whether we must or even can establish fine gradations of judicial review. One school of thought holds that the verbal differences in standards of judicial review (arbitrary and capricious, clearly erroneous, substantial evidence, abuse of discretion, substantial basis, etc.) mark real differences in the degree of deference that the reviewing court should give the findings and rulings of the tribunal being reviewed. The other school holds that the verbal differences are for the most part merely semantic, that there are really only two standards of review — plenary [*de novo*] and deferential — and that differences in deference in a particular case depend on factors specific to the case, such as the nature of the issue, and the evidence, rather than on differences in the stated standard of review.[163]

But perhaps the schools are not so far apart, if it is recognized that "the verbal differences" are just shorthand ways of describing approximately where on a continuum ranging from 100% substitution of judgment to total deference the intensity of review lies for a particular issue.[164] Figure 13-1 presents the resulting spectrum of review[165] in federal courts, showing traditional standards of review above and types of issues below the horizontal line.

---

[162] *Davis v. United States Steel Supply*, 581 F.2d 335 (3d Cir. 1978), *vacated en banc*, 688 F.2d 166 (3d Cir. 1982) (Gibbons, J. dissenting), *cert. denied*, 460 U.S. 1014 (1983).

[163] *Morales v. Yeutter*, 952 F.2d 954, 957 (7th Cir. 1991) (construing standards of review of administrative decisions) (citations omitted).

[164] Childress and Davis remind us that

> [s]tandards of review, though slippery, cannot be dismissed as sheer politics, especially as the court-watcher begins to look at the practical meaning below the surface catchphrase. The ubiquitous standard, either in basic form or as defined and refined, is presented as a meaningful guidepost to frame both the arguments to the appellate court and the court's analytical response. Even when the slogans have no real internal meaning, in many cases it is clear that the issue framing or assignment of power *behind* the words is the turning point of the decision.

1 Steven Alan Childress & Martha A. Davis, Federal Standards of Review § 1.01 (3d 1999) (footnote omitted).

[165] *Cf.* Ellen E. Sward, *Appellate Review of Judicial Fact-Finding*, 40 U. Kan. L. Rev. 1, 5 (1991); Roy A. Schotland, *Scope of Review of Administrative Action — Remarks Before the D.C. Circuit Judicial Conference*, 34 Fed. B.J. 54, 59 (1959).

Figure 13-1

Standards of Review

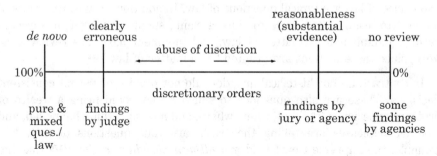

Types of Issues

Location on the spectrum is assigned in accordance with the above-described objectives of appeal and of the procedural system.[166]

[2] The Principal Federal Standards of Review[167]

[a] *De Novo — Questions of Law*

Considerations of comparative institutional competency, described in section 13.09[1], coupled with systemic needs for uniformity and guidance in the application of law, dictate plenary or *de novo* review of questions of law. That is, the appellate court decides whether decision of a question of law was right or wrong, freely substituting its judgment for that of the lower court. For all other issues, the lower court receives some measure of deference, and appellate review is correspondingly less intensive.

Characterization of an issue on appeal as law or fact thus directly affects the likelihood of reversal. But no one has yet formulated a rule or principle that will unerringly make the distinction between law and fact. One useful test is whether consistency among decisions on the issue is necessary. The question is more likely to be one of law if it requires a fixed standard that applies to the

---

[166] One scholar describes the spectrum by assigning hypothetical probabilities to the likelihood of affirmance under each standard:

Standard of Review	Hypothesized Affirmance Rates
No Review	100%
Arbitrary and Capricious	85–90%
Substantial Evidence	75–85%
Clearly Erroneous	70–80%
De Novo	40–50%

Paul R. Verkuil, *An Outcomes Analysis of Scope of Review Standards*, 44 WM. & MARY L. REV. 679, 689 (2002).

[167] *See generally* CHILDRESS & DAVIS, note 164, *supra*; Kelly Kunsch, *Standard of Review (State and Federal): A Primer*, 18 SEATTLE U. L. REV. 11 (1994).

whole community impartially, because then consistency of decision is necessary, which a court can best supply. Questions of statutory intent, sufficiency of a defense, adequacy of jury instructions, admission of evidence, and choice of law are typical questions of law. In addition, trial court grants of motions to dismiss for failure to state a claim, summary judgment, directed verdict, judgment as a matter of law, and judgment n.o.v. are reviewed *de novo*, since these motions are granted "as a matter of law."[168]

In contrast, ad hoc historical questions do not require or permit consistent decisions. These are also questions to which a jury could bring a wealth of ordinary experience.[169] What, when, where, and how something happened, and whether witnesses are telling the truth, are thus questions of fact. For example, the Supreme Court held in *Pullman-Standard v. Swint*[170] that the question of discriminatory intent or actual motive is a question of fact, even when characterized as an ultimate fact,[171] and therefore not subject to *de novo* appellate review.

The problem of characterization is complicated by mixed questions of fact and law: "questions in which the historical facts are admitted or established, the rule of law is undisputed, and the issue is whether the facts satisfy the statutory standard, or to put it another way, whether the rule of law as applied to the established facts is or is not violated."[172] Supreme Court decisions lend some support to *de novo* review of such questions, but the circuit courts are divided and the Court has not yet ruled definitively.[173] Some commentators have urged deferential review under the clearly-erroneous standard discussed in the next subsection, because the application of law to facts will normally generate little of precedential value. Thus it "does not implicate the central function of an appellate court — to exercise control over the development of law."[174] Others have urged bifurcated review, with *de novo* review of legal conclusions and effects and deferential review of determinations of underlying facts and factual inferences.[175]

---

[168] *See* § 12.09[3][c], *supra*.

[169] *See Nunez v. Superior Oil Co.*, 572 F.2d 1119, 1126 (5th Cir. 1978) (if an inference "requires 'experience with the mainsprings of human conduct' and reference to 'the data of practical human experience' " it is for the jury, *quoting Commissioner v. Duberstein*, 363 U.S. 278, 289 (1960)).

[170] 456 U.S. 273, 289–90 (1982).

[171] *See* § 8.03[3] (specificity of code pleading), *supra*.

[172] *Pullman-Standard*, 456 U.S. at 289–90 n.19. *See, e.g., Bogardus v. Commissioner*, 302 U.S. 34, 38–39 (1937) (whether monetary awards given taxpayer were taxable compensation or tax-free gifts is a mixed question of fact and law).

[173] *Pullman-Standard*, 456 U.S. at 289–90 n.19, citing cases. *See generally* Even Tsen Lee, *Principled Decision Making and the Proper Role of Federal Appellate Courts: The Mixed Questions Conflict*, 64 S. Cal. L. Rev. 235 (1991) (finding a four-way split in the circuits on the issue); Wright & Miller § 2589.

[174] Lee, note 173, *supra*, at 236–37 [footnote omitted].

[175] Childress & Davis, note 164, *supra*, § 2.18.

A comparable problem is presented by a fact that is "inseparable from the principles through which it was deduced."[176]

> At some point, the reasoning by which a fact is "found" crosses the line between application of those ordinary principles of logic and common experience which are ordinarily entrusted to the finder of fact into the realm of a legal rule upon which the reviewing court must exercise its own independent judgment. Where the line is drawn varies according to the nature of the substantive law at issue. Regarding certain largely factual questions in some areas of the law, the stakes — in terms of impact on future cases and future conduct — are too great to entrust them finally to the judgment of the trier of fact.[177]

They therefore receive *de novo* review on appeal.

The Court has held that the finding of actual malice necessary to establish liability in a libel action by a public figure against a media defendant falls into this category, because of the courts' special responsibility for preserving First Amendment rights and the close relationship between the finding of such constitutional facts and the scope of the right.[178] "The simple fact is that First Amendment questions of 'constitutional fact' compel this Court's *de novo* review," as Justice Brennan put it.[179]

Some of the same considerations counsel *de novo* appellate review of whether a jury award of punitive damages is constitutionally excessive.[180] Unlike jury determinations of compensatory damages, which are essentially factual, the imposition of punitive damages is not factual, but instead an expression of moral condemnation which is subject to substantive limits imposed by the Due Process Clause. The Due Process standard of "gross excessiveness" is a fluid one which takes its meaning from context and case-by-case application. "Independent review" by appeals courts is therefore necessary to control, clarify, and unify the applicable constitutional legal principles, according to the Supreme Court.[181]

One commentator takes issue with the "mixed question," "application of law-to-facts," and "constitutional fact" rubrics federal courts offer to justify *de novo* review of (at least partially) factual matters. He argues that the intensity of review of such matters should reflect "the intellectual processes" by which the particular determination in question has been made: by observation

---

[176] *Bose Corp. v. Consumers Union of U.S., Inc.*, 466 U.S. 485, 501 n.17 (1984).

[177] *Id.*.

[178] *Id.* at 501. *Cf. Baumgartner v. United States*, 322 U.S. 665, 671 (1944) (whether there is clear, unequivocal, and convincing proof of conduct that justifies denaturalization is a question that "cannot escape broad[] social judgments" justifying independent appellate consideration).

[179] *Rosenbloom v. Metromedia, Inc.*, 403 U.S. 29, 54 (1971) (Brennan, J., joined by Burger, C.J., and Blackmun, J.). See *Roth v. United States*, 354 U.S. 476, 497–98 (1957), for a particularly forceful statement by Justice Harlan of the rationale for this rule.

[180] *Cooper Indus., Inc. v. Leatherman Tool Group, Inc.*, 532 U.S. 424, 431 (2001).

[181] *Id.* at 436.

(warranting substantial deference) or by reflection on record evidence (warranting less).[182]

[b] Clearly Erroneous — Findings by the Court

Historically, the law judge was viewed as a surrogate for the jury, while the equity judge was viewed as the equivalent of a master. Factual findings by the former thus received the same deference on review as findings by a jury, while findings by the latter received no special weight except insofar as they rested on determinations of credibility which only the trial judge could make.[183] With the merger of law and equity in the federal courts, these historical practices have also been merged into Rule 52(a)(6), which provides that judge-made "[f]indings of fact, whether based on oral or other evidence, must not be set aside unless clearly erroneous, and the reviewing court must give due regard to the trial court's opportunity to judge the witnesses' credibility."

The Supreme Court has stated that a finding is clearly erroneous "when although there is evidence to support it, the reviewing court on the entire evidence is left with the definite and firm conviction that a mistake has been committed."[184] It is not enough for the appellate court to conclude that it would have decided the issue differently. The test is not right or wrong, or review would be *de novo*.[185]

How much more is necessary depends not on whether the fact is ultimate or subsidiary,[186] but "on the nature of the materials on which the finding is based"[187] and any other factors that affect the relative competency of trial and appellate courts. Because of the trial judge's unique opportunity to observe the demeanor of witnesses, the presumption of correctness is stronger when the finding is based on oral evidence than when it is based on documentary evidence.[188] Rule 52 expressly reminds the appellate court of this by urging "due regard" for that opportunity. The presumption of correctness becomes stronger as trials become longer and more complex, on the theory that the trial court acquires greater intimacy with the evidence from living with it for weeks or months instead of just a few days or hours.[189] In contrast, the trial court's

---

[182] George C. Christie, *Judicial Review of Findings of Fact*, 87 Nw. U. L. Rev. 14, 56 (1992). *See* § 13.09[2][b] (explaining variability in clearly erroneous standard), *infra*.

[183] JAMES, HAZARD & LEUBSDORF § 12.9; Sward, note 165, *supra*, at 18–20.

[184] *United States v. United States Gypsum Co.*, 333 U.S. 364, 395 (1948).

[185] *See Anderson v. City of Bessemer*, 470 U.S. 564, 573 (1985). On the scope of *de novo* review, see § 13.10[1], *supra*.

[186] *Pullman-Standard*, 456 U.S. at 287 (Rule 52 "does not divide findings into categories"). Categorization of a fact as ordinary fact, mixed question of fact and law, or constitutional fact, on the other hand, can determine whether Rule 52 applies at all. *See* § 13.10[2][a] (*de novo* review), *supra*.

[187] *Baumgartner*, 322 U.S. at 671.

[188] *See Bose Corp.*, 466 U.S. at 497.

[189] 466 U.S. at 497. *See* Jeffrey W. Stempel, *A Distorted Mirror: the Supreme Court's Shimmering View of Summary Judgment, Directed Verdict, and the Adjudication Process*, 49 OHIO ST. L.J. 95, 177–78 (1993).

comparative fact-finding advantage diminishes when the evidence is entirely documentary and the trial short and simple. Then the court of appeals has nearly the same opportunity to acquaint itself with the evidence that the trial court had in making the record. The location of the clearly erroneous standard on the spectrum of review in Figure 13.10[1]-1 then shifts slightly to the left.

Prior to 1985, some federal courts went a step further and reasoned that the presumption in such circumstances was not just weakened but eliminated. They declined to apply the clearly erroneous standard of review to judge-made findings based solely on documentary evidence, instead reviewing them *de novo*.[190] These courts arguably disregarded the conjunctive "due regard" phrase in Rule 52. Moreover, they were wrong by their own reasoning, because they ignored the superiority in fact finding that a trial judge acquires even in documentary cases from his experience in general and his unavoidable exposure to the whole case in particular.[191] They also ignored the systemic interest in finality, which counsels against *de novo* appellate review of findings even when the trial and appellate courts have the same competency.

In 1985, the Supreme Court put an end to this practice in *Anderson v. City of Bessemer*.[192] There it emphasized that the clearly erroneous standard applies to all judge-made findings, although the strength of the presumption of correctness that it embodies may vary.[193] Rule 52(a) was amended thereafter to make clearer its applicability to all "[f]indings of fact, whether based on oral or documentary evidence" (now "oral or other evidence").

[c] Reasonableness — Findings by the Jury and Some Administrative Agencies

The command of the Seventh Amendment ("[N]o fact tried by a jury, shall be otherwise re-examined in any Court of the United States, than according to the rules of the common law") reinforces the considerations noted above and requires more deferential appellate review of jury findings than of judge findings. Logically, too, the jury's greater numbers should enhance its fact-finding ability and dilute its biases, entitling its findings to greater weight on appeal. The standard of review is the same as that employed by the trial judge to decide motions for directed verdict, judgment as a matter of law, or judgment notwithstanding the verdict: whether a reasonable jury could have reached the verdict.[194]

---

[190] *See, e.g., Davis*, 32 Fed. R. Serv. 2d (Callaghan) at 733 ("the Rule 52(a) 'clearly erroneous' standard does not apply to wholly documentary cases where the record discloses no oral testimony"); *Orvis v. Higgins*, 180 F.2d 537 (2d Cir.), *cert. denied*, 340 U.S. 810 (1950).

[191] "The trial judge's major role is the determination of fact, and with experience in fulfilling that role comes expertise." *Anderson v. City of Bessemer*, 470 U.S. 564, 574 (1985).

[192] 470 U.S. 564 (1985).

[193] *Id.*.

[194] *See, e.g., Hersch v. United States*, 719 F.2d 873, 877 (6th Cir. 1983); *Williams v. City of Valdosta*, 689 F.2d 964, 970 (11th Cir. 1982) (*citing Boeing Co.v. Shipman*, 411 F.2d 365, 374–75 (5th Cir. 1969) (*en banc*)). *See* § 12.09[1] (taking the case from the jury), *supra*. The standard of review is nominally the same when the trial judge has denied such motions as when he has granted

Notwithstanding this deferential standard of review, however, there is significant empirical evidence that federal appellate courts are more aggressive in review of jury verdicts for sufficiency of the evidence. They overturned fully half the verdicts appealed in the one-year period from 1984–1985, for example.[195] A large number of these decisions are aimed at so-called excessive jury verdicts.[196]

Statutes subject many administrative agency findings to a reasonableness standard like the standard for deciding motions attacking the jury's verdict.[197] Just as a jury's findings are given deference in part because of its fact-finding abilities, many administrative agency findings receive special weight because of the agencies' expertise in finding particular kinds of facts.

[d]   Abuse of Discretion — Discretionary Orders

Hardest to place on the spectrum of review is the *abuse of discretion* standard for reviewing discretionary orders by the trial court. Certain matters are within the discretion of the trial judge because they are largely ad hoc and situation-specific, closely related to calendar and trial management.[198] Decisions regarding scheduling, amendment by permission, complex joinder, consolidation and separation of claims for trial, order of discovery, order of proof, and sanctions under Rules 11 and 37 are illustrative. A right-or-wrong *de novo* standard of review would be difficult (perhaps impossible) to administer in such cases. Instead, the federal courts apply the abuse of discretion standard, which is tolerant of mistakes in the exercise of acknowledged discretion.

The difficulty in locating this standard on the spectrum of review is well-illustrated by the review of new trial decisions in jury cases. To grant or deny a new trial is in the discretion of the trial judge, who is best positioned to appreciate whether improper influences or argument tainted a jury verdict or whether the verdict is against the weight of the evidence.[199] When a new trial has been denied for any reason, the deference owed the trial court is reinforced by the deference owed a jury verdict. On the other hand, when a new trial is granted, and the issue is preserved for review on appeal from an eventual final judgment,[200] the trial judge receives less deference.

This is because when the jury verdict is set aside usual deference to the trial judge conflicts with deference to the jury on questions of fact.

---

them, but his decision to let the verdict stand may, as a practical matter, add weight to the verdict.

[195] Eric Schnapper, *Judges Against Juries — Appellate Review of Federal Civil Verdicts*, 1989 Wis. L. Rev. 237, 238.

[196] *Id.*, at 313.

[197] The statutory term of art is "supported by substantial evidence," *see* 5 U.S.C. § 706(2)(E), which has been interpreted to mean rational or reasonable. *See generally* BERNARD SCHWARTZ, ADMINISTRATIVE LAW §§ 10.7–10.11 (3d ed. 1991).

[198] *See* Rosenberg, note 161, *supra*, at 643–53 (noting that thirty of the Federal Rules of Civil Procedure involve some area of trial court discretion).

[199] *See* § 12.09 (new trial), *supra*.

[200] *See* § 13.03[1] (final judgment rule), *supra*.

When a new trial is granted on the basis that the verdict is against the weight of the evidence . . . [appellate] review is particularly stringent to protect the litigant's right to a jury trial.[201]

In fact, when the trial is simple, the facts highly disputed, and there is no taint from pernicious circumstances, review should be even more intense because of the correspondingly greater likelihood that the jury verdict was sound.[202]

This is only to suggest that the abuse of discretion standard varies in intensity with the breadth of discretion. Accordingly, abuse of discretion really occupies a band in the middle of the spectrum of intensity of review, its precise locus in any particular case depending upon the nature of the discretionary order under review.[203]

[e]   No Review — Selective Findings by Administrative Agencies

Placing a "standard of review" at the far left hand point of the spectrum of review seemingly poses an anomaly in that zero substitution of judgment — complete deference — is tantamount to no review. But because the intensity of review is issue-specific, the point is not just hypothetical. It is possible to allow review of a decision and still foreclose review of particular issues within it.

This in fact is what Congress has done with respect to certain fact-bound administrative decisions, typically mass justice benefit determinations by social service agencies.[204] Because of the large number of such decisions, their lack of precedential importance, and the arguably reliable adjudicative process by which they are made in the agencies, Congress has made some of the agencies' substantive decisions final and not subject to review outside the agencies. On the other hand, review-denying statutory provisions usually have not been read to foreclose review of associated issues of procedure, regulatory authority, and constitutional law,[205] which are less likely to flood the federal courts and which may carry precedential value.[206]

---

[201] *Hewitt v. B.F. Goodrich Co.*, 732 F.2d 1554, 1556 (11th Cir. 1984).

[202] *See, e.g., Williams v. City of Valdosta*, 689 F.2d 964, 974–75 (11th Cir. 1982).

[203] *Cf. Heat & Control, Inc. v. Hester Indus., Inc.*, 785 F.2d 1017, 1022 (Fed. Cir. 1986). *See generally* Childress & Davis, note 164, *supra*, § 4-154 (asserting that "no single level of deference or scrutiny is intended for the phrase *abuse of discretion*" and that it has a "sliding contextual meaning").

[204] *See, e.g.*, 38 U.S.C. § 511(a) (providing that, "The Secretary shall decide all questions of law and fact necessary to a decision by the Secretary under a law that affects the provision of benefits by the Secretary to veterans. . . . [T]he decision of the Secretary as to any such question shall be final and conclusive and may not be reviewed by any other official or by any court, whether by an action in the nature of mandamus or otherwise.").

[205] The denial of federal court review of bona fide constitutional claims would raise serious questions of due process. *See* Schwartz, note 197, *supra* § 8.40.

[206] *See, e.g., Johnson v. Robison*, 415 U.S. 361 (1974) (statutory review-denying provision does not bar review of constitutional claim); *Carter v. Cleland*, 643 F.2d 1, 3, 5 (D.C. Cir. 1980) (statutory review-denying provisions construed narrowly to allow review of issues of regulatory authority for and constitutionality of agency action).

Chapter 14

REMEDIES

§ 14.01   DAMAGES; SCOPE OF MONETARY RECOVERY[1]

[1]   Types of Damage Awards

[a]   Compensatory Damages

The objective of most civil actions is recovery of damages, a financial award payable from the defendant to the plaintiff. The most common kind of damage formula attaches a monetary value to the difference between what the plaintiff's situation is, and what it would have been if the defendant had performed a legal duty owed to the plaintiff — for example, if defendant had not breached its contract with plaintiff, or had not carelessly caused plaintiff physical injury. When defendant has wronged plaintiff, the measure of the wrong is plaintiff's actual or *compensatory* damages.[2]

This formula requires the fact-finder to resolve two points in plaintiff's favor before awarding damages. First, plaintiff must have suffered harm capable of monetary quantification.[3] Second, the harm must have been caused by defendant's failure to act as he had a legal duty to act toward plaintiff.[4] It is not necessary that harm suffered by plaintiff be susceptible to precise

---

[1] *See generally* DAN B. DOBBS, HANDBOOK ON THE LAW OF REMEDIES §§ 3.1–3.12 (2d ed. 1993); CHARLES T. MCCORMICK, HANDBOOK ON THE LAW OF DAMAGES (1935); Laurens Walker & John Monahan, *Sampling Damages*, 83 IOWA L. REV. 545 (1998); Robert Cooter & Melvin A. Eisenberg, *Damages for Breach of Contract*, 73 CAL. L. REV. 1432 (1985). *See also* § 4.02[2] (prejudgment attachments), *supra*, and § 15.02 (enforcement of money judgments), *infra*.

[2] *Cf.* DOUGLAS LAYCOCK, MODERN AMERICAN REMEDIES — CASES AND MATERIALS 14 (1985) (describing "the essence of compensatory damages" to be "the fundamental principle . . . to restore the injured party as nearly as possible to the position he would have been in but for the wrong.").

[3] Thus, valuation of damage to property is "usually based on the idea that the plaintiff's balance sheet shows a loss of net worth as a result of the defendant's tort or breach of contract." DOBBS, note 1, *supra*, § 3.2.

[4] To consider the points in this order probably makes the formula easier to grasp. In litigation, however, the sequence is usually reversed. This is because issues going to whether defendant owed a duty to plaintiff are much more susceptible to pretrial disposition. For example, plaintiff may have a strong case to make at trial that plaintiff suffered harm from defendant's failure to perform under a contract. But plaintiff will never get to make that case if defendant obtains summary judgment because the contract did not comply with the statute of frauds. Defendant would have established thereby that he owed plaintiff no contractual duty. For discussion of how summary judgments and other procedural devices screen out such cases before trial, see § 12.09[3][c], *supra*.

monetary valuation.[5] At the same time, some wrongs are so difficult to appraise monetarily that courts deny them damage treatment, or permit damages in insignificant amount.[6] When such wrongs can be foreseen, they are often better suited for treatment by preventative (injunctive)[7] relief.

[b] Punitive Damages[8]

In some cases plaintiff will obtain as a substantial element of his total damage recovery a sum unrelated to any actual harm done by defendant. These are *punitive* (exemplary) damages. [9] The object of this form of damages is to deter defendant and others from similar acts in the future. Only exceptional facts will support punitive damages. Usually they must establish either serious and calculated wrong by the defendant or conduct reflecting rank indifference to public safety or welfare.

It is more difficult to generalize a formula for punitive damages than for compensatory damages. As noted above, courts or juries set compensatory damages through a somewhat empirical approach, measuring the difference in plaintiff's situation with and without defendant's wrong. In contrast, punitive damages are more like ad hoc criminal fines. Moreover, while determination of compensatory damages is more or less mandatory upon proof of harm from defendant's wrong, plaintiff has no right to punitive damages.

The United States Supreme Court has in recent years placed significant due process constraints on the availability of punitive damages.[10] The Court's

---

[5] The best example may be damage recovery for intangible pain and suffering in tort cases. *See* Robert L. Rabin, *Pain and Suffering and Beyond: Some Thoughts on Recovery for Intangible Loss*, 55 DePaul L. Rev. 359 (2006); Victor E. Schwartz & Leah Lorber, *Twisting the Purpose of Pain and Suffering Awards: Turning Compensation into "Punishment"*, 54 S.C. L. Rev. 47 (2002). For a comparison of pain and suffering law in the United States with that of foreign countries, see Anthony J. Sebok, *Translating the Immeasurable: Thinking About Pain and Suffering Comparatively*, 55 DePaul L. Rev. 379 (2006); Stephen D. Sugarman, *A Comparative Law Look at Pain and Suffering Awards*, 55 DePaul L. Rev. 399 (2006).

[6] "A plaintiff who loses her pet cat may suffer something that cannot be measured by the market value of the cat." Dobbs, note 1, *supra*, § 3.2.

[7] *See* § 14.02[1], *infra*.

[8] On punitive damages generally, see Thomas A. Eaton, David B. Mustard & Susette M. Talarico, *The Effects of Seeking Punitive Damages on the Processing of Tort Claims*, 34 J. Legal Stud. 343 (2005).

[9] *See* Stephen C. Yeazell, *Punitive Damages, Descriptive Statistics, and the Economy of Civil Litigation*, 79 Notre Dame L. Rev. 2025 (2004); Colleen P. Murphy, *Judgment as a Matter of Law on Punitive Damages*, 75 Tul. L. Rev. 459 (2000); James A. Breslo, Comment, *Taking the Punitive Damage Windfall Away from the Plaintiff: An Analysis*, 86 Nw. U. L. Rev. 1130 (1992); Stephen Daniels & Joanne Martin, *Myth and Reality in Punitive Damages*, 75 Minn. L. Rev. 1 (1990); Dorsey D. Ellis, Jr., *Fairness and Efficiency in the Law of Punitive Damages*, 56 S. Cal. L. Rev. 1 (1982). For a valuable study of the history of punitive damages in English and American courts, see Thomas B. Colby, *Beyond the Multiple Punishment Problem: Punitive Damages as Punishment for Individual, Private Wrongs*, 87 Minn. L. Rev. 583, 614–29 (2003).

Related are statutory provisions for multiple damages — usually a doubling or trebling of compensatory damages. *See generally* Dobbs, note 1, *supra*, § 3.12.

[10] Despite the broad discretion that States possess with respect to the imposition of . . .

modern approach began to take shape in *BMW of North America, Inc. v. Gore*.[11] Gore sued his auto dealer for failing to disclose to him that his car had been repainted after being damaged prior to delivery. Awarding him compensatory damages of $4000, a jury tacked on $4 million in punitive damages. The Supreme Court reversed. It held that the reasonableness of a jury's award of punitive damages depends upon (1) the reprehensibility of defendant's conduct, (2) the disparity between the actual or potential harm suffered by plaintiff and the award, and (3) the difference between an award and the civil penalties authorized or imposed in similar cases. The dealer's failure to disclose the repainting was not notably reprehensible: there was no evidence that it had acted in bad faith or that its nondisclosure had affected the car's performance, safety, or even (initially) its appearance. The punitive damages award was 500 times the amount of Gore's actual harm. Finally, the Court noted that the maximum civil penalty set by state legislatures for deceptive trade practices ranged from $2000 to $10,000, giving the dealer no reason to anticipate the $4 million penalty which the jury had imposed.

The Supreme Court and commentators have attempted to separate the Court's punitive damages decisions into two categories: protection of procedural due process and protection of substantive due process.[12]

In *Honda Motor Co., Ltd. v. Oberg*,[13] the first of three procedural due process cases, the Supreme Court ruled that lack of judicial review of the fairness of a jury's punitive damages award violated due process. Then, in *Cooper Industries, Inc. v. Leatherman Tool Group, Inc.*,[14] the Court required *de novo* review of the trial court's ruling on the constitutionality of a punitive

---

punitive damages, the Due Process Clause of the Fourteenth Amendment . . . imposes substantive limits on that discretion. That Clause makes the Eighth Amendment's prohibition against excessive fines and cruel and unusual punishments applicable to the States . . . The Due Process Claus of its own force also prohibits the States from imposing "grossly excessive" punishments on tortfeasors.

Cooper Indus., Inc. v. Leatherman Tool Group, Inc., 532 U.S. 424, 433–34 (2001).

The appropriate role of the Constitution in regulating punitive damages remains a subject of lively debate. *Compare* A. Benjamin Spencer, *Due Process and Punitive Damages: The Error of Federal Excessiveness Jurisprudence*, 79 S. Cal. L. Rev. 1085 (2006) (urging fewer constitutional constraints on punitive damages), *with* Martin H. Redish & Andrew L. Mathews, *Why Punitive Damages are Unconstitutional*, 53 Emory L.J. 1 (2004) (arguing punitive damages are unconstitutional per se).

[11] 517 U.S. 559 (1996).

[12] *See, e.g.*, Ronald D. Rotunda & John E. Nowak, Treatise on Constitutional Law § 14.6[e] (4th ed. 2007):

The Supreme Court has now ruled that the due process clause of the Fourteenth Amendment requires states to adopt procedures to ensure that punitive damage awards are made through a fair process that include[s] judicial review of jury awards. [The Court] also endorsed the position that the due process clause authorizes review courts to impose a substantive limit on the amount of punitive damages.

[13] 512 U.S. 415 (1994), *discussed in* Ronald D. Rotunda & John E. Nowak, Treatise on Constitutional Law § 14.06[e] (4th ed. 2007).

[14] 532 U.S. 424 (2001), *featured in* R. Shane McLaughlin, *Constitutional Law — Judicial*

damages award. Finally, in *Philip Morris USA v. Williams*,[15] it rejected, as a violation of procedural due process, a determination of punitive damages that included harm to nonparties in the case. *Honda* envisioned the possibility that a punitive damages award might be so great as to violate substantive due process. The Supreme Court thereafter found such a case in *BMW of North America, Inc. v. Gore*,[16] ruling that the differential between $4,000 in compensatory damages and the judgment of $2 million (after reduction from $4 million by the trial court) in punitive damages was so excessive as to violate substantive due process. Similarly, in *State Farm Mutual Automobile Insurance Co. v. Campbell*,[17] the Court stuck down a $145,000,000 punitive damages award when compensatory damages were only $1,000,000. The Court has declined to issue a specific numerical standard for determining the permissible differential between compensatory and punitive damages in cases arising in state court,[18] but did assert in *State Farm*: "Our jurisprudence and the principles it has now established demonstrate . . . that, in practice, few awards exceeding a single-digit ratio between punitive and compensatory damages, to a significant degree, will satisfy due process."[19] This has led two leading constitutional scholars to conclude: "it appears that trial courts will have difficulty justifying any award of punitive damages that is more than 9 times greater than the amount of compensatory damages awarded in a case."[20]

Statutes and rules of civil procedure may also limit punitive damages claims. Statutes may place caps on punitive damages[21] or prohibit them altogether for certain claims. Rules may restrict the discovery of evidence needed to argue punitive damages, the evidence permitted to establish them, or the standard used to supervise them both at the trial court and the appellate levels. Indeed, in *Gore*, three concurring justices emphasized that Alabama's failure to supply either legal or quantitative standards that might "significantly cabin the fairly

---

Review — Appellate Courts Must Review De Novo the Constitutionality of Punitive Damages Awards, 71 MISS. L.J. 711 (2001).

[15] 549 U.S. 346 (2007).

[16] 517 U.S. 559 (1996), *discussed in* Pamela S. Karlan, *"Pricking the Lines": The Due Process Clause, Punitive Damages, and Criminal Punishment*, 88 MINN. L. REV. 880, 905–11 (2004).

[17] 538 U.S. 408 (2003), *discussed in* Joseph J. Chambers, *In re Exxon Valdez: Application of Due Process Constraints on Punitive Damages Awards*, 20 ALASKA L. REV. 195, 212–18 (2003).

[18] In contrast, the Court recently limited punitive damages to the amount of compensatory damages in a federal maritime case. *Exxon Shipping Co. v. Baker*, 128 S. Ct. 2605 (2008). The Court took pains to distinguish *Exxon* from the due process cases discussed in the text.

> Today's enquiry differs from due process review because the case arises under federal maritime jurisdiction, and we are reviewing a jury award for conformity with maritime law, rather than the outer limit allowed by due process; we are examining the verdict in the exercise of federal maritime common law authority, which precedes and should obviate any application of the constitutional standard.

128 S. Ct. at 2626.

[19] 538 U.S. at 424.

[20] RONALD D. ROTUNDA & JOHN E. NOWAK, TREATISE ON CONSTITUTIONAL LAW § 14.06[e] (4th ed. 2007).

[21] For a survey of state statutes imposing caps on punitive damages awards, see *Gore*, 517 U.S. at 614–16 (Appendix to Opinion of Ginsburg, J.).

unbounded discretion" given the jury to decide punitive damages helped to persuade them that the $2 million award was unconstitutionally excessive.[22]

[c]   Nominal Damages

Like punitive damages, *nominal* damages do not reflect real harm, but in contrast they are quite small.[23] When permitted, nominal damages can make possible litigation in which plaintiff either suffered no actual harm or the harm is impossible to prove. They may also play a role when plaintiff seeks but fails to obtain substantial damage recovery, since award of nominal damages often makes the defendant liable for the court costs.[24]

[2]   Added Elements in Financial Awards — Costs, Expenses, and Attorney's Fees

Complaints in damage cases seek compensatory, punitive, or nominal damages (or some combination thereof) in specific amounts. Most such complaints also request court costs. Expenses awarded as court costs to the winning party (plaintiff or defendant) usually are relatively insignificant.[25] While English courts usually require the losing party to pay the victor's attorney's fees,[26] there is still a strong tradition against that practice in this country.[27] There are, however, two types of exceptions.

First, certain forms of litigation (although brought by private parties) are considered sufficiently within the public interest to warrant shifting of attorney's fees from the prevailing party to the losing party as an incentive to suit.[28] Second, the growing expense of legal services and a general apprehension about indiscriminate civil litigation in this country has led to creation of expense-shifting mechanisms in certain procedural rules. These are intended to compensate parties suffering from opponents' litigation abuses and to provide a corresponding incentive for careful and restrained use of civil

---

[22] *Gore*, 517 U.S. at 595–96.

[23] "Nominal damages are damages in name only, trivial sums such as six cents or $1." Dobbs, note 1, *supra*, § 3.3(2). A useful discussion of nominal damages appears in David Schoenbrod, Angus McBeth, David Levine & David Jung, Remedies Public and Private 482–83 (1990).

[24] Dobbs, note 1, *supra*, § 3.8, at 193. *See, e.g.*, Rule 54(d), *discussed in* § 14.01[2] *infra*.

[25] For example, federal Rule 54(d) authorizes courts to allow "costs . . . to the prevailing party . . . ," yet "costs" in this context has been read to cover considerably less than the litigation expenses of the prevailing party.

[26] *Cf. Wright & Miller* § 2665 ("The cardinal principle of the English system has been and continues to be one of total reimbursement.").

[27] Thomas D. Rowe, Jr., *Indemnity or Compensation? The Contract with America, Loser Pays Fee Shifting*, 37 Washburn L.J. 317 (1998); *Symposium on Fee Shifting*, 71 Chi-Kent L. Rev. 415 (1995); *Fogerty v. Fantasy, Inc.*, 510 U.S. 517 (1994); *Key Tronic Corp. v. United States*, 511 U.S. 809 (1994).

[28] Since the Supreme Court's decision in *Alyeska Pipeline Service Co. v. Wilderness Society*, 421 U.S. 240 (1975), federal court authority to award attorney fees on this basis has largely been confined to statute. However, the list of such statutes is quite extensive. *Alyeska Pipeline Serv. Co.*, 421 U.S. at 260 n.33.

procedure. Expense-shifting provisions in federal rules treat the signing of pleadings, motions, and other court papers,[29] discovery abuses,[30] and offers of judgment made prior to trial.[31]

[3] Enforcing Money Judgments

[This topic is discussed in § 15.02, *infra*.]

§ 14.02 EQUITABLE RELIEF; INJUNCTIONS[32]

Injunctions are available in all state and federal courts. They are one of three types of equitable remedies which can be traced to English practice.[33] Injunctions are court decrees which control the behavior of the defendant by ordering him either to act or to refrain from acting in a certain way. While factual elements of damage actions concern the past (what defendant did and what it cost the plaintiff), factual elements in injunction cases concern the future (what the defendant will do to the plaintiff, absent an injunction).

[1] The Shape of Equitable Discretion

Equitable remedies evolved to supplement legal remedies.[34] They were a response to appeals for fairness and justice in what were thought to be especially deserving cases. It continues to be true that equitable remedies

---

[29] *See, e.g.*, §§ 8.05[2] (federal Rule 11) & 10.13[1] (federal Rule 26(g)), *supra*.

[30] *See, e.g.*, § 10.14[2] (federal Rule 37), *supra*.

[31] For example, federal Rule 68 states that, at any time more than 10 days before trial, "a party defending against a claim may serve on an opposing party an offer to allow judgment" in a certain amount. If the offer is refused and "the judgment that the offeree finally obtains is not more favorable than the unaccepted offer, the offeree must pay the costs incurred after the offer was made." On the scope and application of Rule 68, see *Marek v. Chesny*, 473 U.S. 1 (1985); *Delta Air Lines, Inc. v. August*, 450 U.S. 346 (1981). *See generally* WRIGHT & MILLER §§ 3001–3005; Thomas D. Rowe, Jr. & David A. Anderson, *One-Way Fee Shifting Statutes and Offer of Judgment Rules: An Experiment*, 36 JURIMETRICS J. 255 (1996). What "costs" Rule 68 takes in is unclear, although the Court in *Marek* gave the term broader application than it usually has in Rule 54(d). *See* § 14.01, note 25, *supra*. The rule remains a source of controversy. *See* Peter Margulies, *After Marek, the Deluge: Harmonizing the Interaction Under Rule 68 of Statutes That Do and Do Not Classify Attorney's Fees as "Costs,"* 73 IOWA L. REV. 413 (1988); Stephen B. Burbank, *Proposals to Amend Rule 68 — Time to Abandon Ship*, 19 MICH. J.L. REFORM 425 (1986).

[32] *See generally* DOUGLAS LAYCOCK, THE DEATH OF THE IRREPARABLE INJURY RULE (1991); Gene R. Shreve, *Federal Injunctions and the Public Interest*, 51 GEO. WASH. L. REV. 382 (1983); DAN B. DOBBS, HANDBOOK ON THE LAW OF REMEDIES §§ 2.1–2.11 (2d ed. 1993); Note, *Developments in the Law — Injunctions*, 78 HARV. L. REV. 994 (1965); W. DE FUNIAK, HANDBOOK OF MODERN EQUITY (1956).

[33] The other two are specific performance and judicial administration of estates. F.W. MAITLAND, EQUITY 22 (2d rev. ed. 1936).

[34] Writing on English practice in the sixteenth century, a distinguished commentator wrote that it was the "intent [of] equity . . . to temper and mitigate the rigour of the law." C. ST. GERMAIN, DIALOGUES BETWEEN A DOCTOR OF DIVINITY AND A STUDENT IN THE LAWS OF ENGLAND 45 (W. Muchall 18th ed. 1792); *cf.* 4 W. HOLDSWORTH, A HISTORY OF ENGLISH LAW 281 (1924) (equity is necessary in order that the law can do complete justice); PETER HOFFER, THE LAW'S CONSCIENCE 8 (1990) (discussing Aristotle's view of the necessity of equity to lessen the severity of law). *See generally* § 8.02[2] (equity pleading and practice), *supra*.

rarely exist as a matter of right. The discretion of courts to refuse injunctions is well-established. That discretion takes shape from a set of injunctive prerequisites, often called *equitable jurisdiction*, and from a number of maxims, or *equitable defenses*, further limiting the availability of relief.

The concept of equitable jurisdiction[35] encompasses as many as three requirements. Two are keyed on the character of harm plaintiff will suffer without an injunction. First, harm must be immediate and substantial. If the prospect of substantial harm to plaintiff is remote, plaintiff's request for an injunction will usually be denied.[36] Second, harm must be irreparable.[37] This requirement is sometimes stated another way: that plaintiff have no adequate remedy at law.[38] Third and finally, the controversy must provide a manageable setting for injunctive relief. That is, it must be possible for the court to describe the conduct it intends to regulate with sufficient clarity in the decree that it and the parties will not thereafter become ensnared in difficult issues of interpretation and compliance.[39]

Since courts use fairness and justice to support equitable remedies, additional facts showing that plaintiff has been less than fair in his treatment of defendant may render plaintiff ineligible for an injunction. Maxims like "plaintiff must come to the court with clean hands" and "equity aids only the vigilant"[40] thus function as equitable defenses. Courts have also used the technique of "balancing the equities" to deny plaintiffs injunctions, concluding that it would be much harder for defendant to live with the injunction than for plaintiff to live without it.[41]

---

[35] "[T]he equity jurisdiction of the federal courts is the jurisdiction in equity exercised by the High Court of Chancery in England at the time of the adoption of the Constitution and the enactment of the original Judiciary Act, 1789." *Grupo Mexicano de Desarrollo, S.A. v. Alliance Bond Fund, Inc.*, 527 U.S. 308, 318 (1999).

[36] The classic case illustrating this point is *Fletcher v. Bealy*, 28 Ch. D. 688 (1885) (injunction denied because plaintiff failed to establish that the likelihood of harm to its downstream paper processing operation was both substantial and immediate).

[37] *See generally* Douglas Laycock, *Injunctions and the Irreparable Injury Rule*, 57 Tex. L. Rev. 1065 (1979). Whether the irreparable injury rule still has much life in contemporary injunction cases is a matter of debate. *Compare* Laycock, note 32, *supra* (arguing that the rule has little remaining significance), *with* Gene R. Shreve, *The Premature Burial of the Irreparable Injury Rule*, 70 Tex. L. Rev. 1063 (1992) (maintaining that the rule is alive and influential in modern cases).

[38] Owen Fiss, The Civil Rights Injunction 38 (1978). *See generally* Doug Rendleman, *The Inadequate Remedy at Law Prerequisite for an Injunction*, 33 U. Fla. L. Rev. 346 (1981).

[39] *See* Shreve, note 32, *supra*, at 394. *Cf.* de Funiak, note 32, *supra*, at 24 ("Where the court has the theoretical power to grant an injunction but enforcement is impracticable or impossible, the court will not grant the injunction. It would be derogatory of the dignity of the court to enter orders it could not enforce.").

[40] *See generally* Henry L. McClintock, Handbook of the Principles of Equity §§ 26 & 28 (2d ed. 1948) (discussing the development of the clean hands doctrine and the maxim that equity aids only the vigilant). Similar to the latter is the doctrine of laches, "which bars a plaintiff from maintaining a suit if he unreasonably delays in filing suit and as a result harms the defendant." *National R.R. Passenger Corp. v. Morgan*, 536 U.S. 101, 121 (2002).

Not all equitable defenses key on plaintiff's conduct. See for example, discussion of the maxim, "Equity Will Not Enjoin a Crime," in *Developments*, note 32, *supra*, at 1013–18.

[41] *See generally* Elizabeth G. Thornburg, *Litigating the Zero Sum Game: The Effect of*

[2] Procedure for Obtaining and Enforcing Injunctions

The procedure for obtaining a final (permanent) injunction is a trial on the merits of the case much like that for a damages remedy. It takes time, however, to reach judgment on plaintiff's prayer for a final injunction. During the interim, defendant may inflict considerable damage on plaintiff or act to moot the case. All procedural systems thus have provision for provisional (interlocutory) injunctive relief.[42] Federal Rule 65 authorizes both temporary restraining orders and preliminary injunctions.[43] Plaintiff may appeal the denial of a final injunction, and, sometimes, denial of an interlocutory injunction.

What gives interlocutory and final injunctions their force is the prospect that defendants who violate them may be liable for either civil or criminal contempt.[44] Civil contempt adjudications may be either compensatory

---

Institutional Reform Litigation on Absent Parties, 66 OR. L. REV. 843 (1987); W. Page Keeton & Clarence Morris, *Notes on "Balancing the Equities"*, 18 TEX. L. REV. 412 (1940); John L. Mechem, *The Peasant in His Cottage: Some Comments on the Relative Hardship Doctrine in Equity*, 28 S. CAL. L. REV. 139 (1955). *Cf.* David S. Schoenbrod, *The Measure of an Injunction: A Principle to Replace Balancing the Equities and Tailoring the Remedy*, 72 MINN. L. REV. 627 (1988) (proposing changes in the approach).

[42] The leading work on provisional injunctive relief remains John Leubsdorf, *The Standard for Preliminary Injunctions*, 91 HARV. L. REV. 525 (1978). In addition, *see* Richard R.W. Brooks & Warren F. Schwartz, *Legal Undertainty, Economic Efficiency, and the Preliminary Injunction Doctrine*, 58 STAN. L. REV. 381 (2005); Douglas Lichtman, *Uncertainty and the Standard for Preliminary Relief*, 70 U. CHI. L. REV. 197 (2003); Bart Forsyth, *Preliminary Imprimaturs: Prevailing Party Status Based on Preliminary Injunctions*, 60 WASH. & LEE L. REV. 927 (2003); Morton Denlo, *The Motion for a Preliminary Injunction: Time for a Uniform Federal Standard*, 22 REV. LITIG. 495 (2003); Linda J. Silberman, *Injunctions by the Numbers: Less Than the Sum of Its Parts*, 63 CHI.-KENT L. REV. 279 (1987); Ann E. Heiny, Note, *Formulating a Theory for Preliminary Injunctions*, 72 IOWA L. REV. 1157 (1987).

[43] Many courts look to the following factors in determining whether to grant preliminary injunctions:

> (1) the significance of the threat of irreparable harm to plaintiff if the injunction is not granted; (2) the state of the balance between this harm and the injury that granting the injunction would inflict on defendant; (3) the probability that plaintiff will succeed on the merits; and (4) and the public interest.

WRIGHT & MILLER § 2948. The same factors undoubtedly influence decisions whether to issue temporary restraining orders. However, proceedings leading to decision on plaintiff's application for a temporary restraining order tend to be more summary in nature and may, under extraordinary circumstances, be conducted *ex parte*. At the same time, neither Rule 65 nor practice under the rule clearly delineate the two. The Supreme Court has, in fact, downplayed the importance of Rule 65 as a means of defining federal equity practice. *See Grupo Mexicano de Desarrollo, S.A. v. Alliance Bond Fund, Inc.*, 527 U.S. 308 (1999). The distinction between a temporary restraining order and a preliminary injunction may affect the appealability of an order denying relief. *See* § 13.04[1] (statutory appeal as of right), *supra*. On temporary injunctive relief in federal court generally, see WRIGHT & MILLER §§ 2947–2954.

[44] Useful general discussions of civil and criminal contempt and how they differ can be found in Issachar Rosen-Zvi & Talia Fisher, *Overcoming Procedural Boundaries*, 94 VA. L. REV. 79 (2008); Jennifer Fleiscer, *In Defense of Civil Contempt Sanctions*, 36 COLUM. J.L. & SOC. PROBS. 35 (2002); Linda S. Beres, *Games Civil Contemnors Play*, 18 HARV. J.L. & PUB. POLICY 795 (1995); Earl C. Dudley, Jr., *Getting Beyond the Civil/Criminal Distinction: A New Approach to the Regulation of Indirect Contempts*, 79 VA. L. REV. 1025 (1993); Doug Rendleman, *Disobedience and Coercive*

(producing a sum payable to plaintiff for the violation) or coercive (threatening defendant with damages or incarceration if the violations continue). Criminal contempt sanctions are penal (setting fines payable to the sovereign or fixed jail sentences). Two ways in which this difference manifests itself are in the nature of the proceeding necessary to support a determination of contempt[45] and in the gravamen of the wrong.[46]

Choices presented to the addressee of a provisional or permanent injunction[47] are not limited to compliance or contempt. The party may also seek dissolution or modification of the injunction through appeal, or through rehearing before the court that issued it.[48] This factor can either help or hurt addressees of injunctions. On one hand, the concerns of equity and fairness that support issuance of injunctions[49] also support the idea that addressees should have broad court access to argue why injunctions running against them should be dissolved or at least narrowed. Even courts who issued the injunctions will often reconsider that decision, particularly in light of new evidence or changed circumstances. In doing so, courts are more willing than they usually are to revisit matters already decided.[50] On the other hand, the willingness of courts to entertain challenges against the continued operation of injunctions bolsters their authority to impose contempt sanctions against addressees who bypass opportunities for modification or appeal.[51]

Contempt Confinement: The Terminally Stubborn Contemnor, 48 WASH. & LEE L. REV. 185 (1991); Dan B. Dobbs, *Contempt of Court: A Survey*, 56 CORNELL L. REV. 183 (1971); Comment, *Developments*, note 32, *supra*, at 1086–90.

[45] Civil contempt is an adjunct of the main case. It "[i]s prosecuted in the name of the plaintiff, and largely controlled by the plaintiff. He initiates it with a motion, and up to a point he can abandon it or settle it." DOUGLAS LAYCOCK, MODERN AMERICAN REMEDIES — CASES AND MATERIALS 637 (1985). "Criminal contempt," in contrast, "is prosecuted in the name of the sovereign." There are more opportunities for reversible error, since "defendant gets substantially all the protections of criminal procedure." *Id.* at 636.

[46] Criminal contempts represent a kind of defiant disobedience. They are willful in the sense crimes are usually thought of as willful. In contrast, adjudications of civil contempt proceed from the bare fact of noncompliance. *Cf.* ROBERT S. THOMPSON & JOHN A. SEBERT, REMEDIES: DAMAGES, EQUITY AND RESTITUTION § 3.10 (1983) ("Criminal contempts are those which flout the court's authority; civil contempts are those designed to compel enforcement of court orders.").

[47] Here, the "word 'permanent' signifies not the injunction's duration but rather that it is not contingent upon some further finding on the merits." SCHOENBROD ET AL.,, note 23, *supra*, at 166. "A permanent injunction continues to apply unless it expires by its own terms or is later modified or dissolved by a court of competent jurisdiction." *Id.*

[48] For discussion of processes for clarifying, restricting and dissolving injunctions, see Timothy S. Jost, *From Swift to Stotts and Beyond: Modifications of Injunctions in the Federal Courts*, 64 TEX. L. REV. 1101 (1986); Note, *The Modification of Consent Decrees in Institutional Reform Litigation*, 99 HARV. L. REV. 1020 (1986); *Developments in the Law*, note 32, *supra* at 1078–91. The same procedure is available to enlarge injunctions.

[49] *See* note 40, *supra*.

[50] This idea finds support in *Miller v. French*, 530 U.S. 327 (2000), and *Agostini v. Felton*, 521 U.S. 203 (1997). The contrasting reluctance of courts, as a general matter, to return to matters they have already ruled upon is clear from the "law of the case" doctrine, discussed at § 15.14, *infra*.

[51] A graphic illustration of the point can be found in *Walker v. City of Birmingham*, 388 U.S. 307 (1967). The Supreme Court denied defendants an opportunity to raise as a defense to contempt proceedings the unconstitutionality of the state anti-parading law upon which the injunction had

§ 14.03   DECLARATORY RELIEF[52]

[1]   Nature of Declaratory Relief

All judicial remedies proceed from a determination of the rights and obligations of the parties. Courts would otherwise lack the authority to dispense damage awards and injunctions. What sets declaratory judgments apart is that they *only* determine rights and obligations. That may not seem like a lot, but declaratory judgments actually can accomplish a great deal. For example, the fruits of victory for a party threatened with liability are precisely the same in a declaratory proceeding as in a suit for damages — a favorable judgment precluding further litigation.[53]

Requests for declaratory judgments are sometimes made in tandem with requests for damages or injunctive relief. The real significance of the remedy, however, lies in situations where only declaratory relief is available. Frequently the plaintiff in such cases is one who expects eventually to be the target of a claim for damages or an injunction. Plaintiff brings the prospective claimant in as defendant and seeks a favorable adjudication of an issue underlying defendant's prospective claim.[54] Plaintiff's incentive for bringing the declaratory proceeding is to clear the air. The preclusive effect given federal declaratory judgments is typical. "Any such declaration shall have the force and effect of a final judgment or decree and shall be reviewable as such."[55]

---

been based. The Court noted: "This case would arise in quite a different constitutional posture if the petitioners, before disobeying the injunction, had challenged it in the Alabama courts, and had been met with delay or frustration of their constitutional claims." *Walker*, 388 U.S. at 318. For examination of the issues raised in *Walker*, see John R.B. Palmer, *Collateral Bar and Contempt: Challenging a Court Order After Disobeying It*, 88 CORNELL L. REV. 215 (2002); Richard E. Labunski, *The "Collateral Bar" Rule and the First Amendment: The Constitutionality of Enforcing Unconstitutional Orders*, 37 AM. U. L. REV. 323 (1988).

[52] *See generally* WRIGHT & MILLER §§ 2751–71; *Developments in the Law — Declaratory Judgments*, 62 HARV. L. REV. 787 (1949).

[53] Thus,

> declaratory judgment relief creates means by which rights and obligations may be adjudicated in cases involving an actual controversy that has not reached a stage at which either party may seek a coercive remedy or in which a party entitled to a coercive remedy fails to sue.

MOORE § 57.04[3]. For a survey of issues concerning the precise res judicata effects of declaratory judgments, see Elizabeth L. Hisserich, *The Collision of Declaratory Judgments and Res Judicata*, 48 UCLA L. REV. 159 (2000).

[54] In this case, the declaratory judgment action is anticipatory, a kind of preemptive strike. Thus the labels of plaintiff and defendant are the reverse of what they would be if the claimant had been permitted eventually to file suit. *See, e.g.*, *Aetna Life Ins. Co. v. Haworth*, 300 U.S. 227 (1937) (declaratory judgment action filed by insurer against the insured). This reversal may have significant consequences for federal question jurisdiction. *See* § 5.03, *supra*.

[55] 28 U.S.C. § 2201.

[2]　　The Federal Model

Federal courts were slower to dispense declaratory judgments than many state courts. The problem was uncertainty whether suit for declaratory relief alone satisfied the case and controversy requirement of Article III of the Constitution. The Supreme Court finally ruled that such suits were permissible, "so long as the case retains the essentials of an adversary proceeding, involving a real, not a hypothetical controversy . . . ."[56] Congress soon responded by enacting the Federal Declaratory Judgment Act, conferring authority to render declaratory judgments in cases "of actual controversy."[57]

The line between a potential and an actual controversy is not always clear. The best approach is to examine the facts of each case. The Supreme Court's observations in *Aetna Life Insurance Co. v. Haworth* remain a useful guide:

> The controversy must be definite and concrete, touching the legal relations of parties having adverse legal interests. It must be a real and substantial controversy admitting of specific relief through a decree of a conclusive character, as distinguished from an opinion advising what the law would be upon a hypothetical state of facts. Where there is such a concrete case admitting of an immediate and definitive determination of the legal rights of the parties in an adversary proceeding upon the facts alleged, the judicial function may be appropriately exercised . . . .[58]

Even when the prerequisites for a declaratory judgment are satisfied, federal and many state courts have considerable discretion to withhold the remedy. Reasons for doing so include inability of the declaratory judgment to end the controversy, the public interest in delaying suit, and existence of a pending and related action.[59]

Rule 57 extends coverage of the Federal Rules of Civil Procedure to cases under the Declaratory Judgment Act. "The incidents of pleading, process, discovery, trial, and judgment are the same."[60] The parties to a declaratory judgment action have a right to a jury trial, if that right would have existed in the "kind of action in which the issue involved would have been decided if there were no declaratory-judgment procedure."[61] In the usual reversed parties case,[62] this inquiry would require application of the modified historical test for the right to jury trial[63] to the action that the declaratory judgment defendant would have brought had not the declaratory judgment plaintiff filed first.

---

[56] *Nashville, Chattanooga, & St. Louis Ry. v. Wallace*, 288 U.S. 249, 264 (1933).

[57] 28 U.S.C. § 2201.

[58] 300 U.S. 227, 240–41 (1937) (citations omitted).

[59] *See Developments — Declaratory Judgments*, note 52, *supra*, at 805–17.

[60] Wright & Miller § 2768.

[61] Wright § 100.

[62] *See* note 54, *supra*.

[63] *See* § 12.07[1], *supra*.

Chapter 15

RESPECT FOR FINAL JUDGMENTS

§ 15.01 OVERVIEW

[1] Policies That Define and Limit Preclusion

This chapter will examine the manner in which prior adjudications can bind or preclude parties in subsequent lawsuits. The body of law which sets the effect of prior adjudications (judgments) is called *res judicata*[1] or, in modern parlance, *preclusion* doctrine. American courts initially borrowed their law of *res judicata* from English jurisprudence, where the term appears in judicial decisions as early as the thirteenth century.[2] In this country, *res judicata* has always been primarily a creature of judicial doctrine.

The content of preclusion doctrine varies within our system of federal and state courts. The Supremacy Clause of the United States Constitution requires all courts to respect federal law guaranteeing due process to litigants[3] and full faith and credit to the judgments of other states.[4] But these constraints leave each state judicial system a good deal of freedom to fashion its own rules of preclusion. It is clear, for example, that cases decided by the Supreme Court which determine the content of federal court preclusion doctrine are not binding on state preclusion doctrine.[5]

Each system determines how much preclusive effect to give its judgments by weighing policies favoring preclusion against concern that the succeeding case be correctly decided. Commonly accepted policies supporting preclusion derive from the fact that repetitive litigation takes its toll on courts, other

---

[1]

> Res judicata performs the job of delineating the real content of a judgment, doing so by specifying the effects of the decision. Res judicata dictates whether decided matters are subject to reopening, as well as which actually undecided matters nevertheless fall within the bounds of a judgment and so receive treatment as if decided. It thus defines by means of fixing the boundaries of the judgment.

Kevin M. Clermont, *Common-Law Compulsory Counterclaim Rule: Creating Effective and Elegant Res Judicata Doctrine*, 79 NOTRE DAME L. REV. 1745 (2004).

[2] ALAN D. VESTAL, RES JUDICATA/PRECLUSION 28–30 (1969).

[3] *See* § 15.06, *infra.*

[4] *See* § 15.10, *infra.*

[5] Within constitutional limits, the courts of each state determine how preclusive their judgments will be. Yet Supreme Court cases can be influential by example. *See, e.g.*, the discussion of *Parklane Hosiery Co. v. Shore*, 439 U.S. 322 (1979), at § 15.08[2][b], *infra.*

litigants and the public. The objectives of *res judicata* are "to save judicial energy, to prevent harassment of the defendant, to further societal interests in the orderly and expeditious resolution of controversies, and to give repose."[6] The concept of repose is especially important.

> The deepest interests underlying the conclusive effect of prior adjudication draw from the purpose to provide a means of finally ending private disputes. The central role of adversary litigation in our society is to provide binding answers. We want to free people from the uncertain prospect of litigation, with all its costs to emotional peace and the ordering of future affairs. Repose is the most important product of *res judicata*.[7]

Concern for correctness of judicial decision is the prudential counterforce to preclusion in all systems. Judge Learned Hand observed that *res judicata* "must be treated as a compromise between two conflicting interests: the convenience of avoiding a multiplicity of suits and the adequacy of the remedies afforded for conceded wrongs."[8] Granted, courts often say that the incorrectness of a judgment does not diminish its preclusive effect.[9] This maxim is easy to follow when the second suit is merely a replication of the first. The more dissimilar the first and second suits are, however, the more the point loses force. Every system seems to recognize some point where preclusion — although constitutional — is inappropriate because the judgment does not carry a sufficient assurance of correctness to govern the different case as well.

[2]   Contemporary Developments[10]

Three contemporary developments in the law of *res judicata* should be noted.

[a]   The Restatement (Second) of Judgments

In 1982, the American Law Institute published the *Restatement (Second) of Judgments*. It is difficult to overstate its influence. Even in draft form, the work's treatment of the law of *res judicata* shaped many judicial decisions. Like the Restatements generally,[11] it is a combination of what the law currently seems to be and what the writers would like the law to be. Some of its provisions are more controversial than others, yet there is no question that

---

[6] Arthur von Mehren & Donald Trautman, The Law of Multistate Problems: Cases and Materials on Conflict of Laws 1459 (1965). For further discussion of the policies of *res judicata*, see Allan D. Vestal, *Rationale of Preclusion*, 9 St. Louis U. L.J. 29, 31–43 (1964).

[7] Wright & Miller § 4403.

[8] *Lyons v. Westinghouse Elec. Corp.*, 222 F.2d 184, 189 (2d Cir. 1955).

[9] *See, e.g., Federated Dep't Stores, Inc. v. Moitie*, 452 U.S. 394, 398–99 (1981).

[10] For an excellent and comprehensive treatment of the subject, see David L. Shapiro, Civil Procedure: Preclusion in Civil Actions (2001).

[11] *See* Herbert Wechsler, *Restatements and Legal Change: Problems of Policy in the Restatement Work of the American Law Institute*, 13 St. Louis U. L.J. 185 (1968).

it is the most authoritative and influential writing on *res judicata* in American courts.[12]

[b] Changes in *Res Judicata* Terminology

Res judicata law has long consisted of two subdoctrines. The first concerns how a judgment can foreclose subsequent opportunities to bring a claim or cause of action. This used to be referred to as *merger and bar* or simply *res judicata*. While these terms are still employed, the subdoctrine is increasingly described in modern usage as *claim preclusion*. The second subdoctrine concerns how a judgment can prevent relitigation of an issue of fact or law. This used to be referred to as *collateral estoppel by judgment*. That label is in the process of being replaced by the term *issue preclusion*.[13] This chapter will usually refer to the two subdoctrines as claim and issue preclusion.

[c] The Trend of Increased Preclusion

The third modern development in the law of *res judicata* is the tendency of many courts to give greater preclusive effect to judgments.[14] This change is a response to developments elsewhere in modern procedure. First, it has become easier for courts to adjudicate multiple claims and the interests of multiple parties in a single lawsuit.[15] A primary reason for expansion of the permissible scope and complexity of civil lawsuits is to promote more efficient use of judicial resources. By penalizing piecemeal litigation and delay, broadened preclusion pressures litigants to avail themselves of the full range of adjudication opportunities initially provided.[16] Second, many courts and commentators are alarmed that increases in the number of cases filed in federal and state courts[17] will mean that those courts will not be able to handle

---

[12] The *Restatement (Second)* received mostly high marks in *Symposium on the Restatement (Second) of Judgments*, 66 Cornell L. Rev. 401 (1981), and criticism in Robert Ziff, Note, *For One Litigant's Sole Relief: Unforeseeable Preclusion and the Second Restatement*, 77 Cornell L. Rev. 905 (1992).

[13] The modern terminology of claim and issue preclusion has been used by the Supreme Court in several cases. *E.g.*, *Migra v. Warren City Sch. Dist. Bd. of Educ.*, 465 U.S. 75, 77 n.1 (1984). It was adopted by the American Law Institute in Restatement (Second) of Judgments 1 (1982). These changes were brought about primarily through the extensive writing of the late Professor Alan Vestal. *E.g.*, Res Judicata/Preclusion, note 1, *supra*; *Rationale of Preclusion*, note 6, *supra*.

[14] "[T]he trend in the United States is toward increased finality." Roger C. Cramton, David P. Currie & Herma H. Kay, Conflict of Laws: Comments-Cases-Questions 583 (4th ed. 1987). *See, e.g.*, *White v. Allstate Ins. Co.*, 605 N.E.2d 141 (Ind. 1992) (discussing the enlargement of state preclusion doctrine).

[15] *See generally* Chapter 9 (complex pleading and practice), *supra*. The Federal Rules of Civil Procedure and rules governing procedure in many state courts contain liberal provisions for claim and party joinder, pleading amendment and discovery.

[16] Other developments in modern civil procedure also make preclusion easier to justify. For example, broad opportunities for claim pleading, discovery and amendment "enlarge the scope of what might have been litigated by the plaintiff in the first action and should correspondingly enlarge the scope of claim preclusion." James, Hazard & Leubsdorf § 11.16.

[17] For some time now, civil case filings in federal and many state courts have been increasing significantly. *See Report of the Federal Courts Study Committee* 4–10 (1990); *The Role of Courts in*

their cases with the prompt and full attention minimally required in our judicial process. Broadened preclusion may promote conservation of severely-taxed judicial resources.[18]

[3] Litigation Perspectives — Offensive and Defensive Preclusion

The tactical advantages litigants see from preclusion are twofold. First, it is quicker and cheaper to cover ground in the case by incorporating by reference a development that occurred in an earlier case. Second, (and more important) it is better to win by extending a prior judicial victory to your case than to risk the possibility of losing by litigating afresh.

Either plaintiff or defendant may be in a position to argue preclusion. It simply depends on who profits from the prior adjudication.[19] When a litigant argues claim or issue preclusion in order to advance a claim, that is *offensive* preclusion. When a litigant argues preclusion to defeat a claim, it is *defensive* preclusion.[20] Preclusion arguments must be raised in a timely fashion, or they will be waived.[21]

[4] Preclusion Essentials

[a] Claim Preclusion

The basic rule of claim preclusion is that a final judgment on the merits precludes the same parties (and those closely related to them) from litigating the same (or a sufficiently similar) claim in a subsequent lawsuit.[22] Section

---

American Society — The Final Report of the Council on the Role of Courts 3 (1984); PAUL D. CARRINGTON, DANIEL MEADOR & MAURICE ROSENBERG, JUSTICE ON APPEAL 45 (1976).

[18] While some have questioned the relationship between preclusion and judicial economy, *e.g.,* Bruce L. Hay, *Some Settlement Effects of Preclusion,* 1993 U. ILL. L. REV. 21 (1993); Edward W. Cleary, *Res Judicata Reexamined,* 57 YALE L.J. 339, 348–49 (1948); WRIGHT & MILLER § 4403, it is clear that courts' growing aversion to relitigation is tied to concern over the preservation and effective use of judicial resources. Vestal, note 6, *supra,* at 35. *Cf.* Judith Resnik, *Precluding Appeals,* 70 CORNELL L. REV. 603, 611 (1985) ("Resource conservation is a familiar and persistent motif in the literature of courts. Of late, as courts appear both overused and underproductive, interest in economy has increased.").

[19] It is even possible for *both* plaintiff and defendant to make preclusion arguments in the same case. *See* § 15.06, *infra.*

[20] *Cf. United States v. Mendoza,* 464 U.S. 154, 159 n.4 (1984):

Offensive use of collateral estoppel [issue preclusion] occurs when a plaintiff seeks to foreclose a defendant from relitigating an issue the defendant has previously litigated unsuccessfully in another action against the same or a different party. Defensive use of collateral estoppel occurs when a defendant seeks to prevent a plaintiff from relitigating an issue the plaintiff has previously litigated unsuccessfully in another action against the same or a different party.

[21] *See Arizona v. California,* 530 U.S. 392 (2000).

[22] "When suit is brought, the court looks back in time at whatever incident went awry and gave rise to the claims of the action, and requires that any and all other claims arising out of the same

15.02 of this chapter examines how identical claims are precluded. Section 15.03 treats the preclusion of similar though nonidentical claims and defenses. Section 15.04 discusses the identity-of-parties requirement, while § 15.05 treats the requirement that judgments be final and on the merits.

[b]   Issue Preclusion

The doctrine of issue preclusion supplements claim preclusion by giving a final adjudication preclusive effect in a subsequent case which cannot be said, even in the broadest sense, to share the same claim.[23] The basic rule of issue preclusion is that a final judgment precludes relitigation of the same issue of fact or law, so long as (1) the issue was actually litigated, determined and necessary to the judgment in the prior adjudication, and (2) the circumstances of the particular case do not suggest any reason why it would be unfair to invoke the doctrine. Today's issue preclusion usually does not carry the identity-of-parties requirement found in claim preclusion. But due process protects genuine strangers to the original litigation from being bound by issue preclusion. A minority of jurisdictions also still deny strangers use of issue preclusion against original parties by invoking the *mutuality doctrine* — a rule that only one capable of being bound by a prior adjudication may use it to bind another.

The final-judgment requirement of issue preclusion receives no separate attention in this chapter, since it is about the same as the final-judgment requirement for claim preclusion discussed in § 15.05.[24]

Section 15.06 of this chapter discusses how issue preclusion differs from claim preclusion. Section 15.07 treats the basic requirements for issue preclusion: that the same issue be litigated, determined, and necessary to a prior judgment and that application of the doctrine be fair under the circumstances of the particular case. Section 15.08 considers the possible uses of issue preclusion by and against those not parties to the prior case.

Sections 15.09 through 15.12 explore special preclusion problems arising when the judgment of a court system is presented elsewhere for enforcement. Finally, §§ 15.13 through 15.15 examine legal rules similar in function and purpose to preclusion doctrines.

---

incident be pleaded in tandem." Samuel Issacharoff, *The Amercian Law of Repose*, 23 CIVIL JUSTICE Q. 324, 325 (2004).

[23] "[T]he primary purpose of issue preclusion is the completeness of resolution through adjudication, which is an issue of efficiency." Issacharoff, note 22, *supra*, at 329.

[24] *Cf.* RESTATEMENT (SECOND) OF JUDGMENTS, note 11, *supra*, § 13 comment g ("Usually there is no occasion to interpret finality less strictly when the question is one of issue preclusion . . . .").

PART A.
Claim Preclusion

§ 15.02 PRECLUSION WHEN ORIGINAL AND SUCCESSIVE CLAIMS ARE IDENTICAL; DYNAMICS OF JUDGMENT ENFORCEMENT

The most rudimentary application of the principle of claim preclusion prevents parties from pressing a claim or cause of action[25] identical to one presented in a prior adjudication. If the prior case ends with a judgment which is final and on the merits,[26] parties to it[27] are foreclosed from litigating the same claim in any subsequent proceeding. It does not matter whether judgment in the prior suit was for or against the claimant. The function of the judgment is to make the claim disappear.

When a damage claim is successful, the cause of action represented by the claim becomes a cause of action on the money judgment.[28] The successful claimant becomes a *judgment creditor* and the party who unsuccessfully opposed the judgment becomes a *judgment debtor*. If the judgment debtor fails to satisfy the judgment, the judgment creditor may have to sue again — this time in a supplementary proceeding to satisfy the judgment, or as much of it as possible.

Thanks to claim preclusion, the plaintiff-judgment creditor holds most of the cards in the second proceeding. Procedures to enforce money-judgments vary.[29] However, most are summary in nature and usually are limited to the same questions: is the defendant in fact the judgment debtor (the person named in the judgment); how much can the judgment debtor pay toward satisfaction of the judgment; and how soon?[30] Judgment enforcement proceedings usually

---

[25] Courts sometimes use the older term, "cause of action" in place of the term "claim." *E.g.*, *Nevada v. United States*, 463 U.S. 110, 130 (1983).

[26] The requirement that judgments be final and on the merits is discussed at § 15.05, *infra*.

[27] The identity-of-parties requirement for claim preclusion is discussed at § 15.04, *infra*.

[28] *See* Stephen B. Burbank, *Federal Judgments Law: Sources of Authority and Sources of Rules*, 70 Tex. L. Rev. 1551 (1992); Robert L. Haig & Patricia O. Kahn, *Representing the Judgment Creditor*, 16 Am. J. Tr. Advoc. 1 (1992); James J. Brown, *Collecting a Judgment*, 13 Litig. 31 (Fall 1986).

Judgments granting injunctive relief (rather than damages) are enforced differently. *See* § 14.02[2], *supra*.

[29] Rule 69(a) generally requires the supplementary procedure for the enforcement of judgments in federal court to "accord with the procedure of the state where the court is located . . . ." For comparison of procedures in this country with those abroad, see Friedrich K. Juenger, *The Recognition of Money Judgments in Civil and Commercial Matters*, 36 Am. J. Comp. L. 1 (1988).

Even if the judgment debtor has not been sued on the judgment, he may feel pressure to honor it. For example, mere entry of the judgment may act as a lien on real estate held by the judgment debtor in that judicial district. *See, e.g.*, Ind. Code Ann. § 34-55-9-2.

[30] Courts often have authority to compel the judgment debtor to disclose her financial worth and to order that judgment debtor's assets be liquidated or placed in receivership to facilitate payment.

present no opportunity to examine the factual and legal underpinnings of the claim leading to judgment (matters the judgment debtor was free by denials and affirmative defenses to question prior to final judgment).[31] Claim preclusion confines the judgment debtor to a short list of challenges to the validity of the judgment, and it is unlikely that she will be able to raise even these unless the judgment was obtained by default.[32] In short, judgment precludes defendant from improving her position by relitigating the merits.

The claimant may be disadvantaged by claim preclusion in two ways. First, the initial case may end with a judgment on the merits against her. This will preclude (bar) the claimant from relitigating the claim.[33] Less obviously, claim preclusion may also bring adverse consequences to the claimant if she *wins* in the initial case. The damages awarded her in the proceeding may be less than she sought and than she believes she could establish if given another chance to litigate the claim. Yet she will be unable to sue again because her claim *merged* into her judgment.[34] In addition, a final judgment on the merits — whether or not in claimant's favor — may preclude her from presenting claims grounded differently in fact or law from the claim which was the subject of the judgment. The following section discusses how and to what extent judgments preclude such nonidentical claims.

---

[31] It is in this manner that claim preclusion precludes affirmative defenses. *Cf.* RESTATEMENT (SECOND) OF JUDGMENTS § 18(2), at 152 (1982) ("[T]he defendant cannot avail himself of defenses he might have interposed, or did interpose, in the first action."). *See* § 15.03[3], *infra*.

[32] The judgment debtor may attack a default judgment on grounds that she failed to receive adequate notice of the initial proceeding or that the court rendering the default judgment lacked personal jurisdiction to do so. RESTATEMENT (SECOND) OF JUDGMENTS § 1 at 30. For discussion of the requirement of adequate notice, *see generally* Chapter 4, *supra*; of personal jurisdiction, *see* Chapter 3, *supra*.

If the defendant participated in the original proceeding instead of taking a default, she may not use these grounds to attack collaterally a judgment otherwise entitled to claim-preclusive effect. For example, if the defendant elects to question personal jurisdiction initially and is unsuccessful, that decision will preclude reexamination of the question when the judgment is presented for enforcement. *See Baldwin v. Iowa State Traveling Men's Ass'n*, 283 U.S. 522, 525–26 (1931); *Stoll v. Gottlieb*, 305 U.S. 165, 172 (1938); § 10[B][2], *supra*. Theoretically, broadened principles of preclusion, *see* § 15.03, *infra*, should also prevent collateral attack if the defendant omitted her jurisdictional challenge when participating in the initial proceeding. The tendency in such cases, however, is for courts to reach the same result simply by noting that defendant's participation in the initial proceeding operated as a consent to jurisdiction. *Cf. Insurance Corp. of Ireland Ltd. v. Compagnie des Bauxites de Guinee*, 456 U.S. 694, 703–04 (1982) (explaining how defendant can waive her due process challenge by participating in the initial case).

In rare cases, resistance may be permitted when the court rendering the judgment lacked subject matter jurisdiction, or when the judgment is (under the local law of the place rendering it) unenforceable for some reason. *See* § 3.04[2], *supra*.

[33] "A valid and final personal judgment rendered in favor of the defendant bars another action by the plaintiff on the same claim." RESTATEMENT (SECOND) OF JUDGMENTS § 19, at 161. The same is true with reference to a judgment rendered in favor of the plaintiff on defendant's counterclaim. *See* § 15.03[3], *infra*.

[34] "The plaintiff cannot thereafter maintain an action on the original claim or any part thereof, although he may be able to maintain an action upon the judgment . . . ." RESTATEMENT (SECOND) OF JUDGMENTS § 18(1), at 151–52. The same is true with reference to a judgment rendered in favor of defendant on defendant's counterclaim. *See* § 15.02, *infra*.

§ 15.03 PRECLUSION WHEN ORIGINAL AND SUCCESSIVE CLAIMS ARE NOT IDENTICAL

[1]   How and Why Non-Identical Claims are Precluded

Perhaps the most significant feature of claim preclusion is the availability of the doctrine to preclude claims[35] that did not actually appear in the prior adjudication. It has long been accepted that claim preclusion cannot be confined to precluding identical claims.[36] For example, it would be indefensible to permit an automobile accident plaintiff to bring one suit against the other driver for damage to the right fender of plaintiff's car and follow with a second suit for damage to the left fender. All jurisdictions would regard this succeeding property damage claim to be extinguished by judgment in the first suit. This is because the two claims are so related that the doctrine of claim preclusion regards them as parts of what is, in a larger sense, a single claim.

Under modern preclusion law, this expanded concept of a "claim" encompasses all of the alternative legal theories and the full scope of damages or other remedies generated by the facts of the original controversy.[37] Whether all of this broadly conceived claim was actually put forward in the prior case is immaterial. What matters for claim preclusion is whether it *could* have been put forward.[38] If the new material could have been included in a more complete presentation of the initial claim, the succeeding claim is "swallowed by the judgment in the prior suit . . . ."[39] *Jones v. Morris Plan Bank of Portsmouth*[40] is a familiar casebook example. In the first suit, the bank sued Jones and recovered two delinquent car-installment payments. In the second suit, the court held that the prior adjudication extinguished the bank's further rights under the contract, even though Jones had since missed additional payments. The court read the installment contract as creating a right in bank to sue for the entire unpaid balance as soon as Jones missed a payment. For purposes of claim preclusion, the scope of bank's "claim" adjudicated in the first case was what it could have sued for (the entire unpaid balance). Thus defined, that claim (or any part of it) disappeared by merging into the first judgment for the two missed installments.[41]

By holding claimants to the most complete presentation of the claim possible in the initial adjudication, claim preclusion also forecloses alternative

---

[35] The term "cause of action" is sometimes used in place of the term "claim." *See* § 15.02, *supra*.

[36] *E.g., Commissioner v. Sunnen*, 333 U.S. 591, 597 (1948); *Cromwell v. County of Sac*, 94 U.S. 351, 352–53 (1877).

[37] *See* Allan D. Vestal, *Res Judicata/Claim Preclusion: Judgment for the Claimant*, 62 Nw. U. L. Rev. 357, 359–61 (1967); Edward W. Cleary, *Res Judicata Reexamined*, 57 Yale L.J. 339, 343–44 (1948).

[38] "Claim preclusion refers to the effect of a judgment in foreclosing litigation of a matter that never has been litigated, because of a determination that it should have been advanced in an earlier suit." *Migra v. Warren City Sch. Dist. Bd. of Educ.*, 465 U.S. 75, 77 n.1 (1984).

[39] *Commissioner v. Sunnen*, 333 U.S. 591, 598 (1948).

[40] 191 S.E. 608 (Va. 1937).

[41] *See* § 15.02 (merger generally), *supra*.

legal theories in subsequent litigation. Another casebook favorite, *Roach v. Teamsters Local Union No. 688*,[42] illustrates the point. The plaintiffs sued their union local upon the legal theory that the local breached a duty of fair representation imposed by federal statute. After receiving a disappointing recovery, two of the same plaintiffs brought a second suit against the local, this time under a different federal statute which guaranteed them certain rights as union members. The court held that the first suit precluded the second. "We are convinced," stated the court, "that plaintiffs are attempting to recover for a wrong for which they sought recovery" in the prior case.[43] "A party may not litigate a claim and then, upon unsuccessful disposition, revive the same cause of action with a new theory."[44]

[2]   The Emergence of § 24 of the Restatement (Second) of Judgments

Courts once limited the preclusive effect of judgments on nonidentical claims by using several different theories. The first *Restatement of Judgments* embraced the *same evidence* test by which claims are deemed the same "if the evidence needed to sustain the second action would have sustained the first action."[45] Still narrower was the *same right* test, which asked whether the two actions asserted infringement of the same right or sought redress for the same legal injury.[46] This test proved imprecise and difficult to apply[47] and has been justly criticized as question-begging.[48]

Most courts have now adopted more expansive and pragmatic definitions. Section 24 of the American Law Institute's *Restatement (Second) of Judgments* exemplifies this modern approach and has been quite influential. Section 24 advances a *transaction* test. It defines the claim precluded by the judgment to include "all rights of the plaintiff to remedies against the defendant with respect to all or any part of the transaction, or series of connected transactions, out of which the [original] action arose." According to the section, "transaction" and "series" of transactions

> are to be determined pragmatically, giving weight to such consider-
> ations as whether the facts are related in time, space, origin, or
> motivation, whether they form a convenient trial unit, and whether
> their treatment as a unit conforms to the parties' expectations or
> business understanding or usage.

---

[42] 595 F.2d 446 (8th Cir. 1979).

[43] *Id.* at 449.

[44] *Id.* at 450.

[45] RESTATEMENT OF JUDGMENTS § 61 (1942). A few decisions still refer to the test. *See, e.g., Church of New Song v. Establishment of Religion*, 620 F.2d 648, 652 (7th Cir. 1980).

[46] *E.g., Baltimore S.S. Co. v. Phillips*, 274 U.S. 316, 321 (1927) (referring to "single primary right" and to "cause of action" to decide the scope of the judgment).

[47] *See* CHARLES E. CLARK, CODE PLEADING 134 (2d ed. 1947).

[48] *See* JAMES, HAZARD & LEUBSDORF § 11.9.

The transaction test for claim definition set out in Section 24 is only one contemporary approach for articulating the idea that different yet sufficiently related claims should be precluded.[49]

Section 24 is, however, the most influential contemporary claim preclusion test. Many state jurisdictions have adopted it.[50] Many lower federal courts have incorporated Section 24 into federal preclusion doctrine,[51] and the Supreme Court has discussed the section with apparent approval.[52]

[3]   Defendant's Preclusion and Preclusion By Rule

Recall that a final judgment on the merits can preclude not only subsequent claims but also all defenses that were or could have been interposed in the original adjudication.[53] Similarly, a final judgment on the merits of any counterclaim (or cross-claim or third-party claim) asserted by the defendant carries the same claim-preclusive effect as a judgment on plaintiff's claim.[54] Treatment of counterclaims that were available but were not asserted in the prior adjudication is a different and more complicated matter. Under what circumstances is defendant forced to present his claim as a counterclaim or lose it thereafter through preclusion?

When a defendant who has been claimed against intends to make a claim in return which is based on the same subject matter, it is more efficient for the defendant to add the second claim to the original suit than to bring a new suit upon it later. The time and expense taken up in trying the two claims will be significantly reduced if they can be tried together.

---

[49] For example, while a number of lower federal courts have utilized § 24, see note 51, *infra*, "[others] measure the claim by reference to a single transaction or occurrence, all grounds for relief arising out of the conduct complained of, operative facts, or even a 'factual clone.' Two courts of appeals have explained that more traditional tests require search for a common nucleus of operative facts." WRIGHT & MILLER § 4407. For a survey of earlier approaches, see *Developments in the Law — Res Judicata*, 65 HARV. L. REV. 818, 824–25 (1952); Vestal, note 37, *supra*.

Contemporary tests for claim preclusion are thus similar in approach to those for some forms of joinder, see §§ 9.03 (compulsory counterclaims), 9.04 (cross-claims), 9.05[2] (compulsory party joinder); 9.08[1] (intervention of right), *supra*.

[50] *See, e.g., Hadley v. Cowan*, 804 P.2d 1271, 1276 (Wash. App. 1991); *Post v. Schwall*, 460 N.W.2d 794, 797 (Wis. App. 1990); *Kauhane v. Acutron Co.*, 795 P.2d 276, 279 (Haw. 1990). Professor Friedenthal earlier found that a majority of states had already embraced a "same operative facts" test indistinguishable in most respects from the transaction test of the RESTATEMENT (SECOND) OF JUDGMENTS. Jack H. Friedenthal, *Joinder of Claims, Counterclaims, and Cross-Complaints: Suggested Revision of the California Provisions*, 23 STAN. L. REV. 1, 12-13 (1970).

[51] *E.g., Kale v. Combined Ins. Co. of Am.*, 924 F.2d 1161, 1166 (1st Cir.), *cert. denied*, 502 U.S. 816 (1991); *Aliff v. Joy Mfg. Co.*, 914 F.2d 39, 43 (4th Cir. 1990); *Smith v. Safeco Ins. Co.*, 863 F.2d 403, 404 (5th Cir. 1989).

[52] *Nevada v. United States*, 463 U.S. 110, 130 (1983).

[53] *See* § 15.02, *supra*. To this extent, it can be said that the *res judicata* rule applied to the defendant is the "mirror image" of that applied to plaintiff. FRIEDENTHAL, KANE & MILLER § 14.6.

[54] "A defendant who interposes a counterclaim is, in substance, a plaintiff, as far as the counterclaim is concerned, and the plaintiff is, in substance, a defendant." RESTATEMENT (SECOND) OF JUDGMENTS § 23 comment a (1982).

These concerns are reminiscent of those supporting claim preclusion. If the same party held two claims so related, the doctrine of claim preclusion would in most jurisdictions keep him from splitting the claims and withholding one for later suit. A few commentators[55] and courts[56] have also treated a counterclaim sufficiently related to the original claim as within the doctrine of claim preclusion. Because, however, these situations are often expressly covered by rules of civil procedure, it may be more useful to describe the process as preclusion by rule.[57]

For example, Federal Rule 13(a)(1) states:

> A pleading must state as a counterclaim any claim that — at the time of its service — the pleader has against an opposing party if the claim: (A) arises out of the transaction or occurrence that is the subject matter of the opposing party's claim . . . .[58]

A majority of states have adopted Rule 13(a) as part of their local rules of procedure.[59] The relationship between two claims described in Rule 13(a) is much like that required for claim preclusion.[60] Claim preclusion and compulsory counterclaim rules also share common goals. Each is "designed to settle the entire dispute between the parties in one proceeding as fairly as that may be done" and to "conserve judicial resources."[61] At the same time, the claim preclusion and compulsory counterclaim rules do not entirely overlap. It is therefore important to consider how the two sources of law interact in counterclaim cases.

Claim preclusion may supplement the effects of preclusion by rule. A counterclaim insufficiently related to the original claim to meet the test of Rule 13(a) is treated as permissive under Rule 13(b). Omitted permissive counterclaims are not subject to preclusion by rule.[62] They may nonetheless be subject

---

[55] *E.g.*, *Developments in the Law — Res Judicata*, 65 HARV. L. REV., 818, 831–32 (1952).

[56] *See Great Lakes Rubber Corp. v. Herbert Cooper Co.*, 286 F.2d 631 (3d Cir. 1961), and the decisions cited in WRIGHT & MILLER § 1417.

[57] *See generally* ALAN D. VESTAL, RES JUDICATA/PRECLUSION 150–63 (1969). "In many ways this analysis provides a more apposite and useful approach to the problem of omitted counterclaims than does the doctrine of claim preclusion." WRIGHT & MILLER § 1417.

[58] "Although Rule 13(a) does not explain the consequences of failure to plead a compulsory counterclaim, virtually all courts agree that a party who fails to plead a compulsory counterclaim cannot raise that claim in subsequent litigation." Michael D. Conway, Comment, *Narrowing the Scope of Rule 13(a)*, 60 U. CHI. L. REV. 141, 141 (1993).

[59] *See* John B. Oakley & Arthur F. Coon, *The Federal Rules in State Courts: A Survey of State Court Systems of Civil Procedure*, 61 WASH. L. REV. 1367 (1986). *But see* DAVID SIEGEL, N.Y. CIV. PRAC. L. & R. § 3019 commentary (McKinney 1991). "All counterclaims are permissive in New York: D can use his claim as a counterclaim or save it and sue on it separately. D may save it for separate suit even when it is a related counterclaim, i.e., when it arises out of the same transaction or occurrence as P's claim." DAVID SIEGEL, NEW YORK PRACTICE § 224 (4th ed. 2004).

[60] *See, e.g.*, the claim comparison required under § 24 of the RESTATEMENT (SECOND) OF JUDGMENTS, discussed at § 115.03[2], *supra*.

[61] Eugene F. Scoles, *Interstate Preclusion by Prior Litigation*, 74 Nw. U. L. REV. 742, 753 (1979).

[62] Nor, as a general matter, should they be. "The defendant or party who did not choose the

to the doctrine of claim preclusion. For example, defendant may have two claims against plaintiff, neither of which is sufficiently related to plaintiff's claim to be compulsory. Because the counterclaims would be only permissive, defendant could withhold one of them without running afoul of preclusion by rule. If, however, defendant's two claims were sufficiently related to each other and defendant presents only one, he might lose the other by operation of claim preclusion.[63]

On the other hand, at least one of the exceptions built into the compulsory counterclaim rule[64] may limit not only preclusion by rule but also the doctrine of claim preclusion. By this exception, a defendant is not required to replead as a counterclaim a claim he made in earlier, pending litigation. Since the federal rules operate (as statutes typically do) to override judicial doctrine, this exception suspends not only preclusion by rule but also the federal doctrine of claim preclusion.[65]

Some jurisdictions without a compulsory counterclaim rule have declined to preclude unasserted counterclaims as a matter of common law, even when they are transactionally related to plaintiff's claim. For several reasons, however, this generosity may be more apparent than real. First, the common law of preclusion gives preclusive effect to defenses which could have been raised in the first suit,[66] and the facts pertaining to some defenses may also present a potential counterclaim. In such circumstances, defendant cannot always safely predict whether he will be barred from suing on the same facts for an affirmative recovery in a later action.[67] Second, even when claim preclusion poses no bar, issue preclusion may defeat the later action.[68] Finally, some

---

forum or control the litigation, although bound on those matters actually litigated, should not be bound on those claims that, under the law of the first forum, he was not compelled to litigate." Scoles, note 61, *supra*, at 754.

[63] *Cf.* RESTATEMENT (SECOND) OF JUDGMENTS § 23 (1982) (judgment against the defendant on his counterclaim has preclusive effect).

[64] The rule does not apply when the counterclaim requires "adding another party over whom the court cannot acquire jurisdiction." This provision contemplates territorial jurisdiction and not federal subject matter jurisdiction. Rule 13(a) also protects defendant's refusal to plead the counterclaim if, "when the action was commenced, the claim was the subject of another pending action," or when "the opposing party sued on its claim by attachment or other process that did not establish personal jurisdiction over the pleader on that claim, and the pleader does not assert any counterclaim under this rule." *See generally* § 9.03 (counterclaims), *supra*.

[65] The exception "provides defendant with the option of continuing the prior action rather than advancing it as a counterclaim in the second action without fear of it being barred if the second action results in a judgment before the claim has been adjudicated in the first action." WRIGHT & MILLER § 1411.

[66] *See* § 15.02 *supra*.

[67] *Compare, e.g., Mitchell v. Federal Intermediate Credit Bank*, 164 S.E. 136 (S.C. 1932) (judgment on debtor's payment defense to suit on a note precluded debtor's independent action to recover excess payment from creditor), *with Virginia-Carolina Chem. Co. v. Kirven*, 215 U.S. 252 (1909) (judgment in seller's action for payment did not preclude purchaser's subsequent action for damages caused by goods sold). *But see generally* RESTATEMENT (SECOND) OF JUDGMENTS § 22 comment d (1982) (mere defensive assertion of facts should not preclude subsequent use of same facts by defendant in suit for affirmative recovery).

[68] *See* § 15.06 (comparing claim and issue preclusion), *infra*.

jurisdictions that allow defendants to withhold counterclaims for subsequent suit nevertheless bar subsequent suits which are so closely related to the prior suit that they pose a serious risk of logically irreconcilable judgments.[69] The last problem can even occur for federal court defendants who escape rule preclusion.[70]

[4]   Variations from the Norm — Theories of Lesser and Greater Claim Preclusion

Courts share an understanding of the general shape and function of claim preclusion. They do not, however, entirely agree on the limits of the doctrine.

[a]   Lesser Preclusion — Claim-Splitting in Accident Cases

As noted above,[71] a variety of narrower approaches to claim definition once dominated. The narrow approach is perhaps most in evidence today in the minority of jurisdictions permitting claim-splitting in accident cases. There accident plaintiffs can split what would elsewhere be thought of as a single claim into separate suits for property damage and personal injury.[72] Courts in such cases reason that injuries to plaintiff's person and her property give rise to separate and distinct claims or causes of action.

This view is at odds with the modern trend of giving a broader, more functional definition of a claim for purposes of claim preclusion, and jurisdictions still permitting claim-splitting in accident cases[73] may eventually overrule their precedents and adopt the modern approach.

This is what the Ohio Supreme Court did in one well-known case, *Rush v. City of Maple Heights*.[74] Plaintiff suffered a motorcycle accident. She first sued the city for property damage to her motorcycle, alleging that the accident was caused because the city negligently maintained the street. She obtained a final judgment for $100. Thereafter, she sued the city for personal injuries from the same accident and obtained judgment on a verdict for $12,000. The Ohio Supreme Court reversed on the ground that the judgment in the prior case precluded plaintiff's personal injury claim. In so doing, the court

---

[69] *See, e.g., University of N. H. v. April*, 347 A.2d 446, 450–51 (N.H. 1975); *Chicot County Drainage Dist. v. Baxter State Bank*, 308 U.S. 371 (1940).

[70] The problem comes when plaintiff's original suit is dismissed before defendant was obligated to assert an otherwise compulsory counterclaim. *See Martino v. McDonald's Sys., Inc.*, 598 F.2d 1079 (7th Cir. 1979) ("counterclaim exception to the *res judicata* rule" does not permit prosecution of a claim that "would nullify rights established by the prior action").

[71] Notes 46–48 and accompanying text, *supra*.

[72] For an excellent discussion of claim-splitting in accident cases, *see* FLEMING JAMES, ET AL., CIVIL PROCEDURE § 11.10 (5th ed. 2001).

[73] Surveys of state jurisdictions permitting claim splitting under these circumstances include Howard M. Erichson, *Interjurisdictional Preclusion*, 96 MICH. L. REV. 945, 974 n.141 (1998); and Andrea G. Nadel, *Simultaneous injury to person and property as giving rise to single cause of action*, 24 A.L.R.4TH 646, 685–86 (1983).

[74] 147 N.E.2d 599 (Ohio 1958).

abandoned its previous position favoring claim-splitting in accident cases.[75] Claim-splitting, it said, "is in conflict with the great weight of authority in this country and has caused vexatious litigation."[76]

[b]   Greater Preclusion — Claim Preclusion Unlimited by the Nature of the Claim Presented in the First Case, Or by Concerns of Foreseeability

As noted earlier, the generally accepted test for determining preclusion of nonidentical claims involves a comparison between the claim *actually* presented in the prior adjudication and the new claim.[77] Some courts and commentators have taken the position that this requirement of a nexus between the original and succeeding claims is too confining. They would broaden the scope of claim preclusion by also considering whether a nexus exists between the claim to be precluded and a claim which a party had the *opportunity* to bring in the first case.

The Seventh Circuit took this approach in *Marrese v. American Academy of Orthopaedic Surgeons.*[78] The plaintiffs first sued the Academy in state court, alleging that the Academy had breached a state-law duty to consider fairly their applications for membership. After losing that case, plaintiffs sued the Academy in federal court, alleging violations of federal antitrust law. The Seventh Circuit eventually held that the state case precluded plaintiffs from pressing their federal antitrust claims. The court reasoned that (1) plaintiffs had an opportunity to present state antitrust claims against the Academy in the original state proceeding;[79] (2) had plaintiffs done so, the relation between those state antitrust claims and the federal antitrust claims plaintiffs asserted in the subsequent federal case would have been such that the latter would have been precluded by a judgment in the state case; and (3) the result should not change simply because plaintiffs chose not to present state antitrust claims in their state case. Thus, the Seventh Circuit focused on the nexus between federal antitrust claims presented in the federal case and the claims under state antitrust law which plaintiffs *could* have raised in the prior state case.[80]

---

[75] *Vasu v. Kohlers, Inc.*, 61 N.E.2d 707, 712 (Ohio 1945), illustrates the prior position. The Ohio Supreme Court said there: "injuries to both person and property suffered by the same person as a result of the same wrongful act are infringements of different rights, and give rise to distinct causes of action, with the result that the recovery or denial of recovery of compensation for damage to property is no bar to an action subsequently prosecuted for the personal injury."

[76] 147 N.E.2d at 604.

[77] *See, e.g.*, the discussion of Section 24 of the *Restatement (Second) of Judgments* at Section 15.03[2], *supra.*

[78] 726 F.2d 1150 (7th Cir. 1984), *rev'd on other grounds*, 470 U.S. 373 (1985). *See* § 15.11[1], *infra.*

[79] It would have been impossible for the plaintiffs to have presented their *federal* antitrust claims in the original state case. Plaintiffs based their federal claims on Section 1 of the Sherman Act and jurisdiction to hear such claims rests exclusively with the federal courts. *E.g., General Inv. Co. v. Lake Shore & Michigan S. Ry. Co.*, 260 U.S. 261, 287 (1922).

[80] 726 F.2d at 1153, 1154–55.

Given the general trend in *res judicata* developments toward greater preclusion,[81] and the urging of many commentators that expansion continue,[82] other courts probably have been tempted in some cases to dispense with a required nexus between a claim actually presented in the prior adjudication and the claim sought to be precluded.[83] It can be argued that such expansion achieves added judicial economy and evokes a familiar theme in claim preclusion doctrine by focusing on what the claimant could have done in the first case.[84]

On balance, however, it may be unwise to so extend claim preclusion. Such an expansion would sometimes force a claimant to join dissimilar claims in the original proceeding, and benefits to litigants and the courts from forced joinder of dissimilar claims are doubtful.

> Where . . . claims are factually quite distinct so that there will be no overlap in presenting evidence to support them, much less is to be saved by trying them together, or including them in a single lawsuit to be tried separately. Indeed, trying them together may cause confusion and prejudice.[85]

Another enlarged form of claim preclusion occurs when a court uses the doctrine to block a claim related to one presented by the same plaintiff in earlier litigation although the subsequent claim was unforeseeable at the time of the original case. This has occurred in latent disease litigation. Harm from asbestos exposure provides an example. "Typically, victims first suffer asbestosis; many years later, some of the same victims also develop cancer."[86]

Statutes of limitation in such cases evince a fair and sensible trend. The statute is tolled until plaintiff has been able to discover the subsequent and

---

[81] *See* § 15.01[2][c], *supra.*

[82] *See, e.g.,* for arguments expanding the scope of claim preclusion, Michael J. Waggoner, *Fifty Years of Bernhard v. Bank of America is Enough: Collateral Estoppel Should Require Mutuality But Res Judicata Should Not,* 12 Rev. Litig. 391 (1993); Robert G. Bone, *Rethinking the "Day in Court" Ideal and Nonparty Preclusion,* 67 N.Y.U. L. Rev. 193 (1992).

[83] Alternatively, the New Jersey Supreme Court has used its so-called "Entire Controversy" Doctrine, to preclude plaintiffs from later proceeding against different defendants in a later lawsuit when the subsequent claims were related to a claim made against a different defendant in an earlier case. *See Cogdell v. Hospital Ctr.,* 116 N.J. 7, 560 A.2d 1169 (1989); *Mortgagelinq Corp. v. Commonwealth Land Title Ins. Co.,* 662 A.2d 536 (N.J. 1995). The doctrine has been justly criticized. Symposium, *Entire Controversy Doctrine,* 28 Rutgers L.J. 1 (1996)

[84] *Cf.* Robert Ziff, Note, *For One Litigant's Sole Relief: Unforeseeable Preclusion and the Second Restatement,* 77 Cornell L. Rev. 905, 922 (1992) ("Because the benefits of res judicata depend on the expectation of preclusion shaping litigants' behavior, res judicata only makes sense if it is foreseeable.").

[85] James, note 72, *supra,* at 555. Professor James suggested that fear of claim waiver generated by a rule requiring claimant to join dissimilar claims in the first case might defeat judicial economy by forcing parties to introduce claims that would not otherwise have been litigated. At the same time, consequences from the omission of insufficiently related claims would be too severe: "Hardship from oversight would be greatly multiplied if the parties were bound to think of all the aspects of all possible claims against their adversaries." *Id.* at 556.

[86] Note, *Claim Preclusion in Modern Latent Disease Cases: A Proposal for Allowing Second Suits,* 103 Harv. L. Rev. 1989, 1989 (1990).

more serious consequence of asbestos exposure. Yet plaintiff's second case often fares no better than if it had been time barred, if courts invoke claim preclusion to block it.[87]

It is true that, in this setting, the claim making up plaintiff's successive case is often so closely related as to satisfy that requirement for claim preclusion. But to apply claim preclusion disregards another requirement that should be understood as fundamental to the operation of the doctrine — that it was foreseeable to plaintiff when he omitted the claim from the first case that the omitted claim could be the subject of future litigation.[88] Claim preclusion stops making sense and becomes quite unfair when it is used to punish plaintiff's failure to do the impossible.

§ 15.04 THE IDENTITY-OF-PARTIES REQUIREMENT

[1] The Relation Between the Identity-of-Parties Requirement and Limitation of Claim Preclusion to the Same Claim

The general rule has long been that strangers[89] to a prior adjudication can neither bind nor be bound by claim preclusion.[90] The technical reason for this is that different parties cannot be involved in literally the same claim or cause of action.[91] This narrow reading of a claim for purposes of claim preclusion does not seem entirely consistent with the rule that non-identical yet similar claims between the same parties are subject to claim preclusion,[92] and it stands in contrast to the widespread use of issue preclusion *by* strangers to the original proceeding.[93]

Perhaps a better contemporary justification of the identity-of-parties limitation on claim preclusion rests on concerns of party fairness. While issue preclusion usually applies only to fully litigated matters,[94] claim preclusion

---

[87] *Claim Preclusion in Modern Latent Disease Cases: A Proposal for Allowing Second Suits,* note 86, *supra,* at 1990–98.

[88] *See* note 84, *supra.*

[89] In the terminology of *res judicata*/preclusion, those neither parties to nor involved with the prior adjudication are called "strangers" to it.

[90] *See, e.g.,* ALAN D. VESTAL, RES JUDICATA/PRECLUSION 50–51 (1969) (stating American, Canadian and English law to be in accord on the principle that "a judgment against one tortfeasor is not a bar to an action against another.") Notwithstanding this rule, it is possible to bind passive members of a plaintiff class without their active involvement in the case. For discussion of how class actions work and of the special treatment they receive under the Constitution, *see* §§ 4.02[1] (constitutional concerns) & 9.09 (class actions generally), *supra.*

[91] *See, e.g., Developments in the Law — Res Judicata,* 65 HARV. L. REV. 818, 861–62 (1952) ("since a different party is involved in the second action, the cause of action must be different."). *Montana v. United States,* 440 U.S. 147, 154 (1979), makes the same point.

[92] *See* § 15.03, *supra.*

[93] *See* § 15.08[2], *infra.*

[94] *See* § 15.07[2], *infra.*

extinguishes unlitigated claims and attaches even to default judgments.[95] It may be only fair to confine the effects of such broad-spectrum preclusion to parties in the first case or those in close relation to them.[96]

[2]   The Claim-Preclusive Effect of Judgments Upon Those in Close Relation to Parties

Parties not actually named in the original case may be subject to claim preclusion if they are sufficiently related to original parties. Courts often describe the relationship as *privity*.[97]

Privity is a label for situations where courts have been willing to stretch the identity-of-parties requirement in order to find claim preclusion. Professor Vestal wrote: "Involved seems to be the idea that the precluded party's interests were represented in the first suit, or that the precluded party should have no greater interest than did the losing party in the first suit."[98] A classic example of privity is a party's sale or assignment of his interests to a non-party after commencement of the litigation. The transferee of the interest is then considered bound by a judgment affecting the interest.[99] Courts have used the concept of privity to extend preclusion in many other settings.[100] It is possible to express the principle represented by privity without using the term itself.[101] But, in all cases, it is necessary that the closeness of the relationship bear on the claim which was the subject of the first case.[102]

---

[95] *See* § 15.05 and related text, *infra*.

[96] *See, e.g., Taylor v. Sturgell*, 128 S. Ct. 2161 (2008) (refusing to use claim preclusion to bind a nonparty to earlier litigation).

[97] *E.g., Federated Dep't Stores, Inc. v. Moitie*, 452 U.S. 394, 398 (1981) ("A final judgment on the merits of an action precludes the parties or their privies from relitigating issues that were or could have been raised in that action.").

[98] VESTAL, note 90, *supra*, at 121.

[99] VESTAL, note 90, *supra*, at 121.

This same concept is applied in the case of lessor and lessee and mortgagor and mortgagee where the transfer is made after the start of the litigation in Suit I. This same closeness sufficient to ground preclusion is also found in the case of various governmental agencies, guardian and ward, corporation and stockholders, and bankrupt and trustees. In community property states, husband and wife may be held to be in privity. Finally, in the case of a decedent and his successors in interest, the courts have found the closeness so that the label of "privity" may be applied.

[100] VESTAL, note 90, *supra*, at 122–23.

[101] For example, without using the term privity, the American Law Institute's *Restatement (Second) of Judgments* § 48 (1982) describes circumstances under which one member of the family may be precluded by a prior case brought by another family member for damage to a familial relationship. For additional discussion of parties within the reach of mainstream claim preclusion, see Waggoner, note 82, *supra*, at 395–96; Bone, note 82, *supra*, at 197.

[102] *Taylor v. Sturgell*, 128 S. Ct. 2161 (2008).

§ 15.05 THE JUDGMENT MUST BE FINAL AND ON THE MERITS

A lawsuit cannot have preclusive effect until it has been reduced to final judgment.[103]

The law governing finality of a judgment is that of the judicial system where the judgment was rendered. Court systems take different views about what must happen before their judgments become final. Federal courts regard their judgments to be final even if the case is under appeal.[104] In contrast, some state systems do not give finality to their judgments as long as there is a possibility that the outcome will be changed through appeal.[105]

Only judgments on the merits are entitled to claim-preclusive effect. Judgments in favor of the plaintiff are considered to be on the merits. This is true even if the judgment was rendered by default, stipulation between the parties, or summary judgment.[106]

Judgments on the merits for defendants have the same preclusive effect. However, many ways of concluding cases are open to defendants which do not require the court to reach the merits. For example, the defendant may successfully argue that the court lacks personal jurisdiction over him[107] or that an absentee indispensable to the case cannot be brought before the court.[108] Similarly, a defendant in federal court may successfully question the court's subject matter jurisdiction[109] or venue.[110] In such instances, the case is terminated without prejudice to plaintiff's right to refile in a court where the defect which led to initial dismissal can be avoided. Orders dismissing such cases are not judgments on the merits and, hence, do not have claim-preclusive effect.

---

[103] RESTATEMENT (SECOND) OF JUDGMENTS § 13 (1982). For claim preclusion, the significant event is when judgment becomes final, not when the case begins. RESTATEMENT (SECOND) OF JUDGMENTS § 14. This means that a suit filed earlier in time may be subject to the preclusive effects of a subsequent suit when the latter is the first to reach final judgment.

[104] "Should the judgment be vacated by the trial court or reversed on appeal, however, *res judicata* falls with the judgment." WRIGHT & MILLER § 4427.

[105] *See, e.g.*, the discussion of Utah state law in *Chavez v. Morris*, 566 F. Supp. 359 (D. Utah 1983).

[106] *Cf.* RESTATEMENT (SECOND) OF JUDGMENTS § 18 comment a (1982) ("It is immaterial whether the judgment was rendered upon a verdict or upon a motion to dismiss or upon consent, confession, or default."). Courts are divided concerning the preclusive effect of dismissals based on the legal insufficiency of pleadings. Federal decisions generally regard such dismissals under Rule 12(b)(6) to be preclusive. *See, e.g.*, *Federated Dep't Stores, Inc. v. Moitie*, 452 U.S. 394, 399 n.3 (1981). Many state decisions (either styling their motions in the manner of the federal rule or in the earlier form of demurrer) take the same view. But some do not. *See, e.g.*, *In re Estate of Cochrane*, 391 N.E.2d 35 (Ill. App. Ct. 1979).

[107] *See* Chapter 3 (territorial jurisdiction), *supra.*

[108] *See* § 9.05[2] (compulsory party joinder), *supra.*

[109] *See* Chapter 5, *supra.*

[110] *See* Chapter 6, *supra.*

In other situations, the circumstances of the dismissal may not as clearly suggest whether plaintiff's case has been terminated on the merits. Federal and many state courts usually resolve these ambiguities against plaintiff. Thus, Rule 41(b) of the Federal Rules of Civil Procedure states: "Unless the dismissal order states otherwise, a dismissal under this subection (b) and any dismissal not under this rule — except one for lack of jurisdiction, improper venue, or failure to join a party under Rule 19 — operates as an adjudication on the merits."[111]

PART B.
ISSUE PRECLUSION

§ 15.06   ISSUE AND CLAIM PRECLUSION COMPARED

[1]   How Issue Preclusion Supplements Claim Preclusion

The function of issue preclusion (collateral estoppel) is to advance the objectives of *res judicata*[112] beyond the confines of claim preclusion. Thus, it gives a final adjudication preclusive effect in a subsequent case which cannot be said, even in the broadest sense, to share the same claim.

In some cases, issue preclusion operates where claim preclusion obviously could not apply. For example, a criminal proceeding may be capable of generating issue-preclusive effects on a subsequent civil proceeding.[113]

In other cases the distinction between issue and claim preclusion is more subtle. The situation where plaintiff brings successive property damage and personal injury lawsuits arising out of the same automobile accident provides

---

[111] However, the federal rule has not always been applied literally to other dismissals "in which the merits could not be reached for failure of the plaintiff to satisfy a precondition." *Costello v. United States*, 365 U.S. 265, 286 (1961). For example, in *Saylor v. Lindsley*, 391 F.2d 965 (2d Cir. 1968), the court declined to give claim-preclusive effect to a dismissal "with prejudice" for failure to post a bond for costs, reasoning that the defendant had not been put to the burden of preparing a defense to the first litigation and would therefore not be unduly inconvenienced by having to defend the second.

[112] *See* § 15.01[1], *supra*.

[113] *E.g., Allen v. McCurry*, 449 U.S. 90 (1980); *White Earth Band of Chippewa Indians v. Alexander*, 683 F.2d 1129 (8th Cir.), *cert. denied*, 459 U.S. 1070 (1982). However, different burdens of proof for civil and criminal proceedings limit the range of issues which are identical in the sense required by claim preclusion. *See generally* RESTATEMENT (SECOND) OF JUDGMENTS § 85 (1982); Susan W. Brenner, *"Crossing Over": The Issue Preclusive Effects of a Civil/Criminal Adjudication Upon a Proceeding of the Opposite Character*, 7 N. ILL. U. L. REV. 141 (1987); David L. Shapiro, *Should a Guilty Plea Have Preclusive Effect?*, 70 IOWA L. REV. 27 (1984).

Another example of how issue preclusion operates in a sphere separate from claim preclusion may occur in civil litigation, when a prior court decides the identical issue without addressing the merits of plaintiff's claim. *E.g., Deckert v. Wachovia Student Fin. Servs., Inc.*, 963 F.2d 816 (5th Cir. 1992) (preclusive effect given by a Texas federal court to a prior Texas state court ruling that personal jurisdiction for plaintiff's case was lacking in Texas).

an example. A majority of jurisdictions would apply claim preclusion to conclude that a final judgment on the merits in the property case swallows up plaintiff's subsequent lawsuit for personal injury.[114] But the minority of jurisdictions that permit the second suit[115] create opportunities for issue preclusion. Thus, if plaintiff lost the first property damage suit upon a finding of contributory negligence, issue preclusion may deny him the opportunity to relitigate the contributory negligence issue in his subsequent personal injury action. On the other hand, if plaintiff established negligence and recovered in the property damage suit, then plaintiff might argue issue preclusion to advance his personal injury claim.[116]

[2]   How Guarantees of Procedural Fairness Limit Each Doctrine

A fundamental guarantee of our judicial process is that no one may have his rights extinguished by a judgment unless he has first received a full and fair opportunity for a hearing. This idea provides an important check on both claim and issue preclusion.[117] It means that the preclusive weight of a final judgment must be commensurate with the opportunities for litigation which preceded it.

Claim and issue preclusion both prevent parties from raising issues,[118] but they reflect differently the constraints of procedural fairness. Claim preclusion prevents a litigant from raising new issues,[119] but usually only upon a

---

[114] See § 15.03, supra.

[115] See § 15.03, supra.

[116] In that event, defendant might argue claim preclusion, hoping to change the res judicata law of the jurisdiction. This is what happened in Rush v. City of Maple Heights, 147 N.E.2d 599 (Ohio 1958), discussed in § 15.03[4][a], supra. Ohio state trial and intermediate courts ruled in favor of plaintiff on issue preclusion grounds. Given the fairness concerns that should temper applications of issue preclusion, see § 15.08[4], infra, application of the doctrine against the defendant in Rush is open to criticism. The matter became academic when the Ohio Supreme Court reversed and ordered dismissal of the case by invoking claim preclusion.

[117] To preclude parties without affording such fairness protections raises serious questions under the due process clauses of the Fifth and Fourteenth Amendments to the United States Constitution. See Jack Ratliff, Offensive Collateral Estoppel and the Option Effect, 67 TEX. L. REV. 63, 64 (1988); James R. Pielemeier, Due Process Limitations on the Application of Collateral Estoppel Against Nonparties to Prior Litigation, 63 B.U. L. REV. 383 (1983); Robert C. Casad, Intersystem Issue Preclusion and the Restatement (Second) of Judgments, 66 CORNELL L. REV. 510, 517 (1981); Barbara A. Atwood, State Court Judgments in Federal Litigation: Mapping the Contours of Full Faith and Credit, 58 IND. L.J. 59, 69–70 n.54 (1982). See, in addition, the Supreme Court decisions discussed in § 15.08, infra.

[118] While this is literally the province of issue preclusion, claim preclusion also effectively precludes issues. In fact, it operates on a larger scale than issue preclusion. See, e.g., Federated Dep't Stores v. Moitie, 452 U.S. 394, 398 (1981) (emphasis added):

> There is little to be added to the doctrine of res judicata [claim preclusion] as developed in the case law of this Court. A final judgment on the merits of an action precludes the parties or their privies from relitigating issues that were or could have been raised in that action.

[119] Federated Dep't Stores, 452 U.S. 394, 398.

demonstration that the party to be bound could have raised the new matters if she had more fully litigated for or against a claim which was presented in the first case.[120] Issue preclusion extinguishes issues that claim preclusion cannot reach,[121] but only those that were actually litigated in a prior adjudication and necessary to judgment.

§ 15.07   THE SAME ISSUE MUST HAVE BEEN LITIGATED, DETERMINED AND NECESSARY TO THE JUDGMENT IN THE PRIOR CASE

[1]   The Identity-of-Issues Requirement

Issue preclusion (collateral estoppel) can operate only if the issues in the original and the succeeding proceeding are identical. Generally, issues of either law or fact qualify.[122] This is true even though courts have occasionally suggested that issue preclusion is not available for issues of law[123] and might be available only as to issues of "ultimate" fact.[124]

Only issues which reappear in subsequent litigation are subject to issue preclusion. Courts have stressed that the identity-of-issue requirement should be taken literally. For example, in *Commissioner v. Sunnen*,[125] the Supreme Court refused to give preclusive effect to a prior Tax Court determination that a wife's income was not taxable to her husband, even though the original and succeeding cases both involved the husband's practice of transferring rights under patent contracts to his wife. The Court observed that collateral estoppel (issue preclusion) "must be confined to situations where the matter raised in the second suit is identical in all respects with that decided in the first

---

[120] *See* § 15.03, *supra.*

[121] *See* § 15.01[6], *supra.*

[122] RESTATEMENT (SECOND) OF JUDGMENTS § 27 (1982).

[123] *E.g., United States v. Moser,* 266 U.S. 236 (1924). For a critique of this proposition, *see* FRIEDENTHAL, KANE & MILLER § 14.10. The authors note that the principle that issues of pure law should not be subject to issue preclusion has been hard to articulate and to apply consistently, particularly because it is often difficult to distinguish among issues of law, fact, and mixed law and fact. On preclusion of issues of law generally, see RESTATEMENT (SECOND) OF JUDGMENTS § 28(2) (1982); Colin H. Buckley, *Issue Preclusion and Issues of Law: A Doctrinal Framework Based on Rules of Recognition, Jurisdiction and Legal History,* 24 HOUSTON L. REV. 875 (1987); Geoffrey C. Hazard, Jr., *Preclusion as to Issues of Law: The Legal System's Interest,* 70 IOWA L. REV. 81, 86–87 (1984).

[124] The leading case for the latter proposition is *The Evergreens v. Nunan,* 141 F.2d 927 (2d Cir.), *cert. denied,* 323 U.S. 720 (1944). The case attaches importance to the difference between ultimate facts (which support conclusions of law) and factual determinations leading up to ultimate facts (which are only conclusions of "evidentiary" or "mediate" fact). This has not been a very effective tool for limiting issue preclusion, since "[t]he line between ultimate and evidentiary facts is often impossible to draw." RESTATEMENT (SECOND) OF JUDGMENTS § 27 comment j (1982). For the same reason, the distinction caused problems in code pleading and was abandoned in the federal pleading rules. See §§ 8.03[3] (specificity of fact pleading under the codes) & 8.04[1] (specificity of notice pleading), *supra.*

[125] 333 U.S. 591 (1948).

proceeding and where the controlling facts and applicable legal rules remain unchanged."[126]

At the same time, litigants cannot escape issue preclusion by dressing up previously litigated issues to make them appear new. This is true even though a litigant can demonstrate that differences in factual support or legal argument might cause the issue to be resolved differently in the succeeding case.

> Thus, for example, if the party against whom preclusion is sought did in fact litigate an issue of ultimate fact and suffered an adverse determination, new evidentiary facts may not be brought forward to obtain a different determination of that ultimate fact. . . . And similarly if the issue was one of law, new arguments may not be presented to obtain a different determination of that issue.[127]

In this way, issue preclusion is like claim preclusion[128] in pressuring litigants to be complete in their initial presentations.

[2]   The Issue Must Have Been Litigated and Determined in the Prior Case

One feature setting issue preclusion apart from claim preclusion is that the former only precludes matters which were actually litigated and determined in the prior case.[129] Trials provide a frequent but not exclusive means for determining issues. "An issue may be submitted and determined on a motion to dismiss for failure to state a claim, a motion for judgment on the pleadings, a motion for summary judgment . . . , a motion for directed verdict or their equivalents, as well as on a judgment entered on a verdict."[130] On the other hand, there is considerable support for the rule that default judgments, consent judgments and judgments based on stipulations of fact or admissions should not generate issue-preclusive effects because the issues there have not been litigated.[131]

There are important reasons why issue preclusion should operate only on issues actually litigated and determined in the prior proceeding. These reasons

---

[126] 333 U.S. at 599–600. *Accord, United States v. Watts,* 519 U.S. 148, 156 (1997) ("an acquittal in a criminal case does not preclude the Government from relitigating an issue when it is presented in a subsequent action governed by a lower standard of proof." (quoting *Dowling v. United States,* 493 U.S. 342, 349 (1990)).

[127] RESTATEMENT (SECOND) OF JUDGMENTS § 27 comment c (1982).

[128] *See* § 15.03[1], *supra.*

[129] The parties usually will have raised the issues in their pleadings. However, this will not always be the case. Many systems permit their courts to determine upon the evidence at trial issues which go beyond the pleadings. For example, Rule 15(b) authorizes federal trial courts to grant motions to amend pleadings to conform to the evidence at trial but notes that "failure to amend does not affect the result of the trial of that issue." *See* § 8.10[2], *supra.*

[130] RESTATEMENT (SECOND) OF JUDGMENTS § 27 comment d (1982).

[131] *See Arizona v. California,* 530 U.S. 392 (2000) (judgments entered by confession, consent or default should not be entitled to issue-preclusive effect.)

become clear if, for example, we take a closer look at default judgments. The position under federal doctrine appears to be that default judgments carry no issue-preclusive effects.[132] The rule is well-settled in most state court systems.[133] However, New York courts took the opposite view. Their position was that default judgments could support issue preclusion with reference to issues which might have been raised if the lawsuit had proceeded.[134]

This position has been justly criticized.[135] A party's decision to take a default in the initial case is not necessarily a reflection of the strength of his opponent's case. Reasons why a party may default may include "the smallness of the amount or the value of the property in controversy, the difficulty of obtaining the necessary evidence, the expense of the litigation, and his own situation at the time."[136] It is also questionable whether endowing default judgments with issue-preclusive effect even achieves *res judicata's* goal of minimizing controversies.

> It is unfair and unwise to go as far as the New York decisions do in enforcing [issue preclusion] on the basis of earlier defaults. The consequence is to make a default so perilous that a well-advised defendant will be driven to litigate any petty claim asserted against him if there is the slightest prospect that a buried issue may be foreclosed in a subsequent suit. In the end this could frustrate the very purpose of *res judicata,* to reduce contention and dispute. Instead of more litigation later, there will be more litigating now.[137]

[3]   Determination of the Issue Must Have Been Necessary to Judgment

[a]   The Function and Purpose of the Rule

Not only must the same issue have been litigated and determined in the prior proceeding, but the determination must have been necessary to support the judgment there.[138] This added requirement functions with the others to assure that only those who have had a full and fair prior opportunity to litigate issues will be subject to issue preclusion. Insistence that the adjudication be necessary to the judgment "is a protection, for it means that the issue will be

---

[132] *See Nevada v. United States,* 463 U.S. 110, 130 n.11 (1983); *Parklane Hosiery Co. v. Shore,* 439 U.S. 322, 326 n.5 (1979).

[133] *See, e.g., Gwynn v. Wilhelm,* 360 P.2d 312 (Or. 1961); *Watts v. Watts,* 36 N.E. 479 (Mass. 1894); *Ressequie v. Byers,* 9 N.W. 779 (Wis. 1881).

[134] For discussion of these decisions, see Maurice Rosenberg, *Collateral Estoppel in New York,* 44 St. John's L. Rev. 165, 174 (1969).

[135] Rosenberg, note 134, *supra,* at 171–77.

[136] *Cromwell v. County of Sac,* 94 U.S. 351, 356 (1877).

[137] Rosenberg, note 134, *supra,* at 177.

[138] *See, e.g., United States v. Alaska,* 521 U.S. 1, 13 (1997) (issue preclusion "could only preclude relitigation of issues of fact or law *necessary* to a court's judgment." (emphasis in original)).

really disputed and that the loser will have put out his best efforts."[139]

It also means that the party to be bound will usually have an opportunity to appeal the initial adjudication. In contrast, determinations which are not necessary to support the judgment are usually not appealable. "Such determinations have the characteristics of dicta, and may not ordinarily be the subject of an appeal by the party against whom they were made."[140] Issue preclusion is and should be limited to determinations necessary to support the judgment because "the interest in providing an opportunity for a considered determination, which if adverse may be the subject of an appeal, outweighs the interest in avoiding the burden of relitigation."[141]

Rios v. Davis[142] provides an example. Davis sued Rios for negligence in an automobile collision. The jury found Rios negligent, but also found Davis contributorily negligent, requiring judgment to be entered for Rios. Rios then sued Davis for injuries Rios had received in the same collision. Davis defended on the grounds that the jury's finding in the first case established Rios' contributory negligence and precluded him from relitigating it in the second. The court refused to give the earlier judgment issue-preclusive effect. It said of the first case:

> The finding that Rios was negligent was not essential or material to the judgment and the judgment was not based thereon. . . . Since the judgment was in favor of Rios he had no right or opportunity to complain of or to appeal from the finding that he was guilty of such negligence even if such finding had been without any support whatever in the evidence. The right of appeal is from a judgment and not from a finding.[143]

A test useful to determine whether an issue was necessary to support the judgment is to ask whether, if the issue had been decided the opposite way, the same judgment would have been entered. If so, then judgment did not depend on the way the issue actually was resolved. Applying this test to the *Rios* case, we find that, once the jury found Davis to be contributorily negligent, Rios had to win. Thus, the same judgment would have been entered in the case no matter what conclusion the jury reached concerning Rios's own negligence.

[b]   **Alternative Determinations**

A special problem arises when alternative issue determinations support the judgment. If each is independently capable of supporting the judgment, then neither is necessary to the judgment in a strict sense. Applying the test above, if either issue had been resolved differently, the judgment would have been unchanged.

---

[139] *The Evergreens v. Nunan*, 141 F.2d 927, 929 (2d Cir. 1944).

[140] RESTATEMENT (SECOND) OF JUDGMENTS § 27 comment h (1982).

[141] RESTATEMENT (SECOND) OF JUDGMENTS § 27 comment h (1982).

[142] 373 S.W.2d 386 (Tex. Civ. App. 1963).

[143] 373 S.W.2d at 387–88. On the last point, see § 13.08[1] (prejudicial effect as requirement for reviewability), *supra*.

The weakest case for issue preclusion is when it is unclear which of two grounds supports the judgment. Preclusion is unwarranted in such cases.[144] The problem is that it is impossible to determine whether a given issue was determined at all.

A classroom case, *Illinois Central Gulf Railroad Co. v. Parks*,[145] illustrates this difficulty. A husband and wife were injured when their car collided with one of defendant's trains. In the first suit, the wife sued for her injuries and the husband sued for loss of the services and companionship of his wife. The wife recovered against the railroad, but the jury returned a general verdict against the husband. In a subsequent lawsuit, the husband sued defendant railroad for his own injuries. The railroad urged claim and issue preclusion. The court rejected both arguments.[146] The railroad based its case for issue preclusion on the possibility that the first jury returned a verdict against the husband because he had been contributorily negligent as driver of the car. The court noted, however, that it was equally possible that the first jury returned a verdict against the husband because the husband proved no damages for loss of his wife's services and companionship. Under this possibility, the contributory negligence issue would not have been determined in the first case at all.[147]

One influential decision denying preclusive effect to a prior adjudication expressly based on alternative grounds is *Halpern v. Schwartz*.[148] *Halpern* rejected the assumption that alternative grounds were as likely as non-alternative grounds to be thoroughly litigated prior to judgment.

> First, if the court in the prior case were sure as to one of the alternative grounds and this ground by itself was sufficient to support the judgment, then it may not feel as constrained to give rigorous consideration to the alternative grounds. Second, since there are alternative grounds which could independently support the prior judgment, vigorous review of an asserted error as to one ground probably would not occur. The losing litigant would have little motivation to appeal from an alleged erroneous finding in connection with one of several independent alternative grounds, since even if his claim of error were sustained, the judgment would be affirmed on one of the other grounds.[149]

---

[144] *See* RESTATEMENT (SECOND) OF JUDGMENTS § 27, Comment (i) (1982).

[145] 390 N.E.2d 1078 (Ind. Ct. App. 1979).

[146] Whether the husband engaged in a kind of claim-splitting which should have been barred by claim preclusion is an interesting question. Indiana courts appear to be more indulgent on this point than most other jurisdictions. *See* § 15.03, *supra*.

[147] On the issue-preclusion requirement that the issue actually be determined in the prior proceeding, see § 15.07[2], *supra*.

[148] 426 F.2d 102 (2d Cir. 1970).

[149] 426 F.2d at 105–06.

Some courts continued to adhere to the older rule giving effect to issues decided on alternative grounds.[150] But the *Restatement (Second) of Judgments* endorsed the *Halpern* principle, stating that "[i]f a judgment of a court of first instance is based on determinations of two issues, either of which standing independently would be sufficient to support the result, the judgment is not conclusive with respect to either issue standing alone."[151] At the same time, the *Restatement* regards such determinations as preclusive if both grounds are affirmed on appeal. At this point, "the losing party . . . has obtained an appellate decision on the issue, and thus the balance weighs in favor of preclusion."[152]

[4]   Application of Issue Preclusion Must Be Fair in the Given Case

The essential prerequisites for issue preclusion discussed in this section all grow out of a concern of procedural fairness — that litigants have a sufficient opportunity to litigate before they are bound.[153] But issue preclusion's requirement that the same issue be previously determined and necessary to judgment is not always enough to assure procedural fairness.

For example, notwithstanding satisfaction of the above criteria, there should be no issue preclusion if

> [T]here is a clear and convincing need for a new determination of the issue . . . because it was not sufficiently foreseeable at the time of the initial action that the issue would arise in the context of a subsequent action, or . . . because the party sought to be precluded, as a result of the conduct of his adversary or other special circumstances, did not have an adequate opportunity or incentive to obtain a full and fair adjudication in the initial action.[154]

Moreover, the trend, explored in the next section, of relaxing the identity-of-parties requirement for issue preclusion has created a greater need for courts to inquire whether invocation of issue preclusion will be fair under the circumstances of the particular case.[155]

---

[150] *Compare, e.g., Halpern, 426 F.2d 102, with In re Westgate-Cal. Corp.*, 642 F.2d 1174 (9th Cir. 1981); and *Jean Alexander Cosmetics, Inc. v. L'Oreal USA, Inc.*, 458 F.3d 244 (3d Cir. 2006) (giving preclusive effect to an alternate ground supporting a judgment).

[151] RESTATEMENT (SECOND) OF JUDGMENTS § 27 comment i (1982) (citing *Halpern* with approval).

[152] RESTATEMENT (SECOND) OF JUDGMENTS, § 27 comment o (1982).

[153] On the importance of procedural fairness to preclusion law, see § 15.06[2], *supra.*

[154] RESTATEMENT (SECOND) OF JUDGMENTS § 28(5) (1982) .

[155] *See* § 15.08[2], *infra.*

§ 15.08   WHO CAN BIND AND BE BOUND BY ISSUE PRECLUSION?

In most jurisdictions, issue preclusion (collateral estoppel) has no counterpart to the identity-of-parties requirement which limits claim preclusion.[156] It is clear, of course, that issue preclusion can operate when the parties in the succeeding case are the same. Under the right circumstances, however, it may also operate *in favor of* one who was neither a party nor in privity with a party in the earlier case. But issue preclusion is unlikely to operate *against* one who was a complete stranger to the first case.[157]

[1]   The General Rule Against Binding Those Who Were Strangers to the Prior Adjudication

The general rule is that strangers to the prior case cannot be bound by it.[158] After entertaining the possibility of change,[159] the Supreme Court reaffirmed the rule in *Parklane Hosiery Co. v. Shore*, noting that it would be "a violation of due process for a judgment to be binding on a litigant who was not a party or a privy and therefore has never had an opportunity to be heard."[160]

Nonparties are occasionally subject to issue preclusion. But this usually occurs only when they chose to involve themselves significantly in the prior case — whether by becoming unusually active amicus curiae,[161] or by

---

[156] *See* § 15.09, *supra*.

[157] In the terminology of *res judicata*/preclusion, those who had no formal or informal involvement with the prior case are called "strangers" to it.

[158] *See* § 15.06, *supra*, and the authorities surveyed in Jack Ratliff, *Offensive Collateral Estoppel and the Option Effect*, 67 Tex. L. Rev. 63, 64 n.8 (1988).

[159] In *Provident Tradesmens Bank & Trust Co. v. Patterson*, 390 U.S. 102, 114 (1968), the Court wondered whether a person "should be bound by the previous decision because, although technically a nonparty, he had purposely bypassed an adequate opportunity to intervene." *Accord, Richards v. Jefferson City*, 517 U.S. 793 (1996); *National R.R. Passenger Corp. v. Pennsylvania Pub. Util. Comm.*, 342 F.3d 242 (3d Cir. 2003). For the argument that issue preclusion should attach under such circumstances, see ALI, *Complex Litigation Project* § 5.05 (1993); Louis Touton, Note, *Preclusion of Absent Disputants to Compel Intervention*, 79 Colum. L. Rev. 1551 (1979); Michael A. Berch, *A Proposal to Permit Collateral Estoppel of Nonparties Seeking Affirmative Relief*, 1979 Ariz. St. L.J. 511 (1979).

[160] 439 U.S. 322, 327 n.7 (1979). On how the Due Process Clause of the United States Constitution functions to prevent applications of preclusion which compromise a party's right to a hearing, see § 15.06[2], *supra*. For subsequent applications of the rule that strangers to a civil lawsuit may not be precluded by it, see *Georgia v. South Carolina*, 497 U.S. 376, 392 (1990); *Martin v. Wilks*, 490 U.S. 755 (1989). "A judgment or decree among parties to a lawsuit resolves issues as among them, but it does not conclude the rights of stranger to those proceedings." 490 U.S. at 762.

Notwithstanding this rule, it is possible to bind passive members of a plaintiff class without their active involvement in the case. For discussion of how class actions work and of the special treatment they receive under the Constitution, see §§ 4.02[1] (constitutional concerns) & 9.09 (class actions generally), *supra*.

[161] This rarely occurs. "Because the amicus curiae generally lacks party status, or the ability to control the course of the litigation, the private amici can, in most instances, participate in the suit free of the effects of res judicata." Michael K. Lowman, Comment, *The Litigating Amicus Curiae: When Does the Party Begin After the Friends Leave?*, 41 Am. U. L. Rev. 1243, 1260–61 (1992).

furnishing behind-the-scenes assistance to one of the actual parties. For example, in *Montana v. United States*,[162] the Supreme Court held that the United States was bound by issue preclusion even though it was not a party to the prior adjudication. The Court reached this conclusion by noting that the United States subsidized and controlled the actions of one who was a party there. The United States directed decisions to file and to appeal, paid litigation costs, and reviewed and approved papers filed in that case.

For issue preclusion to apply to nonparties, due process probably requires the nonparty to have participated at least informally in the prior adjudication. In contrast, those who did not participate (strangers) probably cannot be bound by issue preclusion. This is true even if a stranger forgoes a clear opportunity to participate in the prior adjudication,[163] and even if the quality of the initial adjudication was so high as to suggest that the stranger will not put on a better case when permitted to relitigate the issue.[164] In this context, due process is not satisfied by adequate or even exemplary representation by another litigant in another case. The sentiment — if not the logic — of due process guarantees strangers some kind of their own day in court before they can be bound, if for no other reason than to cauterize the wounds of defeat.[165]

[2]   When Strangers to the Prior Adjudication May Bind Those Who Were Parties

One question has dominated modern-day developments in issue preclusion. When, if ever, can strangers to the prior adjudication invoke the doctrine? Once the rule was never. Applying the *mutuality doctrine*, courts held, that since strangers were safe from the adverse effects of a prior adjudication, they could not use it to their advantage.[166] In time, however, courts began to attach importance to the difference between binding total strangers to the prior litigation and binding those subject to a prior adjudication of the issue, albeit against a different party. While a minority of jurisdictions continue to adhere to the mutuality doctrine,[167] most courts have now dispensed with it in favor of nonmutual preclusion. They permit strangers to the prior case to invoke issue preclusion against those who were parties, whenever it appears from the circumstances that it is fair to do so, but not the reverse

---

[162] 440 U.S. 147 (1979).

[163] Probably the worst that will happen to a party who deliberately forgoes prior participation will be that he may later be denied use of nonmutual issue preclusion.

[164] *See, e.g., Humphreys v. Tann*, 487 F.2d 666 (6th Cir. 1973).

[165] Thus, in *Taylor v. Sturgell*, 128 S. Ct. 2161, 2171 (2008), the Supreme Court, in a claim preclusion case, rejected an expanded exception for "virtual representation."

[166] *E.g., Bigelow v. Old Dominion Copper Mining & Smelting Co.*, 225 U.S. 111, 127 (1912); *Buckeye Powder Co. v. E. I. DuPont de Nemours Powder Co.*, 248 U.S. 55, 63 (1918).

[167] A study identified eight states that retain the mutuality doctrine: Alabama, Florida, Georgia, Kansas, Louisiana, Mississippi, North Dakota, and Virginia. Howard M. Erichson, *Interjurisdictional Preclusion*, 96 MICH. L. REV. 945, 966–67 (1998) (citing cases).

[a]   The Decline of the Mutuality Doctrine

The mutuality doctrine rests upon two separate propositions. *First*, strangers to a prior adjudication will not be bound by it. *Second*, it is unfair to permit anyone who cannot be bound by a prior adjudication to use it to bind another. That is, one-way preclusion is unfair; the risk of preclusion from the initial case must be mutual.

The first of these two propositions is still true — federal due process law still seems to protect strangers to a prior adjudication from being bound by it.[168] The widespread collapse of the mutuality doctrine occurred because most jurisdictions no longer accept the second proposition. Swelling dockets and a greater appreciation of the benefits of judicial economy led courts to reexamine the assumption that one-way preclusion was invariably unfair. This resulted in a series of significant state and federal decisions repudiating the mutuality doctrine.

The most significant state case was *Bernhard v. Bank of America*.[169] In the first lawsuit, plaintiff, an estate's administratrix, sued her predecessor for failing to include certain funds in his accounting of the assets of the estate. She lost. She then sued the bank in the second lawsuit, claiming that it was indebted to the estate for releasing these same funds without proper authorization. The bank argued that the issue of its authorization had been determined adversely to the plaintiff in the first lawsuit.

The bank was a stranger to the first lawsuit. Thus it could not have been bound[170] had the authorization issue in that case been resolved differently. That is, if the first case determined that the bank released the funds without proper authority, the bank could nonetheless litigate the issue in the second case and attempt to prove that it had been authorized to release the funds. The only way, then, that the California Supreme Court could give preclusive effect to the judgment rendered in the first lawsuit was to dispense with the doctrine of mutuality. It did so, stating that "no satisfactory rationalization has been advanced for the requirement of mutuality."[171]

Two federal cases are also of special importance. In *Blonder-Tongue Laboratories, Inc. v. University of Illinois Foundation*,[172] the Supreme Court extensively criticized the mutuality doctrine.[173] The Court refused to invoke the mutuality requirement in *Blonder-Tongue*, but the breadth of its ruling was uncertain. However, in a subsequent case, *Parklane Hosiery Co. v. Shore*,[174] the Court categorically repudiated the mutuality doctrine and thus

---

[168] *See* § 15.08[2], *supra*.

[169] 122 P.2d 892 (Cal. 1942).

[170] *See* § 15.08[2], *supra*.

[171] 122 P.2d at 895.

[172] 402 U.S. 313 (1971). For additional discussion of this case, see John B. Corr, *Supreme Court Doctrine in the Trenches: The Case of Collateral Estoppel*, 27 Wm. & Mary L. Rev. 35, 37–39 (1985).

[173] 402 U.S. at 322–27.

[174] 439 U.S. 322 (1979). For an extended discussion of the case and the circumstances

ended its use in federal courts.[175]

Parklane faulted the mutuality doctrine for "failing to recognize the obvious difference in position between a party who has never litigated an issue and one who has fully litigated and lost."[176] *Parklane* completes the process, begun by *Blonder-Tongue*, of replacing one fairness test with another. The mutuality doctrine rested on the idea that it was invariably unfair to create risk-free opportunities for preclusion, and that benefits of preclusion were spoils of victory earned through the risk of equally adverse consequences had matters in the original suit turned out differently. Rejecting these ideas, *Parklane* declared that henceforth it would be necessary to adduce some particular reason why it would be unfair to bind a party by nonmutual issue preclusion. Attention under this new approach thus shifted from the position of the party wishing to use the doctrine to the position of the party against whom it was invoked.

[b] Limits on Courts' Discretion to Invoke Nonmutual Issue Preclusion

Nonmutual issue preclusion has not been without its critics. Observers were particularly concerned that, when invoked offensively,[177] the doctrine might give a new claimant an unfair advantage over one who was a defendant in a prior adjudication.[178]

For example, Professor Brainerd Currie put forth what he called the "multiple claimant anomaly."[179] In his hypothetical case, fifty injured passengers bring successive suits against a railroad arising from the same

---

surrounding it, see Lewis A. Grossman, *The Story of Parklane: The 'Litigation Crisis' and the Efficiency Imperative, in* CIVIL PROCEDURE STORIES 405–43 (Kevin M. Clermont, ed., 2d ed. 2008). In addition, see Maurice J. Holland, *Modernizing Res Judicata: Reflections on the Parklane Doctrine,* 55 IND. L.J. 615 (1980).

[175] Judith Resnik, *Tiers,* 57 S. CAL. L. REV. 837, 868 (1984).

[176] 439 U.S. at 327.

[177] Terminology is important here. Effects from a judgment that operate to plaintiff's advantage in the subsequent case are described as "offensive" preclusion, while those operating to defendant's subsequent advantage are described as "defensive" preclusion. For more on the distinction, *see* § 15.01[3], *supra.*

Offensive and defensive classifications apply in the same way to both mutual and nonmutual issue preclusion. Mutual issue preclusion is possible under the mutuality doctrine; nonmutual preclusion is not.

Of the cases discussed in this section, *Bernhard* and *Blonder-Tongue* are examples of defensive nonmutual issue preclusion, while *Parklane* is an example of offensive nonmutual issue preclusion.

[178] *See* Ratliff, note 158, *supra*; Brainerd Currie, *Mutuality of Collateral Estoppel: Limits of the Bernhard Doctrine,* 9 STAN. L. REV. 281 (1957); Edwin H. Greenebaum, *In Defense of the Doctrine of Mutuality of Estoppel,* 45 IND. L.J. 1 (1969); Elvin E. Overton, *The Restatement of Judgments, Collateral Estoppel, and Conflict of Laws,* 44 TENN. L. REV. 927 (1977). *Cf.* Waggoner, note 82, *supra* (rejecting nonmutual issue preclusion but advocating nonmutual claim preclusion); Note, *Exposing the Extortion Gap: An Economic Analysis of the Rules of Collateral Estoppel,* 105 HARV. L. REV. 1940 (1992) (criticizing nonmutual preclusion by contending that it is unfair to subsequent plaintiffs).

[179] Currie, note 178, *supra,* at 285–89.

train accident. In the first case, the railroad wins by establishing that it was not negligent. When the second passenger brings suit, the court will deny the railroad issue-preclusive effect from the prior determination of no negligence, since the second passenger was a stranger to the first suit.[180] The plaintiff in the second suit is thus free to relitigate the question of the railroad's negligence. In Currie's example, twenty-five passenger plaintiffs bring twenty-five successive lawsuits. Each plaintiff is free to relitigate the negligence issue, but each loses. Then, in the twenty-sixth case, a passenger prevails on the negligence issue and recovers. Currie then poses the question:

> Are we to understand that the remaining twenty-four passengers can plead the judgment in the case of No. 26 as conclusively establishing that the railroad was guilty of negligence, while the railroad can make no reference to the first twenty-five cases which it won?[181]

Abuses of nonmutual offensive preclusion might also lead to proliferation of litigation contrary to one purpose of preclusion.[182] For example, passenger B in Currie's hypothetical might forgo an opportunity to join with passenger A in the initial case, taking a "wait and see" attitude. If A wins, B can invoke nonmutual issue preclusion. If A loses, B (a stranger to the first case) is free to relitigate all issues.

The Supreme Court acknowledged all of these concerns in *Parklane*. While it approved offensive nonmutual preclusion for that case, it made clear that the doctrine should not always be available. Federal courts have "broad discretion to determine when it should be applied."[183] They must use their discretion to refuse nonmutual preclusion when circumstances suggest that use of the doctrine against a party to the prior case would be unfair. The Court stated that nonmutual preclusion should be denied when sought by one who deliberately bypassed an opportunity to participate in the original proceeding; when the stake of the party against whom preclusion would be invoked was deceptively small in the original proceeding; when the subsequent proceeding affords significantly more advantageous procedural opportunities for that party; or when there were inconsistent prior judgments.[184]

Of course, *Parklane* is not controlling on state courts.[185] But a large number of state jurisdictions rejecting mutuality have defined and limited nonmutual preclusion in ways similar to Supreme Court's opinion. Since *Parklane* relied in part on a draft provision of the *Restatement (Second) of Judgments*, this consensus is not surprising.

---

[180] *See* § 15.08[1], *supra.*

[181] Currie, note 178, *supra*, at 286.

[182] Promotion of judicial economy is a primary purpose of preclusion doctrine. *See* § 15.01[1], *supra.*

[183] 439 U.S. at 331.

[184] 439 U.S. at 331.

[185] Subject only to the due process and full faith and credit constraints of federal law, state courts are free to devise their own answers to preclusion questions. *See* § 15.01[1], *supra.*

That provision, which became Section 29 of the *Restatement (Second)*, expressly rejects the doctrine of mutuality by making issue preclusion available to strangers to the prior adjudication. But Section 29 makes clear that issue preclusion is unavailable if the party who would be bound "lacked full and fair opportunity to litigate the issue in the first action or other circumstances justify affording him an opportunity to relitigate the issue."

Problems of procedural fairness can arise even if the parties in the successive suits are identical.[186] However, Section 29 notes additional problems which may arise when strangers to the first suit attempt to invoke issue preclusion. These include:

> (2) The forum in the second action affords the party against whom preclusion is asserted procedural opportunities in the presentation and determination of the issue that were not available in the first action and could likely result in the issue being differently determined;

> (3) The person seeking to invoke favorable preclusion, or to avoid unfavorable preclusion, could have effected joinder in the first action between himself and his present adversary;

> (4) The determination relied on as preclusive was itself inconsistent with another determination of the same issue . . . .[187]

Clear acknowledgment in *Parklane* and in Section 29 of situations to which nonmutual issue preclusion should not apply has done much to ease apprehensions over rejection of the mutuality doctrine. For example, both *Parklane* [188] and Section 29[189] seem to offer an answer to the so-called multiple claimant anomaly posed earlier in this discussion. It would clearly be unfair to permit a claimant to exploit one judgment that was inconsistent with twenty-five others, and a court faced with such a case is directed to refuse nonmutual preclusion.[190]

---

[186] *Restatement (Second) of Judgments* Section 28 addresses this. For discussion of Section 28 and how concerns of procedural fairness can prevent application of issue preclusion even when the parties are the same, see § 15.07[4], *supra*. Incorporating Section 28 by reference, Section 29 makes clear that the same factors can be important in ascertaining nonmutual issue preclusion.

[187] Other reasons for refusing nonmutual offensive issue preclusion are listed in § 29 and elsewhere. Partial immunity from issue preclusion extended to government litigants provides an example.

> [B]ecause the government often litigates an issue against different parties in different circuits, an unrestrained use of issue preclusion against the government would allow a decision in one case to bind the government in all subsequent litigation. The result would be to require the government to vigorously contest and appeal every lawsuit in which it is involved, placing an enormous strain on its resources.

LINDA L. SILBERMAN, ALLAN R. STEIN & TOBIAS B. WOLFF, CIVIL PROCEDURE: THEORY AND PRACTICE 888 (2d ed. 2006). For an overview, see Samuel Estreicher & Richard L. Revesz, *Nonacquiesence by Federal Administrative Agencies*, 98 YALE L.J. 679 (1989).

[188] *See* § 15.08[2][a], *supra*.

[189] *See* RESTATEMENT (SECOND) OF JUDGMENTS §§ 29(3) & (4) (1982), quoted in the text of this subsection, *supra*.

[190] In addition, *see* RESTATEMENT (SECOND) OF JUDGMENTS § 29 comment f (1982):

> Giving a prior determination of an issue conclusive effect in subsequent litigation is

Courts are similarly directed to deny nonmutual preclusion to claimants who have adopted a "wait-and-see" attitude toward the initial case.[191]

PART C.
Inter-System Preclusion

§ 15.09   INTRAMURAL AND INTER-SYSTEM PRECLUSION COMPARED

Preclusion law is largely common law. Within limits,[192] each judicial court system is free to fashion doctrine determining how much force its judgments should have. When courts of a system are presented with their own judgments, questions concerning the effect of the judgment arise in an *intramural* [193] context. The intramural law that courts apply is their local preclusion law.

Increasingly, courts must also consider the effect of judgments which were rendered outside their system. Then, questions concerning the effect of the judgment arise in an *inter-system* context.[194] For inter-system cases, which body of preclusion law should determine the force and effect of the judgment? Is it measured by the intramural law of the system rendering the judgment or

---

justified not merely by avoiding further costs of litigation but also by underlying confidence that the result reached is substantially correct. Where a determination relied on as preclusive is itself inconsistent with some other adjudication of the same issue, that confidence is generally unwarranted.

[191] In addition, *see* RESTATEMENT (SECOND) OF JUDGMENTS § 29 comment e (1982) :

A person in such a position that he might ordinarily have been expected to join as plaintiff in the first action, but who did not do so, may be refused the benefits of "offensive" issue preclusion where the circumstances suggest that he wished to avail himself of the benefits of a favorable outcome without incurring the risk of an unfavorable one.

[192] The Due Process Clause of the United States Constitution limits the preclusive effect a court can give to one of its judgments. *See* § 15.06 note 154 and related text, *supra*.

[193] *See* Robert C. Casad, *Intersystem Issue Preclusion and the Restatement (Second) of Judgments*, 66 CORNELL L. REV. 510, 511 (1981); RESTATEMENT (SECOND) OF JUDGMENTS, 2 (introduction) (1982).

[194] An elaboration of many of the points under this heading appears in Gene R. Shreve, *Preclusion and Federal Choice of Law*, 64 TEX. L. REV. 1209 (1986). On the subject generally, see Howard M. Erichson, *Interjurisdictional Preclusion*, 96 MICH. L. REV. 945 (1998); Graham C. Lilly, *The Symmetry of Preclusion*, 54 OHIO ST. L.J. 289 (1993); Gene R. Shreve, *Judgments from a Choice-of-Law Perspective*, 40 AM. J. COMP. L. 985 (1992); Sanford N. Caust-Ellenbogen, *False Conflicts and Interstate Preclusion: Moving Beyond a Wooden Reading of the Full Faith and Credit Statute*, 58 FORD. L. REV. 593 (1990); Jean A. Mortland, *Interstate Federalism: Effect of Full Faith and Credit to Judgments*, 16 U. DAYTON L. REV. 47 (1990); Stephen B. Burbank, *Interjurisdictional Preclusion and Federal Common Law: Toward a General Approach*, 70 CORNELL L. REV. 625 (1985); Barbara A. Atwood, *State Court Judgments in Federal Litigation: Mapping the Contours of Full Faith and Credit*, 58 IND. L.J. 59 (1982); Casad, note 193, *supra*; Ronan E. Degnan, *Federalized Res Judicata*, 85 YALE L.J. 741 (1976).

by the intramural law of the system where the judgment is offered for enforcement?

So long as applicable preclusion law is the same in both systems, the question is academic. The law will often but not always be the same. As noted earlier, systems disagree over whether to permit claim-splitting in traffic accident cases[195] and over whether to refuse nonmutual issue preclusion by invoking the mutuality doctrine.[196] Other differences also exist.[197] When rules conflict, the court where the judgment is presented might have an understandable preference for its own intramural preclusion law. However, federal full faith and credit law severely restricts the court's freedom to disregard the preclusion law of the place rendering the judgment.[198] This appears to be true whether the effect sought from the judgment is claim or issue preclusion.[199]

A different problem exists when foreign-country judgments are presented in the United States for enforcement. Federal full faith and credit law does not reach such cases. The policy arguments for giving preclusive effect to foreign-country judgments are not as strong. At the same time, it would be unwise simply to ignore foreign-country judgments. American courts generally recognize such judgments, but the content of governing law is relatively indistinct.[200]

§ 15.10   THE FEDERAL FULL FAITH AND CREDIT OBLIGATION THAT JUDGMENTS BE GIVEN AS MUCH EFFECT AS THEY WOULD HAVE WHERE RENDERED

To a large extent, federal full faith and credit law determines the enforceability of judgments rendered by a court in the United States and presented elsewhere in this country for enforcement. Full faith and credit obligations appear in the Full Faith and Credit Clause of the United States Constitution[201] and in the full faith and credit statute.[202] The basic requirement of each is that a judgment must be given as much effect where presented for enforcement as

---

[195] *See* § 15.03, *supra.*

[196] *See* § 15.08, *supra.*

[197] For example, compare the federal court view that its judgments are final during appeal with the Utah state view that does not attach finality to its judgments under such circumstances. *See* § 15.05, *supra.* And compare the United States Supreme Court's refusal to give issue-preclusive effect to federal default judgments with the opposing view New York has taken concerning the effect of its state judgments. *See* § 15.07, *supra.*

[198] *See* §§ 15.10–15.11, *infra.*

[199] "Although it has been suggested that issue preclusion may operate with less force than does claim preclusion under [the federal full faith and credit statute] the cases do not support such a distinction." Atwood, note 194, *supra,* at 69. *See Migra v. Warren City School District Board of Education,* 465 U.S. 75, 83 (1984), and *McDonald v. City of West Branch,* 466 U.S. 284, 291 (1984), each equating claim and issue preclusion for purposes of federal court enforcement of state judgments.

[200] *See* § 15.12, *infra.*

[201] U.S. Const. art. IV, § 1.

[202] 28 U.S.C. § 1738.

it would have had where rendered. The Full Faith and Credit Clause imposes the rule on states presented with sister-state judgments. The full faith and credit statute protects state judgments in state or federal courts and has been read to protect federal judgments in state court.

[1]   Preserving the Preclusive Effect of State Judgments in Sister-State Courts

The Full Faith and Credit Clause of the Constitution[203] contains the requirement that "[f]ull faith and credit shall be given in each State to the public acts, records, and judicial proceedings of every other State." Congress passed the full faith and credit statute in 1790.[204] The statute's requirement, that all courts in the United States give "such faith and credit" to state "records and judicial proceedings" as they would have in the courts of that state, dates from 1790.[205] Except in child custody cases,[206] the Full Faith and Credit Clause and statute govern the recognition and enforcement of state judgments in other state courts.[207]

Initially, some lower courts read the Full Faith and Credit Clause and statute to require only that judgments be taken as *prima facie* evidence in subsequent proceedings. This view would have left courts free, at the very least, to apply their own preclusion law to determine the effect of judgments rendered elsewhere. However, the Supreme Court rejected the view in *Mills v. Duryee*.[208] Invoking both Clause and statute, the Court held that the obligation of full faith and credit to a New York state judgment required the application of New York preclusion law.[209] Of the full faith and credit statute, Justice Story wrote, "we can perceive no rational interpretation of the act . . . unless it declares a judgment conclusive when a Court of the particular state where it is rendered would pronounce the same decision."[210]

---

[203] For examination of the Clause, see Katherine C. Pearson, *Common Law Preclusion, Full Faith and Credit, and Consent Judgments: The Analytical Challenge*, 48 CATH. U. L. REV. 419 (1999); Ralph U. Whitten, *The Constitutional Limitations on State-Court Jurisdiction: A Historical-Interpretive Reexamination of the Full Faith and Credit and Due Process Clauses (Part One)*, 14 CREIGHTON L. REV. 499 (1981); Kurt H. Nadelmann, *Full Faith and Credit to Judgments and Public Acts*, 56 MICH. L. REV. 33, 60 (1957); James D. Sumner, Jr., *Full Faith and Credit for Judicial Proceedings*, 2 UCLA L. REV. 441 (1955); Max Radin, *The Authenticated Full Faith and Credit Clause: Its History*, 39 ILL. L. REV. 1 (1944).

[204] Act of May 26, 1790 (now codified as 28 U.S.C. § 1738).

[205] Amendments to the Act of 1790, *reviewed in* Lea Brilmayer, *Credit Due Judgments and Credit Due Laws: The Respective Roles of Due Process and Full Faith and Credit in the Interstate Context*, 70 IOWA L. REV. 95, 95 n.2 (1984), have not altered its basic standard.

[206] *See* note 216, *infra*.

[207] The Revised Uniform Enforcement of Foreign Judgments Act (1964) seeks to expedite compliance with federal full faith and credit law and has been adopted by most States.

[208] 11 U.S. (7 Cranch) 481 (1813).

[209] "[I]t is beyond all doubt that the judgment of the Supreme Court of New York was conclusive upon the parties in that state. It must, therefore, be conclusive here also." 11 U.S. at 484.

[210] 11 U.S. at 485.

When courts simultaneously invoke the Full Faith and Credit Clause and statute, it is often difficult to determine which is carrying the main weight in decisions to follow the preclusion law of the judgment-rendering state. But it may not be terribly important to distinguish between the two in this context. Perhaps it is enough to collapse both — as one distinguished writer has — into "the full faith and credit requirement."[211] While the area is not free of uncertainty,[212] the basic obligation of federal full faith and credit is firm. State courts must give as much effect to sister-state judgments as they would have where rendered.[213]

[2]   Preserving the Preclusive Effect of State Judgments in Federal Court

Congress has always had a variety of legislative options in determining the manner and extent to which it wishes to regulate inter-system preclusion.

At one extreme, Congress could have codified intersystem preclusion law, elaborating a precise, systematic scheme to regulate the inter-system enforcement of state and federal judgments.[214] Commentators have suggested that the idea is worth considering,[215] but Congress has never really acted upon it. Except in child-custody cases,[216] Congress has not used its power to extensively regulate inter-system preclusion.

At the other extreme, Congress could have done nothing. If the Supreme Court had interpreted the Full Faith and Credit Clause as self-applying,[217]

---

[211] Robert C. Casad, *Intersystem Issue Preclusion and the Restatement (Second) of Judgments*, 66 CORNELL L. REV. 510, 520 (1981).

[212] For example, the Supreme Court has had difficulty developing an intelligible standard for determining the effect of state worker's compensation decrees. *See Thomas v. Washington Gas Light Co.*, 448 U.S. 261 (1980); *Industrial Comm'n of Wis. v. McCartin*, 330 U.S. 622 (1947); *Magnolia Petroleum Co. v. Hunt*, 320 U.S. 430 (1943). For a discussion of these cases, see WILLIAM M. RICHMAN & WILLIAM L. REYNOLDS, UNDERSTANDING CONFLICT OF LAWS § 117[c][1]–[5] (3d ed. 2002).

[213] *See, e.g., Underwriters Nat'l Assurance Co. v. North Carolina Life & Accident & Health Ins. Guar. Ass'n*, 455 U.S. 691 (1982); *Durfee v. Duke*, 375 U.S. 106 (1963); *Fauntleroy v. Lum*, 210 U.S. 230 (1908). *See generally* William L. Reynolds, *The Iron Laws of Full Faith and Credit*, 53 MD. L. REV. 412 (1994).

[214] The Full Faith and Credit Clause, U.S. Const. art IV, § 1, expressly authorizes Congress to enact laws elaborating the obligation of states to respect sister-state judgments. Congress' power to impose upon federal courts a duty to recognize state judgments derives from U.S. Const. art. III, § 1. The Commerce Clause (U.S. Const. art. I, § 8) and the Privileges and Immunities Clause (U.S. Const. art. IV, § 2), provide additional support for a broad statutory scheme.

[215] *See, e.g.*, Brainerd Currie, *Full Faith and Credit, Chiefly to Judgments: A Role for Congress*, 1964 SUP. CT. REV. 89.

[216] The Parental Kidnaping Prevention Act of 1980, 28 U.S.C. § 1738A, augments § 1738 with reference to state child custody decrees. Discussions of the Act appear in Barbara A. Atwood, *Child Custody Jurisdiction and Territoriality*, 52 OHIO ST. L.J. 369 (1991); Russell M. Coombs, *Interstate Child Custody: Jurisdiction, Recognition, and Enforcement*, 66 MINN. L. REV. 711 (1982).

[217] After early uncertainty, the Supreme Court adopted the view that the clause is self-applying. Robert H. Jackson, *Full Faith and Credit — the Lawyer's Clause of the Constitution*, 45 COLUM. L. REV. 1, 11 (1945); Elliott E. Cheatham, *Res Judicata and the Full Faith and Credit Clause: Magnolia Petroleum Co. v. Hunt*, 44 COLUM. L. REV. 330, 333 (1944).

congressional inaction might not have diminished state court obligations to enforce sister-state judgments. But federal courts are beyond the textual reach of the Full Faith and Credit Clause.[218] They are probably under no constitutional compulsion to recognize the effects of state judgments created under state preclusion law.[219] Congressional silence, then, would have left federal courts free to determine how much effect to give to state judgments.

Congress decided to steer a middle course. Although the legislative history of the full faith and credit statute[220] is uncertain, it seems clear that Congress intended to impose upon federal courts an obligation to recognize and enforce the judgments of states equivalent to the obligation imposed on states by the Constitution's Full Faith and Credit Clause to recognize and enforce sister-state judgments.[221]

This is how the Supreme Court has read the statute.[222] The Court has made clear that, in cases where the statute applies, "Congress has specifically required all federal courts to give preclusive effect to state-court judgments whenever the courts of the State from which the judgments emerged would do so . . . ."[223]

At the same time, important differences flow from the fact that federal courts' obligation to give effect to state judgments is only statutory. Just as Congress did not have to enact the full faith and credit statute, it is free either to repeal it or to lighten its obligations by amending it to create exceptions. Section 1738 itself contains no exceptions to the obligation of federal courts to honor state judgments, but other federal statutes can suspend that obligation.

Congress has sometimes expressly suspended Section 1738.[224] More often, however, the question will be whether suspension not expressly required is nonetheless necessary to effectuate exclusive federal subject-matter jurisdiction. In short, should an exception to the mandate of Section 1738 be implied from congressional grants of exclusive federal jurisdiction? This question has divided commentators[225] and federal courts.[226]

---

[218] Art. IV, § 1 of the U.S. Constitution imposes a full faith and credit obligation only upon sister states. The Supreme Court noted that federal courts were "not included within the constitutional provision." *Kremer v. Chemical Constr. Corp.*, 456 U.S. 461, 483–84 n. 24 (1982).

[219] *See* Gene R. Shreve, *Preclusion and Federal Choice of Law*, 64 Tex. L. Rev. 1209, 1223 n.77 (1986).

[220] 28 U.S.C. § 1738.

[221] Atwood, note 194, *supra*, at 67; Degnan, note 194, *supra*, at 743–44.

[222] *E.g.*, *Davis v. Davis*, 305 U.S. 32, 40 (1939) ("The Act extended the rule of the Constitution to all courts, federal as well as state.").

[223] *Allen v. McCurry*, 449 U.S. 90, 96 (1980).

[224] The most prominent example is the federal *habeas corpus* statute. 28 U.S.C. § 2254. *See* David P. Currie, *Res Judicata: The Neglected Defense*, 45 U. Chi. L. Rev. 317, 330, 333 (1978).

[225] *Compare, e.g.*, Allan D. Vestal, *Res Judicata/Claim Preclusion: Judgment for the Claimant*, 62 Nw. U. L. Rev. 357, 374–75 (1967), and Note, *The Collateral Estoppel Effect of Prior State Court Findings in Cases Within Exclusive Federal Jurisdiction*, 91 Harv. L. Rev. 1281, 1290–91 (1978) (arguing for preclusion), *with* Stephen B. Burbank, *Afterwords: A Response to Professor Hazard and a Comment on Marrese*, 70 Cornell L. Rev. 659, 664 (1985), and Atwood, note 194, *supra*, at

Marrese v. American Acad. of Orthopaedic Surgeons [227] presented the Supreme Court with the issue whether exclusive federal antitrust jurisdiction operates as an exception to Section 1738. The Court declined to answer the question but did suggest that exclusive federal jurisdiction would not invariably create an implied exception.[228] The Court also offered some guidelines for resolving "the more general question . . . whether the concerns underlying a particular grant of exclusive jurisdiction justify a finding of an implied partial repeal of Section 1738."

> Resolution of this question will depend on the particular federal statute as well as the nature of the claim or issue involved in the subsequent federal action. Our previous decisions indicate that the primary consideration must be the intent of Congress.[229]

[3]   Preserving the Preclusive Effect of Federal Judgments in Other Federal Courts

The preclusive effect to be given to a federal judgment by the court that rendered it, or by any other federal court, is an intramural question of federal preclusion law. The Supreme Court's decisions elaborating federal preclusion doctrine[230] will largely determine the effect of such judgments. When unresolved differences exist among the federal circuits concerning questions which the Supreme Court has not passed upon, one might expect the law of the federal circuit in which the judgment was rendered to control. However, a statute which authorizes federal court registration of a judgment "for the recovery of money or property" rendered in another federal district court[231] suggests a different result. Section 1963 provides that "judgment so registered

---

63 (arguing against preclusion because of the insulating effect of exclusive federal jurisdiction).

[226] *Compare, e.g., RX Data Corp. v. Department of Soc. Servs.*, 684 F.2d 192 (2d Cir. 1982), and *Lektro-Vend Corp. v. Vendo Co.*, 660 F.2d 255 (7th Cir. 1981), *cert. denied*, 455 U.S. 921 (1982) (state court judgment denied preclusive effect when federal court had exclusive jurisdiction), *with Nash County Bd. of Educ. v. Biltmore Co.*, 640 F.2d 484 (4th Cir. 1981), and *Derish v. San Mateo-Burlingame Bd. of Realtors*, 724 F.2d 1347 (9th Cir. 1983) (state judgment given preclusive effect notwithstanding exclusive jurisdiction).

[227] 470 U.S. 373 (1985).

[228] 470 U.S. at 380–81.

[229] 470 U.S. at 386. The Court then cited *Kremer v. Chemical Construction Corp.*, 456 U.S. 461 (1982), and *Brown v. Felsen*, 442 U.S. 127 (1979). In *Kremer*, the Court left open the possibility that jurisdiction over claims under Title VII of the Civil Rights Act of 1964 was exclusive in federal court, but found no support in Title VII or its legislative history for the conclusion that it implied an exception to Section 1738. But the Supreme Court refused in *Brown* to give preclusive effect to a prior state judgment in a subsequent federal bankruptcy proceeding within the federal court's exclusive jurisdiction. The *Brown* Court curiously made no reference to Section 1738, but did declare: "While Congress did not expressly confront the problem created by prebankruptcy state-court adjudications, it would be inconsistent with the philosophy of the [federal statutes] to adopt a policy of *res judicata* which takes these [federal bankruptcy] questions away from bankruptcy courts and forces them back into state courts." 442 U.S. at 136.

[230] *E.g., Parklane Hosiery Co. v. Shore*, 439 U.S. 322 (1979). *Parklane* is discussed at § 15.08[2][a], *supra*.

[231] 28 U.S.C. § 1963.

shall have the same effect" as if it had been rendered where registered, suggesting that the law of the federal circuit where the federal judgment is presented for enforcement will control.

[4]   Preserving the Preclusive Effect of Federal Judgments in State Courts

The Full Faith and Credit Clause of the Constitution and the full faith and credit statute both address state judgments. Neither makes provision for federal judgments in state court. At the same time, "[i]t would be unthinkable to suggest that state courts should be free to disregard the judgments of federal courts, given the basic requirements that state courts honor the judgments of courts in other states and that federal courts must honor state court judgments."[232]

In a series of decisions, the Supreme Court therefore filled the gap by reading the full faith and credit statute to require state courts to respect federal judgments.[233] Congress undoubtedly has the authority to enact legislation protecting federal judgments,[234] but this seems quite beyond the language of section 1738. The Court has never come up with an entirely satisfactory rationale for grafting this requirement onto the statute. After surveying the case law in this area, Professor Ronan Degnan observed that his study did

> not . . . show that the Court was willfully wrong in doing what it did, but that it was wantonly right. By strength of arm and sleight of hand, it achieved a result that is indispensable to federalism. . . . Were there no such rule, it would be necessary to invent one — so invent it the Supreme Court did.[235]

The content of the federal preclusion to be applied by subsequent state (or federal) courts depends on the type of federal judgment offered for enforcement or recognition. Federal question judgments have effect under federal preclusion doctrine. *Parklane* would be an example. Recently, however, the Supreme Court ruled that, by federal common law rule, the preclusive effect of federal diversity judgments must be determined by the intramural preclusion law of the state where the federal court rendering the judgment was sitting.[236]

---

[232] WRIGHT & MILLER § 4468.

[233] *E.g., Embry v. Palmer*, 107 U.S. 3, 9–10 (1883); *Stoll v. Gottlieb*, 305 U.S. 165, 170 (1938).

[234] That authority derives, *inter alia*, from Congress' power to create lower federal courts under Art. III, § 1 of the Constitution. Degnan, note 194, *supra*, at 749.

[235] Degnan, note 194, *supra*, at 749.

[236] *Semtek Int'l Inc. v. Lockheed Martin Corp.*, 531 U.S. 497 (2001). For discussions of *Semtek*, see Patrick Woolley, *The Sources of Federal Preclusion Law After Semtek*, 72 U. CINN. L. REV. 527 (2003); Stephen B. Burbank, *Semtek, Forum Shopping, and Federal Common Law*, 77 NOTRE DAME L. REV. 1027 (2002). On the creation of federal common law, see § 7.07.

§ 15.11 ARE OTHER COURTS FREE TO GIVE JUDGMENTS MORE EFFECT THAN THEY WOULD HAVE WHERE RENDERED?

Conflicts of preclusion law among state and federal courts[237] lead to situations in which the local preclusion law of a court where a judgment is presented would give greater preclusive effect to it than would the law of the court rendering the judgment. For example, a federal court, which permits nonmutual issue preclusion, may be presented with a judgment rendered in a state court which still adheres to the limitations of the mutuality doctrine.[238] Under such circumstances, may the federal court disregard the preclusion law of the rendering forum and apply federal doctrine to give issue-preclusive effect to the state judgment? Supreme Court decisions suggest not. Whether sister-state courts can augment the preclusive effect of other state judgments seems a more open question.

[1] May Federal Courts Give Greater Effect to State Judgments?

There is considerable support for the proposition that the full faith and credit statute[239] prevents federal courts from giving any more preclusive effect to state judgments than they would have under the law of the rendering state. In *Marrese v. American Academy of Orthopaedic Surgeons*,[240] the Supreme Court stated that Section 1738

> directs a federal court to refer to the preclusion law of the State in which judgment was rendered. "It has long been established that § 1738 does not allow federal courts to employ their own rules of *res judicata* in determining the effect of state judgments. Rather, it goes beyond the common law and commands a federal court to accept the rules chosen by the State from which the judgment was taken."[241]

Later in the opinion, the Court read an earlier case[242] to reject "the view that Section 1738 allows a federal court to give a state court judgment greater preclusive effect than the state courts themselves would give to it."[243] The Supreme Court's decisions have not been entirely consistent.[244] However, in

---

[237] *See* § 15.09, *supra*.

[238] For a discussion of these conflicting positions, see § 15.08[2], *supra*.

[239] 28 U.S.C. § 1738.

[240] 470 U.S. 373 (1985).

[241] 470 U.S. at 380, *quoting Kremer v. Chemical Constr. Corp.*, 456 U.S. 461, 481–82 (1982).

[242] *Migra v. Warren City Sch. Dist. Bd. of Educ.*, 465 U.S. 75 (1984).

[243] 470 U.S. at 384.

[244] In *Haring v. Prosise*, 462 U.S. 306 (1983), the Court refused to invoke federal doctrine to give greater preclusive effect to a Virginia judgment, but it discussed the possibility at length. *Haring*, 462 U.S. at 317–23. *Haring* seemed to make clear that, in a deserving case, a federal court could give greater preclusive effect to a state judgment than the state rendering it would. In other cases, the Supreme Court has treated the effect of state judgments in federal court as a matter of

Marrese and in one decision since[245] the Court seems determined that federal courts give state judgments no greater preclusive effect than they would have in the state courts where they originated.[246]

[2]   May State Courts Give Greater Effect to Sister-State Judgments?

It is clear that the federal full faith and credit statute applies to sister-state as well as federal courts.[247] There is little to suggest that the added application of the Constitution's Full Faith and Credit Clause to state courts[248] increases their obligation to respect sister-state judgments. If anything, Section 1738 imposes a more stringent obligation than does the Full Faith and Credit Clause.[249] So the legal obligation should be the same for state and federal enforcement courts.

At the same time, the Supreme Court has confined its strongest statements about the deference due to the preclusion law of the rendering states to cases where their judgments were presented in federal court.[250] A few state courts have flatly refused to honor the confines of the preclusion doctrine of the state where the judgment was rendered.[251] Whether or how the Supreme Court will check the impulse of state courts to give greater preclusive effect to sister-state judgments remains to be seen.

---

federal rather than state law. *Brown v. Felsen*, 442 U.S. 127 (1979); *Montana v. United States*, 440 U.S. 147 (1979). In one case, the Court invoked federal doctrine to permit relitigation in apparent disregard of Section 1738's requirement that a state judgment be given as much preclusive effect in federal court. *England v. Louisiana State Bd. of Med. Exam'rs*, 375 U.S. 411 (1964). The Court did not criticize any of these prior cases in its later *Marrese* decision.

[245] *Parsons Steel, Inc. v. First Ala. Bank*, 474 U.S. 518, 523–25 (1986).

[246] For criticism of this position and for the argument that federal courts should give nonmutual, issue-preclusive effect to judgments rendered by states adhering to the mutuality doctrine, see Shreve, note 219, *supra*, at 1251.

[247] RESTATEMENT (SECOND) OF JUDGMENTS § 86 comment c (1982). *See, e.g., Underwriters Nat'l Assurance Co. v. North Carolina Life & Accident & Health Ins. Guar. Ass'n*, 455 U.S. 691, 694 (1982).

[248] *See* § 15.10, *supra*.

[249] *Cf. Thomas v. Washington Gas Light Co.*, 448 U.S. 261, 270 (1980) (where the plurality opinion observes that the essential obligation to give the same effect to sister-state judgments as they would have where rendered, "[if] not compelled by the Full Faith and Credit Clause itself, is surely required by 28 U.S.C. § 1738.") (citation omitted).

[250] *See* notes 241–43, 246 and related text, *supra*.

[251] *Finley v. Kesling*, 433 N.E.2d 1112, 1116–18 (Ill. App. Ct. 1982) (refusing to honor a mutuality limitation under Indiana law); *Hart v. American Airlines, Inc.*, 304 N.Y.S.2d 810 (N.Y. Sup. Ct. 1969) (refusing to honor a mutuality limitation under Texas law). *But see Columbia Cas. Co. v. Playtex FP, Inc.*, 584 A.2d 1214, 1218 (Del. 1991) (honoring a mutuality limitation under Kansas law). The *Columbia Casualty* court observed that, if Delaware courts were to give "the judgments of a sister state greater preclusive effect than they would have in the rendering jurisdiction," the result would be "at variance with the purpose and spirit of the full faith and credit clause." For further discussion of case developments, see Gene R. Shreve, *Judgments from a Choice-of-Law Perspective*, 40 AM. J. COMP. L. 985 (1992).

[3] Why the Greater-Preclusion Issue Will Rarely Arise Concerning Federal Judgments

Federal doctrine is in the vanguard of the movement to give judgments greater preclusive effect. This is evident from the Supreme Court's rejection of the mutuality doctrine,[252] and from numerous lower federal court decisions giving a broad definition to the "claim" precluded by the federal doctrine of claim preclusion.[253] Therefore, it will be rare for a state court to find the preclusive effect of a federal judgment to be greater under its law than it would be in federal court.

§ 15.12 FOREIGN-COUNTRY JUDGMENTS IN AMERICAN COURTS AND AMERICAN JUDGMENTS ABROAD

[1] Foreign-Country Judgments in American Courts

State and federal courts in the United States take a more receptive view of judgments rendered abroad than the courts of most other nations.[254] It has been suggested that "[m]ost states accord foreign-country judgments essentially the same status as sister-state judgments."[255] This receptiveness is in part a reflection of a strong tradition of inter-system preclusion within the United States.[256] But it is important to note that the compulsion behind judgment recognition in the latter context is missing when American courts are presented with foreign country judgments.

Neither the Full Faith and Credit Clause of the United States Constitution[257] nor the full faith and credit statute[258] apply to judgments rendered in foreign countries.[259] This is due in part to the limited textual reach of these provisions and in part to the interlocking character that the judgment-

---

[252] See § 15.08[2][a], *supra*.

[253] See § 15.03, *supra*.

[254] Arthur T. von Mehren & Donald T. Trautman, *Recognition of Foreign Adjudications: A Survey and a Suggested Approach*, 81 HARV. L. REV. 1601, 1602–03 (1969). For commentary and legal materials on the United States enforcement of foreign judgments generally, see Linda J. Silberman & Andreas F. Lowenfeld, *A Different Challenge for the ALI: Herein of Foreign Country Judgments, an International Treaty and an American Statute*, 75 IND. L.J. 635 (2000); Jeffrey Rabkin, Note, *Universal Justice: The Role of Federal Courts in International Civil Litigation*, 95 COLUM. L. REV. 2120 (1995); Robert E. Lutz, *Enforcement of Foreign Judgments, Part I: A Selected Bibliography on United States Enforcement of Judgments Rendered Abroad*, 27 INT'L LAWYER 471 (1993).

[255] EUGENE F. SCOLES & PETER H. HAY, CONFLICT OF LAWS § 24.6 (2d ed. 1992).

[256] See § 15.10, *supra*.

[257] U.S. Const. art. IV, § 1.

[258] 28 U.S.C. § 1738.

[259] Hans Smit, *International Res Judicata and Collateral Estoppel in the United States*, 9 UCLA L. REV. 44 (1962); WILLIAM L. RICHMAN & WILLIAM M. REYNOLDS, UNDERSTANDING CONFLICT OF LAWS § 122 (3d ed. 2002).

rendering and enforcing forums have when both are courts in the United States. That character is lacking in the international setting. Cautioning against treating foreign country judgments under domestic *res judicata* principles, Professors von Mehren and Trautman have noted some fundamental differences between American and foreign courts:

> [O]ne of the purposes of *res judicata* is to maintain the integrity of the domestic judicial system. The case of recognition of internationally foreign judgments is quite different because it may be proper for different legal systems to come to different results on the same set of facts. [And] there are basic differences in the surrounding circumstances. The economic and cultural relationships within a single jurisdiction tend to be closer, and as a result the practical arguments supporting conclusive effects for domestic judgments are stronger. At the same time, shared traditions and experience and the identity of procedures and standards help reduce doubt about the quality of justice represented by a judgment. For these reasons, treating recognition problems as an aspect of *res judicata* tends to lead to a confusion of concepts which should be kept separate.[260]

By the same token, important interests may be served when American courts recognize foreign-country judgments. "[I]f in our highly complex and interrelated world each community exhausted every possibility of insisting on its parochial interests, injustice would result and the normal patterns of life would be disrupted."[261]

Perhaps the "shared tradition" in American courts which may most clearly set their adjudications apart from foreign-country adjudications is that all proceedings must be in accordance with the constitutional requirements of due process.[262] It is therefore not surprising that judgments of common-law

---

[260] von Mehren & Trautman, note 254, *supra* at 1605–06. Copyright © 1969 by the Harvard Law Review Association. Reprinted with permission.

[261] von Mehren & Trautman, note 254, *supra*, at 1603. The authors suggest that, "at least when judgments emanate from legal systems with well-established legal institutions and traditions," more precise policies supporting recognition of foreign country judgments could be articulated. Their list includes:

> a desire to avoid the duplication of effort and consequent waste involved in reconsidering a matter that has already been litigated; a related concern to protect the successful litigant, whether plaintiff or defendant, from harassing or evasive tactics on the part of his previously unsuccessful opponent; a policy against making the availability of local enforcement the decisive element, as a practical matter, in the plaintiff's choice of forum; an interest in fostering stability and unity in an international order in which many aspects of life are not confined to any single jurisdiction.

Id. at 1603–04. Copyright © 1969 by the Harvard Law Review Association. Reprinted with permission.

[262] For discussion of the effect of due process on personal jurisdiction, notice and *res judicata*, see § 15.02, *supra*.

American courts have also refused to enforce foreign judgments that, on the merits, would have been unconstitutional if rendered in the United States. *E.g., Yahoo!, Inc. v. La Ligue Contre Le Racisme et L'Antisemitisme*, 169 F. Supp. 2d 1181 (N.D. Cal. 2001). For discussion of *Yahoo* and other cases, see Mark D. Rosen, Should *"Un-American" Foreign Judgments Be Enforced?*, 88

countries having a due process tradition close to our own are most open to recognition in American courts. For example, in the well-known case, *Somportex Ltd. v. Philadelphia Chewing Gum Corp.*,[263] the Third Circuit gave effect to an English default judgment.

The *Somportex* court invoked the principle of *comity*, perhaps the most durable of the doctrines addressing the recognition and enforcement of foreign-country judgments.[264] It described comity as

> not a rule of law, but one of practice, convenience, and expediency. Although more than mere courtesy and accommodation, comity does not achieve the force of an imperative or obligation. Rather, it is a nation's expression of understanding which demonstrates due regard both to international duty and convenience and to the rights of persons protected by its own laws. Comity should be withheld only when its acceptance would be contrary or prejudicial to the interest of the nation called upon to give it effect.[265]

Neither Congress nor the executive has acted to create anything approaching comprehensive law governing the recognition of international judgments.[266] Nor has the Supreme Court refined many standards through the development of federal common law.[267] Despite the efforts of individual states,[268] the law

---

MINN. L. REV. 783 (2004); Mark D. Rosen, *Exporting the Constitution*, 53 EMORY L.J. 171 (2004).

[263] 453 F.2d 435 (3d Cir. 1971), *cert. denied*, 405 U.S. 1017 (1972). The Court relied in part on *Hilton v. Guyot*, 159 U.S. 113 (1895), a case that provides much of the framework for modern analysis. For an excellent discussion of *Hilton* and its context, see Louise Ellen Teitz, *The Story of Hilton: From Gloves to Globalization, in* CIVIL PROCEDURE STORIES 445–71 (Kevin M. Clermont ed., 2d ed. 2008).

[264] The doctrine of reciprocity, which limits the effect of judgments of countries to the effect United States judgments would have in their courts, has played a more limited and controversial role in this area. For a discussion of comity, reciprocity and other doctrines, see Smit, note 259, *supra*, at 48–56.

[265] 453 F.2d. at 440.

[266] "Unlike many foreign states, the United States is not a party to any international agreement regarding the mutual recognition of judgments." GARY B. BORN & DAVID WESTIN, INTERNATIONAL CIVIL LITIGATION IN UNITED STATES COURTS 938 (3d ed. 1996).

[267] For discussions of federal common law applicable to the recognition of foreign-country judgments, see Ronald A. Brand, *Enforcement of Foreign Money-Judgments in the United States: In Search of Uniformity and International Acceptance*, 67 NOTRE DAME L. REV. 253 (1991); Albert A. Lindner, Comment, *Judgments Rendered Abroad-State Law or Federal Law?*, 12 VILL. L. REV. 618 (1967).

Thirty-two states have adopted the Uniform Foreign Money-Judgments Recognition Act. The Act states that, subject to exceptions, "[t]he foreign judgment is enforceable in the same manner as the judgment of a sister state which is entitled to full faith and credit." Sec. 3. But the exceptions are more extensive than those for sister-state judgments, and each state's courts are free to vary their interpretation. "The problem is that any system defined by the law of the fifty states is potentially no system at all." RALPH STEINHARDT, INTERNATIONAL CIVIL LITIGATION 615 (2002).

[268] On the experience of states that have adopted uniform judgment-recognition acts, and on guidelines for state court decisions provided by *The Restatement (Third) of Foreign Relations Law*, see Brand, note 267, *supra*, at 265–80.

remains fragmented.[269] This condition is a special cause for concern, because it can affect how courts abroad enforce judgments from United States courts.[270]

United States judgments have not been as well-received abroad as foreign-country judgments have here. Resistance is in part a reaction to the lack of a national standard in the United States for enforcing foreign judgments.[271] Adding to the problem are many traditional features of American litigation that foreign courts find unfamiliar if not distasteful. The late Friedrich Juenger observed:

> No other country routinely tries civil actions to a jury or authorizes discovery to the extent we do. Most outlaw contingent fees, and many follow the "English rule" that loser pays all. These facets of American practice result in judgments that boggle foreign lawyers' minds.[272]

[2] American Judgments Abroad

While attitudes toward American judgments vary from country to country,[273] there is widespread agreement among commentators that "it has often been much more difficult to enforce U.S. judgments abroad that to enforce foreign judgments in the United States."[274] Simply put, "[m]any countries are quite restrictive when it comes to enforcing judgments rendered by courts in the United States."[275]

Resistance abroad is attributable to many important differences between how civil cases are adjudicated United State and foreign adjudications. Numerous idiosyncrasies of American civil procedure account for what one writer has called "the nasty aroma American litigation seems to elicit in much of the rest of the world."[276] Moreover, while the reception given foreign-

---

[269] BORN & WESTIN, note 266, *supra*, at 938 ("There is presently no federal standard governing the enforcement of judgments rendered by foreign courts in the United States.").

[270] SCOLES & HAY, note 255, *supra* § 24.6. On the fate of United States judgments abroad, *see* Brand, note 267, *supra*, at 281–83; Peter Hay, *The Recognition and Enforcement of American Money-Judgments in Germany — The 1992 Decision of the German Supreme Court*, 40 AM. J. COMP. L. 729 (1992).

[271] *See* § 15.12[2], *supra*.

[272] Friedrich K. Juenger, *Traveling to The Hague in a Worn-Out Shoe*, 29 PEPPERDINE L. REV. 7, 11 (2001).

[273] For two examples, see Francisco Ramos Romeu, *Litigation Under the Shadow of an Exequatur: The Spanish Recognition of U.S. Judgments*, 38 INT'L LAWYER 945 (2004); and Alessandro Barzaghi, *Recognition and Enforcement of United States Judgments in Italy*, 18 N.Y. INT'L L. REV. 61 (2005).

[274] Louise Ellen Teitz, *The Hague Choice of Court Convention: Validating Party Autonomy and Providing an Alternative to Arbitration*, 53 AM. J. OF COMP. L. 543, 544 (2005).

[275] Linda J. Silberman, *The Impact of Jurisdictional Rules and Recognition Practice on International Business Transactions: The U.S. Regime*, 26 HOUSTON J. OF INT'L L. 327, 351 (2004). Thus, "companies often do not sue in the United States when the assets are elsewhere because they fear the uncertainty of subsequent enforcement of a United States judgment overseas." Louise Ellen Teitz, *The Hague Choice of Court Convention: Validating Party Autonomy and Providing an Alternative to Arbitration*, 53 AM. J. OF COMP. L. 543, 548 (2005).

[276] Richard L. Marcus, *Putting American Procedural Exceptionalism into a Globalized*

country judgments in the United States is favorable overall,[277] foreign observers find disconcerning the lack of uniform federal law for such cases, as noted above.[278]

PART D.
Beyond Preclusion: Additional Doctrines of Repose

Courts employ doctrines in addition to preclusion to reduce frustration and uncertainty generated by recurrent litigation. None of these focus as much as preclusion on the integrity of prior judgments, but they are sufficiently analogous and complementary to preclusion to merit discussion.

§ 15.13 *STARE DECISIS*

[1] The Nature of the Doctrine

When a legal issue arises for the first time, trial and appellate courts have the latitude to choose from among competing rules of law, declaring and applying the one which seems the best. *Stare decisis*[279] denies courts the same flexibility when the legal issue recurs in subsequent cases, binding them instead to the approach of the prior case (precedent). The doctrine has been described by one commentator as fostering a "blind imitation of the past."[280] In stifling a continuing search for the best legal answers, *stare decisis* bears a considerable burden of justification. It is justified by the fact that our judicial process could not cope with the strains which would be caused if legal re-examination was routinely available.

> [R]outine reconsideration of the correctness or propriety of binding precedents would be enormously destructive. Any one at any time can initiate litigation, and if any litigant on the wrong side of the law could force a full dress reconsideration of settled points simply by filing a

---

Context, 53 AM. J. COMP. L. 709, 709–10 (2005). Professor Marcus lists "relaxed pleading, broad discovery, jury trial, limited cost shifting, potentially remarkable awards for pain and suffering or punitive damages, and heavy reliance on private lawyers to enforce public norms, to name several but not all the distinguishing characteristics" of U.S. procedure. For a similar assessment, see Friedrich K. Juenger, note 272, *supra*, at 11.

[277] *See* § 15.12[1], *supra*.

[278] Linda L. Silberman & Andreas F. Lowenfeld, *A Different Challenge for the ALI: Herein of Foreign Country Judgments, an International Treaty, and an American Statute*, 75 IND. L.J. 635, 636 (2000).

[279] *Stare decisis* defined: "*Stare decisis*" is short for *stare decisis et non quieta movere*, which means 'stand by the thing decided and do not disturb the calm.' . . . At its most basic level . . . *stare decisis* refers simply to a court's practice of following precedent, whether its own or that of a superior court." Amy Coney Barrett, *Stare Decisis and Due Process*, 74 U. COLO. L. REV. 1011, 1016 (2003).

[280] Oliver W. Holmes, *The Path of the Law*, 10 HARV. L. REV. 457, 469 (1897).

complaint, it would not only weaken public reliance on the law, but would require judges to hear endless reargument of the same issues.[281]

Stare decisis thus shares the general aim of preclusion to minimize the assorted costs of relitigation.[282] In particular, *stare decisis* bears a functional resemblance to the preclusion of issues of law.[283] However, *stare decisis* differs from preclusion in that it "relates to the orderly development of law. It does not relate to the finality of judgments."[284] This makes *stare decisis* both broader and narrower in scope than preclusion.

The rule protecting a stranger to the prior adjudication from the effects of preclusion[285] has no counterpart in the doctrine of *stare decisis*. On the contrary, the very purpose of *stare decisis* is to settle future legal controversies. The only way one who expects to be a party in future litigation can avert the possible effects of *stare decisis* is to try to influence the legal decision in the initial case through intervention[286] or *amicus curiae* participation.

On the other hand, the effects of *stare decisis* are often less definite than those of preclusion. There are several reasons for this.

[2]   The Scope of *Stare Decisis*

[a]   Boundaries Set by Legal Analysis

First, the *stare decisis* effect of a case must derive from a well-articulated statement of law that was necessary to explain the decision there. It may be possible to avoid *stare decisis* either by arguing that the court has not yet clearly formed a principle and the law is still in a state of flux,[287] or that the principle offered for *stare decisis* effect is not a rule necessary to explain the decision, but is instead only a rule mentioned in passing — *dictum*.[288]

---

[281] 1B J. Moore, Moore's Federal Practice ¶ 0.402[3.-1] (2d ed.). *Accord*, Benjamin Cardozo, The Nature of the Judicial Process 149 (1921):

> [T]he labor of judges would be increased almost to the breaking point if every past decision could be reopened in every case, and one could not lay one's own course of bricks on the secure foundation of the courses laid by others who had gone before him.

[282] *See* § 15.01[1] (preclusion policies), *supra*.

[283] *See* § 15.07, *supra*.

[284] 1B J. Moore, Moore's Federal Practice ¶ 0.402[2] (2d ed.).

[285] Discussed in § 15.08[1], *supra*.

[286] Some courts have recognized possible prejudice from *stare decisis* as a basis for intervention of right. *See, e.g., Natural Res. Def. Council, Inc. v. United States Nuclear Regulatory Comm'n*, 578 F.2d 1341 (10th Cir. 1978), and the cases cited in Gene R. Shreve, *Questioning Intervention of Right — Toward a New Methodology of Decisionmaking*, 74 Nw. U. L. Rev. 894, 906 (1980); Note, *Federal Civil Procedure: Prejudicial Effects of Stare Decisis Can Compel Intervention of Right Under Rule 24(a)*, 1967 Duke L.J. 1251. On intervention generally, see § 9.08, *supra*.

[287] *Cf.* P.S. Atiyah & Robert S. Summers, Form and Substance in Anglo-American Law 120 (1987) ("Whenever the substantive reasoning in a case seems at all dubious, the case must go through a period of evaluative trial before it can be regarded as settled and therefore valid law.").

[288] "A holding consists of those propositions along the chosen decisional path or paths of

Second, it may be possible to avoid a rule argued for its *stare decisis* effect by challenging the applicability of the rule to the facts of the succeeding case. "[T]he scope of a rule of law, and therefore its meaning, depends upon a determination of what facts will be considered similar to those present when the rule was first announced."[289]

The process of determining whether the facts of two cases are sufficiently similar (apposite) that the first serves as precedent for the second, or sufficiently dissimilar that the first is factually distinguishable and hence without binding effect, is at the heart of legal analysis. One must try to determine what policies supported the rule of the first case and the extent to which those policies are implicated in the facts of the second. Factual differences may take the succeeding case out of the sweep of the prior rule. At the same time, cases are rarely if ever entirely identical. One must be alert to the possibility of extending the prior rule of decision to cover new facts.[290]

[b]　　Boundaries Set by Judicial Structure

Some courts have little choice but to follow apposite precedent. Others are entirely free to disregard it. Still others reserve the authority occasionally to disregard it. These classifications depend on judicial structure, the institutional relationship between the court making the prior decision and the court considering it as precedent.

Precedent is most coercive on the hierarchial inferiors of the court that decided the prior case. Hierarchy is determined by the tiers in a court system's structure. The federal court system and many state systems consist of a trial tier, an intermediate appellate tier and the highest appellate court.[291] In state systems, the last tier is often (but not always) called the state's *supreme* court.[292] In theory at least, the authority of apposite decisions of hierarchial superiors — sometimes called *controlling* precedent — is nearly absolute.[293] The final authority on the meaning of state law is the highest court of that

---

reasoning that (1) are actually decided, (2) are based upon the facts of the case, (3) and lead to the judgment. If not a holding, a proposition stated in a case counts as dicta." Michael Abramowicz & Maxwell Stearns, *Defining Dicta*, 57 Stan. L. Rev. 953, 1065 (2005).

[289] Edward Levi, An Introduction to Legal Reasoning 2 (1948).

[290] "Not only do new situations arise, but in addition peoples' wants change. The categories used in the legal process must be left ambiguous in order to permit the infusion of new ideas." Levi, note 289, *supra*, at 3.

[291] *See* § 13.06 (appellate systems), *supra*.

[292] *See generally* § 13.06 and § 2.01 (state and federal judicial systems), *supra*.

[293] The principle is widely but not universally honored. Atiyah & Summers suggest that, while lower courts entirely lack the authority to overrule precedents of their hierarchial superiors, note 287, *supra*, at 123, they will sometimes ignore them, "even though the American theory of precedent does not fully acknowledge the practice in so many words." *Id.* at 120. In addition, some decisions are designated by appellate courts as non-precedential and thereby not controlling on lower courts. The practice has become widespread in federal courts of appeal. "Today, the vast majority of opinions from the federal appellate courts are designated as non-precedential." Amy E. Sloan, *A Government of Laws and Not Men: Prohibiting Non-Precedential Opinions by Statute or Procedural Rule*, 79 Ind. L.J. 711, 718 (2004).

state.[294] Similarly, the United States Supreme Court is the final arbiter of the meaning of federal law. When federal and state courts decide federal law issues, they are treated as one expanded court system. The Supreme Court's federal law decisions bind federal and state courts alike as controlling precedent.

At the other extreme, precedent may be no more than *persuasive*. This occurs when a decision from one judicial system is offered as precedent in another. Courts may follow such precedent if they agree with it, but they are under no compulsion to do so.[295] Thus a New York state court may reject a rule of decision in a factually indistinguishable New Hampshire case. One federal circuit court may similarly reject the precedent of another federal circuit. State courts may even reject the decisions of lower federal courts concerning the meaning of federal law.[296]

The precedential effect that the decision has on the same court that rendered it falls somewhere between controlling and persuasive precedent. Courts do not control themselves by their cases in the way they control their hierarchial underlings. American courts borrowed their essential conception of *stare decisis* from England but are less reluctant than English jurists to overrule their own decisions.[297] On the other hand, courts cannot regard their own decisions as lightly as would the courts of other systems. If courts do not give their decisions considerably more weight than persuasive precedent, they will be afflicted with the problems that *stare decisis* was intended to avoid.[298]

The resulting rule is that courts usually, but not invariably, follow their own precedents. When courts do discard their precedents, they are said to *overrule* them. The time at which precedent will fall is often difficult to predict and the process frequently controversial.[299] It is possible, however, to identify some of the circumstances in which it is most likely that a court will overrule its own prior decision:

1. If it is seriously out of keeping with contemporary views of what is right and just;
2. if it has been passed by in the development of the law and no longer fits the general principles that govern like cases and overruling it will not require costly or disruptive readjustment of relationships created in reliance upon it; or
3. if the rule has proved to be unworkable or inconvenient in practice and the court is convinced that a different rule will be substantially better,

---

[294] Discussed in § 7.06[1], *supra*.

[295] Under a narrower view of *stare decisis*, the influence of persuasive precedent is so slight as to be outside the doctrine. ATIYAH & SUMMERS, note 287, *supra*, at 115.

[296] *See* David L. Shapiro, *State Courts and Federal Declaratory Judgments*, 74 Nw. U. L. Rev. 759 (1979).

[297] ATIYAH & SUMMERS, note 287, *supra*, at 123–24.

[298] *See* note 281 and related text, *supra*.

[299] *See, e.g.*, Chief Justice Bell's vigorous dissent to the Pennsylvania Supreme Court's overruling of its decisions limiting recovery for negligently inflicted emotional distress. *Niederman v. Brodsky*, 261 A.2d 84, 90 (Pa. 1970).

taking into consideration the dislocation a change may produce.[300]

Courts generally will give greater *stare decisis* effect to their settled interpretations of statutes than to either their constitutional decisions or common law precedents. This view is not universally accepted,[301] but it is defensible. A legislature is presumed to acquiesce in the judicial interpretations of its statutes when it does not overrule them by statutory repeal or amendment. This can be seen as a kind of retrospective legislative intent. Moreover, if courts were more willing to reinterpret statutes, this might sap the legislature's initiative to review and periodically revise statutory law. Therefore, "once a decisive interpretation of legislative intent has been made . . . the court should take that direction as given."[302]

§ 15.14   LAW OF THE CASE

The law-of-the-case doctrine inhibits relitigation of issues of law in the same case.[303] It shares with preclusion the purpose of making litigation more efficient. Unlike preclusion, it operates in advance of final judgment. Since courts have discretion to depart from the law-of-the-case doctrine,[304] it is similar in operation to *stare decisis*.[305] However, the long range purpose of the law-of-the-case doctrine is more modest than that of *stare decisis*, since the former settles law only for the case at hand.

The doctrine is important to judicial administration. At trial,

> the doctrine of the law of the case is little more than a management practice to permit logical progression toward judgment. Prejudgment orders remain interlocutory and can be reconsidered at any time, but efficient disposition of the case demands that each stage of the litigation build on the last, and not afford an opportunity to reargue every previous ruling.[306]

For the trial judge, the law-of-the-case doctrine is one of self-restraint. It offers no protection to the trial court's legal decisions when they are reviewed by an appellate court. But the converse is not true. This is because the law-of-the-case doctrine gives controlling effect to an appellate court ruling if

---

[300] 1B J. MOORE, MOORE'S FEDERAL PRACTICE ¶ 0.402[3.-1] (2d ed.).

[301] *See, e.g.*, criticism of the idea in CARDOZO, note 281, *supra*, at 148.

[302] LEVI, note 289, *supra*, at 32. Correspondingly, since Congress cannot overturn the Supreme Court's constitutional decisions, these are entitled to the least *stare decisis* effect. *Agostini v. Felton*, 521 U.S. 203, 235–36 (1997). *See generally* Amy Coney Barrett, *Statutory Stare Decisis in the Courts of Appeals*, 73 GEO. WASH. L. REV. 317, 317 (2005).

[303] *See* Joan Steinman, *Law of the Case: A Judicial Puzzle in Consolidated and Transferred Cases in and Multidistrict Litigation*, 135 U. PA. L. REV. 595, 597–613 (1987); Brett T. Parks, *McDonald's Corp. v. Hawkins and "The Law of the Case" Doctrine in Arkansas*, 50 ARK. L. REV. 127 (1997).

[304] The law of the case doctrine "cannot prohibit a court from disregarding an earlier holding in an appropriate case . . . ." *Castro v. United States*, 540 U.S. 375, 384 (2003).

[305] Discussed in § 15.13, *supra*.

[306] 1B J. MOORE, MOORE'S FEDERAL PRACTICE ¶ 0.404[1] (2d ed.).

the case is remanded to an inferior court for further proceedings. The doctrine also imposes self-restraint on the appellate court if the case returns by a further appeal.[307]

As with *stare decisis*, the law-of-the-case doctrine permits some flexibility for courts to reconsider their own prior rulings. One court has suggested that reconsideration would be warranted if "the evidence on a subsequent trial was substantially different, controlling authority has since made a contrary decision of the law applicable to such issues, or the decision was clearly erroneous and would work a manifest injustice."[308] In addition, a court is more likely to reconsider one of its legal rulings if it made the ruling when considering a motion for a temporary restraining order or under other hurried circumstances. Similarly, "[e]arly pretrial rulings . . . may often be subject to reconsideration as a case progresses toward trial."[309]

§ 15.15 INCONSISTENT FACTUAL POSITIONS — JUDICIAL ESTOPPEL

Some courts have refused to permit a litigant to take inconsistent positions in successive lawsuits. Doctrine supporting this is sometimes called *judicial estoppel*.[310] While federal courts and virtually all state courts permit litigants to make inconsistent positions in their pleadings,

> courts do not relish the prospect that an adept litigant may succeed in proving a proposition in one suit, and then succeed in proving the opposite in a second. At worst, successful assertion of inconsistent positions may impose multiple liability on an adversary or defeat a legitimate right of recovery. At best, the judicial system is left exposed to an explicit demonstration of the frailties that remain in adversary litigation and adjudication.[311]

---

[307] *Id.*.

[308] *White v. Murtha*, 377 F.2d 428, 432 (5th Cir. 1967).

[309] WRIGHT & MILLER § 4478 (quoting *White v. Murtha*, 377 F.2d 428, 431–32 (5th Cir. 1967)). "Law of the case principles are therefore best understood as rules of sensible and sound practice that permit logical progression toward judgment, but that do not disable a court from altering prior interlocutory decisions in a case." Steinman, note 303, *supra*, at 599.

[310] "Judicial estoppel presently appears under a variety of names, especially in state courts. It is frequently called the doctrine of preclusion against inconsistent positions . . . . Less frequently, courts refer to the doctrine as estoppel by oath." Note, *Judicial Estoppel: The Refurbishing of a Judicial Shield*, 55 GEO. WASH. L. REV. 409, 410 n.8 (1987). *See generally* Kira A. Davis, *Judicial Estoppel and Inconsistent Positions of Law Applied to Fact and Pure Law*, 89 CORNELL L. REV. 191 (2003); Douglas W. Henkin, *Judicial Estoppel — Beating Shields into Swords and Back Again*, 139 U. PA. L. REV. 1711 (1991); Rand G. Boyers, Comment, *Precluding Inconsistent Statements: The Doctrine of Judicial Estoppel*, 80 NW. U. L. REV. 1244 (1986).

[311] WRIGHT & MILLER § 4477. As this quotation suggests, it is necessary not only that the party's successive positions be inconsistent but that "the first position has been accepted by a court." Kira A. Davis, *Judicial Estoppel and Inconsistant Positions of Law Applied to Fact and Pure Law*, 89 CORNELL L. REV. 191, 192 (2003).

Scarano v. Central R.R. Co.[312] is a well-known example. In the first case, plaintiff obtained a substantial damage recovery against his employer for disability resulting from a job-related injury. In the second case against his employer, this time for reinstatement, plaintiff reversed his factual position and sought to prove he was fit for work. The court found the record in the first case insufficiently clear to support collateral estoppel (issue preclusion),[313] but nonetheless refused plaintiff an opportunity to prove a lack of disability in the second case. The court said: "Such use of inconsistent positions would most flagrantly exemplify that playing fast and loose with the courts which has been emphasized as an evil the courts should not tolerate."[314] The court went on to say that plaintiff's maneuver "is more than [an] affront to judicial dignity. For intentional self-contradiction is being used as a means of obtaining unfair advantage in a forum provided for suitors seeking justice."[315]

Judicial estoppel is a controversial doctrine and its boundaries are difficult to chart.[316] Litigants should be free to change factual positions in succeeding cases when new evidence has come to light or in other circumstances which suggest good reasons for a change of position and no injustice to the opposing party. As the *Scarano* court noted, "each case must be decided upon its own particular facts and circumstances."[317] Perhaps the most that can be said is that courts have the power to refuse adjudication under the inconsistent position doctrine and may use that power in a sufficiently compelling case.

---

[312] 203 F.2d 510 (3d Cir. 1953).

[313] Discussed in § 15.07 (requirements for issue preclusion), *supra*. It usually is and should be a requirement for judicial estoppel that the declarant appears to have profited from the first factual position. That is, the court must have relied upon (or ruled consistantly with) the declarant's position in the first case. 203 F.2d at 510. *Cf. Pegram v. Herdrich*, 530 U.S. 211, 228 n.8 (2000) ("Judicial estoppel generally prevents a party from prevailing in one phase of a case on an argument and then relying on a contradictory argument to prevail in another phase.").

[314] 203 F.2d at 513.

[315] 203 F.2d at 513.

[316] It has been described as a "minor but controversial doctrine, which varies widely from jurisdiction to jurisdiction and which is even rejected outright in a good number of states . . . ." RICHARD H. FIELD, BENJAMIN KAPLAN & KEVIN M. CLERMONT, MATERIALS FOR A BASIC COURSE IN CIVIL PROCEDURE 715 (9TH ED. 2007).

[317] 203 F.2d at 513, quoting *Galt v. Phoenix Indem. Co.*, 120 F.2d 723, 726 (D.C. Cir. 1941).

TABLE OF CASES

[References are to sections and footnotes]

[References are to sections and footnotes]

[References are to sections and footnotes]

[References are to sections and footnotes]

[References are to sections and footnotes]

[References are to sections and footnotes]

[References are to sections and footnotes]

[References are to sections and footnotes]

[References are to sections and footnotes]

Q

R

[References are to sections and footnotes]

[References are to sections and footnotes]

[References are to sections and footnotes]

TABLE OF AUTHORITIES

[References are to sections]

[References are to sections]

[References are to sections]

Bator, Paul M., *The State Courts and Federal Constitutional Litigation*, 22 WM. & MARY L. REV. 605 (1981) 5.02 n20

BATOR, P., P. MISKIN, D. SHAPIRO, & H. WECHSLER, THE FEDERAL COURTS AND THE FEDERAL SYSTEM 171 (2d ed. 1981 supplement) . . . . 7.03[5] n45

Bauer, Joseph P., *The Erie Doctrine Revisited: How a Conflicts Perspective Can Aid the Analysis*, 74 NOTRE DAME L. REV. 1235, 1281–99 (1999) . . . . 7.03[3] n32

Baughman, Jr., William H., *Federal Cross-Appeals — A Guide and a Proposal*, 42 OHIO ST. L.J. 505 (1981) . . . . . . 13.09[2] n151

Bauman, John A., *Evolution of the Summary Judgment Procedure*, 31 IND. L.J. 329 (1956) . . . . 11.03[1] n20

Becker, Susan J., *Conducting Informal Discovery of a Party's Former Employees: Legal and Ethical Concerns and Constraints*, 51 MD. L. REV. 239 (1992) 10.01 n3

Beckerman, John S., *Confronting Civil Discovery's Fatal Flaws*, 84 MINN. L. REV. 505, 510–11 (2000) . 10.03[1] n29, n33; 10.12 n257, n267

Beiner, Theresa M., *The Misuse of Summary Judgment in Hostile Environment Cases*, 34 WAKE FOREST L. REV. 71 (1999) . 11.03[3][d] n135

Bell et al., Griffin B., *Automatic Disclosure in Discovery — The Rush to Reform*, 27 GA. L. REV. 1 (1992) . . 10.07[2] n158, n163, n164, n168, n170, n171

Belton, Robert, *Burdens of Pleading and Proof in Discrimination Cases: Toward a Theory of Procedural Justice*, 34 VAND. L. REV. 1205 (1981) . . . . 12.04[2] n128

BENDER'S FORMS OF DISCOVERY (Matthew Bender) 1.05 n67

Benson, David F., *United States v. Dusenbery: Supreme Court Silence and the Lingering Echo of Due Process Violations in Civil Forfeiture Actions*, 78 CHI.-KENT L. REV. 409 (2003) 4.01 n13

Berch, Michael A., *A Proposal to Permit Collateral Estoppel of Nonparties Seeking Affirmative Relief*, 1979 ARIZ. ST. L.J. 511 (1979) . . . . 15.08[1] n159

Beres, Linda S., *Games Civil Contemnors Play*, 18 HARV. J.L. & PUB. POLICY 795 (1995) . . . . 14.02[2] n44

Berger, Robert S., *The Mandamus Power of the United States Courts of Appeals: A Complex and Confused Means of Appellate Control*, 31 BUFFALO L. REV. 37, 86–87 (1982) . 13.04[3] n76

Bergman, Jed I., *Putting Precedent in Its Place: Stare Decisis and Federal Predictions of State Law*, 96 COLUM. L. REV. 969 (1996) . 7.06[2] n141

Berman, Paul Schiff, *The Globalizatiion of Jurisdiction*, 151 U. PA. L. REV. 311, 317 (2002) . . . . 3.12[6] n452

Berry, *Ending Substance's Indenture to Procedure: The Imperative for Comprehensive Revision of the Class Damage Action*, 80 COLUM. L. REV. 299 (1980) . 9.09[1][b] n226

Betten, Alan, *Institutional Reform in the Federal Courts*, 52 IND. L.J. 63, 68 (1976) . 2.02 n15

Bies, John, *Conditioning Forum Non Conveniens*, 67 U. CHI. L. REV. 489 (2000) . 6.02[1] n61

Black, Susan H., *A New Look at Preliminary Injunctions*, 36 ALA. L. REV. 1 (1984) . . . . 13.04[1] n40

Bledsoe, Leighton, *Jury or Non-Jury Trial — A Defense Viewpoint*, 5 AM. JUR. TRIALS 123, 135 (1966) . . 12.06 n158, n161, n162, n163

Blume, *A Rational Theory for Joinder of Causes of Action and Defences, and for the Use of Counterclaims*, 26 MICH. L. REV. 1 (1927) 9.02 n14

Bone, Robert G., *Mapping the Boundaries of a Dispute: Conceptions of Ideal Lawsuit Structure From the Field Code to the Federal Rules*, 89 COLUM. L. REV. 1 (1989) . 3.05[2] n134; 7.04[1] n61

Bone, Robert G., *Rethinking the "Day in Court" Ideal and Nonparty Preclusion*, 67 N.Y.U. L. REV. 193 (1992) . 15.03[4] n82; 15.04[2] n104

Borchers, Patrick J., *Comparing Personal Jurisdiction in the United States and the European Community: Lessons for American Reform*, 40 AM. J. COMP. L. 121 (1992) . . . . 3.01[1] n2

Borchers, Patrick J., *Internet Libel: The Consequences of a Non-Rule Approach to Personal Jurisdiction*, 98 NW. L. REV. 473, 475 (2004) . . . . 3.07[1] n215; 3.09[1] n307; 3.12[5] n438, n448

Borchers, Patrick J., *Jurisdictional Pragmatism: International Shoe's Half-Buried Legacy*, 28 U.C. DAVIS L. REV. 561 (1995) . 3.05[1] n124

[References are to sections]

[References are to sections]

[References are to sections]

[References are to sections]

[References are to sections]

[References are to sections]

G

[References are to sections]

[References are to sections]

[References are to sections]

[References are to sections]

K

[References are to sections]

[References are to sections]

[References are to sections]

[References are to sections]

[References are to sections]

N

[References are to sections]

[References are to sections]

[References are to sections]

[References are to sections]

[References are to sections]

[References are to sections]

[References are to sections]

[References are to sections]

[References are to sections]

[References are to sections]

[References are to sections]

[References are to sections]

Y

Z

TABLE OF STATUTES

[References are to sections and footnotes]

[References are to sections and footnotes]

[References are to sections and footnotes]

INDEX

[References are to section numbers.]

[References are to section numbers.]

[References are to section numbers.]

[References are to section numbers.]

[References are to section numbers.]

[References are to section numbers.]

[References are to section numbers.]

[References are to section numbers.]

[References are to section numbers.]